# An Anglo-Chinese
# Vocabulary of the Ningpo
# Dialect

W. T. Morrison

**Alpha Editions**

This edition published in 2020

ISBN : 9789354045738

Design and Setting By
**Alpha Editions**
www.alphaedis.com
email - alphaedis@gmail.com

AN

# ANGLO·CHINESE

# VOCABULARY

OF THE

# NINGPO DIALECT.

BY

## REV. W. T. MORRISON.

FORMERLY MISSIONARY IN NINGPO.

REVISED AND ENLARGED.

SHANGHAI:
AMERICAN PRESBYTERIAN MISSION PRESS.
1876.

# PREFACE.

Many have expressed surprise on their first arrival at Ning-po, that no Dictionary, or suitable text-book of any kind, has ever been prepared, to facilitate the acquisition of the local dialect ; and those who have wished to learn it, have been compelled to begin *de novo*, to accumulate, by a toilsome process, a vocabulary, or transcribe one already partially prepared. The present work is an attempt to supply this felt want. The author began immediately on his arrival, nearly sixteen years ago, the collection of a vocabulary for personal use. This in process of time grew to a considerable size, and the idea was suggested of putting it into a more permanent and accessible form. The suggestion was taken up, and has resulted in the present work.

During the earlier period of preparation, Lobschied's and Medhurst's Dictionaries, and Williams' and Edkins' Vocabularies were freely consulted. Every word however has been subsequently examined and re-examined with the help of five different Chinese teachers, and no pains have been spared to secure accuracy as far as possible.

Just before his death, the Rev. Dr. Knowlton reviewed the entire manuscript, and added many Chinese words and phrases.

The original plan was to give the equivalents of the English words in the Romanized System, and also in the Chinese character, adhering as closely as possible to the sound of the colloquial. In carrying out this plan great difficulties were encountered. It was found that if characters were used to represent the

precise sound of the colloquial word or phrase, the meaning
would often be sacrificed: if, on the other hand, such characters
were chosen as would fairly express the meaning, the sound
must often be disregarded. Again, no two teachers could be found,
who would agree, as to the character which should be used to represent certain sounds; for example, in the word "*na-hwun*"
which means infant, one teacher would write the *hwun* 歡 to like,
another would write *hwun* 喚 to suck, another, *hwó* 花 a flower;
and, as many such doubtful cases occur in the dialect, ambiguity
and confusion would be the result, were this plan adhered to.
The third and greatest difficulty lay in the fact, that there *are
no characters* to represent a large number of colloquial *sounds*,
as will be seen by the Syllabary following the preface.

No doubt one thoroughly acquainted with the dialect, and
with the *reng-li*, could say absolutely that certain words must be
expressed by certain characters. This field, interesting as it is, has
as yet been quite unexplored in Ningpo, all our books excepting
the Church Prayer-book having been written in the Romanized
System. It would therefore be presumption on the part of the
author, to lay down a system for writing the colloquial in the
character; and this work, with the kindred one of "tracing out
the laws of gradual corruption," is left for those whose attainments better fit them for the task.

The method of giving the sense in the character, and sacrific-
ing the sound where it could not be avoided, has been finally a-
dopted as affording the most satisfactory solution of the many
difficulties, at least so far as the present purpose is concerned.
In cases, therefore, where there is no acknowledged character
corresponding to the colloquial word, borrowed characters, *i. e.*
those having the same sound but not the same meaning, are
avoided, and current *reng-li* is given instead. (Borrowed ones
may have slipped in, but not intentionally.) The example given
above will illustrate this point: the characters, 嫺 歡, 嫺 喚, or

嫺 花, borrowed to represent the word *na-hwun*, infant, mean respectively *liking* or *sucking milk*, and *milk-flower*, and not *infant*; they are therefore discarded, and the veng-li characters 嬰 孩 *(ing-æ)* which mean infant are used. It is hoped that this plan of writing the characters will make the book more generally useful than it otherwise would have been, and that it may also prove a help to Chinese students wishing to learn English.

In a few cases where no *reng-li* equivalents could be found, Mandarin expressions are used.

Sometimes the colloquial phrase expresses a peculiar, and purely local shade of meaning; in such cases the approximate meaning has been given as nearly as possible in the *reng-li*, or the characters have been omitted.

Instances will no doubt occur, where characters will suggest themselves to the student, which, at first sight, seem to be more appropriate than those used. These however may be just the instances in which the characters have been changed over and over again, and those finally adopted have been the result of repeated examinations. A very simple example is the word *siao-nying*, meaning *child* in the colloquial. It would seem self-evident that 小 人 would be the appropriate characters, but in the *reng-li* these signify a bad or mean man: the characters 小 孩 *(siao-æ)* are therefore substituted.

As a Ningpo teacher might not always know whether certain expressions would be current elsewhere, an experienced Shanghai teacher was employed, who read over the work, and in the presence of, and with the approval of the Ningpo teacher, altered such words and sentences as were unintelligible to him.

The late revisions have produced more changes than were anticipated when the system of attaching small circles to the characters was first adopted, and they might perhaps as well have been omitted; but they are allowed to remain, as they may aid the memory in retaining characters.

Tone marks have been omitted, not because tones are deemed unimportant, for they certainly should be observed, especially in some cases, as in distinguishing between *shü* 水 water and *shü* 書 book, between *ping* 氷 ice, and *ping* 餅 cake, &c., &c.; but there seemed to be so much uncertainty about the tones of many words, that it was deemed safer to leave the student to learn them from the teacher, rather than from marks. The marks on the accented syllables will aid the learner in pronouncing correctly. Although great pains have been taken to have the accents correctly marked, yet errors will doubtless be found, and difference of opinion will exist as to their proper location in many words.

Teachers differ so greatly, in accent, in their modes of defining, and in their pronunciation, both of the colloquial, and of the character, that there is room for endless criticism, and, moreover, it is not to be expected that the first book of its kind can at all approach perfection. A perfect vocabulary could only result from the combined wisdom and experience of many. If however this little work shall aid any one in acquiring a knowledge of this widely spoken dialect, or if it should incite some one of greater attainments and experience, to make a perfect Ningpo vocabulary, the labor it has cost will not have been in vain.

We here thank heartily those who have encouraged or aided us in any way, and especially the Rev. J. A. Leyenberger, who has assisted in various ways, and who kindly furnishes the Syllabary, which follows the preface, and also a list of Geographical names, which will be found at the end of the volume.

# LIST OF SYLLABLES

IN THE

# NINGPO DIALECT.

From the following list it will be seen that a large number of the sounds have no character to represent them. From this arises the difficulty of using the Chinese character in the preparation of books in the local dialect, and the consequent necessity of employing some other method. The Roman system is now largely used for this purpose, and thousands of books have been printed in this character, and are in daily use by the people.

Those syllables which cannot properly be represented by Chinese characters, may be subdivided into two classes :—

I. Those which have absolutely no character in the language to express them, as *dza, fœ, gœn, ve.*

II. Those syllables, which may be represented by a character, but their pronunciation has become corrupted, as *kao* for *kyiao, kœn* for *kyin, wœn* for *ngwœn.*

# ALPHABETICAL LIST OF SYLLABLES.

| No. | Syllable | Char | | No. | Syllable | Char | | No. | Syllable | Char |
|---|---|---|---|---|---|---|---|---|---|---|
| 1 | A | | | 34 | Bun | 盤 | | 67 | Ding | 定 |
| 2 | ʻA | | | 35 | Cih | 拙 | | 68 | Do | 駝 |
| 3 | Ah | 阿 | | 36 | Cʻih | 出 | | 69 | Doh | 獨 |
| 4 | ʻAh | | | 37 | Cing | 震 | | 70 | Dong | 同 |
| 5 | Ang | | | 38 | Cʻing | 春 | | 71 | Dô | |
| 6 | ʻAng | | | 39 | Coh | 竹 | | 72 | Dôh | 踱 |
| 7 | Ao | 奧 | | 40 | Cʻoh | 觸 | | 73 | Dông | 堂 |
| 8 | ʻAo | 號 | | 41 | Cong | 中 | | 74 | Dön | 團 |
| 9 | Æ | 愛 | | 42 | Cʻong | 沖 | | 75 | Du | 徒絕 |
| 10 | ʻÆ | 害 | | 43 | Cô | | | 76 | Djih | 蜀 |
| 11 | Æn | 唵 | | 44 | Cʻô | 扯 | | 77 | Djing | |
| 12 | ʻÆn | | | 45 | Công | 掌 | | 78 | Djoh | 蜀 |
| 13 | Ba | | | 46 | Cʻông | 窗 | | 79 | Djong | 重 |
| 14 | Bæ | 敗 | | 47 | Cü | 主 | | 80 | Djô | 搽 |
| 15 | Bæn | 辦 | | 48 | Cʻü | 處 | | 81 | Djông | 常 |
| 16 | Bah | 白 | | 49 | Cün | 專 | | 82 | Djü | 任 |
| 17 | Bang | | | 50 | Cʻün | 穿 | | 83 | Djün | 傳慈 |
| 18 | Bao | 鮑 | | 51 | Da | 大 | | 84 | Dz | |
| 19 | Be | 備 | | 52 | Dæ | 代 | | 85 | Dza | |
| 20 | Beh | 勃 | | 53 | Dæn | 但 | | 86 | Dzæ | 在 |
| 21 | Beng | 盆 | | 54 | Dah | 達 | | 87 | Dzæn | 暫 |
| 22 | Beo | 掊 | | 55 | Dang | 宕 | | 88 | Dzah | 宅 |
| 23 | Bi | 皮 | | 56 | Dao | 道 | | 89 | Dzang | |
| 24 | Biao | 瓢 | | 57 | De | 隊 | | 90 | Dzao | 曹 |
| 25 | Bih | 闢 | | 58 | Deh | 特 | | 91 | Dzeh | 擇 |
| 26 | Bin | 便 | | 59 | Den | 潭 | | 92 | Dzeng | 存 |
| 27 | Bing | 平 | | 60 | Deng | 騰 | | 93 | Dzeo | 愁 |
| 28 | Bo | 婆 | | 61 | Deo | 頭 | | 94 | Dzi | 池 |
| 29 | Boh | 薄 | | 62 | Di | 地 | | 95 | Dzia | |
| 30 | Bong | 蓬 | | 63 | Diah | 疊 | | 96 | Dziah | 着 |
| 31 | Bô | 罷 | | 64 | Diao | 調 | | 97 | Dziang | 長 |
| 32 | Bông | 旁 | | 65 | Dih | 敵 | | 98 | Dziao | 潮 |
| 33 | Bu | 蒲 | | 66 | Din | 田 | | 99 | Dzih | 直 |

| | | |
|---|---|---|
| 100 | Dzin | 漸 |
| 101 | Dzing | 城 |
| 102 | Dziu | 綢 |
| 103 | Dzoh | 族 |
| 104 | Dzong | 從 |
| 105 | Dzô | 茶 |
| 106 | Dzông | 藏 |
| 107 | Dzu | 助 |
| 108 | E | |
| 109 | 'E | |
| 110 | Eh | 遏 |
| 111 | 'Eh | 盒 |
| 112 | En | 暗 |
| 113 | 'En | 汗 |
| 114 | Eng | 恩 |
| 115 | 'Eng | 恒 |
| 116 | Eo | 嘔 |
| 117 | 'Eo | 後 |
| 118 | Fah | 法 |
| 119 | Fæ | |
| 120 | Fæn | 反 |
| 121 | Feh | 弗 |
| 122 | Feng | 分 |
| 123 | Feo | 否 |
| 124 | Fi | 非 |
| 125 | Foh | 福 |
| 126 | Fong | 風 |
| 127 | Fông | 方 |
| 128 | Fu | 富 |
| 129 | Ga | |
| 130 | Gæ | 戲 |
| 131 | Gæn | |
| 132 | Gah | |
| 133 | Gang | |
| 134 | Gao | |
| 135 | Geh | |
| 136 | Gen | |
| 137 | Geng | |
| 138 | Geo | |
| 139 | Go | |
| 140 | Gong | 共 |
| 141 | Gô | |
| 142 | Goh | |
| 143 | Gông | |
| 144 | Gwa | |
| 145 | Gwæn | |
| 146 | Gwah | |
| 147 | Gwang | |
| 148 | Gwe | 葵 |
| 149 | Gweh | |
| 150 | Gweng | |
| 151 | Gwông | 狂 |
| 152 | Gwu | |
| 153 | Gyi | 其 |
| 154 | Gyia | |
| 155 | Gyiæn | |
| 156 | Gyiah | 蹻 |
| 157 | Gyiang | 強 |
| 158 | Gyiao | 橋 |
| 159 | Gyih | 極 |
| 160 | Gyin | 健 |
| 161 | Gying | 近 |
| 162 | Gyiu | 求 |
| 163 | Gyü | 具 |
| 164 | Gyüih | 掘 |
| 165 | Gyüing | 羣 |
| 166 | Gyün | 權 |
| 167 | Gyüoh | 局 |
| 168 | Gyüong | 窮 |
| 169 | Ha | |
| 170 | Hæ | 海 |
| 171 | Hæn | 覔 |
| 172 | Hah | 嚇 |
| 173 | Hang | |
| 174 | Hao | 好 |
| 175 | He | |
| 176 | Heh | 黑 |
| 177 | Hen | 漢 |
| 178 | Heng | 狠 |
| 179 | Heo | 螢 |
| 180 | Ho | 火 |
| 181 | Hoh | |
| 182 | Hong | 烘 |
| 183 | Hô | |
| 184 | Hôh | 霍 |
| 185 | Hwa | |
| 186 | Hwæn | 懁 |
| 187 | Hwah | 豁 |
| 188 | Hwang | |
| 189 | Hwe | 灰 |
| 190 | Hweh | 忽 |
| 191 | Hweng | 昏 |
| 192 | Hwô | 化 |
| 193 | Hwông | 況 |
| 194 | Hwu | 呼 |
| 195 | Hwun | 歡 |
| 196 | Hyi | 喜 |
| 197 | Hyiæ | 駭 |
| 198 | Hyiah | 讘 |
| 199 | Hyiang | 香 |
| 200 | Hyiao | 孝 |
| 201 | Hyih | 歇 |
| 202 | Hyin | 險 |
| 203 | Hying | 與 |
| 204 | Hyiu | 臭 |
| 205 | Hyü | 許 |
| 206 | Hyüih | 血 |
| 207 | Hyüing | 熏 |

| | | | | | | | | |
|---|---|---|---|---|---|---|---|---|
| 208 | Hyün | 喧 | 244 | K'ch | 刻 | 280 | Kwô | 挂 |
| 209 | Hyüoh | 畜 | 245 | Ken | 干 | 281 | Kw'ô | 誇 |
| 210 | Hyüong | 兄 | 246 | K'en | 看 | 282 | Kwông | 光 |
| 211 | Hyüô | 蝦 | 247 | Keng | 根 | 283 | Kw'ông | 曠 |
| 212 | I | 意 | 248 | K'eng | 肯 | 284 | Kwu | 古 |
| 213 | Ia | | 249 | Keo | 苟 | 285 | Kw'u | 苦 |
| 214 | Iæ | 野 | 250 | K'eo | 口 | 286 | Kwun | 官 |
| 215 | Iah | 約 | 251 | Ko | 果 | 287 | Kw'un | 寬 |
| 216 | Iang | 央 | 252 | K'o | 可 | 288 | Kyi | 幾 |
| 217 | Iao | 要 | 253 | Koh | 國 | 289 | Ky'i | 氣 |
| 218 | Ih | 一 | 254 | K'oh | 哭 | 290 | Kyiah | 甲 |
| 219 | In | 烟 | 255 | Kong | 公 | 291 | Ky'iah | 却 |
| 220 | Ing | 因 | 256 | K'ong | 孔 | 292 | Kyiang | 姜 |
| 221 | Iu | 幽 | 257 | Kô | | 293 | Ky'iang | 腔 |
| 222 | Jæ | 惹 | 258 | K'ô | | 294 | Kyiao | 敎 |
| 223 | Jih | 十 | 259 | Kôh | 各 | 295 | Ky'iao | 巧 |
| 224 | Jing | 八 | 260 | K'ôh | 壳 | 296 | Kyiae | 戒 |
| 225 | Joh | 就 | 261 | Kông | 扛 | 297 | Ky'iae | 揩 |
| 226 | Jô | | 262 | K'ông | 康 | 298 | Kyih | 急 |
| 227 | Jông | | 263 | Kun | | 299 | Ky'ih | 乞 |
| 228 | Jü | 樹 | 264 | K'un | | 300 | Kyin | 見 |
| 229 | Jün | 善 | 265 | Kwa | | 301 | Ky'in | 謙 |
| 230 | Ka | | 266 | K'wa | | 302 | Kying | 經 |
| 231 | K'a | 卡 | 267 | Kwæ | 怪 | 303 | Ky'ing | 輕 |
| 232 | Kah | 隔 | 268 | Kw'æ | 快 | 304 | Kyiu | 救 |
| 233 | K'ah | 客 | 269 | Kwah | 括 | 305 | Ky'iu | 邱 |
| 234 | Kang | | 270 | Kwang | | 306 | Kyü | 句 |
| 235 | K'ang | | 271 | Kw'ang | | 307 | Ky'ü | 去 |
| 236 | Kao | 高 | 272 | Kwæn | 關 | 308 | Kyüih | 決 |
| 237 | K'ao | 考 | 273 | Kw'æn | | 309 | Ky'üih | 缺 |
| 238 | Kæ | 改 | 274 | Kwe | 貴 | 310 | Kyüing | 均 |
| 239 | K'æ | 開 | 275 | K'we | 虜 | 311 | Kyü'ing | 窘 |
| 240 | Kæn | | 276 | Kweh | 骨 | 312 | Kyün | 捐 |
| 241 | K'æn | 堪 | 277 | Kw'eh | 闊 | 313 | Ky'ün | 勸 |
| 242 | Ke | | 278 | Kweng | 滾 | 314 | Kyüoh | 鞠 |
| 243 | Keh | 割 | 279 | Kw'eng | 坤 | 315 | Ky'üoh | 曲 |

| | | | | | | | | |
|---|---|---|---|---|---|---|---|---|
| 316 | Kyüong | 迥 | 352 | Lo | | 388 | Mih | 滅 |
| 317 | Ky'üong | 夐 | 353 | Loh | 綠 | 389 | Min | 面 |
| 318 | Kyüô | 嘉 | 354 | Loh | | 390 | Ming | 明 |
| 319 | Kyüôh | 覺 | 355 | Long | 龍 | 391 | Miu | 謬 |
| 320 | Ky'üôh | 確 | 356 | Ló | | 392 | Mo | 慕 |
| 321 | Kyüông | 降 | 357 | Lô | | 393 | Mo | |
| 322 | La | | 358 | Lôh | 落 | 394 | Moh | 木 |
| 323 | La | | 359 | Lông | 浪 | 395 | Moh | |
| 324 | Lah | 蠟 | 360 | Lông | | 396 | Mong | 蒙 |
| 325 | Lah | | 361 | Lön | 亂 | 397 | Mô | 馬 |
| 326 | Lang | | 362 | Lu | 路 | 398 | Mô | |
| 327 | Lang | | 363 | Lu | | 399 | Móng | 忙 |
| 328 | Lao | 老 | 364 | M | | 400 | Mun | 滿 |
| 329 | Lao | | 365 | M | | 401 | Na | |
| 330 | Læ | 來 | 366 | Ma | | 402 | Na | |
| 331 | Læn | 藍 | 367 | Ma | | 403 | Næ | 乃 |
| 332 | Le | 雷 | 368 | Mæ | 買 | 404 | Næ | |
| 333 | Le | | 369 | Mæ | | 405 | Næn | 難 |
| 334 | Leh | 勒 | 370 | Mah | 麥 | 406 | Nah | 捺 |
| 335 | Len | | 371 | Mah | | 407 | Nao | 膠 |
| 336 | Leng | 論 | 372 | Mang | | 408 | Ne | |
| 337 | Leo | 樓 | 373 | Mang | | 409 | Neh | 訥 |
| 338 | Leo | | 374 | Mao | 毛 | 410 | Neh | |
| 339 | Li | 里 | 375 | Mao | | 411 | Nen | 男 |
| 340 | Li | | 376 | Mæn | 慢 | 412 | Nen | |
| 341 | Liah | 屐 | 377 | Mæn | | 413 | Neng | 能 |
| 342 | Liang | 甂 | 378 | Me | 美 | 414 | Neng | |
| 343 | Liao | 了 | 379 | Me | | 415 | Neo | 耨 |
| 344 | Lih | 力 | 380 | Meh | 沒 | 416 | Ng | |
| 345 | Lih | | 381 | Men | 門 | 417 | Nga | |
| 346 | Liu | 連 | 382 | Meng | | 418 | Nga | |
| 347 | Ling | 林 | 383 | Meng | | 419 | Ngæ | 呆 |
| 348 | Ling | | 384 | Meo | 謀 | 420 | Ngæn | 巖 |
| 349 | Liu | 流 | 385 | Mi | 米 | 421 | Ngah | 額 |
| 350 | Liu | | 386 | Mi | | 422 | Ngah | |
| 351 | Lo | 羅 | 387 | Miao | 描 | 423 | Ngang | |

| No. | Syllable | Char | No. | Syllable | Char | No. | Syllable | Char |
|---|---|---|---|---|---|---|---|---|
| 424 | Ngao | 敖 | 460 | Nyiu | 鈕 | 496 | Peng | 本 |
| 425 | Ňgao | | 461 | Ňyiu | | 497 | P'eng | 烹 |
| 426 | Ngeh | | 462 | Nyü | 愚 | 498 | Peo | 襃 |
| 427 | Ngen | 岸 | 463 | Nyüing | | 499 | P'eo | 剖 |
| 428 | Ngeng | 硬 | 464 | Nyün | 元 | 500 | Pi | 比 |
| 429 | Ngeo | 偶 | 465 | Nyüoh | 玉 | 501 | P'i | 批 |
| 430 | Ngo | 峨 | 466 | Nyüong | 濃 | 502 | Piao | 表 |
| 431 | Ngô | 我 | 467 | Nyüông | | 503 | P'iao | 票 |
| 432 | Ňgô | | 468 | O | 窩 | 504 | Pih | 必 |
| 433 | Ngoh | 岳 | 469 | 'O | 禾 | 505 | P'ih | 匹 |
| 434 | Ňgoh | | 470 | Oh | 屋 | 506 | Pin | 變 |
| 435 | Ngông | 昂 | 471 | Ong | 翁 | 507 | P'in | 偏 |
| 436 | Ngwæn | 患 | 472 | 'Ong | 洪 | 508 | Ping | 氷 |
| 437 | Ngwe | 危 | 473 | Ô | | 509 | P'ing | 品 |
| 438 | Ngweh | 兀 | 474 | 'Ô | | 510 | Po | 波 |
| 439 | Ngwu | 吾 | 475 | Ôh | 惡 | 511 | P'o | 破 |
| 440 | Ngwun | 玩 | 476 | 'Ôh | 或 | 512 | Poh | 北 |
| 441 | Ni | | 477 | Ông | 盎 | 513 | P'oh | 撲 |
| 442 | No | 懦 | 478 | 'Ông | 杭 | 514 | Pong | |
| 443 | Noh | | 479 | Pa | | 515 | P'ong | 捧 |
| 444 | Nong | 農 | 480 | P'a | | 516 | Pô | 把 |
| 445 | Ňong | | 481 | Pæ | 拜 | 517 | P'ô | 怕 |
| 446 | Nô | 拿 | 482 | P'æ | 派 | 518 | Pông | 邦 |
| 447 | Nông | 囊 | 483 | Pæn | 班 | 519 | P'ông | |
| 448 | Nön | 曖 | 484 | P'æn | 攀 | 520 | Pu | 補 |
| 449 | Nu | 奴 | 485 | Pah | 百 | 521 | P'u | 鋪 |
| 450 | Nyi | 泥 | 486 | P'ah | 拍 | 522 | Pun | 半 |
| 451 | Nyiah | 虐 | 487 | Pang | | 523 | P'un | 泮 |
| 452 | Nyiang | 仰 | 488 | P'ang | | 524 | R | 耳 |
| 453 | Nyiæn | 念 | 489 | Pao | 報 | 525 | S | 四 |
| 454 | Ňyiæn | 堯 | 490 | P'ao | 抛 | 526 | Sa | |
| 455 | Nyiao | | 491 | Pe | 貝 | 527 | Sæ | 帥 |
| 456 | Ňyiao | | 492 | P'e | 配 | 528 | Sæn | 山 |
| 457 | Nyih | 溺 | 493 | Peh | 不 | 529 | Sah | 薩 |
| 458 | Nyin | 年 | 494 | P'ch | 潑 | 530 | Sang | |
| 459 | Nying | 迎 | 495 | Pen | | 531 | Sao | 掃 |

| No. | Syll. | 字 | No. | Syll. | 字 | No. | Syll. | 字 |
|---|---|---|---|---|---|---|---|---|
| 532 | Se | 雖 | 568 | T'æ | 泰 | 604 | T'oh | |
| 533 | Seh | 色 | 569 | Tæn | 且 | 605 | Tong | 東 |
| 534 | Sen | | 570 | T'æn | 嘆 | 606 | T'ong | 通 |
| 535 | Seng | 生 | 571 | Tah | 搭 | 607 | Tôh | |
| 536 | Seo | 叟 | 572 | T'ah | 塔 | 608 | T'ôh | 託 |
| 537 | Shæ | 奢 | 573 | Tang | 打 | 609 | Tông | 當 |
| 538 | Shih | 失 | 574 | T'ang | | 610 | T'ông | 湯朵 |
| 539 | Shing | 舜叔 | 575 | Tao | 刀 | 611 | Tô | |
| 540 | Shoh | | 576 | T'ao | 討 | 612 | T'ô | |
| 541 | Shong | | 577 | Te | 對 | 613 | Tön | 端 |
| 542 | Shön | 選 | 578 | T'e | 推 | 614 | T'ön | 瑞子此 |
| 543 | Shô | 夏 | 579 | Teh | 德 | 615 | Ts | |
| 544 | Shông | 春 | 580 | T'eh | 脫 | 616 | T's | |
| 545 | Shü | 世 | 581 | Ten | | 617 | Tsa | |
| 546 | Shün | 宣 | 582 | T'en | 貪 | 618 | Ts'a | 再 |
| 547 | Si | 西 | 583 | Teng | 等 | 619 | Tsæ | 朵贊 |
| 548 | Sia | | 584 | T'eng | 吞 | 620 | Ts'æ | 產隻 |
| 549 | Siæ | 寫 | 585 | Teo | 斗 | 621 | Tsæn | 察 |
| 550 | Siah | 削 | 586 | T'eo | 偷 | 622 | Ts'æn | |
| 551 | Siang | 相 | 587 | Ti | 低 | 623 | Tsah | |
| 552 | Siao | 小 | 588 | T'i | 體 | 624 | Ts'ah | |
| 553 | Sih | 錫 | 589 | Tia | | 625 | Tsang | |
| 554 | Sin | 先 | 590 | Tiah | | 626 | Ts'ang | 早草 |
| 555 | Sing | 心 | 591 | T'iah | 貼 | 627 | Tsao | 追翠 |
| 556 | Siu | 手 | 592 | Tiao | 弔 | 628 | Ts'ao | 側測 |
| 557 | So | 鎖 | 593 | T'iao | 挑 | 629 | Tse | |
| 558 | Soh | 宿 | 594 | Tih | 的 | 630 | Ts'e | |
| 559 | Song | 松所 | 595 | T'ih | 鐵 | 631 | Tseh | |
| 560 | Sô | | 596 | Tin | 點 | 632 | Ts'eh | 尊寸 |
| 561 | Sôh | 索 | 597 | T'in | 添 | 633 | Tsen | 走湊 |
| 562 | Sông | 賞 | 598 | Ting | 丁 | 634 | Tseng | 祭妻 |
| 563 | Sön | 算 | 599 | T'ing | 聽 | 635 | Ts'eng | |
| 564 | Su | 數 | 600 | Tiu | 丢 | 636 | Tseo | |
| 565 | Ta | | 601 | To | 多 | 637 | Ts'eo | |
| 566 | T'a | 他 | 602 | T'o | 拖 | 638 | Tsi | |
| 567 | Tæ | 帶 | 603 | Toh | 督 | 639 | Ts'i | |

| No. | Syllable | 字 | No. | Syllable | 字 | No. | Syllable | 字 |
|---|---|---|---|---|---|---|---|---|
| 640 | Tsia | | 676 | U | 烏 | 712 | Wô | 話 |
| 641 | Ts'ia | | 677 | Ü | 於 | 713 | W̌ô | 蛙 |
| 642 | Tsiœ | 者 | 678 | Üih | 懰 | 714 | Wông | 王 |
| 643 | Ts'iœ | 且 | 679 | Üing | 慍 | 715 | W̌ông | 汪 |
| 644 | Tsiah | 爵 | 680 | Un | 宛 | 716 | Wu | 胡 |
| 645 | Ts'iah | 綽 | 681 | Ün | 怨 | 717 | Wun | 綏 |
| 646 | Tsiang | 將 | 682 | Üô | 亞 | 718 | Yi | 移 |
| 647 | Ts'iang | 搶 | 683 | Üôh | 郁 | 719 | Yia | |
| 648 | Tsiao | 照 | 684 | Üong | 永 | 720 | Yiœ | 也 |
| 649 | Ts'iao | 超 | 685 | Vah | 伐 | 721 | Yiah | 藥 |
| 650 | Tsih | 即 | 686 | Væn | 萬 | 722 | Yiang | 羊 |
| 651 | Ts'ih | 切 | 687 | Ve | | 723 | Yiao | 搖 |
| 652 | Tsin | 剪 | 688 | Vch | 佛 | 724 | Yih | 亦 |
| 653 | Ts'in | 千 | 689 | Veng | 文 | 725 | Yin | 現 |
| 654 | Tsing | 進 | 690 | Veo | 浮 | 726 | Ying | 引 |
| 655 | Ts'ing | 親 | 691 | Vi | 維 | 727 | Yiu | 有 |
| 656 | Tsiu | 酒 | 692 | Voh | 伏 | 728 | Yü | 雨 |
| 657 | Ts'iu | 秋 | 693 | Vong | 馮 | 729 | Yüih | 月 |
| 658 | Tso | 做 | 694 | Vông | 房 | 730 | Yüing | 云 |
| 659 | Ts'o | 磋 | 695 | Vu | 輔 | 731 | Yün | 遠 |
| 660 | Tsoh | 捉 | 696 | Wa | | 732 | Yüô | 下 |
| 661 | Ts'oh | 促 | 697 | W̌a | | 733 | Yüoh | 疫 |
| 662 | Tsong | 總 | 698 | Wœ | 懷 | 734 | Yüôh | 育 |
| 663 | Ts'ong | 聰 | 699 | W̌œ | | 735 | Yüong | 榮 |
| 664 | Tsô | 詐 | 700 | Wæn | 還 | 736 | Z | 是 |
| 665 | Ts'ô | 岔 | 701 | W̌æn | 挽 | 737 | Za | |
| 666 | Tsôh | 足 | 702 | Wah | 滑 | 738 | Zœ | |
| 667 | Ts'ôh | 錯 | 703 | W̌ah | 挖 | 739 | Zæn | |
| 668 | Tsông | 章 | 704 | Wang | | 740 | Zah | |
| 669 | Ts'ông | 倉 | 705 | W̌ang | | 741 | Zang | |
| 670 | Tsön | 鑽 | 706 | We | 曾 | 742 | Zao | |
| 671 | Ts'ön | 寶 | 707 | W̌e | 威 | 743 | Ze | 隨 |
| 672 | Tsu | 租 | 708 | Weh | 活 | 744 | Zch | |
| 673 | Ts'u | 初 | 709 | W̌ch | 頗 | 745 | Zen | 鹽 |
| 674 | Tu | 都 | 710 | Weng | 魂 | 746 | Zeng | |
| 675 | T'u | 土 | 711 | W̌eng | 溫 | 747 | Zeo | |

| | | | | | | | | |
|---|---|---|---|---|---|---|---|---|
| 748 | Zi | 徐 | 753 | Zih | 舌 | 758 | Zong | |
| 749 | Zia | | 754 | Zin | 染 | 759 | Zô | |
| 750 | Ziah | 弱 | 755 | Zing | 盛 | 760 | Zóh | 辱 |
| 751 | Ziang | 像 | 756 | Ziu | 受 | 761 | Zông | 上 |
| 752 | Ziao | 兆 | 757 | Zo | | 762 | Zu | |

A comparison of the syllables in the Ningpo Dialect with those of other dialects North and South shows that there is considerable variation in the number. This will be seen from the following table.

| DIALECTS. | INITIALS. | FINALS. | WHOLE No. OF SYLLABLES |
|---|---|---|---|
| CANTON.................... | 23 | 53 | 707 |
| SWATOW.................... | .. | .. | 674 |
| AMOY OR CHANGCHOW........ | 15 | 50 | 846 |
| FUCHOW.................. | 15 | 33 | 928 |
| NINGPO.................. | 30 | 44 | 762 |
| SHANGHAI................ | 33 | 44 | 660 |
| PEKING.................. | 25 | 43 | 420 |

This variation is perhaps partly due to the different methods adopted by foreigners for distinguishing the sounds, and partly perhaps to the fact that two characters which have the same sound in one dialect often have different sounds in another. The great·discrepancy between the number of sounds in the Court dialect and those of the more Southern Provinces is somewhat remarkable. But this difference is explained by the fact that in the former the *jih sing* is suppressed, while it is of very frequent occurrence in the latter.

# EXPLANATIONS.

1. In many cases, an equivalent for the leading word is found immediately after it in Italics; this is not a definition of the English word, but the translation of the Chinese word or phrase following it.

2. The system for spelling the Ningpo sounds, is that used by common consent for printing all the books in the Ningpo dialect, by whatever mission published.

3. Any foreigner who learns the colloquial, should get the sounds from a native who is acquainted with the Romanized system, as quite new sounds are given to many letters, thus— cing is pronounced *ching; i,* has the sound of the English *e, e* of *a,* &c., &c.

4. The classifiers are placed in brackets after nouns.

5. The syllable *veng,* after a word, is a contraction of *veng-li* [wen-li], showing, either that there was no colloquial equivalent, or that while such a sentence might be understood among literary men, it would not be understood by ordinary people.

6. The small circle after a character denotes that the *sounds* of the colloquial, and the character differ; it may be by corruption, or because there being no character for the spoken word, another supposed to have the same meaning is substituted.

7. There are some sounds, in pronouncing which, teachers differ greatly as in saying *sih* or *shih, soh* or *shoh, siang* or *hyiang, cong* or *tsong, djong* or *dzong, keh* or *kah, heh* or *hah,* &c., &c. These differences are often marked in brackets.

8. As the distinction between the sounds *oh* and *ôh* is thought by many to be unimportant, it has been omitted in this work.

# A VOCABULARY

## OF THE

# NINGPO DIALECT.

———•••———

**A**, *usually unexpressed*; *expressed by a numeral followed by its classifier*, thus, *a man*, ih-go nying' 一個°人°; — *pen*, ih-ts pih' 一枝筆; — *book*, ih-peng shü' 一本書. *For classifiers see* The Nyingpo Primer 寧波土° 話°初°學°

**ABACUS**, sön'-bun 算盤 (ih-min); *do you understand the —?* ng sön'-bun hyiao'-teh feh 你°算 盤曉得否°?

**ABANDON**, *to* ky'ï'-diao 棄了; tiu'-diao 丟去°, *or* 丟了°; djih'-diao 絕了°; gwæn'-diao 損去°

**ABANDONED**, *infant — by its mother*, na-hwun' be ah-nyiang' tiu'-diao-de 嬰°孩°被阿娘丟 去°了°; *left off entirely* (as the use of strong drinks, &c.), üong'-yün ka'-de 永遠戒了°; *morally —*, vu-sö'-peh-ts 無所 不至

**ABASE**, *to bring low*, ti-loh'-ky'ï' 低落去°; *to degrade*, kông'-loh 降°落; — *him*, kông' gyi loh' 降°其落

**ABASHED**, *to be —*, dzæn-gwe'-vu-di' 慚愧無地; wông-k'ong'-peh-la' 惶恐之°至

**ABATE**, *to* kæn'-loh 減°落; kæn-ky'ing' 減°輕; — *the price*, kæn'-loh kô'-din 減°落價°錢°; — *the rigor of punishment*, ying-vah' kæn-ky'ing' 刑罰減°輕

**ABATED**, *the wind has —* (somewhat), fong iu'-tin 風小°點; *ditto* (entirely), fong sih'-de 風息了°

**ABBESS**, *Buddhist* tông'-kô-s-t'a 當家°師太°; *Roman Catholic* —, nyü'-siu-dao-tsiang 女修 道長

**ABBOT**, *Buddhist* fông-dziang' 方 丈; *Roman Catholic* —, siu-dao'-yün-tsiang 修道院長

**ABBREVIATE**, *to — strokes in writing*, siao' sia pih' wah 小寫°筆

畫; liao-gying' sia 蹺近寫°;
p'o'-ti sia' 破體寫°; t'eo-læn'
sia 偷懶寫°

ABDICATE, to — the throne, (and
hence office), t'e we' 退位; —
in favor of another, nyiang we'
讓位

ABDOMEN, du'-bi 肚皮

ABDUCT, to—(by deception), kwæ'-
tæ 拐帶; — by force, ngang-
pih'-leh-ky'i 硬逼得°去°

ABED, læ min-zông' li 在°眠床°裡

ABET, to aid, pông-dzu' 幫助; —
in crime, dzu-dziu'-we-nyiah' 助
紂爲虐 (veng); to put one up
to, ts'ön'-teh 攛掇; ditto (something bad), t'iao-so' 挑唆

ABETTOR, cü'-so 主唆

ABHOR, to u'-su 惡愬; dislike excessively, k'eh'-ts'eng' in-tseng'
厭憎

ABIDE, to djü 住; deng 庇; kyin'-
deng 久庵

ABILITY, dzæ-neng' 才能; du'-
dzæ 肚才; dzæ-dzing' 才情;
peng'-z 本事; vu'-nyih-ts 武
藝°子; perfect in mental and
moral character, dzæ-djün' teh'
be 才全德備; give according
to your —, ze lih-liang' dzu-c'ih'
隨力量助出; — tsiao ng'·go
lih-liang' do-c'ih' 照你个°力
量扡出; ze kô fong hyin', 隨
家°豐儉°

ABJECT, mean or poor, bing-dzin'
貧賤; — in condition (as slaves,
&c.), pe-dziu' 身賤

ABJURE, to vah-tsin' ky'i'-djih 罰
咒藥絕; —going, vah-tsiu' feh
ky'i' 罰咒弗去°

ABLE, neng-keo' 能彀; we 會;
has strength equal to, lih tsoh' 力
足; is he — to do it? gyi neng-
keo' tso' feh 其能彀做否°?
he is —, gyi we tso' 其會做;
he is not — to do it, vu lih' neng
we' 無力能爲; lih' sô peh
gyib' 力所不及; an — man,
yin dzæ-dzing-go nying 有才
情个°人°

ABOARD, loh-jün'-de 落船了°;
zông-jün'-de 上船了°; læ-jün'-
li 在°船裡

ABODE, djü-kyü' 住居; djü-oh'
住屋; where is your — ? djü-
kyü' ah-li'住居何°處°? where is
your honorable — ? fu'-zông ah-
li' 府上何°處°?

ABOLISH, to fi 廢; fi'-diao 廢了°;
— law, fi'-diao lih-fah' 廢了°
律法

ABOMINABLE, k'o-'eng' 可恨;
k'o-u'-ts-gyih' 可惡之極

ABOMINATE, to 'eng 恨; ün-'eng'
怨恨; 'eng-gyih' 恨極

ABORIGINES, t'u'-jing 土人°; —
of the middle and South of China,
miao-ts 苗子

ABORTION, siao'-ts'æn 小產; do-
t'æ' 墮胎; do sing' 墮娠; to
cause —, tang t'æ' 打胎

ABOUNDS *in*, ting to' 頂多; fi-væn'-ts to' 非凡之多; — *every where*, c'ü'-c'ü tu yiu' 處處都有; mun' di tu z' 滿地都是; *the Eastern part — in coal*, 'Tong' pin me-t'æn' ting to' 東邊煤炭頂多

ABOUT, da-iah' 大約; iah'-læ 約來; mao 毛; mao-kwu' 毛佔; — *thirty li*,* da-iah' sæn'-jih li' 大約三十里; — *ten*, k'ao jih'; *nearly*, ts'ó'-fch-to' 差弗多; *round* —, s'-tsiu-we' 四周圍; s'-deh-lön'-ky'ün 四圍°團圍; dön-ky'ün' 團圍
  * A li is about one third of an English mile.

ABOVE, zông 上; zông-deo' 上頭; te'-zông 對上; — *the house*, læ oh' te'-zông 在° 屋對上; *over and* —, ling-nga' 另外°; yü-wæ' 餘外; — *me in rank* (one grade), p'ing'-kyih pi ngô' kao' ih-teng 品級比我高一等

ABREAST, bing'-ba 並排°

ABRIDGE, *to* tsah'-tön 摘短; kæn'-liah 減°略

ABROAD, *beyond customs' barriers*, kwæn nga' 關外°; *beyond the frontier*, k'eo' nga 口外°; *spread* —, 'ang-k'æ' 行°開; yiang-k'æ' 揚開; po'-yiang'-k'æ 播揚開; *comes from* —, dzong nga-deo' læ 從外°頭來; *gone* —, c'ih yün'-meng' ky'i'-de 出遠門去°了°

ABRUPTLY, deh-jün' 突然

ABSCESS, doh-dzing-kwun' 毒成瘡°

ABSCOND, *to* dao-tseo' 逃走; tseo'-t'eh 走脫

ABSENT, feh læ'-tong, 弗在°此°; ŏ'-neh læ'-tong 不°在這裏°

ABSENT-MINDED, *forgetting what one is doing*, vông'-gyi-sô'-yi 忘其所以; sing'-feh-dzæ-yin' 心不°在焉 (used in reproach).

ABSOLUTE *power*, gyün-shü' liao-feh-teh' do 權勢極°大°

ABSOLVE, *to* sô 赦°; min 免°; sô'-min 赦°免; — *from sin*, sô zœ' 赦°罪

ABSORB, *to* seng'-tsing 滲°進; heng'-tsing.

ABSTAIN, *to* — *for a time*, gyi 忌; — *entirely*, ka 戒°; — *from food*, gyi zih' 忌食; — *voluntarily*, zi nyün' ka 自°願戒°; zi kying' zi 自°禁自°; — *from wine*, ka tsiu' 戒°酒; — *from opium*, ka a-p'in' 戒°鴉°片

ABSTEMIOUS *in food, and drink*, ing'-zih yiu-tsih' 飲食有節

ABSTRACT, tsah'-iao 摘要 (ih-go)

ABSTRUSE, sing-ao' 深奧

ABSURD, *beyond reason*, ü-li'-feh-'eh' 于理弗合; dzing-li'-ts nga' 情理之外°; — *talk*, hen-wô' 慝話

ABUNDANT, to'-leh-kying' 多得°緊; *more than is needed*, yiu yü' 有餘; *plentiful*, fu'-tsoh 富足;

— (as trees, or fruit), meo-zing′ 茂盛;—crops, or—year, nyin′-koh fong-teng′ 年穀豐登; da-joh′z nyin 大熟時年; — crops, wu′ koh fong teng′ 五穀豐登

ABUSE, to treat badly, long-song′; to injure, 'æ 害; to revile, mô 罵; zoh-mô′ 辱罵; to — by diminish-ing one's due, k'eh′-dæ 刻待; — by soiling (as a book, or one's character), tsao-t'ah′ 蹧蹋; — the weak, ky'i-vu′ 欺侮

ABUSED, who — this book? keh′ peng shü′ be jü′ tsao-t'ah′-diao-de 這°本書被誰°蹧蹋了°?

ABYSS, m̂-ti′-k'ang 無°底坑; m̂-ti′-sing-den 無°底深潭; fathom-less —, væn-dziang′-sing-den 萬丈深潭

ACADEMY, shü-kwun′ 書館; shü-vông 書房

ACCELERATE, to press forward, ts'e 催;— parturition, ts'e-sang′ 催生°; to increase speed gradual-ly, dzin′-dzin kw'a′-ky'i-læ 漸漸快°起來; bu-bu kying′-ky'i-læ 步步緊起來; ih-bu′ kw'a′ ih-bu — 步快° — 步; ih-bu′ kying′ ih-bu — 步緊一步

ACCEDE, to tah-ing′ 答應; ing-jing′ 應認; yüing 允; i 依;* did not —, feh tah′-ing 弗答應; feh yüing 弗允

* These characters usually denote simply a reply, but here they denote an affirmative reply.

ACCEDED, (he) — to what I wanted, ngô sô iao′-go tah′-ing-de 我所要个°答應了°

ACCENT, sing-ing′ djong 聲音重

ACCENT, to sing-ing′ bin ky'ing′ djong′ 聲音辨輕重

ACCEPT, to ziu 受; siu 收; ling′-ziu 領受; pray you — , ts'ing ng′ teng ngô sin′-sin 請你° 與° 我收收; I, having accepted, cannot forget your kindness, ngô ziu-ts′ ko-sing′-feh-ky'i′ 我受了°過心不°去°; — your kind invitation, mong ng′ zing′-dzing ngô læ ling′-ziu 蒙你° 情我來領受

ACCEPTABLE, 'eh-i′-go 合意个°; 'eh-sih′-go 合式个°

ACCESSION to the throne, teng-we′ 登位; — to office, jih tsih′ 襲職

ACCIDENT, to meet with an — (in-jury), p'ong-djoh 'æ 逢°着°害; nyü 'æ′ 遇害′; ditto, (ill luck), p'ong-djoh hwe-ky'i 逢°着° 晦氣

ACCIDENTALLY, ngeo′-jün 偶然; neo′-ts'eo 偶°湊

ACCOMMODATE, to — one's self to, jing′-dzong 順從; ditto (to circumstances), k'en′-ky'i sang′-dzing 隨° 機而° 行°

ACCOMMODATING, (of a person), yün-t'ong′ 圓通; 'o-t'ong′ 和通; — in lending, &c., k'eng t'ong-ytiong′ 肯通融

ACCOMPANY, to dong-de′ ky'i 同隊去°; jü-de′ ky'i 聚隊去°; ih-dong′ ky'i′ 一同去°; dô-kô′ ky'i 大°家°去°; 'eo′-leh ky'i′ 候了°去°; — on the way (or escort), be′-leh ky'i′ 陪了°去°; song′-leh ky'i 送了°去°

ACCOMPLICES, dong-tông′ 同鸞; tso′-tông 佐鸞

ACCOMPLISH, to complete, tso′-dzing 做成; dzing-kong′ 成功; wun-kong′ 完功; to — nothing, sang deng-dæn′.

ACCORDING to, tsiao 照; dziu 就; agreeably, kyü 據; i 依; 'eo 候; jü 如; 'eh 合; — my idea, tsiao ngô′ i′-s 照我意思; — to my seeing, tsiao ngô k'en′-læ 照我看來

ACCOUNT, tsiang 帳; to give in one's — of money entrusted, pao′-siao-diao 報銷了°; ditto, false-ly, hyü-pao′ 虛報; to reckon up an —, sön-tsiang′ 算帳; difficult to — for, nœn ka -shih 難解說; to enter on —, zông tsiang′ 上帳; to draw up an —, k'æ tsiang′ 開帳°; to settle an —, ka tsiang′ 解°帳; fu tsiang′ 付帳; on — of, we 爲°; ing-r′ 因而; on no —, tön′-feh-k'o 斷弗可; ts'ih′-feh-k'o′ 切弗可

ACCOUNT-BOOK, tsiang′-bu 帳簿

ACCOUNTABLE, you are—, hyiang ng′ z veng′ 向你°是問; hyiang ng′ dziah-lôh′ 向你°着落; I am not —, feh′ z ngô′-go kwæn-dzih′ 不°是我个°關涉

ACCOUNTANT, tsiang′-vông 帳房; kwun-tsiang′ cü-kwu 管帳个°人°

ACCUMULATE, to tsih′-jü 積聚; tsih′-hyüoh 積蓄; tsih′-loh 積落

ACCURATE, without faults, 'ao-vu′ ts'o′-c'ü 毫無錯處; bing′-vu ts'o′-ts'oh 並無錯錯; feh-ts'o′ 弗錯; minute, ts′-si 仔細

ACCUSATION, (written), zông-ts′ 狀子 (ih-tsiang); to bring in an — (on both sides), dzing-zông′ 呈狀

ACCUSE, to — before an officer, kao′- zông 告狀; — falsely, hwông′-kao 謊告; he accuses me of stealing, gyi ün ngô t'eo′-go 其屈我偷个°

ACCUSER, nyün-kao′ 原告; the person accused, be-kao′ 被告; your —, kao′ ng-go cü′-kwu 告你°个°人°

ACCUSTOMED, to become —, long-kwæn′ 弄慣°; tso′-kwæn 做慣°; tso′ jing-joh′ 做純熟; — to do, kwæn′-tso-go 慣°做个°; can't become — to hearing (it), t'ing′-feh-kwæn′ 聽弗慣°

ACHE, t'ong 痛; head —, deo-t'ong′ 頭痛; tooth —, ngô-ts′ t'ong′ 牙°齒痛

ACHIEVE, to dzing-kong′ 成功; with fixed aim, (he) will — his

*object,* yiu′ ts kying′-dzing 有志 竟成; — *renown,* kong-ming′ dzing-dziu′ 功名成就

ACKNOWLEDGE, *to own,* jing認; *to confess,* tsiao-jing′ 招認; — *being in the wrong,* jing ts′o′ 認 錯; *unwilling to* —, feh k′eng′ jing′ 弗肯認; *unwilling to* — *a debt,* la tsa′ 賴°債°

ACORN, ziang′-ts 橡子 (ih-ko)

ACQUAINTANCE, siang-joh′-go相 熟个°; joh-nying′ 熟人°; nying-teh′-go nying′ 認°得个° 人°; *mere* —, p′iao′-miao beng-yiu′ 縹緲朋友

ACQUAINTED *with,* joh-sih′ 熟識; *he is well* — *with the business,* keh′-go z-nyih′ gyi ting′ joh-sih′ 這°个° 事業其頂熟識; — *with him many years,* teng gyi′ to nyin′ siang-yü 與°其多年 相與

ACQUIESCE, *to* i依; ing-yüing′應 允; *I certainly* — *in your decision,* ng′ ding - kwe′, ngô vu yiu′ feh i′ 你°定規我無有 弗依

ACQUIRE, *to* tsang 掙°; tsang′-tsing 掙°進; dzæn 賺; djün; — *money,* tsang′ dong-din′ 掙° 銅錢°; — *possessions,* tsang′ kô-kyi′ 掙°家°計; — *knowledge,* kô cü′-sih 加°知識

ACQUIT, *to* — *him,* ding′ gyi, � ze′ 定其無°罪; shü′ gyi, ᇟ ze′ 恕其無°罪

ACRE, (Chinese), meo 畝; m; *an* — *of* (field) *land,* ih meo′ din 一畝田

ACROSS, wang 橫°; *lying* — *the road,* wang′ lu tong 橫°於°路上°

ACT, *to* tso 做; tsoh 作; — *a play,* tso hyi′-veng 做戲文; *to* — *well,* tso nying′ hao′做人° 好; — *benevolently,* we jün′ 爲 善; ′ang jün 行善

ACTIONS, ′ang-we′ 行°爲; tsoh′-we 作爲; sô-tsoh′-sô-we′ 所 作所爲; *bad* —, ẅa ′ang-ts′ 孬行止; *that is a good action,* keh′ z ih-go hao′ ′ang-we′這°是 一个°好行°爲

ACTIVE, *fond of action,* hao′ dong′-go 好°動个°; — *and intelligent,* weh-p′eh′ 活潑; ling-dong 靈動; *quick* (in work), kyih′-tsao 急躁; *strong and* —, mô-lih′.

ACTOR, *stage* hyi′-ts 戲子; pæn-ts 班子

ACTRESS, nyü′-pæn-ts 女班子

ACTUAL, *true,* jih-we′ 實爲; *proved by* — *experiment,* væn′-cing-liao 範準了

ACTUALLY, *really,* jih-dzæ′ 實在; jih-yi′ 實係; ky′üoh′-jih 確實

ACUTE, *sharp,* tsin 尖; — *discernment,* (by figure), ngæn′-lih tsin′ 眼°力尖; — *pain like a knife cutting,* t′ong′ ziang tao′ c′oh ka 痛像刀猎一°樣°

ADAGE, dzoh-wô′ 俗話; *ancient*

—, kwu'-wô 古話; lao'-wô-deo
老話頭 (ih-kyü)

ADAPT, to — one's self to time or
place, tso' tao ah-li', z ah-li' 做
到阿裡是阿裏; ts'' ih-z',
pe' ih-z' 此一時彼一時;
can — himself to circumstances,
neng ky'üih' neng sing' 能屈
能伸

ADAPTED to use, hao'-yüong'-go-
de 好用个°; — to his use, 'eh-
gyi'-go yüong' 合其个° 用

ADD, to kô 加'; t'in 添; tseng
增; ts'eo 湊; kô-ts'eo 加°湊;
t'in-ts'eo' 添湊; tseng-ts'eo'增
湊; — coal, kô me-t'æn' ts'eo'
加° 煤炭湊

ADDITION (in Arithmetic), kô-
fah' 加°法

ADDITIONAL, nga 外°; ling-nga'
另外°; — expense, nga' fi 外°
費; nothing —, bih' vu nga kô'
別無外°加°; — pleasure (as
a new son), t'in hyi' 添喜

ADDRESS, I wish to — you, ngô
iao teng ng kông' 我要與°你
講°; how shall I — him? ts'ing-
hwu' gyi jü 稱呼其誰°? —
a number of people, te cong'-
nying kông' ih-fæn 對衆人°
講°一番

ADDRESS, he made a good —, gyi
fah'-hwe-leh hao' 其發揮得°
好; very good —, do fah'-hwe
大°發揮; — (of a letter, place
only), di-ming' 地名; di-kyiah'-

ing; superscription (on a letter),
sing'-min 信面

ADEPT, joh-siu' 熟手; — (in
that branch), ting' cün-meng'頂
專門

ADEQUATE, enough, keo 够; tsoh
足; is —, keo-de 够了°; do
you feel — (to it)? ng 'ông'-leh-
djü' feh 你°降得°住否°?
ng hao p'e-fu feh 你° 好配
副否°?

ADHERE, to nyin-lao'粘牢; can't
make it —, nyin'-feh-lao 粘弗
牢; will —, we kao-nyin'-go會
膠°粘个°; — (as iron to a
magnet), hyih'-lao 翕牢

ADJACENT, siang-gying' 相近;
— countries, siang-gying'-go koh'
相近个° 國

ADJOINING, ling 鄰; — country,
ling koh' 鄰國; — room, kah'-
pih ih-kæn vông' 隔壁一間°房

ADJUDICATE, to try, sing 審; to
judge, sing'-p'un 審判; p'un'-
tön 判斷

ADJUST, to tsing'-teng 整頓;
tsing-li 整理; — these stones,
keh'-sing zah-deo' iao tsing'-teng
hao 這些° 石頭要整頓
好; — matters, tsing-li' z-ken'整
理事幹; — (or put things in
order), tsing'-zi 整齊; — the
hair, li deo-fah' 理頭髮

ADMINISTER, to bæn 辦; bæn'-li
辦理; — affairs, bæn'-li z-ken'

辦 理 事 幹; *to — medicine to a person,* do yiah' peh nying ky'üoh' 拿°藥 給°人°吃°; — *public affairs,* bæn' kong-z' 辦 公 事

ADMIRAL, se'-s-di-toh 水師提督

ADMIRABLE, gyih-me' 極 美; gyih-hao' 極好; gyih-miao' 極妙

ADMIRE, *to* ky'i'-mo 企慕; cong-æ' 踵愛; (as rare things), hyi-hen' 希罕; — *and long for* (or wish to be like), ky'i'-nyiang 企仰; — *and desire,* nyiang'-vông 仰望

ADMIRED, *I have long — his great reputation,* ngô hyiang'-læ mo' gyi'-go da ming' 我向來慕其°个°大名

ADMIT *him,* peh' gyi tseo'-tsing-læ 俾°其走進來; nyiang' gyi tsing'-læ 讓°其進來

ADMONISH,*to*—(not to do), ky'ün'-kyiæ 勸解; ky'ün'-sih 勸釋; — (to do) ky'ün'-min 勸勉

ADOPT, *to* — (as an outsider), ling 領; ming-ling' 螟蛉; — *a male relative,* (of the same family name), lih-kyi' 立繼; dzing-kyi' 承繼; ko-kyi' 過繼; *ditto from love,* æ'-kyi 愛繼; — *the newest nephew,* ing-kyi' 應繼

ADOPTED *child,* ling'-ts 領子; (of the same family name), kyi'-ts 繼子; — *brother,* (of different family name), nyi hyüong-di' 義°兄弟; kyi'-pa hyüong-di' 結°拜°兄弟

ADORE, *to* kying'- kying - djong-djong pa' 敬 敬 重 重 拜°

ADORN, *to* —(as the person), tsông-pæn' 裝扮; tsah'-kwah 紮刮; — (as houses), tsông-sih' 裝飾; (as things), tsông-wông' 裝潢

These four expressions may be used interchangeably, but according to good usage it is better to distinguish them.

ADRIFT, t'eng'-læ-t'eng'-ky'i' 來 尒 去°; t'eng'-k'æ-de 尒 開了°

ADROITNESS *with the hand,* siu'-fah p'ih'-t'eh 手法狠°快°; siu'-fah c'ih-gyi' 手法出奇

ADULATION, vong'-dzing 奉承; ts'in-vong' 諂奉; shü'-kwu 世故; ts'eo'-c'ü 湊趣

ADULT, *arrived at — age,* zông-ting' 上丁; dzing-ting' 成丁; tsiang'-dzing 長成; dzing-nying'-tsiang'-da 成人°長大

ADULT, do-nying' 大°人°; *school for adults* (of either sex), do shü-vông' 大°書房; — *school for males,* kying-kwun' shü-vông' 經館書房

ADULTERATE, *to* ts'æn-'o' 攪和; ts'æn-tsing' 攪進; ts'æn-long' 攪攏; —*with water,* ts'æn-t'ông' 'o-shü' go 攪湯和水°个°

ADULTERER, kæn-fu' 姦夫; yia'-lao-kong 野°老公

ADULTERESS, kæn-vu' 姦°婦

ADULTERY, kæn-ying' 姦°淫; *a case of —,* kæn-en' 姦°案;

*to commit* —, væn kæn-ying' 犯
姦°淫

ADVANCE, *to* zông-zin' 上 前°;
*price will* —, kô'-din iao kyü'-
zông-de 價° 錢° 要 貴 上 了°;
kô'-din iao tsiang'-zông-de 價°
錢° 要 漲 上 了°; *to improve*,
tsing'-ih 進 益; hao'-ky'i-læ 好
起 來; — *wages* (before the
time), yü-ts' sing-kong' 預 支
辛工; tsæn kong-din' 趲工錢°;
*in* — *of me*, pi ngô' zông-zin' 比
我 上 前°

ADVANCED *in years*, yiu'-sing
nyin-kyi' de 有 些° 年 紀 了°

ADVANTAGE, *profit*, bin-i' 便
宜°; *benefit*, ih'-c'ü 益 處; hao-
c'ü' 好 處; *to take of* — *him*,
tsin gyi'-go zông-fong' 佔 其
个° 上 風; *take* — *of another*,
tsin nying-kô' min-ts' 佔 人° 家°
面 子

ADVENTUROUS, *fond of going into danger*, hwun-hyi' tseo hyin'
lu 歡 喜 走 險 路

ADVERSARY, dziu-dih' 讎 敵;
ün-kô' 冤 家°; te'-deo 對 頭

ADVERSE, feh-jing' 弗 順; feh-
jing'-kying 弗 順 境; feh-jing'-
liu 弗 順 溜; — *day*, nyih-
jing' feh-te' 日° 辰 弗 對; —
*wind*, tông-deo' fong 當 頭 風;
(against the wind), teo' fong 對
風; tao' fong 倒 風; —*current*,
teo'-shü 對 水°

ADVERSITY, (as sickness, fires,

persecution), tsæ-næn' 災 難; —
(in business, &c.), z-yüing' feh-
hao' 時 運 弗 好; tao-yüing'
倒 運; *in* —, loh-boh'-de 落
薄 了°; *in times of* — *trust in
God*, yiu tsæ'-næn z-'eo k'ao'-
djoh Jing-ming' 有 災 難 時 候
靠 着 神 明

ADVERTISE, *to* kao'-bah 告 白°;
— *in a paper*, zông-pao' 上 報;
teng-pao' 登 報; *do you* — *your
goods?* ng'-go ho' yiu zông-pao'-
leh ma 你° 个° 貨 有 上 報
了° 嗎°?

ADVERTISEMENT, kao'-bah 告
白° (ih-tsiang); — *of goods, &c.*,
tsiao-ts' 招 紙; *to put up an.*
— (*i.e.* paste up), t'iah' tsiao-ts'
貼° 招 紙

ADVICE, ky'ün'-hwô 勸 化; *won't
listen to* —, feh k'eng t'ing ky'ün'
弗 肯 聽 勸; feh ziu ky'ün'-hwô
弗 受 勸 化; *I'll give you a
piece of* —, ngô ky'ün'-hwô ng
ih-fæn' 我 勸 化 你° 一 番;
*I will take your* —, ngô t'ing'
ng-go ky'ün' 我 聽 你° 个° 勸;
ling'-kyiao, ling'-kyiao 領 敎
領 敎

ADVISE, *to* ts'-kyiao 指 敎 (not
proper in the first person); —
(or tell) *a person*, kao'-hyiang-
nying-dao 敎° 向 人° 道; *I
beg you to* — *me*, ngô ts'ing' ng
ts'-kyiao ngô 我 請 你° 指 敎
我; *I* — *you not to go*, ngô co

ng vong' ky'i' 我叫° 你° 不°
用° 去°

ADVISER (to one ignorant), hô-
tông-ngæn' 蝦° 當° 眼°

ADVOCATE, *mediator*, cong-pao' 中
保; *attorney*, dzong-s' 訟 師

AFAR, yün'-yün 遠 遠; yiao-yün'
遙 遠

AFFABLE, ky'in-'o' 謙和; 'o-ky'i'
和 氣

AFFAIR, z 事; z-ken' 事 幹; z-
t'i' 事 體; (ih-gyin, ih-ky'i, ih-
tsông, ih-tön); *important* —,
iao'-z 要事; da-z' 大事; *that's
my* — (in anger), dæn'-ming ngô
但 憑° 我

AFFECT, *to influence*, ken' -dong
感 動; kyih'-dong 激 動; —
*to be a scholar*, kô'-s-veng 假° 斯
文; — *to be wise, but thus betray folly*, long-ky'iao'-fæn-cih'
弄 巧 反 拙

AFFECTION *for equals, or infer-
iors*, æ'-sih 愛 惜; — *for superiors*, æ'-kying 愛 敬; *having
great* —, (or affectionate), æ'-
sing djong 愛 心 重; ts'ing-
gying' 親 近; *warm* —, æ'-sing
nyih' 愛心熱; *filial* —, hyiao'
sing 孝 心

AFFINITY, *natural* t'in sing'siang-
lin' 天 性 相 連

AFFIX *to a word*, dang-kyiah'-go
z-ngæn' 宕 脚 个° 字 眼°

AFFLICT, *to* næn 難; næn-næn;
mo-næn' 磨 難; *Heaven afflicts*,

t'in kông tsæ' 天 降° 災; t'in
kông'-loh kw'u'-næn 天 降° 落
苦 難

AFFLICTED, *to be* —, ziu næn'受
難; tsao'-djoh tsæ-næn' 遭着°
災 難; *greatly* —, kw'u'-sah-de
苦 煞 了°; kw'u ky'üoh'-feh-
ko'-de 苦 吃° 弗 過 了°

AFFLICTION, wæn'-næn 患 難;
kw'u'- næn 苦 難; tsæ - næn'
災 難

AFFORD, *can you* — *to buy it?* ng
yiu lih-liang' hao ma' feh 你°
有力量好買° 否°? *I can*
— *it*, ngô hao' ma 我 好 買°;
ngô dong-din' yiu' 我銅錢°有;
*can't* — *to buy*, ma'-feh-ky'i' 買°
弗 起; c'ih'-feh-ky'i' 出 弗 起;
*can't* — ( such expense), lih-
liang' tông-feh-djü' 力量當弗
住; ky'üoh'-feh-loh' 吃° 弗 落

AFFRONT, *to* teh'-ze 得 罪; *to* —
*a person* (by speaking of what he
is jealous of), væn-nying-kô'-go
gyi' 犯 人° 家° 个° 忌; — *unintentionally*, ngwu-væn' 誤 犯

AFFRONTED, kwa'- tih - de 怪°
的 了°

AFLOAT *on the sea*, læ hæ'-li p'iao-
dông' 在°海裡 飄蕩; *floating*,
vu'-tih 浮° 的

AFOOT, *come* bu-'ang' læ 步行°
來; tseo'-leh læ 走得°來

AFRAID, p'ô'-go 怕 个°; læ-tih
p'ô'正在°怕; *don't be* —, hao-
vong p'ô' 不° 用° 怕; feh-dzæ-

wu 弗° 礙 事°; *nothing to be —
of*, ts'-wô lao'-hwu 紙畫老虎
*lit., only a pictured tiger.*

AFTER, 'eo 後; 'eo-deo 後頭;
'eo-læ 後來; yi 'eo 以後; —
*ages,* 'eo'-shü' 後世; — (*you*)
*have finished* (*you*) *can go,* wun-
kong-ts, hao ky'i' 完工了°好°
去°; *after this* (or *that*), dzong-
ts''-ts-'eo' 從此之後; — *this
time,* dzong-kying'-yi-'eo' 從今
以後; ky'i-kó'; — *a month,* ih-
yüih'-ts' 'eo' 一月之後; *come
—* (me), (*i. e.* subsequently), ze-
'eo' læ 隨後來; — *all,* kyin-
kying 究竟; kyiu'-kyiu-kwe-
nyün' 九九歸原

AFTER-BIRTH, pao 胞; pao-i'
胞衣

AFTERNOON, 'ó'-pun-nyih 下°半
日°; tsiu'-ko-'eo' 晝過後; wu'-
'eo 午後; 'ó'-wu 下°午

AGAIN, tsæ 再; yi 又°; djong 重;
*do* (it) —, tsæ' tso 再做; *say*
(it) —, tsæ' wô 再話; *over and
over —,* tsæ'-sæn-tsæ-s' 再三再
四; ih'-r-tsæ', tsæ-r-sæn' 一而
再再而三

AGAINST *me,* teng ngô' tsoh-te' 與°
我作對; *leaning or resting —,*
gæ 戲; gæ'-djoh 戲着°; k'ao'-
djoh 靠着°; *leaning — the wall,*
gæ'-leh ziang' 戲於°墻; *ditto,*
(as a picture), ziang-li hyih-tih;
*touch or strike —,* bang 撞°;
bang-djoh 撞°着°; *brush or rub*

—, ts'ah 擦; ts'ah'-djoh 擦着°;
*the varnish is tender,* (*i. e.* fresh)
*must not rub —* (it), ts'ih neng-
neng'-tih feh k'o ts'ah'-djoh 漆
嫩嫩的弗可擦着°; — *rea-
son,* feh-'eh' ü-li' 弗合乎理;
ü-li' feh-vu' 乎理弗符; —
*the wind,* teo' fong 對風

AGAR-AGAR, hæ'-ts'æ 海菜; zih-
hwô'-ts'ao' 石花草

AGE, nyin-kyi' 年紀; *what is
your —?* (ordinary address), to-
siao' nyin-kyi' 多少年紀?
(more respectful), kwe'-kang 貴
庚°? tseng-kang' 尊庚°? ng to-
siao' kwe'-kang 你°多少貴庚°?
*respectfully ask your lofty —?*
ts'ing' meng kao ziu' 請問°
高壽? *what is his —* (of a
child)? kyi shü' 幾歲°?

AGE, shü 世; *an —* (generation),
shü'-dæ 世代; *through endless
ages,* tao shü'-shü-dæ'-dæ 到世
世代代

AGED, lao 老; nyin-lao'-de 年
老了°; *an — person,* nyin-lao'-
go 年老个°; lao'-nyin nying
老年人°; lao'-dzing nying 老
成人°

AGENT, kying-siu' 經手; tông-
siu' 當手; kwun-tsiang' 管帳;
*to act as an — in selling another's
goods,* kyi'-ma 寄賣°

AGGRANDIZEMENT, *country's —,*
koh'-kô hying-wông' 國家興旺;

*only cares for self* 一, tsih′ iao zi′ hao′ 只要自°好

AGGRAVATE, *to* kô djong′ 加°重 long-leh yüih-fah′ djong′ 弄得° 越發重; *to provoke anger*, pih′-leh sang ky‘i′ 逼得°生氣

AGGREGATE, *the sum total*, tsong′-su 總數; gong 共; t‘ong′-gong 統共; gong-kyi′ 共計

AGGRESSOR, sin dong′-siu-go 先 動手个°; sin ‘ô′-siu-læ tang′-go 先下°手來打个°

AGHAST, hah′-sah 嚇煞; *stupefied with fear*, hah′-ngæ-de 嚇呆 了°; hah′-su-de 嚇酥了°; hah′-hweng-de 嚇惛了°

AGITATE, *to* dong 動; tang′-dong 打動; c‘oh′-dong 觸動; yiao-dong′ 搖動; 一 *the water*, kao′-dong shü 攪動水

AGITATED *by fear, &c.*, sing′ ling-ling′-dong 心懷懷動; 一 *by wind*, be fong′ yiao-dong′ 被風 搖動

AGO, *how long* 一? kyi nyin′ zin 幾年前°? *twenty years* 一, nyiæn nyin′ zin 廿年前°; *not long* 一, feh kyiu′ 弗久; feh yüu′ 弗遠; *long* 一, nyin-dæ′ yün′ 年代遠; dziang-kyiu′-de 長久了°

AGREE, *to* 一 *well together*, ‘eh-deo′ 合頭; te 對; vu 符; siang-nyi′ 相宜; ‘eh-nyi′ 合 宜; teo-deo′ 鬪頭; dô-kô′

siang-te′ 大°家°相對; deo-kyi′ 投機 (used of persons only); *to correspond*, te′-kying 對經; *can't* 一, p‘ing′-feh-long′ 摒弗攏; ‘eh-feh-long′ 合 弗攏; *the two reckonings* 一, liang′-p‘in tsiang, te′-go 兩篇 帳對个°; 一 *together to buy*, iah′-ding iao ma′ 約定要買; 一 *upon a day*, iah′-ding nyih-ts′ 約定日°子; *two parties* 一, liang′ siang dzing-nyün′ 兩相 情願

AGREEABLE *to*, ‘eh-nyi′ 合宜; ‘eh-sih′ 合式; *being in the sun is* 一, sa′ læ nyih-deo-li ‘eh-nyi′-go 曬在°日°頭裏合宜个°; 一 *person*, nying ‘o-ky‘i′-go 八° 和氣个°

AGREEMENT, iah 約 (ih-go); *written* 一 (in trade), nyi-tæn′ 議單; nyi-kyü′ 議據; *to make an* 一, iah′-hao 約好; iah′-jih 約實; wô-hao′ 話好; *to make a written* 一, lih iah′ 立約; sia nyi-tæn′ 寫°議單

AGRICULTURE, nong-z′ 農事 (veng); cong-din′ z-ken′ 種田 事幹

AGROUND, *to run* 一, koh 擱; koh-ts‘in′ 擱淺; *ditto, on sand*, ts‘in sô′ 淺沙; *ditto, on the mud*, ts‘in du′ 淺塗

AGUE, *fever and* 一, nyiah-dzih′ 瘧疾; ma-za′-bing 買柴°病;

fah-'en-nyih' 發寒熱; *tertian*
—, s'-nyih-bing' 四日°病; s'-
nyih-liang'-deo-pæn' 四日° 兩
頭班

AHEAD, læ zin-deo' 在° 前° 頭;
— *of me,* pi ngô' zông-zin' 比
我上前°

AID, *to* pông-dzu' 幫助; vu'-dzu
扶助; siang-pông' 相幫; pông-
ts'eng' 幫襯; — *with strength*
(*i. e.* in labor), dzu lih' 助力;
pông lih' 幫力; —*with money,*
dzu dzæ' 助財; — *the government with money,* dzu hyiang' 助
餉; *ditto, with militia,* dzu üong'
助勇

AIM, *take good* —, k'ô-ding' cing'-
deo tang' 撏° 定準頭打;
miao-deo' k'ô-leh cing' 苗頭
撏° 得準; — *high* (in life),
ts'-hyiang iao lih'-leh kao' 志
向要立得°高; *his* — *is to
excel,* gyi'- go ts'- hyiang du-
zông'-tsing 其°个志向圖
上進

AIR, ky'i 氣; *wind,* fong 風;
*the* — *we breathe,* yiang-ky'i' 陽
氣; seng-ky'i' 生氣; *in the* —,
k'ong' li 空裡; pun'-k'ong
cong 半空中; *birds fly in the*
—, tiao' yün-k'ong'-li fi' 鳥
在懸空裏飛

AIR, *to* t'eo-t'eo ky'i' 透透氣;
t'ong-t'ong fong' 通通風; —
*the room,* vông'-ts peh gyi t'eo-
t'eo ky'i' 房子俾° 其透透

氣; — *clothes in the sun,* i-zông'
sa'-sa gyi 衣裳° 曬° 曬°; *ditto
in the shade,* i-zông' lông-lông'
gyi 衣裳眼眼; — *or cool it,*
liang' ib-liang' 涼一涼

AIR-PUMP, hyih-ky'i'-c'ih-go kô-
sang' 吸氣出个傢° 生°

AIRS, *to put on* —, tsông-mo' tsoh-
yiang' 莊模作樣

ALACRITY, *to do with* —, kao-
hying' tso 高興做; dzing-nyün'
tso 情願做

ALARM, *in a state of* —, hah'-sah-
de 嚇° 煞了°; *must not* — *him,*
m-nao' peh gyi ziu-kying' 弗°
可° 俾° 其° 受驚; m-nao' peh
gyi ky'ih-boh' 弗° 可° 俾° 其°
吃° 嚇°

ALARMED, ky'ih-hoh'-de 吃° 嚇°
了°; *he seemed greatly* —, gyi
yiu kying-hwông' siang'-mao 其
有驚慌相貌

ALARMING *intelligence,* kying-
wông'-go sing'-sih 驚惶个°信
息; hyüong-veng' 凶聞

ALAS! 'æ 唉°! 'a'-yia 哎喲°!

ALBUMEN *in an egg,* dæn-bah' 蛋
白°; — *in hens' eggs,* kyi-ts'
ts'ing' 雞子青

ALCOHOL, *Chinese* siao-tsiu' 燒酒;
*pure ditto,* tsing-tih'- siao 真
滴燒

ALIKE, ih-yiang' 一樣; ih-sih'
一式; ih-seh' ih-yiang' 一色
一樣; t'ih'-seh-vu-r' 貼色無

二；— *in most things,* da dong' siao' yi 大同小異

ALIVE, weh'-go 活个°；— *or dead?* weh'-go si'-go 活个°死°个°？ *is he still* — ? gyi wa dzæ shü' feh 其還°在°世否°？ wa læ-tong' feh 還°在否°？ *he is still* —, wa dzæ' 還°在

ALL, long'-tsong 攏總；tu 都；ih'-gong 一共；ih-kæ' 一概；ih'-t'ong 一統；t'ong'-gong 統共；tu-kyi' 都計；— *men* (or everybody), cong'-nying 衆人°；*take out* — *the things,* tong-si' long'-tsong do-c'ih' 東西攏總拕出；tong-si' ih'-kæ do-c'ih' 東西一概拕出；— *the way,* ih-lu' 一路

ALLAY, *to untie,* ka 解°；— *pain,* ka t'ong' 解°痛；*to check,* ts 止；— *thirst,* ts k'eh' 止渴；— *anger,* sih ky'i' 息氣

ALLEGE, *to* wô-leh kyih'-jih 話得°砝實；*to* — *as an excuse,* ziæ'-k'eo wô 藉口話；tsia' tso yin-nyü' 借°做言語；— *a false reason,* t'oh kwu' 托故

ALLEGORY, nyü'-i 寓意；do-dön'-go pi'-fông 大°段个°比方

ALLEVIATE, *to* — *his burden,* ky'ing' gyi-go tæn'-deo 輕其°个°擔頭；*to* — *pain,* t'ong' ka-ka-bo'少°解°痛勢°；*pain will be alleviated,* t'ong' we siao-tin' 痛會少點；t'ong' we ky'üih'-tin 痛會缺點

ALLEY, *an* —, ih-da-long' 一堺°衕°

ALLIANCE, *to form a family* —, ding-ts'ing' 定親；*to form an* — *between countries,* lih-ming-iah' 立盟約

ALLOT, *to* — *to each his share,* tsiao'-kwu kyüing-feng' 照股均分；— *equally,* bing-feng' 平分；kyüing-feng' 均分

ALLOW, *to* cing 准；hyü 許；ing-jing' 應認；*I do not* — *him to go,* ngô feh cing' gyi ky'i' 我弗准其去°；feh hyü' gyi ky'i' 弗許其去°；— *him to do,* cing' gyi tso 准其做

ALLOWABLE, *proper,* tsoh'-hying 作興；k'o'-yi 可以；*not* —, feh hyü'-go 弗°許个°

ALLOY, *to* ts'æn-kô' 攙假°；ts'æn-'ô' 攙和

ALLUDE, *to* — *to,* di-gyih' 提及；di-ky'i' 提起；*to whom do you* — ? ng' sô di-gyih'-go z jü' 你所提及个°是誰°？

ALLURE, *to* yiu 誘；ying'-yiu 引誘；hong'-yiu 哄誘；— *him to gamble,* yiu gyi tu' 誘其賭

ALLUREMENT, *bait,* nyü-deo' 餌頭；*ditto (for birds),* me-deo' 媒頭；these are both used figuratively, in speaking of persons；thus, *by what* — *was* (he) *caught?* be soh-go nyü-deo' zông keo-go 被甚°麽°餌頭上鈎个°；be soh'-go me-deo'

tsing-long'-go 被甚°麼°媒頭
進籠个°

ALLUSION, *to make an unpleasant*
—, kông ing-wô' 講 陰 話;
k'ao-toh' 拷 聲°; toh lang-djü'
射 冷 鎚°

ALLY, te'-siu 對手; lin-siu' 連手
(ih-go)

ALMANAC, lih-jih' 曆°日; t'ong-
shü' 通書; wông-lih' 皇曆;
*Foh-kien* —, Kyin'-lih 建曆
(ih-peng)

ALMIGHTY, vu-sô'-peh-neng'無所
不能; djün-neng' 全能; yiang-
yiang' neng-keo' 樣樣能毅

ALMOND, 'ang'-nying 杏°仁°; *bit-*
*ter* —, kw'u' 'ang-nying 苦杏°
仁° (ih-lih)

ALMOST, ts'ô'-feh-to' 差弗多;
shü'-kyi-wu 庶幾乎; kyi-kyi'-
wu 幾幾乎; ts'ô-feh-læ'-ky'i
差弗來去°; ts'ô-fông'-feh-to
差仿弗多; siang-ky'ü'-peh
yün' 相去不遠

ALMS, *to give* —, pu'-s dong-din'
佈施°銅錢°; sô dzin' 砂錢°;
*to give* — *to people,* tsiu-tsi'
nying-kô' 賙濟人°家°

ALMS-GIVER, s'-cü 施主; *a great*
—, do s'-cü 大°施主

ALOES, lu-we' 蘆薈

ALOFT, læ zông-deo'在°上頭; *on*
*the mast,* læ we-ken' teng 在°桅°
杆上°

ALONE, doh-zi' 獨自°; doh-ih' 獨
—; *he is there* —, gyi doh-zi'

læ-kæn' 其°獨自°在°彼°;
*person* — *in the world,* kwu-sing'-
nying 孤身人°; tæn-sing'-nying
單身人°

ALONG *with,* ih-dong'一同; dong-
de' 同隊; *come* — *with me,* teng
ngô' ih-dong' ky'i 與°我一同
去°; teng ngô' jü-de' ky'i 與°我
聚隊去°

ALOUD, kao-sing' 高聲; hyiang'-
liang 響亮; *in ordinary tones,*
ze-k'eo' 隨口; *to read or study*
—, doh 讀; ze-k'eo' doh 隨口
讀; *to cry* —, k'oh 哭; *ditto,* (as
an infant) kyiao 叫

ALPACA, yü'-sô 羽紗; *figured*
—, hwô yü'-sô 花羽紗

ALPHABET, *letters of the* —, z-
meo' 字母

ALREADY, yi'-kying 巳經

ALSO, yi 又°; yia 也°; wa-yiu'
還 有; *there is* — *another teach-*
*er,* yi yiu' ih-we sin-sang' 又°
有一位先生°; wa-yiu' ih-
we 還°有一位; *you can come*
—, ng yia' hao læ 你°也°
好來

ALTAR, tsi'-dæn 祭壇

ALTER, *to* kæ 改; kæ'-ko 改過;
kæ'-wun 改換; keng-kæ' 更
改; kæ'-pin 改變; *should* —
*one character,* ih'-go z' iao kæ'
一个°字要改; — *this gar-*
*ment, by making smaller,* keh'
gyin i-zông' iao kæ'-siao' 這°件

衣裳°要改小; *cannot* —,
kæ'-feh-læ 改 弗 來

ALTERCATE, *to* tsang-zao' 相爭°

ALTERNATE, *to* — *with another
in performing*, ling'-leh tso' 輪
了° 做; diao-læ'-wun-ky'i tso'
調 來 換 去° 做; ling-læ'-ling-
ky'i tso' 輪 來 輪 去° 做;
diao-læ'-diao-ky'i tso' 調 來 調
去° 做

ALTERNATE, *on* — *days*, kah'
nyih 隔 日°; kæn' nyih 間 日°

ALTERNATE, *to act as an* —, tso
dæ-siu' 做 代 手

ALTERNATIVE, *to choose one of
two alternatives* (*i. e.* difficulties),
liang'-næn-ts cong kæn ih'-yiang
兩 難 之 中 揀 一 樣; *no* —,
vù tang'-sön 無 打 算; vù fah'-
ts 無 法 子; vu lu' k'o tseo'
無 路 可 走; vu kyi' k'o s' 無
計 可 施

ALTHOUGH, se-tsih' 雖 卽; se-
jün' 雖 然

ALTOGETHER, ih'-kæ 一 概; ih-
zi' 一 齊°; ih-tsong 一 總; 'o'-
jün 全°然°; jih-feng 十 分; —
*bad*, ih'-kæ wa' 一 概 孬°; —
*wrong*, 'o'-jün feh-te' 全°然°不
對; — *unable*, væn'-væn peh-
neng' 萬 萬 不 能

ALUM, ming-væn' 明 攀; bah-
væn' 白°攀

ALWAYS, z-djông' 時 常; peh'-
djông 不 常; djông-djông' 常
常; me'-djông 每 常; dziang-

t'ong' 長 通; coh'-kwun; — *been
so*, lao'-lao z-ka 回°回°如°此°;
lao' kwe-kyü 老 規 矩

AM is often understood; *I — going*,
(in parting), ngô ky'i'-de 我去°
了°; *I — here*, ngô' læ-tong'
我 在°此°; læ-tong' 在°此°;
*I — writing*, ngô' læ-tih sia' 我
現°在°寫

AMALGUM, *to apply a pewter* —,
dông' sih 盪 錫; zông' sih 上 錫

AMANUENSIS, dæ-sia'-go-nying 代
寫°个°人°; dæ-pih' 代 筆;
dæ-shü' 代 書; *copyist*, ts'ao-
sia'-go-nying 抄 寫°个°人°

AMASS, *to* te-tsih' 堆 積; te-tsih'-
jü-sæn' 堆 積 如 山

AMAZED, hyi-gyi'-sah-de 希 奇
煞 了°; *afraid*, kying-hyiæ'-de
驚 駭 了°

AMAZING, *wonderful*, hyi-gyi' 希
奇; gyi-tsæ' 奇 哉; c'ih-gyi'
出 奇

AMBASSADOR, ky'ing-ts'a' 欽 差

AMBER, hwu'-p'ah 琥 珀; *false*
—, mih-lah'-p'ah 蜜 蠟 珀;
— *beads*, hwu'-p'ah cü 琥 珀 珠

AMBIGUOUS, weh-dong' 活 動;
*obscure*, en'-dong-dong 暗 洞 洞;
— *words*, weh-dong'-go shih-wô'
活 動 个°說 話; *words having
double meaning*, sông-kwæn' shih-
wô' 雙 關 說 話

AMBITIOUS, *to be — of fame*, du
ming' 圖 名; — *of gain*, du li'

圖利；— *of false fame*, du hyü ming' 圖虛名

AMEN, üô'-meng 亞孟 (the English word transferred); *so be it*, dzing-sing'-sô-nyün' 誠心所願

AMEND, *to reform*, kæ-oh'-dzong-jün' 改惡從善; kæ'-ko-tso nying' 改過做人°

AMETHYST, kæn-pao'-zah 藍寶石°

AMIABLE, sing'-dzing 'o-nyün' 性情和輭

AMICABLE, 'o-moh' 和睦; siang-æ' 相愛

AMID, cong-nyiang' 中央°

AMISS, ts'o 錯; dzæn 綻; *to speak* —, kông' ts'o 講°錯; kông' dzæn 講°綻

AMMUNITION, ho'-yiah-dæn-ts' 火藥彈子

AMNESTY, eng-sô' 恩赦°; eng-tsiao' 恩詔; — *from the emperor*, wông-eng'-da-sô' 皇恩大赦°

AMONG *them*, dzæ-ne' 在內; dzæ-gyi-cong' 在其中; dzæ-dziang' 在塲; *he also was — them*, gyi yia' dzæ-ne' 其也°在內; ne is also pronounced nen.

AMOUNT, ih-gong' 一共; t'ong'-gong 統共; tsong'-gong 總共; gong'-kyi 共計; tsong'-kyih 總揭; tsong'-su 總數; *what is the* —? ih-gong' to-siao' 一共多少?

AMPLE, *abundant*, ts'iah'-ts'iah yiu'-yü 綽綽有餘

AMPUTATE, *to* tsæn-dön'; kah'-dön 割斷; *to saw off*, ka'-loh 鋸°落

AMULET, bih-zia'-go vu' 辟邪°个°符; wu-sing' vu 護身符; *a silver lock hung about the neck of delicate children to prevent death*, 'ông'-so 項鎖. See CHARM.

AMUSE, *to* — *one's self*, hyi'-hyi 嬉戲; *ditto* (by walking about, &c.), bah-siang' 白相; *ditto* (by drinking, &c.), tsoh-tsoh-loh' 作作樂; — *him* (*i. e.* a child, primarily by deceiving), hong-hong' gyi 哄哄其; *to divert one's mind*, sæn sing' 散心

AMUSED, *pleased*, k'æ-sing'-tih-de 開心的了°

ANALYSIS, *chemical* hwô'-yüoh 化學

ANALYZE, *to* feng-ts'ing' 分清; — *a subject*, p'o' di 破題; — *chemically*, feng-k'æ' peng'-tsih 分開本質; — (as an essay), me moh' feng-ts'ing' 眉目分清; — *logically*, kyiu' gyi peng'-nyün 究其本原

ANARCHY, liao-lön' z-t'i' 繚亂事體; *a time of* —, lön' feng'-feng z-shü' 亂紛紛時世

ANATOMY, *science of the human body*, djün-t'i'-sing-leng' 全體新論; *bones, joints and internal* organs, kweh'-tsih-dzông-fu' 骨節臟腑

ANCESTORS, tsu'-tsong 祖宗; tsu'-sin 祖先; tsu'-zông 祖上

ANCHOR, mao 錨 (ih-meng); to cast —, p'ao mao' 抛錨; to drag —, yin mao' 拽錨; to weigh —, ky'i mao' 起錨

ANCHORAGE, p'ao mao'- go-di'- fông 抛錨个°地方

ANCIENT, kwu 古; — times, kwu- z-tsih' 古時節; men of — times, kwu-z-tsin' nying 古時節人°; tông-ts'u'-ts nying 當初之人°

AND, teng 與°; lin 連; you — I, ng' teng ngô' 你°與°我

ANECDOTE, kwu'-z 故事; tin 典; tell an —, kông ih'-go kwu'-z 講一個°故事; tell an amusing —, kông ih'- go siao'- wô 講一個°笑話

ANGEL, t'in-s' 天使; jing-s' 神使; t'in-jing' 天神

ANGER, ô'-wông; ông; ky'i 氣; nu 怒; to excite —, kyih nu' 激怒; excite him to —, long' gyi ô'-wông 弄其動°怒°; kyih gyi nu' 激其怒; appease —, sih nu' 息怒; ditto by confessing, making a feast, &c., siao-siao ky'i' 消消氣; nursing one's — (i. e. belly-full of — ), ih-du'-ts- ky'i 一肚之氣; eyes standing out with —, nu'-ngæn'-deh-tsin' 怒眼°凸皆°

ANGLE, an ih-koh' 一角°; acute —, tsin koh 尖角°; obtuse —, dzia koh' 斜°角°; right —, dzih koh' 直角°

ANGRY, ông'- de; fah-ông'- de; væn-ông'-de; fak-nao'-de 發惱了°; ô'-wông-de; sang-ky'i'-de 生°氣了°; fah-nu'-de 發怒了°; dong-nu'-de 動怒了°; læ- tih sang-ky'i' 正°在°生°氣; very —, long-do' fah-ông'; ky'i'- sah 氣煞; to grow suddenly — and rude, fæn'-loh min-k'ong' 變°面孔; ziang ts'a'-nying- lin'-ka 像搋°人°个°臉; — and cross, fông-tiao'-de 放刁了°; læ-tih s-sing' 正°在°使性

ANIMAL, cong-sang' 畜°生°; quad- rupeds, tseo'-siu 走獸; (horse, cow, ass) sang-k'eo' 牲°口; wild —, yia'-siu 野°獸; — food, hweng 'ô'-væn 葷下°飯; hweng- sing' 葷腥; to eat — food, ky'üoh hweng' 吃°葷; commence eating — food after abstaining, k'æ hweng' 開葷

ANIMATE, to — him, long' gyi weh-ky'i'-læ 弄其活起來; s'-tch gyi sing nyih' 使得其心熱°

ANISE, star we-hyiang' 茴香; pah koh' 八角°

ANKLE, kyiah'-tsang 脚踭°; kyiah'-bu-lu-den' 脚蒲蘆頭°; — joint, kyiah'-gao 脚餃°

ANNALS, koh'-s 國史; *historical compilations*, kông-kæn' 綱鑑'; — *of the dynasties*, lih-dæ s'-kyi 歷代史記

ANNEX, *to* djoh-zông' 續上; pu'-zông 補上; djoh-pu' 續補; djoh-tseng' 續增

ANNIHILATE, *to* mih-wnn' 滅完; mih ken-zing' 滅乾凈; siao-mih'-wnn 消滅完

ANNOUNCE, *to* pao 報; cü-we' 知會; — *it*, pao' ih-sing 報一聲; *to inform*, t'ong-cü' 通知; t'ong-pao' 通報

ANNOY, *to* væn-nao' 煩惱; tsi-tseo' 嘈° 啁; lo'-so 囉唆

ANNOYED, feh næ'-væn 弗耐煩; væn-nao'-go 煩惱个°; *excessively* —, væn-nao'-sah-de' 煩惱煞了°

ANNUALLY, nyin-nyin' 年年; me'-nyin 每年; djoh-nyin' 逐年; lih-nyin' 歷年

ANNUL, *to* fi 廢; fi'-diao 廢了°

ANOINT, *to* fu-yiu' 傅油; djô-yiu' 搽油; fi-dzông' 非常

ANOMALOUS, gyi-c'ih'-kwu-kwa 奇出古怪°

ANONYMOUS, feh-c'ih'-ming-go 弗出名个°; — *defamatory placard*, ǔ-deo'-pông 無° 頭榜; vu-ming'-kyih'-t'iah 無名揭帖°

ANOTHER, bih'-go 別个°; ling-nga' ih-go 另外°一个°; —

*man*, bih' nying 別人°; *have* —, wa-yiu' ih'-go 還°有一个°; ling-yiu' ih-go 另有一个°; *come again* — *day*, kæ' nyih tsæ' læ 改日°再來; *love one* —, pe'-ts' siang-æ' 彼此相愛; dô-kô' siang-æ' 大°家°相愛

ANSWER, *to* ing 應; ing'-tah 應答; tah'-ing' 答應; — (*more at length*), we-tah' 回答; tah, *also pron.* teh; — *back* (*as when reproved*), ing-cü' 應嘴; *will it* — *or not?* hao'-s-teh feh 好使得否°? *will it* — (*your*) *idea or purpose?* 'eh-i' feh 合意否°

ANSWER, *question and* —, ih-meng' ih-tah' 一問°一答; *verbal* —, we-ing' 回音; *written* —, we-sing' 回信

ANT, wun-hwun' 螻°蟻° (ih-go)

ANTAGONIST, te'-dih 對敵; — *in a game*, dih-siu' 敵手

ANTENNÆ, *of insects*, djong-su' 蟲鬚

ANTICIPATE *pleasure*, siang hying' 想興頭; *not as I anticipated*, peh c'ih' ngô sô liao'-go 不出我所料个°; *did not* —, liao-feh-tao' 料弗到; — *difficulty*, yü-sin' liao' yiu næn-c'ü' 預先料有難處; *you* — *my wishes*, ng sin' teh'-djoh ngô' sing-i' 你先得着°我心意; — *his wishes*, ts'e-djoh' gyi sing-siang' 猜着°其心想; — *and hardly able to wait,* tsông-leh mi'-dao teng'.

ANTIDOTE, (medicine), ka-doh'-go yiah 解°毒个°藥; — *for all poisons,* ka-pah'-doh 解°百°毒

ANTIPATHY, *to have an — to,* gyi 忌; *I have a great — to spiders,* kyih-cü' ting væn ngô' gyi' go 蛣蛛頂犯我忌个°

ANTIQUARY, *one versed in antiquities,* poh-kwu'-go cü'-kwu 博古个°人°; *one fond of antiquities,* æ kwu tong'-go nying 愛古董个°人°

ANTIQUES, kwu'-ky'i 古器; kwu'-tong-wæn'-ky'i 古董玩°器; kwu'-ho 古貨

ANTIQUITY, *times of —,* zông-kwu' z-'eo 上古時候; *of great —,* t'a' kwu 太°古

ANTITHESIS, te'-kyü 對句

ANVIL, t'ih-tsing-den' 鐵槌°頭°; t'ih'-teng'-deo 鐵磴頭

ANXIOUS, *to be —,* tæn-sing-z' 擔心事; iu-li' 憂慮; fông'-sing-feh-loh' 放心弗落'; kwô'-nyiæn 罣念; kyi'-kwô 記罣; *I am — about him,* ngô' dæ gyi iu-li' 我代其憂慮; *don't be too —,* peh pih ko' li 不必過慮; *tired of waiting,* sing'-tsiao 心焦

ANY, *have you — ?* ng yiu' feh 你°有否°? *not —,* m'-teh 沒°有°; *has — one been here ?* yiu soh'-go nying læ-ko' 有甚°麼°人°來過?

ANYTHING, soh'-go or soh'-si 甚°麼°; *do you want — ?* ng iao soh'-si 你°要甚麼? (better to say to a stranger), soh'-go z-ken, or soh' ken 甚°麼°事幹? 'o-ken' 何幹? *I do not want —,* ngô feh iao' soh'-si 我弗要甚°麼°

APART, zi kwun' zi 自°管自°; koh' zi feng-k'æ' 各自°分開; li-k'æ'-liao 離開了; *sit —,* zi kwun' zi zo' 自°管自°坐°; *place* (them) *a little —,* fông'-leh k'æ'-tin 放得°開點; *to pull —,* te'-k'æ 觖開; *ditto with the fingers,* p'ah'-k'æ 擘開

APATHETIC, moh 木; moh-hying-hying'

APE, See MONKEY.

APEX, ting-den' 頂頭°; nao'-tsin 腦尖

APIECE, *how many cash — ?* kyi'-go dong-din ih'-go 幾個°銅錢°一个°? *three cash —,* sæn'-go dong-din ih'-go 三个°銅錢°一个°; *give them a dollar —,* me' nying coh gyi ih-kw'e' fæn-ping' 每人°給°其°一塊番餅; kyin' nying peh gyi ih-kw'e' fæn-ping' 見人°給°其°一塊番餅

APOLOGIZE, *to —* be feh-z' 賠弗是; be li' 賠禮; shü ze' 請°罪; shü ih-go ze' 請°一个°罪

APOLOGY, *to make an —*, be ih′-go feh-z′ 賠 一 个° 弗 是; be ih-go li′ 賠 一 个° 禮

APOSTASY, be-kyiao′ 背° 敎

APOSTATE, be-kyiao′-go nying 背° 敎 个° 人°

APOSTLE, s′-du 使 徒

APOTHECARY, yiah-tin′-kwun 藥 店 夥; k′æ-yiah-tin′-go 開 藥 店 个°

APPARATUS, ky′i′-gyü 器 具; *philosophical —*, keh-veh′-go ky′i′-gyü 格 物 个° 器 具

APPARENT, hyin′-jün 顯然; hyin′-r-yi-kyin′ 顯 而 易 見; hyin′-kyin 顯 見

APPARENTLY *is so*, siang-mao z′-ka 相 貌 如° 此°; —, *but not really*, z-z′-r-fi′ 似 是 而 非

APPARITION, *to see a ghost*, kyin kyü′ 見 鬼°; *any strange sight*, gyi-ying′-kwæ′-ziang 奇 形 怪 狀°; iao-kwa′ 妖 怪°; tsing-kwa′ 精 怪°

APPEAL *to a superior*, ŵông-zông′ su′ 往 上 訴; — *to any one to remove an accusation*, gyiu sing shih′ 求 伸 雪; gyiu sing ün′ 求 伸 寃

APPEAR, *to be manifest*, yin-c′ih′-læ 現 出 來; hyin′-yin 顯現; *very like a man*, tsing′-ziang ih-go nying′ 正 像 一 个° 人°; *this appears larger*, p′e-mo′ ziang keh ih′-go do′ 胚 模 像 這° 一

個° 大°; — (*as a deity*), hyin-sing′ 顯 聖

APPEARANCE, siang′-mao 相 貌; p′e-mo′ 胚 模; kwông-kying′ 光 景; *wears a suspicious —*, ying-tsih′ k′o nyi′ 形 跡 可 疑; *miserably poor* — (*used of persons*), pe-pe′ go siang′-mao 臾 臾 个° 相 貌; *has the* — (*or appears to be*), dzing-ying′ 情 形; *fearful* —, ying-shü′ 形 勢

APPEASE, *to — anger*, sih nu′ 息 怒; *ditto by owning one's fault, &c.*, siao ky′i′ 消 氣

APPEND, *to attach* (*as by a string*), kyih 結; kyih′-zông 結上; — *at the end*, dzoh 續; dzoh-zông′ 續上; *to add to*, pu-ts′eo′ 補 湊

APPENDIX (*to a book*), pu-yi′ 補 遺; dzoh-tsæ′-go shih-wô′ 續 載 个° 說 話; — *to a writing*, tsæ′-p′i 再 批

APPERTAIN, *to — to*, joh-ü′ 屬于; dzæ′-ü 在 于

APPETITE, (*good or bad*) we-k′eo′ 胃 口; — (*great or small*) zih-liang′ 食 量; *good —*, k′æ-we′ 開 胃; *no —*, we-k′eo′ feh k′æ′ 胃 口 弗 開

APPLAUD, *to — with a cheer*, heh-ts′æ′ 喝采; *to praise*, ts′ing-tsæn′ 稱 讚; peo-tsiang′ 襃 獎

APPLE, *a large —*, bing-ko′ 蘋果; *small yellow — with red tinge*, hwô-′ong′ 花 紅. There is no generic term for apples.

APPLICABLE, 'eh-djoh' 合著°; siang-vu' 相符;— to everybody, koh-nying siang-vu' 各人°相符; not — to him, ü gyi' feh vu' 與其弗符; teng gyi' feh 'eh' 與°其弗合

APPLICATION, export c'ih' k'eo pao'-tæn 出口報單; import —, tsing' k'eo pao'-tæn 進口報單

APPLY, to have recourse to, deo 投; — to the customs, pao kwæn' 報關;— to the local constable, deo di-pao' ky'i' 投地保去°;— to the clergyman, deo-tao kyiao'-s di'-fòng 投到敎師地方; — the mind, cün-r'-cü'-ts 專而致°之; cün-sing' 專心

APPOINT, to ming 命; to settle upon, ding 定; who was appointed to go? ming jü' ky'i 命誰°去°? ding jü' ky'i 定誰°去°? — (to each his duties), feng-p'a' 分派°; — a day, ding ih-go nyih-ts' 定一个°日°子; ditto (in the future), ding ih-go gyi' 定一个°期

APPOINTED, time not yet — , vi'-ding gyi' 未定期; who was — to go? ming jü' ky'i 命誰°去°? I was — to come, ngô z vong-ming'-r-kæ'-go 我是奉命而來个°; — by an officer, vong' kwnn'-go ming 奉官个°命; vong-hyin'-go 奉憲个°;— by the emperor, vong-ts'-go 奉旨个°

APPOINTMENT, ming 命; who receives that — ? jü' ziu keh-go ming' ni 誰°受這°个°命呢? a good —, hao' ts'a-s' 好差°使

APPOSITE, 'eh-shing'-go 合榫个°; siang-'eh'-go 相合个°

APPRECIATE, to k'en'-tao 看到; k'en'-tao-kô 看到家°; do not — (it), k'en'-feh-tao-kô 看弗到家°; — fully, k'en'-t'ong-t'eo' 看通透; ts'ih'-ti k'en 澈底看

APPREHEND, to seize, k'ô 拿°; gying 搿; to understand, ming-bah' 明白°; hyiao'-teh 曉得; tong 懂

APPRENTICE, du-di' 徒弟 (ih-go); to be an —, deo s-vu' 投師父; to — lán, peh gyi tso du-di' ky'i 俾°其做徒弟去°; peh gyi 'oh du-di'.

APPROACH, to gying'-long 近攏; — (as a person), tseo'-long-læ 走攏來; gying-sing' 近身; he fears to —, gyi p'ó' gying'-long 其怕近攏; the time approaches, z-'eo' gying'-long læ-de 時候近攏來了°

APPROBATION, cong'-i 中意; jü i' 如意; has my —, jü ngô'-go i' 如我个°意; 'eh ngô' sing-i' 合我心意

APPROPRIATE, to — to one's self, and deny it, la-meh' 賴°沒; ky'üoh'-meh 吃°沒

APRICOT, 'ang'-ts 杏°子 (ih-go)

APRON, (Chinese) *man's* —, yü-pu' 圍°布; *ditto* (*like a skirt*), yü-gyüing' 圍°裙; tsoh'-gyüing 作裙; (Chinese) *woman's large* —, yü-sing-pu'-læn' 圍°身布襴

APT *to learn*, ih-kao' ziu we' 一教°就°會; — *to get angry*, yüong-yi' sang-ky'i' 容易生氣

AQUEDUCT, tsih'-shü-kwun 接水°管°

ARBITRARY, z-yi'-we-z' 自以爲是

ARBOR, liang-bang' 涼棚°; *grape* —, ts'-bu-dao bang' 紫葡萄°棚 (ih-go)

ARBUTUS, *tree-strawberry*, yiang-me' 楊梅

ARCH, gwæn-dong' 環°洞

ARCHED *window*, gwæn-dong' ts'ông 環°洞牕; — *bridge*, gwæn-dong' gyiao 環°洞橋

ARCHER, kong-tsin'-siu 弓箭手

ARCHERY, kong-tsin'-gyi-nyi' 弓箭技藝

ARCHITECT, *head mechanic*, ziang-deo' 匠頭; tsoh'-deo 作頭 The Chinese here have no architect proper.

ARCHIVES, *the place for the* —, koh'-s-kwun 國史館; *the records as just written*, jih-loh' 實錄; *ditto when revised*, kông-kæn'-li tsæ-loh'-go.

ARDENT, nyih-sing' 熱°心

ARDUOUS, sing-k'wu' 辛苦; lao-loh' 勞碌; dziah-lih' 着力

ARE *is generally unexpressed*; *where* — *you?* ng' læ ah-li' 你在°何°處°? *we* — *here*, ah-lah læ-tong' 我°等°在°此°; — *there any?* yiu' m̂-teh 有沒°有°?

AREA, di-dziang' 地塲; *what is the* — *of China?* Cong-koh' di-dziang' yiu dza do' 中國地方°有怎°樣°大°?

ARGUE, *to dispute*, bin'-leng 辨論; *to reason*, nyi-leng' 議論

ARID, *dry*, ken-sao' 乾燥; *parched with the sun*, sa'-sao-de 曬°燥了°

ARISE, *to* bô-ky'i' 爬起; ky'i'-læ 起來

ARISTOCRACY, hyiang-sing' 鄉紳; sing-kying' 紳矜

ARITHMETIC, sön'-yüoh 算學; *rules of* —, sön'-fah 算法

ARM, siu'-kwang 臂°膊° (ih-tsah)

ARMLET, *glass* liao siu'-gyüoh 料手鐲

ARM-PIT, kah'-ts-'ô 腋° 下°

ARMOR, kw'e-kah' 盔甲°

ARMORY, kyüing-gyüoh' 軍局 (ih-zo)

ARMS, (clubs and spears, but not cannon), ky'i'-yiæ 器械°

ARMY, *soldiers*, ping-mô' 兵馬; *to raise an* —, ky'i-ping' 起兵; fah-ping' 發兵

AROMATIC *taste*, lah-ho-ho' mi'-dao 辣阿阿昧°道

AROUND, tsiu-we' 周圍; dön

ky'ün' 團圈; *walk once* —, tsiu-
we' tseo ih'-cün 周圍走一轉;
*all* —, s'-dön-lön'-ky'ün (or s'
deh, &c.), 四圈䢵圈; *walk* —,
d ön-ky'ün' tseo-tæn'-cün 團圈
走轉

AROUSE, *to awaken*, long su'-sing
弄蘇醒; eo diao'-kao'叫°覺°;
— *by reminding of duty*, di-sing'
提醒

ARRAIGN, *to* — *a person*, ta nying'
læ sing'-meng 帶°人°來審問°;
di nying' læ 提人°來

ARRANGE, *to* tsing 整; pa 擺°;
tsing'-teng 整頓; *to* — *properly*, pa' tön-tsing' 擺°端正; —
*in succession*, tsiao ts''-jü tsing'-
tsing hao 照次序整整好;
— *regularly*, tsing tæn'-zi 整
齊°; — *tastefully* (as household
articles), pa'-leh teh-fah' 擺°得°
得法; — (things that have
been displaced), siu-jih'-ko* 收
拾過; — *affairs*, z-ken' en-ba'
hao 事幹安排°好; — *in battle
array*, pa dzing-shü' 擺°陣勢

\* This also means to gather up and
take away, as dishes after eating.

ARREST, *to seize*, k'ô 拿°; k'ô'-
djoh 拿着°; *to stop*, ts'-djü
止住; *to bring a warrant for*
—, ying ba' k'ô nying' 行牌°
拿°人°

ARRIVE, *to* tao 到; *when did you*
—? ng' kyi'-z tao'-go 你°幾時
到个°?

ARROGANT, ngæn'-ka-do' 眼°界°
大°; zi-tseng'-zi-do' 自°尊自°
大°; k'en'-nying'-feh-ky'i° 看
人°弗起

ARROW, tsin 箭 (ih-ts)

ARROW-ROOT, *native* ngeo'-feng
藕粉

ARSENAL *for storage*,kyüing-kong'-
tsong'-gyüoh 軍工總局; —
*for manufacture*, cü'-dzao-gyüoh'
製造局

ARSENIC, p'i-sông' 砒礵; sing'-
zah 信石°

ART, *the* fah'-ts 法子; fông-fah'
方法; *the* — *of bread-making*,
tso mun-deo' go fah'-ts 做饅頭
个°法子

ARTS, gyi-nyi' 技藝; siu'-nyi
手藝; *the six Chinese* —, loh
nyi' 六藝; *viz., etiquette*, li 禮;
*music*, yüoh 樂;*archery*, ziæ 射;
*trades*, nyü 御; *literature*, shü
書; *mathematics*, su 數; *the
hundred* —, pah'-kong-gyi-nyi'
百°工技藝

ARTERIES, hyüih'-mah-kwun 血
脈管; — *and veins*, hyüih'-
kwun 血管; we hyüih'-kwun
迴血管

ARTFUL, diao-bi'; kæn-tsô' 奸°
詐; kwe'-kyi to'-tön 詭計
多端

ARTICLE, *a clause*, or *rule*, ih-diao'
一條; ih-kw'un 一款; ih-'ông'
一項; *an* — (of goods) ih-
gyin' 一件; ih-yiang' 一樣;

the articles *a* or *an* are expressed by classifiers, thus, *a teacher*,
ih-we′ sin-sang 一 位 先 生°;
*an ox*, ih-deo′ yüong-ngeo′ 一
隻° 雄 牛°

ARTICULATION, *distinct* k′eo′-ts′
ts′ing-t′ong′ 口 齒 清 通

ARTIFICE, *trick*, tsô′-kyi 詐 計

ARTIFICIAL, *made by man*, nying
tso′-c′ih-læ-go 人°做 出 來 个°

ARTILLERY, *cannon*, do-p′ao′ 大°
礮; — *men*, p′ao′-sin 礮 手

ARTISAN, s-vu′ 司 務; s-vu′ ziang-
nying 司 務 匠°人°; ziang 匠°

ARTIST, *one who paints pictures*,
tæn-ts′ing′ sin′-sang 丹 青 先 生°

ARTLESS, ve′-tsông-kô′-go 弗°會°
裝 假′个°; *true*, tsing-dzing′-
jih-i′ 眞 情 實 意

As, *for example, like*, or *as if*, hao′-
ziang 好 像; tsing′-ziang 正
像; — *you say*, tsiao ng′ sô wô′
照 你°所 話; — *you please*, ze
ng′ 隨 你°; ze ng′ bin′ 隨 你°
便; ze-bin′ ng 隨 便 你°; —
*much as you please*, ze ng′ to-
siao′ 隨 你°多 少; — *I walked
along*, ngô tseo′-ko z-′eo′ 我 走
過 時 候; — *good — you*, ziang
ng′ ka kwun hao′ 像 你°這°
般 好; *do just — I tell you*,
ngô′ wô dza tso′, ng dza tso′ 我
話 怎 做 你°怎°做; ngô
wô, ih′-z-ih′, wô, nyi′-z-nyi′ 我
話 一 是 一 話 二°是 二°; —
*before*, dzing-gyiu′ 仍 舊; i-

gyiu′ 依 舊; dzing-voh′ 仍 復;
— *usual*, tsiao′ djông 照 常;
tsiao wông′-z 照 往 時; tsiao
′æn-tsao′-ts; *a ball — large —
an egg*, ziang kyi-dæn′, ka kwun
do ih-dön′ 像 鷄 蛋 一 樣 大°
一 團

ASAFŒTIDA, a′-we 阿°魏

ASCEND, *to* sing-zông′ 升 上; —
*by walking*, tseo′-zông 走 上

ASCERTAIN, *to — by inquiry*, meng
dziah′-jih 問°著 實; tang′-
t′ing ming-bah′ 打 聽 明 白°;
*to know certainly*, hyiao′-teh
dziah′-jih 曉 得 着 實

ASCRIBE, *to* kwe-ü′ 歸 于; kwe-
peh′ 歸 與; — *glory to God*,
kwe yüong-wô′ ü Jing-ming′ 歸
榮 華 于 神 明; — *merit to
another*, kwe kong′ ü nying′ 歸
功 于 人°; — *blame to him*, kwe
ze′ ü gyi′ 歸 罪 于 其

ASHAMED, wông-k′ong′ 惶 恐;
dzæn-gwe′ 慚 愧; *slightly —*,
feh-′hao′-i′-s 弗 好 意 思;
næn we′-dzing 難 爲 情; wông-
gwe′ 惶 愧; bao′-ky′in 抱 歉;
weh′-la-siang; weh′-la-tsi-tsi;
*are you not —*? ng yiu feh-hao′-
i′-s ma 你°有 弗 好 意 思
麼°? *you ought to be — of it*,
keh′z ng′ kæ wông-k′ong′-go 這°
是 你°該 惶 恐 个°; (I) *am
— to see you*, kyin ng-go min′
feh læ′ 見 你°个°面 弗 來; te′
ng feh djü′ 對 你°弗 住; *to feel*

—, kyüoh'-teh dzæn-gwe'-siang 覺得慚愧相; p'ô' wông-k'ong' 怕惶恐; — of his appearance (a scholar), 'en-sön'-siang 寒酸相

ASHES, hwe 灰; coal —, me-t'æn' hwe 煤炭灰; wood —, za hwe' 柴灰

ASHORE, læ-ngen-zông' 在°岸上; zông-ngen'-de 上岸了°

ASK, to meng 問°; — and see, meng-meng'-k'en 問°問°看;—indirectly, t'en'-meng-kyi'-k'en' 探探看; — a question, meng ih'-sing 問°一聲;—a favor, k'eng' ih-go dzing' 懇一个°情; t'ao' ih-go kwông' 叩一个°光;—for a cup of water, t'ao' ih-pe' shü' 討一杯水°;—about, bun-meng' 盤問°; — your pardon, ts'ing ng' nyün-liang' ngô 請你°原諒我; to invite, ts'ing 請;— of whom? hyiang' jü' meng 向°誰° 問°? — of me, dziao ngô' meng 向°我 問°; — a girl in marriage (in behalf of one's son or one's ward), gyiu ts'ing' 求親

ASKEW, dzin.

ASLANT, ts'ia or zia 斜°

ASLEEP, kw'eng'-joh-tih 睏°熟°的; foot —, kyiah mô-tseh'-long' 脚麻了°

ASPARAGUS, long-shü'-ts'æ 龍鬚菜 (Mandarin); in Ningpo it is called foreign bamboo, nga-koh' shing 外°國筍

ASPECT, siang'-mao 相貌; ying-yüong' 形容

ASPERITY of manner, oh'-cü-ñgæn-siang' 惡嘴眼°相; — of tone, k'eo'-ky'i zah-ngang' 口氣石° 硬°; p'eng-deo' 嗔頭

ASPIRE, to siang' kao-zông'-ky'i 想高上去°; can't — to union with, kao-p'æn'-feh-læ 高攀弗來 (polite).

ASS, an ih-p'ih li'-ts' 一匹驢子

ASSAIL, to — (in words), tô'-mô 唾°罵; — Confucianism, tô'-mô jü-kyiao' 唾°罵儒敎; to strike, dong'-siu tang' 動手打

ASSASSIN, ts''-k'ah 刺客

ASSASSINATE, to 'ang-ts' 行°刺; en'-di sah nying' 暗地殺人°

ASSAULT, to make the first —, sin long' 先弄; sin dong' siu 先動手

ASSEMBLE, to jü'-long 聚攏; jü'-jih 聚集; we-long' 會攏

ASSENT, to ing - yüing' 應允; tseng 遵; I — to your proposition, ngô' tseng ng'-go ming' 我遵你°个°命; tseng ming' 遵命

ASSERT, to ih-k'eo ngao'-ding 一口齩°定; gyin-k'eo' kyih'-jih 箝口硈實; — that one's self is in the right, tsang zi' yiu' li 爭自°有理; —(one's) rights, tsang yin' veng 爭°有分

ASSESS, to fix customs' tax, ding se' 定稅; estimate ditto, kwu se' 佑稅

ASSEVERATE, *to testify with an oath*, vah-tsiu', tso bing-kyü' 罰咒做憑據

ASSIDUITY, *with* gying-lih' 勤力; *to work with* —, cün-kong'-gyi-z' 專攻其事

ASSIGN, *to* — *duties*, *or employments*, feng-p'a' 'òng-tông' 分派行當; p'a sang-weh' 派生活; — *a day*, 'æn'-ding nyih-ts' 限定日子

ASSIMILATE, *to cause them to resemble*, s'-teh gyi-siang-ziang' 使得其相像; *dispositions gradually* —, sing'-dzing dzin'-'eh 性情漸合

ASSIST, *to* pông-dzu' 帮助; pông-ts'eng' 帮襯; vu'-dzu 輔助; siang-pông' 相帮; — *in managing affairs*, pông-bæn' 帮辦; — *her to her chair*, tông' gyi zông gyiao' 攙其上橋; — *him into the boat*, vu gyi' zông jün' 扶其上船

ASSISTANT, ¡ông-bæn'-go 帮辦个

ASSOCIATE, dong-dé' 同隊; de-ho' 隊夥; *friend*, beng-yiu' 朋友; — *in business*, dong-z' 同事; — *in school*, dong ts'ông 同牕

ASSOCIATE, *to* dong-bun' 同伴; — *in business*, gao-siu' 交手; — (*as friends*), kyih'-kyiao 結交; ts'eo-de' 湊隊; *I was associated with him three years*, ngô' teng gyi dong-bun' sæn nyin' 我

與其同伴三年; — *with the good, forsake the evil*, ts'ing' kyüing-ts', yün siao'-nying 親君子遠小人

ASSOCIATION *for relief of widows*, kwu-sông' we' 孤孀會; — *for giving coffins and medicine*, sô-zæ', s-yiah'-go we' 捨材施藥个會; — *for giving food*, cing'-tsi we' 賑濟會

ASSORT, *to* yiang-tang'-yiang feng k'æ' 樣樣分開; ih-le' ih-le' feng-k'æ' 一類一類分開

ASSUAGE, *to* ka 解; — *sorrow*, ka iu' 解憂; ka meng' 解悶; — *pain*, ka t'ong' 解痛

ASSUME *the liberty of doing*, jün'-cün 擅專; *to* — *another's power*, *or place*, dæ-công' gyün-ping' 代掌權柄; dæ-we'-jing-z' 代爲人事; dæ-we-liao-li' 代爲料理 (công is also pron. tsông).

ASSURANCE, *excess of boldness*, 'eo' ô-lin 厚丫臉; tæ' ô-lin' 默丫臉; si'-bi-la-lin' 死皮賴臉

ASSURE, *to* — *confidently*, kyih-kyih'-jih-jih' wô' 砝砝實實話; sah'-jih wô' 煞實話

ASSUREDLY, pih'-ding 必定; pih'-jün 必然

ASTHMA, hao-bing' 痿病

ASTONISH, *to* kying-hyiæ' 驚駭; *astonished to see* (*it*), ih k'en'-kyin ziu hyi-gyi'-sah-de 一看見就希奇煞了

ASTONISHING *progress* (in study),
ka kwʻaʻ-leh zông tao hyi-gyiʻ-go
習°學°得°快°倒希奇个ʼ

ASTRAY, *gone* tseoʻ tsʻo 走錯; mi-
luʻ-de 迷路了ʼ; tseo tsʻôʻ lu-de
走跤路了ʼ

ASTRIDE, gyi-môʻ-zo 騎馬坐°;
*ought not to sit — the chair*, ü-ts
feh kʻoʻ gyi-môʻ-zo 椅°子弗
可騎馬坐

ASTRINGENT *medicine*, siu-linʻ-go
yiah 收斂个°藥; ts-dzaʻ
yiahʻ 止瀉ʼ藥

ASTROLOGER, ba pahʻ-z cüʻ-kwu
排八字个°人ʼ; kʻen ngʻ-sing
sinʻ-sang 看五°星先生°; sönʻ-
ming sinʻ-sang 算命先生°

ASTRONOMER, tʻin-vengʻ-z 天文
士; *imperial* —, kyʻing-tʻinʻ-
kænʻ 欽天監°

ASTRONOMY, tʻin-vengʻ 天文

ASUNDER, dönʻ-kʻæ-de 斷開了°;
*broken* — (or in two), teʻ ao-
dön-de 對拗斷了°

ASYLUM, *foundling* yüoh - ingʻ-
dông 育嬰堂; — *for the aged*
(really for beggars), kwu-laoʻ-
yün 孤老院

AT, læ or dzæ 在°; — *home*, læ
ohʻ-li 在°家°裡; — *this place*,
læ-tongʻ 在°此°; — *that place*,
læ-kænʻ 在°彼°; — *Peking*,
dzæ Pohʻ-kying 在北京; —
*first*, kyʻi-tsʻuʻ 起初; *arrived*
— *the same time*, tsænʻ-zi tseoʻ-
tao 一齊走到; bingʻ-zi taoʻ

並齊°到; — *this* (or that)
*time*, kehʻ-go z-ʻeoʻ (or læ kehʻ-
go z-ʻeoʻ) 這°個°時候

ATHEIST, feh siangʻ-sing yiu Jing-
mingʻ-go nying 弗相信有神
明个°人ʼ; *the — needs only to
hear the thunder*, "feh singʻ Jing-
mingʻ, dæn tʻingʻ le singʼ" 弗信
神明但聽雷聲

ATLAS, di-duʻ-shü 地圖書
(ih-tsʻah)

ATMOSPHERE, tʻin-kyʻiʻ 天氣;
tʻin-kongʻ-ts-kyʻiʻ 天空之氣

ATOMS, *to divide into* —, fengʻ tao
dzih-siʻ-si 分到極ʼ細細

ATONE, *to* — *for sin*, joh zeʻ 贖
罪; cʻü-joh zeʻ 取贖罪

ATROCIOUS, *cruel*, hyüong-ohʻ 兇
惡; — *crime*, ze do ohʻ-gyih 罪
大惡極

ATTACH, *to* lin 連; lin-longʻ 連
攏; sang-longʻ 生°攏; *to append*, kyih 結

ATTACHED (as a friend, &c.),
lin-longʻ-liao 連攏了°; kao-
nyinʻ-go 膠°粘个°; tsʻih-tʻiah-
go 切貼°个°; tʻiahʻ-sing-go 貼°
身个°

ATTACK, *to* kong-tangʻ 攻打;
tang 打; *to make the first* —
(by striking), sin dongʻ-siu tangʻ
先動手打

ATTAIN, *to* — *one's object*, jü nyünʻ
tehʻ-djoh 如願得著; tsʻingʻ
sing jü iʻ 稱心如意; — *a
good position* (in any thing), tao-

leh hao'-go di-bu' 到得°好个°
地步; — the (Chinese) degree
of A. B., jih 'oh' 入學°; tsing
sin'-dzæ 進秀才; — the
(Chinese) degree of A. M., cong
kyü' nying 中舉人°; teng pông'
登榜; the last is used for any
high literary rank after cong kyü.

ATTEMPT, to try, s'-s-k'en 試試
看; make a trial or — , s-ih'-s
試一試; tso'-tso-k'en 做做看

ATTEND, to heed, yüong-sing' 用
心; liu-sing' 留心; tông-sing'
當心; —, to one's duties, kwu'-
djoh peng'-veng 顧著°本分°;
siu-veng' 守分; tso-veng-ne'-
ts-z' 做分內之事; en-veng'-
siu-kyi' 安分守己°; — the
sick, voh'-z bing-nying' 服事
病人°; tông-dzih' bing-nying'
當值病人°; — a funeral,
song-sông' ky'i 送喪去°; —
another's call, t'ing s'-hwun 聽
使喚

ATTENTION, to pay — to what is
said, liu-sing' t'ing' 留心聽;
yüong-sing' 用心; to pay no
— to the person addressing (i. e.
turn the nose to the wall), bih'
ts'ong' dziao ziang'.

ATTENTIVE, we yüong-sing' 會用
心; k'eng liu-sing' 肯留心;
—(to business), ¡.ô-dziang' 巴亟°

ATTRACT, to hyih'-ying 噏引

ATTRACTION, hyih'-lih 噏力;
hyih'-gying 噏勁

ATTRACTIVE, yiu hyih'-gying 有
噏勁; strongly — , do yiu hyih'-
gying 大°有噏°勁°; hyih'-gying
dza hao' 噏勁甚°好 (used
of persons only in a bad sense).

AUCTION, to sell goods by — , ma
kyiao'-ho 賣叫貨

AUDIENCE, large  ju  t'ing'-go
nying to' 聚聽个°人°多

AUNT, paternal kwu-mô' 姑母°;
maternal — , yi-mô' 姨母°

AUSPICIOUS, kyih'-li 吉利; —
day, nyih-ts' kyih'-li 日°子吉
利; — omen, kyih' ziao 吉兆

AUSTERE, strict, nyin-lah' 嚴辣

AUTHENTIC, k'ao'-leh-jih-go 靠
得°實个°

AUTHOR of a book, cü shü', lih
shih' go nying 著書立說个°
人°; — of a false report, ky'i
yiao-yin'cü-kwu 起謠言个°人°

AUTHORITY, gyün-ping' 權柄;
unjust use of — , gyün-shü' 權
勢; to have official — for doing,
kwun cing' li 'ang' 官准吏行°;
to use —, or threats in oppressing
another, yi shü', ky'i nying' 以
勢欺人°; tang-pô'-shii, long
nying -kô 打霸勢弄人°家°

AUTHORIZE, to  ming 命; — officially, we 委; kao-dæ' gyün-
ping' 交°代權柄

AUTHORIZED by a magistrate,
vong hyin' we' go 奉憲委个°;
has a certificate, yiu tsih'-tsiao
有執照

AUTUMN, Ts'iu-t'in' 秋天

AUXILIARY, pông-dzu'-go 帮助
个°;— troops, kyiu'-ping 救兵

AVAIL, to ts'ing 趁;— one's self
of the convenience, ts'ing bin' 趁
便;— myself of your going, to
send a letter, ts'ing ng'-go bin', ta
ih-fong sing' ky'i' 趁你°个°便
帶° 一封信去°;— one's self
of an opportunity, ts'ing kyi-we'
趁機會;— of this opportunity,
ts'ing'-ts' kyi-we' 趁此機會

AVARICIOUS, t'en-dzæ'-go 貪財
个°; extremely —, iao diu', feh
iao ming' 要錢°弗要命

AVENGE, to pao-dziu' 報讐;—
a brother's injury, pao hyiong-
di'-go dziu' 報兄弟个°讐;
sing-ün' 伸寃

AVENUE, do-lu' 大°路; kwun-
dông'-do-lu' 官塘大°路;
— within an inclosure, üong'-dao
甬道

AVERAGE, t'ong-ts'ô' 通扯;—
price, t'ong-ts'ô' 'ông'-dzing 通
扯行情

AVERSION, have an — to, in 厭;
tseng 憎; u 惡°; in'-tseng 厭
憎; I have an — to him (on
seeing), ngô ih-kyin' ziu tseng'
gyi 我一見就°憎其

AVOID, to bi 避; bi-ko 避過;
— danger, bi hyiu' 避險; to
hide from, to'-bi 躲避;— one's
creditors, to'-bi tsa'-cü 躲避
債°主

AWAIT, to teng'-'eo 等候; teng'-
dæ 等待;— that day, teng'-
dæ keh'-go nyih-ts' 等待這°
個°日°子

AWAKE, to su-sing 蘇醒; diao-
kao' 調覺°; sing 醒

AWAKENED by great noise, do
sing'-hyiang kying sn'-sing-go
大°聲響驚蘇醒个°

AWARD, to ding 定; tön 斷; p'un
判; ding-ding'-k'en 定定看

AWARDING just rewards or punishments, yiu-sông' yiu-vah'-go有
賞有罰个°; yiu en'-fông 有
安放

AWARE, to know, teh'-cü 得知;
hyiao'-teh 曉得; I was not —
(of it) beforehand, ngô yü'-sin
feh teh'-cü 我預先弗得知

AWAY, went — yesterday, zô-nyih'
ky'i'-de 昨°日°去°了°; take
—, do-ko' 挖過; to throw —,
k'ang'-diao 拋°了°; tiu-diao' 丟
去° or 丟了°; ô-diao 掘°了°;
ditto (as liquids), tao'-diao 倒
了°; go —, tseo'-k'æ 走開;
tseo'-ko 走過

AWE, filled with —, kying' we'
敬畏

AWFUL, k'o we'-go 可畏个°

AWKWARD, ao'-siu-ao'-kyiah;
ngang-ky'iang'-dao-bih 作°事°
硬°強°; stiff hands and feet,
ngang-siu'-ngang-kyiah' 硬手
硬腳

AWL, tsön-ts͘ or cün'-ts 鑽子 (ih-me)

AWNING, *to put up an* —, ts'ang tsiang'-bong 撐帳篷; *ditto over a court,* (for some special occasion), mun-t'in-tsiang' 幔天帳

AWRY, hwa 歪; dzin 斜°; *all* —, hwa-cü'-p'ih'-kyiah 歪嘴僻脚

AX, AXE, fu'-deo 斧頭 (ih-pô)

AXIOM, z-jün'-ts-li' 自然之理

AXLE, leng-gyüoh' 輪軸; leng-bun'-sing-ts' 輪盤心子

AZURE, t'in-læn'-seh 天藍色

# B

BABBLE, *senseless talk,* lön-shih'-diao-bin' 亂說ㄕ辮; wu-yin'-lön-dao' 胡言亂道

BABOON, keo-deo-weh-seng' 狗頭猢°孫

BABY, na-hwun' 嬰°孩° (ih-go)

BABYISH, na-hwun i'-tsi-ka 像°嬰°孩°樣°式°

BACHELOR, kw'ông'-fu 曠夫 not common, but used in the Four Books; *very young* —, siao'-kwun-nying 小官人°; kwông-kweng' 光棍 (a term of reproach implying a bad character.)

BACK, *the* pe'-tsih 背脊; *to carry on the* —, pe 背; *behind one's* —, pe'-'eo 背後

BACK, *come* cün-læ' 轉來; kyü'-læ 歸°來; *walk* —, tao'-tseo-cün-læ' 倒走轉來; *when will (he) come* —? kyi'-z kyü-læ' 幾時歸°來?

BACK-BITE, *to* — *a person,* pe'-'eo kông nying' 背後講°人°

BACK-BONE, tsih'-kweh 脊骨

BACK-COURT, 'eo-ming-dông'; 'eo-kyin-t'in' 後天°井°

BACK-DOOR, 'eo'-meng 後門

BACK-STITCH, *to* keo 勾

BACKWARD, *to walk* —, tao'-t'eng'-bu tseo' 倒退°步走; *to fall* —, nyiang' t'in tih'-tao 仰天跌倒; *ditto,* (as in studies), t'e'-loh 退落; *walk* — *and forward,* tseo'-læ, tseo'-ky'i 走來走去°

BACKWARD, *averse to undertake,* p'ô' zông-siu' 怕上手; *late in developing wisdom* (as a child), ts'ong-ming' k'æ-leh dzi' 聰明開得遲; *dull,* dzi-deng' 遲鈍

BACON, *salted pork,* 'æn cü'-nyüoh 鹹猪肉°; *ditto smoked,* in'-cü-nyüoh' 醺猪肉°

BAD, wa 孬°; feh-hao' 弗好; tæ 歹; *thoroughly* — *disposition,* 'ô'-liu p'e'-ts 下°流胚子; 'ô'-tsoh p'e'-ts 下°作胚子; — *name,* wa ming'-sing 孬名聲; *very* — *name,* ts'iu' ming'-sing 醜名聲

BADGE, 'ao 號; kyi'-'ao 記號; *distinguishing* —, pin-'ao' 編號

BAFFLED, tang'-sön feh-t'ong' 打算弗通; tang'-sön-feh-c'ih' 打算弗出

BAG, dæ 袋; *leather* —, bi-dæ' 皮袋 (ih-tsah)

BAGGAGE, 'ang-li' 行李; (*a load*, ih-tæn; *half a load*, ih-deo.)

BAIL, *to give written security for*, gyü pao'-zông 具保狀

BAIT, tiao'-ng-nyü 釣魚餌°

BAKE, *to* p'ang 烹°;—*in hot ashes*, *or coals*, ẁe 煨

BAKER, *bread-maker*, mun-deo' s-vu' 饅頭司務

BALANCE, t'in-bing' 天平; kw'u'-bing 庫平; dzao-bing' 曹平 &c., (ih-kô); the several kinds have different names according to the number of ounces to the lb.

BALANCE, *to — exactly*, ih'-z-bing dæn' 一字平坦°; ih-weh-liang'-bing 一畫兩平; *to — accounts*, kyih tsiang' 揭帳

BALD-HEADED, kwông deo' 光頭; *bald on the crown*, t'ah ting' 禿頂

BALE, *a* ih-pao' 一包; *a — of cotton*, ih-pao min-hwô' 一包棉花; *to do up a —*, tang kw'eng' 打綑; tang pao' 打包

BALL, gyiu 毬; *roll a —*, le gyiu' 擂毬 (ih-go)

BALLAD, ky'üoh'-ts 曲子; siao'-ky'üoh 小曲; siao'-diao 小調 (ih-tsah)

BALLAST, *to take in —*, tang ts'ao'; *stone —*, ts'ao'-zah 壓°舟石°; *for —*, ah-ts'ông yüong 壓°艙用

BALLOON, ky'i'-gyiu 氣毬

BALUSTRADE, ken-ken'欄杆;—

*for stairs*, vu-siu' 扶手; *one or more horizontal bars*, lu-t'æ'-tông 扶°梯檔

BAMBOO, coh 竹; (ih-keng, ih-kwang, ih-ts; *with a root*, ih-cü); —*grove*, coh' ling 竹林;—*for eating*, shing 筍;— *canes*, coh' ken 竹竿; *to whip with a —*, tang pæn'-ts 打板子; *the sacred —*, t'in coh' 天竹

BANANA, ts'ing-kyiao' 青蕉; hyiang-kyiao' 香蕉

BAND, *a tape* or *strip*, ih-keng ta' 一根帶°; — *of drawers*, or *skirt*, iao 腰; *a* — *of men*, ih-de nying' 一隊人°; *a* — *of soldiers*, ih-ts' ping-mô' 一支兵馬; *a* —*of musicians*, ih-pæn' c'ü-'ông 一班吹°手°

BANDAGE, *to* dzin 纏;— *the feet*, dzin kyiah' 纏腳; ko kyiah' 裹腳

BANDAGES, *foot* kyiah'- sô 裹°腳°布°, used by Chinese females.

BANDITTI, dzeh-fi 賊匪; gyiang-dao' 强盜; *local* —, t'u'-fi 土匪 (ih-tông, ih-pæn)

BANG, *to* — *with a stick*, &c., k'ao 拷;—*against*, bang-djoh' 搒着°

BANGING *noise*, bang-bang'-hyiang 嘭嘭°響; dang-dang'-hyiang 宕宕響

BANISH, *to* (1,000 to 2000 *li*) veng-liu' 問流; — (a few hundred *li*), veng-du'問徒; — (beyond the frontier for life, or for posterity), ts'ong-kyüing' 充軍

BANK of earth, na-nyi dông' 泥塘; — of stone, kao-k'en' 高礴; mound, kao-te' 高堆; river —, kông-ngen' 江°岸; kông-dông 江°塘; — for money, nying-'ao' 銀號; — bill, nying-p'iao' 銀票

BANQUET, tsiu'-zih 酒席; tsiu'-yin 酒筵; do-tsiu'; to go to a —, fu zih' 赴席; to partake of a —, zo zih' 坐°席; to prepare a —, shih zih' 設°席; bæn do-tsiu'.

BANTER, to hyi'-hyiah 戲謔; he banters me, gyi' teng ngô hyi'-hyiah 其與°我戲謔

BAPTISM (by sprinkling), si'-li 洗禮; — (by immersion), tsing'-li 浸禮; to receive —, ling si'-li 領洗禮; ziu tsing'-li 受浸禮

BAPTIZE, to —, 'ang si'-li 行°洗禮; 'ang tsing'-li 行°浸禮

BAR, cross wang-tông' 橫°擋; ditto for a door, meng-shün' 門閂; secret —, kyü-shün'; en-shün' 暗閂; upright —, dzih-tông' 直檔; ditto for door, teng'-shün 直閂; sand —, sô-t'æn' 沙灘

BAR the door, shün meng' 閂門; shut the door and — it, kwæn meng', loh shün 關門落閂

BARB, hook with a —, tao'-tsah-keo' 倒紮鈎; barbed spear, keo-lin'-ts'iang 鈎鐮鎗

BARBARIAN, mæn-nying' 蠻人°; yia'-nying 野°人°; outside —, fæn-nying' 番人°; yi-nying' 夷人°; friendly —, joh-fæn' 熟番: strange, and hence unfriendly —, sang-fæn' 生°番

BARBAROUS, cruel, yi-hyüong'-væn-oh' 行°兇作°惡

BARBER who shaves heads, t'i-deo'-s-vu' 薙頭司務

BARE, c'ih 出; kwông 光; — arms, siu'-kwang c'ih'-liao.

BARE-FACED, shameless, tæ-liu' 跴臉; 'eo' min-bi' 厚面皮

BARE-FOOTED, c'ih-kyiah' 出脚

BARE-HEADED, c'ih-deo' 出頭

BARELY, tsih 只; tæn-tsih' 單只; — enough to use, tsih' keo yüong' 只殼用

BARGAIN, to argue the price, leng'-liang kô'-diu 論量價°錢°; kông 'ông-dzing' 講行情

BARGAIN, to agree upon a — (after arguing), kông'-k'æ 講°開; picked up a good —, ts' eh'-læ-go ky'iao'-cong 撮來个°巧拼; hoped to gain, but lost by the —, iao' bin-i, shü bin-i' 要便宜°蝕便宜°

BARK of a tree, jü bi' 樹皮

BARKS, the dog —, keo kyiao' 狗叫

BARLEY, mi'-jing 米 仁; — (as a medicine), i-yi'-jing 薏 苡 仁

BAROMETER, fong-yü'-piao 風 雨 表 (ih-go)

BARRACKS, ying-vông' 營 房

BARREL, dong 桶; *flour* —, min-feng-dong' 麪 粉 桶; — (*i. e.* a drum-shaped tub), hwô-kwu-dong' 花 鼓 桶; *four barreled revolver*, s'-meng-deo siu'-ts'iang 四 門 頭 手 鎗

BARREN *land*, peh' mao-ts di' 不 毛 之 地; — *womb*, zah t'æ' 石°胎

BARRICADE, dza-sah' 寨 柵; — *of earth*, nyi-dzing' 泥 城; — *of stakes*, sah'-lah 柵 欄°

BARRICADE, *to* coh dza-sah' 築 寨 柵; coh nyi-dzing' 築 泥 城 (coh or tsoh)

BARRIER, *customs'* kwæn-k'eo' 關 口; k'a'-ts sah'-lah 卡 子 柵 欄°

BARTER, *to* ho'-diao-ho' 貨 調 貨; yi-ho'-yih ho' 以 貨 易 貨; kao-yih' 交 易

BASE, *of low birth*, pe-zin' 卑 賤°; 'ó'-zin 下°賤; — *morally*, 'ó'-liu 下°流; 'ó'-tsoh 下°作

BASE, *bottom*, or *stand*, zo-ts' 座° 子; bun-ts' 盤 子

BASHFUL, p'ô-siu' 怕 羞; p'ô-wông-k'ong' 怕 惶 恐

BASIN, beng 盆; tseng 額; bun 盤; *wash* — (face), min-beng' 面 盆; min-dong' 面 桶; *bread*

—, mun-deo' bun 饅 頭 盤 (ih-tsah)

BASKET (with a handle), kæn 籃; *clothes* —, lo 籮; *fruit* —, bu 篰; *charcoal* —, leo 簍; — *for washing rice*, dao-lo' 淘 籮; sao-kyi' 筲 箕; *provision* —, ho'-zih-kæn' 火 食 籃; *work* —, tsia-k'ong-kæn' 織°筐 籃 (ih-tsah)

BASTARD, yia'-cong 野°種; zeh-cong' 雜°種; (foreign and Chinese), c'ün-cong' 串 種

BASTE, *to* ting 釘; *first* — (it), sin ting'-ih-ting' 線 釘 一 釘; — *coarsely*, dziang-tsing' ting 長 針 釘

BAT, pin-foh' 蝙 蝠; *bat's dung*, yia-ming'-sô 夜°明 沙 (Med.)

BATH, *to take a* —, gyiang ih-go nyüoh' 洗°一 個 浴°

BATHE, *to* gyiang nyüoh' 洗°浴°

BATHING-TUB, gyiang'-nyüoh-dong 洗°浴°桶

BATTER, *to* k'eh'-bang 磕 撞; — *and spoil*, k'eh'-bang-diao 磕 撞 壞°

BATTERED *by the weather*, (*i. e.* rain and sun), yü tang', nyih sa', wæ'-de 雨 打 日°曬°壞 了°

BATTERY *for mounted cannon*, p'ao'-dæ 礮 臺

BATTLE, *to fight a* —, tang ih' dzing 打 一 陣; *field of* —, tsin'-dziang 戰 塲

BATTLE-AXE, yüih-fu' 鉞斧

BATTLEMENT, *embrasure*, p'ao'-meng 礮門

BAWL, *to* ying-ky'i'-ka-kyiao' 喧° 譁之°聲°

BAY, hæ-wen' 海灣 (ih go); — *horse*, ts'ih' mô 赤馬

BAYONET, heo mi-pô' 鱟尾°巴

BE, *to* — *at home*, læ oh'-li 在° 家°裏; *let it* — *there*, peh gyi læ-kæn' 俾其在°彼°; — (in the imperative), iao 要; yüong 用; — *careful*, iao kwu'-djoh 要顧着°; yüong kwu'-djoh 用顧着°

BEACH, *sea* hæ pin-yiu' 海邊沿

BEACON *in the sea*, hæ'-li-go piao-deo' 海裡个°標頭; *light-tower*, liang-t'ah' 亮塔; *mound from which smoke rises to warn of danger*, in-teng' 烟墩

BEADS, *officers'* dziao-cü' 朝珠; *Buddhist rosary*, sa'-cü 數珠; *aromatic* —, hyiang-cü' 香珠; *common* —, siao-liao-cü' 燒料珠 (*i. e.* burned material); ngô'-cü 瓦°珠; *a string of* —, ih-c'ün cü' 一串珠

BEAK, *bird's* tiao cü-gyin' 鳥° 嘴箝

BEAM, *an important* —, 'ang-diao' 桁°條; *the central* — *in the roof*, tong'-liang 棟梁; — *under the floor*, koh'-sah 閣柵

BEAN, deo 荳 (ih-hh); *the full*

number of beans in a pod, ih-kyih' 一莢

BEAN-CURD, deo-vu' 荳腐; tsiang'-deo-vu' 醬荳腐

BEAN-POD, deo-kyih'-k'oh' 荳莢壳

BEAR, *to* — *on the shoulders*, pe 背; *to sustain*, tông 當; tæn-tông' 擔當; dzing-tông' 承當; *can* — (it), tông-leh'-djü' 當得°住; hao' dzing-tông' 好承當; ky'üoh'-leh-lôh 吃°得°落; 'ông-leh'-djü 降得°住; *can't* — *it*, tông'-feh-djü 當弗住; ky'üoh'-feh-lôh 吃弗落; *I'll* — *the blame*, tsah'-vah ngô', dzing-tông' 責罰我承當; — *fruit*, kyih ko'-ts 結果子; sang ko'-ts 生°果子; kyih ko' 結果; the last is also used in speaking of persons, thus, nying kyih'-ko'-de 人°結果了°, means that the man has come to his end: if he has friends and money, he *has come to a good end*, hao'-kyih-ko' 好結果; *has come to a bad end*, m-kyih'-ko 無結果; — *a child*, sang na-hwun' 生°嬰°孩°; — *the loss*, be-din' ken-z' 賠錢°幹事; — *in mind*, liu dzæ sing'-li 留在心裏; — *on one's heart* (as something at a distance), kyi'-kwô 記罣; *ought to* — *patiently*, ing-kæ' jing'-næ 應該忍耐;

ing-kæ' 'en-jing' 應該含忍；*can't — patiently*, jing'-næ-feh-djü' 忍耐弗住；neh'-feh-djü' 納弗住；— *with* (or be indulgent to), kw'un yüong' 寬容；*ought not to — with*, yüong'-feh-teh'-go 容弗得个°；— *witness*, tso te'-tsing 做對証

BEARD, ngô-su' 髭鬚°

BEARER, *burden* kyiah'-pæn 脚班；kyiah'-fu 脚夫；t'iao-fu' 挑夫；kyiah'-tæn 脚擔；*sedan* —, gyiao-fu' 轎夫；— *of a letter*, song-sing'-go 送信个；ta-sing'-go 帶°信个°

BEAST, cong-sang' 畜生°；*wild* —, yia'-siu 野°獸；— (a term of reproach), ky'üoh'-sang.

BEASTLY *conduct*, cong-sang' 'ang-we' 畜生°行°爲；gying-siu' 'ang-we' 禽獸行°爲

BEAT, *to* tang 打；k'ao 敲°；djü；— *rice*, tang dao' 打稻；gwæn dao' 摜稻；— (as the pulse), t'iao 跳；— *a drum*, k'ao kwu' 敲鼓；— *cotton*, dæn min-hwô' 彈棉花；— *clothes* (in washing), djü i-zông' 搗衣裳；— *the back*, djü pe' 敲背；*down the price*, tang'-loh kô-din 打落價°錢°；— *time*, ah pæn' 拍°板；— *the breast* (meaning. I'll be responsible), tah hyüong' 拍°胸

BEAUTIFUL, hao'-k'en 好看；—

(*lit.*, pleasing), teh-nying'-sih 得°人°惜；zi-tsing'；*very* —, me'-mao 美貌；piao-cü' 標緻

BEAUTIFY, *to* tsông-sih' 妝飾；tsah'-kwah 紮刮；tsông-pæn' 妝扮；tang-pæn' 打扮 (the latter used of the person only.)

BEAVER-SKIN, (or otter-skin), t'ah' bi 獺皮

BECALMED, *no wind*, fong-ky'i', tu m̈'-neh 風氣都沒°有°；*ship is* —, fong m̈'-neh, jün dong'-feh-dong' 風沒°有°船動弗動

BECAUSE, ing-we' 因爲；we'-leh 爲了°；we'-tih-z 爲的是

BECOME, *to* tso 做；dzing 成；pin 變；fah 發；*to — a king*, tso wông-ti' 做皇帝；— *a good man*, dzing ih-go hao' nying' 成一个°好人°；*caterpillar becomes a butterfly*, djong' pin'-hwô wu-diah' 蟲變化蝴蝶；— *rich*, fah' dzæ 發財；— *angry*, fah ông'；*what will* — (of it) *in the end?* dza kyih'-gyüoh 怎結局？dza kyih'-sah 怎結煞？

BECOMING *to him*, (garments), 'eh gyi'-go sing-dzæ' 合其个°身材；*that dress is — to you*, keh' gyiu i-zông, teng ng' siang-nyi' 這°件衣裳與°你°相宜

BED, or BEDSTEAD, min-zông' 眠床° (ih-tsiang)；*want to go to*

—, iao min-zông'-li ky'i-de 要
眠 床°裡°去°了°

BED-BUG, ts'iu'-djong 臭°蟲

BED-CURTAINS, tsiang'-ts 帳子

BEDDING, p'u-kæ' 鋪 盖

BED-FELLOW, p'ing-zông'-go 摒
床°个°; dong zông'-go nying
同 床°个°人°; p'ing-p'u'-go
摒 鋪 个°

BED-ROOM, my ngô'-go vông 我
个°房; sleeping-room, ngo-vông'
卧 房; kw'eng'-vông 睡°房,
rarely used.

BED-TIME, kw'eng'-go z-'eo' 睡°
个°時 候; en-cü' z-'eo 安 置
時 候

BEE, fong-ts' 蜂 子; honey —,
mih-fong' 蜜 蜂 (ih-go)

BEE-HIVE, (tub-shaped), fong-
dong' 蜂 桶 (ih-tsah)

BEEF, ngeo-nyüoh' 牛 肉°; a roast
of —, lo'-s, the English word.

BEEF-STEAK, (beef to be fried),
t'ah'-go ngeo-nyüoh' 爛 个°牛
肉°; the best is from the parts
called, pah'-z-kweh 八 字 骨,
ô-bang-kweh yin', (low), and sæn-
koh-lông 三 角°廊

BEER, bitter wine, kw'u'-tsiu 苦
酒; bi'-tsiu, the English word
combined.

BEES-WAX, mih-lah' 蜜 蠟; yellow —, wông-lah' 黃 蠟

BEET, 'ong-ts'æ'-deo 紅 菜 頭

BEFALL, to ling-djoh' 臨°著

BEFITTING, 'eh-nyi' 合 宜; nyi 宜

BEFORE, some time —, zin-deo'
前°頭; dzong-zin' 從 前; in
front, læ zin-deo' 在°前 頭;
læ min-zin' 在°面 前; — the
flood, 'ong-shü' yi-zin' 洪 水°
以 前°; — and behind, ziu 'eo'
前°後; — the door, læ meng
zin' 在°門 前°; came — me,
sin'-jü ngô' læ'-go 先 我 來
个°; as —, dzing-gyiu' 仍 舊;
i-gyiu' 依 舊; tsiao-gyin' 照
舊; — one's eyes, læ ngæn min-
ziu' 在 眼°面 前

* This expression implies also time
near, whether just past, or just coming,
and also a very short distance; thus:
—if a person died a few days since,
ngæn'-min-zin si'-go 眼 面 前 死°个°

BEFOREHAND, yü'-sin 預 先;
tsao'-tsao 早 早; tsao'-sin 早 先;
to prepare —, yü'-sin be-bæn'
hao 預 先 備 辦 好

BEFRIEND, to tsiao'-ing 照 應

BEG, to t'ao 討; — for, gyiu-
ky'ih 求 乞; to entreat, gyiu-
k'eng' 求 懇; — food (i.e. rice),
t'ao væn' 討 飯; iao væn' 要
飯; ditto (politely) tsia liang' 借
糧; — mercy, or favor (for another on the ground of greater
respectability), t'aodzing' 叨 情;
ma min-k'ong' 賣°面 孔; — you
to excuse me, gyin ng nyün-liang'-
ngô 求 你 原 諒 我; — your
pardon, teh' ze 得 罪 (lit., I have
sinned against you); — (as a
Buddhist priest (or nun) for the

monastery), hwô-yün' 化緣;
ts'ao hwô' 抄化

BEGGAR, t'ao-væn'-go 討飯个';
ky'ih'-kæ 乞丐; *professional*
*male* —, kao'-hwô-ts 叫化子;
*looks like a* —, t'ao'-væn-siang
討飯相

BEGIN, *to* k'æ-siu' 開手; ts'u-
k'æ'-sin 初開手; ky'i'-siu 起
首; dong-siu' 動手; tso-ky'i-
deo' 做起頭; ts'u-ky'i'-deo
初起頭; k'æ-kô'; k'æ-dæ'; k'æ-
deo-meng' 開頭; *beginning to*
*learn*, 'oh ky'i-deo' 學°起頭;
*ditto books*, zông-'oh' 上學°; —
*a journey*, dong-sing' 動身;
*ditto by boat*, k'æ-jün' 開船; —
*a long journey*, ky'i-dzing' 起
程; — *a large work* (as building a house), dong-kong' 動工;
hying-kong' 興工

BEGINNER, *one inexperienced*, nga-
'ông' 外行; *raw hand*, sang-siu'
生°手; *one doing a thing for the*
*first time*, bao-z' tso'-go 暴時
做个°

BEGINNING, ky'i-deó'起頭; ky'i'-
ts'u 起初; bao-z' 暴時; *in the*
—, toh'-fah-ts-deo 元始; *ditto*
*of the world*, k'æ-bih'-go z-'eo
開闢个°時候; k'æ-t'in'-p'ih-
di z-'eo' 開天闢°地時候

BEGONE! ky'i 去°! tseo'-k'æ 走
開! tseo'-ko 走過!

BEGRUDGE *him the possession of*,
pô-feh-nông'-keo gyi 巴°-teh 巴

弗能彀其沒°有°; — *giving*,
feh-sô'-teh, dzn-c'ih' 弗捨°得
助出

BEHALF, *on account of*, we'-leh
爲了°; *I speak in* — *of my*
*younger brother*, ngô we'-leh ah-
di kông'-go 我爲了阿弟講°
个°; *for him*, dæ gyi' 代其; t'i'
gyi 替其

BEHAVES *well*, sih'-sih-ka-go.

BEHAVIOR, 'ang-we' 行°爲; 'ang-
i'-dong-zing 行°意動靜; 'ang-
ts'-kyü'-dong 行°止舉動;
*childish* —, siao'-nying i'-tsi 小
孩°意致°

BEHEAD, *to* sah-deo' 殺頭; tsæn-
deo' 斬頭; c'ü kyüih' 取決;
— *him*, sah-gyi-deo' 殺其頭

BEHIND, 'eo'-pe 後背; — *time*
ko-z'-de 過時了°; — *the times*,
be-z'-de 背時了°; — *one's back*,
pe'-'eo 背後

BEHIND-HAND *with one's work*,
sang-weh' deh-loh'-de 生°活疊°
落了°; sang-weh te'-ky'i-læ-de
生°活堆去°來了°; sang-
weh' tin-ky'i'-tong-de 生°活丟
去了°

BEHOLD! ts'ia'-k'en 且°看! nô!

BELCH, *to* — (from the stomach),
tang-eh' 打呃; — (as a vol-
cano), p'eng' 噴

BELFRY, cong-leo' 鐘樓 (ih-zo)

BELIEVE, *to* siang-sing' 相信; —
*entirely*, toh'-jih siang-sing' 篤

實相信; an exclamation, as much as to say *don't believe it*, 'æ 唉'! yi 咦! expressing both disbelief and surprise, yiu-ka'-t'in-wô'.

BELIEVER, siang-sing'-go cü'-kwu 相信个人°

BELL, *large* cong 鐘 (ih-kô); *small* —, ling 鈴 (ih-go)

BELL-CLAPPER, cong-zih' 鐘舌 (ih-go)

BELLOWS, ky'in-fong'-go tong-si' 牽風个°東西; *Chinese* —, fong-siang 風箱 (ih-bu); *to blow the* —, ky'in fong-siang' 牽風箱

BELLY, dn'-bi 肚皮; — *ache*, du'-bi t'ong' 肚皮痛

BELONGS, joh-ü' 屬于; dzæ-ü' 在于

BELOVED, ts'ing-æ'-go 親愛个°; dzih-din'-go 值錢°个° (primarily worth money).

BELOW, 'ô-deo' 下°頭; ti-'ô' 底下°

BELT, ta 帶°; — *for the waist*, iao-ta' 腰帶° (ih-keng)

BEMOAN, *to* ta'-k'oh-ta-kyiao'帶° 哭帶°叫; æ-dziang' kw'u'-nao k'oh 哀腸苦腦哭

BENCH, teng 凳; pæn'-teng 板 凳; *low* —, a'-teng 矮凳 (ih-keng, ih-kwang)

BEND, *to* ao'-cün 拗轉; ao'-wæn 拗彎; — (*as a bow*), pæn-k'æ' 扳開; — *forward*, eo'-tao 俯°

BENEATH, ti-'ô' 底下°; — *the table*, coh'-teng ti-'ô' 桌凳底下°

BENEDICTION, coh-foh'-go shih-wô' 祝福个°說話

BENEFACTOR, eng-nying' 恩人°

BENEFICIAL, yiu ih'-c'ü 有益 處; — *to him*, yiu ih' ü gyi' 有 益於其

BENEFIT, ih'-c'ü 益處; hao-c'ü' 好處; *favor*, eng-we' 恩 惠; *no* —, vu ih' 無益; *not only no* — *but on the contrary, injury*, fi-dæn' vu ih', fæn'-cün yiu 'æ' 非但無益反轉有害

BENEVOLENT, hao'-we-jün'-z 好 爲善事; — *heart*, jing-æ'-go sing 仁愛个°心

BENT, wæn'-go 彎个°; — *and crooked*, wæn-ky'üoh'-go 彎 曲个°。

BENUMBED, moh'-de木了°; *hands* —, siu moh'-de 手木了°

BEQUEATH, *to* yi-loh' 遺落; gao-loh'; — *property*, yi'-loh ts'æn-nyih 遺落產業

BERATE, *to* joh or zoh 辱; zoh-mô' 辱罵; *to* — *people*, joh-nying'-mô'-tao 辱人°罵倒

BEREAVED *of one's husband*, vi-vông'-jing 未亡人°; ming-æ-neh'-de 命沒°有了°; — *of one's wife*, dön-yin' 斷弦; shih-ngeo' 失偶; — *of a son*, sông-ting' 喪丁; — *of a brother*, siu'-tsoh sông-diao'-de 手足傷 壞°了°

BESEECH, *to* gyiu-k'eng' 求懇;
gyiu 求;— *earnestly*, ts'ih'-sing
gyiu' 切心求; kw'u'-kw'u
gyiu' 苦求

BESIDE, *at the side of*, læ bông-
pin' 在旁邊; tseh'-pin 側
邊;— (himself) *with anger*,
ky'i' hweng-de 氣悷了°

BESIDES, ling-nga' 另外°; djü-
ts'-ts-nga' 除此之外°; *more-
over*, ping'-ts'ia 拜且

BESIEGE, *to* we-kw'eng' 圍困;
dön-dön' we-djü' 團團圍住

BESMEAR, *to* lön-du' 亂塗; lön-
dzô' 亂搽; tsao 遭;— *the wall
with mud*, ziang'-li, lön-du' na-
nyi' 墻裡亂塗爛泥

BESMEARED, *face — with molasses*,
dông-lu' du-leh mun' min-k'ong
糖滷塗得°滿面孔;—
*the hands*, tsao'-leh mun' siu 塗°
得°滿手

BESPEAK, *to* ding-hao' 定好; wô-
hao' 話好; t'ao'-hao 討好°;
*is the chair bespoken?* gyiao-ts
t'ao'-hao ma 轎子討好麽°

BEST, *the* ting'-hao 頂好; gyih-
hao' 極好; ting'-zông-teng 頂
上等; kyü-tsè' 居最; tsè'-
hao 最好; *the very —*, tsæ'-m̄-
tsæ-hao' 再無°再好; *like this
the best*, tsè' hwun-hyi keh'-go 最
歡喜這°个°

BESTIR *one's self*, zi kyih' zi 自
激自°

BESTOW, *to* s'-peh 賜給; sông'-s
賞賜;— *happiness*, sông'-s foh'-
ky'i 賞賜福氣

BET, *to* tu-tong-dao' 賭東道

BETEL-NUT, ping-lông' 檳榔

BETRAY *treacherously*, ma'-loug
賣弄;— *one's master for honor*,
ma-cü' gyiu yüong' 賣主求
榮;— (as a secret), c'ih k'eo'
出口; lu fong' 露風; *Judas
betrayed (i.e. sold) Jesus*, Yiu-da'
ma-Yiæ-su'-diao 猶大賣°耶
穌了°

BETROTH, *to* — (a daughter), hyü-
c'ih' 許出; he'-peh, *or* hyü'-peh
許與°;— (a son), ding-ts'ing'
定親

BETROTHAL *papers*, shü-ts' 禮書
*to exchange ditto*, 'ô-ding' 下°
定; ko-shü' 傳°紅; 'ang-p'ing'
行聘; 'ô-p'ing' 下°聘

BETTER, *a little* hao-tin' 好點;
cün-cü'-tin 精°緻點; *still —*,
keng'-kô hao' 更加°好; yüih-
fah' hao 越發好; veng-nga'-
hao 牙外°好; kah'-nga hao
格外°好;— *than that*, hao-
jü' keh'-go 好如這个°; pi
keh'-go hao 比這°个°好; ko'-
jü keh'-go 過如這°个°;— *that
I should go*, feh jü ngô' ky'i'
hao' 弗如我去°好; *the quick-
er, the —*, yüih kw'a' yüih hao'
越快°越好;— *die*, tao'-feh-
jü si', hao' 到弗如死°好;

ting —, læ-tih hao'-ky'i-læ 正° 在° 好 起 來

BETTER, to make —, tso cün-cü'-tin 做 精° 致 點; long hao-tin' 弄 好 點

BETWEEN, sit — us, zo' læ ah'-lah cong-nyiang 坐 在° 我 等 中 央°; a go — (in marriage), me-nying' 媒 人°; ditto (in business), cong-nying' 中 人°

BEWAIL, to 'ao-li'-da-k'oh' 號 啕° 大 哭

BEWARE, be on your guard, bông-be' 防 備; be careful, tông-sing' 當 心; keep away from, yün'-bi 遠 避

BEWILDER, to mi 迷; mi-djü 迷 住

BEWILDERED, hweng-mi'-de 悟 迷 了°

BEWITCH, to yüong zia-fah' yiu-'oh' 用 邪 法 誘 惑

BEWITCHED, ziu mi'-tih-de 受 迷 了°

BEYOND, yi-nga' 以 外°; ts-nga' 之 外°; — the bridge, gyiao keh' ngen' 橋 那° 岸; — (over) the river, te' kông 對 江°; on that side, keh'-pun-pin 那° 半 邊; — my calculations, c'ih ngô i'-siang ts-nga' 出 我 意 想 之 外°; to live — one's means, vông'-yüong dong-din' 妄 用 銅 錢°

BIAS, to cut —, ts'ia' zæ 斜° 裁; to cut satin on the —, zia'-diao dön'-ts 斜° 條 緞 子

BIASSED, prejudiced, sang-wang-sing'-de 生° 橫° 心 了°

BIB, an infant's —, 'ô-bô-teo' 下° 吧 兜; — used when eating, ky'üoh-væn-pe-tæn' 吃° 飯 背 單; væn-tæn' 飯 單; zih-tæn' 食 單

BIBLE, Sing'-shü 聖 書; Sing'-kying 聖 經

BICKER, to k'eo'-kyüoh 口 角; siang-tsang' 相 爭°

BICKERING, endless to-k'eo'-to-zih' 多 口 多 舌

BID him go, wô-hyiang'-gyi-dao', hao ky'i' 告° 訴 其 好 去°; — him come in, eo gyi tsing' læ 叫° 其 進 來; — adieu, bih'-ih-bih' 別 一 別

BIER, kwun-zæ'kô'-ts 棺 材° 架° 子

BIG, do 大°; to grow —, do-ky'i'-læ 大° 起 來; to talk — (boast), kông do-wô' 講° 大° 話

BIGOTED, tsih'-ih feh t'ong' 執 一 弗 通; tsih'-ih-feh-sing' 執 一 弗 信; tsih'-mi-peh-ngwu' 執 迷 不 悟

BILE, kw'u'-tæn 苦 膽

BILGE-WATER, jün-ing'.

BILL for silver, nying p'iao' 銀 票; — for cash, dzin-p'iao' 錢 票; — of sale, fah'-p'iao 發 票; to make out a —, k'æ fah'-p'iao 開 發 票; — of lading, pao'-ho-tæn 報 貨 單

BILL of a bird, tiao cü-gyin' 鳥° 嘴 筋

BILLET, *note,* bin-z′ 便字; z-den′ 字條°

BILLION, jih væn′-væn 十萬萬

BILLOW, do lông′ 大°浪 (ih)

BIN, *rice* mi′ gyü 米櫃°; *coal —,* me-t'æn′ gyü 煤炭櫃°

BIND, *to* pông 綁; kw'eng 綑; kw'eng′-pông 綑綁; dzin 糧;— *that man,* keh-go nying kw'eng′-pông gyi 這°个°人°細綁其; — *the feet,* dzin kyiah′ 纏脚; — *the head,* pao deo′ 包頭;— *the edge,* pin-yin′, kweng ih′-da 邊沿綑一襟;— *books,* ting shü′ 釘書; *bound firmly,* bo-djü′-liao 縛°住了; *to — as an apprentice,* zông kw'æn-shü′ 上關書

BINDING *of a book,* shü-min′ 書面;— *is bad and must be renewed,* shü-min′ ẅa′, iao wun′-ko 書面孬°要換過

BIOGRAPHY, 'ang-jih′ 行°術 (ih-peng)

BIRD, *a* ih-tsah tiao′ 一隻鳥°

BIRD-CAGE, tiao-long′ 鳥°籠 (ih-tsah)

BIRD'S-NEST, k'o 窠; *edible —,* in′-o 燕窩 (ih-go)

BIRD-LIME, nyin-tiao′-go kao′ 黏鳥°个°膠°

BIRTH, *the time of —,* sang-c'ih-læ′ z-'eo′ 生°出來時侯;*give — to a son,* sang ih-go ng-ts′ 生°一个°兒°子; *of low —,* zin-t'æ′ 賤胎; *of high —,* kwo′-ts 賞子

BIRTH-DAY, sang-nyih′ 生°日°

BIRTH-PLACE, nyün-zih′ 原籍; keng-sang′-t'u-yiang′ 根生°土養; c'ih′-sing-ts-di′ 出身之地

BISCUIT, siao′-ping 小°餅; siao′ mun-deo′ 小饅頭

BISHOP, kyin-toh′ 監督

BIT, *a little —,* ih-tin′ 一點′; ih-ngæn′; *a piece,* ih-kw'ǔ′ 一塊

BITCH, keo-nyiang′ 母°狗°

BITE, *to* ngao 鮫°; *take a —,* ngao ih-k'eo′ 鮫°一口; *ditto* (as an animal), dzæn ih-k'eo′; *pepper bites the mouth,* wu-tsiao′ lah cü′-pô 胡椒辣嘴吧

BITS *of a bridle,* mô′-ziah′-ts 馬嚼子; *— of broken crockery,* un mi-fu′ 磁°屑°

BITTER, kw'u 苦; *very —,* zah kw'u′ 雜°苦

BITUMEN, lih-ts'ing 瀝青

BLACK, heh 黑, u 烏 both used of paint, hair, &c.; ts'ing 青, yün-seh′ 元°色, both used of cloth, garments, thread, and silk; — *cotton cloth,* ts'ing pu′ 青布; — *and blue* (as a bruise), u-ts'ing′ 烏青; — *man,* heh′ nying 黑人°; — *eyes,* ngæn′-cü u′ 眼°珠烏

BLACKING, *shoe* shih-'a′-go-me′ 刷鞋°个°煤; *stove —,* shih-ho′-lu-me′ 刷火爐煤

BLACKEN, *to* long heh′ 弄黑; tsao heh′ 遭黑; — (*i. e. polish*) *the stove,* ho′-lu ts'ah′ gyi yiu kwông′ 火爐擦其有光; — *one's* character, ao-tsao' shü p'eh' 壍 精 水 澂 ; 'en hyüih' p'eng nying' 含 血 嗿 人°

BLACKSMITH, t'ih'-s-vu 鐵 司 務 ; t'ih'-ziang 鐵 匠°

BLADDER, man's bông-kwông', or bông-hwông 膀 胱 ; hog's —, cü shü'-p'aó 猪 尿° 脬°

BLADE, a — of grass, ih-keng ts'ao 一 根 草 ; knife —, tao-sing 刀 身 (rare); edge of —, tao-k'eo' 刀 口 ; shoulder —, væn-ts'iao' kweh 飯 鋬 骨

BLAMABLE, kæ tsah'-vah 該 責 罰 ; yiu ts'o'-c'ü 有 錯° 處 ; he is —, kwe-gyiu' ü gyi' 歸 咎 于 其

BLAME, to s-we'; tsah 責 ; tsah'-be 責 備 ; tsah'-vah 責 罰 ; — mentally, kwa 怪° ; — unjustly, ts'oh'-kwa 錯 怪° ; can — me, kwe gyiu' ü ngô' 歸 咎 于 我 ; need not — me, moh kwa' ngô 莫 怪° 我 ; — another, when guilty one's self, t'e-t'oh' 推 托

BLAMELESS, vu k'o tsah'-go 無 可 責 个° ; vu-tsah'-c'ü 無 責 處 ; 並 ts'o'-c'ü 無° 錯° 處 ; entirely —, 'ao vu' ts'o'-c'ü 毫 無 錯° 處

BLAND, weng-'o' 溫 和 ; no-jün' 懦 善

BLANK, k'ong 空° ; bah 白° ; — book, k'ong bu'-ts 空 簿 子

BLANKET, nyüong-bi' 羢 被° ; nyüong-t'æn' 羢 毯 (ih-diao)

BLASPHEME, to sih'-doh 褻 瀆

BLAST, a ih-dzing fong' 一 陣 風

BLAZE, ho'-yin 火 焰 ; yin-deo' 焰 頭

BLAZE, to — up, ho'-yin ts'ong-zông 火 焰 冲 上 ; — abroad, koh'-c'ü djün-yiang 各 處 傳 揚

BLEACH, to p'iao'-bah 漂 白°

BLEATING, yiang'-kyiao 羊 叫 ; 哶 哶°

BLEED, to c'ih-hyüih' 出 血 ; to — a person, teng nying' fông hyüih' 與 人° 放 血 ; — by lancing quickly, t'iao hyüih' c'ih 挑 血 出

BLED to death, hyüih' liu-sah'-de 血 流 死° 了°

BLEMISH, pæn-pô' 瘢 疤 ; pæn-tin' 瘢 點 ; — (in the flesh, or in one's character), yüô-tin' 瑕 玷 ; fault, mao-bing' 毛 病

BLEND, to mix, 'o-long' 和 攏 ; 'o-tæn'-long 和 打 攏 ; c'ün'-long 串 攏 ; — thoroughly, c'ün'-leh diao-yüing' 串 得° 調 匀 ; to unite, siang-lin' 相 連 ; p'ing-long' 摒 攏

BLESS, to coh-foh' 祝 福 ; — God, coh'-zia Jing-ming' 祝 謝° 神 明 ; — (as priests do), ts'æn'-nyiæn 懺 念

BLESSEDNESS, happiness, foh'-ky'i 福 氣 ; foh'-veng 福 芬

BLESSING, to ask a — upon, coh'-tsæn 祝 讚

BLIGHT *from wet*, læn 爛

BLIGHTED *harvest*, kæn nyin-dzing' 減°年成; nyin-dzing' ẅa' 年成孬°; — *hopes*, sing-hwé'-i'-læn 心灰意懶

BLIND, hah-ngæn' 瞎眼°; — *person*, hah'-ts 瞎子; sông-ngæn' moh-pih' 雙眼°摸壁; kwu'-moh 瞽目; — *in one eye*, doh-ngæn' 獨眼°; *blinded and deceived*, ziu mong pi'-de 受蒙蔽了°

BLIND, *to* mun 瞞; ming-mun'-en'-p'in 明瞞暗騙; mun-sæn'-en'-s 瞞三掩°四; *blinded by love*, be æ'-sing tsô-pi'-de 被愛心遮蔽了°

BLINDS, *window* k'æn'-meng 板°窗°; *venetian* —, fæn-ts'ông' 翻窗; pah'-yih-ts'ông' 百葉窗; *bamboo* —, coh lin'-ts 竹簾子; *let down ditto*, lin'-ts 'ô'-loh 簾子下°落

BLINDFOLD, *to* pao ngæn'-tsing 包眼°睛

BLIND-MAN'S-BUFF, moh-en'-ts 摸暗子

BLINK, *to wink*, ngæn'-tsing sah'-sah 眼°睛眨眨

BLINKING *eyes* (*i.e.* half shut), to-sah-ngæn' 多眨眼°; ziang hô-c'û-ngæn' ka 像瞌眵眼°个°

BLISTER, p'ao 皰; *to raise a* —, ky'i p'ao' 起皰; — *plaster*, ky'i p'ao' kao-yiah 起皰膏藥

BLITHE, p'ao'-c'ing; kw'a'-weh 快°活

BLOAT, *to* fah-hyü' 發虛; fah-cong 發腫

BLOCK *of wood*, ih-kw'é' moh-deo' 一塊木頭; *chopping* —, tsing-deo' 椹頭; *hatter's* —, mao-kw'é' 帽盔; — *for printing*, ing'-pæn 印板; *child's blocks* siao-jü-den' 小樹頭°

BLOCKADE, *to* — *a river*, fong kông' 封港; — *a port*, fong hæ'-k'eo 封海口

BLOCKHEAD, ngæ-moh'-deo 呆木頭; ngæ-nying' 呆人°

BLOOD, hyüih 血; *to shed* —, liu hyüih' 流血

BLOOD-RELATION, ts'ing-kweh'-hyüih 親骨血

BLOOD-SHOT *eyes*, ngæn'-tsing 'ong' 眼°睛紅

BLOOD-THIRSTY, sah'-sing djong' 殺性重

BLOOD-VESSELS, hyüih'-kwun 血管; — *and tendons*, mah-loh' 脈絡

BLOSSOM, hwô 花 (ih-tô)

BLOSSOM, *to* k'æ-hwô' 開花

BLOT, *spot*, tsih'-le 跡累; *ink-spot*, moh-tsih' 墨跡 (ih-go)

BLOT, *to* tang moh-tsih' 打墨跡; — *out*, du-diao' 塗了°

BLOTCH, 'ong-pæn' 紅斑; cü-sô'-pæn 硃砂斑 (ih-tin)

BLOTTER (for daily accounts),

liu-shü′ bu 流水°簿; *paper* —, seng-moh′-go ts′ 沁墨个°紙

BLOW, *to give a* —, tang ih′ kyi 打一記; *give thirty blows* (with a bamboo), tang sæn′-jih pæn′ 打三十板; *a — with the fist*, ih-gyün′ 一拳

BLOW, *to* c‘ü 吹°; — *the trumpet*, c‘ü ‘ao-dong′ 吹°號筒; *the wind blows on me*, fong c‘ü′-djoh ngô′ 風吹°着°我; — *the nose*, hying bih-deo′ 擤鼻°頭; — *out the candle*, c‘ü′ lah-coh′ u 吹°熄°蠟燭; — *hard*, ‘eo-ky‘i′-lih c‘ü′ 俟氣力吹°; — *down*, c‘ü-tao′ 吹°倒; — *away*, c‘ü-ky‘i′ 吹°去°; — *up with gunpowder*, yüong ho′-yiah hong-diao′ 用火藥轟壞°

BLUDGEON, do-deo′-kweng 大°頭棍

BLUE, læn 藍; *light* —, yüih-bah′ 月白°; *very dark* —, sing-læn′ 深藍; ts‘ing-læn′ 清藍; ih′-p‘ing-læn′ 一品藍; *Prussian* —, yiang-ts‘ing′ 洋青; — *vitriol*, tæn′-væn 胆礬

BLUFF *language* (or manner), pæn′-pæn-go k‘eo′-ky‘i 板板个°口氣

BLUNDER, *to* ts‘o′-shih 錯°失; long-ts‘o′ 弄錯

BLUNDERING, ts‘o′-shih to 錯°失多

BLUNT (as an edge), deng 鈍; — *in manner*, dzih-sing′ 直心; — *in manner*, or *language*, sing-k‘eo′-kw‘a 心直°口快°; *very — language*, toh′-fong-deo shih-wô′ 篤鋒頭說話

BLURRED (as print), mo-wu′-de 模糊了°; — (as writing), moh-tsih′ k‘a-k‘æ′ 墨跡揩°開; — *eyes*, ngæn′-tsing hwô′-de 眼°睛花了°

BLUSH, *to* ‘ong-ky‘i′-læ 紅起來; — *easily* (thin skin), min-bi boh′ 面皮薄

BLUSTER, *to talk noisily*, hæ-we′-gyi-dæn′ 海外°奇談

BOAR, p‘oh-cü′; *wild hog*, yia-cü′ 野°猪

BOARD, *a* ih-kw‘e pæn′ 一塊板; *chess* —, gyi-bun′ 棋盤

BOARDS, *the six* —, loh bu′ 六部 *viz*: —

*Board of Civil Office*, li-bu′ 吏部
„ *of Revenue*, wu′-bu 戶部
„ *of Rites*, li-bu′ 禮部
„ *of War*, ping-bu′ 兵部
„ *of Punishments*, ying-bu′ 刑部
„ *of Works*, kong-bu′ 工部

BOARD, *to* kyi′-deng 寄庉; *to take one's meals*, kyi′-væn 寄飯; kyi-zih′ 寄食; — *money*, væn-din′ 飯錢°

BOAST, *to* p‘u-tsiang′ 鋪張; ts‘ing-neng′ 稱能; ts‘ing-hyüing′ 稱勳; *to make an empty* —, c‘ô-dæn′ 詫誕; p‘u-kying′; kw‘ô-k‘eo′ 誇口; kông do-wô′ 講°大°

話; kông kw'eh'-wô 講°鬪話

BOASTING, *always — of one's good deeds*, kwæn'-iao-zông cü' 慣要發°詡°; zông'-cü-zông-teh'.

BOAT, jün 船; t'ing 艇; sæn-pæn' 杉皈 (ih-tsah); *passenger —*, 'ông-jün' 航船; *ferry —*, du-jün' 渡船; *foot-paddle —*, kyiah-wô-jün' 脚划船

BOAT-LOAD, *a* ih-zæ' 一賦°

BOATMAN, *head* lao-da' 老大; *assistant —*, jün'-li-ho'-kyi 船裡夥計

BODY, kyi'-sing; sing-t'i' 身體; *the whole —*, weng'-sing 渾身; 'en kyi'-sing 遍°身°體°

BODILY, kyi'-sing-go 身°體°上°; *— energies*, tsing-jing' 精神

BODY-GUARD, *of the emperor*, z-we' 侍衛; *— of officials*, ming-tsông' 民壯

BOG, wu-nyi'-di 汗°泥°地; læn-din' 爛田

BOIL, ts'ông 瘡 (ih-go); *— caused by heat*, nyih-cih' 熱°瘍; nyih-cih-len' 熱°瘍瘟°

BOIL, *to* ts 煮°; zah 煤; kweng 滾; *— some water*, shü teng'-teng kweng' 水°燉燉滾; *— the milk*, na kweng-kweng' gyi 媔°要°燉°滾; *— sugar*, tsin dông' 煎糖; *— the egg soft*, kyi-dæn' iao ts'-leh dông-wông'-go 雞蛋要煮°得°蕩黃°个°; *— tender*, ts nen' 煮頓'

BOILER, *Chinese* 'oh 鑊 (ih-k'eo); *tin —*, mô'-k'eo-t'ih ko' 馬口鐵鍋

BOILING *water*, kweng' shü 滾水°; k'æ shü 開水°; *— hot (i. e. bubbling)*, dah-dah' kweng 沓沓滾

BOISTEROUS, hæ-we'-gyi-dæn' 海外°奇談

BOLD, *not afraid*, tæn'-ts do' 膽子大°; *presumptuous*, tæn'-ts do yia'-ky'i' 膽子大°野°氣; *not bashful*, feh-p'ô'-wông-k'ong' 弗怕惶恐; 'eo-min'-bi 厚面皮; *— bad woman*, p'eh'-vu 潑婦

BOLDLY, fông'-tæn 放膽; *to speak —*, k'æn-kæn'-r-dæn' 侃侃而談

BOLT *of a door*, meng-shün' 門閂

BOLT *the door*, shün meng' 閂門

BOND *for house*, or *money lent*, pih'-kyü 筆據; *customs' —*, pao'-tæn 保單; *deed*, veng-ky'i' 交契

BONDS, *in —*, or *bound in chains*, be lin-diao' so'-djü-liao 被鏈鎖條住了°

BONE, kweh'-deo 骨頭 (ih-keng)

BONNET, *a hat*, ih-ting mao-ts' 一頂帽子; *man's — for protection from wind*, fong-teo' 風兜; *old woman's ditto*, yü-deo'-mao 圍°頭帽

BONZE, 'o-zông' 和尙

BOOK, shü 書 (ih-peng, ih-bu, ih-ts'ah); *religous* —, kying 經

BOOK-BINDER, ting-shü'-go-nying 釘書個°人°

BOOK-CASE, shü-djü' 書廚; *an open* —, shü-kô' 書架°

BOOK-KEEPER, kwun'-tsiang sin'-sang 管帳先生

BOOK-SELLER, shü-k'ah' 書客; shü-fông'-tin'-kwun 書坊主°人°

BOOK-STORE, shü-fông'-tin 書坊店

BOOR, *countryman*, hyiang-'ô'-nying 鄉下°人°

BOORISH, ts'u-mæn' 粗蠻

BOOTS, hyü 靴; *rain* —, yü'-hyü' 雨靴; ting-hyü' 釘靴 (a pair, ih sông)

BOOTY, *stolen* tsông 贓; zeh-tsông' 賊贓; zeh-t'eo-ho' 賊偷貨; *arms taken in war*, deh-læ'-go ky'i'-yiæ 奪來個°器械; *plunder*, lo'-læ-go tong-si' 攎來個°東西

BORAX, bang-sô' 硼砂; yüih-zah' 月石°

BORDER, *margin*, pin-yin' 邊沿; *boundary*, kao-ka' 交界°; — (of a field), ts'-ka 址界°; — (of a country), we-ka'-go di-fông' 為界°個°地方; — of a garment, i-zông' ken-deu 衣裳衦頭°

BORE, *to* tsön, or cün 鑽; — *a hole*, tsön ngæu'-ts 鑽眼°子

BORN, *when was the baby* — ? na-hwun' kyi'-z sang-go 嬰°孩°幾時生°個°?

BORN AGAIN, *to be* dao'-sing tsæ sang-c'ih-læ 道心再生出°來; *leave the old for the new*, ky'i'-gyiu' wun-sing' 棄舊換新; *begin again to live*, ih'-li-tso-nying' 重新做人°; dzong-sin'-tso-nying' 重新做人°; *as if to cast skin, and change bones*, ziang t'eh'-bi-wun-kweh'-ka 像脫皮換骨個°

BORROW, *to* tsia 借°; *borrowed money*, tsia'-kw'un 借°款; tsia'-'ông 借°項

BOSOM, gwa 懷°; hyüong-kwun'-deo 胸膛°頭; *put in the* —, k'ông læ gwa'-li 园在°懷°裡

BOTANY, *the science of* —, hwô-moh'-gyüong-li-go 'oh-veng' 花木窮理個°學°問; *a Chinese work on* —, Gyüing-fông'-pu 羣芳譜

BOTCH-WORK, sang-weh' liao-ts'ao' 生°活潦草; sang-weh' liao-piao' 生°活潦表; sang-weh' ts'u-ts'ao' 生°活粗糙; feh ziang' sang-weh' 弗像生°活

BOTH, liang-go tu' 兩個°都; 'o-liang'-go; liang-'ô' 兩下°; liang-dzao' 兩造; pe'-ts' 彼此; — *are good*, liang'-k'o 兩可; *they are* — *there*, liang-go tu' kæ'-kæn 兩個°都在°

彼°; *are you — well?* ng-lah ʻo-liang-go tu hao' yia' 你°箏°兩个°都好喲°?

Bother, *to* tsʻao 噪; lo'-so 囉°唆; *do not — me,* m-nao tsʻao ngô' 弗°可°噪我

Bottle, *glass* po-li' bing' 玻璃瓶 (ih-go); *put into a —,* tsi læ po-li' bing'-li 廚在°玻璃瓶裡

Bottom, ti 底

Bottomless, m̄-ti'-go 無°底个°

Bough, ô-ts' 椏°枝 (ih kwang, ih-pʻing, ih-tiao)

Bound, *limit,* ʻæn'-cü 限°制; *without —,* m̄-ʻæn'-liang-go 無°限°量个°

Bound, *tied,* bo-djü'-liao 縛°住了; kwʻeng'-djü-liao 綑住了

Bound, *to set limits,* lih ʻæn' 立限°; — (as a state), kông siang-gyü'-go di'-fông 講°相距个°地方

Bound, *to — upward,* tʻiao'-kyʻi-læ 跳起來; tsæn'-kyʻi-læ 躦起來; *to — back,* pʻong'-cün-læ 搒°轉來; tao'-pʻong-cün' 倒搒°轉

Boundary, feng-ka'-go di'-fông 分界°个°地方; *frontier,* kao-ka' 交°界°; *landmark,* ts'-ka 址界°

Boundless, m̄-ʻæn'-cü 無°限°制; — *ocean,* hæ' m̄-pin' m̄-ngen'-go 海無°邊無°岸个°; — *love,* æ'-sih m̄-gyüong'-dzing-go 愛惜無°窮盡个°

Bountiful, *free in giving,* cʻih'-siu do' 出手大°; — (as God, or as the emperor), kwông'-s-eng-we' 廣賜恩惠; — *feast,* tsiu'-zih fong-fu' 酒席豐盛°

Bounty, ʻeo'-s 厚賜; — (of a superior), sông'-s 賞賜; *imperial —,* wông-eng' 皇恩°

Bow, *to make a —* (with hands together), tsoh-ih' 作揖; *a low —* (in the same way), tang-kong' 打拱; — (bending one knee), tang tsʻin-ts' 打蹉子; tang siao'-gyü 打°小跪°; — *and touch head,* kʻeh-deo' 磕頭; *ditto and worship,* kʻeh'-deo li'-pa 磕頭禮拜°

Bow, kong 弓 (ih tsiang); *to shoot with a —,* zih 射; *to shoot a bird with a —,* zih' ih-tsah tiao' 射一隻鳥°

Bowels, du'-dziang 肚腸; du'-bi 肚皮

Bow-knot, bu-kwu'-kyih 䳕°鴣結; weh kyih' 活結; *tie a —,* tang bu-kwu'-kyih 打䳕°鴣結

Bowl, un 碗 (ih tsah); *finger —,* gyiang'-siu-un 洗°手碗

Bowl-mender, ting-un'-go 釘碗个°

Bow-man, kong-tsin'-siu 弓箭手

Bow-string, kong-yin' 弓弦

Bow-window, pun'-yüih-tsʻông' 半月牕

BOX 51 BRA

Box, siang-ts′ 箱子 (ih-tsah);
small —, 'eh-ts′ 盒子 (ih-go)
Box, to — with the fists, tang gyün-
deo′ 打拳頭;— the ear, tang
r′-kwông 打耳光;— the cheek
tang pô-công 打巴掌;— the
mouth, tang teo-cü′ 打兜嘴; to
inclose in a box, tsông ke siang-
ts′ li 裝在° 箱子裡
Box-wood tree, wông-nyiang′ jü′
黃楊° 樹
Boy, ẇæn孩°; u-ẇæn′; nen-ẇæn′
男孩°; siao-ẇæn′ 小孩°; —
(from ten to sixteen), dong-ts′
童子; a waiting — is called,
ah-siao′ 阿小; a — (serving in
a school), shü-dong′ 書僮
Brace (as in houses), ts'ang-djü′
撐柱; — (as in furniture),
ts'ang-tông′ 撐檔; — resting
on the ground, tsiu′-djü 竪柱
Brace, to — by adding a piece, s′
ih-go t'iah′-boh 使一个° 貼
枕°; t'iah′ ih-kw'e 貼° 一塊
Bracelet, siu′-gyüoh 手鐲
(one, ih-tsah; a pair, ih-te, ih-
sông; a set, ih-fu)
Bracket for supporting a shelf,
ts'ang 撐 (ih-go)
Brackets, to inclose in —, keo-
tsing′ 勾進
Brackish water, 'æn shü 鹹° 水°
Brag, to ts'ing-neng 稱能;
empty boast, kw'ô-k'eo′ 誇口.
See Boast.
Braid, silk s-bin′ 絲辮; dotted

—, cü-zing′ 珠繩°; gold —,
kying-bin′ 金辮; to make —,
tang bin′ 打辮
Braid, to tang-bin′ 打辮; gao-
long′ 絞攏; — the hair, tang
bin′-ts 打辮子; — baskets,
tang læn′ 打籃; gao læn′ 絞° 籃
Brain, nao′-si 膯髓
Bran, wheat fu-bi′ 麩皮; mah-
bi′ 麥皮; rice —, si′-k'ông 細°
糠; — flour, t'ong′ feng 粗°
粉. See Unbolted.
Branch of a tree, ô-ts′ 椏° 枝
(ih-kwang, ih-p'ang); — of a
river, or family, ts-p'a′ 支派°
Branch, to feng ts-p'a′ 分支派°
Brand, ho′-za-deo 火柴° 頭 (ih-
kwang)
Brand, to — (as criminals), ts′-z′
刺字; ts'ih-z′ 刺°字; — with a
hot iron, tang ho′-ing 打火印;
tang ho′-lao-ing′ 打火熔° 印;
—(a priest, or devotee), fu kyiæ′
付戒; to receive such a —, ziu
kyiæ′, or ziu ka′ 受戒
Brandish, to yüih-læ′ yüih-ky'i′
甩° 來甩° 去°
Brandy, nga′-koh siao-tsiu′ 外°
國燒酒; beh-læn′-di, (the
English word.)
Brasier, dong-s′-vu 銅司務;
dong-ziang′ 銅匠; traveling —,
siao′-lu-s-vu′ 小爐司務
Brass, dong 銅
Bravado, yiao-vu′ yiang-ẇe′-go
kông′-shih 耀武揚威个° 講°

式°; c'ô-dæn'-go shih-wô 發°
翻°个° 說話· See BOAST.

BRAVE, üong'-ken 勇敢; *having
great courage,* yiu tæn'-liang 有
膽量; yiu ken-tæn' 有肝膽;
*a — person,* ih-diao hao'-hen 一
條'好漢

BRAWL, *to* ts'ao'-nao 噪鬧; tsang-
zao' 爭°嘈°

BRAWNY, tsah'-ngang 圍硬

BRAYING, *the — of an ass,* li-ts'
kyiao' 驢子叫

BRAZEN, dong'-tso-go 銅做个°;
— *faced* (thick), 'eo'-ô-lin-go
厚丫°臉个

BRAZIER, *a pan for coals with per-
forated cover,* ho'-ts'ong 火燼
See BRASIER.

BREACH, *to make a — in a wall,*
ts'ah ziang-dong' 拆墻洞; *come
in through the —,* ziang-dong'-
li tsön-tsing'-læ 墻洞裏鑽進
來; *there is a — of friendship
between us,* ngô' teng gyi' djih-
kyiao' 我與其絕交; *a — of
morality,* sông fong-hwô' 傷風
化; — *of promise,* shih-sing' 失
信; shih-iah' 失約; — *of marriage contract,* t'e-hweng' 退婚;
*ditto on the woman's part,* la-
ts'ing' 賴°親

BREAD, mun-deo' 饅頭; *a slice
of —,* ih-p'in' mun-deo' 一片
饅頭

BREADTH, kw'eh 闊; *what is the
— of that?* keh' yiu to'-siao

kw'eh' 這° 有多少闊!— *in
cloth* (a little wider than common), foh'-meng kw'eh' 幅門
闊; *a — of cloth,* ih-foh pu' 一
幅布; *less a hair's —,* (*lit.* an
eye-brow hair), ts'ô ih ni-mao'
差一眉°毛; *a hand —,* siu'-
kwông ka kw'eh' 手掌°一
樣°闊

BREAK, *to — in small pieces* (as
cups, tiles, &c.), k'ao-wu' 敲
爛°; — *in pieces,* k'ao-se' 敲
碎; — *apart,* p'ah'-k'æ 擘°開;
— (as a stick or pencil), dön
斷; ao'-dön 拗斷; — *by striking,* tang'-se 打碎; *ditto* (as a
stick), tang'-dön 打斷; — *by
a blow,* k'ao-sông' 敲°傷°; —
*one's word,* shih-sing' 失信;
sông-iah' 爽約; — *land,* k'æ-
k'eng' cong-din' 開墾種田

BREAKFAST, t'in nyiang'-væn 天°
亮°飯; tsao'-væn 早飯

BREAST, hyüong-kwun'-deo 胸°
懷°; *the breasts,* na 嬭; *woman's
—,* na-bu 嬭° 袋° (one, ih-tsah)

BREAST-BONE, hyüong - dông'-
kweh 胸膛骨

BREAST-PLATE, wu- sing'-kying
護心鏡

BREATH, ky'i 氣; k'eo'-ky'i 口氣;
*offensive —,* k'eo'- ky'i ts'iu'
口氣臭°; *can't draw one's —,*
ih' ky'i feh cün' 噎氣弗轉;
*there is not a — of air,* ih tin'

fong tu ǔ'-neh 一 點 風 都
沒 有°; _a_ —, ih hwu' 一 呼;
_out of_ —, ky'i'-kying 氣 緊;
_pant for_ —, t'eo ky'i' 哮 氣;
— _has stopped_, ky'i dön'-do 氣
斷 了°

BREATHE, _to_ hwu-hyih' 呼 吸;
hwun'-tsing hwun-c'ih' 喚 進 喚
出; _to_ —_upon one's hands_, ky'i'
hô læ siu'-li 氣 呵°在°手°裡];
_so warm can't_ —, ka nyih',
ky'i' t'eo'-feh-cün' 這 樣 熱 氣
透 弗 轉

BRED, _well_ kao'-hyüing-hao' 敎°
訓好; _understands politeness_ (said
of a child), sih li'-sing 識 理 性;
_ill_ —, feh sih li'-sing 弗 識 理
性; ǔ kao'-hyüing-go 無° 敎°
訓 个°

BREECHES, kw'u 袴 (ih-diao)

BREED, _to_ — _children_, sang ng'-
bu nön' 生° 兒° 哺 図; _to_ —
_cattle_, yiang ngeo' 養 牛°; _to_ —
_lice_, sang seh' 生° 虱

BREEZE, _gentle_ 'o fong' 和 風;
_there is a little_ —, vi-vi' yiu tin
fong 微 微 有 點 風; _steady,
favorable_ —, ih-dzih' jing-fong'
一 直 順 風

BRETHREN, hyüong-di 兄弟; di'-
hyüong 弟 兄

BREVITY, _with_ — _and clearness_,
kyin'-r-ming' 簡 而 明

BREW, _to_ — _wine_, tso tsiu' 做 酒
zao tsiu' 造°酒; nyiang tsiu' 釀
酒 (veng); _brewing mischief_, læ-

tih hying 'o' de' 正°在°與 禍 了°

BRIBE, hwe'-lu 賄 賂; _to take a_
—, ziu hwe' 受 賄

BRICK, cün-deo' 磚 頭 (ih-kw'e);
_bricks and tiles_, ngô'-yiao-ho 瓦°
窰貨

BRICK-KILN, yiao 窰; siao yiao'
燒 窰 (ih-go)

BRICK-LAYER, _mason_, nyi-shü'-s-
vu' 泥 刷°司 務

BRIDAL-DRESS, kong-tsông' 宮
粧; — (for the second day),
hwô-ao' 花 襖; _head-dress and
robe_, vong-kwun', yün-ling' 鳳
冠 圓 領; _bridal outfit_, kô'-tsông
嫁°粧

BRIDE, sing-læ'-sing-vu' 薪 來 新
婦; sing-nyiang'-ts 新 娘 子;
sing-kwu'-nyiang 新 姑 娘. The
latter is used by the song'-nyiang-
ts. See BRIDES-MAID.

BRIDE-CHAMBER, dong-vông' 洞
房

BRIDEGROOM, sing-lông' 新 郎;
siao'-kwun-nying 小 官 人°

BRIDES-MAID. The Chinese have
none, but instead, have attendants
called, ze-kô'-a-m 隨 嫁°阿°
姆, and song'-nyiang-ts 送 娘

BRIDGE, gyiao 橋; _river_ —,
kông-gyiao 江°橋 (ih-keng, ih-
diao); _floating_ —, veo-gyiao' 浮
橋; — _of the nose_, bih-deo liang'
鼻°樑

BRIDLE. _the reins_, mô' kyiang-zing
馬 韁 繩; _the head gear_, mô'-

long-deo 馬籠頭; *the bits,* mô′ ziah-ts′ 馬嚼子; mô′-k‘eo-t‘ih 馬口鐵

BRIDLE, *to* t‘ao long-deo′ 套籠頭; *saddled and bridled,* mô′ p‘e′-hao-de 馬配好了°

BRIEF, kyin′-kyin-kyih-kyih′ 簡簡潔潔; ling′-kying; kyin′-bin 簡便

BRIER, *thorn bush,* ts‘′-jü 有°刺个°樹

BRIGADE *of troops,* ih-de′ping-mô′ 一隊兵馬; ih-ts′ ping-mô′ 一支兵馬

BRIGHT, kwông-liang′ 光亮; ming-liang′ 明亮; *polish it* —, ts‘ah′gyi liang′ 擦其亮; *dazzling* —, shih′-kwah liang′ 雪光°亮; — *weather,* t‘in′ ts‘ing-kwông′-kyiao-kyih′ 天清光皎潔; væn′-li-vu-yüing′ 萬里無雲

BRIGHTEN, *to rub bright,* mo kwông′ 磨光; ts‘ah′ kwông 擦光; *to illumine,* tsiao′-djoh 照着°; ing′-djoh 映着°; — *one's intelligence,* ts‘ong-ming′ k‘æ-c‘ih′-læ 聰明開出來; *the sky brightens,* t‘in lông′-ky‘i-læ-de 天朗起來了°; — *up, (as an idol, when his eyes are un-covered, or humorously, when a dirty face is washed),* k‘æ kwông′ 開光

BRILLIANT (*as coloring*), kwông-ts‘æ′ 光彩; —(*as light*), kwông-yiao′ 光耀

BRIM, k‘eo 口; pin 邊; *cup's* —, pe-ts′ k‘eo 杯子口; *jar's* —, kông pin′ 江邊

BRIMFUL, mi-mun′ 平°滿; ‘eo-yin′ 㑳沿

BRIMSTONE, liu-wông′ 硫磺

BRINE, ‘æn-lu′ 鹹°滷; lu′-djü; yin-lu′ 盬滷

BRING, *to* do′-læ 拏°來; ta′-læ 帶°來; *the latter has the idea of bringing, at the same time with something else, thus,* — *the eggs and also the sugar,* kyi-dæn′ do-læ′, dông′ hao ta′-læ 鷄蛋拏°來糖好帶°來; — *back* (*something borrowed*), ta-læ wæn′ 帶°來還; — *trouble on one's self,* zi c‘ü′ gyi ‘o 自°取其禍; zi zing′ gyi kw‘u′ 自°尋其苦

BRING FORTH *a child,* sang na-hwun′ 產°嬰孩°; — *fruit,* kyih ko′-ts 結果子; sang ko′-ts 生果子

BRING — (it) *up,* do-zông′-læ 拿°上來; — *up a child,* yiang siao′ nying do′ 養小孩°大°; *ditto, to have every thing it likes,* yiang′ kyiao 養嬌

BRINK, pin-yin′ 邊沿; ts‘ing′-pin 趁邊; *just on the* —, ts‘ing′-pin-dziah-ngen′ 趁邊着岸; — *of a river,* kông pin-yin′ 江°邊沿

BRINY, ‘æn-go 鹹°个°

BRISK, kyih′-tsao 急躁; — *beer,*

tsiu c'ong'-leh kyih' 酒冲得° 急; c'ong is also pron. ts'ong.

BRISTLES, *pig's —* , cü-tsong' 豬鬃

BRITTLE, ts'e'-ts'e; ts'e 脆

BROAD, kw'eh 闊; kwông'-kw'eh 廣闊; *make it broader,* tso gyi kw'eh'-tin 做其闊點

BROAD-CLOTH, do-nyi' 大°呢; *fine —* , siao'-nyi 小呢; to'-lo- nyi' 哆囉呢

BROCADE *silk,* hwô-dziu'花綢; — *satin,* mo-peng'-dön 摹°本緞

BROGUE, t'u'-ing 土音; *cannot speak three words without his —* , sæn kyü' feh li peng'-ky'iang 三句弗離本腔

BROIL, *to* tsih 炙; hong 烘; koh 㸕; *cut* (it) *in pieces and — (it),* ts'ih'-leh p'in tang' p'in, tsih'- ih-tsih' 切得°片打片炙 一炙

BROKER, ma-siu' 買°手; *money —* , t'æn-sin'-sang 聽°行°情° 先生°

BROKER'S-SHOP, (exchange),dzin- tin' 錢店

BRONZE, *old* kwu'-dong 古銅; — *color,* kwu'- dong seh 古銅色

BROOD *of chickens,* ih-k'o' siao kyi' 一窠小鷄

BROOD, *to — on eggs,* bu dæn' 菢° 蛋; u dæn'; *brooding over (as sorrow),* ts'ih-sing'-de 切心了°

BROOK, ky'i-k'ang' 溪坑° (ih- diao, ih-da)

BROOM, sao'-tsin 掃帚; *small —,* or *brush,* shih'-tsin 刷帚 (ih-pô)

BROTH, t'ông湯; *mutton—,* yiang- nyüoh t'ông' 羊肉°湯

BROTHEL, c'ông-kô' 娼家°; meng- k'æn' 門檻°; dông-ming 堂名; — *boat* (at Hangchow), kông- sæn-jün' 江°山船; c'ông is also pron. ts'ông.

BROTHER, *elder* ah-ko' 阿哥; ah-kön'; *younger —* , ah-di' 阿弟

BROTHER-IN-LAW, *elder sister's husband,* tsi'-fu 姊夫; *younger sister's husband,* me-fu' 妹夫

BROTHERLY, jü-hyüong'-ziah-di' 如兄若弟

BROTHERS, hyüong-di' 弟兄

BROW, nao'-k'oh 腦売; *the sides of the —* , ngah-koh' 額角°; *to knit the brows,* zeo mi-deo' 縐° 眉°頭

BROW-BEAT, *to* we'-pih 威逼

BROWSE, *to* k'eng jü'-ô-ts' 齦樹 極°枝

BROWN *color,* tsong-seh' 棕色; *reddish —,* 'ong-tsong' 紅棕; *the color of wet — sugar,* ts'- dông seh 紫糖色; *fry it —* (yellow), t'ah gyi wông' 爛其 黃; *fry it very —,* t'ah gyi ts'- dông seh 爛其紫糖色

BRUISE, sông-'eng' 傷痕; — (where the blood is collected), ü'-hyüih 瘀血; *black and blue*

—, u-ts'ing' 烏靑；— (on fruit, or the mark of a — on flesh), sông-pô' 傷疤

BRUISE, to sông 傷；seng 損；long sông-seng' 弄傷損；to — by falling, tih'-sông 跌傷；— by something falling upon, ah'-sông 壓傷；— by striking against, bang-sông' 撞傷；— by shutting between, gah-sông 夾傷；— by beating, tang'-sông 打傷；to — (as drugs), sông-se', or song-se' 舂碎

BRUSH, shih'-tsin 刷帚 (ih-pô)

BRUSH, to shih 刷；to — teeth, shih ngô-ts' 刷牙齒

BRUTALLY, to treat a person —, oh'-sing-oh'-fi dæ nying' 惡心惡肺待人°

BUBBLES, p'ao 泡；froth, beh 浡 to blow —, c'ü p'ao' 吹°泡

BUBBLE, to — up, ky'i beh' 起浡

BUCK, yüong-loh' 雄鹿

BUCKET, shü'-dong 水°桶 (ih-tsah；a pair, ih-tæn)

BUCKWHEAT, gyiao-mah' 蕎麥；(a grain, ih-lih)

BUD, leaf ngô 芽°；ngô-den' 芽頭°；flower —, nyü 蕊°；hwô-nyü' 花蕊°

BUD, to —, ts'iu ngô' 抽芽°；pao ngô' 苞芽°；fah ngô' 發芽°

BUDGET, a bag of something, ih-dæ veh-gyin' 一袋物件；a bundle in a cloth, pao-voh' 包袱

BUDDHA, veh 佛

BUDDHISM, veh-kyiao' 佛敎；sih'-kyiao 釋敎

BUDDHIST, veh-kyiao'-li-go nying' 佛敎裡个°人°；veh-meng-di'-ts 佛門弟子

BUDDHIST-PRIEST, 'o-zông' 和尙；I, an humble —, sô-mi' 沙彌

BUFF color, dæn' wông 淡黃

BUFFALO, shü'-ngeo 水°牛° (ih-deo)

BUG, djong 蟲；bed —, ts'iu'-djong 臭°蟲 (ih-go)

BUGBEAR, kwa'-ky'i tong'-si 怪°氣東西

BUGLE, nga'-koh 'ao-teo' 外°國號斗

BUILD, to ky'i 起；zao 造°；tang 打；— a house, ky'i ih-tsing oh' 起一進屋；— a boat, zao ih tsah-jün' 造°一隻船；— a wall, tang ih-dao ziang' 打一道墙

BUILDER, ky'i'-zao-go s-vu' 起造°个°司務

BUILDING, oh 屋；oh'-yü 屋宇

BULB, deo 頭；onion —, ts'ong-deo' 葱頭；taro —, nyü-na'-deo 芋芳頭

The Chinese do not distinguish bulbous roots.

BULGING, protruding, deh-c'ih'-liao 凸出了

BULKY, do-gyin'-deo 大°件頭

BULL, yüong ngeo' 雄°牛° (ih-deo)

BULLET, *leaden* k'æn-dæn' 鉛彈

BULLION, veng-nying' 紋銀

BULLOCK, siao' yüong-ngeo' 小雄牛° (ih-deo)

BULLY, *to bluster or swagger*, hah'-sæn-wô'-shü 嚇 山 話 水°

BULRUSH, lu-ken' 蘆 竿; *lamp-wick* —, teng ts'ao' 燈草; *matting* —, zih-ts'ao' 蓆草

BULWARKS, *city walls*, dzing-ziang' 城牆; *earthen rampart*, nyi-dzing' 泥城; *the sides of a ship*, 'en-dông' 旱塘; ken'-dông 趕塘; *a fortification*, p'ao'-dæ 礮臺

BUMP, bang-sông' 揰°傷 (ih-t'ah)

BUMP, *to* k'eh'-bang 磕撞°; k'eh'-djoh 磕着°

BUNCH, *a handful*, ih-pô 一把; *a* — *of grass*, ih-pô ts'ao 一把草; *a* — *of flowers*, ih-nyiah hwô' 一捻花; *a* — *of grapes*, ih-gyiu' ts'-bn-dao 一毬紫葡萄; *a* — *of keys*, ih-c'ün yiah-z' 串鑰匙

BUNDLE, *a* —, ih pao' 一包

BUNGLE, *to* c'ü-ho'; tso' feh loh'-dzih 做弗落直; tso' feh liu'-ky'in 做弗順手°; tso' feh ding'-tông 做弗定當

BUOY, mao-ing' 錨映; vu-dong' 浮°筒 (ih-go)

BUOYANT, *floating*, kying-veo' 輕浮; *buoyant spirits*, t'in-sing 'o-loh' 天性和樂

BURDEN, tæn'-ts 擔 子; tæn'-deo 擔頭; *heavy* —, djong' tæn 重擔; *a* — *for one man to carry with a bamboo*, ih-tæn' 一擔; *a* — *for two men to carry between them*, ib kông' 一扛; *a* — *carried on the back*, ih-kyin' 一肩

BURDENSOME, næn tông' 難當

BUREAU, *a chest of drawers*, ih-tsiang gyü-coh' 一張櫃°桌

BURGLAR *who breaks into houses*, ts'ah ziang-dong' go zeh' 拆墻洞个°賊°

BURIAL *matters*, en-tsông' z-t'i' 安葬事體; — *place*, en-tsông'-go di-fông' 安葬个°地方; — *ground*, veng-di' 墳地; *public ditto*, nyi-cong'-di 義塚地; nyi-sæn' 義°山

BURN, ho t'ông'-sông 火燙傷

BURN, *to* siao 燒; me 煤; dziah 燫; tin 點; — *paper (for the dead)*, siao ts' 燒紙; — *mock-money*, siao sih'-boh 燒錫箔; — *down (as a house)*, me-diao'; dziab-diao' 燫壞°; — *incense*, tin hyiang' 點香; siao hyiang' 燒香; *this oil will not* —, keh'-go yiu, tin'-feh-dziah'-go 這°个°油點弗燫°个°; — *a corpse*, ho'-tsông 火葬; — *the filth off a ship's bottom*, dæn jün' 燂船; *face burns like fire*, min-k'ong nyih', ziang ho' siao' ka 面 孔 熱°像 火 燒 个

BURNED to death, dziah-sah'-de 熄 死°了°

BURNING, smell of something —, in-ho'-ky'i 烟 火 氣; — hot (as with fever), ho'-nyih 火 熱°; fah-siao' 發 燒

BURNISH, to mo-kwông' 磨 光

BURROW, di-dong 地 洞

BURROW, to kong di-dong 打°地°洞; rabbits —, t'u' we kong di-dong' 兔 會 打°地洞

BURST, to — (with a noise), pao'-k'æ 爆 開; to crack open, hwah'-k'æ 豁 開; the cannon —, do-p'ao tsô'-k'æ-de 大°碳 漿 開 了°; p'ao tsô'-de 碳 漿 了°; — out laughing, fah-siao' 發 燒

BURY, to en-tsông' 安 葬

BUSH, siao'-jü 小 樹 (ih-cü)

BUSHEL, sæn teo' 三 斗; three teo equal 30 quarts.

BUSHY tail, mi'-pô bong-song 尾 巴°蓬 鬆; — beard, ngô'-su nyüong' 牙°鬚°濃

BUSINESS, z-ken' 事 幹; z-t'i' 事 體; what is your honorable — ? ng yiu' soh-go kwe'-z 你°有 甚 麼°貴 事? ditto occupation? ng soh'-go kwe-'ông' go 你°甚 麼 貴 行 个°? to mind one's own —, en-veng'-siu-kyi' 安 分 守 己°; what — is it of yours? ng kwun' gyi tso soh' 你°管 其 做 甚°麼°? one's appropriate —, ne-'ông' 內 行; it is not

your —, feh' z ng' veng-ne'-ts-z' 弗 是 你°分°內 之 事; talks constantly of his own —, sæn kyü' feh li peng ky'iang' 三 句 弗 離 本 腔; — hours, bæn tsing'-vu z-'eo' 辦 正 務 時 候

BUSTLE, nao-nyih' 鬧 熱°; —and noise, nao-nyih'-bang-sang.

BUSTLING, nyih-nao' 熱°鬧; — hospitality, dæ nying-k'ah' nyih-zah' 待 客 人°熱°心°

BUSY, employed, yiu z-ken' 有 事 幹; —and hurried, mông-mông'-loh-loh' 忙 忙 碌 碌; harvesting is a — time, keh dao' mông' z-'eo' 割 稻 忙 時 候

BUT, dæn'-z 但 是; only, tæn-tsih' 單 只; tsih'-z 只 是; we were all there — you, djü-liao ng' ah'-lah tu læ'-kæn 除 了°你°我°等°都 在°彼°; — for you, ky'ü-leh ng' 虧 得°你°; ziah feh'-z ng' 若 弗 是 你°

BUTCHER, du-fu' 屠 夫; — of hogs, sah-cü-du' 殺 猪 屠; the seller of meat, tsing-deo'-s-vu' 椹 頭 司 務; to open a butcher's shop, k'æ du-wu' 開 屠 戶

BUTCHER, to sah 殺; — people, sah'-loh pah'-sing 殺 戮 百 姓

BUTLER, one who looks after things generally, kwun-z'-go 管 事 个°; toh-djü 督 廚

BUTT, to gyüih 觝; tiao; ts'oh; — end of a stick, bông'-go do deo' 大° 頭 棒 (deo or den)

BUTTER, na-yiu' 嬭°油; beh-t'ah', transferred from the English.

BUTTERFLY, wu-diah' 蝴 蝶 (ih-tsah)

BUTTOCKS, p'i'-kwu 屁 股

BUTTON, nyiu'-ts 鈕 子 (ih-lih); *cap* —, ting'-ts 頂 子; *common cap* —, mao tih'-ts 帽 結° 子

BUTTON, *to* nyiu'-long 鈕 攏; — *it*, nyiu-ih'-nyiu 鈕 一 鈕; k'eo'-ih-k'eo' 扣 一 扣

BUTTON-HOLE, nyiu'-p'æn 鈕 襻

BUY, *to* ma'-tsing 買°進; ma 買°; ma-læ' 買° 來°; *to — and sell*, ma'-ma 買° 賣°; *to — rice*, dih mi' 糴 米; — *wine*, tang tsiu' 買°酒; — *oil*, iao yiu' 買°油; — *cloth*, ts'ô pu' 買° 布

BUYER, ma'-cü 買° 主

BUZZING, z-z'-hyiang; 'ong-'ong'-hyiang 洪 洪 響; *the — of mosquitoes*, meng-djong' hyiang' 蚊° 蟲 響; du-du'-hyiang.

BY *that road*, dzong keh'-da lu 從 這° 埭 路; *injured — him*, be gyi 'æ' 被 其 害; *close* —, gying 近; — *no means*, bing'-fi 並 非; — *all means*, ts'in-væn' 千 萬; — *what means?* yüong soh'-go fông-fah' 用 甚° 麼° 方 法? — *day*, nyih-li' 日° 裡; — *night*, yia-li' 夜° 裏; — *himself* (there), doh-zi' læ'-kæn 獨 自° 在° 彼°; — *chance*, neo'-ts'eo 偶°湊; ngeo'-jün 偶° 然; *sell — the pound*, leng kying' ma 論 觔 買°; *to say — heart*, be 背°; *come one — one*, ih'-go ih'-go læ' 一 个° 一 个° 來; — *and* —, ko'-leh ih-zông' 過 了° 一 息°; — *and — will come*, deng' ih-zông' ziu læ'; *to pass* —, tseo'-ko 走 過

BY-PATH, tseh'-lu 側 路

BY-STANDER, bông-nying' 旁 人°; *disgraceful for bystanders* (*i. e.* others) *to see*, bông-kwun'-peh-yüô' 旁 觀 不 雅

## C

CABAL, kyih-tông' 結 黨; kæn tông' 奸° 黨

CABBAGE, (native) *yellow* wông-yia'-ts'æ 黃 矮° 菜; *Shantung* —, Sæn-tong' ts'æ 山 東 菜

CABIN *in a vessel*, jün'-li-go k'ah'-ts'ông 船 裡 个° 客 艙; *straw hut*, ts'ao'-oh 草 屋; ts'ao'-ts'iang 草 廠; ts'ao'-sô 草 厙

CABINET *minister*, tsæ'-siang 宰 相; siang'-koh 相 國; addressed as koh'-lao 閣 老 and da yüoh-z 大 學 士

CABLE, ts'ih 大° 繩°; *bamboo* —, mih-ts'ih' 篾 竹° 繩°; *palm husk* —, tsong ts'ih' 棕 篾° 繩°

CACKLE, *to* tô-ts'; *hens — after laying eggs*, kyi-nyiang' pao ts' 雞 娘 報 子

CAGE, long 籠; *bird* —, tiao-long' 鳥° 籠; — *for criminals*,

moh-long' 木籠 (ih-tsah)

CAJOLE, *to* yi vong'-dzing yi hong'-p'in 叉°奉承叉°哄騙

CAKE, kao 糕; *flat* —, ping 餅 (ih-go); — *shop*, dzô-zih' tin 茶食店; kao-ping' tin 糕餅店; *sponge* —, dæn-kao' 蛋糕

CALAMITY, 'o'-se 禍祟; tsæ-næn' 災難; — *changed to blessing*, cün-'o' we-foh' 轉禍爲福

CALCINE, *to* tön-hwe' 煆灰; — *gypsum*, tön zah-kao' 煆石膏

CALCULATE, *to* sön 算; sön-tsiang' 算帳; *you* — *correctly*, ng sön feh ts'o' 你°算弗錯; — *destinies*, sön ming' 算命

CALDRON, do 'oh' 大°鑊

CALENDAR (printed sheet), lih-jih'-tæn 曆日單; tsin-li'-tæn 瞻禮單; li'-pa-tæn 禮拜°單 (ih-tsiang)

CALF, siao'-ngeo 小牛°; *very young* —, siao-ang' 犢° (ih-deo); — *of the leg*, kyiah-nyiang-du'

CALIBER, *size of the bore*, p'ao'-meng ts'ah'-ts'eng 礮門尺°寸; *weight of the ball*, dæn'-ts to'-siao djong' 彈子多少重

CALICO, *white* bah-yiang-pu' 白洋布; *printed* —, hwô-yiang'-pu 花洋布

CALK, *to* seh leo-dong' 塞漏洞; — *a boat*, dzang jün'.

CALL, *to* eo; hwun 喚; kyiao 叫°; — *loudly*, hyiang'-hyiang eo 響響叫°; — *to mind*, ts'eng'-ky'i-læ

忖起來; siang'-ky'i-læ 想起來; *cannot* — *to mind*, ts'eng'-feh-c'ih' 忖弗出; *by what name are you called?* ng' kyiao-leh soh'-go ming'-z 你叫甚°麼°名字? ng eo soh-go ming'-z? *to call out*, eo-tæn'-ky'i 叫°起; hyiang-tæn'-ky'i 響起; — *the cat*, mæn hwun'-leh-læ 猫°呼°得°來; — *on him to pray*, ts'ing gyi' tso tao'-kao 請其做禱告; — *upon* (visit), mông-mông' 望°望°

CALLIGRAPHY, hao-pih'-fah 好筆法

CALLING, *occupation*, z-nyih' 事業; 'ông-nyih' 行業; 'ông-tông' 行當; (polite), kwe'-'ông 貴行; *trade*, siu'-nyi 手藝

CALLOW *bird*, c'ih-k'o'-go tiao° 出窠个°鳥°; *as yet no feathers*, wa m'-neh c'ih mao' 還沒°有°出毛

CALM *weather*, dzing kwông' kyiao kyih' 晴光皎潔; — *wind and wave*, bing fong' zing lông' 平風靜浪; — *mind*, sing' ts'ing-zing' 心清靜; sing en-tæn' 心安耽

CALM, *to* — *the mind*, en sing' 安心; — *his anger*, ah gyi-go ho 壓°其个°火

CALMLY, en-tæn' 安耽; en-en'-zing-zing' 安安靜靜

CALUMNIATE, *to* pông'-hwe 謗毀; tsing dzæn-yin' 進讒言

CALUMNY, dz'en-yin' 譏言

CALVE, to sang siao-ang' 生°犢°

CAMBRIC, zông yiang'-sô 上洋紗; light blue —, kying-læn' si-pu' 京藍細布; coh'-pu 竹布

CAMEL, loh-do' 駱駝 (ih-tsah)

CAMELLIA, dzô-hwô' 茶花

CAMLET, yü'-dön 羽緞; imitation —, yü'-dziu 羽綢

CAMOMILE, dried — flowers, ken-kyüih' hwô 甘菊花

CAMP, ying-za' 營寨°

CAMPHOR, tsông-nao' 樟腦; ping p'in' 冰片; — tree, tsông-jü 樟樹

CAMP-CHAIR, mô'-ü 馬椅°; mô'-tsah-ü 馬杈椅°; leather bottomed (native) —, bi-mô'-ü 皮馬椅° (ih-pô)

CAN, oil yiu-kwun' 油罐 (ih-go)

CAN, neng-keo' 能彀; we 會; — (implying permission, or fitness) hao'-s-teh 好使得; k'o'-s-teh' 可使得; k'o'-yi 可以; — but, feh'-teh-feh 弗得弗; — do (it), tso'-leh-læ 做得來; — not do (it), tso'-feh-læ 做弗來

CANAL, 'o 河; 'o-kông' 河港 small —, siao 'o' 小河; siao' 'o-kông' 小河港; branch — (soon terminating), zao 漕; the Grand —, Yüing 'o' 運河; kông 江° a river, and kông 港 a canal, differ in tone, the former being bing-sing, the latter zông-sing. Tides rise in the former, not in the latter.

CANARY - BIRD, z-zing'-tiao 時辰°鳥°

CANCEL, to blot out, du-diao' 塗壞°; to cross out (as figures), djü-diao' 除去°; keo-siao' 勾銷

CANDID, dzih-sông' 直爽

CANDIDATE (for the lowest literary rank), dong-sang' 童生°; veng-dong' 文童; — to be chosen, 'eo-shün' 候選; — for office, 'eo-pu' 候補 also used in ordinary matters.

CANDIED fruits, dong-ko' 糖菓; honeyed fruits, mih-tsin' 蜜餞; — or honeyed jujubes, (often called dates), mih-tsao' 蜜棗; — oranges, kyüih'-ping 橘餅

CANDLE, lah-coh' 蠟燭 (ih-ts); foreign —, yiang-coh' 洋燭; marriage —, hwô-coh' 花燭; blow out the —, lah-coh' c'ü u' 蠟燭吹°熄°

CANDLESTICK, coh'-dæ 燭臺; lah-coh-dæ' 蠟燭臺° (ih-tsah)

CANDOR, with dzing'-jih-vu-ky'i-go 誠實無欺个°

CANDY, dông 糖; some of the best Ningpo candies are, cowhide —, ngeo-bi'-dông 牛°皮糖; black seed slices, hah-kyiao-ts'ih'黑澆切; lotus-thread —, ngeo'-s-dông 藕絲糖; rice —, tong'-

mi-dông' 凍米糖; *peanut —,*
hwô-seng dông' 花生糖 &c.

CANE, *rattan,* bah-deng' 白籐; —
*seated chair,* deng-min' ü'-ts 籐
面椅°子

CANE, bông 棒; kwa'-dziang 拐°
杖; æ'-dziang 接°杖 (ih-keng)

CANGUE, do-kô' 大°枷° (ih-min);
*to wear the* —, pe do-kô' 背
大°枷°

CANISTER, *tea* dzô-yih'-kwun 茶
葉罐

CANNIBAL, ky'üoh nying'-go nying
吃°人°个°人°

CANNON, do-p'ao' 大°礮 (ih-meng)

CANNON-BALL, do-dæn'-ts 大°
彈子

CANNONADE, *to* yüong p'ao' tang
用礮打

CANNOT, feh neng'-keo 弗能
彀; s'-feh-teh 使弗得, ve, or
feh we 弗會°; — *go,* ky'i'-feh-
læ 去°弗來; *must not go,* ky'i'-
feh-teh 去°弗得; — *on any
account,* væn-feh-k'o' 萬弗可;
ts'ih'-feh-k'o' 切弗可; tön'-wu-
feh-k'o' 斷乎弗可; — *part
with* (or regret to part with),
feh-sô'-teh 弗捨°得; — *spare,*
siao'-feh-teh' 少弗得; hyih'-
feh-læ' 歇弗來; — *reach* (it),
liao'-feh-djoh' 撩弗着°; —
*see* (it), k'en'-feh-kyin' 看弗
見; — *believe* (it), siang-sing'-
feh-læ' 相信弗來; — *find*
(it), zing'-feh-djoh' 尋°弗着°

CANON, *church rule,* kyiao' kwe
敎規

CANONIZE, *to declare a deceased
person to be a saint,* si-ts' ts'ing-
gyi' z sing'-nying 死°之稱其
是聖人°

CANOPY (carried before an officer),
wông-lo'-sæn 黃羅傘; — *pre-
sented for merit,* væn-ming'-sæn
萬民傘

CANTANKEROUS, kæn-ka' 尷尬

CANTHARIDES, pæn-mao' 斑蝥

CANTO, *a division,* ih-p'in' s 一
篇詩; *a book,* ih-peng s' 一本
詩; ih-kyün s' 一卷詩

CANVASS, *to examine,* dzô-ts'ah
查察; k'ao'-kyiu 考究; —
(for votes, pupils &c.), kyiu 糾;
kyiu-long' 糾攏; *sail-cloth,*
fong'-bong pu 風蓬布; sô-pu'
紗布

CAP, siao'-mao 小帽; bin-mao'
便帽; *small silk* —, un'-mao
瓜°皮°帽; si-kwô-bi' 西瓜皮
(ih-ting); *to put on the* —, ta'
mao-ts' 戴°帽子; *take off the*
—, tsoh' mao-ts' 除°帽子

CAPABLE *of doing,* hao'-tso 好
做; ky'üoh'-leh-loh-go 吃°得°
落个°

CAPABILITY, vu-nyih'-ts 武藝;
neng-ken' 能幹; *mental* —, dzæ-
neng' 才能

CAPACIOUS, kw'un-do' 寬大°;
kw'un-ts'iah' 寬綽

CAPACITY, *mental* ts-tsih′ 資質；dzæ 才；*he has a — for something great,* (*i.e.* the main beam), gyi z tong′-liang-ts dzæ′ 其是棟梁之才；*small —,* mah-sin′-ts dzæ 纖線之才

CAPE (of land), we′-koh 匯角°；hæ′-koh 海角°；— (worn by an officer), p′i-kyin′ 披肩；*lady′s —,* yün p′i′-i 圓披衣

CAPER, *to* t′iao′-t′iao 跳跳；t′iao-t′iao, peng′-peng 跳跳奔奔

CAPITAL, *chief,* ting′ do 頂大°；— *crime,* si′ze 死罪；— *scheme,* miao kyi′ 妙計

CAPITAL (of a country), kying-dzing′ 京城；kying-tu′ 京都 (ih-zo)；*stock in trade,* peng′-din 本錢°；*to lose —,* zih peng′ 折°本

CAPITULATE, *to* deo-′ông′ 投降

CAPON, sin′-kyi 騸雞 (ih-tsah)

CAPRICIOUS, ′oh-z′-′oh-pin′ 或是或變；*very —,* kwn-kwa′-deo 古怪°頭

CAPSTAN *for an anchor,* ts′ô mao′-go bun′ 車錨个°盤；— (on land), ts′ô-dong′ 車筒

CAPTAIN, *chief,* cü 主；— *of a boat,* jün′-cü 船主；*military —,* yiu-kyih′ 遊擊；— *of a hundred men,* pah′-tsong 百總

CAPTIOUS, wang p′i-bing, jü′ p′i-bing 橫批評堅批評；zing′-z ts′ao′-nao 尋事譟鬧

CAPTIVATED, *I am — by it,* ngô′ be gyi′ ts′ih-sing′-de 我被其切心了°

CAPTIVE, lo-ky′i′-go nying′ 擄去°个°人；— *soldier,* gying′-ky′i-go ping 擄去°个°兵

CAPTIVE, *to take —,* lo′-ky′i 擄去°；*ditto* (as a soldier), gying′-leh-ky′i 擄得°去°

CAPTURE, *to* k′ô′-djoh 掔°着°；cô-djoh′ 擴°着°

CARCASS, p′oh′-s 仆屍；— *of a man,* s-siu′ 屍首；si′-s 死屍；— *of a horse,* si-mô′ 死馬；— *of a cow,* tao′-ngeo 死°牛

CARD, t′iah′-ts 帖子；— (simply containing one′s name), p′in-ts 片子；— *of invitation,* ts′ing′-t′iah 請帖；*visiting —,* pa′-t′iah 拜帖；— *of thanks,* zia′-t′iah 謝帖；*send a —,* do ih-go t′iah′-ts ky′i′ 掔°一个°帖子°去

CARD-CASE, pa′-t′iah-′eh′ 拜帖盒°；*card-bag* (Chinese), p′in′-ts-dæ 片子袋

CARDAMOM-SEEDS, deo-k′eo′ 豆蔻；bah-k′eo′ 白蔻；sô-jiug′ 砂仁

CARDS, ts-wu-bæn′ 紙糊牌°；*to play —,* c′ô-bæn′ 圖牌°

CARE, *anxiety,* lao-sing′ 勞心；iu-li′ 憂慮；s-li′ 思慮

CARE, *to — for,* kwn′-djoh 顧着°；tsiao′-kwu 照顧；k′en′-kwu 看顧；*take —,* siao′-sing 小心；

tso-gyi' 留 心°; tông-sing' 當
心; dzæ-sing' 在 心

CAREFUL, kying'-jing-go 謹 愼
個°; siao'-sing-go 小心個°; —
(about little things), ts'-si 仔
細; to be — of (as things),
yüong ts'-tsih 要° 小° 心°; æ'-
sih° 愛惜

CARELESS, hweh'-liah 忽 略; feh
siao'-sing 弗 小 心; feh kwu'-
djoh 弗 顧 着°; — (in omit-
ting), shih-kyin'-tin 失 檢 點;
to treat precious things in a —way,
bao'-din - t'in-veh' 暴 殄 天 物

CARGO, jün'-li-go ho'-veh 船 裡
個° 貨 物; jün-ho' 船 貨; to
discharge —, ky'i ho' 起 貨;
zông ho' 上 貨

CARICATURE, to draw a — ridi-
culing a person, sia ih-go du'
tsao-siao nying' 寫° 一 个° 圖
嘲 笑 人°

CARMINE, foreign yiang-'ong' 洋
紅; — (for the face, &c.) in-tsi'
胭 脂°

CARNAGE, sah'-loh 殺 戮; promiscuous —, lön-sah' 亂 殺

CARNAL, joh-ü nyüoh-sing' 屬 于
肉° 身; depraved, zia 邪°; —
desires, nyüoh-sing' s-yüoh' 肉°
身 私 慾

CARNELIAN, mô'-nao 瑪 瑙

CAROUSE, to nao-tsiu' 鬧 熱°
酒 興°

CARP, a fish, li'-ng 鯉 魚° (ih-
kwang)

CARP, to — at, hah' mao-ün 瞎
埋° 怨

CARPENTER, moh-s-vu' 木 司 務;
moh-ziang'-s-vu 木 匠° 司 務
(ih-go)

CARPET, mao-t'æn' 毛 毯; tsin-
t'æn' 氈 毯; t'æn'-ts 毯 子

CARRIAGE, ts'ô-ts' 車 子; mô'-tsô-
ts' 馬 車 子; four-wheeled —, s'-
leng-ts'ô 四 輪 車 (ih-zo, ih-dzing)

CARRIER, burden t'iao-fu' 挑 夫;
kyiah'-pæn 脚 班; letter —,
sing'-pæn 信 班; tseo-sing'-go
走 信 個°

CARRION, ts'iu'-nyüoh 臭° 肉°;
læn-nyüoh' 爛 肉°

CARROT, 'ong lo-boh' 紅 蘿 蔔

CARRY, to — on the head, deo-li
ting' 頭 頂; — on the shoulders
or back, pe 負°; — by a pole,
(one man) t'iao 挑; — (by two
men), dæ 擡; kông 扛; — by
a handle or chain, (as a basket,
teapot, &c.), ky'ih 掣; — in the
hand, do 擎; — away, do'-leh-
ky'i' 擎° 得° 去°; — a child,
siao-nying' bao-leh tseo'-tseo 小
孩° 抱 得° 走 走; only willing
to be carried, lin-siu'-sang 連 手
生°; — in the bosom, gwa'- li
ts'ô'-leh-ky'i 懷° 裏 扠° 得° 去°;
— a letter, ta sing' 帶° 信; —
an umbrella, ta sæn' 帶° 傘; do
sæn' 擎° 傘; — an open ditto,
tæ sæn' 戴 傘; — on the arm
(as a dress), siu-li gwæn' 手 裏

擓;— *on the arm* (by a handle), siu-li t'ao′ 手裏套;— *under the arm*, leh-ts′ 'ô gyih 肐°子下擗;— *on the arm* (as strings of cash), gyiao 撟

CART, liang′-leng-ts'ô′ 兩輪車 (ih dzing, ih-zo)

CARTILAGE, ts'e′-kweh 脆骨

CARTRIDGE, p'e′-hao-liao ho′-yiah-pao′ 配好了火藥包

CARVE, *to* — (ornamentally), tiao-k'eh′ 雕刻; tiao-hwô′ 雕花; — *meat*, ts'ih nyüoh′ 切肉°

CARVER (in wood), tiao-hwô′-s-vu 雕花司務

CARVING *knife*, ts'ih-nyüoh′-go tao′ 切肉°个°刀

CASE, t'ao 套; *pillow* —, tsing′-deo-t'ao′ 枕頭套; 'eh 盒; *watch* —, piao′-'eh 表匣°; *card* —, pa′-t'iah-'en′ 拜帖盒°; k'oh-ts′ 壳子; *spectacle* —, ngæn-kying k'oh′-ts 眼°鏡壳子; dæ 袋; *fan* —, sin′-ts-dæ 扇子袋

CASE *at law*, en′-gyin 案件; *circumstances of a* —, dzing-tsih 情節; dzing-yin′ 情由; *difficult ditto*, ky'üoh′-tsih 曲折; *state of affairs*, kwông-kying′ 光景

CASH, *a* —, ih-go dong-din′ 一个°銅錢°; *a string of* —, ih-c'ün′ dong-din′ 一串銅錢°

CASK, dong 桶; *a wine* —, ih-tsah tsiu′-dong 一隻酒桶

CASKET *for head, and other ornaments*, deo-min-siang′ 飾°箱

CAST, *to* (as metals), cü 鑄

CAST, *to throw down*, gwæn-diao′ 擓去°;— *young*, do-t'æ′ 墮胎; — *the skin* (as a snake), t'eng k'oh° 脫°壳;— *off* (as a bad son), p'i′-t'æn-diao 吒噗了°;— *away*, t'ih′-c'ih 剔出; tin-diao′ 丟去°;— *down in mind*, in-üoh′ 憂鬱

CASTANETS, (bones), ts'oh′-pæn 作°樂°的°綽板

CASTER, ts'ih′-sing-kô′ 七星架°

CASTOR-OIL, pi-mô′-yin 蓖麻油

CASUALLY, neo′-ts'eo 偶°湊; ngeo′-jün 偶°然

CASUALTY, wang-'o′ 橫°禍; fi-læ′-ts 'o 飛來之禍; t'in-li tih′-loh-læ′-go 'o′ 天降°之°禍

CASTRATE, *to* mô; — *an animal*, kyih 羯; *in* 閹

CAT, mæn 貓°(ih-tsah); *let the* — *out of the bag*, shih′-wô kông′-leh c'ih-kyiah′-de 說話講°得°出脚了°

CATALOGUE *of books*, shü-moh′ 書目;— *of names*, ming-moh′ 名目;— *of goods*, ho′-tæn 貨單

CATARACT, boh-pu′ 瀑布; *waterfall*, kwô′-loh-shü;— *in the eye*, zông-tsông 上瘴

CATARRH, *influenza*, sông-fong 傷風; *chronic* —, nao′-liu 腦漏°

CATCH, *to* k'ô 擎°; — *a thief*, k'ô' zeh 擎°賊°; — *fish*, k'ô ng' 捕°魚°; — (as water), zing 盛°; — (as something thrown), tsih 接; — *cold*, sông fong' 傷°風°; — *a disease*, teh bing' 得°病°; *ditto by infection*, bing yin-læ' 病°來延

CATECHISM, veng-teh' 問答° (ih-peng)

CATERPILLAR, *hairy* mao-djong' 毛蟲; — *found on vegetables*, ts'æ' djong 菜蟲

CATHEDRAL, cü'-kyiao-dông'主教°堂°; *bishop's* —, kyin-toh'-dông' 監督堂°

CATHOLIC, kong-gong'-go 公共個°; *a Roman Catholic*, T'in-cü'-kyiao-nying' 天主教°人°

CATTLE, *a herd of* —, ih-dziao ngeo' 一羣°牛°; *beasts of burden*, sang-k'eo' 牲° 口

CATTY, *a* ih-kying' 一斤; *sell by the* —, leng kying' ma 論斤買°

CAUGHT, k'ô'-djoh-de 擎°着° 了°; tsih-djoh-de 接着° 了°; — *in the wrong, and have nothing to say*, loh-gah'-de ; — *in the rain*, nyü-djoh yü' de 遇着° 雨 了°

CAUSE, yün-kwu' 緣故; *ing-deo*' 因頭; keng-yiu' 根由; yün-yiu' 緣由; dzing-yiu' 情由; dzing-tsih' 情節; sô-yi-jün' 所以然; *beginning*, ky'i-ing' 起因; *what is the* — *of it?* soh-go yün-kwu 甚° 麼° 緣故?

dza sô-yi-jün' 怎°樣°所以然? *without* —, vu-yün-vu-kwu' 無緣無故; *to gain a* — (before *a magistrate*), ying kwun'-s 贏官司

CAUSE *me sorrow*, lin-le' ngô iu-meng' 連累我憂悶; ta'-li ngô iu-meng' 帶累我憂悶; s' teh ngô iu-meng' 使得我憂悶; — *one to feel uncomfortable*, cü'-s-teh nying' feh en'-tæn 致使得人°弗安耽

CAUTERIZE *with hot iron*, t'ông 燙; — *with burning herbs, &c.*, kyiu 灸°

CAUTION, *to use* —, tso-gyi' 留心°; — *lest he forget*, di-sing' 提醒; *exhort*, ky'ün 勸

CAUTIOUS, kwu-zin' kwu-'eo' 顧前°顧後°; *circumspect*, ts'-si 仔細

CAVALRY, mô'-ping 馬兵

CAVE, dong 洞; sæn-dong' 山洞; sæn-ngæn'-dong 山巖洞

CAVIL, *to* p'i-poh' 批駁; p'i-siah' 批削

CAVITY, k'ong 孔; dong 洞; ky'iao 竅; *the seven cavities*, (ears, nose, mouth, eyes), ts'ih' ky'iao 七竅

CEASE, *to* hyih 歇; ts 止; deng 停°; — *from*, hyih'-loh 歇落

CEASELESS, feh-hyih' 弗歇; feh-ts' 弗止; feh-deng' 弗停°; ih-zông' feh teh k'ong' 一息° 弗得空

CEDAR, pah'-jü 柏樹

CEILING of boards, t'in-hwô'-pæn 天花板; ting'-kah-pæn 頂隔板; — of lath and plaster, nyi-t'in'-mun 泥天墁; nyi ting'-kah-pæn 泥頂隔板; want a —, iao mun'-ih-mun 要墁一墁

CELEBRATE, to — one's birthday, tso sang' 做生°; what are you celebrating? ng yiu soh'-go hyi'-ky'ing z-ken' 你有甚°麼°喜慶事幹?

CELEBRATED, veng-ming'-go 聞名个°; c'ih-ming'-go 出名个°;—physician, ming i' 名醫; — scholar, ming jü' 名儒;— shop, yiu ming-sing'-go tin' 有名聲个°店

CELL in a prison, nying-vông' 人°房; — for literary condidates, 'ao-ts' 號子

CELLAR, di-ing'-ts 地窨子; di-yüih' 地穴; di-kao' 地窖

CEMENT, lime, zah-hwe' 石°灰; glue, kao 膠°; varnish and flour —, sang ts'ih' min-feng' 生°漆麵粉

CEMETERY, veng-t'æn' 墳灘

CENSER, hyiang-lu' 香爐; swing-ing —, di-lu' 提爐; tiao'-lu 吊爐

CENSOR, nyü-s' 御史

CENSORIOUS, kwæn'-we p'i-bing' 慣會批評

CENSURABLE, kæ tsah'-be 該責備; yiu ts'o'-c'ü 有錯處

CENSURE, he received a great deal of —, gyi' ziu nying-kô' hyü'-to tsah'-be 其受人°家°許多責備

CENSUS, a-wu'-ts'ah 門°牌°冊: to take the —, zao a-wu'-ts'ah 造門°牌°冊;— tables, nying-ting'-ts'ah 人°丁冊

CENTER, or CENTRE, the cong-nyiang' 中央°; tông-cong' 當中°;— of a circle, yün-ky'ün' cong-sing' 圓圈中心

CENTIPEDE, meng-kong 蜈蚣° (ih-kwang); — bite, meng-kong' ngao'' 蜈°蚣°鮫; meng kong' ting' 蜈°蚣°叮

CENTRAL forces, cong-nyiang'-go lih-dao' 中央°个°力道; — road, cong lu' 中路

CENTUPLE, kô ih-pah' be 加°一百°倍

CENTURION, pah'-tsong 百°總

CENTURY, ih-pah' nyin 一百°年

CEREMONIOUS, to-li'-go 多禮个°; do not be so —, feh pih' kyü li' 弗必拘禮

CEREMONY, li 禮; li'-mao 禮貌; li'-tsih 禮節

CERTAIN, ih-ding' 一定; ding-jih' 定實; a — person, mo' nying 某人°; a — day, mo' nyih 某日°

CERTAINLY, pih'-ding 必定; pih'-kying 畢竟; tön'-jün 斷然; kyüih'-ding 決定; jih-dzæ' 實在; — not, ih-ding' peh-yih' 一定不易

CERTIFICATE, *recommendation*, tsin'-shü 薦書; tsiao'-we 照會; *proof*, bing-kyü' 憑據; — *for money*, bing-tæn' 憑單; *customs' general* —, tsong'-tæn 總單

CERTIFY, *to* lib bing-kyü' 立憑據

CESSATION *of work*, deng kong' 停°工; hyih kong' 歇工

CHAFE, *to rub*, soh'-soh 挱挱; no'-no 挪挪; *to rub off the skin*, bi' ts'ah'-t'ah 皮擦脫; bi' ts'ah'-sông 皮擦傷

CHAFED *in mind*, sing'-li ts'iao'-soh-soh'-go-de 中°心°如°刺°

CHAFF (of rice), k'ông 糠; long'-k'ông' 礱糠; *pounded* —, si'-k'ông 細糠; *the inner hull of wheat*, fu-bi' 麩皮; mah-bi' 麥皮

CHAFFER, *to* leng-liang' kô'-din 論量價°錢°

CHAFING-DISH (containing coals for keeping tea warm), nön'-lu 煖爐; — (for vegetables) nön'-ko 煖鍋; *steam heater for food*, t'ông bo'-ts 湯婆子; nön'-un 煖碗

CHAGRIN, *to feel* —, ao'-nao 懊惱

CHAIN, lin-diao' 鏈條 (ih-fu)

CHAIR, ü-ts 椅°子 (ih-pô); *arm* —, ü'-ts yiu k'ao'-siu-go 椅°子有靠手个°; *folding* —, tsih'-diah-ü' 摺疊椅°; *camp* —, mô'-tseh-ü' 馬扎椅°; *sedan* —, gyiao-ts' 轎子 (ih-ting);

*tilt the* —, gyiao-ts' sing-ky'i'-læ 轎子升起來; *set it* (the chair) *down level*, fông gyi bing' 放其平

CHAIR-BEARER, gyiao-fu' 轎夫 (ih-ming); gyiao-pæn' 轎班; gyiao-nying' 轎人°

CHALK, bah-t'u' 白°土

CHALLENGE, *to* t'ao tsin' 討戰; *to reject a* —, min'-tsin 免戰

CHAMBER, *bed* ngo-vông' 臥房; vông-kæn' 房間°; kw'eng-kæn' 寢室°; *a lady's* —, ne-vông' 內房; *officer's* —, zông-vông' 上房; — *pot*, shü-bing' 尿瓶; yia-wu' 夜°壺; bin-wu' 便壺; *wooden ditto*, yia-dong' 夜°桶

CHAMBER-MAID, a-m' 阿°姆°; ah-sao' 阿嫂; *female slave*, ô-deo' 丫頭

CHAMOIS, ling-yiang 羚羊

CHAMOMILE. See CAMOMILE.

CHAMP, *to chew*, ziah 嚼

CHANCE, *by* vu-i'-cong 無意中; neo'-ts'eo 偶°湊; ih'-feh-læ'-kwu 一弗來顧; *met by* —, ngeo'-jün p'ong'-djoh-de 偶°然逢°着°了°; *seize the best* —, tsin bin-i' 佔便宜; tsin siang-ing'; *seize the first* —, tsin zông-fong' 佔上風; tsin min-ts' 佔面子

CHANCELLOR, *literary* 'oh'-dæ 學°臺; — (of the Imperial Academy), da tsong'-dzæ 大總裁; (styled) tsong-s' 宗師

CHANDLER, *tallow* lah-coh'-s-vu 蠟 燭 司 務

CHANGE, to keng-kæ' 更 改; pin 變; pin'-wun' 變 換; pin'-yih 變 易; — *for the worse*, pin'-diao 變 壞°; — *color*, pin seh' 變 色; pin'-wun ngæn-seh' 變 換 顏° 色; — *in appearance*, pin yiang' 變 樣; — *disposition*, sing'-dzing keng-pin' 性 情 更 變; sing'-dzing pin'-hwô 性 情 變 化; — *one's dress*, wun i-zông 換 衣 裳; — *often*, cün-pin' 轉 變; — *a dollar*, de fæn-ping' 儅 番 餅; — *one's mind*, sing cün-diao' 心 轉 調; *to exchange*, wun 換; diao 調; diao-wun' 調 換; *cannot be changed* (altered), keng-kæ'-feh-læ 更 改 弗 來; kæ'-ko-feh-læ 改 過 弗 來; *changed in heart, or mind* (generally for the worse), sing' weh'-de 心 活 了°; sing' weh-dong'-de 心 活 動 了°; sing pin'-de 心 變 了°

CHANGEABLE, hyih'-hyih yiu kyi-pin' 時°時°有 機 變; fæn'-foh-vu-djông 反 覆 無 常 (djông or dzông); — (as weather, or clouds), ts'in-pin'-væn'-hwô 千 變 萬 化

CHANGER, *money* dzin-tin'- kwun 錢 店 中° 人°

CHANNEL, shü'-lu 水° 路; shü'-dao 水° 道; *to dig a* —, k'æ 'o-dao' 開 河 道

CHANT, to — *religious books*, (as Buddhists do), nyiæn kying' 念 經; dzong kying' 誦 經; — *and worship*, pa ts'æn' 拜° 懺

CHAOTIC, weng'-deng 混 沌

CHAP, to — (as the hands), c'ing-ts'ah' 皴 坼; k'æ-kyüing' 開 皺

CHAPEL, li-pa-dông' 禮 拜° 堂 (ih-go)

CHAPTER, a ih-tsông' 一 章; ih-p'in' 一 篇

CHAR, to tön 燉; siao 燒; *this wood is charred*, keh'-go za tön' tso t'æn'-de 這° 个° 柴 燉 做 炭 了°

CHARACTER, *letter*, z 字; z-ngæn' 字 眼° (ih-go); *understands characters*, sih'-teh z' 識 得 字; *a person's* —, p'ing'-'ang' 品 行; nying-p'ing' 人 品; p'ing'-kah 品 格; ming-tsih' 名 節; *his* — *is worthless*, gyi-go p'ing'-'ang feh ky'i'-djong 其 个 品 行 弗 器 重; *lose one's* —, shih ming-tsih' 失 名 節

CHARCOAL, t'æn 炭; *soft wood* —, fu-t'æn' 軟 炭; *hard wood* —, bah-t'æn 白° 炭

CHARGE, *expense*, fi'- yüong 費 用; *I will bear the* —, keh z ngò dzing-dzih'-go 這° 是 我 承 值 个°; *he gave it in my* —, gyi kao-dæ' peh ngô' 其 交° 代 與° 我; *a* — *to be borne*, pe'-tih go tseh'-zing 背 的 个° 責 任; t'iao-tih-go tæn'-deo 挑 的° 个° 擔 頭

CHARGE, *to command*, feng-fu′ 吩
附; — *repeatedly*, ting-eoh′ 叮
囑; *to entrust*, t'oh 託; kao-
dæ′ 交 代 &c.; *to put in — of
another* (as papers of office &c.),
kao-bun′ 交 盤; — *on account*,
zông tsiang′ 上 帳; — *him with
a fault*, wô ze′ kwe′-ü gyi′ 話 罪
歸 于 其; — *falsely*, ün-wông′
冤 枉; ün-ky'üih′ 冤 屈; 'en
hyüih′ p'eng nying′ 含 血 噴
人°; — *the fault to me*, kwe
gyiu ü ngô 歸 咎 于 我; —
*with a fault* (in one's hearing, but not to his face), k'ao-
toh′; — *a price*, t'ao kô′-din 討
價′ 錢°; *to attack*, ts'ong-fong′
衝 鋒

CHARITABLE, yiu jing-æ′-sing 有
仁 愛 心; yiu dz-pe′-sing 有
慈 悲 心; yiu ts'eb-ing′-ts-sing
有 惻 隱 之 心; *very* —, kwông′
tso hao′-z 廣 做 好 事

CHARITABLY, *deal — with him*,
dæ gyi kw'un-shü′ 待 其 寬 恕

CHARITY, jing-æ′ 仁 愛; *to give*
—, tsiu-tsi′ nying-kô 賙 濟 人°
家°; 'ang hao′-z 行 好 事; pu′-s
nying-kô′ 佈 施 人° 家°

CHARM, (paper with characters),
vu 符 (ih-dao); — *for the body*,
wu-sing′-vu 護 身 符; — (for
the wrist), dao-weh′ 桃 核°; —
(for the neck of children), 'ông′-
so 項 鎖; — (for the bed),
ts'ông-bu-'en′ 菖 蒲 孩°; dong-

din′-pao′-kyin 銅 錢° 寶 劍;
— (over the door), pao′-en-ts
保 安 紙; — (in the ancestral
hall), cing′-dzeh-vu 鎮 宅 符;
— (for protecting house furniture and utensils, pasted on at
the New Year), ts'ing-long′-ts 青
龍 紙

CHARM, *to — away bad influences*,
bih zia′ 辟 邪°; — *away disease*
(by incantation), c'ih′-kying′djü-
bing′ 出 經 治 病; *ditto* (by
incantation, and written characters), yüong vu-tsiu′djü bing′ 用
符 咒 治 病; *to captivate*, mi-
weng′ 迷 魂

CHARMED (as by a spell), jib-mi-
weng′-dzing-de 入 迷 魂 陣 了°

CHARMING *person*, gyih-me′-go
nying 極 美 个° 人; — *music*,
byih weng-ling′ go yüoh′ 攝 魂
靈 个° 樂

CHART, *marine* dziu-hæ′-du 籌 海
圖 (ih-tsiang)

CHARTER, *to — a vessel*, tsu jün′
租 船; shü′ jün 賃° 船

CHASE, *the* tang-liah′ 打 獵

CHASE, *to* tse-ken′ 追 趕; ken′-
zông-ky'i 趕 上 去°

CHASM, di′ lih-k'æ′-go di′-fông 地
裂 開 个° 地 方 (ih-da)

CHASTE, ts'ing-kyih′ 清 潔;
tsing-kyih′ 貞 潔, said of women;
tsing-tsih′ 貞 節, used when a
single or widowed woman remains chaste.

CHASTISE, *to punish,* tsah'-vah 責
罰; tang 打; — *severely,* djong'
tsah'-vah 重責罰; ying-vah'
刑罰 is used for legal punishment but not often in school, or
in the family.

CHASTITY (of men), siu-nyi' 守
義; — (of maidens), siu-tsing' 守
貞; — (of women), siu-tsih' 守節

CHAT, *to* dæn'-dæn 談談; jü-jü'
敘敘; kông-kông 講講;
*idle talk,* 'æn wô' 閒話; siao'
wô 笑話

CHATTLES, kô-s'-jih-veh' 家私
什物; kô-yüong'-jih-veh' 家
用什物

CHATTER, *to* ts'ih'-ts'ih-ts'oh-
ts'oh kông' 說話嘈雜講;
kông in' wô 講燕話; *teeth*
—, ngô'-ts' siang-tang' 牙齒
相打

CHEAP, zin 賤; bin-i' 便宜;
(cheaper than it ought to be),
ky'iao 巧; ky'ing-ky'iao' 輕巧;
— (the proper price) siang-ing'
相應; feh-kyü' 弗貴; *can you
sell cheaper?* ng' kô'-din hao weh-
dong'-tin feh 你價錢好活
動點否?

CHEAPEN, *to* kæn kô' 減價

CHEAT, *one who gets by pretence,*
kwa'-ts 拐子; *one who pretends
to be what he is not,* pæn kô'-
nying 扮假人

CHEAT, *to* ky'i 欺; p'in 騙; hong
哄; ky'i-p'in' 欺騙; hong-

p'in 哄騙; *can — men, cannot
— God,* nying' k'o ky'i', Jing,
feh-k'o' ky'i 人可欺神弗可
欺; *to — by asking more than one
pays* (in buying for another), loh
dong-din' 落銅錢; *every trade
has its cheating,* pah' 'ông pah' bi
百行百弊; *to get something
on false pretences,* kwa'-p'in 拐
騙; *to get money ditto,* p'in dong-
din' 騙銅錢; *he can't — me,*
gyi' kwa ngô', kwa'-feh-ky'i' 其
拐我拐弗去

CHECK, *order for money,* nying-
p'iao' 銀票

CHECK, *to stop, or hinder,* tön'-djü
擋住; lah-djü' 拉住; tsu'-
djü 阻住; — *by comparing,*
te'-ko 對過; — *disease,* djü
bing 治病; — *diarrhœa,* ts
dza' 止瀉

CHECKED, *disease is* —, bing ts'ô'-
loh-kæ'-de 病漸差了; bing-
shü' ky'ing-k'o'-de 病勢輕可
了; bing song'-de 病鬆了

CHEEK, cü'-bu 嘴輔 (ih-min);
*the right* —, jing-pin' cü'-bu 順
邊嘴輔

CHEEK-BONES, gyün-kweh' 顴
骨; *high* —, gyün'-kweh kao'
顴骨高

CHEER, *entertainment,* tsiu'-zih 酒
席; — *him up,* kw'un gyi'-go
sing' 寬其个心; k'æ gyi'
go sing' 開其个心; *to en-
courage,* min'-li 勉勵; — *by*

*striking hands and feet*, siu vu tsoh-dao-go ts'ing-tsæn' 手舞足蹈個° 稱讚

CHEERFUL, ken-sing'-go 甘心個°; *always* —, djông-djông' hyi'-siao-yin-k'æ' 常常喜笑顏開

CHEERFULLY, *do* ken-sing'dzing-nyün tso' 甘心情願做; dzing-nyün' do-c'ih' 情願拿°出; *give* —, hyi' dzu 喜助; loh dzu' 樂助

CHEERLESS, m c'ü-hyiang 無趣向; *narrow and — place*, di-fông' 'ah-'ah-tsah-tsah feh sông'-kw'a 地方狹窄弗爽快°

CHEESE, ngeo-na' ping 牛𡡕°餅; jü' ping 乳餅

CHEMISE, t'i-li sæn' 襯°裡衫 (ih-gyin)

CHERISH, *hold as dear*, ziang pao'-pe ka tông-sing' 像寶貝個°當心; — *resentment*, ün'-'eng sing'-li dzeng'-tih 怨恨心裡存的; ün'-ky'i feh sæn' 怨氣弗散; ün'-ky'i k'eo-li 'en'-tih 怨氣口裏含的

CHERRY, ang-dao' 櫻桃; ang-cü' 櫻珠 (ih-go); — *color*, nyi'-'ong seh 二°紅色

CHESS, ziang'-gyi 象棋; — *board*, gyi-bun' 棋盤; — *men*, gyi-ts' 棋子; — *pawns*, ping-tseh' 兵卒; *to play* —, tsiah gyi' 著棋

CHEST, siang-ts' 箱子 (ih-tsah); — *of tea*, ih-siang dzô-yih' 一箱茶葉; *the breast*, hyüong-kwun'-deo 胸管°頭

CHESTNUT, lih-ts' 栗子 (ih-go); — *tree*, lih-ts' jü 栗子樹 (ih-cü)

CHEW, *to* ziah 嚼

CHICKEN, kyi 雞; siao-kyi' 小雞 (ih-tsah)

CHICKEN-POX, shü'-deo 水°痘

CHIDE, *to* tsah 責; tsah'-be 責備; — *in a severe tone*, heng 吒°

CHIEF, *the first*, di-ih-go 第一個°; *the head*, deo 頭; deo-nao' 頭腦; *of — importance*, deo iao-kying' 第一要緊; — *of an army*, nyün-sœ' 元帥; tsiang-kyüing' deo-moh' 將軍頭目

CHIEFLY, di-ih' 第一; *more than half*, ih-do-pun' 一大半; — *indebted to you*, di-ih' to-dzing' ng 第一多承你°

CHILBLAIN, tong'-tsoh 凍瘃 (ih-go); *to have chilblains*, sang tong'-tsoh 生°凍瘃

CHILD, siao-nying' 小孩°; *an infant*, na-hwun' 嬰孩°; *with* —, yiu sing-yüing' 有身孕; *to bear children*, sang na-hwun' 生°嬰°孩°

CHILD-BED, *in* zông zô'-dong 上坐°桶; ling-beng' 臨盆

CHILDHOOD, siao-læ'-z-'eo' 小來時候; in'-nyin 幼年; siao-nyin-z-tsi' 少年時節°

CHILDLESS, m'-teh ng-nô' 沒°有°兒°女°; m'-teh sang-loh'

沒° 有° 生° 落; vu-'eo 無後

CHILDREN, ng-nô' 兒° 女°; ng-ts nön'; *little boys*, siao - wæn' 小兒°

CHILL, *in a* —, 'en seo-seo 寒凍凍

CHILLY, lang'-ts'ing-ts'ing 冷° 清清; *very* —, 'en-gying'-gying 寒噤噤; — *from fear*, hahleh kyiah' siu ping-lang' 嚇得° 脚手冰冷°

CHIMNEY, in-ts'ong' 烟囱 (ih-dao); *lamp* —, teng-tsæn in-dong' 燈盞烟囱° (ih-kwun)

CHIN, 'ô'-bô 下吧°

CHINA, Cong-koh' 中國; Dats'ing'-koh 大清國; Cong-wô' 中華; — *proper*, Jih-pah' sang 十八省°

CHINA-ASTER, kyüih'-hwô 菊°花

CHINA-WARE, dz-ky'î' 磁器; *fine* —, si' dz-ky'î' 細磁器

CHINESE, *native of China*, Cong-koh nying' 中國人°; Hen'-nying 漢人°; — *language*, Cong-koh' wô' 中國話; — *character*, Hen' z 漢字

CHINK, hwah'-lih-vong 豁裂縫 (ih-da); *very small* —, hwah'-u; — *of dollars*, yiang-dzin' sing-byiang' 洋錢聲響

CHIPS, moh-fî' 木屑°

CHIP, *to* — *wood*, siah jü 削樹

CHIRP, *to* — (*as a sparrow*), kyiao 叫; *noisy chirping* (*as of magpies*), ts'ao 診

CHISEL, zoh 鑿 (ih-kwun)

CHIT-CHAT, 'æn - wô' 閒° 話; k'ong'-deo-wô 空頭話

CHOICE, *selected*, kæn'-shün-go 揀° 選个°; t'iao'-shün-go 挑選个°; — *goods*, zông-teng'-go ho'-veh 上等个° 貨物; — *friend*, zông-teng'-go beng-yiu' 上等个° 朋友; *I have no* —, vu sô' kæn'-dzeh 無所揀°擇

CHOIR *of singers*, ih-pæn we ts'ông'-go cü'-kwun 一班會唱个°人°

CHOKE, *to* — *with something in the throat*, gang wu-long' 哽° 喉° 嚨; — *to death*, gang'-sah 哽° 煞; *to* — *to death with the hand*, k'ah'-sah 搕煞

CHOLERA, *vomiting and purging*, hoh'-lön' t'u-sia 霍亂吐瀉; *spasms in the limbs*, kyiah-kying'-tiao 脚筋吊

CHOLERIC *temperament*, sing'-kah ts'ao' 性格躁°; sing'-dzing bao-ts'ao' 性情暴躁°; sing'-ts kyih' 性子急; *temperament like thunder*, sing-ts ziang le ka-go° 性子如°雷

CHOOSE, *to* t'iao 挑; kæn 揀°; shün 選; kæn'-shün 揀°選; kæn'-dzeh 揀°擇; *whichever you* —, ze ng' kæn 隨你°揀°

CHOP, *to* p'ih 劈; *to* — *wood*, p'ih za' 劈柴°; — *meat fine*, nyüob tsæn-se' 肉切°碎°; *a mark*, z-'ao' 字號; *mutton* —, yiang ba'-kweh 羊排°骨

CHOPPING - BOARD, tsing - pæn' 椹板

CHOPPING-KNIFE, boh-tao' 厨° 刀 (ih-pô)

CHOP-STICKS, kw'æn 筷° (a pair ih-sông)

CHORD of a musical instrument, yin-sin' 絃線 (ih-keng)

CHORISTER, choir-leader, ling-deo' ts'ông'-go 領頭唱个°

CHOWDER, ng-kang' 魚° 羹°

CHRIST, Kyi-toh' 基督

CHRISTIAN, siang-sing Yiæ-su'-go nying 相信耶穌个° 人°; disciple of Jesus, Yiæ-su' meng-du' 耶穌門徒; Kyi-toh'-du 基督徒

CHRISTIANITY, Yiæ-su' kyiao 耶穌敎

CHRONICLES, s'-kyi 史記; kông-kæn' 綱鑑°; — (in the Bible), Lih-dæ-ts' liah 歷代志畧

CHRONOLOGY, pin-nyin'-kyi'-loh 編年紀錄

CHRYSALIS, kyin 繭; — of a silk-worm, zen-kyin' 蠶繭

CHURCH, body of christians, kyiao'-we 敎會; kong-we' 公會; kyiao'-meng 敎門; place of worship, li-pa-dông' 禮拜°堂; — member, kyiao'-yiu 敎友; dze-kyiao'-go 在敎个°

CHURLISH, rude, ts'u-lu' 粗鹵; niggardly, pi'-si 鄙細; pi'-seh 鄙嗇

CICATRICE, CICATRIX, pô 疤; — of a wound, sông-pô' 傷疤

CIDER, bing-ko'-tsin 平菓酒

CINDERS, siao-dzing'-go me' 燒剩 个° 煤; pick out the —, siao-dzing'-go me', kæn'-c'ih 燒剩个° 煤揀° 出

CINNABAR, cü-sô' 硃砂

CINNAMON, nyüoh-kwe' 肉° 桂; kwe'-bi 桂皮; the best —, zông-yiao' kwe 上猺桂; —tree, kwe'-jü 桂樹

CIPHER, to sön 算; the word ling 零, a fragment, is used to denote parts of tens, parts of hundreds, &c.; thus 108 is read, ih-pah ling pah 一百° 零八; 1050 is read, ih ts'in ling ng-jih 一千零五° 十

CIRCLE, yün-ky'ün' 圓圈 (ih-go); draw a —, wô ih-go ky'ün' 畫一个° 圈; center of a —, yün-ky'ün'-go cong-sing' 圓圈个° 中心

CIRCLING, dön-ky'ün' yü-tæn'-cün 團圈圍° 轉

CIRCULAR, official tsiao'-we 照會; business —, cü-tæn' 知單; send round a —, feng cü-tæn' 分知單

CIRCULATE, to — (as air &c.) yüing-dong 運動; — (as a person), tseo'-dong 走動; 'ang-dong' 行°動; — (as the blood), cün'-dong 轉動; —(as a report), yiang-k'æ' 揚開

CIRCUMCISION, tsiu-keh'-li 周
割禮

CIRCUMFERENCE, tsiu-we' 周圍；
*what is the — of the earth?* di-
gyiu tsiu-we' yiu to-siao' li 地
球周圍有多少里？

CIRCUMJACENT, tsiu'-we-siang-
gying' 周圍相近

CIRCUMLOCUTION, wæn-wæn'-
ky'üoh-ky'üoh-go kông' 彎彎
曲曲个°講°

CIRCUMSCRIBED *by difficult circumstances,* be kying'-hwông
dzin-djü'-liao 被境况纏住了；
*the space is —,* dæn-dziang' be
di-gyüoh'-æn'-sah-liao 壇塲被
地局限°煞了

CIRCUMSPECT, ts'-si 仔細；siao'-
sing-go 小心个°

CIRCUMSTANCES, kwông-kying'
光景；dzing-ying 情形；kying'-
hwông 境况；*judging from —*
(*as of a country*), k'en'-k'en
ying-shü' 看看形勢；*accom-
modate one's self to —,* ze-kyi'-
ing'-pin 隨機應變；*to act ac-
cording to —,* tso z-ken', k'en'-
ky'i sang'-dzing 做事幹看起
生°情；kyin-kyi'-r-ying' 見機
而行；*yielding to — I let you go,*
ngô dzong-gyün', peh ng ky'i'
我從權俖你去°；*in reduced
—,* gyüong'-de 窮了°

CIRCUMVENT, *to — plans,* p'o fah'
破法

CITE, *to call,* djün-tsing'-ke 傳進

來；—*from a book,* shü'-li ying'-
læ 書裡引來

CITIZEN, dzing-li'-nying 城裏人°

CITRON, *large* (citrus medica),
hyiang-lön 香櫞；*Buddha's
hand,* veh-siu' 佛手

CITY, dzing-ts' or zing-ts' 城子；
(ih-zo)；— *wall,* dzing-ziang' 城
墻；— *moat,* dzing-dzi' 城池

CIVIL, *polite,* yiu li' 有禮；yiu li'-
mao 有禮貌；yiu li'-tsih 有
禮節；— *and military,* veng
vu' 文武

CIVILITY, li 禮；li'-mao 禮貌；
li'-tsih 禮節

CLAIM, *I — your promise,* ng sô
ing-hyü, ngô iao-de 你所應
許，我要了°；— *one's money,*
t'ao dong-din' kyü-læ 討銅錢°
歸°來；*have a right to —,* yiu
meng-veng' hao t'ao' 有名°好
好討

CLAIMANT, t'ao'-cü 討主

CLAM, yün-keh' 圓蛤 (ih-go)

CLAMBER, *to* bô-zông 爬上；weh'-
zông 挖上；hyih'-zông；— *up*
(a rope or pole), jing-zông'-ky'i
循上去°

CLAMOR, *to* nao 鬧；ts'ao'-nao
吵鬧

CLAMOROUS, nao-nyih'-go 鬧熱°
个°；nao-nao'-nyih-nyih-go ts'ao'
鬧鬧熱°熱°个°吵

CLAN, dzoh 族；dzoh-veng 族牙
(ih, and ih-go)；*belonging to the
—,* dzoh cong' 族中；*all of a*

*family,* zi-kô'-nying 自°家°人°; *of the same —,* dong-dzoh'-go 同族个°; dong-sing' go 同姓个°; *of the same family name but of a different —,* dong sing' feh we dzoh' 同姓不°宗°

CLANDESTINE, s-'ô' 私下°; kyü-tao-ih-koh; t'eo-bun' 偷瞒°; en'-me 暗昧

CLANDESTINELY, ing'-dzông 隱藏

CLANK (of a chain), lông-lông'-hyiang 鍞鍞響

CLAP, *to* kwah 摑; *— on the face,* kwah' ih-kwông 摑一掌°; *— the table, &c.*(as if angry), kwah'-coh tang-teng' 摑桌打凳

CLAP *of thunder,* p'ih'-le 霹靂° (ih-go)

CLARIFY, *to* di-ts'ing' 提清; *— it by settling,* ting' gyi-ts'ing' 淀°其清; *— by skimming,* keh' ken-zing' 格乾淨°; *— by straining,* li' ken-zing' 濾乾淨°

CLASH, *to* k'eh'-k'eh-bang-bang' 磕磕撞°撞°; *— in opinion,* i'-s ts'o-p'ing' 意思差摒; i'-s gah-tang'.

CLASP, *n.* k'eo 扣; tah'-k'eo 搭扣

CLASS, *sort,* le 類 (ih); *a — of pupils,* ih-pæn' 'oh-sang'-ts 一班學°生°子; *— (in society),* teng 等; kyih 級

CLASSICS, *Chinese* kying-shü 經書; s'-shü ng'-kying 四書五°經

CLASSIFY, *to* feng le' 分類; feng 'ao-su' 分號數

CLAW, tsao 爪; kyiah'-tsao 脚爪

CLAY, na-nyi' 坭; *potter's —,* wông na-nyi' 黃坭

CLEAN, ken-zing' 乾淨°; kyih'-zing 潔淨°; ts'ing-kyih' 清潔; *— as snow,* kying'-ken-shih-zing' 鏡乾雪淨°

CLEAN, *to* long ken'-zing 弄°乾淨°; *— by washing,* gyiang' ken-zing 洗°乾淨°; *— up (as a place, &c.),* tsin-tsoh'.

CLEAR, ming 明; *very —(as water, glass, &c.),* kwang'-ts'ing 洸清; pih'-po'-s-ts'ing' 碧波四清; *— (as ideas),* ling'-ts'ing 靈清; *— weather,* t'in zing' 天晴°; *— profit,* zing dong'-din 淨°錢'; *—from blame,* 'ao'-vu yüô-tin' 毫無瑕玷; pih'-po'-s ts'ing' 碧波四清

CLEAR, *the weather will —,* t'in we k'æ' 天會開; *— up (by explanation),* kông' ming-bah' 講明白°; *— the way,* nyiang lu' 讓°路; *ditto by calling (before an officer),* heh dao' 喝道; *— one's self,* feng ka' 分解'

CLEARLY, ming-tông'-tông 分°明; ts'ing-t'ong' 清通; t'eo' ming-bah'-go 透明白°个°

CLEARNESS *of vision,* ngæn'-kwông tsin' 眼°光尖; ngæn'-ho tsin' 眼°火尖; ngæn'-tsing liang' 眼°睛亮

CLEAVE, *to* p'ih 劈; p'ih'-k'ae 劈開

CLEAVER *for wood*, za-tao' 柴°
刀; ken-tao' 鋸° 刀 (ih-pô)

CLEFT, vong-dao' 縫道; *crack*,
hweh'-lih-vong 轄裂縫; hweh'-
u 轄裂° (ih-da)

CLEMENCY, *to treat with* —,
kw'un-shü' dæ 寬恕待;
kw'un-dæ' 寬待; *treat a person
with* —, dæ nying kw'un' 待
人°寬

CLEPSYDRA, dong-wu-tih'-leo 銅
壺滴漏

CLERGYMAN, kyiao'-s 教° 師
(ih-we)

CLERK, *writer*, dæ-shü' 代書; dæ-
pih' 代筆; — (in a store), ho'-
kyi 夥計; — (in a ya-men)
shü-bæn' 書辦

CLEVER, l'ing-ky'iao' 靈巧; ling-
li' 伶俐; hwæn 慣°

CLEVERLY *done* (as work), si'-
ky'iao 細巧

CLIFF, zah-pih' 石° 壁; ts'iao'-
pih 峭壁

CLIMATE, shü'-t'u 水° 土; fong-
ky'i' 風氣; *is the — good or
bad?* shü'-t'u hao' ẁa 水土好
孬°? *unfavorable* —, shü'-t'u feh
voh' 水土弗服; fong-ky'i'
feh-te' 風氣弗對

CLIMB, *to* bô 爬; hyih; ẁeh 挖;
— *a tree*, hyih jü' 挖樹; —
*the wall*, bô ziang 爬墻; — *a
hill*, ẁeh sæn' 挖山; — *a rope*,
jing zing' 循繩

CLINCH, *to hold fast*, nyiah lao'
捻牢; — *a nail*, ting-cü' cün-
kyiah' 釘銖轉脚; — (as a
matter), k'ao-ting'-cün-kyiah' 拷
釘轉脚

CLING, *to* hyih'-lao 黏牢; la-lao'
feh fông 拉° 牢弗放; — *to
his mother*, hyih-kying ah-nyiang'
di'-fông 不° 離° 其° 母°

CLIP *off a little* (with scizzors), tsin'-
tin-diao 蕾點去°; zæ-tin'-diao
裁點去°

CLIPPINGS *of cloth*, se-pu-den' 碎
布頭°; pu-tsin'-se 布蕾碎

CLOCK, z-ming'-cong 自鳴鐘
(ih-kô); *what o'clock is it?* kyi
tin'-cong 幾點鐘? *one o'clock*,
ih tin'-cong 一點鐘

CLOCK *and watch maker*, cong-
piao'-s-vu 鐘表司務

CLOD, *a* ih-kw'e na-nyi' 一塊坭

CLOG, *to choke up*, seh'-sah 塞煞;
seh'-djü 塞住

CLOGGED, *shoes — with mud*, 'a,
na-nyi' dong-mun'-de 鞋° 俾° 坭
遭° 滿了°

CLOGS, moh-gyih' 木屐; jü-'a'
樹鞋°; hyiang-'a' 響鞋° (a
pair, ih-sông)

CLOISTER, *Buddhist* z 寺; en 菴;
*Taoist* —, kwun 觀; *nunnery*,
nyi-kwu' en 尼姑菴

CLOSE *of life*, lao'-mæn z-'eo 老
邁時候; sông yü væn'-kying
桑楡晚景 (veng); *sunset*

*of life,* nyih-deo′ loh-sæn′ z-'eo 日°頭落山時候

CLOSE *the door,* kwæn meng′ 關門; — *all the doors and windows,* kwæn-meng′-dong-wu 關門閉戶; — *the eyes,* ngæn′-tsing pi′-long 眼°睛閉攏; *ditto,* (when sleepy), ngæn′-tsing mi-long′ 眼°睛眯攏; — *the mouth,* cü′-pô pi′-long 嘴吧閉攏; — *a letter,* fong sing′ hao 封信好; — *a book,* shü′ siu-long′ 書收攏; — *in* (as with brick), diah-sah′ 疊煞; ts-sah′; seh-sah′ 塞煞; mun-sah′ 壋煞; — (as a wound), sang-long′ 生°攏; — (as a boil), siu-k'eo′ 收口

CLOSE (in texture), si′-kyih 細潔; kyih′-jih 砝實; *niggardly,* pi′-seh 鄙嗇; ky'i′-liang siao′ 氣量小; liang tseh′ 量窄; lin′-kyin 連蹇; gyih-li′-li; — *weather,* t'in-ky'i seh′-meng 天氣塞悶; — *by,* siang-gying′ 相近; — *to,* t'iah′-gying 貼°近

CLOSET, djü 廚; — *in the wall,* pih′-djü 壁廚 (ih-k'eo); *small* — (in a corner, under stairs, &c.), beh-keh-long′ 犇鴿籠; *secret* —, kah-ziang′ 夾°墻; *water* —, siao′-bin vông-ts′ 小便房子; mao-k'ang′ 毛坑°

CLOT, *to* nying-long′ 凝攏

CLOTH, pu 布 (used alone, only for cotton cloth); *good native cotton* —, du′-pu 杜布; *linen*

—, mô-pu′ 麻布; keh′-pu 葛布; coh′-pu 竹布; *nankeen,* ts′-hwô-pu′ 紫花布; *bleached foreign* —, bah-yiang′-pu 白洋布; *grass* —, 'ô-pu′ 夏°布; *twilled cotton* —, zia-veng′ pu 斜°紋布; *oiled* —, yiu-pu′ 油布; *broad* —, nyi 呢; *woolen* — (flannel, &c.), nyüong-pu′ 絨布

CLOTHES, i-zông′ 衣裳; i-voh′ 衣服

CLOTHES, he — me, gyi peh ngô′ c′ün-tsiah′ 其給°我穿着°; ngô i-zông′ z gyi′ kwun′-go 我衣裳是其管个°; ngô c′ün-djoh′ gyi-go 我穿着°其个°

CLOUD, yüing 雲; *red* —, 'ong ngô′ 紅霞°; — *of dust,* hwe, bang-bang′-yiang 灰飛°揚了°

CLOUDLESS, væn-li′-vu-yüing′ 萬里無雲

CLOUDY *weather,* zông-yüing t'in′ 上雲天; ing t'in′ 陰天; ing-a′ t'in 陰靉°天

CLOVES, ting-hyiang′ 丁香

CLOWN (in a play), siao-hwô-lin′ 小花臉; (a) *rustic,* hyiang-'ô′-nying 鄉下°人°

CLOWNISH, *like a clown,* ziang siao-hwô-lin′ ka 像小花臉; *coarse,* ts′n-lu′ 粗鹵; ts'u-ts′ao′ 粗糙

CLOYED, *to be* ky'üoh′-bi-de 吃°疲了°; ky'üoh′-in′-de 吃°厭了°; ky'üoh′-leh in′-tsao-tsao 吃°得°厭遭遭

CLUB, kweng'-ts 棍子 (ih-keng)

CLUB together and hire a boat, tah jün' 搭船; to — together for eating, p'ing ho'-zih 摒火食; — together to live, p'ing-deng' 摒庬; — together to buy, p'ing ma' 摒買°

CLUE, deo-jü' 頭緒; can't find the — (to the idea), moh-feh-djoh' deo-jü' 摸弗着° 頭緒; to trace out a —, jing deng' 攀° 籐; have the —, yiu tsông-tsing' 有賍証; no — to the thief, zeh' ɔ̃-ing' ɔ̃-tsong'-de 賊° 無° 影 無° 踪了°

CLUMSY, dön'-ky'iao-go 不° 入° 竅个°

CLUSTER, ih-gyiu 一毬; ih-p'ang'.

CLUTCH, to c'ô 摢°

COAGULATE, to nying-long' 凝攏; kyih'-long 結攏; tong 凍

COAL, me-t'æn' 煤炭 (a piece, ih-kw'e)

COALESCE, to 'eh-long' 合攏; will not —, 'eh-feh-long' 合弗攏

COAL-MINE, me-t'æn' yüih 煤炭穴; me sæn' 煤山

COAL-SCUTTLE, me-t'æn' dong 煤炭桶

COARSE, ts'u 粗

COAST, hæ'-pin 海邊; all along the —, yin hæ' ih-tæ' 沿海一帶

COAST, to sail along the —, yin-hæ'-pin s' 沿海邊駛

COAT, long — to be worn with a girdle, bao-ts' 袍子; zông-mun', (a country term); long —, kah'-ao 袄襖; do-sæn' 大° 衫; short jacket, mô'-kwô 馬裰; foreign overcoat, do-i' 大° 衣

COAT (of paint or white-wash), ih-du' 一塗; one —, tæn-du' 單塗; two coats of varnish, sông-du ts'ih 雙° 塗漆; first —; deo-ih' du 頭一塗

COAX, to nyün' cü'-du 軟制度; yüong nyün'-kong 用軟工

COB, corn loh-koh sing' 秇穀心

COBWEB, bong-dzing' 逢塵; spider's —, kyih'-cü' mông' 蛞蛛網°; kyih'-cü' lön-mông' 蛞蛛亂網°

COCHINEAL, ngô-læn'-mi 呀嘲米

COCK, yüong-kyi' 雄雞; kong-kyi' 公雞 (ih-tsah)

COCKSCOMB, kyi-kwun' 雞冠; — (a flower), kyi-kwun'-hwô' 雞冠花

COCK-CROWING, kyi-di'-go z-'eo' 雞啼个° 時候

COCKLE, hen-ts' 蚶子

COCKROACH, ts'ông-lông' 蝔螂 (ih-go)

COCOA-NUT, gyia-biao' 茄瓠 (ih-go)

COCOON, kyin 繭; — of silk-worms, zen-kyin' 蠶繭

CODE of laws, lih-li' 律例

CO-EQUAL, bing-teng' 平等; bing'-kyin 並肩; dong-po' 同輩

COERCE, to ah'-cü 壓°制; iah-cü' 挾制; ah'-shü 壓勢

CO-ETERNAL, üong-yün dong-dzæ' 永遠同在

COFFEE, kô'-fi 喫°啡, transferred from the English.

COFFEE-POT, kô-fi wu' 喫°啡壺

COFFER, nying-siang' 銀箱; yiang-siang' 洋箱; — for cash, dzin-gyü' 錢櫃°

COFFIN, kwun-zæ' 棺材°; kwun-moh' 棺木 (ih-k'eo); — containing the corpse, (i.e. the spirit coffin) ling-gyiu' 靈柩; to place in the —, jih-lin' 入殮; jih-moh' 入木; loh lin' 落殮; to see the body placed in the —, song-lin' 送殮

COFFIN-MAKER, kwun-zæ'-s-vu' 棺材°司務; keh'-zæ-s-vu' 合材°司務

COG of a wheel, leng-bun-t3' 輪盤齒 (ih-go)

COGENT, yiu gying-dao'有勁道; — arguments, sô kông' dzing-li'-go 所講°情理个°

CO-HEIR, to be dong ziu ts'æn-nyih 同受產業

COHERE, to kao-nyin' 膠°粘; nyin-long' 粘攏

COIL, a — of iron wire, ih-bun t'ih-s 一盤鐵絲; a — of rope, ih-dön zing' 一團繩°

COIN, cash, dong-din 銅錢°; dollars, yiang-dzin' 洋錢°

COIN, to — cash, cü dong-din' 鑄銅錢°

COIR, tsong-li' 棕櫚

COLANDER, tin sieve, mô'-k'eo-t'ih' s' 馬口鐵篩

COLD, lang 冷°; icy —, ping-lang' 冰冷°; to grow —, lang'-ky'i-læ 冷氣來; to catch —, sông fong' 傷風; very — (as food, or a person), ping-kweh'-s-lang' 冰骨四冷°; seng'-kweh-deo 沁骨頭; to feel—, kyüoh'-teh lang' 覺得冷°; teh'-cü lang' 得知冷°

COLDLY, lang'-dæn 冷°淡; dæn-boh' 淡薄; he treated me —, gyi dæ ngô lang'-dæn 其待我冷°淡

COLIC, sô-ky'i' 痧氣; severe —, kao'-dziang-sô 絞°腸痧

COLLAPSE, in —, t'eh-nyün'-de 脫元了°; to — (as a vessel), ih'-long 凹攏; to shrivel, pih'-long 唎攏

COLLAR, ling 領 (ih-keng)

COLLATE, to compare critically, ts'æn-k'ao' 參考

COLLECT, to — (as persons), jü'-long 聚攏; jü'-jih-long 聚集攏; siu'-jih-long 收拾攏; tsing'-long-læ 整攏來; to — from various places, seo-lo' 搜羅; — (as money), teo 兜; — voluntary small contributions, teo veng-ts' 兜牙子; — large contributions, siu kyün-'ông' 收捐項;

— *revenue*, siu-se′ 收稅; *to make up a sum of money*, kyün-long′ dong-din′ 捐攏銅錢′

COLLECTOR *of land taxes*, siu-zin-liang′-nying 收錢°糧人°; du-ts‘a′ 喬差; liang-ts‘a′ 糧差; — *of customs*, siu-se′ go-nying 收稅个°人°

COLLEGE, shü-yün′ 書院 (ih-go)

COLLIER, gyüih-me-t‘æn′-go-nying 掘煤炭个°人°; k‘æ-me-t‘æn′-go-nying 開煤炭个°人°; *charcoal maker*, siao-t‘æn′-nying 燒炭人°

COLLIDE, *to* te′-deo-n°ong′; dô-kô bang′ 大°家°撞; dô-kô dzông′ 大°家°撞

COLLOCATION (of words), lin-p‘ing-go fah′-ts 連撐个°法子

COLLUDE, *to* dô - kô′ tang′- sön hong′-p‘in 大°家°打算哄騙

COLONEL, ts‘æn-tsiang′ 黎將′; fu′-tsiang 副將

COLONIZE, *to form a new settlement*, sing hying′ ih-go mô′-deo 新興一个°碼頭

COLOR, ngæn-seh′ 顏色; *neutral* —, ts‘in′ seh 淺色; *bright* —, ts‘e′ seh 翠色; *to lose* —, shih seh′ 失色; *to change* —, pin seh′ 變色; *faded* —, ngæn-seh t‘e′-diao-de 顏°色退掉了°; *of the same* —, ping seh′ 拜色; *of nearly the same* —, (when they ought to be alike or quite different), deh seh′ 套色

COLOR, *to* nyin seh′ 染°色; *to* — *red*, nyin ‘ong′ 染°紅

COLUMN, djü′-ts 柱子 (ih-keng); — *of characters*, ih-da z′ 一埭字; ih-‘ông′ z 一行字; — *of smoke*, ih-kwu in′ 一股烟 *large ditto*, ih-bong in′ 一縷烟

COMB, *coarse* s 梳°; *fine* —, bi-kyi′ 筐箕 (ih-kwun); *honey* —, fong-k‘o 蜂窩°

COMB, *to* — *the hair*, s′ deo-fah′ 梳°頭髮; — *and arrange ditto*, s′ deo′ 梳°頭

COMBAT, *to* siang-tang 相打; — (as au army), tang-tsiang 打仗°; — (as people among themselves), tang-nyiug-dzing′ 打人°陣

COMBINE, *to* ‘eh-long′ 合攏; *combined strength*, dong-sing′ yiah-lih′ 同心恊力

COME, *to* læ 來; *coming*, læ-de 來了°; *has* —, læ-ko′-de 來過了°; *came yesterday*, zô-nyih′-ts læ′-go 昨°日°子來个°; *I will* — *immediately*, ngô ziu læ′ 我就°來; — *back the same day*, tông′-nyih cün′-we 當日轉回; *when did you* — (up)? ng kyi′-z zông-læ′ 你幾時上來? — *down* (as Christ), kông′-loh 降落; — *apart*, t‘ah′-k‘æ 脫°開; — *to such an end*, ka′ kyih-ko′ 這°樣°結果; *coming events*, tsiang-læ′-go z-ken′ 將來个°事幹

COMET, sao'-tsiu-sing' 掃帚星; we'-sing 彗星 (ih-lih)

COMFORT, to ky'ün'-ka 勸解°; ka-meng'解°悶; sæn-sing'散心; en-we' 安慰; *he comforted me,* ngô ky'ü-leh gyi ky'ün'-ka 我了°其勸解°

COMFORTABLE, shih'-i 適意; ziu'-yüong 受用; sông'-kw'a 爽快°; hao'-ko; *this chair is very —* (to sit in), zo'-læ keh' pô ü'-ts ting ziu'-yüong 坐°在°這°把椅°子頂受用; *in — circumstances,* weng-pao' 温飽

COMFORTABLY *dressed,* c'ün'-leh pao'-nön 穿得°飽煖

COMFORTLESS, 'ao-vu'c'ü'-hyiang 毫無趣向

COMICAL, hao fah-siao'好發笑; ying nying' siao 引人°笑

COMMAND, feng-fu' 吩附; *an officer's —,* ling 令; 'ao-ling' 號令; *to issue a —,* c'ih 'ao-ling' 出號令

COMMAND, to feng-fu 吩附

COMMANDER, *military—of a province,* di-toh' 提督; *naval —,* se'-s di-toh' 水師提督

COMMANDMENT, kyiæ 誡; *the ten commandments,* jih-diao kyiæ' 十條誡

COMMEMORATE, *to* kyi'-nyiæn記念

COMMENCE, *to* zông sin' 上手; *—for the first time,* k'æ-sin' 開手. See BEGIN.

COMMEND *to your care,* t'oh ng kwun 託你°管; *— him,* ngao' gyi hao' 贊°其好; *to recommend,* kyü'-tsin 舉薦; *to praise,* ts'ing-tsæn 稱讚; pao'-kyü 保舉

COMMENDATION, ts'ing-tsæn' 稱讚; *I am not worthy of that —,* keh'-go ts'ing-tsæn' ngô tông'-feh-ky'i' 這°个°稱讚我當弗起

COMMENT, to kông-ka' 講°解°; cü'-ka 註解°

COMMENTARY, cü'-ka 註解°;*fine print —,* si'-cü 細註 (ih-peng)

COMMENTATOR, cü cü-ka go nying 註註解°个°人°

COMMERCE, kao-yih' 交°易°; ma'-ma 買°賣°; t'ong-sông 通商

COMMISERATE, *to* k'o'-lin 可憐; æ-lin' 哀憐

COMMISSARY, yüing-liang'-kwun 運糧官 (generally the officer who has the care of the rice tribute).

COMMISSON, *officer's* bu'-tsiao 部照; *—for a special service,* we-ba 委牌°; *a factor's percentage,* yüong-din' 用錢°

COMMISSION, *to* we 委;*— him to manage,* we gyi bæn' 委其辦

COMMISSONER, we'-yün 委員; *— of customs,* se'-vu-s 稅務司; *salt —,* yin-yüing'-s 鹽運司

COMMIT, *to* t'oh 託; t'oh'-fu 託
付; kao-dæ' 交代; *to — to an*
*inferior,* fu'-t'oh 付託; *I —*
*this child to your care,* keh-go
siao-nying' ngô t'oh ng kwu'-
djoh 這个小孩我託你顧
着°; — *sin,* væn ze' 犯罪;
*has committed sin,* zo-ze'-liao 坐
罪了; — *to prison,* loh lao-
kæn' 落牢監°; siu kæn' 守
監° or 收監°

COMMITTEE, we'-bæn 委辦;
deh-p'a' cü-kwn 特派个人°

COMMODIOUS, *convenient,* yiang-
yiang' bin-tông 樣樣便當;
*large,* kw'un-ts'iah' 寬綽

COMMON, *ordinary,* bing-dzông' 平
常; bing-su' 平素; — (*every*
*day*) *use,* bing-jih' yüong' 平
日用; dzoh-nyih yüong' 逐
日°用; — *clothes,* bin-i' 便
衣; bin-voh' 便服; — *saying,*
dzoh'-wô' 俗話; *too —,* t'eh
dzoh' 過°於°俗; — *people,*
bing-deo' pah'-sing 平頭百姓;
*in — use,* t'ong-yüong'-go 通用
个°; — *custom,* dzông-kwe' 常
規; dzoh-li' 俗例; *easy to be*
*bought* (or obtained), yüong-yi'
ma 容易買°; sang'-lih ma
省力買°; *to eat in —,* p'ing
ky'üoh 摒吃°; *to live in —,*
p'ing deng 摒定°

COMMONLY *so,* da-kæ' z-ka 大概
如°此; bing-dzông' z-ka 平常
如°此°

COMMON-PLACE, feh c'ih'-seh 弗
出色; feh hyi'-gyi 弗希奇

COMMOTION, nao-nyih' 鬧熱°;
*disturbance,* ts'ao'-nao 吵鬧;
*why is this —?* dza-we' ka nao-
nyih' 如何°這鬧熱°? *to cause*
*a —,* cü'-s-teh nao-nao' nyih-
nyih' 致使得鬧鬧熱°熱°

COMMUNE, *to* dæn-sing' 談心;
fi'-fu-ts dæn' 肺腑之談; *to par-*
*take of the Lord's Supper,* ky'üoh
sing'-væn-ts'æn 吃°聖晚餐

COMMUNICATE, *he communicated*
*it to me,* z gyi' wô-hyiang'-ngô-
dao-go 是其話°向我道个°;
— *news,* pao sing'-sih 報信息;
t'ong-fong'-pao-sing 通風報
信; t'ong-cü' sing'-sih 通知信
息 (*generally something secret,*
*or improper*); — *disease,* bing-
yin-ko' 病延過

COMMUNICATION, læ-læ'-ky'i-ky'i
來來去°去°; *constant —,*
wông'-læ-peh-djih' 往來不絕;
*verbal —,* k'eo'-sing 口信 (ih-
go); *written —,* shü-tsah' 書
札 (ih-fong); *official —,* veng-
shü' 文書; *— from a foreign*
*power, &c.,* tsiao'-we 照會 (ih-
koh)

COMMUNION, *the Lord's Supper,*
sing'-væn-ts'æn 聖晚餐; Cü'
væn-ts'æn 主晚餐; — *of*
*saints,* sing'-du siang-t'ong' 聖
徒相通

COMMUTE, *to — a greater punishment for a less*, kô ze'-ming 加°罪名;— *a less punishment for a greater*, kæn ying-vah' 減°刑罰

COMPACT, *closely united*, kyih'-jih 硈實;— (as the body), kyih'-kweng;— (as cloth), kyih'-tsoh 硈足;— (as a house), kying'-ts'eo 緊礉

COMPACT, *a contract which is torn in two, and given to each party*, 'eh-dong' 合同

COMPANION, de-ho' 隊夥; ts'eo-de' 凑隊; dong-de' cü-kwu 同隊个°人°; tso-de'-go nying 做隊个°人°; *idle companions*, sæn-beng' s-yiu' 三朋四友

COMPANY *of soldiers*, ih-de ping' 一隊兵; *corporation*, kong-s' 公司; *fond of —*, hwun-hyi' nying-k'ah' 歡喜客°人°; *fond of idle —*, hwun-hyi' sæn-beng'-s-yiu' 歡喜三朋四友

COMPARABLE, k'o'-pi 可比

COMPARE, *to* pi 比; pi'-kyiao 比較; pi'-pi-k'en' 比比看;— (as writings or numbers), te'-te-k'en' 對對看; te'-ko 對過

COMPARED, *cannot be —*, pi-feh-læ-go 比弗來个°

COMPARISON, pi'-yü 比喩; pi'-fông 比方; pi'-jü 比如; *to draw a —*, yüong pi'-fông pi-ih'-pi 用比方比一比; *no —*, ing'-tsong pi'-feh-læ 影踪

比弗來; æ-kao' hao pi' 没°有°好比

COMPASS, *to environ*, we-tæn'-cün 圍打°轉;— *with* or *about*, yü-cün' 圍°轉; nyiao-tæn'-cün 繞°打°轉

COMPASS, *the Mariner's* ts'-nen-tsing 指南針; hyiang'-bun 向盤;— *used* (by sorcerers) *in selecting spots of ground*, keh'-hyiang-bun' 格向盤

COMPASSION, æ-lin'-sing 哀憐心; *feel —*, kyüoh'-teh yiu æ-lin'-sing 覺'得有哀憐心; *to excite one's —*, ken'-dong nying-go dz-pe'-sing 感動人°个° 慈悲心

COMPEL, *to* pih'-leb逼勒; ky'iang'-cü 強°制; ngang-iao' 硬要; ngang-k'ò' 硬拿°

COMPELLED, *to be* ngang-ts'-ts.

COMPENDIUM, ts'eh'-iao 撮要; tsah'-iao 摘要 (ih-peng);— *of history*, kông-kæn' ts'eh'-iao 綱°鑑撮要

COMPENSATE, *to* pao'-tah 報答; we-wæn' 回還; *to make a return for some favor*, pao-teh' 報德; pu'-pao 補報; *this compensates for my loss* (in money), keh' hao ti'-dzông ngó'-go su' 這°好抵償我个°數;— *for your trouble*, dziu-pao' ng-go lao-kw'u' 酧°報你°个°勞苦

COMPENSATION, *I expected no —*, ngô feh siang'-vông yiu we-wæn'

我 弗 想 望 有 回 還; *thank money*, zia-din′ 謝°錢°; *reward money*, sông′-din 賞 錢°; *a slight extra* — (*i.e.* tea money or wine money), dzô′-din 茶 錢°; tsiu′-din 酒 錢°; *have given him a — for his trouble*, dziu′-gyi-lao′-ko-de 巳°酬其勞

COMPETE, *to* bih 奪°; bih-gyiao′; tsang zông′-loh 爭°上落; — *for honor and wealth*, tseng-ming′-deh-li′ 爭名奪利; tsang ming-sing′ 爭°名聲; — *in trade*, bih sang-i′ 奪生°意; *able to — with*, k′o′-yi te′-dih 可以對敵; bing′-kyin-go 並肩个°

COMPETENT, *having ability*, yiu dze-′oh′ 有才學°; yiu du′-dze 有肚才; — *to do* (a *certain thing*), nô-siu′-go 拏手个°; — *for*, k′o′-yi tæn-tông′ 可以擔當; ′eh-yüong′-go 合用个°

COMPETITOR, ts′iang ing-yüong′-go nying 爭°英雄个°人°

COMPILE, *to* we′-jih-long 彙集攏

COMPILER, we′-jih-go nying′ 彙集′个°人°

COMPLACENT, *satisfied*, teh′-i-yiang′-yiang 得意揚揚

COMPLAIN *of trouble*, su kw′u′ 訴苦; su t′ong′-kw′u 訴痛苦; — *of grievances*, su ün′ 訴寃; — *of one′s difficulties*, kông zi′-go ræn-c′ü′ 講°自°个°難處

— *of others behind their back*, pe′ ′eo kông ko′-tön 背後講°過短; *to find fault with*, mao-ün′ 埋怨; s-we′.

COMPLEMENT, *full* ngah′-ts tsoh′-de 額子足了°; ngah′-ts mun′-de 額子滿了°; su′-moh zi′-de 數目齊°了°; — *not full*, su′ feh tsoh′ 數弗足

COMPLETE, *not wanting*, djün-be′ 全備; jih-djün′ 十全; jih-tsoh′ 十足; *finished*, wun-djün′ 完全; dzing-dziu′ 成就; dzing-kong′ 成功; — *happiness*, djün foh′ 全福

COMPLETE, *to* tso′-dzing 做成; tso′ wun-djün′ 做完全; *to — arrangements*, bæn′-leh t′o′-tòng 辦得°妥當

COMPLETELY, jih-feng′ 十分; djün-djün′ 十°全; — *consumed by fire*, ho′ dziah-kwông′-de 火燒光了°; — *chilled*, weng′-sing tu lang′-de 渾身都冷°了°

COMPLEX, se′-væn 碎煩

COMPLEXION, min-seh′ 面色; ky′i′-seh 氣色

COMPLIANT, yün-weh′ 圓活; ze-ræn′ tao-ræn′ 隨意而行°

COMPLICATED, *involved*, lin-lin′-ky′in-ky′in 連連牽牽; — *and intricate*, tsi-li′-tseo-leo′ 𠲿哩𠲿嘍; — *affair*, dzin-ziao′-go z-t′i′ 纏繞个°事體

COMPLIMENT, *praise*, ts′ing-tsæn

稱 讚; *to fish for a* —, t'ao nying-kô' vong'-dzing 討人°家° 奉承; la-s' t'iao læ teng'-bun-li; *empty* —, veo-veng' shih-wô' 浮 文 說話; k'eh'-t'ao shih-wô' 客° 套 說話

COMPLIMENTS, *present my* — *to him*, dæ ngô' ts'ing-ts'ing gyi en' 代我請請其安

COMPLY, *to* i 依; *I will* — *with* (*your wishes*), ngô' we i' ng 我 會依你°; tseng-kyiao' 遵教

COMPOSE, *to* cü 著; cü'-tsoh 著 作; — *a book*, cü shü' 著書; — *and collect*, cü-jih' 著述; — *an essay*, tso veng-tsông 做文 章; — *verse*, tso s' 做詩

COMPOSED (*in mind*), sing-ding' 心 定; ding-ding'-sing-sing'; sing t'ih'-ding 心貼°定; sing' feh-dong 心弗動; *perfectly* —, sing-seh'-feh-dong 聲色 弗動

COMPOSED *of two or three things*, liang'-sæn-yiang' keh'-long tso-go 兩三樣合°攏做个°; — *of more than one article*, feh ts' ih-yiang' tso'-c'ih-go 弗止一 樣做出个°

COMPOSITION, *essay*, veng-tsông' 文章

COMPOUND, kah'-dzch-go 夾° 雜个°

COMPRADORE, kông'-bah-bo 岡 勃佗, *transferred from the English; one who buys provisions for*,

ma'-bæn 買°辦; *one who buys goods*, ma'-ho sin-sang 買°貨 先生°

COMPREHEND, *to* ming-bah' 明白; tong 懂; hyiao'-teh 曉得

COMPREHENSIVE, yiu hyü'-to pao-kweh'-tih 有許多包括的

COMPRESS, *to* ah 壓°; — *on both sides*, keh kyih'-jih 夾°砝實

COMPROMISE, *to* tsiah'-wu-gyi cong' 酌乎其中; liang'-tsia 兩借'; liang'-pin tseo-tæn'-long 兩邊走攏

COMPULSION, *by* min'-ky'iang 勉 強

COMPUTE, *to* sön 算; p'a 派°; p'a'-p'a-k'en' 派°派°看

COMRADE, de-bo' 隊夥; dong-de'-nying 同隊人°; *comrades* (*in amusement*), sæn-beng'-s-yiu' 三朋四友

CONCAVE, t'en-tsing' liao-go 凹° 進了个°

CONCEAL, *to* k'ông 囥; — *and deceive*, mun 瞞; — *from another*, mun-sæn'-en-s' 瞞三掩 四; *I can't from* — *you*, mun-ng'-feh-teh-shih' 瞞你°弗得 說; — *one's name*, nyih-ming' nyih-sing' 匿名匿姓

CONCEDE, *to grant*, cing 准; *to yield*, nyiang 讓°

CONCEIT, *a foolish* —, ts'eng'-kong veo-r' peh-jih' 心°思浮 而不實; ts'eng'-deo hyü'-go

想° 頭 虛 个°; ts'eng'- kong, neng-shih' peh-neng-ying' 心 思° 能 說 不 能° 行

CONCEITED, zi sön' dzæ'-'ông 自° 算 在 行；— (in talking), iao ts'ing-neng' 要 稱 能

CONCEIVABLE, ts'eng'-leh-tao'-go 忖 得° 到 个°

CONCEIVE, to — (in the womb) ziu-yüing' 受 孕；ziu-t'æ' 受 胎；— an idea, ky'i-i' 起 意；ky'i-kyin' 起 見；— a purpose, fah sing' 發 心

CONCENTRATE, to kwe-cong' 歸 宗；— the mind, ih-sing c'ong' ih-yüoh' 一 身 充 一 役；sing kwe-long' 心 歸 攏

CONCEPTION, idea, i'-s 意 思；i'-kyin 意 見

CONCERN, siang-ken' 相干；what — is it of mine？ teng ngô soh'-go siang-ken' 與 我 甚° 麼° 相 干？ü ngô' 'o-ken' 于 我 何 干？yü' ngô 'o-dzih' 與 我 何 涉？

CONCERN, to belong to, joh'-ü 屬° 于；ü 于；yü 與；kwæn 關；it does not—me, yü ngô'vu dzih' 與 我 無 涉；feh kwæn'-djoh ngô' z-ken 弗 關 着° 我 事 幹；it does — me, yü ngô' yiu kao-kwæn' 與 我 有 交° 關；ü ngô yiu' kwæn-yi' 于 我 有 干 係；do not — yourself, hao-vong' fi-sing' 弗° 用° 費 心

CONCERNED for, dziah-kyih' 着° 急；tæn-iu' 擔 憂

CONCERT, in p'e' hao-liao-go 配 好 了 个°；siang-p'e'-go 相 配 个°

CONCERT, to dô-kô' tang'-sön 大° 家° 打 算

CONCILIATE, to —(by kindness), teng gyi' 'o-hao' 與 其 和 好；to render friendly, s'-teh gyi 'o-moh' 使 其 和 睦

CONCILIATING, act in a — manner and he will be conciliated, yüong nyün'-kong pa'-pu, peh gyi pa'-pu-tao'-de 用 軟 功 擺° 佈 俾° 其 擺° 佈 倒 了°

CONCISE, kyin'-kyih 簡 潔；tön'-kyih 短 潔；ts'ing-ts'u' 清 楚；ling'-kying 靈 緊；— in speaking tsin'-sao.

CONCH, ngô-lo' 牙° 螺

CONCLUDE, to wun 完；liao 了；wun-kyih' 完 結；— the business, wun z' 完 事；liao z' 了 事

CONCLUSION, kyih'- sah 結 煞；— of a discourse, kyih kyü' 結 句；kwæn-meng' shih-wô' 關 門 說 話

CONCLUSIVE, words are —, shih-wô' kông'-leh loh-shing' 說 話 講° 得° 落 樺

CONCORD, in 'o-moh' 和 睦；kông'-leh-læ 講° 得° 來；— in sounds, sing - ing' tsæn'-zi 聲 音 齊 集°；dong-sing' siang-ing' 同 聲 相 應

CONCOURSE, *a crowd of people,* ih-do'-dziao nying' 一大羣人; *a great many,* vu-ts'in'-da-væn'-go 無千大萬个。

CONCUBINE, ah-yi' 阿姨; siao lao-nyüing' 小老婆; styled, p'in-vông' 偏房; tseh'-shih 側室; jü'-fu-nying' 如夫人°;— *paid by the month,* pao lao'-nyüing 包老婆。

CONCUPISCENCE, yüoh-sing' 慾心; s-yüoh'-sing 私欲心

CONCUR, *I — with him,* ngô teng' gyi dong-i' 我與°其°同意; ngô teng' gyi tso' i-s 我與°其°同°意思; ngô yia' ka i'-s 我也°這°意思

CONCUSSION, *severe* tsing-tsing'-dong li-'æ' 振動利害

CONDEMN, *to* ding ze' 定罪;— *him to death,* ding' gyi si'-ze 定其死°罪;— *the boat as bad,* ding keh' tsah jün wa' 定這°隻船孱°。

CONDENSE, *to* long kyih'-jih 弄硃寳;— *by pressure,* ah kyih'-jih 壓°硃寳;— *by pressure of the hand,* ky'ing kyih'-jih 捺硃寳;— *by pressure of the feet,* dah kyih'-jih 踏硃寨

CONDESCEND, *to* kyüông'-ling 降臨; kông'-loh di-we' 降°落地位;— *to buy of,* s'-kwu 賜顧; 'o'-kwu 下°顧;— *to help in trouble,* kwông'-kwu 光顧

CONDIGN, kæ zin' 該受

CONDIMENTS, liao-li' 料理; pông-deo' 幫頭; *wine as a condiment,* liao-tsiu' 料酒

CONDITION (whether as officer, teacher, or trades-man, &c.), di-we' 地位;— (arrived at), di-bu' 地步;— (whether sick or poor, rich or well, &c.), kying'-di 境地; kying'-hwông 境況

CONDITION, *I make one —,* ngô' lih ih-go 'æn' 我立一个°限';— *must not violate (i. e. step over) the —,* feh-k'o' ko' 'æn' 弗可過限°

CONDOLE, *to — with,* dô-kô' t'æn'-sih 大°家°嘆息

CONDUCT, tsoh'-we 作爲; 'ang-i'-dong-zing 行°意動靜; kyü'-ts 'ang-dong' 舉止行°動; sô-tsoh'-sô-we' 所作所爲; 'ang-we' 行°爲; *very bad —,* 'o'-tsoh 'ang-we' 下°作行°爲; 'o'-liu 'ang-we' 下°流行°爲

CONDUCT, *to* ying'-dao 引導; ta'-ling 帶°領; ling 領

CONDUCTOR, ying'-dao cü'-kwu 引導个°人°; ling-lu'-go nying' 領路个°人°。

CONE, yün ti' tsin deo' 圓底尖頭

CONFECTIONERY, *sugared things* (as fruits), nih-tsiu' 蜜餞. See CANDY.

CONFEDERATE, *adj.* c'ün'-'eh-liao 串合°了; t'ong-dong'-liao 通同了

CONFER, to — (office), fong 封；— (favors), s 賜；sông 賞

CONFER, to consult, siang-liang' 商量；siang-sông' 相商

CONFERENCE, to hold a —, ih-fæn we-nyi' 一番會議；to meet for —, jü'-we siang-nyi' 聚會相議

CONFESS, to jing 認；tsiao-jing' 招認；— something wrong, jing ts'o' 認錯；nying shü' 認°輸

CONFIDANT, n. sing-foh' 心腹

CONFIDE, to instruct, t'oh-sing' 托信；can — in him, gyi t'oh'-sing-leh-ko' 其托信得°過；gyi k'ao'-leh-djü'-go 其靠得°住个°；to believe, siang-sing' 相信

CONFIDENT, certain, yiu'-su 有數；vu nyi' 無疑；self —, zi siang'-sing zi' 自°相信自°

CONFIDENTLY, jih-z'-jih-loh' 實是實落

CONFIDENTIAL, hao'-t'oh-siang-sing' 好托相信；t'oh'-sing-leh-ko 托信得°過；secret, kyi-mih' 機密

CONFINE, to restrict, iah'-soh 約束；tsu'-djü 阻住；— by a guard, kwun'-ah 管押°

CONFINED, close, meng-ky'i' 悶氣；— or narrow quarters, bun-djün'-feh cün'-go di-fông' 盤旋弗轉个°地方

CONFINEMENT, time of — (wo-man's), tso-sang'-m z-'eo' 做產°母°時候；ditto, arrived, ling-ts'æn' 臨產

CONFIRM, to — as true, ding-jih' 定實；— by proof, ying'-tsing 引証；to establish, kyin-kwu' 堅固

CONFIRMATION, the rite of —, kyin-sing'-li 堅信禮

CONFISCATE, to ts'ong kong' 充公；jih kwun' 入官

CONFLAGRATION, ho'-tsong do'-leh-kying' 火鐘大°得°緊；ho'-tsæ 火災

CONFLICT, to gyih-gah' 紏°葛° dzih-kah'-dco / to fight, kao-tsin' 交戰；tang-tsiang' 打仗°

CONFORM to the pattern, tsiao yiang' tso 照樣做；obey, i-dzong' 依從

CONFOUNDED, confused, wu-li'-wu-du' 霧°裏糊塗；perplexed mong'-tong 懵懂 (mong or môong)

CONFRONT, to — with criticism, tông-min' poh' 當面駁；— with threats, tông-min' heng'-hô.

CONFUCIUS, K'ong'-fu-ts 孔夫子

CONFUSE, to lön 亂；weng'-lön 混亂；— his mind, lön' gyi'-go sing' 亂其个°心

CONFUSED, wu-li'-wu-du' 霧°裏糊塗；m-deo'-m-jü 無°頭無°緒；— in mind, sing lön' 心亂；— or in confusion, ô-kohlön'-kying; *very* —, lön-ts'ih-pah-tsao' 亂七八遭

CONFUTE, *to* poh'-tao 駁倒

CONFUTED, *utterly* —, poh'-leh k'æ-k'eo' feh læ' 駁得°開口弗來°; li ky'üih' dz gyüong' 理屈辭窮 (veng.)

CONGEE, coh or tsoh 粥; hyi-væn' 稀飯; — *boiled very smooth and nice*, tsoh' ts-leh dziu-lin' 粥爇°得°綢線

CONGENIAL, yiu yün-veng' 有緣分; sing-i' siang-dong' 心意相同

CONGESTION *of the heart*, byüih' jü'-long læ sing'-li 血聚攏在°心裏

CONGRATULATE, *to* 'o-'o' 賀賀; (I) — *you*, dao ng'-go hyi' 道你°个°喜; kong-hyi' kong-hyi' 恭喜恭喜; 'o ng'-go hyi' 賀你°个°喜

CONGREGATION,jü'-long-go nying' 聚攏个°人°

CONGRESS *of the U. S.*, Da-me' nyi-tsing'-we 大美議政會

CONJECTURE, *to surmise*, ts'æ-doh' 猜度°; — *rightly* (guess), ts'æ-djoh' 猜着°

CONJOINTLY, dong-pông' 同幫; dô-kô' 大°家°

CONJUGAL *love*, fu-ts'i' dzing-veng' 夫妻情分; — *duties*, fu-ts'i' meng-veng' 夫妻名分

CONJURER, pin hyi'-fah-go nying 變戲法个°人°; *one who con-*

*jures by spirits*, yüong vu-jih' go nying 用巫術个°人°

CONNECT, *to* lin-long' 連攏; lin-p'ing' 連摒

CONNECTED, lin-long'-liao 連攏了; siang-lin'-liao 相連了; — (as ideas), kwun'-c'ün 貫串; *can or ought to be* —, siang-lin' 相連

CONNECTION, *one's own family* — *of the same name*, kô-kyün' 家°眷; — *having a different family name*, ts'ing-kyün' 親眷

CONNIVE, *intentionally fail to see* ngæn'-k'æ-ngæn'-pi 眼°開眼°閉; tsông'-leh m-neh k'en'-kyin 糚得°沒°有°看見

CONQUER, *to* tang'-ying 打贏; teh-sing' 得勝; — *self*, k'eh kyi' 克己 (veng.)

CONQUERED, tang'-ba-de 打敗了°; shü-de' 輸了°

CONQUEROR, teh-sing' cü'-kwu 得勝个°人°

CONQUEST, *obtained by* —, tang'-ying teh-læ'-go 打贏得來个°

CONSANGUINEOUS, tih'-ts'ing-go 嫡親个°; ts'ing-kweh'-hyüib 親骨血

CONSCIENCE liang-sing' 良心; t'in-liang' 天良; t'in-li'-liang-sing' 天理良心; z'-fi-ts sing 是非之心; — *smitten*, kw'e sing'-z 愧心事; — *not darkened*, liang-sing' peh-me' 良心不昧

CONSCIENTIOUS, yiu' liang-sing'

go 有 亙 心 个°; — *in conduct,*
tsiao liang-sing′ tso′ nying 照
亙 心 做 人°
CONSCIENTIOUSLY, ʻeh-djoh tʻin-
li′ 合着° 天理 (djoh or dzoh).
CONSCIOUS *of pain,* kyüoh′-teh
tʻong′-go 覺得痛个°; *faculties
clear* (as a sick person), seh′-deo
ts′ing; ts′ing-tʻong 清通
CONSECRATE, *to* tseng-kyʻi′ 尊起;
— (as first fruits &c. to the Emperor), tsing-kong′ 進貢; *the rite
of consecrating ditto, to parents,*
zông-sing′-go li′ 嘗° 新 个° 禮
CONSECRATED (as food), zing′-go
淨° 个°
CONSECUTIVE, lin-kyʻin′-go 連
牽 个°; *come on ten — days,* lin-
kyʻin′ læ jih nyih′ 連 來 十 日°;
*three — years,* deh-lin′ sæn nyin′
疊 連 三 年
CONSENT, *to* ing-yüing′ 應允;
ing-jing′ 應認
CONSEQUENCES, kwæn-yi′ 關係;
kyiao-kwæn′ 交關; *bad —,*
kwæn-ngæ′ 關碍; *if you do not
believe, what will be the —?* ng
feh siang′-sing, yiu soh′-go
kwæn-yi′ 你° 弗 相 信 有 甚°
麼° 關 係?
CONSEQUENTIAL, teng-pʻing′-go
siang′-mao 敦 品 个° 相 貌
CONSIDER, *to* tsing-tsiah′ 斟酌;
— *carefully,* ts-si tsing-tsiah′ 仔
細斟酌; *take time to —,* mæn-
mæn′ tsing-tsiah′ 慢 慢 斟 酌

CONSIDERABLE, feh-kyʻüih′ 弗
缺; feh-siao′ 弗 少; *to* 多
CONSIDERATE, tʻi′-tʻiah-go 體貼
个°; yiu ts′eh-ing′-ts sing′ 有
惻隱之心
CONSIGN *to his hands,* tʻoh′ læ gyi′-
go siu-li′ 托 在° 其 个° 手 裏;
— *for sale,* tʻoh′-ma′ 托 買
CONSIST *in,* dzæ-ü 在于; (Chinese
say) *Life consists in wealth,* "Dzæ,
yü ming′ siang′-lin" 財 與 命
相 連
CONSISTENCY, *no* feh-dzing tʻi′-
tʻong 弗 成 體 統
CONSISTENTLY, *to act —,* yin-
ying′ siang-vu′ 言 行 相 符
CONSOLATION, en-我′ 安慰
CONSOLE, *to* en-我′ 安慰; kwʻun-
sing′ 寬心
CONSPICUOUS, tʻiao′-c′ih-liao 挑
出了; tʻeo′-c′ih-liao 透出了;
tʻiao′-yiang-go 挑 樣 个°; yün-
ling′-ling pa′-c′ih-liao 懸 空 擺 出
CONSPIRACY, kæn-tông′ 奸° 黨;
*to form a —,* kyih tông′ 結黨
CONSPIRE, *to* c′ün′-dong 串同;
tʻong-dong′-tsoh-bi′ 通同作弊;
— *and swear together not to give
up,* kyʻüoh hyiang-hwe′ tsin 吃°
香 灰 酒
CONSTABLE, di-pao′ 地保; politely called, tʻa′-se 太° 歲
CONSTANT, *steadfast,* sing-kyin′
心 堅; *always the same,* nyih-
nyih′ jü-ts′ 日° 日° 如 此

CONSTANTLY, *always*, z-djông′ 時常; djông-djông′ 常常; — *so*, djông-djông′ jü-ts′ 常常如此 (djông or dzông.)

CONSTELLATIONS, *the twenty eight* —, r-jih-pah siu′ 二十八宿

CONSTERNATION, *in* kying-hwông′-de 驚慌了°

CONSTIPATION, do-ka′ feh t′ong′ 大°解°弗通

CONSTITUTE, *to form*, hying 興; *to establish*, lih 立; shih′-lih 設°立; — *by appointment*, fông 放

CONSTITUTION, ti′-ts 底子; peng′ ti-ts 本底子; nyün-ky′i′ 元氣; *strong* —, ti-ts tsah′-cü 底子圓硬°

CONSTRAIN, *to impel*, ts′e-pih′ 催逼; — (him) *to stay*, gyiang′ liu 強留; ngang liu′ 硬°留

CONSTRAINED *to stay*, feh′-teh-feh deng′ 弗得弗停°; *in a* — (contracted) *position*, gyüoh-ts′oh′ 侷促

CONSTRUCT, *to* ky′i 起; zao 造°; tang 打; tsoh 築; — *a house*, zao oh′ 造°屋; ky′i oh′ 起屋; — *a bridge*, zao gyiao′ 造°橋; tsoh gyiao′ 築橋; — *a boat*, tang jün′ 造°船; — *a wall*, tang ziang′; tsoh ziang′ 築墻

CONSTRUE, *to explain*, ka′-shih 解°說; *to translate*, fæn-yih′ 繙譯

CONSUL, ling′-z-kwun 領事官; *British* —, Da-Ing′ ling′-z-kwun 大英領事官; *vice* —, fu′-ling-z 副領事

CONSULATE, ling′-z fu 領事府

CONSULT, *to* siang-liang′ 商°量; siang-sông′ 相商; sông-nyi′ 商議; — *carefully*, tsing-tsiah′ 斟酌

CONSUME *by fire*, me-diao′ 煤壞°; siao-diao′ 燒壞°; — *entirely*, hwô-u-yiu′ 化爲烏有; — *by extravagance*, hwô′-fi-diao 化費了°; — *by decomposition*, hwô′-diao 化壞° (also used for the former).

CONSUMMATE, *to* dzing 成; dzing-djün′ 成全; dzing-dziu′ 成就

CONSUMPTION, (disease), ziah-bing 弱病; lao-ky′ih′-bing 癆怯病

CONSUMPTIVE, yiu ziah-bing′-go ti′-ts læ′-tih 有弱病个°底子

CONTACT, *to come in* — *with*, bang-djoh′ 撞着°; ts′ah′-djoh 擦着°

CONTAGIOUS, iao-yin′-go 要延个°

CONTAIN, *to* tsi 齒; tsông 裝; — (as a boat), tsæ 載; *how much oil will it* —? yiu to-siao yin′ hao tsi 有多少油好齒?

CONTAMINATE, *to* ta′-diao 帶°壞°; ta′-loh 帶°落

CONTEMN, *to* k′en-ky′ing′ 看輕; — *him as worthless*, k′en gyi z ts′æn′-deo 看其是儳懯°

CONTEMPLATE, *to* ngwu 悟; si-si′-go ts′eng′ 細細个°忖

CONTEMPLATION, (Buddhist)

ngwu-jün′ 悟禪; (Taoist) —,
ngwu-dao′ 悟道

CONTEMPORARY, dong z-ʻeo′ 同
時候; tso z-ʻeo′.

CONTEMPT, I treat him with —,
ngô′ kʻen gyi kyʻing′ 我看其
輕; ngô kʻen-gyi-feh-kyʻiʻ 我
看其弗起; ngô kʻen′-feh-
zông-ngæn′ 我看弗上眼;
ngô kyʻing-mæn′ gyi 我輕慢
其; he is treated with —, gyi
peh nying-kô′ kʻen-kyʻing′-liao
其被人°家°看輕了

CONTEMPTIBLE, feh-jih′-nying-
ngæn′ 弗入人°眼; kyʻing
輕; — conduct, kyʻing-zin′ ʻaŋ-
we 輕賤°行°爲

CONTEND, to — (in words), siang-
tsang′相爭°; — (in fight), siang-
tang′ 相打

CONTENTED, cü-tsoh′ 知足;
tsoh′-sing 足心; zi-cü′-veng-
liang 自°知㥆量

CONTENTIOUS, hwun-hyiʻ tsang-
leng′ 歡喜爭°論; pʻô tʻaʻ-
bing 怕太°平

CONTENTS (of a book), moh-loh
目錄

CONTEST, to tsang 爭°; to emulate, piʻ-sæ 比賽

CONTEXT, zông-ʻô-veng 上下°文

CONTIGUOUS, tʻiah′-gying 貼近;
vu-gying′ 附近

CONTINENT, n. da-tsiu′ 大州;
adj. we tsih-yüoh′ 會節欲

CONTINUALLY, z-djông′ 時常;
djông-djông′ 常常 (djông or
dzông); dziang-tʻong′.

CONTINUE, to feh-hyih′ 弗歇;
feh-dön′ 弗斷; — here, dzing-
gyin′ læ′-tih 仍舊在°此°

CONTINUOUS, lin-lin′ 連連; tsih′-
lin 接連; ih′-lin 一連; a
month's — rain, yü lin-lin′ loh
ih-ko′-yüih 雨連連落一個月

CONTORT, to — (as mouth, or
limbs), kyʻin-long′牽攏; kyʻin-
cün′ 牽轉

CONTRABAND goods, kying′ ho
禁貨; — traffic, væn kying′-
go sang-iʻ 犯禁个°生°意

CONTRACT, nyi-tæn′ 議單; iah
約; — for work, dzing-læn′-pʻiao
承攬票; — for marriage, shü-
ts′ 書子

CONTRACT, to shorten, soh 縮;
siu 收; soh′-long 縮攏; ih′-
tsah; — the brows, tseo′-mi-deo′
皺眉°頭; — a habit, jih-kwæn′
習慣; — a habit of drinking or
smoking, kyʻüoh′ nyin 吃°癮°

CONTRACTED mind, kyʻiʻ-liang
ʻah-tsah′ 氣量狹窄; du′-
liang siao′ 度量小; — place,
di-fông′ gyüoh-tsʻoh′ 地方偪促

CONTRADICT, to ing-cü′ 違言°;
— one's self, zin-yin′ feh-te ʻeo′
nyü 前°言弗對後語; — one's
own testimony, fæn-kong′ 翻供

CONTRADICTORY, teo′-deo-feh-

long'-go 對°頭 弗 攏 个°; 'eh-
shing'-feh-long'-go 合 榫 弗 攏
个°; ts'o-gen'; feh-te'; feh-vu' 弗
符; feh-'eh'-deo 弗 合 頭

CONTRARY *ideas*, i'-s siang-fæn'
意 思 相 反; — *in disposition*,
ao'-ky'iang 拗 腔; ao'-diao-
peh-hying' 拗 調 不 馴°; kwæ'-
p'ih 乖 僻; — *wind*, teo' fong
鬬 風

CONTRAST *in quality*, hao' wa
ts'o-yün' 好 歪° 差 遠; —
*in size*, do siao' ts'o-yün' 大°
小 差 遠; — *in height*, dziang
a' da' feh siang'-dong 長 矮 大
弗 相 同; *heightened by* —,
pi'-ih-pi keng'-kô hao'-de 比 一
比 更 加° 好 了°; *worse by* —,
ih-pi'-kyin keng'-kô feh-z'-de 一
比 肩 更 加° 弗 是 了°

CONTRIBUTE, *to* kyün 捐; kyün-
dzu' 捐 助; — *for idolatry*, teo
veng-ts' 兜 牙 子; *like to* —,
hyi' dzu 喜 助; loh dzu' 樂 助

CONTRIBUTIONS, kyün-'ông' 捐
項; kyün-kw'nn' 捐 款

CONTRITE *heart*, sing sông' 心
傷; t'ong'-hwe-ts sing' 痛 悔
之 心

CONTRIVANCE, *ingenious* ky'iao'-
miao tong'-si 巧 妙 東 西

CONTRIVE, *to* shih'-siang-c'ih-læ
設°想 出 來; tang'-mo-c'ih-læ
打 摹 出 來; — *a scheme* (for
injuring &c), shih kyi'-meo' 設°
機 謀

CONTROL, *to* kwun'-soh 管 束; —
*one's self*, zi iah'-soh zi 自°約束
自°; *under his* —, læ gyi siu'-'ô
在°其 手 下°

CONTROVERSY, *fond of* —, hwun-
hyi' bin'-leng 歡 喜 辯 論

CONTUMACIOUS, ngwn-nyih' 忤
逆; — (son), ngwu-nyih'-peh-
hyiao' 忤 逆 不 孝; — *son
and brother*, peh-hyiao'-peh-di 不
孝 不 弟

CONTUMELY, jôh *or* zoh 辱; tsao-
t'ah' 蹧 蹋; *to bear* —, ziu-zoh'
受 辱; *to treat with* —, ying-
zoh' 刑 辱

CONTUSION, sông 傷; *severe* —
(by beating), tang'-sông li-'æ'
打 傷 利 害

CONVALESCENT, læ-tih hao'-ky'i-
læ 現°今°好 起 來

CONVENE, *to* jü 聚; jü'-long 聚 攏

CONVENIENCE, *suit your* —, zeng'-bin' 隨 你°便; ze-bin' ng
隨 便 你°; dzong-ng'-bin' 從
你°便

CONVENIENT, bin 便; bin-tông'
便 當; *while* — (do something
else), jing-bin' 順 便; jing-sin'
順 手; — (*i. e.* without going
out of the way), jing-da' 順 垯

CONVENT, *Buddhist* en 菴; dông
堂; *z* 寺; yün 院; *Taoist* —,
kwun 觀; *Roman Catholic* —,
siu'-dao-yün' 修 道 院

CONVERSANT *with*, joh-sih' 熟

識; *perfectly* —, joh-t'eo'-liao 熟透了

CONVERSE, *to* dæn'-dæn 談談; jü-jü' 叙叙; — *of what is in the heart*, dæn-sing' 談心

CONVERSION, *the time of* —, kæ'-ko z-'eo' 改過時候

CONVERT, we-sing'-liao-go nying' 回心个°人°

CONVERT, *to change*, kæ 改; wun 換; pin'-yih 變易; *to* — *a man*, cih'-cün nying-go ling-sing' 挈轉人°个°靈性; pin'-wun nying'-go ky'i'-tsih 變換人°个°氣質

CONVEX, deh-c'ih' liao-go 凸出了个°

CONVEY *thither* (as letters, presents &c.), kyi'-læ 寄來; ta'-læ 帶來; — *there*, kyi'-ky'i 寄去°; ta'-ky'i 帶去°; — (as goods), yüing-læ' 運來; yüing-ky'i' 運去°; — *there* (as people), peh gyi ts'ing'-leh-ky'i 與°其趁了°去°

CONVICT, *n.* væn'-nying 犯人°

CONVICTED *of sin*, kyüoh'-teh zi'-go ze' 覺得自°个°罪; — *deeply*, c'oh'-sing næn-ko' 趄心難過

CONVINCE, *to* k'æ-dao' 開導 k'æ-t'ong' 開通; — *him of sin*, peh gyi zi kyüoh'-teh yin ze' 俾°其自°覺得有罪; — *him of error*, tsing'-ming gyi-go ts'o' 證明其个°錯°

CONVINCED *by argument*, bin'-leng voh'-de 辯論服了°; *I am* —, ngô' voh-cü'-de 我服制了°

CONVOKE, ts'ing jü'-long 請聚攏; eo-long' 叫°攏; eo-zi' 叫°齊

CONVOY, *to* wu-song' 護送

CONVULSED *with laughter*, siao-leh weng'-sing dong'-feh-gyi 笑得°渾身動弗及°

CONVULSIONS, kying-fong'-bing 驚瘋病

CONVULSIVELY, *crying* weh-djông'-weh-tin' k'oh' 活擅活顛哭

COOK, long-væn'-go 弄飯个°; djü-deo' 廚頭; djü-kong' 廚工; — *in a ya-mun*, djü-ts' 廚子; *head* —, da-s'-vu 大司務; *under* —, 'o'-tsao 下°竈

COOK, *to* long væn' 弄飯; *to boil*, ts 煮°; — (*i. e.* boil) *well*, ts joh' 煮熟; *to bake*, p'ang 烹°; *to steam*, hen 燉; *to fry* (as meat), t'ah 爛; — (as doughnuts), zah 煠°; *to simmer*, teng 燉; *to roast* (as coffee or chestnuts), ts'ao 炒; *to broil*, tsih 炙; koh 烙°

COOL, lang'-ing 冷°陰; ing'-liang 陰涼; — *water*, ing'-liang-go shü' 陰涼个°水°; — *weather*, t'in' ing'-liang 天陰涼; — (breezy), fong-liang' 風涼; *seek a* — *place*, zing fong-liang' 尋風涼; — *it*, long gyi lang' 弄

其 冷°; *let it —*, peh gyi lang'

俟 其 冷°; lang-lang' gyi 冷°

冷° 其; lang kæn'; *wait till it cools*, teng gyi lang'-de 等 其 冷 了°

COOLLY, *to treat a person —*, lang'-dæn nying-kô' 冷° 待° 人°家°

COOLY, or COOLIE, siao'-kong 小 工; c'ih-ts'n'-go nying 出 粗 个°人°; *— for burdens*, kyiah-pæn' 腳 班

COOP, *chicken* kyi-long' 雞 籠; *—* (for day use, with no bottom), kyi-tsao' 雞 罩; *to shut in a —*, kwæn'-tsing long'-li 關 進 籠 裡

COOPERATE, *to* keh'-tso 合° 做; p'ing-tso' 拼 做

COPARTNER, p'ing ho'-kyi 拼 夥 計

COPIOUS, to 多; hyü'-to 許 多; *— rain*, dzing-deo' yü 陣 頭 雨; do yü 大°雨

COPPER, ts'-dong 紫 銅; 'ong-dong' 紅 銅 (a sheet, ih-p'in; a bar, ih-diao)

COPPERAS, loh-væn' 綠 礬

COPPER-SMITH, *brazier*, dong-s'-vu 銅 司 務

COPY, deng 謄; ts'ao 抄; *— neatly*, deng-ts'ing' 謄 清

COPYING-PRESS, ing'-shü-kô 印 書 架°

CORAL, sæn-wu' 珊 瑚

CORD, zing 繩°; soh 索; *strong —*, kyih'-jih-go or tsah'-cü-go

zing' 硈°實° 个°繩°; *to make —*, tang zing' 打 繩°

CORDIAL (to guests), nyih-zah'; *warm-hearted*, nyih-sing' 熱 心

CORD-MAKER, zing-soh'-s-vu' 繩° 索 司 務

CORE, sing 心

CORK, seh'-deo 屑 頭 (ih-go)

CORK, *to — a bottle*, seh bing-k'eo' 屑 瓶 口

CORK-SCREW, k'æ seh'-deo jün-ts' 開 屑 頭 旋 子; cün'-ts 鑽 子

CORN, *Indian* loh-koh' 稑 穀; pao'-r-mi 保 兒 米; *— meal*, (Indian meal), loh-koh' feng 稑 穀 粉

CORN (on the foot), kyi-ngæn' 雞 眼'; kyiah'-tsi 腳 齻°; *to dig out a —*, t'ih kyi-ngæn 剔 雞 眼'

CORNELIAN, mô'-nao 碼 碯

CORNER, koh 角°; koh-loh-den' 角° 落 頭°; *turn a —*, cün-wæn' 轉 彎°; *lonely —*(or place), wæn' koh 彎 角°

CORPOREAL, nyüoh-sing'-go 肉° 身 个°

CORPS, *a — of soldiers*, ih-de ping' 一 隊 兵'; ih-ts ping' 一 支 兵

CORPSE, s-siu' 屍 首; p'oh'-s 仆 屍; s-yia' 屍 骸° (term of reproach).

CORPULENT, vi-p'ông' 肥 膖'; *— from disease*, fah hyü' 發 虛; fah cong' 發 腫

CORRECT, *not wrong*, feh-ts'o' 弗

錯°; feh-dzæn′ 弗綻; *perfectly*
—, ‘ao′-feh-ts‘o′ 毫弗錯; ih-
ngæn′-fsh-ts‘o′ 一點° 弗 錯°;
*upright,* tsing′-dzih 正直; tön-
fông′ 端方; *proper,* kwe-kyü′
規矩

CORRECT, to — (mistakes), kæ′-
hao 改好; kæ-tsing′ 改正; *to
reprove,* tsah′-vah 責罰

CORRESPOND, to — (by letters),
yiu shü-sing′ kæ-wông′ 有書信
來往

CORRESPONDS, te′-go 對个°;
siang-te′-go 相對个°; siang′-
‘eh′-go 相合个°; — *in size,* m-
do′-siao 無° 大° 小

CORROBORATE, *to* s′-teh hao k‘ao-
jih′ 使得好靠實

CORRODE, *to* siu′-wun 銹完; me-
læn′ 霉爛

CORRUPT, *to* wæ-diao′ 壞了°; *to*
— *customs* (and hence morals),
wæ-diao′ fong-djoh′ 壞了°風俗

CORRUPT, *become — in morals,* jih-
‘o′ 習下°; *rotten,* kæn-wu′ 爛腐;
*stinking,* ts‘iu 臭°

CORRUPTIBLE, iao wæ-diao′-go
要壞了°个°

COSMETICS, siu yüong-mao′-go
tong′-si 修容貌个°東西

COST, *price,* kô′-din 價°錢°; kô′-
sæn; — *of living* (is) *high,* kyiao′-
yüong do′ 繳用大°

COSTIVE, do-ka′ sao′-kyih 大°解°
燥結

COSTLY, kô′-din kyü′ 價°錢°貴°

COSTUME, *fashionable* z-sih′-go i-
zông′ 時式个°衣裳°; *to wear
Chinese* —, Cong′-koh tang′-
pæn 中國打扮

COT, *my humble* —, sô′-‘o′ 舍下°;
sô′-pin 舍邊; — *bed,* doh-ze′
min-zông′ 獨睡眠床

COTTAGE, *hut,* sô 廬°; *straw* —,
ts‘ao′-oh 草屋; mao-ts‘ao′-oh
茅草屋 (ih-tsing)

COTTON, min-hwô′ 棉花; —
*cloth,* pu 布; *good native ditto,*
du′-pu 土°布; — *thread,* min-
sô′ 棉紗; *to beat* — (light), tang
min-hwô′ 打棉花

COTTON-GIN, kao-hwô-ts‘o′ 絞°
花車

COUCH, c‘ing-teng′ 春発; t‘ah-
zông′ 榻床°

COUGH, *has a* —, yiu ts‘iang′-bing.

COUGH, *to* ts‘iang; k‘eh′-seo 咳°
嗽; seo 嗽

COULD, neng-keo′ 能殼°; k‘o′-yi
可以; — *not stop,* feh neng′-
keo ts′ 弗能殼°止; hyih′-feh-
læ 歇弗來

COUNCIL, *to hold a* —, kong-nyi′
公議; *to convene a* —, jü kong-
nyi′ 聚公議

COUNCIL-CHAMBER, kong-sô′ 公
所

COUNSEL, *to* lib cü′-i 立主意;
c‘ih cü′-i 出主意; ky‘ün 勸
— *together,* dô-kô′ siang-liang′
大°家°商°量; *he keeps his*

own —, gyi'-go cü'-i feh k'eng
peh nying-kô hyiao'-teh-go 其
個°主意弗肯與°人°家°
曉得個°

COUNSELOR, lih cü'-i-go nying 立
主意个°人°; *officer's* —, mo-
yiu' 幕友; *styled*, s-yia' 師爺°

COUNT, *to* su 數; — *and see*, su'-
su-k'en 數數看; *esteem*, sön 算;
— *no disgrace, but honor*, yi-
joh', we-yüong' 以辱爲榮
(veng)

COUNTENANCE, min-yüong' 面
容; yüong-mao' 容貌; min-
k'ong' 面孔; *looked me out of*
—, k'en'-leh ngô wông-k'ong'-
siang 看得°我惶恐相; *to
keep one's* —, tsông lao'-ky'i
粧老氣; *can't keep his* —,
lao-ky'i tsông'-feh-læ' 老氣粧
弗來

COUNTER, *against*, fæn'-hyiang 反
向; tsoh-teo' 作對

COUNTER *in a shop*, gyü-deo' 櫃
頭 (ih-k'eo)

COUNTERACT, *to make good*, hwô-
hao' 化好; *to make evil*, pin-
wa' 變孬; hwô'-diao 化壞°

COUNTERFEIT, *to* kô'-mao假°冒;
ngwe-zao' 僞造°

COUNTERFEIT *dollar*, kô' fæn-
ping' 假°番餠; kô' yiang-dzin
假°洋錢

COUNTERMAND, *to* — *an order*,
diao cü'-i 調主意; *to* — *an*

*official order*, wun 'ao-ling' 換
號令

COUNTERPANE, *thin cover to be
added*, t'in-kæ-bi' 添盖被°

COUNTLESS, su'-feh-pin 數弗遍;
vu-su'-go 無數个°

COUNTRY, koh 國; *a tract of* —,
di-fông' 地方; (*rural*) —,
hyiang-'ô' 鄉下°; *foreign* —,
nga-koh' 外°國; *your honorable*
—, kwe-koh' 貴國

COUNTRYMAN, hyiang-'ô'-nying
鄉下°人°

COUNTY, *a* ih-fu' 一府

COUPLE, *to* kwe-long' ih-te' 歸
攏一堆; *to join*, lin-long' 連
攏; *to match*, p'e'-long 配攏

COUPLE, *a* ih-te' 一對; *a pair*
ih-sông' 一雙; *a married* —,
liang'-fu-ts'i' 兩夫妻

COURAGE, tæn'-liang 膽量; üong'-
ken 勇敢; tæn'-ts 膽子; ken-
tæn' 肝膽; *great* —, tæn'-liang
do' 膽量大°; tæn'-ts-p'eh' 膽
子潑

COURAGEOUS, yiu' tæn'-liang 有
膽量

COURSE, *road*, lu 路; (*ship's*) —,
hyiang'-dao 向導 (ih-da); —
*hitherto* (*of action*), seng-bing'生
平; *the short* —, liao-gying' lu 踁
近路; *what is the best* — *to take?*
'ah-li' ih da lu hao' 何°處°一揀
路好? *of* — *it is so*, z-jün' z-ka'
自然如°此°; *adopt a* —, yüong'
ih-go fông-fah' 用一个°方法

COURSES, (catamenia),yüih-kying′ 月經; yüih-kô′月家°

COURT (of a Chinese house), ming-dông′ 明堂; *small ditto,* t′in-tsing′ 天井; *place where the Emperor receives his —,* kying-lön′-din 金鑾殿; *to go to —,* zông-dziao′上朝

COURT *officers,* da-dzing′ 大臣; *— dress,* dziao-i′ 朝衣

COURT, *to — favor,* t′ao-hao′ 討好; *to flatter,* vong′-dzing 奉承; shü′-kwu 世故; *— some one's daughter by a middle-man,* teng ling-æ′ tso me°與°令愛作°媒

COURTEOUS, yiu li′-lu 有禮路; ky′in-°o′ 謙和

COURTESY, li 禮; li′-ky′i 禮體°; *he was invited by —* (or out of respect), we-leh tseng-kying′ gyi ts′ing′ gyi læ-go 為了°尊敬其請其來个°; *treat him with —,* long-djong′ gyi 隆重其

COURTIER, bun-kô′-go伴駕°个°; z-dzing′ 侍臣

COUSIN,*male —, by father's brother,* dông-hyüong′-di 堂兄弟, *sons of father's and mother's sisters, and mother's brother's sons,* piao′-hyüong-di 表兄弟; *female —,* dông-tsi′-me 堂姐妹; piao′-tsi-me 表姐妹

COVENANT, iah′ 約; *to make a —,* lih iah′ 立約; ding iah′定約

COVER, kæ 蓋 (ih-go); *take off the —,* kæ′ hyiao-ko′ 蓋拐過; *—*

(as for books, umbrellas, &c.), t′ao 套; *— for letters,* sing′-fong 信封; sing′-k′oh 信壳

COVER, *to* kæ 蓋; *to screen* (as from wind, &c.), tsô 遮°; tsô-kæ′ 遮°蓋; tsô-in′ 遮°掩; *—* (as with a basket), tsao 罩

COVERLET, kæ-min′-go bi 蓋面个°被°; *wadded —,* min-bi′棉被°

COVERTLY, mih-mih′-go 密密个°

COVET, *to* t′en 貪; sang t′en-sing′ 生°貪心

COVETOUS, yiu t′en-sing′有貪心

COW, ngeo 牛°; *yellow —,* wông-ngeo′ 黃牛°; *water buffalo,* shü′-ngeo 水°牛° (ih-deo)

COW *him,* long′-leh gyi′dong′-dæn-feh-læ′ 弄得°其動彈弗來

COW-BEZOAR, ngeo-wông′ 牛°黃

COW-DUNG, ngeo-feng′ 牛°糞; ngeo-o′ 牛°屎°

COW-SHED, ngeo-gyin′ 牛°橛

COWARD, ㄇ tæn′-ky′i-go nying 無°膽氣个°人°; ㄇ tæn′-liang-go nying 無°膽量个°人°

COXCOMB, æ p′iao-yih′-go nying 愛飄逸个°人°; *dissolute —,* hwô-hwô′ kong-ts 花花公子; *— (a flower),* kyi-kwun′-hwô 雞冠花

COY, iu′-siu 幽羞; p′ô iu′-siu 怕幽羞

COZY *room,* (*i. e.* a room for quiet enjoyment),en-loh′-kong 安樂宮

CRAB, ha 蟹°

CRAB - APPLE, hæ'- dông-ko 海棠菓

CRACK, hwah 豁; hwah'-u 豁縫°; hwah'-lih-vong 豁裂縫; *a seam* (as between boards), vong 縫 (ih-da)

CRACK, *to* hwah 豁; k'æ hwah'-lih 開豁裂; — *from heat*, pao'-hwah 爆豁

CRACKED, k'æ hwah' de 開豁了°; — *apart*, hwah'-k'æ de 豁開了°

CRACKERS, *fire* p'ao'-dziang 礮仗; pah'-ts-p'ao 百子礮

CRADLE, *basket* yiao-læn' 搖籃

CRAFTY, kæn-tiao' 奸刁; diao-bi'.

CRAM, *to* seh'-pao 扇飽; seh'-mun 扇滿

CRAMP *of muscles*, kying' geo-long' 筋拘°攏

CRANIUM, kw'u-lu'-deo 骷髏頭

CRAPE, wu-tseo' 湖縐; *thin* — (or gauze), sô 紗

CRASH (as of wall falling), tao'-t'ah sing-hyiang' 倒塌聲響; — (as of dishes falling), tao'-fæn sing-hyiang' 倒翻聲響

CRAVAT, ling'-ta 領帶° (ih-diao, ih-keng)

CRAVE, *to beseech*, gyiu-k'eng' 求懇; *to desire*, siang 想; — *food &c.* (as one destitute), fah-zao' 發糟°; zao-ky'i'-ka 糟°起

CRAVING (at a particular time, as for opium), nyin-deo' 癮°頭

CRAWL, *to* bô 爬

CRAZY, tin'-de 癲了°; veng-tin' 文癲; — *person*, tin-ts' 癲子; tin-nying' 癲人°; *fiercely* —, fah-gwông' 發狂; vu'-tin 武癲

CREAK, ing'-ang 伊呀; *the doors* —, meng' ing'-ang læ-tih hyiang' 門伊呀響; — (as a boat-scull), u'-cih-ga';—(as a chair), kyi'-ka; — (as a wheel), ka-ka-hyiang'.

CREAM, na'-yiu 嬭°油; na'-bi 嬭°皮

CREASE, üih'-u 攣印°; tsih'-u 摺印°; *fold it in the old* —, tsiao lao' u tsih 照老印°摺; tsiao nyün u' tsih' 照原印°摺; *wrinkle*, tseo'-u 皺印°

CREASE, *must not* — (it), m-nao' üih'-diao 弗°可°攣壞°

CREATE, *to* zao 造°; zao'-c'ih-læ 造°出來; zao'-hwô 造°化

CREATION, *the time of* —, k'æ-t'in'-p'ih-di z-'eo' 開天闢地時候; *the things created*, t'in-di'-væn'-veh 天地萬物

CREATOR, *the* zao'-hwô Cü'-tsæ 造°化主宰; zao væn-veh'-go Cü'-tsæ 造°萬物个°主宰

CREATURES, seng-liug' 生靈; yiu hyüih'-ky'i-go tong-si' 凡°有血氣者°

CREDENCE, *to give* —, siang-sing' 相信; *can't give* —, siang-sing'-feh-læ 相信弗來

CREDENTIALS, tsih'-tsiao 執照; bing-kyü' 憑據

CREDIBLE, z'-joh k'o-sing' 似 屬 可 信

CREDIT, *his — is good*, gyi-go bats' hao' 其个°牌°子好; *to his — (praise)*, hao ngao gyi'; *bought on —*, sô-læ'-go 賒 來 个°

CREDITABLE *performance*, ming kòng 名工; iao ngao-ngao' gyi.

CREDITOR, t'ao'-cü 討 主; tsa'-cü 債°主

CREDULOUS, ky'ing-yi' siang-sing' 輕易相信; ih-t'ing' ziu siang-sing' 一聽就°相信

CREED, *apostles* s-du' sing'-kying 使 徒 信 經

CREEK, siao-ts'ô-kông' 小 又 港; siao-kông' 小 港 (ih-da)

CREEP, *to* bô 爬

CREST *of a cock*, kwun'-deo 冠頭

CREW, *sailors*, shü'-siu 水°手

CREVICE, vong 縫; hwah'-vong 豁 縫 (ih-da)

CRICKET, ting-s-ts' 蟋°蟀°; yiu-tih-ling' 油 的 蛉 (ih-tsah)

CRIME, djong'-ze 重罪; *to commit a —*, væn djong' ze 犯 重 罪

CRIMINAL, væn'-nying 犯 人°;

In the 4th month, persons called *ræn-nying* walk in idolatrous processions, dressed in red. These persons had vowed when sick, that if restored, they would be publicly regarded as *criminals*, or *ræn-nying*, as they supposed the sickness was a punishment for some crime.

CRIMSON, ts'-'ong 紫 紅

CRINGE, *to* pe-kong-ky'üih'-tsih 卑 躬 屈 節; *— (as a beggar)*, li-di'-'ô-pe'.

CRIPPLE, væn dzæn'-dzih'-liao-go nying' 犯 殘 疾 个° 人° See LAME.

CRISIS, kwæn 關; kwæn-deo' 關 頭; *— is past*, kwæn' ko'-de 關 過 了°

CRISP *(as cakes)*, su 酥; *— (as pears)*, song-ts'e' 鬆 脆

CRITERION, cing'-tseh 準 則

CRITIC, p'i-bing'-go cü'-kwu 批 評 个° 人°; zing leo-dong'-go nying' 尋°漏 洞 个° 人°

CROAK, *frogs* keh'-pô we kyiao' 蛤 蚆 會 叫

CROAKING, *always (said of a person)*, zeo-shü-bu-kwu' ka 像°愁° 水°鷗°鶻°; zing' kyiao zing', yü kyiao' yü 晴°叫晴°雨叫雨

CROCKERY, *porcelain*, dz-ky'i' 磁 器; *earthen-ware*, ngô'-ho 瓦°貨

CROCODILE, ngoh-ng' 鼉 魚°

CROOKED, wæn 彎; *having many turns*, wæn-ky'üoh' go 彎 曲 个°; *— and twisted*, wæn-nyiao' 彎 繞

CROP *(of a fowl)*, teng 膆; *an abundant —*, nyin-dzing' da-joh' 年 成 大 熟; *spring —bad*, c'ing'-hwô wa' 春 花 孬°; *poor — (i.e. 80 parts out of 100)*, pah'-tsih nyin-se' 八 折 年 歲; *scant —*, kæn nyin-dzing' 減°年 成

CROP, *to bite off*, ngao'-ky'i 齩 去°

CROSS, jih-z'-kô 十 字 架°; *died on the —*, si' læ jih-z'-kô zông' 死°在°十 字 架 上

CROSS, *adj.* kwu'-kwa-deo 古怪頭; kwu-tiao'-deo 孤刁頭; feh-'o'-ky'i 弗和氣; tiao-djü-kwu'-seh 膠°柱鼓瑟; *to put on a — look,* fæn cü'-lin 反嘴臉

CROSS, *to* ko 過; tseo'-ko 走過; — *the ferry,* ko du' 過渡;— *the feet* (or legs), gao kyiah' 交°脚; *to lay across,* wang fông' 橫°放; *must not — him,* feh-k'o ao'-ky'iang gyi 弗可拗强其

CROSS-BAR, wang-shün' 橫°閂 (ih-keng)

CROSS-BEAM, wang-tông' 橫°擋 (ih-keng)

CROSS-EXAMINE, *to* fæn'-foh bun-meng' 反覆盤問; tao'-meng jing-meng' 倒問°順問°; bun-kyih' 盤詰

CROSS-EYED, zia'-bah-ngæn 斜°白眼°

CROUCH, *to* gwu 躬°; — *in hiding,* gwu-leh iu' 躬得°幽

CROUP, 'eo'-fong 喉風

CROW, lao'-ô' 老鴉° (ih-tsah)

CROW, *to* — (as a cock), di 啼; *to* — *over,* ts'ing-üong' 稱勇; *you need not* —, ng hao-vong ying üong'-shü-ts 你°弗°用°行勢

CROW-BAR, gyiao-kweng' 橇棍 (ih-keng)

CROWD, *a* ih-dziao'nying 一羣°人°

CROWD, *to* üong'-tsi 擁擠; a-tsi' 挨°擠; — *together for a bad purpose,* jü'-jih-nying'-cong 聚集人°衆

CROWDED, a-lih'-bah-lang'; *closely* —, a-kyin'-ts'ah'-pe 挨°肩擦背; a-tsi'-feh-k'æ' 挨°擠弗開

CROWN, bing-t'in'-kwun 平天冠; —(worn by a bride, or the wife of a kyü-nying &c.), vong-kwun' 鳳冠; — *of the head,* deo-ti'-sing 頭頂°心

CRUCIFIX, jih-z'-kô 十字架; (Shanghai) kwu-ziang 菩像; *wear a* —, ta' jih-z'-kô 帶°十字架°

CRUCIFY, *to* ting læ jih-z'-kô zông 釘在°十字架°上

CRUDE, sang 生°; feh-joh'弗熟; — *ideas,* i'-s feh dziu'-lin 意思弗綢練

CRUEL, k'eh 刻; k'eh'-doh 刻毒; *very* —, koh-ken'燙乾; *savage,* hyüong-oh'兇惡;—*disposition,* sing-s' k'eh' 心思刻; — *oppression,* bao-nyiah' 暴虐

CRUISE, *to* — *on the rivers,* jing-kông'巡港;—*on the ocean,* jing-yiang' 巡洋

CRULLERS, fæn-kyih' 麪反結; *to boil* —, zah fæn-kyih' 煠反結

CRUMBS, se 碎; — *of bread,* mun-deo' se 饅頭碎; *to drop* —, lông-zih' 狼藉

CRUMBLE, *to* long-se'弄碎; *will* —, iao se' 要碎; — *in the hand,* nyiah-se' 捏碎

CRUMPLE, *to* dön-long' 摶攏; lön-dön' 亂摶

CRUSH, *to* — (as something soft), ah'-pih 壓瘟；— (as something hard), ah'-se 壓°碎；ah'-wu 壓腐°；— *to death*, ah'-sah 壓°殺；*to subdue*, ah'-voh 壓°服

CRUST *of bread*, mun-deo'-bi' 饅頭皮

CRUTCH, lông-t'ông' 榔檔° (ih-go)；*to use crutches*, s lông-t'ông' 使榔檔°

CRY, *to* — (as a baby), kyiao 叫；— *and lament*, k'oh 哭；di-di' k'oh-k'oh 啼啼哭哭；*ready to* — (sour nose), sön-bih' 酸鼻°；*to* — *out suddenly* si' ih-sing；— *out loudly*, wæ-wæ'-hyiang 營° 營°響

CRYSTAL, shü'-tsing or se'-tsing 水°晶

CUB *of a bear*, siao-yüong' 小熊 (ih-tsah)

CUBE, loh-min'-cün-fông' 六面轉方

CUBEBS, dzing-gyia' 澄茄

CUBIT, (Chinese, from elbow to knuckles), ih-tsin' 一肘

CUCUMBER, wông-kwô' 黃瓜 (ih-keng)

CUD, *chew the* —, cün ziao' 轉嚼°

CUDGEL, kweng'-ts 棍子；*to beat with a* —, tang kweng'-ts 打棍子；— *for beating clothes*, lin-djü' 練槌° (ih-go)

CUE, bin'-ts 辮子；fah bin' 髮辮 (ih-kwang)

CUFF, *give him a* —, kwah' gyi ih-kwông' 摑° 其 一 光；sin' gyi ih-kwông' 搧其 一 光

CUFF, *to* kwah 摑°；— *the cheek*, kwah pô-công' 摑巴掌

CUFF, ziu-t'ao' 袖套；*hoof shaped* — *attached to the sleeve*, mô-di-ziu' 馬蹄袖；*a sleeve with* — *turned back*, fæn-ziu' 翻袖；tsao'-ziu 罩袖

CULINARY *utensils*, long-væn' kô-sang' 弄飯家°貨°

CULL, *to pick*, tsah 摘；tsah'-c'ih-læ' 摘出來；*to choose*, kæn 揀°

CULLENDER. See COLANDER.

CULPABLE, k'o-kwa' 可怪°

CULPRIT, yiu-ko'-væn-cü'-kwu 有過犯个°人°；*criminal*, væn'-nying 犯人°

CULTIVATE, *to plough land*, kang din' 耕°田；*to sow*, cong din' 種田；— *the fields*, cong'-din' da-di' 種田藁°地；kang-cong'-din-di' 耕°種田地；— *flowers*, tsæ-cong hwô' 栽種花；— *virtue*, siu teh' 修德；*cultivated land*, joh di' 熟地

CUMBERED *with heavy things*, be djong' sô le' 被重所累

CUMBROUS, t'o le'-go 拖累个°；— *to a person*, le nying' go 累人°个°

CUNNING, *knowing*, kwæ'-ky'iao 乖巧；*deceitful*, diao-bi'; kæn-tsô' 奸°詐；*very* —, kæn-tiao' 奸°刁；*slippery*, weh-t'eng'-weh-kweng' 活氽活滚

CUP, pe-ts' 杯子; large —, cong 盅; tea—, dzô-pe' 茶杯 (ih-tsah)

CUPBOARD for dishes, un'-tsæn-djü' 碗盏廚; — for provisions, ka-djü' 食°廚 (ih-k'eo)

CUPIDITY, t'en-du'-sing 貪圖心; great —, t'en-du'-sing djong'貪 圖心重

CURABLE, hao-i' 好醫; i'-leh-læ' 醫得°來

CURB for a horse, mô'-lah-k'eo'馬 勒口

CURB, to restrain, iah'-soh 約束; to subdue, ah'-cü 壓°制; — the passions, k'eh'-djü s-yüoh' 克治 私慾

CURD, milk nying-long'-liao-go na' 凝攏了个爛°; bean —, deo-vu' 豆腐

CURDLE, to nying-long' 凝攏

CURE, to i 醫; i-hao' 醫好; — disease, i bing' 醫病; — meat with salt, yin nyüoh' 鹽肉°

CURIOSITY, has great —, iao leo-leo'-weh-weh' 要鑢鑢挖挖; desire to find out matters, tang'-t'ing siao-sih'打聽消息; desire to see, iao k'en'-k'en-siang'要看 看; curiosities, hwô-seh' tong'-si 花色東西; antique ditto, kwu'-tong wæn'-ky'i 古董玩°器

CURIOUS, hwun-hyi' tang'-t'ing 歡喜打聽; hwun-hyi' t'eo-k'en' 歡喜偷看; artfully con-structed, hyi-gyi' kwu'-kwa 希 奇古怪°

CURL, to kyün'-long 捲攏; to — the hair, kyün fah' 捲髮

CURLY hair, s-ts' fah' 獅子髮

CURRENCY, money in circulation, t'ong-yüong'-go nying-dzin' 通 用个°銀錢; t'ong-'ang' dong-din' 通行°銅錢°

CURRENT price, da-kæ' kô'-din大 概價°錢'; in — use, t'ong yüong'通用; — expenses, kying-fi' 經費; s'-fi 使費; kyiao-yüong'繳用; dao-yiao'; — rate, 'ông-dzing' 行情

CURRENT, the — is strong, shü'-go læ-long' gyin' 水°个°來龍健

CURRY-POWDER, kyiang-wông'-feng 姜黃粉

CURRY-COMB, mô'-bao 馬刨 (ih-pô)

CURSE, to tsiu'-mô 咒罵; tsiu'-cü 咒咀

CURSORILY, liao-piao'聊表; da-liah' 大略; veo-min' 浮面

CURTAIL, to siu-bo' 收縛; siu-soh'-long 收縮攏; —expenses, fi'-yüong siu-soh'-tin 費用收 縮點; fi'-yüong gyin'-sang 費 用儉省°; — (one's) life, ziu-shü' kæn-tön' 壽歲°減短; kæn ziu' 減°壽

CURTAIN for a bed, tsiang'-ts 帳 子; —for a door, meng-lin' 門 簾; window —, ts'ông-lin' 窓 簾; bamboo —, lin-ts' 簾子

CURVE, to wæn 彎; curving in and out, wæn-nyiao' 彎橈;

curving, *like the moon or a bow,*
yüih-kong' shih 月宮式°

CUSHION, din-ts' 墊子; *pin* —,
tsing-ts'ah' 針插 (ih-go)

CUSTODY, *to take into* —, k'ó'-djoh
擎°著°; *to be in* —, kwun'-ah
管押°

CUSTOM, *usage,* kwe-kyü' 規矩;
— *of a country,* fong-djoh' 風
俗; — *of a place,* hyiang-fong'
or hyiang-fong 鄉風; t'u-fong
土風; *it is the* —, lao'-lao z-
ka' 每°每°如°此°; *it is his* —,
gyi kwæn'-djông z-ka' 其慣
常如°此°; *give him your* —,
'ó'-kwu gyi 下°顧其

CUSTOM-HOUSE, se'-kwæn 稅關;
*to slip the* —, t'eo-ko kwæn'
偷過關

CUSTOMARY, tsiao lao'-li 照老
例; — *presents,* tsiao djông'-
kwe, song-li' 照常規送禮;
— *walk,* tsiao' djông' tseo-tseo'
照常走走

CUSTOMERS, *our* ah'-lah cü'-kwu
我°等°主顧; *old* —, lao' cü'-
kwu 老主顧

CUSTOMS, *Commissioner of* —, se'-
vu'-s 稅務司; *Inspector of* —,
cong' se'-vu-s 總稅務司;
*customs' duty,* se'-din 稅錢°;
*avoid paying ditto,* t'eo se' 偷稅

CUSTOM-STATION, kyün-gyüoh'
捐局; k'a-ts 卡子

CUT, *n.* (with a knife), tao-sông'

刀傷 (ih-da); — *in books,* wô-
du' 畫圖 (ih-go)

CUT, *to* — *with a knife,* kah 割;
tsæn 斬; — *a gash,* kah'-k'æ
割開; — *asunder,* kah'-dön
割斷; tsæn'-dön 斬斷; —
*grain,* kah dao' 割稻; — *or
carve meat,* ts'ih nyüoh' 切肉°;
— *in slices,* ts'ih-p'in' 切片; —
*a slice of bread,* ts'ih' ih-p'in'
mun-deo' 切一片饅頭; —
*with a scizzors,* tsin 剪; — *the
hair,* tsin deo-fah' 剪頭髮; —
*or trim ditto,* tæn deo-fah'; *to* —
*out garments,* zæ i-zông' 裁°衣
裳°; — *or trim off, a little,* zæ-tin'-
diao 裁°點去°; — *a pattern,*
zæ yiang-ts' 裁樣子; *to* — *off
the head,* tsæn deo' 斬頭; —
*down a tree,* tsoh jü' 劚樹; —
*off branches,* tsæn'-diao ô-ts' 斬
了°椏枝; — *in pieces* (as a
pig, &c.), ih-tao ih'-tao, tön-tæn'-
k'æ 一刀一刀斷開; — tön'-
leh tao-tang'-tao 斷得°刀打
刀; — *off an arm,* siu'-kwang
tsæn-loh' 手骨斬落; —
*one's own throat,* zi-veng' 自°刎°;
— *another's throat,* kah wu-long'
割喉°嚨°; — *a capon,* sin kyi'
騙雞; — *glass,* zæ po-li' 裁°
玻璃; *to engrvae,* tiao-k'eh'
雕刻; — *wages,* kæn kong-din'
減°工錢°; — *friendship,* djih
kyiao' 絕交; — *off communication,* dön'-djih læ-wông' 斷絕

來往；— off relationship between parent and child, dön-dzing' djih-yi' 斷情絕義°; — across by a shorter way, liao-gying' lu tseo 蹺近路走; — teeth, c'ih ngô-ts' 出牙°齒; — or give a blow (with a stick), k'ao' ih-kyi 拷一記; — or give a blow (with a sword), tsæn' ih-kyin 斬一劍; — or give a blow (with a whip), tang-ih'-pin 打一鞭

CUTANEOUS, læ bi-fu' li 在°皮膚裏; — diseases, bi-fu'-go bing' 皮膚个°病

CUTCH, r'-dzô 兒茶

CUTLASS, a curved knife worn at the side, iao-tao' 腰刀

CUTLER, tang-tao'-s-vu' 打刀司務

CUTLERY, fong-kw'a'-go kô-sang' 鋒快°个°器皿°

CUTLET, a cut of meat, ih-p'in nyüoh' 一片肉°

CUTTING-BOARD for meat, tsing-pæn' 椹板; cutting-block, tsing-deo' 椹頭

CUTTLE-FISH, moh-ng' 墨魚°; u-zeh' 烏鰂°; dried —, ming-fu' 蝦蛹 (ih-go); — bone, u-zeh'-kweh 烏鰂°骨

CYCLE, (sixty years), kyiah'-ts 甲子; hwô-kyiah'-ts 花甲子; years of a —, nyin-kang' 年庚°

CYCLOPEDIA, poh-veh'-go-shü' 博物个°書

CYLINDER, dziang-yün-t'i' 長圓體; ngô-dong'-shih 瓦°筒式°

CYMBALS, dzô-beh' or ts'ô-beh'; large —, do beh' 大°鈸; smaller —, ts'ih'-ts 小°鈸°; very small —, gen-ts'ön'.

# D

DAB, to throw dirt upon, na-nyi' kwang'-djoh 泥潑°着°

DABBLE in water, long shü' 弄水°

DAGGER, ts'-tao' 刺刀; two edged —, sông-min' kyin 雙面劍 (ih-pô)

DAGUERREOTYPE, tsiao'-siang 照相

DAILY, nyih-nyih' 日°日°; me-nyih' 每日°; djoh-nyih' 逐日°; nyih-dzoh' 日°逐; — food, nyih-nyih'-go ky'üoh'-zih 日°日°个°吃°食

DAINTY as to food, ky'üoh'-zih k'ao'-kyiu 吃°食考°究; ky'üoh'-zih kæn-ka' 吃°食瞰°㕭°; a —, ts'ing-c'ü'-go tong'-si 清㵤个°東西

DALLY, to (the sexes), nen-nyü' o-kyin'-tah-pe' 男女和°肩搭背

DAM for water, ky'i 閘°; — with mud slide for boats, pô 礱; in 堰

DAM, to — up water, kwæn-djü' shü 關住水°

DAMAGE, pay the —, long-diao'-de be-wæn' 弄壞了°賠還

DAMAGE, to — by bruising (as

fruit), ts'ah'-sòng 擦傷; *to spoil,* i'-diao; long-diao' 弄 壞°; wæ-diao' 壞 了°

DAMAGED, *torn or broken,* yiu p'o'-dzæn-go 有 破 綻 个°; *spotted* (*by water, &c.*), yiu tsih'-tsoh-go 有 汁 泥 个°; *goods — by water,* shü'-tsih ho' 水° 汁 貨

DAMASK, dön-pu' 緞 布

DAMN, *condemn him to eternal pun-ishment,* ding' peh gyi ziu üong'-kw'u ying-vah' 定 俾 其° 受 永 苦 刑 罰

DAMNED, *to be* —, vah-loh' di-nyüoh' 罰 落 地 獄; üong' zo di-nyüoh' 永 坐° 地 獄

DAMNED, *the* ziu üong'-kw'n-go nying 受 永 苦 个° 人°

DAMP, dziao-sih' 潮 濕; yiu sih'-ky'i 有 濕 氣; *very* —, sih'-ky'i djong' 濕 氣 重; *to become* —, wæn dziao' 還 潮; cün dziao' 轉 潮; fæn-dziao' 翻 潮

DAMPEN *it,* long gyi' nyüing-tsiu'-go.

DAMSEL, do-kwu'-nyiang 大° 姑 娘; kwe'-nyü 閨 女

DANCE, *to* t'iao-vu' 跳 舞

DANDLE, *to* — *on the knee,* kyiah' teo-teo' 脚 抖 抖; — *in the hand,* siu song-song' 手 聳 聳

DANDRUFF, kw'u'- k'oh - in' 肩 髮 靨

DANDY, p'iao-yih' nying 飄 逸 人°; *an officer's son highly dressed*

*but not of good character,* hwô-hwô'-kong'-ts 花 花 公 子

DANGER, ngwe-hyin' 危 險; *to get into* —, tsao'-djoh ngwe-hyin' 遭 着° 危 險; *in* —, ngwe-hyin' li-hyiang' 危 險 裡 向; *rush into* — *in spite of remon-strance &c.,* weh'-leh feh-næ'-væn 活 得° 弗 耐 煩

DANGEROUS, hyin'-hyin 險 險; ngwe'-go 危 个°; hyin'-hoh 險 霍; hyin'-dao-dao 險 逃 逃; yiu-'æ' 有 害; — *to life,* sing'-ming kao-kwæn' 性 命 交° 關; — *to sit there,* keh'-deo zo, yiu fong-ho' 那° 邊° 坐 有 風 火; keh'-deo zo, yiu ken-yi' 那° 邊° 坐 有 干 係

DANGLE, *to* daug 宕; dang-dang'-dong 宕 宕 動

DAPPLED, pæn-poh'-go 斑 駁 个°

DARE, *to* ken 敢; — *not do,* feh ken tso' 弗 敢 做

DARING, mao do'-tæn-go 冒 大° 膽 个°; — *person,* mao do'-tæn go nying 冒 大° 膽 个° 人°

DARK, en 暗; heh'-en 黑 暗; en'-lih-boh-long'; en'-c'ih-c'ih' 暗 睫 睫°; en'-dong-dong 暗 瞳 瞳; *nearly* —, t'in'kw'a en'-de 天 快 暗 了°; *very* —, moh-ts'eh'-di-en' 墨 漆 地 暗; *afraid of the* —, p'ô en'-go 怕 暗 个°; — *color,* sing seh' 深 色; — *blue,* sing læn' 深 藍

DARKEN, *to* — *slightly,* tsô-ing'

遮°陰°; — *completely,* tsô-en'
遮°暗°

DARLING, *dearly loved,* ting' dzih-din'-go 頂 值 錢° 个°; — *child,* nön-nön' (used for both sexes).

DARN, *to* kang 耕°; — *in ball-stitch,* c'ün 穿; *to mend by imitating the texture of the stuff,* tsih' pu 緝 補; — *stockings,* kang mah' 耕° 襪 (pu mah' 補 襪 which is often used, is incorrect, as it means to mend with a patch); — *slightly,* kang' liang tsing' 耕° 兩 針

DART *carried in the sleeve,* ziu-tsin' 袖 箭

DART, *to forth,* zah-c'ih'-læ.

DASH, *to* — *against,* ts'ong-dzông 衝 撞; dzông-djoh' 撞 着°; *waves* — *up,* lông p'eh-zông-læ' 浪 潑 上 來; — *down,* ts'ong-loh' 衝 落; *ditto, by knocking against,* dzông-tao' 撞 倒

DATE, *time,* z-'eo' 時 候; *what month?* kyi yüih'-li 幾 月 裡? soh'-go yüih-veng' 甚° 麼° 月 孖? *at what date? i. e. in what dynasty?* læ soh'-go dziao-dæ' 在° 甚° 麼° 朝 代? *year of the reign,* nyin-'ao' 年 號; *year of the cycle,* nyin-kang' 年 庚

The date of the year is reckoned by dynasties, reigns, and cycles. The cycle is only used for present time.

DATE, *jujube,* tsao'-ts 棗 子; *honeyed and dried* —, mih-tsao'

蜜 棗; *black* —, heh-tsao' 黑 棗; *red* —, 'ong-tsao' 紅 棗

DAUB, *to* lön-du' 亂 塗; lön-dzô' 亂 搭

DAUGHTER, nön 女°; *how many daughters have you?* ng' yiu kyi'-we ling-æ' 你° 有 幾 位 令 愛? kyi-we' ts'in-kying' 幾 位 千 金? *I have three daughters,* ngô' yiu sæn'-go siao-nyü' 我 有 三 个 小 女

DAUGHTER-IN-LAW, sing-vu' 媳° 婦; *oldest son's wife,* do sing'-vu' 大° 媳° 婦; *second son's wife* (when there are more), nyi-vông' sing-vu' 二° 房 媳° 婦 (if there are only two sons), *the second* —, siao' sing-vu' 小° 媳° 婦

DAUNTED, *nothing* 'ao -vu' gyü-dæn' 毫 無 懼 憚

DAUNTLESS, tæn-da'-jü-t'in' 膽 大 如 天

DAWN, u-long'-song z-'eo' 烏 眼° 曉° 時 候; t'in'-kw'a-liang' 天 快 亮; t'in'-bah-c'ong'-ky'i 天 白 曙° 起; tong-fông'-diao-bah' 東 方 曉° 白

DAY, *a* ih-nyih' 一 日°; *a day's work,* ih-kong' 一 工; *a day's wages,* ih-kong' kong-din' 一 工 工 錢°; *the first* — *of the month,* ts'u-ih' 初 一; *1st and 15th* — *of the month,* soh' vông 朔 望; *what* — *of the month is this?* kying'-tsiao z ts'u-kyi' 今 朝 是 初 幾? kyih-mih' z ts'u-kyi' 今

日°是初幾? *the 15th*, jih-ng′
十五°; yüih-pun′ 月半; *every*
—, me′-nyih 每日°; nyih-nyih′
日°日°; — *and night*, nyih yia′
日°夜°; *all* —, tsing nyih′
覺°日°; dziang nyih′ 長日°;
*half a* —, pun′ nyih 半日°;
*every other* —, kæn′ nyih 間°
日°; *lucky* —, hao′ nyih-ts 好
日°子; *unlucky* —, nyih-ts′
ẇa′ 日°子孬; *the same* —,
tông′ nyih 當日°; — *before
yesterday*, zin nyih′ 前°日°; —
*after tomorrow*, ′eo nyih′ 後日°;
*whatever* — *you please*, ze ng′
′ah-li ih nyih′ 隨你°那裡一
日°; *how many days?* kyi nyih′
幾日°? to-siao′ nyih-ts 多少
日°子? *ten days*, jih nyih′ 十日°

DAY-BOOK, liu-shü′-bu 流水簿
DAY-BREAK, t′in liang′ z-′eo′ 天
亮時候; nyih-deo′ fông-kwông′
z-′eo′ 日°頭放光時候
DAY-LIGHT, nyih-deo′-kwông′ 日°
頭光; nyih-kwông′ 日°光;
t′a′-yiang-kwông′ 太°陽光
DAY-TIME, *in the* —, nyih-li′ 日°
裡; nyih-cong-deo′ 日°中頭;
ts′ing-t′in′-bah-nyih 青天白日°
DAZZLING *light*, kwông′ziang tsing
c′oh′ ka 光如針°猎; kwông′
li-′æ′ 光利害; *my eyes are
dazzled, or overpowered by the
light*, ngô ngæn′-kwông teo′-feh-
djü′ 我眼°光兜弗住; dih-
feh-ko′ 敵弗過

DEAD, si′-de 死°了°; ko′-de 過
了°; vông-ko′-de 亡過了°;
ṁ-neh′-de 沒°有°了°; ky′ü′-
shü-de 去世了°; *just* —, ky′i
dön′-de 氣斷了°; — *tree*, jü ô′-
de 樹殖了°; jü kw′u′-de 樹
枯了°; jü si′-de 樹死了°;
— *body*, s-sin′ 屍首; p′oh′-s
仆屍; si′-s 死°屍; — *cow*, tao′
ngeo 倒牛°; — *fish*, veng-ng′
文魚°; — (*as a backslider in
religion*), dao′-sing si′-liao 道心
死°了°; *the place of the* —,
ing-s′ 陰司; ing-kæn′ 陰間°
DEADLY, iao sah-nying′-go 要殺
人°个°; — *poison*, iao yiah-
sah′-go 要藥殺个°
DEADNESS, ziang si′-liao ka′-go
像死°了°个°; *coldness*, lang′
sing 冷°心
DEAF, long-bang′ 聾聩; ng′-tô
long′ 耳°朵聾; *born* —, sang-
dzing′ long-bang′ 生°成聾
聩; — *and dumb person*, ô′-ts
啞子
DEAFEN, *you* — *me with your
noise*, ngô ng′-tô be ng ts′ao′-
long-de 我耳°朵被你°謅
聾了°
DEAFNESS, *affected* —, *or* — *in
one ear*, tsia′-mi-long′ 借米聾;
*pretended* —, tsông kô′ ng-to
long′ 裝假°耳°朵聾
DEAL, *a great* —, hyü′-to 許多;
*I cause you a* — *of trouble*, tao

iao ng′ ziu hyü′-to lao-loh′ 倒
要 你° 受 許 多 勞 碌 ; to lao′
多 勞 ; fi sing′ 費 心

DEAL *out to them*, feng-feng′ peh
gyi-lah′ 分 分 給° 伊° 等° ;
— *honestly*, kong-dao′ dæ nying′
公 道 待 人° ; — *impartially*,
m̄ p‘in′-sing dæ nying′ 無 偏 心
待 人°

DEALER *in cotton*, tso min-hwô′
sang-i′ go 做 棉 花 生° 意 个°

DEAR, *costly*, kyü 貴 ; kô′-din
kyü′ 價° 錢° 貴° ; *how* —, dza
kyü′ 甚° 貴° ; — *child*, dzih-diu′-
go siao-nying′ 值 錢° 个° 小
孩° ; sing-deo′ nyüoh 心 頭 肉° ;
weh-pao′ 活 寶

In writing letters the address "Dear
friend" is unknown ; Mr. ‘Ong Siao′
Hyiang writing to Mr. Wông, in lieu of
"Dear Mr. Wông" writes, "Wông
Sin′-Sang s-zih′" 王 先 生 史 席
or "veng kyi′" 文 几, and signs himself ‘Ong Siao′-Hyiang z ; to an official's name he adds, "dæ-‘ô′" 臺 下°,
and signs "O. S. H. teng′-siu," 頓
首 *i. e.* bow low ; to a friend's name
he adds "koh′-tô′" 閣 下° ; a pupil
signs by adding "yin-dï′" 賢 弟
(masc.) or "nyü-dï′" 女 弟 (fem.),
to his or her name ; if writing to an
equal or inferior add, "jü-min′" 如 面
or "jü-ngwu′" 如 晤 ; a gentleman
writing to a lady addresses her as "s-
meo′" 師 母 "or tsông-tst′" 粧 次 ;
a youth to father's, mother's or teacher's
name adds, "tseng-zin′" 尊 前

DEARLY *loved*, ts‘ing-æ′-go 親 愛
个° ; *ditto* (of a superior), ting æ′-

kying-go 頂 愛 敬 个° ; *ditto*
(of an equal or inferior), ting æ′-
sih-go 頂 愛 惜 个°

DEARLY *bought*, ma′ kyü-de 買°
貴° 了° ; ma′ ky‘üoh-kw‘e′-de
買 吃° 虧 了°

DEARTH, siu-kah′ feh-zông 收 割
弗 上 ; *great* —, ts‘-lih vu-siu′ 子
粒 無 收 ; *a year of* —, hwông-
nyiu′ 荒 年 ; *a year of scarcity*
(of vegetables or fruit), siao′ nyin
小 年

DEATH, si 死° ; — *of the emperor*,
kô peng′ 駕 崩 ; *the day of one's*
—, si′ gyi 死 期 ; *the time of*
—, ky‘ü-shü′ z-‘eo′ 去 世 時
候 ; ling-cong′ z-‘eo′ 臨 終 時
候 ; ling-si′ z-‘eo 臨 死 時 候 ;
*natural* —, jün′ cong 善 終 ;
bing kwu′ 病 故 ; — *by violence*,
oh′ si 惡 死° ; wang si′ 橫 死° ;
*how old were you at your mother's*
— ? ng′ to-siao nyin-kyi′ sông
meo′-go 你 多 少 年 紀 喪 母
个° ? *the time of your father's*
—, sông vu′ z-‘eo′ 喪 父 時 候

DEATHLESS, ve′ si-go 勿° 會°
死 个°

DEATH-LIKE, ziang si′-yiang ka
像 死 一 樣 ; *to put on a* —
*appearance*, tsông si′-yiang 裝
死° 樣

DEATH-WARRANT, sah nying′-go
tsiao′-shü 殺 人° 个° 詔 書

DEBAR, *to shut out*, kwæn-c‘ih′ 關
出 ; *not to allow*, feh cing′ 弗 准

DEBASED, *to be* jih-'ô' 習下°; jih 'ô'-liu 習下°流

DEBATE *to* bin'-leng 辯論

DEBAUCHEE, tsiu-seh'-ts-du' 酒色之徒

DEBILITATED *in body,* sing-t'i' boh-ziah'-de 身體簿弱了°; peng'-z ŵa'-de 本事孬了°

DEBILITY, ŵ-lih' 無°力; t'eh-nyün' 脫元; bi'-t'ah-lông'-t'ông.

DEBT, tsa 債°; *to owe a —,* ky'in tsa' 欠債°; *to be in —,* pe tsa' 背債'; tsa'-veo 債負; vi wun' 未完; *heavily in —,* kw'e-k'ong' 虧空; *to pay off —* (by borrowing), diu kw'e'-k'ong 墊虧空

DEBTOR, ky'in'-cü 欠主

DECALOGUE, jih-diao kyiæ' 十條誡

DECAMP, *to move a camp,* pun-ying-dza' 搬營寨; bah-ying' 拔營

DECAPITATE, *to* sah-deo' 殺頭; tsæn-deo' 斬頭

DECAY, *to* sæ-ba' 衰敗°; *to rot,* læn-wu' 爛腐°; *decayed tree,* jü læn'-de 樹爛了°; *decayed leaves,* læn-yih' 爛葉

DECEITFUL, kæn-tsô'-go 奸詐個°; *wily,* kwe'-kyi to-tön' 詭計多端

DECEIVE, *to* p'in 騙; hong 哄; ky'i 欺; hong'-p'in 哄騙; ky'i-p'in' 欺騙; kwa'-p'in 拐°騙; *to — by concealing,* mun-p'in' 瞞騙; *cannot — him,* p'in'-gyi-feh-læ' 騙其弗來

DECENCY, *becoming behavior,* lin'-c'ü 廉恥; *no —,* lin'-c'ü ŵ-neh'-de 廉恥沒°有°了°; *he has no sense of —,* gyi lin'-c'ü tu feh æ-go 其廉恥都勿愛個°

DECIDE, *to* ding-kwe' 定規; ding-jih' 定實; kyüih'-ding 決定; *hard to —,* kyüih-tön'-feh-loh 決斷弗落

DECISION, *I leave it to your —,* iao ng' ding-kwe' 要你定規; peh ng' tso cü 俾你作°主; *firm —,* cü'-i k'ô'-ding-de 主意挈定了°; *a person of —,* kyüih'-lih-go nying 決裂個°人°; *of no —,* ŵ-nô'-neh'-go 無°挈捻個°

DECK *of a ship,* ts'ông 艙; ts'ông-min' 艙面

DECK, *to adorn,* tsông-sih' 裝飾; tsông-pæn' 裝扮; tsah'-kwah 紮刮; *— (as a bad woman),* tô'-pæn 朵扮

DECLAIM, *to rant,* kao-dæn' kw'eh-leng' 高談闊論

DECLARE, *to* kao'-su 告訴; wô 話; *to proclaim,* djün-yiang' 傳揚; *— to every one,* vong nying' kao'-su 逢人°告訴; *to — war,* tang tsin'-shü 打戰書

DECLINE, *to refuse,* dz 辭; t'e-dz' 推辭; foh 覆; we-foh' 回覆; *— to see visitors,* dz k'ah' 辭客; *— an invitation,* foh'

ts'ing 覆 請; dz ts'ing' 辭 請;
— *and return*, pih'-wæn 璧 還;
*ditto with thanks*, dz-zia' 辭 謝°;
*to go down*, hyiang 'ô' 向 下°;
*the price has declined*, kô-din
soh'-de 價° 錢° 縮 了°; 'ông'-
dzing t'eng-de 行° 情 余 了°;
*the sun is declining*, nyih-deo'
tang-ts'ia' 日° 頭 打 斜°; —
*years*, nyin'-kyi lao'-mæn-de 年
紀 老 邁 了°

DECORATE, *to* tsông-sih' 粧 飾;
— (*as living things*), tsông-pæn'
粧 扮

DECORUM, li'-cü 禮 制; *to observe*
—, siu li'-cü 守 禮 制; *to*
*violate the rules of* —, be li' 悖
禮 See DECENCY.

DECOY, *to entice*, ying'-yiu 引 誘;
— *to a trap*, p'in' gyüoh 騙 局

DECOY *bird*, me-deo' 媒 頭 (ih-
tsah)

DECREASE, *to* ky'üih'-long-ky'i'
缺 攏 去°; kæn'-loh-ky'i 減
落 去°; — *in size*, siao'-long-
ky'i 小 攏 去°

DECREE, *emperor's* ts'-i 旨 意;
zông-yü 上 諭; tsiao'-shü 詔
書; *official's* —, 'ao-ling 號 令

DECREE, *to* c'ih-ling' 出 令; c'ih
'ao-ling' 出 號 令; — (*as the*
*emperor*), ts'-i pæn'-loh-læ 旨
意 頒 落 來; *to fix or appoint*,
shih'-lih 設° 立

DECREPIT, *forgetful and making*
*mistakes*, lao'-mah-long'-cong 老

邁 龍 鍾; *old, weak, and useless*,
lao'-ziah vu-yüong' 老 弱 無
用; oh'-tsoh 齷 齪

DECRY, *to cry down as worthless*,
wô' ỗ-yüong'-go 話 無° 用 个°;
*to censure and cut down*, p'i-siah'
批 削; — *a person*, kông nying
wa' 講 人° 孬°

DEDICATE, *to* — (*as a child*), hyin
獻; vong'-hyin 奉 獻; — *to*
*God's service*, vong'-z Jing-ming'
yüong-go 奉 事 神 明 用 个°;
tseng-ky'i' peh Jing-ming' 尊
起° 與 神 明

DEDUCE, *to infer*, ying' gyi kwe-
nyün' 引 其 歸 原; kyiu'-kyiu-
kwe-nyün' 九 九 歸 原; t'e-leng'
推 論; t'e-tæn'-k'æ kong' 推 打°
開 講

DEDUCT, *to* djü 除; djü-loh' 除
落; k'eo'-djü 扣 除

DEED, *an action*, ih-tön 'ang-we' 一
端 行 爲; ih-tsông z-t'i' 一 樁
事 體; *his deeds*, gyi sô tso'-go
z-t'i' 其 所 做 个 事 體; —
*of merit*, hao'-z 好事 hao' z-ken'
好 事 幹; *writing*, ky'i' 契
ky'i'-kyü 契 據; — *for land*,
di-ky'i' 地 契; — *for a house*,
oh'-ky'i 屋 契 (ih tsiang)

DEEM, *to* ts'eng-ts'eng' 忖 忖; yi-
we' 以 爲; dao-z' 道 是

DEEP, sing 深; — *well*, tsing sing'
井 深; — *color*, sing-seh' 深 色

DEEPEN, *to* — (*as a hole*), k'æ-leh

sing'-tin 開得°深 點; — color
(by dyeing), nyin sing'-tin 染°
深 點

DEER, loh 鹿; — sinews, loh-kying'
鹿 筋; deer's horns, loh' koh
鹿 角°

DEFACE, to tsao-t'ah' nga-min'蹧
蹋 外° 面

DEFALCATION, See EMBEZZLE.

DEFAME, to pông'-hwe 謗 毀;
hwe'-pông 毀 謗

DEFAULTER, one who fails to appear in court, feh-tao-en'cü'-kwu
弗 到 案 个° 人; one who fails
to account for money, pao-siao'-
feh-c'ih'-go cü'-kwu 報 銷 弗 出
个° 人

DEFEAT, to conquer, ying 贏; tang'-
ying 打 贏; — his plan, ba'
gyi sô meo-we'-go 敗 其 所 謀
爲 个°

DEFEATED, ba'-de 敗 了°; — (in
fight), tang'-ba-de 打 敗° 了°;
tang'-ba-tsiang'-de 打 敗° 仗
了°; tang'-shü-de 打 輸 了

DEFECT, fault, mao-bing' 毛 病;
deformity, dzæn-dzih' 殘 疾;
to have ditto, væn dzæn-dzih 犯
殘 疾; blemish or scar, pæn-
pô' 瘢 疤; — in wearing cotton, t'iao'-sô 挑 紗; ditto in silk,
t'iao'-s 挑 絲; p'o'-dzæn 破 綻;
many defects, tsih'-ky'üih-pah'-
ky'üih 七 缺 八 缺

DEFECTIVE, dzæn-ky'üih'-peh-
djün' 殘 缺 不 全

DEFEND, to protect, pao'-wu 保
護; to prepare for resistance,
bông-tu' 防 堵; to be on guard,
kying'-siu 謹 守; to vindicate,
feng-p'eo' 分 剖

DEFENDANT, (Law) be'-kao 被 告

DEFER, to nga 挨; ah 壓°; — till
to-morrow, nga' tao ming-tsiao'
挨° 到 明 朝; — the day, tsæn
nyih-ts' 趲 日°子; kæ gyi' 改 期

DEFER, to t'e-peh' 推 與; t'e-
nyiang' 推 讓°; — to your opinion, t'e'-peh ng' ding-kwe' 推
與° 你 定 規

DEFERENTIAL, kyü-soh' 拘 束;
kyü'-kyü-jün 拘 拘 然

DEFICIENCY in numbers, ky'üih'-
su 缺 數; there is a —, yiu
ky'üih'-tih 有 缺 的; make up
the —, ky'üih-su iao pu'-tsoh
缺 數 要 補 足

DEFICIENT, ky'in 欠; ts'ô 差;
ky'üih 缺; not enough, feh keo'
弗 彀

DEFILE in the hills, sæn-vong' 山
縫 (ih-da)

DEFILE, to long'-leh lah-t'ah' 弄
得°邋 過; long-leh lah-lih'-lah-
t'ah' 弄 得 邋 裡 邋 過; long'-
leh nyi-siug'-peh-la' 弄 得 泥
腥 不 賴; long-leh ao-lih'-peh-
tsao' 弄°得 璺 裡°百 糟

DEFINE, to — limits, ding 'æn'-
cü 定 限°制; to explain, ka'-
shih 解°說

DEFINITE *words*, shih-wô' ling-ts'ing' 說話靈清; *words not sufficiently* —, shih-wô' ky'in feng-ts'ing' 說話欠分清; shih-wô' feh-loh'-dzih 說話弗落直; shih-wô' yiu zông'-loh 說話有上落

DEFINITION, ka'-shih 解說

DEFORMED, dzæn-dzih' 殘疾; *to become* —, væn dzæn-dzih' 犯殘疾

DEFRAUD, *to* — *of*, ky'üoh'-meh 吃沒; ziah-meh' 嚼沒; t'eng-ky'üoh' 吞吃°

DEFRAY, *to* c'ih出; t'ing 聽; — *the expense*, c'ih fi'-yüong 出費用

DEFY, *to provoke war*, kyih'-dong nying tang-tsiang' 激動人°打仗°; *to challenge*, t'ao-tsin' 討戰

DEGENERATE, *to* wa-loh'-ky'i 孬落去°; sæ-ba'-loh-ky'i' 衰敗°落去°; t'e-pæn'-loh-ky'i' 推板落去°; tao'-tsiang-i-soh' 倒漲又°縮

DEGRADE, *to* ky'ih'-loh 掣落; kông'-loh 降°落; — *to a lower office*, kah-tsih' 革職; kông-kyih' 降°級; *to take away the button*, tsah ting'-ta 摘頂戴°

DEGREE, *grade*, teng-kyih 等級; *the highest literary* —, di-ih' kah 第一甲°; *called*, zông-nyün' 狀元; *the 1st* — (*i. e. lowest*), siu'-dzæ 秀才; *to obtain the* — *of siu-dzæ*, jih 'oh' 入學°; tsing 'oh' 進學°; *the 2nd* —, kyü-

nying 舉人°; *the 3rd* —, tsing'-z 進士; *has he a literary* —? gyi' yiu sing-kying' feh 其有紳衿否°? *what* —? soh'-go sing-kying' 甚°麼°紳衿? *he has the* — *of siu-dzæ*, gyi z dzæ-dziang' 其是在庠; *to obtain the higher degrees*, cong 中

DEGREE, (Geom.), *one* —, ih-du' 一度

DEGREES, *by* dzin'-dzin 漸漸; mæn-mæn' 慢慢

DEIFY, *to* —(when done by the emperor), fong bu-sah' 封菩薩; ts'ih'-fong 勅封; — *him*, tseng gyi' we bu-sah' 尊其爲菩薩

DEIFICATION (when done by the emperor), fong bu-sah'-go ngæn-deo' 封菩薩个°銜°頭°; — *to a higher grade*, tse-fong' 追封; kô-fong' 加°封

DEJECTED *in appearance*, we-t'ah'-t'ah 痿塌塌; — *in mind*, sing-hwe'-i'-læn 心灰意懶

DELAY, *to* tæn-koh' 耽擱; *to ask for* —, iah 約; *ditto in paying debt*, iah-tsa' 約債°

DELEGATE, dæ-li'-go nying 代理个°人°; *to send as a* —, we 委

DELEGATE, *to* — *authority*, kao'-c'ih gyün-ping' 交°出權柄; *to receive delegated authority*, dæ tsông' gyün-ping' 代掌權柄

DELIBERATE, *to* tsing-tsiah' 斟酌; nyi 議; kong-nyi' 公議; siang-nyi' 相議

DELIBERATIVE *body*, we'-nyi 會
議 (ih-go)

DELICATE, *fine*, si 細; — (as
workmanship), si'-ky'iao 細巧;
*tender*, neng 嫩; — *and pretty*
(as a child), neng-æ'-æ 嫩藹
藹; — *food*, ts'ing-c'ü ky'üoh'-
zih 清泚吃°食

DELICIOUS, sông'-k'eo 爽口

DELIGHT, *to — him*, peh gyi kao-
hying' 俾°其高興

DELIGHTED, kao-hying' 高興;
*perfectly —*, kw'a'-weh'-sah-de
快°活煞了°; hwun-t'in'-hyi-
di' 歡天喜地

DELINEATE, *to — by description*,
kông'-tin ying-tsih' 講°點形
跡; kông'-tin ing'-tsong 講點
形踪 (tsong or cong)

DELIRIOUS, nyih-hweng'-de 熱°
昏了°; — *talk*, nyih-wô' 熱話

DELIVER, *to save*, kyiu 救; —
*out of trouble*, kyiu'-kw'u kyiu-
næn' 救苦救難; — *in his*
*extremity*, kyiu' gyi kyih' 救其
急; *to set free*, sih'-fông 釋放;
— (as a letter), kao-dæ'-c'ih 交
代出; — *to him*, kao-dæ' peh
gyi 交°代給°其; — *at the door*,
song'-zông meng 送上門; *have*
*you delivered the message?* keh'
ky'i z-t'i ng yiu wô-ko' ma 這°
件事體你°有話過麼°?
— *by a midwife*, siu-sang' 收
生°; tsih-sang' 接生°

DELUDE, *to cheat*, ky'i-p'in' 欺騙;
tah shih'-gyiao 搭雪橋; —
*by false promises*, ko'-gyiao, bah-
gyiao' 過橋拔橋; *why do*
*you — me?* ng dza'-we peh ngô'
pe moh-sao' 你甚°麼°俾°我
背木稍?

DELUDED, *to be —*, pe moh-sao'
背木稍; pe bô' 背耙

DELUSION, moh-sao' 木稍; *labor-*
*ing under a —*, pe moh-sao' de
背木稍了°

DELUGE, 'ong-shü 洪水°; *the —*
'ong-shü-fæn-tsiang 洪水泛漲

DEMAND, *in great —*, 'ông-ts'iao'
昂°俏

DEMAND, *to* t'ao 討; iao 要; *he*
*demands too much*, gyi t'ao t'eh'
to 其討太°多; — *forcibly*,
ngang-iao' 硬要; — *pertina-*
*ciously*, ts'in-gyiu', væn-gyiu' 千
求萬求

DEMANDED, *grant a little, more*
*will be —*, teh'-bu tsing'-bu 得
步進步

DEMOLISH, *to* ts'ah'-hwe 拆毀

DEMON, oh'-kyü 惡鬼° (ih-go)

DEMONIAC, *one possessed by a*
*demon*, jih-mo'-go nying 入魔
个°人°

DEMONSTRATE *to you*, peh ng
k'ao-jih' 俾°你°靠實; — *step*
*by step*, gyin'-tang-gyin k'ao-jih'
件件靠實; — (as a calcula-
tion), pih'-tang-pih k'ao-jih' 筆
筆靠實

DEMURE, pæn'-pæn go 板板个°; — countenance, lao'-lin 老臉

DEN of thieves, zeh k'o' 賊窠; tiger's —, lao'-hwu k'o' 老虎窠; hwu'-yüih 虎穴; lao'-hwu dong' 老虎洞

DENOTE, to yiu i'-s 有意思; the character ho, denotes riches, ho' z yiu dzæ-veh'-go ka'-shih 貨字有財物个° 解° 說; to indicate, ts'-tin 指點

DENOUNCE, to stigmatize, p'i-siah' 批削; — one really bad, c'ih gyi'-go ts'iu' 出其个° 醜°

DENSE foliage, jü-yih mih-kying' 樹葉密緊; jü-yih' mih-mih'-zeng-zeng 樹葉密密層° 層°; — crowd, nying' mih-kying' 人° 密緊; nying' a-tsi'-feh-k'æ 人° 挨° 擠弗開; — fog, vu-lu nytiong' 霧露濃; — population, nying-in' væn-to' 人° 烟繁多

DENT, a ih-go den' 一个° 潭

DENT, to c'oh-den' 掐潭; c'oh-dong' 掐洞

DENY, to — the truth of, wô feh-z'-ka 話弗是如° 此°; to refuse to grant, feh-cing' 弗准; feh-ing'-hyü 弗應許; to disown, feh-tsiao'-jing 弗招認; feh-jing', or feh-nying' 弗認; to — one's-self, ky'i'-diao zi'-go s-sing' 棄了° 自° 个° 私心

DEPART, to li-k'æ' 離開; bih-k'æ' 別開; — far away, yün'-k'æ 遠開; — on a journey, c'ih-

meng'-ky'i 出門去°; — this life, ky'ü-shü' 去世

DEPARTMENT, sphere of duties, peng'-veng 本分; en-veng'-siu-kyi' 安分守己; — of a prefect, fu 府

DEPEND, to — on, k'ao-djoh 靠着°; i-k'ao 依靠; — on one's parents, k'ao'-djoh do-nying'-go foh'-ky'i 靠着 大° 人° 个° 福氣; what has he to — upon? gyi' yiu soh'-si hao k'ao' 其有甚° 麼° 好靠? no relatives to — upon, loh-ts'ing' vu'-k'ao 六親無靠; a person, &c., upon whom to —, k'ao-sæn 靠山; the man can be depended upon, nying k'ao-leh-djü'-go 人° 靠得住 个°; he cannot be depended upon, k'ao gyi'-feh-jih 靠其弗住

DEPENDENCE, without vu-i'-vu-k'ao 無依無靠; — (but not firm), gæ-deo' 戲頭

DEPICT, to — by drawing, sia' ih-go du' 寫一个° 圖; — in language, kông' ying-kying' 講影° 景

DEPLORABLE, zing-we'-k'o'-sih 甚為可惜

DEPLORE, to pe-t'æn' 悲嘆

DEPOPULATED, nying' siu'-jih-wun'-de 人° 收拾完了°

DEPORTMENT, kyü-ts'-'ang-dong' 舉止行° 動; 'ang-i'-dong-zing' 行° 意動靜

DEPOSE, to — a king, fi'- diao wông-ti' 廢了皇帝；— from office, kah tsih' 革職

DEPOSIT, to lay down, fông'-loh 放落；— money in the bank, nying-ts' dzeng læ dzin-tin'li 銀子存在°錢°店裡；the money deposited, dzeng-'ông' 存項；dzeng-kw'un' 存欵

DEPOT, building for public use, gyüoh 局；— for arms, kyüing-ky'i'-gyüoh 軍器局；open place for storage, ts'iang 廠；— for coal, me-t'æn' ts'iang 煤炭廠；freight —, ko'-dông-'ông' 過塘行°

DEPRAVE, to pin'- diao 變壞；wæ-diao' 壞了°；— the mind, wæ nying' sing-jih' 壞人°心術

DEPRAVED, thoroughly 'ô'-tsoh p'e' 下°作胚；'ô'-liu p'e' 下°流胚

DEPRECIATE, to — others, kông bih' nying feh-tao'-kô 講別人°弗到家°；— one's own merits or abilities (often used in a false sense), ky'in-hyü' 謙虛；do not —yourself, hao-vong' ky'in-hyü' 弗°用°謙虛

DEPREDATE, to plunder, ts'iang'-deh 搶奪；ts'iang'-kyih 搶劫

DEPRESS, to lower by pressure, ah'-loh 壓落

DEPRESSED in spirits, 益 sing'-siang 無°心想；we-we'-ze-ze' 痿痿瘁瘁

DEPRIVE, to take away, do'-leh-ky'i' 拕°得°去°；ditto by force, deh'-leh-ky'i 奪得°去°；— of that, over which we have some control, siu'-leh-ky'i' 收得°去°；— of privilege, ih-tsông me'-z siu-tsing' 一椿美事收進；God has deprived me of my son, Jing-ming' pô ngô ng-ts' siu-leh-ky'i' 神明把我兒子收得°去°

DEPTH, sing 深；what is the — of this well? keh' k'eo tsing' to-siao sing' 這口井多少深？

DEPUTE, to we 委

DEPUTY, we'-yün 委員 (ih-we)

DERANGE, to put out of order, kao'-lön 攪°亂

DERANGED, insane, fah-tin' 發癲；fah-gwông' 發狂；fah-c'ü' 發癡

DERIDE, to sông-ky'üoh' 傷曲；tsao-siao' 嘲笑；kông dæn'-wô 講談話

DERIVATION, peng' ti-ts 本底子；that is of foreign —, keh peng' ti-ts, z nga-koh' læ-go 這°本底子是外°國來个°

DERIVED, whence is it — ? keh'-go ky'i-ts'u' dzong 'o'-r læ' 這°个起初從何而來？it was —from China, peng'-læ z Cong-koh' c'ih'-go 本來是中國出个°

DEROGATORY to one's rank or character, t'eh-p'ing' 脫品；shih'-kw'un' 失欵

DESCEND, *to* loh'-ky'i 下°去°;
loh'-læ下°來; kông'-loh 降°下°;
— *a hill*, tseo'-loh sæn' 走下°山;
— *from heaven*, 'o'-kông' 下°
降°; *Jesus descended from heaven*,
Yiæ-su' 'ô-kông'-de 耶穌下°
降了°; — (as an estate), yi-
loh'-læ 遺下°來

DESCENDANT, 'eo'-dæ 後代; ts'-
seng 子孫

DESCENT, loh'-ky'i 落去°; *the*
— *was dangerous*, keh-go loh'-
ky'i ngwe-hyin'-go 這个°落
去°危險个°; *of honorable* —,
kong-ts' kong-seng 公子公孫;
*direct* —, tih'-p'a 嫡派°

DESCRIBE, *to* ying-yüong'形容;
— *a balloon for me*, ky'i'-gyiu
yiang-shih', hao ying-yüong' peh
ngò t'ing 氣球樣式好形
容俾°我聽; *cannot* — *it*, wô'
feh siang-ziang-go 話弗相
像个°

DESERT, *sandy* sô-di' 沙地; —
*place*, peh'-mao-ts-di' 不毛之
地; *wilderness*, kw'ông-iæ 曠
野 (ih-t'ah)

DESERT, *what is deserved*, ing-kæ'
ziu 應該受

DESERT, *to* ky'i'-diao 棄了°

DESERTER *from the army*, dao-
ping' 逃兵; — *from a ship*,
jün'-li dao-zông'-go 船裡逃
上个°

DESERVE, *to* ing-tông' ziu 應當
受; li' sô tông-jün'-go 理所當

然个°; *he deserves the reward*,
keh'-go sông'-pao, gyi' ing-tông'
ziu 這°个°賞報其應當受

DESIGN, *to* tang'-tsiang 打將; i'-
s iao 意思要; *he designs to
build a house*, gyi tang'-tsiang
ky'i ih-tsing oh' 其打將起
一進屋

DESIGN, i'-s 意思; dzeng-sing'
存心; *my* — *is to give it to a
friend*, ngò i'-s, song-peh beng-
yiu' 我意思送給°朋友

DESIGNEDLY, yiu'-i 有意; kwu'-i
故意; deh-i' 特意; deh-we'
特為

DESIRABLE, *very* meo-ts'-peh-teh'
謀之不得 (primarily too good
to be obtained).

DESIRE, *to* sing'-siang 心想; iao'-
siang 要想 (more intense than
the former); — *earnestly*, hyüih'-
sing siang' 血心想

DESIRE, sing-siang' 心想; sing-
nyün' 心願; *his desires are too
great*, gyi'-go sing-siang' mang'
其个°心想猛; *have long
had that* —, kyiu' yiu-ts' sing'
久有此心

DESIST, *to stop*, hyih 歇; — *from*,
hyih-siu' 歇手; fông-siu' 放手

DESK, *writing-case*, s'-pao-'eh' 四
寶盒; *writing-table*, s'-pao-coh'
四寶桌

DESOLATE, ts'i-liang' 悽涼; vu-
liao' vu-liao' 無聊無聊; ziang-
kwu-tiao'-ka 像孤鳥°樣°式°

DESOLATE, *to* long'-lehling'-ling'-loh-loh' 弄 得° 零 零 落 落

DESPAIR, vu-k'o-vông' 無 可 望; *in utter* —, djih' vu-k'o-vông' 絕 無 可 望

DESPERADO, vông-ming'-ts-du' 亡 命 之 徒; fi'-du 匪 徒; vu-la' 無 賴°; *local* —, dziu-di'-oh'-kweng 就 地 惡 棍

DESPERATE, *I grew* —, ngô oh'-c'ih-de 我 惡 出 了°

DESPERATION, *driven to* —, pih'-leh zông-t'in'-vu-lu', jih-di'-vu-meng' 逼 得° 上 天 無 路 入 地 無 門; *in* —, deo-tseo 益-lu' 投 走 無° 路

DESPICABLE, feh-jih'-ngæn 弗 入 眼°; — *employment*, pe-ziu' 'ông-tông' 卑 賤° 行 當; t'ao'-væn 'ông-tông' 討 飯 行 當

DESPISE, *to* ky'ing-mæn' 輕 慢; k'en-ky'ing' 看 輕; ts'iao-feh-ky'i' 瞧 弗 起; *every one despises him*, ko'-ko nying' k'en'-gyi-ky'ing' 個 個 人° 看 其 輕

DESPONDENT, sing hwe' i'-kæn 心 灰 意 懶; *desire weaker than before*, ts'-hyiang ziah'-de 志 向 弱 了°; sing-i' dæn'-de 心 意 淡 了°

DESPOTIC, bao-nyiah'-go 暴 虐 个°; — *power*, gyün-shü' hyüong' 權 勢 兇

DESSERT, tin'-sing or tia'-sing 點 心, properly a light relish taken to sustain, but not to satisfy.

DESTINED *by the will of Heaven to become great*, t'in-i' s-jün' hying-wông 天 意 使 然 興 旺; — *by fate to decay*, ming-kæ'-jü-ts' sæ-ba' 命 該 如 此 衰 敗°

DESTINY, *end*, kyih'-gyüoh 結 局; *fate*, ming-yüing' 命 運; yüing-dao' 運 道

DESTITUTE *of friends*, kyü-moh'-vu-ts'ing' 舉 目 無 親; 益-beng-yiu' 無° 朋 友; — *of clothing and food*, vu-i, vu-zih' 無 衣 無 食

DESTROY, *to* siao-hwô'-diao 銷 化 壞°; siao-hwe'-diao 銷 毀 了°; — *utterly*, tsao-t'ah' ken-zing' 蹧 蹋 乾 净; — (by fire or otherwise), hwe' ken-zing' 毀 乾 净; — *by tearing down*, ts'ah'-hwe 拆 毀; — (as living creatures), mih-diao' 滅 壞°; — *life*, sah seng', 'æ ming' 殺 生 害 命

DETACH, *to separate*, feng-k'æ' 分 開; *to disunite*, ts'ah'-k'æ 拆 開, ts'ah'-loh 拆 落; *to* — *a body of soldiers*, feng-fah' ih-ts ping' 分 發 一 枝 兵; feng-p'a ih-de ping' 分 派° 一 隊 兵

DETAIN, *to* liu 留; liu-djü 留 住; liu-loh' 留 落; — *forcibly*, ngang-liu' 硬° 留; *it rains and Heaven detains the guest*, " yü' loh, T'in' liu k'ah' " 雨 落 天 留 客

DETECT, *to* k'en'-c'ih 看 出; k'en'-p'o 看 破; — *errors*, k'en'-c'ih ts'o'-c'ü 看出錯°處; *the thief was detected,* zeh' p'o-en'-de 賊° 破案了°

DETER, *to* tsu'-tông 阻當; læn-tsu' 攔阻; tsu'-djü 阻住; — *one from doing,* tsu'-tông nying feh tso' 阻當人°弗做

DETERMINATION, cü'-i 主意; *he has —,* gyi yiu' cü'-i 其有 主意; gyi cü'-i kyüih'-tön 其 主意決斷°; *firm —,* lao cü'-i 牢主意; cü'-i k'ô'-ding-de 主意擎°定了°

DETERMINE, *to* ding-kwe' 定規; ding cü'-i 定主意; kyüih'-ding 決定

DETERMINED, *to be —,* k'ô'-ding cü'-i 拿°定主意; — *to do,* công-dzing' nyiah-ding'-de 章程 捻定了°

DETEST, *to* 'eng 恨; k'o-u' 可惡; *I — him,* ngô ün'-wu gyi' de 我怨乎其°了°

DETESTABLE, *perfectly* k'o-u'-ts-gyih' 可惡之極; 'eng-gyih'-de 恨極了°

DETHRONE, *to — a king,* ts'in' wông-we' 遜皇位; deh wông-we' 奪皇位

DETRACT, *to — from a man's good character,* hwe nying'-ts jün' 毀 人°之善 See DEPRECIATE.

DETRIMENT, 'æ 害; *no —,* m-kao' soh-go 'æ 沒°有°甚°麼° 害; m-'æ'-c'ü' 無°害處

DEVASTATION *by soldiers,* ping-hwông 兵荒; — *by drought,* 'en'-hwông 旱荒; — *by water,* shü-hwông 水°荒

DEVELOP, *to* k'æ-k'æ' 開開; — *one's intellect,* nying'-go ts'ong-ming' k'æ-c'ih'-læ 人°个°聰明 開出來; ts'ong-ming' k'ön-k'æ' 聰明孔°開 (sometimes used of grown people in ridicule); — *ideas,* i'-s t'æn-tæn'-k'æ 意思 攤攤°開

DEVIATE, *to* tseo'-ts'ô 走差; ts'ô'-k'æ 叉開

DEVIATION, *a slight — at first, may amount at last, to a thousand li,* "tseo'-ts'ô 'ao-li, t'e'-pæn ts'in-li" 差以°毫厘謬以°千里

DEVICE, *simple* fông-fah' 方法; *ingenious —,* kyi-kwah' 機括; *crafty —,* kyi-meo' 機謀; kyi'-kao 計較'

DEVIL, *evil spirit,* kyü 鬼°; mo-kyü' 魔鬼; oh'-kyü 惡鬼°; *the —,* Mo-kwe' 魔鬼; *possessed with a —,* jih-mo'-go 入魔个°; *under a devil's influence,* ziu kyü-mi' 受鬼°迷; *been stroked by a —* (and therefore bad), kyü' lo-deo'-de 鬼°攞頭了°; kyü' kwah'-de 鬼°摑°了°; the last two used in reviling.

DEVIOUS, *crooked,* wæn-ky'üoh'-go 彎曲个°

DEVISE, *to* tang'-mo 打摹; — *a way,* tang'-sön ih-go fông-fah'

打算一个°方法; zao' fông-fah' 造°方法; shih fah' 設°法; — a scheme, shih kyi' 設計; ready in devising, pin' t'ong 變通

DEVOLVE, to transfer, sia' peb 卸°與°; my duties — upon him, ngô meng-veng' sia peh gyi' tso' 我名°牙'°卸°與其做; — the responsibility on some one else, sia kyin-ts' 卸肩°子; this devolves on me, keh' kwe ngô' tso' 這歸我做

DEVOTE, to tseng-ky'i' 聳起; liu-ky'i 留起; — to God, tseng-ky'i' peh Jing-ming 聳起與°神明; — six hours a day to study, ih-nyih' li-hyiang' loh tin'-cong kong-fu' tseng-ky'i' doh shü' 一日°裏向六點鐘工夫聳起讀書

DEVOUR, to swallow without chewing, t'eng ky'üoh 吞吃°; to eat rapidly, ziah-loh' sön'-tsiang' 嚼落算帳; — a book, 'o peng' t'eng-loh'-ky'i 和本吞落去°

DEVOUT, gyin-sing' 虔心

DEW, lu-shü' 露水; drops of —, tin' tang tin lu-shü' 點點露水

DEXTROUS, siu weh-p'eh' 手活潑

DIABOLICAL arts, iao-fah' 妖法; great skill in ditto, iao-jih' li-'æ' 妖術利害

DIAGRAM, du'-go da-liab' 圖个大略; du'-go da-tsih'-moh 圖个°大節目; to draw a —, tang' ih-go du' 打一个°圖

DIAL, sun jih-kwe' 日晷; — plate of a clock, cong min-ts 鐘面子 (cong or tsong)

DIALECT, local t'u'-wô 土話; hyiang-dæn' 鄉談; the Ningpo —, Nying-po' wô' 寗波話

DIAMETER, cong-sin' 中線

DIAMOND, kying-kông'-cün 金剛鑽 (cün or tsön) (ib-lih)

DIAPHRAGM, keh'-moh 膈膜 (veng.)

DIARRHEA, dza-bing' 瀉°病; du-foh sia' 肚腹瀉; chronic —, lao' dza-bing' 老瀉°病

DIARY, jih-kyi'-loh 日記錄

DICE, seh'-ts 色子; deo-ts' 骰子; to throw —, dzih seh'-ts 擲色子; — box, seh'-ts 'eh' 色子盒

DICTATE, to k'eo-djün 口傳; to write as dictated, i k'eo' dæ shü' 依口代書; write as fast as dictated, kông' dza kw'a, sia' dza kw'a 講°怎°快寫°怎°快°

DICTIONARY, alphabetical z-meo di-kông 字母提綱; z-nyü' we-ka' 字語彙解°; — arranged according to the radicals, z-tin' 典; z-we' 字彙

DIE, to sì 死; ky'ü-shü' 去世; ling-cong' 臨終; do-kao'kw'eng'-joh 大°覺°睡熟 (coarse); — young, iao ziu' 夭壽; tön' ming 短命; — a natural death, jün'

cong 善終 (cong or tsong);
— *from disease,* bing kwu' 病
故; — *an unnatural death,* wang
si' 橫死°; oh' si 惡死; — *by
starvation,* ngo-sah' 餓殺; —
*satisfied,* ngæn'-tsing pi-leh-ky'i'
眼睛閉得去° (*lit.* with eyes
shut.)

DIET, *to eat sparingly.* ky'üoh' leh
si' 吃得細; tsih ing'-zih 節
飲食; siao shü' ky'üoh' tin 少
些吃°點: *to avoid a certain kind
of food,* gyi zih' 忌食; gyi cü'
忌嘴; *to live on a vegetable —*
(as the Buddhists do), ky'üoh
ts'æ' 吃°菜; kyüoh su' 吃°素

DIFFER, *to* yiu feng-pih' 有分
別; — *greatly,* do' yiu feng-pih'
大°有分別; *differs much,* ts'ô
hyü'-to 差許多; long-do' koh'-
yiang 弄大°各樣; da' feh
siang'-dong 大不°相同; kao-
ti' peh-ih' 高低不一; (it) *differs
very little,* ts'ô yiu'-'æn 差有
限°; ts'ô' feh to' 差弗多; shü'-
vi koh'-yiang 些微各樣

DIFFERENCE, feng-pih' 分別;
*what is the —?* yiu soh'-go feng-
pih' 有甚°麼分別? yiu soh'-
go koh'-yiang 有甚°麼各樣?
*what is the — in length?* dziang
tön' ts'ô' to-siao' 長短差多少?

DIFFERENT, koh'-yiang 各樣;
feh z ih-yiang' 弗是一樣;
*the two are —,* liang' k'æ-dæ'
兩開臺; — *kinds,* koh'-seh

koh-'ao' 各色各樣; *entirely*
—, 'o'-jün koh-yiang' 和然各
樣; — *from the rest,* dzah-ngah'
雜碎

DIFFICULT, næn 難; keh'-tah 糾°
葛°; feh yüong'-yi 弗容易;
*very —,* væn næn' 萬難

DIFFICULTIES, næn 難; næn-c'ü'
難處

DIFFIDENT, yiu hyü-hyih'- bing
有虛怯°病; we fah-neng'-go
會發嫩个°

DIFFUSE, *to spread abroad,* yiang-
k'æ' 揚開

DIFFUSE *in style,* væn 繁; væn-
zeh' 繁雜°; veo-veng' to' 浮
文多

DIG, *to* gyüih 掘; dao 掏

DIGEST, *to — food,* zih' siao-hwô'
食消化

DIGESTION, *bad* bi-we' wa' 脾
胃孬

DIGNIFIED, yiu we-nyi' go 有威
儀个°

DIGNITY, we-nyi' 威儀; *great
—,* we-nyi' djong' 威嚴重;
*assumed —,* kw'un'-shih do' 款
式大°; kô'-ts do' 架°子大°

DIGRESS, *to — in speaking.* ling-
nga' di-ky'i ih-yiang' z-t'i' 零
外°提起一樣事體

DIGRESSION, i-nga'-ts z 意外°
之事

DIKE, *a bank to prevent inundation,*
dông 塘

DILAPIDATED, fong-tao'-ba-loh'

go 風倒敗°落个°; tong-t'æn' si-tao'-go 東坍西倒个°

DILATE, to — (as the eye), fông'-k'æ-læ 放開來

DILATORY, nga-nga' ts'i-ts'i; in'-in tsiang-tsiang'; mæn-t'ang'-t'ang 慢盉盉°; dang宕°; wun-deng'-deng 緩鈍鈍

DILIGENT, pô-kyih' 把急; zông'-kying 上緊; gying-lih' 勤力

DILLY-DALLY, to yiu-dang 遊宕

DILUTE, to 'o'-leh dæn' 和得°淡; to thin, 'o'-leh boh' 和得°薄

DIM, indistinct, feh ts'ing'-t'ong 弗清通; eyesight — (naturally), ngæn'-kwông deng' 眼光鈍; ditto from age &c., ngæn-tsing hwô'-de 眼°睛花了°; — lamp, teng-tsæn' en' 燈盞暗; ngæn'-kwông sæn'-de 眼°光散了°

DIME, ih koh' 一角°

DIMENSIONS, what are its — ? yiu to-siao' do' 有多少大°? yiu dza-kwun' do 有怎°樣°大°?

DIMINISH, to kæn 減°; kæn'-loh 減°落; ky'üih 缺; siao 少; cannot —, kæn' feh-teh 減°弗得; — in size, siao'-long ky'i' 小攏去°; — in number, ky'üih'-long-ky'i' 缺攏去°; ky'üih'-feh-læ, feh-ky'üih' 缺弗來弗缺; — expense, fi'-yüong kæn'-tin-diao 費用減°點去°

DIMITY, liu'-diao-pu 柳條布

DIMPLE, tsiu-den' 酒潭

DIN of voices, zeng-zeng'-hyiang 屑°屑°響; — of hammers, &c., ding-ding'-dang-dang hyiang'.

DINE, to ky'üoh da-ts'æ' 吃大菜; ky'üoh tsiu'-ko-væn' 吃畫過飯; ky'üoh cong-væn' 吃中飯; ky'üoh tsiu'-væn 吃°畫飯

DINGY color, hweng' seh 昏色; — from age, in-t'ang'-t'ang; without polish, deng kwông' 鈍光

DINING-ROOM ky'üoh-væn-kæn' 吃°飯間°; da-ts'æ-vông' 大菜房

DINNER, væn 飯; da-ts'æ' 大菜; noon meal, tsiu'-væn 畫飯; tsiu'-ko-væn 畫過飯

DIP, to — up water, iao' shü' læ' 舀水來; — water with the hands, p'ong shü' 捧°水°; — in water, or immerse, shü'-li tsing' ih-tsing' 水裡浸一浸°; — the pen in ink, pih' weng moh' 筆搵墨; — and wet, weng-weng sih' 搵搵濕

DIPLOMA, certificate, tsiao 照; scholar's —, veng'-bing' 文憑; priest's —, du-diah 度牒 (ih-tsiang)

DIPPER, shü'-zôh 水°瓢; wooden —, ao'-teo 拗斗; 'oh-bin' 鑊瓢°

DIRECT, to manage, kwun'-li 管理; liao-li' 料理; coh'-fu 囑附; to tell or give orders, wô' 話; — (a traveller), ts'-yiug 指引

DIRECT, dzih 直; — *road*, dzih lu' 直路

DIRECTION, *in what* —? 'ah-li' ih-hyiang' 何°處°一向 or 阿裡一向? *in that* —, keh' ih-hyiang' 那°一向; *I do not understand his directions*, sô coh'-fu ngô' feh tong' 所囑附我弗懂; *give him the* — *or address*, ming-moh', wô-hyiang'-gyi-dao' 名目話向其道; — *of a letter*, di-kyiah'-ing 地脚音

DIRECTLY, ziu 就°; *I will come* —, ngô' ziu læ' 我就°來

DIRECTOR *of affairs*, cong'-kwun 總管; cong'-li 總理 (cong or tsong)

DIRGE, pe-sông'-go ko' 悲傷個°歌; *lamentation*, æ-ko' 哀歌

DIRTY, ao-tsao' 壓°糟; lah-t'ah' 邋遢; ao-lih'-peh-tsao' 壓裹°百糟; seh'-deh 塞達; nyi-sing' 泥腥; lah-lih'-lah-t'ah' 邋裏°邋遢; t'i-t'a' 涕汰; — *sweepings*, leh-seh' 垃圾°

DIRTY, *to* long ao'-tsao 弄壓糟, &c.

DISABLED, vu-neng'-we 無能爲; — *intellectually*, tsing-jing' fi'-diao-de 精神廢掉了°

DISADVANTAGE, ky'üoh'-kw'e 吃°虧; *bought at a* —, ma' ky'üoh-kw'e' 買吃°虧; ma' shü-de 買輸了°; *working at a*

—, ka' tso, feh teh'-fah 如°此°做弗得法

DISADVANTAGEOUS, le'-ze-go 累墜个°; feh-bin'-i 弗便宜°

DISAGREE, *to* feh-deo'-kyi 弗投機; — *in opinion*, (*lit.* wrongly joined), i'-s ts'o-p'ing' 意思差°揩; *unsuited*, feh-te' 弗對; feh teo'-deo 弗對°頭; feh 'eh-shing' 弗合榫

DISAGREEABLE, næn-tông' 難當; in'-ky'i 厭氣; *no pleasure*, m-c'ü' 無°趣; *very* —, m-c'ü'-ts-gyih' 無°趣之極; — *weather*, t'in-kô' m-c'ü' 天家°無°趣; — *person*, tseng nying' 憎人°; teh'-nying-væn-tseng' 得人°犯憎; min-moh' k'o-tseng' 面目可憎; — *ways*, i'-tsi tseng' 意致°憎; — *to do*, næn-hyi'; næn we'-dzing 難爲情

DISAPPEAR, *to* — *suddenly*, hweh'-jün feh-kyin' 忽然弗見

DISAPPOINTED, *to be* i'-s shih'-loh 意思失落; shih-vông' 失望; *I was* — *in my expectations*, ngô sô vông' shih'-loh-de 我所望失落了°

DISAPPROVE, *to* feh yüoh'-i 弗欲意

DISARM, *to* kyüing-ky'i' siu-jih'-ko 軍器收拾過

DISARRANGE, *to* kao'-lön' 攪亂; dao-lön' 搯亂; — *so, one can-*

*not do anything*, ts'ao'-lön dæn-dziang' 譟亂壇場

DISASTER, fi-kè'-ts 'o' 飛來之禍; *a* —, ih-go 'o'一個° 禍; ih-ky'i' hyüong z'-t'i 一起凶事體

DISASTROUS, hyüong 凶; li-'æ' 利害

DISBAND, *to*—(troops),ts'ih'-we 撤回;—(school), sæn-kwun' 散館

DISBELIEVES *everything*, pah'-feh-siang'-sing 百弗相信

DISBURSE, *to* do-c'ih' 挓出

DISCARD, *to* tiu-ky'i' 丟去°; *has been discarded*, tsoh'-ko-de 作過了°; koh'-ko-de 擱過了°

DISCERN *clearly by the eye*, k'en' ts'ing-t'ong' 看清通;—*between true and false*, bin'-pih tsing-kô' 辨別° 眞假°

DISCERNMENT, ngæn'-lih 眼°力; kyi-ling' 機靈; liu-liang' 流亮; *great* —, ngæn'-lih hao' 眼°力好

DISCHARGE, *to* — (as firearms), fông 放; *to let out*, fông'-c'ih' 放出;—(as a prisoner), fah-fông' 發放;— *a debt*, tsa' t'eh-c'ih' 債脫出;— *one's duty*, dzing peng'-veng 盡本分°; pô meng-veng' 把名°分°;— *cargo*, ky'i ho' 起貨

DISCIPLE, *learner*, meng-du' 門徒; 'oh-sang-ts' 學°生°子; di'-ts 弟子; meng-seng' 門生

DISCIPLINE *to* — (as a church member), tsiao kyiao'-kwe tsah'-vah 照教規責罰

DISCLAIM, *to* feh-jing' 弗認; feh tsih'-jing 弗接認

DISCLOSE, *to expose to view*, lu-c'ih' 露出; *to leak out*, sih'-leo 洩漏;— *a secret*, tseo'-leo fong-sing' 走漏風聲; sih'-leo kyi-kwæn' 洩漏機關; lu-fong' 露風

DISCOLOR, *to* ngæn-seh' fæn'-diao 顏°色翻壞°; tseo ngæn-seh' 走顏°色; pin seh' 變色

DISCOMFORT, *in* feh ziu'- yüong 弗受用; feh shih'-i 弗適°意

DISCOMMODE, *to* le 累;— *a person*, le nying' feh bin 累人°弗便; ta'-li nying' feh bin' 帶累°人°弗便

DISCONCERT, *to* long-lön' 弄亂; ih-z-li', m-cü'-i 一時裡無°主意

DISCONCERTED, sing-hwông' i-lön' 心慌意亂

DISCONNECTED, feh-lin'-p'ing 弗連摒

DISCONSOLATE, en'-tah-feh-læ' 安搭弗來; vu-k'o' en-we' 無可安慰

DISCONTENTED, feh-mun'-i 弗滿意; pah'-feh-hwun'-hyi 百弗歡喜

DISCONTINUE, *to* hyih'-loh 歇落; ts 止

DISCORD, *variance*, feh tsih'-yiah 弗洽洽;— *in sound*, yüing' feh-'eh' 韻弗合

DISCOUNT *on price of goods,* k'eo'-deo 扣頭; tsih'-deo 折頭; *two out of every hundred,* kyiu'-pah k'eo 九八扣; kyiu'-pah tsih 九八折; *ten out of every hundred,* kyiu' k'eo 九扣; kyiu tsih 九折

DISCOURAGE, *to* long'-leh gyi-sing' lang' 弄得°其心冷°; *to break his inclination to do,* tang-dön'-gyi-go hying'-cü 打斷其個°與致; *discouraged,* ts'-hyiang tih'-tao-de 志向跌倒了°

DISCOURTEOUS, m li'-sing 無°禮性; — *behavior,* ang-we', m li'-sing 行°爲無°禮性

DISCOVER, *to find,* zing-c'ih'-læ 尋°出來; zing-djoh' 尋着° (djoh or dzoh); — *a plot,* kyi-meo' k'en'-p'o 機謀看破

DISCREET, yiu kyin'-sih 有見識; *prudent,* kwu-zin' kwu-'eo° 顧前°顧後

DISCRIMINATE, *to* feng-bin'ts'ing'-t'ong' 分辨清通; feng-ts'ing' dao-bah' 分青道白

DISCUSS, *to* leng 論; — *a subject,* leng' ih ky'i' z-t'i' 論一起事體

DISDAIN, *to* miao'-z 藐視; k'en'-feh-zông-ngæn' 看弗上眼°

DISDAINFUL, k'en'-nying'-feh-zông-ngæn' 看人°弗上眼°

DISEASE, bing 病; bing-tsing' 病症 (ih-dziang); *to have a disease,* sang bing' 生°病; yiu t'ong'-yiang 有痛癢

DISENGAGED *from business,* m-kao' z-ken' 沒°有°事幹; *ut present* —, keh'-zông k'ong'-go 這°時°空个°

DISENTANGLE, *to* ka'-k'æ 解°開; ka'-sæn 解°散

DISFIGURE, *to* siang'-mao kæ'-diao 相貌改壞°; — *the face,* kæ siang' 改相

DISGORGE, *to* t'u'-c'ih' 吐出

DISGRACE, *to* tao-me' 倒楣; — *him,* peh' gyi tao-me' 俾°其倒楣; tao'-gyi-me' 倒其楣; *disgraced,* tao-leh-me'-de 倒得°楣了°; *you not only — yourself but the church,* ng feh tæn'-tsih zi tao'-me yia peh kong-we'-li tao-me' 你弗單只自°倒楣也°俾°公會裡倒楣; — *by berating,* siu'-joh 羞辱; *disgraced by ditto,* zin-joh' 受辱 (joh or zoh)

DISGRACEFUL *affair,* tao-me' z-ken' 倒楣事幹

DISGUISE, *to* tsông-pæn' 粧扮; *to go in* —, zi' tsông-pæn'-leh-ky'i' 自°粧扮得°去°; *the king dressed in the* — *of a subject,* wông-ti' kæ'-wun i-zông' tsông-pæn' pah'-sing 皇帝改換衣裳°粧扮百姓

DISGUSTING, zô'-in 惹°厭; in'-u 厭惡°; væn'-in 犯厭

DISH, beng-ts' 盆子 (ih-tsah); *dishes,* un'-tsæn-diah-ts' 碗盞碟°子

DISH, to — up, beng-ts' tsi'-læ 盆
子舀來

DISHONEST, feh-lao'-jih 弗老
實; feh-dzing'-jih 弗誠實;
kæn-tsô' 奸詐; veo-r'-peh-jih'
浮而不實; feh-cong-'eo' 弗
忠厚 (cong or tsong); nails too
long (i. e. will take a little), ts'-
k'ah hying' 指甲°與

DISHONOR, to — a person, 'æ
nying' m-t'i'-min 害人°無°體
面; disgrace a person, tao-nying'-
me' 倒人°楣

DISHONORABLE business, m-min-
moh' z-t'i' 無°面目事體

DISINCLINED, kæn'-teh 懶得;
— to do, kæn'-teh tso' 懶得做

DISINHERITED, ts'æn'-nyih m-
veng', ken'-c'ih-de 產業無°
分°赶出了°

DISINTERESTED, yiah-ky'i' 俠
氣; — nyi-ky'i' djong' 義氣重

DISLIKE, to feh hwun'-hyi 弗歡
喜; feh cong'-i 弗中意

DISLOCATE, to — a joint, gao'-
kwu t'eh-yüih' 胶°股脫穴

DISLODGE, to drive out, ken'-c'ih
赶出; — (as a miscreant),
ky'ü-djoh' 驅逐

DISLOYAL to the government, feh-
voh' wông-hwô' 弗服王化

DISMAL, m-c'ü'-go 無°趣个°;
ing'-seh-seh 陰煞煞; dark,
en'-c'ih-c'ih 暗黝黝

DISMASTED, we-kæn' sông-diao'-de
檣°杆傷壞°了°

DISMAY, filled with — , mun'-
sing gyü-dæn' 滿心懼憚

DISMISS, to —, (as servants), tang-
fah-ky'i' 打發去°; — him, hyih'
gyi 歇其; — (as a congrega-
tion), peh gyi sæn'-k'æ 俾°其
散開; — (officially), fah'-sæn
發散; — school, fông-'oh' 放
學°; sæn-kwun' 散館; — (as
a teacher), we-foh' 回覆

DISMISSAL, I request a — , ngô
ts'ing' ng, cing' ngô t'e-dz' 我
請你准我推辭; (an of-
ficer) requests — , ts'ing k'æ-
ky'üih' 請開缺

DISMOUNT, to — from a horse, loh
mô' 落馬; t'iao'-loh mô' 跳
落馬

DISOBEDIENT, feh - k'eng'-t'ing'
wô 弗肯聽話; feh ziu kao'-
hyüing 弗受敎°訓; — son,
peh'-hyiao ng-ts' 不孝兒°子;
— and perverse son, wu-nyih'-go
ng-ts' 忤逆个°兒°子

DISOBEY, to we-be' 違背; feh i'-
jing 弗依順; we-nyih' 違逆

DISOBLIGING, feh cing' min-dzing'
弗准面情; very — , 'ao'
feh cing'-dzing 毫弗准情

DISORDERLY, lön-ts'ih'-pah-tsao'
亂七八遭; tossed about east
and west, tong-gwæn', si-gwæn'
東摜西摜; — and noisy as
children, djông' 踵; — and
quarrelsome, seng-z' ts'ông-'o' 生
事闖禍

DISOWN, to feh-jing 勿認; feh tsih'-jing 弗接認;— for fear of consequences, feh tsiao-deo' 弗招頭

DISPARAGE, to u'-tsông 污葬;— him, kông gyi ti 講其低

DISPASSIONATE, ding-ding'-diah-diah' 定定奪°奪°

DISPEL, to hwô'-diao 化去°; ka'-k'æ 解°開; sæn'-k'æ 散開;— doubt, nyi-sing' hwô'-diao 疑心化去°; ka nyi' 解°疑;— sorrow, sæn-sæn meng' 散散悶; ka-ka meng' 解解°悶

DISPENSARY, s'-yiah-gyüoh 施藥局

DISPENSE, to feng-peh' 分給°

DISPENSED, can be — with, k'o'-yi feh-yüong'-go 可以弗用个°; hao-hyih'-go 好歇个°; hao-sang'-go 好省个°

DISPERSE, to tseo'-sæn 走散; sæn'-k'æ 散開

DISPLACE, to fông' ts'o 放差°; en dzæn' 安賺;— repeatedly, lön-fông' 亂放

DISPLAY, to spread out, pa'-k'æ 擺開; t'æn-k'æ' 攤開; to exhibit, hyin'-c'ih 顯出; he displays ability in speaking, gyi hyin'-c'ih k'eo'-dzæ hao' 其顯出口才好;— dress, sæ' voh-seh' 賽服色;— wealth, sæ fu' 賽富;— one's beauty, sæ mao' 賽貌;— the feet, sæ kyiah' 賽脚; empty —, do-ba'-dziang 大°排°塲; p'u-p'a' 鋪派°

DISPLEASE, to long-leh feh hwun'-hyi 弄得°弗歡喜;— me, peh ngô feh hwun'-hyi 俾°我弗歡喜; long' ngô feh yüoh'-i 弄我弗欲意

DISPOSE, to set in order, also to — of, en-ba' 安排°; en-teng' 安頓; how will you — of that unexpected gain? keh'-pih nga-kw'a', dza en'-teng 這°筆外°快°怎°安頓?

DISPOSED, I feel — to give it to him, ngô i'-s z iao peh gyi' 我意思是要給°其

DISPOSITION, sing'-kah 性格; sing'-dzing 性情; sing-dziang' 心腸; hasty —, sing'-kah kyih' 性格急; sing'-dzing bao-ts'ao' 性情暴躁; cross —, sing-ts'ao' 性躁; perverse —, sing'-kah kwæ-p'ih 性格乖僻; bad — (also bad habit pertinaciously adhered to), wa bi'-ky'i 孬°脾氣; make a good — of it, iao tsing'-kying yüong' 要正經用

DISPROPORTIONED, feh siang'-p'e 弗相配

DISPROVE, to prove to be false, feng-ming' z kô'-go 分明是假°个°

DISPUTE, to bin'-leng 辯論;— angrily, tsang-leng' 爭°論

DISQUIETED, feh en'-tæn 弗安

軇；— (as a country), feh t'a'-bing 弗太°平

DISREGARD, *to* peh-yi'-we-i' 不以為意；*pay no attention*, feh liu'-sing 弗留心；ko'-r-peh-liu' 過而不留；— *life*, feh kwu sing'-ming 弗顧性命

DISREPUTABLE, m-ô'-lin-go 無°了臉个°；ti-vi' 低微；— *person*, feh ts'ing'-bah-go nying 弗清白个°人°；feh loh-dzih-go nying 弗落直个°人°

DISRESPECT, *to treat with* — , mao-væn' 冒犯；c'oh'-væn 觸犯；*ditto purposely*, c'ong-dzông' 衝撞；c'ong-væn' 衝犯

DISRESPECTFUL, feh-kong'-kying 弗恭敬

DISSATISFIED, feh-cü'-tsoh 弗知足；feh-tsoh' 弗足；sing'-li feh-jü'-i 心裡弗如意；*I am* — *with him*, gyi feh-'eh' ngô-go i' 其弗合我个°意；gyi feh-jü' ngô-go i' 其弗如我个°意

DISSECT, *to* — *at a Chinese inquest*, siah'-kweh-nyin' 削骨驗

DISSEMBLE, *to pretend to be honest*, tsông lao'-jih 妝老實；kô lao'-jih 假°老實；— *well*, tsông'-leh ziang' 妝得°像；pæn'-leh ziang 扮得°像

DISSEMINATE, *to* po-yiang'-k'æ 播揚開

DISSENT, *to* feh-'eh' 弗合；— *from the crowd*, feh-'eh' jing-

dzing' 弗合人情；— *from one's superiors*, feh-'eh' zông-i' 弗合上意

DISSERTATION, *a* ih-p'in leng' 一篇論

DISSEVER, *to* feng-k'æ' 分開；ts'ah'-k'æ 拆開；— *with a knife*, tsæn-k'æ' 斬開

DISSIMILAR, feh siang'-ziang, 弗相像；*very* —, da' feh-siang'-dong 大弗相同

DISSIPATE *sadness*, ka-ka meng' 解°解°悶；sæn-sæn sing' 散散心

DISSOLUTE, fông'-dông 放蕩

DISSOLVE, *to melt*, yiang 煬；sah 煞；hwô 化；yiang-diao' 煬了°；— *in water*, shü'-li 'o-k'æ 水°裡和開；shü'-li yiang-k'æ 水°裡煬開；— (*i. e.* cut), *friendship*, djih kyiao' 絕交；— *partnership*, feng tsiang' 分帳；feng siu' 分手

DISSUADE, *to exhort and caution*, ky'ün'-kyiæ 勸戒；*exhort him to stop*, ky'ün'-sih gyi hyih' 勸息其歇

DISTANCE, yün 遠；li-yün' 離遠；*what is the* — *apart?* to-siao' yün 多少遠？*the* — *is about five li*, da-iah' ng' li yün' 大約五°里遠

DISTANTLY *connected* (as relatives or ideas), su-yün' 疏遠

DISTASTE, m i'-c'ü 無°意趣

DISTEND, *to* — *with wind*, fah-p'ông', or fah-p'oh' 發膵; *to bloat*, fah-tsiang' 發脹

DISTILL, *to* tsing 蒸; tsing'-ky'i-læ 蒸起來

DISTINCT, *separate*, feh siang'-lin 弗相連; *different*, koh'-bih 各別; *clear*, ts'ing-t'ong 清通 — *articulation*, k'eo'-ing ts'ing-t'ong 口音清通; k'eo'-ing ts'ing-k'oh' 口音清確°

DISTINCTLY, *to see* —, k'en' ts'ing-tong 看清通

DISTINGUISH, *to* bin'-pih 辯別°; feng-pih' 分別°; *I can't — it, therefore it must be hard to discern*, ngô bin'-feh-c'ih'-læ, sô'-yi da-kæ næn feng-bin' 我辯弗出來所以大概難分辯

DISTINGUISHED, yiu ming-vông' 有名望; ming-vông' do' 名望大°

DISTORT, *to* ao'-hwa 拗歪

DISTORTED, hwa 歪; — *mouth*, hwa-cü' 歪嘴

DISTRACT, *to — the mind*, feng sing' 分心

DISTRACTED *mind*, sing-mông'-feh-ding' 心忙弗定; sing-lön' 心亂; *almost* — (crazed), weng-feh'-jih-mo' 魂弗入墓

DISTRESS, kw'u'-ts'u 苦楚; kw'u'-næn 苦難; *suffering*, kw'u'-t'ong 苦痛; *in* —, læ-tih kyüoh' kw'u'-ts'u 來的吃°苦楚; læ'-tih ziu kw'u'-t'ong 來的受苦痛

DISTRESSED (in appearance), zeo-mi' tang-pah'-kyih 愁眉°打百結; *in mind*, sing-li kw'u' 心裡苦; iu-üih' 憂鬱°; iu-iu'-üoh-üoh' 憂憂鬱°鬱°

DISTRIBUTE, *to* feng-p'a' 分派°; — *impartially*, kong-bing' feng' 公平分; kyüing feng' 均分; — *books*, feng shü' 分書; — *type*, wæn z' 還字

DISTRICT, yün 縣; *region*, di-fông 地方; — *magistrate*, cü-yün' 知縣; — *examinations*, yün-k'ao' 縣考; *god of a small* —, t'u'- di-bu'- sah 土地菩薩

DISTRUST *to* nyi-'oh' 疑惑; ts'æ-nyi' 猜疑

DISTURB *to* kying'-dong 驚動

DISTURBANCE, nao-z' 鬧事; *to get up a* —, ts-z' 滋事

DISTURBED *in mind*, sing'-li-yiao-yiao'-peh-ih' 心裡搖搖不一; — *in sleep*, kw'eng'-feh-en'-jün 睡°弗安然

DISUSE, *not to use*, feh-yüong' 弗用; *fallen into disuse*, dziang-kyiu' feh-tsoh' 長久弗作

DITCH, wu-nyi-den' 污°泥潭; yiang-keo-den' 陽溝潭; *to dig a* —, dao keo' 掏溝

DITTY, t'æn-wông' 攤黃 ky'üoh'-ts' 曲子; siao'-diao 小調 (ih-tsah)

DIVE, *to* sah-kong 殺攻; sah-kong'-loh-ky'i' 殺攻落去°

DIVER, sah-kong'-go nying 殺 攻 个° 人°

DIVERGE, to — gradually, dzin'-dzin-ts'ô'-k'æ-ky'i' 漸 漸 义 開 去°

DIVERS, several, kyi-go' 幾 个; hao·kyi'-go 好 幾 个°

DIVERSE, different, koh-yiang' 各 樣; several kinds, hao-kyi'-yiang 好 幾 樣

DIVERSION, for —, siao-ky'in'-yüong-go 消 遣 用 个°

DIVERSITY, koh 各; — in opinion, koh'-nying yiu kob-i'-s 各 人° 有 各 意 思; koh'-tsih-ih-kyin' 各 執 一 見; but little —, sao-we-zông'-loh 稍 爲 上 落; sao'-yiu-feh-dong' 稍 有 弗 同; — in kind, koh-dzong-gyi-le' 各 從 其 類; — in color and pattern, koh'-seh koh-yiang' 各 色 各 樣

DIVERT, to — the mind, sæn-sæn-sing' 散 散 心; siao-siao-ky'in' 消 消 遣; siao-siao-'æn' 消 消 閒°

DIVEST of clothing, kw'un i' 寬 衣; i-zông' t'eh'-loh 衣 裳° 脫 落

DIVIDE, to feng 分; feng-k'æ' 分 開; — by cutting, ts'ih'-k'æ 切 開; ditto (as a fish. melon &c.), p'o-k'æ 破 開; — in halves, te'-feng-k'æ' 對 分 開; te'-ts'ih-k'æ' 對 切 開; — in three parts, feng' tso sæn kwu' 分 做 三 股; — equally, tsiao' kwu kyüing-

feng' 照 股 均 分; — by a partition, lah-k'æ'; kah-k'æ 隔 開

DIVIDED mind, ih sing' ts'ong liang yüoh' 一 心 充 兩 用

DIVIDEND, kæ-feng' 該 分

DIVINATION, ky'i-k'o' sön-ming' 起 課 算 命

DIVINE, to — (with three cash), poh-k'o' 卜 課; ky'i-k'o' 起 課; to settle doubt, kyüih nyi' 決 疑; — (with lettered bamboos), ts'iu-ts'in' 抽 籤; — with a motto, on paper, ts'eh z' 測 字; ditto before an idol, gyiu ts'in' 求 籤; meng ts'in-s' 問° 籤 詩; — with a bird, gyin bæn' 箝 牌; to tell fortunes, sön ming' 算 命; p'i ming-ts' 批 命 呇

DIVINE, belonging to God, kwe'-ü Jing-ming' 歸 于 神 明; proceeding from God, dzæ'-ü Jing-ming' ka læ' 在 于 神 明 而° 來; to become —, dzing Jing' 成 神

DIVINE, a clergyman, kyiao'-s 敎 師; Roman Catholic —, jing-vu' 神 父; a theologian, cü'-ka sing'-shü-go sin-sang' 註 解° 聖 書 个° 先 生°

DIVINER, ky'i'-k'o sin'-sang 起 課 先 生'; — of places, fong-shü' sin'-sang 風 水 先 生'; fortune teller, sön'-ming sin'-sang 算 命 先 生°

DIVINITY, the essence of God, Jing t'i' 神 體; a —, ih'-we Jing-ming' 一 位 神 明; ih-we' bu-sah' 一 位 菩 薩; *treatise on* —, Jing-dao' cong-leng' 神 道 總 論

DIVISION, *Math.* feng-fah' 分 法

DIVISOR, feng-su' 分 數

DIVORCE, *to* li'-diao lao'-nyüing 離 了° 老 女°; *a writing of* —, li-shü' 離 書

DIVULGE, *to* lu-fong' 露 風; sih'-leo 洩 漏; — *a secret*, tseo'-leo fong-sing' 走 漏 風 信

DIZZINESS, deo-yüing' 頭 暈; deo' yüing-yüing'-dong 頭 暈 暈 動

DO, *to* tso 做; tsoh 作; 'ang 行°; we 爲; *when will you* — *it*, ng kyi'-z we tso 你° 幾 時 會 做; *cannot* — (it), tso'-feh-læ 做 弗 來; — *not*, feh-k'o' or m-nao' 弗 可; hao-vong' 弗° 用°; feh iao' 弗 耍; *to* — *evil many times*, tsoh-oh' to-tön 作 惡 多 端; — *good deeds* (or give alms), 'ang jün' 行° 善; tso hao'-z 做 好 事; *whatever we* —, sô-tsoh' sô-we' 所 作 所 爲; *will this* — *or not?* keh' hao'-s-teh feh 這° 好 使 得 否°? *it will* —, hao'-s-teh go 好 使 得 个°; *How do you* —? ng' hao' feh 你° 好 否°? ng' hao' yüe 你° 好 也? *I* — *not know*, ngô' feh hyiao'-teh 我 弗 曉 得

DOCILE, t'iah'-voh 貼° 服

DOCK, *open space for making and repairing vessels*, jün-ts'iang' 船

廠; — *occupied by one vessel*, jün-'ong'; *in* — *for repairs*, jün-ts'iang'-li læ-tih siu' 船 廠 裡 來 的 修

DOCTOR, i-sang' 醫 生°; 'ang-i' sin'-sang 行° 醫 先 生°

DOCTRINE, dao'-li 道 理; — *of religion*, kyiao'-cong dao'-li 教 中 道 理

DOCUMENT, veng-ky'i' 文 契; — *for presentation to the emperor*, tseo'-tsông 奏 章

DODGE, *to* to'-sin 躱 閃 (not an equivalent).

DOE, ts'-loh' 雌 鹿 (ih-tsah)

DOG, keo 狗; wun-kyi' 黄° 犬° (ih-tsah)

DOG-KENNEL, keo-k'o' or keo-k'un' 狗 窠

DOGGED *looks*, min-k'ong' heh'-pong 面 孔 黑 奔°; min vu hyi-seh 面 無 喜 色

DOINGS, tsoh'-we 作 爲

DOLEFUL, *lonely and miserable* (as persons or places), dzih-moh' 寂 寞; kwn-ts'i' 孤 悽; — *sound* (of living creatures), ts'i-ts'æn'-go sing-ing' 悽 慘 个° 聲 音; pe-æ'-go sing-ing' 悲 哀 个° 聲 音

DOLL, 'en 孩° (ih-go)

DOLLAR, fæn-ping' 番 餅; yiang-dzin' 洋 錢 (ih-kw'e); *quarter of a* —, liang'-koh-pun' 兩 角° 半; *ditto, the coin*, s-k'æ' 四 開; *half a* —, pun'-kw'e 半 塊; *ditto, the coin*, te'-k'æ 對 開

DOLT, ngæ-nying′ 呆 人°; ngæ-moh′-deo 呆 木 頭

DOMESTIC *affairs*, kô-vu′ z 家° 務 事; — *use*, kô yüong′ 家° 用; — *produce*, c‘ih′-ts‘æn 出 產; *the six* — *animals*, loh-hyüoh′ 六 畜; sang-k‘eo′ 牲° 口; — or *native cloth*, du′-pu 土° 布

DOMESTIC, *servant*, yüong-nying′ 傭 人°; *male slave*, kô-nying′ 家° 人° (ih-go)

DOMINION, *jurisdiction*, kæ-kwun′ 該 管; *the British* —, Da-Ing′ kæ-kwun′ 大 英 該 管

DOMINEERING, do-yiang′ 大° 樣

DOMINOES, *bone* bæn 牌°; kweb-ba′ 骨 牌° (a set, ih fu); *to play* —, c‘ô bæn′ 扯 牌°

DONE, *finished*, tso′-wun-de 做 完 了°; tso′-ko-tih-de 做 過 的 了°; dzing-kong′-de 成 功 了°; *well cooked*, joh 熟; *insufficiently* —, ky‘in joh′ 欠 熟; *can't be* —, tso′-feh-læ 做 弗 來; long′-feh-læ′ 弄 弗 來; dong′-siu-feh-læ′ 動 手 弗 來; ‘ô′-siu-feh-læ′ 下° 手 弗 來

DONKEY, li-ts′ 驢 子 (ih-p‘ih)

DONOR, s′-cü 施 主; — (of charity), sô′-cü 捨° 主

DOOM, *to condemn*, ding z‘ 定 罪; — *to eternal punishment*, ding zin üong′-kw‘u ying-vah′ 定 受 永 苦 刑 罰

DOOR, meng 門 (ih-deo, ih-sin); *at the* —, meng-k‘eo-den′ 門 口

頭°; *front* —, zin-meng′ 前° 門; *back* —, ‘eo′-meng′ 後° 門; *shut the* —, kwæn meng′ 關 門; *open the* —, k‘æ meng′ 開 門; *lock the* —, so meng′ 鎖 門; *next* —, kah′-pih meng′ 隔 壁 門

DOOR-KEEPER, kwun-meng′-go nying 管 門 个° 人°; *an old* —, kwun-meng lao-den′ 管 門 老 頭°

DOOR-SILL, di-voh′ 地 栿

DORMITORY, vông-kæn 房 間; kw‘eng′-kæn 睡° 間; ngo-vông′ 臥 房

DOSE, *a* ih-voh′ 一 服; *how many doses shall I take?* ngô′ kæ ky‘üoh′ kyi voh′ 我 該 吃° 幾 服?

DOT, *a* ih-tin′ 一 點

DOTAGE, (in his) —, mong′-tong-de 懵 懂 了°; gyi lao′-be-de 其 老 背 了 °(used in reproach).

DOTE, *to* — *upon*, ziang weh-pao′ ka æ′ 像 活 寶 介° 愛; æ′-ju tsông′-zông ming-cü 愛 如 掌 上 明 珠

DOUBLE, sông 雙; — *thread*, sông-keng′ sin 雙 根 線; — *mind-ed*, sæn-sing′ liang-i 三 心 兩 意; — *entendre* sông-kwæn′ shih-wô′ 雙 關 說 話; — *price*, sông-be′ kô-din 雙 倍 價° 錢°; liang-be kyü′ 兩 倍 貴; kô-be to′ 加° 倍 多

DOUBLE, *to* kô′ ih-be′ 加° 一 倍

— *money at interest,* te′-peng te-li′ 對本對利; — *up* (as paper), te üih′-cün 對攏轉; te tsih′-long 對摺攏; — *in trade,* te dzæn din′ 對賺錢°; ′eh-ts din′ 合子錢°

DOUBT, *to* nyi-sing′ 疑心; ts′æ-nyi′ 猜疑; nyi-′oh′ 疑惑; *in* —, nyi-′oh′-peh-kyüih 疑惑不決

DOUBTFUL, *it is* m-su′ 無°數; — (and uncertain), weh-lih′ weh-deh′; 活立活蹋°; iao′-bông feh-ding′ 要防弗定; yün-shü′ 懸勢; yün-shü′-dang-tsiang 懸勢歪將

DOUBTLESS, ih-ding′ 一定; vu-nyi′ 無疑

DOUGH, sang min′-feng 生麵粉; *light* (as —), song′-de 鬆了°; fah-t′eo′-de 發透了°

DOVE, pæn-kyiu′ 斑鳩 (ih-tsah)

DOVETAIL, *to* ô - ts′iah′ - mi′- pô shing′-deo (magpie-tail) 鴉鵲尾巴榫頭

DOWAGER, *the empress* —, wông-t′a′-′eo 皇太后

DOWN, ′ô 下°; loh 落; *walk* —, tseo′-loh-læ 走落來; *take it* —, ′ô-loh′ky′i 下°落去°; *put* (it) —, fông′-loh 放落; en-loh′-ky′i 安落去°; *sit* —, zo-tæn′-loh, 坐打°落; *lie* —, kw′eng′-tao 睡倒; *ditto,* kw′eng′-loh-ky′i 睡°落去°; *lie — a while,* le ih′-zông;

*placed upside* —, fæn′-byiang fông′-tih-de 反向放的°了°; *please sit* —, ts′ing zo′ 請坐°

DOWN, *soft feathers,* nyüong mao′ 絨毛

DOWNCAST, we-deo-t′ah-nao′ 痿頭塌臑; we-we′-ze-ze′ 痿痿瘁°瘁°; pih′-pih-sih-sih.

DOWNHILL, *to walk* tseo′-loh sæn 走落山

DOWNRIGHT, *plainly,* ming-ming′-tông-tông′ 明明當當; — *falsehood,* ming-ming′ z kô′-wô 明明是假°話

DOWRY *of money, lands, houses &c.* (which a woman brings at marriage), ze-kô′ 隨嫁°; ze-lin′-din 隨奩錢°; *furniture and clothing,* tsông-lin′ 粧奩; *furniture,* kô′-tsông 嫁粧; *bedding,* p′u-dzing′ 鋪陳; — (which the husband gives to the wife's father), p′ing′-kying 聘金

DOXOLOGY, dzong-tsæn′-ko 頌讚歌

DOZE, *to* hwô-ky′i′ 花起; tang-k′eh′-c′ong 打磕睡°; gyün-ky′i′ 倦起; *to have a* —, hwô′ ih-hwô 化一化; *just ready to sleep,* kw′eng′-joh kw′a 睡°熟快; *just ready to wake,* tsiang diao-kao′ 將調覺°

DOZEN, *a* jih-nyi′ 十二°

DRAFT, *rough* ts′ao′-kao 草稿 (ih-go); — *of exchange,* we-p′iao′ 匯票 See DRAUGHT.

DRAG, *to* Ia; ky'in 繂; te 舳;
t'o 拖; t'a; — (as a boat), te'-
ky'in or ts'ô-ky'in' 舳繂; — *a*
*net*, t'a mông' 拖°網; — *on the*
*ground* (as a dress), t'o di' 拖地;
— *one into difficulty*, t'o-nying'-
loh-shü' 拖人° 落水°

DRAGGLE, *to* t'o ao'-tsao 拖墾
糟; — *in the mud*, t'o'-djoh na-
nyi' 拖着° 爛°坭; — *and wet*,
t'o sih' 拖濕

DRAGON, long 龍 (ih-keng, ih-
kwang); *dragon's blood*, hyüih-
gyih' 血竭

DRAGON-FLY, ts'ing-ding' 蜻蜓
(ih-tsah)

DRAIN, *covered* —, ing-keo' 陰
溝; *open* —, yiang-keo' 陽溝

DRAIN, *to* — *off water*, keo 溝

DRAKE, yüong-æn' 雄鴨° (ih-
tsah)

DRAMA (in verse), hyi'-ky'üoh 戲
曲; — *for the stage*, byi'-peng
戲本

DRAUGHT, *a swallow of water*,
ih-k'eo shü' 一 口 水; *a* — *of*
*fish*, ih-mông ng' 一網魚°; —
*of wind*, pih'-fong 壁風; leo-
fong' 漏風; *do not let a* —*blow*
(on you), feh-k'o' pih'-fong c'ü
弗可壁風吹°; — *of a ship*,
jün ky'üoh-shü' sing-ts'in' 船
吃°水°深淺; *make a* — *of*
*soldiers*, ts'iu ping' 抽兵; bah
ping' 拔兵

DRAUGHTS, *game of* we-gyi' 圍

棋; *to play* —, tsiah we-gyi' 着
圍棋

DRAW, *to pull*, te 舳; Ia; t'o 拖;
— *up the curtain*, meng-lin' te'-
zông-ky'i 門簾舳上去°; —
*water*, tang shü' 打水°; — *near*,
tseo'-long-læ 走攏來; gying'-
long-læ 近攏來; — *out*, bah-
c'ih' 拔出; tsoh'-c'ih 齣出; —
*out nails*, bah ting-cü' 拔釘銖;
— *out teeth*, tsoh'-loh ngô-ts'' 齣
落牙°齒; — *a picture*, sia wô'
寫°畫; miao-wô'描畫; tang du'
打圖; — *from nature*, i pih'
sia 意筆寫°; — *by looking at a*
*pattern*, ing'-ko-læ 印過來; deo-
ko'-læ 投過來; t'eh'-ko-læ 揭
過來; — *from a pattern through*
*paper*, ing'-leh sia' 印得°寫°;
— *a likeness*, sia ziang' 寫°像;
sia' 'ang-loh' 寫° 行°樂; —
*lots* (by long and short slips),
ts'iu' dziang-tön' 抽長短; *ditto*
(by bits of paper rolled up), ts'ah'
ts-meh-den' 撮紙抹頭°; —
*customers*, Ia ma'-cü 拉°買主;
*I wish to* — *your custom*, ngô' iao
nyiang'-p'æn ng 我要仰攀
你°; — *the hands into the sleeves*,
siu soh'-tsing-ky'i 手縮進去°

DRAWBACK, *customs*' dzeng p'iao'
存票

DRAW-BRIDGE, (to draw up) tiao'-
gyiao 弔橋; *movable bridge*,
weh-gyiao' 活橋 (ih-diao)

DRAWER, ts'iu-teo' 抽斗 (ih-tsah); *pull out a* —, ts'iu-teo yi-c'ih'-læ 抽斗移出來; *push in the* —, ts'iu-teo yi-tsing'-ky'i 抽斗移進去。

DRAWERS, kw'u 褲; *inner* —, t'i'-li kw'u 替裡褲 (ih-diao, ih-iao)

DRAWING, du 圖; sia-go du' 寫个°圖 (ih-go); wô 畫 (ih-tsiang, if mounted, ih-foh); *to make a* —, tang ih-go du' 打一个°圖; miao ih-go du' 描一个°圖; sia ih-go du' 寫一个°圖

DRAWING-PENCIL, miao-hwô'-pih 描花筆 (ih-ts)

DRAWL, *to* kông'-leh, ga-ngô'-ga-teb.

DREAD, p'ô 怕; gyü-dæn' 懼憚; *full of* —, ky'ih'-hyin-ky'ih-hoh' 吃險吃霍

DREADFUL, p'ô'p'ô-go 怕怕个°

DREAM, mong 夢 (also pron. mông); lön-mong' 亂夢

DREAM, *to* tso mong 做夢; *never dreamed of it*, mong'-li siang'-feh-tao'-go 夢裡想弗到个°

DREARY, m-hying'-cü 無°興致

DREDGE *river mud*, nyin' 'o-nyi' 捻河泥; — *with flour*, sen'-tin miu-feng 霰點麨粉

DREGS, tsô 渣; *sediment*, kyiah 脚; — *strained from wine*, tsao 糟

DRENCH, *to soak*, seng'-t'eo 沁°透; heng'-t'eo.

DRENCHED *with rain*, li'-nga tu'

seng'-t'eo 裡外°都沁°透; wu-dah-dah'-go-de 腐°沓沓了°

DRESS, *clothing*, i-zông 衣裳; *every day* —, ts'u-c'ün' i-zông' 粗穿衣裳°; ze-dzông' i-zông' 隨常衣裳°; *visiting* —, c'ih-k'ah' i-zông' 出客衣裳°; si'-c'ün i-zông 細穿衣裳°; *very particular as to* —, c'ün i-zông' tiug k'ao'-kyiu 穿衣裳°頂考究; *careless in* — (dirty), c'ün'-leh lah-t'ah' 穿得°邋遢; *dirty and ragged* (in —), lô-tsô.

DRESS, *to put on clothes*, c'ün i-zông' 穿衣裳°; — *a child*, teng siao-nying' c'ün i-zông' 搭小人°穿衣裳°; *well dressed*, c'ün'-leh, bin k'ah-ky'i-go 穿°得°便客氣个°; *poorly dressed*, c'ün'-leh pe-pe'-go 穿°得°卑卑个°

DRESSING-GLASS, tsiah-i-kying' 着°衣鏡 (ih-min)

DRIBBLE, *to fall in drops*, tin'-tang-tin ti'-loh 點打點滴落; *to slaver*, liu zæn'-dzô-shü' 流涎°沫水

DRIED, ken 乾; — *in the sun*, sa'-ken-de 曬°乾了°; — *fruits*, ken ko'-ts 乾果子; — *apples*, bing-ko ken' 萍果乾; — *grapes*, bu-dao ken' 葡萄乾; fæn-dao' 番萄; — *peaches*, dao-fu' 桃餔; — *persimmons*, z'-ping 柿餅; — *fish*, ng-siang 魚°鯗

DRIFT, *to be driven with the current*, ze shü' t‘eng-læ t‘eng-ky‘i' 隨 水 氽 來 氽 去°; *boat drifting for bad purposes*, t‘eng-kông-jün' 氽 江° 船

DRILL, *to — a hole*, cün dong' 鑽 洞 (cün or tsön); — *a small hole*, tsön ngæn'-ts 鑽 眼° 子; — *as troops*, ts‘ao-lin' 操 練; *going to —*, loh ts‘ao' ky‘i 落 操 去°

DRINK, *to* ky‘üoh 吃°; hah 呷; *he wants to drink a little water*, gyi iao ky‘üoh' ih-tin shü' 其 要 吃° 一 點° 水°; — (as horses), ing 飲

DRINK, *fondness for —*, t‘en tsiu' 貪 酒

DRIP, *to* ti'-loh-læ 滴 落 來

DRIPPING-PAN, *baking-pan*, p‘ang-bun' 烹 盤

DRIVE, *to — cows*, ken ngeo' 赶 牛°; — *him out*, ken' gyi c‘ih' 赶 其 出; — *out mosquitoes*, tæn' meng-djong' 撢° 蚊° 虫; — *a nail*, k‘ao' ih-me' ting-cü' 拷 一 枚 釘 鉄; — *against*, djông-djoh' 撞 着°

DRIVING *rain*, zia-fong' yü 斜° 風 雨

DRIZZLE, *to* loh-yü'-mao-s' 落 雨 毛 絲; *it drizzles*, læ-tih loh-yü-mao-s' 來 的 落 雨 毛 絲

DROLL, hao fah-siao' go 好 發 笑 个°

DROMEDARY, doh-fong-do' 獨 峰 駝 (ih-deo)

DRONE, *the male bee*, yüong-fong' 雄 蜂 (ih-tsah)

DROOL, *to —* (as an infant), c‘ih zæn'-dzô-shü' 出 涎° 沫° 水°

DROOP, *to —* (as a flower), dang-loh' 霆 落; — *the head forward*, deo' eo-tæn'-tao 頭 偃° 打° 倒; — *the head on one side*, deo gwæn-tao'.

DROP, *a* ih tin' 一 點; *a — of water*, ih tin shü 一 點 水

DROP, *to fall in drops*, ti'-loh' 滴 落; *to fall*, tih'-loh 跌 落; *let it drop*, peh gyi tih'-loh 俾° 其 跌 落; — (as ripe fruit), t‘eng'-loh 脫 落; — *by spoon-fuls*, ih diao-kang' ih diao-kang' tao'-tib 一 調 羹° 一 調 羹° 倒 的

DROPSY, shü'-kwu bing' 水° 臌 病; kwu'-tsiang bing' 臌 脹° 病

DROSS, vu'-tong-go tsô' 浮° 當° 个° 渣

DROVE, ih-dziao' 一 羣°; ih-de' 一 隊°; *a — of cattle*, ih-dziao ngeo' 一 羣° 牛°

DROUGHT, ‘en 旱; t‘in ‘en' 天 旱; *Summer —*, ‘en-ô' 旱 夏°; *Winter —*, ‘en tong 旱 冬

DROWN, *to* tsing'-sah 浸 殺; — *one's self*, deo-shü' si' 投 水° 死°; — *one's-self in the canal*, deo ‘o' si' 投 河 死°

DROWSY, hweng-gyün' 昏 倦; gyün-ky‘i' 倦 起

DRUDGE, to   tso kw'u'-kong 做苦工

DRUGGIST, yiah-tin'-kwun 藥店官

DRUGS, yiah-dzæ' 藥材

DRUG-SHOP, (large) yiah-dzæ 'ông 藥材行°; (small) — , yiah-tin' 藥店

DRUM, kwu 鼓; large — , do kwu' 大° 鼓; small —, teo' kwu 斗鼓; — bulging in the middle, hwô kwu' 花鼓 (ih-go)

DRUMMER, kwu-siu' 鼓手 (ih-ming)

DRUM-STICK, kwu-djü' 鼓槌° (ih-tsah)

DRUNK, tsiu' ky'üoh-tse' 酒吃°醉

DRUNKARD, tsiu'-kyü 酒鬼°; tse'-hen 醉漢 (ih-go)

DRY, sao 燥; ken 乾; — as powder, feng'-sao 粉燥; — ground, sao' di 燥地; — wood, ken za' 乾柴°; sao' za 燥柴°; the canals are —, 'o-ken' shü-sao' 河乾水° 燥

DRY, to — in the sun, sa 曬°; — by the fire, hong 烘; ditto something slightly damp, be 焙; — in the open air, lông 朗

DUCK, æn 鴨°; wild — ; yia'-æn 野° 鴨°; shü'-æn 水° 鴨° (ih-tsah); duck's eggs, ah'-dæn °鴨蛋; — meat, ah' nyüoh 鴨肉°

DUCTILE, nying 韌°

DUE, how much is — you? ng' yiu to-siao' tsiang læ nying deo' 你°

有多少帳在°何° 處°? what is required, veng' sô ing-teh'-go 分° 所應得个°; what is proper, li' sô tông-jün' 理所當然; arrived in time, tsiao z-eo' tao'-liao 照時候到了°

DUEL, liang'-'ô siang-tang' 兩下° 相打

DULL, meng-meng'-hweng-hweng' 悶悶昏昏'; — color, hweng' seh 昏色; — of hearing (primarily, affected deafness), tsia'-mi-long' 借° 米聾

DULY, at the time, tsiao z-'eo' 照時候; cing' z-k'eh 準時刻; 'æn' z-k'eh 限° 時刻; letter received, sing, cing'-z-k'eh siu-tao'-de 信準時刻收到了°; — prepared, yü-be' ding-tông' 預備定當

DUMB, ô' k'eo vu-yin' 啞°口無言; — and staring, moh-ding'-k'eo'-ngæ 目定口呆; speechless, ve' kông 弗° 會° 講; a deaf and dumb person, ô'-ts 啞子

DUN color, t'ih' seh 鐵色; to — for money, dong-din' t'ao'-leh lo-so, or dong-din' t'ao-leh tsi-tseo' 銅錢° 討得° 囉° 唆°

DUNCE, one of no capacity, c'ing'-dzæ 蠢才; nyü-c'ü'-peh-dzin'-go nying 愚痴不智° 个°人°

DUNG, o 屎; feng 糞; manure, bi; liao 料

DUNGEON, lao-kæn' 牢監°

DUPE, to keo-ying' 勾引; his —,

gyi'-go zih' 其 个°食 ; ziu gyi-
go nyü' 受 其 个° 愚

DURABLE, næ-kyiu' 耐久 ; kying-
yüong' 經用 ; — (as clothing),
kying-c'ün' 經穿

DURING three years, sæn nyin' li-
hyiang' 三年裡向 ; — the time
I was in Shanghai, ngo' læ Zòng-
hæ' z-'eo 我在°上海時候

DUSK, wông-hweng' 黃昏 cor-
ruptly called wun-hwun-den' ;
sah-en' 雲°暗

DUST, hwe-dzing' 灰塵 ; thick
—, hwe-dzing'-bang-bong' 灰塵
鬅鬡

DUST, to — by wiping, k'a hwe-
dzing' 揩°灰塵 ; — by whip-
ping, tæn hwe-dzing' 撢灰塵

DUST-BRUSH, feather mao-shih'-
tsiu 毛刷帚 (ih-kwun)

DUST-CLOTH, k'a-hwe'-pu 揩°灰
布 (ih-kw'e)

DUST-PAN, peng-teo' 畚斗 (ih-
tsah)

DUTCH, 'O-læn'-koh-go 荷蘭國
个° ; — man, 'O-læn nying' 荷
蘭人°

DUTIFUL, hyiao'-jing 孝順 ; —
son, hyiao'-ts 孝子

DUTY, meng-veng' 名°分° ; one's
own —, peng'-veng 本分° ;
Customs' —, se'-din 稅錢° ; —
memo, zông-se'-tæn 上稅單 ;
wun-se'-tæn 完稅單 ; — proof,
siu-se'-tæn 收稅單

DWARF, a'-ts 矮°子

DWARF, to — by bending branches,
bun-jü' 蟠樹

DWELL, to djü 住 ; deng 庁 ; —
alone, ih-go nying' zi' deng 一
个°人°自庁

DWELLING, where is your honorable —? ng fn'-zông ah-li' 你°
府上何°處°? my humble —,
bi-sò' 敝舍° ; — house, djü-
dzeh' 住宅 ; — place, deng-
sing'-ts-c'ü' 庁身之°處 ; djü-
kyü' 住居 ; ditto of the family,
djü-ko' 住家°

DWINDLE, to grow less by degrees,
dzin'-dzin siao'-long-ky'i 漸漸
小攏去°

DYE, to nyin 染° ; — by dipping,
weh 搵° ; — cotton cloth, nyin pu'
染°布 ; — red, nyin 'ong' 染°
紅 ; — by brushing, shih' nyin
刷染°

DYER, nyin'-s-vu 染°司務

DYE-STUFF, ngæn-liao' 顏°料

DYING, tsiang dön-ky'i' 將斷氣 ;
kw'a ling-cong'-de 快°臨終
了° ; — words, yi-yin' 遺言 ;
— commands, yi-ming' 遺命

DYNASTY, dziao-dæ' 朝代 ; the
present —, peng'-dziao 本朝 ;
the beginning of ditto, peng'-dziao
k'a-koh' 本朝開國

DYSENTERY, 'ong-li' 紅痢 ;
hyüih'-li 血痢

DYSPEPSIA, ky'üoh'-zih feh hwô
吃°食弗化 ; we-kô wa' 胃
家°痎°

# E

**EACH,** koh 各; me 每; — *by himself* or *itself*, koh′-ɒying kwun zi′ 各人°管自°; *they love — other*, gyi-lah′ dô-kô′ siang-æ′ 伊等°大家°相愛; gyi-lah pe′-tsᶜ siang-æ′ 伊等° 彼此相愛; — *end*, liang′ deo 兩頭; *ditto* (of many ends), me′ ih-go deo′ 每一个°頭; — *person has one*, koh′ ɒying yiu ih′-go 各人°有一个°; — *man*, ko′-ko nying 個個人°; koh′ nying 各人°; — *kind*, me′ yiang 每樣; koh′ yiang 各樣; *take three of — kind*, koh′ yiang do′ sæn-go 各樣拿°三个°; me′ yiang do sæn′ go 每樣拿°三个°; *one to* —, ih′-go kah′-kyᶜi 一个°; *a dollar to* — *man*, koh nying′ ih-kwᶜe fæn-ping′ 各人° 一塊番餅

**EAGER,** tsᶜih′-sing 切心; — *expectation*, tsᶜih′-sing siang′-vông 切心想望; hyüih′-sing siang′-vông 血心想望

**EAR,** ng′-tô 耳°朵 (tô or to); *deaf* —, ng′-tô long′ 耳°朵聾; *ringing in the ears*, ng′-tô ᶜong-ᶜong′-hyiang 耳°朵閧閧響; — *ache*, ng′-tô tᶜong′ 耳°朵痛; *in at the right* — *out at the left* (*i. e.* inattentive), jing-tsah′ ng′-tô tsing′ tsia′-tsah ng′-to cᶜih′ 右°隻°耳°朵進左°隻°耳°朵出°; — *brush*, siao-sih′-ts 消息

*子*; — *pick*, leo′ ng-tô w̌æn′ 鏤耳°朵彎; — *ring*, gwænts′ 環子°; — *wax*, ng′-tô ò′ 耳°蒙°; *to lore the ear*, cᶜün′ ng′-tô ngæn′ 穿耳°朵°眼°; *an* — *of corn*, ih-ts′ loh-koh′ 一枝稑穀; ih-be′ loh-koh′ 一穗°稑穀

**EARLY,** tsao 早; — *in the day*, tsᶜing-tsao 清早; — *in the morning*, tsao′ tᶜin-liang 早天亮; — *and late*, or *morning and night*, tsao′-æn 早晏°; *come* —, tsao′-læ 早來

**EARN,** *to* dzæn 賺; — *money*, dzæn′ dong-din′ 賺銅錢°

**EARNEST,** nyih-sing 熱°心; hyüih′-sing 血心; ih′-sing ih′-i 一心一意; cün-sing′ cü-ts′ 專心致志; *in* —, nying′-tsing′ 認眞; *make an* — *effort*, nying′ ih′-kᶜeo kyᶜi′ 忍一口氣; — *at one work*, cün-kong′-gyi-z′ 專攻其事

**EARTH,** *the* di-gyiu′ 地球; *the ground*, di-yiang′ 地陽; *earth*, na-nyi′ 坭; nyi-tᶜu′ 泥土

**EARTHEN-WARE,** ngô′-ho 瓦貨

**EARTH-QUAKE,** di-cing′ 地震; tᶜin-yiao′ di-dong′ 天搖地動

**EARTH-WORM,** tsᶜoh′-zin, cᶜih-zin, or cᶜoh-zin, 曲蟺°; di-zen′ 地蠶

**EASE,** *at* en-tæn′ 安貼; hao 好; *no care*, m-sing′ m-z′ 無°心無°事; *to do with* —, tso leh ky'ing-kæn' 做 得° 輕 泛

EASE, *can you* — *me a little ?* ng' hao' peh ngô kw'un-s'-tin feh 你° 好 俾° 我 寬 舒 點 否°?

EASILY, yüong-yi' 容 易°; sang'-lih 省° 力

EAST, tong 東; — *side*, tong-pin' 東 邊; — *wind*, tong fong' 東 風; — *gate*, tong meng' 東 門

EASTWARD, hyiang-tong' 向 東; dziao-tong' 朝 東

EASY, yüong-yi 容易°; sang'-lih 省力; *not hard*, feh næn' 弗 難; *light*, ky'ing-yi' 輕 易°; *in* — *circumstances*, Weng-pao'-go 溫 飽 个°; keo' ky'üoh, keo' yüong' 彀 吃 彀 用; — *in treating others*, no-jün' 懦 善; — *in manners*, ts'ong-yüong' 從° 容; z-dzæ' 自 在

EAT, *to* ky'üoh 吃°; p'in 骗; — *rice or a meal*, ky'üoh væn' 吃° 飯; — *enough*, ky'üoh pao 吃° 飽; — *only vegetables* (as the Buddhists do), ky'üoh ts'æ' 吃° 菜; *can't* — *it*, ky'üoh'-feh-læ' 吃°弗 來; *don't like to* —, ga' k'co; — (as insects do), cü 蛀; *have eaten*, ky'üoh'-ko'-de 吃° 過 了°; p'in'-ko'-de 骗 過 了°

EATABLE, k'o-yi ky'üoh' 可 以 吃°

EATABLES, ky'üoh'-zih 吃° 食

EATING-HOUSE, tsiu'-kwun-tin' 酒 館 店; *small* —, væn-tin' 飯 店

EAVES, yin-deo' 簷 頭; — *of the house*, oh'-yin-deo' 屋 簷 頭

EAVES-DROPPER, *one who listens at the partition*, ih-pih t'ing' 隔° 壁 聽 (ih-go)

EBB-TIDE, t'e'-dziao 退 潮; loh-shü' 落 水°

EBONY, u-moh' 烏 木

ECCENTRIC *person*, kwæ-p'ih'-go nying 乖 僻 个° 人°; c'ih'-wu-gyi-le'-go nying 出 乎 其 類 个° 人°

ECHO, ing'-ky'i-go sing-hyiang' 應 起 个° 聲 響

ECLIPSE *of the sun*, wu-jih' 糊 日; jih-zih' 日 蝕; — *of the moon*, wu-yüih' 糊 月; yüih-zih' 月 蝕

ECLIPSE, wông-dao' 黃 道

ECONOMIZE, *to* tso-nying-kô 做 人° 家°; gyin'-iah 儉 約

ECONOMICAL, *saving*, gyin'-sang 儉 省; kyin'-sang 儉 省; keh; keh-sön' 合 算

ECSTATIC, hwun-hyi' ko-deo' 歡 喜 過 頭; ko'-ü hwun-hyi' 過 於 歡 喜

EDDY, bun-shü' 盤 水°; jün-shü' 旋 水° (ih-go)

EDGE, bông-pin' 旁 邊; pin-yin' 邊 沿; — *of a knife*, tao-fong' 刀 鋒; tao-k'eo' 刀 口; *has lost its* —, fong-deo' tih'-loh-de 鋒 頭 跌 落 了°

EDGE, *to* — *up*, yi-long'-ky'i 移 攏 去; yi-long'-læ 移 攏 來

EDGEWISE, *can't get a word in*

—, ih-kyü′ tu ts′æn′-feh-tsing′ 一句都申°弗進; ts′ah′ yin feh zông′ 插言弗上

EDGING, kwe′-ts 桂子; siang-diao′ 鑲條

EDICT, kao′-z 告示; *imperial* —, zông-yü′ 上諭; sing′-ts 聖旨; wông-pông′ 皇榜; tsiao′-shü 詔書; *the Sacred* —, Sing′-yü Kwông′-hyüing 聖諭廣訓

EDIFY, *to* — *him*, peh gyi tsing-ih′ 俾°其進益

EDIT, *to* ting′-tsing 訂正

EDITION, *the first* — (printed), di-ih′-ts′ing′- c′ih-go shü′ 第一次印出个°書; *the first* — (cut on blocks), ts′u k′eh′-c′ih-go shü′ 初刻出个°書

EDITOR, ting′-tsing-go cü′-kwu 訂正个°主顧

EDUCATE *him*, dzing-dziu′gyi-go dzæ-′oh′ 成就其个°才學°

EDUCATION, *good* ′oh-jih′ hao′ 學°術好; dzæ-′oh′ kwông′ 才學°廣; *a person of* —, yiu ′oh-veng′ go nying′ 有學°問个°人

EEL, mun 鰻; *field* —, wông-zin 黃鱔; nyi-ts′iu′ 泥鰍; jün′-yü 鱔魚 (ih-keng)

EFFACE, *to blot out*, du-diao′ 塗壞°; —(from the mind), mo-wu′ 模糊

EFFECT, *with what* — ? yiu soh′-go pin′-dong 有甚°麼°變動? yiu soh′-go seng-seh′ 有甚°麼°

生色? *no* —, vu-tsi′-ü-z′ 無濟于事; feh-c′ih′-seh 弗出色; *to have a good* — (as medicine), yiu yiao-nyiæn′ 有效驗; yiu ing′-′ao 有應效°; yiu ing′-nyiæn′ 有應驗; *the* — *of drought*, t′in ′en′-go yün-kwu 天旱个°緣故; *cause and* —, ing-ko′ 因果; *to see no* — *from one's instructions*, sô kao′ feh kyin yiao′ 所敎°弗見效; *bad* — *of misconduct* ( regarded as supernatural), ing-tsih′ 陰隲

EFFECTED, *he has* — *a great deal*, gyi sô tsoh′-we yiu hyü′-to seng-seh′ 其所作爲有許多生色; gyi sô tsoh-we yiu hyü′-to z-ken′ 其所作爲有許多事幹

EFFEMINATE, *womanish*, siao-nyiang′-deo ying 形°如小°娘; nyü′-siang-go 像°女相

EFFERVESCE, *to* p′u-c′ih′-læ; p′eng-c′ih′-læ 噴出來

EFFICACIOUS, ling-ing′-go 靈應个°; — *medicine*, ling-tæn′-miao-yiah′ 靈丹妙藥; — *deity*, ling-ing′ bu-sah′ 靈應菩薩

EFFICACY, gying-dao′ 劝道; lih-dao′ 力道; *has* —, yiu ling-ing′ 有靈應; *owing to the* — *of the medicine*, ky′ü′-leh yiah′-go gying′-dao 虧°得°藥个°劝道;— *of prayer*, tao-kao′-go lih-dao′ 禱告个°力道

EFFICIENT (as a person), vu yiu′ feh tao-kô′ 無冇弗到家; vu yiu′ feh dzing-kong′ 無冇弗成功

EFFIGY, *image*, ngeo′-ziang 偶像°; *straw man*, ts'ao′-kao′ nying′ 草絞°人°

EFFORT, *to make an* —, c'ih lih′ 出力; yüong lih′ 用力; *make a great* —, do′ c'ih′ lih 大°出力; 'eo-ky'i′-lih 盡°氣力; *make a strenuous mental* —, fah-veng′ yüong-kong 發憤用功; *united* —, dong-sing′ yiah-lih′ 同心恊力; dô-kô′ c'ih-lih′ 大°家出力

EFFRONTERY, tæ ô′-lin 厚°臉; 'eo-bi′ ô′-lin 厚皮了°臉; *what* —! ô′-lin tæ′-leh wô′-feh-læ′ 了臉趺得°話弗來!

EGG, dæn 蛋; *hen's* —, kyi-dæn′ 雞蛋; *duck's* —, ah′-dæn 鴨°蛋 (ih go)

EGG-PLANT, gyiæn 茄°

EIGHT, pah 八; — *times*, pah′ tsao, &c. 八次

EIGHTEEN, jih-pah′ 十八

EIGHTH, di-pah′ 第八

EIGHTY, pah′-jih 八十

EITHER *and or are expressed by* 'oh-tsia′ 或者° *or* wa-z′ 還°是 *used twice, thus:* — *great or small*, 'oh-tsia′ do, 'oh-tsia′ siao′ 或者°大或者°小; — *to-day or tomorrow*, wa-z kyih-mih wa-z ming-tsiao 還°是今°日°

還°是明朝; *I would not choose* —, ngô ih′-go tu kæn-feh-cong′ 我一个°都揀弗中 (cong or tsong); — *one*, feh-leng′ ah-li ih′-go 弗論阿裡一个°; ze-bin′ 'ah-li ih′-go 隨便何°處°一个°

EJECT, *to* ken′-c'ih 赶出; (*when done by an officer*) ky'ü-djoh′ 驅逐

ELABORATE, *adj.* si′-cü 細致 dzing-si′ 誠細

ELAPSE, *to* ko 過; *five years have elapsed*, ko′-leh ng′-nyin de 過得°五°年了°

ELASTIC, *springy*, neng-soh′ neng-sing′, 能縮能伸; neng-sing′ neng-geo′; — *tape or band*, kying′-kw'un ta′ 緊寬帶°

ELATED, teh′-i yiang′-yiang 得°意揚揚

ELBOW, siu-tsang-cü-deu′ 手腕°

ELDER, do-jü′ 大°如; — *brother*, ah-ko′ 阿哥; — *sister*, ah-tsi′ 阿姊

ELDER, *an* tsiang′-lao 長老

ELDERLY, kw'a lao′-de 快°老了°; bin-lao-kwun′.

ELDEST *son*, do ng′-ts 大°兒子; tsiang′-ts 長子; — *daughter*, do-nön′ 大°囡; tsiang′-nyü 長女

ELECT, *to* kæn′-shün 揀選; t'siao′-shün 挑選; *God's* —,

Jing-ming′ sô kæn′-shün-go nying′ 神明所揀選个°人°

ELECTRIC, *to receive an — shock,* din-ky′i′ jih-sing′, fah-kying′-de 電氣入身發驚了°

ELECTRICAL *machine,* fah-din′-ky′i-go ky′i′-ming 發電氣个°器皿

ELECTRICITY, din′-ky′i 電氣

ELEGANT, wô-li′ 華麗; me-li′ 美麗; — *colors,* ngæn-seh′ yin-li′ 顏色豔麗

ELEGY, wæn′-dz 輓詞 (ih-p′in)

ELEMENT, *the first principle,* nyün ti′-ts 原底子; peng′-tsih 本質; *the five* (Chinese) *elements,* ng′-ying 五°行; *air is the — we live in,* ky′i′ z ah-lah weh-ming′ go nyün-peng′ 氣是我°等°活命个°原本

ELEPHANT, ziang 象°; *white —* bah-ziang 白象°; *gray — ,* hwe-ziang 灰象° (ih-deo)

ELEPHANTIASIS, do-kyiah-fong′ 大°脚瘋

ELEVATE, *to exalt,* di-zông′-ky′i 提上去°; kao-kyü′ 高舉; kyü′-zông 舉上; sing-zông′ 升上; dæ-ky′ih′-zông 擡掣上; *to — the hand,* siu′ di-tæn′-ky′i 手提打°起; *to —* (something in the hand), di-kao′ 提高; di-zông′-ky′i 提上去°; — *the head,* dæ deo′ 擡頭

ELEVEN, jih-ih′ 十一°; — *o'clock,* jih-ih′ tin-cong 十一點鐘

ELEVENTH, *the* di jih-ih′ 第十一°; *the — month,* jih-ih′ yüih 十一月

ELICIT *to* ying′-c′ih-læ 引出來; — *his ideas,* ying gyi-go i-s′ c′ih′-læ 引其个°意思出來

ELLIPTICALLY, *to speak* ky′ih′-long kông′ 掣攏講°; soh′-long kông′ 縮攏講°

ELM, yü-jü′ 榆樹 (ih-cü)

ELOPE, *to* s-peng′ 私奔; s-dao′ 私逃; *the girl has eloped,* nyiang′-ts keng nying′ tseo′-de 娘子跟人°走了°

ELOQUENT, *having the power of moving the feelings,* we dong nying′-go dzing′ 會動人°个°情; *having the power of expression,* k′eo-neng′-zih-bin′ 口能舌辯; yiu k′eo′-dzæ 有口才

ELOQUENTLY, *to speak* kông′-leh k′eng′-ts′ih 講得°懇切

ELSE, ling-nga′ 另外°; i′-nga 意外°; bih 別; *have you something — ?* ling-nga′ yiu′ feb 另外°有否°? *excluding that, is there anything — ?* djü keh′-go ts-nga′ wa-yiu′ ma 除這个°之外°還°有嗎°? *somebody — ,* bih′ nying 別人°; *nobody — knows,* m′-teh bih-nying hyiao′-teh 沒°有°別人°曉得; *I was laughing at something — ,* sô siao′, ngô yiu bih′ i 所笑我有別意

ELSEWHERE, bih-c'ü' 別處; bih'
t'ah dï'-fông 別塌地方

ELUCIDATE, to kông'-ka ts'ing'-
t'ong' 講解清通

ELUDE, to yüong kyi'-ts'ah to'-bi
用計策躲避

EMACIATED, kweh'-seo jü-za' 骨
瘦如柴°

EMANCIPATE, to sih'-fông 釋放

EMBALM, to hyiang-liao' jih-s'-
foh'- cong 香料實尸腹中
(veng)

EMBANKMENT on a river bank,
kông-dông' 江°塘; — by the
sea, hæ'-dông 海塘; earth-
work, to 壋

EMBARGO, kying c'ih'-k'eo 禁
出口

EMBARK, to loh jün' 落船; zông
jün' 上船

EMBARRASS, to involve in per-
plexity, lin-le' 連累; ky'in-le'
率累; greatly perplexed, le-sah'-
de 累殺了°

EMBARRASSED through fear, gyü
hyih'-de 懼懾了°; — in speaking, kông'-shih gyüoh-gyüoh'-
ts'oh-ts'oh' 講式偈偈促促;
— in funds, siu'-deo kyih'-
kyü 手頭拮据; greatly ditto,
ky'üing-peh' 窘廹

EMBASSADOR, ky'ing-ts'a 欽差;
the persons attending an — , ze-
yün' 隨員

EMBELLISH, to tsông-sih' 裝飾;
tsah'-kwch hao' 紮刮好

EMBERS, smoldering fire, iu-iu' go
ho' 悠悠个°火

EMBEZZLE, to s-'ô' liao-yüong' 私
下°撩用; — money entrusted for
others, liao-yüong' kong-'ông'
nying'-ts 撩用公行銀子; —
the emperor's money, liao-yüong'
hyiang'-nying 撩用餉銀

EMBLEM, piao'-'ao 表號; — of
justice, piao'-'ao en'-dzông kong-
bing'-go i'-s 表號暗藏公平
个°意思

EMBOLDENS me, fông' ngô-go tæn'
放我个°胆

EMBRACE, to — in the arms, o-
tæn'-long; o'-leh bao'; — an opportunity, ts'ing'-kyi-we' 趁機
會; dzing' kyi-we' 乘機會;
embraced within, pao'-kwah dzæ-
ne' (ne or nen) 包括在內;
pao-kwah'-tsing 包括進

EMBROIDER, to siu hwô' 繡花;
tso' hwô' 做花; tso pang-ts' 做
繃子

EMBROIDERY, a piece of — , siu'
hwô p'in'-ts 繡花片子; —
shop, kwu'-siu-tin' 顧繡店; siu'-
hwô-tin' 繡花店

EMBROIL, to be-le' 被累; le'-
tsing-dzæ-ne' 累進在內

EMBRYO, dzing-yüing' 成孕°

EMERGE, to ts'ön-c'ih'-læ 竄出
來; — suddenly, ts'ön-ky'i'-læ
竄起來

EMERGENCY, kying'-kyih z-ken'
緊急事幹; prepare for an

—, bông-be′ wun′-kyih 防備緩
急; be-bæn′ iao′-kying iao′-
mæn 備辦要緊要慢
EMETIC, t′u′ yiah 吐藥
EMIGRATE to a foreign country,
ts′in-kyü′ nga-koh′ 遷居外°
國
EMINENT, kao-tsiah′ 高霄; kao-
kwe′ 高貴; — in scholarship,
kao-dzæ′ 高才; — official, kao-
kwun′-hyin′-tsiah 高官顯霄
EMIT, to fah′-c′ih 發出; to —light
(as a lamp), fah liang′ 發亮;
— light (as the sun or fire), fah-
kwông′ 發光; — sparks, pao′-
c′ih ho′-sing læ 爆 出 火星
來
EMOLUMENTS of office, (unlawful), siu-læ′-go fi′ 收來个°費;
the regular salary of officials,
fong′-loh 俸祿; what is given
outside of salary to prevent squeezing, yiang′-lin 養廉
EMOTIONS, the seven ts′ih′ dzing
七情; viz., pleasure, hyi 喜;
anger, nu 怒; grief, æ 哀;
joy, loh 樂; love, æ 愛; hatred,
u 惡; desire, yüoh 欲; to excite
the —, dong dzing′ 動 情
EMPEROR, wông-ti′ 皇帝; wông-
zông′ 皇上; the present —,
tông-kying′ wông-zông′ 當今
皇上; the present — (is styled),
Kwông-jü′ wông-ti′ 光緒皇
帝; the deceased —, sin-wông′
先皇

EMPHASIZE in reading, sing-ing′
doh-leh djong′ 聲音讀得°重
EMPHATICALLY, kông′-leh sah′-
pô 講°得°煞霸; kông′-leh
kyih′-jih 講°得°砝實
EMPIRE, the Chinese —, Cong-
koh′ 中國; T′in-′ô′ 天下°; Da-
ts′ing′-koh 大清國; Da-dông′-
koh 大唐國
EMPLOY, to yüong 用; — means,
yüong fông-fah′ 用方法; —
one's time, yüong kong′ 用工;
I — my time in study, ngô yüong
kong′ doh shü′ 我用工讀書
EMPLOYMENT, any thing which
engages one's time, z-ken′ 事幹;
z-t′i′ 事體; business, ′ông-tông′
行°當; occupation, z-nyih′ 事
業; ′ông-nyih′ 行°業; in steady
—, tang-dziang′ 打常; dziang-
nyin′-go 長年个°; — for a
short time, ts′eh-tön′ 撮短; tön-
kong′ 短工
EMPORIUM, commercial sea-port,
mô′-deo 馬頭; market-town,
cing′-deo 鎮頭
EMPOWER, to kao′-fu gyün-ping′
交°付權柄
EMPRESS, the wông-′eo′ 皇后;
— dowager, wông-t′a′-′eo 皇
太°后
EMPTY, k′ong 空; hyü 虛; —
place, k′ong di′-fông 空地方;
— talk, k′ong′-deo-shih-wô′ 空
頭說話; hyü-wô′ 虛話 now
means deceitful talk; — or mean-

ingless characters, hyü z′-ngæn 虛字眼°

EMPTY, to tao′-c‘ih 倒 出; tao′-diao 倒 去°; — entirely, tao′-k‘ong 倒空; tao′ ken-zing′ 倒 乾 淨°

EMULATE, to ts‘iang′ zông-zin′ 搶 上 前°; — him, ken′-gyi-zông, ih-yiang′ 趕 其 上 一 樣; — another's skill or strength, pi′-sæ 比賽

ENABLE, to dzu-lih′ 助力; pông-lih′ 帮 力; he enabled me to do it, gyi′ dzu ngô′-go lih′ hao tso′ 其 助 我 个° 力 好 做

ENACT, to — law, lih′ ih-diao fah′ 立 一 條 法; — laws, shih′-lih lih-fah′ 設° 立 律 法

ENAMORED, ts‘ih′-sing-go siang-s 切 心 个° 相 思; ts‘ib-sing-go ky‘i′-mo 切 心 个° 企慕; — till sick, sang siang-s′-bing 生 相 思 病

ENCAMP, to tsah-ying′ 紮° 營; tsah-ying dza′ 紮° 營寨

ENCAMPMENT (of an army), ying-bun′ 營 盤; ying-dza′ 營寨

ENCHANT, to hold by a spell, mi-weng′ 迷 魂; bewitch by giving something, ‘ô-kwu′ 下° 蠱

ENCHANTED, jih mi-weng′-dzing 入 迷 魂 陣

ENCHANTER, one who enchants by sorcery, yüong′-zia-fah′-go 用 邪° 法 个°; — (a priest), yiu-fông′-seng 遊 方 僧

ENCIRCLE, to we-cün′ 圍 轉; we-kw‘eng′ 圍 困; we-djü′ 圍 住

ENCOMIUM, peo-tsiang′ shih-wô′ 褒 獎 說 話

ENCOMPASS, to dön-ky‘ün′ we-djü′ 團 圈 圍 住; dön-ky‘ün′ kw‘eng′-djü 團 圈 困 住

ENCOUNTER, the two armies had an —, liang′ pin tang′ ih-we′ ko′-de 兩 邊 打 一 回 過 了°

ENCOUNTER, to nyü-djoh′ 遇 着°; p‘ong′-djoh 逢 着°

ENCOURAGE, to min′-li 勉 勵; — him, tsông′ gyi-go tæn′ 壯 其 个° 膽

ENCROACH, to dzin′-dzin tsin′ 漸 漸 佔; bu-bu′ tsin-tsing′ 步步 佔進; sea encroaches on the land, hæ′ iao t‘eng di′ 海 要 吞 地

ENCUMBERED, burdened, t‘o-t‘o′-ts‘i-ts‘i 拖 拖 累 累; bound, dzin′-ziao-de 纏 繞 了°

END, deo′ 頭 (ih); both ends, liang′ deo 兩 頭; turn the other —, diao deo′ 調 頭; from one — to the other, dzong-deo′ ts-vi′ 從 頭 至 尾; the conclusion, kyih′-sah 結 煞; from the beginning to the —, dzong ky‘i-deo tao kyih′-sah 從 起 頭 到 結 煞; ditto carefully, i-deo′-ngeng′-tsih 依 頭 痕 節; what will the — be? dza kyih′-sah ni 怎° 結 煞 呢? come to a bad — (death), ̆wa min′ ngæn 姦° 眉′眼; ̆wa kyih′-gyüoh 姦° 結

局；m kyih'-gyüoh 無° 結局

ENDANGER, *to* fông' læ ngwe-hyin' di'-fông 放在° 危險地方；

' — *one's life*, pô' sing'-ming fông' læ ngwe-hyin di-fông 把性命 放在° 危險地方；sing'-ming do'-leh yiang-hyi'-hyi 性命拿° 得° 羊戲戲

ENDEAVOR, *to* dzing sing-lih' 盡 心力；*I endeavored but did not succeed,* ngô sing-lih'-dzing'-ko-de, dæn'-z tso'-feh-tao 我心力 盡過了但是做弗到

ENDLESS, m̄ gyüong'-dzing 無° 窮盡；m̄ dzing'-gyi 無° 盡期； —*quarrelling,* nao-nao'peh-hyin' 嚊° 鬧不休

ENDOW *with a dower,* be kô'-tsông 備嫁° 粧

ENDURANCE, *beyond* 'en-yüong'- feh-djü'-de 含容弗住了°

ENDURE, *to* a 挨；— *a day at a time,* ib-nyih' a' ih-nyih' 一日° 挨一日°；*can't* — *it* (living so), a'-feh-ko'-ky'i 挨弗過去°； *ditto* (can't get along with), ah-feh-ko'- ky'i 壓° 弗過去°； yüong'-feh-ko'-ky'i 容弗過 去°；tông'-feh-djü 當弗住； *ditto* (i.e. can't be patient), neh'-feh-djü 納弗住；næ'-feh-djü' 耐弗住；— *patiently,* jing'-næ ziu 忍耐受；— *suffering,* ziu-kw'u' 受苦；*ditto patiently,* we nying t'ong' 會忍° 痛；— *patiently* (as reproach), jing'-

ky'i t'eng-sing 忍氣吞聲； — *pain,* ngao-t'ong' 熬痛；— *without complaint,* 'en yüong 含 容；— *silently,* neh'-leh sing-deo' ho 納得° 心頭火

ENDURING, *lasting,* næ-kyiu' 耐 久；iu-kyiu 悠久；dziang-kyin' 長久

ENDWISE, *on end,* dzih-teng' 直 竪°；*place* —, teng'-ky'i-fông' 竪° 起放

ENEMY, ün-kô' 寃家°；te'-deo 對頭；dziu-nying 讐人°； *military* —, dziu-dih' 讐敵；*the opposing army,* dib-ping 敵兵

ENERGY, *force,* lih 力；*to work with* —, dzing'-lih tso' 盡力做； *do with whole heart, and strength,* dzing'-sing gyih-lih tso' *or* dzing-sing-dzing-lih tso 盡心竭力 做；*to rouse one's energies,* teng'-ky'i tsing'-jing 頓起精神

ENERVATE, *to* s'-teh nyün'-ziah' 使得軟° 弱；s-teh t'eh-lih' 使得脫力

ENFEEBLED, tsing'-lih sæ'-de 精 力衰了°；*mentally* —, tsing'-jing sæ'-de 精神衰了°

ENFORCE, *to* — *obedience,* pih'-leh i-dzong' 逼勒依從；— *his obedience,* ngang-k'ô' gyi i-dzong' 硬拿° 其依從

ENGAGE, *to* ding-jih' 定實；wô-hao' 話好；iah'-hao 約好； *to promise,* ing-dzing' 應承；*I have already engaged another man,* ih-go nying′ ngô yi′-kying ding-jih′-de 一 个° 人° 我 已 經 定 實 了°; — *three workmen,* ding sæn′-go kong-nying′ 定 三 个 工 人°; — *a boat,* t'ao′ ih-tsah jün′ 討 一 隻 船; *the boat is engaged,* jün t'ao′-loh-de 船 討 落 了°; *I am engaged at present,* keh-zông′-li ngô yiu z-ken′ 這° 時° 裎 我 有 事 幹

ENGINE, *steam* 一, ky'i′-kyi 氣 機; long-deo′ 龍 頭

ENGINE-ROOM, long-deo-kæn′ 龍 頭 間; t'ih-ts'ông′ 鐵 倉

ENGLISHMAN, Da-Ing′ nying 大 英 人°; Ing-kyih′-li nying′ 英 吉 利 人°; *English cloth,* Da-Ing c'ih′-go pu′ 大 英 出 个 布

ENGRAVE, *to* — *on metals,* zen 鏨; k'eh 刻; — *on stone, wood, precious stones, metals,* zoh (or joh) 鑿; k'eh 刻; tiao 雕; — *characters,* k'eh z 刻 字; — *an image,* tiao ngeo′-ziang 雕 偶 像°; — *on the heart,* k'eh læ sing′-li 刻 在° 心 裎; k'eh-kweh′ ming-sing′ 刻 骨 銘 心

ENGRAVER *on metals,* zen′-hwô-s-vu′ 鏨 花 司 務; — *on wood,* tiao-hwô′-s-vu′ 雕 花 司 務; tiao-k'eh′-ziang 雕 刻 匠°; — *of characters,* k'eh-z′-s-vu′ 刻 字 司 務; — *on stone,* hwô-ts'ao′-zah-s-vu′ 花 草 石° 司 務

ENGROSS, *this engrosses my time,*

ngô-go kong-fu′ tsih p'e′-fu keh′-go yüong-dziang′ 我 个° 工 夫 只 配 副 這° 用 塲; — *one's attention,* ih-sing′ ts'ong-ih-yüoh′· 一 身 充 一 役 (ts'ong or c'ong); ih-dzing tsi′-lu 一 程 躋 路

ENIGMA, me-ts′ 謎 子; — *on a lantern,* teng-me′ 燈 謎

ENJOIN, *to* coh′-fu 囑 附; ting-coh′ 叮 囑

ENJOY, *to* hyiang 享; — *the happiness of old age,* hyiang lao′-foh 享 老 福; *to take satisfaction in,* ziu′-yüong 受 用; *I* — *wearing this hat,* keh′ ting mao′-ts ta′-leh ngô ziu′-yüong 這° 頂 帽 子 戴° 得 我 受 用; *I enjoyed the meeting to-day very much,* kyih-mih′ li′-pa ngô ting′ ziu-yüong′ 今° 日° 禮 拜° 我 頂 受 用

ENJOYMENT, kw'a′-loh 快° 樂; — *in absence of care,* kw'a′-weh 快° 活

ENLARGE, *to* tso-leh do′-tin′ 做 得° 大° 點; — *upon,* kông′-leh dziang′-si′ 講 得° 詳 細; t'e-k'æ′ kông 推 開 講°; — *one's experience,* kwông-kyin′-veng 廣 見 聞

ENLIGHTEN, *to* fah′-ming, 發 明; *to* — *the mind,* k'æ-sing′ 開 心; k'æ-ky'iao′ 開 竅; p'o-nyü′ 破 愚

ENMITY, dziu-hyih or dziu-ky'ih 仇 隙; ün′-ky'i 冤 氣

ENNOBLE, *to* hyiang-zông'-ky'i 向上去°

ENORMOUS, ko'-ü do' 過於大°; *enormously wicked*, ôh'-gyih 惡極; ôh' tao pin' 惡到邊

ENOUGH, keo 够; tsoh 足; *is it —?* keo'-de feh 够了°否°? *exactly —*, tsing'-keo 儘°够; *ditto* (hence definite), k'eo-feng'-k'eo-su' 扣分扣數; *— and some over*, fu'-shü 富庶; nông-shü'; yiu-yü' 有餘

ENQUIRE, *to ask*, meng 問°; *go in and —*, tseo'-tsing meng ih'-sing 走進問°一聲

ENRAGE, *to* kyih'-leh nu' fah'-ts'ong-kwun' 激得°怒髮冲冠 *lit.*, so that the hair will rise and lift the hat from the head; nu'-ky'i ts'ong-t'in' 怒氣冲天

ENRICH, *to become rich*, fah dzæ' 發財; *— one's self at others' expense*, seng-jing'-li-kyi' 損人利己; *ditto by foul means*, meo-t'eng' nying-kô' 謀吞人°家°; *— land*, üong din' 壅田

ENROLL, *to — as soldiers' and candidates' names*, zông ts'ah-ts 上册子

ENSIGN, gyi-'ao' 旗號

ENSLAVE, *to* tông nu-boh' yüong 當奴僕用; ts'ong nu' 充奴

ENSNARE, *to — a person*, hong' nying' zông tông' 哄人°上當; long-loh nying 籠絡人°; hong nying' zông keo' 哄人°上鈎; yiu' nying loh ky'ün-t'ao' 誘人°落圈套

ENSUE, *to* keng'-leh-læ 跟得°來; ze'-leh-læ 隨得°來; *bad things certainly will —*, ze'-'eo tsong yiu wa-z' 隨後終有孬事

ENSURE, *to* s'-teh ih-ding' 使得一定; *to guaranty*, pao-hao' 包好; *— a cure*, pao-i' 包醫; *— deliverance from trouble*, pao' c'ih deo' 包出頭

ENTANGLE, *to* dzin-long' tang-kyih' 纏攏打結; *foot entangled in a thread*, kyiah' sin dzin'-tih 脚線纏的; kyiah sin pang'-tih 脚線綳的

ENTER, *to* tseo'-tsing 走進; *— the church*, jih kyiao' 入教; *— on life favorably*, tang gyin-kw'eng' 打乾坤; ting'-t'in-lih-di' 頂天立地; *— the priesthood*, c'ih-kô' 出家°; *— the army*, deo-kyüing' 投軍; deo-ts'ong' 投充; *— on the book*, zông bu'-ts 上簿子; teng bu'-ts 登簿子; *— a name* (of person or ship), kwô 'ao' 掛號

ENTERPRISE, *new undertaking*, sing-hying' z-ken' 新興事幹; *to start an —*, tang'-ih-fæn' gyin-kw'eng' 打一翻乾坤

ENTERPRISING, we sing hying' z-ken' go 會新興事幹个°; yiu cü-üong' 有智勇; be-bun' nying-k'ah 陪伴客人°

ENTERTAIN *guests*, be-bun′nying-k‘ah 陪伴客人°; *to receive*, we 會; tsih′-dæ 接待; — *well (i. e. in talking)*, dæ k‘ah′ dæn-t‘u′ bao 待客談吐好; — *hospitably*, kw‘uu-dæ′ nying-k‘ah′ 欵待客人°

ENTERTAINMENT, *feast*, tsiu′-zih 酒席

ENTHRONE *him*, t‘e gyi′ teng-we′ 推其登位

ENTHUSIASTIC, ky‘i byüih′-sing 起血心

ENTICE, *to* ying′-yiu 引誘

ENTIRE, *perfect*, djün-be′ 全備; *it is* — *(i. e. all here)*, long′-tsong kæ′-tih 攏總在°; *an* — *orange*, tsing-ko′ kyüih′-ts 正個橘子; *an* — *chicken*, tsiung′-tsah kyi′ 全隻雞

ENTIRELY, djün-jün′ 全然; ‘o-jün′ 和然; — *forgotten*, djün-jün′ môung-kyi′-de 全然忘記了°

ENTITLED, ing-kæ′-go 應該个°; — *to receive*, li′-tông zin′ 理當受; ing-tông′ teh-go 應當得个°

ENTOMOLOGY, k‘ao′-kyiu djong-dzi′ ‘oh-veng′ 考究虫豸學問

ENTRAILS, du′-dziang 肚腸

ENTRANCE, tseo′-tsing-go lu′ 走進个° 路 — *of the river*, kông-k‘eo′ 江口; — *and exit*, c‘ih-jih′-ts lu′ 出入之路

ENTRAP, *he wishes to* — *you*, gyi iao ng′ zông-tông′ 其要你° 上當

ENTRAPPED, zông-tông′-de 上當了°; loh-ky‘ün′-t‘ao′-de 落圈套了°

ENTREAT, *to* gyiu-k‘eng′ 求懇 gyiu-ky‘ih′ 求乞

ENTRUST, *to* kao-dæ′ 交代; — *to*, t‘oh′-fu 託付; — *to an inferior*, fu′-t‘oh 付託; — *an important matter*, djong′-t‘oh 重託

ENTRY, *a narrow hall*, long-dông′ 衖堂; *central hall*, cong-kæn′ 中間°

ENTWINE, *to* dzin′-ziao 纏繞

ENUMERATE, *to count*, su′-su-k‘en′ 數數看; kyin′-kyin-k‘en′ 檢檢看

ENVELOP *or* ENVELOPE *for a letter*, sing-k‘oh 信壳; sing-fong 信封; fong-dong′ 封筒; sing-t‘ao 信套

ENVELOP, *to wrap*, pao 包; *to encase*, t‘ao′-tsing 套進

ENVIABLE, *he is* —, peh nying′ ky‘i′-gyi-feh-ko′ 俾° 人° 氣其弗過

ENVIOUS, sang dzih-tu′-sing 生° 嫉妬心; teh-teh-dong′; ky‘i′-feh-ko′ 氣弗過

ENVOY, koh-s′ 國使; ts‘a-kwun′ 差官 (ih-we)

ENVY *n.* tu′-gyi-sing 妬忌心

ENVY, *to* ky‘i′-feh-ko 氣弗過;

*I* — *him*, ngô ky'ï'-gyi-feh-ko' 我 氣 其 弗 過

EPIDEMIC, z-tsing' 時 症; z-yüoh'-bing 時 疫 病; ẃeng-bing' 瘟 病

EPISCOPAL *church*, Kyin-toh' kong'-we 監 督 公 會

EPISTLE, shü-sing' 書 信; sing'-tsah 信 札; *Paul's* —, Pao'-lo shü-sing' 保 羅 書 信

EPITAPH, veng'-li-go pe-kyi' 墳 裡 个° 碑 記

EPOCH, siang-kah'-go z-'eo' 相 隔 个° 時 候

EQUAL, or *about* — *in age*, dong-nyin' siang-shü' 同 年 相 歲°; — *in age and rank*, bing'-teng 並 等; bing'-kyin 並 肩; dong-pe' 同 輩; — *in size*, ih-yiang' do' 一 樣 大°; *ditto* (as potatoes, apples &c.), diao-yüing' 調 勻; — *parts*, kyüing-yüing' 均 勻; — *value*, tso' kô'-din 同° 價° 錢°; — *days and nights*, tsiu'-yia bing 晝 夜° 平; — *weight*, ih-yiang djong' 一 樣 重; *I am not* — *to it*, ngô lih' sô feh-gyih' 我 力 所 弗 及; *you are not* — *to him*, ng feh gyih'-jü gyi' 你° 弗 及 其; *you are* — *to him*, ng sæ'-ko-jü gyi 你° 賽 過 如 其; *make them* — (in size), tso'-ieh diao-yüing' 做 得° 調 勻

EQUALLY, *divide them* —, kyüing-feng' 均 分; feng'-leh diao-yüing' 分 得° 調 勻

EQUANIMITY, sing-seh'-feh-dong' 聲 色 弗 動; *with perfect* —, c'ü'-ts t'æ'-jün 處 之 泰 然

EQUATOR, ts'ih-dao' 赤 道

EQUILIBRIUM, bing-ts'ing' 平 稱; t'in-bing' 天 平

EQINOX, *vernal* —, c'ing-feng' 春 分; *autumnal* —, ts'iu-feng' 秋 分

EQUIPPED, *fully* (arms prepared), kyüing-tsông' zi-be'-liao 軍 裝 齊 備 了

EQUITABLE, kong-dao' 公 道; kong-bing' 公 平

EQUIVALENT, *adj.* te'-diao 對 調; — *expressions*, liang'-kyü shih'-wô i'-s siang-dong' 兩 句 說 話 意 思 相 同; *to return an* — (as for a present received), wæn li' 還 禮

EQUIVOCAL, 'en'-wu-dao'go 含 糊 道 个°; *borrow the shadow of excuse* or *reason*, tsia'-ing go 借° 因 个°

EQUIVOCATE, *to* ing-yiang'-gæ' 陰 陽 戲; kông'-leh 'en-weng'-go 講 得° 含 混 个°; kông tsia'-ing-go shih-wô' 講 借° 因°个° 說 話; kông 'en-wu-dao'-go shih-wô' 講 含 糊 道 个° 說 話; — *in answering*, (lit. lean upon the question), gæ ing' 戲 因

ERA, nyin-'ao' 年 號 (nyin, the year of the reign, 'ao, the year of the cycle); *the Christian* —, Yiæ-su kyüông-shü' 耶 穌 降 世

ERADICATE, *to* lin keng' bah-ky'i' 連根拔去°

ERASE, *to — with a pen*, du-diao' 塗壞°; — *with a knife*, ts'æn'-diao 鑷壞°

ERE, zin 前°; — *he comes*, gyi, vi-læ'-ts-zin' 其未來之前°; — *long*, peh kyiu' 不久

ERECT, *to* jü 竪; jü'-ky'i 竪起; — *a house*, jü oh' 竪屋; — *a shed of matting or branches*, tah bang' 搭棚; — *a stage*, tah dæ' 搭臺

ERECT, dzih 直; pih'-dzih 筆直; *standing* —, pih'-dzih lih'-tong 筆直立當°; *sit* —, 'pih'-t'ing zo' 筆挺坐°

ERMINE *skin*, nying-c'ü'-bi 銀鼠皮

ERR, *to wander from the right way*, tseo ts'ô' lu 走乂路; tseo' ts'o 走錯; — *in judgment*, ts'o'-cü'-i 錯主意; kyin'-sih dzæn 見識賺

ERRAND, *an* ih yiang ts'a-s' 一樣差使; *I want you to do an* 一, ngô yiu ih-yiang ts'a-s' iao ng tso' 我有一樣差使要你°做

ERRAND-BOY, ts'a-dong'-go nying 差動个°人°; ts'a-dong'-kyi-go 差動計个°; ts'a-s' 差使; t'ing-ts'a-go nying 聽差个°人°

ERRATA, ngo-z' 訛字; ts'o' z 錯字

ERRATIC, ying-tsong'-vu-ding' 行踪無定

ERRONEOUS, ts'o 錯; yi-tön' 異端; zia 邪°; — *doctrine*, yi-tön'-go dao'-li 異端个°道理

ERROR, ts'o'-c'ü 錯處; ko'-shih 過失; ko'-tön 過端; sih'-tsiah 失着°

ERUPTION *on the skin*, le 累; *a volcano in* —, ho'-sæn læ-tih p'eng'-c'ih-læ 火山現°在°噴出來

ESCAPE, *to* dao-tseo' 逃走; *already escaped*, dao-t'eh' de 逃脱了°; *to — punishment*, bi-ko ying-vah' 避過刑罰

ESCORT, *to* (*as a mark of attention*), song 送; be 陪; *to protect on a journey*, wu-song' 護送

ESOPHAGUS, zih-kwun 食管

ESPECIAL, di-ih' 第一; deo-ih' 頭一; *of — importance* di-ih' iao'-kying 第一要緊; *you will pay — attention*, ng iao di-ih' liu-sing' 你°要第一留心

ESPOUSE, *to affiance*, ding-ts'ing' 定親; *to wed*, tso ts'ing' 做親

ESSAY, *a literary* —, ih-p'iu leng' 一篇論; *a moral* —, ky'ün' shü-veng 勸世文

ESSAY, *to try*, s'-s-k'en' 試試看; *to make a trial of*, s'-ih-s 試一試;

ESSENCE, *constituent qualities of any thing*, sing'-tsih 性質; — (as of beef), tsih'-shü 汁水°; — *of ginger*, kyiang-tsih' 薑汁; *fragrant —* , hyiang-tsih' 香汁 vulgarly called hyiang-shü' 香水°

ESSENTIAL, *cannot be dispensed with*, ky'üih'-feh-læ-go 缺弗來个°; hyih'-feh-læ-go 歇弗來个°; siao'-feh-teh-go 少弗得个°

ESTABLISH, *to* kyin-kwu' 堅固; *to make him* or *it stable*, peh' gyi lih lao' 俾° 其 立定°; *to institute*, shih'-lih 設 立; kyin'-lih 建立

ESTATE, *condition*, di'-we 地位; *houses and lands*, ts'æn'-nyih 產業; *shops* &c., kyi-nyih' 基業

ESTEEM, *to* k'en'-djong 看重; ky'i'-djong 器重

ESTEEMED, *he is to be —* , gyi dziah-djong'-go 其 着重个°

ESTIMATE, *to* kwu-kwu'-k'en 估估看; — *the price*, kwu kô'-din 估價°錢°; — *present value*, z-dzih' kwu-kô' 時值估價°

ESTRANGE, *to become estranged*, sang su'-ky'i-læ 生° 疏起來; — *entirely*, su 疏; — (another) li-kyin' 離 間

ETERNAL, *without end*, üong'-yün 永遠; üong'-kwu ts'in-ts'iu' 永古千秋; vu gyüong'-dzing

無窮盡; *without beginning or end*, vu-s'-vu-cong' (cong or tsong) 無始無終; — *life*, üong-yün'weh-ming' 永遠活命; *ditto* (in the Taoist sense), dziang-seng' peh'-lao 長生不老

ETHICS, leng-djông'-ts dao' 倫常之道

ETIQUETTE, li 禮; *the rules of —* , li'-fah 禮法; *to observe ditto*, siu li'-fah 守禮法; *book on —* , li'-kyi shü' 禮記書

ETYMOLOGY, *work on —* , shih'-veng 說文 (ih-ts'ah, ih-bu)

EULOGY, *a* ib-p'in' ts'ing-tsæn'-go veng' 一篇稱讚个°文

EUNUCH, t'a-kæn' 太°監°; — *from birth*, dong-ts'-lao 童子老

EUPHONY, diao-'ó' sing-ing'-go 調和聲°音个°

EVACUATE *the city*, t'e'-c'ih dzing' 退出城

EVADE, *to* to 躲; bi 避; to'-ko 躲過; bi'-ko 避過; — *difficulties*, to næn 躲難; — *the payment of debt*, to tsa' 躲債°; — *by putting upon another*, t'e-ẃe 推諉; — *consequences*, sia ken-yi' 卸° 干係

EVANGELICAL *doctrine*, foh'-ing tsing dao' 福音真道

EVAPORATE, *to pass off in vapor*, ky'i sæn'-k'æ siu-zông 氣散開收上; c'ih-ky'i' 出氣; — *by the sun*, sa' sao 曬° 燥; — *by the fire*, hong sao' 烘燥

EVASIVE *answer*, 'en-weng' we-teh' 含混回答

EVEN, *level*, bing 平; bing-dzih' 平直; — *numbers*, sông-su' 雙數; — *tempered*, sing-bing' ky'i-'o 心平氣和; 'o-bing' sing'-kah 和平性格; *now we are* —, næn'-kæn hao tang bing-ts'ih 現°在°好打平尺; ah'-lah ts'ô bing-kyiao'-de, 我°等°扯平交了°

EVEN *you were there*, ng tao' yia we læ'-kæn 你°倒也°爲在°彼°; *he* — *would not wash his hands*, lin siu tu feh-k'eng gyiang 連手都弗肯洗°; — *if you whip him he does not fear*, ziu-z tang' gyi yia feh p'ô' 就是打其也°弗怕

EVENING, yia-deo' 夜°頭; yia-tao' 夜°到; yia-mæn-den' 夜°晚°頭; *toward* —, yia-kw'a 夜°快°; *come this* —, *after you have eaten supper*, kyih-mih' yia'-tao yia'-væn ky'üoh'-ko læ 今°日°夜°到夜°飯吃過來

EVENLY, bing 平; *regularly*, zi 齊°; zi-jih' 齊°集; *smoothly (as paint)*, yüing 勻; yüing-zing' 勻淨; *rub it on* —, k'a'-leh diao-yüing' 揩°得°調勻

EVENT, z-ken' 事°幹; z-t'i' 事°體; *joyful* —, hyi'-z 喜事; *a joyful* — *happened to us to day*, kyih-mih' ah-lah teh'-djoh ih-yiang' hyi'-z 今°日°我°等°得着°一樣喜事; kyih-mih' ah-lah k'æ-sing hwô' 今°日°我°等°開心花; *mournful* —, sông-sing'-go z-ken' 傷心个°事幹; *future* —, vi-læ'z or mi-læ'z 未來事; *at all events, you will come*, se-tsih' z-ka' dæn-z ng' iao læ' 雖只如°此°, 但是你要來

EVENTFUL, *that was an* — *year*, keh ih-nyin' do-siao' z-t'i' væn'-leh-kying 這°一年大°小事體繁得°緊

EVER, *always*, peh'-djông 不常; dziang-t'ong' 長通; *have you* — *met him?* dzong-ziu'yiu we-djoh'-gyi-ko' ma 從前°有會着°其過嗎°? — *since that*, dzong-ts' yi-læ 從此以來; z-ts' ts-'eo' 自此之後; *for* — *and* —, tao shü'-shü dæ'-dæ 到世世代代

EVERGREEN *trees*, feh we kw'u'-go jü' 弗會枯个°樹

EVERLASTING, üong'-yün 永遠; m gyüong'-dzing 無窮盡; — *fire*, üong'-feh-u'-go ho' 永弗熄°个°火

EVERY, me 每; koh 各; — *day*, me' nyih 每日°; nyih-nyih' 日°日°; — *one takes care of himself*, koh' nying kwun zi' 各人°管自°; — *body*, cong' nying 衆人°; — *body says*, da-tsong' wô' 大°衆話; ko'-ko nying 個個人°; *goods of* — *kind*, pah'-yiang

ho'-veh 百樣貨物；— *one
has his own idea,* koh' yiu koh' i
各有各意

EVERY-WHERE, koh'-c'ü 各處；
tao'-c'ü 到處；c'ü-c'ü 處處；
koh-tao'-c'ü 各到處；koh-
tao'-koh-c'ü 各到各處；'en'-
tao-c'ü'; koh'-koh-loh-loh' 角°
角° 落落 (*lit.* in every corner.);
*I have looked* — *and cannot find
it,* ngô koh'-c'ü zing', æu zing'-
feh-d'jh' 我各處尋° 都尋°
弗着°

EVIDENCE, *conclusive proof,* ts'ng'-
kyü 証據；bing-kyü' 憑據；
jih-bing' jih-kyü 實憑實據；
*testimony,* te'-tsing 對証；*ocular*
—, kyin'-tsing 見証；— *in a
case,* k'eo'-kong 口供

EVIDENT, *have proof,* yiu'-bing
yiu-kyü' 有憑有據；*clearly
to be seen,* hyin'-kyin 顯見；
ming-tông'-tông hao k'en'-kyin
明當當好看見

EVIL, oh 惡；*to do* —, troh oh' 作
惡；*forsake* —, oh' z-ken' ky'i'-
diao 惡事幹棄了°；*forsake
the* —, *follow the good,* kæ-oh'-
dzong-jün' 改惡從善；*I
certainly have no* —*inter's against
you,* ngô bing'-m-neh' oh'-i dæ
ng' 我並無° 惡意待你°；
— *spirit,* oh' kyü 惡鬼°；mo-
kwe' 魔鬼 (ih-gɔ)；Mo kwe
in the Bible stands for The Evil
One；*return* — *for* —, yi-oh'

pao-oh 以惡報惡；yiu'-dziu
pao-dziu' 有讎報讐；*return* —
*for good,* yi-oh' pao-teh' 以惡
報德；eng-tsiang' dziu-pao'
恩將讎報；*return good for*
—, yi-teh' pao-oh' 以德報惡；
— *star,* hyüong sing' 凶星；
*carry* — *reports,* pun-teo' z'-fi
搬兜是非；pun-cü' 搬嘴

EWE, ts'-yiang' 雌羊 (ih' tsah)
EWER, miu-shü-bing' 面水瓶
EXACT, *accurate,* cing 准；*my
clock is very* —, ngô go cong'
ting cing' 我個鐘頂准；
*precise,* en'-pæn-ts 摁板子

EXACTLY, k'eo'-k'eo 扣扣；
tsing 真；— *right,* ih-ngæn'-feh-
ts'o' 一點弗錯；'ao-li'-feh-
ts'o' 毫厘弗錯；'ao'-feh-t'e'-
ɪ-en 毫弗推斑；*do not
agree,* shü-vi' ts'o'-ih-ngæn' 些°
微差'一點；sao-we' feh-te'
稍為弗對；*corresponds* —,
'eo-feng'-'eo-su' 侯分侯數；
feng-ngæn'-feng-shing 分眼'分
榫；ky'iah'-k'eo；— *suits my
taste* (as food), keh-go' mi-dao
te ngô zih-sing ky'iah-k'eo 這°
個味° 道對我食性個°；
— *what I wanted,* sih'-vong ngô-
go i' 適逢我個° 意

EXAGGERATE, *to* kông-ko-deo' 講°
過頭；hah'-sæn-wô'-shü 嚇山
話水°

EXAGGERATED *talk,* vu-ky'i'-
deng-deng shih-wô' 霧氣騰

騰 說 話 ; — *boasting,* c'ô'-dæn sbih-kw'ch' 扯 誕 說 闊

EXALT *him,* tseng gyi' zông' 尊 其 上 ; dæ-gyi' kao' 擡 其 高 ; — *above merit,* dæ leh pun' t'io kao' 擡 得° 半 天 高

EXAMINE, *to* dzô-ts'ah' 查察; t'i'-ts'ah 體察 ; nying 膁 ; — *one's-self,* zi dzô'-ts'ah zi' 自° 查 察 自° ; — *for a degree,* k'ao'-s 考 試 ; — *pupils,* k'ao' 'oh-sang-ts' 考 學 生° 子 ; — *into the nature of things,* keh veh' 格 物 ; poh veh' 博 物 ; — (as an offender), keng-dzô' 跟 查 ; bun-dzô' 盤 查 ; — *by asking questions,* bun-kyih' 盤 詰

EXAMINATION *hall* (for examining siu-dzæ), ts'ah-yün' 察 院 ; *ditto* (for examining kyü-nying). kong'-yün 貢 院

EXAMINER, *customs'* nyin'-ho-sin 驗 貨 手

EXAMPLE, pông'-yiang 榜 樣 ; piao'-yiang 表樣 ; *set a good —,* lih' ih-go hao' pông'-yiang 立 一 个° 好 榜 樣 ; *will follow your —,* we keng' ng-go pông'-yiang 會 跟 你° 个° 榜 樣 ; we k'en' ng-go yiang 會 看 你° 个° 樣 ; *give me an —,* yüong ih-go pi'-fông peh ngô t'ing' 用 一 个° 比 方 俾° 我 聽 ; *examples in phrases,* kyü-nyü'-deo 句 語 頭

EXASPERATE, *to* — *him,* kyih' gyi-go nu' 激 其 个° 怒 ; ts'oh' gyi-go nu' (ts'oh or c'oh) 觸 其 个° 怒 ; ts'oh'-væn gyi-go ô'-wông.

EXCAVATE, *to* gyüih-c'ih'-læ 掘 出 來 ; dao ih-go den' 搯 一 个° 潭

EXCEED, *to* ko 過; *to — the appointed time,* nyih-ts' kc-deo' 日° 子 過 頭 ; ko gyi' 過 期 ; *to be greater than,* ko'-jü 過 如 ; do-jü 大° 如 ; *no love exceeds a mother's,* æ'-sih-sing do'-jü ah-nyiang m'-teh-go 愛 惜 心 大° 如 阿 娘 沒° 有° 个° ; — *the bounds of propriety,* yüih-c'ih'-kwe-kyü' 越 出 規 矩

EXCEL, *to* ken' zông-zin' 赶 上 前 ; tseo' zông-zin' 走 上 前° ; *strive to —,* ts'iang'-ts'iang zông-zin' 蹌 蹌 上 前° ; *I cannot — him,* ngô' feh neng'-keo ken' gyi zông-zin' 我 弗 能 殼 赶 其 上 前°

EXCELLENCY, *his or your —,* da-jing' 大 人 ; *his —, Mr. Way,* We' Da-jing' 衛 大 人

EXCELLENT, yin 賢 ; y'u-teh' 賢德 ; — *man,* kyüing s' 君 子 ; nying liang-jün' 人 良 善 ; *thoroughly — man,* yia-liang' fông'-tsing 賢 良 方 正 ; — *flavor,* mi-dao' gyih-miao' 味 道 極 妙 ; — *plan,* miao fah' 妙 法 ; — *idea,* miao i' 妙 意 ; — *penmanship,* miao pih' 妙 筆 ; — *woman,* nyü'-nying sang'-leh miao' 女人°生°得°妙; nyü'-nying sang'-leh kyüô' 女人°生°得° 佳 (in the Chinese sense of excellence, *i. e.* dutiful affable and intelligent).

EXCEPT, *unless*, jü-ziah' 如若

EXCEPT, EXCEPTING, djü-c'ih 除出; djü' 除, with ts-nga' 之外°; *all were there — him*, djü gyi ts-nga' tu læ'-kæn 除其之外° 都在°彼°

EXCEPTIONS, *with few —*, væn cong-ts ih' 萬中之一; ts'in-cong' siao-yiu'-go 千中少有个°

EXCESS, *surplus*, to-deo' 多頭; *good to —*, ko'-ü hao' 過于好; *eat, drink*, or *do anything to —*, ko liang' 過量; ko-du' 過度; ko veng' 過分

EXCESSIVE, EXCESSIVELY, *the heat is excessive*, or *it is excessively hot*, nyih ko-deo' 熱°過頭; *— stupid*, ko'-ü beng' 過于笨; *— angry*, ông' tao gyih-deo' 怒°到極頭; jih-feng' ô-wông.

EXCHANGE, *to* diao-wun' 調換; te'-diao 對調; *— for good and all*, diao-jih' 調實; diao-k'æ' 調開; *— this for a better pen*, diao ih-ts' hao-tin'-go pih' 調一枝好點个筆; wun' ih-ts' hao-tin'-go 換一枝好點个°

EXCITABLE, yüong-yi' fah'-dong 容易發動

EXCITE, *to* dong° 動; kyih' 激;

kyih'-dong 激動; tang'-dong 打動; ts'e-dong' 催動; *— him to anger*, or *to fight*, yüong gyi'-go kyih'-kong 用其个°激工; *— to discord*, t'iao-so' 挑唆; *— to action*, kyih'-li 激勵; *— to gratitude*, ken'-kyih 感激

EXCLAIM, *to cry out*, byiang'-ky'i-læ 響起來; eo-ky'i'-læ 喊°起來

EXCLUDE, *to* djü-c'ih' 除出; djü-ky'i' 除去°

EXCLUDING, djü 除; ts-nga' 之外°; *— this*, djü-ts' ts-nga' 除此之外°

EXCLUSIVE, *not wishing to associate with others*, gah-de'-feh-long' 凑°隊弗攏; kao-p'ing'-feh-long' 交°摒弗攏

EXCOMMUNICATE, *to* ken'-c'ih kong-we' 趕出公會; ken-c'ih kyiao' 趕出教

EXCORIATE, *to rub off the skin*, bi ts'ah'-ky'i 皮擦去°; bi mo-ky'i' 皮磨去°

EXCREMENT, bi 屎°; liao 料; feng 糞; *— of birds*, tiao-o' 鳥°屎°

EXCRUCIATING *pain*, kw'u'-t'ong 苦痛

EXCUSABLE, *very* dzing' yiu k'o nyün' 情有可原

EXCUSE, *to use* or *borrow as an —*, tsia ing-deo' 借因頭

EXCUSE, *to regard with indulgence*, kw'un-shü' 寬恕; 1

beg you to — me, ts'ing' ng kw'un-shü' ngô 請你°寬恕我; ditto for some inadvertency, teh'-ze 得罪; shih-kwu' 失顧; —(as for a fault, or for absence), nyün-liang' 原諒; — me, for not accompanying you (as to the gate), kw'un-shü' ngô feh song' ng 寬恕我弗送你°; ditto to a greater distance (as to the boat), shü ngô' feh yün'-song ng 恕我弗遠送你° — me from doing, min' ngô tso' 免我做; cannot —, min'-feh-læ 免勿來; to feel for and —, t'i'-liang 體諒; — another's fault, pao yüong' 包容

EXECRABLE, k'o'-u-go 可惡个°

EXECRATE, to abhor, 'eng-gyih' 恨極; to curse, tsiu'-mô 咒罵

EXECUTE, to tso 做; — orders, t'ing feng-fu' 聽吩咐; tsiao feng-fu' 照吩咐 (tso may be either expressed, or understood); — for a crime, sah'-ze 殺罪; four criminals are to be executed (by beheading), s'-go væn'-nying iao sah-deo' 四个°犯人°要殺頭

EXECUTION ground, sah'-dziang 殺塲; fah'-dziang 法塲 (ih t'ah)

EXECUTIONER, 'ong-gyi'-siu 紅旗手; kwe'-ts-siu 劊子手 (ih-go)

EXECUTOR, zin coh'-t'oh go nying 受囑託个°人°

EXEMPLARY, hao tso piao'-yiang 好做表樣; tsing' -p'a-go 正派°个°

EXEMPLIFY, to piao'-ming 表明

EXEMPT, to min 免; — from soldier's duty, min' tông-ping' 免當兵

EXEMPTION certificate (customs'), min' se-tæn 免稅單

EXERCISE the body, 'ang-dong' sing'-t'i 行°動身體

EXERT, to c'ih 出; — strength c'ih-lih' 出力; — skill, c'ih siu'-dön 出手段; — one's self, zi' zông'-kying 自°上緊; — one's self greatly, nu' lih 努力; — one's self when weak, ts'ang 撑; ditto (still more), ngang ts'ang' 硬撑; — to the utmost si' ts'ang 死°撑

EXHALATION, vapor, ky'i 氣; noxious —, we'-ky'i 穢氣; tsông ky'i' 瘴氣; poisonous —, doh ky'i' 毒氣; offensive —, ts'iu' ky'i 臭°氣; dzoh ky'i' 濁氣; hurtful — from the earth, t'u' ky'i 土氣

EXHALE from the ground, di-yiang' ky'i' c'ih 地下°氣出; the flowers — their fragrance, hwô t'u'-c'ih hyiang-ky'i' 花吐出香氣

EXHAUST, to use up, yüong-wun' 用完; — the strength, ky'i-lih

yüong-wun' 氣力用完; t'eh lih' 脫力; *exhausted by walking*, ky'i'-lih tseo'-wun-de 氣力走完了°

EXHIBIT, *to show*, lu-c'ih' 露出; hyin'-c'ih 顯出; *exhibits a bad disposition*, lu'-c'ih wa sing'-kah' 露出孬°性格; *he exhibits great patience*, hyin'-c'ih gyi-go jing'-næ feh' siao 顯出其个°忍耐弗少; — *goods*, pa'-k'æ ho'-veh 擺開貨物; — *choice things in temples*, pa-tsi' 擺祭

EXHILARATE, *to* dzn hying' 助興; *he is exhilarated with wine*, gyi hying'-cü z tsiu' dzu' go 其興致是酒助个°; — *with opium*, a-p'in' di tsing-jing' 鴉°片提精神

EXHORT, *to* ky'ün' 勸; — *earnestly*, sah'-k'eo ky'ün' 用°力°勸; kô gying-dao' ky'ün' 加°勸道勸

EXILE, *one exiled for breaking the laws*, kyüing-væn' 軍犯

EXILE, *to* bæn ts'ong-kyüing' 辦充軍 See BANISH.

EXIST *always*, djông-djông' yiu' 常常有

EXISTENT, *self* z-jün'-r-jün yiu'-go 自然而然有个°

EXONERATED, *to be* — *from blame*, ze'-ming t'eh'-diao-de 名脫了°

EXORBITANT, *do* hyü'-deo 大°虛價°; — *charges*, t'ao' kô, hah'-

sæn wô-shü' 討價°嚇山話水°

EXORBITANTLY *dear*, t'æ kyü' 太貴°; kyü ko-deo' 貴°過頭; kah'-nga kyü 格外°貴°; t'ao' kô mông-bah-yiang-yiang 討價°漫°白洋洋

EXORCISE, *to* — *by the Taoist divinity*, vong Nyüoh-wông-da'-ti ts'-i djü zia' 奉玉皇大帝旨意除邪°

EXOTIC *plants*, nga-koh' læ-go hwô'-moh 外°國來个°花木

EXPAND, *to* — (*as rice in boiling, seeds, &c.*) *or to dilate upon*, hwô'-k'æ 化開; — (*as a bird its wings*), tô'-k'æ 撐°開; gwah'-k'æ; — (*as flowers, leaves, &c.*) fông'-k'æ 放開; — *the mind*, k'æ sing ky'iao' 開心竅; k'æ ky'iao'-meng 開竅門; — (*as water in freezing*), kao-k'æ' 膠°開; tsiang 脹; tsiang'-k'æ 脹開

EXPANSE, *a great* mang-yiang'-yiang 漫°洋洋; *the firmament*, ky'üong-ts'ông' 穹蒼

EXPECT, *to* siang'-pih 想必; *suppose*, liao 料; *think*, siang 想; ts'eng 忖; *I* — *guests*, ngô siang'-pih nying-k'ah' læ 我想必客人°來; *I* — *him*, ngô liao-tao' gyi læ 我料到其來; ngô peng'-i zin-deo' siang læ' 我本意前°頭想來; *could not be expected*, i'-siang-feh-tao' 意想弗到; *constantly expecting*, læ-tih yün'-vông 在° 此° 懸 望

EXPECTORATE, *to* t'u dæn'吐痰

EXPEDIENT, *fitting*, ü li' siang-nyi' 于 禮 相 宜；*profitable*, yiu ih' 有 益；yiu bin-i' 有 便 宜°

EXPEDIENT, *an* ih-go fah'-ts 一個° 法° 子；ih-go fông-fah' 一個° 方法

EXPEDITE, *to do quickly*, ken'-kying tso' 赶 緊 做；kw'a'-soh tso' 快° 快° 做

EXPEL, *to* ken'-c'ih 赶出；kah'-diao 革 去°；— *by bad means*, p'ih-c'ih' 撤 出

EXPEND, *to use*, yüong 用；— *much time and strength*, yüong kong-fu' teng sing-lih' feh siao' 用工夫 等 心力 弗 少

EXPENDITURE, k'æ-siao' 開 銷；yüong-dziang 用 埸

EXPENSE, yüong'-du 用度；*great* —, yüong'-du-do' 用 度 大°；*extra* —, to fi' 多 費

EXPENSES, 'æn-fi' 開 費；*profitless* — (as money given to officials), fi'-yüong 費用；— (of any establishment), kyiao'-yüong 繳 用；k'æ-kyiao' 開繳；*family* —, kô-yüong' 家° 用；kô'-li-go kyiao'-yüong 家° 裡 個° 繳° 用 — *that may be cut down*, dao-yiao'；*what are your daily* —? ng' nyih-nyih' iao to-siao' k'æ-kyiao' 你° 日° 日° 要 多 少 開 繳？ *travelling* —,

bun-fi' 盤 費；bun-jün' 盤 纏°

EXPERIENCE, *to pass through*, yüih-lih' 閱歷；kying-lih' 經歷；*has experienced* (as hardships), kying-fong' kying-lông' ko-de 經 風 經 浪 過 了°；sông'-shih ah'-ko de 霜 雪 壓° 過 了°

EXPERIENCE, *of large* —, veng-kwô'-cü to' 聞 寡 知 多；kyiu'-kwông-sih-da' 見 廣 識 大；*tell one's* —, kông tsong-dziang' 講 裏 腸；kông tsong-ky'üoh' 講 裏 曲 (ih-fæn)

EXPERIENCED *man*, nying lao'-lin' 人° 老 練；yüih'-lih-ko'-go nying 閱 歷 過 個° 人°；nying kyiu-lin'-dzing kông' 人° 久 練 成 鋼；— *hand*, joh siu' 熟 手

EXPERIMENT, *to* tsoh'-mo 琢磨；tsoh'-mo-ky'i-k'en' 且 琢 磨 看

EXPERT, jih-kwæn'習慣；*very* —, jih-kwæn' dzing z-jün' 習 慣 成 自 然；nô siu'-hyi 擎 手 戲；— *and then inventive*, joh-neng' seng ky'iao' 熟 能 生 巧

EXPIATE, *to* — *sin*, joh ze' 贖罪

EXPIRATION *of a time*, z-'eo' wun'-de 時 候 完 了°；gyi-deo' mun'-de 期 頭 滿 了°；nyih-ts' mun'-de 日° 子 滿 了°

EXPLAIN, *to* ka'-shih 解 說；— *clearly*, ka'-shih ming-bah' 解 說 明 白；*can you* — *it to me?* ng hao ka'-shih peh ngô t'ing' feh 你° 好 解° 說 俾 我 聽 否°？

EXPLANATION, *verbal* kông'-ka 講° 解°; *written* —, cü'-ka 註 解'; *I cannot understand his* —, gyi'-go kông'-ka ngô t'ing'-leh feh ts'ing-ts'u' 其 个° 講° 解° 我 聽 得° 弗 清 楚

EXPLETIVE, hyü'-z-ngæn 虛 字 眼°; — *for rounding a sentence,* cün'-tsih-go z-ngæn' 轉 折 个° 字 眼°

EXPLICIT, ts'ing-t'ong' 清 通; ming-bah' 明 白; *nothing hidden,* 'o-bun' t'oh'-c'ih 和 盤 托 出

EXPLODE, *to* pao'-k'æ 爆 開

EXPLOIT, fi-dzông'-ts z' 非 常 之 事

EXPLORE, *to* dzô-k'ao' 查 考; — *a region,* dzô-k'ao' di-fông'-go dzing-ying' 查 考 地 方 个° 情 形

EXPORT, *to* ho tsông-c'ih-ky'i' 貨 裝 出 去°

EXPORTS, c'ih'-k'eo ho'-veh 出 口 貨 物

EXPOSE, *to* lu-c'ih' 露 出; c'ih-lu'-lu 出 露 露; — *the face,* min-k'ong' c'ih-lu'-lu 面 孔 出 露 露; — *the person,* c'ih'-sing-lu'-t'i 出 身 露 體; — *one's self to public gaze* (in reproach), c'ih'-kwa-lu-ts'iu' 出 乖° 露 醜; — *his shame,* c'ih' gyi-go ts'iu' 出 其 个° 醜; — *one's faults,* shü' pu'-kæn-kæn 數° 布 襴 襴°; — (another's secrets), toh'-p'o 挑'-破; *the countryman exposes his ignorance of the rules of so-*

ciety, hyiang-'ô'-nying iao ky'in t'u 鄉 下° 人° 顯° 出° 土 氣

EXPOSTULATE, *to* c'ih'-lih ky'ün' 出 力 勸; kw'u'-kw'u ky'ün' 苦 苦 勸

EXPOUND, *to* (in speaking), kông'-ka 講° 解°; — (in writing), cü'-ka 註 解'

EXPRESS, *to* — *in words,* kông'-c'ih-læ 講 出 來; *cannot* —, kông'-feh'-c'ih'-læ 講 弗 出 來; *cannot* — *adequately,* kông'-feh-tao' 講 弗 到

EXPRESS, *to* — *oil,* tsô-yiu' 榨 油

EXPRESS, *footman,* ta-kyih'-sing-go 帶° 急 信 个°; — *who runs by stages* (formerly horseman), ts'in-li'-mô 千 里 馬

EXPRESSION, *an* ih-kyü' shih-wô' 一 句 說 話; *a phrase,* ih-kyü', kyü-nyü'-deo 一 句 句 語 頭; *familiar* —, dzoh-wô' 俗 話; *forced* —, min'-ky'iang shih-wô' 勉 強 說 話

EXPRESSIVE *countenance,* min-k'ong' weh-siang' 面 孔 活 相

EXPRESSLY, *on purpose,* deh-we' 特 爲; deh-i' 特 意; kwu'-i 故 意; *plainly,* ming-ming' 明 明

EXPUNGE, *to* (as an idea), sæn-kæ' 刪 改; — *with a pin,* du-diao' 塗 壞°; *wipe out,* k'a'-diao 揩° 壞°

EXQUISITE, *beautiful,* me'-li 美 麗; *delicate,* si'-cü 細 緻; — *workmanship,* si'-ky'iao' sang-weh' 細 巧 生° 活

EXTEMPORIZE, *to* ze-k'eo kông'-c'ih 隨 口 講° 出 ; ze-i' kông'-c'ih 隨 意 講° 出 ; kông'-c'ih sön'-tsiang 講° 出 算 帳 ; *extemporizes well,* c'ih-k'eo' dziung-tsông' 出 口 成 章

EXTEND, *to* — (as reports, rivers), t'ong-k'æ' 通 開 ; — (as disease, fire, customs), yin-k'æ' 延 開 ; — (as liquids spilt), seng'-k'æ 沁 開 ; — *to every part,* tsiu-tao' 周 到 ; — *the hand,* sing siu' 伸 手 ; — *the arm,* siu' sing-dzih' 手 伸 直 : — (lie) *at full length,* dzih kw'eng' 直 睡°

EXTENSIVE, kwông'-kw'eh 廣 闊 ; *the ruin caused by the flood is* —, tsao'-djoh shü'-tsæ di'-fông kwông'-kw'eh-leh-kying 遭 着° 水° 災 地 方 廣 闊 得° 緊 ; — *learning,* 'oh-veng poh' 學° 問 博

EXTENT, *what is the* — *of his learning?* gyi-go dzæ-'oh' yiu kyi feng' 其 个° 才 學° 有 幾 分 ? *what is the* — *of the flood?* do-shü' tsao'-djoh to'-siao di'-fông 大° 水° 遭 着° 多 少 地 方 ?

EXTENUATE, *to* — (as a fault), kæn ky'ing' 減 輕 ; *will* —, hao ky'ing-k'o' 好 輕 可

EXTERIOR, *the outside,* nga-deo' 外° 頭 ; nga-pin' 外° 邊 ; *the outer surface,* nga min' 外° 面

EXTERMINATE, *to* djih-diao' 絶 壞° ; — *utterly,* mih-wun' 滅 完 ; tsæn-ts'ao' djü-keng 斬 草 除 根

EXTERNAL *appearance,* nga-kwông'-min 外° 光 面 ; nga meng'-min 外° 門 面

EXTINCT, *volcano is* —, ho'-sæn si'-de 火 山 死 了° ; *some species of animals are* —, yiu kyi le' cong-sang' djih-cong'-de 有 幾 類 畜 牲° 絶 種 了°

EXTINGUISH *fire,* mih ho' 滅 火 ; — *the lamp,* teng-tsæn' long gyi u' 燈 盞 弄 其 熄° ; — *a fire,* kyiu ho' 救 火 ; *hopes are extinguished,* siang'-vông ziang ho' p'eh-u'-de 想 望 像 火 澄 熄° 了°

EXTIRPATE, *to* djih-wun' 連 完 lin keng' bah-diao 連 根 拔 去°

EXTOL, *to* dzong'-tsæn 頌 讚

EXTORT, *to force,* pih'-leh 逼 勒 ; — *a confession from him,* pih-leh gyi' tsiao-jing' 逼 勒 其 招 認 ; — *money,* leh-soh dong-din' 勒 索 銅 錢° ; — soh-tsô dong-din' 索 詐 銅 錢°

EXTRACT, *to* bah-diao' 拔 去° ; bah-c'ih' 拔 出 ; bah-loh' 拔 落 tsoh'-diao 劖 壞° ; — *essence* (by soaking), tsih'-shü tsing'-c'ih 汁 水° 浸 出

EXTRAORDINARY, kah-nga' 格 外° ; fi-dzông' 非 常 ; fi-væn' 非 凡

EXTRAVAGANT, *to be* — *in using,* lông'-yüong 浪 用 ; lông'-fi 浪 費 ; *to be wasteful,* hwô'-fi 花 費

EXTREME, gyih-deo' 極 頭 ; *bad*

*in the —*, wa' tao gyih-deo' 燾
到 極 頭; *to be in — poverty,*
gyüong-gyih'-de 窮 極 了°

EXTREMITY, *at the — of the road,*
(also used fig.), tao zing'-deo 到
盡 頭; *in —*, vu lu' k'o tseo'
無 路 可 走

EXTRICATE, *to* t'eh'-c'ih 脫 出;
t'eng'-c'ih; di-bah' 提 拔; —
*from difficulty,* kyiu næn' 救 難;
*he extricated me from difficulty,*
(or owing to him I was &c.),
ky'ü'-leh gyi' keh-go næn-deo'
ngô t'eh'-c'ih-de 虧°得°其 這°
個° 難 頭 我 脫 出 了°

EXUBERANT *spirits,* hyi'- ky'i
yiang-yiang' 喜 氣 揚 揚; *ditto*
*in talking,* hyi'-siao yin-k'æ' 喜
笑 言 開

EXULTANT, hwun-t'in'-hyi-di' 歡
天 喜 地; hwun-hyi' jü-yü'
teh-sc' 歡 喜 如 魚 得 水;—
*triumph of soldiers,* k'ao' teh-
sing' kwu 敲°得 勝 鼓

EYE, ngæn'-tsing 眼°晴 (ih-tsah);
ngæn'-moh 眼°目; *needle's —*,
tsing-ngæn' 針 眼°; *see with one*
—, doh ngæn' k'en 獨 眼°看

EYES, *bright* ngæn'-tsing liang'
眼°晴 亮; *both —*, sông-ngæn'
雙 眼°; *see with one's own —*,
ts'ing ngæn' k'en' 親 眼°看;
*before one's —*, læ ngæn'-zin 在°
眼° 前°; *— open,* ngæn'-tsing
k'æ'-tih 眼°晴 開 的; *— shut,*
ngæn'-tsing pi'-tih 眼°晴 閉 的

EYE, *to — closely,* ngæn'-tsing
ts'ing'-ting k'en' 眼°晴 睜 盯
看

EYE-BALL, ngæn'-u cü' 眼°鳥 珠;
ngæn'-cü 眼°珠

EYE-BROWS, mi-mao' 眉°毛; *the*
*forehead just above the —*, me-
deo' 眉 頭

EYE-LASHES, ngæn'-seh mao' 眼°
睫 毛

EYE-LIDS, ngæn'-p'ao-bi' 眼°泡 皮

EYE-SERVANT, yiu min-zin' pe-
'eo'-go nying 有 面 前°背 後
個° 人°

EYE-SIGHT, ngæn'-kwông 眼°光;
ngæn'-lih 眼°力; ngæn'-fah 眼°
法

EYE-WITNESS, ts'ing ngæn' k'en'-
kyin-go nying 親 眼°看 見
個° 人°; *was an —*, ts'ing-
ngæn'-moh-tu' ko-de 親 眼°目
睹 過 了°

# F

FABLE, yü-yin' 喻 言 (ih-go);
*Æsop's Fables,* I-sô-bo'-go yü-
yin' 伊 沙 婆 個° 喻 言

FABRICATE, *to devise falsely,*
nyiah-zao'-c'ih-læ 揑 造°出 來;
zi' tso yin-nyü' 自°做 言 語

FABULOUS, hwông'- dæn-peh-
kying' 荒 誕 不 經; *— ages,*
miao'-mông z-shü' 渺 茫 時 世

FACE, min-k'ong' 面 孔 (ih-fu);
ô'- lin 丫 臉 (in a bad sense);
*no shame,* m-ô'-lin 無° 臉°恥°;

— to *face*, te' min 對面; *to open the — by pulling hairs* (as for a Chinese bride), k'æ min' 開面; *surface*, min-teng' 面子°

FACE, *to — the south*, dziao nen' 朝南; *in what direction does this house —?* keh tsing oh' hyiang'-dao dziao soh'-go 這° 進屋向道朝甚°麼°? *to turn the — away*, min-k'ong' nyin-cün' bih-hyiang' 面孔側°轉別向

FACETIOUS, we hyiah'-yin 會諧言

FACILITATE, *to* s'-teh yüong-yi' 使得容易; s'-teh sang'-lih 使得省力

FACILITIES, bin-tông' 便當; *many —*, hyü'-to bin-tông' 許多便當; yiang-yiang' bin-tông' 樣樣便當

FACILITY, *he does it with great —*, gyi-go siu'-shü weh-p'eh' 其个手勢活潑; gyi-go siu'-shü jing-dzeh' 其个手勢潤澤

FACING, hyiang'-djoh 向着; — *outward*, dziao nga' 朝外°

FACT, *it is a —*, keh' z jih-z' 這°是實事; *the facts*, jih-dzing' 實情; jih-tsih' 實節

FACTION *having injurious designs*, nyih tông' 逆黨; *that —*, keh' ih tông kyih'-long 這°一黨結攏

FACTOR, tsông-k'ah' 莊客

FACTORY, *manufactory*, do coh'-dziang 大°作塲; — *where*

*factors do business*, siao' z-'ao' 小字號; *The Foreign Factories at Canton*, jih-sæn 'ông 十三行

FACULTY, *mental ability*, dzæ-neng' 才能; — *of speech*, neng shih' neng wô' 能說能話

FADE, *to — (by exposure or age)*, ngæn-seh in' 顏°色薦; — (by washing &c.), ngæn-seh t'e'-diao 顏°色退了°

FAG-END *of a web of cloth*, kyi-deo' 機頭; — *of cotton cloth*, kyi-deo' pu 機頭布

FAGGED *out*, kw'eng'-vah-de 困乏了°

FAGOT, *a bundle of brush with the leaves*, yih-za' 葉柴°; nyün'-za 軟柴° (ih-pô)

FAIL, *to be insufficient*, ky'in 欠; *to grow less by degrees*, dzin'-dzin ky'üih'-long-ky'i' 漸漸缺攏去°; *strength is failing*, lih-ky'i' læ-tih sæ' 力氣將衰; *you have failed in your duty*, ng'-go meng-veng' ky'in tsiu'-tao 你° 个°名°分°欠周到; *to — in doing a thing*, z-ken shih'-ngwu 事幹失悞; *the firm has failed*, 'ông tao'-de 行倒了°; 'ông tao'-diao-de 行倒壞了°

FAIL, *I will come without —*, cing'-ding-feh-ngwu' ngô læ'-gyi; ngô ih-ding læ 我一定來

FAILING, mao-bing' 毛病; oh'-mao-bing 惡毛病

FAILURE, feh' tao'-kô 弗到家';
shih'-ngwu 失悞; — *in an-
swering* (expectations), feh mun'-
i 弗滿意

FAIN, *would — do it*, pô-feh-neng'-
keo tso' 巴弗能殼做

FAINT *from weariness*, ky'i' feh
tsih' 氣弗接; t'eh-lih' 脫力;
— *and fall*, yüing'-tao 暈倒;
*about to* — , hweng-dzing-dzing'
昏沉沉; *to — away*, fah yüing'
發暈; ao'-ky'i 暈去°

FAINT *sound*, sing-hyiang' ing-
ing'-dong 聲響隱隱動; —
*color*, ngæn-seh dæn' 顏色淡;
ts'in' seh 淺色

FAINT-HEARTED, m-tæn'-ky'i-go
無°膽氣个'; gyü-ky'ih' 懼怯

FAIR, *clear* (as water), ts'ing 清;
— *weather*, t'in-zing' 天晴°;
— *complexion*, bi-fu bah-t'oh'
皮膚白; — *wind*, jing-fong'
順風; — *price*, kô'-din bing-
dzih' 價°錢°平直; — *dealing*,
dzih-ky'i' 直氣; dzih sông'
直爽; *beautiful*, me'-mao 美
貌; — *outside, defective within*,
nga yin yü', r ne' peh tsoh' 外°
有餘而內不足 (veng.)

FAIR, *market*, z'-nyih 市日°; *the*
— (held in Ningpo when the
chancellor comes), di-'oh'-da 考°
市°

FAITH, siang-sing'-go sing 相信
个°心; *the virtue of* —, sing'-teh
信德; — *in Christ*, siang-sing'

Kyi-toh'-go sing 相信基督
个心°

FAITHFUL, cong-sing'-go 忠信
个°; — *to one's word*, yin-ying'
siang-vu' 言行相符; —
*words, displeasing to the ear, but
beneficial*, "cong-yin' nyih r' li' ü
ying'" 忠言逆耳利於行
(veng.)

FAITHLESS, *unbelieving*, feh siang'-
sing-go 弗相信个°; — *to
promises*, k'eo'-z, sing-fi' 口是
心非; m sing'-iah 無°信約

FALL, *to — over*, tih'-tao 跌倒; —
*from a higher place*, tih'-loh 跌
落; — *behind*, loh 'eo' 落後;
— *from a horse*, tih'-loh mô' 跌
落馬; — *to pieces, or come
apart*, t'ah'-k'æ 塌開; t'ah loh
塌落; — (as a house), t'æn'-
loh 坍落; t'æn-tao' 坍倒;
— *entirely*, t'æn-t'ah' 坍塌;
tao'-t'ah 倒塌; *ready to — from
rot*, me'-de 霉了°; — (as hair,
teeth, fruit, &c.), t'eng'-loh 脫
落; — (as flowers), zia 謝°;
*the tide is falling*, dziao-shü' t'e'-
de 潮水退了°; dziao-shü' læ-
tih t'e'-loh 潮水°現°在°退
落; — *into sin*, 'æn'-loh ze'-li 陷°
落罪裡; *lest you — into a
bad habit*, k'ong'-p'ô ng wa-
yiang' 'oh-kwæn' 恐怕你°孬°
樣學°慣; — *in love with*,
ngæn'-tsing k'en'-leh tih'-loh,
眼°睛看得°跌落

FALLACIOUS *words*, hyü-sih'- ts dz' 虛 飾 之 詞; tsông-sih'- c'ih-læ-go shih-wô' 裝 飾 出 來 个° 說 話

FALLIBLE, we ts'o' 會 錯

FALLOW, *pale yellow*, dæn wông' 淡 黃; *uncultivated land*, hwông din' 荒 田

FALSE, kô 假°; hyü 虛; vu 誣; ngwe 僞; feh-kwe-jih' 弗 歸 實; *to bear — witness*, kô'-tso te'-tsing 假° 做 對 証; vông'- tsing 妄 証; — *much, true little*, hyü to' jih siao' 虛 多 實 少; — *doctrines*, zia dao'-li 邪° 道 理; — *reputation*, yiu-ming'- vu-jih' 有 名 無 實; — *report*, ngo djün' 訛 傳

FALSEHOOD, hwông'-wô 謊 話; hyü-wô' 虛 話; *tell a —*, kông hwông'- wô 講° 謊 話; kông hyü-wô' 講 虛 話; shih hwông' 說 謊

FALTERING *accents*, ng̃-ng̃'-nga- nga-go shih-wô' 唔 唔 嚘° 嚘° 个° 說 話; — *steps*, kyiah'- bu c'ong'-c'ong-dong; kyiah'-bu k'ô'- feh-w̆eng' 脚 步 拿° 弗 穩

FAME, ming-vông' 名 望; *ambi- tious for —*, t'en ming' 貪 名; (*person*) *of great —*, yiu do ming-vông' 有 大° 名 望

FAMED *places*, yiu'-ming'-go di'- fông 有 名 个° 地 方; *far —*, ming-yiang'-s-bæ 名 揚 四 海

FAMILIAR *with*, joh 熟; — *with the classics*, kying-shü' joh-go' 經 書 熟 个'; — *friend*, siang- hao' beng-yiu' 相 好 朋 友; — *expression*, jing-joh'-go shih- wô' 順 熟 个° 說 話

FAMILY, kô 家°; *a —* or *the head of a —*, ih-veng nying-kô' 一 爿 人° 家; *one's immediate —*, oh'-li 家° 裡; oh'-li-go nying' 家° 裡 个° 人°; kô- kyün' 家° 眷; kô-siao' 家° 小; *the Li —*, Li-kô' 李 家°; *whole —*, 'eh kô' 合 家°; *all of the same — name*, 'eh dzoh' 合 族; zi-kô-nying 自° 家° 人°; — *name*, sing 姓; *have you a —?* tseng-fu' yiu jü 齊 府 有 誰°? yiu kô-siao' m̆'-teh 有 家° 小 沒° 有°? *is your — well?* ng- lah fu'-zông tu hao' feh 你° 府 上 都 好 否°? (*familiarly*) ne'- kyün hao' feh 內 眷 好 否°? *did your — come with you?* ng'-go pao'-kyün dong-læ' feh 你° 个° 寶 眷 同 來 否°? *a rich —*, fu'-kô 富 家°; *ing-wu' 殷 戶; *poor —*, gyüong nying'- kô 窮 人° 家°; *ruined —*, ky'ing'-kô dông-ts'æn' 傾 家° 蕩 產; *he is a disgrace to his —*, gyi' tao ih-kô'-go m̆' 其 倒 一 家° 个° 楣; *all under heaven are one —*, t'in-'ô' ih- kô' 天 下 一 家°; *how many families?* kyi veng' nying'-kô

幾爿人°家°? to-siao′ in-tsao′
多少烟籠? — worship, 'eh-
kô′ li-pa 合家°禮拜°

FAMINE, year of —, hwông-nyin′
荒 年; seven years of —, ts'ih′
nyin do-hwông-nyin′ 七 年 大°
荒 年

FAMISH, to ngo-sah′ 餓 殺

FAMOUS, c'ih-ming′-go 出名个°;
— even to the capital, ming′-cing
ti′-tu 名 震 帝 都

FAN, sin′-ts 扇子 (ih-pô) ; feather —, (i. e. of hawk feathers),
ing-mao′ sin 鷹毛扇; white
folding —, bah-pæn′ sin 白紙°
扇; black ditto, yiu-ts′ sin 油紙
扇; round silk —, yüih-kong′
sin 月宮扇; palm-leaf —, pô-
tsiao′ sin 芭蕉扇; close the —,
sin′-ts hao siu-long′ 扇 子 好 收
攏; open the —, sin′-ts t'æn′
t'æn′-k'æ 扇 子 攤 攤 開

FAN, to tang sin′ 打扇; — one's
self, zi sin-sin 自°扇扇

FANCY, to imagine, i′-ngwu 意
悟; I have a — for that child,
keh′-go siao-nying′ ngô cong′-i
gyi 這°个°小人°我 中意其

FANG, tusk, liao-ngô′ 撩牙°

FANNING-MILL, sin-koh′-mi fong-
siang′ 扇 穀 米 風 箱

FAR, yün′ 遠; how — is it from
here to your place? dông-deo tao
ng-lah keh′-deo to-siao yün′ 這°
邊°到你°那°邊°多少遠?
not very —, feh-da′ li-yün′ 弗

大 離 遠; gone — away, li-
yün′ k'æ-de 離遠關了°; as
— as heaven from earth, t'in-ts'ô′-
di-yün′ 天差地遠; — better,
hao hyü′-to 好許多

FAR-SIGHTED, ngæn′-kwông yün′
眼°光遠

FARCE, all a — (i. e. making a
great show with nothing to back
it), k'ong′-k'oh kô′-ts 空壳架°
子; ditto (as in work), mun sang′-
nying-ngæn′ 瞞 生°人°眼°

FARE, to — well at table, ing′-zih
hao′ 飲食好; ditto, (as a guest),
kong-ing′ hao 供應好; price
of passage, bun-jün′ 盤 櫃°;
bill of —, ts'æ′-moh 菜 目

FARE-WELL, siao-be′ 少陪 (said
only by the person going); to
bid farewell, bih′-ih-bih 別 一
別; ditto (formally before going
on a journey), dz-'ang′ 辭 行°;
to accompany and bid —, song-
'ang′ 送行°; to give a — dinner
to one going, tsin-'ang′ 餞行°

FARINACEOUS food, feng′-zih 粉
食; wheat food, mah-zih′ 麥食

FARM, din-tsông′ 田庄; the Wông
family —, Wông-kô′ tsông 王
家°庄

FARMER, din′-wu 佃戶; cong-
din-tsông′-go nying′ 種田庄
个°人°; the owner of a farm,
tsông-cü′ 庄主; farmer's hired
assistants, tsông-k'ah′ 庄客;
kong-nying′ 工人°

FARRIER, *horse doctor*, i-mô'-go sin'-sang 醫馬個°先生°

FARTHER, *more remote*, yün-tin- 遠點; *go a little* —, ko-ky'i tin 過去°點; *put (it) farther in*, tsæ tsing'-tin 再進點; *still* —, keng-kô yün' 更加°遠; *take no* — *notice of it*, vong to' ky'i ts'æ' gyi 不°要°多睬其°; *have you anything* — *to say?* wa-yiu' shih-wô' m̄-teh 還°有說話嗎°?

FARTHEST, ting-yün' 頂遠; *the* — *shop*, ting yün' keh-bæn tin' 頂遠這°爿店

FASCINATED *by him*, weh-ling' ziang læ gyi siu'-li ka 魂靈像在°其手裡

FASCINATING, we hyih-weng-go 會攝°魂個°

FASHION, *style*, kw'un'-shih 欵式°; *new* —, sing shih' 新式°; *z* shih' 時式°; *old* —, lao' shih 老式°; gyiu kw'un' 舊欵; *out of* —, ko-z'-de 過時了°; *extremely out of* —, be-z' 背時

FASHIONABLE, z-dao' 時道; da-tsoh' 大作; z-kw'un' 時欵°; z-shih 時式°; *not* —, feh-tsoh'-de 弗作了°; feh-z'-de 弗時了°

FAST, *firm*, lao-k'ao' 牢靠; tsah'-cü; — *asleep*, kw'eng sah'-kao 睡°煞覺°

FAST, *quickly*, kw'a'-kw'a 快快°; soh'-soh 速速; 'ao-sao'; — *fellow*, fông'-dông 放蕩

FAST, *to keep a church* —, siu tsa' 守齋°; *a great* —, do tsa' 大°齋°

FAST, *to* kying-zih' 禁食; — *from meat (as the Buddhists do)*, ky'üoh ts'æ' 吃°菜

FASTEN, *to make firm*, long lao-k'ao' 弄牢靠; — *with a nail*, ting' lao 釘牢; — *the door*, meng kwæn-leh lao' 門關得°牢; — *by tying*, bo lao' 縛°牢; pông' lao 綁牢; — *a boat with a stake*, jün' tsông lao 船樁牢

FAT, công 壯 (công or tsông); p'ông 膖; — *and hearty (as a child)*, mi'-p'ông-deo' 肥膖頭°

FAT, *pork* cü-yiu' 猪油; *beef* —, ngeo-yiu' 牛°油

FATAL *to life*, sing'-ming c'ih-t'eh' 性命出脫; — *disease*, si'-tsing 死°症

FATE, ming 命; su 數; T'in-ming' 天命; T'in-su 天數; T'in-i' 天意; *dreadful* —, kyih'-su 劫數; *as* — *would have it*, ming' kæ jü-ts' 命該如此

FATHER, ah-tia' 阿爹; ah-pah' 阿伯; tia'-tia 爹爹; *how is your* —? vu'-lao hao' feh 父老好否°? *my* — *is well*, kô'-vu hao'-go 家父好個°; *(very respectful) your* —, tseng-da'-jing 尊大人; ling-tseng' 令尊; — *and mother*, vu'-meo 父母; *deceased* —, sin-vu' 先父; sin-kyüing' 先君; *Hea-*

venly —, T'in-vu′ 天 父; — in the Catholic church, jing-vu′ 神 父

FATHERS, the we-tsu′ 會祖; ancient bishops, kwu kyin-toh′ 古 監督.

FATHER-IN-LAW on the husband's side, kong-kong′ 公 公; ah-kong′; 阿公; — on the wife's side, dziang′-nying 丈 人; ngoh-vu′ 岳 父

FATHERLESS, m̄-tia′-go 無°爹个°.

FATHERLY man, yiu-ts′-wu vu′-lao 猶之乎父老

FATHOM, to sound, tang sing-ts'in′ 打深淺; tang shü′-deo 打 水頭

FATIGUED, dziah-lih′ 着°力; — and sleepy, bi-gyün′ 疲倦; extremely —, kw'eng′-gyih-liao 困 極了

FATIGUING work, dziah-lih′ sang-weh′ 着°力生°活

FATTEN, to —(as animals), yiang công′ (công or tsông) 養壯; — a goose in close confinement, zeo ngo′ 囚°鵝

FATTY, yiu-nyi′ 油膩; yiu′-go 油个°.

FAULT, mao-bing′ 毛病 (ih-go); moral —, ts'o′-c'ü 錯處; ko′-shih 過失; suffer for one's own —, zi′ tsoh nyih′ 自°作孽; it is not my —, feh′-z ngô′-go mao′-bing 弗是我个°毛病; feh′ z ngô′-go ts'o′ 弗是我个°

錯; good, but has faults, me′ cong′-peh-tsoh′ 美中不足; to find —, mao-ün′ 埋怨; zing leo-dong 尋漏洞; —finding, leh-leh′-gah-gah; kæn-ka′ 尷 尬; give him a duck's egg without a crack, he will find a hole in it, "m̄-vong ah-'ts iao zing dong′" 無°縫鴨°子要尋洞

FAULTLESS, m̄ mao′-bing-go 無° 毛病个°; m̄ p'i′-bing go 無° 批評°个°.

FAVOR (to an inferior), eng-we′ 恩惠; eng-s′ 恩賜; eng-tin′ 恩典; to regard with — (as a superior an inferior), eng-c'ong′ dæ 恩待; to ask a —, t'ao we′ 叫惠; k'eng dzing 懇情; gyiu fông-bin′ 求方便; beg you to grant a —, gyiu ng′ s eng′ 求你°賜恩 (s eng can only be said of a superior); t'ao kwông′ 叫光; k'eng ng′-go dzing 懇你个°情

FAVORITE, teh-c'ong′-go 得寵 个°; c'ong-æ′-go 寵愛个°; sô æ′-go 所愛个°; teh-i′-go 得 意个°.

FAWN, to (as a dog, or as a workman making a great ado, about heaviness of work &c., for the sake of being coaxed), iao jing-mao′-lo 要順毛擡

FEAR, to p'ô 怕; p'ô′-gyü 怕懼; w̆′-gyü 畏懼; — God, p'ô′-gyü Jing-ming′ 怕懼神明;

— *the consequences,* p'ô ken-yi′ 怕干係; p'ô tæn ao-tsao′ 怕担墅糟; *do not —,* hao-vong p'ô 不°用°怕; *nothing to —,* feh-dzæ′-wu 弗礙°事°; feh-fông′-teh 弗妨得; *for — that,* k'ong′-p'ô 恐怕

FEARFUL, *afraid,* p'ô 怕; *inspiring fear* (as a place, &c.), p'ô′-p'ô 怕怕; p'ô′-shü-shü 怕哦哦

FEARING *imaginary things,* sing hyü′ 心虛

FEARLESS, feh p'ô′ 弗怕; *— of death,* feh p'ô′ si 弗怕死°

FEASIBLE, tso′-leh-læ′ go 做得°來个°

FEAST, tsiu′-zih 酒席; tsiu′-yin 酒筵; *to make a —,* bæn tsiu′ 辦酒; *to go to a —,* fu zih′ ky'i 赴席去°; *wedding —,* hao′-nyih tsiu′ 好日°酒

FEAT, gyi-z′ 奇事 (ih-ky'i); gyi-c'ih′-kwn-le′ z-t'i′ 奇出古類事體

FEATHER, mao 毛 (ih-keng); *plumage,* mao-yü′ 毛羽; *fabric made of feathers,* yü′-mao 羽毛; *how beautiful his feathers are,* gyi′ go mao-yü sang′-leh dza hao′-k'en 其个°毛羽生°得°甚°好看; *— bed,* mao-nyüoh′-ts 毛褥子; *— pillow,* (i. e. of goose feathers) ngo-mao-tsing′ 鵝毛枕; *— brush,* mao shih′-tsiu 毛刷篲 (ih-kwm)

FEATURES, kweh′-kah 骨格; *regular —,* kweh′-kah loh-dzih′ 骨格落直; *coarse —,* kweh′-kah ts'u-lu′ 骨格粗魯; *fine —,* ng′-kwun sin′-li 五°官秀麗; *beautiful —* (in a Chinese sense), me-ts'ing′-moh-siu′ 眉清目秀

FEE, FEES, (given to doctors and others), zia-din′ 謝°錢°; *to pay —,* song′ zia-din′ 送謝°錢°; *pen money* (given to teachers), pih′-ts 筆資; *small bribes* (given to officers), fi′-din 費錢°; *entrance —,* k'æ-meng′-fi 開門費; meng-pao′ 門包; *— (given to boatmen, servants &c., for extra services),* dzô-din′ 茶錢°; tsiu′-din 酒錢°

FEEBLE, pih′-t'ah-t'ah 癱極°極°; *— constitution,* ti′-ts tæn-boh′ 底子單薄

FEED, *to* ü 餧; *have you fed the baby?* na-hwun ü′ ko ma 嬰°孩°餧過嗎°? — *, we* 嗯喂 (generally used for animals); *to supply with food* (as masters to workmen), cong væn′ 供°飯; *ditto* (polite), kong-ing 供應

FEEL, *to* moh 摸; *— and see,* moh-moh′-k'en 摸摸看; *— the heat,* teh′-cü nyih′ 得知熱°; p'ô nyih′ 怕熱°; *— the cold,* teh′-cü lang′ 得知冷°; p'ô lang′ 怕冷°; *— happy,* kyüoh′-teh hwun-hyi′-siang 覺得歡喜相; kao-hying' 高興; — *tired*, teh'-cü dziah-lih' 得知着力; — *compassion*, fah dz-pe' sing 發慈悲心; — *angry*, fah ông' 發怒°; — *the pulse*, tah mah' 切°脈; k'en mah' 看脈; — *one's way and then try*, s'-t'en 試探; — *for and excuse*, t'i'-liang 體諒

FEELING, dzing 情; *great —*, dzing 'eo' 情厚; dzing djong' 情重; *no fellow —*, m̄-dzing' m̄-nyi' 無°情無°義°; *to move men's feelings*, tang'-dong nying-go dzing' 打動人°个°情; *tender —*, nyün' sing-dziang' 軟心腸; *to hurt the —*, sông dzing' 傷情

FEIGN, *to* tsông 裝; tsông kô' 裝假°; — *sickness*, tsông bing' 裝病

FELL, tih-tao'-ko 跌倒過; — (*as a person*), tih-ko' 跌過; *to — a seam*, nyiao' ih-da vong' 縫一堆縫; nyiao' ih-da wông-zin'-kweh 縫一堆黃鱔°骨; *to — timber*, tsoh jü' 斷樹

FELL *design*, oh kyi'-kao 惡計

FELLOW *companion*, de-ho' 隊夥 dong-de' 同隊; dong-bun' 同伴; *class —*, dong-ts'ông' 同窗; dong-nyiu' 同硯°; *brave —*, hao'-hen 好漢; *noble —*, da-dziang'-fu 大丈夫; *generous —*, k'ông'-k'æ dziang'-fu 慷慨丈夫; *wicked —*, vu-la' 無賴°

FELLOW, *has a — feeling*, yiu-dzing'-yiu-nyi' 有情有義°

FELLOWSHIP, *to have — with*, siang-kyiao' 相交; kyiao-t'ong' 交通

FELON, *malefactor*, djong'-væn 重犯; iao'-væn 要犯

FELONY, *crime punishable with death*, si'-ze 死°罪; *crime punishable with banishment*, ts'ong-ze' 充罪

FELT, tsin 氈; — *hat*, tsin mao' 氈帽; — *carpet*, tsin t'æn' 氈毯

FEMALE, nyü 女; — *sex*, nyü'-liu-ts-pe' 女流之輩; — *slave*, ô-deo' 丫頭

FEMININE, nyü'-nying go 女人°个°; — *employment*, nyü'-kong-sang-weh' 女工生°活; *womanish*, ziang nyü'-nying ka' 像°女人°

FENCE, *bamboo* ts'iang-pô' 籬°笆; *wooden railing*, læn-ken' 闌干; *very high —*, lu-dzing 木°栅°

FENCE, *to make a bamboo —*, tang ts'iang-pô' 打籬°笆; — *with the sword*, vu-tao' 舞刀; hyi-tao' 戲刀

FENCING-MASTER, kao tao'-fah-go kao'-s 敎°刀法个°敎°師

FERMENT, *to — as dough*, fah kao 發酵°; fah'-ky'i-læ 發起來; — (*as fruit and vegetables*), fæn 泛

FEROCIOUS, hyüong-mang' 兇猛°

FERRIAGE, du-jün'-din 渡船錢°

FERRY, du 渡; — boat, du-jün 渡船; — man, du-jün' lao'-da 渡船老大

FERTILE soil, liang din' 良田; me'-di 美地

FERTILIZE, to tsæ-be' 栽培; üong 壅

FERULE, kao'-fông 戒°方° (ih-kw'e)

FERVENT in heart, nyih-sing 熱°心; ts'ih'-sing 切心

FERVENTLY, hyüih'-sing 血心; very —, ky'i hyüih'-sing 起血心

FERVID, hot, ho'-nyih 火熱°

FESTER, to generate pus, sang nong' 生°膿: tsoh nong' 作膿

FESTIVAL, tsih'-k'eng 節跟°

FETCH, to do-læ' 拿°來; — (when coming), ta'-læ 帶°來; — (as a chair), teh'-leh-læ 掇得°來

FETID, ts'iu 臭°; — breath, k'eu'-ky'i ts'iu' 口氣臭°

FETTER, chain for the feet, kyiah'-liao 脚鐐 (a pair, ih fu).

FETTER, to (both hands and feet), zông liao-k'ao' 上鐐栲; fet-tered, (restrained), ñyin-kyiah' pæn-sin' 黏脚扳手; kyih'-kyü 拮据

FETUS, t'æ-yüing 胎孕; small —, dzing-yüing' 成孕

FEUD, in a state of —, kyih ün-dziu' liao 結冤讐了

FEVER, nyih-bing 熱°病; has

—, læ-tih fah nyih' 正°在°發熱° — is rising, læ-tih nyih-ky'i'-læ 來 的熱 起來; —is going down, nyih læ-tih t'e'-ky'i-læ 熱°正°在°退起來;— is broken, nyih ts'-de 熱°止了°; nyih t'e' ken zing' de 熱°退乾淨了°; intermittent —, dziao-nyih' bing 潮熱°病

FEVER AND AGUE, nyiah-dzih' bing 瘧疾病; ma-za' bing 買°柴病

FEVERISH, kyi'-sing nyih'-go 身°體°熱°个°; very —, kyi'-sing ho'-nyih-go 身°體°火熱°个°

FEW, kyi'-go 幾 个°; yiu-'æn 有限°; m̄ to'-siao 無°多少; a —, m̄-kyi' go 無°幾个°; feh to' 弗多; two, three, or four, liang 兩; I will come after a — days, ko' kyi nyih ngô læ'-gyi 過幾日°我來

FIB, kô'-wô 假°話; hwông-wô 謊話

FIBERS, FIBRES, (as in turnips &c)., kying 經; — (in orange peel), loh 絡; slender rootlets, su 鬚°;— in meat, t'iah'-nyüoh-go si' kying 貼°肉°个°細°筋°

FICKLE, fæn-foh'-feh-ding 反覆弗定; yiao-yiao' peh-jih' 搖搖不實

FICTION, books of siao' shü 小書; 'æn shü 閑°書; siao' shih 小說

FICTITIOUS, kô'-zao-go 假°造个°; hwông-dông' 荒唐

FIDDLE, *two stringed* wu‑gying′ 胡琴; *four stringed* —, bi‑bô′ 琵琶; — *with three strings or more*, yin‑ts′ 絃子; *to play* (the —) *with a bow*, ga; *ditto with the fingers*, dæn 彈; *to tune a* —, diao yin′ 調絃

FIDDLE‑BOW, yin‑kong′ 絃弓 (ih‑go)

FIDDLE‑STRING, yin‑sin′ 絃線 (ih‑keng)

FIDELITY, cong‑sing′ 忠心

FIELD, din 田 (ih‑ky'iu); *battle* —, tsin′‑dziang 戰場 (ih‑go)

FIERCE, mang 猛; — *aspect*, ying‑shü′ üong′‑mang 形勢勇猛; — *as a tiger*, ziang mang′ hwu ka 像猛虎; — *wind*, mang′ fong 猛風; *fiercely angry*, fah′ nu ziang mang′‑tsiang ka 發怒像猛將

FIFTEEN, jih‑ng′ 十五; *the fifteenth*, di jih‑ng′ 第十五

FIFTH, di ng′ 第五; — *month*, — *day*, ng′ yüih ts'u ng′ 五月初五

FIFTIETH, di ng′‑jih 第五十

FIFTY ng′‑jih 五十; — *years old*, ng′‑jih shü′‑de 五十歲了

FIG, vu‑hwô′‑ko 無花果 (ih‑go); *dried figs*, vu‑hwô′‑ko ken′ 無花果乾

FIGHT, *to* (as two or more persons), siang‑tang′ 相打; — (a hundred or more, as clans), tang nying dzing′ 打人陣; — (as

soldiers), tang‑tsiang′ 打仗; kao‑tsin′ 交戰; *to* — *determinedly*, hyüih′‑tsin 血戰; *they are having a* —, gyi‑lah′ læ′‑tih tang siang‑tang′ 伊等現在相打

FIGHTER, tang′‑siu 打手 (ih‑go)

FIGURATIVE *expression*, pi′‑fông shih‑wô′ 比方說話; tsia′ yüong tso pi′‑fông go 借用做比方个

FIGURE, *an image*, ngeo′‑ziang 偶像; ying‑ziang′ 形像 (ih‑go), (of men and animals, as toys), 'en 孩; *he has a fine* —, gyi i‑kô′ hao 其衣架好; *figures* 1,2,3, &c., mô′‑ts 碼子; *by* — *of speech*, weh yüong′ 活用; *without ditto*, jih yüong′ 實用; — *on cloth*, hwô‑deo′ 花頭; *woven* —, tsih′‑c'ih‑go hwô‑deo′ 織出个花頭

FIGURED (as cloth), yiu hwô‑deo′ 有花頭; — *calicoes*, ing′‑hwô yiang′‑pu 印花洋布

FILE, ts′o 鋤 (ih‑pô)

FILIAL, hyiao′‑jing 孝順; — *son*, hyiao′‑ts 孝子

FILINGS, *iron* t'ih′‑sô 鐵沙

FILL, *to* tsi 齒; — *full*, tsi′ mun 齒滿; — *a hole* (as in a wall), seh′ mun 屑滿; — *a hole* (as in the earth) din mun′ 塡滿; *to* — *a boat*, jün′ tsông‑mun′ 船裝滿

FILM, *a* ih‑zeng i 一層翳;

*a — has grown over the eye,*
ngæn'-tsing zông-tsông-de' 眼
睛上瘴了°

FILTER, li-shü'-bing 濾水°瓶;
sô-leo'-kông 沙漏缸° (ih-go)

FILTER, *to* li 濾; *filtered water,*
li-shü' 濾水°

FILTH, ao-tsao' 墾糟; *so much*
—, ka' hyü-to ao-tsao' 這° 許
多墾糟; *sweepings,* leh-seh'
拉扱°; *to remove* —, bô leh-
seh' 扒拉扱; wun leh-seh'
換拉扱°
Countrymen come in and remove filth,
giving a few cash or a coarse broom in
exchange, hence wun.

FILTHY, ao-tsao' 墾糟; lah-t'ah'
邋遢; nyi-sing' 泥腥; — *lan-*
*guage,* ao-tsao' shih-wô' 墾糟
說話

FIN, ts' 翅; *all the lower fins,* wô
shü' 牙鬐; *the thick dorsal fins,*
gyi-ts'iang' 鬐鎗; *shark's fins*
are used for food, and are called
yü-ts'' 魚翅

FINAL, kyih'-sah 結煞; tah'-leh-
meh 末結煞°; — *decision,* tao
kyih'-sah ding-kwe'-hao 到結
煞定規好

FINALLY, tao'-ti 到底; cong-ü'
終於; kwe-keng' 歸根; ts'ih'-
ti 徹底; kyiu'-kying 究竟

FINANCE, *the tribute,* zin-liang'
錢°糧; *customs' revenue,* kwæn-
se' 關稅; *governor of* — (in
each province), pu'-tsing-s' 布
政使; væn-dæ' 藩臺

FIND *by seeking,* zing-djoh' 尋°
着°; zing-c'ih'-le 尋°出來;
*I have found out your idea,* ng'-
go i'-s ngô zing-djoh'-de 你°个°
意思我尋°着了°; *I can-*
*not* — h'm, ngô zing-gyi'-feh-
djoh' 我尋°其弗着°; *to find*
*one's self* (in food), pao væn' 包
飯; *to* — *time,* sang' kong-fu'
省工夫; *ditto, by stealing from*
*other duties,* t'eo-kong'-bah-fu'
偷工夫; *to* — *fault with,* mao-
ün' 埋°怨° See FAULT-FINDING.

FINE, *to pay a* —, do'-c'ih vah-
kw'un' 拿°出罰欵

FINE, *not coarse.* si 細; — (as
meal), t'i'-t'i; dzih-t'i'; *very* —
(good), gyih dao'-di 極道地;
*beautiful,* miao 妙; *very ditto,*
gyih miao' 極妙; — (as workmanship, ornaments, a garden,
&c.) tsing-cü' 精緻

FINE, *to* vah nying-ts' 罰銀子;
vah dong-din' 罰銅錢°

FINELY, si'-si 細細; tsing cü'
精緻; — *written,* sia'-leh tsing-
cü' 寫°得°精緻; — *executed*
*picture,* du si'-ky'iao 圖細巧

FINERY *wanting in taste,* ziang
pô'-byi ka; *wearing fantastic*
—, c'ün ziang' tso hwô-kwu'-
hyi i-zông' 穿像做花鼓戲
衣裳

FINGER, ts'-deo 指頭 (ih-meh);
ts'-meh den' 指拇頭° *the mid-*
*dle* —, cong-ts' 中指; *little* —,

siao′ meh-ts′-deo 小拇指頭

FINGER - BOWL, gyiang′- siu-un′ 洗°手碗 (ih-tsah)

FINGER-RING, ka′-ts 戒°指 (ih-go)

FINISH, to tso-wun′ 做完; tso′-dzing 做成; tso′ loh-dæ′ 做落臺; add to any active verb the particles, hao 好, wun 完; thus: when will you — writing? ng kyi′-z we sia-wun 你°幾時會寫°完? kyi-z sia′-hao 幾時寫°好? to — work, dzing kong′ 成功; liao kong′ 了功; wun kong′ 完功

FINISHED, it is — , hao′-de 好了°; tso-hao′- de 做好了°; wun-kong′-de 完功了°; well finished, tao-kô′ 到家°; ts′-yi dzing′-yi 至矣盡矣

FINITE, yiu ʻæn′-cü 有限°制

FIR tree, sæn-jü′ 杉樹; — wood, sæn moh′ 杉木

FIRE, ho 火; hot or fierce — , ho mang′ 火猛; ho-wông′ 火旺; god of — , ho′-jing bu′-sah 火神菩薩; to make a — , sang ho′ 生°火; to set — to (as a house), fông ho′ 放火; on — (as house, boat, or goods), ho dziah′ 火燔; there was a — last night, zô-yia′ yiu ho-tsong′ 昨°夜°有火鐘; take — , ky′i-ho′ 起火; how did it take — ? dza ky′i-ho 怎°起火? to put out — with water, p′eh ho u′ 潑火熄°; ditto (as a

house on —), kyiu-ho′ 救火; to — a cannon, fông p′ao′ 放砲; to — tea, ts′ao dzô-yih′ 炒茶葉

FIRE-ARMS, ho′-ky′i 火器

FIRE-BRAND, za-deo′-ho 柴°頭火

FIRE-CRACKERS, p′ao′-dziang 爆竹°

FIRE-ENGINE, shü′-long 水°龍; foreign — , yiang shü′-long 洋水°龍

FIRE-FLY, ho-ing-den′ 螢°火 (ih-go)

FIRE-MAN, kyiu′-ho-ping 救火兵 (ih-go)

FIRE-PAN, brass — for warming feet, ho-′ts′ong 腳°爐°; earthen —, ngô′ ho-ts′ong 瓦火熄°

FIRE-SHIP, yüong ho-kong-jün′ 用火攻船 (ih-tsah)

FIRE - WOOD, za-bæn′ 柴°爿; brushwood, nyün za′ 軟柴°; yih za′ 葉柴°

FIRE-WORKS, hwô-p′ao′ ʻeh-ts′ 花砲盒子

Each kind of — has its distinctive name.

FIRKIN, siao′ hwô-kwu dong′ 小花鼓桶 (ih-go)

FIRM, lao-k′ao′ 牢靠; kyih′-jih 砧實; cloth — in texture, pu kyih′-jih 布砧實; — purpose, cü′-i ding-jih′ 主意定實; — footed, kyiah′-dah jih-di′ 腳踏實地

FIRM, ʻông-kô′ 行家; what is the name of your —? ng pao′ ʻao kyiao′-leh soh-go′ tsiao-ba′ 你°

寶號叫甚°麼°招牌°? ng
pao 'ông kyiao-leh soh-go z -'ao'
你°寶行叫得°甚°麼°字號?
FIRMAMENT, ky'üong-ts'ông 穹
蒼

FIRMLY, lao 牢; place —, fông'-
leh lao' 放得°牢; stands —,
lih-leh' lao' 立得°牢

FIRST, the —, di-ih' 第一; deo-
ih' 頭一; the — one, deo-ih'-
go 頭一个°; — ancestor, s'-tsu
始祖; bih-tsu' 鼻祖; —
class, di-ih' pæn 第一班; —
in a class, deo-ih'-ming 頭一
名; — crop, di-ih' kyü 第一
舉; — crop of rice, tsao' dao 早
稻; ditto of tea, deo dzô' 頭
茶; koh yü'-zin dzô' 穀雨前
茶; — story, di-ih' zeng 第一
層; —, of only two stories, leo-
'ô' 樓下°; — fruits, sin kyih'-
loh-go ko'-ts 先結落个°果
子; — head, di-ih' zeng 第一
層; — importance, deo-ih' iao'-
kying 頭一要緊; sin iao'-
kying 先要緊; — month,
tsing yüh' 正月; the — of the
month, ts'u-ih' 初一; — born,
deo sang' 頭生°; — born son,
tsiang'-ts 長子; the 1st, 2nd,
and 3rd sons (corresponding with
the first, second, and third months
of each season of the year), mang
孟°; dzong 仲; kyi 季; — set
the table, then scald the tea, sin' pa
coh'-teng 'eo' p'ao dzô' 先擺

桌橙後泡茶; the — or im-
portant move in chess, di-ih' tsiah
第一着°

FIRSTLY, di-ih' zeng 第一層;
di-ih' dön 第一段; di-ih' tön
第一端; di-ih' diao' 第一條;
di-ih' kw'un' 第一欵; di-ih'
'ông 第一行; di-ih' yiang 第
一樣

FISH, ng 魚° (ih-kwang); fresh
—, sing-sin' ng 新鮮魚°;
fresh water —, dæn' shü ng 淡
水魚°; 'o li'-go ng' 河裏个°
魚°; salt water —, 'æn shü ng
鹹水魚°; hæ-li'-go ng' 海
裏个°魚°; — slightly salted
and dried, dæn'-siang 淡鯗;
(dried but not opened), ng-ken'
魚°乾; very salt, 'æn-siang'鹹
鯗; ng-k'ao 魚烤; — spawn or
roe, ng-ts' 魚°子; very young
ditto, ng-iang' 魚°秧

FISH, to k'ô ng' 捕魚°; — with a
hook, tiao ng' 釣魚°; — with a
net, pæn ng' 扳魚; — in the
sea, k'ô yiang'-sang 洋°內°捕
魚°; to — for praise, kwu ming'
tiao yü 沽名釣舉

FISHERMAN, k'ô-ng'-go nying 捕°
魚°个°人°; yü-ong' 漁翁;
fish-woman, yü-bo' 漁婆

FISH-GLUE, ng-kao' 魚膠°.

FISH-HOOK, tiao'-ng-keo' 釣魚°
鈎 (ih-me)

FISH-MARKET, ma ng' z'-k'eo 買
魚°市口

FISHING-ROD, tiao'-ng-ken' 釣魚° 竿 (ih-kwang)

FISHY *taste*, ng'-go mi'-dao 魚° 个° 味° 道; — *smell*, ng sing-ky'i' 魚°腥氣; sing-ngæn' ky'i.

FISSURE, hwah'-lih-vong 豁 裂 縫 (ih-da); *a crack in rock*, zah-kah u' 石° 楞°

FIST, gyün-deo' 拳頭; *to give a blow with the* —, k'ao' ih-gyün 拷一拳

FIT, *a* — *of ague*, ih-pæn' ma-za'-bing 一班買°柴°病; *a* — *of anger*, ih-dziang ky'i' 一場氣 *to have a convulsion*, fah-kyüih' 發厥; — (with crying like a lamb), yiang-tin' bing 羊癲病; — (with crying like a pig), cü-tin' bing 猪癲病; *by fits and starts*, pæn-zông' pæn-loh' 班上班落

FIT *suitable*, siang-nyi' 相宜; siang-te' 相對; siang-vu' 相符; *not* —, feh siang'-nyi 弗相宜; 'eh'-feh-long' 合弗攏

FIT, *to* — *to*, p'e 配; *fitted to* (as a handle to a pen), p'e'-long liao 配攏了; *this dress fits well*, keh gyin i-zông sing-kô' siang-p'e' 這°件衣裳身架相配; *does not* —, feh tah'-te 弗搭對; *to* — *up a house*, oh' tsông-sih' hao 屋裝飾好

FITLY *spoken*, shih-wô 'eh-shing'-go 說話合榫个°; shih-wô' feng-ngæn' feng-shing' 說話分眼°分寸°

FIVE, ng 五°; *the* — *planets*, ng' sing 五°星; — *elements*, ng' ying 五°行; — *tastes* (sweet, sour, bitter, pungent, salt), wu' vi 五味; — *virtues*, wu' djông 五 常; — *relations*, wu' leng 五倫

FIVE-FOLD, ng'-be 五°倍

FIX, *to fasten* (in the ground, on the floor, &c.) tsông lao' 樁牢; *settle upon*, ding-jih' 定實; ding-kyin' 定見; — *a time*, ding z-'eo' 定時候; — *a day*, 'æn'-ding nyih-ts' 限°定日°子; *to* — *the mind upon, in hearing*, cün-sing' t'ing' 專心聽; — *in the mind*, lao kyi' dzæ sing' 牢記在心

FIXED *determination*, lih-ding' cü'-i 立定主意; — *by fate*, ming cü-ding' 命注°定; ming sang-dzing' 命生成; *eyes* — *upon*, ngæn'-tsing ts'ing'-ting k'en' 眼° 睛睜盯看; — *price*, ding-kô' weh-ih' 定價割一; peh r' kyüô 不二價; — *purpose*, ih-ding' i'-s 一定意思; *not yet* — *or determined*, vi ding' 未定; wa m̄'-neh ding-kwe' 還沒有° 定規

FIZZLE, *to* — *out*, fông c'ü-c'ü.'

FLABBY, (as flesh), c'ô'-c'ô-dong (c'ô or ts'ô).

FLAG, *to* (on the road), tang kyiah'-kweh-nyün' 脚跋°; — *in doing anything*, (by figure), ziang tang kyiah'-kweh-nyün ka' 像

脚°跛° 樣°式°; *indisposed to work*, kæn'-teh tso 懶°得°做

FLAG, gyi 旗 (ih-sin, ih-min); — *or board asking quarter*, min'-tsin ba 勉 戰 牌°; — *of surrender*, 'ông-gyi 降 旗; — *ship*, ta-ling jün' 帶° 令 船; — *staff*, gyi ken' 旗 杆 (ih-ts); — *stone*, zah-pæn 石°版 (ih-kw'e); *to lay ditto*, p'u zah-pæn' 鋪 石°版

FLAGRANT *crime*, ze'-oh t'ao-t'in' 罪 惡 滔 天; ze'-da oh-gyih' 罪 大 惡 極

FLAIL (*used for beating the sesame seeds, &c.*), lin-Wæn' kô 連 環° 枷° (ih-go)

FLAKE, *small — of snow*, shih-hwô' 雪 花; *large — of snow*, shih'-p'in 雪 片

FLAKE, *to — off*, k'oh'-ky'i 戁°起

FLAME, yin-deo' 焰 頭 (ih-bong)

FLANKS *of an animal*, iao-hyih' 腰 脅; — *of an army*, tso-yiu'-kyüing 左 右 軍

FLANNEL, nyüong pu' 絨 布

FLAP, *to* gwah; — *back and forth* gwah-læ' gwah-ky'i'

FLARE, *to — up as flame*, ho'-kwông dzih-ts'ong' 火 光 直 冲; — *into a passion*, ho'-ky'i dzih-ts'ong' 火 氣 直 冲

FLASH, *to* fah'-c'ih liang-kwông' 發 出 亮 光; *to —* (*as lightning*), tang hoh-sin 發 電 光

FLAT, *pin* 扁; *to press —*, ky'ing pin; *level*, bing 平

FLAT-IRON, loh-t'ih' 烙 鐵 (ih-go)

FLATTEN, *to* tso pin' 做 扁; *long-pin* 弄 扁; *ah'-pin* 壓° 扁

FLATTER, *to* vong'-dzing 奉 承; shü'-kwu 世 故; peo-tsiang' 褒 獎 (*lit.* over-praise); — *those higher than one's self*, nyi kao-deo'-pih 戴°高° 帽°子; *thanks, you flatter me*, dzing-peo', dzing peo' 承 褒 承 褒

FLATTERER, vong'-dzing-tsing' 奉 承 精; vong'-dzing-tong' 奉 承 慣° (ih-go)

FLATTERY, vong'-dzing-go shih-wô' 奉 承 个° 說 話

FLATULENCE, ky'i' feh yüing'-dong 氣 弗 運 動; ky'i üoh'-tih 氣 鬱 的; *to relieve —*, li ky'i' 利 氣; yüing ky'i 運 氣

FLAVOR, hyiang 香; ky'i'-mi 氣 味°; *taste*, mi-dao' 味° 道; *has the — of ginger*, yiu sang-kyiang'-go ky'i'-mi 有 生° 薑 个° 氣 味°; *add —* (*as to cake &c.*), kô-hyiang'-ts'eo 加 香 湊

FLAW (*as in glass*), pæn-tin' 斑 點; — (*in cloth*), p'o'-dzæn 破 綻

FLAX, mô 麻; dzi'-mô 苧°麻; — *seed*, mô-ts' 麻 子

FLAY, *to* poh bi' 剝 皮

FLEA, tsao 蚤; t'iao'-tsao 跳蚤; pæn'-tsao 板 蚤 (ih-go)

FLEA-BITE, tsac-ting' 蚤 叮;

*lice and flea-bites many*, hence,
*annoying*, *uncomfortable*, seh-
ting' tsao-ngao' 虱叮蚤鮫

FLEDGED, yiah-sao-kwu' ngang'
翼°翅°股硬 ; *not yet* —, yiah-
sao'-kwu' wa m̄-neh ngang' 翼°
翅°股還°沒°有°硬

FLEE, *to run away*, peng'-tseo 奔
走 ; dao-tseo' 逃走 ; *to* — *from
trouble*, dao næn' 逃難° ; — *from
calamity*, bi 'o'-se 避禍祟

FLEECE, ta'-bi yiang'-mao 帶°
皮°羊毛

FLEECE, *to cut off the* —, tsin
yiang mao' 剪羊毛 ; *to* —
*the people*, poh'-siah pah'-sing
剝削百姓

FLEET *a* — *of fishing boats*, ih-
pông k'ô-ng-jün' 一幫捕°魚°
船 ; *a* — *of war ships*, ih-de'
tsin'-jün 一隊戰船

FLEET, *as if flying*, ziang fi' ka
kw'a' 如°飛之°快°

FLEETING, *time is* —, *or light and
shadow fly like arrows*, kwông'-
ing jü tsin' 光陰如箭° ; —
*and deceitful pleasures*, ngæn'-
zin-hwô' 眼°前°花

FLESH, nyüoh 肉° ; *the body*
nyüoh-sing' 肉°身 ;

FLESHY, vi-p'ông' 肥膹 ; công
or tsông 壯 ; *how* — *you are*,
ng sing'-t'i dza vi-p'ông 你°身
體甚° 肥膹° ; — *person*,
công'-p'ông-ts 壯膹°子 (dis-
respectful).

FLEXIBLE, hao-ao'-go 好拗个° ;
ao'-leh-cün'-go 拗得°轉个°

FLIGHT, *a* — *of stairs*, ih-bu lu-
t'æ' 一步扶°梯° ; *a few steps*,
kah'-bu-kæn' 階°梯°間°

FLIMSY *writing*, veo-boh'-go veng-
li' 浮薄个°文理 ; veng-li
ts'in'-boh 文理°淺薄 ; —
*pretext*, ming-ming'-go ziæ-tön'
明明个°借°端 ; — *cloth* hyi-
pu' 稀布

FLINCH, *to* p'ô-t'ong' p'ô-yiang'
怕痛怕癢 ; *without flinching*,
nying t'ong' 忍°痛

FLING, *to throw*, tiu 丟 ; — *with
force*, k'ang ; ang ; gwæn 撊 ; —
*away*, k'ang-diao ; ang-diao ; tiu'-
diao 丟去°

FLINT, ho'-zah 火石° (ih-kw'e)

FLIPPANT *style of talking*, tih'-tih-
tah-tah lön-kông' lön-wô' 的的
搭搭亂講°亂話

FLIRT, *n.* hong'-nying-tsing' 哄
人°精

FLOAT, *to* vu 浮° ; *floating on the
water*, læ shü' min-teng' vu'-tih
在°水°面上°浮°的

FLOATING-BRIDGE, *or bridge of
boats*, veo-gyiao' 浮橋

FLOCK, ih-dziao' 一羣° ; ih-de' —
隊 ; ih-dzing' 一陣 ; — *of sheep*,
ih-dziao-yiang' 一羣°羊

FLOCK, *to* — *together*, dzing-
gyüing' kyih-de' 成羣結隊

FLOG, *to* — *with a ratan*, tang
deng-diao' 打籐條° ; — *with*

*a lash*, tang pin-ts' 打鞭子

FLOOD, do shü 大°水°; *the Flood*, 'Ong-shü 洪水°; *to* —, fah do-shü 發大°水°; tso do-shü; — *tide*, tsiang'-dziao 漲潮

FLOODING, (menstrual), hyüih'-pong 血崩°

FLOOR, di-pæn' 地板 (properly the lower —); *upper* —, leo-pæn' 樓板

FLOOR, *to* bih di-pæn' 鋪°地板;

FLORA, hwô-ts'ao' 花草; ts'ao'-moh 草木

FLORID *style* (of writing), veng-li' hwô-p'ao' 文理時°新°

FLORIST, k'ao'-kyiu hwô'-go nying 考究花个°人°

FLOSS-SILK, sæn'-sin 散線 (a thread, ih-keng)

FLOUNCE, *to* — *about*, pin-dong pin-t'iao' 徧動徧跳; weh-djông' weh-tin' 活撞活顚

FLOUR, feng 粉; *wheat* —, min-feng' 麪粉; mah-feng' 麥粉; *rice* —, mi'-feng 米粉; *the best or first sifted* —, deo-s' feng 頭篩粉

FLOURISH, *to* hying-wông' 興旺; —'(as trade), hying-long' 興隆; — *luxuriantly* (as foliage), meo-zing' 茂盛; — *a sword*, vu kyin' 舞劍; yüih kyin' 試°劍

FLOW, *to* liu 流; — *down*, liu-loh 流落; — *through*, liu-t'ong 流通; *the tears flowed down*,

ngæn-li'-shü liu'-loh-læ'-de 眼°淚水°流落來了°

FLOWER, hwô 花 (ih-tô); *a cluster of flowers*, ih-gyiu hwô' 一毬花; *a bunch of* —, ih-nyiah hwô' 一捻花; *to pick* —, tsah hwô' 摘花; ao hwô' 拗花

FLOWER, *to* k'æ hwô' 開花

FLOWER-GARDEN, hwô-yün' 花園

FLOWER-POT, hwô-beng' 花盆 (ih-go)

FLOWER-VASE, hwô-bing' 花瓶 (ih-go)

FLOWERY-KINGDOM (*i.e.* China), Cong-wô'-koh 中華國

FLUCTUATE, *to* 'oh-zông' 'oh-loh' 或上或落; zông-zông'-loh-loh 上上落落

FLUENT, jing-liu' 順流; — *in speech*, we-kông'-we-wô' 會講°會話; jing-k'eo' t'eng'-c'ih 順口吶出; — *in replies*, ing'-te jü-liu' 應對如流; pah'-læ-pah-tah.

FLUID, *whatever will flow*, we liu'-go tong-si' 會流个°東西

FLUKE *of an anchor*, mao-ts'' 錨齒 (ih-go)

FLUSH, *to blush*, 'ong-ky'i'-læ 紅起來; fah 'ong' 發紅; — *in money*, dong-din' tsiang-tsong' 銅錢有°餘°

FLUSHED (with wine), min-k'ong' zông lin' 酒°醉°面孔°; —(with anger or shame), 'ong'-min' ts'ih-kying′ 紅面赤筋；— (with heat), ʻong-min′ da-tsiang 紅面大將

FLURRIED, hwông-mông′ 慌忙；læ-loh′-feh-gyi′；hwông-kyih′ hwông-mông′ 慌急慌忙

FLUTE, dih-ts′ 笛子 (ih-kwun)；to play or blow the —, cʻü dih-ts′ 吹°笛子

FLUTED like the lobes of an orange, kyüih′-ts-kæn′ yiang′-shih 橘子稠°樣式

FLUTING-IRON, t′ông i-zông′ ho′-gyin 燙衣裳°火箝 (ih-pô)

FLUTTER, to — without flying, gwah′-kyi gwah′-kyi gwah′-feh-kao′；heart all in a —, sing bih-bih′-t′iao 心關關跳°；sing-hyü′-deh-tsin 心虛肉°顫

FLY, to fi 飛；to — about, fi′-læ fi-ky′i′ 飛來飛去°；— swiftly, fi-p′ao′ 飛跑°；— loose (as dress), geu-gen′-dong.

FLY, the house —, ts′ông-ing′ 蒼蠅 (ih-tsah)；the dragon —, ts′ing-ding′ 蜻蜓

FLY-POISON, ts′ông-ing′-go doh-yiah′ 蒼蠅个°毒藥

FLY-SPECK, ts′ông-ing′ o 蒼蠅屎°

FLYING-FISH, ʻong-nyiang-ng′, (a species found at Ningpo).

FOAL of a horse, siao′ mô 小馬；— of an ass, siao′ li-ts′ 小驢子

FOAM, bah-meh′ 白沫；to —, ky′i bah-meh′ 起白沫；— at

the mouth, nyin-zæn kao′-c′ih 黏涎° 攪 出；c′ü beh′ 吹°沫°

FOCUS, hyüoh-kwông′-go di′-fông 蓄光个° 地方；jü-kwông′-go-di′-fông 聚光个° 地方

FODDER, ts′ao′-liao 草料；to — cattle, ü ngeo′ 飫°牛°

FOE, dziu-nying′ 讐人°；te′-deo 對頭；ün-kô′ 寃家°；a fighting —, dziu-dih′ 讐敵

FOG, vu-lu′ 霧露；dense —, vu-lu djong′ 霧露重；vu-lu nyüong′ 霧露濃

FOGGY (as an explanation), vu-ky′i′-deng′-deng 霧氣騰騰

FOIBLE, bing 病；every man has a —, ko′-ko nying yiu ih-go bing′ 個個人°有 一 個病；old —, lao′ mao′-bing 老毛病；lao′ bi-ky′i 老牌氣

FOIL his plans, p′o gyi′ go kyi-kwæn′ 破其个° 機關

FOIL, leaf, yih-ts′ 葉子；thin —, boh 箔；gold —, kying yih′ 金葉；kying boh′ 金箔

FOLD, sheep yiang-gyin′ 羊棬 (ih-kæn)；crease made in fold-ing, tsih′-u 摺痕°；u 痕°；a plait, ih kæn 一 間°

FOLD, to tsih 摺；— together, tsih-tæn′-long 摺打°攏；— (as a hem, paper &c.), üih 醤；fold it properly, tsih′ gyi hao 摺其好；— the arms, gao siu′ 交°手；the hands, nyiah-siu′ 捻 手；ten —, jih be′ 十倍

FOLIAGE, yih 葉; *luxuriant —*, yih meo-meo'-zing-zing 葉 茂 茂 盛 盛

FOLLOW, *to* keng 跟; keng-leh' 跟 得°; keng-djoh' 跟 着°; *— me*, keng-ngô' læ 跟 我 來; *him* (*i. e.* his example), keng-leh' gyi tso' 跟 得°其 做; keng-leh' gyi 'oh' 跟 得°其 學°; k'en gyi yiang' 看 其 樣; *— immediately*, ze kyiah'-'eo-keng' læ 隨 脚 後 跟 來; *— after a little*, ze-'eo' læ 隨 後 來; *— the pattern*, i yiang' wô weh-lu' 依 樣 畫 葫°蘆; *hence it follows*, sô'-yi yiu' 所 以 有; keh'-lah yiu' 故°此°有; *as follows*, ziu-z' 就°是

FOLLOWER, *one who follows to wait upon*, keng-ze' 跟 隨; keng-pæn' 跟 班; *— of a doctrine*, meng-du' 門 徒

FOLLY, kyin'-sih nyü' 見 識 愚; nyü-kyin' 愚 見

FOND, *to be fond of*, dzih-din' 值 錢° (said of those below us in age, or of things); *very fond of* (as food), ting' hwun-hyi ky'üoh' 頂 歡 喜 吃°; tse' æ ky'üoh' 最 愛 吃°; *weakly — and over-indulgent*, nyih-æ' peh-ming' 溺 愛 不 明; *— of study*, hwun'-hyi doh shü' 歡 喜 讀 書; hao doh' 好 讀; *partially —*, p'in æ' 偏 愛; *— of wine*, t'en tsiu' 貪 酒; *— of lust*, t'en seh' 貪 色; *—*

*of moving about* (*i. e.* unsettled), æ-dong'-go 愛 動 個°

FONT, *baptismal —* (small), 'ang si'-li-go bun'; 行°洗 禮 個 盤; *ditto* (large), 'ang si'-li go kông' 行°洗 禮 個°缸

FONT, *a — of type*, ih-fu' k'æn-z' 一 副 鉛 字

FOOD, ky'üoh'-zih 吃°食; *grain, beans, &c.*, liang-zih' 糧 食; k'eo'-liang 口 糧; *all — eaten with rice*, 'ô-væn' 下°飯; ts'æ'-su 菜 蔬; *— for a journey*, ho'-zih 火 食; ken-liang' 乾 糧; lu-ts'æ' 路 菜; *wheaten —*, mah zih' 麥 食; *nourishing —*, pu' zih 補 食; *excellent —*, zông-p'ing' ts'æ'-su 上 品 菜 蔬; *we have only the plainest —*, ah'-lah, tsih' yiu ts'u dzô, dæn' væn 我 等°只 有 粗 茶 淡 飯; *rich —*, yiu-ky'i' 'ô'-væn 葷°腥 下°飯; *to prepare —*, long væn' 弄 飯

FOOL, do-vu'; hen-deo' 憨 頭; nyü-c'ü' mong'-tong-go 愚 痴 懵 懂 個°; *are you trying to act the —?* ng soh' fah-do hen'-leh ma 你 甚°麼°發 大°憨 嗎°?

FOOL *him*, peh gyi t'æn-ts'ong'倰°其 受°倰°; teng gyi na-'o' 與°其 嬉°戲° (polite); *— and injure him*, teng gyi oh' c'ü'-siao 與 其 惡 取 笑; *fooled by me*, zông' ngô-go ts'ob'-deo 受°我 個 騙

FOOLISH, hen 憨; ngæ 呆; — *affair*, hen' z'-t'i 憨事體; — *words*, c'ing'-c'ing shih-wô' 蠢蠢說話; *like a fool*, do'-vu lin'-ky'i; *ditto* (more severe), ziang fah-c'ü' ka 像發痴; — *hopes*, c'ü-sing vông'-siang 痴心妄想

FOOT, kyiah 脚; *bound* —, dzin-ko'-liao kyiah' 纏過了脚; — *asleep*, kyiah' mô-tsah'-de 脚麻了°; the Chinese divide the feet of animals into *claw-footed*, kyiah-tsao 脚爪, and *palm-footed*, (*i. e.* those that walk on the palms, as bears, and monkeys); kyiah'-tsông 脚掌; *duck's* —, ah' kyiah pæn° 鴨°脚版; *infantry*, bu'-ping 步兵; *a Chinese* — (of ten inches), ih ts'ah' 一尺°; *buy by the* —, leng ts'ah'-deo ma' 論尺° 頭買°; *go on* —, bu-'ang' 步行°; 'ang'-leh ky'i' 行°得°去°; — *of a mountain*, sæn kyiah' 山脚

FOOT-BALL hao t'ih'-go gyiu' 好踢个° 毬; *to kick a* —, t'ih gyiu' 踢毬

FOOT-PATH siao' lu 小路; — *between the fields*, din-zing'-lu 田塍°路; — *across the fields*, din'-li-go liao-lu' 田裡个° 蹻路; liao-din'-koh 蹻田角°

FOOT-PRINT kyiah'-ing 脚印

FOOT-RULE ts'ih 尺 (ih-kwun); *tailor's* —, zæ-ts'ih' 裁° 尺;

*carpenter's* —, lu'-pæn-ts'ih' 魯班尺

FOOT-STOOL, dah'-kyiah-teng' 踏脚櫈 (ih-go); koh'-kyiah-teng' 擱脚櫈 (ih-keng); *native — of plaited straw*, bu-dön' 蒲團

FOOT-STEPS, kyiah'-tsih 脚跡; kyiah'-u 脚印°; *follow in my* —, bu-bu' ing ngô'-go kyiah'-tsih 步步印我个° 脚跡

FOOT-STOVE, ho'-ts'ong 脚° 爐

FOP, p'iao-yih'-nying 飄逸人°; *an officer's son highly dressed but not of good character*, hwô-hwô-kong'-ts 花花公子

FOPPISH, æ-p'iao-yih'-go 愛飄逸个°

FOR, *instead of*, t'i 替; dæ 代; dæ-teng' 代等; *on account of*, we-leh' 爲; — *what reason?* we-leh soh'-go yün-kwu' 爲甚° 麼° 綠故? — *what?* we-leh soh'-si 爲甚° 麼°? — *cash*, we'-tih-z' dong-din' 爲的是銅錢; *as* — *me*, ziah'-z ngô' ni 若是我呢; kông'-tao ngô' 講到我; ts-ü ngô' 至於我; *there is no occasion* — *it*, (to a person asking), keh-z hao-vong' 這是不° 用; keh' z peh-pih' 這° 是 不必; *ditto* (to one doing), keh' z vu-we' 這° 是無爲; — *what price was it sold?* soh'-go kô'-din ma-c'ih'-go 甚° 麼° 價° 錢° 買° 出 个°? *large* — (his) *age*, kw'e-we' 傀偉; *do-*

dao′ 大°道; *buy* — *me*, ng′ teng ngô′ ma′ 你°與°我買°; — *holding tea*, hao tsi dzô′ 好齒茶; *good* — *fever*, hao t′e nyih′ go 好退熱个°; we′ djü dziao-nyih′ 會治潮熱°; — *example*, pi′-fông 比方; — *three hours*, sæn tin′-cong kong-fu′ 三點鐘工夫; *good* — *nothing*, m̄′-kao yüong-dziang′ 無°用場; *to go* —*good*, ky′i′-ts feh læ′-de 去°之弗來了°; ih-ky′ü′ feh we′ 一去弗回; *pray* — *grace*, gyiu eng-we′ 求恩惠; — *ever*, üong′-yün 永遠; — *as much as*, kyi′-kying 旣經; *exchange what is of no use to me but useful to him* — *vice versa*, kying-djü′wun nyüoh-ta′ 金鎚換玉帶°

FORBEAR, *to cease*, hyih 歇; deng loh′ 停°落; *to bear with*, jing′-næ 忍耐

FORBID, *to* kying 禁; kying′-djü 禁住; — *him to do it*, kying′ gyi feh tso′ 禁其弗做; *to do what is forbidden*, væn kying′ 犯禁

FORCE, lih 力; *owing to the* — *of truth*, ky′ü′-leh dao-li′-go lih′ 全°虧°道理个°力; *to use* —, yüong gyiang′ 用强; — *of momentum*, læ-shü′ 來勢; *has* — *of character*, yiu kying-liang′ 有勁°兩; *strength and prowess*, kông-gyiang′剛强; *by* —, miu′-

ky′iang 勉强; *forces* (troops, &c.), ping-mô′ 兵馬; nying-mô′ 人°馬

FORCE, *to* pih 逼; ngang-k′ô′ 硬拿°; ngang iao′ 硬要; — *to do something bad or disgraceful*, pih′ zông liang-sæn′ 逼上梁山; — *him to write*, pih′ gyi sia′ 逼其寫°; *to beg with* — *or* —*one to give*, gyiang′ t′ao 强討

FORCED *to do*, ẇa-feh-læ tso 歇° 弗來做

FORD, *to* liao 蹽; — *a stream*, liao ky′i-k′ang′ 蹽溪坑

FORE, *before, either in position, or in time*, zin 前°; — *before in time*, sin 先

FOREARM, *n.* ′ô′ siu-kwang′ 臂°; siao′ siu-kwang.

FORE-ARM, *to* bông-be′ kyüing-ky′i′ 防備軍器

FOREBODE, *to* — *evil*, bông ′o′-se 防禍祟; bông ′eo′-læ ẇa 防後來孬°

FORE-CAST, *to* yü-sin′ liao-leh-tao′ 預先料得°到; *to contrive beforehand*, sin tang′-sön 先打算; *able to* — *the future*, yiu sin-kyin′ ts-ming′ 有先見之明

FORE-FATHERS, tsu′-tsong 祖宗; tsu′-sin 祖先; sin-tsu′ 先祖

FORE-FOOT, zin kyiah′ 前°脚; *fore-hoof*, zin di′ 前°蹄

FORE-GO, *to* — *a pleasure*, ky′i-diao ih-ky′i hwun-hyi′ z-t′i′ 棄了°一椿°歡喜事體; —

*for another*, nyiang′ peh bih′ nying 讓° 給° 別 人°

FORE-GOING, *the* (what is written), zông-veng′ 上 文

FORE-GROUND, bu′-we gying′ 步 位 近

FOREHEAD, nao′-k'oh 腦 殼; *the middle of the* —, nao′-meng 腦 門; *the corners of the* —, ngah-koh′ 額 角; *high* —, t'in-ding kao′ 天 庭 高

FOREIGN, nga-koh′ 外°國°; yiang′ 洋; — *goods*, nga-koh′ ho′ 外° 國貨; yiang ho′ 洋 貨

FOREIGNER, nga′-koh-nying 外° 國 人°; si-pin-nying 西 邊 人°; 'ong-mao-nying 紅 毛 人° (vulgar); *foreign woman*, nga′-koh nyü′-nying 外°國 女 人°; 'ong′-mao lao′-nyüing 紅 毛 老 女° (vulgar)

FORE-KNOW, *to* yü′-sin hyiao′-teh 預 先 曉 得; sin-cü′ 先 知

FOREMOST, ting′ zin-deo′ 頂 前° 頭; dzih-dzih′ zin-deo′ 極 極 前° 頭

FORENOON, zông-pun′-nyih 上 半 日°

FORE-ORDAIN, *to* yü′-sin cü′-ding 預 先 注 定; yü′-sin ding-kwe′ 預 先 定 規

FORE-RUNNER, sin-fong′ 先 鋒

FORE-SEE. *to* yü′-sin k'en′-kyin 預 先 看 見

FORE-SIGHT, sin-kyin′ ts-dzæ′ 先 見 之 才

FORE-SHADOWING, yü′-sin-go ing′-ts 預 先 个° 影 子

FOREST, dzong-ling′ 叢 林 (ih-c'ü)

FORE-STALL, *to take beforehand*, sin tsin′-leh ky'i′ 先 佔 得 去°; —, *and do one's self*, tsin′-leh zi′ tso′ 佔 得° 自° 做

FORE-TASTE, *have a* — *of heavenly bliss*, T'in-zông′-go foh′-ky'i sin yiu′ ih-ngæn′ zông-djoh′-de 天 上 个° 福 氣 先 有 一 點° 嘗° 着° 了°; *only a small* — *of misery* (or *happiness*), sæn pah′ kying sang-kyiang′ wa tsih′-leh zông′-djob lah ngô-deo′ 三 百 勛 生° 薑 還° 只 得°嘗° 着° 辣 芽° 頭

FORE-TELL, *to* yü′-sin kông′ 預 先 講°; *foretold*, yü′-sin wô-ko′-de 預 先 話 過 了°

FORETHOUGHT, sin liao-tao′ 先 料 到; *owing to his* —, ky'ü-leh gyi′ sin liao-tao′ 虧° 得° 其 先 料 到

FOREVER, üong′-yün 永 遠;

FORE-WARN, *to* yü′-sin kying′-kyiæ 預 先 警 戒

FORFEIT *something good on account of wrong doing*, hao′ z-t'i we-leh ts'o′, shih′- diao 好 事 體 會 錯 失° 了°; — *one's life for another's*, ih ming′, ti′ ih ming′ 一 命 抵 一 命; din ming′ 抵 命

FORGE, *to* — *iron*, tang t'ih′ 打 鐵

FORGE *for iron*, tang- tʻih′- go lu- tsʻ 打 鐵 个° 爐 子

FORGE, *to — a name*, mao ming′ 冒 名 ; *— cash*, s- cü′ dong-din′ 私 鑄 銅 錢° ; *— a name to obtain money,* mao ming′ pʻin dzæ - veh′ 冒 名 騙 財 物 ; *— a seal*, zao kô′ ing 造° 假° 印

FORGERY, *the crime of —*, ngwe- zao′-go zeʻ-ming 僞 造° 个° 罪 名

FORGET, *to* mông-kyi′ 忘° 記 ; *— favors*, mông-kyi′ hao-cʻü′ 忘° 記 好 處

FORGETFUL, m̄ kyi′-sing 無 記 性 ; *very —*, ao- vn′ kyi′-sing 毫 無 記 性 ; cün-ü′ mông-kyi′ 專 于 忘° 記 ; jün-vông′ 善 忘 ; *— of favors*, vông-eng′ veo-nyi′ 忘 恩 負 義° ; kwu-veo′ 辜 負

FORGIVE, *to* nyiao-sô′ 饒 赦° ; sô′- diao* 赦° 了° ; nyiao 饒° min 免 ; kwʻun-shü 寬 恕 ; nyiao-shü 饒 恕 ; *— (as slight offences),* nyün-liang′ 原 諒 ; *I have for- given him*, ngô′ nyiao′-lɛh gyi′ de 我 饒 得° 其 了°

   * Nyiao-sô, and sô-diao, can only be used in speaking of God's or an officer's forgiveness. The other words, may be used more commonly.

FORK, tsʻô 义 ; *silver —*, nying- tsʻô′ 銀 义 (ih-pô°); *— in a road*, tsʻô-lu 义 路 ; *the place where it forks*, s′-tsʻô lu-kʻeo′ 四 义 路 口

FORLORN, kwʻu 苦 ; *destitute*, kwu-gyüong′ 孤 窮 ; *miserable*, kwu-tsʻi′ 孤 悽 ; *— and destitute*

person, kwʻu′-nao-tsʻ 苦 惱 子

FORM, *appearance*, mo-yiang′ 模 樣 ; siang′-mao 相 貌 ; *what — had it?* dza′ mo yiang′ 怎° 模 樣 ? *shape*, yiang-shih′ 樣 式 ; *— (of man)* sing-dzæ′ 身 材 ; jing-dzæ 人 材

FORM, *to — from clay*, su 塑 ; *— in the hand* (as dough), nyiah 揑 ; *— by piling upon* (as snow or mud), te 堆 ; *— an idol*, su bu-sah′ 塑 菩 薩 ; *— a rabbit*, nyiah′ ih-tsah tʻu′ 揑 一 隻 兔 ; *— a snow priest*, te shih′-ʻo- zông′ 堆 雪 和 尙 ; *— with a mould*, su′-ts ing′-cʻih-læ 模° 子 澆° 出 來 ; *— a plan*, tsoʻ-cʻih ih-go fah′-ts 做 出 一 个° 法 子 ; *—a plot*, shih kyi-meo′ 設 計 謀

FORMAL, *having the form without the substance*, yiu′-ming vu-jih′ 有 名 無 實 ; nga′ yiu-yü′, r ne′ peh-tsoh′ 外° 有 餘 而 內 不 足 ; *ceremonious*, to-li′-go 多 禮 个° ; kʻah′-kyʻi 客 氣

FORMALITY, hyü-veng′ 虛 文 ; veo-veng′ 浮 文

FORMER *chapter*, zông-tsông′ 上 章 ; *— occasion*, zin-deo′ ih we′ 前 頭 一 回 ; *— times*, zông- dæ′-go z-ʻeo′ 上 代 个° 時 候 ; *— ages*, zông-kwu′ z-shü′ 上 古 時 世° ; *— life*, (before transmi- gration), zin-seng′ 前 生° ; zin-sɿ′ 前 世°

FORMERLY, yi-zin' 以 前°; dzong
ziu' 從 前°; zin-deo' 前° 頭

FORMIDABLE, fi-dong' siao-k'o'
非 同 小 可; fi-dong' r-hyi' 非
同 兒 戲

FORMLESS, m̄'- neh siang'-mao
沒°有°相貌; vu-ying' vu-ziang'
無 形 無 象°

FORMULA, rule, kwe-tseh' 規 則;
kwe-diao' 規 條; medical prescription, fông-ts' 方 子 (ih-go)

FORNICATION, kæn-ying' 姦 淫°;
biao 嫖

FORNICATOR, kæn-fu' 姦° 夫°;
biao-k'ah' 嫖 客 (ih-go)

FORSAKE, to ky'i'-diao 棄 了°;
tiu-diao' 丟 去°; to leave, li-k'æ'
離 開

FORSWEAR, to deny upon oath,
vah-tsiu' m̄'-teh 罰 咒 沒° 有°

FORT, p'ao'-dæ 礮 臺 (ih-zo); to
guard a —, siu p'ao'-dæ 守礮臺

FORTH, c'ih 出; to go —, c'ih'-
ky'i 出 去°

FORTHWITH, lih-k'eh' 立 刻;
tsih-k'eh' 即 刻; mô'-zông 馬
上; ziu 就°; ze-siu' 隨 手

FORTIFY, to prepare for danger,
bông nyü' 防 虞°; — with soldiers, bông tu 防 堵; — with
embankments, tsoh nyi-dzing' 築
坭 城; to build forts, tsoh p'ao'-
dæ 築 礮 臺

FORTIFIED, small — place, we 衛

FORTNIGHT, jih-s' nyih 十 四
日°; half month, pun'-ko-yüih'
半 個 月; two weeks, liang' li'-
pa 兩 禮 拜°

FORTUNATE, hao zao'-hwô 好造°
化; hao yüing'-ky'i 好 運 氣;
kyih-li'-go 吉 利 个°; yüing'-
dao hao 運 道 好; yiu foh'-ky'i
有 福 氣; — in coming just
when wanted, ts'eo'-ky'iao 湊 巧

FORTUNATELY, ying hyi'-teh 幸
喜 得; ky'ü'-leh 虧° 得°; —
I did not bring him, ying-hyi'-
teh ngô feh ta' gyi læ' 幸 喜
得 吾 弗 帶° 其 來

FORTUNE, yüing-ky'i' 運 氣;
yüing-dao' 運 道; z-yüing' 時
運; good —, yüing-ky'i' hao'
運 氣 好; great good —, foh'-
veng do' 福 牙° 大°; bad —,
boh ming' 薄 命; to enjoy good
—, avoid (the place of) misfortune, "c'ü-kyih,' bi-hyüong'"
趨 吉 避 凶; to make one's —,
fah-dze' 發 財; to seek one's —,
gyiu dzæ' 求 財; depending on a
wife's —, k'ao' lao'-nyüing-go
foh'-ky'i 靠 妻° 个° 福 氣; to
spend a —, ba kô' 敗° 家°

FORTUNES, to tell sön-ming' 算
命; p'i ming' 批 命; ditto, by
drawing slips of paper, gyin bæn'
箝 牌°; ditto with a book, k'en-
hwô kông' 看 花 缸; k'en' liang-
deo' gyin 看 兩 頭 箝

FORTUNE - TELLER, sön'- ming
sin'-sang 算 命 先 生°; gyin-
bæn'-go 箝 牌° 个°

FORTY, s'-jih 四 十 ; *the fortieth,* di s'-jih 第 四 十

FORWARD, *to the front,* hyiang zin' 向 前°; zông zin' 上 前°; ẅông zin' 往 前°; *to bend* —, eo-tæn'-tao 偃° 僂°

FORWARD, *advanced* (as a child), liu'-liang li-lông' ; *putting one's self* —, iao ts'ing-neng' 要 稱 能; *violating propriety,* feh jing' kwe-kyü' 不° 循 規 矩

FORWARD, *to* — (as letters), cün ta' 轉 帶°; cün' kao'-dæ 轉 交° 代

FOSSIL *dug out of the earth,* di-yiang' gyüih-c'ih'-læ-go 地 裏° 掘 出 來 个°

FOSSILS, kyiang-zah' 殭 石°

FOSTER, *to feed,* ü 飫°; *to bring up,* yiang 養

FOSTER-FATHER, kyi'-pa ah-tia' 寄 拜° 阿 爹; nyi-vu' 義° 父

FOSTER-MOTHER, kyi'-pa ah-nyiang' 寄 拜° 阿 娘; yiang'-nyiang 養 娘

FOUL *air,* djoh-ky'i' 濁 氣; — *breath,* k'eo'-ky'i ts'iu' 口 氣 臭°; *to use* — *means,* ẅang te'.

FOUND, *to establish,* shih'-lih 設° 立; — *upon what basis?* k'ao'-djoh soh'-go ti'-ts 靠 着° 甚° 麼° 底 子?

FOUND, *to* — *a bell,* cü' ih-k'eo cong' 鑄 一 口 鐘

FOUND, *tried and* — *guilty,* p'un'-tön-ko', ze ding-jih'-de 判 斷 過

罪 定 實 了°; *three dollars and* —, kong-væn'-ts-nga sæn kw'e' fæn-ping' 供° 飯° 之 外 三 塊 番 餅

FOUNDATION *of a house,* di'-kyi 地 基; — *of a wall,* ziang kyiah' 墻 脚; *lasis,* ti'-ts 底 子; — *to go upon,* keng-kyiah' 根 脚

FOUNDER *of a sect,* kyiao' deo 敎 頭; — *in brass,* cü' dong-s-vu' 鑄 銅 司 務; *to fill with water and sink,* dzing-meh' 沉 沒; dzing-loh' 沉 落

FOUNDLING-ASYLUM, yiang'-yüoh-dông' 養 育 堂; yüoh-ing'-dông 育 嬰 堂

FOUNTAIN, *source,* nyün-deo' 源 頭; *spring,* weh-shü-den' 活 水° 潭; *foreign* —, si-yiang shü'-fah 西 洋 水° 法

FOUR, s 四 ; *the* — *points of the compass,* s' hyiang 四 向 ; s' fông 四 方; — *seasons,* s' kyi 四 季 ; s' z 四 時; — *Books,* S' Shü 四 書; *the fourth,* di s' 第 四

FOUR-CORNERED, s'-koh'-go 四 角° 个°

FOUR-FOOTED, s' kyiah 四 脚

FOUR-FOLD, s' be 四 倍

FOUR-SIDED, s' pin 四 邊

FOUR-SCORE, pah'-jih 八 十

FOURTEEN, jih-s' 十 四; *the fourteenth,* di jih-s' 第 十 四

FOWL, *the domestic* —, kô kyi' 家° 雞 (ih-tsah); *flying creatures,* fi-gying' 飛 禽

Fox, wu-li′ 狐狸 (ih-tsah); —
skin, wu-bi′ 狐皮

Fraction, se′-su 碎數; a —
over, ling-deo′ 零頭; one hundred
and a — over, ih-pah ling tin′
一百°零點

Fracture, to ao′-dön 拗斷;
fractured bone, kweh′-deo dön′-
de 骨頭斷了°

Fragile, feh kying-liu′ 弗經練;
yüong-yi′ se′-go 容易碎个°

Fragments, se′-k′we-deo′ 碎塊
頭; bits, ling-se′ 零碎

Fragrant, hyiang 香; very —
p′eng′-hyiang 噴香; to throw
off fragrance, t′u hyiang-ky′i′
吐香氣

Frail, hyiah′-hyiah 瘦°弱°; —
constitution, ti′-ts hyiah′ 底子弱°

Frame for anything to rest or
hang upon, kô′-ts 架°子; — to be
hung on the wall, kwô′-kying 掛
鏡 (ih-go)

Frame, to zao 造°; — laws, zao
lih-fah′ 造°律法; to — a picture, p′e′ ih-go kw′ông′-ts′ 配一
个°框子 (generally square).

Frank, straight forward, dzih-
sông′ 直爽; honest, lao′-jih 老
實

Frankly, tsiao-dzih′ 照直;
speak —, lao-jih wô 老實話;
tell me —, tsiao dzih′ wô-hyiang′-
ngô-dao 照直話向我道

Frankincense, jü′-hyiang 乳
香

Frantically throwing arms
about, dzông 撞; crying —,
weh-dzông′ weh-tin k′oh′ 活撞
活顛哭

Fraternal love, hyüong-æ′-di-
kying′ 兄愛弟敬

Fraud, bi′-tön 弊端; tsô′-kyi
詐計; kæn-kyi′ 奸°計; to
use —, tsoh bi′-tön 作弊端;
yüong tsô′-kyi 用詐計

Fraudulently obtained, tsoh-
bi′ læ′-go 作弊來个°; obtained
by gross deception, kwa′-p′in læ′-
go 拐骗來个°

Freakish, sing-siang′ moh-feh-
ding′ 心想摸弗定; ze-w̄æn′
tao′-w̄æn 隨彎到彎

Freckle, n. kyiah′-tsi-pæn′ 雀
痣°斑

Free to do as one pleases, zi hao′
tso cü′-i 自好做主意; to
set free, sih′-fông 釋放; too
— and irreverent in speaking,
ky′ing-cü′ boh-zih′ 輕嘴薄舌;
— schools, yi′-′oh or nyi′-′oh′ 義
學°; without charge, bah 白°; to
cross the ferry —, bah′ ko-du′ 白°
過渡; to eat rice —, ky′üoh
bah væn′ 吃白°飯; — from
anxiety, kw′un-sing′ 寬心; —
from customs′ duty, min se′ 免稅;
— in spending money, kw′un-siu′
寬手; song-siu′ 鬆手

Free, to — from all obstacles,
yiu fông-′æ′-go tu djü-diao′ 有
妨害个°都除去°

FREELY, *without fear*, fông'-tæn 放膽; *willingly*, dzing-nyün' 情願; nyün-i' 願意

FREEZE, *to* kyih ping' 結冰°; — *to death*, tong'-sah 凍死°; — *the canals*, kao kông' 膠°港

FREIGHT, *lading of ship*, jün'-li go ho'-veh 船裡个°貨物; *secret* — (for avoiding customs), s-ho' 私貨; — *paid for transportation*, shü'-kyiah 水°脚

FREQUENTLY, le'-ts' 屢次; le'-djông 屢常

FRESH, sing-sin' 新鮮; — *fish*, sing-sin' ng' 新鮮魚°; *not salt*, dæn 淡; *colors* — *and bright*, ngæn-seh' sin-ming' 顏°色鮮明

FRESHEN *it*, (as salt fish), ts'iu'-gyi dæn' 浸°其淡

FRESHET, do shü' 大°水°; *to have a* —, fah do-shü' 發大°水°

FRET, gæn; *to* — *one*, tsi-tseo' 嘈°嘈°; long gyi sing-væn'-tsi-tsao' 弄其心煩嘈°嘈°; — *one's self*, zi-t'æn'-zi 自°嘆自°; p'i-dziang' p'i-tön' 批長批短

FRETFUL, gæn-gæn'tao-tao, used especially of old people.

FRETTED (by something), ông-beh'-tsi-tsao.

FRICTION, feh wah' 發滑; ts'iao'-ts'iao 糙°糙°; *a great deal of* —, ting-ts'iao' 頂糙°

FRIDAY, li-pa-ng' 禮拜°五°

FRIEND, beng-yiu' 朋友; siang-hao' 相好; siang-kyiao' 相交; *intimate* —, cü-kyi' beng-yiu'知己朋友; moh-nyih' beng-yiu' 莫逆朋友; ts'ih'-t'iah beng-yiu' 切貼°朋友; — *in trouble*, wæn'-næn beng-yiu' 患難朋友; *very good friends*, ting kông'-leh-læ beng-yiu' 頂講得°來°朋友; nyi-ky'i' beng-yiu' 義°氣朋友

FRIENDLESS, m̆-beng'- yiu 無°朋友; kwu sing' 孤身

FRIENDLY, 'o-moh'-go 和睦个°; ts'ing-æ'-go 親愛个°; kông'-leh-læ'-go 講得°來个°; — (after a quarrel), 'o-de' 和了°

FRIENDSHIP, kyiao-dzing' 交情; *a* — *exists*, yiu kyiao-dzing' læ-tih 有交情个°; *to break* —, djih kyiao' 絕交

FRIGHTEN, *to* — *one*, long nying' ky'ih-hoh' 弄人吃嚇°; — *away*, hah'-t'e 嚇°退; *to* — *one greatly* (*lit.*, to death), long nying' hab'-sah-de 弄人°嚇°殺了°

FRIGHTENED, ky'ih-hoh'-de吃嚇°了°; ky'ih-kying'-tih-de 吃驚的了°; ziu-kying'-de 受驚了°

FRIGHTFUL *appearance*, p'ô'-p'ô-go siang'-mao 怕怕个°相貌; — *place*, hyin'-hoh-go di'-fông 可°懼°的地方; — *noise*, sing-hyiang' ky'ih-hoh'-go 聲響吃嚇°个°

FRINGE, su-deo' 鬚頭; — *around a mandarin's hat*, ing-ts' 纓子

FRISK, *to jump about*, t'iao-læ'
t'iao-ky'i' 跳 來 跳 去°。

FRITTER, *n.* yiu-zah'-dön 油 煤
糰 (ih-go)

FRIVOLOUS, ky'ing-veo' 輕 浮

FRO, *go to and* —, læ-læ' ky'i-ky'i'
來 來 去°去°; læ-wông' 來 往

FROG, din-kyi' 田 雞 (ih tsah);
*green* —, ts'ing-wô' 青 蛙

FROLIC, do hyi' 大°戲; do na'-'o
大°嬉 戲; *rough play*, mæn tô'
hyi'-deo.

FROM, dzong 從; *hinder him* —
*coming*, tsu' gyi feh læ' 阻 其
弗 來; — *Ningpo to Shanghai*,
dzong Nying-po' tao Zông-læ'
從 寗 波 到 上 海

FRONT, min-zin' 面 前°; *in* —
*of the house*, læ oh' min-zin' 在°
屋 面 前°; — *door* (or *gate*),
zin meng' 前°門; do meng' 大°
門; ziang meng' 墻°門; deo
meng' 頭 門; — *room*, zin vông'
前°房

FRONTIER, pin-kyiang' 邊 疆;
kao-ka' 交°界°; *go to the* —, tao
pin-kyiang' ky'i 到 邊 疆 去°;
*within the* —, kying' ne 境° 內;
*beyond the* —, kying' nga 境°外°

FROST, *white* sông 霜

FROST-BITTEN, tong'-loh-de 凍
落 了°; ziang ngao'-loh-de 像°
皎 落 了°

FROSTY *weather*, t'in' loh sông'
天 落 霜

FROTH, beh 浡

FROWARD, gyüih-gyiang' 倔 强;
gyiang'-deo gyüih-nao' 强 頭 倔
腦; *contrary*, 'aung-deo'-tsoh'-
kying.

FROWN, *to* tseo mi-deo' 縐 眉°
頭; — *from uneasiness or dis-
pleasure*, zeo mi-deo' 愁°眉°頭

FROZEN, kyih-ping'-de 結 氷
了°; *spoiled by freezing*, ping'-
diao'-de 氷 壞 了°; — *to death*,
tong'-sah-de 凍 死 了°

FRUGAL, tso nying-kô' 做 人°
家°; tsih'-gyin 節 儉

FRUIT, ko'-ts 菓 子; *dried* —,
ken ko' 乾 菓; kying ko' 京
菓; *to bear* —, kyih ko'-ts 結
菓 子; *first* — *of the season*, z-
sing' ko 時 新 菓; zông sing'-
ko 上 新 菓

FRUITFUL, kyih'-leh meo-zing'
結 得°茂 盛; sang'-leh to' 生°
得°多; — *tree*, to sang-ko'-ts-
go jü 多 生°果°子 个°樹; *this
year is a* — *one*, kying nyin ko'-
ts do nyin' 今 年 菓 子 熟°年

FRUITLESS, feh kyih'-ko-go 弗
結 菓 个°; *labor proved* —,
kong-fu' loh-k'ong'-de 工 夫 落
空 了°; — (*i. e.* useless) *labor*,
ngô-go siang'-vông p'o'-ba-diao-
de 我 个°想 望 破 敗°了°;
— *attempt*, bah-bah' s' 白°白°試

FRUSTRATE, *my hopes are frus-
trated*, ngô sô' siang'-vông-go
loh-k'ong'-de 我 所 想 望 个°
落 空 了°

FRY, *to* t'ah 爛; — *cakes*, t'ah ping' 爛餅; — *meat*, t'ah nyüoh' 爛肉°; — *fish*, tsin ng' 煎魚°; — *by boiling in fat*, zah 煠 (also boiling in water, in certain ways); — *it brown*, t'ah gyi wông' 爛其黃

FRYING-PAN, t'ah'-bun 爛盤; *the native* —, ngao-bun' 熬盆° (ih-go)

FUEL, *fire-wood*, za 柴°; *good for* —, tông za' siao 當柴°燒; *dried grass, or* — *in general*, za-ts'ao' 柴°草

FUGITIVE, *one flying from trouble*, dao-næn'-go nying' 逃難个° 人°; *escaped criminal*, dao-væn' 逃犯

FULFILL, *he will* — *his promises*, gyi sô ing-hyü' we dzing-kong'-go 其所應許會成功 个°; — *a contract*, jü iah' 如約; *to be* —, yiu ing'-nyiæn 有應 驗; yiu yiao-nyiæn' 有效驗

FULL, mun 滿; mun'-tsoh 滿足; *filled* —, tsi-mun'-liao 齒滿 了; *the* — *time*, z-'eo mun'-de 時候滿了°; z-'eo mun'-tsoh-de 時候滿足了°; *face* — *of joy*, mun'-min hwun-hyi' 滿 面歡喜; *to give a* — *account of*, zing'-yin kông'-c'ih-læ' 盡 言講°出°來; — *grown*, dziang-tsoh'長°足; — *moon*, yüih-liang' yün-mun' 月亮圓滿; *measure of iniquity* —, oh'-kwun

mun-ying' 惡貫滿盈; — *to the brim*, bing k'eo' 平口; — *of flies*, ts'ông-ing' heh'-kyih-kao 蒼蠅甚°多°; — *allowance*, ngah-ts' mun'-de 額子滿了°; — *number*, su'-moh tsoh' 數目 足

FULLER'S-EARTH, wông na-nyi' 黃坭

FULLY, jih-feng' 十分; jih-tsoh' 十足; djün-be' 全備; — *prepared*, jih-feng' be-hao' de 十 分備好了°

FUME, *vapor*, ky'i 氣; *fumes of opium*, a'-p'in ky'i' 鴉片氣; — *of tobacco*, in ky'i' 烟氣

FUMIGATE, *to* hyüing-in' 熏烟; — *with perfume*, hyüing-hyiang' 熏香

FUN, *to have* —, hyi'-hyi 嬉 戲; hyi'-hyiah 戲謔; *to play*, na-'o'; *only in* —(with you), tæn-tsih' teng ng hyi'-hyi 單只 搭°你°嬉戲

FUNCTION, kong-yüong' 功用 (veng.)

FUND, *capital*, peng'-din 本錢°; *public fund*, koh-t'ông' 國帑; t'ông'-nying 帑銀

FUNDAMENTAL, yiu keng-kyi' 有根基; — *principles*, ziang-kyiah' 牆°脚

FUNERAL, *taking out the coffin*, c'ih zæ' 出材°; c'ih sông' 出 喪; *to have a* —, 'ang sông-li' 行°喪禮; c'ih ping' 出殯;

c'ih gyiu′ 出柩；— *ceremonies*, sông-z′ 喪事；*to go through ditto*, bæn sông-z′ 辦喪事；*to attend a —*, song sông 送喪；song zæ′ 送材°；— *expenses*, ping′-tsông-ts fi′ 殯葬之費

FUNNEL, leo′-teo 漏斗；jün-ts′ 旋子 (ih-go)

FUNNY, *laughable*, hao′-fah siao′ 好發笑；we ying′-nying siao′ 會引人°笑

FUR *on the body*, mao 毛；*the skin with —* bi-ts′ 皮子；— *robe*, bi bao′-ts 皮袍子；*sable —*, ts′-tiao-bi 紫貂°皮；*ditto speckled*, (hairs white-tipped), ts-mô′-tiao-bi′芝麻貂皮；*ermine —*, nying-c'ü′-bi 銀鼠皮；*squirrel —*, hwe-tsih′-bi 灰脊皮；*ditto* (with the bellies), hwe-c'ü′ bi 灰鼠皮；*rabbit —*, zih-c'ü′-bi 碩鼠皮；*seal skin*, hæ′-lo-bi 海騾皮；*beaver* or *otter skin*, t'ah′-bi 獺皮；*Astrakhan* (black lamb-skin), heh′ ts-kao 黑紫羔；*white lamb-skin*, kao-bi′ 羔皮；nyi-mao 二°毛；*black and white ditto*, hwô-kao′ 花羔；*unyeaned lamb-skin*, koh-cong′-yiang-bi′各種羊皮；hwe′-koh-cong-bi 灰各種皮；*white ditto*, cü-r-bi 珠兒皮；*fox-skin*, wu-bi′ 狐皮

FURIOUS, dong-da′-nu′-de 動大°怒了°；hyüong mang′ 兒猛°

FURIOUSLY, *quarrel —*, pe ming′ zao 亡°命嘈；pe ming′ tang′ 亡°命打；*beat —*, heng′-sing-go tang′ 狠心个°打

FURL, *to — the sails*, siu bong′ 收蓬；*to pull down the sail*, loh bong′ 落蓬；*ditto partly*, mô bong；tsô bong 遮°蓬

FURLOUGH, *to ask a —*, kao kô′ 告假°；*to grant a —*, cing′ kao-kô′ 准告假°

FURNACE, *portable earthen —*, fong-lu′ 風爐；ngô′ fong-lo′瓦°風爐°；*native kitchen range*, tsao 灶

FURNISH, *to prepare*, be-bæn′ 備辦；— *a house*, be-bæn′ kô-sang′ jih-veh′ 備辦物°件°— *his rice*, kong gyi-go væn 供其个°飯

FURROW *left by a plow*, li gông-s′；— (in the face), veng lu′ 紋路；*furrowed*, tang kæn′-de 打襇了°

FURTHER, *a little —*, yün-tin′遠點

FURTHER, *to —the business*, nyüoh-dzing′ gyi-z′ 玉成其事 See FARTHER.

FURTHERMORE, ping′-ts'ia 拜且°；wa-yiu′ 還°有

FURY, gwông-t'iu′ gwông-di′-go ô-wông 狂天狂地个°怒°

FURY, *virago*, p'eh′-vu 潑婦

FUSE, *to* yiang 煬

FUSIBLE, yiang′-leh k'æ′-go 煬得°開个°

FUSSY, so'-so-se-se' 瑣瑣碎碎 tsi-tsi'-tseo-tseo 嘈嘈嘲°嘲°

FUTILE, k'ong'-deo go 空頭个° m̃-yüong'-go 無°用个°; vu-ih 無益

FUTURE, tsiang-læ' 將來; the uncertain —, mi-læ' 未°來; 'eo'-læ 後來; — event, tsiang-læ'-go z-ken' 將來个°事幹; — misery, 'eo'-læ'-go kw'u'-næn 後來个°苦難; the — life, 'ô'-si 下°世°; to provide for the —, bông'- be tsiang-læ'-go yüong-dziang' 防備將來个°用場

FUZZY, yiu nyüong-deo' 有絨頭

# G

GABBLING noise (as of many talking), zeo-ky'i' ka sing-hyiang'; zeng-zeng' hyiang; ditto, as of geese, ziang ngo kyiao ka sing-hyiang' 像°鵝叫聲响

GADDING about, dziah nying kô' 走°人°家°; ditto, like a cat yiu-hyi'-lông-dông', dziah'- kô - mao ka.

GAG, to — with a stick, ts'ang mih-dæn'-kong 撐篋彈弓; — by stuffing the mouth, seh cü'-pô 塞嘴巴

GAIN, profit, li-sih' 利息; hwô-li' 花利; dzæn'-deo 賺頭; good —, hao dzæn'- deo 好賺頭; hao li'-sih 好利息

GAIN, to get, teh'-djoh 得着°; —

profit, teh li' 得利; — advantage, teh'-djoh ih'-c'ü 得着益處; — (in play), ying 贏; — a victory, teh-sing' 得勝; — bodily strength, diao-yiang sing-t'i' 調養身體; ditto, by rest, tsiang yiang' 將養; gaining upon him, pi' gyi we zông' 比其會上; læ-tih ken'-gyi-zông zin' 正°在°趕其上前°

GAINSAY, to p'i-poh' 批駁; pæn-poh' 翻°駁

GAIT, tseo'-siang 走相

GALA-DAY, k'æ-sing', tsoh-loh'-go nyih-ts' 開心作樂个°日°子

GALE, do fong' 大°風; mang' fong 猛°風; gwông fong' 狂風; bao' fong 暴風

GALL, kw'u'-tæn 苦膽; hence courage, tæn'-ts 膽子

GALL-NUTS, be-ts' 梧子; — and copperas, be-ts', loh-væn' 梧子綠礬

GALLOP, to — or run, p'ao 跑°; — a horse, p'ao mô' 跑°馬

GALLOWS, frame for hanging criminals, tiao væn'-nying-go kô'-ts 弔犯人°个°架°子

GAMBIER, ping-lông'-kao 梹榔膏

GAMBLE, to tu 賭; tu'-poh 賭博; hyi-tu' 戲賭; — with cash by the character pao, tang-pao' 打寶

GAMBLER, tu'-k'ab 賭客; tu'-p'e 賭胚; tu'-kweng 賭棍;

tu'-zeh 賭 賊°; *to arrest gamblers*, k'ô tu 拏° 賭

GAMBLING *stall*, tu-t'æn' 賭 攤：
— *house*, tu'-dziang 賭 塲；tu'-gyüoh 賭 局；— *tools*, tu'-gyü 賭 具

GAMBOGE, deng-wông' 膰 黃

GAME, *play*, hyi-shih' 嬉 耍°；*play a — with dice*, dzih seh'-ts 擲 骰° 子；*to play a — of cards*, ts'ô ts'-wu-bæn' 扯 紙 糊 牌°；*play a — of chess*, tsiah' ih-bun gyi' 搶° 一 盤 棋；*to catch —*, tang-liah' 打 獵；*lost the — (in gambling)*, tu' shü-de 賭 輸 了°；*to make — of one*, hyi'-long nying' 戲 弄 人°

GANDER, yüong-ngo' 雄 鵝

GANG, *a* ih-pông' 一 幫；ih-tông' 一 黨；*a — of robbers*, ih-pông gyiang-dao' 一 幫 强 盗；*the rest of the —*, yü-tông' 餘 黨

GANGRENE *has set in*, læn'-leh li-'æ' 爛 得° 利 害

GAP, k'eo 口；— *in the mountains*, sæn ao' 山 塪；*to mend or stop a —*, pu ky'üih' 補 缺；seh dong' 塞 洞；dong mun-seh' 洞 壂 塞

GAPE, *to* tang hô-hen' 打 呵 㰤

GARBAGE, ka'-dong-leh-seh' 界° 洞 垃 圾

GARDEN, *vegetable* di-yün' 地 園；ts'æ'-yün 菜 園 (ih-ky'iu)；*flower—*, hwô-yün' 花 園；— *bed*, ling 疄 (ih)；— *path*,

siao' lu 小 路；di-gông' (ih-da)

GARDENER *for vegetables*, cong-ts'æ'-go nying 種 菜 个 人°；— *for flowers*, cong -hwô'-go nying 種 花 个 人°

GARGLE, *to — the mouth*, dông k'eo'盪 口；— *the throat*, dông wu-long' 盪 喉° 嚨

GARLIC, da-sön 大 蒜；— *bulbs*, da-sön'-deo 大 蒜 頭

GARMENT, i-zông' 衣 裳°；i-voh' 衣 服 (*a —*, ih-gyin；*a suit*, ih-t'ao)；*to wear only one —*, c'ün tæn gyin' i-zông' 穿 單 件 衣 裳°；*cotton —of a single thickness*, tæn-boh'-tæn 單 薄

GARRISON, siu'-ping 守 兵；— *of a city*, siu-dzing'-go ping 守 城 个° 兵

GARRULOUS, to-djün-z'-go 多 言°

GARTER, mah-ta' 襪° 帶° (ih-tsah；*a pair*, ih-fu)

GAS, ky'i 氣；*coal —*, me-t'æn ky'i 煤 炭 氣

GASH, sông-k'eo' 傷 口；keh'-sông 割 傷 (ih-go)

GASP, *to —for breath*, ky'i t'eo'-feh-cün' 氣 透 弗 轉；ih'-ky'i feh-cün' 噎 氣 弗 轉

GATE, meng' 門 (ih-deo, ih-sin)；*gate in two leaves*, sông-sin' meng 雙 扇 門；— *shutting off a street*, sah'-lah-meng 柵 欄° 門；*to keep the city gates*, siu dzing-meng' 守 城 門

GATHER, *to — up or together*, siu-jih-long′ 收拾攏；— in (as crops), siu-tsing′ 收進；siu hwô-li′ 收花利；— flowers, tsah hwô′ 摘花；ts′æ hwô′ 探花；— (in sewing), ts′oh′-long 撮攏

GATHERS, to push up the — , ts′iu-long′ 抽攏；the —, ts′oh-tih-go kæn′ 撮的个裀°

GAUDY, hwô-seh′ 花色；hwô-p′ao′.

GAUGE, tseh′-moh 準°則°(ih-go)

GAUZE, sô 紗

GAY, free from care and anxiety, kw′a′-weh 快活°；— in laughing, and talking, hyi′-siao yin-k′æ′ 喜笑顏開；— colors, yin′-li ngæn-seh′ 艷麗顏°色

GAYLY dressed, c′ün′-leh-hyin′ 穿得°顯

GAZE, to ts′ing′-ting k′en′ 青叮看

GAZETTE, sing-veng′-pao 新聞報；Peking —, Kying-pao′ 京報

GELATINE, (native), yiang-ts′æ′ 洋菜；fish-glue, ng-kao′ 魚°膠

GEM, pao′-zah 寶石°

GENDER, feng nen-nyü′ 分男女；— of brutes, feng ts′-yüong′ 分雌雄；of the male —, yüong′ ih-le′ 雄一類；of the female —, ts′′ ih-le′ 雌一類

GENEALOGY, pu′-yi 譜系；book of —, kô-pu′ 家°譜(ih-peng)

GENERAL term or designation, tsong′-ming 總名；t′ong-ts′ing′ 通稱；in — use, t′ong-yüong′

通用；t′ong-′ang 通行°；— (opposed to particular), weng′-kweng 渾混；— way of doing, da-kæ′ tso′-fah 大概做法

GENERAL of an army, tsiang-kyüing′ 將軍

GENERALLY, da-kæ′ 大概；da-tu′ 大都；da-væn′ 大凡；da-ti′ 大抵；da-be′ 大備；in the main, da-liah′ 大略

GENERATE, to sang 生°

GENERATION, dæ 代；former —, zông dæ′ 上代；future —, ′ô′ dæ 下°代；preceding generations, lih dæ′ 歷代；the present —, yin-dzæ′ keh dæ 現在一°代；peng′-dæ 本代；from — to —, tao shü′-shü-dæ-dæ 到世世代代

GENEROUS, ky′i′-kæ 氣概；da-kw′æ′ 大快；du′-liang do′ 度量大°；very —, ′ao-yiah′ 豪俠；— treatment, ′eo′-dæ 厚待

GENESIS, the book of —, Ts′ông′-shü-kyi′ 創世記

GENIAL in manner, ′o-ky′i 和氣；lovable, k′o-æ-go 可愛个°；— as the Winter′s sun (used in speaking of a favorite teacher, &c.), ziang tong-t′in′ nyih-deo ka′ ko′-ko nying æ-′go 像冬天日°頭個個人°愛个°；— as (sitting in) the breezes of spring, ziang zo-læ c′ing-fong li′-deo ka 像°坐°在°春風裏頭

GENIUS, t′in-veng kao′ 天分高；

a —, dzæ-ts′ 才子; *a boy* —, jing-dong′ 神童

GENTEEL, yüô′-cü 雅致; veng-yüô′ 文雅; — *dress*, i-zông′ veng-zing′ 衣裳 文靜

GENTLE, no-jün′ 懦善; lao′-jih 老實; — *disposition*, sing′-kah no-jün′ 性格懦善

GENTLEMAN, veng-nying′文人°; sin-sang′ 先生° or 師; *old* —, lao′ sin′-sang 老先生°; *act like a* —, iao tso veng-yüô′-go nying 要做文雅个°人°; iao jih-zông′ feh iao′ jih-′ô′ 要習上弗要習下°

GENTLEMEN! cü-we′ sin′-sang 諸位先生°! lih-we′ sin′-sang 列位先生°!

GENTLY, *lightly*, ky′ing-fæn′ 輕泛; *slowly*, wun′-fæn 緩泛; *speak* —, kông ky′ing-yin′ si′-nyü 講° 輕言細語; *speak more* —, kông ky′ing-sang′-tin 講° 輕省° 點

GENTRY, *Chinese* sing-kying′ 紳衿; hyiang-sing′ 鄉紳; sing-kying′-tông 紳衿黨 (used in reproach); — *who oppress others*, p′o′-hyü-tông′ 破靴黨

GENUINE, tsing 真; — *goods*, tsing ho′ 真貨; *not* —, kô 假°

GENUS, *class*, le 類 (ih)

GEOGRAPHY, di-gyiu′-go ′oh-veng′ 地球个° 學° 問; *book on* —, di-yü′-ts 地輿志

GEOMANCER, fong-shü′ sin′-sang

風水° 先生°; we-k′en-fong-shü′-go 會看風水° 个°; loh-z′ sin-sang′ 六事先生°

GEOMANCY, *the theory of* —, di-li′ 地理; fong-shü′ 風水°; *book on* —, di-li′ shü 地理書; loh-z′ shü 六事書

GERM *of a leaf*, ngô-den′ 芽頭°; — *of flowers*, nyü 蕊°; ′en-nyü′ 合蕊

GERMINATE, *to* pao ngô′ 苞芽; ts′iu ngô′ 抽芽; pao ngô-den′ 苞芽° 頭°

GESTICULATE, *to* tsông siu′-shü 裝手勢; — (more earnestly), tsông kyü′-ts 裝舉止

GET, *to receive*, teh′-djob 得着°; tsih′-ziu 接受; *ditto* (as a package, &c.), do tao′ siu 拿°到手; teh-tao′ siu 得到手; *to take*, do 拏°; — *it for me*, teng ngô′ ky′i do′ 替°我去°拿°; — *nothing by it*, ih′ vu sô teh′ 一無所得; *I can′t* —*in*, ngô tseo′-feh-tsing′ 我走弗進°; *How did the news* — *abroad?* keh sing′-sih dza-djün-k′æ′-go 這信息怎°傳開个°? *It begins to* — *dark*, t′in en′-long-læ-de 天暗攏來了°; — *up*, bô-ky′i′-læ 爬起來; — *rich*, fab-dzæ′ 發財; — *out of* or *rid of*, t′eh′-c′ih 脫出; — *ready* (beforehand) yü-be′-hao 預備好; be-bæn′-hao 備辦好; *go* — (yourself) *ready*, ky′i tsông-hao′ 去°裝好; *can′t*

— *over it* (*i. e.* keep thinking of it), ko'-sing-feh-ky'i' 過意°弗去°; — *down,* tseo'-loh-ky'i' 走落去°; — *angry,* fah ông' 發怒°

GHASTLY, *like a ghost,* kyü'-siang 鬼°相; *death-like,* si'-siang 死°相

GHOST, *spirit,* ling 靈; *Holy Spirit,* Sing-Ling 聖靈; — *of the departed,* kyü 鬼°; *feeding the hungry ghosts,* fông yin-k'eo' 放熖口

GIANT, yi-yiang'-dziang-go nying' 異樣長個°人°; c'ih-kah'-dziang-go nying' 出格長個°人°

GIDDY, *dizzy,* deo-yüing' 頭暈; *to fall from giddiness,* yüing-tao' 暈倒

GIFT, song-go tong'-si 送個°東西; *that is a —,* keh'-z song'-læ-go 這°是送來個°; *this is a — from my father,* keh'-go tong'-si z ah-tia' peh ngô'-go 這個°東西是阿爹給°我個°; *to attend an officer, or literary man who is leaving, with gifts,* tang pô'-shü 打覇勢; *gifts of ceremony,* li 禮; li'-veh 禮物; *to give ditto,* song'-li 送禮; *to give gifts of congratulation,* song 'o'-li 送賀禮

GIFTED, ts-tsih'-hao' 資質好

GIGANTIC, *cannot tell how large,* wô'-feh-læ'-do' 話弗來大°;

feh-tsiao dza do' 了°弗°得°大°

GIGGLE, *to* keh'-keh-siao 哈°哈°笑

GILD, *to* du kying' 鍍金; *to — by plunging,* seng'-kying 沁金; — *with gold leaf,* t'iah kying' 貼金; pao kying' 包金

GILLS, *fish* ng-sæ' 魚°鰓

GILT-EDGED, kying-pin'-go 金邊個°

GIMLET, jün-tsön'-ts 旋°鑽子

GINGER, *fresh* sang-kyiang' 生°薑; *dried —,* ken-kyiang' 乾薑; *preserved —,* dông-kyiang' 糖薑; *powdered —,* kyiang-feng' 薑粉

GINGER-BREAD, sang-kyiang' kao 生°薑糕

GINGHAM, gyi-bun'-hwô-go-pu' 棋盤花個°布

GINSENG, jing-seng' 人參; *foreign —,* yiang-seng' 洋參

GIRDLE, kyiao'-sing-ta 繳身帶; — *with clasp,* k'eo'-ta 扣帶; *bride's —,* koh'-ta 角°帶; *to put on the —,* kyi kyiao'-sing-ta 繫繳身帶

GIRL, nyiang-ts' 小°姐°; kwn-nyiang' 姑娘; *slave —,* ô-deo' 丫頭; s'-nyü 使女

GIRLISH, ziang nyiang-ts' ka 像°小°姐°; ziang nyiang-ts-den'ka.

GIRTH, *horse's* mô'-du-ta 馬肚帶 (ih-keng, ih-diao)

GIVE, *to* peh 給°, 與°, 俾°; — (*to an inferior*), s 賜; s'-peh 賜給°;

—(to any one), s 施; *to present,* song′-peh 送 給°; — *in charge,* kao-dæ 交° 代°; — *leave,* hyü 許; cing 准; — *him an answer,* peh′ gyi we-ing′ 給° 其 回 音°; — *him trouble,* peh gyi keh′-tah 俾 其 疙 瘩° peh gyi we-næn′ 俾° 其 爲 難; — *a daughter in marriage,* kô nön′ 嫁° 囡; — *vent to anger,* c′ih ky′i′ 出 氣; — *place to another,* nyiang 讓°; nyiang-peh′ 讓° 與°; — *up one's life,* pe ming′ 亡° 命; sô′-c′ih sing′-ming 捨° 出 性 命; p′ing ming′ 拚命; — *to the poor,* s′-peh gyüong-nying′ 施° 給° 窮 人°; tsiu-tsi′ nying-kô′ 賙 濟 人° 家°; — *coffins,* sô-s′ kwun-moh′ 捨 施 棺 木; — *up (resistance),* voh 服; shü′-voh 輸 服; *won't* — *in at all,* ting′-cing 訂 準; — *up a thing undertaken,* t′e siu′ 推 辭°; — *up (or lose heart),* sing si′-de 心 死 了°

GIVER, s′-cü 施 主; c′ih-din s′-cü 出 錢° 施 主; eng-cü′ 恩 主, the last so called by the receiver.

GIZZARD, cing 肫; cing-tsông′ 肫 膛

GLAD, hwun-hyi′ 歡 喜; *very* —, fi-væn′ hwun-hyi′ 非 凡 歡 喜; feh′-tsiao dza hwun-hyi′ 了° 弗 得° 歡° 喜

GLADDEN, *to* — *him,* peh′ gyi hwun-hyi′ 俾° 其° 歡 喜; ying′ gyi k′æ-sing′ 引 其 開 心

GLANCE, *a* ih-k′en′ 一 看; *see at a* —, ih-moh′ liao-jün′ 一 目 了 然

GLANCE *to* — *off,* ts′ia′ ts′ah′-ko 斜° 擦°過°; *I have glanced over this book,* keh′ bu shü ngô k′en-k′en ko′-de 這° 部 書 我 看 過 了°

GLANDULAR *swelling,* heng-weh′; dæn-weh′ 痰 核°

GLARE *of light,* kwông li-′æ′ 光 利 害; — *of lightning,* din-kwông′ 電 光; — *from water,* shü teo′-kwông 水° 鬪 光; *glaring eyes,* ngæn-tsing-kwông liu′-liu 眼 睛 光 䁦 䁦°

GLASS, po-li′ 玻 璃; *a pane of* —, ih-kw′e′ 一 塊; ih-p′in 一 片; *to put in a pane of* —, p′e ih-kw′e′ po li′ 配 一 塊 玻 璃; *lest the* — *be broken,* k′ong′-p′ô po-li′ iao k′ao-se′ 恐 怕 玻 璃 要 敲 碎; — *beads,* liao′-cü 料 珠; po-li′ cü 玻 璃 珠; — *bottle,* po-li′ bing 玻 璃 瓶; — *ware,* po-li′ kô′-sang 玻 璃 物° 件°; po-li′ ho 玻 璃 貨; — *maker,* siao po-li′ s-vu 燒 玻 璃 司 務

GLAZING (for pottery, &c.), yiu-shü′ 油 水°; *to put on* —, zông′ yiu-shü′ 上 油 水°

GLEAM, *a* — *of light,* ih-sin′ liang-kwông′ 一 線 亮 光; — *of hope,* ih-ngæn-ngæn′ c′ih-lu′ 一 點° 點° 出 路

GLIB *of tongue,* cü-jing'-bi-boh' 嘴唇皮薄

GLIDE, *to — along,* liu-ko'-ky'i 溜過去°; wah-ko'-ky'i 滑過去°; — *prettily,* ts'ô-ts'ô' tseo dza hao'.

GLIMPSE, *catch a — of,* tsiao-min k'en-kyin 照面看

GLISTEN, *to* t'eo-kwông' 透光; fah-kwông' 發光

GLITTERING, shih'-liang 雪亮; shih'-kwah-liang 雪括亮

GLOBE, gyiu 球; *terrestrial —,* di-gyiu' 地球; *celestial —,* t'in-gyiu' 天球; — (or shade) *of a lamp,* teng-tsao' 燈罩 (ih-go)

GLOOMY, kwu-ts'i' 孤悽; — *and morose,* ziang meng-dong' lao-hwu' ka 像°悶洞老虎

GLORIFY, *to praise,* ts'ing-tsæn' 稱讚; — *God,* kwe yüong-wô' peh Jing-ming' 歸榮華與°神明

GLORIOUS, kwông-wô'-go 光華個; yiu yüong-wô' 有榮華; yiu yüong-kwông' 有榮光 (veng.)

GLORY, yüong-wô' 榮華; kwông-ts'æ' 光彩; *to appropriate the — which belongs to another,* tsin bih'-nying-go kwông 佔別人個°光

GLORY, *to — in,* ts'ing hyüing' 稱勳 See BOAST.

GLOSS, *to — over an affair,* tsông-sih' ih-yiang z-ken' 裝飾一樣事幹

GLOSSY, ts-jing' yiu kwông' 滋

潤有光; ky'i liang-deo' 起亮頭; *not* — , m kwông'-go 無°光個°

GLOVE, siu'-t'ao 手套 (a pair, ih-fu, ih-sông)

GLOWING *charcoal,* siao'-'ong'-go t'æn-ho 燒紅個°炭火; — *heart,* sing ziang ho-döu' ka nyih 心像°火團熱°; *face — with pleasure,* hwun-hyi-teh 'ong-kwông' mun-min 歡喜得°紅光滿面

GLUE, kao 膠; wông'-kao 汪膠°; *Canton —,* Kwông'-kao 廣膠°; *fish —,* ng-kao' 魚膠°; *cow-skin —,* ngeo-bi'-kao 牛°皮膠°

GLUTTONOUS, t'en-cü'-go 貪嘴個°; t'en-zih'-go 貪食個°; t'en-ky'üoh'-go 貪吃°個°

GNASH *the teeth,* ngao ngô' 鉸°牙°; ts'ih' ts'i 切齒

GNAW, *to* k'eng 齦; — *a board,* k'eng pæn' 齦板

GO, *to* ky'i 去; *come and —* , læ-wông' 來往; læ-læ'-ky'i-ky'i 來來去°去°; — *up,* tseo'-zông-ky'i 走上去°; — *out,* tseo'-c'ih-ky'i' 走出去°; — *on a journey,* c'ih-meng' 出門; — *by or over,* tseo'-ko-ky'i 走過去°; *cannot —,* ky'i'-feh-læ 去°弗來; — *aboard,* loh jün' 落船; zông jün' 上船; — *on shore,* zông-ngen' 上岸; — *astray,* mi-lu' 迷路; *the sun goes down,* nyih-deo' loh-sæn' 日頭

落 山；— *out* (as fire), u-long'-ky'i 漸° 漸° 熄 了°；— *away to avoid the heat*, bi shü' ky'i 避 暑 去°；— *your own way then*, dæn'-ming ng' 但 憑° 你°

GOAD, *to force*, pih 逼；*to excite*, kyih 激；*to urge*, ts'e-ts'e bih' 催 促°

GOAT, sæn - yiang' 山 羊 (ih-tsah)

GO-BETWEEN, *mediator*, 'o-z'-nying 和 事 人°；— (in marriage), me-nying' 媒 人°；— (in buying), cong-nying' 中 人°；cong-nyiang'-nying 中 央° 人°

GOD, Jing-ming' 神 明；T'in-cü' 天 主；Zông-ti' 上 帝；*an idol*, bu-sah' 菩 薩；*gods of wood and clay*, nyi-su'-moh-tiao 泥 塑 木 雕；— *of the Buddhists*, Sih'-kyüô-meo'-nyi-veh' 釋 迦 牟 尼 佛：— *of War*, Kwæn-ti'-bu-sah 關 帝 菩 薩；— *of the Taoists*, Nyüoh-wông'-da'-ti 玉 皇 大 帝；*founder of the Taoist sect*, T'æ'-zông-lao-kyüing 太 上 老 君；— *of Wealth*, Dzæ-jiug'-bu-sah' 財 神 菩 薩；—*of the City*, Dzing-wong'-bu-sah' 城 隍 菩 薩；— *who judges departed spirits*, Nyin-lo'-da-wông' 閻 羅 大 王；*gods — of the Earth* (over districts), T'u'-di bu-sah' 土 地 菩 薩；*of the Kitchen*, Tsao'-kyüing bu-sah' 竈 君 菩 薩；*the Ursa Major* (worshipped by scholars),

Veng-ts'ông'-ti'-kyüing 文 昌 帝 君；— *of thunder and lightning*, Le-tsu'-bu-sah' 雷 祖 菩 薩；Le-kong' 雷 公；Le-bo' 雷 婆

GODDESS *of Mercy*, Kwun-ing' 觀 音；Kwun-shü'-ing-bu-sah' 觀 世 音 菩 薩；*Queen of Heaven* (worshipped by sailors), Nyiang-nyiang'-bu-sah' 娘 娘 菩 薩；T'in-'eo'-nyiang'-nyiang 天 后 娘 娘；— *that bestows children*, Song'-ts-nyiang'-nyiang 送 子 娘 娘

GODLY (*lit.* devoted) *person*, gyin-dzing'-go nying 虔 誠 个° 人°

GO-DOWN, dzæn'-vông 棧 房

GOING, *the price is* — *down*, kô'-din læ-tih loh' 價° 錢° 正 在° 落；kô'-din læ-tih tib' 價° 錢° 正 在°, 跌；*where are you* — ? ng'-tao ah-li-ky'i' 你°到何°處° 去°？— *home*, kyü oh'-li ky'i 歸° 家° 去°；*fire is gone out*, ho' u-de' 火 熄° 了°

GOITRE, weh-seng-dæ' 猢 猻 袋

GOLD, kying-ts' 金 子；*pure*, ts'ih'-kying 赤 金；*light colored* —, dæn-kying 淡 金；— *dust*, kying-sô' 金 沙；— *fish*, kying-ng' 金 魚°；— *leaf*, kying yih'-ts 金 葉 子；— *foil*, kying-boh' 金 箔

GOLDEN, kying-ts'-tso'-go 金 子 做 个°

GONG, dong-lo' 銅 鑼 (ih-min)；*to strike the* — k'ao lo' 敲° 鑼；

strike the — for an alarm, k'ao
lön-lo' 敲° 亂 鑼°

GOOD, hao 好; very —, ting hao'
頂好; very — man, kyüing-ts'-
nying 君子人°; ting'-hao
nying' 頂好人°; jün nying'
善人°; liang-jün'-nying' 良
善人°; — medicine, hao'-yiah
好藥; liang-yiah' 良藥; not
so — as, feh gyih'-jü 弗如; —
for nothing, fi'-veh 廢物 (chiefly
used of persons); — bye, (person
going says), siao-be' 少陪; ditto
(person staying says), mæn-mæn'
ky'i 慢慢去°; are you in —
health? ng hao' feh' 你° 好 否°?
ditto (generally to an elderly
person), ng gyin' feh 你° 健 否°?
is the child in — health? siao
nying hwæn' feh 小孩好°
否°? — night (to one going to
bed), ts'ing en-cü' 請安置; in
— order, zi-zi'-tsing-tsing 齊°
齊° 整整; I promise in — faith,
ngô' sò wô' we tso-tao' 我所話
會做到; — natured, &c., sing'-
kah hao' 性格好; — penman-
ship, pih'-fah hao' 筆法好; da
pih' 大筆; much — will come
of it, we sang hyü'-to hao'-c'ü
會生° 許多好處

GOODNESS, virtue, hao' teh'-ky'i
好德氣; thank you for your
great —, to-dzing' ng-go da tch'
多承你个° 大德

GOODS, ho 貨; ho'-veh 貨物;

household —, kô-sang' jih-veh'
家° 中° 物° 件°

GOOSE, ngo 鵝 (ih-tsah); wild
—, t'in ngo' 天鵝; ngang
ngo' 雁° 鵝; — quill, ngo-mao-
kwun' 鵝毛管

GORE, clotted blood, nying-long'-
liao-go hyüih' 凝攏个° 血;
— in a garment, toh-koh' 摒°
角° (ih-go)

GORGEOUS, wô-wô'-li-li 華華
麗麗

GORMANDIZER, dzæn - lao'- go
nying 貪° 饞 个° 人°

GOSLING, siao-ngo'小鵝 (ih-tsah)

GOSPEL, Foh'-ing 福音; preach
the —, djün Foh'-ing 傳福音

GOSSIP, to pun shih-wô' 搬說話

GOSSIP, idle 'æn-yin' 'æn-nyü'閒°
言 閒° 語

GOURD, wu-biao'瓠瓢 (ih-go); the
bottle —, wu-lu' or weh-lu'葫蘆

GOVERN, to kwun'-li 管理; djü
治; công'-kwun 掌管; — China,
kwun'-djü Cong-koh' 管治中
國; — the family, djü' kô 治
家°; công'-kwun kô-vu' z 掌管
家° 務事

GOVERNMENT of a country, koh-
tsing' 國政; — of affairs, koh'-
kô tsing'-z 國家° 政事

GOVERNOR of a province, fu'-dæ
撫臺; — of two or more provinces, tsong'-toh 總督; — of two
or more fu cities, dao'-dæ 道臺;
of one fu, or department, cü-fu'

知府; — *of a district or county,* cü-yün' 知縣°

GOWN, *a Chinaman's long —* (worn girded), dziang-sæn' 長衫; do-sæn' 大°衫; *ditto,* (worn ungirded), bao-ts' 袍子; *China-woman's —,* ao 襖; do-ao' 大°襖; *— worn over another —,* nga-t'ao' 外°套

GRACE, *favor,* eng-we' 恩惠; eng-tin' 恩典; eng-c'ong' 恩寵; eng-s' 恩賜; *to say —,* zia-zia' Jing-ming' 謝°謝°神明

GRACEFUL, *easy in motion,* kyü'-ts yüö'-cü 舉止雅致

GRACIOUS (as a superior), ky'in-ziang' 謙讓; *will grant favor,* we s-eng' go 會賜恩个°; *merciful,* dz-pe'-go 慈悲个°

GRADE, teng'-kyih 等級; *a —,* ih-teng 一等; ih-kyih' 一級

GRADUALLY, dzin'-dzin 漸漸; *step by step,* ih-bu' ih-bu' 一步一步; *— improving,* dzin'-dzin tsing-ih' 漸漸進益; *ditto in health,* or *trade,* dzin'-dzin hao'-ky'i-læ 漸漸好起來

GRADUATE, *to mark by degrees,* feng du'-su' 分度數

GRADUATE, *first literary —,* (*i.e.* lowest), siu'-dzæ 秀才; *— of the second degree,* kyü'-nying 舉人°; *— of the third degree,* tsing'-z 進士; *— of the fourth degree,* 'en-ling' 翰林; *to become a — of the 1st degree,* tsing 'oh' 進學°; *ditto of the 2nd degree,* cong kyü'-

nying 中舉人°; *ditto of the 3rd degree,* cong tsing'-z 中進士; *ditto of the 4th degree,* tin' 'en'-ling 點翰林; *the highest of the graduates,* zông nyün' 狀元

GRAFT, *to — a tree,* tsih jü' 接樹

GRAIN, *five kinds of —,* ng' koh 五°穀; *viz.,* rice, dao 稻, *fine millet,* soh 黍°, *coarse millet,* lu-tsi 稷° (including several varieties), *wheat,* mah 麥 (also including barley and buckwheat), *and beans,* deo 菽°

GRAIN, *texture,* liu 絡; veng 紋; *with the —,* dzih liu' 直絡; *across the —,* wang liu' 橫°絡; wang veng' 橫°紋

GRAIN, *to —* (in painting, &c.), tso hwô-veng' 做花紋

GRAMMAR, veng-yüoh' or veng-'oh' 文學

GRANARY, ts'ông 倉; — *for rice,* koh' ts'ông 穀倉; *two granaries,* liang kæn ts'ông 兩間°倉

GRAND, *high and large,* kao-do' 高大°; — (as an officer's train, or a body of soldiers), we-fong' 威風; — *idea,* i'-s kwông'-kw'eh 意思廣闊; — (as many buildings, or a city), væn-wô' 繁華

GRANDDAUGHTER, *son's daughter,* seng-nyü' 孫女; nön-su' 囡孫°; *daughter's daughter,* nga-sang-nön' 外°孫°囡°; *ditto's daughter,* yün' nga-sang-nön' 玄外°孫°囡°

GRANDFATHER *on father's side,* yia'-yia 爺° 爺°; tsu'-vu 祖 父; *deceased* —, sin-tsu' 先祖; *your ditto,* tseng-tsu' 尊祖; *ditto (in answer),* kô-tsu' 家祖; *mother's father,* nga-kong' 外° 公; wæ tsu'-vu 外 祖 父; *great* — *on father's side,* t'a'-kong 太° 公; tseng-tsu' 曾 祖; *great great* —, kao tsu' 高祖; *great* — *on mother's side,* t'a' nga-kong 太° 外° 公; wæ tseng' tsu 外 曾 祖; *grandfather's older brother,* pah'-kong 伯°公; *grandfather's older brother's wife* pah'-bo 伯° 婆 *grandfather's younger brother,* soh'-kong 叔 公; *grandfather's younger brother's wife,* soh'-bo 叔 婆

GRANDMOTHER *on father's side,* nyiang'-nyiang 娘 娘; tsu'-meo 祖母; *deceased ditto,* sin tsu'-meo 先 祖 母; —, *on mother's side,* nga-bo' 外° 婆; wæ tsu'-meo 外 祖母; *deceased ditto,* sin wæ-tsu' 先 外 祖; *great* — *on father's side,* t'a'-bo 太° 婆; tseng tsu'-meo 曾祖母; *ditto on mother's side,* t'a'-nga-bo 太° 外° 婆

GRANDSON, *son's son,* seng-ts' 孫 子; *daughter's son,* nga-sang' 外° 甥°; *grandson's son,* tseng-seng' 曾孫; *grandson's grandson,* yün-seng' 玄孫

GRANITE, *greenish* ts'ing zah' 石青

GRANT, *to* cing 准; *to bestow,*

s'-peh 賜給°; *to allow,* ing-hyü' 應 許; ing-dzing' 應 承; — *this once, but never again,* 'eo'-peh we-li' 後 不 爲 例

GRAPES, *purple* bu-dao' 葡萄; ts'-bu-dao 紫葡萄; *white* —, se'-tsing bu-dao' 水 晶 葡 萄

GRAPHICALLY, weh-siang' 活 相; — *described,* kông'-leh weh-siang' 講得° 活相

GRAPPLE, *to* — *with hooks,* keo-djü' 鈎 住; *to hold fast,* tsah' djü 紮° 住

GRASP, *to* — *in the hand,* nyiah 捻; *to clutch,* cô 抓; — *firmly,* cô lao' 抓 牢 (cô or tsô)

GRASS, ts'ao 草; *green* —, ts'ing-ts'ao' 青草; *to cut,* — kah ts'ao' 割草

GRASS-CLOTH, 'ô-pu' 夏° 布; (*a piece,* ih-p'ih)

GRASS-HOPPER, koh'-mang 穀 蜢°; keh'-mang 蚱 蜢° (ih-tsah)

GRATE (*in a stove, or furnace*), ho'-lu tsah'-li 火 爐 柵°

GRATE, *to* —, bao 刨; — *nutmeg,* bao nyüoh-ko' 刨 肉° 果; — (*i. e. grind*) *the teeth,* mo ngô-ts' 磨 牙° 齒; — *upon the senses,* seng'-nying-go 塞° 心°

GRATEFUL, yiu peng'-sing 有 本 心; yiu jing-sing' 有 仁 心; *I am* — *to you* (*for great favor*), ngô ken' ng-go eng' 我 感 你° 个° 恩; *he is* —, gyi'-yiu peng'-sing 其有 本 心; *he is* — *to me,* gyi' ken ngô'-go eng 其 感 我 個° 恩

GRATIFIED, hwun - hyi' 歡 喜 _highly_ —, sing'-li to'-siao kw'a'-loh 心 裡 多 少 快° 樂

GRATIFY, _to_ — _one's desire_, dzong sing' sô-yüoh' 從 心 所 欲; _seeking to_ — _another's wishes_, t'i'-sing t'iah-i'-go 體 心 貼° 意 個

GRATITUDE, peng'-sing 本 心; ken-eng'-go-sing 感 恩 個° 心; jing-sing' 仁 心

GRATUITOUSLY, _give_ —, bah-song' 白 送; _to eat rice_ —, bah ky'üoh'-væn 白° 吃° 飯

GRAVE, _tomb_, veng 墳; veng-mo' 墳 墓 (ih-yüih, or ih-ts); _to go to the_ —, _worship, and add earth_, zông-veng' 上 墳; _to make a mound over a_ —, ling-veng' 淋 墳; — _clothes_, ziu-i' 壽 衣; ko'-lao-i' 故° 老 衣; lang'-i 冷 衣; — _stone_, (upright) veng'-li-go pe' 墳 裡 個 碑; veng'-li-go pe-ba' 墳 裡 個 碑 牌°; _ditto_, (laid lengthwise in the side of the mound), læn-t'u' 攔 土; — _yard_, veng-di' 墳 地

GRAVE, lao'-lao 老 老; — _counte-nance_, min-k'ong' lao'-pæn-pæn 面 孔 老 板 板; lao'-lin 老 臉; _weighty_, djong'-jih 重 實

GRAVEL, zah-sô' 石° 沙; — _in the bladder_, sô-ling' 沙 淋

GRAVELY, lao-lao'-ky'i-ky'i 老 氣; — _assured me_, lao'-ky'i-vu-

dih' teng ngô kông' 老 氣 無 敵 與° 我 講°

GRAVITATION, _attraction of_ —, siang-hyih'-ts-shü 相 吸 之 勢

GRAVITY, _tendency to the earth's centre_, di-gyiu hyih'-lih 地 球 吸 力

GRAVY, tsih'-shü 汁 水°; lu 滷; tsih'-lu 汁 滷; — _tureen_, tsih'-shü kwun' 汁 水° 罐

GRAY, hwe-seh' 灰 色; (slightly) — _haired_, deo'-fah hwô-bah'-de 頭 髮 花 白° 了°; _becoming_ —, læ'-tih bah-ky'i'-læ 漸° 漸 白° 起 來

GRAZE, _to rub against_, ts'ah'-djoh 擦 着°; _to eat grass_, ky'üoh ts'ao' 吃° 草

GRAZIER, yiang ngeo'-go cü'-kwu 養 牛° 個 主 顧

GREASE, yiu 油; yiu-nyi' 油 膩

GREASE, _to_ dzô yiu' 搽 油; ts'ah yiu' 擦 油; — _the hair_, yiu' fu deo-fah' 油 傅 頭 髮

GREASY, yiu yiu-nyi' 有 油 膩; _too_ — (_fat_), t'eh' yiu-nyi' 甚° 油 膩; t'eh yiu' 甚° 油

GREAT, do 大; _very_ —, do-leh'-kying 大° 得° 緊; _a_ — _many_, hyü'-to 許 多; — _while_, hyü'-to kong-fu' 許 多 工 夫; _of_ — _advantage_, do' yiu' ih'-c'ü 大° 有 益 處; _of_ — _extent_ (as the sea), mang-yiang'-yiang 漫 洋 洋

GREATER _than_, do-jü' 大° 如; — _than that_, pi gyi' do 比 其

大°; *still* —, keng'-kô do'更 加°
大°; yü-kô' do 愈 加°大°; *the*
— *part*, ih do pun' 一 大° 半
GREATEST, *the* ting'do 頂 大°
GREATLY, do-nyiang' 大° 樣°;
long-do' 弄 大°; — *mistaken*,
do-nyiang' ts'eng' ts'o 大° 樣°
忖 錯
GREEDY, t'en to'貪 多; —*in eating*
t'en ky'üoh' 貪 吃°; dzæn-lao'
貪 饞; lao-zao'; *wants more*
*than he can chew*, "t'en to',
ziah'-feh-se'" 貪 多 嚼 弗 碎
GREEN, loh 綠; pih'-loh 碧 綠;
*bluish* —, shü'-loh 水° 綠; *pea*
—, kyiu'-ngô-seh 韭 芽° 色;
*greenish lemon color*, mih-seh'
蜜 色
GREET, *to* mông-mông' 望° 望°;
'eo-'eo' 候 候; *to wish peace*,
ts'ing-en' 請 安; *to congratulate*,
'o-'o' 賀 賀; *I* — (you), kong-
hyi' kong-hyi' 恭 喜 恭 喜
GRIEF, pe-sông' 悲 傷; *great* —,
t'ong'-sông 痛 傷; *sorrow*, iu-
meng' 憂 悶
GRIEVANCE, *wrong*, we'-ky'üoh
委 屈°; *tell one's* —, su-ün' 訴 冤
GRIEVE *me*, cü'-s ngô tæn iu-meng'
致 使 我 擔 憂 悶; long'-leh
ngô sing' næn-ko' 弄 得°我 心
難 過
GRIEVOUS, *heavy*, djong 重; *af-
flictive*, kw'u 苦; *severe*, li-'æ'
利 害
GRIM, p'o'-siang 怕 相

GRIMACE, *to make crooked mouths*,
tsông hwa-cü' 裝 歪° 嘴°; li-leh
ngô'-ts siao' 齷 得°牙°齒°笑; li-
ngô'-bô-ts' siao' 齷 牙°齯 齒 笑
GRIN, *to draw up the lips, showing*
*the teeth*, c'ih'-jing lu-ts' 出 唇 露
齒 (not necessarily laughing.)
GRIND, *to* mo 磨; — *to powder*,
mo-feng' 磨 粉; — *in a mortar*,
nyin 研: *ditto to powder*, nyin-
meh' 研 末
GRIND-STONE, mo- tao'-zah 磨
刀 石°
GRIPES, du'-dziang kao'-long 肚
腸 絞°攪
GRISTLE, deng-kying' 輭 骨°;
ts'e'-kweh 脆 骨 (veng.)
GRIT, *the coarse part of meal*, feng'-
deo 粉 頭; *sand*, sô-nyi' 沙 泥
GRITTY, *containing sand*, yiu sô'-
go 有 沙 个°
GROAN, *to* üô-üô'-hyiang 呀°呀°
響; — *loudly*, yüô-yüô'-si; *groan-
ing with pain*, t'ong'-teh üô-üô'-
hyiang 痛 得°呀°呀°響
GROCERY, zah-ho'-tin 雜°貨 店
(where wax, alum, thread, ratan,
dye-stuffs, &c., are sold); nen-
poh' zah-ho'-tin 南 北 雜 貨 店
(where sugar, fruits, nuts, &c.,
are sold).
GROIN, kah'-kyiah-vong'夾°脚 縫°
GROOVE, *a* ih-da zao' 一 埭°漕°
GROPE, *to* moh-læ' moh-ky'i'摸
來 摸 去°; — *in the dark*, en'-
moh 暗 摸

GROSS, *coarse and large,* ts'u-do' 粗大°; — *and vulgar,* yiu-ky'iang'-weh-diao' 油腔滑調; — *language,* yiu-wô' 油話; *in the —, or good and bad together,* lin-deo'-ta-kyiah' 連頭帶°脚; — *weight,* lin-bi' 連皮; mao'-kying-liang' 毛勦兩; *buy in the — or large quantity,* teng'-tông ma' 蔓當買°; *price when bought in the —,* t'ong bun' 'ông-dzing' 通盤行情

GROUND, di-yiang' 地; *basis,* keng-kyiah' 根脚

GROUND-FLOOR, di-pæn' 地板

GROUNDLESS, m̃-keng'-kyiah 無°根脚; m̃-ing'-ts'ong 無°影踪

GROUND-NUT, *pea-nut,* hwô-seng' 花生

GROUND-RENT, di tsu'-din 地租錢°

GROUP, de 隊; *in a —,* dzing-de' 成隊; *in groups,* de-tang'-de 隊打隊

GROVE, ling 林; jü-ling' 樹林; *one tree cannot become a — (i. e. one alone cannot do the work of many),* "doh-moh' feh-dzing'-ling" 獨木弗成林

GROW, *to* do-ky'i'-læ 大°起來; *to multiply,* to-ky'i'-læ 多起來; hying'-ky'i-læ 興起來; — *less (as a pencil by use, &c.),* siao mo-long'-ky'i 銷磨攏去°; *to — cold,* dzin'-dzin lang'-ky'i-læ 漸漸冷°起來; — *into a habit* dzin'-dzin tso'-kwæn 漸漸做慣°; *it grew so,* sang-dzing' z-ka'-go 生成如°此; t'in-jün' z-ka'-go 天然如°此°

GROWL, *to* wu-wu'-hyiang 咽咽響

GROWN, *full* dziang-tsoh'; tsoh; tsiang-tsoh' 長足; do-tsoh' 大°足

GRUDGE, *to* (as money), feh-sô'-teh' 弗捨°得; *a —, or to lay up a —,* kyiæ'-i 介意; *don't lay up a — against me,* hao-vong' kyiæ'-i ü ngô 弗°°用°介意於我

GRUEL, *meal* boh-go feng'-wu 薄个°粉糊; *rice —,* boh-coh' 薄粥; ing'-t'ông 飲湯; *make rice —,* lin boh-coh'.

GRUFF *in manner,* oh'-cü-ngæn-siang' 惡嘴眼°相; *to speak gruffly,* wu-long' hyiang-liang kông' 喉°嚨響亮講; yi-li' wæ-ke' kông'; *to reprove gruffly,* heng-hô.

GRUM *looking,* lang'-lin-go 冷°臉个°; lao'-pæn-pæn 老板板; *very —,* heng'-hwu-hwu; — *in face and answer,* lang-min' lang-teh' 冷°面冷°答

GRUMBLE, *to* ün 怨; — *to one's self,* zi gæn' zi 自°慽°自°; — *at heaven and earth,* ün'-t'in 'eng-di' 怨天恨地; — *like a discontented spirit,* ün-w̃ông' kyü'-kyiao 冤枉鬼°叫

GRUNT, *to* ng-ng'-hyiang 嗅 嗅 響; — *as a pig*, nyü-nyü'-hyiang 噥 噥° 響

GUARANTEE, pao-p'iao' 保票; *pledge*, ti'-deo 抵 頭; tông'-deo 當頭; ah'-deo 押 頭

GUARANTEE, *to* pao 保; — *success in a lawsuit*, pao' tang'-kwun-s 包 打 官 司

GUARD, *to* pao'-wu 保 護 ·

GUARD, *to be on one's* —, kying'-bông 謹 防; tso-gyi' 留° 心°; kwu'-djoh 顧 著°

GUARD, *military* pao'-wu-go ping' 保 護 个° 兵; *imperial body* —, z'-we 侍 衛

GUARDIAN, kæ-kwun'-go nying 該 管 个° 人°; — *of a child*, pao'-nying 保 人°; dæ-vu'-meo 代 父 母

GUESS, *to* ts'æ 猜; ts'æ-ts'æ'-k'en 猜 猜 看; *to* — *the meaning*, a i'-nyi 猜° 意° 義; *to estimate*, kwu 佑; — *a riddle*, ts'æ me-ts' 猜 謎° 子; — *one's thoughts*, liao sing-s' 料 心° 思; *guessed rightly*, ts'æ-djoh'-de 猜 著° 了°; *can't* —, ts'æ-feh-c'ih' 猜 弗 出

GUEST, nying-k'ah' 客 人°; *to receive* (meet) *a* —, we nying-k'ah' 會 客 人°; *to entertain a* —, be k'ah' 陪 客; *to accompany a* —, song k'ah 送 客; *belonging to a* —, k'ah'-pin-go

客 邊 个°; — *room or parlor*, k'ah'-vông 客 房·

Guest in the veng-li is *k'ah-nying*; therefore we transpose the characters wherever nying-k'ah occurs.

GUIDE, ling-lu'-go nying 領 路 个 人°

GUIDE, *to* ling 領; *lead the way*, ling lu' 領 路; ying'-dao lu' 引 導 路; *to* — *the pen* (for another), pô pih' 把 筆

GUILD, pông 幫; *Fuh-kien* —, Kyin'-pông 建 幫; *Canton* —, Kwông'-pông 廣 幫

GUILE, kæn-tsô' 奸° 詐; *full of* —, jing'-z kæn-tsô' 純° 是 奸° 詐

GUILELESS, dzih-kwah' 直 鵠; m̆ tsô'-sing 無° 詐 心

GUILT, ze 罪; ze'-ming 罪 名; *to expiate* —, ti ze' 抵 罪; ti'-siao ze' 抵 銷 罪

GUILTLESS, m̆ ze' 無° 罪; m̆ ze'-ming 無° 罪 名

GUILTY, yiu ze' 有 罪; yiu' ze'-ming 有 罪 名; — *of death*, yiu si'-ze 有 死° 罪

GUISE, *man in the* — *of a woman*, nen-tsông'-nyü'-pæn 男裝女扮

GUITAR, *four stringed* —, bi-bô' 琶 琵; *three stringed* —, yin-ts' 絃 子

GULF, ao 墺; wæn 灣

GULL, *sea* kông-mæn' 閗 鷗°

GULL, *to deceive*, ky'i-p'in' 欺 騙; kwa'-p'in 拐° 騙

GULP *down*, t'eng-loh'-ky'i 吞 落 去°; *to* — *up*, t'u'-c'ih 吐 出

GUM, jü-kao′ 樹膠°; — *benjamin*, en-sih′-hyiang 安息香

GUMS, ngô-nyüoh 牙肉°

GUN, ts′iang 鎗; nyiao′-ts′iang 鳥鎗 (ih-kwun); *to fire a —*, fông nyiao′-ts′iang 放鳥鎗

GUN-BOAT, p′ao′-jün 礮船

GUNNER, ts′iang-siu′ 鎗手; *cannonier*, p′ao′-siu 礮手

GUN-POWDER, ho′-yiah 火藥; *to mix —*, keh ho′-yiah 合火藥

GUNSHOT, *within* kong-bu′-li 弓步裡; *beyond —*, kong-bu′-nga 弓步外°; (these terms are principally used in archery).

GUN-SMITH, cü-ts′iang′-go 鑄鎗個°; *a repairer of guns*, siu-ts′iang′ s-vu′ 修°鎗司務

GURGLING *noise*, goh-loh-loh′ hyiang° 榖°轆°轆°響; — *in the throat*, hæ′-ti-dæn zông′ sing-hyiang° 喉°嚨°痰上聲響

GUSH, *to — out*, üong′-c′ih 湧出; piao-c′ih′ 滮出; pao′-c′ih′ 爆出; *tears — out*, ngæn-li pao′-c′ih-læ 眼淚爆出來

GUST, *a — of wind*, ih-zi fong′; ih-dzing fong′ 一陣風

GUSTO, *he told it with —*, gyi-zi′ kông-leh yiu mi-dao′ 其自°講得°有味°道

GUTS, dziang 腸; du′-dziang 肚腸

GUTTER *for conveying water*, shü′-liu 水°溜; *drain*, keo 溝

GUTTURAL *sound*, ′eo-ing′ 喉音

GYPSUM, zah-kao′ 石°膏

# H

HABIT, *in the — of smoking*, kwæn iao ky′üoh′-in 慣°要吃°烟; — *becomes second nature*, jih-kyiu′ dzing t′in-sing 習久成天性; jih-kwæn′ dzing z-jün′ 習慣°成自然; *it is hard to break up an old —*, tso′-kwæn-liao næn kæ′ 做慣°了難改; *careless habits*, wa yiang′-væn 孬°樣式°; *bad —*, wa bi′-ky′i 孬°脾氣

HABITABLE, hao-djü′-go 好住個°; *not —*, djü′-feh-læ 住弗來

HABITUAL, *it is — with him to do so*, gyi su′-djông z-ka′ tso′-fah 其°素常如°此做法; gyi kwæn′ z-ka 其慣°如°此°

HABITATION, *dwelling house*, djü-kyü′ 住居; djü-oh° 住屋

HACK, *to cut irregularly* (with a knife), lön kah′ 亂割; *ditto* (with a knife, or axe), lön tsæn′ 亂斬

HAG, m̄ yiang′-væn-go lao-t′a-bo′ 無°樣式°个°老太°婆

HAGGARD, t′eh-ying′ 脫形

HAGGLE, *to — with scizzors*, tsin′-leh ky′üih-tsing′-ky′üih-c′ih′ 剪得°缺進缺出; — *with a knife*, ts′ih′-leh mao-mao′-ts′ao-ts′ao 切得°毛毛草草; — *about price*, leng-liang kô′-din 論量價°錢°; — (about anything), leng′-kying kwu′-liang 論劬估兩

HAIL, boh-ts′ 雹°子; *to* —, loh boh-ts′ 落雹°子

HAIL, *to call,* eo 叫°; *call loudly,* eo-leh hyiang′ 叫°得°響; *when hailing a stranger, say teacher,* sin-sang′ 先生°; *if* elderly say *older brother,* ah-ko′ 阿哥′; *or uncle,* ah-song′ 阿叔°; *if a mechanic,* s-vu′ 司務

HAIR *on animals,* mao 毛; *on the human body,* ʻen-mao′ 汗毛; — *on the head,* deo-fah′ 頭髮 (ih-keng)

HAIR-BRUSH, deo-fah′ shih′-tsiu 頭髮刷篲; *native* — (for mucilage), ming′-ts 抿子 (ih-kwun)

HAIR-BREADTH, *not the difference of a* —, ʻao-vu koh-yiang′ 毫無各樣; s-ʻao feh-ts′o′ 絲毫弗錯; *within a* — (*i. e.* eyebrow hair) *of being killed,* ts′ô-ih min-mao iao sah′-diao-de 差一眉°毛要殺了°

HAIRY (as a person), ng-′mao to 五°毛多

HALE, k′ông-gyin′ 康健; kyiah′-ky′ing-siu′-gyin 脚輕手健; sing-tsông′ lih-gyin′ 身壯力健 *only used of young people.*

HALF, pun 半; *exactly* —, te′-pun 對半; p′ih-pun′-pin 劈半邊; — *an hour,* pun′ tin-cong 半點鐘; *a dollar and a* —, ih-kwʻe′-pun 一塊半; — *brother,* koh′-meo hyüong-di′ 各母兄弟; *this* —, dông′-pun-

pin 這°半邊; *that* —, keh′-pun-pin 那°半邊; — *cooked,* sang-hwe-boh-loh′ 生灰泊落; pun′-sang-li-joh 半生°裡熟 (also used for a lesson half learned); — *done,* pun′ tso-hao′ 半做好; — *moon,* pun′-pin yüih-liang′ 半邊月亮; *on* — *pay* (soldiers), kyʻüoh pun′-feng zin-liang′ 吃°半分錢°粮; *ditto* (officials), ziu pun′-fong 受半俸

HALL, *central room,* cong-kæn′ 中間°; *an entrance room,* tsing′-c′ih-kæn 進出間°; *the principal room in a Chinese house,* dông-zin′ 堂前°; *ancestral* —, z-dông′ 祠堂; — *of assembly,* kong-sô′ 公所; weʻ-kwun 會舘; — *of audience* (emperor's), din 殿; kying-lön′-din 金鑾殿; — *of examination* (for kyü-nying), kong′-yün 貢院; *ditto* (for siu-dzæ), tsʻah′-yün 察院; kʻao′-bang 考棚; — *of learning,* ʻoh-dông′ 學°堂

HALLOO *there,* ʻe 唉; *to shout,* wæ-wæ eo-hyiang 高°聲°叫°響

HALLOW, *to reverence,* tseng-kying′ 尊敬; *set it apart as holy,* tseng-kyʻi gyi tso sing′-jün-go 尊敬其做聖善个°

HALO *over the head,* deo-zông′ ʻao-kwông′ 頭上毫光; — *of wisdom,* weʻ-kwông 慧光; — *around* the moon, yüih-yüing′ 月暈

HALT, to stop a while, dzæn-z′ deng-loh′ 暫時停°落; halt! lib-loh′ 立落!

HALT, lame, kwa′-kyiah 拐° 脚

HALTER for a horse, mô′-long-deo 馬繮頭

HALVE, to te′-feng-k′æ 對分開

HALVES, two liang′-kô-sang′; liang′-pun-pin′ 兩 半 邊

HAM (salted and dried), ho′-t′e 火腿; salted —, yin t′e 鹹腿; — in man, kyiah′-ao 脚坳

HAMLET, a ih-ts′eng 一村

HAMMER, lông-deo′ 榔頭; iron —, t′ih djü′ 鐵鎚; t′ih′ lông-deo 鐵榔頭 (ih-kwun); — handle, lông-deo′ ping 榔頭柄

HAMMER, to — iron, tang t′ih′ 打鐵; — clothes, djü i-zông′ 搗° 衣裳; — a nail, k′ao ting-cü′ 敲° 釘銖

HAMMOCK, hanging cot, tiao′-zông 弔床°

HAMSTRING, the tendon above the heel, (which the Chinese cut in lieu of the hamstring), kyiah′-kying 脚筋; ′eo′-ts′in-kying 脚° 跟° 筋; to cut ditto, kyiah′-kying fông′-dön 脚筋放斷

HAND, siu 手 (ih-tsah); both hands, liang-tsah siu 兩隻手; sông siu′ 雙手; give him a — (i. e. help), vu gyi′ ih-pô′ 扶其一

把; to stretch forth the —, sing siu′ 伸手; to shake the —, la siu′ 攝°手; draw the —into the sleeve, soh siu′ 縮手; geo siu′; to come to —, tsih tao′ siu 接到手; to carry in both hands, p′ong 捧°; to join both hands, ′eh-công′ 合掌; ditto in salutation, kong siu′ 拱手; the right —, jing′ siu 順手; jing-tsah′ siu; the left —, tsia′ siu 左°手; an experienced —, joh-siu′ 熟手; a raw —, sang-siu′ 生°手

HAND, to di 遞; — up, di-zông′ 遞上°; — to her chair, tông′ gyi zông gyiao′ 扶 其 上 轎; — over, kao-fu′ 交° 付; kao′-dæ 交° 代; — down (as tradition), djün-loh′-læ 傳落來

HAND-BASIN (i. e. face-basin), min-dong′ 面桶; min-beng′ 面盆

HAND-BELL, ling 鈴 (ih-tsah); to ring a —, loh ling′ 摝° 鈴; yiao ling′ 搖鈴

HAND-BREADTH, a ih siu′-min kw′eh′ 一手面闊

HAND-CUFF, siu′-k′ao 手栲 (a pair, ih-fu)

HANDFUL, a ih-pô′ 一把; ih mun′-siu 一滿手

HANDIWORK, siu′-dön 手段

HANDKERCHIEF, kyün-p′æn′ 絹帕°; silk — (carried by Chinese women for ornament), siu′-p′ao 手帕°

HANDLE, *straight* ping 柄; *rounded* — or *bale*, gwæn 鐶° (ih-go); there are a few exceptions thus, *a tea-pot* — (at the side) is either, dzô-wu' ping 茶壺柄 or dzô-wu' gwæn 茶壺鐶°; and a *cup* — is, pe-ts ping 杯子柄; ng'-tô-bi 耳°朵皮 is used, but not properly.

HANDLE, *to* long 弄; *to touch*, mob 摸; *to take in the hand*, do læ siu-li 拏°在°手裡; *to move*, dong 動; *must not* —, m̄-nao' long 弗°可°弄; m̄-nao' dong 弗°可°動

HANDSOME (used of persons, pictures, &c.), me'-li 美麗; ts'ing siu' 清秀; *pretty*, hao'-k'en 好看; *very* — *woman*, me' nyü 美女; — (as dress, places, &c.), wô-li' 華麗; yin-li' 艷麗; — (as work), tsing-cü' 精緻; — *as Si-s* (a beauty of antiquity), ziang Si-s ka me'-mao 像°西施美貌

HANDWRITING, pih'-tsih 筆跡; z'-tsih 字跡

HANDY, ling-long' t'ih-t'eo' 玲瓏剔透; *convenient*, bin-tông' 便當

HANG, *to* tiao 弔; — *against* (as against the wall), kwô 掛; *hang* (it) *up*, kwô'-kwô hao' 掛掛好; *to* — *one's self*, zông-tiao' 上弔; yün-liang' 懸樑; — *a person*, tiao nying sah' 弔人°死; —

*to dry* (properly, in the shade), lông 晾

HANK, ih-kao' 一絞°; ih-siao' 一綃; — *of silk*, ih-kao s-sin' 一絞°絲線; — *of linen thread*, ih-siao-sin' 一綃線

HANKER, *to* — *after*, ts'ih'-sing-go siang' 切心个°想; sah'-k'eo siang'.

HAPPEN, *when will it* — ? kyi-z' yiu' 幾時有? *when did it* — ? læ kyi-z' 在°幾時? *just happened so*, p'ong'-læ we'-su 遇°着°算數; *when walking I happened to have water thrown upon my head*, ngô tseo'-go z-'eo yiu shü', teo'-deo tao'-loh-læ 我走時候有水°兜頭倒落來; *happened so once* (to be bad), ngeo' ih-we ts' 偶一爲之; *there happened* (chanced) *to be*, neo'-ts'eo yiu' 偶°湊有; *happened to be right* (or wrong) *for once*, ts'in tsiao gyi vong 千朝奇逢

HAPPILY, *fortunately*, ying-hyi'-teh —, 幸係°得; ky'ü-leh' 虧°得°; ying-r' 幸而

HAPPINESS, foh'-ky'i 福氣; *peace is* —, bing-en' ziu z foh' 平安就°是福; *had the* — *to meet* (him), yiu ying' yü-djoh-de' 有幸遇着°了; *you have great* —, ng hao' foh-ky'i 你°好福氣

HAPPY, k'æ-sing 開心; yiu foh'-ky'i 有福氣; hao'-foh-ky'i 好福氣; kw'a'-weh 快活; —

*man,* yiu foh'-ky'i-go nying' 有
福氣个人°; foh'-nying 福
人°; *I am very* —, ngô sing'-
li kw'a'-loh-go 我心裡快°
樂个°; ngô ting' k'æ-sing 我
頂開心;—*face,* 'o-yin'-yüih-
seh' 和顏悦色

HARASS, *to* tsoh-næn' 作難;
*harassed,* sing-væn'-tsi-tsao 心
煩嘈°嘈; væn'-meng° 煩悶°;
*greatly harassed,* ng'-mô-loh-deo'-
cün 五°馬六頭鑽

HARBOR, k'eo 口; hæ'-k'eo 海
口; kông-k'eo' 港口; *enter the*
—, tsing k'eo' 進口

HARBORING *resentment,* yiu ün'-
ky'i dzeng'-tih 有怨氣存
的; ün'-ky'i feh-sæn' 怨氣弗
散; —*feelings of dislike,* yiu
'eng'-sing kyi'-tih 有恨心記
的

HARBOR-MASTER, li'-jün-t'ing'
理船廳

HARD, ngang 硬°; *difficult,* næn
難; — *to do,* næn-tso' 難做;
— *water,* sang-shü' 生°水°;
shü sing'-dao ngang 水°性道
硬°; *egg boiled* — *as a stone,*
dæn ts'-leh zah-ngang'-de 蛋煮°
得°石°硬°了°; — *work,* sang-
weh' keh-tah 生°活疙瘩;
*ditto* (heavy), djong'-deo sang-
weh' 重頭生°活; *study* —,
yüong kw'u'-kong doh-shü 用
苦功讀書;— *to get on with,*
(*i. e.* won't bear crossing), næn

ts'ah-ts'o 難作伴°; — *to say*
or *believe,* næn-dao' 難道

HARD-HEARTED, ngang-sing'-go
硬°心个°; sing-dziang-ngang'
心腸硬°

HARDEN, *to become hard* (as the
heart, vegetables, &c.), pin-
ngang' 變硬°; *will* — (as jelly,
&c.), we-ngang' 會硬°; *to grow
hard,* ngang-ky'i'-læ 硬°起夾

HARDLY *enough,* sao-we ts'ô'-tin
稍爲差點°; *I had* — *seated
myself when he came,* ngô wa tsih'-
leh zo'-loh gyi' ziu læ'-de 我還°
只坐°落其就°來了°

HARDSHIP, siao'-kw'u 小苦;
*great* —, næn-deo° 難頭°; *to
suffer* —, ky'üoh siao'-kw'u 吃°
小苦; *suffer great* —, ziu-næn'
受難

HARDWARE, *ironware,* t'ih'-ho
鐵貨; *iron utensils,* t'ih'-ky'i
鐵器

HARDY, kying-kweh'-hao 筋骨
好; *firmly knit,* tsah'-cü 堅°固°;
*can endure it,* tsah'-cü kying'-
leh ky'i 堅固°經得°起

HARE-LIP, ky'üih-cü' 缺嘴

HARK! t'ing'-tong 聽在°此°!

HARLOT, piao'-ts 表子; gyi-
nyü' 妓女; c'ông-vu' 娼嬌
(c'ông or ts'ông)

HARM, *to injure,* 'æ 害; long-
song' 弄唆°; *damage,* sông 傷;
*I will not* — *you,* ngô feh we'
long-song' ng 我弗會弄唆°

你°; *no* —, feh-dzæ'-wu 不
礙°事'; feh-ngæ' 弗碍; feh-
fông'-teh 弗妨得

HARMLESS, feh-'æ-nying'-go 弗
害人°个°; feh-ngæ'-go 弗碍
个°

HARMONIOUS, *agreeing in feeling*,
'o-moh' 和睦; kông'-leh-læ 講
得° 來; dong-sing-'eh-i' 同心
合意

HARMONIZE, *to* — *difficulties*, diao-
'o' 調和; long gy'i 'o-moh' 弄
其和睦

HARMONY *of the Gospels*, Foh'-
ing 'eh-ts'æn' 福音合叅

HARNESS *to a carriage*, tsông
mô-ts'ô 裝馬車°; t'ao' ts'ô-ts'
套車°子

HARP, *seven stringed* —, gying 琴;
*to play the* —, dæn gying 彈琴

HARROW, loh-din'-bô' 落田鈀
(ih-min)

HARSH *to the touch*, ts'ao 糙; —
*voice*, ngang-sing' ngang-ky'i'
硬°聲硬°氣; — *treatment*,
dæ nying k'eh'-li 待人°刻薄

HARTSHORN, *deer's horn*, loh koh'
鹿角°

HARVEST, *to* siu kah' 収割; *the
time of* —, siu-kah'-go z-'eo 収
割个°時候; *harvested not a
grain*, ts' lih vu siu' 子粒無収

HARVEST, *the crops*, nyin-dzing'
年成

HASH, *to* — *meat*, nyüoh tsæn-se'
肉°切°碎

HASP, meng-gying' 門襻° (ih-go)

HASTE, *in* —, kw'a 快°; kw'a'-
soh 快°速; 'ao-sao; *what's your*
— (*flurry*)? ng ky'i soh'-go
mông'-deo' 你°起甚°麼°忙
頭? *make* —, kw'a'-tin 快°
點; soh'-tin 速點; *do quickly*,
tso-leh kw'a' 做得°快°; *why
are you in such* — ? dza-we ka'
læ-feh-gyi' 何°為°如°此°來
弗及°?

HASTEN, *to* — *one's self*, zi ken'-
kying 自°趕緊; — *him*, ts'e'
gyi kw'a' 催其快°

HASTY, kyih 急; ts'ao 躁; *pre-
cipitate*, kyih-ts'ao' 急躁; —
*disposition*, sing'-kah kyih' 性格
急; — *way of doing things*, deo-
gyih'-goh-loh'; — *tempered and
severe*, bao-ts'ao' 暴躁; — *and
stubborn*, ao-pih 執°拗

HAT, mao-ts' 帽子 (ih-ting);
*straw* —, ts'ao' mao' 草帽; bu-
mao' 蒲帽; liang mao' 涼帽;
*felt* —, tsin mao' 氈帽; *to put
on a* —, ta mao' 戴帽; *to take
off the* —, tsoh' mao-ts' 除°帽
子; mao'-ts tsoh'-loh 帽子除°
落

HATCH, *to* — *eggs*, dæn bu-c'ih'
蛋菢出; *ditto* (*by heat*), dæn'
hong-c'ih' 蛋烘出

HATCHET, fu'-deo 斧頭 (ih-
pô.)

HATE, *to* u'-su 惡; k'eh'-ts'eng;
*to detest*, in-tseng' 厭憎

HATEFUL k'o-u'-go 可惡个°; k'eh'-ts'eng-go.

HATRED, *to feel* —, kyi 'eng-sing 記恨心; dzeng u'-su-go-sing' 存惡个°心; *ill-will,* ün'-ky'i 怨氣

HAUGHTINESS *is hard to endure,* jing-ky'i' næn-tông' 神氣難當

HAUGHTY, *to put on* — *airs,* pa kó'-ts 擺°架°子; pa-p'ing' 擺品

HAUL, *to* t'o 拖; — *a great net,* t'a do mông' 拖°大°網°

HAUNCH *of mutton,* yiang t'e' 羊腿

HAUNTED *house,* ing-oh' 陰屋

HAVE, yiu 有; — *you heard the news ?* keh'-go sing-sih ng yiu t'ing'-meng-ko' ma 這°个信息你°有聽聞°過麼? — *you any sugar ?* dông yiu' ma 糖有麼°? (I) — *some,* yiu 有; — *you been to Peking ?* Poh'-kying ng yiu tao'-ko ma 北京你°有到過麼?

HAVOC, *to commit* — *among,* tsao-iang' 遭殃

HAWK, lao-ing' 老鷹

HAY *or straw,* ken-ts'ao' 乾草; *hay-stack,* ts'ao'-bong 草蓬

HAZARD, *danger,* hyin 險; ngwe-hyin' 危°險

HAZARD, *to* mao-hyin' 冒險; — *one's life,* p'un-ming' 拚命; p'un-sô' sing'-ming 拚捨°性命

HAZARDOUS, hyin'-go 險个°;

hyin'-dao-dao 險逃逃; hyin'-teng-teng 險等等; hyin'-ling-ling 險懍懍

HAZE, yüing-in' 雲烟; in-vu' 烟霧

HE, gyi 其; — *says,* gyi wô' 其話; *it is* —, z gyi' 是其

HEAD, deo 頭; *to hang the* —, deo t'ang-loh' 頭垂°落; *to raise the* —, deo-dæ-ky'i' 頭抬起; *leader,* ling-deo' 領頭; deo-siu'; deo-nao' 頭腦; deo-moh' 頭目; *to knock* — *in worship,* k'eh-deo' 磕頭; — *of a bed,* zông-deo' 床°頭

HEAD, *or division,* zeng-ts'' 層°次; tön 端; dön 段; *the first* —, di-ih'-zeng 第一層°

HEAD, *to* — (as an expedition), we-deo' 爲頭; — *a boat to the north,* jün-deo' hyiang-poh' 船頭向北

HEAD-ACHE, deo'-t'ong 頭痛

HEAD-BAND, pao-deo' 包頭 (also a turban)

HEADLONG *way of doing,* deo-gyih'-goh-loh; *acting without thought,* mông'-c'ong 懵衝; mông'-djông 懵撞

HEAD-STRONG *disposition,* gyiang-deo'-gyüih-nao' 強頭倔腦; ang-sing'; cih'-sing 拙性; 'eo-zi' sing'-kah 逞°自°性格

HEAD-WIND, teo'-fong 對風

HEAD-WORKMAN, tsoh'-deo 作頭; ziang'-deo 匠°頭

HEAL, *to* i 醫; i-hao′ 醫 好;
— *disease,* i-bing′ 醫 病; *ditto,
by using sorcery,* yüong fah′-jih
i-bing′ 用 法 術 醫 病

HEALTH, *in good* —, hao 好;
gyin 健; (as an elderly person)
k'ông-gyin′ 康 健; *to injure
the* —, sông tsing-jing′ 傷 精
神; *restored to original* —, voh-
nyün′ de 復 元 了°

HEALTHY *constitution,* ti′-ts tsah′-
cü 底 子 堅° 固°; ti′-ts kyih′-
jih 底 子 砝 實; peng′-ling-bao′
本 領 好; *well,* sông′-kw'a
爽 快°; — *look,* ky'i′-seh-hao
氣 色 好

HEAP, *a* ih-te′ 一 堆; *large* — *of
earth, bricks, &c.,* kao-sæn-te′ 高
山 堆

HEAP, *to* — *up,* te-tsih′ 堆 積;
*to pile in a* —, diah-long′ ih-te′
疊 攏 一 堆

HEAR, *to* t'ing′-meng 聽 聞°;
t'ing′-kyin 聽 見; *cannot* —,
t'ing′-feh-c'ih′ 聽 弗 出; —
*attentively,* si′-t'ing 細 聽; liu-
sing′-t'ing 留 心 聽; *distressing
to* —, t'ing′-ts peh-jing′ 聽 之
不 忍: *pretend not to* —, *or pretend to be deaf and dumb,* tsông′-
long tsoh-ô′ 裝 聾 作 啞°; —
*suddenly, or the first time,* p'ih-
deo t'ing-meng 忽° 然° 聽 聞°;
*how did he* —? gyi′ dza t'ing-
meng-go 其 怎° 聽 聞° 个°?

HEARING, *hard of* ng′-tô moh′

耳° 聾°; r′-be 耳° 背°; (politely
called), ng′-tô feh-bin′ 耳° 朵
弗 便; *pretending to be ditto,*
tsông′-leh m̈′-neh t'ing′-meng
裝 得° 沒° 有° 聽 聞°; tsông kô′
ng-tô′ long 裝 假° 耳° 朵 聾

HEARKEN, *to* tseh′-leh ng-tô t'ing′
側 耳° 朵 聽; si′-r-kong-t'ing′
洗 耳 恭 聽

HEARSAY, fong-sing′ 風 信; *can't
rely on mere* —, fong-sing′-k'ao-
feh-jih′ 風 信 靠 弗 實

HEARSE, (native) zæ-hyin′ 材° 轎

HEART, sing 心; *to search one's
* —, dzô-ts'ah′ zi′-go sing′ 查
察 自° 个° 心; *to gain a person's* —, teh nying sing′ 得
人° 心; *palpitation of the* —,
sing′ bih-bih′-t'iao 心 忟 忟 跳;
— *is broken in pieces,* sing′-li
se′-sah-de 心 裡 碎 煞 了°;
*heart-rending cries,* kyiao-leh se′-
se-dong′ 叫 得° 碎 碎 勳

HEARTH, ho-lu teo′ 火 爐 斗

HEARTILY, dzing-sing′ 誠 心;
*with all the heart,* djün-fu′ sing-
dziang′ 全 副 心 腸

HEARTLESS, m̈-sing′-go 無° 心
个°; *without feeling,* m̈-dzing′
m̈-nyi′ 無° 情 無° 義

HEARTY, *cordial,* nyih-sing-deo′
熱° 心 頭; — (as food), næ-
kyi′ go 耐 飢 个°; *fat and* —
(as a young person), tsah′-công
圓 壯

HEAT, nyih-ky'i′ 熱° 氣; — *of*

*the body,* kyi'-sing'-go nyih-ky'ï'
身° 體° 个° 熱° 氣
HEAT, *to* — (as metals), tsih' nyih
炙 熱°; — *by the fire,* hong-nyih'
烘 熱°; — (as food), nyih'-nyih
熱°熱°; long-nyih' 弄 熱°; —
*in flame,* ho dæn'-dæn 火 燀 燀
HEATHEN, *idolater,* pa bu-sah'
nying 拜° 菩 薩 人°; pa ngeo'-
ziang-go 拜°偶 像 个°; *one out
of the church,* nga-kyiao' nying
外° 敎 人°; *one bound by custom,* shü'-dzoh zông' nying 世 俗
上 人°; *unenlightened people,*
mong'-tong nying' 懵 憧 人°;
HEAVE, *to* — *a sigh,* t'æn ky'ï'
嘆 氣; *the breast heaves,* hyüong-
kwnn'-deo hyih'-kyi, hyih'-kyi
læ-tih dong 胸 膛° 頭 膈 膈
動
HEAVEN, *the expanse of* —, t'ïn
天; ky'üong-ts'ông' 穹 蒼; *the
place of happiness,* T'ïn-dông' 天
堂; T'ïn-zông 天 上; *to go to*
—, T'ïn-dông' ky'ï 天 堂 去°; *returned to* — (commonly said of
one dead), kwe-t'ïn'-de 歸 天
了'; *Heaven's eye is near,* "T'ïn
ngæn gying'" 天 眼° 近
HEAVENLY, T'ïn'-li-go 天 裡
个°; — *bliss,* T'ïn-dông-go foh'-
ky'ï 天 堂 个 福 氣
HEAVY, djong 重; — *burden,*
djong' tæn 重 擔; *how* — *is it?*
yiu to'-siao djong' 有 多 少 重?
— *hands and feet* (said of one

who does things noisily, not
gently), djong'-siu-djong'-kyiah
重 手 重 脚
HEAVILY, *to sleep* —, kw'eng
sah'-kao 睡° 熟°
HEDGE, pô 笆; li-pô' 籬 笆;
*bamboo* —, coh' pô 竹 笆; *a
lamb caught in a* — (*i.e.* in inextricable difficulty), ta koh
yiang' tsing pô-dong' 戴° 角° 羊
進 笆 洞
HEDGED, *way* — *up,* vu lu' k'o
tseo' 無 路 可 走; *completely*
— *in,* djih lu'-dzing 絕 路 程;
we-kw'eng'-sah-de 圍 困 煞 了°
HEDGE-HOG, 'ao-cü 豪 豬
HEED, *to take care,* kying'-jing 謹
愼; kwu'-djoh 顧 着°; siao'-sing
小 心; *to hear and believe,* t'ing'
sing 聽 信 *do not* — *him,* (as a
child playing, &c.) vong kwun'
gyi 不 用° 管 其; *ditto,* (as one
reviling, &c.) hao-vong' ts'æ gyi'
不° 用° 睬 其
HEEDLESS feh tông-sing-go 弗
當 心 个°; bah-mông'-kwông
白 茫 光; — *sport* (as holding
a child in a dangerous place),
mæn-tô hyi'-deo 粗° 戀° 戲
嬉°; mæn-tô'-tô.
HEEDLESSLY, yia'-long-sæn-ts'in
野° 弄 三 千; *to do* —, ts'ao'-
ts'ao liao z' 草 草 了 事; tso
z-ken' feh læ i' li 做 事 幹 弗
在° 意 裏
HEEL *of the foot,* kyiah 'eo-keng'

腳後跟; — *of the shoe*, ʻa-ʻeo-keng′ 鞋°後跟

HEIFER, siao ts′ʻ-ngeo′ 小雌牛° (ih-deo)

HEIGHT, *what is the — of that mountain?* keh′ zo sæn yiu to-siao kao′ 這°座山有多少高?

HEIR, *of the same family name*, dzing-kyi′-go nying 承繼个°人°; tsih-dæ′-go nying 接代个°人°; *one who inherits*, ziu-tsʻæn′-nyih-go nying 受產業个°人°

HEIRLESS, *no posterity*, vu-ʻeo 無後; *the succession is broken*, dön-cong′-de 斷種了°; djih-dæ′-de 絕代了°; djih-dz′-de 絕嗣了°

HELL, di-nyüoh′ 地獄; *to fall into or go to* —, loh di-nyüoh′ 落地獄; *the sufferings of* —, di-nyüoh′-li-go kwʻu′-tsʻu 地獄裡个°苦楚

HELM, *the* do 舵; do′-ngô 舵枒°; *to take the* —, pô do′ 把舵; kʻeh do′-ngô 搿舵枒°; *ditto* (if a small —) pô sao′ 把梢

HELMSMAN, do′-kong 舵工; lao′-da 老大

HELP, *to* pông-dzu′ 幫助; pông-ts′eng′ 幫襯; vu-dzu′ 扶助; pông-vu′ 幫扶; *to — one another*, dô-kô′ siang-pông′ 大°家°相幫; *come and — me*, læ pông′ ngô ih-pông 來幫我一幫; teng ngô′ tso te′-siu 與°我做對手; *I will — you into the boat*, ngô tông′ ng loh jün′ 我扶°你°下°船; — *with money, &c.* (in time of bereavement), tiao hao 弔孝°; tiao-sông′ 弔喪; *there is no — for it*, m̄-shih′-fah 無°設法; m̄-fah′ 無°法; peh-teh′-yi 不得已; w̆a′-feh-læ 歇°弗來; vu-k′o′-næ-ʻo 無可奈何; *cannot — doing it*, feh-neng feh-tso 弗能弗做; feh′-teh feh-tso′ 弗得弗做

HELPER, pông-siu′ 幫手; te′-siu 對手

HELPLESS, kyü′-dong-feh-læ 舉動弗來; dong′-dæn-feh-læ 動彈弗來; vu-lih′-neng-we′ 無力能爲

HELTER-SKELTER, lön-tsʻih′-pah-tsao′ 亂七八遭; *to come in* —, lön tseo′-tsing-læ 亂走進來

HELVE, fu′-deo ping 斧頭柄

HEM, *to* nyiao bin′ 縫°緶; *to turn down a* —, üih bin′ 攣°緶

HEMISPHERE, pun′-gyiu 半球; *the eastern* —, tong pun′-gyiu 東半球

HEMORRHAGE, hyüih-tsing 血症; — *from the womb*, hyüih′-pong 血崩°

HEMP, mô 麻; dzi′-mô 苧麻; *hempen cloth*, mô pu′ 麻布; — *twine*, mô zing′ 麻繩

HEN, kyi-nyiang′ 母°雞°; — *coop*, kyi-long′ 雞籠; — *basket*, kyi-tsao′ 雞罩

HENCE, *from this time,* yi-'eo' 以
後; ts'-'eo' 此後; dz-'eo 嗣後;
dzong-ts'' yi-'eo' 從此以後;
*three years —,* sæn nyin' yi-'eo'
三年以後; ts'-'eo sæn nyin' 此
後三年; *therefore,* sô-yi' 所
以; keh-lah 故°

HENCEFORTH, or HENCEFOR-
WARD, dzong-kying'-yi-'eo' 從
今以後

HER, gyi 其; (*pos.*) gyi-go 其个°

HERALD, *proclaimer,* pao'-z-nying
報事人°

HERBS, ts'ao 草; *medicinal —,*
yiah-ts'ao' 藥草

HERD, ih-de' 一隊; ih-dziao' 一
群°; *a — of cattle,* ih-de ngeo'
一隊牛°

HERDSMAN, k'en-ngeo'-go 看牛
个°; k'en-yiang'-go 看羊个°;
*boy —,* moh-dong' 牧童

HERE, dông-deo 這°裡°; ts'-di 此
地; *to be —,* læ-tong 在°; *have
been — three years,* læ ts'-di sæn
nyin' de 在°此地三年了°;
*bring it —,* do tao dông-deo læ'
拿°到這°裡°來; *I am —,*
ngô læ-tong' 我在°; *— it is,*
dông-deo læ-tong' 在°這°裡°

HEREAFTER, tsiang-læ' 將來;
'eo'-læ 後來; 'eo'-deo 後頭

HEREDITARY *nobility,* shü-jih'
世襲; ing'-kwun 蔭官; *—
(as a trade or profession),* shü'-
djün-go 世傳个°; *— (as pro-
perty, or disease),* zông-dæ' yi-'

loh-læ'-go 上代遺落來个°

HERESY, zia dao'-li 邪°道理;
yi-tön' 異端

HERETIC, zia-kyiao' nying 邪°教
人°; yi-kyiao' nying 異教人°

HERMIT, zo-mao-bong'-go 坐茅
蓬个°; *— who sits in a confined
place and is fed by others,* zo-
kwæn' 坐°關

HERO, ing-yüong' 英雄; 'ao-gyih'
豪傑; da-dziang'-fu 大丈夫;
*strive to be a —,* tsang ing-
yüong' 爭°英雄

HEROINE, nyü'-cong 'ao-gyih' 女
中豪傑; nyü'-cong dziang'-fu
女中丈夫

HESITATE, *to — in deciding,* yiu
yü' peh' kyüih 猶豫不決; *—
in speaking,* ng-ng'-nga-nga kông
嗯°嗯°呀°呀°講; *ditto, as if
holding a walnut in the mouth,*
ziang 'en wu-dao kông' ka 如°
含胡桃講°

HESITATING (in speaking), t'eng-
t'eng-t'u-t'u 吞吞吐吐; ih-
kyü tsing' ih-kyü c'ih' 一句進
一句出

HEW, *to — trees,* tsæn jü' 斬
樹; *— stone,* k'æ zah-deo' 開
石°頭°; *— down a tree,* jü tsoh'-
loh 樹斬落; jü tsoh'-diao
樹斬壞°

HIBERNATE, *to* iu-ko tong' 躲°
過冬

HICCOUGH, *to* tang-eh' 打呃;
tang-ih' 打噎

HIDE, dzông-nyih′ 藏匿; *to — one's self*, iu 幽; — *the head*, dzông deo′ 藏頭; — *the face*, tsô min-k′ong′ 遮°面孔; — *sin*, tsô-in′ ze′ 遮掩罪; tsô-kæ′ ze′ 遮°蓋罪; *he is hidden*, gyi′ iu′-kæn.

HIDE, *skin*, bi 皮; *ox —*, ngeo-bi′ 牛°皮; *cow — candy*, ngeo-bi′ dông′ 牛°皮糖

HIDEOUS *appearance*, siang′-mao ts‛iu′-leo-peh-k‛æn′ 相貌醜陋不堪; p′ô′-p′ô siang′-mao 可°怕相貌; — *sound*, seng′-ngô sah-nying′-go sing-hyiang′.

HIGH, kao 高; *as — as heaven*, ziang-t′in′ ka-kao′ 像°天个°樣°高; *a — price invites the distant trader* (to sell his goods), kô′ kao tsiao yün′-k‛ah 價°高招遠客; — *rank* tsiah′-we kao 爵位高; — *officer*, tsih-veng-do′ 職分大°; — *wind*, mang′-fong 猛°風

HIGH-HANDED, pô′-dao 霸道; gyiang-wang′-pô-dao′ 強橫°霸道; pô′-shü 霸勢.

HIGH-MINDED (principles), p‛ing′-kah kao 品格高

HIGH-PRIEST, tsi′-s-tsiang 祭司長°; tsi′-s-deo′ 祭司頭

HIGH-SPIRITED, ts′-hyiang-kao′ 志向高; ‛ao′-ky‛i 豪氣 (not equivalents.)

HIGH-WATER or *tide*, dziao-tsiang′ tsoh-de 潮漲足了°; bing-dziao′ 平潮

HIGH-WAY, kwun-lu′ 官路; do-lu′ 大°路; kwun-dông′-do-lu′ 官塘大°路

HILL, *a small —*, ih-diao-ling′ — 條嶺; *a larger —*, ih-zo-sæn′ 一座°山; *climb the hills*, bô-sæn′ ‛wah-ling 爬山跨°嶺

HILLOCK, ling 嶺 (ih-diao); *a grave —*, veng-ling 墳陵

HILL-PATH, sæn-lu′ 山路

HILL-SIDE, sæn-pin′ 山邊

HILL-TOP, sæn-ting-den′ 山頂

HILLY *ground*, sæn-di′ 山地; *it is all —*, tu′ z sæn 都是山

HILT, pao′-kyin-ping′ 寶劍柄

HIMSELF, zi 自°; *he — gave* (it) *to me*, gyi-zi′ peh′-ngô 其自°給°我

HIND *feet*, ‛eo′-kyiah 後脚

HINDER, *to* lah-djü′ 攔°住; læn-tsu′ 攔阻; tsu′-tông 阻擋; tsu′-djü 阻住; *hindered by him*, be′ gyi lah-djü′-liao 被其攔°住了 *what's to —*? ‛o-fông′-ni 何妨呢?

HINDRANCE, fông-ngæ′ 妨碍; tsu′-kah 阻隔; tsu′-kah-sing 阻隔星; *without —*, vu-tsu′ vu-ngæ′ 無°阻無°碍; ‛ao′-vu tsu′-kah 毫無阻隔

HINDMOST, meh-‛eo′ 末後; ting-‛eo′ 頂後

HINGES, yiao-bi′; yiao-p‛æn′ 搖襻: *to take a door off the —*, meng-t‛eh′-loh 門脫落

HIP, do-t'e' 大°腿; — joint, do-t'e' gao-kwu' 大°腿骨 交°股; t'e'-kweh kyiao-tsih' 腿骨交節

HIRE, to kwu 偏; to rent, tsu 租; shü 賃; — a boat, t'ao-jün' 討船

HIRE, wages, kong-din' 工°錢°; rent, tsu'-din 租錢'; boat —, jün-din' 船錢°

HIRED, I have — a man, ngô ih-go nying' kwu-hao'-tong-de 我一个° 人° 偏 好 了°; one — for a length of time, dziang-kong' 長工; tang-dziang'-go; one— for a short time, tön'-kong 短工; ts'eh-tön'-go.

HIS, gyi'-go 其 个°; that book is —, keh'-peng shü' z gyi'-go 這° 本書是 其 个°

HISTORIAN, kyi-z'- go cü'- kwu 紀事个°人°; compiler of history, siu-s'-go cü'-kwu 修史个°人°

HISTORY, s 史; official records, kông-kæn' 綱鑑°; — of China (in several hundred vols.), Nyiæn s'-s 廿四史; Natural — of China, Da-ts'ing' ih-t'ong'-ts 大清一統志; origin and — (as of a house, &c.), læ-lih' 來歷

HIT, to — against, bang-djoh' 摐°着°; to — (as a mark), tang'-djoh' 打着°; for fear a brick may — you, k'ong'-p'ô cün-deo' k'ao'-djoh ng 恐怕磚頭敲°着°你°; — a target, tang pô'-ts

打靶子; ditto with an arrow, zih-djoh pô'-ts 射着°靶子

HITHER, dông'-byiang 這°向; to run — and thither, peng'-læ-peng-ky'i' 奔來奔去°

HITHERTO, hyiang'-læ, 向來; ih'-hyiang 一向; dzong-læ' 從來

HIVE, bee-tub, fong-dong' 蜂桶 (ih-go)

HIVE, bees fong-ts' dao'-c'ih dong 蜂子逃出桶; to — the bees, fong-ts' siu-tsing' 蜂子收進

HOAR-FROST, sông 霜

HOARD, to — up money, k'ông' ngæ' dong-din' 囤呆銅錢°; k'ông si' dong-din' 囤死銅錢°

HOARSE, sô wu'-long 嘅喉°嚨; so — unable to speak, wu-long ô' 喉°嚨啞

HOARY hair, deo-fah bah'-de 頭髮白°了°; black and white mixed, hwô-bah' 花白°; — headed man, bah-deo-ong' 白頭翁

HOAX, to — a person, coh ih-go moh-sao' peh nying pe' 給一个° 木梢 俌°人°背; he was hoaxed, gyi pe-moh-sao'-de 其背木梢了°; gyi pe-bô'-liao 其背靶了

HOBBLE, to kwa-kyi' kwa-kyi'tseo 跛走°

HOBBY, that is his —, keh z gyi p'in-æ'-ts-sing 這°是其偏愛之心

HOD, *a mason's bamboo —*, t'u'-kyi 土 箕 (ih-tsah); *coal —*, me-t'æn' dong 煤 炭 桶

HOE, z-deo' 耡 頭 (ih-pô); *to cut weeds with a —*, siah ts'ao' 削 草

HOG, nyi-cü' 泥 猪; *wild —*, yia' cü 野° 猪 (ih-tsah)

HOIST, *to* ts'ô-zông' 扯° 上; *to — a flag*, gyi ts'ô-zông' 旗 扯° 上; *— a sail*, ts'ô bong' 扯° 蓬; bah bong' 拔 蓬

HOLD, *to — in the hand*, do 拿°; nyiah 捻; *— it tight*, do-leh lao 拿° 得° 牢; *— it still*, ding-ding' go do'-tong 拿° 定 當; dong'-feh-dong do'-tong 拿° 定 其° 弗° 動°; *— in both hands*, p'ong 捧; *— in the arms*, bao 抱; *— (or clutch) him fast*, cô gyi lao' 擄° 其牢; *let go one's —*, fông siu'放 手; *— loosely*, kw'un siu' nyiah'-tih 寬 手 捻的; song siu' nyiah'-tih 鬆 手 捻 的; *— a pen*, k'ô pih 揎° 筆; *— on the arm*, gyiao-tih 擤 的; *— under the arm*, gah'-tih 擤° 的; gyih'-tih 挾 的; *— on to something*, p'æn' 扳; *can't — up (no strength)*, ts'ang'-feh-djü 撐 弗 住; *— up the hand*, siu di-ky'i' 手 提 起; *— out the hand*, sing siu' 伸 手; *— one in suspense*, long'-leh gyi tiao'-dang 使° 其 弗° 着° 落°; *— in the mouth*, 'en' læ k'eo'-li 含 在° 口 裡; *— up the*

*dress*, i-zông ky'ih-tæn'-ky'i 衣 裳 挈 起; *how much water will (it) —*? hao tsi to-siao' shü' 好 齒° 多 少 水°?

HOLD, *ship's —*, jün'-li-go ho'-ts'ông 船 裡 個° 貨 艙

HOLE, dong-ngæn' 洞 眼; dong' 洞 (ih-go); *— in a wall*, ziang dong' 墻 洞; *to dig a — in the ground*, gyüih ih-go den' 掘 一 個° 潭

HOLIDAY, *day free from labor*, fông-kô' nyih-ts' 放° 假 日° 子; *day free from study*, fông-'oh' nyih-ts' 放 學 日° 子; *how many holidays have you?* ng fông kyi nyih' kô' 你° 放° 幾 日° 假°?

HOLINESS, sing'-jün teh'-ky'i 聖 善 德 氣

HOLLOW, k'ong 空; k'ong-k'oh'-go 空 壳 個°; k'ong-sing 空 心; *a — place*, den 潭; ao 墺; zao 漕°; t'en-tsing'-go di-fông 凹 進 個° 地 方; *— in an ink stone*, nyin-ngô den' 硯° 瓦° 潭; nyin-ngô zao' 硯 瓦° 漕°; *— of the hand*, siu-sing-den' 手 心 潭

HOLLOW, *to — out*, leo c'ih' 鏤 出; *— slightly*, seo or sin 剜°

HOLLY-HOCK ziang'-vi-hwô 薔 薇 花

HOLY, sing 聖; sing'-jün 聖 善; *— Bible*, Sing'-shü 聖 書; *— Spirit*, Sing'-Ling 聖 靈; *the*

— *Place*, Sing′-sô 聖 所；*the*
— *of Holies*, Ts′-sing-sô 至
聖 所；*God is* —，Jing-ming′
z sing′-jün-go 神 明 是 聖
善 个°

HOME, oh′-li 家°裡°；oh′-lô；kô-
byiang′ 家°鄉；*own* —，zi oh′-
li 自° 家°裡°；*go* —，tao oh′-li
ky′i′；到 家° 裏 去°；*at home* or
*familiar with* (because native to),
ne kô′ gyün-deo′ 內 家° 峯 頭；
peng′-tsoh-ho′ 本 作 貨

HOMELESS, m̄-oh-go 無° 屋 个°；
m̄-neh deng-sing′-ts-c′ü′ 沒°有°
庇 身 之 處；*the* — *who find
shelter anywhere*, (as beggars,
thieves, &c.) deng liang-ding′-go
住°凉° 亭 个°；kw′eng fi-leo′-go
睡°城°樓 个°；tao miao-koh-go′.

HOMELY, *not pretty*, næn-k′en′-
go 難 看 个°；w̌a-k′en′-go 孬
看 个°；sang-leh w̌a-k′en′ 生°
得° 孬 看；*very* —，ts′iu′-leo
醜 陋

HOME-MADE, kô-tsoh′-go 家°作
个°；*home-woven*, peng′-kyi 本
機

HOME-SICKNESS, kyi′ - teh kô-
byiang′-bing 思° 鄉 病

HONE, mo-tao′-zah 磨 刀 石°
(ih-kw′e)

HONEST, *upright and straight forward*, dzing-jih′ 誠 實；ih′-z-ih′
nyi′-z-nyi′ 一 是 一 二°是 二°；
— *man*, weh-ih′-nying 劃 一
人°；teng-′eo′-nying 敦 厚 人°；

cong-′eo′-nying 忠 厚 人°；′eo′-
dao-nying 厚 道 人°；— *and
often simple*, lao′-jih 老 實 ；—
(*won't steal*), siu′-kyiah-w̄eng′-
djong 手 脚 穩 重；—*in trade*,
lao′-siao-vu-ky′i′ 老 小 無 欺

HONESTLY, *speak* jih-we′-kông 實
爲° 講°；kông lao′-jih wô′ 講°
老 實 話

HONEY, mih-dông′ 蜜 糖；*honeyed
fruit*, mih-tsin′-ko 蜜 餞 果；
— *poison* (*i.e.* what seems good,
but injures), mih-tsin′-p′i-sông′
蜜 餞 砒 霜

HONEY-COMB, mih-fong′-k′o′ 蜜
蜂 窠

HONEY-SUCKLE, kying - nying′-
hwô 金 銀 花

HONG, ′ông 行；*foreign* —，
yiang-′ông′ 洋 行 (ih-bæn)

HONOR, *to respect*, k′en′-djong 看
重；kying′-djong 敬 重；tseng-
djong′ 尊 重；kwe′-djong 貴
重；t′e-tseng′ 推 尊；—*parents*,
kying′-djong vu′-meo 敬 重 父
母；hyiao′-jing tia-nyiang′ 孝
順 爹 娘；*reflect* — *upon parents*, tsang-do′-nying-go ky′i′
爭° 大° 人 个° 氣；tsang-fong
ngao-ky′i′ 傲 氣；*you* — *me*,
ng′-peh ngô t′i′-min 你° 俾 我
體 面；ng′-peh ngô lin′-zông yiu
kwông-ts′æ′ 你° 俾° 我 臉 上
有 光 彩

HONOR, *esteem it an* —，sön′ z
yüong-kwông′ 算 是 榮 光

HONORABLE, dziah-djong′-go 鄭° 重 个°; *worthy of honor*, kæ-tông′ kying′-djong-go 該 當 敬 重 个°; *what is your —* *name?* tseng-sing′ 尊 姓? kwe-sing′ 貴 姓? *what is your —* *country?* kwe-koh′ 貴 國? *what* *is your — occupation?* ng-soh′-go kwe-'ông 你°甚°麼°貴行?

HOOD (worn by men), fong-teo′ 風兜; — (worn by old women), kwun-ing′-teo 觀 音 兜 (ih-ting)

HOOF, di-ts′ 蹄 子 (ih-tsah)

HOOK, keo-ts′ 鈎 子 (ih-tsah)

HOOK, *to* keo 鈎; — *up*, keo-ky′i′-læ 鈎 起 來

HOOKED *nose*, ing-cü′ bih-deo′ 鷹 嘴 鼻 頭°

HOOP, ky′iu 箍°; *tub —*, dong′-ky′iu 桶 箍°

HOOP, *to* tang-ky′iu 打 箍°

HOOPING-COUGH, lu′-z-k′eh 鷺 鶿 咳

HOP *on one foot*, doh-kyiah′-t′iao′ 獨 脚 跳

HOPE, *to* siang′-vông 想 望; — *he will prosper*, ts′-vông gyi hying-wông 指 望 其 興 旺; *— in vain*, du-jün′ siang′-vông 徒 然 想 望

HOPE, siang′-deo 想 頭; vông′-deo 望頭; *no —*, m̄-siang′-deo 無°想 頭; *there is —*, yiu-sô-vông′-go 有 所 望 个°; *have* *great —* (of him or it), da-yiu′ sô-vông′ 大 有 所 望; *no — of*

*the man*, nying djih - vông′-de 人°絕 望 了°; *no — of news*, sing′-sih djih-vông′-de 信 息 絕 望 了°; *beyond one's hopes*, hyi′-c′ih-vông-wæ′ 喜 出 望 外; *foolish baseless —*, c′ü-sing′ vông-siang 癡 心 妄 想

HOPEFUL, *promising*, yiu ts′-vông 有 指 望; *he is very —*, gyi vông-deo′ læ-leh ts′ih′ 其 望 頭 來 得° 切

HOPELESS, m̄ siang′-vông go 無° 想 望 个°; sing sah′-de 心 死° 了°; — *disease*, and hence *any* *thing —*, si′-tsing 死°症

HOPES, *his —* *are excited*, gyi siang′-vông bô-ky′i′-tih-de 其 想 望 吧 起 了°; *gyi* vông-deo′ dong′-de 其 望 頭 動 了°; *excite one's —*, ying′-dong nying′-go siang′ - vông 引 動 人°个°想 望

HORIZON, *the sensible —*, t′in-pin′ 天 邊

HORIZONTAL, wang 橫°; *on a* *level*, bing 平

HORN, koh 角° (ih-tsah); *two* *horns*, liang-tsah koh′ 兩 隻 角°; *— for blowing*, so′-na; *shoe —*, 'a-liu′ 鞋 跋° (ih-go).

HORNED, yiu-koh′-go 有 角° 个°; *hornless*, m̄-koh′-go 無°角° 个°

HORNY *skin on the hands*, siu′-bi ky′i-kyin′-de 手 皮 起 皺° 了°

HORRIBLE, iao hah′-sah nying′ go 耍 嚇 殺 人°个°

HORRID, p'ô-p'ô 可° 怕; — to look at (i. e. distresses one), se'-se-dong-go 心 上° 不° 安°; se'-ky'i-siang.

HORRIFIED, sing-hyü'-dah-tsin' 心 虛 肉° 顫; mô-tseh'-tseh-go.

HORSE, mô 馬 (ih-p'ih); a swift or express —, ts'in-li'-mô 千 里 馬 to mount a —, zông-mô 上 馬; to dismount from a —, loh mô' 落 馬; to ride a —, gyi mô'-騎 馬; a saw —, moh-mô' 木 馬; clothes —, i-kô' 衣 架°; towel —, siu'-kying-kô' 手巾架°

HORSE-BACK, on læ mô'-zông 在° 馬 上

HORSE-HAIR (from the tail), mô'-mi 馬 尾° (ih-keng)

HORSE-RACE, do-p'ao'-mô' 大°跑 馬

HORSE-SHOE, t'ih'-ts'ao-'a 鉄草 鞋°; mô'-di-t'ao 馬 蹄 套; — of silver, nyün-pao' 元 寶 (ih-tsah)

HORSE-WHIP, mô' pin-ts 馬鞭子 (ih-go)

HOSE, mah 襪 (ih-sông); water pipe, shü'-kwun 水° 管 (ih-diao)

HOSPITABLE, æ-k'ah'-go 愛客 个°; hwun-hyi' liu nying-k'ah' 歡喜留客人°

HOSPITABLY, to entertain —, dæ k'ah ing-gying' 待客慇懃; ts-nying' dæ-k'ah hao' 支賓待 客好

HOSPITAL, i-gyüoh' 醫局 (ih-go)

HOST, or HOSTESS, tong-dao'-cü 東 道 主; tsih-k'ah'-go 接 客 个°; landlord, or head of the house, cü'-nying-kô' 主 人° 家°; tong-kô' 東家; the Heavenly —, T'in-ping'-T'in-tsiang' 天兵天 將; army, ping-mô' 兵 馬; the whole —, djün-kyüing' 全軍; the — in the Catholic church, sing'-t'i 聖 體

HOSTAGE, pledge, tông-deo' 當 頭; ah'-deo 押° 頭; detain him as a —, liu' gyi tso tông'-deo 留 其 做 當 頭

HOSTILE, kyih-dziu'-liao-go 結讐 了; the two parties are —, liang'-'ô tso ün-kô' 兩 下 做 冤 家°

HOSTILITY, to provoke —, tsiao ün' 招怨; in a state of —, kyih-ün-dziu'-go 結冤讐 个°

HOSTLER, mô'-fu 馬夫 (ih-go)

HOT, ting nyih' 頂 熱°; — (lit. warmer than warm), pi nyih' wa nyih' 熱 上° 加° 熱°; — as fire, ho'-nyih 火 熱°; sun pouring down like fire, nyih-deo' ziang ho' ka p'eh'-loh læ 日°頭 如° 火 逼 落 來°; — (as weather, or fever), ho'-siao-ho-lah' 火 燒 火 辣; — (boiling) water, kweng' shü 滾 水°; boiling —, fah' kweng 發滾; dah-dah' kweng 沓沓滾; very — sun, nyih-deo' dah-dah' kweng. — tempered, ho-ky'i' do 火 氣 大°; sing'-kah ziang ho' ka 性

性格 如 火°; mao-ts'ao' ho'
sing 茅草 火星

HOTEL, k'ah'-nyü 客寓; k'ah'-dzæn 客棧; inn, 'ô-c'ü' 廈處

HOUR, ih tin'-cong 一點鐘; the Chinese —, pun' z-zing 半時辰°; half an —, pun' tin-cong 半點鐘; a quarter of an —, ih k'eh' 一刻; an — and a half, ih tin pun' 一點半; an — ago, ih tin'-cong zin-deo' 一點鐘前°頭; an — hence, deng' ih tin'-cong 停°一點鐘; deng sæn' djü væn' z 停°三餐°飯時

HOUR-GLASS, sô-leo' 沙漏 (ih-go)

HOUR-HAND, ts'-z tsing 指時針; the short hand, tön' tsing 短針 (ih-me)

HOURLY, me' ih tin'-cong 每一點鐘

HOUSE, oh 屋; vông-ts' 房子; oh'-lô; (ih-tsing, ih-t'eo); our — is bad, ah'-lah oh'-lô wa' 我們°房子不°好°; houses joined together, lin-p'ing' keh'-djü-go oh 連摒合°柱个°屋; your lofty —, or mansion? fu'-zông 府上? tseng-fu' 尊府? kwe' fu 貴府? in reply say, our humble —, shæ'-kyin 舍間; sô'-kyin; sô-'ô' 舍°下; sô'-pin 舍°邊; bi-sô' 敝舍°; ice —, ping-ts'iang 冰廠 (ih-go)

HOUSE-BREAKER who forces doors, gyiao-meng'-go zeh' 撬°門个° 賊°; — who breaks through the wall, ts'ah-dong'-go zeh' 拆壁°个° 賊°

HOUSEHOLD, persons of the —, oh'-li-go nying 家°裡个°人°; (ah-lah oh'-li-nying, without the particle go, is my wife); the whole —, 'o-kô' 和家°; 'eh-kô' 合家; every —, veng-veng' nying-kô' 每°界人°家°; a'-kô a'-wu 挨°家°挨°戶; kô-kô' wu-wu 家°家°戶戶; — goods, kô-ho'-jih-veh' 家°貨什物

HOUSE-RENT, vông tsu'-din 房租錢°; oh' tsu-din' 屋租錢°; vông din' 房錢°

HOVEL, mud na-nyi' oh 泥屋; straw —, ts'ao' oh 草屋; oh ziang p'o'-yiao ka' 屋像破窰

HOVERING about, dön-dön'-ky'ün-ky'ün læ-tih fi' 團團圈圈來的飛

HOW, in what manner? dza-go' 怎°樣°? or 怎°个°? — many? kyi'-go 幾个°? ditto (or — much)? to-siao 多少? — can I know? ngô' dza hyiao'-teh ni 我怎°曉得呢? — far is it (from one to the other)? li-yün' to-siao' lu' 離遠多少路? ditto, from here there? dzong dông'-deo tao keh'-deo dza kwun yün' 從這裡°到那°裡°怎°樣遠? — long have you been here? ng' læ-leh'

to-siao′ kong′-fu 你°來了°多
少工夫？— *long* (by measure)?
dza kwun dziang′ 怎°樣°長？
— *are you?* ng hao′ feh 你°好
否°？ hao′ yia 好呀°？— *old
are you?* ng to-siao′ nyin′-kyi
你°多少年紀？(politely) *ditto?*
kwe′-kang 貴庚？ *ditto* (to an
old person)？ kao-ziu′ 高壽？
ng da ziu′ to-siao′ 你°大壽多
少°？ *ditto* (to a child), kyi shü′
幾歲°？ *ditto* (to a young woman)？ ng to-siao′ ts′ing-c′ing′
你°多少青春？

HOWEVER, *although it be so,* se-
tsih′ z-ka′ 雖則°如°此°

HOWL, *when dogs — it is a bad
sign,* keo′ k̇e-tih k′oh′ z peh-
kyih′-ts ziao′ 狗哭是不吉
之兆

HUBBUB, *what is all this —? soh′
z-ken′, ka nao-nyih′-bang-sang′
何°事°如°此°鬧°熱°

HUDDLE, *to — together,* üong′-tsi-
long′ 擁擠攏； tsi-tæn′-long
擠攏； *sit huddled,* a′-tsi zo′ 挨°
擠坐°

HUFF, *in a — of anger,* ho′-ky′i
dzih c′ong′ 火氣直冲 (c′ong
or ts′ong).

HUFFY (from vanity), iao ′ang′
piao-gying′ 要行°彪勁

HUG, *to* o-long′ 抱°攏； o-tæn′-
long.

HUGE, do-leh c′ih-gyi′ 大°得°出
奇； *unusually large,* fi-dzông′ do

非常大°；kah′-nga do′ 格外°
大°

HULL, *the outer — of rice,* long-
k′ông′ 礱糠； *the inner —*, si′-
k′ông′ 細糠； *the — of a ship,*
jün-sing′ 船身

HULL, *to take off the outer — of
paddy,* long koh′礱穀； *ditto the
inner —,* sông mi′ 舂米； ts′ah-
mi′ 碓米； *to take off both hulls
(usually by a buffallo-mill),* nyin
koh′ 碾穀

HUMILIATE, *to — by taunts,* siah-
lin′ 削臉

HUMMING (of insects), ′ong-′ong′-
hyiang 嗡嗡響

HUMAN, nying′-go 人°个； —
*body,* sing-t′i′ 身體； — *relations,*
jing-leng′ 人倫； *what is the
length of — life?* jing-seng′ dzœ
shü′ neng yiu kyi nyin′ 人生
在世能有幾年？ *the seven
— affections,* ts′ih dzing′ 七情
(veng.)

HUMANE, sing-dz′-go 心慈个°

HUMBLE, ky′in-byü′ 謙虛 (has
often a sense of false humility)；
ky′in-seng′ 謙遜； ti-sing′-siao-i
低心小意； *in my — opinion,*
tsiao ngô′ nyü kyin′ 照我愚
見； *of — origin,* c′ih′-sing-ti′出
身低； *my — surname,* bi-sing′
敝姓； (I) *your —* (stupid)
*brother,* nyü-di′ 愚弟

HUMBLE, *to — by placing in a
lower position,* p′ing′-kyih kông′-

loh-ky'i' 品 級 降° 下°; kông-
kyih' 降° 級; — *yourself*, zi'
pe-vi' 自° 卑 微; *to bring down*,
ah'-cü 壓° 制

HUMBLY, ti-sing'-siao-i'-go 低心
小意个°

HUMILITY, ti-sing-siao-i' 低 心
小意; ky'in-hyü-go-sing 謙
虛 个° 心; ky'in-seng'-go-sing
謙遜 个° 心

HUMOR, *in good* — , hwun-hwun'-
hyi-hyi 歡 歡 喜 喜; *in bad*
—, læ-tih-fah sing'-kah 正° 在°
發性格; *to put him in good* —,
peh gyi hwun-hyi' 俾°其歡喜

HUMP, *camel's* do-fong' 駝峰

HUMP-BACKED, do-pe'-go 駝 背
个°

HUNDRED, ih-pah' — 百°; *a* —
*thousand*, ih-pah'-ts'in 一百°千;
jih-væn' 十萬; *a* — *strokes, a*
— *hits* (*i. e.* sure to hit right),
pah'-fah pah'-cong 百° 發 百°
中° (cong or tsong)

HUNGER, *having* du-kyi' 肚飢;
du-pih' 肚饑; *dying with* —,
kw'a-ngo-sah'-de 快°餓死了°;
*to long for*, hyüih'-sing siang' 血
心想

HUNT, *to* — *after a thing*, ts'-si-
zing' 仔細尋°; *ditto, for a long
time*, zing'-leh k'o-lin' 尋得°可
憐; — *it up* (as in a book), dzô-
gyi-djoh' 查其着°; *to* — *wild
animals*, tang-liah' 打獵

HUNTER, liah-wu' 獵戶; tang-
liah'-go 打獵个°

HURL, *to* — *at*, k'ang'-ko-ky'i 摜°
過去°; ang'-ko-ky'i 擲°過去°

HURRICANE, fong-shü' 風水°;
fong-pao' 風暴; *to blow a* —,
tso-fong-shü' 做風水°; tang-
pao' 打颱

HURRIED, *and flurried*, hwông-
mông' 慌忙; hwông-hwông'-
tsiang-tsiang' 慌慌張張; —
*in work*, mông-mông'-loh-loh 忙
忙碌碌

HURRIEDLY, kyih'-mông 急忙;
læ-loh'-feh-gyi' 忙° 碌弗及°

HURRY, *in a* —, læ-feh-gyi' 來弗
及°; *need not be in a* —, hao-
vong' ka læ-feh-gyi' 不°用°
如° 此° 來弗及°; *do not* —,
feh-iao'-mông 弗要忙

HURT, *or wound*, sông 傷

HURT, *to bruise*, sông 傷; long-
t'ong' 弄痛; long-sông' 弄傷;
*to injure*, 'æ' 害; sông-'æ' 傷
害; — *by a cut*, k'eh'-sông 磕
傷; — *by a fall*, tih'-sông 跌
傷; — *by a blow*, tang'-sông 打
傷; *will not* — *you*, feh-wo 'æ'
ng' 弗會害你; *to* — *one's self*,
zi-'æ'-zi 自°害自°; *take care
and not* — *him*, kwu'-djoh long
gyi t'ong' 顧着°弄其痛; *he*
— *my feelings*, gyi sông' ngô'-
go dzing 其傷我个°情

HURTFUL, yiu-'æ'-go 有害个°;
wo-'æ'-go 為害个°

HUSBAND, nen-nyüing' 男子°; tông-kô'-nying 當家°人°; dziang'-fu 丈夫; lao'-kong 老公 (disrespectful); *in what business is your —?* ng'-go nen' tso soh'-go sang-i' 你°个°丈°夫°做甚°麼°生°意? *my —,* ah'-lah tông-kô'-nying 我°們°當家°人°; gyi'-lah-go ah-tia' 彼°等°个°阿爹 (*i. e.* the children's father); *husband's father,* kong-kong' 公公; yia'-yia 爺°爺°; *husband's mother,* nyiang'-nyiang 娘娘; *husband's elder brother,* ah-pang' 阿伯°; *husband's younger brother,* ah-song' 阿叔°; *ah-pang's wife,* a'-m̃' 阿姆°; *ah-song's wife,* ah-sing' 阿嬸; *husband's older sister,* kwu-mô' 姑母'; *husband's younger sister,* siao' kwu' 小姑; *father's sister's — and husband's sister's —,* kwu-dziang' 姑丈; *elder sister's —,* tsi'-fu 姊夫; *younger sister's —,* me-fu' 妹夫; *mother's sister's —,* and *wife's sister's —,* yi-dziang' 姨丈

HUSBAND, *should — your strength,* yin' lih, feh k'o yüong dzing' 有力弗可用盡; ng-go ky'i'-lih iao tsiang-yiang' 你°个°氣力要長養

HUSBANDMAN, cong'-din-nying 種田人°

HUSH, *to — (as a child's crying, or an affair),* en gyi'-go cü'-ṗô pi'

按閉°其嘴巴; — (in the imperative), m̃-nao' hyiang 弗°可°響; — *up privately,* s-'ô kæ ming-bah' 私下°遮醜°

HUSK *of paddy,* long-k'ông' 礱糠; — *of corn,* loh-koh' bǐ 稑穀皮

HUT, siao' oh 小屋 (ih-kæn); *straw —,* ts'ao' oh 草屋; ts'ao' sô 草舍°

HYMN, tsæn'-me-s 讚美詩 (ih-siu)

HYPOCRITE, kô-hao-nying' 假°好人°; veh-k'eo'-dzô-sing' 佛口蛇心

HYSTERICS, dæn-mi', sing-ky'iao' 痰迷心竅, (also suddenly gone on a frolic, &c.).

# I.

I, ngô 我; — *myself,* ngô-zi' 我自°; *it is —,* z ngô 是我; — *your inferior,* væn-pe' 晚輩; — *your pupil,* (in addressing a superior), væn'-sang 晚生°; *ditto* (in addressing one's teacher), meng-sang 門生°; meng-jing' 門人°; — *your humble brother,* nyü-di' 愚弟°; — *your humble sister,* nyü-me' 愚妹

ICE, ping 冰; *a piece of —,* ih-kw'e-ping 一塊冰; *cold as —,* ziang-ping' ka lang 像冰个°冷°

ICE-CREAM, ping-p'oh'-ting (the English word pudding is transferred)

ICE-HOUSE, ping-ts'iang′ 冰 廠

ICE-JELLY, ping-zih′-hwô (native) 冰石花

ICHTHYOLOGY, se′-dzoh-go 'oh-veng′ 水°族學°問

ICICLE, ding-dông′ 冰°柱° (ih-keng)

IDEA, i′-s 意思; *according to my* 一, tsiao-ngô′-go i′-s 照我个°意思

IDENTICAL, *the* — *person,* nyün-gyiu z keh-go-nying 原舊是這个人°; *the* — *place,* dzing′-jün z keh-ten′ 仍然是此°處°

IDIOM, kyü′-fah 句法; lin-p'ing-go kyü-fah′ 連揹个°句法

IDIOT, m̃-ling′-sing-go 無°靈性个°; deo-si′-nying 頭世°人°; ngæ-ts′ 呆子; do′-veh-ling′-sing (in reproach).

IDLE, *not industrious,* feh-gying′-lih 弗勤力; *lazy,* læn′-do 懶惰; *fond of being* 一, yiu-siu′ hao′-'æn′ 遊手好閒°

IDLE, *to* — *away time,* kong-fu′ k'ong′-ko 工夫空過; *to* — *when not watched,* t'eo-læn′ 偷懶

IDLER, k'ong-deo-nying′ 空頭人°; k'ong′-'æn-nying 空閒人°; dang-k'ah′ 宕客

IDOL, *image,* ngeo′-ziang 偶像; bu-sah′ 菩薩; *idols of clay, and wood,* nyi-su′-moh-tiao′ 泥塑木雕

IDOL-PROCESSION, we 會; *to form*

*or have an* 一, nying-we′ 迎會; 'ang-we′ 行會

IDOLATER, pa - ngeo′ - ziang - go 拜°偶像个°; pa-bu-sah-go nying 拜°菩薩个°人°

IDOLATRY, pa-bu-sah′-go z-t'i′ 拜°菩薩个°事體

IF, ziah-z′ 若是; t'eo′-p'ô′; t'ông′-jün 倘然; t'ông′-ziah 倘若; kyüô′-s 假使; jü-ko′ 如果; — *not so,* feo′-tseh 否則; — *not,* ziah-feh-z′ 若弗是; — *it be so,* t'ông′-jün z-ka′ 倘然如°此°; *as* 一, hao′-ziang 好像

IGNITE, *to set on fire,* ying-dziah′ 引燶; tin′-leh-dziah 點得°燶; fah-ho′ 發火; *when ignited,* bo′-sang-dziah′-de 火生燶了°

IGNOBLE (in birth, or station), zin 賤°; pe-zin′ 卑賤°; 'ô′-zin 下°賤°; ti-vi′ 低微; *of* — *birth,* c'ih′-sing zin′-go 出身賤个°; — *actions,* 'ô′-tsoh 'ang-we′ 下°作行°爲

IGNOMINIOUS, *disgraceful,* tao-me′-go 倒°楣个°

IGNOMINY, *consigned to* — 10,000 *years,* yi ts a′ væn nyin′ 遺臭°萬年

IGNORAMUS, bah-du′-bi 白°肚皮; ts'ao′-pao 草包; *one who has never tasted ink,* m̃′-neh ky'üoh-moh-shü′ ko 全°無°墨水°; *a pretender to knowledge,* c'ong dzæ′-'ông nying′ 充在行

人°; kô'-tsoh ts'ong'-ming 假°
作 聰 明

IGNORANT, *not knowing*, feh hyiao'-
teh-go 弗 曉 得 个°; feh ming'-
bah-go 弗 明 白°个°; — *of
rules of propriety, &c.*, feh-sih
shü'-vu 弗 識 世 務; — (*i. e.
stupid*) *people*, nyü pah'-sing 愚
百°姓; nyü ming' 愚 民

IGNORE, *to — one's own words*, zih-
yin' 食 言

ILL, *sick*, yiu bing' 有 病; *slightly
—*, feh sông'-kw'a 弗 爽 快';
feh shih'-i 弗 適°意; næn-ko' 難
過; *must not think — of*, (or take
ill), feh k'o kyin kwa' 弗 可 見
怪°; — *arranged*, pa' feh-hao
擺°弗 好; — *gotten*, keo-ts'ia'
teh'-djoh-go 茍°且°得着°个°;
— *natured*, tiao-cün'-deo-go 刁
尖°頭 个°; kæn-ka' 尷 尬°; —
*will*, du'-bing 肚 病; ün 怨°; ün'-
ky'i 怨 氣; *treat me —*, dæ ngô
Wa' 待 我 孬°; *ditto* (if a guest),
dæ ngô boh' 待 我 薄

ILLEGAL, væn-fah'-go 犯 法 个°;
we-li', væn-fah'-go 違 理 犯 法
个°

ILLEGIBLE, doh-feh-loh'-ky'i 讀
弗 下°去°

ILLEGITIMATE *trade*, væn'-kying-
go sang-i' 犯 禁 个°生°意;
— *birth*, t'eo sang' 偷 生°

ILLIBERAL, ky'i'-liang 'ah-tsah'
器 量 狹°窄; du'-liang tsah'
肚 量 窄

ILLIMITABLE, m̃ 'æn'-cü 無 限°
制; m̃-pin'-m̃-ngen' 無°邊 無°
岸

ILLITERATE, feh sih'-z 弗 識 字

ILLNESS, bing 病; *severe—*, djong'
bing 重 病; *recovered from —*,
bing hao'-de 病 好 了°; bing'
djün-yü'-de 病 全 愈 了°

ILLUMINATE, *to* tsiao'-leh ming-
liang' 照 得°明 亮; kwông'
tsiao'-djoh 光 照 着°

ILLUSTRATE, *to — by example*,
yüong pi'-yü, kông' ming-bah'
用 比 喻 講°明 白'; — *by pic-
tures*, yüong du-wô' peh nying
hyiao'-teh 用 圖 畫 俾°人°曉 得

ILLUSTRIOUS, ming'-sing do' 名
聲 大°; — *for virtue*, teh'-
ky'i kao' 德 氣 高

IMAGE, ziang 像; ngeo'-ziang 偶
像; *small —* (generally a toy),
'en 偶°孩°

IMAGINE, *to* i'-siang 意 想; —
(as something incorrect, or fantastic), du'-djün 杜 撰; du'-
dzao 杜 造; — *something false*,
zia-ho'-ky'i.

IMAGINATION, *the power of —*,
ts'eh'-doh-ts-dzæ' 測 度 之 才;
*it is all his own —*, zi kyin' yiu
kyü 自°見 有 鬼°

IMBECILE, ngæ 呆; — *from age*,
lao'-moh-long'-c'ong 老 邁°龍
鍾°(c'ong or ts'ong),

IMBECILE, *n.* ngæ-moh'-deo 呆
木 頭

IMBEDDED, *buried in*, u'-tsông-tih; — *in mud*, na-nyi-li u'-tsông-tih 臧 在 °泥°中°; *sunk*, 'æn-tsing'-tih 陷°進 的

IMBITTER, *to* long'-leh kw'u'-go 弄 得° 苦 个°; *he imbitters my life*, ngô bing-seng' ky'üoh gyi'-go kw'u' 我 平 生 吃°其 个°苦

IMITATE, *to* — (a person), k'en'-yiang 'oh-yiang 看 樣 學°樣; k'en-nying' 'oh-yiang' 看 人°學°樣; — (as work), tsiao' yiang tso' 照 樣 做; — *others*, nying k'en' nying yiang' 人°看 人°樣

IMITATIVE, we 'oh yiang' 會 學°樣

IMMATERIAL, vu' ying-t'i' go 無 形 體 个°; m̄' ying-tsih' go 無°形 跡 个°; — *to me*, ü ngô' vu dzih' 與 我 無 涉

IMMATURE, m̄'-neh do-tsoh' 沒°有°大°足; m̄'-neh tsiang'-dzing 沒°有°長 成

IMMEASURABLE, liang-feh-læ'-go 量 弗 來 个°; m̄-'æn'-go 無°限°个°

IMMEDIATELY, ziu 就°; ih'-z-li 一 時 裏; tsih'-k'eh 即 刻; lih-k'eh' 立 刻; mô'-zông 馬 上

IMMEMORIAL, *from time* —, dzong-kwu'-yi-læ 從 古 以 來

IMMENSE, *very large*, ting'-do' 頂 大°; do'-leh-kying 大°得°緊; — *quantity*, to'-feh-ko', yi-to' 多 而°又°多

IMMERSE, *to* — *in water*, tsing' læ shü'-li' 浸 在°水°裏

IMMERSION, *baptism by* —, tsing'-li 浸 禮

IMMINENT, *near*, ling-gying 臨 近; *in* — *danger*, ngwe' dzæ tæn' zih 危 在 旦 夕; ngwe-hyin' ling-gying-de' 危 險 臨 近 了°; (*more intense*) ngwe kyih'-de 危 急 了°

IMMODERATE, t'eh' ko-veng' 太°過 歼

IMMODEST, feh-p'ô-siu' 弗 怕 羞; feh-kwu' lin-c'ü' 弗 顧 廉 恥; — *picture*, c'ing kong' 春 宮 (ih-feh)

IMMOLATE, *to sacrifice animals*, yüong sang-k'eo' tso tsi'-li 用 牲 口 做 祭 禮; — *a man, in vengeance*, dziu-nying' sah'-ts tsi' 警 人°殺 了°祭

IMMORAL, *inconsistent with rectitude*, feh-tön'-tsing 弗 端 正; feh-tsing'-kying 弗 正 經

IMMORTAL, ve'-si-go 不°會°死°个°; üong'-weh-go 永 活 个°; — (in the Buddhist sense) dziang-seng'-peh-lao 長 生 不 老

IMMORTALIZE, *to* liu-fông'-pah-shü' 流 芳 百°世

IMMOVABLE, dong'-feh-læ'-go 動 弗 來 个°; yi'-feh-dong'-go 移 弗 動 个°

IMMURED *in a prison*, kwæn' læ lao-kæn'-li 關 在°牢 監°裏;

— *in a convent*, loh ing'-siu-yün-li 落隱修院裡

IMMUTABLE, üong' feh-keng-kæ'-go 永弗更改个°; kæ'-pin-feh-kæ'-go 改變弗來个°

IMPAIR, *to* wæ-diao' 壞了°; — *the health* (*i. e.* body), wæ-diao' sing-t'i' 壞了身體; *bodily energies still unimpaired*, tsing-jing' wa feh sæ' 精神還°弗衰; *impaired fortune*, ts'æn'-nyih ky'üih'-long'-ky'i'-de 產業漸° 缺了°

IMPART, *to* — *instruction*, kao'-hyüing 敎°訓; *willing to* — *to others*, k'eng' peh nying-kó' 肯給°人家; *to* — *the secret* (of making), djün pi'-kyüih 傳秘訣

IMPARTIAL, m̄-p'in-sing' 無°偏心; *just*, kong-dao' 公道; kong-bing' 公平; — *man*, ping'-kong vu-s'-go nying 秉公無私个°人°

IMPARTIALLY, bing-yüing'平允; *treat men* — , kong-dao' dæ nying 公道待人°

IMPASSABLE, tsee'-feh-ko'-ky'i 走弗過去°

IMPATIENT, feh-næ'-væn 弗耐煩; feh-jing'-næ 弗忍耐

IMPEACH *him*, fông' gyi-go shü' 放其个°水°; — *an inferior in office*, ts'æn'-tseo' 叅奏

IMPEACHMENT, *written* tseo'-tsông 奏章

IMPEDE, *to* gah-tang'; *impeded* (by many things, as baskets, &c.), t'o-t'o'-ts'i-ts'i 拖拖㯫㯫°

IMPEDIMENT, gah-tang'; *obstruction*, fông-ngæ' 妨碍; *an* — *in his speech*, kông shih'-wô bun'-zih-keng-go 講°說話拌°舌根个°

IMPENDING *evil*, or *woe*, 'o'-se læ deo-zông' 禍祟在°頭上; 'o'-tsiang ling-deo' 禍將臨頭

IMPENETRABLE, tsing'-feh-læ 進弗來°; — *to the eye* (also used figuratively), k'en-feh-t'eo' 看弗透

IMPENITENT, feh-zing' hwe'-kæ-go 弗曾悔改个°; *obdurate*, t'ih'-tang sing-dziang' 鐵打心腸

IMPERATIVE, pih' ky'iao-leh (or ky'iah-leh) 必須°; vu pih'-ts 務必

IMPERCEPTIBLE *to the eye*, k'en'-feh-c'ih-go 看弗出个°; — *to the touch*, moh'-feh-c'ih'-go 摸弗出个°

IMPERFECT, *not perfect*, feh-djün' 弗全; dzæn-ky'üih'-go 殘缺个°; *faulty*, yiu mao-bing' 有毛病; t'e-pæn' 摧扳; *deficient*, yiu ky'üih' 有缺; feh wun'-djün 弗完全

IMPERIAL, wông-ti'-go 皇帝个°; — (immediate) *family*, wông-kó' 皇家°; — *family or tribe*, tsong-shih' 宗室; — *commands*, zông-yü' 上諭; sing'-ts 聖旨; wông-ming' 皇命; — *proclamation*,

wông-pông′ 皇榜; — *guards,*
z-we′ 侍衛; — *palace,* wông-
kong′ 皇宮; — *censor,* kyin′-
ts‘ah nyü′-s 監察御史

IMPERIOUS, c‘ih′-k‘eo-do - yiang′
出口大°樣; c‘ih′ yin peh
seng′ 出言不遜

IMPERTINENT, *not knowing what
is proper,* feh sih′ siang-t‘i′ 弗
識禮°體; *not caring for ditto,*
s′-vu gyi-dæn′ 肆無忌憚;
*thrusting one′s self into conversa-
tion when not wanted,* iao ts‘ah-
cü′-go 要插嘴个°; — *fellow*
(*i. e.* monkey), to-cü′ weh-seng′
多嘴猢猻

IMPERTURBABLE *in mind,* sing
t‘ih′-ding 心鐵定; — *face,*
min-k‘ong′ t‘ih′-pæn 面孔鐵板

IMPERVIOUS *to water,* shü seng′-
feh-tsing 水°沁弗進; ve′-heng-
shü 弗會°沁水°; feh-ky‘üoh′-
shü 弗吃°水°; — *to air,* feh-
t‘ong-ky‘i′-go 弗通氣个°

IMPETUOUS, *as the moth rushing
into flame,* ziang deo-ho′-ts‘ông-
ing′ ka 像投火蒼蠅; — *tor-
rent,* shü kyih′ 水°急

IMPIOUS, miao-z Jing-ming′-go 藐
視神明个°

IMPLACABLE, seng-s′-feh-‘o′ 至°
死不°和

IMPLANT *love in the heart,* jing-
æ′-go keng-deo′ cong læ sing li′-
hyiang 仁愛个°根頭種在°
心裡向

IMPLEMENTS, kô-sang′; ky‘i′-ming
器皿; — *of all kinds,* siu′-
yüong-kô-sang′ 家°用°物°件°

IMPLICATED, lin-liao′-go 連了
个°; c‘ün′-t‘ong-liao-go 串通
了个°

IMPLICIT, *to place — confidence in,*
ky‘üoh′-jih siang-sing′ 確實相
信; *to give — obedience,* pah′-i-
pah′-jing 百°依百°順

IMPLORE, *to* gyiu-k‘eng′ 求懇

IMPLIED, kwæn′-djoh-tih 關着°
的°; *contained within,* pao-tsing′-
tih 包進的°; ‘en′-tih 含的°;
ko′-tsing-tib 裹進的°; *hidden,*
k‘ông′-tih 囥的°

IMPOLITE, m̃-li′-ky‘i 無°禮體°;
m̃-kwe′-kyü 無°規矩

IMPORT, *meaning,* ka′-shih 解說;
i-s′ 意思

IMPORT *duties,* tsing′-k‘eo se′ 進
口稅; *imported goods,* tsing′-
k‘eo ho′ 進口貨

IMPORT, *to — goods,* ho′ tsông-
tsing′-læ 貨裝進來

IMPORTANT, iao′-kying 要緊;
*weighty,* djong 重; *not —,* m̃-iao′-
teh-kying 無要緊; — *doc-
trine,* do-dön′-dao-li 大°叚道理

IMPORTUNATE, t‘ao′-ko-yi-t‘ao′ 討
過叉°討; iao′-zông-kô-iao′ 要
上加°要

IMPORTUNATELY, sah′-k‘eo t‘ao
着° 實°討; ts‘ih′-sing gyiu′ 切
心求; — *and persist n'ly,* o′-
nyi-bi′-ts‘i t‘ao′,

IMPOSE, to — a customs' tax, k'æ ih-'ông sø' 開一項稅; — (as a burden), djong'-t'oh 重托; he is imposing on you, læ-tih hong' ng zông gyi'-go tông' 正在°哄你°上其个°當

IMPOSSIBLE to do, tso'-feh-læ 做弗來; long'-feh-læ 弄弗來; quite —, tsing-tsing' tso'-feh læ 眞眞做弗來; — to find a seat, zo'-we ih-ngæn' tu zing'-feh-c'ih 坐位一點°都尋弗出

IMPOSTOR, kô'-nying 假人°; one who assumes a false name, mao-ming-go cü'-kwn 冒名个°人°; one who by deception runs off with a child, or property, kwa'-ts 拐°子; an —, ziang kwa'-ts ka 像拐°子

IMPOTENT, weak, nyün'-ziah 輭弱; m̃-lih 無°力; — tao-yiang' 倒陽; — from excess, tsing'-lih-hao'-zing 精力耗盡°

IMPRACTICABLE, tso'-feh-læ 做弗來; long'-feh-læ 弄弗來

IMPRECATE, to tsiu'-mô 呪罵

IMPRECATIONS, mouth full of —, bah-k'eo' tsiu'-cü 滿°口呪咀; oh'-k'eo tsiu'-cü 惡口呪咀

IMPREGNABLE, tang'-feh-tsing' 打弗進

IMPREGNATED, to become — (as animals), zin tsing' 受精; — eggs, ko-shü'-liao-go dæn' 過勢了个°蛋; tang-shü'-liao-go dæn' 打勢過°了个°蛋; infused

into, as in water, ky'i'-mi-jih-ko' 氣味°入過; — with salt, yiu 'æn'-ky'i jih-tsing' 有鹹°氣入進

IMPRESS of a hand, siu'-go ying-tsih' 手个°形跡; siu'-ing 手印

IMPRESS, to engrave on the heart, k'eh' læ sing'-li 刻在°心裡; to — a messenger, k'ô ts'a-s' 捉°差; to — carriers, k'ô fu-ts' 捉°脚°夫

IMPRESSED, to be — on the mind, ts'ih'-ts'ih-dzæ-sing' 切切在心; he — me favorably the first time, ts'u we'-djoh gyi, ngô cong'-i go 初會着°其我中意个

IMPRESSION, the first — in print-ing, ts'u ing' 初印; a bad —, ing'-leh mo-wu' 印得°模糊; take an — of a writing on stone, k'ao pe' 拷碑

IMPRINT, to ing 印; tang-ing' 打印

IMPRISON, loh' lao-kæn'-li 落牢監°裡; kwæn'-leh kæn'-li 關在°監°裏; ky'ih'-loh lao-kæn-li 挈°落牢監°裡

IMPROBABLE, vi-pih' 未必; næn yiu' 難有; cannot be believed, feh' tsoh sing' 弗足信; næn siang'-sing 難相信

IMPROPER, not suitable, feh tsoh-hying 弗作與; fi sô nyi' 非所宜; — (as to make noise in prayers, or walk in with muddy feet), væn gyi' 犯忌

IMPROPRIETY, *where is the —?*
yiu′ 'o feh k'o′ 有 何 不° 可?

IMPROVE, *to* tsing-ih′ 進 益;*to
grow better,* hao′-ky'i-læ 好 起
來;— *the opportunity,* ts'ing-
kyi-we′ 趁 機 會;— *this op-
portunity,* ts'ing′ ts' kyi′-we 乘°
此 机 會;— *the time,* æ′-sih
kwông-ing′ 愛 惜 光 陰

IMPROVED *in looks,* min-seh′ hao′-
jü zin-deo′ 面 色 好 如 前°

IMPROVIDENT, feh-liu-zin′ c'ü-'eo′
弗 留 前° 處 後;*the — are
always poor,* sön′-kyi feh-tao′
ih-si′-gyüong′ 算 計° 弗 到 一
世° 窮

IMPRUDENT, feh-kwu′ zin'eo′ 弗
顧 前° 後;— *with regard to
health,* feh-pao′-yiang 弗 保 養

IMPUDENT, m̄-gyi-dæn′ 無° 忌
憚;— (in reply), ing-cü′ 應 嘴

IMPUGN, *to — one's motives,* k'eh′-
liao gyi 刻 薄° 料 其

IMPULSE, *to give him an —,* ts'e-
dong′ gyi-go hying′-deo 催 動
其 个° 興 頭;dzu′ gyi-go hying′
助 其 个° 興;*ditto* (like giving
a push), yiu-ts-wu′ t'e′-ih-pô 猶
之 乎 提° 一 把;*he acts from
—,* gyi′-go tsoh′-we hyüih-ky'i′
s-jün′ 其 个° 作 爲 血 氣 使
然

IMPUNITY, *with* (without detec-
tion), feh-p'o-en 弗 破 案;*to
steal with —,* tso-zeh′ feh-p'o′-
en 做 賊°弗 破 案;*can do with*

—, *because free from accustomed
restraints,* "T'in kao′ wông-ti
yün′" 天 高 皇 帝 遠

IMPURE, *unclean,* feh-ken-zing′
弗 乾 淨;feh-kyih′-zing 弗 潔
淨;feh-ts'ing-kyih′ 弗 清 潔;
— *thoughts,* nyiæn-deo′ feh kyih′-
zing 念 頭 弗 潔 淨;sing-zia′
心 邪°;— *water,* shü′ dzoh′
水 濁

IMPUTE, *to ascribe to,* kwe-peh′
歸 給°;— *to us,* sön′-tao ah′-
lah ming-'ô′ 算 到 我° 等°
名 下°

IN, læ 在°;dzæ′-li 在 裡;ü 於;
*he is — China,* gyi′ læ Cong-koh′
其 在° 中 國;— *the room,* vông′-
li 房 裡;— *my hand,* læ-ngô′
siu′-li 在° 我 手 裡;*come —,*
tseo′-tsing-læ′ 走 進 來;*go —,*
tseo′-tsing-ky'i′ 走 進 去°;*not
— man,* feh dzæ′-ü nying′ 弗
在 於 人°;— *this manner,* z-ka′
yiang′-shih 如° 此° 樣 式;—
*order,* a-ts'′-jü 挨 次 序;i-ts'′-jü
依 次 序;tsiao-ts'′-jü 照 次
序;— *order to know,* s′-teh hao
hyiao′-teh 使 得 好 曉 得;vu-
fi′ iao hyiao′-teh 無 非 要 曉
得;*small — comparison with
that,* pi′-gyi-siao′ 比 其 小

INACCESSIBLE, tseo′-feh-tao′-go
走 弗 到 个°

INACCURATE, *has mistakes,* yiu-
ts'o′ 有 錯°;yiu-dzæn;— *characters,* ngo z′ 訛 字

INACTIVE, ngæ 呆; ngæ-teng'-
teng 呆等等; ngæ-teh'-poh-loh;
ngæ-c'ing'-c'ing 呆惷惷

INADEQUATE, feh-tsoh' 弗足

INADMISSIBLE, *cannot be received*,
ziu'-feh-læ 受弗來; *cannot be
listened to*, t'ing'-feh-læ 聽弗
來; *cannot be allowed*, ing-byü'-
feh-læ 應許弗來

INADVERTENTLY, feh-læ'-kwu 弗
來顧; ih'-feh-læ'-kwu 一弗
來顧

INANIMATE, feh-weh-dong' 弗活
動; ngæ 呆

INAPPLICABLE, 'eh-feh-læ' 合弗
來; *sometimes applicable, sometimes —*, yiu 'eh'-go di'-fông,
yiu' feh-'eh'-go di'-fông 有合
个°地方, 有弗合个°地方

INAPPROACHABLE, gying'-feh-
long-go 近弗攏个°

INAPPROPRIATE, feh-siang'-nyi
弗相宜; feh-'eh'-li' 弗合理;
feh-te' 弗對

INARTICULATE *sounds*, sing-ing'
feh-ts'ing' 聲音弗清

INATTENTIVE, feh-liu-sing' 弗
留心; feh-kwæn'-sing 弗關
心; feh-tông-sing' 弗當心;
feh-yüong'-sing 弗用心; sing'
feh læ'-tih 心弗在°

INAUDIBLE, t'ing'-feh-c'ih'-go 聽
弗出个°; t'ing'-feh-kyin'-go
聽弗着°个°; *cannot distin-
guish*, bin'-feh-læ'-go 辨弗°來
个°

INAUGURATION *of an officer*,
zông zing' 上任, (also used for
the commencement of anything).

INAUSPICIOUS, feh-kyih'-li 弗
吉利

INBORN, sang-dzing'-go生°成个°

INCAPABLE *of filling the position,
or of doing a certain thing*, dzæ'
peh sing zing' 才不勝任

INCAPACITATED *by sickness*, be
bing' 'æ'-leh feh-neng'-keo 被
病害得°弗能殼; — *by old
age*, be nyin-kyi' sô tsu', feh-
neng'-keo 被年紀所阻弗
能殼

INCAPACITY, m̄-dzæ'-dzing 無°
才情; m̄-peng'-z 無°本事

INCARCERATE, *to* siu'-tsing kæn'-
li 收進監裏

INCARNATE, dzing'-leh nyüoh-
sing' 成得°肉°身; dzing-we'
nyüoh-sing' 成爲肉°身

INCAUTIOUS, feh-tso-gyi' 弗留°
意°

INCENDIARY, fông-ho'-go nying
放火个°人°

INCENSE, hyiang 香; — *sticks*,
bông'-hyiang 棒香; *ditto for
determining night-watches*, ding-
kang'-hyiang 定更°香; *to burn
—*, tin hyiang' 點香; siao
hyiang' 燒香; — *pot*, hyiang-
lo', or hyiang-lu 香爐

INCENSE, *to — one*, kyih' gyi-go
ô'-wông 激其个°怒°; ying'
gyi'-go ô'-wông 引其个°怒°

INCENSED, fah ông'-de 發 怒
了°; ô'-wông fah-tsoh'-de 怒
發 作 了°; *greatly* —, ky'i
gyih'-de 氣 ·極 了°

INCENTIVE, siang'-deo 想 頭

INCESSANT, feh hyih' 弗 歇; feh
ts' 弗 止; — *talking*, kông'-feh-
hyih' 講° 弗 歇; — *flowing of
blood*, hyüih'-c'ih feh-ts' 血 出
弗 止

INCEST, lön-leng' 亂 倫

INCH, ts'eng 寸; *not an* — *wide*,
feh tao' ih ts'eng kw'eh' 弗 到
一 寸 闊

INCIDENT, *a pleasing* —, ih tsông
hyi z 一 椿 喜 事

INCIPIENCY, ky'i-ing' z-'eo 起 因
時 候; ky'i-ing' fah-koh' 起 因
發 覺°

INCIPIENT *stages of disease*, bing'
ts'u-fah-go z-'eo 病 初 發 个°
時 候

INCISORS, *the two middle* —,
meng-zin'-ngô 門 前° 牙°

INCITE, *to* kyih 激; ying 引;
tang'-dong 打 動; *to encourage*, min'-li 勉 勵; — *good* (or
*evil*) *feelings*, ken'-kyih 感 激

INCLEMENT, *severe*, nyin; *very
cold weather*, ping-lang' t'in-kô'
極° 冷° 天; t'in' keh-ti'-ti lang'
天 割 剟° 剟° 冷°

INCLINATION, sing-siang' 心想;
ts'-hyiang 志 向; *to follow one's
own* —, i zi'-go sing-siang' tsu'
依 自° 个° 心 想 做; *he has*

*an* — *for study*, gyi'-go ts'-
hyiang iao doh-shü' 其 个° 志
向 要 讀 書

INCLINE, *to lean to one side*, tang-
pin' 打 邊; — *outward* (*as a
wall*), tang-pin' ts'ia-c'ih nga'
打 邊° 斜 出 外°; — *my heart
to goodness*, s'-teh ngô-go sing'
hyiang'-djoh jün' 使 得 我 个°
心 向 着° 善; — *the ear to hear*,
tseh'-leh ng'-tô t'ing 側 得° 耳°
朶 聽

INCLOSE, *to* (*as with a fence*), we-
djü' 圍 住; yü-cün' 圍 轉; —
(*as in a letter*), fong'-tsing 封
進; — *in an envelope*, t'ao sing'-
fong 套 信 封; — *in an extra
wrapper*, kô fong' 加° 封; —
*in a paper*, yüong ts' pao'-ih-pao
用 紙 包 一 包

INCLOSURE. The Chinese speak
of an inclosure, as that which lies
within the wall, or fence; thus,
the city is *that which lies within
the wall*, dzing-li' 城 裏; *the space
within a bamboo fence*, ts'iang-
pô' li-hyiang 籬 笆 裏 向

INCLUDED *within*, dzæ-ne' or dzæ-
nen 在 內; *ditto as ideas*, pao-
kweh'-tih 包 括 的; pao-'en'-
tih 包 含 的; *is this* —? keh'-
go dzæ-ne' feh 這° 个° 在 內
否°! *not* —, feh dzæ'-ne 弗
在 內

INCOHERENT *words*, (*i. e.* words
without strength), slih-wô' t'eh-

ky'i' go 說話脫氣个°; shih'-wô t'eh-tsih'-go 說話脫節个°

INCOMBUSTIBLE, siao-feh-diao'-go 燒弗壞°个°

INCOME, tsing'-shü 進水°; tsing-nyih' 進業; tsing'-tsiang 進賬; *expenditure exceeds —*, sô-jih' peh-fu' sô-c'ih' 所入不敷所出

INCOMMODE, *do not — yourself to do it*, teng ng feh-bin', hao-vong' tso 與°你°弗便不°用°做

INCOMPARABLE, *transcendent*, pi'-tsong-feh-dong'-go 比衆弗同个°; *cannot be compared with*, pi'-feh-teh'-go 比弗得个°; m̄-kao' pi-deo' 無°比頭

INCOMPETENT, *unequal to a task*, tæn-tông'-feh-djü 擔當弗住; — *as a frog to steady a table leg*, "din-kyi' seh coh'-kyiah si ts'ang'" 田雞扇桌腳死°撐

INCOMPLETE, *not complete*, feh dzing'-kong 弗成功; feh zi'-jih 弗齊°集; *not perfect*, feh djün'-be 弗全備; *unfinished*, feh wun'-djün 弗完全; feh tsiu'-djün 弗周全

INCOMPREHENSIBLE, sih'-feh-t'eo' 識弗°透; moh'-feh-djoh' 摸弗着°; ts'æ'-feh-c'ih' 猜弗出

INCONCEIVABLE, siang'-feh-tao'-go 想弗到个°; ts'eng'-feh-c'ih'-go 忖弗出个°

INCONGRUOUS, feh-siang'-p'e 弗相配; fi-sô-nyi' 非所宜

INCONSIDERATE, feh-li'-we' 弗理會; mông-kyi' li'-we 忘°記理會

INCONSISTENT *talk*, shih-wô' zin-'eo' feh-vu' 說話前°後弗符; *words — with one's heart*, k'eo'-z sing'-fi 口是心非

INCONSOLABLE, feh-zin' en-w̄e' go 弗受安慰个°; feh-k'eng' t'ing ky'ün' 弗肯聽勸

INCONSTANT, fæn'-foh-feh-ding'-go 反覆弗定个°; fæn'-foh-vu-djông' 反覆無常

INCONTINENT, fông'-cong-s-yüoh'-go 放縱私欲个°

INCONTROVERTIBLE, pæn-poh'-feh-tao'-go 駁弗倒个°

INCONVENIENT, feh-bin'-tông 弗便當; feh-bin' 弗便

INCORPOREAL, vu-ying'-vu-ziang' 無形無像

INCORRECT, *has mistakes*, yiu-t'so' 有錯°; yiu-dzæn'; *the characters are —*, z feh-tön'-tsing 字弗端正

INCORRIGIBLE, vu-fah'-k'o-djü' 無法可治°; tsih'-mi-peh-hwô' 執迷不化; — (*as a child*), mæn-bi' 蠻疲; — (*used in reproach*), zah-bi' 賊°疲; bi-gyih'-de 疲極了°

INCORRUPTIBLE, ve'-wæ'-diao-go 弗會°壞个°

INCREASE, *to* hying-wông' 興旺;

*to add to,* kô-ts'eo' 加° 湊; *to grow,* do-ky'i'-læ 大° 起 來; — *his courage,* tsông'-gyi-go-tæn' 壯 其 个°膽; tsiang'-gyi-go-tæn' 長 其 个°膽

INCREDIBLE, siang-sing'-feh-læ' 相 信 弗 來; feh-tsoh-sing' 弗 足 信

INCREDULOUS, pah'-feh-siang'-sing 百° 弗 相 信

INCULCATE *virtue,* cong-teh'-ky'i 種 德 氣; *instruct often,* le'-djông hyüing'-kyiao 屢 常 訓 敎

INCUMBENT, *it is — on me to do,* kwe-ngô'-tso' 歸 我 做

INCUR, væn 犯; væn'-djoh 犯 着°; — *his anger,* væn'-gyi-go ô'-wông 犯 其 个° 怒°

INCURABLE, i'-feh-læ'-go 醫 弗 來 个°; m̄-i'-deo 無° 醫 頭

INDEBTED, *I am — to him,* ngô'-ky'in' gyi tsa' 我 欠 其 債; *ditto, for kindness,* ngô dzing' gyi-go dzing' 我 承 其 个° 情; *ditto, for great kindness,* ngô' ky'in' gyi eng-diu nyi'-tsa 我 欠 其 恩 錢° 義 債

INDECENT, fông'-p'eh-la'-sa 放° 澈襯°褻; *filthy,* ao-tsao' 墺糟

INDECISION, m̄-cü'-i 無° 主 意; m̄-kyüib'-tön 無° 決 斷; hyüong'-vu-dzing-kyin' 胸 無 成 見

INDEED, ko'-jün 果 然; jih-dzæ' 實 在; *is it — so?* ko'-jün z-ka'-feh 果 然 如° 此° 否°?

INDEFATIGABLE, dziang-kyiu' feh-gyün' 長 久 弗 倦; tso'-feh-pih'-go 做 弗 彆 个°

INDEFINITE, weng-teng'-teng 混 滾; feh-feng'-ts'ing 弗 分 清; *the time is —,* vu-ding' gyi 無 定° 期

INDELIBLE, *that will not fade,* t'e'-feh-diao'-go 褪 弗 壞° 个°; *that cannot be rubbed out,* k'a'-feh-ky'i' 揩° 弗 去°

INDELICATE, m̄-t'i'-t'ong 無° 體 統; shih-t'i'-t'ong 失 體 統; — *language,* fi-li'-ts-yin' 非 禮 之 言

INDENTURE, kwæn-shü' 關 書; *to draw up an —,* lih-kwæn-shü' 立 關 書

INDEPENDENT, sing-kao' ky'i-ngao' 心 高 氣 傲; — *and free,* zi-yiu'-zi-dzæ' 自° 由 自° 在; *following one's own will,* 'eo-zi'-go cü'-i 候 自° 个° 主 意

INDEX, *table of contents,* moh-loh' 目 錄

INDIA-RUBBER, k'a-ts'-kao 揩' 紙 膠°

INDIAN-CORN, loh-koh' 稑 穀; pao'-r-mi 保 兒 米; — *meal,* loh-koh'-feng 稑 穀 粉

INDIAN-INK, moh 墨

INDICATES, *points,* ts'-tin 指 點; *shows,* (or can readily see), k'o kyin'-teh 可 見 得

INDICT, *to* kao-zông' 告 狀

INDICTMENT, zông-ts' 狀 紙 (ih-tsiang)

INDIFFERENCE, to hear with —, t'ing'-ts dæn'-jün 聽 之 淡 然; he took it with —, gyi ziu'-ts dæn'-jün 其 受 之 淡 然; dæn'-dæn sing-s t'ing' 不 大° 用° 心 聽; a matter of — (to me), feh-leng' 弗 論; treat one with —, dæ nying' lang'-dæn 待 人° 冷° 淡

INDIFFERENT, not very good, wa hao' 還° 好; wa k'o'-yi 還° 可 以; yia hao' 也° 好; p'o-hao' 頗 好

INDIGESTION, not digesting, feh siao'-hwô 弗 消 化; feh hwô' 弗 化

INDIGNANT, to be — at, ky'i'-veng 氣 忿; I am — at him, ngô teng' gyi dong ky'i'-veng 我 爲° 其 動 氣 忿; too — to endure it, ky'i'-veng-feh-ko' 氣 忿 弗 過

INDIGNITY, to treat with —, tsao-t'ah' 蹧 蹋; ditto (with greater —), sih'-doh 褻 瀆; ditto (with greatest —), ling-joh' 凌 辱

INDIGO, native din'-ts'ing 靛 青; t'u'-din 土 靛; foreign—, yiang-læn' 洋 藍

INDIRECT, feh-tsiao-dzih' 弗 照 直; wæn-ky'üoh' 灣 曲: — answer, feh-tsiao-dzih' we-teh' 弗 照 直 回 答

INDISCREET, kyin'-sih feh tao-kô' 見 識 弗 到 家°

INDISCRIMINATELY, feh-leng' 弗 論; peh-kyü' 不 拘; good or bad —, feh-leng' hao' feh-leng' wa' 弗 論 好 弗 論 孬°

INDISPENSABLE, siao'-feh-teh' 少 弗 得; hyih'-feh-læ' 歇 弗 來

INDISPOSED, not well, yiu' tin feh sông'-kw'a 有 點 弗 爽 快°; — to talk, læn'-teh kông 懶 得 講°; — to work, læn'-teh tso sang-weh' 懶 得 做 生° 活

INDISPUTABLE, poh'-feh-læ' 駁 弗 來; m̄ poh'-deo 無° 駁 頭; m̄-kao wô-deo' 無° 話 頭

INDISSOLUBLE, yiang-feh-k'æ'-go 煬 弗 開 个°; the — bonds of wedlock, kyih'-fah fn'-ts'i' ts'ah'-feh-sæn' 結 髮 夫 妻 拆 弗 散

INDISTINCT, feh ts'ing'-t'ong 弗 清 通; feh ts'ing'-ts'u 弗 清 楚; feh ts'ing'-k'oh 弗 清 確; — as characters, or things in the distance, ing'-ing-dong 隱 隱 動; u-ing'-ing 黑° 隱 隱

INDISTINGUISHABLE, weng-weng'-deng-deng 混 沌; feng'-feh-c'ih-go 分 弗 出 个°; — by sight, k'en'-feh-c'ih-go 看 弗 出 个°

INDITE, to — verses, di s' 題 詩

INDIVISIBLE, feng'-feh-k'æ'-go 分 弗 開 个°; feng'-feh-læ'-go 分 弗 來 个°

INDOLENT, t'en-læn'-go 貪 懶 个°; sang læn'-wông-bing; likes to lie down, t'en-min' læn-do' 貪 眠 懶 惰

INDORSE, *to* tæn-kyin' 擔肩; dæ-kyin' 搭肩

INDUCE, *to* cü'-du 制度; — *him to stay*, cü'-du gyi deng tong 制度其°庒在°此°; kw'un-liu gyi 欶留他°; — *customers to come*, tsiao ma'-cü læ 招買主來

INDUCEMENT, *that is an — to me*, keh z ngô t'en-du' go 這°是我貪圖个°; *there is no — for me to go*, ngô ky'ï' m̄-kao' soh-go t'en-du' 我去°沒有°甚°麼貪圖

INDULGE, *to gratify his wishes*, jü gyi'-go sing' 如其个°心; i' gyi-go sing-siang' 依其个°心想; *to —* (where there should be restraint), yüong-tsong' 容縱; — *the passions*, fông'-tsong s-yüoh' 放縱私慾

INDULGENT, *very* yüong-iang' 容養°; — *and foolish fondness*, nyih-æ'-peh-ming' 溺愛不明

INDUSTRIOUS, gying-lih' 勤力

INEBRIATE, *n.* tse'-hen 醉漢

INEFFECTUAL, feh-tsi'-ü-z' 弗濟于事; — (*as medicine*), feh-kyin yiao' 弗見效; *in vain*, bah-lih'-lih' 空勞°; du-jün' 徒然

INEFFICACIOUS, m̄-ing'-'ao 無°應效°; — (*as an idol, or medicine*), feh ling'-ing 弗靈應

INEFFICIENT, *habitually slack*, tso' z-ken' feh-tao-kô' 做事幹弗到家°; pun-lu'-feh-kyih'-go 半途°而°廢°

INEQUALITY *in surface*, kao-kao'-ti-ti 高高低低; ky'i-ky'i-ky'iao-ky'iao 蹊蹊蹺蹺

INESTIMABLE, vu-kô'-ts-pao 無°價°之寶

INEVITABLE, peh-min'-go 不免个°; *cannot be escaped*, min'-feh-ko 免弗過

INEXCUSABLE, nyün-liang'-feh-læ 原諒弗來

INEXHAUSTIBLE, vu-gyüong'-go 無°窮个°; yüong'-feh-wun'-go 用弗完个°

INEXORABLE, m̄-wæn'-we-go 無°挽回个°; — (*person*), tsih-ih' feh-k'eng' 執一弗肯; feh-cing' dzing; — *in carrying out law*, tsih-fah' feh-liu dzing 執法弗留情

INEXPERIENCED, m̄'-neh yüih-lih'-ko 沒°有°閱歷過°; sang-sn'-go 生疏个°; — *in the ways of the world*, feh-sih shü'-lu 弗識世路

INEXPERT, feh jing'-joh 弗純熟

INEXPLICABLE, i'-s ka'-shih-feh-c'ih' 意思解°說弗出

INEXPRESSIBLE, kông'-feh-c'ih'-go 講弗出个°; wô'-feh-læ'-go 話弗來个°

INEXTRICABLE *tangle*, kyih', ka'-feh-c'ih' 結解弗出; — *difficulty*, ka'-feh-k'æ'-go keh'-tah 解弗開个°疙瘩

INFALLIBLE, ve-ts'o' 弗會°錯;

*the* — (the emperor), sing′-zông 聖上

INFAMY, ts'iu′ ming′-sing 醜名聲; *eternal* —, yi-ts'iu′-væn-nyin′ 遺臭°萬年

INFANT, na-hwun′嬰°孩° (ih-go); ing-r 嬰兒 the veng-li for a male infant.

INFANTICIDE, long-sah′ na-hwun′ 弄殺嬰°孩°; *custom of killing girls*, nyih nyü′ fong-djoh 溺女風俗

INFANTRY, bu′-ping 步兵

INFATUATED, jih-mi-weng′-dzing-de 入迷魂陣了°; hweng′-tih′-de 惛的了°

INFECT, *to* — *the air*, yiang′-ky'i long′-leh doh′-go 陽氣弄得°毒个°; *to bring disease*, long-c'ih′ bing læ 弄出病來; *whole body is infected*, weng′-sing yiu ts'iu′-ky'i 渾身有臭°氣; *bad influences will* —, jih-ky'i′ iao jih-ko′ 習氣要染°

INFECTION, *I took the* —, ngô bing′ be ts'iu′-ky'i jih-tsing′-go 我病被臭°氣入進个°; ngô bing′ z heh′ ts'iu′-ky'i saug′-go 我病是嚇°臭°氣生°个°

INFECTIOUS, *disease is* —, bing′ iao-yin′-go 病要延个°

INFER, *to* t'e-k'æ′-ky'i 推開去°; *I* — *that it was you who took it*, ngô t'e-leng′-k'æ-ky'i z ng′ do′-go 我推論開去°是你拿°个°; *from one truth to* — *the*

*second*, veng ih′ cü r′ 問 一 知 二 (veng.)

INFERENCE, t'e-leng′-k'æ-go ï′-s 推論開个°意思; *draw a wrong* —, t'e-leng′ ts'o′ 推論錯; ï′-ziang bông′-pih 倚墻傍壁

INFERIOR *in quality*, t'e-pæn′ tin 推扳點; wa′ tin 孬°點; ts'ô′ tin 差點; *the lowest grade*, mah teng′ 末等; 'ô′ teng 下°等; — *in age*, siao ih′-pe 小一輩; 'ô′ ih′-pe 下°一輩; *under another's jurisdiction*, (as officers, or servants), 'ô′-joh 下°屬; — *in learning*, 'oh-veng′-ts'in′ 學°問淺; — *to him*, pi-gyi′-ti 比其低

INFESTED, *the seas are* — *with robbers*, yiang-wu′ dao′-hyin to 洋湖盜險多

INFIDEL, *disbeliever in the Scriptures*, feh-siang′-sing Sing-shü-go-nying′ 弗相信聖書个°人°

INFINITE, m̄-'æn′-cü 無限°制; m̄′-'æn′-liang 無限°量

INFIRM, *enfeebled*, ky'i′-hyüih sæ′-de 氣血衰了°

INFLAME, *to* — (as a desire), dong-ho′ 動火; — *the passions*, ying′-dong yüoh-ho′ 引動慾火; *to grow hot, and painful*, ziang-ho′ dziah-c'ih′ ka 像火燶°出°

INFLAMED *eyes*, nyih-ngæn′ 熱°眼; ho′-ngæn 火眼°

INFLATE, *to blow up*, c'ü-p'ông' 吹°膨

INFLEXIBLE, *that will not bend*, ao'-feh-cün'-go 拗弗轉个°; — *in purpose*, cü'-i m̄-w̄æn'-we-go 主意無°挽回个°

INFLICT, *to — punishment*, tsah'-vah 責罰; *ditto* (by an officer), dong ying-vah' 動刑罰; — *a fine*, vah-nying-ts' 罰銀子

INFLUENCE, *yield to his* —, tsiao-gyi'-go dong'-zing tso' 照其个°動靜做; k'en gyi siu'-tsang-cü-den' 看其手法°; *use the — of an official*, i'-kwun t'oh-shü' 倚官托勢; *trusts to foreign* —, gæ nga'-koh shü' 靠°外°國勢; *to ward off evil* —, bih-zia 辟°邪°

INFLUENCE, *to* ken'-dong 感動; ken'-hwô 感化; — *for good*, ying'-dao 引導; — (generally for evil), ying'-yiu 引誘; *easily influenced*, ng-tô nyün' 耳°朵軟

INFLUENTIAL, hyüing'-hyiang 薰香

INFLUENZA, shü'-sông-fong' 水°傷風

INFORM, *to* t'ong-cü' 通知; t'ong-pao' 通報; kao'-su 告訴; cü-we' 知會; — *friends of a death*, pao fu'-ing 報訃音; pao si'-sing 報死°信

INFORMANT, t'ong-pao'-go cü'-kwu 通報个°人°; t'ong-fong' pao-sing'-go-nying 通風報信个°人°

INFORMER, *one who informs for selfish ends, &c.*, liu'-long-ky'ing'.

INFREQUENT *times*, m̄'-to-siao we-su' 無°多少回數; m̄-kyi'-we 無°幾回; yiu'-tsao'-su 有遭數

INFRINGEMENT *of law*, væn-kying' 犯禁; — *of rules*, væn-kwe' væn-kying' 犯規犯禁

INFURIATED, nu'-fah-ts'ong'-kwun 怒髮冲冠 (ts'ong or c'ong).

INFUSE, *to extract qualities by steeping*, tsing' gyi tsih'-shü c'ih' 浸其汁水°出

INGENIOUS, yiu zao'-tsoh-ts dzæ' 有造°作之才; yiu kyi-ky'iao'-go 有機巧个°; — *contrivance*, ling-ky'iao'-go kô-sang' 靈巧个°器°皿°

INGENUOUS, dzih-sông' 直爽

INGOT *of sycee*, veng-nying' 紋銀; nyün-pao' 元寶

INGRAFT, *to — a tree*, tsih-jü' 接樹

INGRATITUDE, SEE UNGRATEFUL.

INGREDIENT, *mix together three ingredients*, sæn-yiang' liao-tsoh' p'e-tæn-long 三樣料作配攏; — (in a medical prescription), ih-vi' 一味

INHABITANTS, *how many* — ? to-siao'-nying deng'-tih 多少人°庉的? to-siao' ting-k'eo' 多

少丁口? to-siao' nying'-ting 多少人°丁?

INHABITED, *this house is* —, keh' tsing oh' yiu nying' deng'-tih 這°進屋有人°庶的

INHALE, *to* — *the air*, ky'i hwun'-tsing 氣噢進; byih'-tsing 噏進

INHERIT, *to* — *property*, tsih'-ziu ts'æn'-nyih 接受產業; — *an office* (trade, &c.), jih tsih' 襲職

INHERITANCE, yi - loh'- læ - go ts'æn'-nyih 遺下來个產業; yi-loh'-læ-go kô-kyi' 遺下°來个°家°計

INHOSPITABLE, *afraid of entertaining*, p'ô tsih k'ah' 怕接客; *to treat guests badly*, ky'ing-boh' dæ nying'-k'ah 輕薄待客人°

INHUMAN, oh'-doh 惡毒; — *disposition*, doh-sing' 毒心; sing ziang za-lông' ka 心像豺貔; lông'-sing keo'-fi 狼心狗肺

INIMITABLE, 'oh'-feh-siang-ziang'-go 學°弗相像个°; 'oh'-feh-læ-go 學°弗來个°

INIQUITY, ze 罪; ze-oh' 罪惡; oh'-nyih 惡孽

INJECT, *to* — *water*, shü' zih-tsing'-ky'i 水°射進去°

INJUDICIOUS, *acting without thought, or intelligence*, hwông-dông' 荒唐; mông-bah' 茫白°; *an* — *act*, ih-dziu'-ts-kyin' 一籌之見

INJURE, *to* 'æ 害; sông-'æ 傷害; *to treat wrongfully*, kw'e-dæ' 虧待; *ditto* (in a greater degree), long-song' 弄唆°; *to treat unjustly*, wĕ'-ky'üoh 委曲; — *secretly*, s' ing-sön' 使陰算; en' tsiu-coh' 暗弄°; — *reputation*, sông-'æ' ming-vông' 傷害名望; wæ-diao' ming'-sing 壞了°名聲; — *the health*, tsao-t'ah' tsing-jing' 蹧蹋精神

INJURIOUS, *very* ting we-'æ'-go 頂會害个°

INK, moh-shü' 墨水°; *a stick of* —, ih-ding moh' 一錠墨; *carmine* —, in-tsi' shü 胭脂水°; ts-pin' shü 脂邊水°; *vermilion* —, nying-cü' 銀硃

INKSTAND, mch-kwun' 墨罐 (ih-go)

INKSTONE, nyin-ngô' 硯瓦° (ih-kw'e).

INLAID, k'æn'-siang-go 嵌鑲个°; — *table*, k'æn-siang-go yün-coh 嵌鑲个°圓桌

INLAND, *the inner land*, ne-di' 內地 (ne or nen); *gone* —, tao ne-di' ky'i-de 到內地去°了°; — *rivers*, li'-kông 裡港; li'-'o 裡河; — *trade*, ne-di' sang-i' 內地生°意

INMATES, *persons within*, li'-deo nying 裡頭人°; *how many* — *are living here?* li'-deo to-siao' nying deng'-tih 裡頭多少人°庶的?

INN, 'ô-c'ü' 厦°處; k'ah'-nyü 客
寓; *rice and lodying shop*, væn-
tin' 飯店 (ih-go)

INNER, li-deo' 裏頭; li-hyiang'
裏向; — *room for women*, ne-
vông 內房 (nen or ne)

INNKEEPER, tin'-cü 店主; (master) laung'-z; tong-kô' 東家°

INNOCENT, feh ing'-kæ kyin-kwa'-
go 弗應該見怪个°; —
*people*, ts'ing-bah' liang-ming'
清白亮民 (also not ignoble
as to birth, or employment); *no
distinction between — and guilty*,
dzao'-bah feh-feng' 皂白弗分

INNOCUOUS, ve'-'æ-go 弗會害
个°; m̂-'æ-c'ü'-go 無°害處个°

INNUMERABLE, su'-feh-pin'-go 數
弗遍个°; sön'-feh-læ'-go 算
弗來个°

INOCULATE, *to — with small pox*,
cong deo-ts' 種痘子; 'ô miao'
下°苗

INODOROUS, m̂ ky'i'-mi-go 無°氣
味°个°; *no fragrance*, m̂ hyiang-
ky'i'-go 無°香氣个°

INOPPORTUNE, feh-ts'eo'-ky'iao
弗湊巧

INORDINATE *to excess*, ko-veng' 過
孖; ko-deo' 過頭; — *appetite*,
zih-liang' do ko-deo' 食量甚°
大°

INQUEST, *to hold an —*, nyin s'
驗屍

INQUIRE, *to ask*, meng 問°; —
*into*, bun-meng' 盤問°; tang'-
t'ing 打聽; dzô-meng' 查問°;
— (as an officer, into the state of
the people), ts'ah'-fông 察訪

INQUIRER, *religious* bun-meng'
dao'-li-go nying' 盤問° 道理
个° 人°; k'ao'-kyiu dao'-li cü'-
kwu 考究道理个° 人°

INQUISITIVE, dzô-dzô'-k'ao-k'ao-
go 查查考考个°; *prying*, to-
bo'-go 多啵°言°个°; bo-bo'-
tah-tah; *excessively —*, leo'-zing
kweh'-si 問°入骨髓

INSANE, tin 癲; *has become —*,
tin-de' 癲了°; *raving*, fah-
gwông' 發狂

INSATIABLE, m̂-ti'-ts-go 無°底
止个°; — *avarice*, t'en-sing' m̂-
ti'-ts 貪心無°底止; t'en-
sing' feh tsoh' 貪心弗足

INSCRIPTION, sia'-tih-go kyi' 寫°
的个° 記; — *of praise*, ming-
yin' 銘言; *a board, or stone with
an —*, pin 匾; ba-pin' 牌°匾;
*ditto* (over one's door or in a
garden), pin-ngah' 匾額; *a
wide scroll with an —*, z-wô' 字
畫; *a pair of narrow ditto*, z-
te' 字對

INSCRUTABLE, *cannot be searched
into*, dzô-feh-c'ih' 查弗出;
*cannot be thought out, or measured,*
ts'eh'-doh-feh-læ' 測度弗來

INSECTS, djong 蟲; *flying —*, fi-
djong 飛蟲

INSECURE, feh-Weng'-tông 弗穩
當

INSENSIBLE, moh-dzih'-dzih 木直直; — *from cold*, tong'-moh-de 凍木了°; *not knowing, or feeling*, feh-kyüoh'-teh 弗覺得; — (*like one dead*), jing'-z feh-cü' 人事弗知

INSEPARABLE, *cannot be divided*, feng'-feh-k'æ' 分弗開; — (*as friends*), li-sing'-feh-kæ 離身弗來

INSERT, *to* en-tsing'-ky'i 安進去; — *a character*, k'æn' ih-go z ts'eo' 嵌一个字湊; pu'-tsing ih-go z' 補進一个字

INSIDE, li-hyiang' 裡向; li'-deo 裡頭; *the inner surface*, li'-min 裡面

INSIDIOUS, weh-long'-weh-yin' 活龍活現; *crafty*, diao-bi'; *treacherous*, kæn-weh' 奸°猾

INSIGNIA *carried before a Chinese officer*, tsih'-z 執事

INSIGNIFICANT (*as a person, or words*), vu-yüong-vu-joh'-go 無榮無辱个

INSINCERE, feh-dzing'-jih 弗誠實

INSINUATE, *to — by remote allusion*, en'-di-li ts'-tin 暗地裡指點

INSIPID, m̄-mi'-dao 無°味°道; dæn 淡 (*generally wanting salt.*)

INSIST, *will not stop*, feh k'eng'-hyih 弗肯歇; *must have*, ih-ding' iao' 一定要; — *upon the full price*, kô'-din ngao'-ding

feh-k'eng ky'üih' 價°錢°嶔°定弗肯缺

INSNARE, *to* — (*as an animal*), gyiang-djoh' 擒着°; *wishes to — you*, iao ng loh' gyi-go 'æn' 要你落其个陷°; iao ng loh' gyi-go ky'ün'-t'ao' 要°你落其个°圈套°

INSOLENT, *to treat in an — manner*, c'ong-væn' 衝犯; c'ong-djông' 衝撞; — *language*, s'-vu-gyi-dæn'-go shih-wô' 肆無忌憚个說話

INSOLUBLE, yiang'-feh-k'æ'-go 煬弗開个°

INSPECT, *to* k'en 看; *to go about to* —, jing 巡; jing-dzô' 巡查; — *troops*, k'en-ts'ao' 看操

INSPECTION, *come on a tour of* —, jing-dzô' læ-go 巡查來个°

INSPECTOR-GENERAL OF CUS-TOMS, tsong'-se-vu-s 總稅務司

INSPIRE, *to* — *others*, ta'-zông bih'-nying 帶上別人°; *inspired by him* (*i. e.* warmed), sing peh gyi ta'-nyih-de 心被其帶熱了°; — *by Heaven*, T'in meh-ky'i'-go 天默啟个°; — *by the Holy Ghost*, be Sing'-ling ken-dong 被聖靈感動

INSTALL, *to* — *a person as pastor*, lih mo'-nying tso moh-s' 立某人°做牧師

INSTALLMENTS, *to pay by* —, bah-wæn' 拔還; bah-fu' 拔付

INSTANCE, *for* pi'-fông 比方;
pi'-jü 比如; kyüô'-jü 假如

INSTANT, *an* ih-sah'-z, *or* ih'-seh-
z 一霎時; *in an* —, tsih'-
k'eh' 即刻; *on the tenth* —,
ts'u-jih' keh-nyih' 初十日°

INSTANTLY, ih-sah'-z 一霎時;
tsih'-k'eh' 即刻; lih-k'eh' 立
刻

INSTEAD OF, t'i' 替; dæ 代; —
*me*, t'i' ngô 替我; *one who works*
— *another*, t'i'-kong 替工

INSTEP, kyiah'-min 脚面; kyiah'-
pe 脚背

INSTIGATE, *to* — *to evil*, t'iao-so'
挑唆

INSTILL, *to instruct by little and
little*, yüong-yin-yiang'-go kong'-
fu kao'-hyüing 用涵養个工
夫教°訓

INSTINCT, t'in-sing' 天性; t'in-
sang'-dzing-go cü'-kyüoh 天生°
成个°知覺

INSTITUTE, *to found*, lih 立; shih'-
lih 設立; — *an asylum*, lih' ih-
go gyüoh' 立一个°局

INSTITUTION *of learning*, shü-
yün' 書院

INSTRUCT, *to* kao 教°; kao'-
hyüing 教°訓

INSTRUCTION, *primary (i. e.* what
is first learned), ts'u-ts'u'-'oh 初
學°

INSTRUCTOR, sin-sang' 先生°;
kao'-shü sin'-sang 教°書先生°

INSTRUMENTS, kô-sang 家°生°;

ky'i'-ming 器皿; *surgical* —,
nga-k'o' kô'-sang 外°科所°用°
之°物°; *musical* —, tsoh-yüoh'-
go ky'i'-ming 作樂个°器皿

INSTRUMENTAL, *he was* — *in
bringing it about*, dzong gyi'
seng-kwô' k'æ-ky'i' 從其生
化開去°; dzong gyi' seng-fah'-
c'ih-læ' 從其生發出來

INSUBORDINATE, feh-k'eng'-voh
弗肯服; — (as subjects of the
emperor), feh-voh' wông-hwô'
弗服王化; — (as soldiers),
feh-voh' kyüing-ling' 弗服軍
令; — (as pupils), feh-voh'
kyiao'-hwô 弗服教化

INSUFFERABLE, *cannot be endur-
ed with patience*, jing'-næ-feh-
djü' 忍耐弗住; *detestable*,
peh-k'æn 不堪

INSUFFICIENT, feh-keo' 弗够;
feh-tsoh' 弗足; ky'in-to'.

INSUFFICIENTLY, ky'in 欠; —
*thick*, ky'in 'eo' 欠厚

INSULT, *you* — *me*, ng siah ngô'-
go lin' 你°削我个°臉; *to
treat with abuse*, tsao-t'ah' 蹧蹋;
siu'-joh 羞辱; — (a woman),
u-zoh' 污辱

INSUPERABLE *difficulties*, næn-c'ü'
kying-lih'-feh-læ 難處經歷
弗來

INSUPPORTABLE, tông'-feh-djü'
當弗住; tông'-feh-ky'i' 當弗
去°; — *pain*, t'ong' ngao'-feh-
djü' 痛熬弗住

INSURANCE *money*, pao-hyin'-go nying-ts' 保險个° 銀子

INSURMOUNTABLE, See INSUPER-ABLE.

INSURRECTION, *in a state of —*, lön 亂; tsoh-lön' 作亂; *in re-bellion*, fæn 反; dzao-fæn' 造反; *to plot —*, meo-fæn' 謀反

INSUSCEPTIBLE *of impression* (heart), sing dong'-feh-læ 心動 弗來

INTANGIBLE, moh-feh-djoh'-go 摸弗着°个°; cô-feh-djoh'-go 攃弗着°个°

INTEGRITY, *a man of —*, tsing'-dzih-go nying 正直个°人°

INTELLECT, ling-sing' 靈性; *fine —*, jing z' ling-sing' 純是靈性; *scanty —*, ling-sing' ky'üih' 靈性缺; *— or capacity*, ts-tsih' 資質

INTELLIGENCE, *great natural —*, t'in-ts'ong'-t'in-ming 天聰天明

INTELLIGENT, (naturally) ts'-tsih-ling' 資質靈; *knowing*, ts'ih'-t'ong-pah-dah' 七通八達; ts'ong-ming' 聰明; *— and clever*, ts'ong-ming' ling-li' 聰明伶利; ling-ky'iao' 靈巧

INTELLIGIBLE, hao' ming-bah'-go 好明白°个°

INTEMPERATE, *he is — in the use of liquors*, gyi' ky'üoh tsiu' ko-liang'-go 其吃°酒過量个°

INTEND, cü'-sing 主心; ding-kyin' 定見; *what do you — to do?* ng ding-kyin' tso soh'-si ni 你°定見做甚°麼°呢°? ng cü'-sing tso soh'-go z-ken' 你°主心做甚°麼°事幹?

INTENSE *in the extreme*, tao gyih-deo' 到極頭; tao-toh'; *— cold*, lang tao-toh' 極°冷°; *— admiration*, (and sometimes long-ing), dza ih'-cong ky'i'-mo 極°企慕

INTENTION, i'-s 意思; *no such —*, 'ao-vu' keh'-go i'-s 毫無這°个°意思; *fixed —*, lih-ding' cü'-i 立定主意; kyüih-i' 決意

INTENTIONAL, deh-i' 特意; kwu'-i 故意; deh-wo' 特爲

INTENT UPON ⎫ ih-dzing-tsi'-lu
INTENTLY, ⎭ 專°務; tsih'-kwu 只顧

INTER, *to* en-tsông 安葬

INTERCALARY *month*, yüing-yüih' 閏°月

INTERCEDE *for*, dæ gyiu' 代求; cün' gyiu' 轉求; *Christ intercedes for our pardon*, Kyi-toh' dæ teng' ah-lah t'a-nyiao' 基督代我° 等°討°饒°

INTERCEPT, *to —* (as persons, or letters), pun'-lu yi-shih 半路 遺失

INTERCESSOR, dæ-k'eng'-gyiu'-go nying 代懇求个°人°; cün'-gyiu-go nying' 轉求个°人°

INTERCHANGE (of courtesies, &c.) yiu-læ'-yiu-ky'i' 有 來 有 去°; — of goods, yi-ho'-yih-ho' 以貨 易貨; diao ho' 調 貨

INTERCOURSE, læ-ẁông' 來往; the two countries have a great deal of —, keh' liang koh læ-ẁông' to' 這° 兩 國 來 往 多

INTEREST, for your —, ng' do yiu ih'-c'ü 你° 大° 有 益 處; ng' do yiu li'-sih 你° 大° 有 利 息; I have an — in it, ü ngô' yiu kyiao-kwæn' 於 我 有 交 關; takes — in (as a servant in his work, &c.), tso z-ken' kwæn-sing'-go 做 事 幹 關 心 个°; — (on money), li'-din 利 錢°; li'-sih 利息; to pay —, fu-li' 付利

INTEREST, to — a person, t'iao-dong' nying-go sing' 挑動 人° 个° 心

INTERESTED, yiu c'ü'-hyiang 有 趣 向; yiu mi-dao' 有 味 道; yiu i'-c'ü 有 意 趣; — by him, be' gyi t'iao-dong'-de 被 其 挑 動 了°

INTERESTING child, siao nying' we ying nying' hwun-hyi' 小 囝° 會 引 人° 歡 喜; that was an — discourse, keh p'in kông'-ka tao c'ih-seh'-go 這° 篇 講° 解° 到 出 色 个°

INTERFERE, will it — with you (i. e. your plans)? ü ng' yiu ngæ' feh 於° 你° 有 碍 否°?

it will not —, peh-fông' 不妨; (you) need not —, hao-vong' kwun'-tsiang 弗 用° 管 賬

INTERIOR, the inside, li'-deo 裡頭; li-hyiang' 裡 向; — of a country, koh tông'-cong 國 之° 中

INTERLOPER, one who has forced himself in, ts'ông'-tsing-go-nying 闖 進 个° 人°; one who has no right, m̄-veng'-go nying 無° 分 个° 人°

INTERMARRY, to liang'-ʿô kyih-ts'ing' 兩 下° 結 親

INTERMINABLY, m̄-dzing'-gyi 無° 盡 期

INTERMISSION, time of cessation, hyih'-go z-'eo 歇 个° 時 候; noon —, hyih tsiu' 歇 晝; — (of fever), t'e z-'eo' 退 時 候; feh-fah'-go z-'eo' 弗 發 个° 時 侯

INTERMITTENT hyih'-hyih-deng'-deng 歇 歇 停° 停°; — in do-ing, t'eh'-t'eh-ga - ga tso'; — fever, dziao-nyih'-bing 寒° 熱° 病

INTERNAL, li'-deo 裡頭; li-hyiang' 裡 向; ne 內; — disease, nen bing' 內 病 (nen or ne)

INTERPOLATE, to pu'-zông 補 上; djoh-ts'eo' 續 湊; — a pas-sage, pu'-zông ih-tsih 補 上 一節

INTERPOSE, to — obstacles, tsu'-tông 阻 擋; — between parties at variance, ky'ün'-ka 勸 解°

INTERPRET, to (usually a native dialect) djün wó' 傳 話; — (a

foreign language), tso t'ong-z′ 做 通 事; *to translate*, fæn-yih′ 繙 譯; *to explain*, ka′-shih 解° 說

INTERPRETER (usually of a dialect), djün-wô′-go 傳 話 个°; *ditto to an officer*, dzih-dông-vông′-go 值 堂 个°; — *of a foreign language*, t'ong-z′ 通 事; — *of dreams*, ziang-mong′-go nying 詳° 夢 个° 人°

INTERROGATE, *to examine by questions*, meng 問°; dzô-meng′ 查 問°

INTERROGATION, *signs of* — *in the colloquial are*, m? ma 嗎°? ni 呢? yia 呀°? feh 否°? *have you any*? yiu 而 有 沒° 有? yiu ma 有 嗎°? *how is it*? dza′-go ni 怎° 樣° 呢? dza-go yia′ 甚° 麼 呀°?

INTERRUPT, *to* gab-tang′; *to break off*, tang′-dön 阻° 隔°; — *work*, tang′-dön kong-fu′ 工 夫 被° 阻°

INTERRUPTION, *without* m̄′-neh hyih′-loh 沒° 有° 歇 落

INTERSECT, *to divide in parts*, feng-tæn′-k'æ 分 開; — *at right angles*, jih-z′ feng-k'æ 十 字 分 開; — *by a cross line*, wang sin′ feng-k'æ′ 橫° 線° 分 開

INTERSECTION, *the point of* —, ts'ô′-k'æ-go di′-fông 叉 開 个° 地 方

INTERSTICES, li-vong′ 離 縫

INTERTWINE, *to* liang′-'ô gao-long′ 兩 下° 絞° 攏; liang′-'ô dzin-long′ 兩 下° 纏° 攏

INTERVAL *in space*, kah′-k'æ 隔 開; li-yün′ 離 遠; *an — of three feet*, kah-k'æ sæn-ts'ah′ 隔 開 三 尺°; *an — of a year*, teo-deo′ ih-nyin′ 週° 年; *an — of two years*, kah′ liang-nyin′ 隔 兩 年

INTERVIEW, *to have an* — (*i. e. mutual view*), we-kyin′ 會 見; *to confer with*, kyin′-min kông′ 見 面 講°

INTESTINES, du′-dziang 肚 腸

INTIMATE, cü-kyi′ 知 己; moh-nyih′ 莫 逆; ts'ih′-t'iah 切 貼°; ts'ing-mih′ 親 密

INTIMIDATE, *to* hah 嚇; — *him*, hah′ gyi 嚇 其; long gyi p'ô′-gyü 弄 其 怕 懼

INTO, læ 在°; li 裡; tsing 進; li′-deo 裡 頭; li-hyiang 裡 向; *pour — a bowl*, sia′ læ un′-li 舄° 在° 碗° 裡; *take* (*it*) — *the house*, do-tsing′ oh′-li 拿° 進 屋 裡

INTOLERABLE, *that cannot be borne*, tông′-feh-djü′ 擋 弗 住

INTOLERABLY *bad*, ẅa-r′-vu-tông′ 孬° 而 無 當

INTOLERANT, feh-k'eng′ yüong-nying′-go 弗 肯 容 人° 个°

INTOXICATE, *to* tse 醉; *wine will* — *people*, tsiu′ we tse nying′ 酒 會 醉 人°

INTOXICATED, tsiu-tse′-tih-de 酒 醉 的 了°

INTRACTABLE, gyüih-gyiang′ 倔強

INTREAT, See ENTREAT.

INTRENCHMENT, camp, ying-bun′ 營盤; earth-work, nyi-dzing′ 泥城; to make an —, tah′ ying-bun′ 搭營盤

INTREPID, üong 勇; üong′-tsiang 勇將

INTRICATE, ao′-gao 坳境°; yiu ky‘üoh′-tsih 有曲折; having many windings, wæn-nyiao′to′ 彎繞多

INTRIGUES, kæn-kyi′ 奸計; tsô′-kyi 詐計

INTRODUCE, to — them, ts′-ying gyi ts‘ing-hwu′ 指引其稱呼; — me, ts′-hyiang-ngô-dao′ 指向我道; to begin to speak, k‘æ-k‘eo′ 開口; — a subject, di-ky‘i′ ih-yiang′ z-ken′ 提起一樣事幹

INTRODUCTION, a letter of —, t‘oh-shü′ 託書; — to a book, siao′-ying 小引 (veng); væn-li′ 凡例 (veng); ditto (generally not written by the author), jü-veng′ 序文; — to a discourse, tsong-mao′ 總冒

INTRUDE, to ts‘ah-tsing′, 插進; gah-tsing′; cün-tsing′ 鑽進; c‘ông-tsing 闖進 (also pron. ts‘ông′-tsing); — remarks, ts‘ah-cü′ 插嘴; ts‘ah-yin′ 插言

INTRUSIVE, we ts‘ah-tsing′ 會插進

INTRUST, to t‘oh 託; t‘oh′-fu 託付; kao-dæ′ 交代; I — this business to you, keh′-yiang z-ken′ ngô t‘oh′-fu ng′ de 這°樣事幹我託付你 了°

INTUITIVE, seng-r′-cü-ts′ 生而知之 (veng.)

INUNDATE, to tso do′-shü′; fah-shü′ 發水°

INUNDATION, there is an —, yiu′ do-shü′ 有大°水°; great — (like the Flood) ziang ‘Ong-shü′-fæn-tsiang′ ka 像洪水°氾漲

INURED to hardships, kw‘u kwæn′-liao 苦慣°了

INVADE, to — another's borders, væn-ka′ 犯界°; to — a place with hostile intentions, ts‘ing-tsin′ di-fông′ 侵佔地方

INVALID, sick person, yiu-bing′-go-nying 有病个°人°

INVALIDATE his will, fi-diao gyi-go yi-coh′ 廢了°其个°遺囑 (coh or tsoh)

INVALUABLE, vu-kô′-ts-pao 無價°之寶°; ts‘in-kying′-næn-ma′ 千金難買°

INVEIGLE, to keo′-leh 勾勒; ying′-yiu 引誘; ying′-zô 引惹°

INVENT, to shih′-siang-c‘ih-læ 設想出來; tang′-mo-c‘ih-læ 打摹出來; — a new pattern, zao′ sing yiang′-shih 造°新樣式°

INVENTOR, shih-siang′-c‘ih-læ′ cü′-kwu 設想出來个°人°; ky‘i-deo′ zao′-go cü′-kwu 起頭造°个°人°

INVERT, *to* fæn-hyiang′ 反向；
— *it,* foh′-ts 覆之

INVERTED, tao′-toh-go 頂°倒个°；
*leave it* —, fæn′-hyiang en′-tih
反向安的； — (*when it
ought not to be*), tao′-hyiang-go
倒向个°; foh′-ken-go 覆蓋°
个°

INVEST, *to* — *with the ostrich-
plumed hat,* sông′ ta′-ling-mao′
賞°戴°翎枝; — *a city,* we-
kw'eng′-dzing-ts′ 圍困城子;
— *safely* (*as money*), fông′-leh
t'o′-tông-go 放得°妥當个°

INVESTIGATE, *to*— (*as belief, &c.*),
k'ao′-kyiu 考究; dzô-k'ao′ 查
考; — (*as business*), tse-kyiu′
追究; — *with rigor,* nyin-kyiu′
嚴究; nyin-dzô′ 嚴查

INVESTMENT, *good* hao c'ih′-sih
好出息

INVETERATE, kwu′-tsih feh-hwô′
固執弗化; *deep-rooted,* keng-
sing′-ti′-kwu 根深底固; —
*disease,* bing′ we dzin-sing′ 病
會纏身

INVIDIOUS, *making an* — *distinction,* feng′-c'ih bin′-pih-læ 分別
出來; *exciting envy,* long′-leh
yiu tu′-gyi-sing 弄得°有妒
忌心

INVIGORATE, *to* — *the body,* diao-
yiang′ sing-t'i′ 調養身體; —
*by rest,* tsiang-yiang′ 長養

INVIGORATING, yiang-jing′-go 養
神个°; — *medicine,* pu′-yiah

補藥; *it is* — *there,* keh′-deo we
k'ông-gyin′ 那°裏°會康健

INVINCIBLE, tang′-feh-ying′-go
打弗贏个°; ying′-feh-læ′-go
贏弗來个°; — *foe,* vu-dih′-
siu 無敵手

INVISIBLE, k'en′-feh-kyin′-go 看
弗見个°

INVITATION, *I accepted his* —,
ngô ing-hyü′ gyi sô ts'ing′ 我
應許其所請; *card of* —,
ts'ing′-t'iah′ 請帖 (ih-go)

INVITE, *to* ts'ing 請; siang-ts'ing′
相請; siang-iao′ 相邀; — *with
formality* (*as a man to be a
pastor, &c.*), p'ing′-ts'ing 聘請

INVOICE, ho′-tæn 貨單 (ih-tsiang)

INVOKE, *to* gyiu-kyiao′ or gyiu-
kao′ 求敎

INVOLUNTARY, feh-yiu′ zi′-go cü′-
i 弗由自个°主意; tso-gyi′-
feh-læ 留°意弗來

INVOLVE, *to* ta′-li 帶°累°; ky'in-
le′ 牽累; lin-le′ 連累; — *in
evil consequences,* ta′-li yiu kwæn-
ngæ′ 帶°累°有關碍; — *one
in trouble by dying on his hands,
&c.,* du-vu′ 誣詐

INWARD, *seated within,* li-deo′ læ-
tih 在裡頭; *toward the inside,*
hyiang-li′ 向裡; dziao-li′ 朝裡

INWARDS, *the* dzông-fu′ 臟腑;
ng-dzông-loh-fu′ 五°臟六腑;
*disease has gone to the* —, bing′-
jih kao-hwông′ 病入膏肓

IOTA, *an* ih-tin′ 一點

IRKSOME, in'-væn 厭煩; in'-ky°i 厭棄

IRON, t°ih 鐵; — wire, t°ih'-s 鐵絲; — filings, t°ih'-sô 鐵沙

IRON heated by charcoal within, ing'-teo 熨斗; — heated on coals, loh-t°ih' 熔鐵 (ih kwun); to heat (or light) the first—, sang ing'-teo 生° 熨° 斗; to heat the second, we loh-t°ih' 煨熔鐵; fluting — (or pincers), t°ông'-gyin 燙箝

IRON, to — clothes, t°ông i-zông' 燙衣裳°

IRON-CLAD, t°ih'-kah ping-jün' 鐵甲° 兵船 (ih-°ao)

IRONICAL words, gyiao wô' 搭°橋話; words the opposite of what one means, diao-deo' wô 調頭話; fæn wô' 翻話

IRRATIONAL, without knowledge, m̄-cü'-sih-go 無° 知識个°; without intelligence, m̄ ling'-sing-go 無° 靈性个°

IRRECLAIMABLE, siu'-feh-kyü-læ 收弗歸° 來; — (as a person), siu-liu'-feh-læ' 收留弗來

IRRECONCILABLE, °o-feh-long' 和弗攏

IRRECOVERABLE, that cannot be restored, wæn-nyün'-feh-læ' 還原弗來

IRREGULAR, not uniform, feh zi'-jih 弗齊° 集; ts°æn-ts°æn'-ts°-ts° 參參差差; not straight, dzin'-mô-liu; hwa-ts°ia' 歪斜°;

— (in doing), feh cn'-pæn 弗按板; zông-zông'-loh-loh' 上上落落

IRRELEVANT, feh siang-te' 弗相對; ts°o-gen'-go; feh °eh vong' 弗合縫; very —, do'-feh-te' 大°弗對; da' feh-vu' 大弗符

IRREMEDIABLE, m̄-yiah' k°o-i' 無° 藥可醫; liao'-feh-teh'-go 了弗得个°

IRREPARABLE, that cannot be repaired, siu-li'-feh-læ' 修理弗來; that cannot be made up, m̄-siu'-dziang 無° 收場

IRREPROACHABLE; m̄-p°i'-bing-go-hao' 無° 批評个° 好

IRRESISTIBLE, feh-neng' feh-pa'-voh 弗能弗拜° 服; — (as power), kæn-tsu'-feh-djü 攔阻弗住; tsu-tông'-feh-djü 阻擋弗住; irresistibly charmed, voh-lah'-go 拜° 服° 个°

IRRESOLUTE, yiao-yiao'-°oh-°oh 搖搖惑惑; cü'-i feh-ding' 主意弗定; sing-feh-kyin' 心弗堅

IRRESPONSIBLE, he is —, feh kwe' gyi-go sing-zông' 弗歸其个° 身上

IRRETRIEVABLE, voh-feh-cün' 復弗轉; voh-nyün'-feh-læ 復原弗來

IRREVERENT, feh kong'-kying 弗恭敬

IRREVOCABLE law, tsih-fah'-jü-sæn' 執法如山; — word

(*i. e.* a word once spoken four horses cannot bring it back), ih-yin′ kyi-c′ih′ s′-mô-næn-tse′ — 言旣出駟馬難追

IRRIGATE, *to* kyiao shü′ 澆水°; — *by chain pump,* ts′ô shü′ 車水°

IRRITABLE, næn ts′ah′-ts′o-go 難擦挫个°; *very* —, ziang yiang-lah′-mao′ ka 像刺毛°蟲°; — *from inflamed liver,* ken-ho′ t′eh wòng′ 肝火太°旺

IRRITATE, *to provoke him,* pih′ gyi sang-ky′i′ 逼其生°氣; c′oh′ gyi nu′ 觸其怒; — (as a sore spot), væn nyün-pô′ 犯原疤; — *extremely,* sông-bi′ dong′-kweh 傷皮動骨

IRRITATING *words,* c′oh′-sing-c′oh-ti′ shih-wô′ 猎心猎肺說話

IS, z 是; yiu 有; — *it good?* keh′ z hao′ feh 這°是好否°? — *there any?* yiu′ m̄ 有沒°有°?

ISINGLASS (made from fish-bellies), yü-tu′ 魚肚°; — (made from sea-weed), yiang-ts′æ′ 洋菜

ISLAND, hæ′-tao 海島; hæ′-sæn 海山 (ih-zo)

ISOLATED (as a person), kwu-sing′ 孤身; — (as a house), kwu-ts′ing′ lang-loh′ 孤清冷°落; yün-ling′-ling 懸零零

ISSUE, *result,* kyih′-gyüoh 結局; *what was the* —? dza kyih′-gyüoh 怎°結局? dza kyih-

en′ 怎°結案? dza liao-z′ 怎°了事?

ISSUE, *to* — *forth as water,* liu c′ih′ 流出; *to* — *forth secretly,* liu-c′ih′-ky′i; *to* — *a proclamation,* c′ih kao′-z 出告示; — *a warrant,* c′ih ba′ 出牌°

ISTHMUS, in-′eo′ 咽喉; t′u′-iao 土腰

IT (generally unexpressed), gyi 其; *bring* — *here,* do′ gyi læ′ 拿°其來; — *snows,* loh-shih′-de 落雪了°; — *rains,* loh-yü′-de 落雨了

ITCH, *the* keh′-lao 疥癩°

ITCH, *to* yiang 癢

ITEM, *an* —, ih diao′ 一條; ih kw′un′ 一欵; ih-yiang′ 一樣; *an* — *of news,* ih′-go sing-veng′ 一个°新聞; — *by* —, yiang-tang′-yiang 一°樣一°樣

ITINERATE *for preaching,* ih-c′ü′ ih-c′ü′ djün kyiao′ 一虛一虛傳教

ITSELF, zi 自°; *will move of* —, zi′ we dong′ 自°會動; *by* —, doh zi′ 獨自°

IVORY, ziang-ngô′ 象牙°; — *ware,* ziang-ngô′ tong′-si 象牙°東西

## J

JABBER, *to* kyih′-lih-kwah′-lah kông′; kông in′-wô 講°燕話

JACKET, mô′-kwô 馬褂 (primarily, a riding jacket)

JADED, tso′-vah-liao 做乏了：

vah-lih'-de 乏力了°; — *horse*, mô tseo'-vah-liao-go 馬走乏了°

JADE-STONE, fi'-ts'e 翡翠; *pure green, or serpentine —*, pih'-nyüoh 碧玉

JAGGED, ky'üih-tsing'-ky'üih-c'ih' 缺進缺出; — *like a saw*, ziang ken'-ts' ka' 像鋸°齒

JAIL, lao-kæn' 牢監°

JAILER, lao-deo' 牢頭; kying'-ts 禁子; *an official —*, s-nyüoh'-s 司獄°使

JAM *of people*, nying te-sæn'-tsib-hæ'-go 人°堆 山積 海个°; ziang diah'-nying-sæn'-ka go 像 疊人°山个°

JAM, *preserved fruit*, ko'-ts tsiang' 果子醬

JAM, *to crowd closely*, a-tsi'-feh-k'æ 挨擠弗開; — (*as one's finger*), gah-sông' 軋傷

JAR, *large water —*, shü'-kông 水°缸 (ih-k'eo); *small-mouthed —*, bing 瓶; bang 甏; *wine —*, tsiu'-dzing 壜° (ih-tsah)

JAR, *to shake*, tsing'-tsing-dong 怔怔動; — *against*, bih-djoh' 蹤了°一°蹤°

JASMINE, (Jasminum Sambac), meh-li'-hwô 茉莉花

JAUNDICE, wông-tæn'-bing 黃疸病; *to have the —*, sang' wông-tæn'-bing 生°黃疸病

JAUNT, *to take a journey*, c'ih-meng' ky'i 出門去°; *to go for pleasure*, ky'i hyi'-hyi 去°嬉戲

JAVELIN, ts'iang 鎗 (ih-ts)

JAW, *the upper —*, zông-bæn'-ngô-zông'上爿牙°床°; *the lower —*, 'ô'-bæn-ngô-zông' 下爿牙°床

JAW-BONE, 'ô'-bô-kweh' 下吧骨

JEALOUS, yiu ts'u'-i 有酷意; ky'i'-feh-ko' 氣弗過; dzih-tu' 嫉妒; ngæn'-k'ong-ts'in' 眼孔淺; tu'-gyi 妒忌; hwah-ts'u'-bing 損°酷瓶 (only used of women in ridicule)

JEAN, *twilled foreign cloth*, zia'-veng yiang-pu' 斜°紋洋布

JEER, *to* tsao-siao' 嘲笑

JEHOVAH, Yiæ-'o'-wô 耶和華

JELLY, *very stiff —*, kao 膏

JELLIFY, *to* nying-long' 凝攏; kyih'-long 結攏; tang-tong 結°凍

JERK, *to* yih 易; *to — away*, yih-ko'-ky'i 易過去°; — *open*, wah'-k'æ 用°爪開

JEST, *to* kông siao'-wô 講°笑話; kông hyiah'-wô 講譀話

JESUS, Yiæ-su' 耶穌; *Jesus Christ*, Yiæ-su Kyi-toh' 耶穌基督

JET *of water from a pipe*, kwun'-ts piao-c'ih'-go shü 管子澆出个°水

JET, *to spout*, piao-c'ih' 澆出; — (*as gas*) tsön-c'ih' 鑽出

JETTY, dao'-deo 街頭; *ferry —*, du'-deo 渡頭; — *for washing*, &c., bu-deo' 埠頭

JEW, Yiu-t'a'-nying 猶太°人°

JEWELS (in general), tsing-cü'pao'-pe 珍珠寶貝

JEWELER, one who sells jewels, cü-pao' k'ah'-nying 珠寶客人°; one who cuts precious stones, nyüoh-ky'i' s-vu' 玉器司務

JINGLING, ting-ting' tông-tông' 丁丁瑲瑲; sing'-sing-sang'-sang.

JOB, a piece of work, ih'-go sang-i' 一个°生°意; ih-yiang' sang-weh' 一樣生°活

JOCOSE, given to jesting, ting'-we hyi'-hyiah-go 頂會戲謔个°

JOG, to — his elbow, or hand, dzoh gyi-go siu' 觸其个°手; — one's memory, di-sing' 提醒; di-deo' 提頭; ky'ih'-gyi lin'-ts 挈其令°子

JOGGLE, to dong 動; yiao-dong' 搖°動

JOIN, to — in doing, 'eh-long'-tso 合攏做; dong-tso' 同做; — together (as pieces), p'ing-long' 摒攏; tsih'-long 接攏; sang-long' 生°攏; — (as words or ideas), lin-long' 連攏; can be joined, siang-lin' 相連; — successively (as links), tsih'-lin 接連; — (as premises), t'iah'-lin 貼連

JOINT, junction, gao-kwu' 鉸股 incorrectly called, yüih-dông° 穴堂; the space between joints, tsih 節; out of —, gao-kwu' t'eh-yüih'-de 鉸股脫穴了°

JOINT-PARTNER, p'ing-ho'-kyi 摒夥計

JOKE (at some one's expense), hyiah'-yin 謔言; hyi'-hyiah-go shih-wô' 戲謔个°說話

JOKE, to kông-siao'-wô 講笑話

JOKER, kông-siao'-wô-go-nying' 講笑話个°人°

JOLLY, hyi'-siao-yin'-k'æ 喜笑顏開

JOLTING in a carriage, zo ts'ô-ts', gyih-lih'-goh-loh 坐°車子栗六°顛簸°

JOSTLE, to a 挨; — through (i. e. in), a-tsing'-ky'i 挨進去°

JOSS-STICKS, bông'-hyiang 棒香 SEE INCENSE.

JOT, a ih-tin' 一點; ih-weh' 一畫

JOURNAL, private jih-kyi'-bu 日記簿; jih-kyi'-loh 日記錄; day-book, ts'ao'-bu 草簿; the —, ts'ing-bu' 清簿

JOURNEY, to go on a —, c'ih-meng' ky'i 出門去°; go on a long —, c'ih yün'-meng 出遠門; to start on a —, dong-sing' 動身; ky'i-sing' 起身; ditto on a long —, ky'i dzing' 起程; to — by land, ky'i 'en' ky'i 起旱去°; loh lu' ky'i 陸路去°; — by water, shü'-lu ky'i' 水°路去°; — rapidly on foot, p'ao-lu' or bao-lu' 跑路

JOURNEYMAN, sæn-kong' 散工; one hired for a job, tön'-pông ho'-kyi 短幫夥計

JOY, *to have* —, yiu do hwun'-hyi 有 大° 歡 喜；hwun-hyi'-feh-sah' 歡 喜 弗 煞

JOYOUS, kw'a'-weh 快° 活；— *news*, kyüô ing' 佳 音；hao' ing 好 音

JOYLESS, 'ao-vu' hying'-cü 毫 無 興 致

JUDGE *of a district*, cü-yün' 知 縣；— *of a province*, en'-ts'ah-s 按 察 司

JUDGE, *to* — (a case), sing'-p'un 審 判；tön'-hao 斷 好；tön'-ding 斷 定；*to pass sentence*, p'un'-tön 判 斷, — *between* (as compositions, men, &c.), zæ-deh' 裁° 奪；ding-leng' 定 論；— *from circumstances*, gwe'-doh 揆 度；*come see and* — (said of an officer), loh-k'en' tön'-hao 查° 勘 而° 斷 好

JUDGMENT, *he has good* —, gyi'-go kyüih'-tön kao ming' 其 个° 決 斷 高 明；gyi ming' kyüih'-go 其 明 決 个°；gyi-go kyin'-sih feng-ming' 其 个° 見 識 分 明

JUDGMENT, *the— day*, sing'-p'un nyih'-ts 審 判 日° 子

JUDICIOUS *counsel* (*i. e.* safe), sô ky'ün' t'o'-tông-go 所 勸 妥 當 个°

JUGGLE, *to* pin hyi'-fah 變 戲 法

JUGGLER, tso-hyi'-fah-go nying' 做 戲 法 个° 人°

JUICE, tsib 汁；tsih'-shü 汁 水°

JUICY, yiu tsih' go 有 汁 个°

JUMBLE, *to* dao-lön' 搯 亂；tang-weng' 打 混；*jumbled* (good and bad together), weng'-dzeh 混 雜

JUMP, *to* t'iao 跳；— *about*, t'iao-t'iao' 跳 跳；— *down*, t'iao'-loh-læ' 跳 下° 來；— *up and down* (in play, anger, &c.), t'eo-ky'i-læ 趐 起 來；— *up*, t'iao'-zông-ky'i' 跳 上 去°；— *over*, t'iao'-ko-ky'i 跳 過 去°

JUNCTURE, *critical point*, iao'-kying kwæn'-deo 要 緊 關 頭；ky'ih'-kying z-'eo' 吃 緊 時 候

JUNIOR *members*, nyin-ky'ing' cü'-kwu 年 輕 个° 人°；*I your* — (*i. e.* inferior), væn'-pe 晚 輩

Mr. Wòng Junior may be styled Wòng Sin-sang, and Mr. Wòng Senior, T'a Sin-sang or Lao Sin-sang；Siao Wòng Sin-sang for the Junior, which is often used, is disrespectful.

JURISDICTION, kæ-kwun' 該 管；*official* —, joh-yün' 屬 員；*under his* —, z gyi' kæ-kwun' go 是 其 該 管 个°；læ gyi siu'-'ô 在° 其 手 下°

JUST, kong-bing' 公 平；kong-dao' 公 道；— *price*, kong-bing' kô'-din 公 平 價° 錢°

JUST *as, or* — *at the time*, k'eo'-k'eo；kông-kòng' 剛 剛；ts'ing'-mi-mao'；'eo-mi'-mao；— *at that time*, sih'-vong gyi-z' 適 逢 其 時；*has come* — *at the right time*, ky'iah'-hao læ-de 恰 好 來 了°；

— *as I was coming it rained*, k'eo'-k'eo ngô læ', loh-yü'-de 恰° 恰°我來落雨了°; — *as you treat me I'll treat you*, ng dza læ', ngô dza ky'i' 你怎°來我怎去°; *when so anxious to have it right*, — *the opposite*, p'in-p'in' feh-te' 偏偏弗對; — *like*, tsing'-ziang 正像; k'eo'-k'eo ih-yiang' 貼°準°一樣; — *now*, dzæ'-s 纔始; dzæ-fông' 纔方; fông'-dzæ 方纔; kông-kông' 剛 剛; — *what I want*, k'eo-k'eo 'eh'-djoh ngô'-go yüong 正°好° 合着°我个°用

JUSTLY, *to treat men* —, dæ nying' kong-dao' 待人公道; *to receive* —, ing-tông' ziu 應 當受

JUSTIFY, *to treat as just, though guilty*, sön tsing'-dzih 算正直

JUT OUT, *to* deh-c'ih' 凸出

JUVENILE *pupils*, din-kyi' 'oh-sang' 小°學°生°; *ditto* (boys), mong-dong' 蒙童; *to teach ditto*, en din-kyi' 訓°蒙°; — *sports*, siao nying' hyi'-deo 小孩°嬉 戲°

## K

KALEIDOSCOPE, væn-hwô-dong' 萬花筒 (ih-go)

KALENDAR, See CALENDAR.

KEEL *of a ship*, jün'-go long-sing' 船个°龍身

KEEN, *sharp*, kw'a 快°; fong-li'

鋒利; — *eyes*, ngæn'-tsing tsin-li' 眼°睛尖利; *ditto* (in a bad sense), lao-ing' ngæn 老鷹 眼°; — *blast*, fong' ziang tao kah' 風像刀割°

KEEP, *to* siu 守; pao'-siu 保守; — *the sabbath*, siu li'-pa-nyih' 守禮拜°日°; — *watch at night*, siu yia' 守夜°; — *shop*, kwun tin' 管店; — *a secret*, siao'-ho-shih-wô' ve' lu-fong' 私°話 弗會°露風; cü'-pô kying'-jing 嘴巴謹慎; — *back some-thing, which one is unwilling to tell*, 'en-hyüoh' 合蓄; — *off the wind*, tsô fong' 遮風; — *in memory*, kyi'-nyiæn 記念; *must* — *away from*, yüong li-k'æ' 要°離開; *keeping house*, læ-tih tông-kô 正°在°當家°; — *ac-counts*, zông-tsiang' 上賬; kwun tsiang'; *will* — (or *last well*), kying-k'ông'; næ'-kyiu-go 耐 久个°; *will not* —, feh næ'-kyiu 弗耐久; — *order*, ah'-djü 壓 服°; — *the rules*, siu kwe' 守規

KEEPER, *gate* kwun-meng'-go 管 門个°; *prison* —, kwun-lao-kæn'-go 管牢監°个°

KEEPSAKE, *I give you this for a* —, keh'-go peh ng, tso piao'-kyi 這°个°給°你°做表記

KENNEL, keo-k'o' 狗窠 (lit. dog's nest)

KERNEL (of a fruit stone), jing or nying 仁; — *of a nut*, nyüoh

肉°; *peach* —, dao-jing' 桃仁; *apricot* —, 'ang'-nying 杏仁°; *walnut* —, wu-dao' nyüoh 胡桃肉°; *a* — *of rice*, ih-lih' mi' 一粒米

KEROSENE, ho'-yiu 火油; me-yiu' 煤油

KETTLE, *iron* t'ih'-kwun 鐵鑵 (ih-go); *tea* —, dzô-wu' 茶壺 (ih-pô)

KEY, yiah-z' 鑰匙 (ih-kwun)

KEY-HOLE, yiah-z'-ngæn 鑰匙眼° (ih-go)

KICK, *to* t'ih 踢; — *one another*, t'ih-læ'-t'ih-ky'i' 踢來踢去°; *gave me a* —, t'ih'-ngô ih-kyiah' ko 踢我一脚過; — *a shuttle-cock*; t'ih in'-ts 踢燕子

KID, siao' sæn-yiang' 小山羊 (ih-tsah)

KIDNAP, *to* kwæ'-tæ 拐°帶; *to take anything by false means*, kwa 拐°

KIDNAPPER, kwa'-ts 拐°子

KIDNEYS, iao-ts' 腰子

KILL, *to* sah 殺; — *by striking, &c.*, tang'-sah 打殺; — *one's self*, zi-zing'-si 自尋°死°; — *one's self with a knife*, zi-veng' 自刎

KILN, yiao 窰; *brick* —, cün-yiao' 磚窰; — *for tiles*, ngô'-yiao 瓦窰

KIMBO, *arms a* —, siu' iao'-li t'oh'-tih 手腰裡托的; siu' t'oh-iao' 手托腰

KIND, *a sort*, ih-yiang' 一樣; ih-

'ao' 一號; ih-cong' 一種; *ten different kinds*, jih-yiang'-sang' 十樣生°; *many kinds*, hyü'-to yiang'-su 許多樣數; *a class* (of things), ih-le' 一類

KIND, sing hao' 心好; sing-din'-hao' 心田好; sing-jih'-hao 心術好; *has — feelings*, yiu-dzing'-yiu-nyi' 有情有義°; *very* —, djong-nyi'-go 重義°个°; dzing-djong' 情重

KINDLE, *to — a fire*, sang-ho' 生°火; — *up* (from a little), ho'-sang-dziah' 火生°熗; — *one's anger*, sing'-ho tin'-dziah 心火點熗; sing'-ho ying'-dziah 心火引熗

KINDLINGS, ying-ho-za' 引火柴°; *to split* —, p'ih'-ying-ho-za' 劈引火柴°

KINDNESS, dzing 情; nyi-ky'i' 義氣; *thank you for your* —, dzing ng' hao'-c'ü' 承你°好處; dzing ng' me'-i 承你°美意; *owing to your* —, t'oh'-ng-go-foh' 托你°个°福; mong-ng' dæ-æ' 蒙你°擡愛; *I appre-ciate your* —, ngô kyin ng'-go-dzing' 我見你°个°情

KINDRED, *near* ts'ing-dzoh 親族; *distant* —, yün-dzoh 遠族; *re-lations in general*, ts'ing-kyün' 親眷

KING, wông 王; kyüing-wông 君王; *the emperor*, wông-ti' 皇帝; — *or prince*, wông-yia'

王爺; *the —* *of kings,* væn-wông'-ts-wông' 萬王之王

KINGDOM, koh 國; *— of Great Britain,* Da-Ing'-koh 大英國; *the animal and vegetable kingdoms* dong'-dzih-ts veh 動植之物 (veng.)

KINGLY *roles,* dziao-voh' 朝服; long-bao' 龍袍; nyü'-i 御衣

KISS, *to* ts'ing-cü' 親嘴; *to smell the lips,* hyüong-cü' 齅嘴; hyiang'-cü 向嘴

KITCHEN, tsao'-keng 竈下°; djü' vông' 厨房; djü-'o' 厨下°

KITE, yiao-ts' 鷂紙 (ih-ting); *to fly a —,* fông-yiao-ts' 放鷂紙; *— whistle,* yiao-mang' 鷂鞭°

KITTEN, siao-mæn' 小貓° (ih-tsah)

KNACK, *has* we diao-du' 會調度; we diao-deo' toh-koh'; we ẅeh-tang 會挖打

KNAVE, vu-la' 無賴°; di-kweng' 地棍; *great,* —, do-vu'-la 大°無賴°; di'-deo-oh'-kweng 地頭惡棍

KNEAD, *to — dough,* nyüoh-feng' 攪°粉; *— thoroughly,* nyüoh-leh t'ong-t'eo' 攪°得°通透

KNEE kyiah'-k'o-deo 脚髁頭 or 膝° (ih-tsah) *to bend one —,* tang-ts'in-ts' 打踜子

KNEEL, *to* gyü'-loh 跪落; gyü'-tao 跪°倒; *— on one knee,* tang-siao'-gyü 打小跪°

KNIFE, tao 刀; *pocket —,* siao'-tao-ts' 小刀子; *paper —,* lih-ts'-tao 裁°紙刀; *chopping —,* boh-tao'; djü-tao' 厨刀; *—for splitting wood,* za-tao' 柴°刀; ke-tao' 鈎°刀 (ih-pô)

KNIT, *to — stockings,* kyih-mah' 結襪; *to — the brows,* zeo-mi-deo' 皺°眉頭; zeo-mi-pah'-kyih 愁眉°百°結

KNOB *of a door,* meng-cih'; *— of a — drawer,* cih'-siu.

KNOCK, *to* tao 搞; *to — at a door,* tao-meng' 搞門; *to strike, or pound,* k'ao 拷; *— against,* bang-djoh' 撞°着°; gah-djoh' 軋着°; djông-djoh' 撞着°; *— down,* bang-tao' 撞°倒; *ditto from a high place,* bang-loh' 撞°落; *— (a person) down* bang*-tih' 撞°跌; tang'-tao-di '打倒地; *— intentionally,* kwu-i' bang 故意撞°; *— head on the ground, &c.,* k'eh-deo' 磕頭
    * Bang, means *to knock unintentionally.*

KNOCK, *give a —,* bang-ih'-kyi 撞°一記; bang-ih'-bang 撞°一撞°; *give another — (at a door),* tsæ tao'-ih-kyi 再搞一記

KNOCKER, k'ao-meng'-go tong'-si 敲門个°東西

KNOLL, te 堆 (ih-go)

KNOT, kyih 結; *hard —,* si' kyih 死°結: *to tie in a —,* tang-kyih' 打結; *— in wood,* jü-tsang' 樹椿; tsang-cü' 椿株

KNOTTY, kyih'-deo hyü'-to 結頭許多；— (as wood), yiu tsang-cü' to 有掙楪多

KNOW, to hyiao'-teh 曉得；sih'-teh 識得；nying'-teh 認°得；teh'-cü 得知；I do not —, ngô feh hyiao'-teh 我弗曉得；do you — me？ ng' nying'-teh ngô'-feh 你°認°得我否°？ng min-jing ngô feh 你面善°我否？he is gone, did you — it？ gyi ky'i'-de, ng teh'-cü feh 其去了°你°得知否°？— one's self that it is wrong, zi' cü m̄ li' 自°知無°理

KNOWINGLY to do wrong, ming-cü'-kwn'-væn 明知故犯；sih'-fah væn'-fah 設法犯法

KNOWLEDGE, cü'-sih 知識；his — is extensive, gyi-go cü'-sih to 其个°知識多；gyi' kyin'-kwông-sih-da' 其見廣識大；to extend one's —, kwông-kyin'-veng, to cü'-sih 廣見聞多知識

KNUCKLES, siu'-ts-tsih 手指節

KORAN, T'in-kying' 天經

# L

LABEL, ts'in-deo' 簽頭；— on goods, tsiao-deo'-ts 招頭紙；ts'in-ts'in-deo' 簽簽頭

LABEL, to — by pasting, t'iah ts'in-deo' 貼簽頭；t'iah tsiao-deo'-ts 貼招頭紙；to — by placing a slip, kyih' ts'in-deo' 揭簽頭

LABOR, hard work, kw'u' sang-weh' 苦生°活；djong'-næn sang-weh' 重難生°活；toil, lao-loh' 勞碌；lao-kw'u' 勞苦；sing-kw'u' 辛苦；with great — (as when unnecessary, or not accomplishing much), dziah'-kying tô'-lih；nu'-kying-bah-hæn'；to be in —, zông-zo'-dong 上坐°桶；ling-beng' 臨盆 (veng.)

LABOR, to yüong kong' 傭工；tso kw'u'-kong 做苦工；to work, tso sang-weh' 做生°活；— so that perspiration flows, 'en-bô'-yü-ling tso' 汗爬雨淋做；to begin —, zông kong' 上工；to leave off —, hyih kong' 歇工；loh kong' 落工；hyih tsoh' 歇作；to finish —, wun kong' 完工；dzing kong' 成工 liao kong' 了工；— in vain, lao-r'-vu-kong' 勞而無功；bah-bah' lao-loh' 白°白°勞碌；— (as a student), 'ô kw'u'-kong' 下°苦功；yüong kw'u'-kong' 用苦功

LABORED, or forced construction, kông'-fah ky'ih'-lih go 講°法吃力个°

LABORER, kong-nying' 工人°；tso-kong'-go 做工个°；tso-sang-weh'-go 做生°活个°；permanent —, dziang-kong' 長工；dziang-yüong'-go 長用个°；temporary —, tön'-kong 短工；ts'ah-tön'-go 拆短个°

LABORIOUS, *toilsome*, kw'u 苦; sing-kw'u' 辛苦; lao-kw'u' 勞苦; lao-loh' 勞碌

LABYRINTH, *place where one may lose his way*, iao mi-lu'-go di'-fông 要迷路个°地方; *labyrinthine roads*, lu-kying' m̄-deo'-jü-go 路徑無°頭緒个°

LACE, cü-lo' 珠羅; — *edging*, cü-lo'-bin 珠羅辮; *any bordering to be tacked on*, kwe'-ts 桂子; *gold* —, kying kwe'-ts 金桂子

LACE, *to* — *with a string*, zing, c'ün-tæn'-ko 繩穿打°過

LACERATE, *to* — *the flesh* (as with a knife), bi-nyüoh' lih-k'æ' 皮肉°裂開; bi-nyüoh' kah'-k'æ 皮肉°割開

LACK, LACKING, ky'in 缺; ky'üih 缺; siao 少; ky'üih'-siao 缺少; — *a little* ts'ó'-tin 差點

LACKER or LACQUER, yiang-ts'ih' 洋漆; — *ware*, yiang-ts'ih'-go tong'-si 洋漆个°東西; *inlaid* — *ware*, yiang-ts'ih', k'æn' lo-diu'-go tong-si' 洋漆嵌螺鈿个°東西

LAD, dong-ts' 童子; siao'-kwun-nying 小官人°; *a large* —, cong-nying' 中人°; siao 'eo-sang' 小後生°

LADDER, t'æ-ts' 梯°子; lu-t'æ' 扶梯° (ih-bu)

LADLE, zoh 瓢°; *soup* —, t'ông' diao-kang' 湯調羮° (ih-go)

LADY, dông-k'ah' 堂客; nyü-dông-k'ah' 女堂客; fu-nying'* 夫人°; *the wife of a teacher*, or *gentleman*, s-meo' 師母; *an old* —, lao'-bo-bo 老婆婆; *ditto* (in an officer's family), lao-t'a'-t'a 老太太°; *ditto* (in a teacher's family), t'a'-s-meo' 太師母; *where a gentleman is styled*, lao'-yia 老爺, *the gentleman's wife* may be styled, na'-na 孄孄°; *young* —, do-kwu'-nyiang 大°姑娘
* This term answers for any lady, but properly belongs only to ladies of the 1st and 2nd rank.

LAG, *to* — *behind*, loh-'eo' 落後; — *purposely*, t'eng'-loh 'eo' 退°落後

LAIR *of a wild beast*, yia'-siu k'o' 野°獸窠

LAKE, wu 湖 (ih-go); *red paint*, in-tsi' 胭脂°

LAMB, siao-yiang' 小羊; — *skin with curled wool*, kao-bi' 羔皮; *native ditto*, t'u'-kao 土羔

LAME, *slightly* tin'-kyiah 蹎脚; *weak in the feet*, nyün'-kyiah 軟脚; *very* —, kwa'-kyiah 拐脚; *limping*, zeh-kyiah'-go 趏脚个°; *one foot, or both turned out*, dzin'-kyiah 斜°脚; — *from crooked feet*, p'ih'-kyiah 併脚; *flinging out the feet in walking*, hwang'-kyiah 甩°脚

LAMENT, *to* kông'-leh pe-pe'-ts'ih-ts'ih 講得°悲悲切切;

t'ong'-k'oh 痛 哭; di-k'oh' 暗
哭; — *with a loud noise*, 'ao-
li'-da-k'oh' 號 啕 大 哭
LAMENTABLE, k'o'-sih 可 惜;
k'o'-lin 可 憐; k'o'-lin-siang
可 憐 相; — *death*, si'-leh k'o-
sông' 死 得° 可 傷
LAMP, teng-tsæn' 燈 盞 (ih-kwun);
*light the* —, tin teng' 點 燈;
— *light*, teng-kwông' 燈 光; *by*
— *light*, teng-kwông' 'ô 燈 光
下°; — *black*, teng-me' 燈 煤;
— *chimney*, teng-t'ao' 燈 套; —
*shade*, ing'-kwông 映 光; —
*wick*, teng-sing' 燈 心; *ditto of*
*pith*, teng-ts'ao' 燈 草
LANCET (for discharging matter),
lang'-tao or lang-ten' 冷° 刀°;
*surgeon's* —, nga-k'o' siao'-tao
外° 科 小 刀
LAND, di 地; *cultivated* —, din
田; ·*uncultivated* —, sang-di'
生° 地; *a piece of* —, ih-kw'e-
di' 一 塊 地; ih-tseh'-di 一 則
地; *an acre of* —, ih-meo-din'
一 畝 田; *dry* —, sao'-di 燥
地; *to travel by* —, 'en'-lu ka-
tseo' 旱 路 而° 走
LAND, *to* zông-ngen' 上 岸; —
*goods*, ky'i-ho' zông-ngen' 起 貨
上 岸
LAND-OWNER, nyih-cü' 業 主
LAND-TAX, zin-liang' 錢° 糧;
*to pay the* —, deo-zin-liang' 完°
錢° 糧
LANDING-PLACE, bu'-deo 埠 頭

LANDLORD *of a lodging house*,
*&c.*, tin'-cü 店 主; *one who lets*
*houses*, *&c.*, vông-tong' 房 東;
oh cü'-nying-kô' 屋 主 人° 家°;
vông' cü'-nying-kô' 房 主 人°
家°
LANDMARK, *stone* ts'-ka-zah 址
界° 石°
LANDSCAPE, kying'-cü 景 致;
*fine* —, hao kying'-cü 好 景 致
LANE, siao'-lu 小 路; *long* 衖;
'ông 巷 (ih-da); — *that has no*
*outlet*, toh-sah-long' 不° 通° 之°
衖; si long' 死° 衖
LANGUAGE, wô 話; shih-wô' 說
話; *the English* —, Da-Ing'-wô
大 英 話; *strong or emphatic* —,
djong'-deo shih-wô' 重 頭 說
話; *bad*—, Wa-wô' 孬° 話; Wa-
shih-wô' 孬° 說 話
LANGUID, nyün'-yiang-yiang 軟
洋 洋; nyün'-bi-bi 軟 疲 疲
LANTERN, teng-long' 籠 橙 (ih-
kwun)
LAP, *sit on the* — (lit., on the
knees), kyiah'-k'o-deo zông zo'
脚 髁 頭 上 坐°; *in the* —,
kyiah'-k'o-deo teo'-tih 脚 髁 頭
兜 的; *gathered in the* —, teo-
tih 兜 的
LAP, *to* — *the edge over*, deh-zông'
疊 上; *one edge lapping over*
*another*, pin-yin dzông'-zông'-tih
邊 沿 撞° 上 的
LAP, *to* — *up water*, shü t'ah'-t'ah-
ky'üoh' 水° 嗹 嗹 吃°

LAPIDARY, nyüoh-ky'i'-s-vu' 玉器司務

LARD, cü-yiu' 猪油

LARGE, do 大°; *how —?* dza-kwun'-do 怎樣大°? —*number of people*, hyü'-to nying 許多人°; nying' to 人°多; *largest*, ting'-do 頂大°; tsæ'-m̀-tsæ-do 再無°再大°; gyih-do' 極大°; — (as if bloated), p'ông 膨; p'oh'-do; *very —*, do-leh'-kying 大°得緊; — *for one's age*, sang-leh dziang-do' 生°得°長大°; kw'e-we' 傀偉; —*hearted*, sing-di'-k'æ-kw'eh' 心地開闊 *Jam-m-sin*

LARK, pah-ling' 百°鴒 *kiao*

LARYNX, ky'i'-kwun-k'eo 氣管口

LASCIVIOUS, t'en-seh'-go 貪色個°

LASH, *a whip*, pin-ts' 鞭子; *to beat with the —*, tang pin-ts' 打鞭子

LASSITUDE, *he suffers from —*, gyi kyüoh-teh nyün-yiang'-yiang 其覺°得軟洋洋; gyi teh'-cü nyün-ky'i ka.

LAST, kyih'-sah 結煞; meh 末; teh-leh-meh; *to the very — degree*, tao-pin' de 到邊°了°; — *night*, zô-yia' 昨°夜°; zô-nyih' yia'-tao 昨°日°夜°到; — *year*, gyiu nyin' 舊年; zông-nyin' 上年; *year before —*, zin nyin' 前°年; — *month*, zin-ko' yüih 前°個月; zông

yüih' 上月; — *day of the year*, nyiæn-kyiu'-yia 廿九夜°; *the — but one*, kyih'-sah yi-zông'ih'-go 結煞以上一个°; *ditto* (sometimes in a bad sense), 'ô' shü zông di nyi' 下°數上第二°; *the — day of the world*, shü'-kæn-zông meh'-go nyih'-ts 世界°上末个°日°子

LAST, *to — well*, kying-yüong' 經用; næ-kyiu' 耐久; *ditto in wear*, ziu-c'ün' 受穿; *how long will it —?* to-siao' kong-fu' hao yüong' 多少工夫好用?

LAST, *shoe-maker's —*, 'a hyün'-deo 鞋楦頭; *stretch on a —*, hyün 楦

LASTING, *durable*, dziang-kyiu' 長久; næ-kyiu' 耐久; iu-kyiu' 悠久

LASTINGS, yü'-ling 羽綾

LASTLY, tsong-kyiu' 終究; kyih'-sah 結煞; *finally*, tao'-ti 到底

LATE dzi 遲; æn 晏°; *past the time*, z-'eo' ko-deo' 時候巳°過; *the — emperor*, sin-wông' 先皇; — *father*, sin-vu' 先父

LATELY, gying'-læ 近來; keh'-liang-nyih 這°兩日°

LATENT, hyüoh'-tih 蓄的; — *heat*, nyih-ky'i' hyüoh'-tih 熱°氣蓄的

LATH, pih-ts'' 壁刾; — *and plaster* (properly ceiling), nyi-t'in-mun' 泥天墁

LATHE, ts'ô 車

LATHER, *soap* bi-zao' beh 肥°皂°浮

LATIN, *the — language,* Lah-ting' wô 辣丁話; Lo-mó' wô 羅馬話

LATITUDE, *lines of —,* we'-sin 緯線

LATTER, 'eo'-deo-go 後頭个°; 'eo'-læ-go 後來个°

LATTERLY gying'-læ 近來; gying'-z 近時

LAUDABLE, k'o-yi ts'ing-tsæn' 可°以°稱讚

LAUGH, *to* siao 笑; — *aloud,* keh'-keh-siao 呵°呵°笑; da-siao' 大笑; *to —* (when amused), fah-siao' 發笑; *need not — at me,* hao-vong' siao' ngô 弗°用°笑我; *to make a person —,* ying' nying siao' 引人°笑; — *derisively,* lang-siao 冷笑

LAUGHING-STOCK, kyin'-siao-da-fông' 見笑大方

LATER, *a little —,* dzi'-tin 遲點; *afterward,* 'eo'-deo 後頭; *the latest,* ting' 'eo'-deo-go 頂後頭个°; ting' kyih'-sah 頂着°末°; *a year —,* ko' ih nyin 過一年; *the latest fashion,* sing' c'ih-læ'-go z-dao' 新出來个°時道; djün-z'-go 全時个°

LAUGHABLE, hao-siao'-go 好笑个°; hao-fah-siao'-go 好發笑个°

LAUGHTER, kah-kah-siao 呵°呵°笑: ga-ga-siao; ha-ha-siao'.

LAUNCH, *to — a ship,* sing-jün loh-shü 新船落水°

LAVISH, ky'i-p'ah' do' 氣魄°大°; kw'un siu' 寬手; yüong'-leh m̃-tsih'-cü-go 用無°節制; — *in giving,* c'ih-siu'-do 出手大°

LAW *of the country,* fah 法; lih-fah' 律法; lih-li' 律例; wông-fah' 王法; koh-fah' 國法; *to break the —,* væn fah' 犯法; *international —,* væn-koh' kong-fah 萬國公法; *to go to —,* tang kwun-s' 打官司; ky'üoh kwun-s' 吃°官司

LAWFUL, tsiao lih-fah' 照律法

LAWLESS, wang-ying'-peh-fah' 橫行不法 vu-fah'-vu-t'in' 無法無天

LAWN, (grass) bing-bing'-go ts'ao'-di 貼°平个°草地

LAWSUIT, kwun-s' 官司; dzong z' 訟事 (ih-ky'i); *to have a —,* tang kwun-s' 打官司; *the — is settled,* kyih-en'-de 結案了°

LAWYER, dzong s' 訟師; (in reproach) tang-tao'-go 打刀个°; *writer of indictments,* sia-zông-ts'-go 寫°狀紙个°

LAX, song 鬆; kw'un 寬; — *in principle,* dao'-li k'en-leh ky'ing-song 道理看得°輕°鬆

LAXATIVE *medicine,* sia'-yiah or dza-yiah' 瀉藥

LAY, *to — down,* fông'-loh 放落; en-loh' 安落; — *or spread a cloth, bricks &c.,* p'u 鋪; — *the*

*table-cloth*, p'u coh'-pu 鋪桌布 ;
— *the foundation* (native), ding
sông-bun' 定礎盤 ; — *upon
another* (as blame, &c.), t'e-t'oh'
peh bih'-nying 推托與°別人°;
— *by*, liu-ky'i' 留起; *ditto money
for a purpose*, dzeng-ky'i' dong-
din' 存起銅錢 ; — *up money*,
tsih'-loh dong-din' 積聚°銅錢°

LAY, to — *eggs*, sang-dæn' 生蛋

LAYERS, *in* ih-zeng' ih-zeng' 一
層°一層°; zeng-tang'-zeng 層°
夾°層°

LAZY, læn'-do 懶惰 ; — *and fond
of ease*, t'en-læn'-go 貪懶个°

LEAD, k'æn 鉛 ; *a sheet of* —, ih
p'in k'æn' 一片鉛

LEAD-PENCIL, k'æn-pih' 鉛筆

LEAD, *red* 'ong tæn' 紅丹 ; *white*
—, bah-tæn 白丹 ; k'æn-feng'
鉛粉

LEAD, *to take the* —, tang zin' 打
前°; we-deo' 爲頭

LEAD, to ling 領; ying 引; ying'-
dao 引道; ta'-ling 帶°領; —
*by the hand*, siu ling'-leh-ky'i 携°
手°而°去°; — *the way*, ling lu'
領路; ying lu' 引路; — *me*,
ying'-dao ngô 引導我; ta'-ling
ngô 帶°領我; — *by the hand, or
by a string*, ky'in-leh tseo' 牽了°
走; *one who leads another into
mischief*, sông-mông' 喪門°

LEADER, deo 頭; we-deo'-go 爲
頭个°; deo-siu'; deo-nao' 頭
腦; *to be a* —, tso deo' 做

頭; — *of an army*, tsiang-kyüing'
將軍; nyün-sæ' 元帥

LEAF, *a* — (of plants), ih-bæn yih'
一辮葉; — (of a door), ih-
sin meng' 一扇門; — (of a
book), ih yih' 一頁

LEAFLESS *trees*, kwông jü' 光樹

LEAGUE, iah 約 (ih-go); *to make
a* —, lih iah' 立約

LEAK, to leo 漏 ; *the water leaked
out*, shü' leo-c'ih'-de 水°漏出
了°; *to* — *out* (as news), sih'-
leo 洩漏

LEAN, *to depend upon*, i'-k'ao 倚
靠; k'ao-djoh' 靠着°; — *on for
support*, gæ-djoh' 戤着°; — *the
arm on the table*, siu k'ao'-leh
coh'-teng 手靠在°桌上°; —
*the head on the hand*, deo siu
t'oh'-tih, 手托頭; siu t'oh sæ'
手托顋; — *against the wall*,
gæ-djoh ziang' 戤着°墙; —
*forward*, eo'-tao 俯°; — *backward*, nyiang'-ky'i 仰起

LEAN, *thin*, seo 瘦; — *meat*, tsing
nyüoh' 精肉

LEAP, to t'iao 跳; — *down*, t'iao'-
loh-læ 跳落來; — *over a wall*,
t'iao'-ko ziang' 跳過墙

LEARN, to 'oh 學°; — *by practice*,
'oh-jih' 學°習; *has learned*, 'oh-
we'-de 學°會了°; — *easily*,
ih-kao' ziu we' 一敎°就°會;
*commencing to* —, ky'i-deo' 'oh
起頭學°; k'æ-deo'-meng 'oh';
— *thoroughly*, 'oh'-tao tsing-
t'ong' 學°到精通

LEARNED, poh'-yüoh-go 博學
个°; a — person, poh'-lao 博士°
LEARNER, 'oh-jih'-go nying 學°
習个°人°
LEARNING, 'oh-veng' 學°問;
dzæ-'oh' 才學°; profound —,
'oh-veng' sing 學°問深
LEASE, n. tsu-ky'i 租契
LEASE, to — for a term of years,
dziang-tsu' 長租; dziang-shü'
長賃°; — and refund the money
at the expiration of the lease,
tin 典
LEAST, ting' siao 頂少; gyih'
siao 極少; at the very —, ts'
siao 至少; ting ky'üih' 頂缺;
not in the — afraid, ih-ngæn' tu
feh p'ó' 一點都弗怕; 'ao-
vu' p'ó'-gyü 毫無怕懼
LEATHER, bi 皮; joh bi 熟皮;
— shoes, bi 'a' 皮鞋; — dresser,
siao-bi'-s-vu 硝皮司務; made
of —, bi' tso-go 皮做个°;
tough as —, ziang bi' ka nying
像皮个°韌; — articles, bi-go
kô-sang 皮个°器皿°
LEATHERY, tough, nying-bi'-tiao-
tsi 韌疲刁牵° (also used for
a child which clings to one, and
cannot be pulled off, &c.)
LEAVE, ask meng, k'o feh k'o' 問°
可弗可; meng, cing' feh cing'
問°准弗准; t'ao k'eo' ky'i
討口氣; — of absence, meng
k'o' hyih' feh 問°可歇否°;
meng hyih kong' 問°歇工; to

grant —, ing-hyü' 應許; cing
准 (when granted by a superior).
LEAVE, to depart from, li-k'æ' 離
開; bih-k'æ 別開; I — it to
you, kwe ng' tso cü' 歸你°做
主; — it for supper, dzing-ky'i'
tao yia' ky'üoh' 剩起到夜°吃°;
— it here, liu'-tong 留在°此°;
nothing left, m̄-neh dzing' 沒
有°剩; — out, or omit, ts'o'-loh
錯落; — me to be killed by the
robbers, 'eo ngô', peh gyiang-
dao' tang-sah 任°我俾°强盗
打殺; cannot —, li-sing'-feh-
k'æ' 離身弗開; to take —
of, dz 'ang' 辭行°; come to take
— of you, læ dz ng'-go 'ang' 來
辭你°的行°
LEAVEN, kao'-shü 酵°水°; to raise
with —, fah-kao' 發酵°
LEAVINGS, dzing-loh'-go ling-sé'
剩落个°零碎; — of food,
dzing-kang'-dzing-væn' 剩羹
剩飯
LECTURE, to — from a moral book,
kông jün'-shü 講°善書
LEDGER, tsong'-ts'ing-bu 總清簿
LEE, 'ó'-fong 下°風
LEECH, mô'-wòng 螞蟥 (ih-keng)
LEEK, kyiu-ts'æ' 韭菜
LEER, to ts'ia-leh ngæn'-tsing-
k'en' 斜視°
LEES, kyiah 腳
LEFT hand, tsia'-siu 左°手; —
side, tsia'-siu-pin 左°手邊;
steer to the —, pæn.

LEFT, *a little* —, dzing-leh yiu'-'.en 剩 得° 有 限°; —, or *forgotten*, ts'o'-loh-de 錯° 落 了°; shih'-loh-de 失 落 了°

LEFT-HANDED, tsia'-siu zông-ziu' 左° 手 上 前°; — *in holding chopsticks*, tsia'-siu k'ô'-kw'æn 左° 手 拿° 筷

LEG, kyiah'-kwang 腿° (ih-tsah); — *is broken*, kyiah'-kw'ang dön'-de 脚 骨° 斷 了°

LEGACY, kô-ts'æn'家° 產; — *to an adopted son*, ko'-kyi kô-ts'æn' 承 繼° 產° 業°

LEGAL, tsiao lih-fah' 照 律 法

LEGEND, kwn'-tin 古 典

LEGERDEMAIN, pin hyi'-fah 變 戲 法

LEGGIN (worn by Chinese women), ngô-dong' 瓦° 笱; *worsted* —, nyüong ngô-dong' 海° 絨 瓦° 笱 (a pair, ih-sông)

LEGIBLE, k'en'-leh-c'ih-go 看 得° 出 个°

LEGISLATE, *to* zao lih-fah' 造° 律 法; ding lih-fah' 定 律 法

LEGITIMATE, 'eh-li'-go 合 理 个°; — *child*, ts'ing-sang' 親 生

LEISURE, k'ong 空, *nothing to do*, k'ong'-'æn vu-z' 空 閒° 無 事

LEISURELY, *slowly*, mæn-mæn' 慢 慢; wun'-wun 緩 緩; mæn-t'eng'-t'eng; wun-t'ang'-t'ang 緩 宕° 宕°

LEMON, nying-mong 檸 檬 (Cantonese name); — *color*, dæn-hyiang-seh 沉° 香 色; *greenish* — *color*, mih-seh' 蜜 色; *brownish* — *color*, hyiang'-seh 香 色

LEND, *to* tsia'-peh 借 給°; *will you* — *me your pen?* ng'-go pih k'o tsia' peh ngô feh 你° 个°筆 可 借 給° 我 否°?

LENDER, *money* fông dong-din'-go 放 銅 錢° 个°

LENGTH, *what is its* —? to-siao dziang' 多 少 長? dza kwun' dziang 怎° 樣° 長°? *days and nights of equal* —, nyih-yia' ih-yiang dziang' 日° 夜° 一 樣 長; tsiu-yia bing' 晝 夜° 平

LENGTHEN, *to* — *by piecing*, tsih-dziang' 接 長; — *the time*, z-'eo t'o-dziang' 時 侯 拖 長; *to grow longer*, dziang-ky'i'-læ 長 起 來

LENIENT, kw'un-shü' 寬 恕

LENIENTLY, *to treat* —, kw'un-dæ' 寬 待; *hard to treat* —, dzing-li' næn-yüong'情 理 難 容

LEOPARD, pao 豹 (ih-tsah)

LEPROSY, da-mô'-fong 大 麻 瘋; fah'-la-bing 發 癩° 病

LEPER, sang-da-mô'-fong-go 生° 大 麻 瘋

LESS *in size*, siao-tin' 小 點; — *in quantity*, siao-tin' 少 點; ky'üih'-tin 缺 點; *a little* —, siao ih'-ngæn 少 一 點°; *still* —, keng'-kô siao 更 加° 少; — *than twenty*, feh tao nyiæn' 弗 到 廿; *can you take* —? ng yiu ky'üih'-deo feh

你有讓°頭否°? *how much — can you take?* yiu to-siao' hao ky'üih' 有多少好讓°? *in — than an hour,* feh tao' ih tin'-cong 弗到一點鐘; kw'a' ih tin'-cong 快°一點鐘; *to grow —,* siao-long'-ky'i 少攏去°

LESSEN, *to* kæn 減°; kæn-siao' 減°少; kæn-loh' 減落

LESSON, *or task,* kong-k'o' 功課; ih-tsông-shü' 一章書; *show me your —,* ng' shü-li kong-k'o' fæn' peh ngô k'en' 你°書裏功課翻典°我看; *to recite a —* (by rote), be-shü' 背°書; *ditto by answering,* ing'-tah 應答

LEST, k'ong'-p'ô 恐怕; zông-k'ong'-p'ô 倘恐怕; vi-k'ong'-p'ô 惟恐怕

LET, peh 任°, *or* 俾°; *— him go,* peh gyi ky'i' 任°其去°; *— him alone,* ze' gyi læ-kæn' 任°其在°彼°; *— go* (as a bird), fông' 放; *— in,* fông'-tsing 放進; *— down* (as a curtain), fông'-loh 放落; *— a house,* tsu-c'ih' 租出; *— to,* tsu-peh' 租與°; *—out what one wishes to keep secret,* dzi-kyi' bun-deo', p'i'-kwn c'ih nga-deo' 雉雞盤頭屁股出外°頭; dzông-deo' lu-vi' 藏頭露尾

LETTER *of the alphabet,* z-meo' 字母; *Roman letters,* Lo-mô' z 羅馬字

LETTER, sing 信 (ih-fong); *to direct a —,* sia sing'-min 寫°信面; *to send a —,* ta ih-fong sing' 帶°一封信

LETTUCE, sang-ts'æ' 生°菜

LEVEE, *to go to the emperor's —,* zông-dziao' 上朝; *the emperor has a daily —,* wông-ti' nyih-nyih' zo-dziao' 皇帝日°日°坐朝

LEVEL, bing-bing' 平平; bing-dzih' 平直; *— road,* bing lu' 平路; *to lay or spread —,* p'u bing' 鋪平; *beat —,* tang-leh bing' 打得°平; tang bing-ts'ih; *to make — by putting something under,* din 墊

LEVER, gyiao'-kweng 撬棍 (ih keng); *to raise by a —,* gyiao 撬

LEVITY *in behavior,* ky'ing-veo' 'ang-we' 輕浮行°爲; *— and coarseness in behavior,* ky'ing-p'iao' 'ang-we 輕飄行°爲; *— in words,* ky'ing-boh' shih-wô' 輕薄說話

LEVY, *to — taxes, or contributions,* lih kyün-kw'un' 立捐欵; *— troops,* tsiao ping' 招兵

LEWD, t'en-ying'-go 貪淫个°; *— fellow,* ying-fu' 淫夫; *— woman,* ying-vu' 淫婦

LEXICON (arranged according to the radicals), z-we' 字彙; z-tin' 字典. SEE DICTIONARY.

LIABLE *to punishment,* li'-tông'-voh-ying' 理當服刑; ze'-ming pe'-tih 負°罪; zo-ze'-go 坐°罪个°

LIAR, shih-hwông'-go nying 説
謊个° 人°; kông-hwông'-wô-go
講° 謊 話 个°

LIBEL, (anonymous) ṅ-deo'-pông
無° 頭 榜; vu-ming'-kyih-t'iah'
無 名 揭 帖

LIBERAL, do du'-liang 大° 度量;
kw'un-'ong' du-liang 寬 宏 度
量; 'ao-yiah' 豪 俠; — reward,
djong'-sông 重 賞; djong'-zia
重° 謝

LIBERALLY, to treat — , kw'un
dæ' 寬 待; 'eo' dæ 厚 待

LIBERATE, to sih'-fông 釋 放;
fông'-c'ih 放 出

LIBERTINE, debauchee, seh-kwe 色
鬼; ying-fu 淫 夫; wild, rude
fellow, fông'-dông-go-nying 游°
蕩 个° 人°

LIBERTY, at — to follow one's in-
clinations, dzong-sing' sô-yüoh'
從 心 所 欲; zi' tso-cü'-i 自°
做 主 意; zi-yiu'-zi-dzæ' 自° 由
自° 在°; at — to think, or do as
one pleases, z-cü'-ts-gyün 自 主
之 權; at — to suit your convenience, dzong ng'-go bin' 從
你° 个° 便; ze ng'-go bin' 任°
你° 个° 便; you are taking liberties with my things, ngô-go tong'-
si ng-zi tso-cü-i' 我 个° 東 西 你°
自° 做 主 意; taking liberties
with others' things, jün'-cün-go
擅 專 个°; take — with one of
another sex, &c., peh-nen-peh-nyü
不 男 不 女; take — (as of

coming into women's apartments,
&c.), nen kah vu nyü 男 女 混°
雜°

LIBRARIAN, kying-kwun'-shü-zih'-
go 經 管 書 籍 个°

LIBRARY (large), shü-koh' 書 閣;
shü-leo' 書 樓

LICENSE, tsiao 照; tsih'-tsiao 執
照; t'iah 帖; to take out a —,
ling tsiao' 領 照; ling-t'iah'
領 帖; to grant a —, kyih
tsiao' 給 照

LICENSE, to — a preacher, fông
cing-s' 放 准 試

LICENTIOUS, tsong'-fông-yüoh-
ho' 縱 放 慾 火; shing-tsong'-
s-yüoh' 狗 縱 私 慾; ying-
yüoh-vu-du 淫 慾 無 度; —
books, ying shü' 淫 書; — plays,
ying hyi' 淫 戲; — songs, ying
dz' 淫 詞

LICHEES, fresh sin li'-tsi 鮮 荔 子°;
dried —, ken li'-tsi 乾 荔 子°

LICK, to t'in 舔, or 餂

LICORICE-ROOT, ken ts'ao' 甘 草

LID, kæ 該 (ih-go); eye —, ngæu-
p'ao-bi' 眼 朦 皮

LIE, n. hwông'-wô 謊 話; kô'-wô
假 話; hyü-wô' 虛 話 (ih-
kyü)

LIE, to kông hwông'-wô 講° 謊
話; shih-hwông' 説 謊

LIE, to kw'eng 睡°; — down,
kw'eng'-loh 睡° 落; — on the
back, nyiang' t'in kw'eng' 仰
睡°; — on the face, foh'-ken-

kw'eng 覆 睡 ; — on the side,
tseh'-leng-kw'eng' 側 睡°; —
curled up, geo-leh kw'eng'; (it)
lies on the table, læ coh'-teng
en'-tih ; læ coh'-teng fông'-tih.
放° 在° 桌° 上°

LIFE, seng-ming' 生命 ; weh-
ming' 活命 ; ming 命 ; sing'-
ming 性命 ; save —, kyiu ming'
救命 ; to risk —, p'un ming'
拚命 ; a litter, or hard —,
kw'u' ming 苦命 ; happy —,
hao ming' 好命 ; — before we
came into this world, zin-si' 前°
世°; zin-seng' 前° 生 ; the present —, kying'-si 今世°; kying-
seng' 今生 ; the future —, 'o'-
si 下° 世°; læ-seng' 來生 ; to
lose one's —, sing'-ming e'ih'-
t'eh' 性命休° 矣 ; one's whole
—, ih-sang'-ih'-si 一生°一世°;
bing-seng' 平生 ; we-nying'-
dzæ-shü' 爲人° 在世° ; ih-si'-
we-nying' 一世° 爲人°; cong-
sing' 終身 ; one's — until now,
seng-bing' 生平 ; ih'- hyiang
tso'-nying 一向做人°; eternal
—, üong'-seng 永生 ; dziang-
seng' 長生 ; üong'-yün weh-
ming' 永遠活命 ; to be restored
to —, si'-ky'i wæn-weng' 死°
去° 還魂 ; has seen much of —,
shü'-min tu kyin'-ko 經° 歷°世°
事°; short —, tön'-ming 短命 ;
iao-ziu' 天壽 ; long —, dziang-
ming' 長命 ; dziang-seng' 長

生 ; dziang-ziu' 長壽 ; dziang-
ming'-pah'-shü 長命百° 歲°
(complimentary ) ; full of — (i.e.
always moving ), feh-tch-hyih-
go 弗得歇个

LIFELESS, ve'-weh-de 弗° 活了°;
m-sing'-ming 無° 性命 ; (as if
glad of it) teo'-ti si'-le 實° 在°
死° 了°

LIFETIME, weh'-tong-go z-'eo' 活
在° 的° 時候 ; dzæ'-shü we-
nying' 在世爲人°

LIFT, to — (with both hands), teh
撅 ; — up, teh-tæn'-ky'i 撅起 ;
— (one or more persons), ts'iah
擦 ; cannot — it, do'-feh-dong'
拏° 弗動 ; ts'iah'-feh-dong' 擦
弗動 ; — (two or more persons),
kông 摑 ; — with string, or lever,
kông 扛 ; dæ 擡 ; — up, ts'iah-
tæn'-ky'i 擦起 ; — and take
away, ts'iah'-leb-ky'i.

LIGATURE for binding blood vessels, tsah hyüih'-mah-go pu' 紮
血脈个布

LIGHT, kwông 光 ; liang-kwông'
亮光 ; sun —, nyih-kwông 日°
光 ; dim —, liang'-kwông u-
teng'-teng 亮光暗° 洞° 洞°;
how — it is ! dza-liang' 甚° 亮!
insufficiently —, kwông ky'in
liang 亮光不足°; bring a
—, do-liang'-læ 携燈° 來

LIGHT (in color), dæn 淡 ; a
little lighter, dæn-tin' 淡點 ; not
heavy, ky'ing 輕 ; ky'ing-k'o'

輕可; — *wind,* ky'ing-fong' 輕
風; vi-fong' 微 風; *eat a —
meal,* ih-djü' siao ky'üoh' tin —
餐°少吃°點; — *matter,* ky'ing-
k'o' z-t'i' 輕 可 事 體; —
*work,* ky'ing-k'o' sang-weh' 輕
可 生°活; — *bread,* mun-deo'
ky'ing-song' 饅 頭 輕 鬆

LIGHT, *to* — *a candle,* tin lah-coh'
點 蠟 燭; — *a lamp,* tin teng'
點 燈; *light a* —, tin liang' 點
亮; *will not* —, tin'-feh-dziah'-
go 點 弗 爠 个°; —(as a cigar),
tin-ho' 點 火; — *the fire,* sang-
ho' 生 火; *I will* — *you* (in
going), ngô-tsiao'-leh ng ky'i'我
照 了°你°去°

LIGHTED, *well* tsiao'-leh shih'-
liang 照 得°甚°亮; *brightly*
— (lamps or candles), teng-coh'-
hwe-wông' 燈 燭 輝 煌; *eye —
upon,* ngæn'-tsing kwæn-djoh'-
go 眼°睛 看°過; *bird — upon
a tree,* tiao' jü'-li ding-ko' 此°
鳥°會°集 於°樹°

LIGHTEN, *to make it light,* peh
gyi ky'ing' 俾°其 輕; *to —
*(as lightning), fah-sin' 發 閃;
long-kwông' sin-din' 龍光 閃電

LIGHT-FINGERED *person,* siao-
ts'eh-ts'eh' 小 撮 撮; ts'eh'-lao
扒°手°

LIGHT-FOOTED, kyiah'-deo ky'ing-
fæn' 脚 步 輕 泛

LIGHT-HEADED, *thoughtless,* ky'ing
輕; feh-djong'-jih 弗 重 實;

— (as when on a high place),
yiao-ling'-ling 頭°搖懍懍; —
(as in delirium), hweng-tih'-de
惛 了°

LIGHT-HEARTED, kw'un-sing' 寬
心; m-sing'-m-z 無°心 無°事

LIGHT-HOUSE, liang-t'ah' 亮塔;
teng-t'ah 燈 塔 (ih-zo)

LIGHTLY, ky'ing 輕; ky'ing-
kw'un' or ky'ing-kun.

LIGHTNING, sin'-din 閃 電

LIKE, ziang 像; siang-ziang' 相
像; siang-dong' 相 同; fông-
feh' 仿彿; *somewhat* —, tao'-
ziang 倒像; *exactly* —, ih-
yiang' 一 樣; tsing'-ziang 正
像; ih-seh'-ih-yiang' 一 色 一
樣; *seems* —, or *seems as if,* oh'-
ziang; hao-ziang 好°像; — (as
a picture to a person), weh'-t'eh-
ko'; *just* — (his) *father,* tsing'-
ziang ah-tia' 正像阿爹°; teng
ah-tia tso su'-ts (inelegant).

LIKE, *to* hwun-hyi' 歡 喜; cong'-
i 中意; *as you* —, ze ng' 任°
你°; *choose which you* —, ze
ng' hwun-hyi kæn ih'-yiang 任°
你°歡喜揀一樣; *what I*
—, ngô sô sing-miao'-go 我
所合°意 个°; *just what one
likes,* jü-sing' ziang-i' 如心像
意; *I* — *him,* ngô cong'-i' gyi
我 中意其; gyi cong ngô'-
go i' 其 中我个°意

LIKELY, liang-pih 諒必; bông-
tao' 防到; jih-r-kyiu' 十面

九; jih'-yiu-kyiu' 十 有 其°
九; *very* —, kyiu'-feng kyiu'-li
九 分 九 釐

LIKENESS, *there is a slight* —, yiu
tin' siang-ziang' 有 點 相 像;
*portrait*, siao'-tsiao 小 照; 'ang-
loh' 行° 樂 圖°; hyi'-yüong 喜
容; *to draw a* —, sia siao'-tsiao
寫° 小 照; *to photograph a* —,
ing siao'-tsiao 映 小 照; — *taken
in old age*, ziu-yüong 壽 容; —
*hung in the ancestral-hall after
death*, ziang 像

LIKEWISE, *also*, yia 也°; *in like
manner*, yia' z-ka 也° 是 如 此°

LILAC (called in Peking), ting-
hyiang'-hwô 丁 香 花; — *color*,
'o-hwô' seh 荷 花 色; shih-ts'ing'
雪 青

LILY, *golden* kying-tsing'-hwô 金
針 花 (when dried, it is often
used for food); *wild pink* —,
tsông-lông'-hwô 蟑 螂 花

LIMB, *the four limbs*, s'-ts 四 肢;
*four limbs and one hundred mem-
bers*, s'-ts-pah'-t'i 四 肢 百 體;
— *of a tree*, ô-ts' 了 枝; *cut off
a* —, ô-ts' tsoh'-diao 了 枝 斷
去°; *limbs spread out*, p'ah'-
kyiah dô'-siu'.

LIMBER, nyün 軟; mi-nyün' 綿
軟; *bamboo when heated becomes*
—, coh ho'-li dæn-dæn we mi-
nyün' 以° 竹° 燻° 之° 爲° 軟

LIME, *stone* zah-hwe' 石° 灰; *the
best* — comes from Fu-yiang

and is called Fu-yiang' hwe 富
陽° 灰; *shell* —, koh'-hwe 壳°
灰; *unslaked* —, sang zah'-hwe'
生° 石° 灰; *slaked* —, joh hwe'
熟 灰; *to mix* —, c'ün hwe'
串 灰; *to pound* —, sông hwe'
舂 灰

LIME-KILN, hwe-yiao' 灰 窰 (ih-
go)

LIMIT, 'æn'-cü 限° 制; *boundary*,
ka'-'æn 界° 限°; *no* —, m̄ 'æn'-
cü 無° 限° 制; *to settle the* —,
ding ka'-'æn 定 界° 限°; *to pass
the* —, ko-'æn' 過 限°; *has a*
—, yiu' 'æn 有 限°

LIMIT, *to* — *the time*, 'æn' nyih-ts'
限° 日° 子; *I* — *you to a dol-
lar*, ngô teng ng 'æn'-ding ih-
kw'e' fæn-ping' 我 與° 你° 限°
定 一 塊 番 餅

LIMP, *wanting stiffness*, nyün'-joh
軟 熟

LIMP, *to* kwa-kyi'-kwa-kyi tseo'
跛 走; ih-kwa', ih-dih' 一 拐°
一 敧; — *slightly*, zeh-kyiah'-
go tseo.

LIMPID, kwang'-ts'ing 光° 清;
pih'-ts'ing 碧 清

LIGHTNING, sin'-din 閃 電; *a
flash of* —, sin'-din ih-sin 閃
電 一 閃; *sheet* —, long'-sæn
龍 閃°; *that house was struck
by* — (lit. thunder), keh' tsing
oh' le tang'-diao-de 這 進 屋 雷
打 壞° 了°; *killed by* —, (*i. e. a*
thunder-bolt), p'ih'-lih tang'-sah

霹靂打殺; T'in-lc' tang'-sah
天雷打殺; T'in-li' tang'-sah
天理打殺

LINE, sin 線; *straight* —, dzih-sin'
直線 (ih-da); *to divide by cross*
—, tang wang kah' 打橫°格;
*to divide by straight* —, tang dzih
kah' 打直格; *curved* —,
w̅æn-ying'-go sin 彎形个°線;
*crooked ink* —, w̅æn-w̅æn'-
ky'üoh-ky'üoh'-go moh-sin' 彎
曲个°墨線; *the spaces enclos-
ed by cross lines*, kah'-ts 格子;
*draw a* —, weh ih-da sin' 畫一
埭線; *carpenter's ink* —, moh-
sin' 墨線; *tailor's powder* —,
feng'-sin 粉線

LINE, *to fit a lining*, p'e li'-ts 配
裡子; p'e-keh'-li.

LINED *garments*, kah'-i 袷衣；
*unlined ditto*, tæn-i' 單衣

LINEAGE, *race*, ts-p'a' 支派°; *of
the* — *of David*, Da-bih' dzoh'-li
keh p'a' 大闢族裡這°派

LINEN, coh'-pu 竹布; *hempen
cloth*, mô-pu' 麻布; *grass cloth*,
'ô-pu' 夏布; *hemp*, or — *thread*,
mô-sin' 麻線

LINGER, *to delay*, tæn-koh' 就擱;
*to loiter*, yiu-lu' 遊路; deng-
deng'-tah-tah 或°行°或止°

LINGERING, *fond of* — (*as a visitor*), deng ih-zông z' ih-zông 停
一息°是一息°; — (*as dis-
ease*) in-dzi' 淹滯

LINGUIST, *one who speaks several*

*languages*, we tang loh'-koh-
hyiang'-dæn 會說°六國鄉談

LINING, keh'-li; li'-ts 裡子

LINK, lin-w̅æn-ky'ün' 連環圈
(ih-go)

LINK, *to* lin-long' 連攏; *can be
linked*, hao siang-lin' 好相連

LINSEED, (*hemp seed*) wu'-mô'-ts
胡麻子

LION, s-ts' 獅子 (ih-tsah)

LIP, *the upper* —, zông'-bæn-cü'-
jing 上爿嘴唇; *the lower* —,
'ô'-bæn-cü'-jing 下爿嘴唇;
*lips*, cü'-pô 嘴巴

LIP-SERVICE, yiu' k'eo' vu sing'
有口無心

LIQUID, we liu'-go tong'-si 會流
个°東西

LIQUOR, tsih 汁; *distilled* (*Chinese*) —, siao'-tsiu' 燒酒; *strong
ditto*, tih'-siao 元°燒酒

LIQUORICE, SEE LICORICE.

LISP, *to* kông-leh ngao'-zih-keng-
go 講°得°齩舌根个°

LIST, *a* — (*of articles, prices, &c.*),
ih-p'in tsiang' 一片帳; ih-p'in'
ts'ing-tsiang' 一片清帳; — *of
names*, ming-moh' 名目; *ditto*
(*on a sheet*), kyi'-ming-tæn' 記
名單; — (*of baggage, &c.*),
ky'i'-mô-tæn' 起馬單; — *of
places on a journey*, lu-dzing'-tæn
路程單; — *of characters*, tsah'-
c'ih-go' z 摘出个°字; — *of
goods*, ho'-tæn 貨單 (ih-p'in, or
ih-tsiang)

LISTEN, *to* t'ing 聽; *must —,* yüong t'ing' 要聽; *— attentively,* tông-sing' t'ing' 當心聽; *— secretly,* t'eo-bun' t'ing' 私°下°聽

LISTLESS, feh liu'-sing 弗留心; læn'-teh t'ing' 懶得聽

LITERALLY, *to translate —,* tsiao nyün ti'-ts fæn-yih' 照原底子繙譯

LITERARY *man,* yiu-'oh-veng'-go nying 有學°問个°人°; veng-moh'-go-nying 文墨个°人°; *— chancellor,* 'oh-dæ' 學°臺°; *the — dialect,* veng-wô' 文話; veng-li' 文理; *— composition,* veng-tsông' 文章; *— reputation,* veng-ming' 文名, *—title,* kong-ming' 功名; *the god who presides over — men,* Veng-ts'ông'-ti'-kyüing 文昌帝君; *inferior ditto,* Kw'e-sing' bu-sah' 魁星

LITERATI, doh-shü-nying' 讀書人°; Confucianists, jü-kô' 儒家°

LITHOGRAPH, *to* t'ah shü 搨書; *lithographic plates,* zah-deo' k'eh-go t'ah'-shü-pæn 石°刻搨書版

LITIGATE, *to* tang kwun-s' 打官司

LITIGIOUS, jün'-ü hying-dzong' 善于興訟; hao-dzong' 好訟

LITTER *of pigs,* ih-k'o' siao'-cü 一窠小豬

LITTLE, siao 小; *— child,* siao-nying' 小孩°; *— matter,* siao-z-ken' 小事幹; siao'-i-s 小意思; *a —,* ih-ngæn'; ih-ngæn'-ngæn; ih-tin' 一點; ih-tin-tin' 一點點; ih-ti' 一渧; ih-ti'-ti 一渧渧; yiu'-'æn 有限°; *very —,* kyin'-liang' 見量; *a — more,* to'-tin 多點; to'-ih-ngæn; *a very — more,* sao'-we to'-tin 稍爲多點; siao-shü' to'-tin 少些多點; liah-liah' to'-tin 略略多點; shü-vi' to'-tin 些微多點; *add a —,* kô ih-tin' ts'eo' 加一點湊 &c. &c.; *a — longer,* dziang'-tin 長點; *a — better,* hao-tin' 好點; *differs but — (or is about right),* ts'ô-feh-to' 差弗多; zông'-loh vu-kyi' 上落無幾; siang-ky'i' ying-kwun' 相去仿°彿° (kwun or kun)

LITURGY, p'a'-ding-go kyiao'-kwe 派°定个°敎規

LIVE, *to dwell,* djü 住; deng 庇; *where do you —?* ng'-djü læ 'ah-li' 你°住在°何°處°? ng djü-kyü' soh-go di-fông 你°住居甚°麼°地方? (polite) ng fu'-zông djü-'ah-li' 你°府上住何°處°? *to be alive,* weh 活; *to spend one's days,* ko nyih-ts' 過日°子; du-nyih' 度日°; du kwông-ing' 度光陰; *only enough to — on,* tsih'-keo wu-k'eo' 只穀餬口; dziang-ming'-pah-shü 長命百歲°；— long, ziu-shü dziang′ 壽歲°長；wants to 一, iao sing′-ming 要性命；to — by pen and ink, yi pih-moh′ du kwông-ing′ 以筆墨度光陰；— according to one's means (lit. knows where to stop), sih′-k'o′-r-ts 適可而止

LIVELIHOOD, du nyih′ 度日°; du kwông-ing′ 度光陰；how do you make a —? ng yi soh-si du kwông-ing 你°以甚°麼度光陰? ng soh′-go du-nyih′ 你°甚°麼度日°? ng k'ao soh′-si du nyih′ 你°靠甚°麼°度日°?

LIVELONG, the — day, ih-nyih′ tao-yia′ 一日°到夜°；tsing-nyih′ 儘日°；dziang-nyih′ 長日°

LIVELY in motion, weh-dong′ 活動；weh-loh′ 活絡；— in talking, kông′-leh weh-loh′ 講°得活絡

LIVER, ken 肝；beef —, ngeo-ken′ 牛°肝

LIVERY, 'ao′-i 號衣

LIVID, ts'ing-heh′ 青黑；— bruise, u-ts'ing′ 烏青

LIVING things, weh′-go tong-si 活個°東西；weh-veh′ 活物；while —, weh′-tong z-'eo′ 活在°時候；dzæ-shü′ we-nying′ 在世為人°

LIVING, how do you make a —? ng dza du nyih 你°怎度日? ng tso soh-go sang-i 你°作何°

生°意? ditto (to a gentleman) ng-kwun-di′ læ ah-li′ 你°就°館°在°何°處°?

LIZARD, in′-deo-dzô′ 蝘蜓°蛇°；s′-kyiah-dzô′ 四脚蛇°

LOAD for a man, ih-tæn′ 一擔；— for two men, ih-kông′ 一扛；boat —, ih-zæ′ 一臟；ih-jün′ 一船；having a — on the mind, læ′-tih tæn′-sing-z′ 正在°擔心事

LOAD, to tsæ 載；ts'ông 裝；kwun 管；— a boat, jün′ tsông ho′ 船裝貨；— a cannon, tsông p'ao′ 裝礮

LOAD-STONE, hyih′-t'ih-zah′ 吸鐵石°；dz-zah′ 磁石°

LOAF, a — of bread, ih-go mun-deo′ 一個饅頭

LOAFER, yiu-dang′-go-nying 游宕个°人°；yiu-hyi′-lông-dông-go nying′ 遊戲浪蕩个°人°

LOAM, yiu-lih′-go na-nyi′ 有力个°坭

LOAN, to tsia-peh′ 借給°；to — a large sum, fông nying-bun′ 放銀盤

LOATH or LOTH (to give up), feh-sô′-teh 弗捨°得；— to go, feh-dzing′-nyün ky'i′ 弗情願去

LOATHE, to tseng 憎；tseng-sah′ 憎極°；I — the thing, k'eh′-go tong-si ngô tse k'o-u′-go 這个°東西我最可惡个°

LOBSTER, great crab, long-hô′ 龍蝦 (ih-tsah)

LOCAL, *peculiar to one place*, ih-t'ah di'-fông yiu'-go 一處°地方有个°; ih-c'ü' yiu-go 一處有个°; — *products*, t'u'-ts'æn 土產; — *custom*, hyiang-fông; hyiang-fong' 鄉風; t'u'-fong 土風; t'u'-dzoh 土俗; — *banditti*, t'u-fi' 土匪; — *customs differ*, hyiang-fong c'ü'-c'ü bih 鄉風處處別

LOCK *of a door*, so 鎖 (ih-kwun); *canal* — *with gates*, ky'i 閘; — *with inclined plane*, pô 壩; — *of hair*, ih-lu' deo-fah' 一縷°頭髮

LOCK, *to* so 鎖; so'-loh 落鎖; — *a door*, so-meng' 鎖門; meng so'-loh 門落鎖; — (*as with padlock*) zông-so' 上鎖

LOCKED-JAW, ngô' kwæn-kying'-pi 牙°關緊閉

LOCUST, wông-djong' 蝗蟲 (ih-tsah)

LODGE *in a field*, sô 厍

LODGE, *to* deng 庑; *dwell for a time*, dzæn'-deng 暫庑; — *for the night*, soh-yia' 宿夜°; hyih-yia' 歇夜°

LODGING-PLACE, deng-sing'-ts-c'ü' 庑身之處; *lodging-shop*, soh'-yia-tin 宿夜°店

LOFT, *a low* —, koh'-teng 上°擱; *house has a* —, oh' yiu koh-teng'-go 屋有上°擱个°

LOFTY, kao-kao' 高高; — *and large*, kao-do' 高大°

LOG *of wood*, moh-deo' 木頭 (ih-dön)

LOGICAL, yiu diao-li'-go 有條理个°; jing-jü'-go 循序个°

LOGWOOD, su-moh' 蘇木

LOINS, *the upper part*, iao-hyih' 腰脇; iao-bo' 腰間°; *at the hips*, do t'e' pin 大°腿邊

LOITER, *to* yiu-dang' 遊宕; *to* — *on the way*, yiu-lu' 遊路

LOLL, *to* — *about*, t'en-min' kæn-do 貪眠懶惰; — *the tongue*, zih-deo' t'a-c'ih' 舌頭伸°出

LONELY, lang'-loh 冷°落; dzih-moh' 寂寞

LONG, dziang 長; *four feet* —, s' ts'ah dziang 四尺°長; *not long enough*, ky'in dziang 弗殼°長; *a* — *time*, dziang-kyiu' 長久; dziang-yün' 長遠; *how* — *shall I wait?* ngô iao' teng' to-siao' kong-fu' 我要等多少工夫? — *period of years*, nyin-yün' jih-kyiu' 年遠日久; *how* — *ago did the Rebels come?* dzong Dziang-mao' læ', tao jü-kying' to-siao' z-'eo' 從長毛來到如今多少時候?

LONG, *to* — *constantly*, k'eh'-k'eh-neng'-neng siang'-vông 時°時°刻刻想望; — *ardently*, ts'ih'-sing siang' 切心想; yün-vông' 懸望; — *for something superior, or above one*, ky'i'-mo 企慕; *I* — *to see my mother*, ngô ky'i'-mo kyin ah-nyiang' 我企慕

見 毋, (ky'i-mo cannot be used in the sentence, my mother longs to see me); — for (as for food), siang 想; s-ts'eng' ziang k'eo-k'eh' ka 思 忖 渾° 如 口 渴

LONG-SUFFERING, næ'-leh dziang-kyiu' 耐 得° 長 久; lenient, kw'un-shü' 寬 恕

LONGER, a little —, dziang'-tin 長 點; still —, keng'-kô dziang' 更 加° 長; want it —, wa-iao dziang 還° 要 長; to wait a little —, tsæ' teng-leh dziang' ih-zông 再 等 得° 長 一 息°

LONGEVITY, dziang-ziu' 長 壽; ziu-shü' dziang 壽 歲° 長

LONGITUDE, lines of —, kying-sin' 經 線

LOOK or LOOKS, siang'-mao 相 貌; shü'-seh 水° 色; ts-seh' 姿 色; has an honest —, min-yüong' k'en'-læ dzing-jih'-go 面 容 看 來 誠° 實 個°

LOOK, to k'en 看; siang 相; take a —, k'en'-ih-k'en' 看 一 看; k'en'-k'en-siang 看 看 相; mông-mông'-k'en 望° 望° 看; — around, dön-ky'ün' k'en 周° 圍° 看; — up, dziao zông' k'en 朝 上 看; dæ-ky'i' k'en 抬 起 看; — down, k'en-'ô' 看 下°; hyiang-'ô' k'en' 向 下° 看; stoop and —, co'-tao k'en' 偏 倒 看; — lack, nyin-cün' k'en' 回° 轉 看; we-deo' k'en 回 頭 看; — down upon, or

have contempt for, k'en'-feh-zông-ngæn' 看 弗 上 眼°; — askance, zia'-k'en 斜° 看; tseh'-k'en 側 看; — for, or find, zing 尋; — for it, zing-zing' k'en 尋° 尋° 看; dzô-dzô' k'en 查 查 看; I have looked every where, ngô tao'-c'ü' zing-pin' ko 我 到 處 尋° 遍 過°; — for, or expect p'æn'-vông 盼 望; — carefully, ts'-si k'en' 仔 細 看; — after, or take care of, kwun 管; you — after things here, ng' kwun-tong 你° 管 在° 此°; this dress looks well, keh' gyin i-zông' siang'-mao tao hao'-go 這° 件 衣 裳 樣° 式° 倒 好 個°

LOOKING, she is fine —, gyi'-go shü'-seh sang-leh hao' 其 個° 水° 色 生° 得° 好

LOOKER on, bông-pin' k'en'-go cü'-kwn 旁 邊 看 個° 人°; bông-kwun'-tsiæ 旁 觀 者

LOOKING-GLASS, kying'-ts 鏡 子 (ih-min)

LOOKOUT, on the —, læ'-tih tsiao'-liao 正° 在° 瞧瞭°; platform for observing enemies, liao-dæ' 瞭 臺; — on city wall, fi-leo' 飛 樓; turret, vông-leo' 望 樓; — for cool air, jü'-fong-ding 聚 風 亭

LOOM, kyi 機; — for cotton cloth pu'-kyi 布 機 (ih-tsiang)

LOOP, p'æn 襻; — for a button, nyiu'-p'æn 鈕 襻

LOOP-HOLE for cannon, p'ao'

dong-ngæn′ 砲洞眼°; *find a* — *for escape,* zing leo-dong′, hao zah-c‘ih 尋漏洞好逃°出

LOOSE, *not tight,* song 鬆; kw‘un 寬; *unfastened,* sæn-de 散了°

LOOSEN, *to* fông song′-tin 放鬆點; — (bound) *feet,* fông ky‘iah′ 放脚

LOOSENESS *of bowels,* du′-li læ-tih dzæ′ 腹°中°作°瀉°

LOP, *to* — *off an ear,* siah′-loh ng′-to 削落耳°朶; — *a branch,* tsoh-diao ô-ts′ 斫去°了枝

LOQUACIOUS, shih-wô′ to′ 說話多; to-kông′-to-wô′ 多講°多話; to-cü′-tah-zih′ 多嘴搭舌; — (because thin-lipped), cü′-jing-bi-boh′ 嘴唇皮薄

LOQUAT, bi-bô′ 枇杷

LORD, cü′ 主; — *of Heaven,* T‘in-Cü′ 天主; *Lord's Supper,* Cü-go væn′-ts‘æn 主个晚餐

LORD, *to* — *over,* we-deo′, we-nao′ 爲頭爲腦

LOSE, *to* shih′-diao 失了°; tiu-diao′ 丟去°; — *one's life,* shih′-diao sing′-ming 失了性命; sông sing′-ming 喪性命; sing′-ming c‘ih′-t‘eh 性命休°矣; — *heart,*\* kæn-t‘æn′ sing-deo ky‘i′ 可°歎°可°氣°; — (opposed to win), shü′-diao 輸了°; — *courage,* tæn ‘en′ 膽塞;

\* *It should be observed that,* shih sing′ 失心 *means to lose one's mind, and not one's heart;* shih′-loh 失落 *means also to leave behind, or forget.*

tæn ky‘iah′ 膽怯°; — *interest* (in), sing′ lang′ 心冷°; sing-s′ dæn′-dæn 心思淡然°; sing ga′; — *flavor,* c‘ih ky‘i′ 出氣; — *savor,* tseo mi′ 走味°; *to suffer loss,* ky‘üoh′-kw‘e 吃°虧; ky‘ih′-kw‘e; ky‘ih-ky‘ü′; — *capital, or* — *in trade,* zih-peng′ 折本; kw‘e-peng′ 虧本; kw‘e-zih′ 虧折°; *how much did you* —? ng′ zih to-siao′ peng 你°折多少本?

LOST, shih′-diao-de 失了°; (as a ship), tso′-diao-de 做壞°了°; — *in trade,* sô tseo′, tsong′-go 不°符°總个°; sô zih′, diao-go 蝕出°个°; — *to shame,* sông′ lin-c‘ü′ 傷廉恥; fæ-gyi ô-lin′ 弗要°臉; — *time,* kong-fu shih′-loh-de 工夫失落了°; — *appetite,* we-k‘eo′ t‘e-pæn′-de 胃口不°佳°了°; — *memory,* kyi′-sing t‘e-pæn′-de 記性差°了°; *missing,* feh-kyin′-de 弗見了°; — *the way,* mi-lu′-de 迷路了°

LOT, *a* — *of land,* ih-kw‘e-di′ 一塊地; *the whole* — (of things), ih′-kwu-nao-r 一概

LOTS, *to draw* — (bamboo splints), ts‘iu-ts‘in′ 抽籤; *ditto* (bits of paper), ts‘eh-ts′-meh-den′ 拈°鬮°; *to cast* — *with dice,* dzih-seh′-ts 擲骰°子

LOTUS, ‘o-hwô′ 荷花; lin-hwô′ 蓮花; — *seeds,* lin-ts′ 蓮子; — *roots,* ngeo 藕

LOUD, hyiang 響; *speaks—*, kông-leh-hyiang' 講得響; — *voice,* sing-ing'-do' 聲音大°; sing-ing'-djong' 聲音重; wu-long'-do' 喉°嚨大°; *a little louder,* hyiang-tin' 響點

LOUNGER, *idler,* k'ong'-ʻæn-nying' 空閒人° See Loafer, Loll.

LOUSE, seh 虱; *the nid of a —,* seh-ts' 虱子; kyi'-ts 蟣子; *to kill lice,* k'eh seh' 剋虱; *to kill lice by biting,* ngao seh' 鮫虱

LOUSY, seh' sang'-leh-to' 虱生°得°多; seh sang'-leh kao-kao-dong'.

LOVE *of wine,* t'en-tsiu' 貪酒; — *of wealth,* t'en-dzæ' 貪財; — *of lust,* t'en-seh' 貪色; — *of eating,* t'en-ky'üoh' 貪吃°; t'en-zih' 貪食

LOVE, *to* æ'-sih 愛惜; — *greatly,* c'ong'-æ 寵愛; *to — a superior,* æ'-kying 愛敬; — *an inferior* (as a child), dzih-din' 値錢°; — *one another,* dô-kô'-siang-æ' 大°家°相愛; — *and pity,* æ-lin' 愛憐; *he is much loved,* gyi teh-c'ong'-go 其得寵个°; — *and treat partially,* p'in-æ' 偏愛; — *blindly,* nyih-æ' 溺愛

LOVELY, k'o-æ' 可愛; me 美; — *woman,* me'-nyü 美女

LOW, *not high,* ti 低; — *coast lands,* du 渡; t'æn 灘; — *land,* di'-sbü ti' 地勢低; — *voice,* sing-ing' ti 聲音低;

sing-ing' ky'ing 聲音輕; wu-long iu' 喉°嚨細°; — *birth,* c'ih-sing' ti-vi' 出身低微; — *tide,* dziao t'e'-zing 潮退盡; dziao loh-ken' 潮落乾; *vulgar,* ts'u-c'ing' 粗蠢; — *in price,* kô'-din ti 價°錢°低; — (*i. e.* poor) *diet,* ky'üoh'-zih dæn'-boh 吃°食淡薄; ts'u-ts'æ' dæn-væn' 麤菜淡飯

LOWER, *to — one's self,* zi-ky'ing', zi-zin' 自°輕自°賤

LOWER, *a little —,* ti'-tin 低點; — *side,* 'ô'-min 下°面; — *classes,* mæn pah'-sing 頑民°; siao pah'-sing 小百°姓

LOWEST, ting-ʻô'-deo-go 頂下°頭个°; — *class* or *rank,* meh-teng'-go sing-veng' 末等个°身分°; ting 'ô' pe 頂下°輩

LOWLY, *mean,* ti-vi' 低微, pe-vi' 卑微; *humble,* ky'in-hyü' 謙虛

LOW-SPIRITED, sing-hwe i'-læn 心灰意懶

LOYAL, cong-sing' 忠心; — *officer,* cong-dzing' 忠臣

LUBRICATE *it,* long gyi wah' 弄其滑

LUCID, ming-ts'ih' 明澈; ming-liang' 明亮

LUCK, zao'-hwô 造°化°; yüing'-ky'i 運氣; yüing'-dao 運道; z-yüing' 時運; *good —,* hao yüing'-ky'i 好運氣; hao zao'-hwô 好°得°意°; *when in good*

—, 'ang yüing' z-'eo 行運時候; *bad* —, zao-hwô ẅa' 勿°得°意°; tao-yüing' 倒運; yüing'-dao feh-t'e' 運道弗通°; *that was your good* — (no right to expect), keh z ng'-go ngah'-koh kao 這°是你个°額角高; iao-ying' 僥°倖

LUCKY, yiu zao'-hwô 有造化; yiu ying' 有幸; — *omen*, hao ts'æ'-deo 好兆°頭; — *day*, hao nyih-ts' 好日子; — *star*, kyih' sing 吉星

LUCRABAN SEED, da-fong-ts' 大楓子

LUCRATIVE, hao fah-dzæ' 好發財

LUDICROUS, hao fah'-siao'-go 好發笑个°

LUG, *to* dzing'-lih do' 盡°力拿°; *to drag with all one's strength*, 'eo-ky'i'-lih t'o' 儘°氣力拖

LUGGAGE, 'ang-li' 行°李; *how many pieces of* —? kyi gyin' 'ang-li' 幾件行°李?

LUKEWARM, feh-lang'-feh-nyih' 弗冷°弗熱°; nyih-ẅeng-ẅeng' 熱溫溫°; ẅeng'-t'eng 溫和°

LULL, *the wind lulls*, fong' iu-loh'-ky'i 風聲°漸°靜°; *wind lulled*, fong sih'-de 風息了°

LUMBER, *old things*, hyiu'-gyiu tong-si 朽舊東西; *wood*, moh-deo' 木頭

LUMP, gyi-ts'-kw'e 棋子塊; *a ball*, ih-dön' 一團; *a piece*, ih-

kw'e' 一塊; *to buy in the* —, (not in powder), weh-leng' ma 囫圇買°

LUMP, *to form lumps*, dzing-kw'e' 成塊; — *together*, tang t'ong-bun' 打通盤; *to* — *the prices*, t'ong-ts'ô' kô'-din 通扯價°錢°

LUNAR *month*, yüih-veng tsiao yüih-liang'ding'-go 月牙°照月亮定个°

LUNATIC, tin-ts' 癲子; fong-tin'-go 瘋癲个°

LUNCH, tin'-sing, or tia'-sing 點心

LUNG-NGAN, kwe'-yün 桂圓; yün ngæn' 圓眼°

LUNGS, fi 肺

LURE, *to entice*, ying-yiu' 引誘; *to tempt*, mi-'oh' 迷惑; — *away*, kwa'-tæ 拐°帶°; kwa'-p'in 拐騙

LURK, *to* tong-iu'-si-iu' 東避°西避°; tong-tsiang'-si-ẅông' 東賬西望°

LUSCIOUS, ken-din' 蜜°甜

LUST, *desire for possession*, s-yüoh' 私欲; *concupiscence*, yüoh-ho' 慾火

LUSTING, yüoh-ho' kæ-tih dong' 慾火動; yüoh-ho' fah'-dong 慾火發動

LUSTFUL, t'en-seh' 貪色; *extremely* —, hao'-seh-ko-du' 好色過度; — *person*, hao'-seh-ts-du' 好色之徒

LUSTER or LUSTRE, kwông 光

LUSTY *fellow*, hao'-hen-ts 好漢

LUXURIANT, meo-zing' 茂 盛

LUXURIOUS, shiæ-wô', or sô wæ
奢 華

LYE, kæn'-shü' 碱 水°

# M

MACE, *the coat of nutmegs,* nyüoh-
ko' bi 玉 菓 皮 ; *a tenth of a
Chinese ounce,* ih-din' 一 錢°

MACERATE, to — *in water,* shü'-
li tsing-t'eo' 水° 裏 浸 透

MACHINATION, tsô'-kyi 詐 計

MACHINE, kyi-ky'i' 機器

MACKEREL, ts'ing-tsön' 青 鱄 ;
*horse* —, mô'-kao-ng 馬鮫°魚°;
*very coarse ditto,* hwô-lin-djü' 花
鏈 鎚°

MAD, vu'-tin 武 癲 ; gwông 狂 ;
fong-tin' 瘋 癲 ; — *dog,* fong
wun-kyi' 瘋 黃°犬° ; tin keo'
癲 狗 ; — *with evil desire,* hwô-
tin' 花 癲 ; *to become* —, fah
tin' 發 癲 ; fah gwông' 發 狂

MADAM, (to a lady of rank), na'-
na 奶°奶° ; t'a'-t'a 太° 太° ; (to
the wife of teacher), s-meo' 師-母

MADE *of wood,* jü' tso-go 樹 做
个° ; *well* —, sang-weh' tso-leh
hao' 生° 活 做 得° 好

MADEIRA-NUT, or *English walnut,* wu-dao' 胡 桃

MADMAN, vu'-tin-ts 武 癲 子

MADNESS, tin-bing' 癲 病 ; *to
feign* —, tsông tin' 裝 癲

MAGAZINE, *powder* ho'-yiah gyüoh'
火 藥 局

MAGENTA, (a color), ngô-læn-
'ong' 一°品° 紅

MAGGOTS, *to breed* —, c'ih djong'
出 蟲 ; sang djong' 生° 蟲

MAGIC, fah'-jih 法 術

MAGICIAN, yiu fah'-jih go jih-z'
有 法 術 个° 人°; yiu fah'-lih-
go cü'-kwn 有 法 力 个° 人°

MAGIC-LANTERN, ing'-wô-kying'
映 畫 鏡 (ih-go)

MAGISTRATE, kwun 官 ; kwun-
fu' 官 府 ; styled, lao'-yia 老
爺° ; *magistrate's office,* or *residence,* ngô-meng 衙 門 ; *magistrate's hall,* kong-dông 公 堂 ;
do-dông' 大° 堂

MAGNANIMOUS, 'ao-yiah' 豪 俠 ;
k'ông'-k'æ 慷 慨

MAGNET, hyih'-t'ih-zah 吸 鐵 石°

MAGNIFICENT, wô-li' 華 麗

MAGNIFYING-GLASS, hyin'-vi-
kying' 顯 微 鏡 ; the same word
is used for microscope.

MAGNOLIA, *purple* moh-pih'-hwô
木 筆 花 ; *white* —, nyüoh-
dông'-hwô 玉 堂 花

MAGPIE, ô-ts'iah' 鴉 鵲 (ih-tsah) ;
— *robin,* hyi'-ts'iah 喜 鵲

MAHOMETAN, See MOHAMMEDAN.

MAID, MAIDEN, *girl,* nyiang-ts'
娘 子 ; *miss,* do-kwu'-nyiaug
大° 姑 娘 ; *old* —, lao do-kwu-
nyiang 老 大° 姑 娘 ; *slave,* ô-
deo' 丫 頭 ; s'-nyü 使 女

MAIDENLY, *modest,* iu'-siu 幽 靜°;
p'ô wông-k'ong' 怕 惶 恐

MAIL-BAG, sing'-dæ 信袋;—
boat, sing-pæn-jün' 信船;—
carrier, tseo-sing'-go-nying 走
信个° 人°; official ditto, tseo-
veng-shü'-go-nying' 走文書
个° 人°

MAIMED, dzæn-dzih'-go 殘疾个°;
to become —, væn dzæn-dzih'
犯殘疾

MAIN, the — reason, do yün-kwn'
大° 緣故;— idea, tsing'-i 正
意; da i' 大意; good in the —,
da kwe'-mo hao' 大規模好

MAINTAIN, to hold, siu 守; to keep,
pao'-siu 保守; can — it, siu'-
leh-djü' 守得° 住; to support,
yiang 養; cong 種; cong-yiang'
種養 (commonly pron. tsong-
yiang);— one's family, cong-
kô' yiang-kyün' 養家活°口°

MAJESTY, his wông-zông' 皇上;
sing-zông' 聖上; cü'-ts 主子;
his, or your —, væn'-se 萬歲;
his — the present Emperor, tông'
kying' wông-zông' 當今皇上

MAJOR (in the army), ts'æn-tsiang'
參將; siu'-be 守備

MAJOR-GENERAL, tsong'-ping 總
兵; cing'-dæ 鎮臺; di-toh'
提督

MAJORITY, ih-do'-pun' 一大° 半;
eight parts (out of ten), pah'-
feng 八分

MAJORITY, to reach one's —, zông
ting' 上丁; already attained —,
dzing-ting' 成丁

MAKE, to tso 做; to build, zao
造;— clothes, tso i-zông' 做
衣裳;— a tower, zao t'ah'
造塔;— a road, k'æ lu' 開
路;— it better, long' gyi hao'-
tin 弄其好點; to cause, long
弄; s'-teh 使得; cü'-s-teh 致
使得; peh 俾°;— him afraid,
long' gyi p'ô' 弄其怕; s'-teh
gyi p'ô' 使得其怕;— a bill,
or account, k'æ tsiang' 開帳;
— a bed, p'u' min-zông' 鋪眠
床°;— it good, t'ing'-djông 聽
償; pu'-wæn 補還;— up (the
difference), din 墊;— a league,
lih-iah' 立約;— or compel
him to do, ah' gyi tso' 押其做;
kwun' gyi tso' 管其做; p'in-
sang' iao gyi tso' 偏要其做;
— believe, tsông kô' 裝假°;
— believe cry, tsông kô' kyiao
裝假哭°;— peace, ka 'o' 解°
和;— up one's mind, cü'-i
kyüih'-tön 主意決斷; it makes
no difference, m̄-kao'; ditto which,
feh-leng' 弗論;— (form) an
association, hying we' 興會;—
rules, lih' fah-tseh' 立法則;
lih' kwe-kyü' 立規矩

MAKER, tso'-go cü'-kwu 做个°
人°; flower —, hwô'-s-vu 花司
務; God, Hwô'-kong 化工

MALARIA, doh-ky'i' 毒氣; vu-
doh'-ts-ky'i 腐毒之氣

MALAYS, Mo-lu'-nying' 嚤囉人°

MALE, nen 男;— child, siao'-

wæn' 小兒°; u-wæn'; — *of animals*, yüong 雄

MALEDICTION, tsiu'-mô 咒罵

MALEFACTOR, væn'-nying 犯人°; ze'-væn 罪犯

MALEVOLENT, oh'-doh 惡毒; *likes others to have trouble*, hwun'-hyi bih'-nying ky⟨üoh'-kw⟨u 歡喜別人°吃°苦

MALICIOUS, *injuring without cause*, vu-kwu' 'æ'-nying 無故害人°; — *accusation*, vu-kao' 誣告

MALIGN, *to* pông'-hwe 謗毀

MALIGNANT, hyüong-hyüong'-go 兇个°人°; *very —*, hyüong sah'-sah 兇煞; — *disease*, hyüong-bing' 凶病

MALLEABLE, hao' tang boh'-go 好打薄个°

MALLET, moh-djü' 木鎚; *heavy —*, lông-deo-djü' 榔頭鎚; jü'-lông-deo' 樹榔頭 (ih-go)

MALTREAT, *to* long-song' 弄唆°; tsiu-tsoh' 收拾°; — *greatly*, tsao-t⟨ah' 蹧蹋

MAMMALIA, ky⟨üoh-na' keh' ih-le' 吃°嬭這°一類

MAN, nying 人°; *every —*, ko'-ko-nying 個個人°; *all men*, cong'-nying 衆人°; — *of propriety or influence*, do-nying'-do-mô' 大°丈°夫°

MAN OF WAR, ping'-jün' 兵船; p⟨ao'-jün 礮船; tsin'-jün 戰船 (ih-tsah)

MANACLE, *to* ting siu'-k⟨ao 釘手栲; k⟨ao siu'-k⟨ao 栲手栲

MANACLES, siu'-k⟨ao 手栲 (ih-fu)

MANAGE, *to* bæn 辦; kwun 管; liao-li' 料理; diao-du' 調度; — *affairs*, bæn-z' 辦事; *manages well*, diao-du'-leh hao' 調度得°好; *I can — it*, ngô'-hao liao-li' 我好料理; — *a family*, djü kô' 治家°; kwun' kô' 管家°

MANAGEMENT, *has good —*, yiu hao en'-fông 有好安頓°

MANAGER, we-deo' 爲頭; — (of larger affairs), tong'-z 董事; siu'-z 首事

MANCHU, Mun'-tsiu nying' 滿洲人°; — *language*, Mun'-tsiu wô' 滿洲話; — *characters*, Mun'-tsiu z' 滿洲字

MANDARIN, kwun 官; kwun-fu' 官府; kwun-yün' 官員 (ih-we); — *dialect*, kwun'-wô' 官話; — *ducks*, ün'-iang' 鴛鴦

MANDATE, *imperial —*, wông'-ming' 皇命; zông-yü' 上諭; sing'-ts 聖旨

MANE *of a horse*, mô'-tsong-mao' 馬鬃毛

MANFULLY, *bravely*, üong'-ken 勇敢; kông-üong' 剛勇

MANGER, *horse's* mô'-zao 馬槽

MANGY *dog*, fah-la'-keo 發癩狗

MANGLED, keh'-wu-de 割爛°了°; ng'-hwô pao'-lih-de 五°花爆裂了°.

MANHOOD, *arrived at —*, zông'
ting'-de 上丁了°; dzing-nying'-
tsiang- da'- de 成人°長大
了°; *ditto* (in reproach), ts'ih'-
dziang'-pah-do' 七長八大°

MANIAC, vu'-tin-ts 武癲子

MANIFEST, *ship's* jün-cü' pao'-tæn
船主報單; ho'-tæn 貨單

MANIFEST, *to* hyin 顯; lu 露;
piao 表; hyin'-c'ih-læ 顯出
來; lu'-c'ih-læ' 露出來

MANIFESTLY, ming-tông'-tông
分°明°; hyin'-jün 顯然; hyin'-
kyin 顯見

MANIFESTO, *imperial* wông-pông'
皇榜; *official —*, kao'-z 告示

MANIFOLD *varieties, or changes,*
ts'in-pin'-væn'-hwô 千變萬化;
*many forms,* to'-leh-kying'-go
yiang'-shih 多得緊个°樣式

MANKIND, nying' ih-le' 人°一類;
*all —*, 'en'-t'in-'ô nying' 合°天
下°人°

MANLY, ziang hao-hen' ka 正°
像好漢

MANNER, *fashion,* t'æ'-du 態度;
t'i'-t'æ 體態; yiang 樣; *in like
—*, ih-yiang'-go 一樣个°; *do it
in this —*, ka' siang-mao tso'
如°此°做; *his — is pleasing,*
gyi'-go t'æ'-du hao' 其个°態度
好; *his — of speaking is good,*
gyi'-go dæn-t'u' hao' 其个°談
吐好; *of expressing one's self,*
kông'-fah 講°法; *has no manners,* m-li'-ky'i 無°禮體°

MANNERS, *or customs,* fong-djoh'
風俗; hyiang-fông' 鄉風°

MANSION, fu'-zông 府上; fu'-di
府第; tseng-fu' 奪府

MANTEL or MANTLE-PIECE, ho'-
lu-teng; ho'-lu zông-go koh'-kyi
火爐上个°擱几

MANUFACTORY, tsoh'-dziang 作
場; fông 坊; *silk —*, kyi-fông'
機坊; *powder —*, ho'-yiah-
gyüoh' 火藥局

MANUFACTURE, *to* cü'-zao 製造

MANURE, bi 肥°; feng 糞; liao
料; *exchange money for —*, wun
bi' 換糞°; *— cakes,* k'ông'-sô
坑沙

MANURE, *to — land,* üong din'
壅田; *to water with —*, kyiao
bi' 澆糞°

MANUSCRIPT, *rough draft,* ts'ao'-
kao 草稿; *the improved —*,
ts'ing'-kao 清稿

MANY, hyü'-to 許多; yiu'-ho;
to 多; zing'-kyi; to-siao'; *very
—*, to-to' 多多; ting-to 頂
多; to-to'-ih-jün' 多多益善:
*how — men?* to-siao' nying'
ni? 多少人°呢; *not —*, m'-
to-siao 無°多少; feh-to' 弗
多; hao-kyi'-go 好幾个°; *—
times,* hyü-to' tsao'-su 許多回°
數; *too —*, t'eh' to 太°多; *—
thanks, to* zia' 多謝°; *so —*,
keh-tang'; ka-sing'.

MAP, di-li'-du 地理圖 (ih-go, or
if for hang-ing, ih-foh); *— of the
world,* di-gyiu'-du' 地球圖

MAP 288 MAR

MAPLE, fong-jü' 楓樹 (ih-cü)

MAR, to damage, seng'-sông 損傷; her beauty is marred by the blemish, gyi'-go me'-mao be yüô'-tin ta'-loh 其个°美貌被瑕玷滅色°; gyi'-go me'-mao be yüô'-tin sô 'æ' 其个°美貌被瑕玷所害

MARBLE, Da-li'-zah 大理石°; T'a'-wu-zah 太°湖石°; yüing-zah' 雲石°

MARBLED paper, yüing-zah'-tsin 雲石°箋

MARCHING, tired with —, (or walking), tseo'-vah-liao 走乏了

MARE, ts'-mô' 雌馬 (ih-p'ih)

MARGIN, pin 邊; pin-yin' 邊沿; — of a river, kông' pin-yin' 江邊沿; — of a leaf, pin-da' 邊; upper — ditto, zông'-kah 上格; t'in-deo'; lower ditto, 'ô'-kah 下格; ti'-kah 底格

MARK, or sign of something, kyi'-nying 記認°; kyi'-'ao 記號; trace, or the — of a sore, 'eng-tsih' 痕跡; trace, u 痕°; finger —, ts'-tsih u 指跡痕°; — of folding, tsih'-u 摺痕°; üih'-u 攦痕°; ink — (spot), moh-tsih' 墨跡; one's private —, hwô-iah' 花押; hwô-z' 花字; receive the — of a Buddhist priest, ziu ka' 受戒°; marks of having been moved, ying-tsih' hao'-ziang dong'-ko-liao 形跡好像動過了

MARK, to make a — as a sign, tso' kyi'-nying 做記認°; tso' kyi'-'ao 做記號; to make or leave a mark (or spot), tang tsih' 遭°跡; — perpendicularly (as an incorrect character), dzih 直; — with a hot iron, t'ông kyi'-'ao 燙記號; — with attention, and remember, sing'-li tang' ih-go kyih', kyi'-tih 牢°牢切°記

MARKET, z'-min-zông' 市面上; z'-k'eo 市口; country —, z'-cing 市鎮; — day, z'-nyih 市日°; to come into —(as fruit), zông-z' 上市; have cherries come into —? ang-dao' zông'-leh ma 櫻°桃出了°嗎? to go to —, c'ih z' ky'i 出市去°; ditto early in the morning, c'ih tsao' z ky'i' 出早市去°; — price, z'-kô 市價°; — street, ka z' 街°市; no — (for it), z' zông m̄ siao-dziang' 市上無°銷塲

MARKETABLE, yiu siao-dziang' 有銷塲; siao'-leh-diao'-go 銷得°去°个

MARKET-MAN, (the seller), 'ông-fæn' 行販; (the buyer), ma'-bæn 買辦

MARKING-LINE, carpenter's ink —, moh-sin' 墨線; tailor's powder —, feng-sin 粉線

MARRIAGE, tso-ts'ing' 做親; dzing-ts'ing' 成親; hao'-nyih 好日°; to consult about a —,

nyi-ts'ing' 議親; — contract,
hweng-shü' 婚書; shü-ts' 禮
書°; — dower from the father,
tsông-lin' 粧奩; kô'-tsông 嫁°
粧; kô'-ts 嫁°奩°;—, from the
bridegroom, or his father, p'ing'-
li 聘禮

MARRIED, hao'-nyih-ko'-de 完°
姻°過了°; not yet —, feh-
zing' hao'-nyih-ko 弗曾完°
姻°; (said of the man), feh-zing'
c'ü-ts'ing' 弗曾娶親; (said
of the woman), feh-zing' ko'-
meng' 弗曾過門; vi-dzeng'
c'ih-kô' 未曾出嫁°

MARROW, kweh'-si 骨髓

MARRY, to — a wife, c'ü-ts'ing'
娶親; t'ao-ts'ing' 迎°親; c'ü
lao'-nyüing 娶妻°; dæ lao'-
nyüing 擡新°人°;—a husband,
c'ih-kô' 出嫁°; c'ih-koh' 出閣°;
tso sing-vu' 做新婦;— a
second wife, dzoh c'ü' 續娶;
— a second husband, tsæ' tsiao
再醮

MART, busy mô'-deo 馬頭

MARTIAL, vu 武; — appearance,
vu' siang 武相;— law, kyüing
fah' 軍法

MARTYR for one's religion, we
dao'-li cü-ming'-go 爲道理致
命个°

MARVELOUS, gyi-kwa' 奇怪°;
hyi-gyi' 希奇

MASCULINE, yüong 雄;— gen-
der, yüong' ih-le' 雄一類

MASH, to sông-wu' 舂腐°, nyin'-se
研碎; to crush, ah'-wu 壓腐°

MASK, yia'-wu-lin'; to wear a —,
ta kyü'-lin 帶°鬼°臉

MASON, nyi-shü'-s-vu' 泥水°司
務; nyi-ziang' 泥匠; stone —,
zah'-s-vu' 石°司務; zah-ziang'
石°匠

MASS, a lump, ih-dön' 一團; to
say —, tso' mi'-sah 做彌撒;
the masses, cong' pah'-sing 衆
百°姓

MASSACRE, to sah'-loh 殺戮;
—all in a city, du-dzing 屠城;
— a village, mih ts'eng' 滅村°

MASSIVE, yi-do' yi-djong' 又°大
又°重

MAST, we 桅; we-ken' 桅杆
(ih-ts)

MASTER of a house, cü'-nying-
kô' 主人°家°; tông-kô' 當°
家°; — workman, tsoh'-deo 作
頭,; — of a shop (hired), pô'-
dæ sin'-sang 當°手°先生°;
ditto who has the capital, lang'-z;
tong-kô' 東家°; teacher, sin-sang'
先生°; (politely styted) lao'-fu-
ts 老夫子; (native) —of Arts,
kyü'-nying 舉人°

MASTERS, he who— great difficulties, will become a great man, ziu'-
teh kw'u' cong kw'u', fông-we
jing-zông'-jing 受得苦中苦
方爲人上人

MASTERY, strive for —, pih-gying'
比劢

MASTICATE, *to* ziah 嚼

MAT, zih 蓆; zih-ts' 蓆子 (ih-diao); *rattan table* —, deng-din' 籐墊; — *made from palmetto fibres,* tsong-tsin' 棕荐; *foot* —, t'ô-kyiah'-go din'-ts 刷°鞋°泥°的°墊子; — *awning,* liang'-bang' 涼棚; — *shed,* bong-ts' 蓬子

MATCH, *lucifer* z-læ'-ho 自來火; — *box,* z-læ'-ho 'eh-ts' 自°來火盒子; — *paper,* ho'-ts 火紙

MATCH, *a happy* — *is made in Heaven,* T'in-s' liang-yün' 天賜艮綠

MATCH, *to* p'e 配; p'e'-long 配攏; p'e'-dzing 配成; p'e'-zông 配上; — *colors,* p'e'-long ping'-seh 配攏拜色; — *this color,* p'e'keh'-go ngæn-seh' 配這°个°顏°色; *the two are well matched,* liang'-go p'e'-dzing ih-te' 兩个°配成一對

MATE, *companion,* bun 伴; dong-bun' 同伴; *first* — *on a ship,* da-fu' 大副; *second* —, nyi-fu' 二°副; *school* —, dong-ts'ông' 同窓; *lost her* — (the pair parted), ts'ah te'-de 拆對了°

MATERIALS, liao-tsoh' 料作; tsoh'-liao 作料

MATERNAL *love,* ah-nyiang'-go dz-sing' 母之°慈心; ah-nyiang-go æ'-sing' 母之°愛心; — *uncle,* nyiang-gyiu' 娘舅; gyiu'-gyiu

舅舅; — *grandfather,* nga-kong' 外°公; *grandmother,* nga-bo' 外°婆

MATHEMATICIAN, *the imperial* — *and astronomer,* ky'ing-t'in'-kæn 欽天監°

MATHEMATICS, sön'-yüoh or sön'-'oh 算學

MATTER, *the essence of* —, tsih 質; *properties of* —, væn-veh'-go sing'-tsih 萬物个°性質; *what's the* —? soh'-go z-ken' 甚°麼°事幹? *trifling* —, siao' z 小事; *pus,* nong 膿; ao-tsao' 墾精

MATTING, di-zih' 地蓆; — *in the long piece,* do-bæn'-deo, tsing-kw'e' zih 一°大°爿°正塊之°蓆; *a roll of* — (large), ih-dön' zih; ih-kw'eng' zih 一捆蓆; *coarse* — *for wrapping,* bu-pao' 蒲包

MATURE *in knowledge,* cü'-sih joh' 知識熟; — *fruit,* ko'-ts joh' 菓子熟; *that child is very* —, keh'-go siao nying' yiu do nying' t'ï'-liao 這個小孩°有大°人°體統°

MATURITY, *arrived at years of* —, do-tsoh'-de 大°足了°; dziang-tsoh'-de 長足了°

MAXIM, keh'-yin 格言

MAY *do it,* k'o-yi tso' 可以做; hao' tso 好做; hao'-s-teh 好使得; — *be so,* 'oh-tsia' z-ka' 或者°如°此°

ME, ngô 我; *he told* —, gyi' wô-

hyiang-ngô'-ko'-de 其 向 我 話
過 了°; gyi teng' ngô' wô-ko'-de
其 與° 我 話 過 了°

MEAL, a ih-djü' 一 筯; ih-ts'æn'
一 餐; ih-teng' 一 頓; — of
rice, ih-djü væn' 一 筯 飯

MEAL, feng 粉; corn, loh-koh'
feng 稑 穀 粉; wheat flour, min-
feng' 麪 粉

MEAN about little things, si'-si se-
se' 細 細 碎 碎; low, ti-vi' 低
微; pe-zin' 卑 賤°; 'ô'-zin 下°
賤°; stingy, sing'-jih pi'-si 心
術 鄙 細; — action, 'ô'-tsoh
'ang-we' 下°作行°爲; —spirit-
ed, ky'i'-liang 'ah-tsah' 氣 量 狹
窄; k'æn-kyiang'.

MEAN, to intend, siang 想; what
do you — to do? ng' siang tso
soh'-si 你° 想 做 甚° 麼°? 
what do you —? ng' yiu soh'-go
i'-s 你°有 甚° 麼° 意 思?

MEANING, i'-s 意 思; ka'-shih
解 說; saying one thing, — another, k'eo' feh te' sing 口 弗
對 心; yiu' k'eo m̄ sing' 有 口
無° 心

MEANLY, to treat a person —,
boh-dæ' nying-kô' 薄 待 人°家°

MEANS to an end, fông-fah' 方 法;
fah'-ts 法 子; no — of attaining,
m̄'-neh fah'-ts hao teh'-djoh 沒°
有° 法 子 好 得 着; by no —,
bing'-fi 並 非; bing'-feh-z 並
弗 是; by all —, vu-pih'-ts 務
必

MEAN-TIME, in the—, ts'ing wông'
feh tsih-gao' z-'eo' 青 黃 不°接°
時 侯

MEASLES, ts'u'-ts 瘄 子; sick with
the —, c'ih' ts'u'-ts 出 瘄 子

MEASURE, to — in feet and inches, liang ts'ah'-ts'eng 量 尺°
寸'; — and see, liang-liang'-k'en
量 量 看; — in pints, liang
sing-teo' 量 升 斗

MEASURE and compare length, in
眶; — and see, in'-in k'en' 眶
眶 看; — by the foot, &c., liang
量; — by the eye, kwu'-kwuk-
k'en' 估 估 看; — land, or boats,
dziang'-liang 丈 量; — the person*, liang sing-kô' 量 身 架
* The Chinese do not measure the
person except in the case of criminals.

MEASURE, quart — (nearly), ih-
sing' 一 升; 10 quarts, ih-teo'
一 斗; 10 teo, ih-zah' 一 石;
do according to the — of your
ability, liang-lih' r-ying' 量 力
而 行 (veng.)

MEASURING, the art, or way of
—, liang-fah' 量 法

MEAT, nyüoh* 肉°; lean —,
tsing-nyüoh' 精 肉°
* Nyüoh used alone signifies pork.

MECHANIC, s-vu' 司 務

MEDDLE, to — with other people's
affairs, kwun 'æn-tsiang 管 閒°
帳; need not — with my af-
fairs, hao-vong' kwun ngô'-go
'æn-tsiang 不° 用° 管 我 个°

閒帳；— *in conversation*, ts'ah-cü' 譌 嘴；ts'ah-yin' 譌 言
MEDDLESOME *in affairs*, to-kwun' 'æn-tsiang' 多管閒°帳；to-z'-go 多事个°；— *in touching*, ts'ih'-siu pah-kyiah' 七手八脚；— *in answering when not wanted*, ts'ih-tah' pah-tah' 七嗒八嗒
MEDIATE, *to* ts'ah-ky'ün' 譌勸
MEDIATOR, Cong-pao' 中保；*to act as a* — *in making peace*, tso 'o-z' nying 做和事人°
MEDICINE, yiah 藥；*to take* —, ky'üoh yiah' 吃°藥；*feel the effect of* —, teh' yiah lih' 得藥力；*the study of* — (*healing*), i-yüoh' 醫學
MEDITATE, *to think quietly*, zing-zing'-go ts'eng' 靜靜个°忖；*secretly* — *doing*, en'-di shih-siang' 暗地設°想
MEDIUM, *observe a due* —, tsiah'-wu-gyi-cong' 酌乎其中
MEDLEY *of things*, tong-si' se'-zeh 東西碎雜；zeh'-keh-leng'-teng tong-si' 雜件°東西
MEEK, w̌eng-ziu' 溫柔；w̌eng-'o' 溫和
MEET, *to* p'ong'-djoh 逢°着°；nyü-djoh' 遇着°；we-djoh' 會着°；— *accidentally*, ngeo'-jün p'ong'-djoh 偶然逢°着°；— *suddenly*, *or for the first time*, p'ih-min k'en-kyin 劈面看見；— (*again*) *tomorrow*, ming-tsiao' we' 明朝會；*to go to* —,

nying-tsih' 迎接；*failed to* —, we'-feh-kyin' 會弗見；*to assemble*, jü'-long 聚攏；kwe-long' 歸攏；*to befall one*, tsao-djoh' 遭着°；ling-djoh' 臨着°；— *with an accident*, tsao'-djoh hwe'-ky'i 遭着°晦氣
MELANCHOLY, iu-üoh' 憂鬱；meng-meng'-peh-loh' 悶悶不樂
MELLOW, nen-joh' 軟°熟
MELODY, ing-yüing' diao-'o' 音韻調和；— *of instruments*, ing-yüoh' diao-'o' 音樂調和
MELON, kwô 瓜；*water* — *seeds*, kwô-ts' 瓜子
MELT, *to* sah；yiang-k'æ' 煬開；hwô'-k'æ 化開；— *silver*, sah nying'-ts 煬°銀子
MEMBERS *of the body*, ts-t'i' 肢體；*all the ditto*, s'-ts-pah'-t'i' 四肢百°體；*church* —, kyiao'-yiu 教友
MEMOIR, 'ang-jih' 行述；*brief* —, djün 傳；*the* — *of Confucius*, K'ong'-fu-ts-go 'ang-jih' 孔夫子个°行述
MEMORABLE, üong' feh mông-kyi' 永弗忘°記；ts'ih'-kyi-dzæ-sing' 切記在心
MEMORANDUM-BOOK, dzeng-kyi'-bu 存記簿
MEMORIAL (*to officials*), dzing-dz' 呈詞；ping'-tæn 稟單；— *from higher officers, to the emperor*, tseo'-tsông 奏章；peng'-tsông 本章

MEMORY, kyi'-sing 記性; excellent — (see, then remember), ko'-moh-peh-vông' 過目不忘

MENCIUS, Mang'-fu-ts 孟°夫子

MEND, to ts'eh'-dzæn 撮綻; siu-pu' 修補; to patch, pu 補; — (darn), kang 耕°; to repair, siu 修; siu-li' 修理; — stockings, kang mah' 耕襪; ditto by patching, pu mah'; — bowls, &c. (with nails), ting un' 釘碗; If we do not — the little holes, the big holes will cry out bitterly, "siao dong' feh pu', do dong kyiao kw'u" 忽 小害°大°; — by stitching together, vong-tæn'-long 縫攏

MENSES, yüih-kying' 月經; yüih-kô' 月°家°; to have —(at first), kyi-sing cün 身體°轉; suppression of —, yüih-kying' ding-tsih' 月經停積

MENTAL ability, dzæ-neng' 才能; dzæ-'oh' 才學°; — effort, lao-sing' 勞心; to use ditto, yüong sing-kyi' 用心機

MENTION, to di-ky'i' 提起; need not — names, feh pih' di-ky'i' ming-deo' 弗必提起名頭

MERCENARY, tsih-ts'eng' dong-din' 只忖銅錢°; li'-sing djong' 利心重

MERCHANDIZE, ho'-veh 貨物; foreign —, yiang ho' 洋貨

MERCHANT, sông 商; sông-kô' 商家°; traveling —, k'ah'-sông 客商; k'ah'-nying 客人°;

silk —, s-sông'-kô 絲商; he is a traveling —, gyi tso k'ah we sông 其出°門°爲商

MERCIFUL, dz-pe'-go 慈悲个°; nyün'-sing-dziang'-go 軟心腸个°

MERCILESS, sing oh' 心惡; sing-heng' 心狠; vu dz-sing' go 無慈心个°

MERCURY, shü'-nying 水°銀

MERCY, dz-pe' 慈悲; the goddess of —, Kwun-ing' bu-sah' 觀音菩薩

MERELY, tæn-tsih' 單只; peh-ko' 不過; tæn-z' 單是; tsih'-z 只是; kwông'-z 光是

MERIDIAN, (noon), cong-wu'-sin 中午線; — of longitude, kying-sin' 經線

MERIT, kong-teh' 功德; kong-lao' 功勞; reputation on account of —, kong-ming' 功名

MERIT, to ing-kæ' teh'-djoh 應該得着°; merits reward, li kæ ts'ing-sông' 理°該請賞

MERITED, ing-teh'-go 應得个°

MERRY, p'ao'-c'ing 不°勝°歡°喜°; kw'a-weh siao-yiao' 快活逍遙

MESHES, ngæn'-ts 眼°洞°; small —, ngæn'-ts mih-kying' 眼°洞°密緊; large —, ngæn'-ts hyi 眼°洞°稀

MESSAGE, verbal k'eo'-sing 口信; want you to take a —, iao ng' ta ih-go k'eo'-sing 要你°

帶°一个°口信；*take a —* *for me,* teng ngô' djün ih-kyü wô' 替°我傳一句話

MESSENGER, ts'a-s' 差使；— *with letters,* di-sing'-go-nying 遞信个°人°

METALS, ng'-kying keh-le' 五° 金這°一°類

METAMORPHOSIS, pin'-hwô 變 化；— *of insects,* hwô'-seng 化生

METAPHOR, tsia'-yüong-go pi'- fông 借°用个°比方

METEMPSYCHOSIS, loh-dao' 六 道；(one kind of) —, deo' t'æ 投胎；*the six kinds of* —, loh'- dao leng-wé' 六道輪迴

METEOR yi-sing' 移星；ti-sing' 飛星；liu-sing' 流星

METHOD, fông-fah' 方法；fah'- ts 法子；fah'-tseh 法則； *excellent* —, miao' fah 妙法

METHODICAL, en'-bu-dziu-pæn' 接部就班；— *in time,* or *order,* en'-pæn-ts 接班子

METROPOLIS, *the capital,* tu-dzing' 都城；kying-tu' 京都；kying-dzing' 京城

MEW, *to* ñyiao.

MIASMA, ẅeng-ky'i' 瘟氣；tsông'- ky'i 瘴氣

MICA, *foliated* ts'in'-zeng-ts' 千層紙

MICROSCOPE, hyin'-vi-kying' 顯 微鏡 (ih-go, ih-kô)

MIDDAY, tông tsiu'-ko 當晝；

tsing'-wu-z 正午時；*just at* —, jih-tông' cong wu' 日當中午

MIDDLE, cong-nyiang' 中央°； tông-cong' 當中；tông-cong-nyiang' 當中央°；— *of any thing,* cong-sing' 中心；*in the* — *of them,* ne cong' 內中；— *aged,* cong-nyin' 中年；— *man,* cong-nying' 中人°；*ditto in planning a marriage,* me-nying' 媒人°

MIDDLING, cong-teng' 中等； tsiah'-cong 酌中；pun'-cong-tsiah 半中；cong-bing' 中平； bing-teng' 平等

MIDNIGHT, pun'-yia-ko 半夜°過

MIDWIFE, siu-sang'-bo 收生°婆； tsih-sang'-go 接生°个°；(styled) lao'-nyiang 老娘；nga-bo'.

MIGHT, *power,* gyün-ping' 權柄； — *of body,* lih-ky'i' 力氣； gying-dao' 劢道

MIGRATE, *to* tao bih' c'ü ky'i 到別處去°；*birds* — *to the south,* tiao ti-ko nen' 鳥飛過南

MILD, ẅeng-'o' 溫和；— *disposition,* sing'-dzing ẅeng-'o' 性情溫和；sing-ky'i' 'o-bing' 性氣和平；næ-sing'-næ-siang' 耐心耐想；— *weather,* t'in 'o-nön' 天和暖

MILDEW, *to* fæn 翻；fah 發； fah-me' 發霉；*time for* —, tso me' z-'eo' 做霉時候；*to spoil with* —, me'-diao 霉壞； *rot with* —, me'-læn 霉爛

MILDEWED, fah'-c'ih-de 發出了°; fah-pæn'-de 發斑了°; fah-pæn-tin'-de 發斑點了°

MILE (Chinese, about one third of an English —), ih li' 一里

MILITARY *officers*, vu'-kwun 武官; — *art*, vu' nyi 武蓺

MILITIA, hyiang-yüong' 鄉勇

MILK, na 嬭 or 圝: *yellow cow's* —, wông-ngeo' na 黃牛嬭; *buffalo's* —, shü'-ngeo na 水°牛°嬭; *deer's* —, jü'-loh 乳酪

MILK, *to* dziu-na' 挼°嬭; te-na' 滴嬭

MILKMAN, ma - ngeo - na'- nying 賣牛°嬭人°

MILKY-WAY, t'in-'o' 天河

MILL, *stone* mo 磨; *wooden — for hulling grain*, long 礱 (ih-djü'); *buffalo ditto*, nyin'-ts 碾子 (ih-go); *flour —, and — room*, lo-mo'-fông 羅磨坊

MILLET, (generic name) kao-liang' 膏粱 *fine yellow —*, soh 粟; siao'-mi 小米; *red —*, lu-tsi' 穭穄

MILLION, *a* ih-pah' væn 一百°萬; ih-ziao 一兆; *ten millions*, ts'in væn 千萬

MIMIC, *to* k'en-yiang'-'oh-yiang' 看樣學°樣; *mimics well*, 'oh-leh ziang' 學°得°像; tsông-leh ziang' 裝得°像

MINCE, *to hash fine*, tsæn se' 切°碎; *minced meat*, tsæn-leh se'-se-

go nyüoh' 切°得°細°碎个°肉°

MIND, *the intellect*, sing-kyi' 心機; *fine —*, sing-kyi' ling-ky'iao' 心機靈巧; — *or heart*, sing 心; sing-di' 心地; — *made up*, cü'-i ding'-de 主意定了°; *out of one's —*, shih-sing'-de 失心了°; sing wu'-de 心糊了°; *engraven on the —*, sing'-li k'eh'-tih 心裡刻的; — *confused*, sing lön' 心亂; wu-li'-wu-du' 霧裡糊塗; *to put him in —*, di-gyi deo' 提其頭; *to keep in —*, fông' læ sing zông 放在°心上; dzæ sing' 在心

MIND, *to obey*, t'ing'-dzong 聽從; t'ing 聽; i 依; i-dzong' 依從; *do not — it*, k'o-yi feh pih' dzæ i' 可以°弗必在意; *to attend to*, tông-sing' 當心; liu-sing' 留心; yüong sing' 用心; dziah' læ i'-li 着意; — *your own business*, siu ng'-go peng'-veng 守你°个°本弅; *ditto, in a good sense*, en-veng'-siu-kyi' 安弅守己

MINE, ngô'-go 我个°; *that book is —*, keh'-peng shü z ngô'-go 這°本書是我个°

MINE, *gold* kying sæn' 金山; *coal —*, me-k'ang' 煤坑; me-yiao' 煤窰; me-sæn' 煤山

MINER *in coal*, k'æ me-t'æn'-go nying' 開煤礦°个°人°; —*for gold*, dao-kying-sô'-go 淘金沙个°

MINERALOGY, kying-zah'-go 'oh-veng' 金石°个°學°問; kying-zih' ts-yüoh' 金石之學 (veng.)

MINGLE, to 'o-tæn'-long 和攏; to blend, diao-'o' 調和

MINISTER of state, da-dzing' 大臣; prime —, tsæ'-siang 宰相; cong-dông' 中堂; — of religion, kyiao'-s 教師

MINISTER, to serve, voh-z' 服事; to wait upon, tông-dzih' 當值; — to one's wants, tsiao'-ing 照應; tsiao'-kwun 照管; tsiao'-kwu 照顧

MINOR, under age, nyin-ky'ing'-go 年輕个°; nyin-siao'-go 年少个°; nyin-iu'-go 年幼个°

MINSTREL, dæn-ts'ông'-go nying 彈唱个°人°

MINT (for cash), cü'-dzin-gyüoh 鑄錢局; peppermint, bo-ho' 薄°荷°

MINUTE (in time), ih feng' 一分; — hand, dziang-tsing' 長針; minutes of a meeting, tsông-dzing' 章程;

MINUTE, si'-si 細細; dzih-si'-si 極°細; mi-mi kwun' do ziang hwe' ka 細°如°灰

MINUTELY, ts'-si 仔細; dziang-si' 詳細; to investigate —, ts'-si dzô-ts'ah' 仔細查察

MIRACLE, jing-tsih' 神跡; ling-tsih' 靈跡; to work a —, 'ang jing-tsih' 行°神跡

MIRE, wu na-nyi' 糊坭; wu-nyi-tsiang' 糊°坭漿

MIRROR, kying'-ts 鏡子; large —, tsiah'-i-kying 著衣鏡 (ih-min)

MIRTH, hyi'-siao-yin-k'æ' 喜笑顏開; noisy —, ho-lo'-da-siao' 呵呵°大笑

MISANTHROPIC, u'-su cong'-nying-go 惡衆人°个°

MISAPPREHEND, to li'-we-ts'o' 理會錯; — (in hearing), t'ing ts'o' 聽錯

MISBEHAVE, to feh-siu-veng' 弗守孖; feh-en-veng' 弗安孖; — one's self, feh en-veng' siu-kyi' 弗安孖守己

MISCALCULATE, to sön'-ts'o 算錯; iah'-ts'o 約錯

MISCALL, to eo-ts'o' 叫°錯; eo-dzæn 叫°綻

MISCARRIAGE, siao'-ts'æn 小產; do-loh' 墮產°

MISCELLANEOUS, koh-seh' koh-yiang' 各色各樣; zeh'-keh leng'-teng 雜件°; zeh-leng-kwu'-teng 零°星°什°物°; — articles, zeh-gyih' tong-si 雜°件° 東西; small ditto, se'-gyin tong'-si 碎件東西

MISCHIEF, to do — to things, sông-'æ' tong-si' 傷害東西; to make — (or great trouble), tsiao-'o' 招禍; jô 'o' 惹禍; seng-z'-ts'ông-'o' 生事闖禍; tattling is sure to make —, pun-teo shih'-wô pih' to z'-fi 搬說話必多是非

MISCHIEVOUS, nyih-siu', nyih-kyiah' 開° 手 閉° 腳; *will do harm*, iao ts'ông 'o' go 要 鬧禍 個°; — *disposition*, ts'ông 'o' p'e 鬧禍胚; — *like a monkey*, ziang weh-seng' ka 像猢°猻°樣°式°

MISCONDUCT, peh-tön' 'ang-we 不 端 行°爲; 'ang-we' feh loh'-dzih 行°爲弗直

MISCOUNT, *to* su-ts'o' 數錯; su-dzæn' 數綻

MISER, k'en'-dzæ-nu' 看財奴

MISERABLE, kw'u'-leh k'o'-lin 苦 得°可憐

MISERLY, pi'-si-go 鄙細個°

MISERY, kw'u'-næn 苦難; wæn'-næn 患難; tsæ-næn' 災難; 'o'-næn 禍難

MISFORTUNE, feh kyih'-li z-ken' 弗吉利事幹; feh jing'-liu z'-t'i 弗順溜事體; *to meet with a* —, p'ong'-djoh hwe'-ky'i z-ken' 逢°着°晦氣事幹

MISGIVINGS, ts'æ-nyi' 猜疑; *have* —, yiu ts'æ-nyi' sing 有猜疑心

MISGOVERN, *to* kwun'-li feh hao' 管理弗好; — (as an official), djü-li' pah'-sing ky'in' hao 治 理百姓弗好

MISINTERPRET, *to* ziang'-diao 詳壞°

MISJUDGE, *to* liao-ts'o' 料錯; k'en-ts'o' 看錯; *I misjudged him*, ngô ts'o', liao-gyi-feh-tao' 我錯料其弗到

MISLAY, *to place wrongly*, fông'-ts'o 放錯; fông'-dzæn 放綻;

*to forget* or *not know where laid*, feh'-tsiao en' læ 'ah-li' 弗知° 安在°何°處°

MISLEAD, *to* ta'-li-ts'o' 帶累錯; *he misled me*, gyi ta'-li ngô ts'o' 其帶累我錯; gyi 'æ'-ngô-ts'o' 其害我錯

MISMANAGE, *to* diao-du' feh hao' 調度弗好; bæn-li' feh-hao' 辦理弗好

MISPLACE, *to* fông'-ts'o 放錯; en-ts'o' 安錯

MISREPRESENT, *to* lön-shih'-tiao-pi' 亂說刁疲; wu-yin'-lön-dao' 胡言亂道

MISS, kwu-nyiang' 姑娘; *an officer's daughter*, siao'-tsia 小姐

MISS, *to* — *in throwing*, tiu feh-djoh' 丟弗着°; —*in firing, &c.*, tang'-feh-djoh 打弗着°; — *by omitting*, ts'o'-loh 錯落; — *an opportunity*, ts'o'-ko kyi-we' 錯 過機會

MISSING, feh-kyin'-de 弗見了°; m̃-dziah'-loh 無°着°落

MISSPEND, *to* yüong-ts'o' 用錯; *to squander money*, lông'-fi 浪 費; — *time*, ts'o'-ko kwông-ing' 錯過光陰

MIST, vi-vi'-si'-yü 微微細雨; yü'-mao-s' 雨絲; — *is falling*, læ-tih loh yü'-mao-s' 正在°下° 雨絲

MISTAKE, ts'o 錯; ts'o'-c'ü 錯 處°; dzæn 綻; *has many mistakes*, ts'o'-c'ü to-leh-kying' 錯

處多得°緊; ts'ih'-dzæn pah-
dzæn' 七綻八綻; ts'ih'-ts'o
pah'-ts'o 七錯八錯

MISTAKE, to ts'o'-ts'oh 錯錯°;
siang'-ts'o 想錯 (See Wrong);
k'en'-ts'o 看錯; — in recogniz-
ing a person, nying-ts'o' 認°
錯; — in speaking, kông'-ts'o
講°錯

MISTER, or MR., (to teachers, and
generally to all but artizans),
Sin-sang' 先生°; (to officers),
lao'-yia 老爺°; (to mechanics),
s-vu' 司務

MISTRESS, or MRS., (to a teacher's wife), s-meo' 師母; (to an
officer's wife), na'-na 奶奶; (to
an officer's mother), t'a'-t'a 太
太°; — of a house, nyü tong'-kô
女東家°; tong-kô' 東家'; lang-
z-bo'; Mrs Wông, Wông-s-meo'
王師母; Wông'-kô-sao 王家°嫂

MISTRUST, to sing'-li nyi-'oh' 心
裡疑惑; half trust, half —,
pun'-sing pun-nyi' 半信半疑

MISUNDERSTAND, to i'-s feh-
tong' 意思弗懂; to hear wrong,
t'ing'-ts'o 聽錯

MISUSE, to dæ-wa' 待壞°; k'eh'-
boh dæ 刻薄待; 'æ 害

MITIGATE, to kæn-ky'ing' 減°輕

MIX, to 'o-long' 和攏; 'o-tæn-
long'; c'ün'-long 攙攏; — (as
medicines), keh'-long 合°攏;
— smoothly, 'o-leh diao-yüing'
和得°調勻; diao-'o' 調和

MIXED, jumbled, kah'-dzeh 夾°
雜; — as men and women sitting
together, weng'-dzeh 混雜; —
confusedly, zeh-ts'ih' zeh-pah' 雜
七雜八

MOAT, city 'ao-'o' 濠河; dzing-
'o' 城河; wall and —, dzing-
dzi' 城池

MOB, to nao-z' 鬧事; the —, yia'-
ky'i pah'-sing 野°民°; the ex-
pedients of a — are numberless,
mæn'-fah sæn'-ts'in 蠻法三
千

MOCK, to tsao-siao' 嘲笑; c'ü'-
siao 取笑

MOCK elephant, tsông-bah-ziang'
裝扮°白°象

MODEL, form, or mold, mo-ts' 模
子; mo-yiang' 模樣; pattern,
yiang'-ts 樣子

MODEL, to form after a —, tsiao
mo'-ts tso' 照模子做; —
in clay, su 塑

MODERATE, is yiu tsih'-cü 有節
制; be —, yüong-tsih'-cü 用節
制; not too much, nor too little,
feh-to' feh-siao' 弗多弗少

MODERATE, to restrain, ah'-djü
壓°住; tsu'-djü 阻住; — the
fire, ho' long-leh iu'-tin 火弄
得°幽點

MODERATION, siu-lin' 收斂;
tsih'-cü 節制; prudence, kying-
we' 經緯; person of —,
nying yiu tsih-cü 人°有節
制; fond of —, æ siu-lin-go 愛

收 歛 个°; *having no* —, 卬-tsih'-cü-go 無° 節 制 个°; 卬-kying-we'-go 無° 經 緯 个°

MODERN *style*, z-shih' 時 式°; z-kw'un' 時 款; — *times*, tông kying' z-shü 當 今 時 世; — *times are not equal to the ancient*, kying-næn'-kæn peh-jü kwu-z-tsin' 今 不 如 古

MODEST, yiu lin-c'ü' 有 廉 耻; iao lin-c'ü' 要 廉 耻; min-bi boh' 面 皮 薄; — (as a girl), p'ô in'-siu 怕 羞

MODULATE, *to* — *the voice, singing* p'e'-teh diao-yüing' 聲 音 配 搭 調 勻

MOHAMMEDAN, We-ts' 回子 (ih-go) not respectful.

MOHAMMEDANISM, We-we'-kyiao 回 回 敎

MOIST, dziao 潮; dziao-sih' 潮 濕; *just* — *enough, as fresh food, &c.*, ts-jing' 滋 潤; *to become* —, fæn dziao' 氾 潮; wæn dziao' 還 潮

MOISTEN, *to* long-long' sib 弄 弄 濕; peh gyi ts-jing' 俾° 其 滋 潤; *to be moistened by rain*, ling-sih' 淋 濕

MOISTURE, dziao-sih' 潮 濕; sih'-ky'i 濕 氣; *much* —, dziao-sih' to' 潮 濕 多

MOLASSES, dông-lu' 糖 滷

MOLD, MOULD, *soft earth*, hao' nyi-nyüoh' 好 泥; *thick skinny* — (from damp), bah-fu' 白° 殕; pæn-mao' 斑 毛; *spoiled*

*from* —, me-læn'-de 霉 爛 了°

MOLD, MOULD, mo'-ts 模 子; mo'-yiang 模 樣; su'-ts 塑 子

MOLD, MOULD, *to* fah'- c'ih 發 出; —(with hairs), fah-pæn-mao' 發 斑 毛; fah hwô' 發 花; *to* — *a vessel*, dzing ky'i' 成 器; — (as clay), nyiah 捏; su'-c'ih-læ 塑 出 來; *to cast*, cü'-c'ih-læ 鑄 出 來; kyiao-c'ih'-læ 澆 出 來

MOLDER, MOULDER, *to* — *away*, (as wood, stone, &c.), dzin'-dzin siao-mo' 漸 漸 消 磨; — (as dead bodies, &c.), dzin'-dzin siao-hwô' 漸 漸 消 化

MOLDY, MOULDY, fah'- c'ih-de 發 出 了°; fah-bah-fu'-de 發 白° 殕 了°; fah-pæn-mao'-de 發 斑 毛 了°

MOLEST, *to* næn-we' 難 爲

MOLT, MOULT, *to* t'eng mao' 褪 毛; wun-mao' 換 毛

MOMENT, *a* ih-hyih' kong-fu' 一 歇 工 夫; ih-sin' kong-fu' 一 綫 工 夫; ih-tin' kong-fu' 一 點 工 夫; *wait a* —, teng' ih-hyih' 等 一 歇

MONARCH, kyüing-wông' 君 王; wông-ti' 皇 帝

MONARCHY, kyüing-cü'-ts koh' 君 主 之 國

MONASTERY, *Buddhist* z 寺; en 菴; *Taoist* —, kwun 觀

MONDAY, li-pa-ih' 禮 拜° 一; (according to the Roman Catholics), tsin-li-nyi' 瞻 禮 二°

MONEY, *silver*, nying-ts' 銀子；
nying-dzin' 銀錢；*cash*, dong-
din' 銅錢°；*dollars*, fæn-ping'
番餅；*travelling* —, bun-jün'
盤纏°

MONEY-BOX, dzin-dong' 錢筒；
dzin-teo' 錢斗

MONEY-CHANGER, dzin-tin'-kwun
錢店主°人°；*ditto's shop*, dzin-
tin' 錢店；*ditto small*, yin-de'-
tin 現兌店

MONEY-LENDER, fông - nying -
bun'-go 放銀盤利°；fông-dong-
din'-go 放銅錢个°；fông-tsa'-
go 放債°个°

MONGOLIAN, Mong-kwu'-nying'
蒙古人°；Dah-ts' 韃子

MONK, *Buddhist* seng-kô' 僧家°；
'o-zông 和尚；*Taoist* —, dao'-z
道士；dao'-kô 道家°；siu-dao'-
z 修道士；*Roman Catholic
monks* are styled, siang'-kong
相公

MONKEY, weh-seng' 猢°猻；'eo
猴

MONOPOLIZE, *to* — (in trade),
deng'-tsih 囤積

MONOPOLY, *to have a* — *of*,
doh-kwæn', doh-sah' 獨關獨
塞

MONSOON, *S. W.* si-nen' fong 西
南風；*N. E.* — tong-poh' fong
東北風

MONSTER, (departing from the
usual type), gyi-ying'-kwæ-ziang'
奇形怪°狀°

MONSTROUS, *large*, c'ih'-kah do
出格大°

MONTH, *a* ih-ko yüih' 一個月；
*the first day of the* —, ts'u-ih'
初一；*the beginning of the* —,
yüih-ts'u' 月初；*the middle of
the* —, yüih-pun' 月半；yüih-
pun-keng' 月半跟；yüih-cong'
月中；*the end of the* —, yüih-
ti' 月底

MONTHLY, yüih-yüih' 月月；me'-
yüih 每月

MONUMENT, pe 碑；*slab*, pe-ba'
碑牌；— *of antiquity*, kwu'-
tsih 古蹟

MOOD, *temper*, sing'-dzing 性情；
*in pleasant* — (time), hwun-hyi'
z-'eo' 歡喜時候

MOON, yüih-liang' 月亮；*new* —,
ngo-me' yüih 蛾眉月；*full* —,
yüih-liang' dön-yün' 月亮團
圓；yüih-liang' tsing'-dön-yün'
月亮正團圓

MOONLIGHT, yüih-kwông 月光

MOOR, *to* — *a boat*, boh jün' 泊°
船

MOPE, *to* kæn'-we-jing-z' 懶爲
人事

MORAL, *agreeing with the right*,
tsing'-kying 正經；tön-tsing' 端
正；tsing'-p'a 正派°；*the* —
(of a tale), ih-go yüong-dziang'
一個用塲；*the Chinese* —
*law*, ng'-dzông 五°常 viz. love,
justice, politeness, knowledge,
and truth.

MORAL *essays,* ky'ün'-shü-veng' 勸世文; jün-shü' 善書

MORALITY, *to exhort to —,* ky'ün nying' we jün' 勸人爲善; *to practise —,* 'ang jün' 行°善

MORE, *to* 多; *a little —,* to' tin 多點; to' ih-ngæn 多一點; liah-liah' to'-tin 略略多點; sao'-we to'-tin 稍爲多點; siao-shü' to'-tin 少許多點; shü-vi' to'-tin 些°微多點; *have* (you) *any —?* wa-yiu' ma 還° 有嗎°? *— than ten,* jih to 十多; *still —,* yüih-fah' to 越發多; yü-kô' to 愈加°多; keng'-kô to' 更加°多; *still — difficult,* yüih-fah næn' 越發難; *— than one,* feh ts' ih'-go 弗止一個°; *the — the better,* yüih to' yüih hao' 越多越好; *how much —,* (also how much less), 'o-hwông' 何况; *if I can walk it how much — should you* (be able to), ngô' tseo-leh-ky'i', 'o-hwông' ng' ni 我走得°去何况你° 呢

MOREOVER, hwông'-ts'ia 况且°; ping'-ts'ia 幷且°; r-ts'ia' 而 且°; tsæ-wô' 再話

MORNING, t'in-liang' or t'in'-nyiang 天亮; *early in the —,* tsao'-t'in-liang 早天亮; *ditto* (seven or eight o'clock), ts'ing-tsao' 清早; *the forenoon,* zông-pun'-nyih 上半日°; *the middle of the —,* tsao'-pun-zông' 早半

日°; *— star,* ng'-kang-hyiao 五°更°曉

MOROSE, *sour tempered,* geng-cü'-cü; *— in countenance,* min-k'ong' pæn'-pæn-go 面孔板 個°

MORROW, ming-tsiao' 明朝

MORSEL, ih tin-tin' 一點點; ih ti'-ti 一淸淸; *a mouthful,* ih-k'eo' 一口

MORTAL, we-si'-go 會死°个°

MORTAR, nyin-bu-tsu' 石°臼°; *large —,* tao'-gyiu 搗臼 (ih-bu); *— for mixing medicines,* jü-peh' 堅鉢; *the pestle,* but used for either pestle or —, tao-ts-den' 杵° (ih-go); *lime cement,* diao-hao'-liao-go zah-hwe' 調 好个°石°灰

MORTGAGE, ti'-ah ky'i' 抵押° 契; ti'-ah kyü 抵押°據; tin'-ky'i 典契

MORTGAGE, *to — as security for debt,* ti'-ah 抵押°; *to lease for a certain time and sum, and, at the end of the time, give up the pro-perty and receive the money back,* tin 典; *— a wife,* tin lao'-nyüing 典女°人°

MORTIFIED *flesh,* si nyüoh' 死° 肉°; wu nyüoh' 腐°肉°

MORTIFY, *to — him,* peh gyi t'æn-dæ 俾其坍臺; *extremely mor-tified* (ashamed), wông-k'ong'-vu-di' 惶恐無地; wông-k'ong-ŭ-c'ü-ky'i' 惶恐無°處去°

MORTISE, shing'-deo 榫頭; —
*fitting exactly,* teo shing' 合°榫

MOSQUITO, meng-djong 蚊°蟲;
— *curtain,* tsiang'-ts 帳子; —
*brush,* meng-djong' tæn'-tsiu 撣
蚊°蟲个°帚

MOSS, i; ts'ing-i; ts'ing-dæ 青苔

MOST, *very,* ting 頂; tse 最;
gyih 極; — *excellent,* ting' hao
頂好; gyih hao' 極好; dzih
miao' 絕妙; kyü tse' 居最;
kyü ting' 居頂; *he* (has) *the —,*
gyi, ting' to' 其頂多; *the —,*
or *the greater part,* ih do pun'
一大°半; — *of the night,* pun'
yia to' 半夜°多

MOSTLY *good,* kyiu' feng hao'
九分好; jih-yiu-kyiu' hao'
十有九好

MOTH, *any insect which eats clothes,
wood, &c.,* cü-djong 蛀蟲; *candle —,* fi-ngo'; p'i-sông'- wu-
diah' 撲°燈°蛾

MOTHER, ah-nyiang' 阿娘; ah'-
ṁ 阿媽°; ṁô' or ṁ-ṁô; (res-
pectful) meo'-lao 老母; (in
writing) meo'-tsing 母親; *my
deceased —,* sin-meo' 先母;
*my —,* kô-meo' 家°母; *your
—,* ling-dông' 令堂; lao' t'a-
t'a 老太°太°; *mother's older
sister,* yi-ṁô' 姨媽; *mother's
younger sister,* siao'-yi 小姨;
*mother's brother,* gyiu'- gyiu 舅
舅; *wife's—,* dziang'-ṁ 丈母°;
ngoh-meo' 岳母; *husband's —,*

ah-bo' 阿婆; nyiang'-nyiang
娘娘

MOTHER OF PEARL, yüing-meo'
k'oh' 雲母壳; — *shell,* lo-
din 螺鈿

MOTION, *in* læ'-tih dong' 正在°
動; (as a man, boat, &c.), læ'-
tih 'ang-dong' 正°在°行°動

MOTIONLESS, ih-ngæn' feh-dong'
一點弗動; dong-'a'-feh-dong'
動也'弗動; *sit perfectly —,*
zo'-jü T'a'-sæn 坐如泰°山

MOTIVE, i'-kyin 意見; i'-s 意
思; *has a —,* yiu sing 有心

MOTLEY, ng'-ngæn-loh-seh' 五°
顏°六色

MOULD, MOULDER, MOULDY,
MOULT, See MOLD, MOLDER,
MOLDY, MOLT.

MOUND, teng 墩; te 堆; — *of
earth and rubbish,* kao-sæn'-te
高山堆 (ih-go)

MOUNT, *to* tseo'-zông 走上; —
(as a scroll, or map), piao wô'
裱畫

MOUNTAIN, sæn 山; sæn-ling' 山
嶺 (ih-go); *the top of a —,* sæn-
ting-deu' 山頂頭°; *the foot of
a —,* sæn-kyiah-'ô' 山脚下°; —
*pass,* sæn-k'eo' 山口; sæn'-cü-
den'-go lu' 山嘴頭个°路

MOURN, *to bewail,* k'oh' 哭; *to
utter sorrowfully,* kông'-leh pe-
ts'ih' 講得°悲切

MOURNERS, yiu sông-z' cü'-kwu
有喪事主顧; —*following a*

*coffin,* song-sông'-go nying 送
襄 个°人°

MOURNFUL, sông-sing'-siang 傷
心相; *very* —, peh'-jing-siang'
不忍相

MOURNING, *to wear* — (properly
on the head, but used for all),
ta-hao' 帶孝°; *ditto* (properly for
distant relatives), c'ün-su' 穿素;
*to wear deep* —, ta djong' hao
帶重孝°; *to wear* — *for parents,* siu-cü' 守制; *white* — *dress,*
hao'-i 孝衣; *other* — *dress,*
su'-i 素衣; *to put on* —, (first
sackcloth, and then other garments), dzing-voh' 成服; *to
put off* —, mun-voh' 滿服 k'æ-
hweng' 開葷; *for whom do you
wear* —? ng' c'ün jü'-go su' 你°
穿誰°个素? (I) *wear* — *for
my father,* ta ah-tia'-go hao' 帶
阿爹个°孝°

MOUSE, *little rat,* siao lao-ts'' 小
鼠 (ih-tsah)

MOUTH, cü 嘴; cü'-pô 嘴巴; k'eo
口; k'eo'-deo 口頭; *tea-pot* —
(or spout), dzô-wu' cü' 茶壺嘴;
*tea-pot* — (or opening at the
top), dzô-wu' k'eo' 茶壺口

MOVABLE, hao-dong'-go 好動
个°; weh-dong'-go 活動个°

MOVABLES, dong'-yüong-jih-veh'
動用什物

MOVE, *to* dong 動; yi 移; pun
搬; *why do you not* —? ng dza'-
we ih-dong' feh-dong' 你°爲何°

一動弗動? — *a little,* yi'
ih-pô' 移一把; — *it away a
little,* yi-ko'-ky'i 移過去°; *can't
— (it),* dong'-feh-læ 動弗來;
dong'-feh-teh' 動弗得; — *to
another place,* tsæn-tsæn u' 移°
於別°處°; tsæn dæn'; — *to
another house,* pun oh' 搬屋; —
*to action,* ken'-dong 感動;
kyih'-dong 激動; — *to gratitude,* ken'-kyih 感激; *will* —
*the feelings,* we dong nying'-go
dzing 會動人°个情

MOW, *to* kah 割; — *grass,* kah
ts'ao' 割草

MUCH, *to* 多; yin'-ho; *not* —,
feh-to' 弗多; yiu-'æn 有限;
kyin'- liang 見量; kyin'-siao
見少; *too* —, t'eh to' 太多;
*a great deal too* —, to-zông'-
kô-to' 多上加°多; *so* —,
keh-tang'; ka-sing'; *how* —? to-
siao 多少? *as* — *as you please,*
ze ng' to-siao' 任你°多少;
*no matter how* —, feh-leng' to-
siao' 弗論多少; peh'-kyü to-
siao' 不拘多少; — *obliged
to you,* to-dzing' ng 多承你°;
to-zia' ng 多謝°你°; to-mong'
ng 多蒙你°; *ditto, or trouble
you* —, to-lao' ng 多勞你°

MUD, na-nyi-tsiang' 泥漿; wu-
nyi-tsiang' 腐°泥漿

MUDDY, *the road is* —, lu' ziang
tsiang ka 路如泥°漿; *dress is*
—, i-zông' tsao na-nyi dô' 衣

裳遭坭了°; *all —*, jing'-z na'-nyi 純是坭

MULBERRY *tree,* sông-jü' 桑樹; *mulberries,* sông-ko' 桑菓; sông-ts 桑子

MULE, lo-ts' 騾子 (ih-p'ih)

MULTIPLICAND *and multiplier,* siang dzing' 相乘

　　Taken from W.A.P. Martin's Ningpo Arithmetic.

MULTIPLICATION, dzing-fah' 乘法

MULTIPLY, *to* dzing-long' 乘攏

MULTITUDE *of people,* ih do'-dziao nying 一大°羣°人°; cong'-nying 衆人°

MUMPS, tô'-sæ 朶腮; *to have the —,* sang tô'-sæ 生°朶°腮

MUNITIONS *of war,* kyüing-tsông-ky'i'-kyiæ 軍裝器械

MURDER, *to* long-sah 弄°殺; tang'-sah 打殺; *— with a knife,* sah 殺; c'oh'-sah 㓬殺; *to plot —,* meo-sah' 謀殺

MURDERER, hyüong-siu' 兇手 (ih-go)

MURIATIC ACID, yin-gyiang'-shü 鹹強水°

MURMUR (*of water*), ts'ô'-ts'ô hyiang' 沒沒響; *— (of voices),* zeng-zeng'-hyiang; *to complain,* mao-ün' 埋°怨; *grumbling,* gæn-gæn'-tao-tao læ'-tih ün'.

MUSCLE, *or tendon,* kying 筋; *flesh,* nyüoh 肉°

MUSCLE *or* MUSSEL, (a shellfish), bang 蚌 (ih-go)

MUSCULAR, *great — strength,* kying'-lih tsông'-do 筋力壯大°

MUSHROOM, dzing 菌°; *dried —,* hyiang-dzing' 香菌°

MUSIC, yüoh 樂; tsoh-yüoh' 作樂 (veng.); *do you like to hear instrumental — ?* ng hwun-hyi' t'ing s-ing' kô'-sang feh 你°歡喜聽絲絃否°? — (blowing and beating), c'ü-c'ü tang-tang 吹°吹°打打; seng-siao'-kwu-dih' 笙簫鼓笛 (veng.)

MUSICAL *instruments,* yüoh-ky'i' 樂器; *brass ditto,* hyiang'-ky'i 响器; *— boxes,* pah'-ing-gying' 八音琴

MUSICIANS, tsoh-yüoh'-go nying 作樂个°人°; *trumpeters,* c'ü-sin' 吹°手; *players and singers,* dæn'-ts'ông-go nying 彈唱个°人°

MUSK, zô-hyiang' *or* dzô-hyiang' 麝香

MUSK-DEER, hyiang-tsông' 香麝 (veng.); *commonly called,* hyiang-li-mæn' 香狸貓°

MUSKET, nyiao'-ts'iang 鳥鎗; *foreign —,* yiang-ts'iang' 洋鎗; *breech-loader,* 'eo'-deo-meng 後頭門 (ih-kwun)

MUSLIN, *foreign bleached* p'iao'-bah yiang-pu' 漂白洋布; *unbleached foreign —,* peng'-seh yiang-pu' 本色洋布; *mull —,* yiang sô' 洋紗

MUST, pih'-iao 必要; tsong'-iao 總要; vu-pih'-ts-iao' 務必

要; ding-iao' 定要; — *have,*
siao'-feh-teh' 少弗得; — *not,*
m-nao'; feh-k'o 弗可; *certainly*
— *not,* ts'ih'-feh-k'o' 切弗可;
tön'-feh-k'o 斷弗可; tön'-jün
feh-k'o' 斷然弗可; tön'-wu
feh-k'o 斷乎弗可

MUSTACHE, zông'-bæn ngô-su'
上爿鬍°鬚°

MUSTARD (the plant), ka'-ts'æ
芥菜; — *seed,* ka'-ts'æ-ts 芥
菜子; *ground —,* ka'-lah-feng
芥°辣粉

MUSTER *strength, and press for-*
*ward,* nu'-lih zông-zin' 努力上
前°

MUSTY, *grown* ah'-ko-de 過過了
— *smell,* ah'-boh-ky'i 過°蒸°氣

MUTE, *deaf* ô'-ts 啞°子; ô'-pô-
ts 啞°吧子; *clock is —* (*i. e.*
stopped), z-ming'-cong ô'-de 自
鳴鐘啞°了°

MUTILATE, *to — the body,* long'-leh
s'-t'i feh djün' 弄得四體弗全

MUTINY, *to revolt,* meo-nyih'
kyih-tông' 謀逆結黨

MUTTER, *to — to one's self,* zi-wô-
deo-bun' 自言°自°語°

MUTTON, yiang-nyüoh' 羊肉°

MUTTONY SMELL (said by the
Chinese to be peculiar to some
foreigners), yiang-sao'-ky'i 羊
臊氣

MUTUAL, pe'-ts' 彼此; liang'-'ô
兩°下°; dô-kô' 大°家°; siang
相; — *pleaure,* pe'-ts' hwun-hyi'

彼此歡喜; — *recognition,*
liang'-'ô nying-teh' 兩下°認°
得; — *love,* dô-kô' siang-æ' 大°
家°相愛

MY, ngô-go' 我个°; — *older*
*brother,* kô-hyüong' 家°兄; —
*younger brother,* sô-di' 舍°弟; —
(humble) *cottage,* sô-'ô' 舍下°;
bi-sô' 敝舍°; sô'-kyin 舍°間;
— *country,* peng'-koh 本國;
— (humble) *country,* bi'-koh 敝
國; — *relatives* (of the same
surname), ah'-lah peng'-kô 我°
等°本家; — *own son,* ts'ing-
sang' ng-ts' 親生°兒°子

MYRIAD, ih-væn' 一萬

MYRRH, meh-yiah' 沒藥

MYSELF, ngô-zi' 我自°; *I saw*
*it —* (with my own eyes), ts'ing-
ngæn' k'en'-kyin-ko' 親眼°看
見過; ts'ing-ngæn moh'-tu 親
眼°目視

MYSTERIOUS, næn-ts'eh' næn-
ziang' 難測難詳; ao'-miao
奥妙 sing-ao' 深奥

MYSTICAL, *dark,* en'-dong-dong
暗洞洞

# N

NAIL, ting-cü' 釘銖 (ih-me);
*finger —,* ts'-k'ah 指甲°; *toe*
—, kyiah'-ts-k'ah' or kyiah'-
tsib-k'ah' 脚指甲°; *nails too*
*long,* ts'-k'ah hying' 指甲°興
(also used for pilfering).

NAIL, *to* ting 釘; yüong ting-cü′, ting′-ih-ting′ 用 釘 銖 釕 一 釕; *to drive a* —, k‘ao ting-cü′ 拷 釘 銖

NAKED, c‘ih′-sing-lu-t‘i′ 出 身 露 體; kwông-sing′ 光 身; c‘ih′-liao-siao 赤 條 條; c‘ih-lön-c‘ih-poh′ 出 卵° 出 膖 (vulgar); *upper part* —, c‘ih-poh′ 裸 體; *strip* —, i-zông′ poh-kwông′ 衣 裳 剝 光

NAME, ming-z′ 名 字; ming-deo′ 名 頭; *what is the* — *of this* (called)? keh′ kyiao soh′-go ming-z′ 這° 叫 甚° 麼° 名 字? *a man has three names, viz, ming* 名, z 字; ‘ao 號; *ming is given by parents; z is given by teachers;* ‘ao 號; bih-‘ao 別 號 *are chosen by himself, and changed at will; milk* — (only used by parents) na-ming 嬭 名; jü-ming 乳 名; *siao-ming*′ 小 名; *book or school* —, shü-ming′ 書 名; k‘ao′-ming 考 名; *family* —, sing′-su 姓 氏°; *what is your family* —? ng′ sing soh′ 你° 姓 甚° 麼? *your honorable ditto?* kwe′ sing 貴 姓? tseng sing′ 尊 姓? *a good* — (reputation), hao′ ming-sing′ 好 名 聲

NAME, *to* cü ming-z′ 取 名 字; lih ming′ 立 名; — *him John,* c‘ü′ gyi ming Iah′-‘en 取 其 名 約翰; *to call,* kyiao 叫 eo; ts‘ing-hwu′ 稱 呼; *how shall I* — *your teacher?* ng-go sin-sang′

ngô′ dza ts‘ing′-hwu gyi 你° 个° 先生° 我° 怎° 樣° 稱 呼 其?

NAMELESS, 씨 ming′-z 無° 名 字; *undistinguished,* 씨-ming′ 씨-sing 無° 名 無° 姓

NAMELY, ziu-z′ 就° 是

NANKEEN, ts′-hwô-pu′ 紫 花 布

NAP, *to take a short* —, hweh′-ih-hweh 眠°一°眠; hweh-ih-zông′; *ditto sitting,* tang-k‘eh′-c‘ong 打 瞌睡°; *take a long* —, kw‘eng′-ih-k‘ao 睡° 一 覺°; — *of cloth,* nyüong-deo′ 絨 頭

NAPKIN, *table* ky‘üoh′-væn siu′-kying 吃° 飯 手 巾

NARRATE *at length* or *particularly,* dziang-si′ kông′ ih-fæn′ 詳 細 講° 一 番

NARROW, ‘ah 狹°; ‘ah-tsah′ 狹° 窄; — *minded* (not liberal), ky‘i′-liang ‘ah-tsah′ 器 量 狹° 窄; sing-di′ ‘ah-tsah′ 心 地 狹° 窄; — *experience,* kyin′-sih ‘ah-tsah′ 見 識 狹° 窄

NASTY, *filthy,* nyi-sing′-pah-la 泥 腥 百 邋°; nyi-sing-pah-kyü′

NATION, koh′-kô 國 家; *all nations,* t‘in-‘ô′ væn-ming′ 天 下 萬 民

NATIONAL *expenditure,* koh′-kô-go yüong-du′ 國 家° 用 度

NATIVE, *n.* peng′-di-nying′ 本 地 人°; dziu-di′-nying′ 當°地 人° (ih-go)

NATIVE *dialect,* peng′-di wô′ 本 地 話; — *place,* peng′-hyiang

本鄉; peng'-t'u 本土; peng'-c'ü 本處; peng'-zih 本籍; — *productions*, t'u'-ts'æn 土產; — *cotton cloth*, du'-pu 土°布

NATIVITY *of Christ*, Yiæ-su' sing'-dæn 耶穌聖誕

NATURAL, t'in sang'-dzing-go 天生°成个°; — *disposition*, peng-sing sang'-dzing 本性生°成; *great* — *abilities*, t'in-ts'ong' t'in-ming' 天聰天明

NATURALLY, t'in-sing' s-jün' 天性使然

NATURE, *the course of* —, t'in-di' z-jün'-ts li' 天地自然之理; t'in-di' ts ky'i'-hwô 天地之氣化; *to investigate the* — *of things*, keh-veh' gyüong-li' 格物窮理; *human* —, nying'-go peng'-sing 人°个°本性

NAUSEATE, *will* — *him*, we peh gyi oh'-sing 會俾°其欲°嘔°

NAVAL *officer*, se'-s-kwun' 水°師官; — *commander*, se'-s di-toh' 水師提督

NAVEL, du'-dzi-ngæn' 肚臍眼°; — *cord*, dzi-ta' 臍帶°

NAVIGABLE, s'-leh-t'ong'-go 駛得°通个°

NAVIGATE, *to* — *a ship*, s jün' 駛船; 'ang jün' 行°船

NAVIGATOR, s-jün'-go-nying 駛船个°人°; 'ang-jün'-go-nying 行°船个°人°

NEAR, gying 近; siang-gying' 相近; dziu-gying' 就近; *very* —,

ting'-gying 頂近; *so* — *as to touch*, t'iah'-gying 貼近; vu-gying' 附近; — (like one's own friends, hence affectionate), ts'ing-gying' 親近; *nearer*, gying-tin' 近點; *nearest, or next*, kah-pih' 隔壁; *time drawing* —, z-'eo' ling-gying' 時候臨近; — (and therefore practicable), dzæ'-gying we-gying' 隨°近爲°事°

NEARLY, ts'ô'-feh-to' 差弗多; kyi-wu' 幾乎; — *alike*, siang-ky'ü' 相去; da-iah' ih-yiang' 大約一樣; zông'-loh vu-kyi' 上落無幾; liah-dong' 略同; — *there*, ziu hao' tao' 就°好到; kw'a tao'-de 快°到了°; — *night*, kw'a yia'-de 快°夜°了°; — *noon*, kw'a tsiu'-ko 近°午°; tsao' tsiu'-ko' 早°午°

NEAR-SIGHTED, gying'-z-ngæn' 近視眼°

NEAT, ts'ing-c'ü' 清泚; — (primarily, clear as water), pih-po'-s-ts'ing 碧波四清; ts'ing-kyih' 清潔

NEATLY *done*, tso'-leh ts'ing-c'ü' 做得°清泚

NECESSARIES, *all the* ih-ts'ih' sô yüong'-go 一切所用个°; *the seven* —, *viz., wood, rice, oil, salt, sauce, vinegar, and tea*, za, mi, yiu, yin, tsiang, ts'u, dzô, ts'ih'-go-z' 柴米油鹽醬醋茶七个°字

NECESSARY, pih'-iao 必要;

hyih'-feh-læ' 歇 弗 來; siao'-feh-teh' 少 弗 得; — or *important*, iao'-kying 要 緊; *very — to do*, feh'-teh-feh tso' 弗 得 弗 做

NECESSARILY, peh-teh'-yi 不 得 巳; m̄-fah' 無° 法; pih'-shü 必 須; m̄-næ'-'o 無° 奈 何; ẁa'-feh-læ 歇° 弗 來.

NECESSITY, *what is the —?* 'o-pih' ka iao'-kying 何 必 如° 此° 要 緊; 'o-yüong' ka dziah-kyih' 何 用 如° 此° 着 急; *there is a — in his going*, gyi pih' ky'iao-leh ky'i' (or ky'iah-leh.)

NECK, deo-kying' 頭 頸

NECKLACE, 'ông'-cü-c'ün' 項 珠 串; *mandarin's —*, dziao-cü' 朝 珠

NECK-TIE, ling'-ta 領 帶° (ih-diao)

NECROMANCER, kông-du'-sin-go 講° 肚 仙 个°; *female —*, du'-sin-bo' 肚 仙 婆

NECROMANCY, kông-du'-sin 講° 肚 仙

NEED, *in — of*, ky'üih'-siao 缺 少; ky'üih'-ky'in 缺 欠; ky'üih'-siao dziang-tön' 缺 少 長 短; *in — of fuel*, ky'üih'-siao za' 缺 少 柴°

NEED NOT, hao-vong' 不° 用°; feh-yüong' 弗 用; peh-pih' 不 必

NEEDFUL, iao'-kying 要 緊; iao-yüong' 要 用

NEEDLE, tsing 鍼 (ih-me); *to thread a —*, c'ün tsing-ngæn' 穿 鍼 眼°; *magnetic —*, ts'-nen'-tsing 指 南 鍼

NEEDLE-WORK, tsing-ts' sang-weh' 鍼 黹 生° 活; tsing-ts' 鍼 黹

NEEDLESS, hao hyih'-go 好 歇 个°; *quite —*, ih-ngæn' hao-vong' 一 點 不° 用°; — *work* (can be saved, or spared), sang-weh' hao sang'-go 生° 活 好 省° 个°

NEEDY, kyih'-pah 急 迫; kyih'-kyü 拮 据; siu'-deo tön'-ts'oh 手 頭 侷 促

NEGLECT, *to — duty*, feh-pô meng-veng' 弗 守° 名° 分; — *work*, sang-weh' yiu'-iao'-m̄-kying' tso' 生° 活 有 要 無° 緊 做; — *trade*, sang-i' feh kwu'-djoh 生° 意 弗 顧 着°; — *unintentionally*, shih kyin'-tin 失 檢 點; kwu'-tsih feh-tao'-kô 侍° 值° 弗 到 家°; *died from —*, kwu'-tsih feh-tao'-kô si'-de 侍° 值° 弗 到 家° 死 了°; *to slight*, shih-kwu' 失 顧

NEGLIGENT, ts'o-ts'o'-do-do' 蹉 蹉 跎 跎; *not diligent*, yiæ-dæ' 懈 怠; *careless*, hweh'-liah 忽 略; *inattentive*, feh-liu-sing' 弗 留 心

NEGOTIATE, *to transact business*, bæn z-t'i' 辦 事 體; — *peace*, nyi 'o' 議 和

NEGOTIATOR, bæn-z'-go 辦事
个°; *middle-man,* cong-nying'
中人°

NEGRO, heh'-nying 黑人°

NEIGH, *the horse neighs,* mô læ-tih
kyiao' 馬正°在°叫

NEIGHBOR, ling-sô'-kô 隣舍°家°;
ling-kyü' 隣居; *near—,* gying'-
ling 近鄰; *next —,* kah'-pih
t'iah'-ling 隔壁貼°鄰; *sur-
rounding neighbors,* s'-ling 四隣

NEIGHBORHOOD, s'-gying-s-yün'
di'-fông 四近四遠地方;
gying'-fông-zông 近个°地°方°;
zin-zin' 'eo-'eo di'-fông 前°前°
後後地方; *— just at the door,*
meng-zin'-meng-wu' 門前°
門戶

NEIGHBORING, in-ho'-siang-lin'
人°烟°凑°集°

NEITHER, NOR, feh 弗; yia feh
也°弗; yi feh 又°弗; *neither
cold, nor hot,* feh'-lang-feh-nyih'
弗冷°弗熱°; *neither here nor
there,* yia feh læ dông'-deo, yia
feh læ keh'-deo 也°弗在°這°
裡°也°弗在°那°裡°; *— will
go,* ih-go tu feh ky'i 一個都
弗去°; *neither one th'ing nor the
other,* feh ts'eng' feh gao.

NEPHEW, *brother's son,* dzih-ts' 姪
子; *sister's son,* nga-sang' 外°
甥°; *a sister calls her brother's
son,* ne-dzih' 內姪

NERVE, nao'-kying-sin 腦筋線
(coined).

NEST, k'o 窠; *edible swallows' —,*
in'-o 燕窩; *— of th'eves,* zeh-
k'o' 賊窠; zeh-o-kô' 窩賊°家°

NESTORIANS, Kying'-kyiao 景教

NET, *fishing* mông 網°; *small ditto,*
pæn-tseng' 扳罾; *— for the
hair,* mông'-kying 網°巾 (formerly worn by Chinamen); *mosquito —,* tsiang'-ts 帳子; *—
weight,* jih kying liang' 實勘
兩; *how much is the — weight?*
zing' djong to-siao' 淨重多少?
djü zing' to-siao djong' 除淨多
少重? djü bi' to-siao djong' 除
皮多少重? *—profit,* zing' dzæn
淨賺; *—goods,* zing' ho 淨貨

NEUTER, *to remain neutral,* liang'
feh-siang-dzu' 兩弗相助;
*neither male nor female,* peh'-nen-
peh-nyü' 不男不女

NEVER, dzong m̄'-neh 從沒°有°;
dzong-læ m̄'-neh 從來沒°有°;
tsong m̄'-neh 終究°沒°有°
(tsong or cong); *— (hereafter),*
üong'-feh 永弗; *— can,* cong'
feh-neng'-keo 終弗能彀; *—
saw,* dzong m̄'-neh k'en'-kyin-ko
從沒°有°看見過; *— heard
of it,* 'ao-vu t'ing'-meng-ko 毫
無聽聞°過; *— heard of such
a thing,* dzong sang ng' to m̄'-
neh t'ing'-meng keh'-cü-ka z-t'i
從生耳°朶以°來°沒°有°
聽聞°這°些°事體; *will —
come again,* üong'-feh tsæ læ' 永
弗再來; *— gets angry,* üong'-

feh sang ky'i' 永 弗 生°氣;—
yct, dzong feh zing' 從 弗 曾

NEW, sing 新; *just* —, ts'oh' sing
礐 新; ts'oh'-kwah-sing 礐 刮
新; ts'oh-tsæn'-sing 礐 蕿 新;
— *fashioned*, z sing' 時 新;—
*pattern*, sing yiang'-shih 新 樣
式; — *comer*, bao'-z læ'-go 暴
時 來 个°; ts'u læ'-go 初 來
个°; — *Testament*, Sing-iah'-shü
新 約 書

NEW-YEAR'S *day*, tsing'-yüih ts'u-
ih' 正 月 初 一; — *eve*, sæn-
jih nyin yia' 三 十 年 夜°;
nyiæn-kyin' yia' 廿 九 年°夜°;
— *money* (given to children, or
servants), ah-shü-din' 謁 歲
錢°; — *gifts*, nyin-yia' li-veh
年 夜°禮物; ko-nyin'-go li 過
年 个°禮

NEWS, sing'-sih 信息; siao-sih' 消
息; sing-veng' 新 聞; *to let out
the* —, t'ong-fong' pao-sing' 通
風 報 信

NEWSPAPER, sing'-veng-pao 新
聞 報; sing-veng-ts' 新 聞 紙

NEXT, *the second*, di-nyi' 第 二°;
— *day*, di-nyi' nyih 第 二°日°;
— *month*, 'o'-ko yüh 下°個月;
— *year*, ming nyin' 明 年; nen
nyin'來°年°; *sit* —, t'iah'-gying
zo 貼°近坐; *ditto, or in the same
row*, bing-ba' zo 並 排°坐; —
(house, &c.), t'ih'-kah-pih 貼°隔
壁; — *neighbor*, t'iah'-ling 貼°
隣; *do that* — (after doing

this), keh'-go mæn' ih-bu tso'
這°个°慢一步做

NIBBLE, *to* k'eng 齦; k'eng'-
ky'üoh 齦吃°

NICE, *pleasing*, cong'-i 中 意;
hao 好

NICELY *done*, tso'-leh tsing-cü' 做
得°精 緻

NICHE, *hole made in a partition*,
pih-dong' 壁 洞

NICKNAME (given in derision),
ts'iao-'ao' 綽 號; weng'-'ao 混
號; *to* —, c'ü'-ming-ts'iao-'ao'
取 名 綽 號

NIECE, *brother's daughter*, dzih-
nyü' 姪 女; *sister's daughter*,
nga-sang-nön' 外°甥°女°; *wife's*
—, ne'-dzih-nyü' 內 姪 女;
*niece's husband*, dzih-si' 姪 壻;
ne'-dzih-si 內 姪 壻

NIGHT, yia-tao' 夜°到; *in the* —,
yia-li' 夜°裡; yia-deo' 夜°頭;
*spend the* —, soh-yia' 宿夜°; ko-
yia' 過夜°; hyih-yia' 歇夜°;
djü-yia' 住夜°; *nearly* —, kw'a-
yia' 快°夜°; *dark* —, heh'-yia
黑夜°; *last* —, zô yia' 昨夜°;
*tomorrow* —, nning-tsiao' yia'-tao
明朝夜°到; *to do at* —, lin
yia' tso 連夜°做; *all* —, ih-
yia' 一夜°; tsing'-yia 正夜°;
*late at* —, yia-sing' 夜°深; yia-
zing'-kang'-sing 夜°盡更深;
*up all* —, ngao yia'; tæn-koh
yia' 玁擱夜°; *watch at* — *with
the sick*, be-yia' 陪夜°; *to watch*

at —, siu-yia′ 守夜°; *to sit up all* —, zo-yia′ 坐夜°

NIGHT-DRESS, kw'eng′-i 睡°衣

NIGHTLY, yia-yia′ 夜°夜°; me-yia′ 每夜°

NIGHT-MARE, fah-in′ 發魘; *shü*- t'ah ah 水獺壓; *has the* —, læ-tih fah-in′ 正°在°發魘

NIMBLE, ky'ing-kw'a′ 輕快°

NINE, kyiu 九; — *fold*, kyiu′-be 九倍; — *tenths*, kyin′ feng 九分

NINETEEN, jih-kyiu′ 十九

NINETY, kyiu′-jih 九十

NINTH, *the* di-kyiu′-go 第九个°

NIP, to — *with the fingers*, tih 摘

NIPPERS, gyin 箝; gyin-ts′ 箝子 (ih-kwun)

NIPPLE, na-deo′ or na-den′ 媽°頭; na-ts′ 媽°子 (ih-go)

NIT *of a louse*, seh′-ts 蝨子; kyi′-ts 蟣子 (ih-go)

NITRE, siao 硝; yin-siao′ 鹽硝

No, feh 弗; m̄ 無°; (I cannot) feh-neng′ 弗能; — (not willing) feh-k'eng′ 弗肯; — *one*, m̄-nying′ 無°人°; — *matter*, m̄-kao′; m̄-kwæn′-dzih 無°關涉; — *use*, m̄-yüong′ 無°用; — *matter which*, feh-leng′ 弗論; — *help for it*, m̄-fah′ 無°法; m̄-shih′-fah 無°設法; shih′-fah-næ′-'o 失法奈何

NOBILITY, yiu tsiah′-we cü′-kwu 有爵°位人°; *the five ranks of* — *viz*, kong, 'eo, pah, ts, nen, 公, 侯, 伯, 子, 男

NOBLE, *of* — *rank*, yiu tsiah′-we 有爵°位; *disinterested*, yiah-ky'i-go 俠氣个°; *will not stoop to anything dishonorable*, üong′-feh tao ze′-ky'i 永弗倒銳°氣; *generous*, k'ông′-k'æ 慷慨

NOBODY, m̄-nying′ 無°人°; — *is there*, m̄-nying′ læ′-kæn 無°人°在°彼°

NOD, to — eo′-eo deo′ 僞°僞°頭; tin-tin deo′ 點點頭

NOISE, hyiang 響; sing-hyiang′ 聲響; *no* —, m̄-sing′-hyiang 無°聲響; m̄ hyiang′-dong 無°響動; — *of the sea*, hæ′-shü hyiang 海水°響

NOISY, nao-nyih′ 鬧熱°; *very* — ziang loh-ying′-fæn′-ky'i ka 像°六營反起; nao-nyih′-bang-sang′ 鬧熱°非常°; — *voices*, da-sing′ hen′-kyiao 大°聲喊叫; — *and troublesome to neighbors*, ts'ao′-ling′-mô′-sô 噪鄰罵舍

NOMINAL, *only in name*, yiu-ming′-vu-jih′ 有名無實

NONE, *have* m̄-neh 沒°有°; m̄′-teh; — *or no one could do*, m̄-nying′ neng′-keo tso 無°人°能彀做

NONSENSE, *talk half in play, half in earnest*, pun′-byi-pun-tso-shih-wô′ 半嬉半眞°說話; *foolish talk*, wu-du′ shih-wô′ 糊塗說話; *wild talk*, lön wô′ 亂話; yia′ wô 野°話

NOON, tsiu′-ko 當°晝; tsing′-wu-

z 正午時; nyih-deo dzih' 日°
頭直; cong-wu' 中午; *past*
—, tsiu'-ko ko'-de 畫午過
了°; *rest at* —, hyih tsiu' 歇
畫; *before* —, tsao tsiu'-ko 早
午°

NOR, See NEITHER.

NORTH, poh 北; poh'-pin 北邊;
*to go* —; hyiang poh' ky'i 向
北去°; *nose to the* —, *or dead*,
(because corpses were formerly
so placed), bih-deo' dziao poh'
鼻頭朝北

NORTH-EAST, tong-poh' 東北;
— *west*, si-poh' 西北

NORTH-STAR, poh'-teo-sing 北
斗星

NOSE, bih-deo-kwun' 鼻頭管;
— *bleed*, bih-deo c'ih 'ong' 鼻°
頭°出紅; *follow your* —, (*i.e.*
go straight ahead), bang bih'-
deo' 撞鼻°頭

NOSEGAY, ih-nyiah hwô'一紮°花

NOSTRIL, bih-deo-kwun ngæn 鼻°
孔°

NOT, feh 弗; m̀ 無°; m̀'-neh;
— *understand*, feh tong' 弗懂;
*is it so or* —? z-ka' feh 如°此°
否°; — *so*, feh' z-ka' 弗如°此°;
*if* — *so*, feh-jün' 弗然; *must*
—, m̀-nao'; *ought* —, feh-k'o'
弗可; *have* —, m̀-yiu' 沒°
有; — *a cash*, ih'-go dong-diu'
tu m̀'-teh 一個銅錢°都沒°
有°; — *yet*, feh-zing' 弗曾;
*have you finished or* —? tso'-hao-

leh feh' 做好了°否°? tso-
hao'-liao m̀-'teh 做好了嗎°?
— *finished*, m̀'-teh tso'-hao 沒°
有°做好; — *at all sick*, ih-
ngæn' m̀-neh næn-ko' 一點沒°
有°難過

NOTABLE, c'ih-ming'-go 出名
个°; veng-ming'-go 聞名个°

NOTCH, *cut a* —, kah' ih-go ky'üih
割一个°缺; *notched* (like
teeth), keo-ky'üih-ngô' 像°鋸°
齒°; *knife-blade is notched*, tao
t'eng-ky'üih'-de 刀殘°缺了°

NOTE, *billet*, bin-z' 便字; z-den'
字條° (ih-go); *bank* —, p'iao'-
ts 票紙; dzin-p'iao' 錢°票;
nying-p'iao' 銀票; — *of hand*,
we-p'iao' 匯票; — *in music* (a
character), ing'-ao 音號; *ditto*
(a sound), yüoh'-ing 樂音;
*native ditto*, pæn'-ngæn 板眼°

NOTE, *to* — *down*, kyi 記; loh
錄; — *in a* — *book*, kyi'-læ kao'-
peng-li 記在°稿本裡; *to
take notes*, ts'ao-loh' 抄錄; *brief*
(or culled) *notes*, tsah-ts'ao 摘抄

NOTE-BOOK, *scholar's* kao'-peng
稿本; *memorandum book*, dzeng-
kyi'-bu 存記簿

NOTHING, m̀-kao' soh-go 沒°有°
甚°麼°; ih-ngæn' m̀-kao'; — *to
say*, m̀-kao' soh-go hao wô' 沒°
有°甚°麼°好話; — *to me*,
teng-ngô' m̀-kwæn-dzih' 與°我
無°關涉; ü-ngô' vu-kwæn'
於我無關; *good for* —, fi'-

veh 廢 物; hyiu'-moh 朽 木;
*produced from* — (as unfounded
tales), vu cong' seng yiu' 無 中
生 有; — *to fear*, feh-fông'-
teh 弗 妨 得; feh-dzæ'-wu; —
*else*, m̄-kao bih'-yiang 沒° 有°
別 樣; — *but this*, djü-ts'-ts
nga m̄-kao' bih'-yiang 除 此
之 外° 沒 有° 別 樣

NOTICE, kao'-bah 告 白°; cü-
tæn' 知 單; cü-tsiao' 知 照
(ih-tsiang)

NOTICE, *to* li'-we 理 會; *to perceive*, kyüoh'-teh 覺 得; *to see*,
k'en'-kyin 看 見; *did you —
the eclipse?* wu-jih' ng yiu li'-we
ma 蝕° 日 你° 有 理 會 嗎°?
*I noticed it*, ngô li'-we-ko-de 我
理 會 過 了°; *I did not — it*,
ngô feh-læ'-kwu 我 弗 來 顧;
·ngô shih-kwu'-de 我 失 顧
了°

NOTIFICATION, *an official* —,
kao'-z 告示; — (of literary advancement), pao'-tæn 報 單; —
(of the death of a friend), fu'-ing
訃 音

NOTIFY, *to* t'ong-pao' 通 報; cü-
we' 知 會; *to inform*, t'ong-cü'
通 知; — *officially*, c'ih kao'-z.

NOTION, *I have some* — (of it)
ngô' yiu tin i'-s 我 有 點 意 思

NOTIONAL, kæn-ka' 尷 尬

NOTORIOUS, cong'-k'eo-næ'-næ 衆
口 喃° 喃°; cong'-nying tu
byiao'-teh 衆 人 都 曉 得;

*notoriously bad*, ba-ts' ts'iu' 醜°
名°

NOTWITHSTANDING, dæn'-ming
但 憑°; sih'-t'ing 悉 聽°; zing'-
bing 任 憑; — *his prohibition,
I will gamble*, sih'-t'ing gyi-dza'
kying'-djü ngô we tu' 悉 聽°
其 怎° 禁 住 我 會 賭

NOUN, jih-z'-ngæn 實 字 眼°

NOURISH, *to* tsiang' tsing-lih' 長
精 力; — *the body*, yiang sing-
t'i' 養 身 體

NOURISHING, yiu-lih'-go 有 力
個°; we-sang-lih'-go 會 生° 力
個°; we-tsiang'-kying-kweh' 會
長 筋 骨

NOVEL *and strange*, sing gyi' 新
奇; — *mode*, sing-tsoh' veng-
fah 新 作 文 法

NOVEL, *n.* 'æn-shü' 閒° 書; siao'-
shü 小 書 (ih-peng)

NOVICE, *beginner*, ts'u-'oh'-go 初
學° 個°; sang-siu' 生° 手; —
*in religion*, sing' jih-kyiao'-go
新 入 教 個°

NOW, næn'-kæn 刻° 下°; keh-zông'
這° 息°; yiu-dzæ' 現 在; moh-
yüo' 目 下; mô; jü-kying' 如
今; ngæn'-zin 眼 前°; tsih'-
moh 卽 目

NOW-A-DAYS, kying-næn'-kæn
當 今° 之° 世° or 今 日° 者°;
— *it is different*, kying-z'-koh'-
bih 今 時 各 別

NOWHERE *to be found*, tao'-c'ü
zing-pin' zing'-feh-djoh' 到 處

尋°遍尋°弗着°; *is* —, ɑ̄-c'ü' yiu 無°處有°; ih-c'ü' tu ɑ̄'-teh 一處都沒°有°

NOWISE, bing'-fi 並非; tön'-tön-feh 斷斷弗

NOXIOUS *vapor*, doh-ky'i' 毒氣

NUISANCE, ngæ-nying'-ts-veh 碍人°之物; *commit no* —, (*i. e.* forbidden to pollute), kying'-ts u-w̄e' 禁止污穢

NULL, ɑ̄-tso'; vu yüong' 無用

NUMB, mô-moh' 麻木; mô tseh'-long; *perfectly* —, moh dzih'-dzih 木直直

NUMBER, su'-moh 數目; *the whole* —, tsong' su 總數; *the science of numbers* sön'-fah 算法; *in great numbers*, su'-moh to' 數目多

NUMBER, *to* su'-su-k'en 數數看; su-ih'-su 數一數

NUMBERLESS, su'-feh-pin 數弗遍; peh-kyi'-gyi-su' 不計其數; vu-ts'in'-da-væn 無千大萬; leng'-ts'in-leng-væn' 論千論萬

NUMBERS, mô'-ts 碼子; su'-moh 數目

| | | | | | |
|---|---|---|---|---|---|
| 1. | one, | ih. | 一 | 壹 | 丨 |
| 2. | two, | nyi. | 二 | 貳 | 丨丨 |
| 3. | three, | sæn. | 三 | 叁 | 丨丨丨 |
| 4. | four, | s. | 四 | 肆 | ㄨ |
| 5. | five, | ng. | 五 | 伍 | ㄡ |
| 6. | six, | loh. | 六 | 陸 | 丄 |
| 7. | seven, | ts'ih. | 七 | 柒 | 丄丨 |
| 8. | eight, | pah. | 八 | 捌 | 丄丨丨 |
| 9. | nine, | kyiu. | 九 | 玖 | ㄨ |

| | | | | |
|---|---|---|---|---|
| 10. | ten, | jih. | 十, 拾, | 什 |
| 100. | ih-pah'. | | 一百, 壹佰 | |
| 1000. | ih-ts'in'. | | 一千, 一阡 | |
| 10,000. | ih-væn. | | 一萬, 壹萬 | |
| | | | 万 | |

NUMEROUS, to'-leh-kying 多得°緊; hyü'-to 許多; yiu'-ho

NUN, *Buddhist* nyi-kwu' 尼姑; nyü' 'o-zông' 女尼°; *long haired* —, s-kwu' 師姑; — *who makes no change in dress*, ta'-fah-siu-'ang' 帶°髮修行°; *Taoist* —, dao'-kwu 道姑; *Roman Catholic* —, siu-dao' kwu-nyiang' 修道姑娘

NUNNERY, *Buddhist* en 菴; en-dông' 菴堂; *Roman Catholic* —, nyü' siu-dao-yün' 女修道院

NUPTIAL *ceremonies*, kô'-c'ü-go li'-tsih 嫁°娶禮節; *to perform ditto*, 'ang kô'-c'ü-go li' 行°嫁°娶禮; 'ang hweng-ing'-go li' 行°婚姻禮; tso-ts'ing' 成親; hao'-nyih 好日°; dzing-hweng' 成婚; — *presents*, jing-dzing' 人情; *ditto* (to groom), 'o-li' 賀禮; *ditto* (to bride), song-kô' 送嫁°

NURSE *for children*, ling siao-nying' go a-ɑ̄' 領小人°个阿姆; — *for sick person*, z'-dzih bing-nying' go 侍值病人°个; tông-dzih'-go cü'-kwu 當值个人°; *wet* —, ah-bu' 阿婷; na'-ah-bu 嬭阿婷

NURSE, *to suckle*, ü na' 餧嬭; *to*

*— the sick,* z'-dzih bing-nying' 侍
值病人°; tông'-dzih bing-nying'
當值病人°
NUT, *kernel,* nyüoh 肉°; *walnut
meat,* wu-dao nyüoh' 胡桃肉°
Nuts are considered as fruits.
NUT-GALL, ng'-be-ts 五°倍子
NUTMEG, nyüoh-ko' 肉°菓
NUTRITIOUS, we-sang-lih' 會生°
力; we-pu-hyüih'-ky'i 會補
血氣
NUT-SHELL, k'oh 壳

## O

OAK, ziang'-jü 橡樹 (ih-cü)
OAKUM, mô-kying' 麻筋
OAR, tsiang 槳 (ih-ts)
OATH, vah-tsiu' 罰咒; *to make a
great —,* vah-zing do-tsiu' 罰
甚大°咒 *to violate an —,* vah-
tsiu' feh-tsoh'-cing 罰咒弗作
準; vah-tsiu' feh-sön-su' 罰咒
弗算數; *violates oaths with ease,*
vah-tsiu' tông ko'-ts ky'üoh' 輕°
於°罰°咒°
OATMEAL, yiu'-mah-feng 油麥粉
(Mandarin)
OATS, yiu'-mah 油麥
OBDURATE, sing-dziang' ngaug'
心腸硬; *disposition — as iron
and stone,* t'ih'-zah sing-dziang'
鐵石心腸; t'ih'-tang sing-
dziang' 鐵打心腸
OBEDIENT, k'eng t'ing wô' 肯聽
話; we-i-jing'-go 會依順个°;
ao-ao'-ing-go 諾°諾°之°聲°;

*— to the letter,* i'-diao-dzih-vong'
依條直縫; *— in all respects,*
pah'-i-pah-jing' 百°依百°順;
vi-ming'-z-dzong' 惟命是從
OBEISANCE, *to make* ts'ing-ts'ing'
請請; *— with folded hands,*
tsoh-ih' 作揖; *— by falling on
the ground,* p'oh-tao pa' 仆倒
拜°; *— by knocking the head,*
k'eh deo' 磕頭
OBEY, *to* i-jing' 依順; i-dzong'
依從; t'ing 聽
OBJECT *in coming,* læ-i' 來意;
*— in going,* ky'i'-i 去°意; *attained the — of desire,* sô siang'-
vông, tao-siu'-de 所想望到
手了°
OBJECT, *to* p'i-bing' 批評; p'i-
poh' 批駁
OBJECTION, *have you any —* (to
offer)? ng yiu soh' go p'i-bing'
ni 你有甚°麽°批評呢°? 
*ditto to my going out?* 'o-fông'
peh ngô tseo'-c'ih 何妨俾我
走出呢? *no —,* peh-fông'
不妨
OBLATION, *sacrifice,* tsi'-veh 祭
物; kong'-vong-go tong-si' 供
奉个°東西
OBLIGATION, *you are under no —
to do it,* ng' k'o, peh-pih' tso 你°
可不必做; *cannot forget my
—,* ko'-sing-feh-ky'i 過意弗
去°; ken'-kyih-feh-zing' 感激
弗盡; *no end to my —,* ken-
eng-feh-zing' 感恩弗盡

OBLIGATORY, li'-tông-kæ' 理當
該;— *upon men to keep the Sab-*
*bath,* nying siu li'-pa, li sô tông-
jün'-go 人°守禮拜理所當
然个°。

OBLIGE, *to compel,* ngang-k'ô' 逼°
勒°; min'-ky'iang-iao' 勉强要;
gyiang'-iao 强要; — *him to*
*write,* ngang-k'ô' gyi sia 逼°勒°
其寫; leh' gyi sia 勒其寫°。

OBLIGED, ǎ-næ'-'o 無°奈何;
shih'-fah-næ'-'o 失法奈何;
peh-teh'-yi 不得已; — *to use*
*it,* shih'-fah-næ'-'o yüong' 失法
奈何用; *much* — *to you* (*i. e.*
see your kindness), kyin ng'-go
dzing' 見你个°情; *ditto* (see
your great kindness), tsoh'-kyin-
zing'-dzing 足見盛情; *ditto,*
fi-sing' 費心; fi-jing' 費神; to-
mong' 多蒙; *ditto* (have put you
to much trouble), to-lao' 多勞;
*I will be much* — *to you, if you*
*will go to the city for me,* ngô iao
fi ng'-go jing' tao dzing-li' ky'i
ih-da' 我要費你°个°神到
城裡去°一揀

OBLIGING, kwun-min' 冠冕; pah-
min'-kwông 八面光; iao-t'ao'-
hao' 要討好; we-t'ao'-hao' 會
討好; (the last two have a
selfish motive.)

OBLIQUE, zia 斜°; ts'ia; dzia;
hwa 歪

OBLITERATE, *to blot out,* du-diao'
塗壞°

OBLONG, dziang-fông' 長方

OBLOQUY, zoh-mô' 辱罵; *to*
*endure* —, ziu zoh-mô' 受辱罵

OBSCENE, yiu-ky'iang'-weh-diao'
油腔滑調; — *talk,* yiu wô' 油
話; — *books,* ying shü' 淫書;
— *pictures,* c'ing kong' 春宮

OBSCENITY, ying-lön' z-ken 淫
亂事幹

OBSCURE, heh'-en 黑暗; moh-
ts'eh'-di-en' 墨漆°地暗; —
*ideas,* i'-s k'en' feh-ming'-bah-go
意思看弗明白°个°; —
*by clouds,* be yüing' tsô-djü' 被
雲遮°住

OBSCURITY, *to retire into* —
(usually leaving one's family,
&c.), ing'-loh 隱落; *in* — (*i.e.*
don't know any thing about
him), ing'-sæn loh-dao'-de 隱山
避°世了°; *ditto, as an officer,*
feh-c'ih-z' 弗出仕

OBSEQUIES, sông-li' 喪禮; sông-
z' 喪事

OBSEQUIOUS, pe-kong'-ky'üih-tsih'
卑躬屈節; — *and designing,*
li to' pih tsô' 禮多或詐

OBSERVANT, we liu-sing' k'en'
會留心看; *not* —, kwu'-tsih
feh-tao'-go 侍°值°弗°到个°

OBSERVATIONS, *to take* —, (of
the stars, &c.), ts'eh'-liang 測量

OBSERVATORY, *astronomical* kwun
t'in-ziang'-dæ 觀天象臺

OBSERVE, *to see,* k'en 看; *to take*
*notice,* li'-we 理會; *not to* —

(when one ought to —), shih-kwn' 失顧; — *the laws*, sin koh'-fah 守國法

OBSOLETE, feh-tsoh'-de 弗作了°; tsoh'-ko-de 不° 行° 了°; — *as fashions, &c.*, ko-z'-de 過時了°

OBSTACLE, fông-ngæ' 妨礙; tsu'-ngæ 阻礙; *serious* — , kwæn-ngæ' 關礙; *in spite of all obstacles*, fong-yü', vn-tsu' 風雨無阻; *meets with many obstacles*, p'ong'-djoh hyü'-to fông-ngæ' 逢°着° 許多 妨礙

OBSTINATE, tsih-ih' 執—; kwu'-tsih 固執; nying-dzih' feh-cün-wæn' 認°直弗轉彎; —(as a child, servant, or inferior), sah-gyiang' 撒强

OBSTRUCT, *to hinder*, læn-tsu' 攔阻; tsu'-djü 阻住; *to stop up*, seh'-sah 塞煞; üong'-sah 壅煞

OBSTRUCTED, feh-t'ong' 弗通; — *breath*, ky'i' feh-t'ong'-de 氣弗通了°

OBTAIN, *to* teh'-djoh 得着; teh'-tao-siu 得到手; *difficult to* —, næn teh'-go 難得个; *have obtained my wish*, ngô sô siang'-vông tao-siu'-de 我 所 想望到手了°

OBTRUSIVE, gah-gah'-dong'-go 辯辯動个°; iao gah-long'-læ 要辯攏來; (duck wants to be goose), æn'-gah-ngo'-de' 鴨°鵝隊

OBTUSE, *blunt*, deng 鈍;— *mind*, ts'-tsih deng 資質 鈍; *stupid*, nyü 愚; nyü-beng' 愚笨

OBVIATE, *to* pa'-pu 擺°佈; ts'a'-bæn 措辦; *these difficulties can be obviated*, keh'-sing næn'-c'ü hao pa'-pu 這 些° 難處 好擺°佈

OBVIOUS, hyin'-kyin 顯見; ming-tông'-tông 分° 明°

OCCASION, *opportunity*, kyi-we' 機會; *take* — , ts'ing' kyi-we' 趁機會; *on this* — , keh' ih-ts'' 這° 一次; keh ih-vah'; *on a previous* — , zin' ih-we' 前° 一回; *on a succeeding* — , 'eo ih-we 後 一 回; 'ô'-ih-we' 下° 一回; zin vah' ts 前° 回°; *there is no — for your paying*, ng k'o' feh-pih' do-c'ih' 你° 可 弗 必 拿° 出

OCCASION, *to cause*, s'-teh 使得; long 弄; — *pleasure* (to him), s'-teh gyi hwun-hyi 使得其歡喜; — *a loss, or injury by delay*, tæn-ngwu' 耽悞; *this occasioned trouble*, be keh'-go sô 'æ' 被這个° 所害

OCCASIONALLY, *comes* yiu'-teh læ 有 得 來; *meet* — , p'ong'-djoh'-p'ong' 偶°然而遇°; *do* (it) —, yiu'-teh z-'eo tso' 有得時候做

OCCUPATION, z'-nyih 事業; 'ông-nyih' 行業; 'ông-tông 行當; *what is your respect-*

*able* — ? ng soh'-go kwe' nyih 你° 甚° 麼° 貴業? *my mean — is selling cloth*, ngô bi'-nyih ma-pu'-go 我 敝 業 賣° 布 个°

OCCUPIED, *always* feh-teh'-k'ong 弗 得 空

OCCUPY, *to — one's time*, ko nyih-ts' 過 日° 子; du kwông-ing' 度 光 陰; *how do you — your time?* ng' dza ko' nyih-ts' 你° 怎° 過 日° 子?

OCCURRENCE, *a strange* ih-ky'i' gyi-z' 一 椿° 奇 事; *there has been no other —*, bing'-vu bih' dzing 並 無 別 情

OCCUR, *when did it —?* læ kyi'-z yiu' 在°幾 時 有? *if a difficulty —*, ziah p'ong'-djoh yiu keh'-tah 若 逢° 着° 有 疙° 瘩°

OCEAN, do-yiang' 大° 洋; hæ'-yiang 海 洋; *western —*, si-yiang' 西 洋

OCULIST, ngæn'-k'o siu'-sang 眼° 科 先 生°; cün-meng' ngæn'-k'o 專 門 眼° 科

ODD, koh' c'ih koh-yiang' 各 出 各 樣; t'iao'-c'ih-liao 超°出°了°; c'ih-gyi' 出奇; *strange*, gyi-kwa' 奇 怪°; *— number*, tæn-su' 單 數; *— jobs*, ling-se' sang-weh' 零 碎 生° 活

ODDS *and ends*, ling-se' tong'-si 零 碎 東 西

ODES, s 詩; s-ko' 詩 歌; *Book of Odes*, S-Kying' 詩 經

ODIOUS, k'o-u' 可 惡; k'o-'eng' 可 恨

ODOR, (often unpleasant), ky'i'-min 氣味°; *pleasant —*, hyiang 香; *fragrant —*, p'eng'-hyiang 噴 香; *bad —*, we'-ky'i 穢 氣; wa ky'i'-sih 孬 氣息; ky'i'-sih 氣 息

ODORIFEROUS *vapor*, hyiang'-ky'i 香 氣; *— wood*, hyiang-moh' 香 木

ŒSOPHAGUS, we-kwun' 胃 管; zih-kwun' 食 管

OF (sign of the possessive), go 个°; *friend — mine*, ngô'-go beng-yin' 我 个° 朋 友; *the Lord —, Heaven*, T'in-cü' 天主; *—what is it made?* z-soh'-si tso'-c'ih-læ-go' 是 甚° 麼° 做 出 來 个°? *made — wood*, jü tso'-go 樹 做 个°; moh-deo' tso-go 木 頭 做 个°; *— course*, z-jün' 自 然

OFF, *far* li-yün' 離 遠; yün'-leh-kying 遠 得° 緊; *how far —?* li-yün' to-siao' 離遠多少? ts'ô to'-siao yün' 差多少遠? *take — clothes*, t'eh i-zông' 脫 衣 裳; t'ch'-diao i-zông'; *take — (as beads from a string)*, leh-c'ih' 捋 出; *break — a piece (as wood, &c.)*, ao ih-t'ön 拗 一 段°; *ditto (as bread)*, p'ah' ih-kw'e 擘° 一 塊; wah' ih-tin 挖 一 點

OFFENCE, See OFFENSE.

OFFEND, *to — him*, peh gyi kwa

俾°其怪°; peh gyi′ tsiao-kwa′
俾°其招怪°; peh gyi kyin-
kwa′ 俾°其見怪°; *to displease,*
long′-leh gyi feh 'eh-shih′ 弄得°
其弗合式°; peh gyi feh yüoh′-
i 俾°其弗欲意; s′-teh gyi
kyiæ′-i 使得其介意; —
*against* (propriety, or law), teh′-
ze′ 得罪; væn 犯; væn′-djoh
犯着°; — *unwittingly*, ngwu-
væn′ 悮犯

OFFENDED, *is* kwa′-de 怪°了°;
kyin-kwa′-de 見怪°了°; *dis-
pleased*, feh yüoh′-i-de 弗欲
意了°; sing′-li ts′iao′-soh-soh
心裡糙°粟粟; *you are —
at me*, ng kyin ngô′-go kwa′ 你°
見我个°怪°; *not —* , ú́-teh
kwa′ 弗°怪°

OFFENDER *against law*, we-lih′-
væn-fah′-go 違律犯法个°;
væn′-nying 犯人°; væn-fah′-go
nying 犯法个°人°

OFFENSE, *what — has he committed ?* gyi væn soh′-go en′ 其犯
甚°麼案? væn soh′-go kwe′
犯甚°麼規? *to commit an
— against propriety*, shih li′ 失
禮

OFFENSIVE *language*, feh cong
t′ing-go shih-wô′ 弗中聽个°
說話; feh-jih′ ng′-tô shih-wô′
弗入耳°个說話; *disgust-
ing*, we-u-go 穢污个

OFFER, *to* tang′-tsiang peh 意°欲°
給°; *I offered him* $7. *but he was*

*unwilling*, ngô tang′-tsiang peh
gyi ts′ih-kw′e′ fæn-ping′, gyi feh
k′eng′ 我意°欲°給°其七塊
番餅其弗肯; *how much do
you — ?* ng he′ to-siao 你°許°
多少? ng hen′ to-siao′ 你°允°
多少? — *to a superior*, vong-
hyin′ 奉獻; hyin′-zông 獻上;
— *to an idol*, *or ancestor*, kong′-
vong 供奉; — *tribute*, tsing kong′
進貢; — *presents*, song li′-veh
送禮物; — *a lower price*, kô′-
diu he′-leh ky′üih 價°錢°許°
得缺; — *him a chair*, ü′-ts
teh′ peh gyi′ 椅°子撥與°其

OFFERING, *or sacrifice*, tsi′-veh 祭
物; — (whole, in platters before
an idol), foh′-li 福禮; — (smaller, in bowls), kong′-ts′æ 供菜;
— *to ancestors*, kang-væn′ 羹飯;

OFFICE, tsih′-veng 職分; ngæn-
deo′ 衙頭; *to decline —* , t′e-
dz′ kwun-tsih′ 推辭官職;
*to enter —* , zông zing′ 上任;
*to degrade from —* , kah tsih′
革職; kông kyih′ 降級

OFFICER, kwun 官; kwun-fu′ 官
府; kwun-yün′ 官員; *princes
and great officers*, wông-kong′ da′-
dzing 王公大臣; *civil —* ,
veng-kwun′ 文官; *military —* ,
vu′-kwun 武官; *civil and military —* , veng-vu′-pah-kwun′ 文
武百°官; *great ditto*, kong-'eo′-
tsiang′-siang 公侯將相; *to
become an — by fair means*, (i. e.

by examination), tsing'-du c'ih-sing' 正途出身; *ditto through merit*, kyüing-kong' c'ih-sing' 軍功出身; *ditto by purchase*, kyüin-pæn' c'ih-sing' 捐納°出身

OFFICIAL, *to attend to — duties*, bæn kong-vu' 辦公務; — *documents*, kong veng' 公文; — *residence*, ngô-meng' 衙門; *embroidered satin square denoting — rank*, pu'-ts 補子; — *jacket and robe*, môug'-bao pu'-kwô 蟒袍補褂;

OFFICIOUS, ô'-zông-meng 掗上門; dzoh-zông'-meng 擉上門; *meddling*, ts'ih'-siu-pah-kyiah' 七手八脚; to-z'-go 多事个°

OFTEN, le'-ts' 屢次; *how —?* to-siao' we'-su 多少回數? *very* —, hyü'-to we'-su 許多回數

OIL, yiu 油; *bean* —, deo-yiu' 荳油; *fragrant* —, hyiang-yiu' 香油; *tallow-tree* —, ts'ing'-yiu 青油; *rape-seed* —, ts'æ'-yiu 菜油; *sesamum* —, ts-mô'-yiu 芝蔴油; *pea-nut* —, seng-yiu' 生油; mô-yiu' 麻油; *kerosene* —, ho'-yiu 火油; *castor* —, pi-mô'-yiu 蓖蔴油; — *paint*, yiu ts'ih' 油漆

OIL, *to* dzô yiu 搽油; *to rub on* —, k'a-yiu' 揩°油; — *it*, yiu-yiu' gyi 抹°其°油; — *the hair*, fu deo' 傅頭

OILMAN, yiu-k'ah'-nying 油客人°

OILY *taste*, yiu'-go mi-dao 油个°味°道; — *flavor*, yiu yiu'-ky'i læ-tih 有油氣; *too* —, t'eh' yiu 太°油; — *lips, slippery tongue*, yiu-cü' weh-zih 油嘴滑舌

OINTMENT, kao 膏; kao-ts' yiah 膏子藥; *mercurial* —, shü'-nying kao' 水°銀膏

OLD, *not new*, gyiu 舊; — *clothes*, gyiu i'-zông 舊衣裳; *not fresh*, dzing 陳; — *bread*, dzing mun'-deo 陳饅頭; *not young*, lao 老; *aged*, lao'-de 老了°; — *person*, lao'-dzing nying 老成人°; — *man*, lao' kong-kong 老公公; lao-den' 老頭°兒°(not respectful); lao ziu-sing' 老壽星 (used jokingly); — *woman*, lao' bo-bo 老婆婆; lao-t'a-bun' 老太婆° (not respectful); *how — are you?* ng to-siao' nyin-kyi' 你多少年紀? *ditto* (very respectful), to-siao' kwe'-kang 多少貴庚°? — *and worn*, kwu'-nyin-pah-dæn' 古年百°代; *antique*, kwu'-lao 古老; zông-kwu'-fong-go 尙古風个°; — *fashioned*, (out of date), be-z-de 背時了°; — *friend*, lao' beng-yiu 老朋友; lao' siang-hao 老相好; kwu'-kyiao 故交; — *and experienced*, lao'-lin 老練

OLDER *than I*, nyin-kyi' do-jü' ngô 年紀大°如我; *a year — than I*, tsiang' ngô ih nyin' 長

我一年; do ngô′ ih nyin′ 大°
我一年; pi ngô do′ ih nyin′ 比
我大°一年; *this is —, that is
newer,* keh′ z sing′-tin keh′ z
gyiu-tin′ 這°是新點這°是
舊點

OLEANDER, keh′-coh-dao 夾°竹
桃

OLIVE, ts'ing-ko 青果; ken′-læn
橄欖 (veng.); *— seeds,* ts'ing-ko
nying 青果仁°; kæn′-nying 欖
仁° (veng.)

OMEN, ziao-deo′ 兆頭; *good —,*
kyih′ ziao 吉兆; dziang ze′ 祥
瑞; *bad —,* hyüong ziao′ 凶兆;
wa ziao′ 孬兆; *strange and bad
—,* iao nyih′ 妖孽

OMIT, *to* ts'o′-loh 錯落; shih′-loh
失落; *— what one ought to have
seen,* or *done,* shih-kyin′-tin 失
檢點

OMNIPOTENT, vu-sô′-peh-neng 無
所不能; djün-neng′ 全能; m̄-
yiu′ ih-yiang feh neng′ 無°有
一樣弗能; yiang-yiang′ tu
neng-ken′ 樣樣都能幹;

OMNIPRESENT, vu-sô′ peh-dzæ 無
所不在; m̄-yiu′ ih-c'ü′ feh læ-
tong′ 無°有一處弗在°

OMNISCIENT, vu-sô′-peh-cü′ 無
所不知; m̄-yiu′ ih-yiang′ feh
hyiao′-teh 無°有一樣弗曉得;
yiang-yiang′ tu hyiao′-teh 樣樣
都曉得; djün-cü′ 全知

ON, læ 在; læ-zông′ 在°上; *—
the table,* læ coh′ zông 在°桌

上; *— the water,* læ shü min-
teng′ 在書面上; *— the pa-
per,* læ ts′ zông-teng 在°紙上;
*— account of,* we′-leh 爲了°;
*— purpose,* deh-we′ 特爲; deh-
i′ 特意; *— no account must,*
ts'ih′-feh-k'o′ 切弗可; *— the
contrary,* fæn′-cün 反轉; tao′-
hyiang 倒向; *— the way,* jing-
da′ 順堰; *retired from office —
account of age,* kao lao′ de′ 告
老了°; *— foot,* bu-'ang′ 步
行°; *did you come — foot ?* ng′
bu-'ang′-læ, ma′ 你°步行°來
的嗎°? ng tsco′-leh-læ, soh′
你°走°來了°嗎°?

ONANISM, nen-seh′ 男色

ONCE, ih-we′ 一回; ih-tsao′
遭; ih-ts'′ 一次; ih-pin′ 一
遍; *at one time* or *formerly,* yiu
ih′-we 有一回; *all at —,* ih-
zi′ 一齊; ih-t'ong′ 一通; ih-
dong′ 一同; tsæn′-zi 並°齊°;
tsæn′-pô-s zi′ 一°樣°齊°; *go
all at —,* ih-zi′ ky'i′ 一°齊°去°;
*sing all at —,* tsæn′-zi ts'ông′
並齊唱; *the whole at —,* teng′-
cü 會°齊°; *write all at —,* teng′-
cü sia′ 會°齊°寫°

ONE, ih 一; *— by one,* ih′-go
个 一个°; ih′-tang-ih′ 一打
一; *every —,* dzoh-ih′ 逐 一;
me′-go 每个°; *every — is good,*
ih′-tang-ih′ tu hao′-go 一打一
都好个°; *— and all,* ih′-ping
一併; t'ong′-gong 通統; 一

*thir d*, sæn-feng′-ts-ih′ 三 牙 之
一; sæn-kwu′-li′-hyiang-ih-kwu′
三 股 裡 向 一 股; *receive —
third*, sæn-kwu′-teh-ih′ 三 股
得 一; *of — language*, ih′-go
k′eo′-ing 一 个° 口 音; dong
k′eo′-ing 同 口 音; — *sheep*,
ih-tsah yiang′ 一 隻 羊; —
*knife*, ih-pô tao′ 一 把 刀; *any
—*, feh-leng′ ‛ah-li ih-go 弗 論
何 處 一 个°; ze-bin′ ‛ah-li
ih′-go 隨 便 何° 處° 一 个°;
*every —*, ko′-ko 個 個; *bring
every —*, ko′-ko do′-læ 個 個
拿° 來; — *eyed*, doh-ngæn′-go
獨 眼° 个°

ONE'S *self*, zi 自°; — *own*, zi′-go
自 个°; — *own child*, ts‛ing-
sang′-go 親 生° 个°; — *own
brother*, tih′-ts‛ing hyüong-di′
嫡 親 兄 弟; — *own mother*,
tih′ meo 嫡 母

ONENESS *of purpose*, tso sing′-
siang 同° 心 想; ih-sing′-ih′-
i 一 心 一 意 (used of one or
more persons); *the same heart,
one purpose*, doug-sing′-‛eh-i′ 同
心 合 意 (used of many).

ONION, ts‛ong 葱; — *bulb*, ts‛ong
deo′ 葱 頭; *Shantung —*, Sæ:-
tong′ ts‛ong 山 東 葱

ONLY, tæn-tsih′ 單 只; tsih′-z
只 是; peh′-ko 不 過; — *one*
tæn′-tsih ih′-go 單 只 一 个°;
tæn-tæn′ ih′-go 單 單 一 个°;
doh-doh′ ih′-go 獨 獨 一 个°;

— *have*, tsih′-yiu 只 有; — *can
or — good for*, tsih′-hao 只 好;
— *need one*, tsih′-siao ih′-go 只
須 一 个°; tæn-ts‛ô ih-go 單
差 一 个°; *not —*, feh tæn′-
tsih 弗 單 只; feh-doh′ 弗 獨;
feh-ts′ 弗 止; — *son*, doh-yiang′
ng-ts′ 獨 養 兒° 子

ONSET, kong-tang′ 攻 打; c‛ong-
fong 衝 鋒

ONWARD, *to go* hyiang zin′ ky‛i
向 前 去°; wông zin′ ky‛i 往°
前° 去°; zông zin′ ky‛i 上
前° 去°

OOZE, *to — out*, seng′-c‛ih 沁 出;
heng′-c‛ih; — *in drops*, ti′-loh
滴 落

OPAQUE, ing′-feh-ko-go 映 弗 過
个°; feh-t‛eo-kwông′ 弗 透
光

OPEN, *uncovered*, k‛æ′-tong; k‛æ′-
tih 開 的; — (*as a letter,
&c*), k‛æ-k‛eo-go′ 開 口 个°; —
*to view*, t‛æn-k‛æ′-tong 攤 開 的°;
*free from obstructions*, t‛ong 痛;
*clear, frank*, tsing′- da-kwông′-
ming 正 大 光 明; *straight forward*, kông′- leh hyiang; *in —
day*, ts‛ing-t‛in′-bah-nyih′ 青 天
白 日°; — *in texture*, hyi 稀;
lông 鬆; ga.

OPEN, *to* k‛æ 開; — *the door*,
k‛æ meng′ 開 門; — (*as bundles,
or bedding*.) tang′-k‛æ 打 開; —
*a letter*, k‛æ-fong′ 開 封; *sing*
ts‛ah′-k‛æ 信 拆 開; — *a shop*,

k'æ-tin' 開店; — *a school,* k'æ-kwun' 開館; k'æ-'oh' 開學°; — *a book,* shü' fæn-k'æ'-læ 書翻開來; *to push* —, t'e-k'æ' 推開; — *the bowels,* li da-bin' 利大便; t'ong-da-bin' 通大便; *to free* (as a drain), peh gyi t'ong 俾其痛; *commence,* k'æ-siu' 開手; k'æ-deo'-meng 開頭; *mouth is still* — (*i.e.* the matter is still unsettled), wa k'æ-k'eo'-go 還開口個°; *cannot* —, k'æ'-feh-k'æ' 開弗開; *how can* (I) — *it ?* dza-hao' k'æ 怎好開? *must not* —, *or don't know how to* —, k'æ'-feh-læ' 開弗來

OPENING, k'æ'-go di-fông 開個°地方; *hole,* dong-ngæn' 洞眼°; *a crevice,* ih-da vong' 一埭縫; — *for work, trade, &c.,* meng-lu' 門路; deo-lu' 頭路

OPENLY, ming-tông'-tông 分°明; hyin'-jün 顯然; c'ih-lu'-lu 露出

OPERA-GLASS, sông-ngæn'-kying 雙眼°鏡

OPERATE, *to* — *with a knife,* k'æ tao' 開刀

OPERATED, *has the medicine* — ? yiah yiao'-feh-yiao' 藥效弗效? *it has* —, kyin-yiao'-de 見效了°

OPERATION, *he has skill in surgical operations,* gyi'-go tao-fah' hao' 其個刀法好

OPHTHALMIA, nyih-ngæn' 熱°眼°

OPIATE, en-zæ'-yiah 安睡藥

OPINION, i'-s 意思; i'-kyin 意見; *decision,* cü'-kyin 主見; *according to my* —, tsiao ngô' go i'-s 照我個意思; dziu ngô' k'en' læ 就我看來; *according to my humble* —, tsiao ngô' nyü kyin' 照我愚見; *every one has his own* —, koh' nying yiu zi'-go i-s' 各人°有自個°意思

OPINIONATED, *he is* —, gyi' go i'-s tsih-ih'-go 其個意思執一個°; *self* — *person,* cih' nying 固°執個人°

OPIUM, a-p'in' 鴉°片; yiang-yiah' 洋藥; yiang-in' 洋烟; t'u 土°; *native* —, T'æ-tsiang' 台土°; *to smoke* —, ky'üoh a-p'in' 吃鴉片; *more commonly,* ky'üoh in' 吃烟 (lit. to smoke tobacco); tsao in' ; *to swallow* —, ky'üoh sang a'-p'in 吃°生°鴉片; *to stop smoking* —, ka a-p'in' 戒鴉片; ka in' 戒烟; *addicted to* —, a-p'in' nyin'-de 鴉片癮了°; a-p'in' zông ying'-de 鴉片上癮了°

OPIUM-SHOP, t'u'-tin 土店; t'u'-'ông 土行; — (where it is both sold and smoked), a-p'in tin' 鴉片店; a-p'in t'æn' 鴉片攤

OPPONENT, te'-dih 對敵; te'-deo 對頭; *equal opponents,* dih-siu' 敵手

OPPORTUNE, ky'iah'-hao 恰好;
*to meet accidentally something very*
一, nyü-ky'iao' 遇巧

OPPORTUNELY, ky'iao 巧; ts'eo'-
ky'iao 湊巧; *you have come*
*quite* —, ng' læ-leh ky'iao' 你°
來得°巧

OPPORTUNITY, kyi-we' 機會;
*improve the* —, ts'ing kyi-we'
趁機會; *improve this* —,
ts'ing'-ts' kyi-we' 趁此機會;
*ditto when some one else is send-*
*ing*, or *going*, jing-bin' 順便;
dziu-bin' 就便; *to improve ditto*,
ts'ing-bin' 趁便

OPPOSE *läm* (*i. e.* cover up his
light), kæ gyi'-go tsiao' 蓋其
个°面°子°; — *one's views*, or
*propositions*, gyiang'-bin 强辯;
— *in fight*, &c., ti'-dih 抵敵;
ti'-tông 抵當

OPPOSED, *mutually* siang-fæn' 相
反; *ditto* (persons only), teo-deo'-
feh'-long 對頭弗攏; — *as ice*
*and hot coals*, yiu jü', ping t'æn'
猶如冰炭

OPPOSITE, *in front*, siang-tè' 相
對; *facing*, te'-min 對面;
— *door*, te' meng 對門; *the*
*two are opposites*, liang'-go siang-
fæn' 兩个°相反; liang' feh-
siang-tè' 兩弗相對; — *forms*
*of expression*, fæn-foh'-go shih-
wô' 反覆个°說話°

OPPRESS, *to* — *those in one's power*
(as slaves), mo-næn' 磨耀; —

*a people*, bao-nyiah' pah'-sing 暴
虐百°姓; tsô'-ziao ming-kyin'
詐擾民間; *ditto in exacting*
*money*, k'eh'-poh (or k'eh-boh)
pah'-sing 刻薄百°姓; —
*in requiring too much*, pih'-p'ah
逼迫; *to use strength* or *authority*
*in oppressing*, tang-pô'-shü 打霸
勢; yi-shü'-ky'i-nying' 以勢欺
人°; *ditto* (as an underling relying on the power of an official),
yi'-kwun-t'oh'-shü 倚官托勢

OPPRESSIVE *government*, koh'
tsing' bao-nyiah'-go 國政暴
虐个°

OPPRESSIVELY *hot*, ôh'-tsi-tsi-go
nyih' 熱°甚°

OPPROBRIOUS (abusive) *language*,
zoh-mô'-go shih-wô' 辱罵个°
說話

OPTIC *nerve*, ngæn'-tsong-kying'
眼°總筋

OPTICS, kwông-yüoh' 光學(veng.)

OPTION, *at your* bing-ng'-sô-yüoh'
憑你°所欲; ze-bin' ng 任°
憑°你°

OR, wa-z' 還°是; 'oh'-tsia 或者°;
ih'-'oh 抑或 (for the second
connective); *will you go* — *stay?*
wa-z ky'i', wa-z læ-tong 還°是
去°還°是在°此°? *I will*
*either go* — *not, as you deter-*
*mine*, 'oh ky'i', ih'-'oh feh-ky'i'
ze ng' ding-kyin' 或去°抑或
弗去° 隨你°定見; — *not*,
feh 否°? *will you do* (it) —

*not?* ng' we tso' feh 你°會做否°? *will you go — not?* ng' ky'i'-feh-ky'i' 你°去°弗去°

ORACLE, *to inquire of an —* (or in China of an idol), meng ts'in-s' 問°籤詩; gyiu ts'in' 求籤

ORALLY, *to comunicate —,* k'eo'-djün 口傳

ORANGE, kyüih'-ts 橘子; *Fok-kien, or Mandarin —,* Foh'-kyüih 福橘; *Canton, or cooly —,* Kwông'-kyüih 廣橘; *bitter —,* (from Weng-tsiu), ken-ts' 柑子; *cumquat —,* kying-ken' 金橘°; *— peel,* kyüih'-bi 橘皮; *— color,* yü-'ong'-seh 榆紅色; kying-wông'-seh 金黃色; *red-dish ditto,* kyüih'-'ong 橘紅

ORATOR, *good speaker,* jün'-ü kông'-go nying 善於講°个°人°

ORBIT *of a planet,* 'ang-sing'-go kwe'-dao 行°星个°軌道

ORDAIN *a law,* shih'-lih lih-fah' 設°立律法; zao lih-fah' 造°律法; *— an elder,* lih' ih-go tsiang'-lao 立一个°長老

ORDER, *in* ts'-jü 次序; ts'-di 次第; *without —,* ɯ-ts'-jü 無°次序; *in regular —,* a-ts'-jü 換次序; *give it to them in —,* a-ts'-jü feng-peh' gyi 換次序分給°其; tsiao-ts'-jü feng' 照次序分; *out of —, or disar-ranged,* lön-tsia'-bong ka 亂°鬆鬆; *military —,* 'ao-ling' 號令; *— for money,* p'iao'-ts 票紙;

dzin-tæn' 錢單; dzin-p'iao' 錢票; *put the room in —,* siu'-jih vông-kæn' 收拾房間°; vông'-ts tsiu-coh'-hao 房子收°拾°好; vông'-ts tsông-tsih-hao 房子裝飾°好; *put in —, or repair,* siu-li' hao 修理好; *to regulate* (things in disorder), tsing'-teng 整頓

ORDER, *to —, or dispose,* en-ba' 安排°; *to command,* feng-fu' 吩附

ORDERLY, en'-pæn-ts-go 按班子个°; en'-bu-dzin-pæn 按部就班; jing-kwe'-dao'-kyü 循規蹈矩; *— and prettily,* zi-tsing 齊整; *— and precise,* doh-fông-bu' 踱方步

ORDINAL *numbers,* 1*st,* di-ih' 第一; 2*nd,* di-nyi' 第二°; 3*rd,* di-sæn' 第三

ORDINARY, bing-djông' 平常; 'æn djông 閒°常; cong-cong' 中中; da-kæ' 大概

ORDINARILY, bing-su'-kyin, or bing-su'-kæn 平素間

ORE, *gold* kying-kw'ông' 金礦; *silver —,* nying-kw'ông' 銀礦

ORGAN, *wind* fong-gying' 風琴; *the five organs of sense,* ng'-kwun 五°官

ORGANIZE, *to* en-ba' 安排°

ORIFICE, *mouth of a tube,* k'eo 口; *hole,* dong-ngæn' 洞眼°; *the seven orifices,* ts'ih'-ky'iao 七竅

ORIGIN, læ-lih' 來歷; læ-keng' 來根; læ-yiu' 來由; keng-yiu'

根 由; nyün-yiu′ 緣° 由; ing-
yiu′ 因 由

ORIGINAL, peng 本; nyün 原;
*the — text*, peng′-veng 本 文;
nyün ti′-ts 原 底 子; peng′ti-ts
本 底 子; — *cargo*, nyün-ho′
原 貨; *he is quite —*, gyi ling
yiu′ ih-diao ts′ong-ming′ 其 另
有 一 樣° 聰 明

ORIGINALLY, peng′-læ 本 來; *at
first*, ky′i′-ts′u 起 初; *he was —
from Peking*, gyi peng′-læ z
Poh-′-kying læ-go′ 其 本 來 是
北 京 來 个°

ORIGINATE, c′ih 出; *where did it
—?* soh′-go di-fông c′ih′-go 甚°
麽° 地 方 出 个°? c′ih′-c′ü læ
′ah′-li′ 出 處 在° 何° 處°? *who
originated?* jü′ tsoh′-c′ih-læ′ go
誰° 作 出 來 个°? *ditto this
plan?* keh′-go fah′-ts jü c′ih′-go
這 个° 法 子 誰° 作° 出 个°?

ORNAMENT, *to* tsông-sih′ 裝 飾;
— *the person*, tsah′-kwah 紥 刮;
tang′-pæn 打 扮

ORNAMENTED, yiu hwô-deo′-go
有 花 頭 个°

ORNAMENTS, hwô-deo′ 花 頭;
— *for the head*, (others are often
included), siu′-sih 首 飾

ORPHAN, m̄ - tia′ m̄-nyiang′-go
無° 爹 無° 娘 个°; kwu-æ′-ts
孤 哀 子; *one who has lost one
or both parents*, hao′-ts 孝° 子

ORTHODOX, tsing′-kyiao 正 教;
*in China Confucianism is the —*

*belief*, Cong-koh′-go Jü-kyiao′ z
tsing′-kyiao 中 國 个° 儒 敎
是 正 敎

OSCILLATE, *to* dang - læ′ - dang-
ky′i′ 宕 來 宕 去°

OSTENTATIOUS, pa-p′ing′ 擺
品; pa-do-kw′un′ 擺 大° 欵;
kw′un′-shih do′-go 欵 式 大°
个°; deo′-do-go 大° 模 大°樣°
(in ridicule.)

OSTENSIBLY *for a good object, but
really for a bad one*, yi-ts′′ we-
ming′ yi-pe′-we-li′ 以 此 爲 名
以 彼 爲 利; — *to teach*, kao-
shü′ tso ing-deo′ 敎° 書 做 因
頭; — *to teach, but really to do
business*, ming′- go kao-shü′ en′-
go tso sang′-i 明 係 敎° 書 暗
却° 做 生° 意

OSTRICH, do-nyiao′ 鴒 鳥

OTHER, bih 別; — *persons*, bih′-
nying 別 人°; bih′- go nying′
別 个° 人°; — *kinds*, bih-
yiang′ 別 樣°; *love each, —*, dô-
kô′ siang-æ′ 大°家°相 愛; pe′-
ts′ æ′-sih 彼 此 愛 惜; *the others*,
gyi-yü′ 其 餘

OTHERWISE, feh′-z-ka′ 弗 如°
此°; feh′-jün 弗 然; *if it be
—(you) need not come*, ziah feh′-
z-ka′ k′o′-yi feh-læ′ 若 弗 如°
此° 可 不° 必° 來

OTTER, t′ah 獺; *sea —*, shü′-t′ah
水° 獺; — *skin*, t′ah′-bi 獺 皮

OUGHT, kæ 該; ing-kæ′ 應 該;
ing-tông′ 應 當; kæ-tông′ 該

當; tông-kæ′ 當該; ky′iah-leh (or ky′iao-leh) 却要°; *it — to be so*, tsiao li′ ing-kæ′-go 照理應該 个°.

OUNCE, *an* ih-liang′ 一兩; *sixteen (Chinese) ounces make a catty*, jih-loh′-liang sön ih kying′ 十六兩算一觔; *an — and a half*, ih-liang-pun′ 一兩半; *an —*, *or tael of silver*, ih-liang′ nying-ts′ 一兩銀子

OUR, OURS, ah-lah′-go 我等° 个°;— *country*, peng′-koh 本國

OURSELF, *the emperor*, dzeng 朕; kwô′-jing 寡人; *ourselves*, ah-lah zi 吾° 輩° 自°

OUT, c′ih 出; *to walk —*, tseo′-c′ih 走出; *gone —*, tseo′-c′ih-ky′i′-de 走出去° 了°; *— of doors*, t′in-nga′ 天外°; *the fire is —*, ho n′-de 火熄° 了°; *walked till — of breath*, tseo-leh ky′i′-kying bi-hyü′ 走得° 氣急° 皮虛; *— of employment*, zo lang′-pæn′-teng′ 坐冷° 板凳

OUTCAST (*as a vagabond*), ky′i′-diao-go-nying 棄了° 个° 人°; (*as a child*, &c.), loh-shü′-nying 失°意° 个° 人°; loh-liu′-go nying 流落 个° 人°.

OUTCRY, *to make an* fah-hæn′ 發喊; *make a great —*, do-sing bæn-kyiao′ 大°聲 喊叫; wæ-wæ′-si.

OUT-DO, *you — me*, ng ko′-jü ngô′ 你° 過 如 我; ng sing′-jü ngô′ 你 勝 如 我

OUTER, nga-deo′ 外°頭; *the — surface*, nga-min′ 外°面; *— skin*, nga-deo′-go bi 外°頭 个° 皮

OUTERMOST, ting′ nga-deo′ 頂外°頭

OUTLANDISH *fashion*, gyi-c′ih′-kwu yiang′ 奇出古樣

OUTLINE, *to draw an —*, wô ih′-go da′-kwe′-mo 畫一个°大規模; *write a brief — (of a subject)*, sia ih-tin′ da-liah′ 寫° 一點大畧; *an — of history*, kông-moh′ 綱目; kông-kæn′ 綱鑑

OUTRAGEOUS, ying-hyüong-pô-oh′ 行兇作° 惡; ying-hyüong pô-dao′ 行兇覇道

OUTSIDE, nga-deo′ 外°頭; nga-pin′ 外°邊; nga-min′ 外°面; *— show*, k′ong-k′oh′ 空売; *ditto, not real*, k′ong′-k′oh kô′-ts 空売架° 子

OUTWARD, dziao-nga′ 朝外°; hyiang-nga′ 向外°

OVAL, dziang-yün′ 長圓; *kidney shaped*, iao-ts′ shih 腰子式°; *egg-shaped*, dæn′-go yiang′-shih 蛋 个° 樣 式° (little used).

OVEN, p′ang-lu′ 烹爐; *native or Dutch — (where coals are placed above and below)*, p′ang-′oh′ 烹鑊; *lake in the —*, lu-li p′ang′ 爐裏烹°

Over, zông 上; — *your head*, læ ng' deo zông' 在°你°頭上; *to cross* or *pass* —, tseo'-ko-ky'i' 走過去°; *to turn* — *and* —, fæu-læ'-foh-ky'i 翻來覆去°; *in excess*, ko'-ü 過於; — *much*, ko'-ü to' 過於多; *there is a little* —, yiu tin tsiang-tsong 有點積°蓄°; yiu tin ling-nga' 有點另外°; *ditto* (remaining), yiu tin yü'有點餘; yiu tin dzing' 有點剩; — *ten*, jih to' 十多; — *forty*, s'-jih to 四十多; s'-jih yiu yü' 四十有餘; *to boil* —, p'u-c'ih' 溢°出; kweng'-c'ih 滾出

Over-anxious, ko'-ü zeo' 過於愁°; *to* zeo' 多愁°

Overawe *a person*, yi-shü' ah nying' 以勢壓°人°

Overawed, gyü-hyih'-go 懼懾个°

Overburdened *with work*, lao-loh' ko-deo' 勞碌過分

Overcast, *the sky is* —, t'in' ing-t'en'-t'en; t'in' ing-a'-de 天陰翳了°; *ditto with clouds*, t'in', yüing tsô-djü'-liao 天雲遮°住了°; t'in', zông-yüing'-de 天漫°雲了°; — *a seam*, nyiao-zông'.

Overcome, *to conquer*, ying 贏; *Prussia has* — *France*, P'u-lu'-z tsin-go z-'eo pi Veh-læn'-si ko-deo' 普魯士戰个°時候比法°蘭西勝°; — *difficulties*, næn'-c'ü kying-lin'-ky'i 難處經練起

Overdone (as food), job ko-deo' 過於°熟; t'eh joh' 太°熟

Overestimate *the importance of*, sön t'eh' iao'-kying 算太°要緊

Overflow, *to* kah'-c'ih 溢°出; — (as a river), kah'-zông 溢°上; üong'-zông 湧上; tsiang'-zông 漲上; *full to over-flowing*, mi-mun-kah'-c'ih 彌滿溢°出

Overhanging *rocks*, sing-c'ih'-liao-go zah-deo' 伸出了个°石°頭; p'oh'-c'ih-liao-go zah-deo' 撲出了石°頭

Overhead, læ deo-zông' 在°頭上

Overhear, *to* — (without intention), vu-i'-cong t'ing'-meng 無意中聽聞°; *take care, your neighbors will* —, kwu'-djoh kah'-pih t'ing'-meng 顧着°隔壁聽聞°

Overjoyed, hwun- t'in'-'hyi-di' 歡天喜地; hwun-hyi'-sah-de 歡喜巳°極°

Overland, 'en'-lu 旱路; loh-lu' 陸路

Overlay, *to* t'iah 貼°; du 鍍; — *with gold*, t'iah kying' 貼°金

Overload, *to* — (as a box, or boat), tsông'-leh t'eh djong' 裝得°太°重

Overlook, *to* — *from above*, zông-k'en-loh 上望°下°; *to* — *by inadvertence*, kwu'-feh-tao' 顧弗到; feh-læ'-kwu 弗來顧; *to*

*excuse,* feh-kyi'-kyiao 弗計較;
— *little faults,* feh kyi' siao ko'
弗計小過

OVERPLUS, to-deo' 多頭; yü-
deo' 餘頭

OVERPOWER *lăm,* ah'-gyi-voh'
壓°其服

OVERPRESSED, dziah-kyib' 着急

OVERSEE, *to* tsiao'-kwu 照顧;
— (work), toh'-bæn 督辦

OVERSEER *of work,* toh-kong'
督工

OVERSIGHT, *he has the —,* tsiao'-
liao z gyi'-go meng-veng' 照瞭
是其个° 名° 分°

OVERSLEEP, *to* shih-kao' 失覺°

OVERSPREAD *the country,* vu-
c'ü'-feh-tao' 無處弗到

OVERREACH *one's self,* (the heart
too fierce will hold only an empty
cup.), sing'-li mang' we-nyiah
k'ong' coh-kwun' 心裡猛會
揸空竹管, or 心裡懵撞
反落空

OVERSTEP *the bounds of propriety,* yüih-li'-væn-veng' 越禮犯分

OVERTAKE, *to* tse-djoh' 追着°
ken'-tao 趕到

OVERTASK, *to — one's strength,*
yüong lih t'æ'-ko 用力太過

OVERTHROW, *to* t'e-tao' 推倒;
tang'-tao 打倒; — *a kingdom,*
mih-diao' koh'-kô 滅掉國家°

OVERTHROWN, *government* koh'
peng'-de 國崩了°

OVERTURN, *to* fæn'-tao 翻倒

OVERWHELMING, (like waters
rising overhead), meh-deo'-meh-
nao' 沒頭沒腦; — *sorrow,*
meh-deo'-meh-nao'-go iu' 沒頭
沒腦个° 憂

OWE, *to* ky'in 欠; kæ 該; —
*a person* (without intending to
pay), la-tsa' 賴債°; siao nying-
kô' dong-din' 少人°家°銅錢°;
*how much do you — me?* ng
ky'in ngô' to-siao' 你°欠我
多少? — *and have nothing to
pay,* k'we k'ong' 虧空

OWL, djoh-weng' 貓頭鷹° (ih-
tsah)

OWN, zi'-go 自°个°; — *hand,*
ts'ing siu' 親手; — *family,*
peng'-kô 本家°

OWN, *to —* (as property), ken or ke
掙; *do you — this?* keh z ng-go
feh 這°是你°个°否°? *he is
unwilling to — his son,* gyi feh-
k'eng' jing ng-ts' 其弗肯認
兒°子; *to confess,* tsiao-jing'
招認; — *one's self in the wrong,*
be feh-z' 賠弗是; be li' 賠禮

OWNER, cü 主; ken-cü' or ke-cü'
掙主; cü'-nying-kô 主人°
家°; *who is the —of this?* keh'-
go, cü z jü' 這个°主是誰°?
— *of houses,* or *land,* nyih cü'
業主; vông-tong' 房東

OX, ngeo 牛°; — *house,* ngeo-gyin'
牛欄

OYSTER, li-wông' 牡°蠣°; —
*shells,* li-wông k'oh' 牡°蠣°壳

# P

PACE, ih-bu′ 一步

PACIFY, to — *his anger*, long′ gyi ky′ı̆′ bing 弄其氣平; long′ gyi ky′ı̆′ sih′ 弄其氣息; — *anger by some ceremony*, be-li′ sih-ky′ı̆′ 賠禮息氣; *get up theatricals and a feast to* — *anger*, hyi′-veng tsiu siao-ky′ı̆′ 戲文酒消氣

PACK, *bundle*, pao-voh′ 包袱 (ih-go); *a* — *of cards*, ih-fu ts-bæn′ 一副紙牌°

PACK, *to* — *in a box*, tsông′-loh siang-ts′-li 裝落箱子裡; tsing′-loh siang-ts′-li 整落箱子裡; *to* — *or wrap in a bundle*, pao-hao′ 包好

PACKED, *it is already* — *up* (in a box), yi′-kying loh-siang′-de 巳經落箱了°; *is your baggage all* — ? ng′-go 'ang-li′ siu-jih-hao′ ma 你°个° 行李收拾好嗎?

PACKAGE, *a* ih-pao′ 一包; *a* — *of letters*, ih-pao sing′ 一包信

PADDY, koh 榖; — *in the field*, dao 稻; — *field*, dao′- din 稻田

PADLOCK, *foreign hanging lock*, nga-koh tiao′-so 外國弔鎖

PAGE, *a* ih-min′ 一面; *the second* —, di-nyi′ min 第二°面

PAGEANT, *a fine* yi wô-li′ yi t′ı̆′-min-go z-ken′ 華麗而°又°體面之°事

PAGODA, *a* ih-zo t′ah′ 一座塔;

*the Ningpo* —, T′in-fong′-t′ah 天封塔

PAIL, *water* ky′ih-shü-dong′ 挈水桶; *large* —, *or bucket*, t′iao-shü′-dong 挑水°桶 (ih-tsah)

PAIN, t′ong 痛; *to feel* —, teh′-cü t′ong 得知痛; kyüoh′-teh-t′ong′ 覺得痛; — *in the limbs*, kyiah′-kweh sön′ 脚骨酸

PAINFUL, t′ong′-go 痛个°; *very* —, t′ong′-leh li-′æ 痛得°利害; *extremely* —, gyih t′ong′ 極痛

PAINS, *take* gying lao′ 勤勞; yüong sing-k yi′ 用心機; *one's trouble for one's* —, bah-bah′ yiao-lao 空°勞; wông′-fi sing-kyi′ 枉費心機; — du lao′ 徒勞

PAINTER, *varnisher*, ts′ih′-s-vu′ 漆司務; — *of pictures*, tæn-ts′ing′ sin′-sang 丹青先生°

PAINT, *green* loh yiu′ 綠油; *yellow* —, wông yiu′ 黃油; *foreign yellow* —, yiang-wông′ 洋黃

PAINT, *to* (with oil paint, or simply with oil), yiu 油; yiu-ih′-yiu 油一油; k′a yiu′ 揩°油; — *with foreign green*, yiu yiang-loh′ or k′a′ yiang-loh′ yiu 揩°洋綠油; — *lead color*, yiu hwe-seh′ 油灰色; — *pictures*, ts′æ′-seh sia-wô′ 彩色寫°畫; *to color, as maps, &c.*, tsiah′-seh 着色; *to* — *the face* (with carmine), dzô in-tsi′ 搭臙脂°

PAINTINGS, ts'æ'-seh-go wô' 彩
色个° 畫; ts'æ' wô 彩畫

PAINTS, ngæn-liao' 顏°料; *dishes
of —,* ngæn-liao' diah 顏° 料
牒

PAIR, *a* ih-te' 一對; ih-sông' 一
雙; ih-fu' 一 副 (also means a
set); *in pairs* (as men, or animals
in procession), pa te'-ts 擺° 對
子; *a — of flower jars,* ih-te
hwô-bing' 一 對花瓶; *a — of
shoes,* ih-sông 'a' 一雙鞋°; *a —
of bracelets,* ih-fu siu'-gyüoh 一
副 手鐲; *a — of scizzors,* ih-
pô tsin'-tao 一把剪刀

PAIR, *to match,* p'e-te' 配對; —
*off in couples,* p'e'-tah 配搭

PALACE, wông-kong 皇宮

PALATABLE, sông'-k'eo-go 爽 口
个°; yiu ts-mi' go 有滋味°个°

PALATE, (soft) siao zih-deo' 小
舌頭

PALE, bah-liao'-liao 白° 了 了;
—(from sickness, or fright), liao'-
bah 了白°; leh-bah' 鑞 白°; —
*as death,* ziang si' seh ka bah'
像死° 色一° 樣° 白°; *to grow
—,* min-seh' pin-bah'-de 面色
變 白° 了°; shih-seh' 失色

PALL *for a coffin,* kwun-zæ'-t'ao
棺材套

PALLIATE, *to* veng-ko'-sih-fi' 掩
過飾非; — *his sin,* tsông-sih'
gyi-go ze' 裝飾其个° 罪;
long gyi-go ze' ky'ing'-k'o 致°
其个° 罪輕可

PALM *of the hand,* siu'-ti-sing' 手
心; siu'-công 手掌; *the coir
— or palmetto,* tsong-li' jü 棕櫚
樹; — *leaf fan,* (miscalled) pô-
tsiao sin' 芭蕉扇; gwe-sin' 葵
扇 (ih-pô)

PALPITATION *of the heart,* sing'-
li bih-bih'-t'iao 心裡蹕蹕跳

PALSY, fong-t'æn'-bing 瘋癱病

PALTRY, t'æ'-si-siao 太細小

PAN, *dish,* beng 盆; *earthen —,*
ngô-beng' 瓦° 盆; *shallow —
or platter,* bun 盤; *tin —,* mô'-
k'eo-t'ih bun' 馬口鐵盤

PANCAKES, *to fry* t'ah ping' 爛
餅

PANE, *a — of glass,* ih-kw'e po-li'
一塊玻璃

PANEL, nyin-ngô-zao 視 瓦° 槽°

PANG, teng'-z t'ong' 頓時痛;
*one — after another,* zi'-tang-zi
t'ong' 一°陣°一°陣°; *pangs frequent* (before delivery), kying'-zi
t'ong 緊齊痛

PANIC, *in a* hwông'-de 慌 了°;
kying-wông'-de 驚惶了°

PANT. *to* t'eo-ky'i' 透氣; ky'i
t'eo'-feh-cün' 氣透弗轉; —
(from disease, or anger), ky'i'
kying 氣緊; *panting sound,* hyi-
hyi' hwu-hwu' 嘻嘻呼呼

PANTALOONS, kw'u 褲 (ih-iao)

PANTHER, (a kind of leopard), pao
豹 (ih-tsah)

PANTOMIME, tsông-kyü'-ts 裝舉
止; tsông i-tsi 裝意致°; 一

*by gesticulation,* tsông siu'-shü 裝
手勢

PANTRY, ho-zih-kæn' 伏食間°

PAPA, pah'-pah 伯°伯°; ah-pah'
阿伯°; tia-tia' 爹°爹°

PAPER, ts 紙; *a sheet of* —, ih-
tsiang ts' 一張紙; *letter* —,
sing' ts 信紙; — *used for
Chinese writing,* mao-loh' 毛六;
mao-pah' 毛八; *strong wrapping*
—, sông-bi-ts' 桑皮紙; *coarsest
ditto,* ts'ao'-ts 草紙; *match, or
touch* —, ho'-ts 火紙; me-deo'-
ts 煤頭紙; *flowered* —, hwô-
tsin' 花箋; *gold sprinkled* —,
sa'-kying-tsin' 灑°金箋; *thin
white* —, lin-s-ts' 連史紙;
— *sized with alum,* væn-ts'
攀紙; *thick alum dressed* —,
djong'-væn-ts' 重攀紙; *very
large sized ditto,* cong-wô'-sing
畫心紙°; *waxed* —, lah-
tsin' 蠟箋; — *utensils, &c., for
the dead,* ts' ky'i 紙器; ts'-shü
紙賃; — *clothing ditto,* ming-i'
冥衣; — *ingots for burning,*
nyün-pao' 元寶; nying-ding'
銀錠; *tinseled paper used for
the latter,* sih'-boh 錫箔; —
*clippings* (for mortar, and for
packing coffins), ts'-kying 紙
筋; — *flowers,* ts'-hwô 紙花

PAPER *maker,* ts'- s-vu 紙司
務

PAPERS, *documentary* en'-kyün 案
卷

PARABLE, pi'-fông 比方; pi'-yü
比喩

PARADE, ba-dziang' 排°塲; *fond
of* —, hao' ba-dziang 好排°
塲; — *of militia,* hyiang-yüong'
pa deo ka tseo' 鄉勇成隊而°
行°; — *of authority,* hyin-we-
shü' 顯威勢; *false ditto,* tsông
we-shü' 裝威勢; — *ground,*
kao'-dziang 敎°塲

PARADISE, *Buddhist* Si-t'in'-gyih-
loh-shü'-ka 西天極樂世界°;
*Christian* —, T'in-dông' 天堂;
T'in-zông' 天上; *Eden,* Yiæ-
din' yün 埃田園

PARAGRAPH, ih-dön' 一段; ih-
p'in' 一篇; *newspaper* —, ih-
dön sing-veng' 一段新文

PARALLELS, bing-siu' 平線; —
*of latitude,* we'-sin 緯線

PARALLELOGRAM, dziang-fông'
長方

PARALYSIS, fong-t'æn'-bing 瘋
癱病; — *of one side,* pun'-ts-
fong 半肢瘋

PARAPHRASE, kyin' ming kông'-
ka 簡明講°解°

PARASITE, *trencher friend,* tsiu'-zih
beng-yiu' 酒肉°朋友; *sponger,*
kwæn' ky'üoh bah-zih'-go 慣吃°
白°食个°; — *who follows, and
likes just what you like,* ts'eo-
c'ü' 湊趣

PARASOL, liang-sæn' 凉傘

PARBOIL, *to* ts-leh pun'-joh 羹
得°半熟

PARBOILED, *half cooked*, pun'-sang-li-joh' 半生° 半° 熟; *very slightly cooked*, sang-hwe'-boh-loh 外° 焦° 裏° 勿° 熟°

PARCEL, *a* ih-pao' 一 包

PARCEL, *to — out*, feng-hao' 分好

PARCH, *to — corn*, ts'ao loh-koh' 炒稑穀

PARCHED, *very dry*, feng'-ken-sao' 粉乾四燥; *— ground*, di-yiang' feng-sao' 地下° 粉燥; *— (as a tree)*, kw'u-sao' 枯燥

PARCHMENT, yiang-bi-ts' 羊皮紙

PARDON, *to* nyiao 饒°; sô 赦°; sô'-diao 赦 了°; nyiao-sô' 饒° 赦°; sô'-min 赦° 免; *a general — from the Emperor*, wông-eng'-da-sô' 皇恩大赦°; *beg your —*, ts'ing ng' nyün-liang' ngô 請你° 原諒我; teh'-ze ng 得罪你°, (lit, have sinned against you).

PARDONABLE, k'o'-yi sô'-go 可以赦° 个°

PARE, *to* siah 削; *in* 削°; *— nails*, siah ts'-k'eh 削指甲°; *— the skin of a pear*, in li-deo' bi 削° 梨皮

PARENTAGE *for three generations*, sæn-dæ li'-lih 三代履歷

PARENTAL *love*, æ-ts' ts sing 愛子之心

PARENTS, do-nying' 大° 人°; tia-nyiang' 爹娘; vu'-meo 父母

PARLIAMENT, *British* Da-Ing' nyi-tsing'-we 大英議政會;

*— house* (or large place of assembly), nyi-tsing-yün' 議政院

PARLOR, k'ah'-vông 客房; *—* (on the first floor), k'ah'-t'ing 客廳, or, to distinguish it from a guest's sleeping room, we-k'ah-vông' 會客房

PARROT, ang-ko' 鸚鵡° (ih-tsah)

PARRY, *to turn aside*, kah'-ko 格° 過

PARSEE, Po'-s-koh nying' 波斯國人°; bah-deo-da'-pæn 白° 頭大班

PARSIMONIOUS (in using, and in treating others), k'æn-k'eh' 鄙° 刻; gyih-li' li 竭利利; 'eo-teo'-teo 猴抖抖; gying - gying'-dong 懔懔動; *— fellow*, k'æn-kyü'.

PART, kwu'-ts 股子; veng'-ts 分子; tsih 接; *give me a —*, kwu'-ts feng peh' ngô 股子分給° 我; *a —*, ih-feng' 一分; ih-kwu' 一 股; *divide in four parts*, tso s'-kwu k'æ' 做四股開; *give him a fourth —*, peh gyi s'-kwu-teh-ih' 給° 其四股得 *—*; *the greater —*, ih do pun' 一 大半; ih do kwu' 一大° 股; *the upper —*, zông döu' 上段; zông-gyüih'; zông-pun'-gyüih; *lower —*, 'ô döu' 下段; *take the — of one injured*, tang bao'-feh-bing 打抱弗平; gyiang' c'ih deo' 強出頭; *the latter — of the book is better than the first —*, 'ô'-pun

peng', pi zông' pun peng' hao'
下°半本比上半本好; *in
two parts*, liang'-k'æ-dæ 兩分°
開; *two parts joined*, liang'-tsih-
sang 兩接生°; *division* (as
a book of the Bible), peng 本;
kyün 卷

If nothing is said as to the number
of parts, ih-peng and ih-kwu mean one
of ten parts.

PART, *to divide*, feng 分; feng-
k'æ' 分開; — *in portions*, feng
kyi feng' 分幾分; *to — from*,
li-k'æ' 離開; bih-k'æ' 別開;
*can't — with*, feh-só'-teh' 弗捨°
得; — *with reluctantly*, lin-lin'-
peh-shiæ 戀戀不捨° (veng.)

PARTAKE, *to participate in*, dô-kó'
yüong' 大°家°用; dô-kô ziu'
大家°受; *will you — of a little?*
ts'ing ng' dô-kó' yüong tin' 請
你大°家°用點? *share another's
abundance*, dong-byiang' fu'-kwe
同享富貴

PARTIALITY, p'in-sing' 偏心;
p'in-dzing' 偏情; tæn pin'-sing;
tseh'-sing 側心; *to have a
special fondness for*, p'in æ' 偏
愛; *to show — in befriending one's
own*, pao-pi' 包庇°; we-kwu'
迴顧

PARTICIPATE, See PARTAKE.

PARTICLE, *Gram.* byü' z-ngæn 虛
字眼°; — (grain) *of dust*, ih-
lih hwe' 一屑灰; *the least —
(thread, or hair)*, s-'ao' 絲毫;
'ao-li'-s-hweh 毫厘絲忽

PARTICULAR, ts'-si 仔細; *over
— and fault-finding*, su'-se 瑣
碎; kæn-ka' 尷尬

PARTICULAR, *give every —*, ih-
dzing' ih-tsih kông' 一情一節
講°; ih-tsih' ih-tsih kông' 一節
一節講°

PARTICULARIZE, *to* kông'- leh
dziang-si' 講°得°詳細

PARTICULARS, *state the* ih-ih'
kông'-c'ih-læ 一一講°出來

PARTICULARLY, *notice* k'en ts'-si
看仔細; *notice more —*, keng'-
kô ts'-si k'en 更加°仔細看;
veng-nga' ts'-si k'en' 分外°仔
細看; — *remember this*, keh' ih
tün' ts'ih'-ts'ih yüong kyi'-teh
這一端切切要°記得

PARTING *feast* (given to one going), tsin-'ang' 餞行°; — *gifts
or attendance*, song-'ang' 送行°;
— *words*, song' bih-go shih-wó'
送別個°說話; li-bih'-go shih-
wô' 離別個°說話

PARTITION, pih 壁; iao-tsih' 腰
壁°; — *of boards*, pæn'-pih 板
壁; — *of bricks*, cün-pih' 磚壁;
*mud —*, nyi-pih' 泥壁; *to make
a —*, tsông' ih-dao pih' 裝一
道壁; *to separate by a —*, kah'-
k'æ 隔開; lah-k'æ' 拉開; *the
room separated from this by a —*,
(or the next room), kah'-pih vông'
隔壁房; pin 遍; i-pin' 依遍

PARTLY, pun 半; kyi-feng 幾
分; *garment — new, partly old*,

i-zông' pun'-sing-gyiu' 衣裳半
新舊; *words — true, — false*,
shih'-wô pun'-tsing-pun-kô' 說
話半眞半假°; — *brass —
silver*, kyi'-feng dong' kyi-feng
nying' 幾分銅幾分銀; —
*to see, — to hear*, pin-k'en', pin-
t'ing' 遍看遍聽

PARTNER (who supplies capital),
p'ing-cü' 拼主; p'ing ho'-kyi 拼
夥計; — (who has no capital),
kying-siu' 經手; tông-siu' sin-
sang' 當手先生; dæ sin'-sang.

PARTURITION, sang-yiang' 生
養; *difficult —*, sang-yiang næn'
生°養難

PARTY, pæn 班; pông 幫; tông
黨 (always has a bad sense); *of
the same —*, dong-pæn' 同班;
dong-pông' 同幫; *of our —*,
ah'-lah ih-pông' 我°等°一幫;
ah'-lah dong-pæn' 我°等°同
班

PASS, *mountain* ling 嶺; — *for
admission, &c.*, tsih'-tsiao 執照
See PASSPORT.

PASS, *to* ko 過; tseo'-ko 走過;
*he passed the gate*, gyi ts'ing'
meng-k'eo tseo'-ko 其沿門口
走過; — *under one's hand*, ko-
siu' 過手; — *under one's eye*,
ko-ngæn' 過眼°; ko-moh' 過
目; *must necessarily — that way*,
pih'-yiu-ts-lu' 必由之路;
*will not —* (as counterfeit money),
yüong'-feh-ko'-ky'i 用弗過

去°; — *through a hole*, dong-
ngæn' c'ün-ko'-ky'i 洞眼°穿
過去°; —*through Yentai*, kying'-
ko In'-dæ 經過烟臺; tseo'-
ko In'-dæ 走過烟臺; — (as
food), di-ko' 遞過; — *the dish
to me*, di beng-ts' peh ngô' 遞
盆子給°我; — *tea in a tray*,
pun dzô' 搬茶; *passed through*,
(or experienced), kying-lih'-ko
經歷過

PASSABLE, ko'-leh-ky'i'-go 過得°
去°个°; k'o'-yi 可以; peh'-ko
z-ka' 不過如°此°

PASSAGE, *a — way*, ih-da tseo'-lu
一垛走路; *to take — in a
boat*, or *to hire a boat*, ts'ing jün'
趁船; — *money* (by boat), jün-
din' 船錢°; *fare in general*, bun-
jün' 盤川°

PASSENGER, k'ah'-nying 客人°;
— *on a boat*, ts'ing-jün'-k'ah'-
nying 趁船客人°; — *boat*,
'ông-jün' 航船

PASSION, *feeling*, dzing 情; sing'-
dzing 性情; *he has a passion
for books*, gyi sing'-ts sô æ' z
shü 其性之所愛是書;
dzing'-ts sô cong' z' shü 情之
所鍾是書; *in a —*, fah do-
ông' de 發大°怒°了°; *the
seven lower passions*, s-dzing' 私
情; ts'ih'-dzing 七情

PASSIONATE, *he is very —*, gyi
ho'-ky'i do'-go 其火氣大°个°;
— *disposition*, sing'-kah kyih'-

ts'ao 性格急躁; sing'-dzing mao-ts'ao' 性情暴°躁

PASSOVER, yü-yüih'-tsih 踰越節; djü-kao'-tsih 除酵°節

PASSPORT, lu-bing' 路憑; lu-tsiao' 路照; wu-tsiao' 護照; — given by the Rebels, lu-p'iao' 路票; — to the other world, (Buddhist) lu-ying' 路引

PAST, ko'-de 過了°; — the time, ko-z'-de 過時了°; — ages, ko'-ky'i-go shü'-dæ 過去°个°世代; yi-wông'-z-shü' 巳往時世; to repent of — offences, t'ong'-k'æ zin-fi' 痛改前°非; — noon, dzi tsiu'-ko 遲晝過; signs of the — tense, ko 過; de; liao 了

PASTE, to tsiang-wu' 漿糊; to make —, diao tsiang-wu' 調漿糊; liu-wu' 冲°漿; to — together, s wu' nyin-long'-ky'i 以°糊粘攏去°; to — upon (as on the wall), t'iah 貼°; — for pies, &c., feng 粉; diao-hao'-liao-go min-feng' 調好了个°麵粉

PASTEBOARD, ts'-pah 紙栢; pe'-pah-ts 背栢紙 (ih-tsiang)

PASTE-BRUSH, wu - shih'-tsiu 糊刷篱 (ih-pô)

PASTOR of a church, moh-s' 牧師

PASTRY, feng' tso-go tin'-sing 粉做个°點心

PASTURE-GROUND for cattle, k'en-ngeo'-dziang 看牛°塲; grass land, ts'ao'-di 草地

PAT, to tah'-tah 搭搭

PATCH, to pu 補

PATH, siao' lu 小路; — between fields, din-dzing' lu 田塍路; stone —, zah lu' 石°路; my — is cut off (i. e. there is nothing for me to do), ngô lu' djih'-de 我路絕了°; vu-lu'-k'o-tseo' 無路可走

PATIENCE, jing'-næ-sing 忍耐心

PATIENT, næ'-sing-go 耐心个°; næ-sing' næ-siang'-go 耐心耐想个°; can't be —, jing'-næ-feh-djü 忍耐弗住; neh'-feh-djü' 納弗住; very —, ting' we jing-næ'-go 頂會忍耐个°; how — you are, ng sing' dza næ-hæ' 你°心怎°耐

PATIENTLY, do it —, næ'-sing tso 耐心做; bear —, næ-loh'-ky'i 耐下去°; try to bear —, ts'ia neh'-ih-neh 且°納一納

PATRIARCH, early ancestor, s-tsu' 始祖; — in the family, kô-tsu' 家°祖

PATRIMONY, vu'-yi-go ts'æn'-nyih 父遺个°產業

PATROL, to jing-lo' 巡邏; jing-dzô' 巡查; — at night, jing kang' 巡更; jing yia' 巡夜°

PATRON, s'-cü 施主; —who gives money, c'ih'-din s'-cü 出錢施主; — (the Emperor, &c.), eng-cü' 恩主; — of a store &c., ma'-cü 買°主

PATRONIZE by taking interest in

k'en'-kwu 看顧; — *by buying one's goods*, s'-kwu 賜顧; 'ô'-kwu 下°顧

PATTER, *to* tih'-tih-tah-tah' 遆遆霥霥; tih'-lih tah-lah' 遆遆霥霥

PATTERN, yiang-ts' 樣子; yiang-shih' 樣式°; *old* —, lao' yiang-ts' 老樣子; lao'-shih 老式°

PAUPER, vu-i' vu-k'ao'-go gyüong-nying' 無依無靠个窮人°; loh'-ts'ing vu-k'ao'-go 六親無靠个°

PAUSE, tin 點; *full* —, *or period*, tin'-dön 點斷; *a ditto* (in Chinese), ih-ky'ün' 一圈

PAUSE, *to* hyih'-ih-hyih 歇一歇; hyih'-ih-zông 歇一息°; deng'-ih-hyih 停°一歇

PAVE, *to* p'u 鋪; *to* — *with stones*, p'u zah-deo' 鋪石°頭

PAVEMENT *of stone*, zah-deo'-di 石°頭地; — *of brick*, cün-deo'-di 磚頭地

PAW, *foot*, kyiah 脚; *foot with claws*, kyiah'-tsao 脚爪

PAWN, *pledge*, tông'-deo 當頭

PAWN, *to* — (at a licensed shop), tông 當; — (at a place unlicensed), ah 押°; *to give in pledge*, ti'-ah 抵押°; *to take out of* —, c'ü-tông' 取當; *to prolong the time* (for three months, for an article pawned), tin li' 典°利; *to prolong the time* (for a year), cün p'iao' 轉票

PAWN-BROKER, tông'-sông 當商; *pawn-broker's clerk*, dziao-vong' 朝奉

PAWN-SHOP, tông'-tin 當店; *do*-tông' 大°當; *small* —, siao' tông 小當; — (generally small), ah' tông 押°當

PAWN-TICKET, tông'-p'iao 當票; ah'-p'iao 押°票

PAY, *wages*, kong-din' 工錢°; sing-kong' 辛工; *salary*, soh'-siu 束修; *officer's* —, fong'-loh 俸祿; *soldier's* —, zin-liang' 錢°糧; *soldier's half* —, pun'-feng zin-liang' 半分錢°糧; *to stop an officer's* —, vah fong' 罰俸

PAY, *to* — (as wages, or for what is bought), fu 付; kyih 給; — (out of politeness, or for something injured, &c.), t'ing; kwe 歸; *we* 匯; be-c'ih' 賠出; *I will* — *your chair hire*, ng'-go gyiao-din' ngô t'ing' 你个轎錢°我出°; — *off an account*, fu tsiang' 付賬; ka tsiang' 還賬; kyih tsiang' 給賬; *to* — *debts*, wæn tsa' 還債°; — *lack the worth of*, t'ing'-dzông 聽債; dzông-wæn' 償還; be 賠; — *the remainder*, tsao 找; tsao'-wæn 找還; wæn-tsao-den' 還找頭°; — *in instalments*, bah wæn' 拔還; bah-fu' 拔付; — *his debt*, teng'gyi dæ wæn' 與其代還; din'-fu 墊付; — *a visit*, mông-mông'

望° 望°; (or more ceremonious-
ly), pa'-mông 拜°望; 'eo-'eo'候
候; — *rows*, wæn nyün' 還願;
wæn nyün'-sing' 還願心; liao
nyün' 了願; dziu nyün' 酬願;
— *attention*, (or listen), liu-sing'
t'ing' 留心聽; — *a life for
a life*, ih-ming' ti' ih-ming' 一
命抵一命; — *him a debt*,
(with houses, or goods), ti'-siao
peh' gyi 抵銷給°其

PEA, zən-deo' 蚕苣; lo-hen'-deo
羅漢苣

PEACE, bing-en' 平安; en-tæn'
安耽; *at* — (as a place), t'a'-bing
太°平; *at* —, *in rest*, or *in
safety*, en-weng' 安穩; *to make,
or exhort to* —, ky'ün 'o' 勸
和; — *has been brought about,*
'o-sih'-de 和息了°; *to wish one*
—, ts'ing en' 請安

PEACEFUL, en-tæn'-go 安耽个°;
*in comfort*, en-loh'-go 安樂个°;
*very* — (no sorrow), t'ih'-t'a-
vu-iu' 極°穩無憂

PEACE-MAKER, 'o-z'-nying 和事
人°; kông-'ô'-go nying' 講°和
个°人°

PEACH, dao-ts' 桃子 (ih-go);
*luscious* (from Shanghai), shü'-
mih-dao' 水°蜜桃

PEACOCK, k'ong'-ts'iah 孔雀; *to
wear a pair of* — *feathers*, ta
sông-ngæn' hwô-ling' 帶°雙眼°
花翎

PEAK, *mountain* sæn-fong' 山峰

PEAKED, tsin-tsin'-go 尖尖个°;
pih-tsin' 筆尖

PEAL, *a* — *of thunder*, ih-go p'ih'-
lih 一聲霹靂

PEANUT, hwô-seng' 花生; dziang-
seng'-ko 長生菓 (ih-kyih);
— *candy*, hwô-seng dông' 花
生糖; — *oil*, seng yiu' 生油

PEAR, li-deo' 梨子° (ih-tsah)

PEARL, cü-ts' 珠子; *real* —,
tsing cü' 真珠; *false* —, kô'
cü-ts' 假°珠子; — *beads*, (false),
cü-k'oh' 珠壳; —, *brilliant at
night*, yia'-ming-cü' 夜°明珠

PEARL *barley*, mi'-jing 米仁;
*ditto* (as a medicine), i-yi'-jing
薏苡仁

PEBBLE, zah-ts' 石子; zah dæn'-
ts 石°彈子; — (large as a
goose egg), ngo-lön'-zah 鵝°卵°
石°

PECK, *a Chinese* — (of ten sing, or
about ten pints), ih teo' 一斗

PECK, *to* teh 啄°; — *and eat*, teh'-
teh ky'üoh' 啄°啄°吃°

PECUL, *a* ih tæn' 一擔

PECULATE, *to* s-yüong' koh'-t'ông
私用國帑

PECULIAR, *that fashion is* — '*to
Ningpo*, keh'-go yiang'-shih tsih'
yin Nying-po' tsoh' 這°个°樣
式只有寧波行°个°; —
*person*, gyi-bih'-go nying 奇別
个°人°

PEDANTIC, t'u'-lu dzæ-'oh'-go 吐
露才學°个°

PEDDLE, *to* — (as vegetables, fish, &c.), tso ʿông-fæn' 做行販; tso siao'-sang-i 做小生°意; t'iao weh-lu' tæn 挑活路擔; — *silks, needles, &c.*, tso ho-lông' sang-i' 做貨郎生°意

PEDDLER, tso ʿông-fæn'-go 做行販个°; ho-lông' 貨郎; *peddler's baskets*, bu'-tæn 藍°擔; *peddler's pack*, ho'-lông tæn' 貨郎擔

PEDESTAL, zo'-ts 座子; zo-bun' 座盤; *stone — for a pillar*, sông'-bun 礎磐; sông'-teng 礎礅

PEDESTRIAN, bu-ʿang'-go nying 步行个°人°; *good —*, tseo-kyiah'-go nying 善於°走个°人°

PEDIGREE, *register of* kô-pu' 家°譜; dzoh-pu' 族譜

PEEL, bi 皮; *orange —*, kyüih'-ts bi' 橘子皮; *dried ditto* (in the shops), dzing bi' 陳皮

PEEL, *to* in bi' 剝°皮; siah bi' 削皮; *to tear off skin with the fingers*, poh bi' 剝皮

PEEP, *to* — *at*, tsiang-tsiang'-k'en 睍睍看; — *secretly*, t'eo tsiang' 偷睍; — *through the crack in a partition*, pih'-vong-li tsiang' 壁縫裡睍; *to play bo-peep*, tsiang-mao' 睍貌

PEEVISH, wang' feh-z' jü' feh-z'-go 橫弗是豎弗是个°; tsi-tseo'-go 嘈鬧个°

PEG, *wooden* moh ting' 木釘; *bamboo —*, coh ting' 竹釘

PEKING, Poh'-kying 北京; — *Gazette*, Kying-pao' 京報

PELT, *to* ang 拋°; k'ang 擲°; — *him with snowballs*, yüong shih-dön' ang' gyi 用雪團擲其

PEN, pih 筆 (ih-ts); *steel —*, kông pih' 鋼筆; *quill —*, ngo-mao' pih 鵝毛筆; *the nib of a —*, pih'-fong 筆鋒; pih'-deo 筆頭; — *rack*, pih'-kô 筆架; — *knife*, siao' tao-ts' 小刀子

PEN, gyin 槤; *cattle —*, ngeo-gyin' 牛°槤; *pig —*, cü-gyin' 豬槤

PENAL *laws*, ying-lih' 刑律

PENANCE, *to do* tso pu'-joh 補贖其°罪°; zi' kw'u' zi 自°苦自°; *ditto* (as Buddhists), kw'u'-lin siu-ʿang' 苦煉修行°

PENATES, *family gods*, kô-jing' 家°神; *the six ditto*, kô-dao loh-jing 家°道六神

PENCIL, k'æn-pih' 鉛筆 (ih-ts)

PENDULUM, cong-pa' 鐘擺° (ih-go)

PENETRABLE, t'ong-leh-ko 通得°過; c'oh'-leh-ko' 掐得°過; — *by boring*, cün'-leh-ko' 鑽得°過

PENETRATE, *to* tsing'-ky'i 進去°; — *by boring*, cün-tsing' 鑽°進; *the wind penetrates the bones*, fong' jih kweh'-go 風入骨个°; *the eye cannot —*, ngæn'-tsing k'en'-feh-t'eo' 眼° 睛看弗透

PENITENT, *adj.* læ-tih ao' 來的 懊悔°; *truly* —, dziah-jih' læ-tih hwe' 着實來的悔

PENMANSHIP, pih'-fah 筆法; pih'-ts 筆子; *your* — *is good,* ng'-go pih'-fah hao' 你个°筆 法好; ng-go da-pih' tsing hao' 你°个°大筆眞好 (without the tsing, da-pih' 大筆, is used in a flattering way, when the — is not good).

PENSION, tsiang'-sông 獎賞; — *for great merit,* dzæ'-kyüô zih-fong' 在家食俸

PENSIONER *living on others' bounty and doing nothing,* ky'üoh bah-fong' bah-loh' 受°空°俸°祿

PENTAGON, ng'-koh-ying' 五° 角形

PENTECOST, wu-shing'-tsih 五 旬節

PENURIOUS, *excessively saving,* gyin'-sang ko-deo' 過°於°儉 省°; gyin'-p'oh 儉樸

PEOPLE, pah'-sing 百°姓;—*say,* nying-kô' wô' 人°家°話; *how many* — *were there?* yiu to-siao' nying læ-kæn' 有多少人° 在°彼°?

PEPPER, wu-tsiao' 胡椒, (*a grain,* ih-lih); *ground* —, wu-tsiao' feng 胡椒粉

PEPPER-BOX, ( bottle ) wu-tsiao bing' 胡椒瓶

PEPPERS. lah gyiæn' 辣茄; *very small,* or *button* —, nyiu'-ts lah-gyiæn' 圓°小°辣茄

PEPPERMINT, bo-ho' 薄荷°; — *oil,* bo-ho' yiu' 薄荷°油

PERCEIVE, *to be conscious of,* kyüoh'-teh 覺得°; *not to* — *or be conscious of,* peh'-cü-peh-kyüoh' 不知不覺; *to understand clearly,* t'eo'-ts'ih 透澈; — *by the eye,* k'en'-leh-kyin 看得°見; k'en'-leh-c'ih 看得°出

PERCENTAGE, me pah k'eo-deo 每百°扣頭 See DISCOUNT, and PERQUISITE.

PERCEPTIBLE (by the eye), k'en'-leh-c'ih'-go 看得°出个°; — (to the touch), moh'-leh-c'ih'-go 摸得°出个°

PERCH, *to* ding 停

PERCH, (a fish), lu-ng' 鱸魚°; (ih-kwang); *hen* — , kyi ding'-go tông' 鷄停个°檔

PERDITION, mih-vông 滅亡; leng-vông 淪亡 (veng.); *going to* —, læ'-tih tsco' si' lu 正在° 走死°路

PEREMPTORY, kyüih'-lih 決裂; sah'-tsoh 煞足; sah'-bo; kyih'-jih 砧實; *his commands are very* —, gyi'-go feng-fu' dza kyüih'-lih 其个°吩咐甚° 決裂

PERFECT, djün-be' 全俗; *complete,* wun-djün-go' 完全个°; *absolutely* —, jih-siang'-yü-tsoh'

十相餘足; jih-tsoh′ 十足; dzing-kong′-go 成功个°; dzing-dziu′-go 成就 个°

PERFECT, to tso′ dzing-djün′ 做成全; tso′ dzing-kong′ 做成功; — what is lacking, pu′-tsoh 補足

PERFECTLY done, tso′-leh tsiu-djün′-go 做得°周全个°; — good, jih-feng′ hao 十分好; djün-be′ hao′ 全備好; learn —, doh′-leh joh′-go 讀得°熟个°; iao joh-t′eo′ 要熟透; — understand, ts′ih′-ti ming-bah′ 徹底明白°; t′co′-ti ming-bah′ 透底明白°

PERFIDIOUS, we tao′-toh′-long-ts 明°瞞°暗°騙°; t′oh′-sing-feh-læ′ 托信弗來

PERFORATE, to — by boring, cün-ko′ 鑽過; — by punching, toh-ko 豬°過

PERFORM, to tso′ dzing-kong 做成功; — one's duty, dzing peng′-veng 盡本分; — acts of merit, 'ang hao′-z 行°好事

PERFUME, hyiang 香; p′eng′-hyiang 噴香; — materials, hyiang-liao′ 香料; perfumed essence, hyiang-shü′ 香水°

PERFUNCTORY, done in a — manner, tso′-leh liao-ts′ao′ sah-tsah′ 做得°潦草塞責

PERHAPS, iao′-bông 要防; 'oh-tsia′ 或者°; k′ong′-p′ô 恐怕, (usually signifies lest); væn-ih′

萬一; vi-min′ 未免; yia vi′-k′o-cü 也°未可知

PERIL, ngwe-hyin′ 危險; in 一, ling-hyin′ 臨險

PERILOUS, hyin′-hyin-go 險險个°; hyin′-dao-dao 險逃逃; in a — position, yiao-ling′-ling 搖懍懍

PERIOD, time, z-′eo′ 時候; age, z-shü′ 時世; cycle of sixty years, kyiah′-ts 甲子; — of prosperity, bying-wông′ z-′eo 興旺時候; —, or sentence, ih-kyü′ 一句; kyü-deo′ 句讀; a dot or 一, ih-tin′ 一點; 一, or circle (as used in the veng-li), ih-ky′ün′ 一圈

PERIODICAL, en′-z-′eo-go 按時候个°; — wind, en′-z-′eo-go fong′ 按時候个°風; time of ditto, pao′ gyi 颮期

PERISH, to be destroyed, mih-diao′ 滅境°; mih-vông′ 滅亡; to die, si 死°; — with cold, tong′-sah 凍死°

PERISHABLE, iao wæ-diao′ go 要壞个°

PERJURE, to — one's self, vah-kô′-tsiu 罰假°咒

PERMANENT, dziang 長; dziang-kyiu 長久; kyiu-dziang′ 久長; dzông-z 常時

PERMEATE, to t′ong-t′eo′ 通透; jih-t′eo′ 入透

PERMIT, n. tsiao 照; tsih′-tsiao 執照 (ih-go); a — to do (from

an official), we'-ba 委牌°; — (to consignee), ky'i'-ho-tæn 起貨單; — (to shipper), 'ó'-ho-tæn 下° 貨單; di-ho'-tæn 提貨單

PERMIT, to peh 與°; to allow, hyü 許; ing-jing' 應允°; to grant, cing 准; will you — me to enter ? hao peh ngô tseo'-tsing læ feh 好俾°我走進來否°? he would not — me to go, gyi feh byü' ngô' ky'i 其弗許我去°

PERNICIOUS, yiu-'æ'- go 有害個; yiu-seng'-vu-ih'-go 有損無益個°

PERPENDICULAR, [ dzih 直; to raise to a —, jü'-ky'i-læ 堅起來; jü' gyi dzih' 堅其直

PERPETRATE evil, 'ang ôh'-z 行°惡事; who perpetrated this deed ? keh ôh'-z jü' 'ang-go 這°惡事誰° 行 個°?

PERPETUAL, feh-dön' 弗斷; üong'-yün 永遠; üong'-feh-hyih 永弗歇; — inheritance, üong'-yün ts'æn'-nyih 永遠產業; — motion, feh hyih' go læ-tih dong' 時°時°而°動

PERPETUATE, to shü'-dæ liu-djün' 世代流傳; s'-teh üong'-kwu-ts'in-ts'iu, liu-djün' 使得永古千秋流傳

PERPLEX, to long'-leh ǹ-deo'-ǹ-jü' 弄得°無°頭無°緒; long-leh weng-teng'-teng 弄得°混濁°

PERPLEXED in mind, sing lön' 心亂; sing lön'-jü-mô 心亂如麻

PERQUISITES, i'- nga-ts-dzæ 意外° 之財; nga-ts'eh'-hwô 外°撮 花; nga-peh' 外° 撥; nga-kw'a' 外° 快°; — on wood, and ashes, shü'-deo-din 賞頭錢°; — of runners bringing presents, k'æ-fah'-go dong-din' 開發個°銅錢°

PERSECUTE, to pih'-næn 逼難; mo-næn' 磨難

PERSECUTORS, your pih'-næn ng-go cü'-kwu 逼難你°個° 人°

PERSEVERANCE, dziang-yün'-ts sing 長遠之心

PERSEVERE, to s'-cong, jü-ih tso' 始終如一做; — to the end, tso tao-ti' 做到底; yiu-s' yiu-cong' tso 有始有終做; hyih-sin'-feh-læ 歇手弗來; having begun must —, sih'-siu tsao min-feng' iao tso-tao-ti' 濕手遭麵粉要做到底; — in spite of difficulties, sing-kyin'-zah c'ün' 心堅能使°石°穿; t'ih tao'-ts-deo' mo siu'-tsing 若°要°功°夫°深°鐵杵磨綉針 (lit., from an iron pestle, to grind an embroidery needle).

PERSIMMON, z'-ts 柿子; tiao-'ong 火°柿°; large —, fông-z' 方柿; dried —, z'-ping 柿餅

PERSIST, to — in doing, p'in iao' tso 偏要做; p'in-sang' iao tso' 偏偏°要做; dzing-gyiu' iao tso' 仍舊要做

PERSON, a ih-go nying' 一 个°人°; a certain —, mo' nying 某人°; other persons, bih' nying 別 人°; go in —, ts'ing-sing' ky'i 親身去°; on the — (body), læ kyi'-sing zông' 在°身°體°上; (receives) in his own —, læ zi'-go sing zông' 在°自°己°个°身上; three persons in one, sæn we' ih-t'i' 三 位 一 體; call when speaking to a —, or in the second —, tông-min' ts'ing'-hwu 當面稱呼; call when speaking of a —, or in the third —, pe'-'eo ts'ing'-hwu 背後稱呼

PERSONIFY, tsia veh ky'i hying' 借物起興; — a rare flower, as if it were a beautiful woman, tsiang z-hwô' pi tso me-'nyü 將時花比作°美女

PERSPICUOUS, feng-ming' 分明; hyin'-jün 顯然; ming-tông'-tông.

PERSPIRATION, 'en 汗; to be in a —, læ-tih c'ih-'en' 正°在°出汗; — rolling down, 'en-c'ih'-t'ô-liu 汗出如流

PERSPIRE, to c'ih-'en' 出汗; — from drink —, or medicine, fah-'en' 發汗; fah-piao' 發表

PERSUADE him to come, ky'ün-gyi-sing' hao læ' 勸其信好來; he tried hard to — me but could not, gyi kw'u'-kw'u ky'ün' ngô, ky'ün'-feh-sing' 其苦勸我勸弗信; — kindly, un'-

cün ky'ün'-hwô 婉轉勸化

PERSUADED by him, be gyi ky'ün'-sing 被其勸信

PERTAIN, dzæ-ü' 在於; joh-ü' 屬於; pertains to God, dzæ'-ü Jing-ming' 在於神明

PERTINACIOUS, obstinate, nying dzih' feh cün-wæn' 認°直弗轉彎; ih-li' kang tao deo' 一犁耕°到頭; sticking to one's own way, 'eo-zi' 自°用°; — beggar, gyiang'-t'ao-væn' 強討飯

PERTURBED in mind, sing-hwông', i-lön' 心慌意亂

PERVADE, to fill, c'ong-mun' 充滿

PERVERSE, ao'-ky'iang 拗強; ao'-diao-peh-sing' 拗調不馴°; diao - bi' 刁疲; wang-pang' hyüing-liu' 橫°七°竪°八°; naturally —, kwæ-p'ih' 乖僻

PERVERT, to — the right, or the true, yi-dzih'-we-ky'üoh' 以直爲曲; he perverts my words, gyi pô ngô'-go shih-wô' tin-tao' z-fi' 其把我說話顛倒是非; perverted mind, sing'-jih yia'-de 心入邪了°

PESTILENCE, weng-bing' 瘟病; weng-yüoh' 瘟疫

PESTLE, jü'-peh 研°鉢; nyin'-ts 研子; tao-ts-den' 杵° (ih-go)

PET, to tseng-æ' 珍愛; o-lo.

PET, weh-pao' 活寶 (ih-go)

PETAL, a ih-bæn' 一 瓣; flower —, hwô bæn' 花瓣

PETITION, *written* ping'-tæn 稟單; *to present a* —, di ping'-tæn 遞稟單; — *signed by many*, kong-dzing' 公呈; *grant my* —, cing' ngô sô gyiu' 准我所求

PETITION, *to* ping'-gyiu 稟求; ping'-ts'ing 稟請; *to pray*, gyiu 求

PETRIFY, *to* pin'-we zah-deo' 變爲石°頭

PETROLEUM, ho'-yiu 火油; me-yiu' 煤油; zah-yiu' 石°油

PETTICOAT, gyüing 裙 (ih-diao)

PETTY *matters*, ky'ü-ky'ü'-siao z 區區小事; vi-vi-si' z 微微細事; — *reason*, si' kwu 細故

PETULANT, ô'-wông-tsi-tsao' 悭惶嘖嘈; ông-beh'-tsi-tsao' 勃°然°變°色°

PEWTER, *native* lah 鑞; sih 錫

PEWTERER, lah-s-vu' 鑞司務

PHANTOM, iao-kwa' 妖怪°; iao-ky'i' 妖氣; iao-nyih' 妖孽

PHARMACY, keh-yiah'-go fông-fah' 合°藥方法

PHEASANT, dzi'-kyi 雉雞; sæn-kyi' 山雞; yia'-kyi 野°雞; *golden* —, kying-kyi' 金雞 (ih-tsah)

PHILANTHROPIST, yiu jing-æ'-sing-go nying 有仁愛心个°人°

PHILOLOGIST, cü'-ka-z-nyi'-go 註解字義°个°

PHILOLOGY, *the science of* z'-yüoh, or z'-'oh 字學

PHILOSOPHER, poh-veh'-go cü'-kwu 博物个°人°; *learned man*, t'ong-dah'-go nying 通達个°人°; *very learned man* (in a Chinese sense), poh'-yüoh-'ong-jü' 博學鴻儒

PHILOSOPHY, *the Science of Natural* —, keh-veh'-go 'oh-veng' 格物个°學°問; *moral* —, sing'-li 性理

PHLEGM, dæn 痰; *to raise* —, t'u-dæn' 吐痰

PHOTOGRAPH, *to take a* —, ing siao'-tsiao 映小照; *photograph*, siao'-tsiao 小照

PHRASE, *a* ih-kyü djün-be shih-wô 一句全備說話; *a sentence*, ih-kyü shih'-wô 一句說話; *common phrases*, djông-yüong' shih-wô' 常用說話; — *that one is always using*, lao wô'-deo 老話頭

PHRASEOLOGY, kông'-fah 講°法; *good* —, dæn-t'u' hao 談吐好

PHYSIC, yiah 藥; *a dose of* —, ih-voh yiah' 一服藥

PHYSICIAN, 'ang-i' sin-sang' 行°醫先生°; i-sang' 醫生°; *clever* —, liang i' 頁醫; — *of repute*, ming i' 名醫; *I am a* —, ngô'-'ang i-dao' 我行°醫道; *travelling* — (quack), ma-yiah'-lông'-cong 賣°藥郎中; — *who heals by charms, &c.*, coh'-yiu-k'o' 祝由科; *physician's occupation*, i-dao' 醫道

PHYSIOGNOMIST, *and fortune teller*, k'en-siang'-go 看相个°

PHYSIOLOGY, *the science of* leng-sing-t'i'-go 'oh-veng' 論身體个°學問

PIAZZA, nao-dông'-teng 鬧塘等; nao-lông' 洋°臺°; nao-lông'-teng 西°洋°樓°; nao-leo' 鬧樓; *lower* —, yiu-jing'-k'eo 廊°下°

PICK, *to — rice* (as birds), teh-mi' 啄米; — *apart*, (as hair, wool, &c.,), p'ah'-k'æ 擘開; — (as fruit, or flowers), tsah 摘; ts'æ 探; — *tea leaves*, tsah dzô-yih' 摘茶葉; — *over tea* (taking out sticks, &c.), kæn dzô-yih' 揀茶葉; — *up*, ts'eh'-ky'i-læ 拾°起來; *will — out other's faults*, we t'ih' nying-kô'-go ko' 會提人°家°个°過; we t'ih'-bi t'ih'-kweh-go 會剔皮剔骨个°; — *out*, or *choose*, t'iao 挑; t'iao'-shün 挑選; kæn'-dzeh 揀擇; kæn'-shün 揀°選; — *out stitches*, ts'ah sin'-kyiah 拆線脚; — *out* (as nut-meats, eyes, &c.), leo-c'ih' 鏤出; wah-c'ih' 挖出; — *a fowl*, t'e kyi' 燒鷄; — *out feathers*, bah mao' 拔毛

PICKLE, *to — meat* (in brine), yin nyüoh' 鹽肉°; — *in vinegar*, ts'u'-tsing 醋浸

PICKLED *fruits*, sön-ko' 酸果; — *garlic*, ts'u'-tsing da-sön' 醋浸大蒜

PICK-POCKET, tsin-liu'-zeh 剪綹賊°

PICTURE, du 圖 (ih-ko); *Chinese picture*, or *scroll*, wô 畫 (ih-foh); — *of men and things*, jing-veh' du 人物圖; — *of scenery*, sæn-se' du 山水圖; — *of flowers*, hwô-hwe' du 花卉圖; —*frame*, and sometimes *a framed* —, kwô'-kying 掛鏡

PICTURE, *to — in one's imagination*, i'-ngwu 意悟

PIE, p'æn (the Chinese sound for the English).

PIECE, ih-kw'e' 一塊; *a slice*, ih-p'in' 一片; *a — of cloth*, ih-p'ih-pu' 一疋布; *a roll of cloth*, ih-dön pu' 一段布; —*by* —, kw'e-tang'-kw'e 一塊一塊; *divide in pieces*, (as a stick, fish, or something round), gyüih-tang-gyüih (or t'ön-tang'-t'ön) feng-tæn'-k'æ 一段°一段°分開; *cut pieces* (with scizzors), tsin se'-kw'e-deo 剪碎塊頭; *pieces*, ling-se' kw'e-deo 零碎塊頭

PIECE, *to — out*, tsih-dziang' 接長; — *together*, p'ing-long' 摒攏

PIECE-MEAL, ih-kw'e, ih'-kw'e 一塊一塊

PIER, mô'-deo 馬頭 (ih-go)

PIERCE, *to* c'oh'-tsing 猎進; ts'-tsing 刺進; — (with a boring instrument), cün-tsing' 鑽進

PIETY *toward God*, kying'-we Jing'-ming 敬 畏 神 明; *filial* —, hyiao'-jing do-nying' 孝 順 父 母°

PIG, siao'-cü 小 豬 (ih-tsah); *full grown* —, c'ong cü' 綜 豬

PIGEON, beh-kah' 鵓 鴿 (ih-tsah); — *whistle* (tied over the tail), beh-kah-ling' 鵓 鴿 鈴

PIGMY, a'-ts 矮 子; — (in ridicule), a-dong-djü' 矮 銅 鎚°; — *country*, a'-nying-koh' 矮 人°國

PIKE, dziang-ts'iang' 長 鎗; — *staff*, ts'iang-ken' 鎗 杆; *bamboo* —, kw'u' - coh - ts'iang' 竹 鎗; *ditto with iron point*, dziang-miao' 長 矛 (ih-kwun)

PILE, *to* — *up*, te-zong'-ky'i 堆 上 去°; te-diah' 堆 疊; — *in order*, diah-zong'-ky'i 疊 上 去°

PILES, tsông 椿; *to drive* —, tang tsông' 打 椿; *to drive* —, *and at the same time sing a song*, song-sông', or sông-hông'.

PILES, (a disease), dzi'-ts'ông 痔 瘡; *outward* —, nga dzi' 外° 痔; *inward* —, ne dzi' 內 痔

PILFER, *to* tso siao'-ts'ih 做 小 竊; tso siao'-zeh 做 小 賊°

PILFERER, siao'-ts'ih 小 竊; siao'-zeh 小 賊°; (more polite term, *lit.* a three handed person), sæn-tsah'-siu 三 隻 手

PILGRIM, *traveller*, c'ih-meng'-go nying 出 門 个° 人°; — *to a temple*, hyiang-k'ah' 香 客

PILGRIMAGE, *to go on a* — (*i. e.* to offer incense), tsing-hyiang'-ky'i 進 香 去°; *ditto to the sacred hill*, dziao sæn' ky'i 朝 山 去°; — *to the four mountains*, dziao s da ming sæn 朝 四 大 名 山

PILL, wun-yiah' 丸 藥; yiah-yün' 藥 圓 (ih-lih)

PILLAGE, *to* ts'iang'-kyih 搶 刦; tang'-kyih 打 刦; lo 擄; *to fire houses for* —, fông'-ho ts'iang'-ho 放 火 搶 火; *wholesale* — (as of a city), lo'-liah 擄 掠

PILLAR, djü'-ts 柱 子 (ih-keng); — *of state*, koh'-kô-go tong'-liang 國 家 棟 梁

PILLOW, tsing'-deo 枕 頭 (ih-tsah); *feather* —, ngo-mao'-tsing 鵝 毛 枕; *hair* —, mô-mi tsing 馬 尾°枕

PILLOW-CASE, tsing'-deo-t'ao' 枕 頭 套; tsing'-t'ao 枕 套 (ih-tsah)

PILOT, ling'-kông lao'-da 領 港 老 大 (ih-we)

PILOT-BOAT, ling'-kông-jün' 領 港 船 (ih-tsah)

PIMPLE, le 瘤; ts-mô-le' 芝 麻 瘤; *many fine pimples*, 'ong-tin' 紅 點; 'ong-pæn' 紅 斑 (ih-lih); — *from heat*, fi'-ts 疿 子

PIN, bih-tsing' 闊 針 (ih-me); *hair* —, fah'-ts'a 髮 釵 (ih-ts)

PIN, *to* yüong bih-tsing' kyin' 用 闊 針 緘; *to* —, *or tack*, bih 闊; *pin it*, bih'-ih-bih 闊 一 闊

PIN-CUSHION, tsing-ts'ah' 針插 (ih-go)

PINCERS, gyin 箝; *iron* —, t'ih-gyin' 鐵箝; *crab's* —, ha gyin' 蟹°箝

PINCH, *to* nyiu 扭; — *with the finger tip*, tih 摘; *put in a* — *of salt*, fông liang'-go ts'-deo, ih-ts'eh yin' 將°兩°个°指頭撮一屑°鹽

PINE *tree*, sæn-jü' 杉樹 (ih-cü)

PINE, *to* — *away*, in-üih'-leh, bi-wông'-kweh-seo' 憂鬱得°皮黃骨瘦

PINE-APPLE, po-lo'-mih 波羅蜜 (ih-go)

PINION, *to* — *the wings*, bo yiah-sao' 縛°翼°翅; — *the arms*, siu bo' læ iao-hyih'-li 手縛°在°腰脊裡; *tie his hands together*, siu, pông'-leh gyi 反°綁其手

PINK, (*the flower*), Loh-yiang'-hwô 洛陽花; *a deep* — (*or cherry color*), nyi-'ong' 二紅; *peach color*, dao-'ong' 桃紅; *light* —, dæn' dao-'ong' 淡桃紅; *feng'-'ong* 粉紅; *shü'-'ong* 水°紅

PINNACLE, ting-den' 巔°頂°; nao'-tsin' 頂°尖

PINT, *a* — (*dry meas.*), ih'-sing 一升; *half a bottle*, ih-pun' bing 一半瓶

PIOUS, *devoted*, gyin-sing' 虔心

PIPE, kwun'-ts 管子 (ih-ts); *water* —, shü'-kwun 水°管; *tobacco* —, in-kwun' 烟管;

— *stem*, in-kwun' ken'-ts 烟管杆子; *musical* — *with six holes*, siao 簫; *vong-wông'-siao* 鳳凰簫

PIRATE, hæ'-yiang gyiang-dao' 海洋強盜 (ih-go); *a boat for catching pirates*, ts'ih'-fi jün' 緝匪船

PISTOL, siu'-ts'iang 手鎗 (ih-kwun)

PIT, k'ang 坑°; di-k'ang' 地坑°

PITCH, lih-ts'ing' 瀝青; *to fill in with* —, din lih-ts'ing' 塡瀝青

PITCH, *to* — (*as cash, balls, quoits*), p'ao 抛; — *a tent*, tah tsiang'-bong 搭帳蓬

PITCHER, shü'-bing 水°瓶 (ih-go)

PITCH-FORK, kông-ts'ô' 鋼义; dao'-ts'ô' 稻义 (ih-pô, ih-kwun)

PITEOUSLY, *crying* kyiao'-leh k'o'-lin-siang 叫得°可憐相; k'oh-leh sông-sing'-siang 哭得°傷心相

PITH *of grasses*, ts'ao-sing' 草心; — *of trees*, jü-sing' 樹心; — *paper*, t'ong-ts'ao'-ts 通草紙

PITIABLE, k'o'-lin-siang 可憐相; — *condition*, kw'u'-kying 苦景

PITTED *with small pox*, mô-bi'-go 麻皮个°

PITY, *to* k'o'-lin 可憐; æ-lin' 哀憐; *what a* —! k'o'-sih 可惜!

PIVOT, *scissor* gao-kwu'-ting 交°股釘; — *on which a boat scull rests*, lu-cü' 櫓鈕°

PLACARD, *official* kao'-z 告示；
*notice,* kao'-bah 告白°；*adver-
tising —,* tsiao-ts' 招紙；pao'-ts
報紙 (ih-tsiang)

PLACE, di-fông' 地方；u-sen' 所°
在°；u-dông 戶蕩, (ih-t'ah or
ih-c'ü); *in what—?* læ soh'-go di-
fông' 在°甚°麼°地方？*no —,*
ꞗ-c'ü' 無°處；ꞗ di'-fông 無°
地方；*native —,* peng' hyiang
本鄕；peng' hyiang 本鄕；peng
t'u' 本土；c'ih sing' ts di' 出
身之地；*belonging to the same
—,* dong hyiang' 同鄕；*every
—,* koh'-tao-koh-c'ü' 各到各
處；*shady —,* tsô-ing' di-fông
遮°陰地方；*standing —,* lih-
kyiah'-go di'-fông 立脚个°地
方；*in the first —,* ih'-læ 一來；
ih'-tseh 一則；deo-ih' yiang 頭
一樣；di-ih' zeng 第一層

PLACE, *to* fông 放；en 安；—
*on a shelf, or stool,* koh 閣；*to
give — to,* nyiang-peh' 讓°給°；
t'e-nyiang' peh 推讓°給°；*— it
on top,* fông'-læ zông-deo' 放在°
上頭；*when does it take —?*
kyi-z yiu' 幾時有？*— the hand
upon,* siu en' ih-en' 手按一按

PLACID, en-zing' 安靜；en-jün'
安然；*— sea,* hæ bing-fông'
zing-lông 海平浪靜

PLAGIARIZE, *to copy and use
another's composition,* ts'ao-læ'
dzing-veng' sön zi'-go 抄來陳
文算自°个°

PLAGUE, *to* næn-we' 難爲；*the
—,* z-tsing' 時症；ẅeng-bing'
瘟病

PLAICE, *or sole,* nyiah-t'ah 鮭鰻

PLAIN, *level,* bing 平；*—ground,
or a plain,* ih-p'in' bing-yiang' 一
片平地°；*easily understood,*
hyin'-jün ming-bah' 顯然明
白°；*— words,* shih-wô' ts'in'-
gying 說話淺近；*unadorned,
or simple,* su'-zing 素淨；p'oh'-
jih 樸實；tsih'-p'oh 質°樸；
the last two also signify, respectable, and well behaved；*—
spoken,* sing-dzih' k'eo'-kw'a 心
直口快°

PLAINLY, *openly,* ming'-tông-tông
分°明°：*— dressed,* c'ün'-leh
p'oh'-jih 穿得°樸實

PLAINTIFF, nyün-kao' 原告

PLAINTIVE *voice,* sing-ing' pe-
ts'ih' 聲音悲切；sing-ing'
kw'n'-ts'ih 聲音苦切

PLAIT, *to lay in plaits,* kæn 裀°；
tsih-kæn' 摺裀°；tang-kæn' 打
裀；*to braid,* tang 打；gao-long'-
ky'i 絞°攏去°；*— the cue,* tang
bin'-ts 打辮子

PLAN *of a house,* oh'-yiang 屋樣
圖°；*to draw up a ditto,* tang ih'
go-oh'-yiang 寫°一个°屋樣；
*mode of doing,* fah'-tseh 法則；
fông-fah' 方法；*to devise a —,*
mo-nyi ih-go fah'-tseh 摹擬一
个°法則；tang'-ꞗo ih-go fông-
fah' 打摹一个°方法；*our —*

*works well,* ah'-leh fông-fah 'eh'-gyi-nyi' 我等方法合其宜; *what are your plans?* ng-sö' meo-we 'o-z' 你所謀爲何事? *intention,* dzing-i' 成意; cü'-sing 主心; *purpose,* cü'-kyin 主見; *that is a good —,* keh'-go siang'-deo hao' 這个想頭好

PLAN, *to* meo-we 謀爲; tang'-mo 打幕; tang'-sön 打算; sön'-kyi 算計; — *mischief,* meo-'œ 謀害

PLANE, bao 鉋 (ih-go)

PLANE, *to — it smooth,* bao gyi kwông' 鉋其光

PLANET, 'ang-sing' 行星; *the five planets,* ng'-sing 五星

PLANK, pæn 板 (ih-kw'e); *thick,* —, 'eo'-pæn 厚板; *teak —,* lih-jü-pæn 栗樹板

PLANT, *to* cong 種; tsæ-cong' 栽種; 'ô 下'; 'ô-cong' 下°種'; *to scatter seed,* tsah 撒'; *to stick in the ground,* ts'ah 插; — *a tree,* cong' ih-cü jü' 種一株樹

PLANTS, *grass, and herbs,* ts'ao 草; *ditto, and trees,* ts'ao'-moh 草木

PLANTAIN, pô tsiao' 芭蕉

PLASTER *for walls,* hwe 灰; hwe-feng' 灰粉; joh-feng' 熟粉; *medicinal —,* kao-yiah' 膏藥 (ih-tsiang); — *of Paris,* joh zah'-kao 熟石膏

PLASTER, *to* feng 粉; zông-hwe' 上灰; — *outside walls,* feng ziang' 粉墙; — *partitions,* feng

pih' 粉壁; *to put on a —,* t'iah kao-yiah' 貼膏藥

PLAT, *a grass* ih-kw'e ts'ing-ts'ao' di 一塊青草地

PLAT, *to* tang 打; gao 絞°

PLATE, beng-ts' 盆子; *soup —,* t'ông-beng' 湯盆; *dessert —,* cong-beng' 中盆; *small preserve* —, tsiang'-beng 醬盆 (ih-tsah)

PLATE, *to* pao 包; t'iah 貼; du 鍍; — *with silver,* pao nying'-ts 包銀子

PLATFORM, dæ 臺; — *for theatricals,* hyi'-dæ 戲臺 (ih-zo)

PLAUSIBLY, z'-wu-gying-dzing' 似乎近情; z-wu-'eh-li' 似乎合理; z'-wu-ziang' 似乎像

PLAY, *game,* hyi-kying' 嬉景; *gentle —,* veng hyi' 文戲; *coarse, or rough —,* ts'u hyi' 粗戲; mæn-tô hyi'-deo 蠻做°戲頭; — *for the stage,* hyi'-veng 戲文 (ih-peng); *one act of a* —, ih-c'ih hyi' 一齣戲; — *actor,* hyi'-ts 戲子; pæn-ts'-nying 班子人°; kyiah'-seh 脚色; — *fellow,* hyi-de' 嬉隊; hyi-yiu' 嬉友; — *thing,* na-'o' tong'-si 嬉戲東西; *toys* hyi-djü' 嬉具°

PLAY, *to* hyi'-hyi 戲嬉; na-'o' 𡞡和; hyi'-mæn 戲蠻; *to — on an instrument with the fingers,* dæn 彈; *to — by blowing,* c'ü 吹°; — *cards,* c'ô ts'-wu-bæn'

闒° 紙牌；— *for money*, tu dong-din′ 賭銅錢°；— *fairly*, ngang-dziang′ 硬場；*to cheat in* —, nyün-dziang′ 軟場；nyün′-gyüoh 軟局；— *checkers*, tsiah we-gyi′ 着圍棋；— *chess*, tsiah ziang′-gyi 着象棋；— *tricks of hand*, pin hyi′-fah 變戲法；— *with water*, long shü′ 弄水°；*fishes* — *in water*, ng hyi shü′ 魚戲水°；— *truant*, la-°oh′ 賴學°；— *for a day*, hyi′ ih nyih 戲一日°

PLAYFUL, tse′ æ hyi-mæn′ 最愛戲孌；oh′ we na-°o′ 極會嬉°戲°

PLEA, *to make a* — *in defence*, su 訴；— *on paper*, su′-ts 訴紙°；— *in court*, k°eo′-kong 口供；*apology*, feng-ka′ 分解°；feng-p°eo′ 分剖

PLEAD, *to entreat*, gyiu-k°eng′ 求懇；— *for another*, kông-dzing′ 講°情；wæn-dzing′ 挽情；— *a false reason*, or *excuse*, t′oh-kwu′ 托故；— *sickness as an excuse*, t′oh bing′ 托病

PLEASANT, yiu′-c°ü 有趣；*what* — *weather it is!* t′in′ dza yiu-c°ü′ ni 各°人°喜°見°天°晴°！

PLEASANTLY *playing*, hao′-tön-tön, læ-tih hyi′ 好好°而戲

PLEASE, *to* — *him*, s′-teh gyi hwun-hyi 使得其歡喜；peh gyi cong′-i 俾°其中意；*please* (I invite you to) *sit*, ts°ing zo′ 請坐；— *take tea*, ts′ing dzô′ 請茶；— *let me go* (can or not)？k°o′-feo peh ngô ky°i′ 可否俾°我去°？；*as you* —, ze-bin′ ng 隨便你°；ze-ng-bin′ 隨你°便；zing′-bing ng′ 任憑你°；ze ng′ i′-s 隨你°意思；dzong ng′ i′-s 從你意思；dzong ng′-go bin′ 從你°个°便；— *help yourselves* (at a meal), ze′ i′ ts°ing′ 隨意請；*tries to* —, we moh nying′-go sing-siang′ 善°合°人°意°

PLEASED, *greatly* gyih-gyi′ hwun-hyi′ 極其歡喜；hwun-hyi′-feh-sah 甚°歡喜；*not* — *with*, feh cong′-i 弗中意；feh jü-sing′ 弗如心

PLEASING, cong′-i-go 中意个°；— *and beloved*, (i.e. according to one′s mind) teh-i′-go 得意个°；— *to the sight* (as a landscape, a party of children, &c.), yiu kying′-cü 有景致

PLEASURE, *take* — *in*, yiu hying′-cü 有興致；*enjoyment*, kw°a′-weh 快°活；kw°a′-loh 快°樂；*to give one′s self to* —, tsoh-loh′ 作樂；*to spend time in* —, kw°a′-weh siao-yiao′ 快°活逍遙；*spoil my* — (lit. sweep away), sao ngô′-go hying′-cü 掃我个°興致；*cut off my* —, tang′-dön ngô-go i′-cü 打斷我个°意致；*I have long had the* — *of knowing and admiring*,

(him), ngô kyiu' nyiang, siang
yü' go 我久仰相與个°

PLEDGE, to pawn, tông 瞥; ah
押°; to — a garment, ti'-ah i-
zòng 抵押衣裳; i-zông' tso
tông'-deo 衣裳°做當頭

PLEDGE, tông'-deo 當頭; ah'-deo
押° 頭 (ih-yiang)

PLENIPOTENTIARY, ky'ing-ts'a'
da'-dzing 欽差°大臣

PLENTEOUS, PLENTIFUL, fong-
fu' 豐富; prepare a — supply,
be'-leh fong-fu' 備得°豐富

PLENTY, fong-tsoh 豐足; to-to'
多多; ts'iah'-ts'iah yiu-yü' 綽
綽有餘; — of food, liang-
zih' fong-tsoh' 糧食豐足;
year of —, da-joh' z-nyin 大
熟年°成°; fong nyin' 豐年;
successive years of —, lin-nyin'
da-joh' 連年大熟

PLIABLE, easily bent, ao'-leh-wæu'-
go 拗得°彎个°; nyün 軟;
yielding to others, jing nying'-go
i'-s 順人°个°意思; a —
person, ze-fong'-tao 隨風倒; ze-
zông'-ze-loh 隨上隨落; ziang'
ziang-deo'-ts'ao ka' 像牆上°
之°草

PLIERS, nyiah-ts'-gyin 揑指箝
(ih-pô)

PLOD, to — (as a student), kw'u-
kw'u' yüong-kong 苦苦用功;
— (as a laborer), tso kw'u'-kong
做苦功

PLOT, kyi'-kao 計巧°; kyi-meo'

機謀; kyi'-ts'ah 計策; (ih-go)
dark —, en' kyi 暗計

PLOT, to — injury, s ing-cü' 使陰
謀; s en-sön' 使暗算; en'-tsin
sông nying' 暗箭射°人°; —
mischief, meo-'æ' 謀害; —
murder, meo-sah' 謀殺; — rebellion, meo-fæn' 謀反; — for
money, meo-dzæ' 謀財; —
against the king in order to seize
the throne, meo wông' ts'ön we'
謀王篡位

PLOUGH, a ih tsiang li' 一張犂;
—share, li-zæn' 犂鑱°; — handle,
li-mi-pô' 犂尾巴

PLOUGH, to—the ground, kang din'
耕°田

PLUCK, to — (as flowers, or fruit),
tsah 摘; ts'æ 探; — up, bah-
ky'i'-læ 拔起來; —up by the
roots, lin keng' bah-ky'i' 連根
拔起; — hen-feathers, bah kyi'-
mao' 拔雞毛

PLUG, to seh 塞; din 塡; tsing-
seh' 鑕煞; stopple, seh'-deo 屗
頭; a wooden —, jü seh'-deo 樹
屗頭

PLUM, li'-ts 李子; sour —, me
梅; red —, in-tsi' li 胭脂李;
purple —, gyia-bi' li' 茄皮李

PLUMAGE, mao-yü' 毛羽; it has
beautiful —, gyi'-go mao-yü'
sang'-leh hao'-k'en 其个°毛
羽生°得°好°看

PLUMB, perpendicular, pih'-dzih
筆直; kweh'-dzih 骨直

PLUMMET, *weight*, djü 錘°; *car-penter's* —, cing'-tseh sin' 準則線; — (on ship), tang-shü'-zing 打水繩°; *to measure depth by a* —, tang sing-ts'in' 量°深淺

PLUMP, công 壯°; công'-mun 壯°滿

PLUNDER, *n.* tsông 贓; tsông-tsing' 贓証

PLUNDER, *to* ts'iang'-kyih 搶刦; — *on the road*, pun-lu tang'-kyih 半路打刦

PLUNGE, *to* — *into water*, t'iao'-loh shü-li' 跳落水°裏; *ditto to drown one's self*, deo-shü' 投水°; deo 'o' 投河; — *into water* (as the hand), tsing'-loh shü-li 浸落水°裡

PLUNGED *into poverty*, loh'-pe'-de 落悲了°; — *in great poverty*, loh-boh' de 落泊了°; — *into difficulty*, loh-næn'-de 落難了°

PLY, *to* — *one's self to study*, ts'ih'-sing yüong-kong' 切心用功; *plies between Ningpo and Shanghai*, ŵông'-læ Nying-po' Zông-hæ' 往來寧波上海

PNEUMATICS, ky'i'-yüoh or ky'i-'oh' 氣學

POACH, *to* — *eggs*, shü'-t'eng dæn' 水°余蛋

POCKET, dæ 袋; — *in a garment*, i-zông'-dæ 衣裳°袋; bin-dæ' 便袋; *Chinaman's small bag*, 'o-pao' 荷包; *tobacco* —, in-dæ' 烟袋; in-'o'-pao 烟荷

包; *long* — *for cash*, dzin-dæ' 錢袋; sông-bun' 錢搭°; — (tied on in front with the drawers), du-pang' 肚兜°; *long cloth* — *tied about the loins*, tah'-poh 搭膊

POD, k'oh 殼; *bean* —, deo-k'oh' 豆殼

POEM, *a* ih-siu-s' 一首詩

POET, yiu-s-dzæ'-go 有詩才个°; s-ong' 詩翁

POETIC *talent*, s-dzæ' 詩才

POETRY, *to write*, or *make* —, tso-s' 做詩

POIGNANT, *stinging*, ts'iang 鎗; — *words*, shih-wô' ts'iang 說話如°鎗; shih'-wô tsin-li' 說話尖利; — *distress*, c'oh'-sing næn-ko' 猎心難過

POINT, *sharp* tsin-den' 尖頭°; — *of a pen*, pih'-fong 筆鋒; — *of a knife*, tao-tsin-den' 刀尖頭°; tao-deo' 刀頭; *a* — (in writing), ih-tin' 一點; *to the* —, ky'üoh'-ts'ih 確切; *not to the* —, dz-i' feh-'eh' 詞意弗合; dz-i' veo-fæn' 詞意浮泛

POINT, *to* — *to*, tin 點; ts'-tin 指點; ts'-ying 指引; — *upward*, tin zông-deo' 點上頭; — *with a stick*, yüong bông' tin' 用棒點; — *off sentences*, tin kyü-deo 點句讀; — *mortar*, ming zah-hwe' 抿石°灰

POINTED, tsin-deo'-go 尖頭个°; yiu' fong-deo' 有鋒頭; — 一

*words,* shih'-wô ts'ih-cong' 說°
話切中

POINTLESS, m̄-tsin-deo'-go 無°尖
頭°个; m̄-deo'-go 無°頭°个;
*blunt,* toh'-fong-deo 言°; *his talk
is* —, gyi'-sô kông' m̄-fong-
deo'-go 其所講°是蠢°个°

POISED *on the head,* deo'-li ting-
leh weng' 頭上°頂得°穩

POISON, doh-yiah' 毒藥; *poisoned food,* doh-zih' 毒食; *to take*
—, voh doh' 服毒; *to put* —
*into,* 'ô doh' 下°毒; *fông doh'*
放毒; 'ô kwu'.

POISONOUS, doh-go 毒个°; yiu
doh' 有毒

POKE, *to* t'in'-toh 揣撥°; *to* — *the
fire,* t'in ho' 揣火; — *him,* toh'
gyi ih-kyi' 撥其一撥°

POKER, t'in'-ho-bông 揣火棒;
ho'-t'in 火揣 (ih-keng)

POLE, kông 杠; ken 杆; kao 篙;
*sedan* —, gyiao-kông' 轎杠;
*round* — *for carrying,* kông'-
kweng 扛棍; *flat ditto,* pin'-
tæn 扁擔; — *for drying clothes,*
lông-ken' 眼杆; — *of steelyards,*
ts'ing'-ken 秤杆; — *for a boat,*
kao-ts' 篙子; ts'ang-kao' 撐°
篙; *the North* —, Poh'-gyih
北極; *the South* —, Nen-gyih'
南極; — *star,* poh'-teo-sing
北斗星

POLE, *to* — *a boat,* ts'ang jün' 撐°
船; toh kao-ts' 揣篙子

POLICE *officer,* bu-t'ing' 捕廳;

— *runners,* bu-yüoh' 捕役;
*thief catchers,* bu-pæn' 捕班

POLICE-MAN, jing-bu' 巡捕 (ih-
go).

POLISH, *to make bright,* ts'ah liang'
擦亮; *to make smooth,* mo
kwông' 磨光; tsoh'-mo 琢磨;
ts'ih'-ts'o 切磋

POLISHED *in manners,* ky'i'-du
ts'ong-yüong' 氣度從容°

POLITE, yiu-li' 有禮; yiu li'-sing
有禮心; yiu li'-mao 有禮
貌; yiu li'-tsih 有禮節; yiu
li'-ky'i 有禮氣; *be* —, iao
dzing-li' 要成禮; feh-k'o' shih-
li' 弗可失禮

POLITENESS, li 禮; li'-mao 禮
貌; li'-ky'i 禮氣; li'-tsih 禮
節; *affected* — k'ah'-ky'i 客氣;
*true* —, k'ah'-dzing 客情; *understands* —, cü li' 知禮; sih
li' 識禮

POLITICS, koh-kô z-t'i' 國家°
事體; *the people ought not to
meddle with* —, pah-sing lön
kông dziao ding 百°姓亂講°
朝°廷事°

POLLUTE, *to* u-we' 污穢

POLYGON, to-koh'-ying 多角°形

POMFRET, ts'ô ng' 鯧魚°; ts'ông
鯧 (veng.)

POMEGRANATE, zih-liu' 石榴 (ih-
ko)

POMPOUS, we-pa-p'ing'-go 會擺°
品个°; do-moh'-do-yiang' 大°
模大°樣; deo'-do'-go, (slang);

— *show,* ba-dziang′ 排° 塲;pa-kô′-ts 擺° 架° 子;— *manner,* siang′-mao z′-wu ih-kying′ 相 貌 似 乎 一 景;i′-tsi-pah′-kyü 意 致 各° 別°

POND, dzi 池 (ih-k′eo);*fish —,* ng-dzi′ 魚° 池;ng-dông′ 魚° 塘

PONDER, *to — right and left,* tso′-s-yiu-siang′ 左 思 右 想;— *many times,* ts′in-s′ væn-siang′ 千 想 萬 想

PONGEE, kyin′-dziu 繭 綢;*gray* —, hwe′-seh kyin′-dziu 灰 色 繭 綢

POOR, gyüong 窮; *very* —, gyüong-kw′u′ 窮 苦;kw′u-li′-loh-boh′ 苦 裡 落 泊;— *cloth,* sô-ho pu′ 娑 貨 布

POOR-HOUSE, (for the poor, and crippled), yiang′-tsi-yün′ 養 濟 院

POP, *to — in,* zah-tsing′ 闖°進°; *to — out,* zah-c′ih′-læ 闖°出°來

POPE, kyiao′-hwô-wông′ 敎 化 王

POPPY, ang′-seh′-hwô 罌° 粟 花; ′a-p′in′ hwô 鴉 片 花

POPULACE, pah′-sing 百° 姓;*the vulgar —,* mæn pah′-sing 蠻 百° 姓

POPULAR, *is* teh nying′-go sing 得 人° 个° 心;*he is —,* gyi′ nying′-sing hyiang′-hwô-go 其 人° 心 向 化 个°

POPULATION, nying-ting′ 人° 丁; wu-k′eo′ 戶 口;*what is the — of China?* Cong-koh′ yiu to-

siao′ nying-ting′ 中 國 有 多 少 人° 丁 ?

POPULOUS, nying ts′ông-zing′ 人° 丁 昌 盛

PORCELAIN-WARE, dz-ky′i′ 磁 器;*fine —,* si′ dz-ky′i′ 細磁器

PORCH (has no equivalent);*shed, or arbor,* meng-k′eo-go bong-ts′ 門 前° 遮° 篷;*wooden projection over doors, or windows,* p′i-shü′- pæn 披 水° 板. See VERANDAH.

PORCUPINE, tsin-cü′ 箭 豬 (ih-tsah)

PORES *of the skin,* ′en′-mao′-kwun 汗 毛 管

POROUS, song 鬆;— *wood,* jü-moh song′ 樹 木 鬆

PORK, cü-nyüoh′ 豬 肉°

PORT, bæ′-k′eo 海 口;— *clearance,* ′ong-tæn′ 紅 單;jün-tsiao′ 船 照;— *for gun,* p′ao′-meng 礮 門

PORTABLE, hao-do′-go 好拿个°; do-leh-læ′-go 拿 得° 來 个°

PORTENTOUS, m̄-li′-z 無° 利 市; m̄-ts′æ′-deo 無° 彩 頭;— (ill) *omen,* peh-kyih′-ts ziao′ 不 吉 之 兆

PORTER, *door-keeper,* kwun-meng′-go 管 門 个°

PORT-FOLIO, wu-shü-kah′ 護 書 匣° (ih-go)

PORT-HOLE (in a ship of war), p′ao′-ngæn 礮 眼°; (window) liang-dong′ 亮 洞

PORTICO, yiu-jing′ 遊巡; yiu-jing′ k'eo 簷°前°

PORTION, a part, ih-feng′ 一分; ih-kwu′ 一股; to divide in equal portions, tsiao′-kwu kyüing-feng′ 照股均分

PORTRAIT, hyi′-yüong 喜容; zin-yüong′ 壽容; tsing yüong′ 真容; 'ang-loh′ 行°樂; siao′-tsiao 小照; to draw a —, sia hyi′-yüong 寫°喜容; — paint-er, sia-tsing-yüong′-go 寫°真容个°; tæn-ts'ing sin-sang′ 丹青先生°

POSITION in life, sing-veng′ 身分; in high —, sing-veng kao′ 身分高; great respect for one's —, sing-kô′ djong′ 聲價°重

POSITIVE, sure, ih-ding′ 一定; one — price, kô′-din weh-ih′ 價°錢°割一; peh-r′-kyüô 不二價; — in asserting, zi tsang′ yiu li′ 自爭°有理; zi wô′ zi z′ 自°話自°是; — in opinion, kwu′-tsih kyi′-kyin 固執己見

POSITIVELY, certainly, dziah-jih′ 着實; ts'ih′-jih 切實; to deter-mine —, k'eo′-jih 扣實; to as-sert —, gyin-k'eo′ kyih′-jih 箝口給實

POSSESS, to yiu 有

POSSESSED with a devil, jih-mo′-go 入魔个°

POSSESSION, in dzæ siu′ 在手; læ siu′-li 在°手裡; obtained —, tao′-siu-de 到手了°; why is it in your —? dza-we′ læ ng′-go siu′-li 怎°麼 在°你°手裡?

POSSESSIONS, houses, lands, &c., ts'æn′-nyih 產業; kô-kyi′ 家°計; kyi-nyih′ 基業; kô-ts'æn′ 家°產; — of money, dzin-dzæ′ 錢財 ·

POSSIBLE, practicable, neng-keo′-go 能殼个°; tso′-leh-læ′-go 做得°來个°; although —, it is not probable, se neng-keo′, r vi pih′ 雖能殼而未必

POST, pillar, djü′-ts 柱子; stake, tsông ts'ün (ih-go) 椿 (一個); to drive a —, tang tsông′ 打椿; go — haste, kying′-kyih-fi-pao′ 緊急飛報; to — a placard, t'iah ih-tsiang′ tsiao-ts′ 貼°一張招紙

POST for carrying letters, sing′-gyüoh 信局; shü-sing′-kwun 書信館

POSTAGE, sing′-din 信錢; also called wine money, tsiu′-din 酒錢°, and foot money, kyiah′-din 脚錢°

POSTAGE-STAMP, sing′-p'iao 信票; deo-ts′ 頭子

POSTERIOR, pe′-'eo 背後; be′-min 背面

POSTERIORS, p'i′-kwu 屁股; rump, deng-tsin′ 臀尖; — of an animal, zo-deng′ 坐°臀

POSTERITY, 'eo′-dæ 後代; ts′-seng 子孫; without —, or cut off, djih-'eo′ 絕後; dön′-cong′ djih-dæ′ 斷種絕代, the latter is used in cursing); *to descend to* —, djün-loh' peh 'eo'-dæ 傳 於°後代

POSTHUMOUS *son*, yi-foh'-ts 遺腹子; — *title*, z-fah' 諡法 (veng.)

POSTMAN, tsco-sing'-go 走信个°; ta-sing'-go 帶信个°

POSTPONE, *to* — *the day*, kæ gyi' 改期; tsæn nyih-ts' 趲日°子; *to put off*, dzi-wun' 遲緩; kw'un-wun' 寬緩; iah 約

POSTSCRIPT, nga-kô'-go shih-wô' 外°加°个°說話; *to write a* —, tsæ' tsiæ 再者; *a* —, ih-go ling'-p'i 一个°另批, disrespectful if addressed to a superior.

POSTURE, kw'un'-shih 欵式°; — *in sitting*, zo'-siang 坐相; — *in standing*, lih-siang' 立相

POT, iron t'ih'-kwun 鐵罐; *native* —, t'ih-ko' 鐵鍋; 'ôh 鑊 (ih-k'eo); — *lid*, kwun'-k:e 罐蓋 (ih-go); *earthen* —, tseng 甑; bing 瓶; bang 罌; *tea* —, dzô-wu' 茶壺; *flower* —, hwô-beng' 花盆 (ih-tsah); *water* —, shü-bing' 水瓶; *night* —, shü-bing' 尿瓶; *ditto* (used by Chinamen), yia-wu 便°壺 (ih-go)

POTATO, *foreign* nga-koh fæn-jü' 外國山°芋°; *sweet* —, fæn-jü' 山°芋° (ih-go)

POTTER, ngô'-yiao-s vu 瓦°窰司務; siao yiao' s-vu 燒窰司務

POTTER'S-FIELD, nyi-cong'-di 義°塚°地

POTTERY, ngô'-ho 瓦貨; *place for making* —, ngô'- yiao 瓦°窰; *place for selling* —, yiao-fông' 窰坊

POUCH, dæ 袋; *monkey's* —, weh-seng dæ' 獅°孫袋

POULTICE, *to* p'i 披; ah 壓°; — *with bread*, yüong mun-deo' p'i'-tih 用饅頭披的

POULTRY, kyi-ngo-æn' keh'-sing 雞鵝鴨°一°頖°

POUNCE, *to* — *upon*, boh-djoh' 伏°着°

POUND, *a* (borrowed from the English), ih-pông' 一磅; *Chinese* —, or *catty*, ih-kying' 一觔; *we buy beef by the* —, ah'-lah ngeo-nyüoh' leng pông' ma 我°們° 牛°肉°論磅買°

POUND, *to* — (as lime), sông 舂; — (as rice), ts'ah 舂; — (as clothes), djü 椎°; k'ao 敲°

POUR, *to* — *from an open vessel* (as a pail, or pot), tao 倒; — *out*, tao'-c'ih 倒出; — *upon*, tao-zông 倒上; — *from a spout*, sia 篩°; *to* — *tea*, sia dzô' 篩°茶; *to* — *water into, from a spout*, ts'ong-shü 冲水°; ts'ong-dzô' 冲茶; *to* — *in*, sia'-tsing 篩°進; ts'ong-tsing' 冲進; — *into one bowl* (the contents of two bowls), ping' ih-tsah' un 併一隻碗

POUTING *out the lips,* cü'-pô ky'iao-tæn'-ky'i 嘴 巴 翹 起 ; cü'-pô tu-tæn'-ky'i ; tu'-cü-bang'-sang.

POVERTY, *in a state of extreme —,* kying'-hwông gyüong-gyih'-de 境況窮極了° ; *does not fear —* (*wasteful &c.*), gyüong feh p'ô' 窮弗怕

POWDER, feng 粉 ; *medicinal —,* yiah-feng' 藥粉 ; yiah-meh' 藥末 ; *gun —,* ho'-yiah 火藥 ; *— for the face,* shü'-feng 香°粉 ; p'oh'-feng 宮°粉 ; *to make —,* sông feng' 舂粉 ; mo feng' 磨粉

POWDER, *to —* (*the face*), tsông feng' 粧粉 ; *—* (*elsewhere*), dzô feng' 搽粉 ; *— with a puff,* p'oh feng' 撲粉

POWER, *authority,* gyün-ping' 權柄 ; gyün-shü' 權勢 ; *might,* (*as that given by friends, money, &c.*), shü'-dao 勢道 ; shü'-fong 勢風 ; *ability,* neng-ken' 能幹 ; dzæ-neng' 才能 ; *strength,* lih-liang' 力量 ; gying-dao' 力道 ; *—* (*both mental, and physical*), vu'-nyih-ts' 武藝子° ; *in one's —,* læ siu-li' nyiah'-tong 揑在°手裡

POWERFUL, *having great authority,* yiu do' gyün'-ping 有大°權柄 ; *having great strength,* yiu do' gying-dao' 有大°力道

POWERLESS, shü'-sô-feh-neng' 勢所不°能 ; lih'-sô-feh-neng' 力所不°能

POX, *chicken* shü'-deo 水°痘 ; *small —* (*natural*), t'in-deo' 天痘 ; t'in-hwô' 天花 ; *to inoculate small —,* cong deo-ts' 種痘子 ; cong-hwô' 種花 ; *to have the small —,* c'ih t'in-deo' 出天痘 ; *ditto* (*by inoculation*), c'ih deo-ts' 出痘子

PRACTICABLE, tso'-leh-læ-go 做得°來个° ; hao'-tso-go 好做个°

PRACTICE, *usage,* kwe-kyü' 規矩 ; *— of a place,* hyiang-fong' 鄉風 ; fong-djoh' 風俗 ; *bad ditto,* jih-ky'i' 習氣 ; *an injurious —,* yiu-'æ'-go jih-ky'i' 有害个°習氣

PRACTICE, *to* jih 習 ; jih-lin' 習練 ; 'oh-jih' 學習 ; *— in order to be perfect,* kyiu' lin s'-teh hao dzing-kông 久鍊成鋼

PRACTICED *hand,* lao'-siu 老手

PRAISE *to* ts'ing-tsæn' 稱讚 ; tsæn'-me 讚美

PRAISE, *worthy of* ing'-teh ts'ing-tsæu' 應得稱讚

PRANCE, *to* t'iao 跳 ; ts'ön 竄

PRAWNS, *and shrimps,* hô 蝦° ; *— dried,* hô-ken' 蝦°乾 ; *ditto dried without shells,* hô-mi' 蝦°米

PRAY, *to* gyiu 求 ; tao'-kao 禱告 ; *— for another,* dæ gyiu' 代求 ; cün' gyiu 轉求 ; *— for clear weather,* gyiu zing' 求晴°

PRAYER, tao'-kao 禱告; — *for special mercy*, coh'-veng 祝文; *to make a* —, tso tao'-kao 做禱告

PRAYER-BOOK, *a* ih-peng tao'-kao-veng' 一本禱告文; *Buddhist* —, kying'-kyün 經卷; kying-ts'æn' 經懺

PREACH, *to* — *religion*, kông dao'-li 講°道理; djün kyiao' 傳敎; djün dao' 傳道; — *the Sacred Books*, kông kying' 講°經

PREACHER, kông dao'-li-go nying 講°道理个°人°; djün kyiao cü'-kwu 傳敎个°人°

PRECARIOUS, yün-shü'-dang-tsiang 懸勢宕槳; yiao-yiao'-peh-jih 搖搖不實; — *footing*, dah'-tih feh-ẃeng'-tông 踏的弗穩當

PRECAUTION, *to take* yü-sin' bông-be' 預先防備

PRECEDE, *you will* — (us), ng' sin ky'i' 你°先去°; ng' dzæ zin' 你°在前°

PRECEDENCE, *one who takes* — *in age*, zin-pe' 前°輩; zin-pæn'-pe 前°班輩; tsiang'-pe 長輩

PRECEDENT, pi'-kyin 比肩; *quote as a* —, ying'-læ tso lao-li' 引來做老例; *to establish a* —, tso' ih-go pi'-kyin 做一个°比肩

PRECEDING *month, or months* — *this*, keh'-yüih ts-zin' 這°月之前°; *the* — *verse*, zông-deo' ih-tsih' 上頭一節

PRECEPT, feng-fu' 吩附; kwe-kyü' 規矩

PRECIOUS, pao'-pe 寶貝; kwe'-djong 貴重; hyi-gyi' 希奇; — *stones*, pao'-zah 寶石°; *it is very* — *to me*, z ngô ting' pao'-pe-go 是我頂寶貝个°; z ngô' ting kwe'-djong-go 是我頂貴重个°; z ngô ting' hyi-gyi'-go 是我頂希奇个°

PRECIPICE, sæn-ngæn' 山巖; ts'iao'-pih 峭壁 (veng.); *standing on the brink of a* —, lih'-læ sæn'-ngæn pin-yin' 立在°山巖邊沿

PRECISE, *exact*, ting'-cing 訂準; *accurate*, ts'ih'-jih 切實; *minutely careful*, ts'-si 仔細

PRECISELY, *exactly*, feng-ngæn'-feng-shing 分眼°分櫱; k'eo'-k'eo 剛°剛°

PRECLUDE, *to* — *one from doing*, long'-leh gyi zông-siu'-feh-læ' 弄得°其上手弗來°; *the necessity for that is precluded*, keh' lu z-t'i', ts'-djü-de 這椿°事體不°通了°

PRECOCIOUS, *the* — *child is hard to rear* (*i. e. may die early*), siao-nying' t'eh ling', næn yiang'-go 小孩°太伶難養个°

PREDECESSOR *in office*, zin-zing 前°任; — *on the throne*, zin-deo' wông-zông 先°皇帝; *which is better, the present officer or his* —? wa z yin-zing' kwun hao,'

zin-zing kwun' hao' 還°是現
任°官好呢°前°任°官好？
PREDESTINATE, *to* ding-su' 定
數; dzin-ding' 前定
PREDICAMENT, *in a bad* zi we'-
u 自°穢污; gyi ngeo p'ong-
djoh ts'ing-kô'-kong 騎牛逢
着°親家°公; feh-seh'-deo 弗
色頭
PREDICT, *to* yü-sin' kông 預先講°
PREDICTION, yü-sin' shih-wô' 預
先說話; yü yin' 預言 (veng.)
PREDOMINANT, ziang yiu gyün'
tsông'-tih ka 如°掌權°一°
般°; — *desire*, deo-ih'-go sing-
nyün' 頭一个°心愿
PRE-EMINENT, c'ih-cong' 出衆;
c'ih-kah' 出格; ts'iao-c'ih-ü-
cong' 超出於衆
PRE-EMINENTLY *beautiful*, c'ih-
cong'-go hao'-k'en 出衆个°
好看
PREFACE, jü-veng' 序文; siao'-
ying 小引
PREFECT *of a department*, cü-fu'
知府; do-fu'.
PREFECTURE, ih-fu' 一府
PREFER, *to* — (*in choice*), neng'-
k'o or nying'-k'o 甯°可; *rather*,
neng'-s 甯°使; — *in rank*, kô
p'ing'-kyih 加°品級; — *in
office*, sing-zông'-ky'i 陞上去°;
— (*or set one above another*),
t'e-tseng 推尊
PREFIGURE, *to* yü-sin' piao'-ming
預先表明

PREFIX, *to* kô' læ zông-deo' 加°
在°上頭
PREGNANT, sông-sing' 雙身; yiu-
sing' 有娠°; yiu-yüing' 有孕°;
yiu-t'æ' 有胎; do-du' 大°肚
PREJUDGE, *to* yü'-sin tön' 預先
斷; *to blame severely beforehand*,
sin p'i-siah' 先批削
PREJUDICE, p'in-kyin' 偏見;
*to harbor* —, dzeng p'in-kyin' 存
偏見; *willing to believe only one
side*, t'ing' tæn-min'-ts-yin 只°
聽°一°面之言
PREJUDICIAL, *injurious*, we-'æ'-
go 爲害个°
PREMATURE, *time not arrived*, z-
'eo' wa feh-tao' 時候還°弗
到; *too early*, t'eh' tsao 太°早
PREMEDITATE, *to* hyüoh-i' 蓄
意; hyüoh'-i iao 'æ 蓄意要
害; cü-sing iao 'æ 存°心要害
PREMEDITATED *injury*, yiu'-i meo-
'æ 有意謀害; — *murder*,
dzeng-sing' meo-sah' 存心謀
殺; hyüoh'-i sah-nying' 蓄意
殺人°
PREMIUM (*generally from an officer*), sông'-kah 賞格; *to give a
reward*, sông tong-si' 賞東西
PREMONITION, *had notice*, r'-fong
t'ing-meng-ko-de 風聞過了°;
fong'-sing kwah'-djoh-ko-de 風
信得°着°過了°
PREOCCUPIED *mind*, sing'-læ bih'
u-sen' 心在°別處°; sing' feng-
k'æ'-de 心分開了°

PREPARE, *to* be-bæn′ 備辦; — *beforehand,* yü-be′ 預備; — *without fail,* ih′-cing be-bæn′ 準備辦; — *against,* bông-be′ 防備; — *for emergency,* yi′-be wun′-kyih 以備緩急; be-r′-peh-yüong 備而不用; — *food* (rice), long væn′ 弄飯

PREPARED, *all* — (or ready), be-zi′-de 備齊了°; be-hao′-de 備好了°

PREPOSSESSING, we teh nying′ hwun-hyi′ go 會°得人°歡喜個°

PREPOSTEROUS, ky'i - yiu′-ts'-li 豈有此理

PREROGATIVE, z-cü′-ts-gyün′ 自主之權; *my* —, ngô-go veng-ne′-ts-z′ 我个阼內之事

PRESBYTERIAN *church,* tsiang′-lao kong′-we 長老公會

PRESBYTERY, lao′-we 老會

PRESCRIBE, *to* — (in medicine), k'æ fông-ts′ 開方子; — *rules,* shih′-lih kwe-tseh′ 設°立規則

PRESCRIPTION, *medical* yiah-fông′ 藥方; fông-ts′ 方子

PRESENCE, *in the* — *of,* læ tông-min′-zin 在°當面前°; læ min-zin′ 在°面前°; *speak in his* —, te′-min-kông′ 對面講°; *in* — *of all,* sæn-kyin′-loh-ming′ 三見六面; *has* — *of mind,* yiu ling-kyi′; 有靈機; seh′-deo ts'ing′ 見°識°快°; sing′ feh hwông′ 心弗慌

PRESENT, *here,* 在°; læ-tong′ 在此°; — *life,* kying′-si 今世°; kying-seng′ 今生; — *comforts,* ngæn′-zin bao-c'ü′ 眼°前°好處; — *dynasty,* peng′-dziao 本朝; — *emperor,* tông′-kying wông-ti′ 當今皇帝; *at* —, yin-dzæ′ 現在; moh-yüô′ or moh-'ô′ 目下; ngæn′-zin 眼°前°

PRESENTS, li′-veh 禮物; jing-dzing′ 人情; — *of congratulation,* 'o-li′ 賀禮; — (on visiting a superior), ts′-kyin-li′ 贄儀°; — *given to employees, usually at the three festivals,* hwô-'ong′ 花紅; *a small present to those one visits,* seh′-hwô 色花

PRESENT, *to* — (as a gift), song 送; vong-song′ 奉送; — (to a superior), vong′-hyin 奉獻; — (to one going on a journey), gwe′-song 餽送; — *at court,* ying′-kyin 引見; — *a document to the emperor,* zông peng′ 上本

PRESENTLY, *coming* ziu læ′ 就°來; mô-zông′ ziu læ′ 馬上就°來

PRESENTIMENT, (and also a sign), ts'eng′-z 識事; *to believe in a* —, siang-sing′ ts'eng′-z 相信識事

PRESERVE, *to keep from harm,* pao′-wu 保護, pao′-djün 保全; pao′-yiu 保佑; tô′-hwô 眷顧°; (the last two refer only to God); — *from decay,* s′-teh feh wæ′-diao 使得弗壞了°

PRESERVED, *fruits — in sugar,* dông-ko′ 糖果; *fruits — in honey,* mih-tsiu′ 蜜餞;—*ginger,* tsiang′-kyiang 醬薑

PRESIDE, *to — over,* kyin-ling′ 監臨 (veng.)

PRESIDENT, *the head,* siu′-z 首事; — *of a college,* yün-tsiang′ 院長;— *of one of the six Boards,* zông-shü 尙書;—*of a republic,* siu′-ling 首領; tsing′-siu-ling′ 正首領; *vice —,* fu′-siu-ling′ 副首領

PRESS, *machine for squeezing wine,* tsô′-zông 榨床; —, tsiu′-tsô 酒榨; *clothes′ closet,* i-djü′ 衣櫥; *printing —,* ing′-shü kô′-ts 印書架子

PRESS, *to urge,* ngang-ky′ün′ 硬勸; — (another) *forward,* pih′-leh kying′ 逼得緊; ts′e′-leh kyih′ 催得急;— *down,* ky′ing′-loh-ky′i 撳落去;— *down with a weight,* ah′-loh-ky′i 壓落去; — *to the front,* a-zông-zin′ 挨上前;— *oil,* tsô yiu′ 榨油; —, or *push against the door,* t′e meng′ 推門;— *one to eat,* iang nying ky′üoh′ 極意請人吃; iang nying-k′ah′;— *to take wine,* iang tsiu′ 敬酒不停

PRESSED *in spirit,* dziah-kyih′ 着急; — *for money,* siu′-deo kyih-kyü′ 手頭拮据

PRESSING *affairs,* kyih′-ts′ih z-t′i′ 急切事體; *he is in — need,* gyi-go dzing′ kyih′-tih-de 其个情急了

PRESUME, *I — so,* ngô kwu′ læ z ka′ 我估來是如此; tsiao ngô k′en′ z-ka′ 照我看是這樣; ngô bông-bông′ z-ka′ 我恐防是如此; *to dare,* ken 致; — *on one′s strength to injure,* or *demand,* tang-pô′-shü 打覇勢;— *on one′s strength* (in being wilful), i′- z gyiang-wang′ 依恃强横

PRESUMPTUOUS, mông-bah′-go 茫白个; tæn′-ts do′ yia′-ky′i 胆子大野氣;— *in thinking one willing* (when he may not be), ih′-siang dzing-nyün′ 一相情願

PRETEND, *to — to be,* tsông 裝; tsông-kô′ 裝假; pæn 扮; — *with craft,* tsô 詐;— *to be a doctor,* tsông i-sang′ 裝醫生; — *to be sick,* tsông bing′ 裝病 — *to be willing,* or— *not to want,* tsông-ky′iang′ 裝腔; *to allege a reason which is false, but which has a shadow of truth,* tsia′-ing 借因; *to use another′s name falsely,* tsia ming-deo′ 借名頭; — *that another is at fault,* t′e-we′ 推諉; t′e-t′oh′ læ bih′-nying sing-zông′ 推托在別人身上; *to pass off the false for the true,* mao-c′ong′ 冒充

PRETERNATURAL, (as a cat or fox changing into a person &c.), tsing-kwa′ 精怪

PRETEXT, *to rely upon a false* —, ziæ-kwu' 藉 故°; *to use a false* —, ziæ-k'eo' 藉 口

PRETTY, hao-k'en' 好 看; teh-nying'-sih 得 人° 惜; *very* —, ts'iao 俏; ts'iao-li' 俏 麗; me'-mao 美 貌; piao-cü' 標 緻; (these four are only used of persons); —(as colors), sin ming' 鮮 明; *tolerably* —, p'o' hao'-k'en 頗 好 看; *how* — *you are!* (ironical), ng dza hao yiang-væn 你 怎 好 樣 範!

PRETTY, *tolerably*, p'o 頗 (not in common use); —*well* p'o' sông'-kw'a 頗 爽 快; — *well to do*, k'o' ko nyih-ts' 可 過 日°子; — *near*, p'o'-gying 頗 近

PREVAIL, *to conquer*, teh-sing' 得 勝; *perhaps will* —, ying-min' 贏 面; *I could not* — *on him to go*, ngô' ky'ün-gyi-feh-cün', z-feh k'eng ky'i' 我 勸 其 弗 轉 是 弗 肯 去°

PREVALENT, kwông'-'ang-go 廣 行 个°; t'ong-'ang'-go 通 行 个°; *that is a* — *belief*, keh'-go dao'-li kwông-'ang-liao-go 這° 个° 道 理° 廣 行° 个°; *what disease is* — *now?* yin-dzæ' yiu soh'-go tsing'-'eo 現 在 有 甚 麼° 症 候? *colds are very* —, sông-fong' da-li ting-t'o 傷 風 之°症 頂 多, sông-fong' kwông 傷 風 廣

PREVARICATE, *to* kông'-leh t'eng-t'eng'-t'u-t'u 講°得°吞 吞 吐 吐; kông'-leh pun'-tsing pun-c'ih' 講°得°半 進 半 出

PREVARICATION, ts'ih'-gæ-pah'-gæ shih-wô 七 戲 八 戲 說 話; *to say what in heart is not believed*, k'eo'-z-sing-fi' 口 是 心 非;

PREVENT, *to* tsu 阻; læn-tsu' 攔 阻; læn-djü' 攔 住; zih-djü' 截 住; tsu'-djü 阻 住; these are all used with feh, thus; — *him from coming*, tsu'-gyi-feh-læ 阻 其 弗 來, (this also means, cannot prevent him); min'-teh gyi læ' 免 得 其 來; — *trouble afterwards*, min 'eo'-wæn 免 後 患; — *sleep* (as strong tea), su-sing k'eh'-c'ong 蘇 醒 睏 睡; — *his telling* (by giving him something, &c.), en gyi cü'-pô pi 按 其 嘴 巴 閉; seh gyi cü'-pô 塞 其 嘴 巴

PREVIOUS, sin 先°; zin 前°; *the* — *day*, sin'-ih-nyih 先 一 日°; zin'-ih-nyih 前° 一 日°; *the* — *month*, zin-ko'-yüih 前° 個° 月; *on a* — *occasion*, zin-deo' ih-we 前° 頭 一 回

PREVIOUSLY, yü-sin' 預 先; yü-tsao' 預 早; bông-tsao' 防 早

PRICE, kô'-din 價° 錢°; *market* —, 'ông-dzing' 行 情; z-kô' 時 價°; *to rise in* —, kô'-din tsiang'-zông 價° 錢° 漲 上; *to fall in* —, kô'-din tih'-loh 價° 錢° 跌 落; *what is the* —? to siao' kô'-din 多 少 價° 錢°? *high* —, kô'-din do' 價 錢° 大°; kô'-din kyü' 價° 錢° 貴°; kô'- din kao' 價錢高 (seldom used); *I cannot afford that*—, ka kô'-din ngô c'ih'-feh-ky'i 如° 此° 價° 錢° 我 出 弗 起

PRICELESS *treasure*, vu-kô'-ts-pao 無 價° 之 寶

PRICK, *to* c'oh 撮; — *like a needle*, ziang tsing c'oh' ka 像 針 撮; *to* — *up the ears*, ng'-tô jü'-ky'i-læ 耳° 朵 竪 起 來

PRICKLES, ts' 莉; *has* —(or roughness), ts'-c'oh ling-ting 莉 撮 零丁; *full of* —, jing-z ts' 純 是 莉; ts'-kyih kao 莉 結 交°

PRICKLY *heat*, fi'-ts 痱 子

PRIDE, kyiao'-ngao 驕 傲; — (usually proper), sing-kao' ky'i-ngao' 心 高 氣 傲; *take* — *in* (anything proper), tsang ih k'eo ky'i' 爭° 一 口 氣

PRIEST, *Buddhist* 'o-zông' 和 尙; veh-meng' di'-ts 佛 門 弟 子; *head ditto*, fông-dziang' 方 丈; fah'-s 法 師; *Taoist* —, dao'-z 道 士; *Lama* —, na'-mô-seng' 喇° 嘛 僧; *itinerating* — (bad), yiu-fông-seng' 遊 方 僧; *Catholic* —, jing-vu' 神 父; *Jewish* —, tsi'-s 祭 司; *Mahometan* —, lao'-s-vu 老 師 父; — (with long hair, and band on the head), deo-do' 頭 陀; *chief* —, tsi'-s-deo 祭 司 頭; *high* —, tsi'-s-tsiang' 祭 司 長; *to become*

*a Buddhist* —, c'ih-kô' 出 家°

PRIESTESS, *Buddhist* nyi-kwu' 尼 姑; *Taoist* —, s-kwu' 師 姑

PRIESTHOOD, *Buddhist* sih'-kô 釋 家°; seng-kô' 僧 家°; *Taoist* —, dao'-kô 道 家°

PRIESTLY *garment*, (Buddhist), kô-sô' 袈 裟; *Taoist ditto*, dao'-bao 道 袍

PRIME, *first*, di-ih' 第 一; — *importance*, di-ih' iao'-kying 第 一 要 緊; *excellent*, ting'-hao 頂 好; gyih-miao' 極 妙; gyih-me' 極 美; *just in their* —, (whether persons, or fruits), tsing'-tông - shü 正 當 時°; — *cost*, nyün-kô' 原 價°; — *minister*, siu'-siang 首 相

PRIMER, *Ningpo* Nying-po' ts'-'oh' 甯 波 初 學°; *Trimetrical* —, Sæn-z kying' 三 字 經; — *of Juvenile verse*, Jing-dong-s' 神 童 詩; — *of Hundred names*, Pah'-kyüô-sing 百° 家° 姓

PRIMITIVE *times*, t'æ'-kwu z-'eo' 太 古 時 候

PRIMOGENITURE, *possession by* —, tsiang'-ts-go ts'æn'-nyih 長 子 个° 產 業

PRINCE, *sovereign* kyüing-wông' 君 王; *princes in general*, wông-yia' 王 爺°; *king's sons*, t'a'-ts 太 子; shü'-ts 庶 子; *the one appointed to be heir apparent*, lih'-go t'a'-ts 立 个° 太 子; — *of the blood*, ts'ing-wông' 親 王; *other princes,* gyüing'- wông 郡王

PRINCESS, *king's daughter,* kong-cü' 公主; *king's sister, or daughter,* gyüing'- cü 郡主

PRINCIPAL, deo 頭; cü 主; — *importance,* deo-ih' iao'-kying 頭一要緊; — *wife,* kyih'-fah 結髮; nyün-p'e' 元配; ts'i 妻; *capital in trade,* peng'-din 本錢°

PRINCIPALLY, da-tu' 大都; da-iah' 大約

PRINCIPLE *of order,* li 理; — *which arranges matter,* li'-ky'i 理氣; *the dual — in nature,* ing 陰, and yiang 陽; *inborn —,* t'in-sing' 天性; *a universal —,* c'ü-c'ü ih-yiang'-go li 處處一樣個理; T'in-'ô', tsih' yiu ih-li' 天下只有一理; *fundamental —,* deo-ih'-zeng-go dao'-li 頭一層° 个道理

PRINT, *to* ing 印; — *from blocks,* yüong moh-pæn' ing 用木板印; — *with type,* yüong k'æn-z-pæn ing 用鉛字板印

PRINT, *impression,* 'eng-tsih' 痕跡; ying-tsih' 形跡; *foot —,* kyiah'-tsih 腳跡; — *of a hand,* siu'-tsih 手跡; *to make the — of one's hand in token of divorce,* tang siu'-ing 打手印; *that book is out of —,* keh' ih-bu shü' dön'-de 這一部書斷絕°了°; *calico,* ing'-hwô yiang-pu' 印花洋布

PRINTED, ing'-c'ih-liao 印出了;

—*pictures,* ing'-go du' 印个°圖

PRINTER, ing'-shü-go nying 印書个° 人; ing'- shü s-vu' 印書司務

PRINTING-INK, ing'-shü-moh' 印書墨

PRINTING-OFFICE, ing'-shü-vông' 印書房; ing'-shü-kwun' 印書館

PRINTING-PRESS, ing'-shü-kô'印書架°

PRISON, lao-kæn' 牢監°; kæn-lao' 監° 牢 (ih-go); *to be in — three years,* zo sæn nyin' lao-kæn' 坐°三年牢監°; *put him in —,* ky'ih'-gyi-loh lao-kæn'-li 擎其落牢監° 裏; *to escape from —,* dao-c'ih-kæn' 逃出監°

PRISONER, kæn'-li væn'-nying 監° 裏犯人°; — *of war,* weh-gying'-go nying 活擒个° 人

PRIVATE, *opposed to public,* s 私; — *business,* s-z' 私事; — *land,* s-kyi' din 私田; *secret,* s-'ô' 私下°; — *place,* en'-djông n-sen' 暗藏之° 所; lang'-koh-loh-deo' 冷° 角° 落頭; — *room,* mih-shih' 密室; mih-feh-dong-fong vông' 密弗通風之° 房; — *families,* loh-kô' 住° 家°; *I have a word to say to you in —,* ngô yiu ih-kyü shih-wô' iao teng ng s-'ô kông' 我有一句說話要與°你°私下°講°

PRIVILEGE, *benefit,* hao-c'ü' 好處; *favor bestowed by a superior,*

eng-we′ 恩惠; sông′-s 賞賜;
*peculiar* —, kah′-nga hao-c′ü′
格外°好處; *having ditto, meo-*
ts′ peh-teh′ 謀之不得; *con-*
*fer privileges upon him,* sông′-
s gyi 賞賜其; *deprive of a*
—, ih-tsông me′-z siu-tsing′ —
樁美物° 收進
PRIVY *to, or knowing,* siang-t′ong′
相通; zi hyiao′-teh 自°曉得
PRIVY, mao-k′ang′ 茅坑°; k′ang-
ts′ 坑°子; zah-zao′ 石漕°;
*to go to the* —, ka-siu ky′i′ 解°
手去°; c′ih-kong′ ky′i 出恭
去°
PRIVY *council,* ky′ü-mih-yün′ 樞
密院
PRIZE, sông′-go tong-si′ 賞个°東
西; — *given by the emperor, or*
*by an officer,* tsiang′-sông 獎賞
PRIZE, *to* k′en′-leh djong′ 看得°
重; kwe′-djong 貴重; hyi-gyi′
希奇; *I* — (*it*), ngô dziah-
djong′-go 我着重个°
PROBABLE, liang-pih′ 諒必; iah′-
ding 約定; jih′-yiu-kyiu′ 十
有九; *not* —, feh kyin′-teh 弗
見得; vi-pih′ 未必
PROBATION, *time of* s′-t′en z-′eo′
試探時候
PROBE, *to* — *with a needle,* tang-
tsing′ teo-ti′ 打鍼兜底; —
*the heart,* ziang tsing′ c′oh sing′
像鍼猎心
PROBOSCIS, *elephant's* ziang′-bih
象鼻°

PROCEED, *to go forward,* zông-zin′
ky′i 上前°去°; — *from the*
*mouth,* dzong k′eo′ c′ih-læ′ 從
口出來; c′ih′-ü k′eo-li′ 出於
口裏; *whence does it* — ? dzong
′ah-li′ c′ih-læ′ 從何°而出?
PROCESSION, *idolatrous* we 會;
*to have a* —, nying we′ 迎
會; ′ang we′ 行°會; nying-
jing′ sæ-we′ 迎神賽會; *to*
*contribute toward a* —, c′ih-we′
出會; *funeral* —, song-sông′-
go-nying 送喪个° 人°
PROCLAIM, *to* djün-yiang′ 傳揚;
— *abroad,* djün-yiang′-k′æ′-ky′i
傳揚開去; djün-k′æ′ 傳開;
— *by writing,* or *engraving,* pu′-
kao 布告
PROCLAMATION, *official* kao′-z 告
示; *to issue a* —, c′ih kao′-z 出
告示; *imperial* —, wông-pông′
黃榜; (written) — *of war,* tsin′-
shü 戰書
PROCRASTINATE, *to* t′ah′-t′ah-
wu; — *from day to day,* ih-
nyih′ nga ih-nyih′ 一日°捱°
一日°; — *beyond the time,* ngwu
z-′eo′ 誤時候
PROCURE, *to find,* zing-djoh′ 尋°
着; — *for me,* bæn′-læ peh ngô′
辦來給°我; *to obtain,* teh′
tao-siu′ 得到手; — *for me,*
bæn′-læ peh ngô′ 辦來給°我
PROCURED, *cannot be* zing feh-
tao′-siu-go 尋°弗到手个°; teh′
feh-tao-siu′-go 得弗到手个°

PRODIGAL, *n.* ba-ts′ 敗° 子；lông-dông′-ts 浪子

PRODIGAL, *to use in a — way*, lông-yüong′ 浪用；p′eh-t′ông′ p′eh-shü yüong′ 潑湯潑水°用；— *expenditure*, lông′-fi 浪費；— *living*, vông′-ky′üoh vông-yüong′ 妄吃° 妄用

PRODIGIOUS *in size*, gyi-yiang′ do 異° 樣 大°；wô-feh-læ′ do 話弗 來大°；— *quantity*, c′ih′-kah to′ 出格多

PRODIGY, kwa′-z 怪° 事

PRODUCE, *to* sang-c′ih′-læ 生°出來；*clouds — rain*, yüing′ sang yü′ 雲騰° 致° 雨

PRODUCT *in multiplication*, gong′-dzing 共乘

PRODUCTIONS, c′ih′-ts′æn 出產；*native —*, t′u′-ts′æn 土產

PRODUCTIVE, we sang′ 會生°；sang-leh to′ 生′ 得° 多

PROFANE, *to blaspheme*, sih′-doh 藝瀆；*to use lightly*, ky′ing-yi′ yüong 輕易用；*to treat with disrespect*, ky′ing-mæn′ 輕慢；*to pollute*, tsao-t′ah′ 蹧蹋；*to violate God's name*, væn′-djoh Jing-ming′-go ming-deo° 犯着° 神明个° 名頭

PROFESS, *to confess*, jing ′認；tsiao-jing′ 招認；— *openly*, ming-ming′ tsiao-jing′ 明明招認；-- *one thing and mean another*, k′eo′ feh te sing′ 口弗對心

PROFESSION, *the literary* veng-mah′-cong′ 文墨中人°；s-veng′-pe 斯文之°輩；*the medical —*, i-kô′ 醫家°

PROFESSOR *of Astronomy*, kaot′in-veng′ sin-sang′ 敎°天文先生°

PROFFER *him a fan*, sin′-ts song′ gyi yüong′-ih-yüong′ 扇子送其用一用

PROFILE, *to draw a* sia tseh′-min 寫° 側面

PROFIT, *gain*, li-sih′ 利息；c′ih′-sih 出息；c′ih′-hwô；dzæn′-deo 賺頭；*to receive advantage*, teh′-djoh bin-i′ 得着° 便宜°；*benefit*, ih′-c′ü 益處；li-ih′ 利益；*receive benefit*, teh ih′ 得益

PROFITLESS, vu-ih′ 無益；ṅ ih′-c′ü 無°益處；bah-bah′ tso 白° 白° 做

PROFLIGATE, vu-sô′-peh-we 無所不爲；ky′ing-kweh′-deo 輕骨頭；ṅ-kweh′-ky′i 無°骨氣°

PROFOUND, *deep*, sing 深；— *and mysterious*, sing-ao′ 深奧

PROFUSE *in thanks*, zia-feh-hyih′-go zia 謝° 弗歇个°謝°；ts′in-ko′-væn zia′ 千謝° 萬謝°；*in promises*, mun′-k′eo ing-dzing′ 滿口應承

PROGENITOR, lih-dæ′ tsu′-tsong 歷代祖宗

PROGENY, *descendants*, ts′-seng 子孫；*offspring of man, or animal*, cong 種；jang 秧

PROGNOSTIC, ziao-deo′ 兆頭

PROGNOSTICATE, to — by three cash, ky'i-k'o' 起 課; poh-k'o' 卜 課; — by bamboo slips, gyin-ts'in' 求 籤; ts'iu-ts'in' 抽 籤

PROGRESS, to — in travel, ken-lu' 趕 路; ditto, or in study, zông-zin' 上 前°

PROGRESSING, not m'-neh ken-lu' 沒° 有° 趕 路; tseo' feh zông-zin' 走弗上前°; — a little every day, ih-nyih' hao' ih-nyih — 日° 好 一 日°; — toward the end, tsiang iao' dzing-kong'-de 將 要 成 功 了°

PROHIBIT, to kying 禁; kying'-ts 禁 止; kying'-djü 禁 住; — opium smoking, kying ky'üoh' a-p'in' 禁 吃°鴉 片; — gambling, kying tu'-poh 禁 賭 博

PROHIBITED, lih-li' kying'-liao 律 例° 禁 了°; strictly —, nyin-kying'-liao 嚴 禁 了°

PROJECT, he has many projects, gyi meo-we' hyü'-to z-t'i' 其 謀 爲 許 多 事 體; gyi weh-ts'ah' hyü'-to z-t'i' 其 畫 策 許 多 事 體; to engage in a visionary —, bu'-fong tsoh-ing' 捕 風 捉 影; k'ö tong-fong' 捉° 東 風

PROJECT, to jut out, deh-c'ih' 凸 出

PROJECTILE force, tiu ky'i'-go shü'-lih 丟 去°个° 勢 力; ditto (from cannon), hong'-c'ih-læ-go shü'-lih 轟 出 來 个° 勢 力

PROLIX in discourse, wô-deo' t'eh dziang' 話 頭 太° 長

PROLONG, to kô-to' 加° 多; kô-dziang' 加° 長; — a stay, to deng'-deng 多 住° 幾° 時°

PROMINENCE, raised place, kao-ky'i' 高 起

PROMINENT men, kao-tsiah'-go nying 上° 等° 个° 人°

PROMISCUOUS, zeh-lön' 雜° 亂; kah'-dzeh 夾° 雜; zeh'-kah-leng'-teng 雜 夾° 零 等; zeh-ts'ih'-zeh-pah' 雜° 七 雜° 八; — lot of things, zeh-gyin' 雜° 件

PROMISE, to ing-hyü' 應 許; ing-dzing' 應 承; ing-yüing' 應 允; to break one's —, shih-sing' 失 信; shih-iah' 失 約; zih-yin' 食 言; — can't be depended upon, ing-hyü' feh-tsoh'-cing 應 許 弗 作 準; ing-dzing' feh-sön-su' 應 承 弗 算 數

PROMISING, yiu ts'-vông 有 指 望

PROMONTORY, hæ'-sæn-deo 海 山 頭

PROMOTE, to — the increase, or advancement of, s'-teh hying'-ky'i-læ 使 得 興 起 來; — trade, dzu sang-i' hying-wông 助 生 意 與 旺; ü ming' hying-li' 與 民 興 利; — learning, cing'-coh veng-fong' 振 作 文 風; — to office, fong-tsih' 封 職; — one in office, kô-kyih' 加° 級; sing-kwun' 陞 官

PROMPT, to di 提; — one reciting, &c., di sbü' 提 書; — me, dingô-deo'; — *lam to action*, di-sing' gyi 提醒其

PROMPT *answer*, ze-k'eo' ing 隨口應; — *or obedient*, ao'-ao ing' 噯°噯°應

PROMPTER *in matters of etiquette*, hô 蝦°

PROMPTLY, *at the time*, cing'-ding z-'eo' 準定時候; *quickly*, soh 速; kw'a'-soh 快速

PROMULGATE, or PROMULGE, djün-k'æ' 傳開; djün-yiang' 傳揚; po-yiang' 播揚; — *every where through the world*, djün pin'-t'in-'ô' 傳遍天下°

PRONE, *heart — to evil*, sing' hyiang'-djoh oh' 心向著°惡

PRONOUNCE, *to* kông-c'ih-læ 講° 出來; *distinctly —*, kông ts'ing-t'ong' 講°清通

PRONUNCIATION, k'eo'-ing 口音; k'eo'-ts' 口齒°; — *bad, or indistinct*, k'eo'-ing feh-ts'ing' 口音弗清; k'eo'-ing 'en-wu-dao' 口音如°含胡桃

PROOF, bing-kyü' 憑據; tsih'-tsiao 執照; *positive —*, tsing'-kyü 証據; — (*of crime*), tsông-tsing' 贓証; *no —*, m̆-bing' m̆-kyü' 無°憑無°據; *reliable —*, ky'üoh'-jih-go bing'-kyü 確實个°憑據; jih-bing' jih'-kyü 實憑實據; *what — have you?* yiu soh'-go bing-kyü' læ ng'-go siu'-li 有甚°麼°憑據在°你手裡? *to put to the —*,

s'-lin 試鍊; — *against water, fire, &c.*, ziang t'ih-dong-kwu' ka 像鐵桶之°固; — *sheets*, yiang-ts' 樣子; *to correct —*, kyiao-te shü' 校對書; kæ shü' 改書

PROP, cü'-bông 拄棒°; ts'ang'-bông 撐棒°; — *of the family*, kô'-li-go tong'-liang 當°家个° 棟梁

PROP, *to* cü 拄; ts'ang 撐; tsin 伞

PROPAGATE, *to* djün 傳; 'ang 行°; — *religion*, djün-kyiao' 傳教

PROPER, tsoh'-hying 作興; *befitting*, 'eh-li' 合理; siang-nyi' 相宜; tsiao kwe-kyü' 照規矩; ing-kæ'-go 應該个°

PROPERTIES, sing'-tsih 性質

PROPERTY, (*houses, lands, and goods*), kô-kyi' 家計; *uncertain —* (*as boats, bridges, &c.*), veo-ts'æn' 浮產; *landed —*, jih-nyih' 實業

PROPHECY, yü-sin' shih-wô' 預先說話; yü-yin' 預言 (veng.)

PROPHET, sin-cü-nying 先知人°; kông-yü-yin'-go 講°預言个°

PROPHETESS, nyü'-sin'-cü 女先知

PROPHETIC *dream*, mong-ziao' 夢兆

PROPHESY, *to* kông vi-læ'-go z-t'i' 講°未°來个°事體; —

*without divining,* vi-poh' sin'-cü 未°卜先知

PROPITIATE, *to* sih-nu' dzing-kwe 'o-hao' 息怒仍歸和好

PROPITIATORY *sacrifice,* joh-ze'-go tsi'-veh 贖罪个°祭物

PROPITIOUS *winds,* jing fong' 順風

PROPORTION, *in* siang-ing'相應; siang-ts'ing' 相稱; *in good* —, deo-mi' siang-ing' 頭尾°相應; *the rule of* — pi'-li 比例

PROPOSE, *to — one's ideas,* kông'-c'ih peng'-i 講°出本意; — *a plan,* kông'-c'ih fah'-ts læ 講°出法子來; *do you — to go to-day?* ng' siang kying-tsiao' ky'i' feh 你°想今朝去°否°？

PROPOSITION, ming 命, pro-perly, something appointed, but by politeness, can be used here; thus, *I assent to your* —, ngô' tseng ng'-go ming' 我遵你命; *very polite,* ngô vong ng-go yü' 我奉你个°諭; *consider my* —, ngô' sô kông'-go i'-s, ng hao tang'-mo 我所講个°意思你°好揣摹; *I cannot consent to your* —, ngô feh tseng'-kyiao 我弗遵敎; næn tseng'-kyiao 難以°遵敎

PROPRIETOR, cü'-nying-kô 主人°家; tong-kô' 東家°; lang-z.

PROPRIETY, li 禮; kwe-kyü' 規矩; *act in accordance with* —, tsiao li' s-'ang' 照禮施行°;

*not in accordance with* —, feh 'eh-li' 弗合禮; feh i-li' 弗依禮

PROROGUE, *to* t'e-pæn' 退班; t'e-dông' 退堂

PROSE, *classical* kwu'-veng 古文; *recent writings,* z-veng' 時文

PROSECUTE, *to — continuously,* lin-liu' tso 連連做; tsih'-lin tso 接連做; *to accuse,* kao-zông' 告狀

PROSELYTE *to Christianity,* kæ' dzong Yiæ-sn' kyiao' 改從耶穌敎

PROSPECT, *view,* kying'-cü 景致; *fine* —, hao kying'-cü 好景致

PROSPECTS, *his — are good,* gyi-go kying'-ziang feh wa 其景象弗孬

PROSPER, *to be prosperous,* jing-liu' 順溜; — *in making money,* fah-ky'i-læ 發起來; fah'-dzæ 發財; — *in examinations,* fah-dah 發達; — *and increase,* hying-wông' 與旺; — *in trade,* hying-long 與隆; hying-fah' 與發; *to be fortunate,* yüing-ky'i' t'ong-dah' 運氣通達

PROSPEROUS, jing-liu' 順溜; jing-kying' 順境; — *country,* koh'-kô bing-en' kyih-ky'ing' 國家°平安吉慶

PROSTITUTE, *n.* piao'-ts 婊子; ts'ông-vu' 娼婦; hwô-lao' 花老; t'iao-ts'; gyi-nyü' 妓女

PROSTRATE, *to — one's self* (as a suppliant), boh-tao' 伏°倒; p'oh'-tao 仆倒; pa'-tao 拜°倒

PROSTRATE *on the face*, foh-ken' kw'eng'-tih 覆蓋°睡°的

PROTECT, *to* wu 護; pao'-wu 保護; we-wu' 廻護; we-kwu' 廻顧; we-gyih' 廻及; — *the weak,* we-kwu' no-ziah'-go nying 廻顧懦弱个°人°; *may God* — *you,* dæn'-nyün Jing-Ming pao'-wu ng' 但顧神明保護你°

PROTEST, *to — against,* ming-ming' wô' feh ing'-kæ 明話弗應該; ming-ming' p'i-bing' 明明批評

PROTRACT, *to — the time,* z-'eo' kô-leh dziang' 時候加°得°長

PROTRUDE, *to* deh-c'ih' 凸出; sing-c'ih' 伸出; t'a-c'ih' 拖出; t'u'-c'ih 吐出

PROTRUDING *out of the pocket,* dæ-k'eo'-deo sing-c'ih'-tong 袋口頭°伸出了°; dæ-k'eo-deo t'a-c'ih'-tong 袋口頭°拖出了°

PROTUBERANCE, *a* ih-go cih' 一個疙°瘩°

PROUD, kyiao-ngao' 驕傲; do-dao' 大道; zi-tseng' zi-do' 自穿自°大°

PROVE *that I am a thief,* ngô tso zeh' wæn-c'ih te'-tsing tso bing-kyü' 我做賊°還出°對証

做憑據; — *that the earth is round,* di-gyiu' z yün'-go do-c'ih tsing'-kyü læ 地球是圓个°拿°出証據來

PROVED *by measurement,* te'-tsing-c'ih-kæ'-de 對証出來了°; yiu te'-tsing-de 有對証了°; kao-cing'-liao 較°準了

PROVENDER, zih-liao' 食料; — *and rations,* liang-ts'ao' 糧草

PROVERB, *old saying,* dzông-yin'-dao 常言道; lao'-wô 老話; kwu'-wô 古話; *familiar —,* dzoh-wô' 俗話 (ih-kyü); *the Book of Proverbs,* Tseng-yin' 箴言

PROVIDE, *to* yü-be' 預備; be-bæn' 備辦; — *against,* bông-be' hao 防備好; di-bông'-hao 提防好; *in plenty — for want,* yiu'-z bông 㐬-z' 有時要°防無°時

PROVIDENT, yiu sön'-kyi 有算計; *saving some for after use,* lin-zin'-c'ü-'eo' 留前取後

PROVINCE, *a* ih-sang' 一省°; *the eighteen provinces,* jih-pah' sang 十八省°

PROVINCIAL *capital,* sang'-dzing 省°城; — *dialect,* t'u'-wô 土話; hyiang-dæn' 鄉談

PROVISIONS, liang-zih' 糧食; k'eo'-liang 口糧; ky'üoh'-zih 吃°食; — *for man, and beast,* liang-ts'ao' 糧草; *dry — for a journey,* ken-liang 乾糧

PROVOCATION (either to good, or bad), kyih'-kong 激功; *to be provoked by me*, (*i. e.* receive my —), zông ngô'-go kyih'-kong 上我个° 激功

PROVOKE, *to* kyih 激; ying 引; zô 惹°; ying'-zô 引惹°; yüong kyih'-kong 用激功; *he cannot be provoked* (or incited), gyi' feh ziu' kyih'-kong 其弗受激功; kyih'-kong yüong'-feh-tsing' 激功用弗進; — *him to anger*, kyih'-dong gyi ô'-wông 激動其怒°; kyih'-gyi-nu' 激其怒; væn' gyi ô'-wông 犯其怒°; ts'oh'-væn gyi nu' 觸犯其怒; — *him to vomiting*, ying'-gyi t'u' 引其吐; long gyi t'u'-c'ih 弄其吐出; — *him to laughter*, ying'-zô gyi siao' 引惹° 其笑

PROVOKED, *easily* ziang liu-sing' ho'-p'ao ka 像流星火爆°; — *beyond endurance*, ün'-sing tsæ-dao' 怨聲載道

PROVOKING *man*, dao-ky'i'-go nying 陶氣个人°

PROW, jün-deo' 船頭

PROWL, *wild beasts — about for food*, yia'-siu jing-lo' ky'üoh 野° 獸尋° 找° 吃° 物°

PRUDENT, yiu kying-we' 有經緯; kyin'-sih tao-kô'-go 見識到家°; — *in managing*, liang-lih' r-ying 量力而行; *cautious*, we-bông-'eo' 會防後

PRUNE, *to — trees*, yüong tao' siu-li' jü-moh' 用刀修理樹木

PRUNES, *dried plums*, me-ken' 梅乾

PRUSSIAN-BLUE, yiang-din' 洋靛; yiang-ts'ing' 洋青

PRY, *to — by looking*, t'eo-k'en' 偷看; — *by asking*, dao'-t'ing 道聽; — *by asking secretly*, ts'ih'- t'ing 竊聽; t'en'- t'ing 探聽

PSALMS, sing'-s 聖詩; s-p'in' 詩篇

PUBERTY, *the time of* fah-sing' z-'eo 發身時候; fah-tsiang'-z 'eo 發長時候 (coarse).

PUBLIC, kong 公; *in* —, c'ih-kwun 出官; — *business*, kong-z' 公事; — *opinion*, kong-leng' 公論; cong'-leng 衆論; — *examination*, (whether right, or wrong), kong-p'ing' 公評°; — *use*, kong-yüong' 公用; — *road*, kwun-lu' 官路; *the* —, cong'-nying 衆人°; cong' pah'-sing 衆百°姓; *known to the* —, kong'-kô hyiao'-teh 公家曉得; cong'-nying teh'-cü 衆人° 得知

PUBLISH, *to — abroad*, yiang-k'æ' 揚開; djün-k'æ' 傳開; — (by telling what one wishes kept quiet), t'ong-hyiang kwun' 通鄉貫

PUCKER, *to* ts'oh'-long 縐攏; — *the lips*, cü'-pô ts'oh'-long 嘴巴

纈攏; *puckering to the mouth,* we seh k'eo' 會潲口

PUDDLE, shü-den' 水° 潭; — *in a court, or any where,* shü-ming-dông 水° 明堂

PUFF, *a — of wind,* ih-kwu fong' 一縷° 風; *to blow a — of smoke,* p'eng' ih-k'eo in' 噴 一 口 烟; *to — up, or inflate,* c'ü-p'ông' 吹° 脿; *to praise,* ts'e-hyü' 吹 嘘

PUGILIST, gyün-s' 拳師; *to exercise as a —,* tang-gyün' 打拳

PULL, *to —along,* la 拉; ky'in 牽; 劧 te; — (*as a boat, or anchor*), ts'ô 扯; — *up,* (*as roots, or nails*), bah-ky'i'-læ 拔起來; — *up* (*as a weight, or curtain*), la-zông' 拉上; te'-zông 劧上; ts'ô-zông' 扯上; — *out,* la-c'ih' 拉出; te'-c'ih 劧出; — *out teeth,* tsoh ngô-ts' 捉牙°齒; bah-c'ih' ngô-ts' 拔出牙°齒; — *out* (*as a drawer*), ts'iu-c'ih' 抽出; — *down* (*as a house*), ts'ah'-diao 拆了°; te'-gyi-tao' 劧其倒; *give a —,* la-ih-la 拉一拉; la ih-pô 拉一把; te ih'-pô 劧一把; — *up out of water,* shü-li' liao-ky'i'-læ 水° 裡撈起°來; — *apart,* p'ah'-k'æ 擘開

PULLET, *a* ih'-tsah siao-kyi' 一隻小雞

PULLEY, ts'ô-bun' 車盤; ts'ô-leng' 車輪

PULP *of fruits,* ko'-ts nyüoh' 果

子肉°; *to pound to a —,* sông-wu' 春°糊

PULPIT, kông'-kying-dæ 講°經臺; kông'-shü-dæ 講°書臺

PULSATE, *to* dong 動; t'iao 跳

PULSATIONS *of the heart stopped,* sing si'-de 心死°了°

PULSE, mah 脈; mah-sih' 脈息; *to feel the —,* tah mah' 搭脈; k'en mah' 診°脈

PULVERIZE, *to — by grinding,* mo feng' 磨粉; nyin meh' 研末; — *by pounding,* sông feng' 春°粉; — *by rolling,* le feng' 擂粉

PUMELO, p'ao; veng-tæn' 文膽 (ih-go)

PUMICE-STONE, veo-zah' or vu-zah' 浮石°

PUMP, hyih'-dong 吸筒; hwun'-dong 喚筒 (ih-kwun); *a chain —,* ih-bu shü'-ts'ô 一步水°車°

PUMP, *to — water,* hyih shü' 吸水°; hwun shü' 喚°水°

PUMPKIN, *squash,* væn-kwô' 飯瓜; nen-kwô' 南瓜

PUN, sông-kwæn' shih-wô' 雙關說話

PUNCH, *to give a poke,* djoh-ih'-pô 搠一把; — *a hole,* toh ngæn'-ts 督眼°子

PUNCTILIOUS, to-li'-go 多禮个°; — *and only cares for one thing,* ü-vu'-deng-deng-go 迂腐騰騰个°; ü-vu' ts dao 迂腐之道;

*too* — (as a teacher), sön-ky'i' 酸氣; — *man*, ü-nying' 迂人; *ditto* (in ridicule), dzing-djong'-ts 陳仲子

PUNCTUAL *to the day*, tsiao nyih-ts' 照日°子; — *to the time*, tsiao z-'eo' 照時候; *doing regularly*, feh ts'o-yi' 弗差°移; — *to appointment*, cing gyi' 準期

PUNCTUATE, *to* tin kyü'-deo 點句讀

PUNGENT, lah 辣; *slightly* —, lah-ho'-ho 辣阿阿; — *taste*, lah'-go mi'-dao 辣个味°道; — *remarks*, c'oh'-sing-go shih-wô' 豬°心个°說話 (c'oh or ts'oh)

PUNISH, *to* vah 罰; tsah'-vah 責罰; — (officially), ying-vah' 刑罰

PUNISHMENT (official), ying-vah' 刑罰; ze 罪; ze'-ming 罪名; *to recive ditto*, ziu ying-vah' 受刑罰; ziu ze' 受罪; *to receive* — (as from parents, or teacher), ziu tsah-vah 受責罰; *to determine what* —, ding ze'-ming 定罪名; *instruments of* —, ying-gyü' 刑具; — *by bambooing*, tang pæn'-ts 打板子; — *by rattaning*, tang deng-diao' 打籐條; — *by compressing the feet, and extending the arms*, t'in-bing'-kô 天平架°; — *by compressing the fingers*, tsæn'-ts 榜子; — *by beating the face*, tang pô-công' 打巴掌; — *by beating the ankles*, k'ao kyiah'-tsang 敲°脚脛°; — *by compressing the*

*ankles between upright bars*, kah'-kweng 夾°棍; — *by strangling*, kao 絞°; — *by beheading*, sah-deo' 殺頭; c'ü-kyüih' 處決 — *by standing in a cage with the head out*, lih dong' 立籠°; — *by cutting to pieces*, se'-kwô-ling-dzi' 碎剮凌遲; *by wearing the cangue*, ta do-kô' 帶°大°枷°; — *by banishment* (to a distance, or in one's own city), du-ze' 徒罪; *ditto* (from one to two thousand li), liu-ze' 流罪; *ditto* (beyond the frontier), kyüing-ze' 軍罪

PUNKAH, fong-sin' 風扇 (ih-min,

PUNY, *thin and small*, seo'-siao 瘦小

PUPIL, 'oh-sang-ts' 學°生°子; meng-du' 門徒; meng-sang' 門生°; di'-ts 弟子; — *of the eye*, ngæn'-u-cü 眼°烏珠; *the image reflected in the* —, dong-jing' 瞳神

PUPPET, *wooden* moh-deo 'en' 木頭°孩°; — *show*, moh-deo hyi' 木人°戲; tsiang-deo 'en'-hyi 帳頭孩°戲

PUPPY, siao'-keo 小狗; siao wun-kyi' 小黃°犬° (ih-tsah)

PURCHASE, *to* ma 買°; — *office*, kyün tsih' 捐職; — *rice*, dih-mi' 糴米; — *wine*, tang tsiu' 沽°酒; — *oil*, iao yiu' 買°油; — *merchandize*, cü ho' 置貨; ma ho' 買°貨; bæn ho' 辦貨

PURE, ts'ing 清; ts'ing-tsing' 清正; *clean*, ts'ing-kyih' 清潔; kyih'-zing 潔净; *the — article*, tsing ho' 真貨; — *silver*, tsoh' nying 足 銀; — *sugar*, jing dông' 純糖; — *milk*, jing na' 純嬭°; — (as water), pih'-po'-s-ts'ing 碧波四清

PURGATIVE *medicine*, sia' yiah or dza yiah' 瀉藥

PURGATORY, lin-nyüoh' 煉獄

PURGE, *to — from sin*, gyiang'-diao ze' 洗°掉°罪; — *the bowels*, du'-bi sia'-gyi-ih-sia' 肚 皮 瀉° 其 一 瀉°

PURIFY, *to make clean*, long ken-zing' 弄乾净; long kyih'-ziug 弄潔净; —*by washing*, gyiang-ken-zing' 洗° 乾 净; — (as metals) *by fire*, tön'-lin 煅煉

PURPLE, *dull reddish —*, in'-ts'ing-seh' 燕青色; *bluish —*, ts'ing-lin'-seh' 青蓮色; *grape —*, bu-dao'-seh 葡萄色

PURPORT, i'-s 意思

PURPOSE, cü'-i 主意; *fixed —*, lih-ding' ts'-hyiang 立定志向; lih-ding' cü-i' 立定主意; *on —*, kwu'-i 故意; deh-i' 特意; deh-we' 特爲; *for what —?* we'-leh soh'-go i'-s 爲了°甚°麼°意思? we'-leh soh'-go yüong-dziang 爲了°甚°麼° 用塲? *a good — changed for a bad*, sing weh'-de 心活了°; sing web-dong'-de 心活動了°

PURPOSELY, *brought — for you*, deh-i' do-læ' peh ng' 特意拿° 來給°你; *to do wrong —, and knowingly*, ming-cü' kwu-væn' 明知故犯

PURSE, *bag which may be used for money*, (or snuff), 'o-pao-dæ' 荷包袋; s'-hyi-dæ 四喜袋; *wu-*bing'-dæ 壺瓶袋; *my — is empty*, nông'-t'oh k'ong-hyü' or nông'-t'oh k'ong-k'ong' 襄囊空虛

PURSUE, *to* tse 追; ken 趕; tse'-ken' 追趕; —*and overtake*, tse-zông' 追上; tse-djoh' 追着°

PUS, nong 膿

PUSH, *to* t'e 推; — *over*, t'e-tao' 推倒; — *aside*, t'e-k'æ' 推開; — *him down*, t'e gyi tih' 推其跌; t'e-gyi-loh' 推其落; — *in*, t'e-tsing' 推進; *he gave me a —*, gyi t'e' ngô ih-pô ko'-de 其推我一把過了°; — *back and forth*, t'e'-læ-nông'-ky'i 推來攘去°

PUSILLANIMOUS, 无 tæn'-ky'i 無°膽氣; 无 tæn'-liang 無°膽量; 无 ken-tæn' 無°肝膽; tæn'-ts siao' 膽子小

PUSTULE, gweng-nong le' 作°膿瘰; *a — in small pox*, ih-lih deo-ts' 一粒痘子

PUT, *to lay*, en; fông 放; fông'-læ 放在°; — *down*, fông'-loh 放落; — (it) *on the table*, fông-læ coh'-teng zông' 放在°

桌上；— on clothes, cʻün i-zông' 穿衣裳°；tsiah i-zông' 着衣裳°；— off clothes, tʻch i-zông' 脱衣裳°；— away, kʻông'-ko 囥過；— on the hat, ta mao-ts' 戴°帽子；— off the hat, coh' mao-ts' 除°帽子 (coh or tsoh); to — in order, pa'-hao 擺°好；ditto or repair, siu-li' 修理；tsing-teng' 整頓；— a room in order, siu-jih' vông-ts' 修葺°房子；—forth strength, yüong ky'i'-lih 用氣力；kô gying-dao' 加°勁道；—forth great strength, sah'-kʻeo dziah-lih' 着意°用°力；'eo-ky'i'-lih 候氣力；— him in mind, di-sing' gyi 提醒其；— into, tsi 齒；tsông装；—into a dish, tsi' beng-ts' 齒盆子；to — out a fire (as a house, &c.), kyiu ho' 救火；— out (ordinary) fire, ho long-u' 火弄熄°；— (blow) out a lamp, cʻü-u' teng-tsæn' 吹°熄°燈盞；— together, fông'-long 放攏；en-tæn'-long；— something against the door to fasten it, meng' a-ih'-a 門挨°一挨°；— to my account, sön' z ngô'-go tsiang' 算是我个°帳；sön' ngô' ming'-'ô 算我名下°；can't — up with it, jing-næ'-feh-djü 忍耐弗住；to — out the hand, siu' sing-cʻih'-læ 手伸出來；— on airs, pa kô'-ts 擺°架子；— lam to

flight, ken'-gyi-tseo' 趕其走；ken'-gyi-ky'i' 趕其去°；—one up to a thing, tsʻön-teh' 攛掇；— one up to (a bad thing), t'iao-so' 挑唆；— up a notice, t'iah tsiao-ts' 貼°招紙；— forth buds, tsʻiu ngô' 抽芽°；pao ngô' 苞芽°；— in charge of another, kyi' læ bih-nying'-go siu'-li 寄在°別人个°手裡：ditto (a child), kyi'-yiang 寄養

PUTREFY, will we læn' 會爛
PUTRID, rotten, læn-wu'-de 爛腐°了°；læn'-de 爛了°；bad smelling, tsʻiu'-de 臭°了°
PUTTY, dong-yiu'-hwe 桐油灰
PUZZLE, yüong-sing-s'-go hyi-deo' 用心思个°戲玩°(ih-t'ao)；— of seven blocks, tsʻih'-ky°iao-pæn 七巧板；chain — kyiu'-lin-gwæn 九連環
PUZZLE, to yüong sing-s' 用心思；long-hweng' 弄惛
PUZZLED, I am —with this account, ngô' be keh'-go tsiang' long-hweng'-de 我被這°个°帳弄惛了°

# Q

QUACK doctor, ma-yiah'-lông'-cong 賣°藥郎中
QUADRANGULAR, four-sided, s'-fông-go 四方个°；having four angles, s'-koh-go 四角°个°
QUADRUPED, tseo'-siu 走獸；the class of quadrupeds, tseo'-siu ih-le 走獸一類

QUAIL, *n.* en-jing' 鵪鶉 (ih-tsah)

QUAIL, *to* sông-tæn' 傷膽; *lose spirit,* shih-sing' 失心

QUAINT *style of talking,* lao-kwu'-ky'iang kông'-fah 老古腔講° 法

QUAKE, *to tremble,* fah-teo' 發抖; gwah-gwah·teo' 搰°搰°抖; — *with fear,* fah-kying' hah'-leh fah-teo' 發驚嚇得°發抖; *the earth quakes,* di-yiang' cing'-dong 地陽震動

QUALIFY, *to* — *one's self,* 'oh'-leh tau-kô' 學°得°到家°; 'oh-we' 學°會

QUALIFIED *to teach others,* 'oh-veng' neng-keo' kao bih'-nying 學°問能敎敎°別人°

QUALITY, *best* zông-teng' 上等; *poorest* —, 'ô'-teng 下°等; *middle* —, cong-teng' 中等

QUALITIES, *properties,* t'i'-tsih 體質; peng'-tsih 本質

QUANTITY, *what* —? to-siao' 多少? *a large* —, hyü'-to 許多; to-to' 多多; *estimate the* —, iah'-læ yiu to-siao' 約來有多少; p'a'-læ yiu to-siao' 派來有多少; sön'-læ yiu to-siao' 算來有多少

QUARREL, *to* tsang-leng' 爭°論; siang-tsang' 相爭°; tsang-teo' 爭°鬥; k'eo'-kyüob, or k'eo-koh 口角; k'eo-zih 口舌; siang-mô' 相罵; — *noisily,* tsang-zao' 爭°嘈; zao-nyih';

— *arising from rivalry,* teo-ky'i 鬥氣; *to get up a* —, zing zao-nyih' 尋相罵°; *to seek a cause for a* —, zing pæn'-deo 尋錯處°; zing ts'iah'-deo 尋齰頭

QUARRELSOME hao k'eo'-kyüoh 好譁°; hwun-hyi' tsang-leng' 歡喜爭°論; we tsang-teo' 會爭°鬥

QUARRY, zah-dông' 石°膛

QUARRYMAN, k'æ zah-deo' nying 開石頭人°

QUART, *nearly a* — (dry measure), nyi sing' 二°升; *a* — *of milk,* ih-bing na' 一瓶爛°

QUARTER, s'-kwu-teh-ih 四股得一; s'-feng-ts-ih' 四分之一; — *of a dollar,* liang'-koh-pun' 兩角°半; *a* — (coin), ih-go s'-k'æ 一個四開; — *of an hour,* ih-k'eh' 一刻; — *of a catty,* s'-liang 四兩

QUARTER, *to* s'-kwu-feng-k'æ' 四股分開

QUARTERLY *payments,* (as rents, &c.), s'-kyi fu'-ts'ing 四季付清; en'-kyi kyiao-ts'ing 接季交清

QUARTZ, *white* bah ho'-zah 白°火石°; — *crystal,* sæn-tsing' 山晶

QUEEN, nyü'-wông 女皇; *king's wife,* wông-'eo' 皇后; — *mother,* t'a'-'eo 太°后; — *of England,* Da-Ing' nyü'-wông 大英女皇

QUELL, to — a disturbance, bing-lön' 平亂; — rebellion, bing-fæn' 平反

QUENCH, to — thirst, ts-k'ah' 止渴; — fire, p'eh-u ho' 潑熄火; kyiu ho' 救火; ho' long-u' 火弄熄°

QUERULOUS, gæn-gæn'-tao-tao 煩°言°

QUESTION, to ask a —, meng ih-kyü shih'-wô 問°一句說話; I have a — to ask you, ngô' yiu ih-kyü shih'-wô iao meng' ng 我有一句說話要問°你°; iao meng' ng ih-sing' 要問°你°一聲; — and answer, ih-veng' ih-tah' 一問一答; — him, meng-meng' gyi 問°問°其; — and see, meng-meng' k'en 問°問°看

QUICK, QUICKLY, kw'a 快°; kw'a'-kw'a 快°快°; kw'a'-soh 快速; soh'-soh 速速; ao-sao'; p'ih'-t'eh 霹脫; zah-zah; ts'oh 屁; ts'oh'-ts'oh-kyiao 屁屁交; (as fire), ho'-soh 火速; a little quicker, kw'a'-tin 快°點; 'ao-sao'-tin; — eye, ngæn' kw'a 眼°快°; — hand, siu kw'a 手快°; — of hearing (ears bright), ng'-tô liang 耳°朵亮; — and severe, bao-ts'ao' 暴躁; — of apprehension, ling-li' 伶俐; get through quickly, tsin'-sao 箭稍; ky'i-kw'a-loh'-dzih 氣快°落直

QUICKEN me, su-sing' ngô 蘇醒我; — the dead, s'-teh si'-nying weh' 使得死人活

QUICKLIME, sang-hwe' 生°灰

QUICKSILVER, shü'-nying 水°銀

QUIET, not noisy, pih'-zing 謐靜; iu-zing' 幽靜; ts'ing-zing' 清靜; zing'-væn; zing'-cü 靜致; — and peaceful, en-zing' 安靜; bing-en' 平安; not moving, t'ih'-ding 鎮定; — your anger, ky'i' næ-tæn'-loh 氣耐下去°; — place, pih'-zing-go di'-fông 謐靜个°地方; — man, nying' iu-zing' 人°幽靜; all —, dzih-jün'-feh-dong' 寂然弗動; t'ih'-t'a-s-bing' 鎮太°四平

QUILL, goose ngo-mao'-kwun 鵝毛管 (ih-ts)

QUILT, to 'ông; ing 紉; thick —, min-bi' 褊被; — for the dead, dzing-bi' 殮被; djong'-bi 重被; lang'-bi 冷°被°

QUINCE, moh-kwô' 木瓜

QUIT, to leave, li-k'æ' 離開; to have done with, hyih 歇; — a place entirely, ih'-ky'ü peh-we' 一去不回; — doing favors, üong' peh we li' 永不回禮; — the Buddhist priesthood, wæn-djoh' 'o-zông' 還俗和侚

QUITE, tsing 儘; jih-feng 十分; — good, tsing' hao 正好; jih-feng' hao' 十分好; — right, ting' z 頂是; feh ts'o' 弗錯;

gyih z' 極是; — *ready*, tsing zi'-de 整齊了°

QUIVER *for arrows*, kong-ts'ô'-sah-dæ; tsin'-dæ 箭袋

QUIVER, *to* tsing'-tsing-dong 震°震°動; — *with rage*, ky'i'-leh gwah-gwah-teo' 氣得°撈°撈°抖

QUOTATION *from a book*, ying'-læ-go shü-kyü' 引來个°書句 (ih-kyü).

QUOTE, *to* — *from a book*, ying shü' 引書; — *as proof*, ying tsing' 引証

# R

RABBIT, t'u 兎; zih-c'ü' 鯑鼠 (ih-tsah.)

RABBLE, mæn pah'-sing 蠻百°姓; *the lowest* —, 'ô'-teng nying 下°等人°

RABID *dog*, fong wun-kyi' 瘋黃°犬°; tin keo' 顛狗 (ih-tsah)

RACE, dzoh 族; le 類; *the human* —, nying' ih-le' 人°一類; *contest in running*, pi peng'-gying 比奔勁; sæ peng'-gying 賽奔勁; — *horses*, p'ao mô' 跑馬; — *course*, p'ao'-mô-dziang' 跑馬塲

RACK, *frame*, kô-ts 架°子 (ih-go)

RACKET, zi-zi'-zao-zao' 嘈°嘈°嘈°嘈°; loh-ying-fæn'-ky'i 像°六營反起

RADIANT, fah-kwông'-de 發光了°; — *face*, min-k'ong' yiu

kwông-ts'æ' 面孔有光彩

RADIATE, *to* — *heat*, fah'-c'ih nyih-ky'i' 發出熱°氣; fah'-c'ih liang-kwông' 發出亮光

RADICAL *change*, t'eh'-bi wun-kweh' 脫皮換骨

RADICAL, bu 部; *under what radical?* læ soh'-go bu'-li 在°甚°麽°部裡?

RADISHES, *red* 'ong lo-boh' 紅蘿蔔; *white* —, bah lo-boh' 白°蘿蔔
Carrots are also called 'ong lo-boh'.

RAFT, *wooden* moh-ba' 木排; jü-ba' 樹排; *bamboo* —, coh'-ba 竹排 (ih-ba)

RAFTER, djün-ts' 樣子 (ih-ken)

RAG, p'o'-pu 破布; se'-pu 碎布; *rags*, se-pu-den' 碎布頭°; *old rags*, gyiu pu-den' 舊布頭° (ih-kw'e)

RAGE, *in a* ho'-ky'i dzih-c'ong'-de 火氣直冲了°; nu-ky'i' c'ong-t'in'-de 怒氣冲天了°; *white with* —, ky'i'-leh leh-bah'-go 氣得°鐵白°了°

RAGE, *to* fah-ho' 發火; fah-doông' 發大°怒; fah-gyih' 發極

RAGGED, p'o'-li-p'o'-sa 破裂破褫°; — *and dirty*, læn-li' 襤褸 (may be also used for soiled only); — *shoes*, p'o' 'a-bæn' 破鞋°月; — *shoes and stockings*, 'a-t'ah'- mah-t'ah' 鞋°脫襪脫°

RAIL, to — at, zoh-mô' 辱罵;
zoh 辱;— at people, zoh-nying'-
mô'-tao 辱人°罵倒

RAILING, kæn-ken' 欄杆

RAIMENT, i-voh' 衣服 (veng);
i-zông' 衣裳°

RAIN, to loh-yü' 落雨; it is rain-
ing, læ'-tih loh-yü' 正°在°落
雨; it is going to —, iao loh-
yü' 要下°雨; looks like —,
yü'-mong-mong 雨濛濛; a
shower of —, ih-dziao yü' —
陣°雨;— for a long time, kyiu'
yü 久雨

RAIN water, t'iu-shü' 天雨水°

RAINY season, me-t'in 霉天

RAINBOW, heo 虹° (ih-da)

RAISE, to dæ 擡; dæ-ky'i' 擡
起; gying-ky'i' 擎起;— the
hand, sin di-ky'i' 手提起; sin
di' ih-di 手提一提;— the
head, dæ deo' 擡頭;— a little
higher, dæ kao'-tin 擡高點;
— (as heavy furniture), dæ-ky'i-
læ 擡起來;— him up, tông'-
gyi-ky'i'-læ 擡°其起來; vu'-
gyi-ky'i'-læ 扶其起來;—
the price, tsiang kô'-din 漲價°
錢°;— to a better condition, di-
bah'-ky'i-læ 提拔起來;—
his hopes, ying'-ky'i gyi'-go
siang'-vông 引起其个°想
望; ky'i' gyi'-go nyiæn-deo' 啟
其个°念頭;— militia, tsiao-
mo' hyiang-üong 招募鄉勇;
— chickens, yiang siao-ky'i 養

小雞;— wheat, cong mah' 種
麥;— (or scatter) dust, yiang
hwe-dzing' 颺灰塵;— the hat,
mao'-ts t'ing-ih'-t'ing 帽子挺
一挺;— money, tang'-sön dong-
din' 打算銅錢°; dziah'-loh
dong-din' 着落銅錢°

RAISINS, bu-dao-ken' 葡萄乾

RAKE, bô 鈀; bamboo — (for
grass), la'-ts'ao-bô, or la-ts'a-bô'
拉草鈀; paddy —, t'æn-
koh'-bô' 攤穀鈀 (ih-pô)

RAKE, to bô 鈀;— even, bô bing'
爬平;— open (as grass), bô-
tæn-k'æ 爬開

RAKE, a vicious fellow, seh-kyü'
色鬼°; t'en-hwô-lóng'-ts 貪花
浪子; (polite), fong-liu-k'ah'
風流客

RALLY, to — for another fight
(after defeat), voh-dzing' 復陣;
tang'-wæn weng'-dzing 打還
魂陣

RAM, yüong-yiang' 雄羊 (ih-tsah)

RAM it in well, tsing gyi lao' 揕
其牢

RAMBLE, to yiu-wun' 遊玩°; yiu-
hyi' 遊戲;— in the hills, yiu-
sæn' 遊山; hyi-sæn' 嬉山

RAMIFY, to feng-ts-p'a' 分支派°

RAMPARTS, city walls, dzing-ziang'
城牆; opposite — (in fight),
te'-le 對壘

RANCID, yiu-hao'-ky'i-de 油嗃
氣了°; yiu-hông'-ky'i' 油; yiu-ih'
ky'i.

RANDOM, *to do in a — manner*, hah'-ts'ih-hah-pah' lön-tso' 黑七黑八亂做 ; — *talk*, keh-ts'ih'-keh-pah' shih-wô' 夾°七夾°八説話

RANK, *grade*, teng'-kyih 等級 ; *official —* , p'ing-kyih' 品級 ; the first and second of the nine ranks are divided in two, the second being but a trifle lower than the first, *viz., first —* , tsing'-ih-p'ing 正一品 ; djong ih-p'ing 從一品 ; *second —* , tsing' nyi-p'ing 正二°品 ; djong-nyi'-p'ing 從二°品. The insignia for the several ranks are :—
1st rank, *ruby*, 'ong - pao'-zah 紅寶石°
2nd, *coral*, sæn-wu' 珊瑚
3rd, *sapphire*, læn-pao'-zah 藍寶石° , or ming-læn 明藍
4th, *lapis-lazuli*, ts'ing-kying-zah 青金石°, or en'-læn 暗藍
5th, *crystal*, shü'-tsing 水°晶
6th, *white stone*, bah-zah' 白石°, or ts'ô-gyü 硨磲
7th, *gold button*, kying-ting' 金頂
8th, and 9th, *gilded silver button*, du-kying' nying-ting' 鍍金銀頂
*position*, sing-veng' 身分 ; *unbecoming* or *overstepping one's —* , sing-veng' feh-p'e' 身分弗配 ; *literary —* , sing-kying' 紳衿 ; *the five ranks of nobility*, ng'

teng tsiah 五°等爵 ; *viz.*, kong-tsiah' 公爵, 'eo-tsiah' 侯爵, pab'-tsiah 伯°爵, ts'-tsiah 子爵, nen-tsiah' 男爵 ; *to place* (soldiers) *in rank*, pa dzing-shü' 擺°陣勢

RANK *smell belonging to mutton*, yiang sao'-ky'i 羊臊氣

RANSACK, *to* dao 掏 ; fæn 翻 ; — *a drawer*, dao ts'iu-teo' 掏抽屜° ; — *in order to find*, seo-zing' 搜尋°

RANSOM, *to* c'ü 取 ; joh 贖 ; — *a person*, c'ü nying' 取人° ; — *from sin*, joh ze' 贖罪 ; — *money*, c'ü nying'-go kô'-din 取人°个°價錢°

RAP, *to* tao 搗 ; k'ao 敲° ; — *at the door*, tao meng' 搗門 ; k'ao meng' 敲°門 ; *give another —* , tsæ k'ao' ih-kyi 再敲°一記

RAPACIOUS, ziang lông-hwu' ka 像狼虎樣°式°

RAPE, *to commit* gyiang-kæn' 强姦°

RAPE-SEED, ts'æ'-ts 菜子

RAPIDS, kyih'-shü 急水° ; *catch fish in the —* (*i. e.* busy time in trade), k'ô kyih'-shü ng 捕°急水°魚°

RAPTUROUS, hao' feh hwun'-hyi 大°大°歡喜

RARE, hyi-hen' 希罕 ; næn-teh' 難得 ; siao-yiu' 少有

RARELY *met with*, næn-teh p'ong-djoh 難 得 逢°着°; hyi-vong' 希 逢; — *happens*, ts'in-tsiao gyi vong 千 朝 奇 逢; *he is — angry*, gyi sang-ky'i siao-yiu-go 其 動°氣 少 有 个°; — *heard*, næn'-teh t'ing'-meng 難 得 聽 聞° (also means unpleasant to hear).

RASCAL, p'in'-zeh 騙 賊°; vu-la' 無 賴°; 'ô'-tsoh p'e-ts' 下°作 胚 子; *a bold —*, di-deo-oh'-kweng 地 頭 惡 棍

RASH, t'eh mao hyin' 太°冒 險; lao'-hwu k'eo za yiang' 老 虎 口 搔°癢

RASH *broken out over the body*, weng'-sing fah'-c'ih 'ong-tin' de 渾 身 發 出 紅 點 了°

RASPBERRIES, miao-ts' 苗 子 (so called at T'in-dong)

RAT, lao'-ts' 老 鼠°; *water —*, shü lao-ts'' 水°老 鼠 (ih-tsah)

RATE, *fixed —*, (allowance, or number), ih-ding'-go ngah-ts' 一 定 个°額 子; *a fixed price*, ih-ding'-go kô'-din 一 定 个°價 錢°; *not two rates*, peh-r'-kyüô 不 二 價; *estimating at the present —*, z'-dzih kwu'-kô 時 值 佔 價°

RATHER, neng'-s 寧°使; nying'-k'o 寧 可; *moderately*, p'o 頗; *I would — not go*, ngô neng'-s feh ky'i' 我 寧 使 弗 去°; — *pretty*, p'o' hao'-k'eu 頗 好 看

RATIFY, *to —* (as a treaty, &c.), ding li' 定 例

RATIONAL, *endowed with reason*, yiu li'-sing 有 理 性

RATIONS *to soldiers*, ping-liang' 兵 糧; — *given by the Emperor to Manchus*, wông-liang' 皇 糧

RATTAN, deng 籐 (*a strand*, ih-keng); — *seated chair*, deng-min' ü'-ts 籐 面 椅°子

RATTLE, *a candy peddler's —*, or *a child's —*, yiao-teng-kwu' 搖 鼕 鼕

The rattle of each kind of peddler has its distinctive name.

RATTLE, loh-loh'-hyiang 轆 轆 響

RAVAGE, ts'iang'-kyih 搶 劫; lo'-liah 據 掠; *place ravaged by the rebels*, di'-fông be dziang-mao' ts'iang'-kyib-ko'-de 地 方 被 長 毛 搶 劫 過 了°

RAVEL, *to —* (as the edge of cloth), mao-c'ih-læ 毛 出 來; sih'-c'ih-læ; — *out* (as sewing), t'ah'-k'æ 脫°開

RAVENOUS, hwông zao'-ky'i 荒 糟°起; — *appetite*, we'-k'eo hwông-ky'i' 胃 口 大°開°

RAVINE, *a* ih-da k'ang' 一 埭 坑°; ih-go ao' 一 條 墺

RAVISHED *with delight*, gyih'-gyi kao-hying' 極 其 高 興

RAW, sang 生°; *good to eat —*, sang ky'üoh' hao 生°吃°好; *partly cooked*, feh-joh' 弗 熟

RAY *of light*, ih-sin' liang-kwông' 一 綫 亮 光

RAZE, *to* hwe'-diao 毀壞°; — *to the ground*, hwô'-we bing-di' 化爲平地

RAZOR, t'i'-deo-tao 薙頭刀 (ih-pô)

REACH, *to extend to*, tao 到; 'ang-tao' 行° 到; t'ong-tao' 通到; liu-tao' 流到; — *after, or to*, liao 撩; pæn 扳; *cannot — it*, liao-feh-djoh' 撩弗着°; *within —*, liao-leh-djoh' 撩得° 着°; pæn-leh-djoh' 扳得° 着°; — *out the hand*, sing'-c'ih siu' 伸出手; sing-k'æ' sin' 伸開手; — *out the head*, deo' sing-c'ih' 頭伸出; *cannot — up to the branches*, p'æn'-feh-djoh ô-ts' 攀弗着° 椏° 枝

READ, *to — silently*, k'en shü' 看書; — *or study aloud*, doh shü' 讀書; *I have read this whole book*, keh'-peng shü ngô dzong-deo'-ts-vi' k'en'-ko-de 這本書我從頭至尾看過了°; — *prayers*, (and other Buddhistic words), nyiæn-kying' 念經; dzong kying 誦經; — *other's hearts by one's own*, yi kyi'-ts sing' doh jing'-ts sing 以己之心度人之心

READILY, ken-sing' 甘心; *willingly*, dzing-nyün' 情願

READY *speaker*, k'eo'-neng-zih-bin' cü'-kwu 口能否辯个°人°; pah'-læ-pah-te'-cü'-kwu 百° 來百° 對个°人°; *quick*, (because accustomed to), jing-joh' 純熟;

— *with the pen*, pih' nyiah-leh jing-joh' 筆捏得° 純熟; — *prepared*, yü-be'-hao-liao 預備好了; *all —*, zi-be'-de 齊備了°; — *money*, yin' dong-din 現銅錢°; — *money on hand*, yin t'ông' 現帑; *buy with — money*, yin ma' 現買°; *to trade for — money*, yin'-dzin kao-yih' 現錢交易; *make —*, be-bæn' hao 備辦好; yü-be'-hao 預備好

READY-MADE, yin-dzing' or yin-zing'; 現成; *bought —*, yin-dzing' ma'-go 現成買个°

REAL, tsing 眞; — *pearls*, tsing cü'-ts 眞珠子; — *facts*, jih-dzing' 實情; *true*, jih-dzæ' 實在; ky'üoh'-jih 確實; tib'-ky'üoh 的確

REAL-ESTATE, jih-din'-jih-di' 實田實地; jih-nyih' 實業

REALLY, jih-dzæ' 實在; tsing-z' 眞是; ko'-jün 果然; nying-tsing' 認° 眞

REAP, *to — rice*, kah dao' 割稻; — *wheat*, kah mah' 割麥

REAR, *the* 'eo 後; — (*of an army, flock of sheep*, &c.), 'eo' de 後隊

REAR, *to —* (as children), iang 養°; yiang 養

REASON, yün-kwu' 緣故; kông'-kyiu 講° 究; *what is the — ?* dza kông'-kyiu 甚° 麽° 講° 究? *oh! that is the — of it* (or that cannot be so), kwa'-dao-z 怪° 道是; *the original — of*, nyün yiu' 原

由; keng yiu 根由; *right principle*, li 理; dao′-li 道理; *to accord with* —, ‘eh li′ 合理; *what* — (*or* sense) *is there in that?* ky‘i′-yiu ts‘′-li′ 豈有此理? vu-ts‘′-dzing-li′ 無此情理? *by* — *of*, we-leh′ 爲了°; we 爲

REASON, *to* leng 論; nyi-leng′ 議論; bin′-leng 辯論; kông′-leng 講°論; *to* — *out with one's self*, zi fah′-hwe ih-fæn nyi-leng′ 自°發揮一番議論

REASONED *well*, fah′-hwe-leh hao′ 發揮得°好

REASONABLE, yiu-li′ 有理; ‘eh-li′-go 合理个°; li′ sô tông-jün′-go 理所當然个°

REBEL, zeh-fi′ 賊匪; fæn-zeh′ 反賊°; *long haired* —, dziang-mao′ 長毛

REBEL, *to* bun′-nyih 叛逆; dzao-fæn′ 造反

REBELLION, *to plot* meo-fæn′ 謀反

REBOUND, *to* tao′-bang-cün-læ 倒撞轉來; tao′-p‘ong-cün-læ.

REBUILD, *to* tsæ-ky‘i′ 再起; tsæ′-zao 再造°

REBUKE, *to* tsah′-vah 責罰; tsah′-be 責備; heng.

RECALL, *to* we-s′ kyi′-teh 回思記得; — *him*, eo gyi cün′-læ 叫°其轉來; *cannot* — (*it*), ‘a′-feh-c‘ih′ 回想°弗出; kyi′-feh-læ 記弗來; *try to* — (*it*), ‘a-‘a′-k‘en′ 回頭°想°想°

看; (I) — *it*, ‘a-deo′ tao-de 想°到了°

RECANT, *to* zih-yin′ 食言; be yin′ 背言; kæ-k‘eo′ 改口; cün-yin′ 轉言

RECEDE, *to* t‘e-‘eo′ 退後; tao′-t‘e 倒退

RECEIPT *for payment*, siu-p‘iao′ 收票; siu-diao′ 收條 (ih-tsiang); *a* — *for making*, ih-yiang fông-fah′ 一樣方法

RECEIVE, *to* siu 收; ziu 受; tsih′-ziu 接受; teh′-djoh 得著; tao′-siu 到手; — (*from a superior*), ling 領; — (*something sent*), tsih′-tao 接到; tsih′-djoh 接著°; — *and open*, siu-ts‘ah′ 收拆; — *a guest politely*, tsih′-dæ nying-k‘ah′ 接待客人°; — *favors*, mong eng′ 蒙恩 (too strong an expression for ordinary use).

RECENT, sing-gying′-go 新近个°; gying-læ′-go 近來个°; gying-z′-go 近時个°; gying-nyih′-go 近日个°; — *news*, sing-gying′-go sing′-sih 新近个°信息; — *years*, gying′ nyin 近年; dzæ-s′ kyi nyin′ 纔始幾年

RECENTLY, gying′-læ 近來; — *come*, sing-læ′-go 新來个°; bao′-z læ.

RECESS, *noon* hyih tsiu′ 歇晝; *ditto at school*, fông tsiu′-‘oh 放晝學°

RECIPE *for medicine,* yiah fông′
藥 方; fông-ts′方子; *give* (tell)
*me the* —, keh′-go fông′-ts djün
peh′ ngô 這°个°方子傳給°
我

RECIPROCAL *love,* dô-kô′ siang-
æ′ 大°家°相 愛; ngwu-siang′
ts′ing-′æ′ 互相親愛

RECIPROCALLY *willing,* liang′-
siang dzing-nyün′ 兩相情願;
pe′-ts‛ dzing-nyün′ 彼此情願

RECITE, *to* — *lessons, &c.,* be shü′
背°書; — *stories* (in public),
kông siao′-shih 講°小說; —
*ditto with gestures,* kông do-shü′
講°大°書

RECKLESS, mông 莽; bah-mông′-
kwông 白°漫光; feh-kwu′-
ziu-‛co′ 弗顧前°後

RECKON, *to* sön 算; sön-tsiang′
算帳; p′a-tsiang′ 派°帳; —
*and see,* p′a′-p′a-k‛en 派°派°看;
*to count,* su 數; su′-su-k‛en′ 數
數看; *want to* — *with you,* iao
teng ng′ sön-tsiang′ 要與°你°
算帳; tsiang′ teng ng sön′-sön-
k‛en′ 帳與°你°算算看; —
*to my account,* sön ngô′-go ming
‛o′ 算我个°名下°

RECKONING, tsiang 帳 (ih-go; if
it is written, ih-p‛in); *your* — *is
wrong,* ng-go tsiang ts‛o-go 你°
个°帳錯个°; ng-go tsiang′
sön ts‛o′-de 你°个°賬算錯了°

RECLAIM *the wanderer,* ling mi-
lu′-go nying we-deo′-de 領迷

路个°人°回頭了°; *to claim
back,* t′ao-wæn′ 討還

RECLINE *on a couch,* gæ tao′ c‛ing-
teng′-li 戲°倒春凳裏; —
*against the wall,* gæ′-djoh ziang′
戲°著°墻; — *on a staff,* k‛ao′-
djoh kwa′-dziang 靠著°拐
杖

RECOGNIZE, *to* min-jün′ 面善;
nying-teh′ 認°得; *do you not*
— *me?* ng′ feh min-jün′ ngô′ yia
你°弗面善°我喲°? — *and
claim as one's own,* nying-kyü′
認°歸°

RECOLLECT, *to remember,* kyi′-teh
記得; *to think of,* siang′-ky‛i-
læ 想起來; *try to* —, ts‛eng′-
ts‛eng-siang 忖忖相; ‛a-‛a′-
siang 挰挰°相

RECOMMEND, *to* tsin 薦; kyü′-
tsin 舉薦; *one who recommends
another,* tsin′-deo nying′ 薦頭
人°; læ′-deo nying 來頭人°;
*to advise,* ky‛ün 勸

RECOMMENDATION, tsin′-shü 薦
書; tsin′-sing 薦信; *write a* —
sia ih-fong tsin′-shü 寫°一封
薦書

RECOMPENSE, *to* pao 報; wæn
還; — *favor,* pao eng′ 報恩;
— *evil,* pao dziu′ 報讐; — *evil
for good,* eng-tsiang′ dziu-pao′
恩將讐報; yi-oh′-pao-teh′ 以
惡報德; — *good for evil,* yi-
teh′-pao-oh′ 以德報惡

RECONCILE, *to* ‛o-hao′ 和好;

siang-ʻoʹ 相 和 ; tsæ ʹo-longʹ 再
和 攏 ; — *by exhorting,* kyʹün-ʻoʹ
勸 和 ; — *by speaking,* kông-ʻoʹ
講° 和

RECORD, *to* siaʹ-loh 寫°錄 ; kyiʹ-
loh 記 錄 ; tsæʹ-loh 載 錄 ; —
(as something omitted, &c.), din-
lohʹ 塡 錄°

RECORDS *of statistics, &c.,* tsʹ-shü
志書 ; — *of one's ancestors, for
three generations,* liʹ-lih 履歷 ; —
*of criminal cases,* enʹ-kyün 案 卷

RECORDER, shü-bænʹ書辦 ; tông
laoʹ-s 當 書° 吏° ; *to be a —,*
tông shü-bænʹ 當 書 辦

RECOVER, *to —* (an article), kwe-
wænʹ 歸 還 ; tsæ tehʹ-djoh 再
得 着°

RECOVERED (quite) *from sickness,*
voh-nyünʹ-de 復 元 了° ; bingʹ
djün-yüʹ-de 病 全 愈 了°

RECREATE, *to — one's self,* yiang-
yiang jingʹ 養 養 神

RECRIMINATE, *to* liang - ʻoʹ to-
kʻeoʹ-ko 兩 下°多 口 過 ; liang-
ʻoʹ gyi-gwu 兩 下° 譏 誚° ; —
*with abusive language,* zoh-læʹ zoh-
kyʻiʹ 辱 來 辱 去°

RECRUIT, *to — one's strength,* pu
kyʻi-lih 補 氣 力 ; pu nyün-
kyʻiʹ 補 元 氣 ; pu hyüihʹ-veng
補 血 牙 ; — *an army,* puʹ-tsoh
ping-ngahʹ 補 足 兵 額 ; *raw
—,* singʹ tsʻong-go pingʹ 新 充
个° 兵

RECTANGLE, dziang-fôngʹ 長 方

RECTIFY, *to — mistakes* (of words,
or deeds), nying-cünʹ-læ 認° 轉
來 ; — (as mistakes in writing),
kæʹ-hao 改 好 ; kæ tön-tsingʹ
改 端 正 ; — *spoken mistakes,*
kôngʹ-cün 講° 轉

RECTITUDE, tsingʹ-dzih-vu-sʹ 正
直 無 私 ; — *in administration,*
pingʹ-kong-vu-sʹ 秉 公 無 私

RECTUM, kông 肛 ; koh-daoʹ 穀
道 ; *the outer mouth of the —,*
fengʹ-meng 糞 門

RED, ʻong 紅 ; *blood —,* hyüihʹ-
ʻong 血紅 ; *tinged with —,* ʻong-
hyüihʹ-hyüih ; *bright —,* do-
ʻongʹ 大° 紅 ; *to dye —,* nyin-
ʻong 染° 紅 ; — *haired person,*
or *foreigner,* (vulgar), ʻong-mao-
nyingʹ 紅 毛 人°

REDDEN, *to* fah -ʻongʹ 發 紅 ;
ʻong-kyʻiʹ-læ 紅 起 來

REDEEM, *to* cʻüʹ-joh 取 贖 ; —
*from sin,* joh-zeʹ 贖 罪 ; — *sin-
ners,* cʻüʹ-joh zeʹ-nying 取 贖 罪
人° ; — *the time,* æʹ-sih kwông-
ingʹ 愛 惜 光 陰 ; — *a pledge,*
cʻü-tôngʹ 取 當

REDEEMER, joh-zeʹ-go cüʹ-kwu
贖 罪 个° 人° ; *the Redeemer,*
joh-zeʹ-go Cü 贖 罪 个° 主

REDRESS, *to — grievances,* ka ünʹ
解° 冤° ; shih ünʹ 雪 冤° ; ka-ünʹ
sih-kyihʹ 解° 冤° 釋 結

REDUCE, *to — the price,* kæn kôʹ-
din 減 價° 錢° ; *ditto so much out
of every hundred,* tang tsihʹ-deo

打折頭; tang k'eo'-deo 打
扣頭; See Discount. — ex-
penses, sang fi'-yüong 省°費用;
— unnecessary expenses, sang
'æn-fi' 省° 閒° 用; — to subjection, ah'-voh 壓° 服; — (as
rebels), bing-voh' 平服

REDUCED in circumstances kwông'-
kying loh'-de 光 景 衰° 了°;
a person ditto, loh-boh'-go nying
落 泊° 个° 人°

REDUNDANCY in words, shih-wô'
t'eh to' 說 話 太° 多; to-yin'-
to-nyü' 多 言 多 語

REED, a ih-ts lu-ken' 一 枝 蘆
竿; ih-ken lu' 一 根° 蘆; a bamboo —, ih-ken coh' 一 根° 竹

REEL, ts'ô 車; — for winding
from the cocoon, dziu s'-ts'ô 抽°
絲 車 (ih-bu)

REEL, to stagger, ts'ih'-ts'ong-pah-
tih' 七 瞥 八 跌; — from
drunkenness, tseo' ziang sia do-
z ka' 像 寫° 大° 字 樣° 子°
的° 走°

RE-ESTABLISH, to tsæ shih'-lih
再 設 立; — a government, tsæ
tsing'-teng kông-sæn' 再 整 頓
江° 山

RE-EXPORT, to nyün-ho' c'ih-k'eo'
原 貨 出 口

REFER, to point to, ts'-tin 指 點;
quote, ying 引; — to his example,
ying gyi'-go pông'-yiang 引 其
个° 榜樣°; to — another, ts'ing'-
kao 請敎°; — to a higher official,

dziang-zông' 'eo-p'i' 詳 上 候
批; — the decision to you, peh
ng' tso-cü' 俾° 你° 作° 主

REFINE, to lin 煉; — by fire,
tön'-lin 煅 煉

REFINED in manners, ts'ing-siu'
siang 清 秀 相; veng-sih' 文
飾; veng-yüô' 文 雅; — in
heart, iu-yüô' 幽 雅; — sugar,
dông' di-ts'ing'-liao-go 糖 提
清 了 个°

REFIRE, to — (as tea), fæn ts'ao'
翻 炒

REFLECT, to fæn'-tsiao 反 照;
tao'-tsiao 倒 照; ing 映; —
light, we-kwông' fæn'-tsiao 迴
光 反 照; — upon the past, (or
on the absent), tse-siang' 追想;
to think, s-siang' 思 想; —
calmly, si'-sing-go ts'eng' 細 心
个° 忖

REFORM, to we-deo' 回 頭; kæ'-
ko 改過; — in heart and thought,
we-sing'-cün-i' 回 心 轉 意;
ling-sing-coh'- cün 靈 心 回
轉; to turn from the evil to the
good, kæ-oh'-dzong-jün' 改 惡
從 善; ky'i'-zia-kwe-tsing' 棄
邪° 歸 正

REFORMED, already yi'-kying we-
deo'-de 巳 經 回 頭 了°

REFRACTION of light, kwông cün'-
zih 光 轉射

REFRACTORY, ao'-diao-peh-hying'
拗 調 不 馴°

REFRAIN, to — from singing, feh

ts'òng'-de 弗 唱 了°; —*from*,
ka 戒°; — *for a long time*,
dziang ka' 長 戒°; —*for a short
time*, tön' ka 短 戒°; —*from
eating*, gyi zih' 忌 食; gyi cü'
忌 嘴

REFRESH, *to* — *one's mind*, sing-li'
k'æ-wæ' 心 裏 開 懷; k'æ'-
k'æ sing' 開 開 心; kw'un sing'
寬 心; — *one's strength*, yiang
lih' 養 力; yiang-jing' 養 神

REFUGE, *a place of* — dzông-
sing'-ts-c'ü' 藏 身 之 處; to'-bi
u'-sen 躲 避 之° 所; bi næn'
di'-fông 避 難 地 方

REFUGEES, dao-næn'-go nying'
逃 難 个° 人°; næn-ming' 難 民

REFUND, *to* wæn 還; t'ing'-wæn
聽 還; —(for an article injured),
be-wæn' 賠 還; be-djông' 賠 償

REFUSE, vu-yüong'-ts-veh 無 用
之 物, fi'-veh 廢 物; *lime* —,
zah-hwe-deo' 石 灰 餘° 屑°; —
*tea*, dzô-yih'-meh 茶 葉 末

REFUSE, *to* foh 覆; dz 辭; we-
deo' 回 頭; we-foh' 回 覆; t'e-
dz' 推 辭; — *for a false reason*,
t'e-t'oh' 推 托; *cannot* — (to
do), t'e-feh-t'eh' 推 弗 脫; *ditto*
(to admit), t'e-feh-k'æ 推 弗
開; — *consent*, feh-hyü' 弗 許;
feh ing-dzing' 弗 應 承; —
*with thanks*, dz zia° 辭 謝°; *affect
to* —, kô' t'e-dz 假° 推 辭

REFUTE, *to* poh-tao 駁 倒

REFUTED, *cnnnot be* poh'-feh-tao'-

go 駁 弗 倒 个°; *utterly* —,
poh'-sah-de 駁 煞 了°

REGAIN, *to* voh-cün'-læ 復 轉 來;
yi teh'-djoh 又° 得 着°

REGAINED (by the government),
kw'e-voh'-de 恢 復 了°; siu-
voh'-de 收 復 了°

REGARD, *to care for*, kwn'-djoh
顧 着°; ts'æ 睬; kwun 管;
ts'iu-ts'æ' 愀 睬: *do not* — *him*,
hao-vong' ts'æ gyi 好 不° 用°睬
其; *speak and* (he) *regards not*,
wô-feh-ts'æ' 話 弗 睬; *in* — *to
this matter*, kông'-tao keh'-go z-
ken' 講° 到 這 个° 事 幹;
— *as improper*, yi'-we feh-k'o'
以 爲 弗 可

REGARDLESS *of danger*, feh-kwu'
ngwe-hyin' 弗 顧 危 險; — *of
cost*, feh-leng to-siao' dong-din'
弗 論 多 少 銅 錢°

REGARDS, *present my* — *to him*,
dæ ngô' mông-mông' gyi 代 我
望° 望° 其; læ gyi' di-fông dæ
ngô cü-i 在° 其 地 方 代 我
致 意; t'i ngô' ts'ing gyi en' 替
我 請 其 安

REGENCY, *to govern by a* —, dæ
djü' koh tsing' 代 治 國 政;
*ditto during the minority of the
heir apparent*, bao t'a'-ts zo long-
ding' 抱 太 子 坐 龍 廷

REGIMEN, *follow a prescribed* —,
ing'-zih iao tsiao fah' 飲 食 要
照 法

REGIMENT, *a* ih-ts ping' —

枝 兵; ih-de ping′ 一 隊 兵

REGION, a ih-tæ di-fông′ 一 帶 地 方

REGISTER of names, or of lands, ts'ah′-ts 冊 子; — of population, a-wu′-ts'ah 挨° 戶 冊

REGISTER, to cü-ts'ah′ 註 冊; zông-ts'ah′ 上 冊; — the census, zao a-wu′-ts'ah 造° 門° 牌° 冊; — the males, zông nying-ting′- ts'ah 造° 人° 丁 冊

REGRET, to ao-nao-siang′ 懊 惱 相; sing′ næn-ko′ 心 難 過; — to part with, feh-sô′-teh 弗 捨° 得

REGRETTED, to be k'o′-sih 可 惜; always to be —, ao′-feh-cün′-go 懊 弗 轉 个°

REGULAR, tsæn′-zi 整 齊°; zi-jih′ 齊° 集; in — order (or succession), a-ts′-jü 挨° 次 序; — (as persons sitting, or standing, &c.), pai-pai′-shing 挨° 排° 排°; — in eating, and drinking, ing′-zih diao-yüing′ 飲 食 調 勻; risen in the — way, (i. e. by examinations), sæn-k'ao′ c'ih-sing′ 三 考 出 身; tsing′-du c'ih-sing 正 途 出 身; not risen in the — way, (i. e. bought), kyün-pæn′ c'ih-sing′ 捐 班 出 身

REGULARLY, a-ts′′-jü 挨° 次 序; i-ts′′-jü 依 次 序; tsiao′-ts′′-jü 照 次 序

REGULATE, to — what is in disorder, tsing′-teng 整 頓; djü-li′

治 理; cannot — his family, how can he govern a kingdom? peh neng dzi kyüô′ in neng djü koh′ 不 能 齊 家 焉 能 治 國?

REGULATIONS, công-dzing′ 章 程 (công or tsông); diao-li′ 條 例; kwe-kyü′ 規 矩; kwe-diao′ 規 條 (ih-diao); to make —, shih′-lih tsông-dzing′ 設° 立 章 程

REIGN, to tso wông-ti′ 做 皇 帝; zo-we′ 坐° 龍° 廷°; zo tin-'ô′ 坐° 天 下°; begin a —, teng-we′ 登 極°; in the 8th year of T'ung-chih, Dong-Djü′ pah′-nyin 同 治 八 年

REITERATE, to ts'in-ting-væn′-coh-go wô′ 千 叮 萬 囑 个° 話; wô-ko′ yi-wô′ 話 過 又° 話

REJECT, to ky'i′-diao 棄 了°; tiu-diao′ 丟 了°; — finally, ky'i′-djih 棄 絕

REJECTED by every one, we nying′ sô ky'i′ 爲 人° 所 棄

REJOICE, to be pleased, hwun-hyi′ 歡 喜; — together, dô-kô′ hwun-hyi′ 大° 家° 歡 喜; greatly pleased, kw'a′-loh 快 樂; to be delighted, kao-hying′ 高 興; — exceedingly, hwun-t'in′-hyi-di° 歡 天 喜 地

RELATE, to tell, kông 講°; djün 傳; I will — (it) to you; ngô kông′ peh ng t'ing′ 我 講 與° 你° 聽; ngô kông′-hyiang-ng-dao′ 我 講 向 你 道; —

*particulars,* kông′-leh dziang-be′ 講°得°詳備

RELATED, *is he —* *to you?* gyi′ z ng′-go zing-dzoh′ soh′ 其 是 你° 个° 貴° 族 麼°? *he is distantly —,* z ah-lah yün′-vông ′en-dzoh′ 是 我° 等° 遠 房 寒 族; *we have the same surname, but are not —,* dong-sing′ feh we-dzoh′ 同 姓 不°宗°

RELATIONS, *and* RELATIVES, *nearest —,* ts′ing-nying′ 親 人°; *distant —,* yün′-ts′ing 遠 親; *— of the same surname,* dong-dzoh′ 同 族; zi-kô-nying′ 自° 家° 人°; *— of a different surname,* ts′ing-kyün′ 親 眷; *near — (whether by affinity, or consanguinity),* kweh′-joh-ts-ts′ing′ 骨 肉 之 親; hyüih′-ts′ing 血 親; *the five —,* ng′ leng 五°倫

RELAX, *to — (as a cord),* fông-song′ 放 鬆; *— (as muscles, &c.),* kw′un-shü′ 寬 舒

RELAXATION, *take* sing′-li en-yih′-kyi 心 裡 安 逸; *— (after* (sorrow or trouble), sæn-sæn sing′ 散 散 心; kw′un-kw′un sing′ 寬 寬 心

RELEASE, *to* fông 放; fông′-c′ih 放 出; *— from confinement,* fah-fông′ 發 放; sih′-fông 釋 放; *pardon and —,* nyiao-fông′ 饒 放

RELENT, *to* sang nyün′-sing-dziang 生°軟 心 腸

RELIABLE, t′oh′-leh-ko 托得°過; k′o-t′oh′-go 可 托 个°; k′ao′-leh-djü′-go 靠 得°住 个°; hao′ siang-sing′-go 好 相 信 个°; *to receive — information,* teh′-djoh jih-loh′ 得 着°實 在°; *— news,* jih-jih′-loh-loh-go sing′-sih 實 實 在°在°个°信 息

RELICS, *ancient* kwü′-tsih 古 蹟; *— of Buddha,* shiæ′-li 舍 利; *— of saints, &c.,* sing′-doh 聖 簪°

RELIEF, *can give no —,* lih feh neng-dzu′ 力 弗 能 助; vu lih neng we 無 力 能 爲

RELIEVE *pain,* kæn-kæn t′ong′ 滅°痛; ka-ka t′ong′ 解°痛; ka-ka bo; ts-ts t′ong 止 痛; *— the poor,* tsiu-tsi′ gyüong-nying′ 賙 濟 窮 人°; sô′-s gyüong-nying′ 捨 施 窮 人°; *ditto (on a more extensive scale),* tsi-bing′ 濟 貧

RELIGION, kyiao 敎; kyiao′-meng 敎 門; *Confucian —,* Jü kyiao′ 儒 敎; *Buddhist —,* Sih′ kyiao 釋 敎; *Taoist —,* Dao′ kyiao 道 敎; *Mahommedan —,* We-we′ kyiao 回 回 敎; *Catholic —,* T′in-cü′ kyiao 天 主 敎; *Protestant —,* Yiæ-su′ kyiao 耶 穌 敎

RELIGIOUS, gyin-dzing′ 虔 誠; *— newspaper,* ′ang kyiao′ sing-pao′ 行 敎 新 報; kyüoh′-shü sing-pao′ 覺 世 新 報

RELINQUISH, *to — with regret,* p′i′-diao 譬 了°; p′i-t′æn′-diao

罾 嘆 了°;— (as an undertaking), t'e-diao' 推 了°; t'e-k'æ' 推 開; hyih siu' 歇 手

RELISH, *to eat with a —*, ky'üoh'-leh yiu ts-mi' 吃°得°有 滋味°

RELUCTANT, feh-dzing'-nyün 弗 情 願; feh-yüoh'-i 弗 欲 意

RELY, *to — upon*, i'-t'oh 倚 托; t'oh'-læn 託 賴°; k'ao'-djoh 靠 着°; *can — upon*, k'o k'ao'-go 可 靠 个°; *I am well, relying on your happiness*, (a polite answer), t'oh-ng-foh' 託 你° 福 or t'oh-foh' 託 福

REMAIN, *to stay*, deng 停; deng-loh' 停 了°; *— long*, dziang deng' 長 停°; *— for a short time*, dzæn deng' 暫 停°; *— over* (as food), dzing-loh' 剩 落

REMAINDER, yü-to' 餘 多; gyi-yü' 其 餘; to-deo' 多 頭

REMARKABLE, fi-dzông' 非 常; c'ih-gyi' 出 奇; *— wisdom*, fi-djông'-go ts'ong-ming' 非 常 个° 聰 明

REMEDY, *efficacious* ling yiah' 靈 藥; ling-tæn'-miao yiah' 靈 丹 妙 藥; sin-tæn' 仙 丹; *no — for*, m̄ yiah' k'o-i' 無° 藥 可 醫

REMEMBER, *to* kyi'-teh 記 得; kyi' læ sing'-li 記 在° 心 裏; kyi læ hyüong-cong' 記 在° 胸 中; fông' læ sing'-li 放 在 心 裡; dzng' læ sing'-li 存 在° 心 裏; *— and constantly think of*, kyi'-nyiæn 記 念; *— after once*

seeing, ko'-moh peh-vông' 過 目 不 忘

REMIND, *to* di-ky'i' 提 起; di-deo'; *— of something forgotten*, di-sing' 提 醒; *— him*, di-gyi-deo, or di-ky'i gyi deo 提 醒° 其

REMISS, yiæ'-dæ 懈 怠; *— in business*, tso' z-ken' ky'in gying-lih' 做 事 幹 少° 勤 力

REMIT, *to pardon*, sô'-diao 赦° 了°; miu'-diao 免 了°; *— the land tax*, hweh'-min zin-liang' 豁 免 錢° 糧; *— money to a distance*, ta nying-sing' c'ih-ky'i 寄° 銀 信 出 去°

REMITTENT *fever*, sih'-nyih-tsing 濕 熱° 症

REMNANT (of cloth), t'ön-den' 段 頭°; ling-deo'-ling-mi' 零 頭 零 尾°

REMONSTRATE, *advise him not to do*, ky'ün' gyi feh-k'o' tso 勸 其 弗 可 做; *ditto* (with a superior), kyin' gyi feh-k'o' tso 諫 其 弗 可 做

REMORSE *on account of one's sin*, di-sing' tiao'-tæn, we-leh zi'-go ze' 提 心 吊 膽 爲 了 自°罪; we-leh zi-go ze' sing'-li ngao-tsin' 爲 了° 自° 罪° 心 裏 熬 煎

REMOTE, yün 遠; liao-yün' 遼 遠; nyiao-yün' 窵 遠; *very —*, ting'-yün 頂 遠; yiao-yün' 遙 遠

REMOVE, *to* yi-ko' 移 過; tsæn'-ko 趲 過; *— to another house*, pun-oh' 搬屋; ts'in-kyü' 遷居; *ditto temporarily,* tsæn-oh' 趲屋

REMUNERATE, *to* — (with a present), dziu-zia' 酬謝; — *for trouble,* dziu-lao' 酬勞

REND, *to* — (as rocks), hwah'-k'æ 豁開; — (as cloth), c'ô'-k'æ 撦開; *to split,* lih-k'æ' 裂開

RENDER *an account of matters,* we-pao' z-t'i' 回報事體; *to pay back,* wæn 還; pao'-wæn 報還; — *thanks* (to God), coh'-zia 祝謝°

RENDEZVOUS, *to* we-zi' 會齊°

RENEW, *to* kæ-sing' 改新; tso-sing' 做新; — *the heart,* ky'i gyiu' wun-sing' 棄舊換新

RENOUNCE, *to* djü-diao' 除去°; djih-diao' 絕了°; ky'i'-djih 棄絕; dön'-djih 斷絕; — *one's allegiance,* be-fæn' 背反

RENOWNED, yiu do ming'-sing 有大°名聲; — *even to the capital,* ming'-ciing ti'-tu 名震帝都

RENT, *n.* tsu-din' 租錢°; vông-din' 房錢°; vông tsu-din' 房租錢°; tsu-kô' 租價°; *to raise the* —, tsiang tsu-kô' 漲租價°; *money, paid down as security for* —, t'eu' tsu-din 賠租錢°; ah' tsu-din 押°租錢°

RENT, *to* tsu 租; shü 賃; *to* — *out,* tsu-c'ih' 租出; shü'-c'ih 賃出

REPACK, *to* — (in a box), kæ-siang' 改箱; — (in a bundle), kæ-pao 改包

REPAIR, *to* siu-li' 修理; siu-gyiu' 修舊; — *by patching,* siu-pu' 修補; — *and embellish,* siu-sih' 修飾; — *bridges, and roads,* siu-gyiao' p'u lu' 修橋補°路

REPAY, *to* wæn 還; ti'-siao 抵銷; — (for an article injured, or lost), be-wæn' 賠還; ti'-dzông 抵償

REPEAL, *to* — *a law,* djü-diao' lih-fah' 除去°律法; k'æ-diao' lih-fah' 開去°律法

REPEAT, *to do again and again,* tsæ'-sæn tso' 再三做; *to say again and again,* kông'- ko-yi-kông' 講過又°講; wô-ko'-yi-wô' 話過又話; — *the same thing in discourse,* bun-zông'-bun-loh' 盤上盤落; — *after another,* djün 譔; — *after me,* keng'-leh ngô djün' 隨°我譔; — *Buddhist prayers,* nyiæn kying' 念°經; — *a lesson,* be shü' 背°書

REPEATEDLY, tsæ'-sæn-tsæ-s' 再三再四; *charge* — (by words), ting-coh' 叮囑; coh'-t'oh 囑託

REPENT, *to* ao'-hwe 懊悔; — *and turn from,* hwe'-kæ 悔改; we-sing'-cün-i 回心轉意; t'ong'-kæ zin-fi' 痛改前非; ao'-hwe kæ-ko' 懊悔改過; hwe'-ze kæ-ko' 悔罪改過; — (in a Buddhist sense, by paying the priests to pray for), ts'æn'-hwe 懺

悔; *to change one's mind*, sing fæn'-hwe 心 翻 悔

REPETITION *of words*, djün-ko'-yi-djün' 譔 過 叉° 譔; bo-bo'-nao-nao'-go shih-wô' 重 叠° 个° 說 話; *endless* —, djün-feh-hyih'-go 譔 弗 歇 个°

REPINE, *to* — *at*, ün 怨; 'eng 恨; — *at Heaven and Earth*, ün'-T'in 'eng-Di' 怨 天 恨 地; — *at poverty*, ün gyüong' 怨 窮

REPLACE, *to place as before*, dzing-gyiu en' 仍 舊 安 放°; — *as if it had not been moved*, nyün-fông' feh dong' 放° 在° 原 處° 弗 動

REPLENISH, *to fill again*, kô-mun' 加° 滿; *fill completely*, s'-teh mun'-tsoh 使 得 滿 足

REPLY, *to* we-tah' 回 答; te'-tah 對 答; tah'-ing 答 應; *a* —, we-ing' 回 音; we-wô' 回 話; — *to a letter*, we-sing' 回 信; *ditto* (unsealed), we-z' 回 字

REPORT, *rumor*, fong-siug' 風 聲; *idle* —, yiao-yin' 謠 言; *to create ditto*, nyiah-dzao' yiao-yin' 揑 造° 謠 言; *ditto and make trouble*, dzao-yin'-seng-z 造° 言 生 事; fah kyü'-lông; ky'i mông-deo'; *the* — *is*, nying-kô wô' 人° 家° 話; — (*of expenses*, &c.), ts'ing-tæn' 清 單; ts'ing-tsiang' 清 帳; — *of a cannon*, p'ao'-go hyiang'-sing 礮 个° 響 聲

REPORT, *to* t'ong-pao' 通 報; — *to him*, pao'-hyiang-gyi-dao 報

向 其 道; — *to a superior*, ping'-cü 稟 知; — *to the Emperor*, tseo'-ming wông-zông' 奏 明 皇 上; — *to the officers*, ping-kwun' 稟 官

REPOSE, *quiet*, en-zing' 安 靜; *to seek* —, zing en-zing' 尋° 安 靜; *I wish you sweet* —, ts'ing' en-cü' 請 安 置

REPOSE, *to* hyih-sih' 歇 息

REPRESENT, *you* — *him as a bad man*, gyi'-go dzing-ying', tsiao ng' kông'-læ z ẁa'-go 其 个° 情 形 照 你° 講 來 是 孬 个°; — *typically*, piao'-ming 表 明; —, *or act a part*, tsông-pæn' 裝 扮; *to act for another*, dæ-we' jing-z' 代 爲 人 事; *one represents ten*, ih' tông jih' 一 當 十; — *the people* (as in Congress), dæ pah'-sing cü z' 代 百 姓 調° 處°

REPRESS, *to* ah'-djü 壓 住; ah'-cü 壓° 制; ah'-jih 壓 習; ts'-djü 止 住; — *anger*, ah'-djü ô'-wông 壓° 住 怒 氣°; jing-ky'i-t'eng'-sing 忍 氣 吞 聲; *could not* — *laughter*, nying'-feh-djü' siao' 忍 弗 住 笑; — *bad disposition*, k'eh'-djü ẁa sing'-kah 克 治 孬 性 格

REPRIEVE, *to* ying-vah' kw'un-wun'-tin 刑 罰 寬 綏 點

REPRIMAND, *to* tsah'-be 責 備; — (generally in a loud tone), heng,

REPRINT, *to* tsæ ing' 再 印; dzong ing' 重 印

REPROACH, to s-we' 施為; p'i-bing' 批評; to — severely, ba; wô; siah gyi lin' 削其臉; to humiliate him (extremely) by —, siu-joh' gyi 羞辱其; da gyi ô-lin' 抓其丫臉; suffer —, ziu siu'-joh 受羞辱; ziu tsao-t'ah' 受蹧蹋; without —, 嬎 p'i'-bing 無批評; ditto (blemish), 嬎 yüô'-tin 無瑕玷

REPROVE, to tsah'-be 責備; — (generally in a loud tone), heng; — and threaten, tsah'-vah 責罰

REPROBATE, vu-sô'-peh-we'-go 無所不為个; peh-k'æn'-ts-gyih' 不堪之極

REPROOF, ba-deo'; severe —, do' ba-deo'; receive a —, for the verb say either, t'ing 聽, ky'üoh' 吃, or ziu 受; thus, I to-day received a —, ngô kyih-mih' t'ing ba-deo' ko-de 我今日聽埋怨過了; give him a —, ba' gyi ib-we' 埋怨其一回

REPTILES, bô'-go djong' 爬个蟲

REPUBLIC, ming-cü'-ts-koh 民主之國

REPUDIATE, to dön'-djih 斷絕; ky'i'-diao 棄了; t'ih'-c'ih-læ 剔出來; —(as an affair), t'eng'-c'ih-læ 佘出來; — acquain-tance, dön'-djih-læ-wông' 斷絕來往; — a wife, ky'i'-diao lao'-nyüing 棄了妻子; ditto (for misbehavior), li'- diao lao'-nyüing 離了妻子

REPUGNANT to a person, long nying' we'-wu-go 弄人穢污个

REPULSE, to tang'-t'e 打退

REPULSIVE countenance, min-k'ong' p'ô-nying'-sah-la' 面孔可怕; cold and disagreeable, lang'-ts'ih-ts'ih 冷澈澈

REPUTABLE, yiu-ming'-go 有名个; — employment, t'i'-min-go 'ông-nyih' 體面个行業

REPUTATION, ming-sing' 名聲; ming-ky'i' 名器; ming-vông' 名望; character, ming-tsih' 名節; to lose or injure —, tsao-t'ah' ming-sing 蹧蹋名聲; wæ-diao' ming-sing' 壞了名聲; ditto another's —, wæ nying'-go ming-tsih 壞人名節; his — is good, gyi'-go ming-sing' hao' 其个名聲好; an indifferent —(i.e. not very good), ming-sing' biug-djông' 名聲平常

REQUEST, to ts'ing 請; siang-ts'ing' 相請; siang-iao' 相邀; — him to come, siang-iao' gyi læ' 相邀其來; ts'ing gyi læ' 請其來; respectfully — and entrust, pa'-t'oh 拜托; I will comply with your —, tseng kyiao', tseng kyiao' 遵敎遵敎

REQUIRE, to shü iao' 須要; vu-pih'-ts-iao 務必要; pih'-shü iao 必須要

REQUISITE, how many are — ?

ing-yüong' ky'iah'-leh to-siao' 應
用却耍° 多少？ pih'-ky'iah-
leh to-siao' 必 須° 多 少？
(ky'iah-leh or ky'iao-leh).

REQUITE, to pao 報；pao'-tah 報
答；— favors, pao-eng' 報恩；
pao-peng' 報木

RESCUE, to save, kyiu 救；come
to the —, læ kyiu' 來 救；—
from fire, ho-li' kyiu'-c'ih-læ 火
裏 救 出 來；kah ho' kyiu'-
c'ih-læ 夾°火救出來；— (as
one who has fallen into something), tsing-kyiu' 拯救；kyiu'-
yün 救援；— out of trouble, or
difficulty, kyiu'-kw'u kyiu-næn'
救苦救難

RESEARCHES, to make —, (i. e.
seek diligently), seo-zing' 搜
尋°；ditto by examining, k'ao'-
kyiu 考 究

RESEMBLING, ziang 像；siang-
ziang' 相 像；jü-dong' 如同；
fông'-feh 仿彿

RESEMBLES, yiu-ts'-wu 猶之乎；
z'-wu 似 乎；— in countenance,
tso' min-ngæn' 同° 眉 眼°；—
his father, yiu-ts'-wu ah-tia' 猶
之乎阿爹°；ziang tia' 像爹°；
teng ah-tia' siang-ziang'-go 與°
阿 爹° 相 像 個°；— exactly,
weh-t'eh'-ko 活揚過；t'ih'-
seh-vu-r' 貼色無二

RESENT, to dong ky'i 動氣；kô
ky'i 加° 氣；(polite) kyin ky'i
見氣

RESENTMENT, ün 怨；ün'-ky'i 怨
氣；bitter —, ün'-ky'i-beh-beh'
怨氣勃勃；ün-dzin' 冤讐；
— and hatred, ün'-'eng-go sing
怨恨個°心；should not cherish
—, ün' feh-k'o kyih' 冤弗可
結；ün' feh-k'o' dzeng 怨弗
可存；implacable —, ka'-feh-
k'æ'-go ün' 解弗開個° 冤

RESERVE, to liu-loh' 留落；dzing-
loh' 剩落；dzeng-loh' 存落；
— a little, liu-tin'-loh 留些°；
dzing-tin'-loh 賸些°

RESERVED in words, kwô'-yin-
kwô-nyü'-go 寡言寡語個°

RESIDE, to djü 住；deng 居°；
where do you —? ng'-djü læ
'ah-li 你° 住在° 何° 處°？

RESIDENCE, djü-c'ü' 住處；deng-
c'ü' 庶 處；deng-sing'-ts-c'ü' 庇
身之處；en-sing'-ts-c'ü' 安身
之 處；where is your honorable
—？ tseng fu' 'ah-li 尊府何°
處°？ fu'-zông 'ah-li 府上那°
裡？ fu'-zông 'o-c'ü' 府 上 何
處？ my humble —, sô-'ô' 舍
下°；sô'-kyin 舍間；bi-sô' 敝舍

RESIDUE, the gyi-yü'-go 其餘
個°；yü-to'-go 餘多個°

RESIGN, to give up, dz 辭；zia
謝°；t'e 推；t'e-diao 推 了°；
— a situation, dz di - fông' 辭
缺°；— one's office, dz kwun' 辭
舘；zia z' 謝° 事；zia zing 謝°
任；ditto on account of old age,
kao'-lao 告老；— to another,

nyiang 讓°; *ditto by writing,* sia z' 卸事

RESIST, *to* ti'-tông 抵擋; tông'-djü 擋住; — *an enemy, &c.,* ti'-dih 抵敵; — *paying taxes* (in a body), nao liang' 鬧漕°

RESOLUTE, kyin-sing' 堅心; ts'-hyiang lih-lao'-liao 志向立牢了; *be —*, sing' iao kyin' 心要堅

RESOLUTION, *unshaken firmness,* lih-sing' 烈心

RESOLUTIONS (passed by an assembly, &c.), công-dzing' 章程 (công or tsông).

RESOLVE, *fixed* k'ô'-ding cü-i' 掔°定主意; cü'-i lih-lao'主意立牢

RESOLVE, *to* ding cü'-i 定主意; lih cü'-i 立主意

RESORT, *many — thither,* læ-ky'i'-go nying to' 來去個人多°; *a place of —*, jü'-jih-nying'-cong di'-fông 衆°人聚集之°地°; *the last —*, (figurative, from chess), meh-tsiah'-gyi-ts' 末著棊子

RESOURCE, fông-fah' 方法; fah'-ts 法子; *no —* (but this), m̄-fah' 無°法; shih'-fah-næ'-'o 失法奈何; vu-k'o'-næ-'o 無可奈何

RESPECT, *to* kying'-djong 敬重; kong-kying' 恭敬; tseng-djong' 尊重; — *one's parents,* kying'-djong vu'-meo 敬重父母;

*ditto,* (or reflect honor upon), tsang do'-nying-go ky'i' 爭°大°人個°氣; — *this,* (official), ling-tseng' 憐遵; — *written paper,* kying'-sih z-ts' 敬惜字紙

RESPECT, *with — to,* kông'-tao 講到; ts'-ü 至於; *no — for superiors,* moh'-vu tseng-tsiang' 目無尊長; m̄-do' m̄-siao' 無°大°無°小; *self —* (as flowing from — for one's parents), tsang-ts'-ky'i 爭志氣; ze-ky'i' 銳氣; *to endure trouble from ditto,* tsang-fong' ngao'-ky'i 爭°風傲氣; *lost all self—* —, ze-ky'i' tih'-tao-de 銳氣跌倒了; tao ze-ky'i' de 倒銳氣了°; *no — for self,* or *for parents,* m̄- tsang'-m̄-ky'i' 弗°爭°氣; *a good man respects him-self,* kyüing-ts' z-djong 君子自重

RESPECTS, *to pay one's —*, mông-mông' 望望; pa' mông 拜°望°; *in some — alike, in some — not alike,* yiu-sing dong', yiu sing feh-dong 有些°同有些弗同, (also means some are alike and some are not).

RESPECTABLE, t'i'-min 體面; yiu t'i'-min 有體面; — *people,* zông kô'-ts nying' 上等°人°

RESPECTFUL, kong-kying' 恭敬; — *to his master,* dæ cü'-nying-kô kong-kying' 待主人°

恭 敬 ; *be* — , tso nying' iao ky'in-kong' 做 人°要 謙 恭

RESPECTING, leng-tao' 論到; ts'-ü 至 於

RESPIRE, *to* ih-hwu' ih-hyih' — 呼一吸; hwun-tsing' hwun-c'ih' 喚 進 喚 出; hwu-hyih' 呼 吸

RESPITE, *no* ih-hyih'-feh-k'ong' 一 歇 弗 望

RESPLENDENT, ming-liang' 明 亮; kwông-liang' 光 亮; — (as snow), sbih'-kwak-liang 雪 亮

RESPOND, *to* ing'-tah 應 答; ing'-te 應 對; we-tah' 回 答

RESPONSIBILITY, tseh'-zing 責 成°; kyin-ts' 肩 子; *the — rests on you,* z ng'-go tseh'-zing 是 你°个°責 成'; z ng' tæn-tông' 是 你°擔 當; dzæ-ü ng' 在 于 你°; *the —* (consequence), *rests on you,* z ng'-go ken-yi' 是 你° 个°干 係; (*the burden*) *ditto,* z ng'-go tæn'-deo 是 你° 个°擔 頭; hyiang ng' z veng' 向 你° 是 問; læ ng' sing zông' 在°你° 身 上; *to bear the —,* pe' ken-yi' 背 干 係; *to devolve the — on some one else,* sia' kyin-ts' 卸° 肩 子

RESPONSIBLE, *to be — for another,* tso pao' 做 保; tso-cong'-tsoh-pao' 做 中 作 保; *a — situation,* zing-djong'-tseh-da' 任 重 責 大

REST, en-tæn' 安 耽; en-sih' 安 息; bing-en' 平 安; en-yih' 安 逸; *day of —,* en-sih' nyih 安 息 日°; *remainder,* gyi-yü' 其 餘; yü-to' 餘 多

REST, *to* tsiang-sih' 將 息; — *from labor,* hyih-kong' 歇 工; deng kong' 停 工; — *a while,* deng' ih-hyih' 停°一 歇; *ditto from effort,* hyih lih' 歇 力; hyih' ih-zông lih' 歇 一 歇°力; *won't* (you) — *a while?* ts'ia' hyih'-ih-hyih 且°歇 一 歇? — *or lean upon,* gæ-djoh' 戲 着' ; a-djoh' 挨 着°; — *on the wall,* gæ-djoh ziang' 戲 着°牆; — *your heart,* (or be easy), fông'-sing 放 心; *can't — my heart,* (or can't be easy), fông'-sing-feh'-loh' 放 心 弗 下°

RESTING-PLACE, tsiang-sih'-go di'-fông 將 息 个 地 方; — (by the way), liang-ding' 涼 亭

RESTLESS, zo'-lih-feh-en' 坐°立 弗 安; sing-mông'-feh-ding' 心 忙 弗 定

RESTORE, *to give back,* kwe-wæn' 歸 還; — *to original owner,* kwe-wæn' nyün-cü' 歸 還 原 主; *to bring back,* wæn'-we 挽 回; — *tea* (that has been used), wæn-weng' dzô-yih' 還 魂 茶 葉; — *paper,* wæn-weng' ts' 還 魂 紙

RESTORED *from sickness,* djün-yü'-de 全 愈 了; zông-hao'-nyiang-de; — *to original health and strength,* voh-nyün'-de 復 元 了°; wæn-nyün'-de 還 元 了°

RESTRAIN, *to* iah'-soh 約束;
kwun'-soh 管束; 'en 含忍'; —
*one's bad behavior*, 'ang-we' siu-
lin' 行°爲收歛; — *one's self*,
zi iah'-soh zi' 自°約束自°; —
*anger*, neh-leh sing-ho' 耐°下°
心火; — *anger, and keep quiet*,
jing'-ky'i t'eng'-sing 忍氣吞
聲; *not to* — *one's lust*, fông'
tsong 放縱; *could not* — *tears*,
ngæn'-li 'en'-feh-djü'-de 眼°淚
含弗住了°

RESTRAINT, *under* — (*uneasy*),
kyü-soh' 拘束

RESTRICT, *to* 'æn 限°; 'æn'-cü
限°制; 'æn'-ding 限°定°; —
*him to one bowl*, 'æn'-ding peh
gyi ih un 限°定°給°其一碗

RESTRICTIONS, *many* —, *or re-*
*stricted in many ways*, hyü'-to
kyü-soh'-liao 許多拘束了°;
kyü-kyü'-soh-soh 拘拘束束

RESULTS, kyih'-gyüoh 結局; siu-
dziang' 收場; *bad* —, ẘa
kyih'-gyüoh 孬°; 結局; *what*
— ? dza-go kyih'-gyüoh 怎°樣°
結局?

RESULTS *from*, kwe-keng'-kyih-ti'
歸根結蔕; c'ih'-ü 出於;
*this* — *from the medicine*, keh z
yiah'-go kwe-keng-kyih-ti' 這°
是藥个°歸根結蔕; keh'
c'ih-ü yiah' 這°出於藥

RESUME, *to* dzing-gyiu' tso 仍舊
做; — *the duties of office*, voh-
zing' 復任

RESURRECTION, *the doctrine of the*
—, veo-weh'-go dao'-li 復活
个°道理; *the* — *day*, weh-cün'-
læ-go nyih-ts' 活轉來个°
日°子

RESUSCITATE, *to* — (*from ap-*
*parent death*), long sing'-cün-læ
弄醒轉來

RETAIL, *to sell at* —, ling-ts'ah'
零拆; ts'ah-ma' 拆賣; *to do*
*small* — *trade*, tso siao' sang-i'
做小生°意; tso siao' peng'-
kying-kyi 做小本經紀

RETAIN, *to* liu 留; liu-loh' 留
下°

RETALIATE, *to* wæn-li' 還禮;
yiu'-li-wæn-li' 有禮還禮; yiu'-
pao-wæn-pao' 有報還報

RETARD, *to* wun 緩; tso'-leh
wun-fæn'-tin 做得°緩點; *a*
*painful foot retarded my walking*,
be kyiah' t'ong wun'-wun tseo'
爲°腳痛緩緩走

RETINUE, *attendants*, ze-dzong' 隨
從; keng-ze'-go-nying; 跟隨
个°人°; *those who wait upon,*
*and follow*, keng-pæn' 跟班;
*Emperor's* —, z-we' 侍衞

RETIRE, *to withdraw*, t'e 退; —,
*or get out of an officer's way*, we-
bi' 廻避; bi-ih'-bi 避一避; —
*a step*, t'e'-ih-bu 退一步; *go*
*out*, t'e'-c'ih-ky'i 退出去°; —
*from office*, zia-z' 謝°事; *ditto,*
*and live in seclusion away from*
*one's home*, ing'-loh 隱落

RETIRED *spot*, iu-zing′ di′-fông 幽靜地方

RETIRING, *liking to drop behind*, hwun-byi′ loh ‛eo′ 歡喜落後°; *preferring others before one's self*, tseng nying′ zông zin′ 遜°人; 上前°

RETORT, *to* we-k‛eo′ 回口; we-yin′ 回言; — *improperly*, ing-cü′ 應嘴; ing lang′-wô 應冷°話; *to — wittily*, ing-ky‛iao′ wô 應巧話

RETRACT, *to — one's words*, shih-wô′ fæn-diao′ 說話翻調; cün-yin′ 轉言; — (*as in court*), cün-kong′ 轉供; fæn-kong′ 翻供

RETREAT, *to* t‛e 退

RETREATED, *the army* ping t‛e′-de 兵退了°

RETRIBUTION, pao′-ing 報應; ko′-pao 果報; ken′-ing 感應; *just —* , pao′-ing ‛ao-li′ feh-ts‛o′ 報應°毫厘弗錯°

RETURN, *to —* (*thither*), kyü-læ′ 歸來; cün′-læ 轉來; we-læ′ 回來; —(*there*), kyü-ky‛i′ 歸°去°; cün-ky‛i′ 轉去°; we-ky‛i′ 回去°; — *home*, kyü oh′-li ky‛i′ 歸°家°去°; *in haste to —* , kwe-sing′-ju-tsin′ 歸心如箭; *to turn back*, tao′-tseo-cün 倒走轉; — *a present*, (*i. e. send it back with thanks*), pih′ zia 璧謝°; — *to bad ways*, væn nyün′ ts‛ông-pô′ 犯原瘡疤; — *to old* (*bad*) *habits*, væn lao′ mao-

bing 犯老毛病; — *to old crimes*, væn gyiu en′ 犯舊案; — *visits*, we-pa′ 回拜°; *ditto and thank for attention*, zia bu′ 謝°步; —*things*, we-wæn′ tong-si′ 回還東西; *returned to Peking*, we Poh′-kying ky‛i′-de 回北京去°了°

RE-UNITE, *to —* (*persons*), tsæ′-jü 再聚; — (*things*), tsæ-‛eh′ 再合; tsæ′-tsih′-long 再接攏

REVEAL, *to open*, k‛æ-c‛ih′-læ 開出來; *to disclose*, lu′-c‛ih-læ 露出來; *to manifest*, hyin′-c‛ih-læ 顯出來; — *a matter*, lu fong-sing′ 露風信

REVELATION, meh-z′ 默示; *the Book of —* , Meh-z′-loh 默示錄

REVENGE, pao-dziu′ 報讐; (*in a less degree*), pao-ün′ 報怨

REVENUE, hyiang′-nying 餉銀; — *from customs*, se′-din 稅錢°; — *from lands*, zin-liang′ 錢°糧

REVERE, *to* tseng-kying′ 尊敬; kong-kying′ 恭敬

REVERENCE, kying′-djong 敬重

REVERENTIAL, gyin-kying′ 虔敬

REVERIE, *in a* ts‛eng′-leh c‛ih-jing′ 忖得°出神

REVERSE, *to turn over*, fæn-cün′-læ 翻轉來; *to turn end for end*, diao-deo′ 調頭; *to turn the other side*, fæn-hyiang′ 翻向; fæn-min′ 翻面

REVERT, *to — to the original,* kwe-nyün′ 歸原; voh-nyün′ 復原; — *to the old practice,* tsiao nyün′ tso 照原而°做

REVIEW, *to — studies,* li shü′ 理 一°理書; — (as a critic), bing-shü′ 評書; — *troops,* k'en ts'ao′ 看 操; yüih ping′ 閱兵

REVILE, *to* zoh-mô′ 辱罵; lön-zoh′-lön-mô′ 亂辱亂罵; zoh-nying-mô′-tao 辱人°罵倒

REVISE, *to — and correct,* kyiao′-ting 校訂

REVIVE, *to — strength,* tsih lih′ 接力; — (as from a swoon), sing′-cün-læ 醒轉來

REVIVED, *trade* sang-i′ hying′-ky'i-læ′-de 生°意興起來 了°; *strength —,* lih′ wæn-cün′-læ-de 力還轉來了°

REVOKE, *to —* (a decision, or promise), fæn-diao′ 翻調; fæn-tsiao′ 翻招; — *a law,* kæ′-diao lih-fah′ 改了°律法; kæ-diao is more often used than fi-diao, as the latter implies disrespect to a former ruler.

REVOLT, *to* dzao-fæn′ 造反; bun′-nyih 叛逆; liao-lön′ 擾°亂

REVOLUTION, ih-cün′ 一轉; *to make a —,* tsiu-we′-ih-cün′ 周 圍一轉; *political —,* (i. e. change of dynasty) wun dziao-dæ′ 換朝代

REVOLVE, *to* cün 轉; dön-dön′-cün 團團轉; *the earth revolves*

*around the sun,* di-gyiu′ hyiang nyih-deo′ ih-cün′ 地球向日°頭一轉; — *in the mind,* sing-li′ dziu-djü′ 心裏躊躇

REWARD, *to* sông 賞; —(for services), k'ao′-sông 犒賞; — *the good, punish the wicked,* sông jün′ vah oh′ 賞善罰惡

REWARD, *official* sông′-kah 賞格; — *of money given to servants,* or *employees,* sông′-fong 賞封; *notice of — promised,* sông-diao 賞條; *a —* (whether good or bad), pao′-ing 報應

RHEUMATIC *pains,* fong-ky'i′-t'ong 瘋氣痛; *ditto in the shoulders,* leo-kyin-fong′ 漏肩瘋

RHINOCEROS, si-ngeo′ 犀牛°(ih-deo); — *horn,* si-ngeo′ koh 犀牛°角 (ih-go, ih-tsah)

RHOMBUS, zia′-fông 斜方°

RHUBARB, da-wông′ 大黃

RHYME, yüing 韻; yüing-kyiah′ 韻腳; *to make rhymes,* ah yüing′ 押°韻

RIB, leh-ba-kweh′ 肋膀°骨 (ih-keng); *mutton —,* or *chop,* yiang ba′-kweh 羊膀°骨; *a — of the fin is broken,* ih-keng sin′-kweh, dön′-de 一根扇骨斷了°

RIBALDRY, *wine talk,* tsiu′-wô 酒話; tsiu′-tse-wu-du′ shih-wô′ 酒醉糊塗說話; *lewd talk,* ying-wô′ 淫話

RIBBON, s-ta′ 絲帶° (ih-keng)

RICE, *growing* dao 稻; — *in the*

*hull,* koh 穀; *uncooked* —, mi 米; *cooked* —, væn 飯; *a grain of* —, ih-lih mi' 一粒米; — *sprouts,* dao iang-ts' 稻秧子; — *gruel,* coh 粥; hyi-væn' 稀飯; *very smooth ditto,* dziu-lin'-go coh 綢黏°个°粥; *boiled* —, *with water added,* t'ông'-væn 湯飯; *must not waste* (or soil) —, væn' 飯-nao' tsao-t'ah' 飯弗可°蹧蹋; — *weevil,* mi'-djong 米蟲

RICH *person,* yiu'-lao nying-kô' 有錢°人°家; yiu'-lao dzæ-cü' 有錢財主; ing-wu' 殷戶; fu'-wu 富戶; do-nying-kô' 大°戶人°家°; — *and honorable,* fu'-kwe 富貴; *to become*—, fah-dzæ' 發財; *if* (you) *wish to be* — (fear not) *to walk a dangerous way,* ziah-iao-fu' tseo-hyin'-lu 若要富走險路; — *dress,* fu'-kwe i-zông 富貴衣裳; — *tasted,* (as food), 'eo'-vi 厚味; — *soil,* di-t'u' 'eo-jih 地土厚實; nyi-nyüoh 'eo 泥土°厚

RICHES, dzæ-veh' 財物; dzin-dzæ' 錢財; *god of* —, dzæ-jing' bu-sah' 財神菩薩

RID, *to get* — *of,* t'eh'-diao 脫了°; t'eh'-c'ih 脫出; t'eh-siu' 脫手; tiu-siu' 丟手; *glad to get* — *of him,* pô'-feh-neng'-keo t'eh'-diao' gyi 巴弗能彀脫了°其

RIDDLE, me-ts' 謎°子; — *on a lantern,* teng-me' 燈謎°; *to guess a* —, ts'æ me-ts' 猜謎°子

RIDE, *to* —*a horse,* gyi mô' 騎馬; — *in a sedan,* zo gyiao' 坐轎; — *in a carriage,* zo ts'ô-ts' 坐°車°子

RIDGE *of a house,* oh'-tsih 屋脊; — *pole,* tong'-liang 棟樑; — *of mountains,* lin-keng'-go sæn 連亘°个°山

RIDICULE, *to* tsao-siao' 嘲笑; c'ü'-siao 取笑; siao 笑

RIDICULOUS, hao-siao'-go 好笑个°; kyin-siao'-go 見笑个°

RIGGING, *sail-ropes,* bong-soh' 蓬索

RIGHT, *according with* —, li'-ing z-ka' 理應如°此; li'-kæ jü-ts'' 理該如此; ing-tông'-go 應當个°; ing-kæ'-go 應該个°; *reasonable,* yiu'-li 有理; *not wrong,* feh-ts'o' 弗錯°; *straight, or upright,* tsing 正; — *doctrine,* tsing' dao'-li 正道理; *not* —, *not up to the* —, *or crooked,* feh-tsing'-kying 弗正經; *the* — *hand,* jing-tsah' sin 順隻手; — *side,* jing-siu'-pin 順手邊; — *angle,* dzih-koh' 直角°; *is it* —? z-ka' feh-z-ka' 是如°此°不°是如°此°? *it is* —, feh-ts'o' 弗錯°; *it is not* —, feh'-z-ka' 弗是如°此°; *quite* —, tsing'-z 正是; — *side,* (as of cloth), tsing'-min 正面; — *side up,* jing-hyiang' 順向

RIGHT, *my* li'-ing peh ngô' 理應給°我; ngô li' sô ing-teh'-

go 我 理 所 應 得 个°: ngô veng′ sô tô g-jün′-go 我 牙 所 當 然 个°; ngô ing-veng′ sô teh′-go 我 應 牙 所 得 个°

RIGHTS, *put to* —, tsing-li′-hao 整 理 好; tsing′-teng-hao 整 頓 好; *ditto* (by taking away), tsin-coh′-ko; siu-jih′-ko 收 拾 過

RIGHTEOUS, jün 善; liang-jün′ 良 善; tsing′-dzih 正 直; jih-djün′ 十 全

RIGID, *hard*, ngang 硬°; — *in adhering to rules*, kwe-kyü′ siu′-leh nyin′ 規 矩 守 得° 嚴; *too ditto*, kyiao-djü′-kwu-seh′, or tiao-djü′-kwu-seh 膠 柱 鼓 瑟

RILL, siao′ ky′i-k′ang 小 溪 坑 (ih-da).

RIM, pin 邊; — *of a cup*, uu′ pin 碗 邊; *to put on a* —, siang ih-go pin′ 鑲 一 个° 邊

RING, ky′ün 圈 (ih-go); — (attached to something), gwæn 環°; *finger* —, ka-ts′ 戒° 指; *ear* —, gwæn-ts′ 耳´ 環´ (a pair, ih-fu)

RING, *to* — *a bell*, k′ao cong′ 敲° 鐘; — *a small bell*, yiao ling′ 搖 鈴; loh ling′ 捵 鈴; — *by beating*, djông cong′ 撞 鐘

RINGING *in the ears*, ng′-tô ′ong-′ong′-hyiang 耳° 朵 鬨 鬨 響

RINGLEADER, we-deo′-we-nao′ 為 頭 為 腦; deo-nao′ 頭 腦; — (in something bad), ′o′- ts-siu′ 禍 之 首; ze′-ts-kw′e′ 罪 之 魁

RINGWORM, ky′ün-sin′ 圈 癬

RINSE, *to* — (as cups &c.), dông 盪; — (as clothes), dzah; — *it*, dông′ gyi ih dông′ 盪 其 一 盪; *to shake back and forth in the water*, da; — *the mouth*, dông k′eo′ 盪 口; — *in clear water*, ts′ing shü′ dzah′ ih-du′ 清 水° 浸 一 回°

RIOT, ts′ao′-nao 譟 鬧; nao-z′ 鬧 事; — *in time of famine*, hwông-lön′ 荒 亂

RIP, *to* ts′ah-k′æ′ 拆 開; ts′ah′-diao 拆 了°; — *seams*, ts′ah′-k′æ vong-ts′ 拆 開 縫 子; — *open*, p′o′-k′æ 破 開; — *up the bowels*, p′o foh′ 破 腹

RIPE, joh 熟; *insufficiently* —, ky′in joh′ 欠 熟

RIPPLES, shü po-lông′ 水 波 浪; — *in circles*, shü yüing′ 水° 暈

RISE, *to get up*, bô-ky′i′ 爬 起; ky′i-sing′ 起 身; *to stand up*, lih-ky′i′-læ 立 起 來; — (to higher office), kao-sing′ 高 陞; sing-zông′-ky′i 陞 上 去°; —, (step by step), sing-deng′ 陞 等; — *in life*, fah′-dah 發 達; or *be promoted in literary examinations*, cong′- k′o-fah-kah′ 中 科 發 甲°; *smoke will* —, in′ we ts′ong-zông′-ky′i 烟 會 冲 上 去°; — (as dough), fah′-ky′i-læ 發 起 來; — *from the dead*, si-ts′ weh-cün′-læ 死 後° 活 轉 來; *market price has risen a little*, ′ông-dzing′ tsiang′-tinko-de 行情漲點過了°; *when will the tide —* ? kyi'-z dziao tsiang' 幾時潮漲? soh'-gɔ z-'eo dziao-shü tsiang' 甚°麼°時候潮漲? *sun* —, nyih-deo' c'ih ky'i' z 'eo' 日°頭出起時候

RISE, *origin,* keng-yiu' 根由; ky'i-ing' 起因; ky'i-deo' 起頭

RISK, *danger,* or *run the* —, mao-hyin' 冒險; — *life,* p'un-ming' 拚命; pe sing'-ming 拚°性命; *if not run some — how can one catch the tiger's cub,* "peh-jih hwn'-yüih in'-teh hwu-ts'" 不入虎穴焉得虎子

RITE, li 禮; *the mode of administering a —,* li'-cü 禮制; li'-tsih 禮節; *marriage and funeral rites,* hweng-sông' li'-tsih 婚喪禮節

RIVAL, te'-sin 對手; *antagonist,* te'-deo nying 對頭人°

RIVAL, *to* tsang-zin' 爭°前°; — *in display,* sæ-fu' 賽富; *the two — each other,* liang'-go bih kao ti' 兩个°別高低

RIVER, ( where there are tides ), kông 江°; — ( where there are no tides ) kông 港; 'o 河 (ih-da); *the —,* 'ô'-kông 下江°, so called as compared with the canals.

RIVULET, ky'i - k'ang' 溪坑° (ih-da)

RIVET, liang'-deo-bing'-go ting' 兩頭平个°釘; — (of scissors, or fan), gao-kwu' 交°股

ROAD, lu 路; lu-du' 路途; dao'-lu 道路 (ih-da); — *that does not go through,* toh'-sah-lu 不通°之°路; lu' feh-t'ong' 路弗通; — *that one knows,* joh-lu' 熟路; *strange —,* sang-lu' 生°路; *unfrequented —,* hwông-lu' 荒路; lang'-lu 冷°路; *on the —,* lu-zông' 路上; *what —?* 'ah-li' ih-da lu' 何°處°一垛路?

ROAM, *to* 'æn-tseo' 閒°走°; yiu-hyi' 遊戲

ROAR, *to* — (as a tiger), wu-wu'-hyiang 嗚嗚响; — (as wind, or falling water), nga-nga'-hyiang 颮°颮°响

ROAST, *to bake,* p'ang 烹°; — *beef,* p'ang ngeo-nyüoh' 烹°牛°肉°; — *chestnuts,* ts'ao lih-ts' 炒栗子; — *or five tea leaves,* ts'ao dzô-yih' 炒茶葉

ROB, *to* ts'iang'-deh 搶奪; — *when travelling,* tang'-kyih 打刼

ROBBER, zeh-heo' 賊°; do-zeh' 大°賊°; *one who robs with violence,* da-dao' 大盜; ts'iang'-væn 搶犯; *a bold —,* (often) *a pirate,* gyiang - dao' 強盜; *mounted —,* hyiang'-mô gyiang-dao' 响馬強盜

ROBE *worn with a girdle,* bao-ts' 袍子; *imperial ditto,* long-bao' 龍袍; *official —,* mông'-bao 蟒袍; *long Summer —,* (not girded), dziang-sæn' 長衫; *lined —,* kah'-ao 袷袄

ROBUST, gyin 健; tsông'-gyin 壯
健

ROCK, do zah'-deo 大°石°頭; *fixed*
—, bun-zah' 磐石°; — *work*,
kô'-sæn 假°山; *to make ditto*,
te kô'-sæn 堆假°山

ROCK, to yiao 搖; — *back and
forth*, yiao-læ'-yiao-ky'i' 搖來
搖去°; *to* — *a chair*, kwa' ü-ts
拐椅°子

ROCKING-CHAIR, yiao-dong'-go
ü'-ts 搖動个°椅°子; yiao'-
ü 搖椅°; kwa'-ü-ts 拐椅°子
(ih-pô)

ROCKET, liu-sing'-ho'-p'ao 流星
火爆

ROCKY *hills*, zah sæn' 石°山; —
*precipice*, zah pih' 石°壁

ROD, ken'-ts 釣°竿; *fishing* —,
tiao'-ng-ken' 釣魚°竿 (ih-
keng)

ROE, *female deer*, ts' loh' 雌鹿;
*fish* —, ng-ts' 魚°子

ROGUE, we-fi'-tsoh-tæ'-go-nying
爲非作歹个°人°; *one who
goes about deceiving*, tong'-kwa-
si-p'in-go 東拐西騙个°

ROLL, *a* ih-kyün' 一卷

ROLL, *to* le 擂; kweng 滾; kyün
捲; *the ball will* —, gyin we
le 球會擂; — *dough*, le min'
擂麵; *will* —*off*, iao le'-ko-ky'i'
要擂過去°; — *the ground
even*, di-yiang' le bing' 地上°擂
平; — *over and over*, fæn-læ'
foh-ky'i' 翻來覆去°; — *up*

*the sleeves*, ziu-ts' kyün-tæn'-zông
袖子捲上

ROLLER *for maps*, gyüoh 軸; *stone*
—, le-zah' 擂石° (ih-go)

ROLLING *pin*, ken'-djü 桿鎚; le-
djü 擂鎚° (ih-keng)

ROMAN *letters*, Lo-mô' z 羅馬字

ROMANCE, *book of leisure moments*,
'æn-shü 閒°書 (ih-peng)

ROOF, oh'-teng 屋上°; *tile* —,
oh'-ngô-teng 屋瓦°上°; *to mend
the* —, kæ leo' 蓋漏; coh leo'
築漏; ts'eh leo' 搣漏

ROOM,. vông 房; *the next* —, kah'-
pih vông' 隔壁房; *sleeping* —,
vông-kæn' 房間; kw'eng'-vông
臥房 (ih-kæn); *make* — (by
putting things closer), tsing'-leh
kw'un-k'ong'-tin 整得°寬空
點; *no* — *to sleep*, kw'eng'-u
m̄-teh 睡處°沒°有°; m̄-di-
fông hao kw'eng' 無°地方可
睡°; *no* — *to put it*, m̄-c'ü' hao
fông 無°處好放

ROOST, *perch*, tông'-ts 檔子;
*roosting place* (used figuratively
for men), ts'i-sing'-ts-sô' 棲身
之所

ROOST, *to* ts'i 棲; —*in the branches*, ts'i' læ jü-ô-ts' li 棲在°樹
極枝上°

ROOT, keng 根; keng-deo' 根頭;
*to take* —, sang keng' 生根

ROOT, *to* — *up*, keng bah-diao'
根拔出°; — *with the nose*,
ky'üing.

ROPE, zing 繩°; soh 索;* *cable,*
læn 攬; ts'ih 箞° 繩°; *to make*
—, tang zing' 打 繩; *to walk a*
—, 'ang zing' 走 繩 索°
  * Zing and soh are used for string,
  or rope, of whatever size.

ROPE-MAKER, zing-soh'-s-vu 繩°
索 司 務

ROPY, (as boiled sugar), we ky'i
s-go 會 起 如° 絲

ROSARY *Buddhist,* (108 beads),
shü'-cü or su-cü 數° 珠; *Romanist*
—, nyiæn-cü' 念 珠

ROSE, *dark red* —, me-kwe'-hwô
玫 瑰 花; du-me'-hwô 茶 蘼°
花; *monthly red* —, yüih-yüih-
'ong' 月 月 紅; *seven sisters* —,
ts'ih'-tsi'-me 七 姊 妹; *white
Banksia* — , bah-moh'-hyiang
白 木 香

ROSE-WATER, me-kwe'-lu' 玫 瑰
露

ROSEWOOD, (red wood), 'ong-moh'
紅 木; (more expensive), ts'-
dæn 紫 檀

ROSIN, song-hyiang' 松 香

ROSY, 'ong-feng'-si-bah 粉 紅; —
*faced,* dao-hwô-min' 桃 花 面;
*ditto and healthy-looking,* 'ong'-
c'ih-hen'-hen 紅 出 酣 酣

ROT, *will* we læn-wu' 會 爛 腐°;
iao læn-wu' 要 爛 腐°

ROTATE, *to go out and be succeeded
by others,* leng-cün' 輪 轉; —
*in order,* a-ts' leng-liu' 挨° 次
輪 流

ROTE, *to recite by* —, be shü 背°
書

ROTTEN, læn-wu'-de 爛 腐° 了°;
— *teeth,* (*i. e.* have worms in
them), cü'-ngô 蛀 牙°

ROUGE, in-tsi' 胭 脂°

ROUGH, ts'ao or ts'iao 糙; ts'ao'-
siu, or ts'iao'-siu 糙 手; — *draft,*
ts'ao'-kao 草 稿

ROUND, yün 圓; kweng'-yün 窺°
圓; *to walk* — *the table,* coh'-
teng-yin dön-ky'ün' tseo'-cün 桌
子° 邊 團 圈 走 轉; *turn* —
*a corner,* cün-wæn' 轉 彎

ROUND-SHOULDERED, hong-pe'
盎° 背

ROUSE *him from sleep,* eo gyi' su-
sing' 叫° 其 穌 醒; eo gyi diao'-
kao 叫° 其 醒 覺°; *to excite,*
kyih 激; dong 動; — *to anger,*
kyih nu' 激 怒; — *to effort,*
min'-li 勉 勵; — *one's self to
effort,* teng'-ky'i tsing'-jing 頓
起 精 神; tsing-jing' teng-tæn'-
ky'i 精 神 頓 起

ROUT, *to* da-ba' 大 敗°

ROUTE, *are you acquainted with
that* —? keh' da lu-dzing' ng
joh-sih' feh 這° 堹 路 程 你°
熟 識 否°?

ROVE, *to* — *about,* yüing-yiu'-s-
fông' 雲 遊 四 方

ROVER, *an idle* —, yin pin wu
逍 遙° 河 上°

ROW, *a* ih-da — 堹; ih-ba or
ih-bi' — 排; *sit in a* —, bing'-

ba zo 並 排° 坐°; *sit in rows,*
ih-ba′ ih-ba zo′ 一 排° 一 排°
坐°; bi-tang′-bi zo.

ROW, *to use oars,* pæn-tsiang′ 扳
槳

ROW-BOAT, pæn-tsiang′-jün 扳槳
船; *eight oared* —, pah tsiang-
jün′ 八 槳 船

ROYAL *family,* wông-kô 皇 家°.
— *will,* sing′-ts 聖 旨

RUB, *to* ts‘ah 擦; — *it bright,* ts‘ah
gyi liang′ 擦 其 亮; — *in both
hands,* ts‘o-ts‘o′ 搓 搓; *cannot*
— *off,* ts‘ah′-feh-diao 擦 弗 起°;
— *against* (as an animal against
a post), za; — *on* (as medicine,
or oil), dzô 搭; du 塗; k‘a 揩°;
— *the hands,* ts‘o-siu′ 搓 手; —
*it in the hands,* siu-li′ ts‘o′-ts‘o
gyi 手 裡 搓 搓 其; — *with the
hand,* soh′-soh 挼 挼; — *the
eyes,* nyü ngæn′-tsing 揿 眼° 睛;
— *ink,* mo moh′ 磨 墨

RUBBISH, p‘o′-ba tong′-si 破敗°
東 西

RUBY, ‘ong-pao′-zah 紅寶° 石°

RUDDER, do 舵 (ih-min)

RUDE, yia 野°; yia′-ky‘i 野° 氣;
— *and daring,* tæn′-ts sah′-yia
膽 子 撒野°; ts‘u-lu′ 粗 鹵;
i-læ′-peh-te′; fông′-s 放 肆; ts‘u-
mæn′ 粗 蠻; — *child,* yia′-ky‘i
siao-nying′ 野° 氣 小 孩°

RUDELY, *to treat one* —, yia′-ky‘i
beh-c‘ih′ dæ nying′ 野° 氣 勃 出
待 人°

RUDENESS, *treat one with* —,
c‘ong-væn′ nying′ 衝 犯 人°;
yia′-tsih yia-pah′ dæ nying′ 野°
七 野° 八 待 人°

RUDIMENTS *of learning,* ‘oh-veng′-
go keng-kyi′ 學° 問 个 根 基

RUE, *to lament,* iu-zeo′ 憂 愁°; *to
regret,* ao′-nao 懊 惱

RUEFUL *looks,* zeo yüong′ 愁 容;
zeo-mi′-tang-pah′-kyih 愁° 眉°
百° 結

RUFFIANLY, p‘o′-dao 覇道; *will
not stop at any crime,* vu-sô′-peh-
ts 無 所 不 至

RUG *of skin,* bi t‘æn′-ts 皮 毯子;
*carpet* —, tsin-diao′ 氈 條;
tsin-t‘æn′ 氈 毯 (ih-bæn)

RUIN, *to* ba-diao′ 敗 壞°; p‘o′-
diao 破壞°; *to destroy,* mih-diao′
滅 壞°

RUINS, *a house in* —, tao′-t‘æn-
liao-go oh′ 倒 坍 了 个° 屋;
t‘æn-t‘ah′-liao oh′ 坍 塌 了 屋;
*ditto from fire,* ho′-siao dziang
火 燒 墻; ho′-siao t‘æn′ 火 燒
灘

RULE, diao-kw‘un′ 條款; diao-
iah 條約; kwe-tseh′ 規 則;
kwe-kyü′ 規 矩; *regulations,*
công-dzing′ (công or tsông) 章
程; (ih-diao, ih-kw‘un, or ih-
‘ông); — *with a penalty attached,*
fah′-du 法 度; — *of etiquette,*
nyi-cü′ 儀 注; *to transgress
ditto,* væn′-djoh nyi-cü′ 犯 著°
儀 注

RULE, to kwun 管; kæ-kwun' 該
管; — in small matters, kying-
kwun' 經管; — in large matters,
kwun'-li 管理; dju-li' 治理;
dju 治; — the family, djü-kô'
治家; to — paper, wah kah'-ts
畫格子

RULED paper, ts' yiu kah'-ts 紙
有格子 (See LINES.)

RULER, cü'-tsæ 主宰; the rulers,
pah'-kwun 百官; kwun-fu' 官府

RUMBLING sound, 'ong-'ong'-hyiang
閧閧響; lah-lah'-hyiang 轆°
轆°響

RUMINATE, to cün-ziao' 轉噍;
— upon, sing'-li tsin-cün' 心
裡輾轉

RUMOR, report, fong-sing' 風信;
— says (or we hear), fong-veng'
風聞; r'-veng-teh 耳聞得;
idle —, yiao-yin' 謠言

RUMP, deng-tsin' 臀尖; p'i'-kwu
屁股

RUMPLE, to —, peh-gyi-tseo' 俾°
其縐; long'-gyi-tseo' 弄其縐

RUN, to peng 奔; — swiftly, fi
peng' 飛奔; p'ao 跑; — away,
peng'-leh-ky'i 奔得去°; to —
(as water), liu 流; to — out, liu-
c'ih' 流出; — together (as water),
we-long' 匯攏; — over (the
brim), kah'-c'ih-læ 溢°出來;
— (as vines), yin-k'æ'-ky'i 延
開去°; — hither and thither,
(troubled), loh-deo'-loh-peng' 無°
路°投°奔; lön ts'ön' 亂竄; on

the — (or going hither and thither) to earn money, peng-po' dzæn
dong-din' 奔波賺銅錢°; —
against, bang-djoh' 撞着°; —
against each others' heads, teo'-deo
p'ong' 兜頭撞°, (hence simply
to meet); — a risk, yiu fong'-ho
有風火; yiu ken'-yi 有干
係; — through (as a thread),
c'ün-ko' 穿過

RUNAWAY, dao-tseo'-go-nying 逃
走個°人°

RUPTURE of a blood vessel, hyüih'-
kwun pao'-k'æ 血管爆開;
hernia, shün'-ky'i-bing 疝氣
病; siao'-dziang-ky'i-bing 小
腸氣病

RUSH lu-ken' 蘆竿; bu 蒲; —
mats, bu-zih' 蒲席; — shoes,
bu-'a' 蒲鞋°; — used for lamp-
wick, teng-sing'-ts'ao 燈芯草;
— used for cording, 'æn-ts'ao'
薔°草

RUSH, to c'ong 衝; ts'ông 闖; —
in, ts'ông'-tsing-læ 闖進來;
— at once, ih-deo ts'ông'-ko-læ
忽°然°闖過來; — against,
djông-djoh' 撞着°

RUST, to siu 銹; fah-siu' 發銹;
rusted out, siu'-me-de 銹黴了°

RUSTIC, hyiang-'ô'-go 鄉下°個°;
— people, hyiang-'ô'-nying 鄉
下°人°

RUSTLE, to — (as garments), wah-
wah'-hyiang 劃劃響; — (as
leaves), sah'-sah-hyiang 颯颯響

RUSTY siu′-de 銹了°; fah-siu′-de 發銹了°

RUT *of a wheel,* leng-bun′ loh-'æn′-go lu′ 輪盤落陷°个°路; *fallen into his old way, or* —, moh gyiu lu′ de 摸舊路了°

## S

SABBATH, li′-pa-nyih 禮拜°日°; en-sih′-nyih 安息日°; cü′-nyih 主日°; tsin′-li-ih′ 瞻禮一

SABLE-SKIN, ts′-tiao-bi 紫貂皮; *ditto* (hairs white-tipped), ts′-mô-tiao bi′ 芝蔴貂皮

SACK, dæ 袋 (ih-tsah); *a garment,* mô′-kwô 馬掛 (ih-gyin)

SACK-CLOTH, ts'u-mô′-pu 粗蔴布; *to put on* —, c'ün mô-i′ 穿蔴衣

SACKING (used for wrapping), dæ pu′ 袋布; (better quality) pao-bi′-pu 包皮布

SACRAMENTS, *the* sing′-li 聖禮

SACRED, sing 聖; — *books,* sing′ kying 聖經; — *Edict,* Sing′-yü Kwông′-hyüing 聖諭廣訓

SACRIFICE, tsi′-veh 祭物; — *placed before an idol,* foh′-li 福禮; *to offer up a* —, hyin tsi′ 獻祭; zông tsi′ 上祭; tsi 祭; — *to one's ancestors,* tsi tsu′-tsong 祭祖宗; *to take one's turn in ditto,* tông tsi′-z 當祭祀; — *at the grave,* tsi′-sao veng-mo′ 祭掃墳墓; zông veng 上墳; (these expressions are also some-times used for simply keeping the grave in order); — *one's life,* sô′-c'ih sing′-ming 捨°出性命

SACRILEGE, *to commit* —, sih′-doh 褻瀆; *to commit* — *against the gods,* c'ong-væn′ bu-sah′ 衝犯菩薩; c'oh′-væn bu-sah′ 觸犯菩薩

SAD, iu-meng′ 憂悶; iu-zeo′ 憂愁°; iu-li′ 憂慮; zeo-meng′ 愁°悶; — *looking,* min tæ′ iu-yüong′ 面帶憂容; *looks very* —, mun′-min iu-zeo′ 滿面憂愁°; — *in heart,* sing-li′ ts'i-ts'æn′ 心裏悽慘; *both* — *and joyful,* pe-hyi′-kyiao-jih′ 悲喜交集

SAD-IRON, loh-t'ih′ 烙鐵 (ih-go)

SADDEN, *to* s′-teh iu-meng′ 使得憂悶; — *him,* peh′ gyi iu-meng′ 俾°其憂悶

SADDLE, en-ts′ 鞍子 (ih-go)

SADDLE, *to place the* — *upon,* zông en-ts′ 上鞍子; — *and bridle a horse,* p'e mô′ 配馬

SAFE, weng′-tông 穩當; t'o′-tông 妥當; ding-tông′ 定當

SAFE *for provisions,* sô-djü 紗櫥 (ih-k'eo); *iron* —, t'ih′-gyü 鐵櫃; *native money* —, yiang-siang′ 洋箱

SAG, *to* den 凹; ah′-den 壓°凹; den′-loh 凹°落

SAGACIOUS, tsing-ming′ 精明; t'eo′-ts'ih 透澈; — *in affairs,* tsing-ming′ shü′-vu 精明世務;

— *in discerning character,* t'eo'
ts'ih jing-dzing' 透徹人情;
— *person,* pah'-k'æn pah-liang'-
go nying 料事如神个°人°
SAGES, sing'-nying 聖人°
SAGO, si-koh'-mi 西國米
SAIL, fong-bong' 風篷 (ih-tsiang,
ih-sin); *to* —, s-jün' 駛船; s-
bong' 駛篷; s-fong' 駛風; *to
take in* —, siu-bong' 收篷; *to
let down the* —, 'ô-bong' 下°篷;
loh-bong' 落篷; *to hoist* —,
t'sô-bong' 义篷; *to reef a* —,
mao bong, *or* mô bong' 冒篷
SAIL-CLOTH, bong-pu' 篷布
SAILING-VESSEL, fong-bong-jün'
風篷船
SAILOR, shü'-siu 水手 (ih-ming,
ih-go); *on native boats,* lao'-da'
go ho'-kyi 老大个°夥計
SAINTS, sing'-du 聖徒
SAKE, *for the* — *of,* we-leh'
爲了; *for the* — *of fame, and
gain,* we-ming'-we-li' 爲名爲利
SALAD, sang-ts'æ' 生°菜
SALARY, *officer's* fong'-loh 俸祿;
*teacher's* —, soh'-siu 束修; soh'-
kying 修°金; sing-fong' 辛俸;
sing-se' 薪水
SALE *at auction,* kyiao'-ma 叫賣°;
ma kyiao'-ho 賣叫貨; *on* —
*for another,* kyi'-ma 寄賣°; *for*
—, fah'-ma 發賣°; c'ih-ma'
出賣°
SALEABLE, ma'-leh-c'ih'-go 賣°
得°出个°; siao-leh-diao'-go

销得°去°个°; *not* —, m-
siao-dziang' 無°销塲
SALESMAN, ma-siu' 賣手
SALIVA, zæn-t'u' 涎°唾
SALLOW *countenance,* min-seh'
tsiao-wông' 面色焦黃
SALT, yin 鹽; — *taste,* mi-dao
'æn' 味°道鹹°; *too* —, t'eh
'æn' 太°鹹°; *put in a little* —,
fông ih-tin yin' 放一點鹽;
*add* —, kô-yin'-ts'eo 加°鹽
湊; — *water,* 'æn-shü' 鹹°水°;
— *provision store,* 'æn-ho'-tin
鹹貨店
SALT-CELLAR, yin-diah' 鹽碟°;
yin-beng' 鹽盆 (ih-tsah)
SALT-MERCHANT, yin-sông'鹽商
SALT-PEDDLER, ma-yin'-go 賣°
鹽个°
SALT-PETER, ) siao 硝; yin-siao'
SALT-PETRE, ) 鹽硝; p'oh'-siao
朴硝
SALUBRIOUS *climate,* shü'-t'u hao'
水土好
SALUTATION, *words of* —, tsiao-
hwu'-go shih-wô' 招呼个°說
話; k'ah-t'ao-go shih-wô' 客套
个°說話
SALUTE, *to* — *with folded and
uplifted hands,* kong-kong-siu'
拱拱手; — *with folded hands
and a bow,* tsoh-ih' 作揖; *to
fire a* — (*for a certain event,*) 'ao
p'ao' 號礮; *ditto for an officer,*
fông p'ao' kying kwun' 放礮敬
官; — *and part,* kong'-siu bih-
k'æ' 拱手別開

SALVATION, kyiu'-sing 救星；
*the doctrine of* —, kyiu-nying'-
go dao'-li 救人个°道理

SALVE, dzô-yiah' 搭藥

SAME, *the* ih-yiang' 一樣；tso'-
yiang；siang-dong' 相同；*ex-
actly the* —, ih-seh'-ih-yiang' 一
色一樣；t'ih'-seh-vu-r' 貼
色無二；ping'-seh 拚色；*the*
— *as before*, dzing-gyiu' ih-
yiang' 仍舊一樣；*of the* —
*age*, dong nyin' 同年；dong
kang' 同庚；*at the* — *time*,
bing'-zi 並齊；veng'-zi 會齊°；
ts‹en'-zi 整°齊°；— *rank*, dong
p'ing' 同品；*on the* — *day*,
tông' nyih 當日°；*make the* —
*as the pattern*, tsiao' yiang tso'
照樣做；*have the* — *meaning*,
tso' i'-s；i'-s siang-dong' 意思
相同

SAMPLE, yiang-ts' 樣子 (ih-go)

SANCTIFIED, *to become* dzing-dziu'
sing'-jün-go 成就聖善个°

SANCTIFY, *to* — *a person*, s'-teh
nying' dzing-sing' 使得人°成聖

SANCTION, *to obtain his* —, ts'ing
gyi'-go z' 請其个°示；t'ao'
gyi-go k'eo'-ing 討其个° 口
音；*to give one's* —, cing 准；
yüing 允

SAND, sô 沙；sô-nyi' 沙泥；*fine*
—, hwe-sô' 灰沙；— *bank*, or
*bar*, sô-t'æn' 沙灘；*there is a*
— *storm*, t'in' loh wông-sô' 天
落黃沙

SANDALS, t'o-'a' 拖鞋°；*straw*
—, ts'ao'-'a 草鞋° (a pair, ih-
sông, or ih-shông)

SANDAL-WOOD dæn-hyiang-moh'
檀香木

SANGUINARY *disposition*, sah'-sing
djong 殺性重；— *luttle*, (ground
filled with blood), hyüih' liu
mun di' 血流滿地

SANGUINE *temperament*, sing ho'-
nyih-go 心火熱°个°；sing'-li
ziang ho-dön' ka 心裡像火
團一°樣°

SANSCRIT, or SANSKRIT *characters*, Væn-z' 梵字；— *language*,
Væn-yin' 梵言

SAP (of trees), jü-tsiang' 樹漿

SAPAN-WOOD, su-moh' 蘇木

SAPPHIRE, læn-pao'-zah 藍寶石；
en'-læn 暗藍

SARCASM, tsin-k'eh'-go shih-wô'
尖刻个°說話；shih-wô ziang
tao' ka 說話像刀

SASH, iao-ta' 腰帶°；*an ornamental belt*, 'en-kying 汗巾 (ih-
diao)

SASH, *window* ts'ông 窗；*raise the*
—, ts'ông, zông'-leh gyi 好°上°
了°窗；*put down the* —, ts'ông'
ô-loh' 好°下°了°窗

SATELLITE, vu-'ang-sing'-go siao'-
sing 附行°星个°小星；*the
moon is the earth's* —, yüih-liang'
z vu di-gyiu'-go siao'-sing 月
亮是附地球个°小星

SATIATE, *to eat to the full*, ky'üoh'

pao 吃° 飽; *to eat to loathing,* ky'üoh in' 吃° 厭

SATIN, dön-ts' 緞子; *superior —,* kong'-dön 貢 緞; *inferior —,* ling-ts' 綾子

SATIRICAL, *to give a — name,* c'ü ts'ih'-'ao 取 綽° 號

SATIRIZE, *to* kyi ts'' 譏 刺

SATISFACTION, *to one's —,* jü-sing'-ziang-i' 如心像意; *to make — to one,* be-li' 賠 禮; pu'-pao gyi 補報其; be-wæn' gyi 賠 還其; be-pu' gyi 賠補其

SATISFIED, sing mun'-tsoh 心滿 足; i-sing' mun-tsoh' 依心滿 足; *contented,* cü-tsoh' 知足; tsoh'-sing 足心; sing-tsoh' 心足

SATISFY, *will — man's heart,* neng'-keo mun'-tsoh nying'-go sing' 能 殼滿足人° 个° 心 or 能懷 人°心

SATISFYING, (as certain kinds of food), næ-kyi' 耐 饑

SATURATE, *to* seng'-t'eo 沁° 透

SATURATED, sih'-t'eo-de 濕透 了°

SATURDAY, li-pa-loh' 禮拜°六; tsin-li-ts'ih' 瞻 禮七

SATURN, t'u'-sing 土 星

SAUCE, *pungent* lah-tsiang' 辣醬; *sweet —,* din lu' 甜 滷; *soy,* tsiang'-yiu 醬 油

SAUCE-PAN, kwun 罐; *earthen —,* ngô'-kwun 瓦罐; ing'-teo-kwun 熨°斗罐

SAUCER, *tea* dzô-beng'-ts 茶 盆

子; *boat shaped —,* dzô-jün' 茶 船

SAUCY, c'ih'-yin-vu-zông'-go 出 言無狀个°

SAUNTER, *to stroll idly about,* tong-tseo'-si-tseo' 東走西走; tong-dang'-si-dang' 東宕西宕

SAUSAGE *meat,* tsæn-wu'-liao-nyüoh' 作°膽°个°肉°

SAUSAGES (flat), nyüoh-ping' 肉° 餅; *round —,* nyüoh-yün' 肉圓

SAVAGE, *cruel,* hyüong-oh' 兇惡

SAVAGES, yia'-nying 野°人°

SAVE, *to* kyiu 救; —*out of trouble,* kyiu-næn' 救 難; — *the soul,* kyiu weh-ling' 救 魂°靈; — *from imminent danger,* kyiu-jün-me'-ts-kyih' 救燃眉之急; —*from death,* dzong-si' li-hyiang' kyiu'-c'ih-læ 從死°裡救 出來; — *trouble,* sang z' 省 事; — *time,* sang kong-fu' 省 工夫; — *money* (but not put it by), sang dong-din' 省°銅錢°

SAVING, *frugal,* kyin'-sang 簡 省°; gyin'-sang 儉省°

SAVIOR, SAVIOUR, Kyiu'-cü 救 主; Kyiu'-shü-cü 救世主

SAVORY, yiu ts-mi' 有滋味°; yiu mi-dao' 有味°道

SAW, ken 鋸°(ih-pô)

SAW, *to* ka 鋸°; — *firewood,* ka za-bæn' 鋸°柴爿; *did see,* k'en'-kyin-ko 看見過; k'en'-kyin-ko'-de 看見過了°

SAW-DUST, ken'-sih 鋸°屑

SAY, to kông 講°; wô 話; *what do you* —? ng dza wô' ni 你° 怎° 話 呢? ng dza kông'-fah ni 你° 怎° 講° 法 呢? *I was just saying,* ngô dzæ-s' læ-tih wô' 我 纔 始 話; *can you* — *so?* z-ka' hao wô' feh 如° 此° 好 話 否°, *or* 可° 說° 否°; *can* — *it,* hao' wô-go 可° 話 个°; k'o'-yi wô' 可 以 話; — *a word to him,* teng gyi wô' ih-kyü' 與° 其 話 一 句; teh gyi kông' ih-sing' 對° 其 講° 一 聲; — *it again,* tsæ' wô 再 話; *cannot* — *it, cannot pronounce, or must not* — *it,* kông'-feh-c'ih'-go 講° 弗 出 个°; *people* — *so,* nying-kô' z-ka wô' 人° 家° 如 此 話; *you don't* — *so, or who says so?* jü wô' 誰° 話; *nothing to* —, m̄-kao' hao wô' 沒° 有° 好 話; m̄-kao' hao kông' 沒° 有° 好 講°

SAYING, *common* dzông-yin' 常 言; dzông-yin'-dao 常 言 道; *old* —, lao'-wô 老° 話°; kwu'-wô 古 話 (ih-kyü)

SCAB, *in* 靨; *to form a* —, kyih in' 結靨; *vaccine* —, ngeo-deo'-in 牛° 痘 靨

SCABBARD, t'ao 套; k'oh'-ts 壳 子; *for a sword,* pao'-kyin-k'oh'-ts 寶 劍 壳 子

SCAFFOLDING, ing-kô' 鷹 架; kô'-ts 架 子; *to put up a* —, tah kô'-ts 搭 架° 子

SCALD, t'ông'-sông 燙 傷

SCALD, *to* t'ông 燙; * — *to a blister,* t'ông ky'i-p'ao' 燙 起 皰
  * The colloquial is the same for burning by fire, or scalding by hot water, but the characters are different.

SCALE, *fish* —, ng-ling' 魚° 鱗 (ih-bæn)

SCALE, SCALES, *balance,* t'in-bing' 天 平 (ih-kô); *the dish of a balance,* teng'-bun' 戥 盤; *a balance with one* —, teng'-ts 戥 子; *ditto (for weighing very small things),* li-teng' 厘 戥

SCALE, *to* — *city walls,* bô zing'爬 城°; zông zing', *or* zông dzing' 上 城°

SCALE, *to* — *off,* p'in' tang p'in' k'oh'-ky'i 片 片 變 起

SCALP, deo-bi' 頭 皮

SCANDAL, *to talk* c'ih nying-kô'-go ts'in' 出 人° 家° 个° 醜

SCANDALOUS *affair,* ts'iu'-z 醜 事; — *affairs in the women's apartment,* kwe' cong ts'iu' z 閨 中 醜 事 (cong *or* tsong)

SCANT, feh-keo' 弗 彀; ts'ô'-tin 差° 點; ky'in'-ih-ngæn 欠 一 點°

SCAR, pô 疤; *blemish,* pæn-pô' 瘢 疤 (ih-go)

SCARCE, ky'üih'-siao 缺 少; *difficult to procure,* næn-teh' 難 得; *this year cherries are* —, kying-nyin' ang-dao' ky'üih'-siao 今 年 櫻 桃 缺 少

SCARCELY *enough,* kyih'-pah 急 廹; *ditto, but will make it do,*

ün-pang'; — (but just) *obtained,*
ts'ô ih-ngæn' feh teh'-djoh 差 一
點° 勿 得 着°

SCARCITY, *year of* — , siao'-nyin
小 年 ; *ditto* (a small crop, two
parts instead of ten), nyi-feng'
nyin-se' 二 ° 分 年 歲

SCARE, *to* — *him,* hah' gyi ih-deo'
嚇 其 一 嚇°

SCARE, *a great* — *about nothing,*
da-kying'-siao-kwæ' 大 驚 小 怪

SCARED, *he* — *me,* gyi' long ngô'
ky'ih'-ih-hoh' 其 弄 我 吃° 一
霍 ; — *to death,* hah'-sah-de 嚇
殺 了°

SCARE-CROW, *straw man,* ts'ao-
kao-nying' 草 絞 人°

SCARLET, do-'ong' 大° 紅° ;—*paint,*
cü-'ong' ts'ih 朱 紅 漆

SCATTER, *to* sæn'- k'æ 散 開 ;
sæn'-lön 散 亂 ; tsah'-k'æ 撒° 開 ;
— *seed,* tsah iang-ts' 撒° 秧 子

SCATTERED *about* (in every direction), tong-si' lön-gwæn' 東 西
亂 摜 ; *in disorder* (at sixes and
sevens), wang-ts'ih'-jü-pah' 橫°
七 竪 八

SCAVENGER, bô-lah-sah'-go 爬
垃° 圾° 个° ; wun-bi'- go (in
Shanghai, leh-sah'-fu 垃 圾 夫)

SCENERY, *fine* hao kying'-cü 好
景 致

SCENT, hyiang 香 ; hyiang-ky'i'
香 氣 ; *the dog follows the* — ,
keo' i lu' hyüong ky'i'-mi 狗 依
路 嗅° 氣 味°

SCEPTRE, *the golden* — , kying
kwe' 金 圭 (Esther 5 : 2.)

SCHEME, kyi'-ts'ah 計 策 ; kyi-
meo' 計 謀 ; kyi'-kao 計 較° ;
the last two usually have a bad
sense ; *to devise a* — , tang'-sön
kyi-meo' 打 算 計 謀 ; *to carry
out a* — , yüong kyi' 用 計

SCHISM *in the church,* kyiao'-we
feng-lih'-k'æ 敎 會 分 離° 開

SCHOLAR, *pupil,* 'oh-sang-ts' 學°
生° 子 ; *very small* — , mong-
dong' 蒙 童 ; *educated man,* doh-
shü-nying' 讀 書 人° ; z'-ts 士
子 ; *accomplished* — , poh'-lao
博 士° ; *the class of scholars,* jü-
kyiao' 儒 敎

SCHOLARSHIP, *good* hao nen-dzæ'
好 內 才 ; hao du'-dzæ 好 肚
才 ; *poor in* — , bah du'-bi 白
腹° ; ts'ao'-pao 草 包

SCHOOL, shü-vông' 書 房 ; shü-
kwun' 書 館 (ih-kwun) ; —
*room,* shü-vông-kæn' 書 房 間° ;
'oh-dông' 學° 堂 ; *to teach a* —
(or one person), zo shü-vông' 坐
書 房 ; zo kwun' 坐 館 ; *to go to*
—, or *to enter* — , zông 'oh' 上
學° ; *to open a* — , k'æ kwun' 開
館 ; k'æ shü-vông' 開 書 房 ; *boy's*
—, nen shü-vông' 男 書 房 ;
*family* — , ts'ing'- kwun shü-
vông' 供 饌° 書 房 ; *girl's* — ,
nyü' shü-vông 女 書 房 ; *public*
(charity) — , nyi-'oh' 義 學° ;
— *of little boys,* mong-kwun' 蒙

館; — *of boys who study Chinese classics*, kying-kwun' 經館; — *teacher*, or *master*, kao' shü sin'-sang 敎°書先生°; — *mistress*, nyü' sin-sang' 女先生°; —*fellow*, dong shü-vông' 'oh-sang'-ts 同書房學°生子°; — *friend*, dong-ts'ông' beng-yin' 同窻朋友; *to board at the* —, kyi'-zih ü shü-vông' 寄膳°於房書

SCIENCE, 'oh-veng' 學°問; yüoh 學 (veng); *natural* —, keh-veh'-go 'oh-veng 格物學°; — *of numbers*, sön'-yüoh 算學; — *of Astronomy*, T'in-veng' 天文; — *of medicine*, I-yüoh' 醫學

SCISSORS, tsin'-tao 剪刀 (ih-pô); — *grinder*, mo-tsin'-tao-go 磨剪刀个°

SCOFF, *to* — *at*, tsao-siao' 嘲笑; vu-siao' 侮笑

SCOLD, *to* wô 話; mao-ün' 埋怨; — *in loud tones*, heng 哼; — *with abuse*, zoh-mô' 辱罵; *your mother will* —, a'-nô iao wô'-go 阿°娘°要話个°

SCOLDING, *don't mind a* —, wô, feh-ts'æ'-go 話弗睬个°; zoh, feh-p'ô'-go 辱弗怕个°; — *woman*, dziang-zih'-vu 長舌婦

SCOOP *for bailing water*, biao 瓢; zob 勺° (ih-tsah); ao'-teo 拗斗 (ih-go); *to* — *up water (if much)*, dao-shü'-c'ih' 掏水°出; iao'-shü'-c'ih' 舀水°出; *ditto* (if little), kwah-shü'-c'ih' 括水°出

SCOPE, *general* da-i' 大意; tsong-i 總意

SCORCH, *to* — (as food), tsiao 焦; — *in ironing*, t'ông'-tsiao 燙焦; — *in frying*, t'ah'-tsiao 爛°焦; — *at the fire*, hong-tsiao' 烘焦; koh'-tsiao 擱焦; tsih'-tsiao 炙焦

SCORN, *to* miao'-z 藐視; k'en'-feh-ky'i' 看弗起; ky'ing-hweh' 輕忽; *look upon with* —, k'en'-feh-zông-ngæn' 看弗上眼°

SCORPION, byih'-ts 蠍子 (ih-tsah)

SCOUNDREL, ú-keng'-kyiah-go 無°根脚个°; *a low unprincipled fellow*, oh'-kweng 惡棍; kwông-kweng' 光棍; di-kweng' 地棍

SCOUR, *to* ts'ah 擦; mo 摩; — *it bright*, ts'ah' gyi liang' 擦其亮

SCOURGE, pin-ts' 鞭子 (ih-keng); *to* —, yüong pin-ts' tang' 用鞭子打

SCOUT, t'en'-ts 探子; *to act as* —, tso t'en'-ts 做探子; t'en'-t'ing 探聽; *to sneer at*, kyi-siao' 譏笑

SCOWL, *to* zeo mi-deo' 皺眉°頭; — *at him*, dziao' gyi zeo nî'-deo' 朝其皺°眉°頭

SCRAMBLE, *to* — *up*, bô zông'-ky'i 爬上去; wah-zông'-ky'i 挖上去°; — *for* (things), ta'-ts'iang-ta-deh' 亂°搶亂°奪

SCRAP, or SCRAPS, siao'-kw'e 小塊; se'-kw'e 碎塊; se'-deo-senao' 碎頭碎腦; *pork —*, cü-yiu-tsô' 豬油渣

SCRATCH, *to* kwah 刮; *— by rubbing*, ts'ah 擦; *— it clean*, kwah' gyi ken-zing' 刮其乾凈; *— the skin off*, bi ts'ah'-ky'i 皮擦起; *— potatoes*, bao fæn-jü' bi 刨山°芋°皮

SCRATCH, *a* ih-da 'eng' 一壨痕 ih-da ky'i.

SCRATCH, *to* tsao 搔; *— (as a dog)*, da

SCRAWL, *to* sia'-leh hwô-liu'-dzô' ka 寫得°花柳蛇°一°般°

SCREAM, *to* wæ, si-ih-sing' 吶喊°一°聲; *to call loudly*, do-sing'-hæn'-kyiao 大°聲喊叫

SCREEN, bing 屏; bing-fong' 屏風; ing'-bing 映屏 (ih-sin); *a folding —*, we-bing' 圍屏 (ih-dông); *split bamboo —* (for doors or windows), coh'-lin 竹簾 (ih-tsiang); *bead —* (for ladies' apartments), cü-lin' 珠簾

SCREEN, *to — from*, lah 攔; tsô-djü' 遮住; tsô-in' 遮掩; tsô-kæ' 遮°蓋; *— from the sun*, tsô-djü' nyih-deo' 遮°住日頭; *— a fault*, tsô-kæ' ts'o'-c'ü 遮°蓋錯處; *— the light*, liang-kwông' lah-djü' gyi 亮光蘭°住其; *— from the light*, liang-kwông' tsô-ing' 亮光遮°陰

SCREW, jün-ting' 旋°釘; lo-s-ting' 螺螄釘 (ih-me); *cork —*, tsin'-tsön-ts 酒鑽°子 (ih-go); *—*

*driver*, jün-joh' 旋°鑿° (ih-ρô)

SCREW, *to — in*, jün-tsing'-ky'i 旋進去°; *— together*, jün-long'-ky'i 旋攏去°

SCRIBBLE, *to* lön-dô' 亂塗°; lön-sia' 亂寫°

SCRIPTURES, *the Holy* Sing'-kying 聖經; Sing'-shü 聖書

SCROFULA le-lih' 瘰癧

SCROFULOUS *swelling*, lih-c'ün' 癧串 (ih-go)

SCROLL, *a written* ih-kyün shü'— 卷書; *ornamental —* (for hanging), ih-gyüoh wô' — 軸畫; *a pair of scrolls*, ih-fu te'-lin — 副對聯

SCRUB, *to* ts'ah 擦

SCRUBBING-BRUSH ts'ah'di-pæn'-go shih'-tsiu 擦地板个°刷箒

SCRUPULOUS, *exact and careful*, tsing-si' 精細; *over —*, tsing-si' ko-deo' 精細過牙°; si'-si se'-se 細細碎碎; so'-so-se'-se 𤞤𤞤碎碎; *to-*veng'-to-li' 多文多禮

SCRUTINIZE, *to* ts'-si k'ao'-kyiu 仔細考究

SCUFFLE, *to* siang-tang' 相打

SCULL, (oar in the stern), lu 櫓 (ih-ts); *— rope*, lu'-ta 櫓帶°; *— pin*, lu-cü' 櫓鈕°; *to —*, yiao-lu' 搖櫓; *— to the right*, t'e 推; t'oh 托; *— to the left*, pæn 扳; sao 捎

SCULPTOR *who carves wood*, or *stone*, tiao-k'eh'-s-vu 雕刻司務

SCUM, vu-ky'i'-læ-go ao-tsao' 浮
起 來 个° 堊 精, veo-nyi' 浮
泥

SCURF on the head, kw'u-k'oh-in'
肩° 燙 歷

SCUTTLE, coal me-t'æn' dong 煤
炭 桶 (ih-tsah)

SEA, hæ 海; yiang 洋; hæ'-yiang
海 洋; bottom of the —, hæ ti'
海 底

SEA-FIGHT, shü'-tsin 水° 戰

SEA-HORSE-TEETH hæ'-mô-ngô
海 馬 牙°

SEAL, hæ'-keo 海 狗 (ih-tsah)

SEAL, any private —, du-shü' 圖
書 (ih-k'o); officer's —, ing
印; ing'-sing 印 信; kwen-ing'
官 印; Imperial —, nyüoh-si'
玉 璽; to affix a —, tang ing'
打 印; the — character, djün
veng' 篆 文

SEAL, to — a letter, fong sing' 封
信; fong k'eo' 封 口; to break
the —, ts'ah fong' 拆 封; k'æ
fong' 開 封; — a door, fong
meng' 封 門; — or close the
ya-mun for the New Year, fong
ing' 封 印; to open the ya-mun
—, k'æ ing' 開 印

SEALING-WAX, ho'-ts'ih 火 漆

SEAM (in cloth), vong-ts' 縫 子 (ih-
da); — (in wood, &c.), vong-dao'
縫 道; the mark of the —, vong-
u' 縫 痕°; straight —, dzih vong'
直 縫; felled —, wông-zin'-
kweh 黃 鱔 骨; rip the —,

vong-ts' ts'ah'-k'æ 縫 子 拆 開

SEA-MAN, shü'-siu 水° 手

SEA-PORT, hæ'-k'eo 海 口

SEARCH, to look for, zing 尋; to
investigate, k'ao'-kyiu 考 究;
tse-kyiu' 追 究; — through the
house, oh' li-hyiang' seo-kyin'
屋 裡 向 搜 檢; examine, dzô-
dzô'-k'en 查 查 看; — one's
heart, dzô-ts'ah' zi'-go sing' 查
察 自° 个° 心; — everywhere,
koh'-tao-c'ü zing' 各 到 處 尋;
seo zing' 搜 尋

SEA-SHORE, hæ-pin-yin' 海 邊 沿

SEA-SICK, cü-lông'暈 浪; yüing-
jün' 暈 船; do you get —? ng
we cü-lông' feh 你° 會 暈 浪
不° 會°? I do become —, ngô
iao yüing jün' 我 要 暈 船

SEASON, in —(as fruit, &c.), gyih-
z' 及 時; came just in —, 'eo-
feng'-'eo-su læ'-de' 候 分 候 數
來 了°; the four seasons, s'-kyi
四 季; s'-z 四 時; a dry —, t'in
'en' 天 旱; very dry —, t'in
da 'en' 天 大 旱

SEASON, to p'e liao-li' 配 料 理;
— boards, pæn' lông gyi' sao' 板
眼 其 燥

SEASONABLE weather, t'in-ky'i',
teng z-ling' siang-te' 天 氣 與°
時 令 和 對; — rain, gyih-z'
yü 及 時 雨; z yü' 時 雨; ken
yü' 廿 雨

SEASONING, liao-li' 料 理 (the
Chinese implies more than the

English, as seasoning is usually restricted to salt and pepper);
*wine as a* —, liao-tsiu′ 料酒
SEAT, zo′-u 坐處°(ih-go); zo′-we
坐位；— *of a chair*, ü′-ts min
椅子面；*will — how many?*
kyi′-go nying′ hao zo′ 幾个°人°
好坐？yiu to′-siao′ zo-deo′有多
少坐頭？*cannot — so many*,
zo′-feh-ko 坐弗過；*there are
no seats*, zo′-u zû′-teh 坐處°
沒°有°
SEATED, *please be* —, ts'ing zo′
請坐
SEA-WEED, hæ′-ts'æ 海菜；ts′-
ts'æ 紫菜；dæ-diao′ 苔條
SECLUDED, p'ih′-zing 僻靜；*quiet*,
iu-zing′ 幽靜；zing′-ts'iao-ts'iao
靜悄悄
SECOND, *the* di-nyi′ 第二°；*in
the — month*, di-nyi′ ko yüih′-li
第二°个°月裡；nyi-yüih′-li
二°月裡；— *son*, ts'′-ts 次子；
*a* — (*of time*), ih-miao′ 一秒
SECOND-HAND *clothing*, ts'ah′-i
拆衣；— *clothing-shop*, ts'ah′-i
tin 拆衣店；di-tsông′ 提庄；
*to buy — goods* (lit. old), ma
gyiu-ho′ 買°舊貨
SECRET, mih 密；pi′-mih 秘密；
kyi-mih′ 機密；s 私；s-'ô′ 私
下°；— *deeds*, s-z′ 私事；*a*
—, siao′-ho z-t'i′ 私下°事體；
siao′-ho shih-wô′ 私下°說話；
— *for making something*, pi′-
kyüih 秘訣；*to let out a* —, sih′-

leo kyi-kwæn′ 洩漏機關；lu
fong′ 露風；*he can keep a* —,
kyi-kwæn′ gyi ve sih′-leo 機關
其不°會°洩漏；*to tell one a*
—, ngao ng′-tô 鉸耳°朶
SECRETLY, s-'ô′ 私下°；s ti-'ô
私底下°；en′-di-li 暗地裡；
be-di′-li 背°地裡；*to plot* —
s-'ô′ yüong kyi-meo′ 私下°用
計謀
SECRETARY, *private* shü-kyi′ 書
記；— *to a Mandarin*, shü-kyi′-
s-yia′ 書記師爺°；tsih-pih′ s-
yia′ 執筆師爺°
SECRETE, *to* dzông-k'ông′ 藏囥；
—*well*, k'ông′-leh mih-lah-kying′
囥得°密緊
SECRETIONS, (of animals, or
plants), tsing-yih′ 津液
SECT, kyiao′ 教；kyiao′-meng 教
門；*to found a new* —, sing lih′
ih-go kyiao′ 新立一个°教
SECTION (of a book), ih-tsông′ 一
章；ih-p'in′ 一篇；—(of a treaty),
diao-kw'un′ 條款 (ih-diao)
SECULAR, shü′-kæn-zông′-go 世
間°上个°；— *affairs*, shü′-z 世
事；shü′-vu 世務；—*newspapers*,
shü′-dzoh sing-pao′ 世俗新報
SECURE, weng′-tông 穩當；t'o′-
tông 妥當
SECURE, *to make fast*, tso′-leh lao-
k'ao′ 做得°牢靠；*to insure*,
pao 保
SECURELY, *to dwell* —, deng′-leh
weng′-tông-go 停得°穩當个°

SECURITY, *to become — for another,* tso-pao' 做 保; *one who becomes —,* pao'-nying 保 人°; *— (evidence of debt, &c.),* bing-kyü' 憑 據

SEDAN, gyiao-ts' 轎子 (ih-ting); *mountain —,* teo-gyiao' 兜 轎; *ditto (very rude),* bô-sæn-hwu' 爬 山 虎; *bride's —,* hwô-gyiao' 花 轎; ts'æ'-gyiao 彩 轎; *Imperial —,* lön-kô' 鑾 駕°; *to ride in a —,* zo gyiao' 坐 轎; *I came in a —,* ngô' zo gyiao' læ'-go 我 坐 轎 來 个°; *to lift a —,* gyiao-ts' sing-ky'i'-læ 轎 子 陞 起 來; *to set down a —,* gyiao-ts' fông'-loh 轎 子 放 落; *— poles,* gyiao-kông' 轎 杠; *(a pair of ditto, ih-fu),— bearer,* gyiao-fu' 轎 夫

SEDATE, tön-tsông' 端 莊; z-z'-dzæ-dzæ 自 自 在 在

SEDENTARY, zo'-kong to 坐 工 多

SEDIMENT, kyiah 腳; ting'-loh-go kyiah' 定° 落 个° 腳

SEDITIOUS, we-tsoh-lön'-go 會 作 亂 个°

SEDUCE, *to* ying'-yiu 引 誘; t'eo 偷

SEDULOUS, gying-kying' 勤 謹; *never idle,* feh-teh-k'ong' 弗 得 空

SEE, *to* k'en 看; k'en'-kyin 看 見; *let him —,* peh gyi-k'en 俾° 其 看; *— another making a mistake, or getting into trouble and not* tell *him,* k'en-ts'ing-beng' 冷° 看; *easy to — through,* ih-moh liao'-jün 一 目 了 然); *— through,* k'en'-t'eo 看 透; *ditto, (as a deception),* k'en'-p'o 看 破; *— after, or to,* k'en'-siu 看 守; *sees quickly what ought to be done,* ngæn'-deo weh-loh' 眼° 頭 活 絡; *I have come to — you,* ngô' læ k'en' ng 我 來 看 你; læ mông-mông' ng 來 望 望° 你°; *— (one) off,* song-'ang' 送 行°; song dong-sing' 送 動 身

SEEN, *cannot be —,* k'en'-feh-kyin'-go 看 弗 見 个°; *have not — for a long time,* dziang-kyiu' feh-kyin' 長 久 弗 見; kyiu'-we 久 違; *nothing to be —,* m̆-kao' k'en'-deo 沒° 有° 看 頭

SEED, cong 種; ts 子; iang-ts' 秧 子; *— or planting time,* hao cong'-go z'-'eo 好 種 个° 時 候; *the stony — of fruit,* weh 核; *the inner kernel of ditto,* jing 仁; *save for —,* liu tso cong' 留 做 種; *gather a little — for me,* siu' ih-tin ts' peh ngô 收 一 點 子 給 我; *to plant —,* 'o cong 下° 種: cong 種; cong'-tsoh 種 作; *descendants,* ts'-seng 子 孫

SEEDSMAN, ma-cong'-go 賣° 種 个°; *seller of vegetable seed,* ma-ts'æ'-ts-go 賣° 菜 子 个°

SEEING THAT, kyi'-jün 既 然; kyi'-kying 既 經

SEEK, to zing 尋°; — *and find,* zing-djoh'尋°着°; —*gain,* tang'-mo dong-din' 打摹銅錢°; — *favor* (by gifts, or doing what one need not do), t'ao-hao' 討好; — (or pray for) *happiness,* gyin foh' 求福; —*employment,* zing deo-lu' 尋°頭路; zing 'ông-nyih' 尋°行業

SEEMS, oh'-ziang 阿°像; hao'-ziang 好像; z'-wu 似乎; *this — the larger,* keh'-go oh'-ziang do-tin' 這°个°阿°像大°點; *it — to me,* ngô' kyüoh-teh ziang' 我覺得像; dziu ngô k'en-læ 就我看來; —*unwilling,* oh'-ziang feh dzing'-nyün 阿°像弗情願

SEIZE, to k'ô 拿°; gying 擒°; 'oh 獲

SEIZED, *already* yi'-kying k'ô'-djoh-de 巳經拿°着°了°

SELDOM, hyi-vong' 稀逢; feh-da'-li 弗常°; ǎ-kyi'-tsao 無°幾遭; —*comes,* hyi-vong' læ-go 稀逢來个°; feh-da'-li læ-go 弗常°來个°; *happens very —,* ts'in-tsiao'-gyi-vong' 千朝奇逢

SELECT, to kæn 揀°; shün 選; t'iao 挑; t'iao'-shün 挑選; kæn'-shün 揀°選; kæn-'dzeh 揀°擇; — *a day,* ding nyih-ts' 定日°子; — *a lucky day,* kæn nyih-ts' 揀°日°子; *to divide off, and —materials,* c'ü liao-tsoh' 取料作

SELF, zi 自°; ts'ing-sing' 親身; *he went him —,* gyi zi' ky'i'-de 其自°去°了°; *examine one's —,* zi' dzô-ts'ah zi' 自°查察自°; — *respect,* zi-djong' 自重; *has ditto,* yiu ts'-ky'i 有志氣; yiu ts'-hyiang 有志向; tsang-fong' ngao'-ky'i 爭風傲氣; — *conceit,* zi-tseng'-zi-do' 自°尊自°大°; zi-tseng'-zi-djong' 自°尊自°重; *to lower one's —* (as by doing something wrong), zi-ky'ing'-zi-zin' 自°輕自°賤; *reproach one's —,* zi tsah'-vah zi' 自°責罰自°; — *existent,* z-jün'-r-jün-yiu'-go 自然而然有个°; — *willed,* zi-lih'-ih-koh'-go 自°立一國个°; zi-ih'-go cü'-i 自°一个°主意

SELFISH, t'en-s' 貪私; — (*i. e.* first helps himself and then divides), iao'-leh ih-un bing-feng' 舀得°一碗平分; *takes care of himself not of others,* tsih'-kwu zi,' feh-kwu' nying-kô' 只顧自°弗顧人°; *not —,* feh t'en-s'-go 弗貪私个°; ǎ s-sing' 無°私心

SELL, to ma 賣°; ma-diao' 賣°了°; siao-t'eh' 銷脫; fah'-ma 發賣°; —*at auction,* ma kyiao'-ho 賣°呌貨; — *by the catty,* leng kying' ma 論劤賣°; — *by the single one,* leng ko'-deo ma 論個數°賣°

SEMI-CIRCLE, pun'-ky'ün 半圈

SEMINARY, (college), do shü-yün' 大°書院; *Theological* —, Sing'-Kying shü-yün' 聖經書院

SEND, *to* ts'a 差; tang'-fah 打發; — *a letter*, ta' ih-fong sing' 帶° 一封信; — *ditto by a friend*, t'oh bœng-yiu' ta 托朋友帶'; — *back*, t'e'-wæn 退還; — *to my house*, song' tao ngô oh'-li-ky'i 送到我家裏去°; — *troops*, ky'i ping' 起兵; — *him word* (by some one), ts'a nying' t'ong-cü' gyi 差人通知其; — *for him*, ts'a nying' ky'i eo' gyi 差人去°叫°他°

SENIOR, *my* — *in age*, nyin-kyi' pi ngô' do' 年紀比我大°; nyin-kyi' tsiang'-jü ngô 年紀長於我; — (by 30 or more years), tsiang'-pe 長輩; zin-pe' 前輩; *Mr.* — *Senior*, T'a' sin-sang 太°先生°

SENSE, *meaning*, i'-s 意思; *talks* —, kông'-leh yiu-dzing'-yiu-li' 講得°有情有理; *no* — *of propriety*, feh-sih' siang-t'i' 弗識禮°體; *ditto* (as in using other people's things, &c.), i'-læ-peh-teng' 擅自°; *use your own good* —, zi-dzæ'-jing-we' 事°在人爲; *having good* —, ling-bin'-go 靈便個°; ts-tsih' hao' 知質好; kyin'-sih hao' 見識好; *no* — *of shame*, ᴍ lin'-c'ü 無°廉耻; *the five senses*, ng' kwun 五°官

SENSELESS, *meaningless*, ᴍ i'-s 無°意思; *no understanding*, ᴍ ling-sing' 無°靈性; *stupid*, ngæ-teng'-teng 呆瞪瞪; ts-tsih moh' 知質木

SENSIBLE *to the eye*, k'en'-leh-kyin'-go 看得°見個°; — *to the touch*, moh'-leh-c'ih'-go 摸得°出個°; —*person*, t'ong dzing' dah-li'-go nying 通情達理個°人; — *of favors*, we ken eng' 會感恩

SENSUALIST, hao'-seh-go 好色個°; seh-kyü' 色鬼°; tsiu'-seh ts-du' 酒色之徒

SENSUALITY, seh'-yüoh 色慾

SENSITIVE (heart), sing nyün' 心軟; — *to others' woes*, sing sang'-leh dœ' 心生°得°慈

SENSITIVE-PLANT, p'ó'-yiang-ts'ao' 怕癢草

SENTENCE, *a* ih-kyü' shih-wô' 一句說話

SENTENCE, *to* ding-en' 定案; ding-ze' 定罪; p'un'-tön 判斷; — *him to death*, ding gyi si'-ze 定其死°罪

SENTIMENTS (of one's heart), sing-jih' 心術

SENTINEL, bông-siu'-go 防守個°; — *going the rounds*, jing-lo'-go nying 巡邏個°人°

SEPARATE, *to divide*, feng-k'æ' 分開; *to* — *from* (as friends, &c), li-k'æ' 離開; bih-k'æ' 別開; — *by placing something between*, kah'-k'æ 隔開; lah-k'æ' 拉開;

to — *by a line* (of ink), yüong moh'-sin kah'-k'æ 用 墨 線 隔 開; *to — friends*, gyiao'-k'æ beng-yiu' 離 人° 朋 友; — (because of some difficulty), ts'ang-k'æ' 撑 開; *the time to —*, li-k'æ'-go z'-eo 離 開 个° 時 候

SEPARATE, *a — one*, ling-nga' ih'-go 另 外° 一 个°

SEPARATELY, koh'-nying-kwun-zi' 各 人° 管 自°; koh-kwun-koh' 各 管 各; liang-k'æ-dæ' 兩 分° 開°

SERENE, bing-en' 平 安; — *sky*, t'in-ts'ing 天 青

SERGEANT, pô'-tsong 把 總

SERIES *of misfortunes*, tsih'-lin-go 'o'-se 接 連 个° 禍 祟; lin-ky'in'-go 'o'-se 連 牽 个° 禍 祟; *through a — of years*, lih-nyin' 歷 年

SERIOUS, *sedate*, tön-tsông' 端 莊; *grave beyond one's years*, siao'-nyin lao'-dzing 少 年 老 成; *important*, kying'-kyih 緊 急; — *illness*, bing djong' 病 重; bing' li-'æ' 病 利 害; — *consequences*, djong'-deo kwæn-yi' 重 頭 關 係

SERMON, kông'-ka 講° 解°(ih-p'in)

SERPENT, dzô 蛇; (ih-kwang, ih-keng)

SERPENTINE *path*, bun-dzô lu' 盤 蛇° 路; yiang-dziang lu' 羊 腸 路

SERVANT yüong-nying' 傭 人°; *followers*, keng-pæn' 跟 班; nyi yia' 二° 爺; ti'-'ô-nying 底 下°

人°; — *who splits wood, and carries water*, p'ih-za' t'iao-shü'-go 劈 柴° 挑 水° 个°; — *boy*, ah-siao' 阿 小; siao-wæn' 小 使°; — *woman*, a-m̄ 阿 姆; ah-sao' 阿 嫂

SERVE, *to* voh-z' 服 事; *stand and wait orders*, z'-'eo 侍 候; —, *or wait upon* (as on a sick, or old person), tông-dzih' 當 值; z'-dzih 侍 值; — *tea to guests*, di dzô' peh nying-k'ah' 遞 茶 給° 客 人°; — *in a tray*, pnn 搬; — *a warrant*, 'ang ba' 行° 牌°

SERVICEABLE, yiu yüong-dziang° 有 用 場; teh-yüong'-go 得 用 个°; — *goods*, meng-z'-ho 門 市 貨

SERVILE, pe-kong'-ky'üih'-tsih 卑 躬 屈 節; mô'-wông kyin lu'-djü 螞 蝗 見 鹵 䱱°

SESAME, *or* SESAMUM (*plant*), ts-mô' 芝 蔴; — *oil*, mô-yin' 蔴 油

SESSION *of a church*, dông-we° 堂 會; *to have a meeting of —*, jü dông-we' 聚 堂 會; — *of a trial before an officer*, dông 堂; *morning —*, tsao'-dông 早 堂

SET, *a — of small boxes*, ih-t'ao' 'eh-ts' 一 套 盒 子; *a — of five buttons*, ih-fu nyiu'-ts 一 副 鈕 子; *a — of four or eight chairs*, ih-dông ü'-ts 一 堂 椅° 子; *a — of men*, ih-pæn nying' 一 班 人°; *a — of books*, ih-ts'ah shü' 一 冊 書

SET, to — down, fòng 放; en; to fix, ding 定; to establish, shih'-lih 設立; — about (doing), k'æ-siu' 開手; dong-siu' 動手; — out on a journey, dong-sing' 動身; to inlay, k'æn 嵌; k'æn'-siang 嵌鑲; — fire to, fòng ho' 放火; — table, pa coh'-teng 擺桌子°; — out (as plants), cong 種; does not — well, feh-'eh sing' 弗合身; — the heart at rest, fòng'-sing 放心; the sun sets, nyih-deo'-loh-sæn' 日°頭落山; — a joint, gao'-kwn yiao-tsing' 鉸股落°樺°; — a watch, piao' te-te-cing' 表對對准; piao' te-te tsing' 表對對正

SETTEE, c'ing-teng' 春橙 (ih-dziang)

SETTLE, to determine, ding-kwe' 定規; — a price, ding kô'-din 定價°錢°; — disturbances, bing-lön' 平亂; bing-fæn' 平反; — quarrels, li-c'ü' z-t'i' 理處事體; — a quarrel, ka-ün' sih-kyih' 解冤釋結; — for, ko'-kah 過割; ditto with ready money, yin ko'-kah 現過割; to adjust accounts, kyih-tsiang' 揭賬; ditto (by paying), kyih ts'ing' 揭清; — (a fluid), ting'-loh 淀落; — till clear, ting'-gyi-ts'ing' 淀其清; — (by hollowing down), t'en-loh' 凹°落; — (as a bird), ding-loh' 停落

SETTLED, (by talking), shih'-t'o'-de 說妥了°; wun-kyih'-de 完結了°; wô ding'-tông-de 話定當了°; the affair is — , z-ken' bæn-t'o'-de 事幹辦妥了°; reckoned and —, sön'-ky'ih-de 算訖了°; — (as a place for a person, goods &c.), dziah-cü'-hao-de 安°置好了°; wait till I am —, teng ngô' en-teng'-hao-ts 待°我安頓好之

SEVEN, ts'ih 七; — fold, ts'ih'-be 七倍

SEVENTEEN, jih-ts'ih' 十七

SEVENTH, the di-ts'ih'-go 第七個°; — of the month, ts'u-ts'ih' 初七; the — day after a death, deo-ts'ih' 頭七; the 5th — after death, (when the spirit of the deceased is supposed to visit the family), ng'-ts'ih 五°七; the 7th — (when the seven weeks of mourning end), dön'-ts'ih 斷七

SEVENTY, ts'ih'-jih 七十

SEVERAL, hao-kyi' 好幾; deh-ma' 幾許°; — times, hao-kyi' tsao 好幾遭

SEVERALLY, ih-ih' 一一; ko'-ko 個個

SEVERE, li'-æ' 利害; djong 重; hyüong 凶; strict, nyin-kying' 嚴禁; — illness, bing li'-æ' 病利害; — punishment, ying-vah' djong' 刑罰重; have a — cold, djong' sông-fong' 重傷風; — rules, kwe'-kyü nyin' 規矩嚴

SEW, *to* vong 縫; vong-lin′縫連; *can you —?* ng′ we vong-lin′-feh 你°曾縫連否°? *— together,* or *seam,* vong′-ih-vong 縫一縫

SEWING, (work), tsing-ts′ sang-weh′ 鍼帶生°活; *the style of —,* tsing-ts′ 鍼帶; *good —,* tsing-ts′ hao 鍼帶好

SEWING-MACHINE, t′ih-tsing-zông′ 鐵鍼床; (incorrectly called) t′ih-zæ-vong′ 鐵裁縫

SEWING-WOMAN, *who sews by the wayside for any one,* vong-gyüong′ 縫窮 (Shanghai and Su-chow).

SEWER, *drain,* keo 溝; *covered —,* ing-keo′ 陰溝; *open —,* yiang-keo′ 陽溝 (ih-da)

SEXTANT, liang-t′in ts′ah′ 量天尺

SEXTON, *chapel-keeper,* kwun-li-pa-dông′-nying 管禮拜°堂人°; *cemetery-keeper,* kwun-veng′-go 管墳个°

SHABBY, *old and faded,* gyiu-læn′-tsæn 舊襤襂°; in-dza′-dza 蔫; læn-in′ 襤蔫; *worn,* or *ragged,* yiang′-de; yiang-yi′-de 破°壞°了°

SHABBILY, *to treat persons —,* bob-dæ′ nying-kô′ 薄待人°家; dæn′-boh dæ nying 淡薄待人°

SHACKLE, *to — the feet,* so kyiah′ 鎖腳

SHACKLES *for the feet,* kyiah′-k′ao 腳栲; *— for the hands,* siu′-k′ao 手栲

SHAD, z-ng′ 鰣魚 (ih-tsah)

SHADE *for a lamp,* ing-kwông′ 隱光; teng-t′ao′ 燈套; *paper ditto,* ts′-t′ao 紙套; *glass ditto,* po-li′ tsao 玻璃罩; *hang in the —* (as a dress), lông læ ing′ di′-fông 眼在°陰地方

SHADE, *to* tsô 遮°; tsô-in′ 遮°掩; tsô-djü′ 遮°住; *— from wind,* tsô fong′ 遮°風

SHADOW, ing 影

SHADOWY, *and fleeting,* kying′-hwô-se′-yüih 鏡花水月

SHADY *place,* ing di′-fông 陰地方; tsô-ing′ di′-fông 遮°陰地方; *— and cool,* ing′-liang 陰凉

SHAGGY *and curly dog,* s′-ts keo 獅子狗

SHAKE, *to* t′eo 褪°; *—one's clothes,* i-zông′ t′eo-ih′-t′eo 衣裳褪一褪; *— a child,* siao-nying′ t′e-t′e′-nông-nông′ 小孩°推推攎攎; *—* (as a house, windows, &c.), tsing′-tsing-dong 怔怔動; yiao-dong′ 搖動; *—* (as an old man), fah-kying′ 發驚; kying-kying′-dong 驚驚動; *—* (as in ague), fah-gying′ 發懍; *hands,* siu la-leh ts′ing-ts′ing′ 手携°得°請請; *—* (as from fear), gwah-gwah′-teo′ 捐捐抖

SHAKY, *or uncertain,* weh-deh-shing 活脱°桦

SHALL, pih′-iao 必要; pih′-shü 必須

SHALLOW, ts′in 淺; ts′in-gying

淺近；— learning, 'oh-veng' ts'in' 學°問淺

SHAM, to tsòng-kô' 裝假°; kô' hyi-deo tso-tang'-c'ih-læ' 假°意做出來; it is all —, keh tu z tsô'-i 這°都是詐意; tu z tsô'-kyi 都是詐計

SHAME, wông-k'ong' 惶恐; sense of —, lin'-c'ü 廉恥; no sense of —, feh-p'ô' wông-k'ong 弗怕惶恐; ǹ-lin'-c'ü 無°廉恥; feh iao min-moh' 弗要面目

SHAMEFUL, wông-k'ong'-go 惶恐个°

SHAMEFULLY, to treat —, ling-joh 凌辱; tsao-t'ah' 蹧蹋

SHAMELESS, ǹ-lin'-c'ü 無°廉恥; ǹ-ô-lin' 無°了臉; thick skinned, min-bi 'eo' 面皮厚; 'eo'-bi ô'-lin 厚皮了臉

SHANK-BONE, kyiah'-li ding'-kweh 脚裡脛骨

SHAPE, ying 形; round —, yün-ying'-go 圓形个°; leaf —, jü-yih' ying'-go 樹葉形个°; — or pattern, yiang-shih' 樣式°; what —? soh-go ying'-go 甚°麼°形个°!

SHAPE, to c'ih-yiang' 出像°; tsô'-c'ih siang'-mao 做出相貌; to mold, su'-c'ih-læ 塑出來

SHAPELESS, ǹ-siang'-mao 無°相貌; ill-formed, ǹ-yiang'-væn 無°樣範

SHARE, a ih feng' 一分; ih kwu' 一股; how many shares? tso kyi-kwu' feng 做幾股分? a — in the business, ih kwu' sang-i' 一股生°意; to have a — in, yiu veng-ts' 有分子; yiu kwu'-deo 有股頭

SHARE, to tsiao'-kwu feng 照股分; — alike, kyüing-feng' 均分; to — grief, feng-iu' 分憂

SHARK, sô-ng' 鯊魚°; — fins, yü-ts' 魚翅; — skin, sô-ng' bi 鯊魚°皮

SHARP, kw'a 快°; very —, fong-li' 鋒利; how — these scissors are, keh'-pô tsin'-tao dza fong-li' 這°把翦刀甚°鋒利; — pointed, tsin 尖; tsin-li' 尖利, (also sharp in looking after one's interests); — pointed scissors, tsin'-tao-deo kw'a' 翦刀頭快°; — taste, lah'-go mi'-dao 辣个°味°道

SHARPEN, to — (as knives, &c.), mo kw'a' 磨快°; — (as a pencil), siah' tsin 削尖; — the appetite, k'æ we' 開胃

SHARPER, kwa'-ts 拐°子; p'in'-zeh 騙賊°

SHATTERED to pieces, k'ao'-leh feng'-se 敲°得°粉碎; pah'-meh-kæn'-se 百°末爛碎; — constitution, ti'-ts tang'-loh-de 精°神°衰°弱了°; ti'-ts ky'ih'-loh-de 底子吃落了°

SHAVE, to siah 削; t'i 薙; — off a little, siah'-tin-diao 削點了°; — the head, t'i deo' 薙頭; — the beard, t'i ngô-su' 薙

鬚°;—*on becoming a priest*, loh fah′ 落髮

SHAVINGS (of wood), moh-fi′ 木柿; *to make* —, bao′ moh-fi′ 刨木柿; bao-hwô′ 刨花

SHAWL, p‘i-i′ 披衣

SHE, gyi 其

SHEAF, *a small* —, ih-shoh′ 一束°; ih-bo′ 一縛; *large* —, ih-kw‘eng′ 一綑

SHEAR, *to* — *sheep*, tsin yiang-mao′ 剪羊毛

SHEARS, tsin′-tao 剪刀; — *for cutting metal*, kah′-tsin 夾°剪

SHEATH, k‘oh 壳; t‘ao 套; — *for a knife*, tao-k‘oh′ 刀壳 (ih-go); — *for a fan*, sin′-dæ 扇袋 (ih-tsah)

SHEATHE *the sword*, kyin, t‘ao′-tsing k‘oh′-li 劍套進壳裡

SHED, bang 棚; bong 蓬; ts‘iang 廠; — *of pine branches*, song-mao′ bang 松毛棚; *a cool shelter*, liang bang′ 涼棚; *straw* —, *or lodge*, ts‘ao′-ts‘iang 草廠; *to make a* —, tah bang′ 搭棚

SHED, *to* — *tears*, c‘ih-ngæn′-li 出眼°淚; c‘ih ngæn-li′-shü 出眼°淚水; ngæn′-li beh-c‘ih′ 眼°淚流出; — (as skin), t‘eng-diao 褪了°; *the snake sheds its skin*, dzô′ t‘eng k‘oh 蛇蛻°; — *teeth, and get new ones*, wun ngô-ts′ 換牙°齒;— *blood*, liu hyüih′ 流血

SHEEP, yiang 羊; wu-yiang′ 胡羊; (ih-tsah)

SHEEP-FOLD, yiang-gyin′ 羊樫

SHEET, bi-tæn′ 被單; (ih-diao, ih-keng); —, (or cover for a quilt used by Chinese when travelling), bi-t‘i′ 被替; *a* — *of paper*, ih-tsiang ts′ 一張紙; *a* — *of iron*, ih-p‘in t‘ih′ 一片鐵

SHELF, koh′-pæn 擱板 (ih-kw‘e); *two, three,* or *four shelves*, sæn-koh-lông′ 三角°架°子°; *the third* —, (counting from the top downward as Chinese do), di-sæn′-kah 第三格

SHELL, k‘oh 壳; *a spiral* —, s-lo′-k‘oh 螺蛳壳; *egg* —, dæn k‘oh′ 蛋壳

SHELL, *to* — (as peas, eggs, &c.) poh-k‘oh′ 剝壳

SHELTER *from rain, to* yü′ di′-fông 躲雨地方; — *from wind*, bi fong′ di′-fông 避風地方; o fong′ di′-fông 矮風地方; *no* —, æ tsô-lah′-go 無遮攔个°

SHELTER, *to* tsô-lah′ 遮攔°

SHEPHERD, k‘en-yiang′-go nying 看羊个° 人°; yiang-moh′ 羊收; *styled*, moh′-s′ 牧師

SHIELD, *rattan* deng-ba′ 籐牌°; *skin* —, bi-ba′ 皮牌° (ih-min)

SHIELD, *to* — *from wind*, tông′-djü fong′ 擋住風

SHIFT, *to* — *about* (as wind), cün hyiang′ 轉向

SHIFTLESS *person,* ǎ-ky'i' ǎ-p'ah-go 無°氣無°魄个°; vu-yüong' vu-joh'-go 無榮無辱个°; ǎ-yüong'-nying 無°用人°

SHINE, *to* — (*independently, as the sun, fire, &c.*), fông kwông' 放光; — (*by reflected light, as brass, mirrors, &c*), fah-c'ih liang-kwông' 發出亮光; — *upon,* tsiao'-djoh 照着°

SHINING, t'eo'- kwông 透光; kwông-liang' 光亮; liang-liang' 亮亮; dzang-liang, (*sometimes used ironically*).

SHIP, jün 船 (ih-tsah); *merchant* —, sông-jün' 商船; k'ah'-jün 客船; — *captain,* lao'-da 老大; — *master,* jün-cü' 船主; *to build a* —, tang jün' 造°船; ting jün' 釘船; *to knock a hole in a* —, jün' ngô-leo'船矴漏; —*broken apart,* jün' t'ah'-k'æ-de 船脫開了°;—*broken to pieces,* jün' sæn-pæn'-de 船散板了°

SHIP, *to* —*goods,* tsông bo' 裝貨

SHIPBOARD, *on* læ-jün'-li 在°船裡; læ jün' zông' 在°船上

SHIPWRECK, jün' tso'-diao-de 船傲壞°了°; — (*by running on rocks*), jün' ngô-tsiao'-de 船矴礁了°; — (*by being upset in a storm*), jün' tao'-meh-de 船倒沒了°; jün foh'-meh-de 船覆沒了°

SHIP-YARD, jün-ts'iang' 船廠

SHIRT, pu'-sæn 布衫 (ih-gyin);

— *with plaited bosom,* kæn'-sæn 裥衫

SHIVER, *to* — *with cold,* tang 'en-tsin' 打寒顫

SHOCKED, se'-se-dong 碎碎動; mô-tseh'-tseh 麻唶唶; *too* — *to move,* hah'-leh su-ngæ'-ky'i 嚇得°酥呆起; ngæ-ih-ngæ' 呆一呆; hah'-ngæ 嚇呆

SHOCKING *news,* hyüong sing' 凶信; — *affair,* (*i. e. obscures the heavens*); hweng-t'in' heh-di' z-ken 昏天黑地事幹; *ditto* (*upsetting heaven and earth*), t'in-pong' di-tao'-go z-ken 天崩地裂°个°事幹

SHOE, 'a 鞋°; (*one,* ih-tsah; *a pair,* ih-song); *straw* —, bu-'a' 蒲鞋°; ts'ao'-'a 草鞋°; *fine ditto,* (*cool*), liang-'a' 涼鞋°; *to put on a* —, c'ün-'a' 穿鞋°

SHOE-HORN, 'a-liu' 鞋°籬

SHOE-MAKER, 'a-s'-vu 鞋°司務; bi-'a' s-vu 皮鞋°司務

SHOE-SOLE, 'a-ti' 鞋°底

SHOE-STRING, 'a-ta' 鞋°帶 (ih-keng); *your* — *is untied,* ng-go 'a-ta' sæn'-de 你°个°鞋°帶散了°

SHOOT, *to* — *with bow and arrow,* zih-tsin' 射箭; — *birds,* zih tiao' 躲鳥°;—*with a gun,* fông ts'iang' 放鎗; *ditto birds,* tang-tiao' 打鳥°;— *at a target,* tang-pô'-ts 打靶子

SHOOTS, ngô 芽°; miao 苗;—*for*

*planting*, iang 秧 ; *bamboo —* ,
sbing 箵

SHOP, tin 店 (ih-bæn); *— keeper*,
tin'-cü 店主 ; *lang'-z* 東° 人°;
*— tender*, tin'-kwun 店夥°

SHORE, ngen 岸; *to go on —* ,
zông ngen' 上 岸; *on —* , læ-
ngen-zông' 在° 岸上 ; *sea —* ,
hæ-pin-yin' 海邊沿

SHORT, tön 短 ; *— road* (or cut
across), liao-lu'躂路; liao-gying'
lu 躂 近 路 ; *— of breath*, iao-
ky'i'-kying 氣 緊 ; *a — time*,
ih-zông' 一息°; ih-hyih' 一 歇 ;
dzæn-z 暫 時 ; feh dziang'-kyiu
弗 長久; *the — way* (of doing a
thing), kyin'-bin 簡便 ; dzong-
bin' 從便; gying'-bin 近便 ;
*— life*, tön' ming 短命 ; *to have
ditto*, ziu-shü' feh dziang' 壽歲°
弗 長

SHORTEN, *to* long tön tin' 弄短
點;— (by sawing), zih' ih-gyüih
loh' 截 一段° 落;— (by cut-
ting), ze tön' 裁短;— *by a few
days*, kæn liang' nyih 減° 兩日°

SHORT-COMING, feh-tao'-ts-c'ü弗
到之 處; tön'-c'ü 短處

SHORT-SIGHTED, *near - sighted*,
gying' z-ngæn 近視眼°; — *as
to the future*, kyin'-sih tön' 見
識 短; siao-nying' kyin-sih' 小
孩° 見識; tön'-kyin 短見

SHOT, *small* sô-ts' 砂子 ; *bullet*,
dæn-ts' 彈子; *small ditto*, sô-
dæn' 砂彈 (ih-k'o, ih-lih)

SHOULD *he*, (if he), ziah'-z gyi' 若
是 其; *— or not ?* nyi' feh nyi'
宜 弗宜?

SHOULDER, kyin-kah'-deo 肩 胛
頭 (ih-tsah) ; *— of mutton*,
zin-t'e' yiang-nyüoh' 前° 腿羊
肉; *thrown over the —* , kyin-
deo' gwæn'-tih; *even shoulders*,
(*i. e.* on a level, or of the same
rank), bing kyin' 平 肩

SHOUT, *to* wæ-wæ'-hyiang 啞 啞
響; da-sing'-hæn'-kyiao 大 聲
喊 叫; wu-long' hyiang'-liang
喉° 嚨響 亮

SHOVE *to* t'e 推 ; *— away*, t'e-
k'æ' 推 開

SHOVEL, ts'iao 鍫 ; ts'æn 鏟 ;
*large —* , wô-ts'iao' 划 鍫 ;
gông-hyin' 鉄° 鍫°; *coal —* ,
ho'-hyin 火 掀; me-t'æn' ts'iao
煤 炭 鍫 (ih kwun)

SHOVEL, *to* ts'iao 鍫

SHOW, *false* pang t'i'-min 綳 體
面 ; *fond of —* , æ' hwô-hyin' 愛
奢° 華°; *making a —of not wanting*, (as money), tsông-ky'iang'
裝腔; *ditto of not being in want*,
tsông-p'ông' 裝胮; *ostentatious
—* , ba-dziang' 排° 塲; *making
a — of being great*, pa-p'ing'
擺° 品 ; *a fine —* , pa'-shih
kông'-kyiu 擺設 講° 究; *—
of strength*, hyü-tsiang' sing-shü'
虛張聲 勢

SHOW, *to disclose*, lu-c'ih'-læ 露
出 來; hyin'-c'ih-læ 顯 出 來;

— (it) *to me,* peh ngô k'en' 俾°
我看; — *how to do,* di-peh' 提
撥'; *to point out,* ts'-tin 指點; —
*great kindness to him,* 'eo' dzing
dæ' gyi' 厚 情 待 其

SHOWER, *a* ih-dziao yü'; *a little*
—, ih-bong yü' 一 蓬 雨; *a
heavy* —, ih-dzing yü' 一 陣
雨; — *from a passing cloud,* ko'-
yüing-yü 過 雲 雨

SHOWMAN, *travelling* tseo-kông-
wu'-go 走 江° 湖 个°

SHOWY, SHOWILY, hyin 顯;
*dressed* —, c'ün'-leh hyin' 穿
得°顯; *ditto* (as a bad woman),
hyin'-dô-dô.

SHREWD, hwæn-ky'iao' 儇 巧;
k'en'-fong s-jün'看 風 駛 船; —
(calculating, and underhanded)
*person,* we ẁeh-tang'-go nying
會° 挖 打 个° 人°

SHRIEK, *to* wæ si ih-sing 吶 喊°
一 聲; djoh-sing' si tæn'-ky'i
突° 然° 一° 聲°

SHRILL *sound,* sing-hyiang' tsiu'
聲 響 尖; — *voice,* wu-long'
pih'-tsin 喉° 嚨 筆 尖

SHRIMP, hô, or hön 蝦° (ih-tsah);
— *meat out of the shell,* hô-jing'
蝦°仁; *dried* —, hô-mi' 蝦°米°

SHRINE, (whether ancestral, or
otherwise), dông 堂; jing-dông'
神 堂; *idol* —, sing'-dông' 聖
堂; — *of a large idol,* nön'-koh
暖 閣; — *of the god of wealth,*
dzæ jing-dông' 財 神 堂

SHRINK, *to* — *from,* t'e'-soh 退縮;
soh'-dzoh 縮 侷'; p'ò 怕; *if he
sees water, he shrinks from it,* gyi
k'en'-kyin shü' ziu t'e'-soh'-de
其 看 見 水° 就 退 縮 了°; —
(as fruit), kyiang-long'-ky'i 殭
攏去°; pih-long'-ky'i 癟攏去°;
ken-long'-ky'i 乾 攏 去°; — (as
cloth), geo-long'; soh'-long 縮
攏; soh'-tön' 縮 短

SHRIVELLED (as fruit, &c), pih-
pih'-go-de 癟 癟 个°; pih-cü'-
pih-tah' 癟 嘴 癟 臉°; *skin* —,
bi' tseo'-long-de 皮 皺 攏 了°

SHROFF, k'en'-nying-yiang' sin'-
sang' 看 銀 洋 先 生°

SHROUD, *burial dress,* ziu-i' 壽衣;
lang-i' 冷° 衣 (disrespectful);
Ningpo people wear seven, or at
least five garments in the coffin,
called, ts'ih'-z-i' 七 事 衣; ng'-
z-i' 五° 事 衣

SHRUB, siao'-jü 小 樹; *dwarf
tree,* a'-jü 矮 樹 (ih-cü)

SHRUG, *to* — *the shoulders,* song'
kyin-kah' 聳 肩 胛

SHUDDER, *cause one to* —, seng'-
ngao sah-nying' 沁° 煞 煞 人°;
song'-jün 悚 然 (veng.)

SHUN, *to* bi-ko' 避 過; to'-bi
躲 避

SHUT, *to* kwæn 關; — *the door,*
kwæn meng' 關 門; — *up shop,*
kwæn tin' 關 店; zông-ba-meng'
上 排° 門; — *him in,* kwæn-
gyi'-tsing 關 其 進; — *him out,*

kwæn-gyi-c'ih' 關其出; —
*the eyes,* ngæn'-tsing pi'-long 眼°
睛 閉 攏; — *the mouth,* cü'-pô
pi'-ts 嘴 吧 閉 了°; — *the
book,* shü' siu-long' 書收攏;
— *the door, and not bolt it, (i. e.
to do things by halves),* kwæn
meng' feh-loh shün' 關門弗
落閂

SHUTTER, *window* ts'ông - meng'
牕 門; k'æn'-meng 檻° 門
(ih-siu)

SHUTTLE, so 梭; *to pass the —,*
c'ün so' 穿梭; *days and months
pass like a —,* jih-yüih' jü-so'
日月如梭

SHY (*as a girl*), iu'-siu 幽羞; *unwilling to speak before others, or
show what one has done,* pa'-feh-
c'ih'-go 擺° 弗出个°

SICK, *slightly* næn-ko' 難過; feh
sông'- kw'a 弗 爽 快°; feh
shih'-i 弗適° 意; *is —,* yiu
bing' 有病; *to become —,* sang
bing' 生°病; — *at the stomach,*
dæ-dæ'-dong; oh'-sing 欲° 嘔°
iao mao' 要 吐°; — *people, or
person,* bing nying' 病人°; —
*of it,* in'-sah-de 厭煞 了°; *the
— day in ague,* pæn-gyi' 症°
候° 个° 班期

SICKLE lin-tao' 鐮刀 (ih-pô)

SICKLY *person,* to'-bing'-go nying
多病个°人°; ziang bing-mæn'
ka 像 病 貓° 一° 樣° (slang).

SICKNESS, bing 病; bing-tsing'

病症; yiang 恙; *prevalent —,*
tsing'-'eo 症 候; *severe* ·, —,
djong' bing 重病; *your honorable —,* kwe' yiang 貴恙; *my
mean —,* zin yiang' 賤恙

SIDE, pin 邊; *the — of,* bông-
pin' 旁邊; pin-yin' 邊沿; *the
right —,* jing-siu'-pin 順手
邊; *the left —,* tsia'-siu-pin 左°
手 邊; *this —,* dông' pin 這°
邊; *that —,* keh' pin' 那° 邊;
*on the —,* tseh'-go-de 側 个°
了°; tseh'-pin 側邊; tseh'-leng
側輪; *place on the —,* tang'
tseh-fông 打側放; *only on
one —,* tæn' pin 單邊; tæn
pun'-pin 單半邊; *the — (of the
body),* hyih 脅; *pain in the right
—,* jing-siu'-pin hyih' t'ong 順
手邊脅痛; *to turn from —
to —,* fæn-læ' foh-ky'i' 翻來
覆去°

SIDEWAYS, SIDEWISE, wang
橫; ts'ia 斜°; hwa 歪; *crabs
move (creep)—,* ha' wang bô' 蟹
橫 爬; *to roll —* (as an animal), tang kweng' 打䠀

SIEGE, *to lay — to a city,* we-
kw'eng' dzing-ts' 圍困城子

SIEVE, sô-s' 紗篩; *very fine —,*
kyün'-s 絹 篩 (ih-min); *bamboo
—for grain,* s'-koh-dza' 篩穀籮

SIFT, *to* s 篩; — *by throwing up,
and blowing off chaff,* yiang 揚
po 簸; po-yiang' 簸揚; po-
long' 播弄

SIGH, to t'æn-ky'i' 嘆氣; to heave a —, t'æn ih-k'eo ky'i' 嘆 一 口氣; deep —, 'æn-sing' t'æn'-ky'i 咳聲嘆氣; — from pity, t'æn'-sih 嘆息

SIGHT, in k'en'-leh-kyin-go 看 得°見个°; pleasing to the —, hao'-k'en 好看; the first —, ts'u k'en'-kyin 初看見; bao'-z k'en'-kyin 暴時看見; deo ih-we' k'en'-kyin 第° 一 回看 見; good (eye)—, ngæn'-lih hao' 眼°力好; ngæn'-ho tsin' 眼 光°尖; ngæn'-kwông liang' 眼° 光亮

SIGN, kyi'-nying 記°認; kyi'-'ao 記號; piao-deo' 標頭; to make a —, tso kyi'-nying 做記認'; — agreed upon, we-'ao' 爲號; secret —, en'-'ao 暗號; en'-nying 暗認'; shop —, tsiao-ba' 招牌'; z-'ao' 字號; twelve signs of the zodiac, jih-r'-kong 十 二 宮; good —, kyih'-ziao 吉兆; hao ts'æ'-deo 好彩頭; a bad —, hyüong-ziao' 凶兆; to make a —, or omen, coh-ts'eng'作 識; good ditto, hao' ts'eng'-z好識事; — of the future tense, we 會; iao 要; — of the past tense, de; ko 過; hao'- de 好 了°; liao 了; hao'-liao 好了; the — of the possessive, go 个°; man's, nying'-go 人° 个°

SIGN, to — one's name, loh ming-z' 錄名字; loh kw'un' 錄欵;

ditto as evidence, c'ih-ming' 出 名; gyü-ming' 具 名; tang' hwô-z' 打花字; tang' hwô-iah' 打花押

SIGNAL, we-'ao' 爲號; to fire a gun as a —, fông-p'ao'we-'ao' 放 礮爲號; to hoist a flag as a—, tang' gyi-'ao' 打旗號; ts'ô' gyi-'ao' 扯旗號; to raise a — of distress, ts'ô t'ao-kyiu'-go gyi-'ao' 扯討救个° 旗號

SIGNIFICANT, it is very — (of something else), gyi cong-ling' yia' bih' dzing 其中另有別情

SIGNIFICATION, meaning, i'-s 意 思; i'-nyi 意義; ka'-shih 解° 說; — of individual characters, z-nyi' 字義

SIGNIFY, what does it —? yiu sob'-go i'-s 有甚°麼°意思? it signifies little, (or is of little consequence), m̃-kao' kao'-kwæn 沒° 有°交°關; 'ao-vu' ken-dzih' 毫 無干涉

SILENCE, to keep —, feh k'æ' k'eo 弗開口; — one's own complaints, zi' ka zi'-go ün' 自°解°自个° 怨

SILENT, no sound, m̃-sing'-hyiang 無°聲響; feh-sing' feh-hyiang' 弗聲弗響; m̃eng-sing' feh hyiang' 悶°聲弗響; no words, meh-meh' vu-yin' 默默無言; pi'-k'eo vu-yin' 閉口無言

SILENTLY, hardships borne —, meh-ts'eh'-ts'eh-go siao'-kw'u

喑°受°个°苦; *to think* — (as the Romanists do), meh-siang′ 默想

SILK, *raw* s 絲; *ditto from Wu-tsiu*, Wu′-s 湖絲; *native* —, t‘u′-s 土絲; *wild raw* —, yia′-zen s′ 野°蠶絲; *woven* —, dziu 綢; *poorer ditto*, kyün 絹; *pongee*, (from Shantung), fu′-dziu 府綢; kyin′-dziu 繭綢; *gray ditto*, hwe-seh fu′-dziu 灰色府綢; *buff ditto*, (of the natural color), peng′-seh fu′-dziu 本色府綢; *sewing* —, s-sin′ 絲線; i-sin′ 衣線; *floss* —, sæn′-sin 散線; — *wadding*, min-teo′ 絲°綿; — *cocoon*, kyin 繭; — *worm*, zen 蠶; *ditto in chrysalis*, zen-ngo′ 蠶蛾; — *worm's eggs*, zen-ts′ 蠶子; *to reel* —, dziu-s′ 抽°絲

SILK-SHOP, (*i. e.* silk, and satin), dziu-dön′ tin 綢緞店

SILK-WEAVER tsih′-kyi s-vu′ 織機司務

SILK-WEAVING *establishment*, tsih′-kyi fông 織機坊

SILL, *door* di-voh′ 地栿; *window* —, k‘æn-deo 檻°頭

SILLY, m̆-lông′-go; hen′-deo lin′-ky‘i 憨頭臉氣; ziang m̆-lông′ ka; m̆-deo′-jü 無°頭緒

SILVER, nying-ts′ 銀子; — *shop*, nying-leo′ 銀樓; — (jewelry) *shop*, siu′-sih tin 首飾店; — (money) *shop*, nying-‘ao′ 銀號 — (thread), nying-sin′ 銀線

SILVER-SMITH, siu′-sih s-vu′ 首飾司務; nying s-vu′ 銀匠°

SIMILAR, siang-ziang′ 相像; hao′-ziang 好像; weh′-t‘eh-ziang 活搨像; oh′-ziang 阿°像; fông′-feh 仿彿; ih-yiang′ 一樣; *this is — to that*, keh′-go teng keh′-go siang-ziang′-go 這°个°與°那°个°相像个°; *in a — manner*, ih-yiang′ tso′-fah 一樣做法

SIMMER, *to boil slowly*, mæn-mæn′ ts′ 慢慢煮°; — *over a slow fire*, iu-iu′ ho′ ts 幽幽火羨°; veng ho′ ts 文火煮°

SIMPLE, *easy to understand*, kyin′ r yi ming′ 簡而易明; — *and honest*, lao′-jih 老實; *of one kind*, doh-yiang′ 獨樣; jing-z′ 純是; — *and plain*, tsih′-p‘oh 質樸; p‘oh′-jih 樸實; su′-zing 素淨; — *clothing*, tsih′-p‘oh-go i-zông′ 質樸个°衣裳°; — *food*, su′-zing-go ky‘üoh′-zih 素淨个°吃°食; *how — you are!* ng hen-deo′ nying 你°憨頭人°!

SIMPLETON, hen-deo′ 憨頭; ngæ-ts′ 呆子

SIMPLIFY, *to make more easy*, tso kyin′-bin-tin 做簡便點; — (to the understanding), tso kyin′-ming-tin 做簡明點

SIMPLY, *merely*, doh-doh′ 獨獨; tæn-tsih′ 單只

SIMULTANEOUS, tso′z-‘eo′ 一°樣°个°時候; dong z-‘eo′ 同時候

SIN, ze 罪; ze'-ko 罪 過; ze'-ky'in 罪 愆; ze'-nyih 罪 辜; *original —*, peng' ze 本罪; nyün ze' 原罪; *great —*, do ze' 大° 罪; djong' ze 重罪; ze'-oh 罪 惡; *add — to —*, ze'-zông kô-ze' 罪 上 加° 罪; *to commit a — worthy of death*, væn si'-ze 犯 死° 罪

SIN, *to* væn ze' 犯罪; *— against God*, teh'-ze Jing-ming' 得 罪 神 明; *— knowingly, and purposely*, ming-cü' kwu-væn' 明 知 故 犯

SINCE, kyi 既; kyi'-jün 既 然; kyi'-kying 既 經; *— then*, dzong-ts'-yi-'eo' 從 此 以 後; *— I was a child*, dzong-siao' 從 小; z'-siao 自小; *— you are here, I will go*, kyi' ng læ-tong' ngô ky'i'-de 既 你 在° 此° 我 去 了°

SINCERE, dzing-jih' 誠 實

SINCERITY, dzing-sing' 誠 心

SINEWS, kying 筋 (ib-kwang); *deer —*, loh kying' 鹿 筋

SING, *to* ts'ông 唱; *— without an instrument*, ts'ing' ts'ông' 清 唱; *— hymns*, ts'ông tsæn'-me-s 唱 讚 美 詩

SINGE, *to* tsih'-tsiao 炙 焦

SINGER, we-ts'ông'-go nying 會 唱 个° 人°

SINGLE, tæn 單; doh 獨; *— thickness*, tæn zeng' 單 層; *a — garment*, tæn gyin' i-zông' 單 件 衣 裳°; doh gyin' i-zông' 獨

件 衣 裳°; *a — flower* (on a stem), doh tô' hwô 獨 朵 花; *— flower* (not double), tæn zeng' hwô-bæn' 單 層 花 瓣

SINGLY, *one by one*, ih-tsah'ih-tsah' 一 隻 一 隻; ih'-go ih'-go 一 个° 一 个°; *standing — and alone*, doh ih'-go lih'-tong 獨 一 个° 立 在° 此°

SING-SONG, *read in a — tone* (as the Chinese do), lông'-lông-doh' 朗 朗 讀; *ditto indistinctly*, nyi'-li-ngwu'-lu doh 咿° 哦° 之° 聲°

SINGULAR, *uncommon*, fi-væn' 非 凡; fi-dzông' 非 常; c'ih-cong' 出 衆; *—, or strange*, c'ih-gyi' 出 奇; *— affair*, c'ih-gyi'-go z-t'i' 出 奇 个° 事 體

SINK, *to —* (in water), dzing-loh'-ky'i 沉 下 去°; *—* (in mire, &c), 'æn-loh'-ky'i 陷 下 去°; *— and be lost*, dzing-meh' 沉 沒; *— in the mud*, 'æn-loh' nyi-du'-li 陷° 下° 泥 塗 裏

SINNER, ze'-nying 罪 人°; væn-ze'-go nying 犯 罪 个° 人°

SIP, *to* hwun 嚘; *— and try*, hwun'-hwun'-k'en 嚘 嚘 看

SIR, *respected —*, (to a stranger), tseng kô' 尊 駕°; (to an officer), lao'-yia 老 爺; (to a young person in an officer's family), siao'-yia 少 爺; siang'-kong 相 公; (to a teacher), sin-sang' 先 生°

SIRLOIN, li'-nyüoh 裡 肉°

SISTER, *elder* ah-tsi′ 阿姊; *younger* —, ah-me′ 阿妹; me′- me
妹妹; *elder sister's husband*, tsi′-
fu 姊夫; *younger sister's husband*,
me-fu′ 妹夫

SISTER'S *son*, nga-sang′ 外甥;
— *daughter*, nga-sang-nön′ 外
甥女

SISTERS, tsi′-me 姐妹

SISTER-IN-LAW, *man's older brother's wife*, hyüong-sao′ 兄嫂;
*man's younger brother's wife*, di′-
sing-vu 弟媳婦; *a wife calls
her husband's brothers' wives*,
dzob-li′ 妯娌; *she calls her
husband's older brother's wife*, a-
m′ 阿姆, *and the younger brother's wife*, ah-sing′ 阿嬸; *her
husband's older sister*, kwu-mô′
姑媽; *husband's younger sister*,
siao′-kwu 小姑

SIT, *to* zo 坐; — *still*, ding-ding′
zo′ 坐定; — *a la Turque*, bun-
kyiah′ zo 盤脚坐; bun-k‘ong′
zo′ *or* bun-k‘o′ zo′ 盤空坐; tang
zo′ 打坐; *please* —, ts‘ing zo′
請坐; ts‘ing zo-tæn′-loh 請坐
下; — *up straight*, dzih-ky‘i′
zo 直起坐; zo′-leh dzih′ 坐
得直; — *up, and* — *still*, pih′-
t‘ing zo 筆挺坐; —*at a feast*,
zo-zih′ 坐席; — *up all night*,
zo yia′ 坐夜; — *on a chair*,
zo ü′-ts 坐椅子; — *on a
bench*, zo teng′ 坐櫈; — *on
eggs*, bu dæn′ 菢蛋

SITUATED *on the North Bank*, zo′-
loh Kông-poh-ngen′ 坐落江
北岸地方

SITUATION, yüih-dông′ 穴堂;
*a well chosen* —, yüih-dông′ tin-
leh hao′ 穴堂點得好; —
(*of a house*), dzeh-kyi′ 宅基;
*position*, di-we′ 地位; — *better
than before*, di-we′, pi zin-deo′
hao′ 地位比前頭好; — *or
circumstances*, kwông-kying′ 光
景; *what is his* — *now?* yin-
dzæ′ gyi-go kwông-kying′ dza′-
go 現在他的光景怎个?

SIX, loh 六; *the* — *Boards*, loh
bu′ 六部

SIXTEEN, jih-loh′ 十六

SIXTH, di-loh′ 第六

SIXTY, loh-jih′ 六十; — *years
old*, nyin-kyi′ zông loh-jih′ 年
紀到六十; — *years make a
cycle*, loh-jih′ nyin ih′-go kyiah′-
ts 六十年爲一甲子

SIZE, kw‘un-do′ 寬大; kw‘eh′-
do 闊大; *large* —, do-dao′
大道; *what* —? dza-kwun′-do
怎麼大? dza kwun-kw‘eh′-
do 怎麼闊大? to-siao′ do
多少大?

SIZE, *to* (prepare with glue water),
zông kao-shü′ 上膠水

SIZING, *glue-water*, kao-shü′ 膠
水; *alum-water*, ming-væn′ shü′
明礬水

SKATE, *ice shoe*, ping-‘a′ 冰鞋;
(*a fish*), hwu-ng′ 虎魚 (ih-kwang)

SKEIN *of silk*, ih-ts-sin′ 一 枝 線; — *of thread*, ih-kao sin′ 一 絞° 線; — *of linen thread*, ih-siao sin′ 一 綃 線

SKELETON, ih-fu kweh′-deo 一 副 骨 頭; *a human* —, ih-fu nying-kweh′ 一 副 人° 骨; *thin as a* —, kweh′-seo-jü-za′ 骨 瘦 如 柴°; lu-kying′-lu-kweh′-go 露 筋 露 骨 个°; *to prepare a* — *of a discourse*, ao kweh′-ts 拗 骨 子

SKETCH, kao′-ts 稿子; *to draw a* —, tang ih′-go kao′-ts 打 一 个° 稿 子

SKETCH, *to* — *with pen, or pencil,* miao 描; wô 畫; sia 寫°

SKILL, hao siu′-dön 好 手 段

SKILLED *in*, joh-sih′ 熟 識

SKILLFUL, yiu-hao′ siu′-dön 有 好 手 段; — *hand*, joh-siu′ 熟 手

SKIM, *to* kah′-c′ih-læ 溢° 出 來; — *cream*, na′-yiu kah′-c′ih-læ 嬭° 油 滿° 出 來

SKIN, bi 皮; — (of a person only), bi-fu′ 皮 膚; *squirrel* —, hwe-c′ü′-bi 灰 鼠 皮; *silver ditto,* nying-c′ü′-bi 銀 鼠 皮; *rabbit* —, t′u′-bi 兔 皮; *doe* —, kyi′-bi 麂 皮; *otter* —, t′ah-bi 獺 皮; shü′-t′ah-bi 水° 獺 皮; *marten* —, ′oh-bi′ 貉 皮. See FUR.

SKIN, *to* — *with the hand*, poh-bi 剝 皮; poh-diao′ bi 剝 了° 皮; — *rubbed off,* bi ts′ao′-ky′i-de 皮 擦° 去° 了°; bi ts′ao′-t′eh-de 皮 擦° 脫 了°

SKIP, *to* fah-t′iao′ 發 跳; — *for joy,* hwun-hyi′-leh fah-t′iao′ 歡 喜 得° 發 跳; — *over*, t′iao′-ko 跳 過; — (a page), kah′-tông t′iao′ ih-min 跳 過 了° 半° 頁°

SKIRT, gyüing 裙 (ih-diao)

SKULL, *bony case of the brain*, deo-ting′-kweh 頭 頂 骨; t′in-ding′-kweh 天 庭 骨; *the brainless head*, kw′a-lu′-deo 詁 顱 頭

SKY, t′in 天; *clear* —, ts′ing-t′in′ 青 天; *blue* —, læn-t′in′ 藍 天; *dark* or *clouded* —, ing-a′ t′in 陰 靉° 天

SKY-LIGHT, t′in-tsing′ 天 井; — (Chinese, of shell), t′in-tsing′-pæn 天 井 板 or 天° 窓°

SLAB *of stone*, zah-pe′ 石 碑; zah pe-ba′ 石° 碑 牌°

SLACK (in doing), ts′u-sing′ 粗 心; *not tight*, kw′un 寬; den 潭; song 鬆; kw′un-den′-den 寬 潭 潭; kw′un-jah′-jah; den-den′-dong 潭 潭° 動; (these are also used of persons); — *water,* bing shü′ 平 水°

SLACKEN, *to* fông′-leh kw′un′-tin 放 得° 寬 點; — *speed,* kw′un-song′-tin 寬 鬆 點; mæn-tin′ 慢 點; mæn-fæn′-tin 慢 泛 點; kw′un′-tin 寬 點; kw′un-wun′-tin 寬 綏 點

SLAKE, *to* — *thirst*, ts k′eh′ 止 渴; *to* — *lime*, fông shü′, diao hwe′ 放 水° 調 灰

SLAM, *to* gwah; bang - bang′-

hyiang 澎°聲°響°; *must not —
the door*, meng' 㐫-nao gwah'.

SLANDER, *to* kông dzæn-yin' 講°
譏言; pông'-hwe 誹謗

SLANDER, *to believe a —*, t'ing
dzæn-yin' 聽譏言

SLANDERER, zeh-cü' 賊°嘴

SLANG, ts'u-ts'u'-go shih-wô' 粗
个°說話

SLANTING, ts'ia 斜°; *— to one side*
(*as a boat*), tseh'-go 側个°; —,
*will upset*, iao tseh'-cün 要側
轉; iao tseh'-fæn 要側翻

SLAP *him*, tang gyi' ih-kyi' 打其
一記; *— on the face*, kwah'-
ih-kwông 摑一光; tang pô-
công' 打巴掌 (công or tsông);
*— on the mouth*, tang teo-cü' 打
兜嘴

SLATE, nga-koh' feng'-pæn 外°
國粉板; *native — for native
ink*, feng'-pæn 粉板; k'æn-pæn'
鉛板 (ih-min)

SLATE-PENCIL, zah-pih' 石°筆
(ih-ts).

SLATS *running lengthwise*, dzih
tông' 直檔; *— running cross-
wise*, wang tông' 橫檔

SLATTERN, t'i'-t'i-t'a-t'a-go nyü-
nying 浠浠汰°汰°个°女人

SLAUGHTER, *met with great —*,
tsao sah'-loh 遭殺戮; *— of a
city*, du-dzing' 屠城; *to prohibit
— of animals*, kying du' 禁屠

SLAUGHTER-HOUSE (*for cattle*),
sah'-ngeo-dziang 殺牛°塲

SLAVE, nu-boh' 奴僕; nu-dzæ'
奴才; *called*, kô-nying' 家°
人°; *— girl*, ô-deo' 丫頭; s'-nyü
使女; *— boy*, dong-boh' 僮僕

SLEAZY, hyi 稀; *light and thin*,
biao-boh', or byiao-boh' 杪薄

SLEDGE-HAMMER, lông-deo-djü'
榔頭鎚° (ih-go)

SLEEK, kwông-wah' 光滑; kying'-
kwông shih-wah' 鏡光雪滑

SLEEP, kw'eng'-joh 睡°熟; *cannot
—*, kw'eng'-feh-joh 睡°弗熟;
*— soundly*, kw'eng sah'-kao 熟°
睡°; sah'-k'eo kw'eng'-joh; *—
lightly*, kw'eng'-leh kying-sing'
睡得°瞥醒; *— in one's clothes*,
ta' i-zông kw'eng' 連°衣裳°
睡°; *— and dream much*, lön-
mong' tin-tao; 亂夢顛倒; *cry
out in —*; lön-mong' hæn-kyiao
亂夢喊叫; *sleeping-room*,
vông-kæn' 房間°; *to — the long
— (i.e. death)*, do-kao' kw'eng'-
joh 大°覺睡°熟

SLEEPY, iao kw'eng'-joh 要睡°
睡°, or 要睡°熟°; k'eh'-c'ong-
mi-mong' 瞌饛眯矇; mi-hwô'-
ky'i-de 眯眦去了°; *— eyes*,
ngæn'-tsing mi-long'-ky'i 眼睛
眯攏去°

SLEET, shih'-ts 雪珠°

SLEEVE, ziu-ts' 袖子 (ih-tsah)

SLEIGHT *of hand*, kyiah'-kw'a
siu-kw'a' 脚°快°手°快°; *to use
ditto*, long-siu'-kyiah 弄手脚;
yüong siu'-kyiah 用手脚; pin

hyi'-fah 變戲法; *to perform
a ditto*, pin ih-t'ao' hyi'-fah 變
一套戲法

SLENDER, (as persons), dziang-
liao'-siao 長敧篠°; bah-dziang'
勃°長

SLICE, *a* ih'-p'in 一片

SLICE, *to* ts'ih-leh p'in'-tang-p'in
切得°片打片

SLIDE, *to* wah 滑; — *down*, sô'-
loh-ky'i; *to slip*, wah-loh'-ky'i
滑落去°; — *back and forth*,
(move), yi-læ' yi-ky'i' 移來移
去°; — *up and down*, ts'iu-zông'
ts'iu-loh' 抽上抽落

SLIGHT *matter*, si'-si-siao'-z 些
些小事; ky'ü-ky'ü-siao'-z 區
區小事; — *wound*, sông
ky'ing-k'o' 傷輕可; *not the
slightest mistake*, ih-ngæn' feh-ts'o'
一點°弗錯

SLIGHT, *to* —(a person), lang'-dæn
冷淡; ts'iao'-feh-ky'i' 瞧°弗
起; — *unintentionally*, shih'-kwu
失顧; *to do carelessly*, tso'-leh
hweh'-liah 做得°忽略; tso'-leh
peh-yi' we-i' 做得°不以爲意

SLIGHTLY, ih-tin' 一點°; p'o'-p'o
頗頗; — *acquainted*, p'o'-p'o
nying-teh' 頗頗認°得

SLING, *to put the arm in a* —, loh
siu'-kwang 絡手膀°; *to throw
a stone with a* —, yüong ta'
dæn zah'-ts 用帶彈石子

SLIP, *a* — *of paper*, ih-p'in ts'
一片紙; ih-da ts' 一揲紙;

— *of bamboo*, coh'-bæn 竹爿;
(ih-kw'e)

SLIP, *to* wah 滑; liu 溜; — *down*,
wah-loh' 滑落; — (as a person),
wah-tao' 滑倒; *to lose footing*,
shih-kyiah' or sib-kyiah' 失腳,
(also to speak words that cannot
be trusted); — *and almost fall*,
tang wah-t'ah' 打滑°脫; —
*and fall*, web-tih' 滑跌; liu-tih'
溜跌

SLIPPER, bin-'a' 便鞋 (a pair,
ih-sông)

SLIPPERY, wah-lih'-wah-t'ah' 滑
立滑脫° (also used of persons);
*not easily caught*, wah-wah'-dah-
dah 滑脫°脫°; — *in making
promises, and not fulfilling*, tang-
wah'-t'ah'-de 打滑脫了°

SLIT, lih-vong' 裂縫 (ih-da); —
*made purposely in a garment*,
ts'ô'-ts 衩子 (ih-da)

SLOPING, ts'ia'-min 斜°面; ts'ia'-
shing 斜°响

SLOPPY, *wet*, sih'-sih-go 濕濕
個°; wu-dah-dah'-go 腐脅脅
個°; wu-gyih'-gwah-lah.

SLOUGH, na-nyi-den' 爛坭潭

SLOUGH, *to* — *off*, t'eng-diao' 褪
去°; *ditto skin*, or *shell*, t'eng
k'oh' 褪壳

SLOVENLY, fông'-p'ah-la'-sa 放
潑賴撒°; *dirty*, t''i'-t''i-t'a-t'a
涕°涕太太; lah-t'ah' 邋遢

SLOW, mæn 慢; wun 緩; mæn-
t'ang'-t'ang 慢宕°宕°; wun'-

deng-deng 綏鈍鈈; — fire,
wun'-ho 綏火; veng-ho' 文火;
iu-iu' ho 幽火

SLOWER, a little mæn-tin' 慢點

SLOWLY, mæn-mæn' 慢慢; wun'-
wun 綏綏; kw'un-wun'-diao-da
寬綏; walk — (said to a guest
on leaving), mæn-mæn' tsco 慢
慢走

SLUGGISH, læn-r' vu-tông'-go 懶
而無當个°; sang læn'-wông-
bing 生°懶黃病 (in reproach);
too — to get up to eat, kæ min-
feng' min-bi' go 盖麵粉縣
被个°

SLUICE, ky'i 閘°; — gate, ky'i'-
meng 閘°門; mud —, pô 礴;
stone —, in 堰

SMALL, siao 小; si'-siao 細小;
vi-si' 微細; siao'-so; very —,
ting'-siao 頂小; ih-ngæn'-ngæn'
do 一點°點°大°; siao'-siao-
kwun do; dzih-si' do 極些大°;
— quantity, ih-ngæn'-ngæn 一
點°點°; yiu'-'æn 有限°

SMALTS, da-ts'ing' 大青

SMALL-POX, inoculated deo-ts' 痘
子; — taken naturally, t'in-deo'
天痘; has the —, c'ih-deo-
ts'-go 出痘子个°; to inoculate
the —, cong deo' 種痘; cong
hwo' 種花; 'ô miao' 下°苗;
marked with —, mô-bi'-go 麻
皮个°

SMART, clever, hwæn 僝; hwæn-
ky'iao' 僝巧; — in reply, tah'-

leh ky'iao' 答得°巧; — and
active, weh-loh' 活絡

SMARTING pain, tsih'-lah-lah-go
t'ong' 炙辣辣个°痛; —
like fire, ho' siao ho'-lah-go t'ong'
火燒火辣个°痛

SMASH, to k'ao-se' 敲碎; tang'-
se 打碎; — accidentally, p'ong-
se, or bang-se' 撞碎

SMATTERING, veo-min' 'oh'-tin
浮面學°點

SMEAR, to dzô 搭

SMELL, to hyüong 齅; hyüong'-
hyüong-k'en 齅齅看; — some-
thing sweet, veng hyiang-ky'i' 聞
香氣; meng hyiang-ky'i' 吻°
香氣

SMELL, fragrant hyiang-ky'i' 香
氣; a strong —(generally bad),
ky'i'-mi 氣味°; a bad —, ky'i'-
ts 氣子; ky'i'-sih 氣息; flowers give forth a sweet —, hwô
læ-tih p'eng'-hyiang 花噴香;
sweaty —, 'en-sön'-ky'i 汗酸
氣; fishy —, sing-ky'i' 腥氣;
musty —, eh'-boh-ky'i' 霉蒸
氣; slightly musty — (as damp
clothes), ze-nong-ky'i' 歪膿氣;
sour — (as of bread, or meal),
sön tsiang'-ky'i 酸漿氣; strong
— (as of mutton), sao-ky'i' 臊
氣; rank — (of certain persons),
lao'-ô ky'i' 老鴉氣

SMELT, to melt, yiang 煬; sah
煞; yiang-k'æ' 煬開; sah'-k'æ
煞開

SMILE, *to* mi-mi'-siao 眯眯笑；
mi-ko'-ngæn-siao 眯花°眼°笑

SMILING, *wears a — face*, ta siao'-
lin 帶°笑臉

SMOKE, *in* 烟；*the smell of —,*
in-ho' ky'i 烟火氣；*in* ky'i'-
mi 烟氣味°

SMOKE, *to — meat*, hyüing nyüoh'
燻肉°；*— tobacco*, ky'üoh in'
吃°烟；*— opium*, ky'üoh a-p'in'
吃°鴉片；(more polite), ky'üoh
in' 吃°烟

SMOKED (as things in cooking),
in-ho'-ky'i-de 烟火氣了°

SMOKY *place*, in-hyüing ho'-dæn
n-sen' 烟燻火燀

SMOOTH, kwông 光；wah 滑；
kwông-wah' 光滑；*very —,*
kying'-kwông shih-wah' 鏡光雪
滑；tih-wah-lin' ka 滴滑臉
個°；wah-liu-cü' ka' 滑流嘴個°

SMOOTH, *to — with the hand*, t'ô'
kwông 抹°光；*— with a plane*,
bao kwông' 刨光

SMOOTH-TONGUED, (not to be depended upon), yiu-cü'-t'ah'-zih
油嘴諜舌；cih'-læ-bin-ky'i
啜來辯去°

SMOOTHING-IRON (to be heated
from within), ing'-teo 熨°斗
(ih-kwnn)；— (to be heated on
the fire), loh-t'ih' 烙鐵

SMOTHER *to death*, meng-sah' 抆
煞；*— out fire*, meng-u' 抆熄

SMUGGLE *to* t'eo-se' 偷稅；leo-
se' 漏稅

SMUGGLING, *to detect one in —,*
k'ô leo-se'-go 拿°漏稅個°

SMUTTY, yiu in-me' tsao'-tih 有
烟煤遭的；*—face*, heh'-moh
du-lin' 黑墨塗臉

SNAIL, *common* (either with or without a shell), yin-yiu'-lo' 涎游
螺；*fresh water —*, s'-lo 蛳螺；
*sea —*, hæ' s-lo' 海蛳；*field —,*
din-lo' 田螺 (ih-keng)

SNAKE, dzô 蛇° (ih-kwang, ih-
keng)；*poisonous —*, doh dzô'
毒蛇°；*Buddha's mouth, snake's
heart*, (*i.e.* fair words coming from
a bad heart), veh-k'eo' dzô-sing
佛口蛇°心；*tiger's head, snake's
tail*, (said of anything which
commences with a great flourish,
and ends in nothing), hwu'-deo
dzô-vi' 虎頭蛇°尾

SNARE, ky'ün'-t'ao' 犬韜；gyiang
弶；kw'n-t'ao'-ky'ün 箍套圈；
*to set a —*, tsông ky'ün-t'ao' 裝
圈套；tsông gyiang' 裝弶

SNARL, *all in a —*, lön-tsia'-bong
亂絨°鏬

SNATCH, *to* ta'-ts'iang ta'-deh；
帶°搶帶°套；ts'iang'-ts'iang-
deh-deh 搶搶套套；*— with
violence*, deh, 套；deh-ky'i' 套
去°；ts'iang 搶；ts'iang'-ky'i 搶
去°

SNEER, *to — at*, lang'-siao；冷
笑；*to turn up the nose at*, bih-
deo'-kwun siao nying' 鼻°孔°
笑笑人°

SNEEZE, *to* tang p'eng'-t'i 打噴嚏

SNORE, *to* yiu min-hen' 有眠鼾; *he snores loudly*, gyi'-go min-hen' do' 其个°眠鼾大°

SNOUT, dziang cü-bu' 長嘴輔°; — *of a tea-pot*, dzô-wu-cü 茶壺嘴; *to work the — under* (as a hog), ky'üing.

SNOW, shih 雪°; *white as* —, shih'-bah-go 雪°白个°; shih'-lin-bah'-go 雪°練白个°; — *in scattering flakes*, shih'-hwô-fi 雪°花飛; *snowing fast and thick*, p'iao'-p'iao-dong shih' 飄飄動雪°; — *in large flakes*, læn-shih'-p'in 雪°片

SNOW *to* loh-shih' 落雪

SNOW-BALL, *to throw a* —, tiu shih-dön 丟雪團; — (the flower), moh-siu'-gyiu-hwô 木繡毬花

SNOW-BALL, *to* ô shih'-dön; ting shih-dön.

SNUFF, bih-in' 鼻烟; *to take* —, soh bih-in' 齅°鼻烟 (soh or shoh); ky'üoh bih-in' 吃°鼻烟; — *bottle*, bih-in'-wu 鼻烟壺

SNUFF, *to* — *a candle*, tsin (or gyin) lah-coh'-me 翦蠟燭煤

SNUFFLE, *to* soh (or shoh) bih-deo' 縮鼻°聲°

SNUFFERS, coh'-tsin 燭翦; lah-coh'-gyin 蠟燭箝 (ih-pô)

SO, ka 如°此°; z-ka'; ziang-ka 像如°此°; ka'-siang-mao 如°此°相貌; — *that there be no mistake*, sang-leh long-ts'o' 省°得°弄差; — *that will not*, sang-leh 省°得°; — *many*, ka'-to 如°此°多; ka' hyü'-to 如°許多; keh-tang'; *is it — every day?* nyih-nyih' z-ka feh 日日如°此°否°? *about* —, ka' kwông'-kying 如°此°光景

SOAK, *to* seng'-t'eo 沁透; tsing'-t'eo 浸透; *soaked with perspiration*, 'en' seng'-t'eo-de 汗沁透了°; — *in water over night*, shü tsing' ko yia' 水°浸過夜; shü'-li sah-ko yia'.

SOAP, bi-zao' 肥皂 (a bar, ih-diao); properly native soap, or the fruit of the soap-tree.

SOAP-TREE, zao'-kyih-jü 皂°莢樹; bi-zao'-jü 肥°皂°樹 (ih-cü)

SOAP-STONE, væn-zah' 礬石°; Ts'ing-din zah' 青田石°

SOAR, *to* gwah-zông'-ky'i 飛°上去°

SOB, *to* hyih'-hyih-hoh'-hoh k'oh' 吸吸鼾°鼾°哭; hyih'-hyih'-hyiang k'oh' 吸吸響哭

SOBER, *sedate*, tön-tsông' 端莊; z-dzæ' 自在; djong 重

SOCIABLE, we kao-nyin'-go 會膠°黏个°; hwun-hyi' kyih'-kyiao-go 歡喜結°交个°; æ-beng-yiu'-go 愛朋友个°; *easy to associate with*, hao' ts'eo-de' 好湊隊

SOCIALLY, *to talk* —, ts'ông'-dæn 暢談; ts'ông'-jü 暢叙

SOCIETY, we 會 (ih-go)

SOCKS, tön mah-cü' 短襪子; (a pair, ih-sông), — *covers*, mah-t'ao' 襪套; mah-tsao' 襪罩

SODA, *impure native* —, zah-kæn' 石°鹼°

SODA-WATER, 'O-læn' shü 荷蘭水°

SOFA, c'ing-teng' 春櫈

SOFT, nyün 軟; mi-nyün' 綿°軟; nyün'-joh 軟熟 nyün'-siang; — (as fruit, or cooked food), nen; wông; *very* —, wông'-t'ah-t'ah; nen-bu'-bu; *that is a — boiled egg*, keh'-go dæn ts'-leh liu-wong'-go 這°个°蛋煑得°流黄°个°; z dông-wong'-go dæn 是蕩黄°个°蛋; — *voice*, sing-ing' 'o-nyün' 聲音和軟; *too* — (as cloth, or paper), nyün-t'ah'-bi 軟脫皮

SOFTEN, *to — it*, s'-teh gyi nyün' 使得其軟; *soften by soaking*, tsing' gyi nen' 浸其軟°; — *by scalding*, p'ao' gyi nen' 泡其軟°

SOFTLY, ts'iao'-ts'iao 悄悄; *talk* —, ts'iao-ts'iao' kông 悄悄講°; ky'ing-ky'ing' kông' 輕輕講°

SOIL, di-t'u' 地土; nyi-nyüoh' 泥肉°; *good* —, di-t'u' 'eo'-jih 地土厚實; hao nyi-nyüoh' 好泥肉°

SOIL, *to* long ao-tsao' 弄垩糟

SOLDER, 'en-yiah' 釬藥

SOLDER, *to* 'en 釬

SOLDIER, ping 兵; ping-ting' 兵丁 (ih-go); *soldiers*, ping-mô' 兵馬; *volunteer* —, t'u-ping 土兵; (a body, ih-ts, ih-de, ih-dzing)

SOLE *of the foot*, kyiah'-ti 脚底; — *of the shoe*, 'a-ti' 鞋底

SOLE, (a fish), nyiah-t'ah'-ng 鮎°鰈魚°

SOLELY, doh-meng' 獨門; tæn-tsih' 單只

SOLEMN, nyin-soh' 嚴肅; soh'-jün 肅然 (veng); *still*, zing'-ts'iao-ts'iao 靜°悄悄

SOLICIT, *to* gyiu 求; — *a reward*, gyiu sông'-fong 求賞封; — *a favor*, gyiu dzing' 求情; k'eng dzing 懇情

SOLICITOUS *to obtain*, ts'ih'-sing iao 切心要; *anxious* or *troubled*, fông'-sing-feh-loh' 放心弗落; ky'ih'-du kwô'-dziang 挈肚掛腸; tæn sing-z' 擔心事

SOLID, jih-sing', zih-sing', or dzih-sing' 實心; — *piece of stone*, tsing-kw'e' zah-deo' 正塊石°頭; — *wall*, jih-diah'-go ziang' 實疊个°墻; — *silver*, jih-sing' nying-ts' 實心銀子; tsoh' nying-ts' 足銀子

SOLITARY, doh-ih' 獨一; doh-ling'-ling 獨零零; —(as a person), tæn-sing' 單身; kwu-sing' 孤身; — *and alone*, tæn-sing' doh gyi' 單身獨騎; *without relatives*, kwu-ling'-ting 孤零丁; *no relatives to depend upon*, loh-ts'ing' vu-k'ao' 六親無靠; —

place, kwu-ts'ing' lang'-loh-go di-
fông' 孤 清 冷° 落 个° 地 方
SOLSTICE, *Winter* tong-ts' 冬 至;
*Summer* —, 'ô-ts' 夏 至
SOLUBLE, we yiang'-go 會 煬 个°
SOLVE, *to* ka 解°; — *doubts,* ka
nyi' 解° 疑; — *a difficult matter,* ka'-c'ih næn-z' 解° 出 難 事
SOME, *a few,* kyi'-go 幾 个°; yiu'-
sing 有 些°; yiu'-teh-go 有 得
个°; *a little,* ih-tin' 一 點; ih
ngæn'; *buy* — *sugar, and peaches,*
ma tin dông', ma kyi'-go dao-ts'
買° 點 糖 買° 幾 个° 桃 子;
— *years ago,* kyi' nyiu zin-deo'
幾 年 前° 頭; — *people say so,*
yiu'-sing nying z-ka' wô' 有 些°
人° 如° 此 話; — *other person,*
ih-go bih'-nying 一 个° 別 人°
SOMEBODY, mo'-nying 某 人°;
yiu-nying' 有 人°; — *certainly
did it,* pih'-ding yiu nying tso'-
ko-de 必 定 有 人° 做 過 了°
SOMETHING, *I have* — (*i. e.* one
thing), ngô' yiu ih-yiang' tong-
si' 我 有 一 樣 東 西; *have
to eat, and* — *to wear,* yiu'-leh
ky'üoh' yiu'-leh c'ün' 有 得 吃°
有 得° 穿; *I have* — *to tell you,*
ngô' yiu z-ken' t'ong-cü' ng 我
有 事 幹 通 知° 你°; *talk of
* — *else,* kông bih-yiang' z-ken'
講° 別 樣 事 幹
SOMETIMES, yiu'-z-'eo 有 時 候;
yiu'-teh-z'-'eo 有 的° 時 候; —
*there is, and* — *not,* yiu'-z-'eo

yiu', yiu'-z-'eo m̄'-teh-go 有 時
候 有, 有 時 候 沒° 有°
SOMEWHAT, *is* yiu'-tin 有 點; yiu
kyi-feng' 有 幾 分; — *damp,*
yiu'-tin dziao-sih' 有 點 潮 濕;
liah yiu'-tin dziao-sih' 略 有 點
潮 濕
SON, ng-ts' 兒° 子; ts'-sih 子 息;
*another's* — *taken to rear,* kyi'-pa
ng-ts' 寄 拜° 兒° 子; *adopted*
—, ling'-ts 領 子 (See ADOPT);
*your* —, ling-lông' 令 郎; lông-
kong' 郎 公; ah-lông' 阿 郎;
*my* —, ah-lah siao'-r 我 們° 小
兒°; ngô'-go siao'-r 我 个° 小
兒°; ah'-lah siao'-ky'ün' (*i. e.*
little dogs) 我 們° 小 犬; *eldest*
—, do ng'-ts 大° 兒° 子; tsiang'-
ts 長 子; *the second* —, ts''-ts 次
子; *only* —, doh-yiang' ng-ts'
獨 養 兒° 子; *sister's,* or *daughter's*
—, nga-sang' 外° 甥°
SON-IN-LAW, nyü-si 女 壻
SONG, ky'üoh'-ts 曲 子; *comical*
—, t'æn-wông' 灘 黃; *vulgar*
—, siao'-diao 小 調 (ih-tsah);
— *book,* ts'ông'-shü 唱 書 (ih-
peng)
SONOROUS, hyiang'-liang 響 亮
SOON, *early,* tsao 早; *quickly,* kw'a
快°; *come as* — *as called,* ih-eo'
ziu læ' 一 叫° 就 來; *as* — *as he
came I went,* gyi' ih-læ' ngô ziu
ky'i'-de 其 一 來 我 就 去° 了°
SOONER *than I,* pi ngô tsao' 比
我 早; *a little* —, tsao-tin' 早

點; kw'a'-tsao-tin' 快° 早 點

SOOT, in-me' 烟 煤

SOOTHE, to — (by consoling), en'-
tah 安 搭; — him, kw'un-gyi-
sing' 寬 其 心; ky'ün'-ka-gyi
勸 解° 其

SORCERER ( who divines with
spirits), kông-du-sin'-go 講° 肚 仙
个°; — (who chants, and wor-
ships for another), nyæn-bun'
sin-sang' 念 䇔 先 生°

SORCERESS (who divines with
spirits), du-sin-bo' 肚 仙 婆°;
(who chants, &c., for others),
dao-z-bo' 道 士 婆°

SORCERY, zia-jih' 邪° 術; zia-fah'
邪° 法; to practise —, yüong
zia-jih' 用 邪° 術

SORDID, meanly avaricious, ts'-ts-
we-li' 孳 孳 爲 利; niggardly,
k'æn; k'eh'-li 刻 厲

SORE, bruise, sông-t'ong' 傷 痛;
boil, or ulcer, ts'ông 瘡; doh 毒

SORE, slightly ing'-ts'ih-ts'ih-go
t'ong' 隱 戚 戚 个° 痛; — to
the touch, bang-djoh' t'ong' 揼°
着° 痛; — (pain in the flesh, not
in the bones), nyüoh'-li t'ong'
kweh'-li feh'-t'ong' 肉° 裡 痛 骨
裏 弗 痛

SORROW, iu-meng' 憂 悶; zeo-
meng' 愁° 悶

SORROWFUL, sông-sing' 傷 心;
pe-sông' 悲 傷; — countenance,
min' ta iu seh' 面 帶 憂 色

SORRY, I am — for you, ngô t'i

ng iu' 我 替 你° 憂; dæ ng'
næn-ko'-siang 代 你° 難 過 相;
very — for you, t'i ng' peh'-
jing-siang 替 你° 不 忍 相;
— for it, k'o'-sih 可 惜; sih'-wu
惜 乎

SORT, a ih yiang' 一 樣; ih 'ao'
一 號°; ih cong' 一 種; the same
—, tso' yiang; tso' 'ao; every
—, yiang-yiang' 樣 樣; cong'-
cong 種 種

SORT, to ih-yiang ih-yiang' kwe-
de' 一 樣 一 樣 歸 隊

SORTED, 'ao-tang'-'ao feng-k'æ'-
liao 號 打 號 分 開 了°

SOUL, weh-ling' 活 靈; weng-
ling' 魂 靈; ling-weng' 靈 魂;
man has three spiritual and six
animal souls, nying yiu sæn-
weng' loh-p'ah' 人° 有 三 魂 六
魄 (Buddhist idea); rational
—, ling-weng' 靈 魂; ling-sing'
靈 性; animal —, kyüoh'-weng
覺 魂; vegetable —, seng-weng'
生 魂

SOUND, sing-hyiang' 聲 響; sing-
ing' 聲 音

SOUND, to hyiang 響; does not
—, ve' hyiang 弗 會° 響

SOUND, to — the depth, tang sing-
ts'in' 量° 深 淺

SOUND in health, gyin 健; k'ông-
gyin' 康 健; ditto (as a young
person), tsông'-gyin 壯 健

SOUNDLY, to sleep kw'eng sah'-kao
睡° 煞° 覺

SOUP, t'ông 湯; *to ladle out* — , iao t'ông' 舀湯

SOUP-LADLE, t'ông-diao-kang' 湯調羹° (ih-tsah)

SOUP-TUREEN, t'ông-kwun' 湯罐 (ih-tsah)

SOUR, sön 酸; *to become* — , fah sön' 發酸; — (as food that has turned), seo'-ky'i 餿氣; *ditto* (as the stomach, &c.), tsoh-sön' 作酸

SOURCE (of affairs), læ-yiu' 來由; keng-yiu' 根由; nyün-yiu' 原由; — *and ending*, læ-keng' ky'ü-mah' 來根去脉; — (of man, principles, &c.), nyün-peng' 原本; keng-nyün' 根原; keng-peng' 根本; — (of water), nyün-deo' 源頭; læ-nyün' 來源; læ-mah' 來脉

SOUTH, Nen 南; *toward the* — , hyiang Nen' 向南; dziao Nen' 朝南; *come from the* — , dzong Nen' læ-go 從南來个°; — *East*, tong nen' 東南; — *West*, si nen' 西南

SOW, cü-nyiang' 豬娘; *old* — , lao'- cü-nyiang 老豬娘 (ih-tsah)

SOW, *to* — *seed*, tsah iang-ts' 撒°秧子

SOY, tsiang'-yiu 醬油

SPACE *above us*, hyü-k'ong' 虛空; *empty* — , k'ong di'-fông 空地方; *great unoccupied* — , di-fông sæn'-dæn 地方散°淡; *the* —

*between fingers*, ts'-deo vong 指頭縫

SPACIOUS, kw'un - do' 寬大°; kw'eh'-do 闊大°; kwông'-kw'eh 廣闊

SPADE, wô-ts'iao' 划鍫 (ih-pô)

SPAN, (Chinese, from the end of the thumb, to the end of the middle finger), ih-t'oh' 一庹

SPAN, *to measure by the hand*, t'oh'-t'oh-k'en 庹庹看

SPANISH-STRIPE, pih'-kyi 嗶嘰

SPARE, *to* — *life*, nyiao-ming' 饒°命; — *one for me*, liu ih'-go peh ngô' 留一个°給°我; *can you* — (*i.e.* sell one) *for me?* hao we' ih'-go peh ngô' feh 好匯一个°給°我否°? *can you* — *it a day?* keh, hao sang' yüong ih-nyih' feh 這°好省°用一日°否°? *can't* — *it*, hyih'-gyi-feh-læ 歇其弗來; siao'-gyi-feh-teh' 少其弗得; *can't* — *the time*, kong-fu' bah'-feh-c'ih 工夫拔弗出; *does not* — *his strength*, gyi feh-sih'-lih'-go 其弗惜力个°; *can you* — *me for a while?* ng' hao sang ngô' ih-zông' feh 你°好省°我一息°否°?

SPARING, *using frugally*, feh-sô'-teh yüong 弗捨°得用; — *in diet*, ky'üoh'-leh sang 吃°得°省°

SPARK, *a* ih-lih ho'-sing 一粒火星

SPARKLING, t'eo'-kwông-go 透

光个°; — *like the stars*, ziang sing-kwông' ka 像星光

SPARROW, mô-tsiang' 麻雀° (ih-tsah)

SPASM, kying-fong'驚瘋; kyih'-kying-fong 急驚瘋

SPATTER, *to* tsæn 濺; tsæn-sih' 濺濕; — *with mud*, na-nyi' tsæn'-ky'i 搵°泥濺°起

SPAWN, ng-ts' 魚°子

SPEAK, *to* kông 講°; wô 話; *need not* — *of it*, hao-vong kông'-c'ih 好不°用°講°出; — *louder*, kông-leh hyiang-tin' 講°得°響點; — *the truth*, kông-leh jih-dzæ'-go 講°得°實在个°; tsiao dzih' kông 照直講°; *I want to* — *to you*, ngô iao teng ng kông 我要與你°講°; — *on the spur of the moment, or without previous thought*, kông'-c'ih sön'-tsiang 講°出算賬; ze-k'eo' kông'-c'ih 隨口講°出; *we do not* — *to one another*, ah-lah feh kao' k'eo 我°等°弗交°口; *cannot* — *of it*, wô-feh-c'ih'-go 話弗出个°

SPEAKER, *able* k'eo-neng'-zih-bin'-go nying' 能言°舌辯个°人°

SPEAR, ts'iang 鎗 (ih-ts)

SPECIAL, deh-we' 特爲; deh-i' 特意; — *proclamation*, deh-z' 特示; *a* — *business*, ih-yiang deh-i' z-ken' 一樣特意事幹; *needs* — *care*, iao kah'-nga kwu'-djoh 要格外°顧著

SPECIALLY *for*, cün-meng' we 專門爲; tæn-tsih' we 單只爲; doh-doh' we 獨獨爲

SPECIES, le 類; cong 種; *the same* —, tso' cong; dong-le' 同類; *each according to its* —, koh'-tsiao gyi le' 各照其類; cong'-cong koh-bih' 種種各別

SPECIFY, *to* dzoh 逐; — *each one*, dzoh-yiang' kông'-c'ih-læ 逐樣講°出來; dzoh-ih' pao'-zông-læ 逐一報上來

SPECIMEN, yiang-ts' 樣子 (ih-go)

SPECIOUS, *deceitful*, z-z'-r-fi'似是而非; *superficially fair words*, hwô-yin' ky'iao'-nyü 花言巧語

SPECK, *a* ih-tin' 一點; — *of dust*, ih-tin hwe' 一屑°灰

SPECKLED, hwô-tin'-go 花點个°

SPECTACLES, ngæn'-kying 眼鏡 (ih-fu)

SPECTATORS, k'en'-k'ah 看客; k'en'-go nying 看个°人°

SPECULATION, *a good* —, hao' dzæn'-deo 好賺頭; *a good investment*, hao' c'ih'-sih 好出息

SPEECH, *talk*, shih-wô' 説話; *fluent in* —, liu'-c'ih sön'-tsiang 巧°言°如°流; t'ông-bing' sia-shü' 湯瓶倒°水° (sometimes used in reproach); *clever in* —, jün'-ü shih'-dz 善於説詞; we-kông' we-wô' 會講°會話

SPEECHLESS, *cannot speak*, feh-neng' kông 弗能講; soh'-k'eo deng' 縮口鈍; meh-meh' vu yin′ 默默無言 ;—(as if dumb, used in reproach), ó′-k‛eo vu-yin′ 啞° 口無言

SPEED, *with great —* , ting′-kw‛a 頂 快°; fi-kw‛a′ 飛 快°; fong-kw‛a′ 風 快°; ho′-soh 火 速 ; (their) *— is not equal*, kw‛a′-mæn feh-dong 快° 慢 弗 同

SPEEDILY, *go* tseo′-leh ziang fi′ ka 走 得° 像 飛 个°; *return —*, kw‛a′-kw‛a ziu-læ′ 快° 快° 就° 來; ‛ao-sao′ læ 快° 燥 來

SPELL, *to* p‛ing z-meo′ 摒字母

SPELLING, *Chinese phonetic* fæn-ts‛ih′ 反切

SPELTER, bah-k‛æn 白鉛

SPEND, *to — money*, yüong dong-din′ 用銅錢°; *— wastefully*, fi 費; fi′-diao 費了°; *— to no purpose*, hwô-fi′ 花費; bah fi′-diao 白費了°; *— the day with a friend*, beng-yiu′ di′-fông deng′ ih nyih′ 朋友地方庳一日°; *— the night*, soh yia′ 宿夜°; hyih yia′ 歇夜°; ko yia′ 過夜°; *— one's life in*, tso′-leh ih-si′ 做了°一世°; *ditto laboriously*, lao-loh′ ih-si′ 勞碌一世°; *— one's time idly*, hyü-du′ kwong-ing′ 虛度光陰; nyih-kyiah′ k‛ong′-ko 日°腳空過

SPEND-THRIFT, ba-ts′ 敗子; *to live as a —*, vông′-ky‛üoh vông′-yüong 妄吃°妄用

SPERMACETI, zông-teng′ gying-ng′ yiu 上等鯨魚°油

SPHERE, gyiu 毬

SPHERICAL, ziang gyiu′ ka 像 毬 樣° 式°

SPICES, hyiang-liao′ 香料

SPIDER, (the one which makes a large web), kyih′-cü 蜘°蛛; *flat —* (found in partitions), hyi′-ts 蟢子; pih′-hyi 壁蟢; *very large house —*, pih′-ha 壁蟹° (ih-tsah)

SPIDER-WEB, kyih′-cü-mông′ 蜘° 蛛°網°; kyih′-cü lön′-mông 蜘° 蛛°亂網° (ih-go)

SPIKE, *iron* bao′-djü-ting′ 抱柱 釘; do t‛ih′-ting 大°鐵釘; *bamboo —*, coh′-ting 竹釘;—*of wheat*, ih-cü mah′ 一株 麥

SPILL, *to* yiang′-c‛ih 漾 出; kwông′-c‛ih 洸出;—*by upsetting*, yiang-fæn′ 漾翻; tao′-fæn 倒翻;—(because on a slant), tseh′-c‛ih 側出; *to overflow*, kah′-c‛ih-læ 溢°出來

SPIN, *to — cotton yarn*, fông hwô′ 紡花; fông-sô′ 紡紗

SPINACH, SPINAGE, po-leng′-ts‛æ 菠菜

SPINAL *marrow*, tsih′-kweh-si′ 脊 骨髓

SPINDLE, ding°-ts 錠子 (ih-me)

SPINE, pe′-tsih-kweh 背脊骨

SPINNING-WHEEL, fông′-hwô-ts‛ô′ 紡花車 (ih-tsiang)

SPIRAL, ziang lo-s′ ka 像螺蜥 樣°式°; s′-lo dzin′ 蜥螺旋; *— stair-case*, bun-t‛æ′ 盤梯°

SPIRIT, ling靈; *the Holy—*, Sing'-Ling 聖靈; *pure —*, jing' z ling' 純是靈; *—of love*, jing-sing' 仁心; jing-æ'-sing 仁愛心; *departed —*, ing-weng' 陰魂; kyü 鬼°; kwe'-se 鬼祟; *evil —*, oh'-kyü 惡鬼°; *— of ancestors*, kô-sin' 家°先; *in fine spirits*, (*i. e.* delighted and playful, said in fun), p'ao'-c'ing 快°樂°; *in low ditto*, üoh'-beh-tsky'i' 鬱勃之氣

SPIRITED, *full of life*, jing-ky'i' tsoh' 神氣足; *high —*, sing-kao'-ky'i-ngao'-go 心高氣傲個°; *— talk*, kông'-leh c'ih-jing' 講°得°出神

SPIRITLESS, 尚 jing'-ky'i 無°神氣; pih'-t'ah-t'ah go 肭塌塌個°; ziang pih-gyiæn' ka 像肭茄

SPIRITUAL, ling'-leh-kying-go 靈得°緊個°; ling-weh'-go 靈活個°

SPIT, *to* t'u-zæn-t'u' 吐涎°唾

SPITE, ün'-sing 怨心; 'eng-sing' 恨心; *done out of —*, we'-leh 'eng' tso'-go 為了°恨做個°; *in — of you*, ze ng' læn-tsu' 隨你°攔阻; dæn'-ming ng' tsu'-feh-tsu' 但憑你°阻弗阻; sih'-t'ing ng tsu'-feh-tsu' 悉聽你°阻弗阻; (I'll do it) *in — of you*, dæn'-ming ngô' 但憑我

SPITTLE, zæn-t'u 涎°唾

SPITTOON, dæn-bing' 痰瓶; *small —*, dæn-kwun' 痰罐

SPLENDID, wô-li' 華麗; *bright*, or *showy*, kwông-liang' 光亮

SPLENDOR, kwông-ts'æ' 光彩

SPLICE, *to* tsih'-zông, dzin-long' 接上糶攏

SPLINTER, *a* ih-me ts'' 一根莿; ih-go sang'; *finger has a —*, ts'-deo ts''-c'oh-de 指頭莿猎了°

SPLINT, moh-p'in'-pông 木片綁 (a set, ih t'ao)

SPLIT, *to* p'ih 劈; lih 裂; p'ih-k'æ' 劈開; lih-k'æ' 裂開; *— or burst open* (as a melon, &c.), hwah'-k'æ 豁開; *— in two*, te'-p'ih-k'æ 對劈開; *— the difference*, te'-la-la.

SPOIL, *to* i'-diao; long-diao' 弄壞; wæ-diao' 壞了°; *—(as preserves, honey, &c.)*, fæn-diao' 反掉; *— by indulgence*, i-yiang'-diao; yüong yiang'-diao 容養壞°; *— by altering*, kæ'-diao 改壞°; *—by inadvertence*, bih-ts'iah' 辟散; *ditto* (more intense), tso c'ong'-p'ang; *— by wanting too much, &c.*, tsing-hweh' 棋豁; *to plunder*, tang'-kyih 打叔; lo'-liah 撈掠

SPOIL, *booty*, tsông 臟; *thief's —*, zeh-tsông' 賊臟; *piratical —*, dao'-tsông 盜臟

SPOKEN, *what was — about*, (but not settled), sô yüing'-go 所云個° (veng.)

SPONGE, hæ'-min-hwô 海緜花 (ih-go)

SPONGE-CAKE, dæn-kao' 蛋糕 (ih-go)

SPONTANEOUS, zi sang'-c'ih-læ 自°生°出來; zi fah'-c'ih-læ 自°發出來; c'ih'-ü-z-jün' 出於自然

SPOOL, or *ball of thread*, min-sô dön' 緜紗團

SPOON, diao-kang' 調羹°; kang-z' 羹°匙; *large* or *table* —, do diao-kang' 大°調羹°; *middle* or *dessert* —, cong diao-kang' 中調羹°; *small* or *tea* —, siao' diao-kang' 小調羹°; *native brass ditto*, dzô-z' 茶匙 (ih-tsah)

SPOONFUL *of*, ih diao-kang' 一調羹°; *a tea — of medicine*, ih siao' diao-kang' yiah' 一小調羹°藥

SPORT, hyi'-mæn z-ken'戲蠻事幹; *to make* —, (or make others laugh), ying-siao' 引笑

SPOT, tsih'-le 漬痕°; *oil* —, yin-tsih' 油漬; *black* —, heh'-tin 黑點; heh'-pæn 黑斑; *ink* —, moh-tsih' 墨跡; moh-n' 墨痕°; *to make a* —, tang tsih' 遭°漬

SPOTTED, yin-tsih 有漬; —(as clothes that have laid away), fah pæn-tin'-de 發斑點了°

SPOTLESS, ŭ-tsih'-le-go 無漬痕°个°; — *white*, zing-bah' 淨白°

SPOUT, *pipe*, kwun'-ts 罐子; *tea-pot* —, dzô-wu cü' 茶壺嘴

SPOUT, *to* p'eng'-c'ih-læ'噴出來; ts'ong'-c'ih-læ' 衝出來

SPRAIN, bih-sông' 蹴傷; üih'-sông 攔傷

SPRAINED *ankle*, kyiah'-tsang bih-sông'-de脚脛蹴傷了°; kyiah-bu-lu-den' bih-ih-bih'-de 脚蒲蘆頭°蹴一蹴了°

SPREAD, *to* p'u 鋪; — *out*, (as matting &c.), p'u-k'æ' 鋪開; t'æn-k'æ' 攤開; — (as wings), tô'-k'æ 排°開; — *the table*, pa coh'-teng 擺桌子°; — *food*, pa væn' 擺飯; — *abroad*, 'ang-k'æ' 行°開; — *the Gospel*, Foh'-ing 'ang-k'æ' 福音行°開; — *abroad*, yiang-k'æ' 揚開; po-yiang' 播揚; — (by words), djün-k'æ' 傳開; — *reputation*, ming-sing' yiang-k'æ' 名聲揚開; — (as water spilled), seng'-k'æ' 沁開; — (as disease), yin-k'æ' 延開

SPRIGHTLY, weh-p'eh' 活潑; weh-sin' weh-kyiah' 活手活脚

SPRING, *the season of* —, C'ing-kyi' 春季; C'ing-t'in' z-'eo' 春天時候; *watch* or *clock* —, fah'-diao 法條; *elastic* —, t'e-neh'-diao 捱捺掉; *source of water*, shü'-nyün 水°源; — *of living water*, weh-shü-den' 活水°潭

SPRING, *to start up*, c'ün-ky'i'-læ 竄起來; *to — forward*, t'iao'-ko-ky'i 跳過去°; c'ün-ko'-

ky'i 竇過去° (tsön or c'ün);
mông-zin'-t'iao 望前°跳; *ditto*
(as an animal); boh-ko'-ky'i 撲°
過去°; — *up* (as a plant), c'ih
出; pao'-c'ih 苞出; *will* —
(*i. e.* is elastic), neng-shoh'-neng-
sing' 能縮能伸

SPRINKLE, *to — water about*,
tsah shü' 撒°水°; — *over* (as
from a watering pot, &c), ling
shü' 淋水°; *to — a little salt*,
tsah ih-tin yin' 撒一點鹽

SPROUTS, ngô-den' 芽°頭°; *vegetable —*, ts'æ'-iang 菜秧; *paddy
—*, koh'-ngô 穀芽°; *bean —*,
deo-ngô' 荳芽°; *tender bamboo
—*, neng-shing-den' 嫩筍頭°

SPROUT, *to* ts'iu ngô' 抽芽°; *fah
ngô' 發芽°

SPUNGE, SEE SPONGE.

SPURIOUS, kô 假°:— *dollar*, kô'
fæn-ping' 假番餅; *ditto* (brass
in the middle), ka'-pæn 鉎°版;
*ditto*, (no sound), ô-pæn 啞版;
*ditto* (having a hollow sound),
moh-pæn' 木版

SPURN, *to* *to disdain*, k'en' feh-ky'i
看弗起; *to reject*, ky'i'-diao
棄了°

SPURT, *to — out*, piao-c'ih-læ' 澎
出來

SPY *who watches others*, t'en'-ts 探
子:— *sent to inspect an enemy's
movements, &c*, kæn-si' 奸°細

SPY, *to — into one's movements, &c*,
k'en dong'-zing 看動靜

SQUABBLE, *to — over a petty matter*, siao' z-ken nao-do'-de 小事
幹鬧大°了°

SQUALL *of wind*, ih-dziao fong'
一陣°風; *violent —*, u-'fong-
mang-pao' 烏風猛°颮; — (*as a
child*), sah'-k'eo kyiao' 竭力°
叫; — *of wind and rain*, zi-fong'-
zi-yü 橫°風橫°雨; *ditto in the
hills*, sæn ts'iah' fong 山帕°風

SQUARE, s'-koh-fông' 四角°方;
tih'-koh-fông' 的角°方; *a —*,
ih'-go cün-fông' 一个°轉方;
ih-fông' 一方; *two feet —*,
nyi ts'ah' cün-fông' 二°尺轉
方; — *table*, fông-coh' 方桌;
— *board*, fông pæn' 方板;
*carpenter's —*, koh'-ts'ih 角°尺

SQUASH, nen-kwô' 南瓜; væn-
kwô' 飯瓜 (ih-go)

SQUASH, *to — by a fall*, tih'-wu
跌廢°

SQUAT, *to —*, t'ah'-di-zo 塌地
坐; ts'ing'-di-zo 趁地坐

SQUEEZE, *to — in the hand*, nyiah-
long'-ky'i 捻攏去°; — *out
juice*, tsih'-shü tsô'-c'ih 汁水°
榨出; — *through*, a-c'ih' 挨
出; *ditto a hole*, zah'-c'ih dong-
ngæn'-li 圆°出洞眼°裡; —, *or
hug*, gyih-long' 扱攏; — *money*,
tsô dong-din' 詐銅錢; soh'-tsô
dong-din' 索詐銅錢°; tsô'-ziao
dong-din' 詐擾銅錢°; *to be
squeezed* (as to money), zông-
tsô'-zông 上酢床

SQUINT, to —, zia k'en 斜看;
— with eyes half shut, mi'-leh-
k'en' 眯了°看
SQUINTING eyes, zia'-bah-ngæn
斜白眼; half shut eyes, mi'-
ts'i-ngæn' 眯呲眼°
SQUIRREL, song-c'ü' 松鼠 (ih-
tsah); gray — fur, hwe-c'ü' bi
灰鼠皮
STAB, to pierce, c'oh 猎; c'oh'-
tsing 猎進
STABLE for a horse, mô'-vông 馬
房; — for cattle, ngeo-gyin'-kæn
牛楗間°
STABLE, firm, kyin-kwu' 堅固;
lao-k'ao' 牢靠
STACK of straw, ts'ao'- bong 草
蓬
STAFF, stick, kweng'-ts 棍子;
old person's —, æ'-dziang 按°
杖; kwa'-dziang 拐°杖
STAG, yüong-loh' 雄鹿 (ih-tsah)
STAGE of a journey, ih-dzæn' lu —
站路; the first ditto, deo-dzæn'
頭站; platform for play-acting,
hyi'-dæ 戲臺; to erect a —, tah
hyi'-dæ 搭戲臺
STAGGER, to c'ong'-c'ong-dong'衝
衝動; ts'ih-c'ong'-pah-tih 七衝
八跌
STAGNANT water, si'-shü 死°水°
STAGNATION in trade, sang-i' feh-
dong' 生°意弗來°
STAIN, to spot, tsao tsih' 遭漬;
tang tsih'; hands are stained, siu'
yiu ngæn-seh' tsao'-tih 手有

顏°色遭的; — (as wood be-
fore varnishing), tang ti'-ts 打
底子; ts'eng ti'-ts 襯底子;
— (as glass), 'o ngæn-seh' 和
顏°色
STAIRS, lu-t'æ' 扶°梯° (a flight,
ih-bu); go up —, leo-teng' ky'i
樓上°去°; zông-leo' 上樓;
down —, leo-'ô' 樓下°
STAKE, công 椿 (ih-keng)
STALE, dzing 陳; excessively —,
dzing-nyin'-pah-kwu 陳年百°
古; — bread, dzing mun'-deo 陳
饅頭
STALK, a — of corn, ih-cü' loh-
koh' 一棵稑穀; a — of wheat,
ih-kwang mah' 一根°麥°; —
of a flower, hwô-kwang' 花莖°
(ih-ts).
STALK, to — with long steps, do-bu'
doh 大°步躠; — proudly, tseo'-
leh do-mo' do-yiang' 走得°大°
模大°樣
STALL for merchandize, t'æn 攤;*
ma-ho'-t'æn 買°貨攤; — for
cattle, ngeo-gyin' 牛°楗
* T'æn generally refers to goods
spread out on boards, or by the road-
side without shelter.
STALLION, yüong-mô' 雄馬 (ih-
p'ih)
STAMMER, to kông-leh t'a-ngô'-
gying-k'eo' 講得°拖°牙禁口
STAMMERING, hesitating, ngao'-
zih-keng-go 齩舌根个°; bun'-
zih-keng-go 絆舌根个°; —
speech, k'eo'-ts' deng 口齒鈍;

k'eo'-ts' ngao'-zih-keng-go 口齒
齦 舌 根 个°

STAMP, to — the foot, teng kyiah'
蹬 脚; to — a seal (officially),
tang ing' 打印; — one's name,
tang du-shü' 打圖書

STANCH in heart, sing kyin' 心
堅

STANCH, to — blood, ts hyüih' 止
血

STAND, kô'-ts 架°子; clothes —,
i-kô' 衣架°; wash —, min-kô'
面 架°; pen —, pih-kô' 筆架°

STAND, to lih 立; —up, lih-ky'i'-
læ 立起來; — erect, pih'-dzih
lih'-tong 筆直立在°此°;
— firm (don't fall), lih-leh-lao'
立得°定°; lih - leh - ẅeng' 立
得°穩; cannot — firm, lih-feh-
lao' 立弗定°; lih-feh-ẅeng'
立弗穩; can neither sit nor —
in peace, (i. e. restless), zo'-lih
feh-en' 坐立弗安; can't —
it, ün'-tsæ-wu-yiæ' 寃哉何°奈°

STANDARD, banner, gyi 旗; —
of comparison, tseh'-ts 則子;
cing'-tseh 準則

STAR, sing 星; sing-siu', or sing-
soh' 星宿; fixed —, 'eng-sing'
恒星; evening —, wông-hweng'-
hyiao' 黃昏曉; morning —,
ng'-kang-hyiao 五更曉; shoot-
ing —, liu-sing' 流星; yi-sing'
移星 (ih-lih)

STAR-LIGHT, sing-kwông' 星光

STARCH, tsiang'-feng 漿粉; to

make —, (by pouring water
upon), ts'ong tsiang'-feng 冲漿
粉

STARCH, to — clothes, tsiang i-
zông' 漿衣裳°; — (it) stiff,
tsiang'-leh ngang' 漿得°硬;
tsiang'-leh gyin' 漿得°健

STARE, to ts'ing'-ting-k'en' 睚°
叮看

START, to commence, k'æ-siu' 開
手; — or light a fire, sang ho
生°火; — or kindle fire, ying
ho 引火; — business, k'æ z' 開
市; going to — an enterprise, iao
tang' ih-fæn' gyin-kw'eng' 要
做°一番事°業°; when does the
boat —? jün' kyi'-z k'æ' 船幾
時開? — on a journey, dong-
sing' 動身; to — (in alarm),
ky'ih'-ih-kying 吃一驚; — in
sleep, kw'eng'-joh, kying diao'-
kao 睡熟°驚覺

STARTLE, to kying-dong' 驚動;
must not — him, feh-k'o' kying-
dong' gyi 弗可驚動其

STARTLED, to be ziu-kying' 受驚;
were you —? ng ziu-kying' feh
你° 受驚否°?

STARTLING intelligence, kying-
hyiæ'-go sing'-sih 驚駭个°信
息

STARVE, will iao ngo-sah'要餓死°

STARVED to death, ngo-sah'-de餓
死了°

STARVING, ngo'-leh hyih'-hyih-
dong' 餓得°吸吸動

STATE, *circumstances*, kwông-kying′ 光景; ying-kying′ 形景; *in a good* —, kwông-kying′ hao′ 光景好; *condition*, di-we′ 地位; *to such a* — (*i. e.* bad), tao ka′-go di-bu′ 到如°此°地步; *a* —, *or country*, koh′-kô 國家°; *the state of ditto*, ky′i′-ziang 氣象; *in a declining* —, ky′i′-ziang sæ′-de 氣象衰了°; *to live in great* —, shæ-wô′ ko kwông-ing′ 奢華過光陰

STATE, *to* kao′-su 告訴; t′ong-cü 通知; — *particulars*, dziang-si′ kông′-c′ih-læ 詳細講出來; — *grievances*, su ün′ 訴冤; — (*to an inferior*), ping′-cü 禀知; ping′-ming 禀明

STATELY (*as a person*), kw′e-we′ 傀偉; — (*as an official*), we-nyin′-go 威嚴个°

STATEMENTS *vary according to circumstances*, shih-wô cih′-læ biu-ky′i′ 說話嬰來辯去°

STATESMAN, *high officer*, da-dzing′ 大臣; do-kwun′ 大°官; *styled*, da-jiu′ 大人

STATION *in life*, sing-veng′ 身分°; sing-kô′ 身家°; *official* —, we-ts′ 位子; *high* —, we-ts′ kao′ 位子高; *military* — (*place*), ying-sing′ 營汛; siu′-di 汛地

STATISTICAL *account* (of money), ts′ing-tæn′ 清單; (*of persons*), ts′ing-ts′ah′ 清册; *statistics of*

STATUE, *image*, ngeo′-ziang 偶像; *stone image*, zah-deo-′go ngeo′-ziang 石°頭个°偶像; zah′ dzing-siang 石°丞相

STATUETTE, ′en′ 孩°; *soap-stone* —, væn-zah ′en′ 礬石°孩°; *jade* —, nyüoh ′en′ 玉孩°

STATURE, sing-dzæ′ 身材; *of great* —, sing-dzæ′ dziang-do′ 身材長大°; *of small* —, sing-dzæ′ a′-siao 身材矮小

STATUTE, *a* ih-diao lih-fah′ 一條律法

STAY, *to* deng 停°; — *here*, deng′-tong 停°在°此°; — *a while*, deng′ ih-zông 停°一息°; — *a long time*, deng′-leh dziang-kyiu′-de 停°得°長久了°

STEADFAST, kyin-kwu′ 堅固

STEADY, djong′-jih 重實; weng′-djong 穩重

STEAK, *meat for frying, &c.*, t′ah-go nyüoh′ 爛个°肉°; *the best beef* — *is called* pah′-z-kweh-li-go nyüoh′ 八字骨裡个°肉°, sæn-koh-lông′, *and* ô-bang-kweh-yin′.

STEAL, *to* t′eo 偷; *to* — *time from one′s proper duties*, t′eo-kong bah′-fu 偷工夫; *will not* —, siu′-kyiah′ weng′-djong 手脚穩重

STEALTHILY, t′eo-bun′ 偷瞞; en′-di-li 暗地裡

STEAM, shü′-go ky′i 水°个°氣

STEAM, *to* tsing 蒸; tsing-hen' 蒸
熯;— (over something else that
is cooking), hen 熯; — *rice,*
tsing væn' 蒸飯

STEAM-BOAT, ho-leng-jün' 火輪
船 (ih-tsah)

STEAM-CAR, ho-leng-ts'ô' 火輪車
(ih-dzing)

STEEL, kông 鋼; — (for striking
fire), ho'-tao 火刀; ho'-p'in 火片

STEELYARDS, ts'ing 秤; *small* —
(for silver, and medicines), teng'-
ts 戥子; *very small* —, li teng'
厘戥

STEEP, shing 峋; toh 督 or song-
dzih 聳°直°; *precipitous,* ts'iao-
pih 峭壁 (veng.)

STEEP, *to* — *in water,* tsing' læ
shü'-li 浸在°水°裡; — *in hot
water,* p'ao' læ shü'-li 泡在°水°
裡
　　This signification of p'ao is peculiar to Ningpo.

STEER, *to* pô do' 把舵; pô sao'
把艄

STEM, *a* ih-kwang' 一梗°

STEP, *a* ih-bu' 一步; *to take a* —,
tseo' ih-bu' 走一步; — *quickly*
(as when in an official's presence),
tseo ts'iang'-bu 走蹌步; *keep*
—, kyiah'-bu tseo'-leh tsæn'-zi
脚步走得°整°齊; — *by* —,
bu-tang'-bu 步打步; *long* —,
do bu' 大°步

STEP, *to* ky'i-bu' 起步; — *over,*
bæn-zông' 蹖上; bæn-ko' 蹖

過; — *down,* bæn-loh'-ky'i 蹖
下去°; tseo'-loh 走下°; *be
careful in stepping in, and out,*
(as of a boat), bæn-zông' bæn-
loh' tseo-leh hao' 蹖上蹖下°
走得°好; *can't* — (as an old
person), bæn-feh-dong' 蹖弗動

STEPS, *short* si' bu 細步; *a woman's steps are short,* nyü'-nying-
go kyiah'-bu siao' 女人°个°
脚步小; *stone* — (long flight),
pah'-bu-kæn 百°步階°; *ditto*
(four or five), kah'-bu-kæn 隔
步階°; — *at the water's edge,*
'o-bu'-deo 河埠頭

STEP-MOTHER, in' ah-nyiang' 寄°
阿娘; politely called, 'eo'-meo
後母; dzoh-meo' 續母; mæn'-
nyiang 晚°娘 (coarse).

STEP-FATHER, nyi-vu' 義父;
mæn'-tia 晚°爹

STEREOSCOPE, si-yiang-kying' 西
洋景

STERILE *land,* hwông-di' 荒地;
di-t'u boh' 地土薄

STERN *of a ship,* 'eo'-sao 後艄

STERN, nyin-nyin'-go 嚴嚴个°;
we-nyin' 威嚴; hyüong-sah'-
sah 兇煞煞

STEW, *to* teng燉; u 焗; — *meat,*
teng nyüoh' 燉肉°

STEWARD (of money, food, &c),
pô-tsong'-go 把總个°

STICK, *a* ih-keng bông'一根棒;
*a bit of board,* ih-tin pæn-den' 一
點板頭°; ih-tin pæn'-pin-bi'

一點板邊皮; *a large round —,*
ih-keng kweng'-ts 一 根 棍 子
STICK, *to — in,* ts'ah'-tsing 插進;
*ditto,* (as staves in a tub, a padlock in its place, &c.), siao-tsing'
銷 進;— *a candle* (in its place),
ts'ah lah-coh' 插 蠟 燭; *to —*
*with paste,* (or as a plaster), t'iah
貼°; nyin 粘;— *together,* nyin-
long' 粘 攏;—(it) *tight,* t'iah'-
leh-lao' 貼 得° 牢; nyin'-leh-
lao' 粘 得° 牢; *sticks to his own*
*way,* kyü-nyi' feh-t'ong' 拘 泥 弗
通; *in the wrong, but sticking to*
*it,* ky'iang'-bin 強 辯
STICKLAC, ts'-keng 紫 梗
STICKY, nyin 粘; nyin-kao'-kao
粘 膠° 膠°; nyin-cü'-keh-tah,
(also applied to persons).
STIFF, ngang 硬;— (in opinion),
zah-ngang' 石° 硬; gyiang 強;
sang-gyiang' 生° 強
STIFF-NECKED, gyiang-deo'-gyüih
nao' 強 頭 個 膓
STIFLING, meng-ky'i' 悶 氣
STIGMATIZED, ming-sing' u-wæ'-
diao-de 名 聲 污 壞 了°; p'ing-
'ang tsao-tsih'-de 品 行° 遭 迹 了°
STILL, *no sound,* soh'-zing 肅 靜°;
pih'-zing 謐 靜°; 無-sing-hyiang'
無° 聲 響; zing'-ts'iao-ts'iao
靜° 悄 悄; *not moving,* feh-dong'
弗 動; *sit —,* zo-leh ding' 坐
得° 定; *the wind and waves are*
—, bing-fong' zing'-lông 平 風
靜° 浪

STILL, *yet,* wa; yia 也°; yi 又°;
wæn 還;— *as before,* dzing-
gyiu' z-ka' 仍 舊 如° 此°;—
*more,* 'o-hwông' 何 況;— (used
with the comparative), yü'-kô
愈 加°; keng'-kô 更 加°; yüih-
fah' 越 發;— *better,* yü-kô' hao
愈 加° 好
STIMULATE, *to urge,* ts'e 催; ts'e-
ts'oh' 催 促; *to encourage,* min'-li
勉 勵
STIMULATED *to effort,* (by seeing
another better than ourselves, or
by our own dispraise), tsang' ih-
k'eo' ky'i' 爭° 一 口 氣
STIMULATING *to strength,* dzu-lih'-
go 助 力 个°
STING, *to* ting 叮
STING *of a bee,* wông-fong-ts'' 黃
蜂 刺; *the place stung* (swollen),
ting'- go tsing' 叮 个° 痕° 迹°;
*ditto* (red but not swollen), pæn 斑
STINGY, kyü-seh'-seh 鬼° 嗇 嗇;
lin'-kyin 歛 簡; gyih-li'-li 竭 厲
厲; 'eo-teo'-teo 猴 抖 抖; pi'-
si 鄙 細; pi'-nying 鄙 吝; pi'-
seh 鄙 嗇; nying'-seh 吝 嗇;
k'æn-kyiang' 鉛 僵
STINKING, ts'iu 臭°; zeh-ts'iu'
雜 臭°
STINT, *to* k'æn'-k'ah-loh 苛° 刻°;
*to — rations,* ky'üih'-kæn kyüing-
liang' 缺 減° 軍 糧
STIPULATIONS, iah'-hao-liao-go
tsông-dzing' 約 好 了° 个° 章
程 (tsông or công)

STIR, *to move*, dong 動; — *up by talking*, ts'ön-teh' 攛掇; — *up (as something forgotten)*, t'iao-peh' 挑撥; *to agitate*, yiao-'oh' 謠惑; — *and render turbid*, dao-weng' 搯混; *the wind stirs the leaves*, fong dong' jü'-yih 風動樹葉; *to* — *(as food)*, liu-lin' 摟摟; diao-long' 調攏; kao-kao' 攪攪; diao-diao' 調調; *one who stirs up trouble*, liu-ho'-coh-bông' 㑪摟火竹棒个° 人°

STIR, *great* nao-nyih' fi-væn' 鬧熱° 非凡

STIRRING, *is anything* — *(i. e. in a town, &c.)*? yiu soh'-go kyü-dong' feh 有甚°麼°舉動否°?

STIRRUP, mô'-dah-teng 馬踏鐙 (ih-tsah; *a pair*, ih-fu)

STITCH, tsing-kyiah' 針脚; sin'-kyiah 線脚 (ih-go); *take a* —, ting' ih-tsing 釘一針; *take small stitches*, tsing-kyiah' iao si' 針脚要細; *grinning stitches*, sin'-kyiah li-ngô'-bô'-ts' 線脚齜牙°齜齒

STITCH, *to sew*, vong 縫; *to back-* — *(like machine work)*, keo 勾; ts'ih 緝; — *finer*, vong-leh si'-tin 縫得°細點; — *together*, keo-long' 勾攏; — *(by over-handing)*, nyiao-long'; — *a book together*, ting shü' 釘書

STOCK *in trade*, peng'-din 本錢°; *to take account of* —, bun ts'ing-

tsiang' 盤清賬; *gun* —, ts'iang ken'-ts 鎗杆子

STOCK-FISH, ts'-ng 紫魚°

STOCKINGS, mah 襪 (*a pair*, ih-sông)

STOCKS *for the feet*, kyiah'-kô 脚柳

STOMACH, we 胃; we-un' 胃腕; bi-we' 脾胃; zih-pao' 食包; *pit of the* —, sing-o-den' 心窩° 潭°; hyüong-o-den' 胸窩°潭°; *pain in the* —, we t'ong' 胃痛; — *(or belly) ache*, dü'-bi t'ong 肚皮痛

STONE, zah-deo' 石頭 (*a piece*, ih-kw'e); *a flat* —, zah-pæn' 石版; *small* — zah-ts' 石子; *precious* —, pao'-zah 寶石°; — *(of fruit)*, weh 核°

STONE, *to* — *a person*, yüong zah-deo' k'ang nying' 用石°頭丟人°

STONE-CUTTER, zah-s-vu' 石°司務; zah-ziang 石°匠

STONE-SHOP, zah-tsoh'-tin 石°作店

STONE-QUARRY, zah-dông' 石°宕°

STOOL, *long wooden* —, pæn'-teng 板櫈; *bamboo* —, coh' fông-teng 竹方櫈; *foot* —, dah-kyiah'-teng' 踏脚櫈; *drum shaped stone or porcelain* —, zah-kwu' 石°鼓; — *(for night use)*, yia-dong 夜°桶; mô'-dong 馬桶; *ditto for travelling*, sæn′-dong 杉桶; *ditto*, (a box), yia-dong′-siang 夜°桶箱; *to go to —*, c‘ih-kong′ 出恭; ka-siu′ 解手; *evacuation*, do-bin′ 大°便; do-ka′ 大°解°

STOOP, *to* eo 傴°; — *the head*, eo deo′ 傴°頭; — *down*, eo-tæn′-tao 傴°倒; — *in walking*, eo deo tseo′ 傴°頭走

STOP, *to hinder*, lah-djü′ 攔住; tsu′-djü 阻住; ts′-djü 止住; — *in walking*, lih-loh′ 立住°; — *a minute*, lih′-ih-lih′ 立一立; — *talking*, hyih k‘eo′ 住°口; — *by filling up* (as a hole), seh′-mnn 塞滿; din-mun′ 填滿; — (as a window), cü′-sah; ts′-sah; — *up the way*, læn lu′ 攔路; *will soon —*, ih-zông′ ziu hyih′-go 一息°就歇个°; — *doing*, hyih-siu′ 歇手; — *over night*, hyih′-ko yia′ 歇過夜°; *can't —* (it, or him), ts′-feh-djü′ 止弗住

STOPPED, hyih′-loh-de 歇落了°; — *talking*, kông′ hyih-de 講°歇了°; *clock has —*, cong′ ve tseo′-de 鐘不°會°走了°; cong si′-de 鐘死了°; cong ngæ′-de 鐘呆了°; cong′ ve cün′-de 鐘不°會°轉丁°; cong hyih′-de 鐘歇了°; cong deng′-de 鐘停了°

STOPPING, *where are you —?* ng tæn-koh′ ah-li′ 你°就攔何°處°? — *place*, hyih′-loh-go di-

fông′ 歇落个°地方; deng-loh′-go di-fông 停°落个°地方

STOPS (in punctuation), tin′-dön 點斷; *ditto* (in Chinese), ky‘ün-tin′ 圈點

STORE, ‘ông 行; tin 店 (or 鋪); — *for foreign goods*, yiang-ho′-‘ông 洋貨行; kwông′-ho-tin 廣貨店; *book —*, shü-fông′ 書坊 (ih-bæn)

STORE, *to — away*, k‘ông′-loh 囷落; deng-tsih′ 囤積; dzeng-tsih′ 存積; — *up* (by constant addition), tsih′-loh 積落; tsih′-jü 積聚; tsih′-hyüoh 積蓄

STORE-HOUSE, dzæn′-vông 棧房; *tea —*, dzô-dzæn′ 茶棧; — *for grain*, ts‘ông 倉

STORK, ngôh 鶴; *sacred —*, sin-ngôh′ 仙鶴 (ih-tsah)

STORM, do-fong′-do-yü′ 大°風大°雨; *sudden —*, (black sky), u-fong′-mang-pao′ 烏風猛颮; — *of wind*, gwông-fong′ 狂風; bao′-fong 暴風

STORY, *one — house*, bing oh′ 平屋; bing-vông′ 平房; *two — house*, leo-oh′ 樓屋; *three — house*, sæn-zeng′-leo 三層樓

STORY, kwu′-z 故事; *tell you a —*, kông ih-yiang kwu′-z peh ng t‘ing′ 講°一樣故事俾°你°聽; *ditto — of olden times*, kông kwu′-tin 講°古典; *tell* (or *quote*) *a — in illustration*, ying ih′-go kwu′-z 引一个°故事

STOUT, *fat,* công'-do 壯大°; *of
— arm,* siu'-gying do' 手勁大°
STOVE, ho'-lu 火爐; t'ih'-lu 鐵
爐; *cooking —,* t'ih'-tsao 鐵竈
STOW, *to — away,* tsông 裝; dzông
藏; k'ông 囥; *— goods,* tsông
ho' 裝貨; *— away in the mind*
(also not to tell), dzông' læ du'-
bi-li 藏在肚皮裡
STRADDLE, *to* pa zo-mô'-shü 擺
坐馬勢
STRAGGLER, 'æn-nying' 閒人°
STRAGGLING *in one after another,*
ts'iu-ts'in' læ 鞦韆來; *— behind,* loh 'eo' 落後
STRAIGHT, dzih 直; pih'-dzih 筆
直; pih'-lih-dzih 筆立直;
kweh'-dzih 骨直; *go — ahead,*
ih-dzih'-bah-deo 對°鼻°頭一
直去°
STRAIGHTEN, *to — it,* long gyi
dzih' 弄其直
STRAIGHT-FORWARD, sing'dzih'-
go 心直个°;* — (in action),
li'-dzih-ky'i-công' 理直氣壯
(công or tsông); *— in speaking,*
dzong dzih' kông' 從直講°;
tsiao' dzih kông' 照直講°; *—
talk,* dzih wô' 直話; tsiao' yin-
dzih dæn' 照言直談
    * Observe that dzih-sing'-go 直心
    个° has not this sense, but the bad
    sense of blunt, or abrupt.
STRAIN, *to —* (as milk, &c.), li 濾;
*to over-exert one's strength,* lih'
yüong ko-deo' 力用過頭; *to*

*exert to the utmost,* nu'-lih 努力;
'eo-ky'i-lih 候氣力
STRAIN, *the — is too great,* (i. e.
pulled too tightly, as cloth, &c.),
te'-leh t'eh kyih' 㧁得太°急;
*ditto* (as in mental effort), kong-
k'o' bih'-leh t'eh kying' 功課
逼°得太°緊
STRAITENED, *in — circumstances,*
kying'-hwông kyih'-pah 景况
急廹
STRAND, *a* ih-kwu' sang 一股
生°; *a single —,* doh-kwu'-deo
獨股頭; *three strands,* sæn-
kwu'-sang 三股生°
STRANGE, hyi-gyi' 希奇; gyi-
kwa' 奇怪°; kwu'-kwa 古怪°;
hao gyi-kwa' 好奇怪°; *not
at all —,* kwa'-feh-teh 怪弗
得; *not according to the common
way,* yi'-yiang 異樣
STRANGER, *unacquainted person,*
sang-deo' nying 生°人°; sang-
su'-go nying 生°疏个°人°;
*— whose home is in another place,*
yi'-hyiang nying 異鄉人°;
gyiao-yüа' nying 隔°縣人°
STRANGLE, *to* ts'eh'-sah 拼殺;
leh-sah' 勒殺; *—* (as a punishment), kao'-sah 絞°殺
STRAP, *leather* bi-ta' 皮帶°; *Chinese barber's —,* kwah'-tao-pu
刮刀布
STRATAGEM, tsô'-kyi 詐計; kyi-
mco' 計謀; kyi'-kao 計較
STRAW, ts'ao 草; *rice —,* dao'-

ts'ao 稻草; *wheat —*, mah-ken' 麥稈; *new —*, sing ts'ao' 新草; *old —*, dzing ts'ao' 陳草; *— braid*, ts'ao'-mao bin 草帽辮; *— tied together for a mattress*, ts'ao'-tsin 草氈

STRAWBERRY, *tree—*, or *arbutus*, yiang-me' 楊梅 (ih-go)

STRAW-COLORED, dæn'-wông 淡黃

STRAY, *to deviate from the right*, tseo ts'o' lu 走差路; *to lose the way and become bewildered*, mi-lu' 迷路; *— lamb*, mi-lu'-go yiang 迷路个°羊

STREAKED, yiu hwô-veng' 有花紋

STREAKY, hwô-kying'-da 花輕埭; hwô-yüing'-da 花雲埭

STREAM *of water*, ih-liu shü' 一溜水°; *rivulet*, ky'i-k'ang' 溪坑; *mountain —*, sæn-loh-shü' 山落水° (ih-da)

STREET, ka 街; lu-ka' 路街°; ka-lu' 街°路; ka-dao' 街°道; (ih-da); *great —*, do ka' 大街°; *narrow —*, long 衖 (ih-diao)

STRENGTH, lih 力; ky'i'-lih 氣力; lih-dao' 力道; gying-dao' 勁道; *— (used principally of medicines)*, sing'-dao 性道; sing 性; *to do according to one's —*, liang'-lih-r-ying 量力而行; *with all one's heart, and —*, dzing-sing' gyih-lih' 盡心竭力; *united —*, dong-sing' yiah'-lih' 同心協力; *no —*, 㿺 ky'i'-lih 無°氣力; 㿺 gying'-dao 無°勁道; *no — to do*, vu-lih'-neng-we' 無力能為; *(person's) — exhausted*, ky'i'-lih dziah-wun'-de 氣力用°完了°; *its — is gone*, sing'-dao ko'-de 性道過了°; *no —*, (used either of body or mind), nyün'-bi-bi 軟疲疲; pih'-hyi-hyi 胹希希; *but little —*, lih boh' 力薄; lih feb-tsoh' 力弗足

STRENGTHEN, *to —him*, kô-zông' gyi-go lih' 加上其个°力; dzu' gyi'-go lih' 助其个°力; pông' gyi-go lih' 幫其个°力; *— it*, dzu'-ih-dzu lih' 助一助力; *— one's faith*, kyin-kwa' gyi siang-sing'-go sing' 堅固其相信个°心; *— (as by a tonic)*, pu lih' 補力

STRENGTHENING (as food, or medicine), pu-lih-dao'-go 補力道个°; pu-hyüih'-ky'i-go 補血氣个°; pu-tsing-jing'-go 補精神个°

STRENUOUS, *to make — effort*, sah'-k'eo c'ih-lih' 煞口出力; 'eo ky'i'-lih 候氣力

STRESS, *to lay — upon*, djong-k'en' 重看; *lay — on that sentence*, keb kyü shih-wô' iao djong-k'en' 這°句說話要重看

STRETCH, *to* te'-k'æ-læ 捱開來; la-k'æ'-læ; *— out*, sing-dziang' 伸長; *to — out the hand*, sing sin′ 伸手; *can't — it*, te′-feh-k′æ 刨弗開; ĺa-feh-k′æ′; — *a bow*, ĺa kong′ 拉弓; pæn kong′ 扳°弓

STRICT, nyin 嚴; nyin-kying′ 嚴禁; *too —*, t′eh nyin′ 太°嚴; kwe′-kyü tso ko-deo′ 規矩甚°嚴°; *the — teacher turns out good scholars*, nyin-s′ c′ih kao-du′ 嚴師出高徒; *not — enough*, iah′-soh peh-nyin′ 約束不嚴

STRIFE *of words*, k′eo′-kyüoh siang-tsang′ 口角相爭°; *ditto with abuse*, zao-nyih-oh-cü; *at —*, kæ′-tih siang-tsang′ 正°在°相爭°

STRIKE, *n.* (because of a stern master, &c.), sæn-dông′ 散堂

STRIKE, *to* k′ao 敲°; tang 打; *— a blow*, k′ao′-ih-kyi′ 敲°一記; tang ih-kyi′ 打一記; *— against*, bang-djoh′撞着′; djông-djoh′ 撞着°; *— fire*, k′æ ho′ 開火; tang ho′ 打火; *the clock strikes*, cong′ læ-tih k′ao′ 鐘正°在°敲°; *— dead by lightning*, le tang′-sah 雷打殺; le kyih′ 雷趷

STRING, zing 繩° (ih-keng); *cash —*, dzin-c′ün′ zing 錢串繩°; *a — of cash*, ih-c′ün′ dong-din′ 一串銅錢°; *a — of fire crackers*, ih-c′ün′ pah′-ts-p′ao 一串百°子爆

STRING, *to* c′ün 穿; *— porcelain beads*, c′ün ngô′-cü 穿瓦°珠

STRIP, *a — of paper*, ih-da ts′ 一埭紙; ih-diao ts′ 一絛紙; *cover with a —*, kæ′ ih-zeng zông′ 蓋一層°上

STRIP, *to — off clothing*, t′eh i-zông′ 脫衣裳°; *to — another*, poh′ nying-kô′ i-zông′ 剝人°衣裳°; *— off bark*, poh bi′ 剝皮; *to — off a garment and pawn it, in order to gamble*, poh′ bi tu′ 剝皮賭; *— naked*, i-zông′ poh′-kwông 衣裳°剝光; poh′-leh kying′-kwông 剝得°精光

STRIPE, dzih-veng′ 直紋 (ih-da)

STRIPED *cloth*, (of one color), liu′-diao pu′ 柳絛布; *ditto* (in colors), hwô-dzih′-veng pu′ 花直紋布

STRIPES, *beat with many —*, tang hyü′-to pæn′-su 打許多板數 tang hyü′-to kyi′-su 打許多記數

STRIVE, *to* tsang 爭°; *— with*, siang-tsang′ 相爭°; te′-toh 對敵°; *— to get ahead of*, pih gying′ 逼勁; *— to be first*, tsang zông-zin′ 爭上前°; *— for a prize*, ts′iang sông′ 搶賞; *— for the goal*, ts′iang′ piao-deo′ 搶標頭; *— to enter in*, zing′-lih ts′ang′-tsing 盡°力撐進

STROKE, *n.* kwah 摑; *give a —*, kwah′ ih-kwah 摑一摑; *pen —*, pih′ wah 筆畫; *how many strokes?* kyi pih′ 幾筆?

STROKE, *to* lo 攞; lo′-kwah 攞

刮; — *with the hair*, or *the right way*, jing'-mao lo' 順毛擺;— *the wrong way*, tao' ts'iah lo 倒散擺

STRONG, yiu gying-dao' 有勁道; yiu lih' 有 力; yiu ky'i'-lih 有氣力; yiu vu'-nyih-ts 有武蓺子; — *flavor*, mi-dao' pô'-lah 味道濃°辣;—(as tobacco, or wine), ts'iang 鎗; hyüong 兇; — (as tea), nyüong 濃; ts'ih 赤; kw'u 苦; — *and firm*, lao-k'ao' 牢靠; kyih'-jih 結實; tsah'-cü; — *breeze*, mang' fong 猛°風; — *bodied*, (said of a young person), tsông'gyiu 壯健 (tsông or công).

STRUGGLE, *to make violent efforts*, weh-djông'-weh-tin' 活蹚活蹚

STRUT, *to* tseo'-leh do-mo' do-yiang' 走得°大°模大°樣

STUBBLE, keng-cü' 根株; *rice* —, dao' keng-cü' 稻根株

STUBBORN, tsih'-ih 執 —; ih-tsông'-kying-k'ah'-sah-liao 一掌經搭煞 了; kyiao-djü-kwu'-seh, or tiao-djü'-kwu'-seh 膠柱鼓瑟; *stupid and* —, nyü-cih' 愚拙

STUDENT, *pupil*, 'oh-sang'-ts 學°生°子; *one devoted to books*, doh-shü-nying' 讀書人°; *fellow* —, dong-bun' doh-shü 同伴讀書

STUDIOUS, gying doh'-shü-go 勤讀書个°

STUDY, *book-room*, shü-vông' 書房 (ih-kwun)

STUDY, *to* doh-shü' 讀書; yüong-kong' 用功; — *silently*, meh-nyiæn' 默 念°; — *deeply*, ts'in'-s-væn'-siang 千思萬想;— *and yield to his disposition*, coh gyi-go sing'-kah 琢其个°性格; — *it out*, du-bi koh'-loh-den zing-zing'-k'en' 肚皮角°落頭°尋°尋°看

STUFF, *materials*, liao-tsoh' 料作; dzæ-liao' 材 料; *household* —, kô-ho' 家°伙; kô-sang'-jih-veh' 家°伙°什物

STUFF, *to* tsi 齒; seh 屬; — *full*, seh'-leh pao' 屬得°飽

STUMBLE, *to* pæn-kyiah' 扳脚 — *and fall*, pæn-tih' 扳跌

STUMP *of a tree*, jü keng' 樹根; (ih gyüih)

STUNNED *by the blow*, k'ao'-leh u-yüing'-en-tao' 敲°得°昏暈; *ears* — (by noise), ng-to si-long'-de 耳°朵震°聾了°;— (by a blow), kwah'-long-de 摑聾了°

STUNT, *to* — *trees by twisting*, bun jü' 盤樹

STUNTED *trees*, a'-siao-go jü 矮小个°樹

STUPEFIED, jing-z'-feh-cü' 人事弗知; hweng-ky'i'-de 昏去°了°

STUPID, beng 笨; nyü-beng' 愚笨; nyü-c'ing' 愚蠢; moh-do'-jün 木舵船; moh-moh' 木木; ngæ-ts'i'-ts'i 呆痴; ngæ-teng'-teng 呆等等; — *from*

*fright*, moh-ding′ k‘eo′-ngæ 目
定°口呆;—(as when one does a
foolish thing; *lit.* seven out of the
nine souls dead), ts‘ih′ deo-weng
si′ 七魂°巴°死°; *very* —, (all
the cavities stopped), ih-ky‘iao′
feh-t′ong′ 一竅弗通

STUTTER, *to* shih′-wô keh′-feh-
c‘ih 說話格弗出

STUTTERER, keh′-zih-deo-go, or
keh′-zih-den-go 格舌頭个°

STY (on the eye), t‘eo-tsing′ 偷針
眼°; *to have a* —, sang t‘eo-tsing′
生°偷針眼°

STY, *pig* cü-gyin′ 豬楗

STYLE *of composition*, veng-fah′ 文
法; veng-li′ 文理; *bad* —,
veng-li′ feh-hao′ 文理弗好;
*strong*—, pih′-ky‘i lao 筆氣老;
*flowing* —, veng-ky‘i′ jing′ 文
氣順; *abstruse* —, veng-li′
sing-ao′ 文理深奧; *modern*
—, z-dao′ yiang′-shih 時道樣
式°; *modern* — (of writing), z-
veng′ 時文; *ancient* —, kwn′-
lao yiang′-shih 古老樣式°;
*ancient* — (of writing), kwu′-veng
古文; (done) *in good* —, teh-
fah′ 得法; teh-ky‘iao′-meng 得
竅門

STYLE, *to* ts‘ing′-hwu′ 稱呼; co
呌°; *the Tao-ti is Styled Da-jing*,
Dao′-dæ ts‘ing′-hwu Da-jing′ 道
臺稱呼大人

SUAVITY, mun′-min c‘ing-fong′ 滿
面春風

SUBDIVIDE, *to* feng-ko′ yi-feng′
分過义°分

SUBDUE, *to*—(as a country), tsing-
voh′ 征服; tsin′-voh 戰服;
— (as a person, or animal), cü′-
voh 制服; siu-voh′ 收服; —
*by force*, ah′-voh′ 壓°服

SUBJECT *to him*, læ-gyi′ sin′-‘ô 在°
其手下°; voh-gyi′ kæ-kwun′ 服
其該管;— *to illness*, bing′ ta′-
leh tseo′ 有°病纏°身°; — *to
Great Britain*, joh′-ü Da-Ing′-koh
屬於大英國

SUBJECT, *theme*, di-moh′ 題目

SUBJECT, *to* — *him to suffering*,
peh′ gyi ziu kw‘u′ 俾°其受
苦

SUBJECTION, *cannot bring into* —,
ah′-feh-voh′ 壓°弗服; *in good*
—, sing′-voh′-go 心服个°;
*brought into* —, sing tsih′-voh-
go 心折服个°

SUBJUGATE, *to* tsing-voh′ 征服

SUBLIME, kao-do′ 高大°; — *idea*,
ting′-kao i′-s 頂高意思

SUBMERGE, *to plunge under water*,
tsing′-loh shü′-li 浸在水°裏;
*to sink*, dzing-loh′ 沉落

SUBMISSIVE *to God's will*, ken-
sing′ t‘ing Jing-ming′-go ts‘-i 甘
心聽神明个°旨意; —(to
*authority*), voh-cü′ 心°服; voh-
lah 服力°

SUBMIT, *to* voh 服; kwe-voh′ 歸
服; deo-voh′ 投服; — *willingly*,
dzing-nyün′ voh′-go 情願服

个°;— *to injury,* k'eng ky'üoh kw'e' 肯 吃° 虧

SUBSCRIBE, *to write one's name,* loh ming-z' 錄 名 字；— *money,* sia kyün' 寫° 捐；*how much did he* —*?* gyi' sia to-siao' kyün' 其 寫° 多 少 捐? gyi' kyün-kw'un' to-siao' 其 捐 款 多 少?

SUBSCRIBERS, loh-ming-z-go nying 錄 名 字 个° 人°；*a poster containing names of* — *to charity, &c.,* piao-'ong' 標° 紅

SUBSCRIPTION (*of money*), kyün-'ông' 捐 項；kyün-kw'un' 捐 款；— *paper,* kyün-tæn' 捐 單

SUBSEQUENT, 'eo'-deo 後 頭；— *age,* 'eo' shü 後 世

SUBSIDE, *to* t'e'-loh-ky'i 退 下° 去°；'ô'-loh-ky'i 下° 去°；bing-loh'-ky'i 平 下° 去°；*wait till his anger* —, teng'-tao gyi'-go nu' t'e'-loh-ky'i 等 到 其 个° 怒 退 落 去°

SUBSIST *day by day,* djoh nyih' tso nying 逐 日° 做 人°；*they* — *on rice,* væn, z gyi-lah' yiang' ming' go 飯 是 伊° 等° 養 命 个°

SUBSISTENCE, *means of* yiang'-seng-ts veh' 養 生° 之 物；du-nyih'-ts liang' 度 日° 之 糧；*to make a* —, wu k'eo' 餬 口；wu cü'-pô 餬 嘴 吧；du-weh' 度 活；du-nyih' 度 日°

SUBSTANCE, tsih 質；peng'-tsih 本 質；ti'-ts 底 子；ying 形；*as the shadow follows the* —, jü

ing', ze ying' 如 影 隨 形；*a man of* —, yiu kô-dzæ'-go 有 家° 財 个°

SUBSTANTIAL, 'eo'-jih 厚 實；*firm,* lao-k'ao' 牢 靠；tsah'-cü.

SUBSTITUTE *for a teacher,* gyün' sin'-sang 權 館° 先 生°；— *for a servant, or workman,* t'i'-kong 替 工；*one who dies as a* —, t'i-si'-go 替 死° 个°

SUBSTITUTE, *to* gyün 權；diao 調；wun 換；— *another pen for that,* keh'-ts pih gyün'-ih-gyün' 這 枝 筆 權 一 權；diao' ih-ts' pih' 調 一 枝 筆；wun' ih-ts' pih' 換 一 枝 筆

SUBTERFUGE, *to resort to a* —, kô'-t'oh 假°托；*to use something true, but not the real cause as a* —, tsia'-ing 借° 因

SUBTERRANEAN, di-'ô'-go 地 下° 个°；di ti'-'ô-go 地 底 下° 个°

SUBTILE, *delicate and fine,* tsing-si' 精 細°

SUBTLE, *cunning,* diao-bi' 刁° 疲°；diao-wæn' 刁° 頑°

SUBTRACT, *to* djü - loh' 除 下°；djü-c'ih' 除 出；kæn'-loh 減° 落

SUBTRACTION, djü-fah' 除 法

SUBURB, dzing-meng-'ô 城 門 下°；*the Eastern* —, Tong-meng-nga' 東 門 外°

SUBVERT, *to* fæn'-tao 翻 倒；*he subverts my authority,* ngô'-go gyün-ping' tao'-fæn gyi siu'-li' 我 个° 權 柄 倒 翻 其 手 裡

SUCCEED, to — in doing, tso' tao siu' 做到手; tso' dzing-kong' 做成功; to prosper, jing'-liu 順溜; — (by getting hold of the right way), teh-fah' 得法; teh ky'iao'-meng 得竅門; does not — (i. e. is not according to my mind), feh ts'ing' ngô-go sing 弗稱我个心; feh jing'-liu 弗順溜; — in every thing, pah'-z-heng-t'ong 百事亨通; deo-deo'-jing'-liu 頭頭順溜; he who is in earnest will —, yiu' ts kying dzing' 有志竟成

SUCCEED, to follow after, tsih 接; to take the place of, dæ tso' 代做; who will — me! jü' we teng ngô dæ-tso' 誰會與我代做! — to the throne, tsih-we' 接位; teng-we' 登位

SUCCESSFUL, jing-tông' 順當; jing-kying' 順境; always —, ih-lu'-jing-fong 一路順風; in obtaining one's desire, ts'ing'-sing-jü-i' 稱心如意; jü-sing' 如心; this is a — year (in trade, or literary examinations), keh' nyin da-fah'-go 這年大發个; who is the — candidate, (i.e. who enjoys the happiness)? keh'-go foh' jü hyiang'-de 這个福誰享了!

SUCCEEDING, the — days, tsih'-lin-go nyih-ts' 接連个日子

SUCCESSION, in —, or in order, a-ts'-jü 挨次序; tsiao ts'-jü 照次序; i ts''-jü 依次序; in — (each taking his turn, as the spokes of a wheel), leng-liu' 輪流; ling 輪; enter in —, yü-kwun'-r-jih' 魚貫而入; ngao' mi'-pô tsing-læ' 皎尾巴進來

SUCCESSIVE years, lih nyin' 歷年; four — years of famine, lih-nyin' s'-go hwông nyin' 歷年四个荒年; four — days, deh-lin' s' nyih 疊連四日

SUCCINCT, kyin'-kyih 簡潔

SUCCOR, to help, pông-dzu' 幫助; pông-ts'eng' 幫襯; — the poor, tsiu-tsi' nying 睭濟人; k'en'-kwu gyüong-nying 看顧窮人

SUCCUMB, to deo-voh' 投服

SUCH, keh'-cü-ka or keh'-cong-ka 這種樣; keh'-sing-ka 這些樣; z-ka' 是如此; — as he, ziang gyi' nying' ka 像其人一樣个

SUCK, to cih 啜; — (as wind), hwun 唤; — milk, cih na' 啜嬭; ky'üoh na' 吃嬭

SUCKLE him, ü' gyi na-na' 餵其嬭嬭; peh' gyi ky'üoh ñæ'-næ 給其吃嬭嬭

SUDDENLY, hweh'-r-jün 忽然; deh-jün' 突然; p'ih'-min 劈面; p'ih'-deo 劈頭; p'ih'-k'ong 劈空

SUE, to kao-zông' 告狀; to prosecute (on both sides), tang-kwun-s′ 打官司; ky′üoh kwun s′ 吃官司

SUET, *beef* ngeo-yiu′ 牛°油; *mutton* —, yiang-yiu′ 羊油

SUFFER, *to* ziu næn′ 受難; ziu kw′u′ 受苦; — *great pain,* ziu kw′u′-t′ong 受苦痛; — *injury,* ziu ′æ′ 受害; ky′üoh kw′e′ 吃°虧; — *hunger,* t′eng-kyi′-ziu-ngo 吞饑受餓; — *persecution,* ziu pih′-næn 受逼難

SUFFER, *to let,* peh 任°; — *him to talk,* peh gyi kông′ 任°其講°

SUFFICIENT, keo′-de 够了°; tsoh′-de 足了°

SUFFOCATE, *to* ih′-sah 噎煞; ih′-ky′i-feh-cün′ 噎氣弗轉; *I was nearly suffocated,* ngô ts′ô′-feh-to ih′-sah-de 我差弗多噎煞了°; ngô ih′-sah kw′a′-de 我噎煞快°了°

SUFFUSED, *eyes* — *with tears,* ngæn-li′ ′en′-tih 眼°淚含的; ngæn′-li ŵông-ŵông′ 眼°淚汪汪

SUGAR, dông 糖; *white* —, bah dông′ 白°糖; *dark brown* —, wông dông′ 黃糖; *raw* —, sô dông′ 沙糖; *rock* —, *or rock candy,* ping dông′ 冰糖

SUGAR-BOWL, dông-kwun′ 糖罐 (ih-tsah)

SUGAR-CANE, ken-tsô′ 甘蔗°; dông tsô′ 糖蔗°

SUGGEST, *to* — (to another), di-ky′i′ 提起; — *a subject,* c′ih

di·moh′ 出題目; *to cause another to remember,* di-sing′ 提醒; *to give a hint* (of something forgotten), di-deo′ 提頭

SUGGESTIONS, *to make* — *to,* ts′-kyiao 指教; ts′-ying 指引

SUICIDE, *to commit* —, zi-veng′ 自°刎; zing-tön′-kyin 尋°短見; zi-zing′-si 自°尋°死°; zi-sah′-zi 自°殺自°; *wishing to commit* —, zing-si′-ming-weh′ 尋°死°覓°活

SUIT, *a* —*of clothes,* ih-t′ao′ i-zông′ 一套衣裳; ih-sing′ i-zông′ 一身衣裳

SUIT, *to* —, *or be suitable,* cong′-i 中意; ′eh-i′ 合意; ′eh-sih′ 合式; *do not* — *each other,* (persons), feh deo′-kyi 弗投機; *it suits me exactly,* tsing′-hao cong-ngô′-go i′ 正好中我个°意

SUITABLE, te′-go 對个°; siang-te′-go 相對个°; ′eh-shih′ 合式 (shih or sih); ′eh-i′ 合意

SULLEN, fông-tiao′ 放刁; — *countenance,* min-k′ong′ moh-heh′ 面孔墨黑; min-k′ong′ heh′-pông 面有°怒°容°

SULPHUR, liu-wông′ 硫磺

SULTRY, nyih′-leh meng-ky′i′-go 熱°得°悶氣个°; *very hot,* tsih′-lah-lah-go nyih′ 炙辣辣个°熱°; *close and oppressive weather,* t′in′-ky′i seh′-meng 天氣塞悶

SUM, *the* — (of numbers), gong′-

kyi 共計; tsong'-su 總數;
t'ong'-gong 統共
SUM, to — up, kyih tsong'-tsiang
揭總賬; to — up the whole,
tsong'-r-yin'-ts 總而言之
SUMMER, 'Ô-t'in' 夏°天; the festival at the beginning of —, lih-
'Ô' tsih 立夏°節
SUMMIT of a hill, sæn-ting-den'
山頂
SUMMON, to djün 傳; — the spirits, dziao kyü' læ 召°鬼°來
SUMMONS, a — to appear, djün-
p'iao'傳票; ditto (official), gyün-
sing'-ba 傳訊牌°
SUMPTUOUSLY, live ky'üoh'-c'ün
tu shæ-wô' 吃°穿都奢華
SUN, nyih-deo'日°頭; t'a'-yiang
太°陽; the — is shining brightly,
(i.e. strongly), mang'-mang nyih-
deo' 盯°盯°日°頭; put (it) in
the —, fông' læ nyih-deo' 'ô 放
在°日°頭下°
SUN, to sa 曬°; sa'-djoh 曬°者°;
— a while, sa'-ih-sa' 曬°一曬°;
— (something damp), tsiao'-ih-
tsiao' 照一照
SUNBEAM, a — entered, ih-da'
nyih-kwông' zih-tsing'-læ 一揀
日°光射進來
SUNBURNT, dark colored, sa'-heh-
go 曬°黑个°; reddish brown,
sa'-'ong-joh'-de 曬°紅熟了°
SUNDAY, li'-pa-nyih 禮拜°日°;
en-sih'-nyih 安息日°; Cü'-nyih
主日°

SUN-DIAL, jih-kwe' 日晷
SUN-FLOWER, gwe-hwô' 葵花;
hyiang'-jih-gwe 向日葵
SUNDRY, kyi-yiang' 幾樣; —
goods, zah ho' 雜貨
SUNRISE, nyih-deo' c'ih-ky'i' 日°
頭出起
SUNSET, nyih-deo' loh-sæn' 日°
頭落山
SUNSHINE, nyih-kwông' 日°光
SUPERANNUATED, lao'-joh 老
弱; (polite), lao'-moh-long'-cong
老邁°龍鍾; to be excused from
office on account of being—, kao'-
lao wæn-hyiang' 告老還鄉
SUPERCARGO, ah'-ho 押°貨
SUPERCILIOUS, ngæn-kao' 眼°高;
moh-cong'-vu-jing' 目中無人;
ngæn'-tsing sang-læ mi-mao-
teng' 眼°睛生°在°眉°毛上°
SUPERFICIAL, veo-min' 浮°面;
shallow, ts'in 淺: ts'in'-gying 淺
近; — learning, 'oh-veng' ts'in'-
go 學°問淺个°; — (as work),
tsih'-du nga-kwông'-min 只圖
外°光面; tsih' pang nga-meng'-
min 只繃外°門面; deo-vu'-
bi t'iah ngæn'-tsing 荳腐皮貼°
眼°睛
SUPERFLUOUS, vu-kwæn'-kying-
iao' 無關緊要; what is left
after using, yüong-ko' yiu-yü'
用過有餘; what is over and
useless, to'-go feh 'eh-yüong' 多
个°弗合用
SUPERINTEND, to tin'-toh 點督;

— (as an officer), toh'-li 督理；
to control, kwun 管；kæ-kwun'
該管；tsih'-tsông 職掌；tsông'-
kwun 掌管

SUPERINTENDENT, tin - toh' - go-
nying 點督个°人°；one who
helps another by superintending a
particular department, yü-z'-go 與
事个°；— of work, toh-kong'-
go 督工个°

SUPERIOR, zông 上；zông-deo'
上頭；zông-teng' 上等；ts'iao-
teng' 超等；— to him (or that),
k'yü-gyi'-ts-zông' 居其之上；
— to other men, dzæ-nying'-ts-
zông' 在人之上；bih'-nying
iao peh gyi gah-loh 別人要
俾°其軋落；a — pen, zông-
p'ing'-go-pih' 上品个°筆；a
— man, zông-teng'-ts nying' 上
等之人°；— goods, zông-teng'-
ts ho' 上等之貨；ting'-ho 頂
貨；— officers, zông-s' 上司；—
talent, kao-dzæ' 高才；— scholar,
dzæ-ts' 才子；—in age, tsiang'-
pe 長輩；ziu-pe' 前°輩；zông-
pe' 上輩

SUPERLATIVE, the signs of the
—are, ting 頂, tse 最, heng 狠,
gyih 極, di-ih' 第一, jih-feng'
十分；the best, ting'-hao 頂好

SUPERNATURAL, (appearing and
disappearing suddenly, &c.),
jing-c'ih'- kwe'- meh - go 神出
鬼沒个°

SUPERSCRIPTION, zông-min'-go z

上面个°字；— of a letter,
sing'-min 信面

SUPERSEDE, to diao-wun' 調換；
— (as affairs, or things), kah'-
diao 革去°；the old regulations
are superseded, gyiu' công'-dzing
kah'-diao-de 舊章程革去°
了°；the new supersedes the old,
gyiu'-kæ-sing' 舊改新；ky'i-
gyiu-wun-sing' 棄舊換新

SUPERSTITIOUS, kyin'- kyü - fah
diah'-go 見鬼°發牒个°；siang-
sing' zia-ky'i' z-ken' 相信邪°
氣事幹

SUPPER, yia-væn 夜°飯；yia-
dzô' 夜°茶；the Lord's —, Cü'-
væn-ts'æn 主晚餐；Sing'-væn-
ts'æn 聖晚餐

SUPPLE, joints easily bent, gao-
kwu' weh-loh' 餃°股活絡；—
limbs, or bones, kweh'-deo nyün'-
siang 骨頭軟相；— limbed
fellow (as in theatres), gwæn-
lao' 跌°打个°戲°子°

SUPPLEMENTARY, vu-zông'-go 附
上个°；djoh-tseng'-go 續增个°

SUPPLICATE, to entreat, gyiu-k'eng'
求懇；— (the Deity), gyi-tao'
祈禱

SUPPLY, to minister to, kong-ing'
供應；kong-kyih' 供給；—
with food, kong-zih' 供食；
my need, s'-peh ngô' ing-yüong'-
go 賜°給°我應用个°；to an-
ticipate and —(one's) wants, t'i'-
t'iah 體貼°；— when needed,

tsih-ing′ 接應; — *troops*, fah
ping′ tsih-ing′ 發兵接應; —
*the deficiency*, pu ky‘üih′ 補缺;
pu ts‘eo′ 補湊; pu tsoh′ 補足

SUPPORT, *to* iang or yiang 養;
cong 種; — *one's family*, iang
kô′ 養°家°; cong-iang′-kô-siao
養家°小; *he supports himself
by teaching*, gyi kao-shü′ wu-
k‘eo′ 其教°書飼口; *to up-
hold*, *or keep from falling*, vu
扶; tông; ts‘æn 撐

SUPPORT, *something to lean upon*,
(but not a firm —), gæ-deo′
戤頭; — (whether property, or
friend), k‘ao′-sæn 靠山; *to use
such —*, tông tso k‘ao′-sæn 當
作靠山

SUPPORTABLE, hao-tông′-go 好
擋个°, tông′-leh-djü′ 擋得°住

SUPPOSE, *to* i′-we 意會; dao or
tao 度°; *guess*, ts‘æ 猜; *I supposed*,
ngô dao-z 我°度°是; *I — so*,
ngô′ liang-dzing′ z-ka′ 我諒情
如°此°; *I supposed he was at
home*, ngô′ tao gyi′ læ oh′-li 我
度°其在°家°裡

SUPPOSING, (when there is great
probability), liang-pih′ 諒必;
— (if, or in case that), t‘ông′-jün
倘然; t‘eo′-p‘ô 仍恐°; kyüö′-
s 假使; kyüö′-jü 假如; shih′-
s, or sih′-s 設使; — *for example*, pi′-fông 比方; pi′-jü 比如

SUPPRESS, *to* ah′-loh 壓落;
ah′-djü 壓住; neh-loh′ 納落;

nying 忍°; — *your anger*, ô′-
wông ah′-gyi-loh-ky‘i′ 怒°氣°
壓其下°去°; — *rebellion*,
bing-fæn′ 平反; *could not —
anger*, ky‘i′ neh′-feh-djü′ 氣納
弗住; *could not — a smile*,
nying′-feh-djü′ siao′ 忍弗住笑

SUPPURATE, *to* sang nong′生°膿;
tsoh nong′ 作膿; gweng nong′.

SUPREME, ting′ kao 頂高; *the
— Ruler*, Zông-ti′ 上帝; *ditto*
(Taoist), Nyüoh-wông′-da-ti 玉
皇大帝

SURE, *true*, ky‘üoh′-jih 確實; tih′-
ky‘üoh 的確; væn-vu′-ih-shih′
萬無一失; *to be — of*, nô′-
leh-djü′ 拿得°住; jih-nô-kyiu′-
weng 十拿九穩; *made —* (as
a prophecy, promises, &c.), pih′-
fah-pih-cong′ 必發必中; —
*footed*, kyiah′-bu weng′脚步穩;
en′-kyiah-tseo′-go 按脚走个°

SURELY, ih-ding′ 一定; pih′-ding
必定; z-jün′ 自然

SURETY, (a person), pao′-nying
保人°; —*and go between*, cong-
pao′中保; *to become —*, tso pao′
做保; tsoh pao′ 作保

SURFACE, min-teng′ 面上°; *floating on the —*, veo-min′ 浮面

SURGEON (for cuts, and bruises),
sông-k‘o′ sin′-sang 傷科先生°;
—(for ulcers), nga-k‘o′ sin′-sang
外°科先生°; — (for internal
diseases), nen-k‘o′ sin′-sang 內
科先生°

SURMOUNT, *to— difficulties*, kying-lin' næn-c'ü '經練難處

SURNAME, sing 姓; sing'-su 姓氏°; *what is your honorable —?* tseng sing' 尊姓? kwe' sing 貴姓? kao sing' 高姓? *my humble* —, bi sing' 敝姓

SURPASS, ko'-jü 過 如; *surpasses him*, ko'-jü gyi 過 如 其

SURPASSING *all*, c'ih-cong' 出衆; — *talent*, dzæ-neng' c'ih-cong' 才能出衆; — *every thing in the world*, (but used in a more limited sense), kæ'-shü 蓋世

SURPASSINGLY *beautiful*, me'-mao kæ'-shü 美貌蓋世

SURPLUS, to-deo' 多頭; yü'-to 餘多; *enough and a —*, fu'-shü 敷舒; nông-shü' 小°康°

SURPRISE, *to — a person*, s'-teh nying kwa'-ky'i 使得人°怪°氣; long'-teh nying' c'ih-gyi' 弄得°人°出奇; long-teh nying' gyi-kwa' 弄得°人奇怪°; peh nying' c'ih-gyi' 俾人°出奇; *I am surprised*, ngô tao' c'ih-gyi'-go 我到出奇个°

SURPRISING, kwa'-ky'i 怪°氣; *not —*, feh sön' kwa'-ky'i 弗算怪°氣; *strange*, gyi-kwa' 奇怪°; *could not have been expected*, liao'-feh-tao'-go 料弗到个°; siang'-feh-tao'-go 想弗到个°; —(as something suddenly disappearing), jing-c'ih'-kwe'-meh 神出鬼沒

SURRENDER, *to* deo-'ông' 投降; deo-voh' 投服; — *one's self up*, zi deo'-tao 自°投到

SURROUND, *to* we-djü' 圍住; — *on all sides*, s'-pin we-djü' 四邊圍住; tsiu-we,' we-djü' 週圍圍住; —, *or hem in* (as by soldiers), we-kw'eng' 圍困; *to — by a wall*, tsiu-we' tang ziang' 週圍打墻

SURVEY, *to* k'en'-cün 看轉; k'en'-pin 看遍; *to measure land*, liang din-di' 量田地

SURVIVED *him a year*, pi gyi' to weh' ih nyin' 比其多活一年; pi gyi' to tso' ih-nyin' nying' 比其多做一年人°

SURVIVING, *still* wa' læ-tong' tso nying' 還在°此°做人°

SURVIVES *till now*, tao' jü-kying' wa læ-tong' 到如今還在°此°

SUSCEPTIBLE, (used of persons), ih-ts'oh' ziu dong' 一觸就動

SUSPECT, *to* nyi 疑; ts'æ-nyi 猜疑; *I — him*, ngô' nyi-sing z gyi 我疑心是伊°

SUSPECTED, *that man is to be —*, keh'-go nying' k'o nyi 這°个°人°可疑

SUSPEND, *to hang*, tiao 弔; kwô 掛; — *work*, sang-weh' deng-kong' 生°活停°工; *ditto*, (for an indefinite time), dang-ky'i' 宕起°; yün-ky'i' 懸起°; —*from office*, kah'-tsih wæn-hyiang' 革職還鄉

SUSPENSE, *to be in —*, kwô′-sing 掛心; kwô′-ky′in 掛牽; kwô′-nyiæn 掛念; *I was in — for a month,* ngô kwô′-sing ih-ko yüih′ de 我掛心一个°月了°

SUSPICIOUS, *inclined to suspect,* nyi-sing′ djong′ 疑心重; — *circumstance,* dzing yiu′ k′o nyi′ 情由可疑; *wears a — appearance,* ying-tsih′ k′o nyi′ 形跡可疑; dzing-tsih′ k′o nyi′ 情跡可疑

SUSTAIN, *to* tông 擋; *can —, or bear it,* tông-leh′-djü′ 擋得°住; *cannot long — life,* yiang weh′ feh dziang′-kyiu 養活弗長久

SWALLOW, in′-ts 燕子 (ih-tsah)

SWALLOW, *to* in′-loh 嚥落; ky′üoh′-loh 吃°落; *to gulp down,* t′eng-loh′ 吞落; *can′t —the pill,* wun-yiah′ t′eng′-feh-loh′-ky′i 丸藥吞弗落去°

SWAMP, kæn-diu′ 爛田; *swampy place,* ′æn-nyi-den′ 陷°泥潭

SWARM, ih-tsong′-sang 一種; *a — of bees,* ih-tsong′-sang mih-fong′ 一種蜜蜂

SWATHE, *to* dzin 纏; tsah 紮

SWAY, *to bear rule,* tsông′-kwun 掌管 (tsông or công); *to have authority,* tsông-gyün′ 掌權

SWEAR, *to* vah-tsiu′ 罰呪

SWEAT, ′en 汗

SWEAT, *to* c′ih-′en′ 出汗; *to bring out —* (as by medicine),

fah-′en′ 發汗; *to — profusely,* ′en-bô-yü-ling′ 汗如°雨淋; ′en′-c′ih-t′ô′-liu 汗出如°漿°

SWEEP, *to* sao 掃; — *the ground,* sao di′ 掃地; — *and brush off dust,* tæn′-sao 撢掃; sao-shih 掃刷; *sweeping assertion,* kô′-deo shih-wô′ 過忿° 說話

SWEET *to the taste,* din 甜; — *to the smell,* hyiang 香; *has a — perfume,* yiu hyiang-ky′i′ 有香氣; — *and deceitful words,* shih-wô′ din-dông′-mih-ti′-go 說話甜糖蜜滴个°

SWEET-WILLIAM, jih-yiang′-kying hwô 十樣景花

SWEETEN, *to* fông′ ih-tin din′ tih 放一點甜的

SWEETMEATS, dông-ko′ 糖菓; *peach preserves,* dao-tsiang′ 桃醬; *sugared and honeyed fruits,* mih-tsin′ 蜜餞

SWELL, cong 腫; cong′-ky′i-ke 腫起來

SWELLING *has gone down,* cong pih′-loh-de 腫瞞落了°; cong t′e′-diao-de 腫退去°了°

SWERVE *from the right way,* li-k′æ′ tsing′-lu 離開正路

SWIFT, kw′a 快; — *as if flying,* ziang fi′ ka kw′a′ 像飛樣°快; fi-kw′a′ 飛快°; — *as the wind,* fong-kw′a′ 風快°

SWILL, ken-shü′ 泔水°; *exchange lamp-wick for —,* teng-sing′-wun-ken′ 燈芯換泔水°

SWIM, to yiu 泅; — in the canal, yiu-'o' 泅 河; fortunately, he knows how to —, (or understands the water), ky'ü'-leh gyi sih shü' 虧° 得° 其 識 水°

SWINDLE, to kwa'-p'in 拐° 騙; tso kwa'-ts 做拐° 子; — every where, tong-kwa' si-p'in' 東拐° 西 騙

SWINE, nyi-cü' 泥 豬 (ih-tsah); a herd of —, ih-dziao' nyi-cü' 一 羣° 泥豬

SWINE-HERD, yiang nyi-cü'-go 養 泥豬 个°

SWING, to dang-dang' 宕 宕; — back and forth, dang-læ' dang-ky'i' 宕 來 宕 去°; — the arms (in walking), siu-kwang hwah-kyi hwah-kyi; — over and over, (as a mouse in a cage), tang ts'iu-c'ün' 打 鞦 韆°

SWITCH of false hair, ih-ts kô'-fah 一 枝 假° 髮

SWOON, to fah-kyüih' 發厥; ao'-ky'i 暈 去; fah-hweng' 發 惛

SWORD, pao'-kyin 寶 劍; double-edged —, sông-min'-pao'-kyin 雙 面 寶 劍; charmed —, ts'ih'-sing-kyin 七 星 劍 (ih-pô)

SYCEE, veng-nying' 紋 銀; horse-shoes of —, nyün-pao' 元 寶

SYCOPHANT, vong'-dzing-tong' 奉 承 个°; p'ah-mô'-p'i-go 拍° 馬 屁 个°

SYMMETRICAL proportions, do-

siao' siang-ts'ing' 大°小,相稱; deo-mi' siang-ing' 頭 尾° 相 應

SYMBOL, piao'-yiang 表樣; piao-pông' 標 榜

SYMPATHIZE, to — with another'' trouble, cü' nying-kô'-go kw'us 知人°家°个°苦; cü-kw'u' cü-lah' 知苦知辣; — with (be-cause of like suffering), dong-bing' siang-lin' 同 病 相 憐

SYMPATHIZING (with a friend), dzing'-læ-tih dong 正° 在°動° 情°; — heart, ts'eh-ing'-ts sing' 惻 隱 之 心; — and helping, ti'-t'iah-go sing 體 貼 个° 心; — and excusing, t'i'-liang 體諒

SYMPATHY, in — with one an-other, sing'-dzing 'eh'-leh-long'-go 性 情 合 得 攏 个°; lone-ly and without —, ts'i-liang' 淒涼

SYMPTOMS of disease, bing-shü' 病勢; bing-kying' 病景; bing'-go siang'-mao 病 个° 相 貌; — violent, or severe, bing-shü' li-'æ' 病 勢 利害

SYNONYMS, equivalent characters, tso' ka'-shih-go z' 一° 樣° 解° 說 个° 字; equivalent words, i'-s siang-dong'-go shih-wô' 意思 相 同 个° 說 話

SYRINGE, zib-shü'-kwun 射 水° 个° 管

SYRUP, dông-lu' 糖 滷; peach —, dao-tsih' 桃 汁

TAB 469 TAK

## T

TABERNACLE, tsiang'-bong 帳蓬 (ih-ting)

TABLE, coh'-teng 桌子°(ih-tsiang); round —, yüih-coh' 月桌; yü'-sæn coh' 小°圓°桌; small tea —, dzô-kyi' 茶几 (ih-go); — cloth coh'-teng pu' 桌布 (ih-kw'e)

TABLET, upright ancestral —, jing-we' 神位; ditto, (and for idols), jing-cü' 神主; jing-cü'-ba, or jing-cü-bæn 神主牌°; ba-we' 牌°位 (ih-we); horizontal inscribed —, pin 匾; pin-ngah' 匾額 (ih-kw'e)

TACK, kwu'-ting 鈄釘;—with two prongs, for matting, mô'-wông-gying 螞蝗鐵°襻° (ih-me)

TACK, to — with nails, ting 釘; — by sewing loosely, dziang-tsing' vong 長針縫; — together, (by sewing), ting-tæn'-læ 釘攏°來; — on (as trimming), tsa-ih-tsa 釘°一釘°; —a ship, diao ts'iang' 調向°; cün bong' 轉蓬

TACTICS, military ping-fah' 兵法

TADPOLE, n'-kyü-deo-djong' 烏龜°頭蟲; — character, k'o-teo' veng 料蚪文

TAEL, (1⅓ oz. av.), ih-liang' 一兩; — of silver, ih-liang' nying-ts' 一兩銀子; one Ningpo —, kông-bing' ih liang' 江°平一兩; the Hong Kong —, kwæn-bing'

關平; Shanghai —, deo-kwe' nying' 豆規銀; kwe-yün' 規圓

TAIL, mi'-pô, or mi'-pun 尾巴° (ih-keng)

TAILOR, zæ-vong'-s-vu 裁縫司務: dzing-i' 成衣

TAINTED meat, nyüoh in'-de 肉°宿了°; — (i. e. kept over its time), tah-dziao'-de.

TAKE, to do 拿°; — away, do'-leh-ky'i 拿°了°去°; gather together and — away, siu'-leh-ky'i 收了去°; — (properly at the same time with something else), ta'-leh-ky'i 帶°了°去°; —in the hand, nyiah 捏; — with both hands, p'ong 捧°; — care of, kwu'-djoh 顧着; ditto (or look after), tsiao'-kwu, or tsiao'-kwun 照顧; ditto (another's child, or animal), kyi'-yiang 寄養; — care of yourself, zi yüong pao'-djong 自°要°保重; — upon one's self the care of, zi dzing dzih' 自°承值; — in charge (properly a person), siu-liu' 收留; — a walk, ky'i tseo-tseo' 去°走走; — a turn (for one's own business), tang ih-go wang' 走一°回°; — a written inventory, k'æ ho'-tæn 開貨單; — one's leave, kao'-bih 告別; ditto (when going on a journey), dz-'ang' 辭行°;—medicine, ky'üoh yiah' 吃°藥; — out (of water), liao-ky'i'-læ 撩起來; — off

*one's clothes,* t'eh i-zông' 脱衣
裳°; — *off the hat,* coh mao-ts'
除° 帽子 (coh or tsoh); — *off
the cover,* hyiao-k'æ' 揭開; —
*off a coverlid,* kyih'-k'æ min-bi'
揭開棉被°; — *breath,* (*i. e.*
stop a while), t'eo-ky'i' 透氣;
— *a look,* k'en'-ih-k'en 看一
看; — *a disease* (by infection),
bing' yin-læ' 病延來; — *cold,*
sông-fong' 傷風; — *pains,*
yüong-sing 用心; — *by force,*
ts'iang'-deh 搶奪; — *to heart,*
tæn-sing-z' 擔心事; — *alive,*
weh gying' 活擒°; — *percentage,*
ts'iu' yüong-din' 抽用錢°; k'eo'
yüong-din' 扣用錢°; (in buying
for another), *to — more than was
paid,* keh-fi-deo'; loh dong-din'
落銅錢°; tang-'eo'-siu 賺°後
手; (in buying for another) *to
— a percentage promised by the
seller, &c,* do bah-deo' 扡扣°頭;
*ditto* (secretly) *in cloth, goods,* or
*money,* loh deo' 落餘°頭. See
Discount. — *a little out for one's
self* (from what one is expected
to give to another), k'a' bih-deo'
貪°扡頭; leo bih-deo-o ky'üoh
(slang); *to — the part of one's
own,* pao pi' 保庇; — *advantage of your going, doing, &c,*
ts'ing ng'-go bin' 趁你°个°便;
— *a little relaxation,* weh-dong'
ih-zông 活動一息°; — *your
studies* (in school), zông kwun'

上舘; — *a chair in the hand,*
teh ü'-ts 掇椅子

TAKEN *in, in buying,* ma-c'ong-de-
買貴了° (c'ong or ts'ong).

TALE, kwu'-z 故事; *ancient —,*
kwu'-z 古事; *unfounded —,*
vu-kyi'-ts-dæn 無稽之談

TALE-BEARER, pun-cü'-go nying
搬嘴个°人°; pun-cü'-long-
zih 搬嘴弄舌; — *and mis-
chief maker,* pun-teo' z'-fi-go
nying 搬兜是非个°人°

TALENT, dzæ-neng' 才能; dzæ-
dzing' 才情; du'-dzæ 肚才;
*natural —,* t'in-dzæ' 天才;
*man of —,* dzæ-ts' 才子; *he
has great —,* gyi'-go dzæ-dzing'
kao' 其个°才情高

TALISMAN (of paper), vu 符; —
*of the seven stars,* ts'ih'-sing-vu
七星符; — *of words,* tsiu'-
nyü 咒語; (ih-dao); *to drive
out evil influences with a —,*
bih-zia' 辟邪

TALK, *to* kông 講°; — *together,*
kông-kông' 講°講°; dæn-dæn'
談談; *to chat,* p'æn-dæn' 攀談;
*talks well,* jün'. we shih'-dz 善爲
說詞; *he ditto, or can — one into
believing what is not true,* gyi
shih'-kwah hao' 其談吐°好; —
*idle words,* kông 'æn-wô' 講開
話; *to — foolish or useless words,*
kông bah-wô' 講°白°話; kông
liao-t'in' 講°遼天話°; — *when
not wanted,* to cü' 多嘴; *to cü'*

tah-zih' 多嘴搭舌; ts'ih'-tah-pah'-tah 七嗒八嗒; — *too much*, to-kông'-to-wô' 多講°多話; *I want to — to you*, ngô iao' teng ng kông' 我要與°你°講°

TALKATIVE *person*, to-kông'-to-wô'-go nying 多講°多話个°人°

TALL, dziang-liao-siao 長鼓簫; — *person*, nying dziang' 人°長; *ditto*,(contemptuous), dziang diao-ts' 長條子; — *in stature*, sing-diao' dziang' 身條長; — *and slender*, ( contemptuous), lang-hwang'-dziang; dziang-hwang-hwang.

TALLOW, yiu 油; *mutton* — , yiang-yiu' 羊油; *vegetable* — , gyiu'-yiu 桕油; bah-yiu' 白°油

TALLOW-TREE, gyiu'-jü 桕樹 (ih-cü)

TALONS, *caught in his* — , kyiah'-tsao gyin'-leh-ky'i'-go 脚爪箝得°起°个°

TAME, *to* — *him*, iang gyi joh' 養其熟

TAME, joh 熟; — *bird*, joh tiao' 熟鳥°

TAN, *to* — *skin*, siao bi' 硝皮

TANNER, siao-bi' s-vu 硝皮司務

TANNED *leather*, job bi' 熟皮

TANGLE, *in a* —, lön-tsia'-bong 亂績鬓

TANGLE, *to* da-lön' 抓°亂; *all tangled together*, long'-leh ky'in-s'-bong, da-s-bong' 弄得°寨絲鬓抓°絲鬓; ky'in-ky'in-pang'-pang 牽牽絆絆

TANK, *water* shü'-gyü 水°柜; — (on boats), shü'-tsing, or shü-ts'ông' 水°井

TAP, *to* tah 搭; — *on the shoulder*, kyin-kah'-deo tah'-ih-tah' 肩胛°上°搭一搭

TAP, *to pierce*, tsön dong-ngæn' 鑽洞眼°

TAPE, ta 帶°

TAPERING *fingers*, ts'-deo tsin' 指頭尖

TAR, pah'-yiu 栢°油

TARDY, *slow*, mæn 慢: mæn-t'ang'-t'ang 慢宕°宕°; wun'-deng-deng 緩鈍鈍; wun'-t'o-t'o 緩拖拖; *late*, dzi 遲°

TARE, djü bi' 除皮

TARES (found in rice), bô-ts'ao' 稗°草

TARGET, pô'-ts 靶子 (ih-go); *to fire at a* —, tang pô'-ts 打靶子; *ditto*, *with arrows*, zih pô'-ts 射靶子

TARIFF, se'-tsch 稅則; se'-kw'un 稅款

TARNISH, *to* t'e-kwông' 退光

TARNISHED, kwông t'e'-de 光退了°

TARO, nyü-na' 芋°芀°

TARTAR, or *Bannerman*, gyi-'ô-nying 旗下°人°; Tah'-ts 韃子; Dah-ts' 韃子; *Manchu*, Mun'-tsiu-nying 滿洲人°; — *language*, Mun'-tsiu-wô 滿洲話

TASK, *work*, meng-veng′ sang-weh′
名外生°活;—(usually in
study), kong-k′o′ 功 課; *daily*
—, (*i .e.* studies, or chantings),
djoh-nyih′ kong-k′o′ 逐日°功
課

TASSEL, *a* ih-p′ang′ su-deo′ 一掛°
鬏°頭

TASTE, mi-dao′ 味°道;— *just*
*right,* jih-mi′ 入味°; *in bad —*
feh teh′-fah-go 弗得法个°

TASTE, *to* zông mi-dao′嘗°味°道;
— *and see*, zông-zông′-k′en 嘗°
看

TASTELESS, *without taste*, m̄-mi′-
dao 無°味°道; *flat, or without*
*salt*, dæn 淡: m̄-yin-dæn′-tsiang
無°鹹淡醬;—(as meat, or
fish), m̄-sin′-mi 無°鮮味°

TATTERED, p′o′-li-p′o-sa′ 破褸
破褸°; p′o′-p′o 破破; zah-p′o
紛°破

TATTLE, shih-wô′ k′ông′-feh-lao′說
話困弗牢. See TALE-BEARER.

TATTOO, *to — the skin*, ts′ih bi-fu′
刺皮膚

TAOISM, Dao′-kyiao 道敎; Dao′-
kyiao dao′-li 道敎道理

TAOIST, Dao′-kô-li-go nying′ 道
家°个°人°;— *priest*, Dao′-z
道士

TAUNT, *to* siu-joh′ 羞辱; tsao-
t′ah′ 嘲嗒; *to humiliate by taunt-*
*ing*, siah-lin′ 削臉

TAUTOLOGICAL *expressions*, djong-
foh′ shih-wô′ 重複說話

TAVERN, *eating and lodging house*,
væn-tin′ 飯店; k′ah′-nyü 客
寓; *inn*, ′ô-c′ü′ 厦處: *lodging*
*house*, hyih′-yia-tin′ 歇夜店

TAX, kyün 捐; *salt —*, yin-kyün′
鹽捐; *land —*, zin-liang′ 錢°
糧 *house —*, vông-kyün′ 房捐;
— *on goods*, kwæn-se′ 關稅;
se′-din 稅錢°; *pay taxes*, deo
liang′ neh se′ 投糧納稅: *to*
*pay land —*, deo zin-liang′ 投
錢°糧; *pay — on goods*, deo-se′
投稅; *to collect the land taxes*,
siu′ zin-liang′ 收錢°糧; *to pay*
*ditto*, wun koh′-k′o 完國課

TAX, *to* ding se′-tseh 定稅則;
*to — houses*, lih′ vông-kyün′ 立
房捐

TAX-OFFICE, kyün-gyüoh′ 捐局

TEA, dzô 茶; *tea-leaf*, dzô-yih′ 茶
葉; *broken ditto*, se′ dzô-yih′ 碎
茶葉; *green —*, loh-dzô′ 綠茶;
*black —*, ′ong-dzô′ 紅茶; *strong*
—, nyüong dzô′ 濃茶; ts′ih′
dzô 赤茶; *weak —*, dæn′ dzô
淡茶; ts′ing-dzô′ 清茶; *to scald*
—, p′ao dzô′ 泡茶; *pour —*,
sia dzô′ 斟°茶; ts′ong dzô′ 冲茶;
*pass —*, di dzô′ 遞茶; *ditto in a*
*tray*, pun dzô′ 搬茶; *to drink —*,
ky′üoh dzô′ 吃°茶; hah dzô′ 喝
茶; *to pick —*, tsah dzô-yih′ 摘
茶葉; *to pick over —* (*i. e.* pick
out refuse, &c.), kæn dzô-yih′ 揀°
茶葉; *to finish up —* (by rolling,
and coloring), tso dzô-yih′ 做茶

葉; *to fire* —, ts'ao dzô-yih' 炒
茶葉; *a great* — *drinker,* dzô-
tsu'-s 茶 祖 師; — *dust,* dzô-
meh' 茶末;— *stems,* dzô-kwang'
茶 梗; — *seeds,* dzô-ts' 茶 子;
*Congo* —, Kong-fu' dzô 工 夫
茶; *Souchong* —, Siao-cong' dzô
小 種 茶; *Oolong* —, U-long'
dzô' 烏 龍 茶. The kinds of tea
exported from Ningpo are as
follows.

*Gunpowder,* 1st *grade,* Pao'-cü 寶
珠; *do.* 2nd *grade,* Ts-cü' 芝珠;
*Hyson,* 1st *grade,* Me-hyi' 眉熙;
*do.* 2nd *grade,* Hyi-c'ing' 熙春;
*Young Hyson,* 1st *grade,* Ngo-
me' 娥 眉; *do.* 2nd *grade,* Yü'-
zin 雨 前; *Imperial,* 1st *grade,*
Yün-cü' 圓 珠; *do.* 2nd *grade,*
Fu'-yün-cü' 副 圓珠; *Hyson-
skin,* Bi-dzô' 皮 茶: *Leaf-tea,*
Mao-dzô'毛茶; *Twankey,* Song-
lo' 松 蘿

TEA-CUP, dzô-pe' 茶 杯; *covered*
—, kæ'-nn 蓋 碗; meng-nn'捫
碗 (ih-tsah)

TEA-KETTLE, dzô-wu'茶壺; teng'-
dzô-wu' 燉 茶 壺 (ih-pô)

TEA-POT, dzô-kwun' 茶罐; dzô-
wu' 茶 壺; ts'ong'-dzô-wu' 冲
茶 壺 (ih-pô)

TEA-POY, dzô-kyi' 茶 儿 (ih-
tsiang)

TEA-SPOON, diao-kang' 調 羹°;
*native brass* —, dzô-z' 茶 匙
(ih-tsah)

TEA-TRAY, dzô-bun'茶盤(ih-min)

TEACH, to kao 教°; *to instruct,*
kao'-hyüing 教° 訓; — *a child
to read,* kao'siao-nying' doh-shü'
教°小 孩° 讀 書

TEACHABLE, hao-kao'-go 好教°
个°; k'o-kao'-go 可 教°个°.

TEACHER, sin-sang' 先 生° (ih-
we); *to call,* or *employ a* —,
ts'ing sin-sang' 請 先 生°; *my*
—, ngô'-go nyih-s 我个°業 師

TEACHING, *I live by* — *young
children,* hyüing mong' we nyih'
訓 蒙 爲 業

TEAR, to c'ô'-k'æ, or ts'ô-k'æ 撑
開; c'ô'-p'o 撑 破; — *to pieces,*
c'ô'-se 撑 碎; c'ô' wu 撑 腐;
— (as on a nail), keo-p'o' 勾
破; tsah'-p'o 扎 破; — *one's
self* (or something) *away,* ngang
feng'-k'æ 硬分開; ngang ts'ah'-
k'æ 硬 拆 開; — *off the skin,*
poh bi' 剝 皮; — *open,* poh'-
k'æ 剝 開

TEARS, ngæn'-li 眼 淚; ngæn'-
li-shü 眼 淚 水°; *to shed* —,
c'ih ngæn'-li 出 眼 淚; ngæn'-
li beh-c'ih' 眼 淚 勃 出; *burst
into* —, ngæn'-li pao'-c'ih-læ'-
de 眼 淚 爆°出 來 了°

TEASE, *to* ts'ao 噪; — *continually,*
tsi-tseo' 嘈啁; *won't stop teasing,*
ts'ao'-feh-ko 噪 弗 過; tsi-tseo'-
feh-ko 嘈 啁 弗 過

TEAT, na-di' 嬭 頭°

TEDIOUS, in'-væn-go 厭 煩 个°;

*tediously slow*, mæn'-leh m̄-liao'-liang 慢得°無°量;—*talk*, kông'-leh dziang-p'in' 講°得°長篇

TEETH, ngô-ts' 牙°齒 (ih-lih); *irregular* —, ngô-ts' feh-zi' 牙°齒弗齊°; *to cut* —, c'ih ngô-ts' 出牙°齒; *to lose the* —, ngô-ts' t'eng'-loh 牙°齒脫落; *incisor* —, meng-zin'-ngô 門前牙°; *molar* —, do-ngô' 大°牙°

TELEGRAM, din-pao' 電報(ih-go)

TELEGRAPH, *to* ta din-sing' 帶°電信

TELEGRAPH *wire*, din-sin' 電線

TELESCOPE, ts'in-li'-kying 千里鏡 (ih-min, ih-kô)

TELL *him*, teng gyi' wô, or teh' gyi wô 與°其話; pao'-hyiang-gyi-dao' 報向其道; wô-hiang'-gyi-dao 話向其道; kao'-su gyi 告訴他°; *charge not to* —, mun-cü' 瞞嘴; *don't* —, m̄-nao' wô soh' 弗可°話甚麼°; feh-k'o' kông'-c'ih 弗可講°出; *bribe not to* — *him*, en gyi cü'-pô pi' 按其嘴吧閉; — *the news*, t'ong-cü' sing'-sih 通知信息; pao sing' 報信; — *a secret*, t'ong fong' pao sing' 通風報信

TEMERITY, tæn'-ts p'ah' 膽子潑; tæn'-ts sah'-yia 膽子撒野°; *to show* —, mao do'-tæn 冒大°膽

TEMPER, *disposition*, sing'-kah 性格; sing'-ky'i 性氣; sing-dzing 性情; *even*—, sing'-ky'i 'o-bing'

性氣和平; *to give way to one's* —, fah sing'-kah 發性格; sing-kyih' 性急, implies too great haste in doing, but is a polite term for *quick* or *hasty* —, (which is also), sing'-kah ts'ao' 性格躁; ky'i'-tsih tön' 氣質短; ky'i kying' 氣緊; ziang mao-ts'ao' bo-sing' ka 像茅草火星樣式°; *easy* —, ky'i'-tsih dziang' 氣質長; ky'i-kw'un' 氣寬

Bi-ky'i' 脾氣 is sometimes used for temper, but in Ningpo it generally implies an evil nature, so that all one's bad behaviour, such as gambling, drinking, &c. are attributed to his wa bi-ky'i; hao bi-ky'i is sometimes used, but it implies only a temporary goodness.

TEMPERAMENT *sluggish*, or *slow*, sing'-dzing sang'-leh dzi-deng' 性情生°得°遲鈍; *mercurial* —, sing'-dzing sang-leh liu-dong' 性情生°得°流動

TEMPERATE, tsih'-cü 節制; — *in eating, and drinking*, ing'-zih yiu-tsih' 飲食有節

TEMPEST, fong-pao' 風颺

TEMPLE, miao 廟; miao-yü' 廟宇; *Buddhist* —, z 寺; z-yün' 寺院; *small ditto*, en 菴; *Taoist* —, kwun 觀; *the large central hall of ditto*, da-din' 大殿; *ancestral* —, z-dông 祠堂; kô-miao' 家°廟; *ditto of one branch of a family*, ts-dz' 支祠 (ih-go)

TEMPLES (of the head), t'a'-yiang 太陽

TEMPORAL *affairs*, (of this world),

shü'-kæn-zông'-go z-t'i' 世界
上个°事體; shü'-z 世事;
*affairs of this life*, seng-zin'z-ken'
生前°事幹

TEMPORARY, dzæn-z'-go 暫時个°

TEMPORARILY, dzæn-ts'ia' 暫且';
gyün-ts'ia' 權且°

TEMPORIZE, *to* ze shü'-dao tseo'
隨勢道走; k'en' fong-deo' tseo
看風頭走

TEMPORIZING, ze-fong-tao'-go 隨
風倒个°

TEMPT, *to persuade to evil*, ts'ön-
teh' tso-wa' 攛掇做孬'; *to
deceive, and persuade*, yiu-'oh' 誘
惑; — *and blind*, mi-'oh' 迷惑;
*to entice*, ying'-yiu 引誘

TEMPTED *by the Devil*, be Mo-kwe'
mi-'oh'-de 被魔鬼迷惑了';
— *by him*, ziu gyi'-go mi' 受其
个°迷; ziu gyi'-go nyü' 受其
个°愚; — *and fallen*, ta-diao-
de 帶°壞°了°

TEN, jih 十; — *to one it will be
spoiled*, (nine out of ten), jih'-yiu
kyiu' iao tso'-diao-go 十有九要
做壞个°; — *out of every hundred*,
kyiu' k'eo 九扣; kyiu' tsih 九折

TENACIOUS *of one's own opinion*,
nyiah-sah' zi'-go cü'-i 捻煞自°
个°主意

TENANT, tsu-wu' 租戶; tsu-cü'
租主

TEND, *to* kwun 管; k'en 看; — *a
child*, kwun siao-nying 管小孩';
— *sheep*, k'en yiang' 看羊

TENDENCY, z-jün'-ts shü 自然
之勢

TENDER, neng 嫩; *to boil it —*,
ts' gyi nen' 羹°其軟°; — *heart*,
nyün' sing-dziang' 軟心腸;
sing dz'-go 心慈个°; *to rear
tenderly*, kyiao-iang' 嬌養

TENDON, kyiing 筋 (ih-kwang)

TENON, shing'-deo 榫頭

TENT, tsiang'-bong 帳蓬; *to pitch
a —*, tah tsiang'-bong 搭帳蓬

TENTH, *the —*, di-jih' 第十; *a
— of*, jih-kwn'-ts-ih' 十股之
一; *the —* (usually added by
Chinese storekeepers, and which
they will deduct), k'eo'-deo 扣
頭; tsih'-deo 折頭; *have you
deducted the —*, k'eo'-deo k'eo'-
loh-leh ma 扣頭扣落嗎°?

TEPID, nyih-weng-weng' 熱溫
溫; nyih-dong'-dong 熱烘°烘°

TERM, *name*, ming-z' 名字; — *of
three years*, (official), sen nyin'
ih-dzing' 三年一任°; *to collect
bills at the three terms*, siu tsih'-
tsiang 收節賬

TERMINATE, *to end*, wun 完; pih
畢; liao'-kyih 了結; *to stop*, ts'-
djü 止住

TERM, *to* ts'ing-hwu' 稱呼; co
叫°

TERMINATED, *the war is —*, tang-
tsiang tang-kyih'-gyüoh-de 打
仗結局了°

TERMINATION, meh-kyih'-sah 末
結煞

TERRACE, *platform*, dæ 臺; *flat*
— *on the roof*, sa'-dæ 曬° 臺

TERRIBLE, p'ô'-siang-go 怕 相
个°; p'ô'-shü-shü 怕 勢 勢

TERRIFIED, kying-hoh'-de 驚嚇°
了°; ziu kying-hoh' de 受驚
嚇° 了°; hah'-sah-de 嚇 煞
了°; kw'a'-tæn hah'-se 苦膽嚇
碎

TERRIFY, *to* — *him*, long gyi hah'-
sah 弄 其 嚇 煞; s'-teh gyi
ky'ih-hoh' 使 得 其 吃 嚇°

TERRITORY, pæn'-du 版 圖; di-
fông' 地 方

TERSE, kyin'-kyih 簡 潔

TERTIAN *ague*, s'-nyih-bing' 四
日° 病; s'-nyih liang-deo pæn'
四 日° 兩 頭 班

TEST, s'-fah 試 法; s'-væn-fông-
fah' 試 範 方 法

TEST, *to* s'-væn 試 範; *to experiment*, s'-nyiæn 試 驗; — *as by
fire*, s'-lin 試 煉; *to try*, s'-s-k'en
試 試 看; — *one's learning by
examination*, k'ao-s' 考 試

TESTAMENT, yi-coh', or yi-tsoh'
遺囑; *to make a* —, lih' yi-coh'
立 遺 囑; *Old* —, Gyiu-yi'-
tsiao'-shü 舊 遺 詔 書; Gyiu-
iah'-shü 舊 約 書; *New* —,
Sing-yi'-tsiao'-shü 新 遺 詔 書;
Sing-iah'-shü 新 約 書

TESTIFY, *to* tso te'-tsing 做對証;
te'-tsing 對 証; — *of what has
been seen*, tso kyin'-tsing 做 見
証

TESTIMONY, te'-tsing shih-wô' 對
証 說 話

TEXT, bah-veng' 白° 文; — *of a
discourse*, di-moh' 題 目

TEXTURE, sing-veng' 身 分; *firm*
—, sing-veng' kyih'-jih 身 分
砥 實

THAN, jü 如; pi 比; *greater* —
*I*, do-jü' ngô 大° 如 我; pi
ngô do' 比 我 大°; *better* —,
hao'-jü 好 如; *more* — *once*, feh-
ts' ih-we' 弗 止 一 回; *less* —
*three catties*, feh tao' sæn-kying'
弗 到 三 勛; feh-mun' sæn-kying'
弗 滿 三 勛

THANK, *to* zia 謝°; — *you*, zia-
zia' ng 謝°謝°你°; ze-ko; teh-ze
得罪; — *much*, or *many thanks*,
to-zia' 多 謝°; to-dzing 多 承;
*cannot express my thanks*, ken'-zia-
feh-zing' 感謝°弗盡°; zia'-feh-
wun' 謝°弗完°; — *you very much*,
to-to' cü'-i ng 多 多 致意你°;
*return a present in thanks for
favor received*, dziu-zia' 酬 謝°

THANKFUL *heart*, sing'-li ken'-
kyih 心 裡 感 激; ken'-zia-go
sing' 感 謝° 个° 心; *ditto* (for
great favor), ken-eng'-go-sing
感 恩 个° 心; *I am very* — *to
you*, ngô jih-nyi' feng ken'-kyih
ng 我 十 二° 分 感 激 你°

THANKLESS, vông-eng'-veo-yi'-go
忘 恩 負 義 个°; m̄-liang'-sing
無° 良 心; m̄ peng'-sing 無°
本 心

THAT, keh'-go 這°个°; — *man*, keh'-go nying 這°个°人°; — *gentleman*, keh'-we sin-sang 這°位先生°; — *pen*, keh-ts pih' 這°枝筆; — *which*, sô 所; — *which he said*, gyi' sô wô' 其所話; — *night*, tông'-yia 當夜°; lin-yia' 連夜°; keh'-yia 這°夜°; *so —*, s'-teh 使得; *this and —*, pe'-ts' 彼此; *I heard —you were sick*, ngô t'ing'-meng ng sang-bing'-ko'-de 我聽聞你°生病過了°; *Oh! —'s it, or I don't believe —*, kwa'-dao-z 怪道是

THATCHED *house*, ts'ao-kæ'-go oh' 草葢个°屋

THAW, *to* sah 煞°; yiang 烊; hwô 化; siao 消

THEATRE, (a building), hyi'-kwun 戲館; *open place where plays are enacted*, hyi'-veng-dziang' 戲塲

THEFT, *the sin of —*, t'eo-tong-si'-go ze' 偷東西个°罪; *a case of —*, ts'ih' en 竊案; *lost by —*, shih ts'ih'-de 失竊了°; *guilty of —*, væn ts'ih'-en go 犯竊案; *— væn'-djoh zeh'-go ze'-ming 犯着賊个°罪名

THEIR, gyi-lah'-go, or gyi-go 伊°等°个°

THEM, gyi-lah' 伊°等°; *— selves*, gyi-lah zi' 伊°等°自°

THEME, di-moh' 題目

THEN, ziu 就°; ze-tsih' 隨即; ze-siu' 隨手; *following after*, ze-'eo' 隨後

THENCE, *from that place*, dzong keh'-deo 從那°邊°

THENCEFORTH, dzong-ts'' yi-'eo' 從此以後; dzong keh' z-'eo yi-læ' 從這°時候以來

THERE, keh'-deo 那°邊°; *— it is*, na; nô; læ-kæn' 在°彼°

THERE is, yiu 有; *there is none*, m-yiu' 無有; m-neh-go 沒有°个°

THEREABOUTS (in quantity), ts'ô' feh-to' 差弗多; — (in place), ts'ô'-feh-to' di-fông' 差弗多地方; ts'ô'-feh-to' lu' 差弗多路; *Ningpo —*, teng Nying-po' siang ky'ü' vu-kyi' 與°寗波相去無幾

THEREFORE, sô'-yi 所以; keh'-lah 是°以°; kweh'-lah 故以°; *on account of that*, we'-leh ka 爲此°; kwu'-ts' ka 故此

THEREIN, dze-gyi-nen' 在其內; dze gyi-cong' 在其中

THERMAL *springs*, weng-djün' 溫泉 (veng.)

THERMOMETER, 'en-shü'-piao 寒暑表

THESE, keh'-sing 這°些°; dông-deo keh'-sing.

THEY, gyi-lah' 伊°等°

THICK, 'eo 厚; 'eo'-jih 厚實; *— fog*, vu'-lu nyüong' 霧露濃; vu'-lu djong' 霧露重; *— and tangled* (as hair, bushes), bong-bong-dong' 亂蓬鬆°

THICKEN, *to become thick*, 'eo'-ky'i-læ 厚起來

THIEF, zeh 賊; sæn-tsah'-siu 三隻手; yia'-mæn 夜°孿; sô-lao'-ing; siao'-ts'ih 小竊; — *who steals, in day-light,* bah-nyih'-djông' 白°日°撞; — (who cuts and snatches watches, &c.), tsiu-liu'-go zeh 剪綹个'賊°

THIEF-CATCHER, mô'-kw'æ 馬快; bu-kw'æ' 捕快

THIEVISH, *addicted to stealing,* kwæn' t'eo go 慣偷个°; *naturally— hearts,* zeh-sing' sang-dzing'-go 賊°心生°成个°; *fond of picking,* ts'eh' siu ts'eh kyiab' 撮手撮脚; — (hands and feet), zeh-siu' zeh-kyiah' 賊°手賊°脚

THIGH, do-t'e'大°腿; do-kyiah'-p'ông 大°脚膀°

THIGH-BONE, do-t'e'-kweh大°腿骨 (ih-keng)

THIMBLE, ti'-tsing 抵針 (ih-go)

THIN, boh 薄; *spare,* seo 瘦; *wan,* bah-liao'-liao 白'嫽嫽; — *blooded,* ts'ing-bi' boh'-hyüih 青皮薄血

THINNER, *a little* boh'-tin 薄點; *much —,* bob hyü'-to 薄許多; *ditto,* (of a person), seo hyü'-to 瘦許多

THING, tong-si' 東西 (ih-yiang, ih-gyin); *all things,* pah' yiang tong-si' 百°樣東西; væn-veh' 萬物

THINK, *to* ts'eng 忖; siang 想; s 思; s-siang' 思想; s-ts'eng' 思忖; — *carefully,* yüong sing-

s' 用心思; *ditto over it,* tso'-s-yiu-siang' 左思右想; *can't —it out,* ngwu'-feh-tao' 悟弗到; ts'eng'-feh-c'ih' 忖弗出; — *of,* or *recall suddenly,* ngwu-tao' 悟到; —*constantly of,* kyi'-nyiæn 記念; — *of, and not forget,* nyiæn-nyiæn' peh-vông' 念念不忘

THIRD, *the* di-sæn' 第三; *a —,* sæn-kwu'-ts-ih' 三股之一; *divide in thirds,* sæn-kwn' k'æ 三股開

THIRDLY, sæn-læ' 三來; sæn-tseh' 三則

THIRST, *to quench —,* ts-k'eh' 止渴; ka-k'eh' 解°渴

THIRSTY, k'eo-k'eh' 口渴; *very —,* k'eo-pah' 口乾°; — (dry), k'eo'-ken zih-sao' 口乾舌燥

THIRTEEN, jih-sæn' 十三

THIRTEENTH, di-jih-sæn'第十三

THIRTY, sæn-jih' 三十

THIS, keh'-go 這个°; — *month,* keh'-ko yüih 這°個月; peng'-yüih 本月; — *year,* kying-nyin' 今年; peng'-nyin 本年; — *or the same year,* tông'-nyin 當年; — *day,* kyih-mih' 今°日°; kying-tsiao' 今朝; — *morning* (early), kyih-mih t'in-nyiang' 今°日°天亮°; — *book,* keh'-peng shü' 這°本書; — *shop,* keh' bæn tin' 這° 爿店; — *time,* keh'-go z-'eo' 這° 个°時候; — *life,* kying'-si z-'eo' 今世°

時候;— *and that*, dông' ih-go, keh' ih-go 這°一个°, 那°一个°;— *time and that are different*, ts<sup></sup> ih-z pe' ih-z 此一時彼一時; *on — account*, we-leh keh'-go yün-kwu' 爲了這个° 緣故

THITHER, *go* tao keh-deo' ky'i 到那°邊°去°

THONG, bi-ta' 皮帶 (ih-diao).

THORN, ts' 刺 (ih-me)

THOROUGH, (*i. e.* through and through), t'eo 透; t'ong-t'eo' 通透; t'eo-ti' 透底;— (*i. e.* from the bottom to the top), teo-ti 兜底; ts'iah-ti 撤°底

THOROUGHLY, *understand* t'eo' ming-bah' 透明白°; *ditto or to be — dry*, feng'-sao 粉燥; feng'-kweh-sao 粉骨燥; sao-ko-keh' 燥過牙°; feng'-ken s-sao' 粉乾四燥;— *acquainted with*, joh-t'eo' 熟透; *to do* —, nying-tsing' tso 認°真做

THOROUGH-FARE *a street running through*, t'ong-lu' 通路; *a frequented way*, kwun-dông' do-lu' 官塘大°路; t'ong-'ang' do-lu' 通行°大°路

THOSE, keh'-sing 那°些°; keh'-deo keh'-sing 那°邊°那°些°

THOUGH, se 雖; se-tsih' 雖只; se-tseh' 雖則; se-jün' 雖然; *as — (he) did not notice*, hao'-ziang feh-læ'-kwu 好像弗來顧

THOUGHTS, ts'eng'-deo 忖頭; siang'-deo 想頭; (deeper —), nyiæn-deo' 念頭;—, *or way of thinking*, ts'eng'-shih 想°法°

THOUGHTFUL, we yüong sing' 會用心; we yüong ts'eng'-kong 會用心思

THOUGHTLESS, mông-bah'忙白°; mong 懞; bah-mông'-kwông白°忙光; bah-du'-du 虛°度;— *heedless person*, mông'-fu 懞夫

THOUSAND, *a* ih ts'in' 一千; *ten* —, ih væn' 一萬; jih ts'in'十千

THRASH. See THRESH.

THREAD, sin 線; *hempen* —, mô-sin' 麻線; *cotton* —, min-sò' 棉紗 (ih-keng)

THREAD *a needle*, c'ün tsing-ngæn' 穿針眼°

THREAD-BARE, *worn* yiang-yi'-de 希°散°了°; nyüong-deo' yi-kwông'-de 絨頭散°光了°

THREATEN, *to* kying'-kyiæ禁戒; heng-hô' 哼哈; ngô-heng' 砑哼; *to frighten*, hah 嚇. See WARN.

THREE, sæn 三;— *times — are nine*, sæn-sæn' kyin kyiu' 三三見九;— *times as much*, (*i.e.* add two parts), kô liang'-be ts'eo' 加二°倍湊;— *cornered*, sæn-koh'-go 三角°个°;— *stranded cord*, sæn-kwu'-deo-zing' 三股頭繩°;— *highest* (in this Empire) *in literary rank*, sæn-ting'-kah 三鼎甲

THRESH, *to — paddy*, tang dao′ 打 稻; gwæn dao′ 摜 稻

THRESHING-FLOOR, dao′-dziang 稻塲; dao′-di 稻地;—, and also *drying-floor*, sa′-dziang 曬°塲

THRESHOLD, *door-sill*, di-voh 地柣; *stumbled over the —*, di-voh′ pæn-tih′-go 地柣失° 跌个°

THRICE, sæn tsao′ 三遭; sæn we′ 三 回; sæn pin′ 三 遍

THRIFTY, *increasing in wealth*, nyih-tsing′ feng-feng 日° 進 紛 紛; *— in growing*, nyih-tsiang′ yia-do′ 日° 長 夜° 大°

THRIVE, *to* hying-wông′ 興 旺; *will not —*, (as a tree, or child), yiang′-feh-hying 養 弗 興 起°

THROAT, wu-long′ 喉° 嚨; *to cut one's —*, zi-ming′-sah 自° 抿 殺

THROB, *to* t′iao 跳; dong 動; *heart throbs*, sing bih′-bih-t′iao 心 闢 闢 跳

THRONE, we 位; *the Imperial —*, wông-we′ 皇 位; long-we′ 龍 位; da-pao′ 大 寶; *to ascend the —*, teng we′ 登 位; *ditto* (the first of a dynasty), teng kyi 登 基; *to succeed to the —*, tsih we′ 接 位; *to abdicate the —*, t′e we′ 退 位

THRONG, *a* ih-do-dziao nying′ 一 大° 羣° 人°

THRONG, *to* üong′-tsi 擁 擠; a-tsi′ 挨 擠

THROTTLE, *to* k′ah wu-long′ 搭 喉° 嚨

THROUGH, *to pass —*, c′ün-ko′ 穿 過; *pass — the city*, c′ün-zing-ko′ 穿 城° 過; *wet —*, sih′-t′eo-de 濕 透 了°; *come — the rain*, kah′-yü kæ′ 冒° 雨 來; *read a book —*, shü′ doh-wun′ 書 讀 完; *look — a hole*, dzong dong-ngæn′-li k′en′ 從 洞 眼° 裏 看

THROUGHOUT, *that book is circulated—China*, keh-peng shü′ Cong-koh′ t′ong-′ang′-go 這° 本° 書 中 國 通 行° 个°; *good —*, ih-kæ′tu hao′ 一 概 都 好; dzong deo′-ts-vi tu hao′ 從 頭 至 尾 都 好

THROW, *to* tiu 丟; k′ang; gwæn 摜; *— away*, tiu-diao′ 丟 去°; k′ang′-diao; gwæn-diao′ 摜 了°; ô′-diao 揶° 了°; ang′-diao; *— about*, k′ang′-sæn 丟° 散; lön gwæn′ 亂 摜; *he threw stones at me*, gyi do zah-deo′ k′ang′ ngô 其 拿 石° 頭 丟° 我; *— bricks, or broken tiles*, ô ngô′-bæn 揶° 瓬 爿; *— away one's life*, song-si′ 送 死°; song sing′-ming 送 性 命; *ditto, or reputation, for a noble object*, si′ djong′-jü T′a′-sæn 死° 重 如 泰° 山; *ditto, for a very small object*, si′ ky′ing′-jü ′ong-mao′ 死° 輕 如 鴻 毛°; *— him down* (playfully), k′ô-gyi-tao′ 捉° 其 倒; *ditto* (in anger), tang′-gyi-tao 打 其 倒; *— away* (or waste money), k′ang′-loh shü′-den-li 丟° 在° 水 潭 裏; *—*

over the head (as a cloth), 'o-deo'-t'ao 和 頭 套；— off (as covering), hyiao-diao' 拐 去°；kyih'-diao 揭 去°；dip up, and — out (as specks in food), peh'-diao 撥 去°；— blame upon some one else, yi-hwô'-tsih-moh' 移 花 接 木

THRUST, to push, t'e 推；— out the head, sing'-c'ih deo' 伸 出 頭；—out the tongue, t'a'-c'ih zih-deo' 霪° 出 舌 頭；— through with a knife, tao' c'ün-ko' 刀 穿 過

THUMB, do ts'-meh-den' 大° 指 拇 頭

THUNDER, le 雷；the noise of —, le-sing' 雷 聲；le'-hyiang 雷 響；a clap of —, ih-go p'ih'-lih 一 聲 霹 靂；— shower, loh le-yü' 下° 雷 雨；there will be a — shower, iao loh le-yü' 要 下° 雷 雨

THUNDER, to hyiang le' 響 雷

THURSDAY, li-pa-s' 禮 拜° 四；tsin-li ng 瞻 禮 五°

THUS, z-ka' 如° 此°；ka'-siang-mao 如°此°相 貌；ka' yiang-ts 如° 此° 樣 子；jü-ts' 如 此 (veng.)

THWART his plans, p'o gyi-go fah' 破 其 个° 法；— my wishes, ao'-ky'iang ngô-go sing-siang' 拗 强 我 个° 心 想

TICK, to tah'- tah-hyiang 得° 得° 響；tsah'-tsah-hyiang 耷 耷 響

TICKET, siao'-p'iao 小 票；p'iao 票；p'iao'-deo 票 頭；pawn —, tông'-p'iao 當 票

TICKLE, to hô-yiang'-c'ü-c'ü' 吷 癢 哦° 哦°

TICKLISH, p'ô-yiang'-go 怕 癢 个°

TIDE, dziao-shü' 潮 水；— contrary (i.e. against), t'eo' shü 問 水：dziao-shü' feh-te' 潮 水° 弗 對；— is rising, dziao tsiang'-de 潮 漲 了°；dziao læ-tih tsiang' 潮 正 在° 漲；full flood —, dziao-tsiang' tsoh'-de 潮 漲 足 了°；— eight parts full, tsiang'-pah 漲 了 八 分°；ebb —, loh-dziao 落 潮；t'e'-dziao 退 潮；slack —, bing dziao 平 潮；dziao-shü' bing' 潮 水°平°；— is favorable, jing-dziao' jing-shü' 順 潮 順 水°；to go with the—, ze dziao' ky'i 隨 潮 去°；the — follows the moon, dziao-shü' ze yüih-liang' go 潮 水° 隨 月 亮 个°

TIDE-WAITER, ah'-sia 押° 卸°

TIDINGS, fong-sing' 風 信；siao-sih' 消 息；sing'-sih 信 息；ing-sing' 音 信

TIE, to bo 縛°；— together, bo-tæa'-long 縛 攏；— or bind tightly (as bales), kw'eng 細；— (as bundles), tsah 紮；—a man, pông nying' 綁 人°；kw'eng'-pông nying' 細 綁 人°；— in a hard knot, cannot untie, tang si'-kyih ka'-feh-k'æ 打 死 結 解° 弗 開

TIER, zeng 層°；dæ 臺；— above —, zeng tang' zeng 層 層°；ih-dæ' ih-dæ' 一 臺 一 臺

TIGER, hwu 虎; lao'-hwu 老 虎
(ih-tsah)

TIGHT, kying 緊

TIGHTEN, to tang kying-tin' 打
緊點; siu kying-tin' 收緊點

TILE, ngô'-p'in 瓦 片 (ih-tsiang);
square —, fông-cün' 方 磚

TILE, to — a roof, kæ ngô'-p'in 蓋
瓦° 片

TILL, tao 到; ih-dzih' tao — 直
到; wait — I come, teng' tao
ngô læ' 等 到 我 來

TILL, to — the ground, cong din'
種 田; kang-cong' 耕° 種

TILT on one side, din' ih-pin ky'i'
墊 一 邊 起

TIMBER, moh-deo' 木 頭; moh-
liao' 木料; (a piece, ih-keng, ih-
cü), —merchant, jü-k'ah'-nying
樹 客 人'; moh-k'ah' 木 客

TIME, kong-fu' 工 夫; z-'eo' 時 候
(if speaking of hours); nyih-ts'
日°子 (if speaking of month, or
day); what —, soh'-go z-'eo' 甚°
麼° 時 候; how much —? to-
siao' kong-fu' 多 少 工 夫? no
—, m-kong'-fu 無 工 夫; no
leisure, (or empty — ), m'-neh
k'ong 沒 有° 空; to fix a —,
ding z-'eo' 定 時 候; ditto in
the more distant future, ding gyi'
定 期; to limit the — (when to
be done, or to arrive), 'æn' z-
zing' 限° 時 辰°; what — is it?
(i. e. of the clock), kyi-tin'-cong
幾 點 鐘; a long —, dziang-

kyiu' 長 久; to-z' 多 時; hyü'-
to kong-fu' 許 多 工 夫; a short
—, dzæn-z' 暫 時; at the —,
tsiao z-'eo' 照 時 候; en' z-'eo'
按 時 候; — has arrived, z-'eo'
tao'-de 時 候 到 了°; ditto (implying no chance for preparation),
ling-z' k'eo'-tsih 臨 時 適°節;
any — you please, zé-bin' soh'-
go z-'eo' 隨 便 甚°麼° 時 候;
feh-leng' soh'-go z-'eo' 弗 論
甚°麼° 時 候; at the same —,
tso' z-'eo' 同 時 候; in the day
—, nyih-li' 日° 裏; at the present —, yin-dzæ' 現 在; tông'-
z 當 時

TIMELY, teh-z' 得 時; seasonable,
gyih-z' 及 時; your coming is
very —, ng' læ-leh ting' teh'-z
你° 來 得° 頂 得 時

TIMES, tsao 遭; we 回; pin 遍;
vah; ts' 次; many —, hyü'-to
tsao su' 許 多 遭 數; hao-kyi'
we 好 幾 回; three or four —,
sæn s' pin 三 四 遍; hard times,
kyin-næn' z-'eo' 艱 難 時 候;
kæn-ka' z-'eo' 尷 尬 時 候; these
are hard — (i.e. are bad),— shü'-
k'eo gyih' 世 口 竭; shü'-k'eo
wa' 世 口 磊; good —, z-shü'
hao' 時 世 好; z-kwông' hao'
時 光 好

TIME-SERVING, ze-zông' ze-loh'-
go 隨 上 隨 落 个°; loh-meh'-
ts-den' tsao-yiang' 六 拇 指 頭°
搔 癢

TIMID, tæn′-ts siao′-go 膽 子 小
個°; tæn-ʻen′ go 膽 寒 個°; ɯ-
tæn′-kyʻi-go 無° 膽 氣 個°

TIN, mô′-kʻeo-tʻih 馬 口 鐵

TINDER, ho′-nyüong 火 絨; —
paper, me-deo′-ts 煤 頭 紙; ho′-
ts 火 紙 — bag, or box, ho′-lin
火 鏈; — bag, ho′-lin pao 火
鏈 包

TINGED with green, loh-ang′-ang
綠 影° 影°; — with red, ʻong-
hwe′-bwe 紅 輝 輝; — with yellow,
wông-bang′-bang 有° 些° 黃

TINKER, travelling brass-mender,
siao′-lu-s-vu′ 小 爐 司 務; kettle
mender, puʻ-ʻoh-ziang′ 補 鑊 匠°

TINKLING sound, ting-ting′ tông-
tông′ sing-hyiang′ 丁 丁 當 當
聲 響

TINSEL, gold kying-boh′ 金 箔;
silver —, nying-boh′ 銀 箔; brass
—, dong-boh′ 銅 箔; pewter —,
lah-boh′ 鑞 箔; sih′-boh 錫 箔

TIP, tsin 尖; — of the finger, ts′-
deo tsin′ 指 頭 尖; stand on —
toe, kyiah′ tin′-tæn-kyʻi′ 脚 顚° 起

TIPSY, (manifest in talking), yin-
tsin′-i 有 酒 意; yiu tseʻ-i 有
醉 意; tottering, ts′ih′-ts′ong-
pah′-tih-go 七 衡 八 跌 個°

TIRE, to — one's self, vah-lih′ 乏 力

TIRED, dziah-lih′ 着 力; kyʻih′-
lih 怯 力; slightly —, dziah-
lih-kwun′ 着 力 相°; kyʻih′-lih-
siang 怯 力 相; — and sleepy,
bi-gyün′ 疲 倦; tsing-jing′ gyün′-

kyʻi 精 神 倦 去°; — of wait-
ing, sing′-tsiao 心 焦; very —,
vah-lih′-de 乏 力 了; tso′-bi-
de 做 疲 了; vah′-de 乏 了;
quite — out, tʻeh-lih′-de 脫 力
了; — of, in′-tsao-tsao 厭 遭
遭; — of eating, (as a certain
kind of food), kyʻüoh′-leh in′-
tsao-tsao 吃 得° 厭 遭 遭; ditto
(in a less degree), kyʻüoh′ in′-de
吃° 厭 了; kyʻüoh-bi′-de 吃°
疲 了

TIRESOME, in′-væn-go 厭 煩 個°;
zô′-in, or jô′-in 惹° 厭; — (as
something often repeated), shü′-
væn 絮 煩

TITHE, a jih-feng′-ts-ih′ 十 分 之
一; jih-kwu′-ts-ih′ 十 股 之 一;
to take out a —, jih-feng′ li′-
hyiang do′-c′ih ih-feng′ 十 分 裏
向 扸 出 一 分

TITLE of an officer, kwun-ngæn′ 官
銜; ngæn-deo′ 銜 頭; — of
nobility, tsiah′-we 爵 位; to
confer ditto, fong tsiah′-we 封 爵
位; to confer a — (upon one
deceased), fong dzing′ 封 贈;
— of a book, shü ming′ 書 名;
(you) call (me) by a higher —
than (I) deserve, tseng-ts′ing′ feh-
ken′ 尊 稱 弗 敢; he has a —,
or right to it, gyi yiu′ veng′ 其 有
分; he has the exclusive ditto, gyi′
doh zi′ yiu′ veng 其 獨° 自° 有 分

TO, tao 到; teng 等; — Shanghai,
tao Zông-Hæ′ 到 上 海; say

— *him*, teng gyi wô' 與°其話;
*give* (it) — *me*, peh ngô' 給°我;
*go* — *a trade*, 'oh siu'-nyi ky'i'
學°手藝去°

TOAD, keh'-pô 蛤蚆; la-s (ih-tsah)

TOAD-STOOL, doh-dzing' 毒菌°

TOAST, *to* koh 烤°; *to* — *bread*,
koh mun-deo' 烤°饅頭

TOBACCO, in 烟; *to smoke* —,
ky'üoh in' 吃°烟; *ditto in a water
pipe*, ky'üoh shü' in 吃°水°烟;
*ditto in a dry pipe*, ky'üoh 'en'-
in 吃°旱烟; *to cultivate* —,
cong in-yih' 種烟葉; — *pipe*,
in kwun' 烟管

TO-DAY, kyih-mih' 今°日°; kying-
tsiao' 今朝

TOE, kyiah'-ts-meh-den' 脚指拇
頭; kyiah'-meh-den' 脚拇頭';
kyiah-ts-deo' 脚指頭 (ih-ko,
ih-go)

TOGETHER, dô-kô' 大°家°; 'eo'-
leh 候得°; *sing all* —, tsæn'-zi
ts'ông' 並°齊唱; tsæn'-pô-s'-
zi ts'ông' 並°排°會°齊唱; jü-
de' 聚隊; tso-de'; *go* —, dô-
kô' ky'i 大°家°去°

TOIL, lao-kw'u' 勞苦; sing-kw'u'
辛苦; *life of* —, lao-kw'u'
ih-si' 勞苦一世°; *anxious* —,
lao' sing fi'-lih 勞心費力

TOIL, *to* tso sing-kw'u' sang-weh'
做辛苦生°活; tso djong'-
deo sang-weh' 做重頭生°活

TOILSOME, lao-kw'u'-go 勞苦个°;
*laborious*, lao-loh'-go 勞碌个°

TOILET, *to make one's* — (as a
lady), su-tsông' 梳妝; tsah'-
kweh 紮°束°

TOKEN, *memorial*, piao'-kyi 表記

TOLERABLE, *that may be borne*,
næ'-leh-djü' 耐得°住; *passable*, ñong'-leh-ko 將°就°得°過;
p'o'-hao 頗好; yia-hao 也°好°;
wa'-hao 還°好

TOLERABLY *well done*, tso'-leh
p'o'-hao 做得°頗好

TOLL, *bridge* ko'-gyiao-din' 過橋
錢°; — *for mending a road*, siu-
lu' fi 修路費

TOMATO, called in Ningpo *foreign
egg-plant*, fæn-gyiæn 番茄°; and
*foreign peppers*, nga-koh lah-
gyiæ' 外°國辣茄°; in Shanghai
called fæn-z 番柿°

TOMB, veng 墳; veng-mo' 墳墓;
*the place of the* —, veng-deo' 墳
頭; veng-keng 墳跟; *to worship
at, and repair the* —, zông veng'
上墳

TOMB-STONE, mo-pe' 墓碑; pe-
ba' 碑牌°; *stone surrounding a
mound*, læn-t'u' 攔土

TO-MORROW, ming-tsiao' 明朝;
*day after* —, 'eo-nyih' 後日°;
— *or the day after*, ming 'eo'-
nyih 明後日°

TON, teng 噸

TONNAGE, teng-su' 噸數; —*dues*,
jün ts'ao' 船鈔

TONE, *sound*, sing-ing' 聲音

TONES, *the four* —, bing-tseh'-sing

平仄聲; *viz.,* bing-sing' 平聲, zông'-sing 上 聲, ky'ü'-sing 去 聲, and jih-sing' 入 聲

TONGS, ho'-gyin 火箝 (ih-pô)

TONGUE, zih-deo' 舌 頭 (ih-go); *to put out the* —, sing'-c'ih zih-deo' 伸 出 舌 頭; t'a'-c'ih zih-deo' 垂° 出 舌 頭

TONIC *medicine,* pu'-yiah 補 藥

TO-NIGHT, kyih-mih' yia'-tao 今° 日° 夜° 到; kying-yia' 今 夜°; tông'-yia 當夜°; lin-yia' 連夜'

TOO, t'eh or t'o 太°; —*cold,* t'eh' lang or t'o lang 太°冷; —*many,* t'eh to' 太° 多; *quite —much,* t'eh' ko-deo' 太° 過 頭; —*far beyond what is proper,* t'eh' ko-veng' 太°過分; —*young,* nyin-kyi' t'eh-ky'ing' 年 紀 太° 輕

TOOL, kô-sang 傢°伙°; *tools,* siu'-yüong kô'-sang 手 用 傢° 伙°

TOOTH, ngô-ts'' or ngô-ts'; 牙°齒; — *of a saw,* ken'-ts 鋸° 齒

TOOTH-ACHE, ngô-ts'' t'ong 牙° 齒 痛

TOOTH-BRUSH, ngô-shih' 牙°刷

TOOTH-PICK, t'ih'-ngô-ziang 剔 牙° 杖°

TOOTH-POWDER, ngô-feng 牙°粉

TOP, *apex,* ting'-deo 頂 頭; *the upper surface,* zông' min 上面; — *of a hill,* sæn ting-den' 山頂 頭°; — *of a tree,* jü ting-den' 樹 頂 頭°; jü nao-tsin' 樹 杪°

TORCH, ho'-pô 火把 (ih-ts); *many torches,* lah-za'ho'-pô 雜 柴 火把

TORMENT, *to* yüong sing-s' 用心 思; næn-we' 難 為; s-ing-sön' 使 陰 算

TORMENTED *with pain,* t'ong'-leh kw'u'-feh-ko 痛 得° 苦 弗 過

TORMENTOR, sing-s kyü' 心思鬼°

TORN, p'o'-de 破 了°; c'ô-k'æ-de 撦開 了°

TORRENTS, *rain falls in* —, c'ong t'in do yü 冲 天 大° 雨; yü loh ziang tao' ka 落° 雨 像 倒 下° 一° 般°

TORTOISE, *black* u-kyü' 烏 龜°; — *shell,* dæ-me k'oh 玳 瑁 壳°; *broken do,* dæ-me sih 玳 瑁 屑; *black — shell,* pih'-kah 鱉 甲°

TORTUOUS, wæn-ky'üoh'-go 彎 曲 个°

TORTURE, (as a punishment), ying-vah hyüong 刑罰兇; gyih-ying 極° 刑; *in perfect* —, kw'u'-t'ong ky'üoh'-feh-ko 苦 痛 吃° 弗 過

TOSS, *to* — *up,* tiu-zông'-ky'i 丟 上去°; —*about,* tiu-læ' tiu-ky'i' 丟 來 丟去°; —(as one unable to sleep), cün-tsch' 轉 側

TOTAL, t'ong'-gong 統共; *sum* —, tsong'-su 總數; gong-kyi' 共計; —*eclipse of the sun,* nyih-deo' djün-zih' 日頭全蝕; nyih-deo djün-ko wu-sah 日頭 全個 食° 去°

TOTALLY *spoiled,* long'-tsong i-diao-de 攏總 壞° 了°; djün-djün' long-wæn'-de 全弄壞°了°

TOTTERING, (a person), ts'ong'-ts'ong-dong 衝 衝 動; ts'ih'-ts'ong-pah-tih' 七 衝 八 趺; — *wall*, ziang' yiao-yiao'-dong 墻 搖 搖 動

TOUCH, *to* bang 搪; bang-djoh' 搪着'; *cannot be touched*, bang'-feh-teh'-go 搪 弗 得 个°; — *and feel*, moh 摸; moh-djoh' 摸 着°; *must not —, or move*, siu' m̄-nao' dong gyi 手 弗° 可° 動 其; *to place the hand upon*, siu en'-ih'-en 手 按 一 按

TOUCHING, *close to*, t'iah'-gying 貼° 近

TOUCH-STONE, s'-kying-zah' 試 金 石°; mo-kying'-zah 磨 金 石°

TOUGH, nying 靭; nying-bi'-tiao'-ts'i 靭 疲 刁 氣°; *able to endure*, mæn-ky'i' 蠻 氣

TOW, *to — a boat* (as by a steamer), ta jün' 帶° 船— *by a rope*, ts'ô-ky'in' 拉° 縴; te-ky'in' 背° 縴

TOWARD, hyiang 向; dziao 朝; — *the South*, hyiang Nen' 向南

TOWEL, siu'-kying 手巾; min-pu' 面布; *dish —*, k'a' beng'-ts pu' 揩° 盆 子 布; k'a-pu' 揩° 布 (ih-keng, ih-kw'e)

TOWER, t'ah 塔; *drum —*, kwu'-leo 鼓 樓; — *on the city wall*, dzing-leo' 城 樓; fi-leo' 飛 樓

TOWN, *walled* dzing-ts' 城子 (ih-zo); *market —* (unwalled), cing'-deo 鎮頭; z'-cing 市鎮 (ih-go)

TOYS, byi-djü' 戲具°; sô'-ho 要貨

TOY-SHOP, sô'-ho tin 要貨店; *toy-stall*, sô'-ho t'æn 要 貨 攤; *toy-image-shop*, 'en'-tin 泥° 孩° 店

TRACE, ying-tsih' 形 跡; ing'-tsong 影 踪; *mark*, 'eng-tsih' 痕 跡; — *of footsteps*, kyiah'-tsih 脚 跡; tsong-tsih' 踪 跡; kyiah'-u 脚 痕°

TRACE, *to — on paper*, ts-li' miao' 紙 裡 描; — *over a pattern*, ing'-leh sia' 引 了° 寫°; — *his footsteps*, keng'-leh gyi kyiah'-tsih tseo' 跟 得° 其 脚 跡 走

TRACK *of carriage wheels*, ts'ô-leng'-go ying-tsih' 車 輪 个° 形 跡

TRACT *on religion*, siao peng'-deo dao'-li shü 小 本 个° 道 理 書

TRADE, sang-i' 生°意; kying-ying' 經營; — *is dull*, sang-i' ts'ing-dæn' 生° 意 清 淡; sang-i ga'; sang-i' diao-da'; — *is diminished*, sang-i' siu-soh'-de 生° 意 收 縮° 了°; *to curtail one's —*, sang-i' siu-bo'; *what is your —?* ng soh'-go kying-ying' 你° 甚° 麼° 經 營?

TRADE, *to* kao-yih' 交°易; *to do business*, tso sang-i' 做 生° 意; — *at our shop*, teng ah'-lah tin'-li kao-yih' 與 我° 等° 店 裡 交° 易; *with whom do you —?* ng jü'-lah kao-yih'-go 你° 誰° 交° 易 个°?

TRADER, sang-i' nying 生° 意 人°; tso-m̄a'-ma-nying' 做° 賣 買 人°; *travelling —*, k'ah'-nying 客 人°

TRADITION, kwu'-djün-yin' 古傳
言 (veng); djün'-loh-læ'-go shih-
wô' 傳下°來个°說話; shü'-
dæ siang-djün'-go 世代相傳
个°; djün-yin' 傳言

TRADUCE, to po-long' 播弄

TRAFFIC in tea is large, dzô-yih'
zža'-ma to' 茶葉買°賣°多;
unlawful —, væn-kying'-go
sang-i' 犯禁个°生°意; —
in human beings, fæn'-ma sang-
nying-k'eo' 販賣°人°口; — in
fattening girls for bad purposes,
yiang seo'-mô 養瘦馬

TRAGEDY, mournful play, pe-sông'-
go byi'-veng 悲傷个°戲文;
mournful event, ts'æn'-sông-go z-
t'i' 慘傷个°事體

TRAIN, to instruct, kao 教°; to bring
up, iang 養

TRAIN of followers, keng-dzong'-
go cü'-kwu 跟從个°人°; ze-
dzong'-go 隨從个°

TRAIT, a good ih-yiang hao'-c'ü
一樣好處; many good traits,
hyü'-to hao-c'ü' di-fông 許多
好處地方

TRAITOR, one who informs the enemy, li'-t'ong nga-koh'-go 裏通
外°國个°; an officer who turns
—, kæn-dzing' 奸°臣; a Chinese
—, Hen'-kæn 漢奸°; one who
sells his country, ma-koh'-go 賣
國个°

TRAITOROUS, kæn-tsô'-go 奸°詐
个°; kæn-wah-go 奸°滑个°

TRAMPLE, to dah 踏; nao 踏°;
— to death, dah-sah' 踏死°

TRANQUIL, en-tæn' 安貼; bing-
en' 平安; t'a'-bing 太°平;
all — (nothing to disturb), en'-
jün' vu-z' 安然無事

TRANQUILIZE, to — him, s'-teh
gyi ding-diah' 使得其定奪°;
long gyi bing' 弄其平

TRANSACT, to — business, bæn z-
t'i' 辦事體; ditto diligently,
ken'-bæn z-t'i' 幹辦事體; —
another's business, dæ'-we jing-z'
代為人事

TRANSACTION, sô-bæn'-go z-ken'
所辦个°事幹

TRANSCENDS all our ideas, c'ih'-
ü i'-nga 出於意外°

TRANSCRIBE, to ts'ao-sia' 鈔寫°;
deng-sia' 謄寫°; ts'ao sia'-ko-
ky'i 鈔寫°過去°; — distinctly,
deng-ts'ing' 謄清

TRANSCRIBED copy, ts'ao-bah'抄
白°

TRANSFER, to tsæn 趲; ts'in 遷;
pun 搬; yi 移; — to another
place, tsæn-u' 趲地°方°; — to
that box, tsæn'-ko keb'-tsah siang-
ts'-li 趲過這隻箱子裏; —
to another person, kao-c'ih' 交
出; ditto entirely, kao'-siao 交°
銷; — the capital, ts'in-tu' 遷
都; — a coffin, ts'in-zæ' 遷材°;
— baggage, 'ang-li'pun'-ko'-ky'i
行李搬過去°; — an official
to another place, diao-zing' 調任

TRANSFORM, to pin-yiang 變樣;
— (by some internal law, as
from a worm to a butterfly), pin'-
hwô 變 化

TRANSGRESS, to væn 犯; — the
law, væn fah' 犯 法; to sin, væn
ze 犯 罪

TRANSGRESSION, ze 罪; ze'-ky'in
罪 愆; ko'-shih 過 失; ko'-tön
過 端

TRANSGRESSOR, ze'-nying罪人°;
væn'-nying 犯 人°; væn-fah'-
go 犯 法 个°

TRANSIENT, ziu we ko'-ky'i 就°
會 過 去°; dzæn-z'-go 暫時个°

TRANSIT, inward jih ne'-di 入 內
地; outward —, c'ih nen'-di 出
內地; inward —pass, (Customs),
jih ne-di se-tæn 入 內 地 稅 單

TRANSITORY, ko'-r-peh-liu'過而
不 留

TRANSLATE, to fæn 繙; fæn-yih'
繙 譯; — (completely), fæn-
c'ih' 繙 出; how do you — this
sentence into English? keh'-kyü
Da-Ing'-wô dza fæn'-go 這° 句
大 英 話 怎° 繙 个°?

TRANSLATION of the Four Books,
fæn-yih'-go S'-Shü 繙譯个°四
書

TRANSLATOR, fæn-yih'-go cü'-kwu
繙 譯 个° 人°

TRANSMIGRATION of souls, cün-
si' 轉世°; deo-t'æ 投 胎

TRANSMIT, to — money, ta dong-
din' 帶° 銅 錢°; ditto through

others (as bills of exchange), we
匯; — (as words), djün 傳;
— to posterity, djün' peh 'eo'-
dæ 傳 與° 後 代; djün-loh'-
læ 傳下° 來; — the throne to a
successor, djün we' 傳 位

TRANSPARENT, kwông' we t'eo'-
ko-go 光 會 透 過 个°

TRANSPIRED, the secret has —,
tseo'-leo fong-sing'-de 走 漏 風
聲 了°; lu-fong'-de 露 風 了°

TRANSPLANT, to ts'in-ko' ky'i-
cong' 遷過去°種; — rice, cong
dao' 種 稻

TRANSPORT, to yüing 運; pun-
yüing' 搬 運; — goods, yüing
ho'-veh 運 貨 物

TRANSPORT for carrying rice to the
capital, yüing liang jün' 運糧船

TRANSPORTATION a few hundred
li, du 徒; — 1000 to 2000 li, liu
流; — beyond the frontier, c'ong-
kyüing' 充 軍

TRANPOSE, to diao zin-'eo' 調前°;
後; tsæn zông'-loh 趲 上 落

TRAP, gyiang 弶°; rat —, lao'-
ts' gyiang 老 鼠 弶° (ih go);
iron ditto with teeth, t'ih-mæn'
鐵 貓° (ih tsah); to set a —,
tsông gyiang' 裝 弶°

TRASH, vu-yüong'-ts veh 無 用
之 物

TRAVAIL, to ky'üoh seng-ts'æn'-
go kw'u'-deo 吃° 生 產 个° 苦
頭

TRAVEL, to c'ih-meng' 出 門;

— *a distance*, c'ih yün'-meng 出 遠 門;— *every where*, koh'-tao-c'ü tseo-pin' 各到處走遍; — *to learn*, yin-'oh' 遊 學°

The last expression refers primarily to a *siu-dzæ* 秀 才 going abroad for study, but is now used in a wider signification.

TRAVELLER, *one passing on*, ko-lu'-go-nying 過 路 个°人°; *one away from his home*, c'ih-meng'-nying 出 門 人°; *one who has travelled far*, c'ih-yün'-meng-go 出 遠 門 个°

TRAY, bun 盤; *tea* —, dzô-bun' 茶 盤 (ih-min)

TREACHEROUS, *violating trust, and injuring*, tao'-toh-long'-ts-go 反° 背° 前° 言° 个°; fông-tao'-deo-p'ao'-go 放 倒 頭 礮 个°; *faithless by nature*, ǔ-sing'-'ang-go 無° 信 行° 个°

TREAD, *to* — *upon*, dah 踏; nao 蹈°; *must not* — *on it*, ǔ-nao' dah-gyi'-zông' 弗°可°踏 其 上

TREASURE, *a* ih-go pao'-pe — 个°寶 貝; ih-yiang pao'-pe — 樣寶貝; gyi-ho' k'o-kyü' 奇 貨 可 居; *wealth*, dzæ-veh' 財 物; *silver*, nying-liang' 銀兩; *royal* —, kw'n' nying 庫 銀

TREASURE, *to* — *with care*, kying'-kying kwu'-djoh 兢 兢 顧 着°; *to put*, or *store away*, k'ông 囥; *ditto safely*, dzông-k'ông' 藏 囥

TREASURER, tsông nying-bun'-go 掌 銀 盤 个°

TREASURY, kw'n 庫; dzin-kw'n' 錢 庫

TREAT, *to* dæ 待; k'en'-dæ看 待; — *slightingly*, ky'ing-dæ' 輕 待; ky'ing-mæn' 輕 慢; dæ'-mæ 怠 慢; — *ill*, ts'ô'-tô 剿° 諷°; — *shabbily*, boh-dæ' 薄 待; — *one well*, dæ nying hao' 待人°好; — *kindly*, or *pet*, we'-wu 衛 護; o'-lo 捼 擺;— *a person well*, dæ nying 'eo' 待 人°厚; *as you* — *me*, I'll — *you*, ng dza læ', ngô' dza ky'i' 你°怎°來我怎°去; — *with disrespect*, mao'-væn 冒 犯; — *with irreverence*, sih'-doh 褻° 瀆; *ditto purposely*, c'ong-dzông', or ts'ong-dzông 衝 撞

TREATY, *contract*, iah 約; — *of peace*, 'o-iah' 和 約; *to make a* —, lih iah' 立 約; *to violate a* —, be iah' 背 約

TREBLE. *first* — (in music), tsing'-p'ing 正品; *second* —, fu'-p'ing 副 品. See MRS. J. B. Mateer's Musical Instructor.

TREBLE, *to* kô-liang'-be-ts'eo' sæn-be' 加 兩 倍 湊 三 倍

TREE, jü 樹 (ih-cü)

TREES, jü-moh' 樹 木

TREMBLE, *to* teo 抖; fah-teo' 發 抖; gwah-gwah'-teo 撊°撊°抖; — *with fear*, or *cold*, gying 噤; fah-gying' 發 噤; 'en-gying' 寒 噤; lang'-gying 冷°噤; *heart trembling with fear*, sing hyü'-dah-tsin' 心 虛 肉°顫°

TRENCH, keo 溝; *open a* —, k'æ' ih-da keo' 開一堵溝

TRESPASS, ze'-ko 罪過; ko'-shih 過失

TRESPASS *over another's boundary*, (by building, &c.), tsin di-ka' 佔地界'; —*on your time*, tæn-ngwu' ng-go kong-fu' 躭悮你个°工夫; — *against*, teh'-ze 得罪

TRIAL, *give* (him or it) *a* —, s' ih-tsao k'en 試一遭看; s-ih'-s 試一試; *to bring to* —, *&c.*, dzing-dzong' 成訟; *have a* —, yiu dzong-z' 有訟事; *ditto* (*i.e.* both sides going to law), tang kwun-s 打官司; ky'üoh kwun-s' 吃°官司; yiu kwun-s' 有官司; (ih-ky'i); *won the* —, kwun-s' tang'-ying-de 官司打贏了°; *is the* — (of a case) *over?* en'-gyin yiu liao'-kyih-feh 案件有了結否°?

TRIALS, *afflictions*, wæn'-næn 患難

TRIANGLE, sæn-koh'-ying 三角形

TRIBE, *race*, tsong-dzoh' 宗族; *barbarous* —, bu'-loh 部落; *divisions of a* —, ts-p'a' 支派°; *the twelve tribes of Israel*, Yi-seh'-lih jih-nyi' ts-p'a' 以色列十二支派°

TRIBULATION, næn-deo' 難頭; kw'n'-næn 苦難; wæn'-næn 患難

TRIBUNAL, *before the* —, dæ yin' 臺前°; we yin' 位前°; *place of the* —, fah'-dông 法堂; *the*

*six tribunals* (at Peking), loh-bu' 六部

TRIBUTARY *kingdoms*, joh-koh' 屬國

TRIBUTE, *to bring* tsing-kong' 進貢; *things offered as* —, tsing-kong'-go li'-veh 進貢个°禮物

TRICK, kwe'-kyi 詭計 (ih-go); *to play a trick upon*, hyi'-long 戲弄

TRICKS, *full of* —, kwe'-kyi to-tön'-go 詭計多端个°

TRICKLE, *to* — *down*, ti'-loh-læ 滴落來; jing'-loh-læ 潤下°來

TRIFLE, siao'-z 小事: ky'ü-ky'ü'-siao'-z 區區小事; *to* — *with*, r-hyi' 兒戲; *to make sport of*, hyi'-long 戲弄

TRIFLING *behaviour*, 'ang-we'ky'ing-veo' 行°爲輕浮; 'ang-we feh djong'-jib 行°爲弗重實

TRIGGER, wông鑕; long-deo' 龍頭

TRIM, *to* — *a lamp* (wick), tsin' teng-sing'-me 翦燈芯煤; — *even*, tsin bing' 翦平; — *the beard*, tæn ngô-su' 剝髭°鬚

TRIMMING, *to put* or *tack on* —, ting kwe'-ts 釘桂子; tsa kwe'-ts.

TRINITY, sæn we'-ih-t'i 三位一體

TRINKETS *for the head*, (principally, but others may be included), siu'-sih 首飾; *box for* —, deo-min-siang 頭面箱

TRIP, *take a* —, c'ih ih-go meng 出一次°門

TRIP, *to* — *along*, tseo'-leh ky'ing-fæn' 走得°輕泛; *ditto* (as a child), ky'ing-t'iao' 輕佻; *to lose footing*, shih-kyiah' 失 脚; *to cause to stumble*, keo-tih' 鈎 跌; pæn-tih' 扳 跌; *your foot tripped me*, ng-go kyiah' keo ngô tih' 你 个° 脚 鈎 我 跌

TRIUMPH, *beat the drum of* —, k'ao teh-sing'-kwu 敲 得 勝 鼓; *sing —over victory*, ts'ông' teh'-sing'-ko' 唱 得 勝 歌

TROOP, *a — of horse*, ih-de' mô'-ping 一 隊 馬 兵; *a — of infantry*, ih-de' bu-ping' 一 隊 步 兵; *many troops*, da-ping' 大 隊° 兵 馬°

TROPIC *of Capricorn*, nen-ta' 南 帶°; — *of Cancer*, poh'-ta 北 帶°

TROPICS, *the* nyih-ta' 熱°帶°; jih-ts'-sin 日 至 線

TROT, *to* siao'-p'ao 小 跑°

TROUBLE, *to* le 累; kying-dong' 驚動; — *many times, or in many ways*, væn 煩; væn-zeh' 煩 雜°; *to annoy*, væn-ky'i' 煩 起; *may I — you*, væn' ng 煩 你°; siang-væn' ng' 相 煩 你°; *can I — you to do it?* hao væn-lao' ng tso' feh 好 煩 勞 你° 做 否°; *to worry*, ts'ao 嘈; ts'ao'-ziao 嘈 擾; *tired of* (*your*) *troubling*, ts'ao'-feh-ko' 嘈 弗 過; — *to come* (or go), lao-kyüô' 勞 駕; *I put you to too much* —, (or, thank you), næn-we' ng 難 爲 你°; fi-sing' fi-sing' 費 心 費 心; fi-ng-sing' 費 你° 心

TROUBLE, *to make* —, sang'-c'ih z-ken' læ 生° 出 事 幹 來; *I have a great deal of* — *in teaching him*, ngô læ-tih kao' gyi yiu hyü'-to keh'-tah 我 教°其 有 許 多 疙 瘩; *to have one's* — *for one's pains*, ky'in' k'ong-mo' 牽 空 磨

TROUBLED *in mind*, sing ông'-de; sing' væn-meng' 心 煩 悶; — *and worried*, væn-nao' 煩 惱; — *looks*, zeo-mi' tang-pah'-kyih 愁° 眉° 百° 結; *the more I thought, the more I was* —, yüih-ts'eng' yüih-ông' 愈°想 愈°煩

TROUBLESOME, *how* dza væn' 甚° 煩; dza næn-we' 甚° 難 爲

TROUGH, zao 槽°; *pig* —, cü-zao' 豬 槽°; *horse* —, mô'-zao 馬 槽° (ih-go)

TROUSERS, kw'u 袴 (a pair, ih-iao); *the bottom of* —, kw'u' kyiah 袴 脚

TROWEL, *mason's* nyi-tao' 泥 刀; nyi-kah' 泥 夾° (ih-pô)

TRUANT, *one who shirks study, and deceives*, la-'oh tsing' 賴°學° 精

TRUCE *to hostilities*, dzæn-ding' tang-tsiang' 暫 停 打 仗; *board begging a* —, min'-tsin ba 免 戰 牌°

TRUE, tsing 眞; jih-we' 實 爲; jih-dzæ' 實 在; ky'üoh-jih 確 實; dzing-jih' 誠 實; *something — to act upon*, jih-loh' 實 落; — *to his word*, gyi'-go shih'-wô sing'-

jih-go 其个° 說話信實个°;
— *and no mistake,* tsing-tao'-wô
真實° 話

TRULY, jih-dzæ' 實 在; tsing-
tsing' 真真; ko'-jün 果然

TRUMPET, (Chinese) 'ao-dong' 號
筒; 'ao-teo' 號斗 (ih-kwun)

TRUNK, siang-ts' 箱子 (ih-tsah);
— *for clothes,* i-siang 衣箱;
*leather* — , bi-siang' 皮箱;
*board covering to protect a* —,
kah'-pæn 夾° 板; — *of a tree,*
jü'-sing 樹身; *elephant's* —,
ziang bih 象鼻°

TRUST, *to rely upon,* k'ao'-djoh 靠
着; i'-k'ao 依靠; i'-z 倚恃;
*to believe in,* siang-sing' 相信;
*cannot* — *what he says,* gyi'-go
shih-wô' feh-tsoh'-cing 其个°
說話弗作準; gyi'-go shih-
wô' sön'-su-feh-læ 其个° 說話
算數弗來; gyi'-go shih-wô'
k'ao'-feh-jih' 其个° 說話靠
弗實; — *in Christ,* k'ao'-djoh
Yiæ-su' 靠着° 耶穌; — *to
one's self,* i'-z zi' 倚恃自°; —
(something) *to another,* kao-dæ'
交° 代; kao-fu' 交° 付; *ditto,
expecting him to look after,* t'oh'-
fu 託付; *can't* —*him,* k'ao'-feh-
djü'-go 靠弗住个°; t'oh'-sing-
feh-ko 託信弗過

TRUST, *responsible* tsah'-zing djong'
責任重; ken-yi' do' 干係大°

TRUSTY, t'o'-tông 妥當; weng'-
tông 穩當; tih'-tông 的當

TRUSTWORTHY, t'oh'-sing-leh-ko
託信得° 過; k'ao'-leh-djü 靠
得住

TRUTH, *the* tsing dao'-li 真道理;
*speak the* —, kông tsing-wô' 講°
真話; kông jih-wô' 講°實話;
tsiao dzih-li' kông 照直理講°;
kông lao'-jih wô' 講°老實話;
*absolute* —, z-jün' tsing'-go 自
然真个°

TRY, *to* s'-s 試試; s'-s-k'en' 試
試看; — *once,* s'-ih-s' 試一
試; — *at first,* or *beforehand,* s'-
t'en 試探; — *to sleep,* s'-s hao
kw'eng-joh 試試好睡°熟否°;
— *the taste of,* zông-zông'-k'en
嘗° 嘗° 看; zông mi-dao' 嘗°
味° 道; — *various means to
make better,* cü'-du 制度; —*all
means possible and fail,* wang cü'-
du jü' cü-du, cü'-du feh-hao'
橫°制度竪制度制 度弗好;
— *a case,* sing'-meng en'-gyin
審 問° 案件; — (as by fire),
s'-lin 試煉

TUB, dong 桶; *wash* —, kyiah'-
dong 脚桶; *bath* —, gyiang'-
nyüoh-dong' 洗°浴°桶; nyüoh-
dong' 浴°桶 (ih-tsah)

TUBE, kwun'-ts 管子; *bamboo* —,
coh'-kwun-dong 竹管筒 (ih-
diao, ih-keng)

TUCK, *to* — *in order to shorten* (as
a dress), soh'-leh tön' 束短;
— *it,* or *make a* —, soh'-ih-soh
束一束; —*in* (as bed covering),

seb'-tæn'-cün 扆 進° 去°; —
or *pull up the sleeves*, ziu-ts' leh-
zông'-ky'i 袖 子 挦 上 去°
TUFT, *a* ih-soh' 一 束; ih-lu' 一
縷°; — *of feathers*, ih-soh tiao'-
mao 一 束 鳥° 毛; — *of hair*,
ih-lu deo-fah' 一 縷° 頭 髮
TUFT, *to* — (as a cushion), ih-soh'-
ih-soh ting' 一 束 一 束 釘
TUMBLE, *to* — *down*, tib'-tao 跌
倒; le-tao'; —*over*, fæn'-tao 翻倒
TUMBLER, po-li'-pe' 玻 璃 杯 (ih-
tsah)
TUMOR, *swelling*, cong 瘇 (ih-go)
TUMULT, nao-z' 鬧 事; nying-to'
k'eo'-hyiang 人° 多 口 響; *to
raise a* —, nao'-c'ih z' læ 鬧 出
事 來
TUMULTUOUS, *to be* —, ts'ao'-nao
譟 鬧
TUNE, ky'iang-diao' 腔 調
TUNE, *to* — (as a fiddle), diao-yin'
調 絃
TUNNEL *for discharging liquors*,
leo-teo' 漏 斗 (ih-go); — *in
the ground*, di-dao' 地 道; —
*through a hill*, sæn-dong' lu 山
洞 路; *to make a* —, k'æ ih-
go di-dao' 開 一 个° 地 道
TURBAN, pao-deo'-pu' 包 頭 布
(ih-kw'e)
TURBID, weng-weng'-go 混 混
个°; weng-djoh'-go 混 濁 个°
TURBULENT, sing'-dzing yia'-ky'i
性 情 野° 氣

TUREEN, t'ông-kwun' 湯 罐 (ih-
tsah)
TURF, *sod*, ts'ao'-bi 草 皮 (ih-kw'e)
TURKEY, ho'-kyi 火 雞 (ih-tsah)
TURMERIC, kyiang-wông' 薑 黃
TURN, *to* — *around* (as a wheel),
cün 轉; cün'-dong 轉 動; yüing-
dong' 運 動; — (as a key, or
screw), cih'-cün 折° 轉; — *the
head*, deo' nyin-cün' 頭 回° 轉;
deo nyin-hyiang' 頭 側° 向; —
*upside down*, fæn'-cün 反 轉; —
*back* (in walking), tao' tseo-cün
倒 走 轉; — *a corner*, cün-wæn'
轉 彎; wæn-cün' 彎 轉; —
*wrong side out*, fæn-min' 翻 面;
— *the back* (in going), fæn' pe
反 背; — *the back towards*, be
hyiang' 背 向; — *out* (as from a
bowl), tao'-c'ih 倒 出; *the tide
is turning*, dziao-shü' we-deo'-de
潮 水° 回 頭 了°; dziao-shü'cün'-
de 潮 水° 轉 了°; *to* — *bad* (as
food), tseo-mi' 變° 味; *ditto* (as
sweet-meats, &c.), fæn 泛; fæn-
diao 泛 壞°; — *sour*, pin'-leh
sön'-de 變 得° 酸 了°; tsoh-sön'
作 酸; — *to oil*, pin'-leh yiu de
變 得° 油 了°; — *against one
for slight cause*, we'-leh siao'-z
fæn-lin' 為 了° 小 事 翻 臉; —
*away*, nyin-cün'-ky'i 側° 轉 去°;
— *back and forth*, fæn-læ' fæn-
ky'i' 翻 來 翻 去°; — *over and
over*, fæn-læ' foh-ky'i' 翻 來 覆
去°; — *out well* (as a child, &c.),

dzing-ky‘i′ 成 器 ; *to take a* —,
or *short walk,* tseo′ ih-cün 走 一
轉 ; *ditto, for one's own business,*
tang ih-go wang′ ;—*with a lathe,*
ts‘ô 車

TURNS, *to do by* —, ling′-leh tso′
輪°得°做 ; ling-wun′ tso 輪°換
做 ; ling-læ′ ling-ky‘i tso′ 輪°來
輪°去°做 ; *ditto,* (by exchange),
diao-læ′ wun-ky‘i tso′ 調 來 換
去°做 ; *cold and hot by* —, ih-zi
lang′, ih-zi nyih′ 一 齊°冷 一
齊°熱 ; dziao-lang′ dziao-nyih′
潮°冷 潮°熱°

TURNIP, *radish,* lo-boh′ 蘿蔔

TURTLE, *small* u-kyü′ 烏 龜° ;
kyiah′-ng 甲 魚° ; do-ng′ 大
魚° ; pih 鱉 ; *large* —, la-deo-
nyün′ 癩°頭°黿 (ih-tsah)

TURTLE-DOVE, pæn-kyiu′ 斑 鳩
(ih-tsah)

TUSK, liao-ngô′ 獠牙° ; *elephant's*
—, ziang′-ngô 象 牙° (ih-ts)

TUTELARY *deity* (of a place), t‘u′-
di bu′-sah 土 地 菩 薩

TUTOR, *teacher,* sin-sang′ 先 生°
(ih-we)

TWEAK, *to* — *the nose,* nyiu bih-
deo′ 扭°鼻°頭

TWEEZERS, nyiah-ts-gyin′ 揑指
箝 (ih-pô).

TWELVE, jih-nyi′ 十 二°

TWELVTH, *the* di jih-nyi′ 第 十
二° ; — *part,* jih-nyi′-feng ts-ih′
十 二° 分 之 一

TWENTY, nyiæn 廿

TWENTIETH, *the* di-nyiæn′ 第廿 ;
— *of the month,* nyi-jih′ 二°十 ;
—*part,* nyiæn-feng′ ts-ih′ 廿 分
之 一 ; nyiæn-kwu′ li-hyiang′
ih-kwu′ 廿 股 裏 向 一 股

TWICE, liang′ tsao 兩 遭 ; liang′
we 兩 回 ; liang′ pin 兩 遍 ; liang′
vah.

TWIG, *a* ih-tiao ô-ts′ 一 條°椏°枝

TWILIGHT ( in the morning), u-
long′-song 烏 眼°臊° or 矇°矇°
亮°; — (in the evening), wông-
hweng-den′ 黃 昏 時°

TWILLED *cotton cloth,* zia′-veng-pu′
斜°紋 布 ; *gray ditto,* hwe-seh′
zia-veng 灰 色 斜°紋

TWINE, *hemp* mô-sin′ 麻 線

TWINE, *to* — *about,* dzin 纏 ; nyiao
繞°

TWINKLING *of an eye,* ngæn′-tsing
ih-sah′ 眼 睛 一 瞤 ; — *of a*
*star,* sing-kwông′ t‘eo′-t‘eo-dong
星 光 透 透 動

TWIN, sông-sang′ 雙 生°

TWIRL, *to* — *with the fingers,* mih
轉° ; — *a cash,* mih dong-din′
轉° 銅 錢°

TWIST, *to* cih′-cün 折°轉 ; *to* —
*with the hand,* ts‘o 搓 ; — *with the*
*fingers,* tsih 織 ; mih 搐 ; —*hem-*
*pen thread,* ts‘o mô-sin′ 搓蔴線 ;
t‘oh mô-sin′ ; — *ropes,* kao læn′
絞°纜 ; tang zing′ 打繩°

TWISTED, *neck bone is* —, deo-
kying′-kweh cih′-c‘ih-de 頭 頸
骨 折° 出 了° ; — *or twined,*

*together*, nyiao-long'-liao 繞°攏
了°; gao-long'-liao 絞°攏了

TWITCHING, *muscles are* —, kying'
læ-tih te 筋°適°轉°

TWO, nyi 二°; liang 兩,(also means
a few); — *catties*, nyi kying' 二°
斤; — *hundred*, nyi pah' 二°百°;
— *men*, liang'-go nying' 兩 个°
人°; — *months*, liang'-ko yüih'
兩 個月; — *or three cash*, ko'-
pô dong-din' 個巴 銅 錢°; *cut
in* —, te' p'o'-k'æ 對 破 開;
*ditto* (with scissors), te' tsin-k'æ'
對 剪 開

TYPE, ing'-ts 影子; — *of Christ*,
Yiæ-su'-go ing'-ts 耶 穌 个° 影
子; *lead* —, k'æn-z' 鉛 字;
*movable* —, web-z'-pæn 活字版

TYPE-SETTER, pa-z'-go 排°字°个°

TYPHOON, fong-pao' 風颮; gyü'-
fong 颶 風

TYRANNICAL, bao-nyiah'-go 暴
虐 个°; byüong-ôh' 兇 惡

TYRANT, bao-nyiah'-go wông-ti'
暴 虐 个° 皇 帝; Gyih-Dziu'-
ts-kyüing' 桀 紂 之 君.*

* So called from two ancient Chinese
kings named Gyih and Dziu.

TYRO, sang-siu' 生° 手

## U

UBIQUITOUS, vu-sô'-peh-dzæ' 無
所 不 在; c'ü'-c'ü læ-tong' 處
處 都 在°

UDDER, na-dæ 嫺° 袋; na-lu.

UGLY, ẁa-k'en' 歪 看; *very* —,

p'o'-nying-sah-la 怕人°檄 頓°;
ts'iu'-leo 醜 陋; — *and uncouth*,
jing'-feh-c'ih-cong', mao'feh-c'ih-
siang'人 弗 出 衆 貌 弗出 相

ULCER, ts'ông 瘡; ts'ông-doh'瘡
毒; *malignant* —, doh ts'ông'
毒 瘡; *to have an* — , sang
ts'ông' 生° 瘡; sang doh 生° 毒

ULTIMATELY, tao'-ti 到 底; kwe-
keng' 歸根; kyin'-kying 究竟;
tao kyih'-sah 到 結 煞; cong-
ü' 終 于

UMBRELLA, sæn 傘 (ih-ting); *rain*
—, yü'-sæn雨傘; *sun*—, liang-
sæn' 涼傘; —*of state*, wông-lo'-
sæn 黃 羅 傘; *to open an* — ,
ts'ang sæn' 撐傘; *to shut an* —,
siu sæn' 收 傘

UMBRELLA-MAKER, sæn'-s-vu傘
司 務

UMPIRE, kong-tön' cü'-kwn 公斷
个°人°

UNABLE, feh neng'-keo 弗能殼;
— *to remember*, kyi'-feh-teh 記
弗得;— *to use*, yüong'-feh-djoh'
用 弗 着°; yüong'-feh-teh' 用
弗得; yüong'-feh-læ' 用弗來;
— *to bear*, tông'-feh-djü 擋弗
住; — *to eat, to do*, or *to endure*,
ky'üoh-feh-loh 吃° 弗 下°; —
*to overtake*, ken'-feh-zông 赶弗
上; — *to stand*, dzæn-feh-djü'
站 弗 住; — *to stand firmly*,
lih'-feh-ẁeng' 立 弗 穩; lih'-
feh-lao' 立 弗 牟

UNACCOMMODATING, feh-yün'-

t'ong 弗圓通; feh-t'ong'-yüong
弗通融

UNACCOUNTABLE, soh'-go yün'-
kwu, feh-tong'甚°麼°緣故, 弗
懂; næn-ts'eh' næn-ziang' 難測
難詳

UNACCUSTOMED, feh-kwæn' 弗
慣; long-feh-kwæn' 弄弗慣;
— to do, tso'-feh-kwæn 做弗
慣 — to wear, c'ün'-feh-kwæn'
穿弗慣

UNACQUAINTED with, feh-nying'-
teh 弗認°得; feh-min'-jing 弗
面認; — with the ways of the
world, feh-sih shü'-vu 弗識世務

UNADULTERATED, m̄'-neh ts'æn-
kô' 沒°有°攙假°; feh-tsiah-
kô' 弗攙假°;— goods, tsing
ho' 眞貨

UNALTERABLE, keng'-kæ-feh-læ-
go 更改弗來个°

UNANIMOUS, dong-sing'-'eh-i' 同
心合意

UNANSWERABLE, pæn-poh'-feh-
læ 扳駁弗來

UNANSWERED (as letters), feh-
zing' we-teh'-de 弗曾回答了°

UNANTICIPATED, liao'-feh-tao'
料弗到; siang'-feh-tao' 想弗
到; liao-siang'-feh-tao' 料想
弗到; i'-siang-feh-tao' 意想
弗到

UNAPPROACHABLE, gying-sing'-
feh-long'-go 近身弗攏个°

UNARMED, feh-ta' bông-sin'- go
kô'-sang 弗帶°防手个°傢伙°;

— soldiers, feh-ta'-ky'i-yiæ'-go
ping' 弗帶器械°个°兵

UNATTAINABLE, teh'-feh-djoh'
得弗着°; teh'-feh-tao-sin' 得
弗到手

UNAUTHORIZED, gyüoh-nga' 局
外°; veng-nga'牙外°

UNAVOIDABLE, cannot be shunned,
min'-feh-teh 免弗得; cannot get
rid of, t'e'-feh-diao' 推弗去°;
no help for it, peh-teh-yi' 不得
巳; shih'-feh-teh' 設法奈°何°

UNBECOMING, feh-siang-nyi' 弗
相宜; feh-siang-'eh' 弗相合

UNBELIEVING, feh-siang-sing'-go
弗相信个°

UNBENDING, tsah'-ngang 圓硬;
— (in a good purpose), ngang-
lah' 硬辣; kông-gyiang' 剛强;
— (in a bad thing), sang-gyiang'
生°强

UNBIASED, m̄-p'in'-go 無°偏个°;
m̄-p'in-ky'üoh'-go 無°偏曲个°;
— opinion, m̄-p'in-ky'üoh'-go
i'-s 無°偏曲个°意思;—
mind, kong-dao' sing 公道心

UNBIND, to t'eo 抖°; t'eo'-k'æ 抖
開; t'eo'-sæn 抖散; ka'-k'æ 解
開;—the feet, t'eo kyiah' 抖脚

UNBLAMABLE, kwa'-feh-læ'- go
怪°弗來个°; m̄-p'i-bing'-go
無°批評个°

UNBLEMISHED, m̄-yüô-tin' 無°瑕
玷

UNBOLT the door, bah meng-shün'
拔門閂

UNBOLTED *flour*, ta'-bi min-feng' 帶°皮麪粉; ts'u min'-feng 麤麪粉

UNBOSOM *the heart*, dæn-dæn sing' 談談心; — *one's troubles*, kông sing-z' 講 心事

UNBOUNDED, ʊ̆-ꞌæn'-cü 無°限°制; ʊ̆-ꞌæn'-liang 無°限°量; ʊ̆-pin'-ʊ̆-ngen' 無°邊無°岸

UNBRIDLED, fông'-tsong 放縱

UNBROKEN, ʊ̆'-neh k'ao'-se 沒°有°敲碎; — *line*, lin-ky'in' feh-dön 連牽弗斷; — *succession*, mah-mah' siang-lin' 脈脈相連; *ditto* (as living things), seng-seng'-peh-sih' 生生不息; — *horse*, sang mô' 生°馬

UNBURIED (as a person), ʊ̆'-neh en-tsông' 沒°有°安葬; — (as animals), ʊ̆'-neh tsông' 沒°有°葬; ʊ̆-neh bu-loh' 沒°有°理°落

UNBURNT *bricks*, cün-deo' p'e-ts' 磚頭胚子

UNBUTTON, *to* coh nyin'-ts 解°鈕子; *unbuttoned*, nyiu'-ts coh-k'æ-tih-de 鈕子解°開了°

UNCEASING, feh-byih' 弗歇; — *by day, or night*, nyih-yia' feh-hyih' 日°夜°弗歇

UNCERTAIN, vi-ding' 未定; vi-k'o'-cü 未可知; yün-shü' 懸勢; yün-r-vu-poh' 懸而無薄°; *not determined*, weh-deh' 滑突; ʊ̆-su' 無°數; ʊ̆-su'-moh-tsiang 無°數目賬

UNCHAIN, *to* k'æ lin-diao' 開鏈條

UNCHANGEABLE, üong' feh-piɳ'-yih 永弗變易; *cannot be changed*, k'æ'-pin-feh-læ 改變弗來

UNCHARITABLE, ʊ̆-jing-sing'-go 無°仁心个°, or ʊ̆-jing-sing'-go 無°人心个°

UNCHASTE *thoughts*, nyiæn-deo' feh-kyih'-zing 念頭弗潔凈

UNCIVIL, ʊ̆-li'-go 無°禮个°

UNCLE, *father's older brother*, ah-pang' 阿伯; *father's younger brother*, ah-song' 阿叔'; *mother's brother*, gyiu'-gyiu 舅舅; nyiang-gyiu' 娘舅

UNCLEAN, feh-kyih'-zing 弗潔凈; — *thoughts*, nyiæn-deo' feh kyih'-zing 念頭弗潔凈; ao-tsao' i'-s 墅糟意思

UNCOMFORTABLE, feh-ziu'-yüong 弗受用; feh-shü'-voh 弗舒服; — *in mind*, sing'-li feh teh'-ko 心裡弗得過; feh sông'-kw'a 弗爽快; feh-shih'-i 弗適°意

UNCOMMON, fi-dzông' 非常; feh'-z z'ing-dzông' 弗是尋常

UNCOMMONLY, fi-væn' 非凡; — *good*, fi-væn' hao 非凡好; c'ih'-kah-go hao' 出格个°好

UNCONCERNED, feh-læ' i'-li 弗在°意裡; *perfectly* —, 'ao'-feh-dzæ i' 毫弗在意; *to look* —, feh-ts'iu'-ts'æ 弗偢睬

UNCONSCIOUS, feh'-cü-feh-koh' 弗知弗覺; peh'-cü-peh-kyüoh'

不知不覺；— of wrong, ü-sing'-vu-kw'e' 於心無虧

UNCONSTRAINED, ts'ong-ts'ong'-yüong-yüong' 從從容容; z-z'-dzæ-dzæ 自自在在

UNCOURTEOUS, 齭-li'-go 無°禮个°; shih-li'-go 失禮个°

UNCOUTH, 齭-yiang'-væu 無°樣範

UNCOVER, to open a cover, hyiao-k'æ' 拐開; — (as by removing a cloth, &c.), kyih'-ky'i 揭起

UNCULTIVATED land, hwông di' 荒地; — in manners, t'u'-lao 土老兒°

UNDECIDED, feh-zing' ding-kwe' 弗曾定規; wa vi-ding' 還°未定; wa vi-kyüih' 還°未決; — in purpose, cü'-i k'ô'-feh-ding' 主意拿°弗定; cü'-i lih'-feh-ding' 主意立弗定; — (as a battle), sing'-ba-vi-feng' 勝敗未分

UNDECEIVE, to k'æ-ngæn' 開眼°; di-p'o' 點°破

UNDER, 'ô 下°; ti-'ô' 底下°; 'ô-deo' 下°頭; — side, 'ô'-min 下°面; — the table, læ cuh'-teng 'ô 在桌下°; — his control, læ gyi' siu'-'ô 在°其手下°; — fifty, ng'-jih yi-'ô' 五十以下°; ng'-jih yi-ne' 五十以內

UNDER-DONE, ky'in joh' 欠熟

UNDERGO, to ziu 受; ziu'-teh 受得; — suffering, ziu'-kw'u zin-næn' 受苦受難; — great changes, do keng'-kæ 大°更改; ditto (as places), kæ'-zao-ko 改造°過

UNDER-GROUND, læ di-'ô' 在°地下°; di-'ô'-go 地下°个°

UNDERHAND, to do things in an — way, en'-di-li tso' z-t'i' 私°下°行事°; secretly to use unfair means, t'eo-bun' yüong siu'-kyiah 偷瞞°用手腳; ying-s'-tsoh'-bi 行私作弊

UNDER-LET, to cün' tsu-c'ih' 轉租出; gyiao tsu-c'ih' 僑租出

UNDERLING (as an inferior officer), 'ô'-joh 下°屬; — (as a servant), ti-'ô'-nying 底下°人°; siu-'ô'-nying 手下°人°; polite, nyi-yia' 二°爺°

UNDERMINE, to — a wall, ziang-kyiah' gyüih-song' 牆腳掘鬆

UNDERNEATH, læ ti'-'ô 在°底下°; læ 'ô'-deo 在°下°頭

UNDERRATE, to k'en'-feh-tao' 看弗到; kwu'-liang-feh-tao' 估量弗到; yiu-ngæn' feh-sih' T'a'-sæn 有眼°弗識泰°山; — the price, kô'-din kwu'-leh zin' 價°錢估得°賤°

UNDERSELL others, pi bih'-nying ma'-leh zin' 比別人°賣得°賤°; t'eng'-kô ma 減°價賣°;

UNDERSTAND, to tong; 懂 hyiao'-teh 曉得; — clearly, ming-bah' 明白°; do you —? ng' ming-bah' feh 你°明白°否°? ng tong' feh-tong' 你°懂弗懂? I —, ming-bah'-go 明白°个°; tong'-go 懂个°; he understands his business, gyi'-go 'ông-tông joh-sih' 其 个° 行° 業° 熟 識; *he understand his trade,* gyi'-go vu'-nyi tsing-t'ong' 其 个° 武 藝 精 通; gyi dzæ-'ông' 其 在 行'

UNDERSTOOD, *I — you to say so,* ngô i'-we ng z-ka' wô' 我 意 會° 你° 如° 此° 話

UNDERTAKE, *to* tæn-tông' 擔 當; dzing-tông' 承 當; *I dare not — it,* ngô' feh-ken' tæn-tông' 我 弗 敢 擔 當; *to begin,* k'æ-siu' 開 手

UNDESERVING OF, feh-kæ'-tông ziu' 弗 該 當 受; feh-ken' tông 弗 敢 當

UNDESIGNEDLY, vu-i'-cong 無 意 中; z'-c'ih-vu-sing' 事 出 無 心

UNDETERMINED, See UNDECIDED.

UNDIGESTED, feh-siao-hwô' 弗 消 化; feh-k'eh'-hwô 弗 尅 化; feh-'ang'-hwô 弗 行 化

UNDISCERNIBLE, k'en'-feh-c'ih'-go 看 弗 出 个°

UNDISCIPLINED, m̄'-meh ts'ao-lin'-ko 沒° 有 操 練 過

UNDISTINGUISHABLE, feng-ming feh-læ 分 明 弗 來; feh-kyin'-teh feng-ming' 弗 見 得 分 明

UNDIVIDED, *to give — attention,* cün-r' cü'-ts tso' 專 心° 致 志 而° 做

UNDO, *to — (what has been done),* sông-diao' 傷 壞°; *to untie, or unfasten,* ka'-diao 解° 去°; ka'-k'æ 解 開

UNDOUBTEDLY, ih-ding' 一 定;

ih-ding-peh-yih' 一 定 不 易; vu-nyi' 無° 二°

UNDRESS, *to* t'eh i-zông' 脫 衣 裳°

UNDULATING (like waves), ziang shü-po-lông' ka 像 水° 波 浪 一° 樣°; *— ground,* di-yiang ih'-kao, ih-ti' 地 下° 一 高 一 低

UNDUTIFUL, peh-hyiao' 不 孝°; peh-hyiao'-peh-di' 不 孝 不 弟

UNEASY, sing feh-en' 心 弗 安; fông'-sing-feh-loh' 放 心 弗 下°; sing-mông'-feh-ding' 心 忙 弗 定; *— and anxious,* ky'ih'-du kwô'-dziang 挈 肚 掛 腸; *— and worried,* sing'-li tsiao-ts'ao' 心 裏 焦 躁; *— (without knowing the reason, &c.),* bông-wông'-tsi-tsao' 徬 徨 嘈 嘈

UNEMBARASSED, ts'ong-ts'ong'-yüong-yüong' 從 從 容 容

UNEMPLOYED, zo'-siu 坐 守; k'ong'-æn 空 閒°; hyih'-nyih-tong' 閒° 居° 無° 事

UNENLIGHTENED, mong'-tong 懵 懂

UNEQUAL, *not regular,* feh-zi'-jih 弗 齊° 集; ts'æn-ts', or ts'en-ts' 参 差; *not uniform,* feh' z ih-pæn' sang 弗 是 一 班 生°; *— proportions,* feh-kyüing-yüing' 弗 均 匀; *— to a task, (in talent, strength, &c.),* dzæ-lih' peh-gyih' 才 力 不 及

UNEVEN, *not level,* feh-bing' 弗 平; feh bing'-dzih 弗 平 直; ky'i-ky'iao' 踦 蹺; *— (as stones* jutting out, &c.), ngæn-ngæn'-ngô-ngô' 嚴 巖 砑 砑; ts'ih'-kao-pah-ti' 七 高 八 低

UNEVENLY *put on*, or *mixed* —, feh-diao-yüing' 弗 調 勻

UNEXPECTEDLY, liao-feh-tao'-go 料 弗 到 个°; siang'-feh-tao'-go 想 弗 到 个°; ts'eng'-feh-tao'-go 忖 弗 到 个°; i'-nga'-go 意 外° 个°; *to meet* or *happen* —, peh'-gyi-r nyü' 不 期 而 遇

UNEXPLORED *place*, di-fông' 𢫦'-neh dzô-ts'ah'-ko 地 方 没 有° 查 察 過

UNFAIR, *unjust*, feh-kong'-dao 弗 公 道; *to be* — (in play, &c.), long nyün'-gyüob 弄 軟 騙° 局; *to use* — *means*, yüong siu'-kyiah 用 手 脚

UNFAIRLY, *money* — *obtained*, fi-li'-ts dzæ' 非 禮 之 財; ao-tsao' dong-din' 非° 義° 之 錢°

UNFAITHFUL, feh-cong'-sing 弗 忠 心

UNFASHIONABLE, feh-'eh-z' 弗 合 時; feh-z'-dao 弗 時 道; feh-tsoh' 弗 作 興; *out of date*, be-z' 背 時

UNFEELING, *hard-hearted*, t'ih'-tang-sing-dziang' 鐵 打 心 腸; sing-dziang ngang' 心 腸 硬; 𢫦-dzing'-veng 無° 情 分; boh dzing' 薄 情

UNFINISHED, vi wun'-de 未 完 了°; feh-zing tso'-wun 弗 曾° 做 完; vi' liao-kong' 未 了 工; feh-

zing tso'-hao 弗 曾° 做 好; vi tso'-dzing 未 做 成; vi-dzeng liao'-kyib 未 曾° 了 結

UNFIT *for use*, 𢫦-tso' ; feh-teh-yüong' 弗 得 用; feh-'eh-yüong' 弗 合 用; — *for eating*, ky'üoh'-feh-teh 吃° 弗 得

UNFOLD, *to* t'eo'-k'æ; ka'-k'æ 解° 開; — (as a flower), k'æ 開; fông'-k'æ 放 開

UNFORESEEN *difficulties*, ts'eng'-feh-tao'-go næn-c'ü' 忖 弗 到 个° 難 處; peh-i'-ts z' 不 意 之 事

UNFORGIVING, kyi-'eng'-sing-go 記 恨 心 个°; feh-kw'un-shü-' go 弗 寬 恕 个°

UNFORTUNATE, shih-z', or sih-z' 失 時; peh-ying' 不 幸; hyiao-fæn' 鵁 泛; *very* —, da' peh - ying' 大 不 幸; — *lot*, yüing-ky'i' kæn-ka' 運 氣 尷 尬; ming-yüing' feh-hao' 命 運 弗 好; yüing-dao' seh'-deh 運 道 失 達

UNFOUNDED, 𢫦-keng'-go 無° 根 个°; 𢫦-keng-kyiah'-go 無° 根 脚 个°; yüing-læ' vu-ky'i'-go 雲 來 霧 去 个°; — *words* (as reports, &c.), hwông-dông' shih-wô' 荒 唐 說 話; *it is quite* —, keh'-z ts'ah'-c'ih-læ-go z-ken' 這° 是 造° 出 來 个° 事 幹

UNFREQUENTED *road*, 𢫦-nying' dza-tseo'-go lu' 無° 甚 人 走 个° 路; *lonely* —, lang'-loh-go lu' 冷° 落 个° 路

UNFRIENDLY, tsoh-te'-go 作鬧
个°;— *persons,* te'-deo nying 仇°
讐°人°; *he is* —, gyi' yiu du'-
bing 其有肚病; *he treated me
in an* — *manner,* gyi feh tông'
ngô beng-yiu' k'en-dæ' 其弗當
我朋友看待

UNFRUITFUL, ve'-kyih-ko'-ts-go
不會°結果子个°; ṁ-dao'-
dzing-go 無°道成个°

UNGOVERNABLE, kwun'-feh-djü'-
go 管弗住个°; kwun'-feh-
voh'-go 管弗服个°

UNGRATEFUL, feh-dzeng' ken'-
zia-go-sing' 弗存感謝°个°心°;
ṁ-jing-sing 無°仁心; hyiao'-
go 楛个°; feh-kyin-dzing' 弗見
情;— *for great favors, or mer-
cies,* ṁ-peng'-sing 無°本心;
feh-ken'-eng' 弗感恩; veo-eng'-
go 負恩个°; vông-eng'-veo-
yi' 忘恩負義; hyiao-nyiao'
鴞鳥

UNHAPPY, sing-kw'u'心苦; sing-
feh-en' 心弗安; *very*—, sing'-
li meh'-deh-deh-go kw'u' 心裡
默沓沓个°苦

UNHEALTHY, (as a place disagree-
ing with one), shü'-t'u feh-voh'
水°土弗服; *a place having
miasma,* yin tsông'-ky'i-go di'-
fong 有瘴氣个°地方; *having
a poor constitution,* t'i'-tsih tæn-
boh' 體質單薄; ti'-ts hyiah'
體質°弱; — *appearance* (as a
person), ky'ih'-boh-siang 怯薄

相; *ditto,* (as children), ts'ing-bi'
boh-byüih 青皮薄血

UNHULLED, lin-k'ông'-go 連糠
个°; lin-bi'-go 連皮个°

UNHURT, ṁ'-teh sông 沒°有°傷;
vu-'æ' 無害; — (by a fall),
ṁ'-neh k'eh-t'ong' 沒°有°磕
痛; ṁ-neh k'eh-sông' 沒°有°
磕傷

UNIFORM, ih-pæn'-sang 一班生°
ih-t'i'-s-sang' 一體樣°式°; *of
— color,* ih-seh'-go 一色个°;
*to dress in*—, c'ün 'ao-i' 穿號衣

UNIMPORTANT, feh iao'-kying 弗
要緊

UNINHABITABLE, deng-nying'-
feh-læ'-go 庵人°弗來个°

UNINHABITED *house,* k'ong' oh
空屋; — *place,* ṁ-nying'-deng'-
go di-fong 無°人庵个°地方;
ṁ-nying'-in'-go di-fông' 無°人°
烟个°地方

UNINTELLIGIBLE, ming-bah'-feh-
læ 明白°弗來; kwun'-t'ong-
feh-læ' 貫通弗來

UNINTENTIONAL, vu-i'-cong 無
意中; feh'-z deh-we' 弗是特
爲; ṁ-sing 無°心

UNINTERRUPTED, siang-lin' feh-
dön' 相連弗斷; — *rain for
a month,* yü', lin-loh' ih-ko yüih'
de 雨連落一個月了°

UNINVITED *guest,* ṁ'-neh ts'ing'-
go nying-k'ah' 沒°有°請个°
客人°; peh'-soh-ts k'ah' 不速
之客°

UNION (of two or more in one), 'eh'-r-we-ih' 合而爲一; *the — of many states in one,* hyü'-to sang' 'eh-we' ih-koh' 許多省° 合爲一國

UNIT, *one,* ih 一; *units occupy the first place, tens the second place, and hundreds the third,* tæn-su'di-ih' we, jih-su' di-nyi' we, pah'-su di-sæn'we 單數第一位十數第二位百°數第三位

UNITE, *to* 'eh-long' 合攏; siang-'eh' 相合; ping'-long 併攏; *to join,* siang-lin'相連; lin-long' 連攏; *to mix,* 'o-long'和攏; — (as a wound), siu k'eo'收口; *oil and water will not —,* shü' teng yiu' 'eh'-feh-long 水°與油合弗攏;—*all the numbers,* tsong'-su 'eh-tæn-long' 總數合攏;— *the contents of two bowls in one,* ping'-long ih-tsah un' 併攏一隻碗; — *in one pair,* (man and wife), p'e' ngeo 配偶; p'e'-long ih-te' 配攏一對

UNITED, 'eh-long'-liao 合攏了°; ping'-long-liao 併攏了°; *to be — with a superior in rank, or wealth,* kao-p'æn' 高攀; *put forth — strength,* do-kô''ô gying-dao' 大°家°用°勁道; dô-kô' dziah-lih' 大°家°着力; — *purpose, and effort,* dong-sing'-yiah-lih' 同心愶力

UNITED-STATES, *the* 'Eh-cong'-koh 合衆國; Hwô-gyi'-koh

花旗國; *America,* Da-me' koh 大美國

UNITY, *the church is one,* kyiao'-we dong-ky'i'-lin-ts'-go 敎會同氣連枝个°;—*of design,* ih-ky'i' kwun'-t'ong 一氣貫通; 'eh-dzing'-ih i' 合成一意;—*of the races,* t'in-'ô' dzoh-veng' tu z ih'-go keng-mah' 天下°族牙都是一个°根脈

UNIVERSAL, p'u'-t'in-'ô' go 普天下° 个°; 'en-t'in-'ô'-go 合° 天下° 个°; — *reputation,* kæ'-shü-go ming-sing 蓋世个° 名聲; — *peace,* t'in-'ô' t'a'-bing 天下° 太° 平

UNIVERSE, t'in-di'-væn'-veh 天地萬物; væn-yiu' 萬有

UNJUST, feh-kong' 弗公; feh-kong'-dao 弗公道; feh-kong'-bing 弗公平

UNKIND, sing-jih' feh-hao' 心術弗好; sing-jih' 'ah-tsah' 心術狹窄; sing-di' feh-hao' 心地弗好

UNKNOWN, m̆-nying' hyiao'-teh 無° 人° 曉得

UNLADE, *to* ky'i-ho' 起貨; zông-ho' 上貨; — *a vessel,* sia-zæ' 卸載°

UNLAWFUL, lih-fah'kying'-liao-go 律法禁了个°; we-lih' væn-fah'-go 違律犯法个°; — *trade,* væn-kying'-go sang-i' 犯禁个° 生°意; væn-fah'-go sang-i' 犯法个° 生°意

UNLEARNED, *not knowing letters*, feh-sih-z'-go 弗 識 字 个°; *not having learned*, m̆'-neh 'oh-ko' 沒° 有° 學° 過

UNLIKE, feh-ziang' 弗 像; koh'-kiang 各樣; koh'-bih 各別; feh-dong' 弗同; *very* —, kyüong'-kyüong koh'-bih 迥迥 各別; 'o'-jün koh-yiang' 一° 概° 各樣; da'-feh-siang-dong' 大 弗 相 同

UNLIKELY, vi-pih' 未 必; feh-kyin'-teh 弗 見 得; siang'-pih ve' 想 必 不° 會°; — *that he will go*, gyi vi-pih' ky'i' 其 未 必 去°; siang'-pih ve'ky'i 想 必 不° 會° 去

UNLIMITED, m̆-'æn'-go 無° 限 个°; m̆-'æn'-cü-go 無° 限 制 个°; m̆-pin'-m̆-ngen' 無° 邊 無° 岸; — (*as space*), m̆-ka'-'æn 無° 界° 限°

UNLOAD, *to* ky'i-ho' 起貨; zông-ho' 上 貨; sia-bo' 卸 貨; — *a ship*, sia-zæ' 卸 艙

UNLOCK, *to* k'æ-so' 開 鎖

UNLOOSE, *to* fông-kw'un' 放寬; fông-song' 放 鬆; — *a knot*, ka-kyih' 解° 結

UNLUCKY, hwe'-ky'i 晦氣; tao-yüing' 倒 運; peh-ying' 不 幸; feh-seh'-deo 弗 色 頭; feh-kyih'-li 弗 吉 利; feh-jing' 弗 順; zao'-hwô-wa' 勿° 得° 意°; *to become* —, 'ang-mo' kw'u'-yüing 行 暮 庫 運

UNMANAGEABLE, feh-yiu'-nying-kwun' 弗 由 人° 管; — *pupil*, 'oh-sang'-ts feh-yiu'-nying-kwun' 學 生° 弗 由 人° 管; — *horse*, mô' feh-yiu-nying' 馬 弗 由 人°; — *therefore let them do as they like*, yiu-mô' feh-yiu-nying' 由 馬 弗 由 人°

UNMANLY, feh-ziang' nen-ts'-hen 弗 像 男 子 漢

UNMARRIED *man*, feh-zing' c'ü-ts'ing'-go 弗 曾° 娶 親 个°; feh-zing' dæ lao'-nyüing-go 弗 曾° 完° 姻° 个°; siao'-kwun-nying 小 官 人°; dong-ts' 童 子; *ditto* (who yields to evil desires, not being deterred by family restraints), kwông-kweng' 光 棍; — *woman*, feh-zing' c'ih-kô'-go 弗 曾° 出 嫁° 个°; feh-zing'tso sing-vn'-go 弗 曾° 做 新 婦 个°; do-kwn'-nyiang 大 姑 娘; politely termed, kwe-nyü' 閨 女

UNMEANING, *confused*, m̆ - ka'-shih-go 無° 解° 說 个°; wu-du' 糊 塗; *light* (often false) *words*, veo-yin' 浮 言; wu-yin' lön-dao' 胡 言 亂 道

UNMERCIFUL, m̆-dz-sing' 無° 慈 心; sing-heng' 心 狠; *hardhearted*, sing-ngang' 心 硬

UNMERITED, feh-kæ' zin'-go 弗 該 受 个°; feh-ing'-teh ziu' 弗 應 得 受

UNMINDFUL, feh-dziah' læ i'-li 弗 着 在° 意 裡; feh-liu'-i 弗 留 意; feh-dzæ'-i 弗 在 意; *you are* — *of what I say*, ngô' sô wô'-go, ng' feh-dziah læ i'-li 我 所 話

个° 你° 弗 着 在° 意 裡；— *of his own safety*, (*i. e.* death or, life), feh kwu' zi-go si'-weh 弗 顧 自° 个° 死° 活

UNMIXED, jing 純；feh keh'-dzeh 弗 夾° 雜；ṁ'-neh c'ün'-long-go 沒° 有° 串 攏 个°；— *or pure milk*, jing na' 純 嫲°；*with — pleasure*, jing' z hwnn-byi' 純 是 歡 喜

UNMOLESTED, ṁ-kao'næn-we' 沒° 有° 難 爲

UNMOVED(by temptation,&c.),feh-dong'-sing 弗 動 心；— *countenance*, min' feh pin-seh' 面 弗 變 色；*perfectly —*, sing seh' feh dong' 聲 色 弗 動

UNNATURAL, t'in sang' - dzing, siang-fæn'-go 天 生° 成 相 反 个°；—*disposition*,t'in-sing'siang-fæn' 天 性 相 反

UNNAVIGABLE *river*, 'o-kông' s'-jün'-feh-læ-go 河 港 駛 船 弗 來 个°

UNNECESSARY, hao-vong' 好 不° 用°；feh-yüong 弗 用；peh-pih' 不 必；*quite —* (to do, or say), to-li'-shü 多 禮 數°

UNOCCUPIED *house*, k'ong' oh 空 屋；— *time*, k'ong'-'æn z'-'eo 空 閒° 時 候；—*person*, k'ong' 'æn nying 空 閒° 人°；*ditto* (who happens in), 'æn nying' 閒° 人；*sitting* (there) —, k'ong'-deo zo-kæn' 空 閒° 坐 在° 彼

UNOBSERVED, ṁ nying'k'en'-kyin 無° 人° 看 見

UNPAID, *wages still —*, kong-din'-feh-zing' kyih-fah' 工 錢° 弗 曾° 給 發；kong-din' feh-zing ka'-fah 工 錢° 弗 曾° 開 發；*salary still —*, soh'-siu feh-zing' fu' 束 修 弗 曾° 付；— *debts*, tsa' feh-zing' fu' 債 弗 曾° 付；tsa' feh-zing' wæn' 債 弗 曾° 還

UNPALATABLE, wa-ky'üoh' 歪 吃°；næn-ky'üoh' 難 吃°

UNPARDONABLE, nyiao-sô'-feh-læ 饒 赦° 弗 來；* sô'-feh-læ 赦° 弗 來；sô-feh-diao；*the ten — crimes* (in China), jib-oh'-feh-sô' 十 惡 弗 赦°

* Used for lighter offences, as those not against the laws of the country.

UNPERCEIVED, nying' feh-teh'-cü 人° 弗 得 知；*I entered —*, ngô tseo'-tsing, nying' feh-teh'-cü 我 走 進 人° 弗 得 知

UNPLEASANT, ṁ-c'ü' 無° 趣；ṁ-i'-cü 無° 意 趣；ṁ-hying'-cü 無° 興 致；ṁ-c'ü'-hyiang 無° 趣 味°；feh-cong'-i 弗 中 意；— *man*, tseng-nying 憎 人°；— *business*, ṁ-i'-c'ü-go z-ken' 無° 意 趣 个° 事 幹；ṁ-hying'-cü-go z-ken' 無° 興 致 个° 事 幹；— *weather*, t'in-kô' ṁ-c'ü-hyiang 天 不° 晴° 霽°；— *to eat*, feh-cong ky'üoh-go 弗 中 吃° 个°；— *to hear* (as a truth), feh-cong t'ing'-go 弗 中 聽 个°；*ditto* (as sounds), næn t'ing' 難 聽；— *smell*, ky'i'-mi næn tông' 氣 味°

難 當 ; ts'iu' peh-k'o tông' 臭 不 可 當

UNPOLISHED, (as a stone, or person), ᴢ'-neh tsoh'-mo-ko 沒°有°琢 磨 過; —(as metals, &c.), ᴢ'-neh mo-ts'ah'-ko 沒°有°磨 擦 過; *anything* —, ᴢ-neh bao-siah'-ko 沒°有°刨 削 過; mao-sæn-jü' 毛 杉 樹; mao-p'e'-ts 毛 胚 子

UNPOPULAR, cong'-nying feh-'eh' go 衆 人°弗 合 个°; cong'-nying feh-voh' 衆 人 弗 服

UNPRECEDENTED, dzong-læ' ᴢ'-neh-go 從 來 沒°有°个°

UNPREJUDICED, kong-bing'-go sing' 公 平 个°心; *impartial*, ᴢ-p'in'-ky'üoh'-sing-go 無 偏 曲 心 个°; ᴢ-p'in'-sing-go 無°偏 心 个°

UNPREPARED, ᴢ'-neh bông-be' 沒°有°防 備; ᴢ'-neh yü-be'-hao 沒°有°預 備 好

UNPROFITABLE, vu-ih'-go 無° 益 个°; —*business*, vn-ih' ts-kyü' 無 益 之 舉; —*trade* (very little profit), li-sih' boh 利 息 薄; *ditto* (no profit), ve-c'ih-hwô'-go 不°會°出 化 个°; ᴢ-c'ih'-sih 無°出 息; *hard*, —*work*, bah yiao-lao' 白°効 勞

UNPROTECTED, (as a child, or female), ᴢ nying' dzing-kwun'-go 無°人°承 管 个°

UNPUBLISHED, *not printed*, ᴢ'-neh ing'-pæn-de 沒°有°印 板 了°

UNPUNISHED, ᴢ'-neh vah-ko'沒° 冇°罰 過

UNQUENCHABLE, long'-feh-u'-go 弄 弗 熄°个°; — (with water), p'eh'-feh-u'-go 潑 弗 熄°个°; —(by smothering), p'oh'-feh-u'-go 撲 弗 滅°个°; — *thirst*, ts feh-djü-go k'eh 止 弗 住 个°渴

UNRAVEL, *to* —(as edges of cloth), seh-c'ih-læ 毛 出 來; —(as knitting), sæn'-c'ih-læ 散 出 來; —(as a snarl), ka'-k'æ 解°開; fông'-k'æ 放 開

UNREASONABLE, feh-dzing'-li-go 弗 情 理 个°; ᴢ-li'-sing-go 無° 理 性 个°; — *hopes*, vông'-siang 妄 想

UNREDEEMABLE, (as a hostage), c'ü'-feh-læ 取 弗 來

UNRECONCILED, ᴢ'-neh 'o-long' 沒°有°和 攏; ᴢ'-neh siang-'o' 沒°有°相 和

UNREQUITED *favors*, vi-pao'-go eng 未 報 个°恩

UNRESERVEDLY, *not concealing anything*, 'ao' feh-ing'-mun 毫 弗 隱 瞞; *not withholding anything*, 'o-bun' t'oh'-c'ih 和 盤 托 出; zing'-du-dziang t'eo'-c'ih 盡 肚 腸 顯 出

UNRIGHTEOUS, feh-tön'-tsing 弗 端 正; feh-tsing'-dzih 弗 正 直; feh-kong-dao' 弗 公 道

UNRIPE, feb-joh' 弗 熟; sang 生°

UNROLL, *to* k'æ kyün' 開 卷

UNSAFE, feh-ẇeng'-tông 弗穩當；
feh-t'o'-tông 弗妥當

UNSALABLE, ṁ-siao-dziang' 無
銷塲

UNSATISFACTORY, feh-te'-kying
弗對徑；— to me, feh-mun' ngô-
go i' 弗滿我个°意

UNSATISFIED, feh-mun'-i 弗滿
意；feh-cü-tsoh' 弗知足

UNSEASONABLE, z-'eo-fæn-djông'
時候反常；feh-gyih'-z 弗及
時；t'in-z' feh-tsing' 天時弗
正；z-ling' feh-te' 時令弗對

UNSEEN, ṁ'-neh k'en'-kyin-ko 沒°
有°看見過；— (or dark) world,
ing-kæn' 陰間°；ing-s' 陰司

UNSETTLED in heart, sing feh-
ding' 心弗定；sæn-sing' liang'
i' 三心兩意；sing weh' 心
活；undecided, cü'-i feh kyüih'
主意弗決；cü-i' k'o'-feh-ding'
主意拿°弗定；can't deter-
mine, yiu-yü' peh-kyüih' 猶豫
不決；kyüih-tön'-feh-loh' 決
斷弗落

UNSHAKEN, feh-dong'-go 弗動个°；
ṁ'-neh dong'-ko 沒°有°動過

UNSHAVED (as a Chinaman), ṁ'-
neh t'i-deo'-ko 沒°有°薙頭過

UNSKILLED, siu'-dön ẇa' 手段
孬°；feh joh'-sih 弗熟識；one
just learning, and therefore —,
bao-c'ih-long' 暴出籠

UNSOCIABLE, kao-nyin'-feh-long'
膠°黏弗攏；feh teng nying'
siang-yü' 弗同°人°相與；feh

teng nying' kyiao-tsih' 弗與°
人°交接

UNSOLD, ṁ'-neh ma'-diao-de 沒°
有°賣去°了°

UNSOUND, yiu mao-bing' 有毛
病；has hidden faults, yiu en'
mao'-bing 有暗毛病

UNSPEAKABLE, wô-feh-læ'-go 話
弗來个°；kông'-feh-c'ih'-go
講°弗出个°；cannot be de-
scribed, wô'-feh - siang'-ziang-go
話弗相像个°；feh-k'o' yin-
djün' 弗可言傳

UNSTEADY hand for holding a pen,
pih' k'o'-feh-ẇeng' 筆揑弗穩；
—foot (in standing), kyiah' lih'-
feh-ding' 腳立弗定；kyiah'-bu
lih-feh-ẇeng' 腳步立弗穩；—
(as a person), ṁ-ding'-diah-go
無°定奪°个°

UNSUBDUED as before, dzing-gyiu'
feh-voh' 仍舊弗服；—(primarily
in war, but used frequently in
other connections), tsing' feh-
voh' 征弗服；— by whipping,
tang'-feh-voh' 打弗服

UNSUBSTANTIAL (as work), hyiah'-
hyiah; feh kyin'-kwu 弗堅固；—
and false, hyü-veo' 虛浮；— and
worthless goods, 'ang-ho' 次°等貨

UNSUCCESSFUL, not fortunate, ṁ-
zao'-hwô 無°造°化；feh-jing'-
tông 弗順當；labor all in vain,
bah-bah' lao-loh' 白°白°勞碌；
— in obtaining what one desires,
feh teh' i 弗得意

UNSUITABLE, feh-siang'-nyi 弗相 宜; feh-te' 弗對

UNSULLIED, ts'ing-bah' 清白°; ts'ing-kyih' 清潔; — *reputation*, ts'ing-bah'-go ming-sing 清白° 个° 名聲

UNSURPASSED, *it is* 㑚-yiu' hao'-jü gyi' 沒°有好如他°; 㑚-yiu' ko'-jü gyi' 沒°有過如他°; 㑚-yiu gyih'-jü gyi' 沒°有及如 他°; c'ih' wu-gyi-le' 出乎其類

UNSUSPECTING, feh-ts'æ'-nyi-go 弗猜疑个°; feh-nyi-sing'-go 弗疑心个° (veng.)

UNTEACHABLE, feh - ziu' kao'-hyüing 弗受教°訓; feh-t'ing' wo' 弗聽話

UNTHANKFUL, feh-dzeng' ken'-zia-go sing 弗存感謝°个°心; hyiao-nyiao' vu-dzing' 鵁鳥無° 情; hyiao-dzing' boh-nyi' 梟情 薄義

UNTHINKING, feh-ts'eng'-go 弗忖 个°; *heedless*, mông-bah'-go 茫° 白°个°

UNTIE, *to* ka 解°; ka'-k'æ 解°開° — *a knot*, ka kyih' 解°結

UNTIL, tao 到; ih-dzih'-tao — 直到; teng'-tao 等到; — *now*, tao-jü-kying' 到如今; ih-dzih'-tao næn'-kæn 一直到如°今°; *wait —I come*, deng tao' ngô læ' 庵到我來

UNTIMELY *birth*, yüih-veng' feh-tsoh' 月孖弗足; — *death*, iao-ziu' 天壽; tön'-ming-si' 短命

死°; *plucked before his time*, ngang-ao' si'-de 硬拗死°了°

UNTOUCHED, 㑚'- neh dong'-ko 沒°有°動過; — (*i.e.* just as it was), nyün-fông' feh-dong' 原 放弗動; 㑚'-neh bang'-ko 沒° 有°捫過

UNTRUE, feh-jih' 弗實; feh-jih'-we 弗實為; hyü'-go 虛个°; feh-tsing' 弗真

UNTRUTH, hwông'- wô 謊話; hyü-wô' 虛話; — (boasting, &c.), do-wô' 大°話

UNUSUAL, feh-tsiao dzông' 弗照 常; dzah-ngah'; *it is* —, bing-djông' feh z-ka' 平常弗如° 此°; su'-djông feh z-ka' 素常 弗如°此°

UNUSUALLY, c'ih-keh' 出格; — (never was so), fi-djông' 非常; — *cold*, c'ih'-keh lang' 出格 冷°; yi-wu' zing-djông'-go lang' 異乎尋常个°冷°; pi-'æn-djông' lang 比𨵦°常冷°

UNUTTERABLE, kông'-feh-c'ih'-go 講°弗出个°; wô'-feh-læ'-go 話 弗來个°; 㑚-wô'-deo-go 無°話 頭个°; *too much to be expressed*, kông'-feh-tao-kô' 講°弗到家°

UNVARYING, feh-keng'-kæ 弗更 改; — (as appearance, sounds, &c.), feh-pin'-yiang' 弗變樣

UNWARY, *not cautious*, feh-tso'-gyi 弗留°意°; *not watchful*, feh-kying'-jing 弗謹慎; *not careful*, feh-siao'-sing 弗小心

UNWAVERING, feh-yiao'-dong-go 弗搖動个°

UNWEARIED, feh-p'ô' lao-kw'u' 弗怕勞苦; feh p'ô in'-væn 不° 怕厭煩

UNWELL, feh-sih'-i, or feh-shih'-i 弗適意; feh-sông'-kw'a 弗爽 快°; næn-ko' 難過; yiu yiang' 有恙; a little —, yiu-tin' feh-shih'-i 有點弗適°意; yiu siao'-yiang 有小恙

UNWHOLESOME food, yiu-ngæ'-go ky'üoh'-zih 有碍个°吃°食; — climate, (i. e. water and soil not serving), shü'-t'u feh-voh' 水° 土弗服

UNWILLING, feh-k'eng' 弗肯; feh yüoh'-i 弗欲意; feh dziing'-nyün 弗情願; loth to part, feh-sô'-teh bih-k'æ' 弗捨°得離°開

UNWIND, to dziu-c'ih'-læ 紬出來

UNWORTHY to fill that office, dzæ' peh sing zing' 才不勝任; — to receive, or bear, tông' feh-ky'i 當 弗起; not daring to bear, feh-ken-tông' 弗敢當; not good enough, ky'in-hao' 欠好; conduct — of a teacher, 'ang-we' teng sin-sang feh-p'e' 行°為與先 生°弗配; — to sit with, sing-kô' feh-p'e zo'-long 身家°弗 配坐攏; — to do (lest I spoil it), veo-nyi' sô-t'oh' 負你所托; — of you, teng ng p'e'-fu-feh-long 與°你°配副弗攏; — of mention, peh-tsoh' dao' 不足

道; — of use, peh-tsoh' yüong' 不足用

UNYIELDING, zah-fông-shing' 若° 板°方°; kwu'-pæn-lin'-ky'i 古板 臉氣; heart — as iron, (in a bad sense), sing' ziang t'ih' ka 心似° 鐵一°般°; sang'-leh'eo zi' 生°得 執己°; — man, nying dzih' feh cün-wæn'-go 認直弗轉彎个°

UP, zông 上; come —, tseo'-zông-læ 走上來; push it —, t'e-zông'-ky'i 推上去°; the sun is —, nyih-deo' zông-sæn'-de 日°頭 上山了°; — on the hill, læ-sæn-zông' 在°山上; — to this time, dzih-tao' jü-kying' 直到如今

UPBRAID, to mao-üu' 埋°怨; to reprove, tsah'-vah 責罰; — one for a fault, p'i'-bing' gyi-go ts'o' 批評其个錯

UPHOLD, to vu 扶; vu-dzi' 扶持°

UPLIFTED hand, siu'di-zông-tih 手 提上的°; — eyes, ngæn'-tsing dao-zông'-tih 眼睛朝上的°

UPON, læ zông-deo' 在°上頭; — my head, læ ngô'deo zông 在° 我頭上; dependent — salary, k'ao soh'-siu du-nyih' 靠束修 度日°

UPPER, zông 上; — layer, zông zeng' 上層°; — lip, zông-bæn' cü'-jing 上爿嘴唇; — room, leo-teng' vông-kæn' 樓上°房間°

UPPERMOST, ting'-zông-go 頂上 个°; ting-kao'-go 頂高个°

UPRIGHT (in position), pih'-dzih

筆直; *stand* —, pih'-dzih lih'-
tong 筆直立在°此°; — (*in
character*), tsing'-dzih-go 正直
个°; tön-tsing' 端正; tön-fông'-
go 端方个°; tsing'-dzih-vu-s'
正直無私

UPROAR, *great noise*, ts'ao'-nao 謅
鬧; *ditto, with trouble*, nao-z' 鬧事

UPROOT, *to* lin keng' bah-diao' 連
根拔去°; *to dig up roots of
trees*, dao za-cü' 掘°柴°株

UPSET, *to* fæn'-tao 翻倒; *to turn
over*, fæn-cün' 翻轉; — *by push-
ing*, t'e-tao' 推倒; *be careful, or
you will be —, &c., (i. e.* be sick
yourself, — said to one taking care
of the sick), yüong kw'u-djoh zi'
fæn-tao' 要顧着自°翻倒; — (as
plans, work, &c.), tin-tao' 顛倒

UPSIDE *down*, tao'-toh-go-de 頂°
倒°个°; tao'-deo-go-de 倒頭
个°; tao'-hyiang-de 倒向了°

UPSTAIRS, leo-teng' 樓上°

UPWARD, hyiang-zông' 向上;
dziao-zông' 朝上

UPWARDS, *thirty years and* —,
sæn'-jih nyin' yi-zông' 三十年
以上; sæn'-jih nyin' yi-nga' 三
十年以外°

URGE, *to* ts'e-song' 催慫; ky'ün
勸; — *to speed, or diligence*, ts'e
催; ts'e-ts'oh' 催促; — *with
forcible means*, pih 逼; ts'e-pih',
or ts'e-bih 催逼; bih-bih'-ts'e'
辟辟催; — *a man to buy*, ts'e-
song' nyiu ma' 催慫人°買°

URGENT, *instantly important*, kying'-
iao 緊要; kyih'-ts'ih 急切; *in
— need*, kyih'-soh iao' 急速要

URINAL, shü-bing 尿°瓶; yia-wu'
夜°壺; bin'-wu 便壺 (ih-tsah)

URINE, shü 尿°; siao'-shü 小尿°;
siao'-bin 小便; *to pass* —, c'ih
siao'-bin 出小便; dza shü 撒°
尿°; ka siu' 解°手; c'ih siao'-
kong 出小恭; siao' ka 小解°

USAGE, kwe-kyü 規矩; *long estab-
lished* —, lao' kwe'-kyü 老規
矩; lao' li 老例; *regulation*,
tsông-dzing', or công-dzing' 章
程; *receive bad* —, ziu we'-ky'üoh
受委曲

USE, yüong-dziang 用塲; *don't
waste, you may find — for it*,
peh'-fi-ts-we' 不費之惠
The veng-li means that it is not
necessary to waste money in order to
bestow favors.

USE, *to* yüong 用; s 使; s'-hwun
使唤; s'-yüong 使用; — *in common*, kong-yüong' 公用; tsong'-
yüong 衆用; — *chopsticks*, yüong
kw'æn' 用筋°; s kw'æn' 使筋°;
— *carefully*, ts'-tsih yüong' 仔°
細用; *want to — a man*, iao ih'-
go nying s'-hwun 要一个人°
使唤; *I cannot — it* (as a machine, *i.e.* it will not obey me), feh
t'ing' ngô s'-hwun 弗聽我使唤

USED *much* (as words), nyih 熱°;
*not ditto*, lang 冷°

USEFUL, yiu yüong-dziang' 有用
塲; *very* —, jih-feng'-teh-ih' 十

分 得 益; — *to me*, yiu-ih' ü-ngo' 有 益 于 我

USELESS, m̄-yüong'-dziang 無°用 塲; m̄-yüong'-go 無°用 个°; — (*because not good, or spoiled*), m̄-tso' 沒°做; — (*because not suitable*), feh-teh'-yüong 弗 得 用; — *labor*, k'ong'-deo yüong-kong 徒°然°用 功

USHER, *to* — *in*, ying'-tsing 引 進

USUAL, djông 常; bing-su' 平素; zing-djông' 尋°常; djông-z' 常時; *as* —, tsiao' djông 照 常; jü-djông' 如常; *the same as* —, tsiao' 'æn-djông' ih-yiang' 照朋°常 一 樣

USUALLY, bing-su'-kyin, or bing-su'-kæn 平素間°

USURP, *to* tsin 佔; — *by force*, po'-tsin 覇 佔; gyiang-tsin' 强 佔; — *the throne*, tsin we' 佔 位

USURY, djong li'-din 重利錢°; *to exact* —, fông djong' li 放 重 利; *ditto in the extreme*, djong' li bun-poh' 重利盤剝; *heavy* — *paid daily*, ing'-ts-din 印子錢°; pe'-din 負°利°錢

UTENSILS, kô sang'傢伙°; ky'i'-gyü 器 具; ky'i'-ming 器 皿; *farming* —, cong'-din kô'-sang 種田傢伙°; nong gyü' 農具; — *in general*, kô-sang'-jih-veh' 傢 伙° 什 物; *household and sewing* —, siu'-yüong kô'-sang 手用傢伙°

UTMOST, *to the* —, tao gyih-deo'

到 極; tao-piu'-de 到 邊 了°; *put forth* — *strength*, 'eo-ky'i'-lih tso' 盡氣°力做; nu'-lih tso' 努力做; *ditto* (whole heart, and strength), dzing'-sing gyih-lih' 盡心竭力

UTTER, djih 絕; gyih 極; — *stranger*, djih-feh-nying'-teh-go nying' 絕弗認°得个°人°

UTTER *words*, wô-c'ih shih-wô læ 話 出 說 話 來; *to* — *an oath*, vah-zing do'-tsin 罰 咒

UTTERANCE, *indistinct* k'eo'-ing feh ts'ing'-t'ong 口音弗清通; 'en-wu-dao' 含糊道; *impeded* —, ngao'-zih-keng-go kông'-fah 齩舌根个°講°法

UTTERLY *unwilling*, weh-ih' feh-k'eng' 劃 一 弗 肯

UTTERMOST *parts of the earth*, di'-ts gyih' 地之極; di'-go zing'-deo 地个°盡頭

## V

VACANCY, ky'üih 缺; *wait for a* —, teng'-'eo ky'üih-c'ih' 等 候 缺 出; 'eo-pu' 候補; 'eo-ky'üih 候缺; *to fill a* —, pu ky'üih'補 缺; *when a* — *occurs*, yiu ky'üih-k'ong' 有缺空; yiu ky'üih-c'ih' 有 缺 出; yiu ky'üih'-veng k'ong 有 缺 外 空

VACANT, k'ong 空; — *house*, k'ong' oh 空屋

VACATION, fông-ko' 放假; — (*for a longer time*), sæn-kwun'

散舘; — *during Summer*, hyih 'Ô' 歇夏'

VACCINATE, *to* cong ngeo-deo' 種牛痘'; cong yiang-deo' 種羊痘

VACCINE *matter*, deo-tsiang' 痘漿; *to take — from one to another*, djün-tsiang' 傳漿; —*scab*, ngeo-deo iu' 牛° 痘靨

VACILLATE, *to* fæn'-fæn-foh-foh' 反反覆覆; tsiao-sæn'-mo'-s 朝三暮四

VAGABOND, liu-loh'-go nying 流落個'人'; *idler*, dang-k'ah' 蕩客; lông-dông'-ts 浪蕩子

VAGUE, *muddled*, weng-teng'-teng 混濁°濁°; *cannot distinguish black from white*, heh'-bah feh-feng' 黑白° 弗分

VAIN, *having no real substance*, hyü 虛; *delusive*, hyü-hwô' 虛花; *in —*, bah-bah' 白°白°; bah'-lih-lih'; wông'-jün 枉然; du-jün' 徒然; *labor in —*, bah-bah' lao-loh' 白°白° 勞碌; *use one's energies in —*, wông'-fi tsing-jing' 枉費精神; wông'-fi sing-kyi' 枉費心機; *to spend one's life in —*, hyü-du' ih-si' 虛度一世°; *to take God's name in —*, vông'-ts'ing Jing-Ming -go ming-deo' 妄稱神明個°名頭

VAIN, piao-piao'-go 彪彪個'; iao ts'ing-piao' 要稱彪 — *of one's person, or accomplishments*, iao ts'ing-üong' 要稱勇; zi-sön' z'-wu-ih-kying' 自算似乎一衿

VALID, t'o' t'iah 妥貼°; k'ao'-leh jih'-go 靠得° 實個°

VALLEY, ao 墺; bing 坪; sæn koh' 山谷 (ih-go)

VALUABLE, dzih dong-din' 値銅錢°; kwe'-djong-go 貴重個°

VALUE, *to* djong 重; — *highly*, long-djong' 隆重; tse'-djong 最重; kwe'-djong 貴重; *I — it highly*, keh z ngô' sô long-djong'-go 這° 是我所隆重個°

VALUE, *price*, kô'-din 價°錢°; *true —*, jih-kô' 實價°; *to estimate the —*, kwu kô'-din 估價°錢°; *what is its —?* dzih to-siao' kô'-din 値多少價°錢°? *you do not know the — of the goods*, ng' feh sih' bo 你°弗識貨

VANISH, *to* — *suddenly*, hweh'-jün feh-kyin' 忽然弗見; ngæn'-tsing ih-sah 眴-neh'-de 眼°睛一眴 沒°有了°; — (go) *quickly*, ts'ong-ts'ong' ky'i 忽忽去°

VANITY, hyü-veo'-go z-ken 虛浮個°事幹; hyü hwô'-z 虛花之°事; vu-ih'-ts-z' 無益之事

VANITY, *he has a great deal of —*, gyi' yiu ih-kwu' piao-ky'i 其有一皷彪氣

VANQUISH, *to* tang'-ying 打贏; *to be vanquished*, shü 輸; ba 敗°; shü-diao' 輸了°; ba-diao' 敗了°

VAPID, *having lost life and spirit*, (*as wine*), sing'-dao kô'-de 性子過了°

Vapor, ky'i 氣 : — *rises*, ky'i'-tsing-ky'i'-læ 氣蒸起來

Variable, kæ'-pin 改變; wun-yiang' 換樣

Variance, *at* yiu du'-bing 有肚病; *not agreeing*, feh-deo'-kyi' 弗投機; feh-siang-'eh' 弗相合

Varied *talents*, to-dzæ' to-nyi'-go 多才多藝个°; — *uses*, yüong-dziang' væn'-go 用塲繁个°

Variegated, ng'-ngæn'-loh-seh' 五顏°六色; hwô-lih'-peh-lang' 花麗°斑° 爛;* hwô-hwô'-loh-loh' 花花綠綠

\* Also signifies, figured, changeable, or having various kinds. Cloth of one color, figured, may be hwô-lih-peh-lang, a changeable person who cannot be trusted, and the various goods in a shop irrespective of color, may be the same.

Variety, a — of, or Various, pah'-yiang 百°樣; koh'-yiang 各樣; koh' seh 各色; zeh'-keh-leng'-teng 雜°夾零°等; zeh gyih' 雜°劇; *various matters*, pah'-yiang z-t'i' 百°樣事體

Varnish, *Ningpo* ts'ih 漆; *unboiled ditto*, sang ts'ih' 生°漆; *ditto* (boiled with dong-yiu' 桐油), kying ts'ih' 金漆; *false* —(more oil, and less ts'ih), kô'-kying ts'ih' 假°金漆; *vermilion* —, cü-'ong' ts'ih' 硃紅漆; *to be poisoned with* —, sang' ts'ih'-ting' 生°漆疔

Varnish, *to* ts'ih 漆; k'a ts'ih' 揩° 漆; ts'ah' ts'ih 擦漆; —

*only with oil*, k'a yiu' 揩°油; — *with shining oil*, k'a liang-yin' 揩°亮油; — *an untruth*, shih'-long wô'-hwn 說龍話虎

Vary, *to* — *in form*, kæ-yiang' 改樣; pin-yiang' 變樣; wun-yiang' 換樣; — *in color*, pin-seh' 變色

Vase, (bulging in the middle, and small at the top), wu-bing' 壺瓶; *flower* —, hwô-bing' 花瓶 (ih-tsah)

Vast, ting'-do 頂大°; kwông'-kw'eh 廣闊; — *expanse*, (as the sky, or ocean), mang-yiang'-yiang 茫°洋洋

Vaulted, *arched*, gwæn-dong'-shih-go 環°洞式个°

Vaunt, *to* p'u-hæ'-kying 舖海景; kông-hæ'-wô 講°海話; *to boast*, c'ô-dæn' 詫誕; kw'ô-k'eo' 誇口; kông do-wô' 講°大°話 See Boast.

Veal, siao'-ngeo nyüoh' 小牛°肉°

Vegetable, ts'æ 菜; *vegetables* (in general), su'-ts'æ 蔬菜; *to live on vegetables only*, (as the Buddhists often do), ky'üoh ts'æ' 吃°菜; ky'üoh dziang-su' 吃°長菜; — *kingdom*, ts'ao'-moh ih-le' 草木一類

Vehement, ts'u - bao' 粗暴; mang'-tsiang 猛°將, these characters only have a good meaning, as brave, &c.; *quick, and severe*, bao-tsao' 暴躁; — *gestures*,

vu'-siang 武 相; ti'-kyiah vu-
siu' 手° 舞° 足° 蹈°

VEIL, *thin* tsao'-sò 罩 紗; — *for
the face,* tsao'-min-sô' 罩 面 紗

VEIL, *to* —, *or cover,* tsao-zông'
罩 上; — *the face,* tsô' min-
k'ong' 遮° 面 孔; *Chinese bridal*
—, tæ'-deo-bong' 兜 頭 纔

VEIN, byüih'-kying 血 筋

VELOCITY, *what is the* —? to'-siao
kw'a' 多少快°? dza kwun' kw'a
怎° 樣° 快°?

VELVET, nyüong 絨; tsin'-nyüong
剪 絨; *silk* —, s nyüong' 絲絨

VELVETEEN, min nyüong' 綿 絨

VENERABLE *appearance,* nyin-kao'
yiu-teh'-go siang-mao 年 高 有
德 个° 相 貌; lao'-dzing-ky'i-
ziang 老 成 氣 象

VENERATE, *to* tseng-kying' 尊 敬;
tseng-djong' 尊 重

VENEREAL *ulcer,* yiang-me ts'ông'
楊 梅 瘡; ao-tsao' ts'ông 垩 糟
瘡; yiang-me' kyih'-doh 楊 梅
結 毒

VENETIANS, pah'-yih-ts'ông' 百°
葉 牕; fæn-ts'ông' 翻 牕

VENGEANCE, *to take* —, pao-dziu'
報 讐

VENISON, kyi'-nyüoh 麂 肉°; loh-
nyüoh' 鹿 肉°

VENOMOUS, doh 毒

VENT, *to—feeling,* su cong-dziang'
訴 衷 腸; — *sorrow,* t'æn kw'u'-
cong (cong or tsong) 歎 苦 衷; —
*anger,* c'ih ky'i' 出 氣; sih veng'

澳 忿; fah sing'-kah 發 性 格

VENTILATE, *to* t'ong ky'i' 通 氣;
t'eo ky'i' 透 氣; — *the room,*
vông-kæn' t'ong-t'ong ky'i' 房
間° 通 通 氣

VENTURE, *to* mao do tæn' 冒 大°
膽; *to dare,* ken 敢; *to run the
risk,* mao hyin' 冒 險; *if unwilling to* — *into the tiger's den,
how can you catch her cub,* peh jih
hwu'-yüih, in teh hwu'-ts (veng.)
不 入 虎 穴 焉 得 虎 子

VERANDAH, *upper* nga-leo' 外° 樓;
nao-lông' 走° 廊; nao leo'-teng
月° 臺'; *lower* —, yiu-jing k'eo'
檐° 廊° 口; yiu-jing-di' 檐° 廊°
地; yiu-jing' 遊廊'; *a very long*
—, (around two or more houses,
in Chinese style), tseo'-mô-leo
走 馬 樓

VERB, weh-z'-ngæn 活 字 眼°

VERBAL, k'eo'-djün-go 口 傳 个°;
*take a* — *message,* ta k'eo'-sing
帶° 口° 信

VERBATIM, *repeat* tsiao' yiang
djün' 照 樣 譔; *ditto* (by figure
of speech), i yiang', wô wu-lu'
依 樣 畫 葫 蘆

VERBOSE *style,* veng-dz' dzing-
dziang' 文 詞 太° 長; *lengthy
speech,* wô-deo dziang' 話 頭 長

VERDICT (of an official), dông-
tön' 堂 斷; *the* — *is, guilty,*
tön'-ding gyi kw'e li' 斷 定 其
處 理

VERDIGRIS, dong-loh' 銅 綠

VERIFY, to — (by seeing), nyin
驗;— the amount of cargo, nyin
ho' 驗貨; to bring out proofs,
do'-c'ih bing-kyü kæ 拿° 出 憑
據來;— it (to me), peh ngô
nyin' ming-bah' 俾我驗明白

VERMICELLI of wheat or rice flour,
min 麫; ken-min' 乾麫; (transparent) — of bean flour, feng'-
ken 粉乾

VERMILION, nying-cü' 銀硃;
— pencil, cü-pih' 硃筆

VERSE, a — (of a hymn, or from
the Bible), ih tsih' 一節

VERSED in (as books), joh-doh'-
go 熟讀个; well acquainted
with, (not persons), joh-sih' 熟
識;— in the classics, sing'-kying
joh-doh'-go 聖經熟讀个°

VERSION of the Bible, fæn-yih'-go
Sing'-shü 繙譯个°聖書; which
ditto do you prefer? fæn-yih' go
Sing'-shü ng ting'hwun-hyi' 'ah-
li' ih-cong' 繙譯个°聖書你°
頂歡喜那° 裡° 一種?

VERTEBRA, tsih'-kweh 脊骨; pe'-
tsih-kweh 背脊骨

VERTEX, ting 頂; ting-deo' 頂頭;
tsin-fong-den' 尖峯頭°; nao'-
tsin 腦尖

VERTICAL line, dzih sin' 直線;
(ih-da); the sun is —, nyih-deo'
dzih'-de 日° 頭直了°

VERTIGO, deo-yüing' 頭暈

VERY, ting 頂; gyih 極; djih 絕;
tse 最; altogether, jih-feng' 十分;

— good, (the best). ting'-hao 頂
好; gyih-hao' 極好; jih-feng'
hao' 十分好; tsæ'-m̄-tsæ' hao'
再無° 再好; — large indeed,
ngæ-do'-do 極大°;— lately, —
soon, or — near, ngæn' min-zin'
眼° 面前; the — least (price),
ky'i-mô' 起碼; ky'i-kô' 起價°;
ky'i-cü' 起注;— hot weather,
t'in da-nyih' 天大熱°;—dif-
ferent, ts'ô-yün' 差遠; ts'ô-to'
差多; da-ts'ô' gyi yün' 大差
其遠: t'in-ts'ô' di-yün' 天差
地遠; long-do' koh-yiang' 大°
相° 懸° 遠°; da' feh-siang-dong'
大弗相同; this — day, tông'-
nyih 當日°; tsih'-nyih 卽日°;
I am — sorry you cannot go, ng'
feh ky'i', ngô tao' k'o'-sih 你°
弗去° 我倒可惜; k'o'-sih
ng' feh ky'i' 可惜你° 弗去°;
for, — well, hao', hao' 好好, or
substitute, owing to you I have
happiness, t'oh-ng-foh' 托你°福;
t'oh-foh' 托福

VESSEL (for holding anything),
tsi'-go kô'-sang 齒个°傢伙°;
— (for the sea), hæ'-jün 海船;
— with a sail, fong-bong jün'
風篷船

VESTIBULE, meng-vông' 門房
See PORTICO.

VETERAN officer (military), tsing-
liu'-go kwun-ping' 精練个官
兵;— soldier, tsing-ping' 精兵

VEX, to irritate, ts'ao 譟; to make

*angry by repeated provocations,* væn-nao' 煩惱; *to harass (as if by tying, or pulling back),* dzin'-ziao 纏擾

VEXATIOUS, t'in-væn-nao' 添煩惱;— *petty cares,* se'-se væn-væn z-t'i' 碎繁事體

VEXED, sing'-li væn-nao' 心裡煩惱; — (because one has done something wrong), ao'-nao 懊惱

VIAL, siao' po-li' bing' 小玻璃瓶 (ih-tsah)

VIBRATING, tsing'-tsing-dong 怔怔動; *swinging,* dang-dang'-dong 宕宕動

VICE, *bad practices,* oh'-jih 惡習; *sink into —,* 'æn'-loh oh-nyin'-dao lu 陷°落惡孽道路

VICE, (smith's) ngang-cü'-pô' 鐵°夾°箝°

VICE, (second in rank), fu 副; — *president,* fu'-siu 副手

VICEROY *of two provinces,* tsong'-toh 總督; styled, cü'-dæ 制臺; ts-kyüing 制軍; — *of one province,* fu-dæ' 撫臺; styled, jing-fu' 巡撫

VICINITY, *in the — of,* siang-gying' 相近; *in the — of Peking,* læ Poh'-kying siang-gying' 在°北京相近

VICIOUS, *having — propensities,* 'ô'-liu p'e'-ts 下°流胚子;— *person,* 'ô'-tsoh-nying' 下°作人

VICISSITUDES, ky'i'-tao-to'; fæn'-foh to' 反覆多; *he has passed through many —,* gyi' din sön kw'u lah tu zông-ko' 其甜酸苦辣都嘗過; gyi hyü'-to kying-hwông' kying-lih'-ko 其許多境况經歷過

VICTIM, *three* (important) *sacrificial victims,* sæn-sang' foh'-li 三牲°福禮; *a human sacrificial —,* nying' tông tsi'-veh 人°當祭物; *men become victims to wealth, birds to food,* nying' we dzæ-s', tiao' we zih-vông' 人爲財死鳥°爲食亡

VICTOR, teh-sing'-go-nying 得勝个°人°; ying'-go cü-kwu 打°贏个°人°

VICTORIOUS, *were you*—(or how)? sing'-ba jü-'o' 勝敗°如何? *returned —,* teh-sing' kyü-læ' 得勝歸來; *to be —,* tang teh-sing'-tsiang 打得勝仗°; tang-sing'-tsiang 打勝仗°

VICTORY, *to gain a —,* teh-sing' ih-ts' 得勝一次; ih-tsao tang'-ying 一遭打贏

VICTUALS, ky'üoh'-zih 吃°食; — (prepared for a journey), ho'-zih 伙食; *light ditto* (as cakes &c.), ken-liang' 乾糧; *vegetables and rice,* ts'æ'-væn 菜飯; *to have plenty of — and warm clothes,* ts'æ'-væn pao, pu'-i nön' 菜飯飽布衣煖

VIEW, *to see,* k'en 看; — *carefully,* ts'-si k'en' 仔細看; — *the prospect,* k'en kying'-cü 看景致

VIEW, *according to this* —, ka'-k‘en'-ky‘i-læ 如°此°看起來；*to take a narrow* —, zo-tsing' kwun-t‘in' 坐井觀天

VIGILANT, bông-siu' nyin-mih' 防守嚴密

VIGOR, *in full mental* nyin'-lih tsing-tsông' 年力精壯；*strength*, ky‘i'-lih 氣力；lih-liang' 力量

VIGOROUS, *firm and strong*, tsah'-tsông 圍壯 (tsong or cong)；tsah'-cü；— (used only of youth), tsông'-gyin 壯健；gyin 健*
\* Not usually applied to a young person unless he has recently been ill.

VILE, *despicable*, zin 賤°；pe-zin' 卑賤°；‘ô'-zin 下°賤°；*bad*, ‘ô'-tsoh 下°作；‘ô'-tsoh-peh-k‘æn' 下°作不堪

VILIFY, *to* hwe'-pông 毀謗；pông'-hwe 謗毀

VILLAGE, *a* ih-ts‘eng' 一村；ih'-go hyiang-ts‘eng' 一个°鄉村

VILLAGERS, ts‘eng' li-hyiang'-go nying' 村裏向个°人°；ts‘eng-tsông-zông'-go nying 村庄上个°人°

VILLAIN, kweng'-du 棍徒；vu-la' 無°賴°；di-kweng' 地棍；*bold* —, kwông-kweng' 光棍；fi'-du 匪徒

VILLAINOUS *fellow*, liang-sing'-ts‘eh'-hah-go-nying' 俍心漆°黑个°人°；hah'-sing-hah-fi'-go nying 黑°心°黑肺个°人°；— *affair*, feh-kyin'-t‘in-nyih'-go z-ken' 弗見天日°个°事幹；

*ditto* (darkening heaven), heh'-t‘in-heh-di'-go z-ken' 黑天黑地事幹°

VINDICATE, *to* feng-ts‘ing'-dao'-bah 分青道白°；si-ts‘ing' 洗清；— *another*, dæ-we' feng-ts‘ing' dao'-bah 代爲分青道白°

VINDICTIVE, yiu pao-dziu'-go sing 有報仇个°心

VINE, *creeper*, yin-deng' 延籐；*grape* —, bu-dao'-jü' 葡萄樹 (ih-cü)

VINEGAR, ts‘u 醋

VINEYARD, bu-dao-yün' 葡萄園 (ih-zo)

VIOLATE, *to* væn 犯；— *the law*, væn fah' 犯法；— *the Sabbath*, væn en-sih'-nyih 犯安息日°；— *a promise*, shih iah' 失約；shih sing' 失信；— *an oath*, vah-tsiu' we la'-go 賴°罰咒个°；*to commit rape on*, gyiang-kæn' 强姦°

VIOLENCE, *to use* —, ying-hyüong' 行兇；*to take by* —, gyiang do' 强拿°；*to borrow with* —, *or snatch*, gyiang tsia' 强借°；*to rob with* —, gyiang-deh' 强奪；gyiang-ts‘iang' 强搶；ts‘iang'-kyih 搶刼

VIOLENT, ying-hyüong' 行兇；*wind*, gwông-fong' 狂風；*long fong* 龍風；fong pao' 風颷

VIOLIN, (native 4 stringed) bi-bô' 琵琶；*three stringed* —, yin-ts' 絃子；sæn-yin' 三絃；*two stringed* —, wu-gying' 胡琴；*violins*, (in-

general), s-yin' kô'-sang 絲絃
傆°伏°

VIPER, doh-dzô' 毒蛇° (ih-diao,
ih-keng, ih-kwang)

VIRGIN, dong-nyü 童女 (ih-go)

VIRILE, we sang-yiang' 會生°
羕°; nyün yiang'-tsoh'-de 元陽
足了°

VIRTUE, teh'-ky'i 德氣; teh'-
'ang 德行; the five virtues, wu'
djông 五常; — of medicine,
yiah'-go kong-yiao' 藥个功效

VIRTUOUS, yiu teh'-ky'i 有德
氣; yin-teh'-go 賢德个°; —
widow, tsih'-vu 節婦; tsing-
tsih'-vu 貞節婦

VIRULENT, oh'-doh 惡毒;hyüong'-
feh-ko', yi hyüong' 兇而°叉°兇

VISAGE, yüong-mao' 容貌; min-
yüong' 面容; fearful —, ô-lin'
p'ô'-p'ô 可°怕°之°相°

VISCERA, dzông-fu', or djông-fu
臟腑

VISCID, nyin-kao'-kao 黏膠°; —
(like snails), nyin-zæn' 黏涎°

VISIBLE, k'en'-leh-kyin'-go看得°
見个°

VISION, yi'-ziang 異象 (ih-go);
to be in a state for seeing a —,
(i.e. soul out of the body), jing-
yiu' ziang-wæ' 神遊象外
(veng.)

VISIONARY, catching the sun's shadow, k'ô nyih-deo-ing' 捉°日頭
影; catching the east wind, k'ô
tong-fong' 捉°東風; catching

the wind that blew off the hat, k'ô
loh-mao'-fong 捉°落帽風; to
engage in —projects, ky'in-k'ong-
mo' 牽空磨

VISIT, to pa'-mông 拜°望; to — a
friend, mông-mông' beng-yiu'望°
望°朋友; k'en beng-yiu' 看朋
友; — the sick, k'en bing-nying'
看病人; do you — one another ?
ng-lah yiu mông-læ' mông-ky'i
ǎ'-teh ? 你等°有往°來°拜°
望°嗎°

VISIT, to make a ceremonious —,
pa'-we 拜°會; to return ditto,
we-pa' 回拜°; to make ditto to a
superior, pa'-kyin 拜°見; to miss
a —, shih-'eo' 失候;shih-nying'
失迎

VISITOR, nying-k'ah'客人°; lady
—, nyü'-k'ah 女客 (ih-we); to
receive a —, we k'ah' 會客; not
to receive a —, feh we' k'ah' 弗
會客; feh we' 弗會; to meet a
—, tsih k'ah' 接客; to await (a
—), teng'-'eo 等候; kong'-'eo
恭候;attend a — to the door, or
to the gate, song k'ah 送客; to
go with a —, be k'ah' 陪客

VITAL, of—importance, iao'-kying
kwæn'-deo 要緊關頭

VITALS, ky'iao'-meng竅門; ming-
meng' 命門

VITIATE, to wæ-diao' 壞了°

VITIATED by it, be gyi' sô 'æ'被其
所害; — appetite, we-k'eo' pin'-
diao-de 胃口變壞°了°

VITRIOL, *blue* tæn'-væn 胆礬;
*green —*, loh-væn' 綠礬
VIVACIOUS, weh-siang' 活相;
weh-loh' 活絡; ling-long' 玲瓏
VIVIPAROUS, t'æ-sang' 胎生°
VOCABULARY, z-nyü'-we'-ka 字
語彙解° See DICTIONARY.
VOCIFERATE, *to* 'eo wu-long' si'
竭聲而° 喊; wu-long'
hyiang'-liang 喉° 嚨嚮亮
VOICE, sing-ing' 聲音; tæn din' 丹
田; wu-long' 喉嚨; *loud —*,
sing-ing' do' 聲音大°; wu-long'
do' 喉° 嚨大°; *soft —*, sing-ing
si' 聲音細; *low —*, ti sing 低聲
VOLATILE, *capable of passing off,*
we tseo'-diao 會走去°; *— (light)*
*person,* ky'ing p'iao'-go nying' 輕
飄个° 人°; *ditto,* kying-kweh'-
deo-go 輕骨頭个°, this usually
means a bad person.
VOLCANO, ho'-sæn 火山 (ih-zo)
VOLUME, *a* ih-peng shü' 一本書
VOLUNTARILY *enter a net,* (or into
sin), zi-deo' lo-mông' 自° 投羅網°
VOLUNTARY, (as giving, &c.),
c'ih'-ü zi'-go i'-s 出° 於自个°
意思; c'ih'-ü zi'-go peng'-sing
出於自个° 本心; *of one's own*
*accord,* zi dzing'-nyün 自° 情願
VOLUNTEER, *to offer one's self,*
deo-tao' 投到; song'-zông-meng
送上門; *he volunteered to go,*
gyi deo-tao' we ky'i 其投到
會去°; gyi song'-zông-meng'
we-ky'i' 其送上門會去°; *—*
(as a soldier without pay), deo-

ying'-yiao-lih' 投營効力; *—*
*to help him,* song'-zông-meng'
pông-dzu' gyi 自° 願° 幫助其
VOLUPTUOUS, *ministering to sens-*
*ual pleasures,* du-hwun-loh'-go
圓歡樂个°; *fond of ditto,* æ
hwô-loh' go 愛花綠个°
VOMIT, *to* t'u 吐; mao 嘔°; *hav-*
*ing an inclination to —*, oh'-sing
yiang-yiang' 欲嘔°; iao'-siang
t'u'-c'ih-læ 要想吐出來
VORACIOUS, du'-ts do' 肚子大°;
tsiu'-nông-væn-dæ 酒甕飯袋;
*— person,* do-zih-vu 食量大°
个° 人°
VOW, *to make a —* (to God, or an
idol), hyü nyün-sing' 許願心;
hyü nyün' 許願; (more often), he
nyün-sing; *to return a —*, wæn
nyün-sing' 還願心; wæn nyün'
還願; *to promise solemnly, calling*
*God to witness,* fah nyün' 發願
VOYAGE, *to go on a —*, zo jün'
ky'i 坐船去°; *a —* ih-t'ông
jün' 一躺船:* ih-shü' ky'i 一
水去°; ih-t'ông' 一躺; *the last*
*— was a successful one,* zin-shü'
da-fah'-go 前° 次° 大° 發个°
This term is used by the crew, and
those constantly passing and repassing,
for voyages made by fishing-boats.
In asking about a friend's voyage use
the word journey, which see.
VULGAR, *coarse and common,* ts'u
粗; ts'u-dzoh' 粗俗; zah-t'u' 極
土; *— language* (the vernacular),
t'u'-wô 土話; hyiang-dæn' 鄉
談; *— eyes,* djoh-ngæn' 俗眼°

# W

WAD, to — (as a garment), ts'eng′ min-hwô′ 襯棉花; si′ min-hwô′ 翻°棉花

WADDED garments, min-i′ 棉衣

WADDING, cotton dong′-hwô 筒花; a roll of —, ih-kyün′ dong-hwô′ 一卷筒花

WADE, to — through water, liao-shü′ 蹽水°

WAG, pô′-hyi-nying 善°戲謔°个°人°; ying-nying′-siao′-go 引人°笑个°

WAG, to yiao 搖; hwæn 甩; — head and tail, yiao-deo′hwæn mi′-pô 搖頭甩尾°巴

WAGER, to lay a —, tang-tu′ 賽°賭; to lay a — for food, tn tong-dao′ 賭東道; to lose a —, tu′-shü 賭輸; to win a —, tu′-ying 賭贏

WAGES, kong-din′ 工錢°; to pay out —, c′ih kong-din′ 出工錢°; give him his —, fu kong-din′ peh′-gyi 付工錢°給°伊

WAGON, s′-leng-ts′ô′ 四輪車° (ih-bu, ih-dzing).

WAILING, 'ao-li′-da-koh′ 號啕°大哭

WAIST, iao 腰; — slender (as a willow stem), liu′-iao 柳腰

WAIST-BAND of drawers, kw'u′-iao 褲腰; — of a skirt, gyüing-iao′ 裙腰; a girdle, kyiao-sing′-ta 緊°身帶°; soh′-iao-ta′ 束腰帶° (ih-diao)

WAIT, to teng 等; teng′-'eo 等候; 'eo 候; deng 庵*; — a little, teng-ih′-teng 等一等; deng′-ih-zông′ 庵一息°; (to an inferior), lao-ih′-lao; lao-ih-zông′; z′-'eo or ts″-'eo 侍°候; — for an answer, teng we-sing′ 等回信; I — here for you, ngô teng-ng′-tong 我在°此°等你°; — for one till out of patience, (or till the heart burns), teng′ nying sing′-tsiao 等人°心焦

*Deng properly has only the sense of stopping or remaining, therefore for wait, teng is preferable, though deng is sometimes used.

WAIT, to — upon (as the table, &c.), z′-dzih 侍值; — upon (as on a sick person), tông-dzih′ 當值

WAITER, attendant, z-dzih′-go-nying 侍值个°人°; si-tsæ′ 細崽西价′; tray, bun 盤 (ih-min).

WAKEN, to cease to sleep, diao-kao′ 調覺°; su-sing′ 蘇醒; — after a nap, hwah 豁; — (another), eo′ diao-kao′ 叫°醒°; eo su-sing′ 叫°蘇醒

WAKEFUL, sleeping but little, ve′-da-li kw'eng′-joh 不°甚°睡°熟; — and restless (as a child), tin-min′-joh 顛眠熟

WALK, to tseo 走; take a walk, tseo′ ih′-we 走一回; sæn-sæn bu′ 散散步; ky'i tseo-tseo′ 去°走走; did you come in a chair, or did you —? ng wa-z zo gyiao′ læ wa-z tseo′ læ 你°還°是坐

轎 來 還° 是 走 來? — *erect,
and dignified,* tseo-leh yin ẁe-shü
走 得° 有 威 勢; — *gracefully,*
(said of a woman), tseo' yin fong-
deo' 走 得° 飄° 逸°; — *quickly,*
ky'i diao'-diao 去 蹀 蹀; — *leisurely along,* doh-soh' kyi 踱 踱

WALKER, *he is a good* —, gyi'
tseo'-gying hao' 其 走 勁 好

WALL, ziang 墻 (ih-dao); *dividing*
—, iao-ziang' 腰 墻; *partition*
— (of a house), pih 壁; *surrounding* —, ziang-yü' 墻 宇;
*city* —, dzing-ts' 城 子; dzing-
ziang' 城 墻; *the Great* —, Væn-
li' dziang-dzing' 萬 里 長 城

WALLOW, *to* — *in mud,* le'-nyi-
wu'-tsiang 擂 泥 糊 漿

WALNUT, *English* wu-dao' 胡 桃
(ih-go); *to crack walnuts,* k'ao-
k'æ' wu-dao' 敲° 開 胡 桃;
*cracked walnuts,* k'ao dao' 敲° 桃

WANDER, *to* tseo-læ' tseo-ky'i' 走
來 走 去°; *to* — *idly about,*
k'ong'-deo tseo' 空 頭 走; 'æn
tseo' 閒° 走; — *in quest of amusement,* yiu-hyi' 遊 戲

WANDERING *in delirium,* kông
nyih-wô' 講 熱° 話; kông weng'-
wô' 講° 混 話; *to have* — *thoughts,*
feng-sing' 分 心

WANT, *deficiency,* ky'üih'-siao 缺
少; ky'in'-ky'üih 欠 缺; ky'üih'-
siao dziang-tön' 缺 少 長 短; *in*
— *of wood and rice,* m̄-za' m̄-mi
無° 柴 無° 米; feh-dong-ho'-in

弗 動° 火 烟; — *of food,* m̄-kao'
ky'üoh'-de 沒° 有° 甚° 吃°

WANT, *to* iao 要; *do not* —, feh
iao' 弗 要; fæ'-gyi; — *very much
to do,* pô'-feh-neng'-keo tso' 巴
弗 能 彀 做; *what do you* —?
ng' iao soh' si 你° 要 甚° 麽°?
*don't* — *to be there* (as a servant
leaving a place), sang t'eng'mao-
de 計° 欲° 脫° 身° (slang).

WANTING, ky'üih 缺; ky'in 欠;
ts'ô 差; *five o'clock,* — *five minutes,* ng' tin-cong ky'üih ng' feng
五° 點 鐘 缺 五° 分

WAR, tang-tsiang' z-ken 打 仗°
事 幹; *the art of* —, kyüing-kyi'
軍 機; ping-fah' 兵 法; *gone
to the* —, c'ih'-ping tang-tsiang'
出 兵 打 仗°; *to go to* —, dong
ken-ko' 動 干 戈; *at* —, læ-tih
kyiao-tsin' 正° 在° 交 戰; læ-
tih tang-tsiang' 正° 在° 打 仗°;
*implements of* —, kyüing-ky'i'
軍 器

WARD, *to* — *off a blow,* ih-kyi kah'-
ko 遮° 攔° 其° 打°

WARDROBE, *closet for clothes,* i-
djü' 衣 廚 (ih-k'eo); *complete*
—, s'-kyi i-sæn' 四 季 衣 衫

WARE-HOUSE, dzæn-vông' 棧 房
(ih-t'eo)

WARES, ho'-veh 貨 物; *porcelain*
—, dz-ky'i' 磁 器; *earthen* —,
ngô'-ho 瓦° 貨°; *miscellaneous* —,
zah-ho' 雜 貨

WARM, nyih 熱°; — *water,* nyih-

shü' 熱° 水°; — *weather,* t'in-
kô nyih 天 熱°; *to grow — by
degrees,* dzin'-dzin nyih-ky'i'-læ
漸 漸 熱° 起 來

WARM, *to* — (as food), nyih-nyih'
熱°一熱°; nön'-ih-nön' 煖一煖°;
we'-ih-we' 回一回; — *the soup,*
t'ông' nyih-nyih' gyi 湯 熱° 一
熱°; t'ông' nön-ih-nön' 湯煖一
煖; — *the wine,* (genteel), tsiu'
p'ao'-ih-p'ao 酒 泡 一 泡; —
*one's self* (at a fire), k'ao ho' 烤
火; *one's hands* (at a fire), hong
siu' 烘 手

WARM-HEARTED, nyih sing-
dziang' go 熱° 心 腸 个°; nyih
sing'-go 熱° 心 个°

WARMING-PAN, *Chinese* (for the
feet), ho'-ts'ong 脚° 爐°; *very large
ditto,* kyiah'-dah 大° 脚 爐°; —
*for the hands,* siu'-lu 手 爐; *very
small egg shaped ditto,* ah'-dæn
siu-lu' 鴨° 蛋 手 爐; ziu-lu' 袖 爐;
— *to keep tea warm,* nön-dzô'-go
lu' 煖 茶 个° 爐; ngao-lu' 熬 爐

WARN, *to* — *and threaten* (a superior to an inferior), kying'-kyiæ
警 戒; — (an equal), ky'ün'-
min 勸 勉

WARP, kying-sin' 經 線; — *and
woof,* kying-we' 經 緯; *long
threads in the loom,* or *thread on
the shuttle,* kying-sô' 經 紗; yü-
sô' 緯° 紗

WARP, *to* ho-gyiao' 彎° 橋; *warp-*

ed, dzin-mô'-liu 橾 蔴 縷; gyiao-
gyiao'-goh-goh 橋 橋° 搁° 搁°

WARRANT, ba 牌°; ba-p'iao' 牌°
票 (ih tsiang); — *for immediate
seizure,* ho'-ts'in 火 籤; *to issue
a* —, c'ih ba' 出 牌°

WARRANT, *to guaranty,* pao 包;
— *for a year,* pao t'ao'-hao ih-
nyin' 包 討 好 一 年; — (that
a man will do well), pao'-kyü
保 舉

WARRIOR, *experienced* tsing-ping'
精 兵

WASH, *to* gyiang 洗°; — *the face,*
gyiang min' 洗° 面; — *the body,*
gyiang nyüoh' 洗° 浴°; — *dishes,*
gyiang-un'dông-tsæn 洗° 碗 盪 盞

WASH-BASIN, min-dong' 面 桶 )
min-beng' 面 盆 (ih-tsah)

WASHER-MAN, gyiang i-zông'-go
nying 洗° 衣 裳 个° 人°

WASH-STAND, min-kô' 面 架 (ih-zo)

WASP, yia' fong-ts' 野° 蜂 子;
dang-kyiah' wông-fong' 宕 脚
黃 蜂 (ih-tsah)

WASTE *land,* hwông di' 荒 地;
— *paper,* fi'-ts 廢 紙; — *lettered
paper,* z-ts' 字 紙

WASTE, *to* fi 廢; fi'-diao 廢 了°;
wông-fi 枉 費; bah-fi' 白° 費;
du-fi' 徒 費; — (money), hwô-
fi' 花 費; lông-fi' 浪 費; mi-fi'
糜 費; — *time,* tang'-loh kong-
fu' 誤° 工 夫; fi kong-fu' 費
工 夫; ts'o-do' kwông-ing' 蹉
跎 光 陰; *mis-spend time,* byü-

du′ kwông-ing′ 虛度光陰；
*lay — the land,* tsao-t′ah′ din-di′
蹧蹋田地

WASTEFUL, we tsao-t′ah′ tong-si′
會蹧蹋物°件°；*lavish,* kw'un-
sin′-go 寬手个°；song-sin′-go 鬆
手个°；ky'i′-p'ah do′ 氣魄大°

WATCH, z-ming′-piao 自鳴表；
z-jing-piao′ 時辰表 (ih-tsah);
*gold —,* kying piao′ 金表；—
*crystal,* (glass cover), po-li-kæ′ 玻
璃蓋；*to fit a — crystal,* p'e ih-
go piao′-kæ 配一个°表蓋；*to
wind a —,* k'æ piao′開表 *first
— (of the night),* ib-kang 一更；
*the five night watches,* (from 7 P.
M. to 5 A. M.), ng′ kang 五°更

WATCH, *to* kying′-sin 謹守；—
*over,* k'en′-kwu 看顧；*to look after,*
k'en′-siu 看守；— *and prepare
against,* kying′-bông 謹防；—
*for thieves* (at night), kwun yia-
mæn′ 防°賊个°；*to — a chance*
(as a thief), gyiang z-'eo′ 弶時
候；— (as a night-watchman),
jing kang′ 巡更°；jing yia′ 巡
夜°；dzih kang′ 值更°；dzih yia′
值夜°；— *the house,* k'en′-siu
oh′-li 看守家裡；k'en vông-
ts′ 看房子；kwun oh′ 管屋；
— *over,* or *for* (as some one expected), tsiao′- liao 照嘹；—
*from a high place* (as an enemy),
liao-vông′ 嘹望

WATCHFUL, kying-sing′ 警心；
kying′-jing 謹慎

WATCH-MAKER, cong-piao′ s-vu′
鐘表司務

WATCHMAN, *night* dzih-yia′- go
nying 值夜°个°人°；*day —,*
dzih-nyih′-go 值日°个°；— *who
strikes the watches,* ts-kang′-go
nying 支更°个°人°

WATCH-TOWER, kang-leo′更°樓；
kwu′-leo 鼓樓 (ih-zo)

WATCH-WORD, k'eo′-'ao 口號；
*secret sign,* en′-'ao 暗號

WATER, shü 水°；*rain —,* t''in-
shü′ 天雨水°；*salt —,* 'æn-shü′
鹹水°；*warm —,* nyih shü′ 熱°
水°；*boiling —,* kweng′ shü 滾
水°；dah-dah′ kweng′ shü 杏杏
滾水°；*to make —* (*i.e.* urinate),
dza shü′ 撒尿°

WATER, *to irrigate,* kyiao shü′ 澆
水°；*to go by —,* teng shü′-lu ky'i
從°水°路去°；— *the flowers,*
kyiao hwô′ 澆花；*ditto* (*i. e.* let
them drink), ing hwô′ 飲花；
— *the horse,* peh mô′ ing shü′ 給°
馬飲水°；*mouth waters,* k'eo
dzæn′ 口饞；cü′-pô dzæn′ 嘴
吧饞；*make the eyes —,* (with
something pungent), lah′-leh
ngæn′-li-c'ih′ 辣得°眼°淚出*

* Play actors and impostors sometimes have a piece of fresh ginger-root
(instead of an onion) in their hand-
kerchiefs, so as to bring tears when
they wipe their eyes.

WATER-CHESTNUT, bu-dzi′ 荸
薺；di-lih′ 地栗 (ih-go)

WATER-FALL, kw'ô′-loh-shü′ 跨
落水°

WATER-GATE, shü'-meng 水°門；(ih-dao)

WATER-LILY, *lotus*, 'o-hwô' 荷花；lin-hwô' 蓮花 (ih-tô)

WATER-MELON, si-kwô' 西瓜 (ih-go)

WATER-SPOUT, long-hwô'-shü 龍取°水°

WAVE, lông 浪；*little* —, po 波；po-lông' 波浪；lông-hwô' 浪花

WAVE, *to* — (as a flag, or the hand, when a thing is not wanted), yüih'-yüih 搖°手°；yüih-dong' 搖動

WAVERING, fæn'-fob feh-ding'反覆弗定；fæn'-fæn fob-foh' 反反覆覆；c'ih'-wu-r', fæn'-wu-r' 出乎爾反乎爾

WAX, lah 蠟；*white* —, bah-lah' 白°蠟；*yellow* —, wông-lah' 黃蠟；*ear* —, ng'-tô o' 耳蠟°

WAY, lu 路 (ih-da)；*to make* — *for*, k'æ lu' 開路；*on the* —, læ lu-zông' 在°路°上°；*without going out of the* —, jing-da' 順埭；jing-lu' 順路；*in the* — (obstructing), gah-tang' 軋打；*get out of the* —, tseo'-k'æ 走開；nyiang lu' 讓°路；*the same* —, dong lu' 同路；*to leave the right* —, li-k'æ' tsing'lu 離開正路；*the wrong* —, ts'ô' lu 跂路；*come this* —, tseo dông' ih-da lu' 走這°一埭路；*stop half* — *and lose all*, pun'-r-feh-kyih' 半路°弗結；pun'-du-r-fi' 半途而廢；—

*of acting*, i'-tsi 意致°；*pretty* — (of a child), i'-tsi bao'-k'en 意致°好看；*method*, fah'-ts 法子；fông-fah' 方法；*do it in this* —, ka'-siang-mao tso' 如°此°樣°式°做；ka tso'-fah 如°此°做法

WAYLAY, *to* tön-lu' 斷路；*will* — *us*, we tön-ah-lah'-go-lu' 會斷我等°个°路：*one who waylays to rob*, tön' lu gyiang-dao' 斷路強盜

WAYS, *all sorts of* —, ts'in-fông' pah-kyi' 千方百°計

WAYWARD, gyüih-gyiang' 個强mæn-bi' 蠻疲

WE, ah-lah' 我等°；*you and both*, pe'-ts' 彼此

WEAK, nyün'-ziah 軟弱；no-ziah' 懦弱；ɔ-ky'i'-lih 無°氣力；pih-bi' 罷癏；*too* — *to bear*, or *do*, ts'ang'-feh-dong 撐弗動；— *tea*, dæn'-dzô 淡茶

WEAKEN, *will* — *the body*, ti'-ts iao tang'-loh 身°體°漸弱°；— *the tea a little* (by pouring in water), dzô' ts'ong'-leh dæn-tin' 茶冲得°淡點

WEAKLY *constitution*, ti'-ts tæn-boh' 身°體°單薄；ti'-ts hyiah'-hyiah 身°體°弱°个°；ti'-ts ky'ih'-boh 身°體°怯°薄

WEALTH, dzæ-veh' 財物；kying-nying' dzæ-veh' 金銀財物；*to gain* —, fah-dzæ' 發財；*God of* —, Dzæ-jing bu'-sah 財神菩薩

WEALTHY, *a* — *person*, fu'-wu

富戶; fu'-ong 富翁; dzæ-cü'
財°士; ing-wu' 殷戶; yiu'-lao.

WEAN, to tsah-na' 摘嬭°; *must*
—(it), yüong tsah-na' 要°摘嬭°

WEAPONS *of war*, kyüing-ky'i'
軍器; —*of self-defence*, bông-
siu' kô'-sang 防手傢°伙°

WEAR, to — *clothes*, c'ün i-zông'
穿衣裳; — *shoes*, c'ün 'a' 穿
鞋°; —*a hat*, ta mao-ts' 戴°帽
子; —*a collar*, kyi ling' 戴°領;
— *mourning*, ta hao' 戴°孝°;
c'ün su'穿素;—*away*, yi; yiang;
yiang-yi' 希°散°; — *out*, c'ün-
wu' 穿腐°; c'ün-diao' 穿壞°;
— *to tatters*, c'ün-p'o'穿°破; —
*well*, kying-c'ün' 經穿; ziu-c'ün'
耐°穿

WEARY, dziah-lih' 着力; vah'-
de 乏了°; ky'ih'-lih 怯力;
*exceedingly* —, vah-lih'-de 乏力
了; t'eh-lih'-de 脱力了°; —
*and sleepy*, bi-gyün' 疲倦; su-
nyün'-ky'i-de 酥軟了°

WEASEL, wông-ts'-lông' 黃鼠
狼; wông-lông' 黃狼 (ih-tsah)

WEATHER, t'in 天; t'in-kô' 天
時°; t'in-ky'i' 天氣; *dry* —,
'en'-t'in 旱天; *clear* —, t'in
zing' 天晴°; *rainy* —, loh-yü'
t'in' 落雨天; *mild* —, t'in-kô'
'o·nön' 天時°和暖

WEATHER-COCK, ding-fong'-piao'
定風標; — (*a flag*), ding-fong-
gyi' 定風旗; fong-sing'-gyi' 風
信旗

WEAVE, *to* tsih 織; — *silks*, tsih
dzin-ling' 織綢綾

WEAVER, tsih'-kyi s-vu' 織機
司務; — *of cotton cloth*, iao-kyi'
s-vu' 布機司務: *silk-weaver's
shop*, tsih'-kyi fông' 織機坊

WEB *of cotton cloth*, ih-kyi pu' 一
機布; *spider's* —, kyih'cü-mông',
or cü'-cü-mông' 蜘蛛°網°;
kyih'-cü lön'-mông蜘蛛°亂綱°

WEB-FOOTED, kyiah' yiu pæn' go
脚有版个°; *the duck is* —,
æn' yiu kyiah'-pæn 鴨°有脚版

WEDDING, *to celebrate a* —, hao'-
nyih 好日°; kyih-hweng' 結婚;
dzing-ts'ing'成親; *to partake of
a* —*feast*, ky'üoh hao'-nyih-tsiu
吃°好日°酒; —*day*, hao'-nyih
好日°; *golden* —, kying-hweng'
金婚; — *sedan*, hwô-gyiao' 花
轎; ts'æ'-gyiao 彩轎 (ih-ting)

WEDNESDAY, li-pa sæn' 禮拜°
三; (according to the Roman
Catholics), tsin-li s' 瞻禮四

WEEDS, yia'-ts'ao 野草; — *in
paddy* or *wheat*, bô-ts'ao' 稗°草°;
*to pull up* —, bah yia'-ts'ao 拔
野°草

WEEK, ih li'-pa 一禮拜°;(according to the Roman Catholics), ih-
cü' nyih 一主日°; ih-tsin li'
一瞻禮

WEEKLY, me li'-pa 每禮拜°;
me li'-pa yiu' 每禮拜°有; ts'ih'-
nyih ih-we' 七日°一回

WEEP, *to shed tears*, c'ih ngæn'-li

出 眼° 淚; liu ngæn'-li 流眼°
淚; *to cry,* or *lament,* k'oh 哭°
— *bitterly,* k'oh'-leh sông-sing'
哭 得° 傷心

WEIGH, *to* ts'ing 稱; ts'ing kying-
djong' 稱輕重; — *pounds and
ounces,* ts'ing kying-liang 稱觔
兩; — *and see,* ts'ing-ts'ing'-
k'en 稱稱看; *it weighs ten catties,* ts'ing'-ko' jih kying' djong'
稱過十觔重; — *accurately,*
ts'ing cing'-tsoh 稱準足; —
*a matter* (by measuring), liang-
doh' 量度

WEIGHER, ts'ing'-siu 秤手

WEIGHT, djong 重; *what is the
—?* yiu to-siao' djong' 有多少
重; *oranges sell by —,* kyüih-'
ts leng veng-liang' ma 橘子論
分兩賣°; *compare the —,* kao
ky'ing-djong' 較輕重; *ask the
—,* meng' kying-liang' 問°觔兩

WEIGHTS for steelyards, ts'ing'-
djü 秤錘°; — for scales, fah'-mó
法°碼

WEIGHTY, djong'-da 重大; —
*matter,* djong'-da z-ken' 重大
事幹

WELCOME *letter,* sing' læ-leh 'eh-
i' 信來得合意; *you are —,*
(*i. e.* I give it cheerfully), ngô
nyün-i' peh' ng 我願意給°
你; *you are — here,* (*i. e.* we like
to have you here), ah'-lah yüoh-i'
ng læ-tong' 我°等°欲意你°
在°此°

WELD, *to* tang'-long 打攏

WELL, tsing 井 (ih-k'eo)

WELL, *in health,* sông'-kw'a 爽
快°; bing-en' 平安; z-dzæ' 自在;
*are you —?* ng hao' 你好? ng
hao yia' 你°好呀; (the last sometimes has a tinge of disrespect);
(*I*) *am —,* hao'-go 好个°; hao'
hao' 好好; t'oh-foh' 托福;
t'oh-ng-foh' 托你°福; *tolerably —,* wa hao' 還°好; p'o' hao
頗好; yiu-tin' hao 有°點好;
*you look —,* ng min-seh' tao hao'
你°面色倒好; hao' ky'i'-seh
好氣色; *colors — (i.e.* accurately) *matched,* ngæn-seh' p'e'-leh
t'o-tông 顏色配得° 妥當;
— *done,* tso-leh hao' 做得°好;
— *written,* sia-leh hao' 寫得°
好; — *dressed,* i-zông' c'ün-leh
hao'-go 衣裳°穿得° 好个°;
c'ün'-leh 'ao-yiah'-go 穿得°豪
俠个°; sing pe'-zông t'i'-min-go
身上體面个°; — *bred,* (taught
well at home), kyüô-kyiao' hao'
家教好; kô-kwe' hao' 家°規
好; *the — day in ague,* k'ong'-
nyih 空日°

WEST, si 西; *in the —,* læ si-pin'
在°西邊; læ si-pun'-pin 在°
西半邊; *toward the —,* dziao
si' 朝西; hyiang si' 向西

WET, sih 濕; — *with rain,* ling-
sih' 淋濕; — *through,* sih-t'eo'
濕透; *ditto* (by being in water),
tsing'-sih 浸濕

WET-NURSE, ah-bu′ 阿婷; na′ ah-bu′ 嬭 阿 婷

WHARF, jün mô′-deo 船 碼 頭 (ih-go)

WHAT, soh′-go 甚° 麽; soh′-si 爲° 甚°; *for — did you come?* ng′ we-leh soh′-go z-ken′ læ′ 你° 爲了°甚°事幹來? (polite), ng′ yiu soh′-go kwe z′ 你°有甚° 麽°貴事; — *do you want?* ng′ iao soh′-si? 你°要甚°麽; — *business?* soh′ ken? 何°事°? — *farther?* wa-yiu soh′-si 還° 有 甚°麽°? — *is your name?* ng′ kyiao soh′-go ming′-z 你° 叫 甚°麽°名字? — *is your family* — *?* sing soh′ 姓甚°麽°? (more polite), kwe sing′ 貴姓? — *is it to you?* yü ng′ ′o-ken′ 與 你° 何干! teng ng′ yiu soh′-go siang-ken′ 與你°有甚°麽°相干?

WHATEVER, feh-leng′ soh′-go 弗 論 甚°麽; peh′-kyü soh′-go 不拘甚°麽°; — *ever you please,* ze-bin′ ng iao soh′-go 隨便你° 要甚°麽°; — *he does is well done,* gyi′ feh leng′ tso soh′-go tn hao′ 其 弗 論 做 甚°麽°都 好

WHEAT, mah 麥; — *cakes,* mah ping′ 麥餅; — *flour,* min-feng′ 麵 粉; — *straw,* mah ken′ 麥 稈

WHEEDLE, *to* nyün′-pa-pu 軟 擺 佈

WHEEL, leng-bun′ 輪 盤 (ih-go)

WHEEL-BARROW, siao′-ts′ô 小

車; *one wheeled carriage,* doh-leng′-ts′ô 獨 輪 車° (ih-go)

WHEN, kyi′-z 幾 時? soh′-go z-′eo′ 甚° 麽° 時 候? — *I was sick,* ngô bing′-go z-′eo′ 我 病 个° 時 候; — *you were here,* ng læ-tong′ z-′eo′ 你°在°此°時 候

WHENCE, dzong ′ah-li′ 從 那° 裏? dzong ′o-c′ü′ 從 何 處? — *do you come?* ng dzong ′o′-r læ′ 你° 從 何 而 來?

WHENEVER, feh-leng kyi′-z 弗 論 幾 時; ze-bin′ kyi′-z 隨 便 幾 時; peh′-kyü kyi′-z 不 拘 幾 時

WHERE? ah-li′ or ′ah-li′ 那°裡°? ′o-c′ü′ 何 處? soh′-go di′-fông 甚° 麽°地 方? ′o-fông′ 何 方? soh′-go u-sen 甚° 麽° 所° 在°? — *is* (it)? læ ah-li, or læ ′o-c′ü′ 在°何 處? — *are you going?* ng′ tao ah-li′ ky′î′ 你°到 那° 裡去°? *place* — *I live,* ngô ɛ̂ô deng′-go di′-fông 我 所 庄 个° 地 方

WHEREAS, *since,* kyi′-jün 旣 然; kyi′-kying 旣 經

WHEREVER, feh-leng′ ah-li′ 弗 論 那°裏; feh-leng′ ′o-c′ü′ 弗 論 何 處, &c.

WHEREFORE? *for what reason?* we ′o yün-kwu′ 爲 何 緣 故? we-leh soh′-go yün-kwu′ 爲了°甚° 麽° 緣 故? ′o kwu′ 何 故? *why?* dza-we′ 何° 爲? we dza′ yün-kwu′ 爲 甚° 緣 故? *for what business?* we-leh soh′ ken?

WHETHER, *I do not know* — (*I*) *shall go,* feh'-tsiao ky'i'-feh-ky'i 不°知°去° 弗 去°; *do you know* — *he has come or not?* ng hyiao'-teh gyi læ'-leh 峃 -teh 你°曉得 其 來 了° 嗎? — *cold or hot,* feh-leng' lang feh-leng' nyib' 弗 論 冷° 弗 論 熱°

WHET-STONE, mo-tao'-zah 磨刀 石° (ih-kw'e)

WHICH *one?* 'ah-li ih'-go 那°裡 一 个°? — *boat?* 'ah-li ih-tsah jün' 那°裡一隻船? *do not know* — *road is right,* feh'-tsiao 'ah-li' ih-da lu z' 不°知°那°裏一墂路 是; — (the relative), sô 所; *that* — *I said,* ngô sô wô 我 所 話

WHIFF *of smoke* (from the mouth), ih-k'eo in' 一 口 烟

WHILE, *a little* —, ih-zông kong-fu' 一 息° 工夫; hao'-to kong'-fu' 好 多 工 夫; *a long* —, dziang-kyiu' 長 久; pun'-pun-jih-nyih'; yiu'-ho z-tsih' 許°多° 時 候; *such a long* —, ih-veh' ts'ih-shü' 這°許°多°工°夫; *wei a* —, teng ih'-zông 等 一 息°; *not worth* — *to go,* feh dzih'-teh ky'i' 弗 值 得 去°; feh væn'-djoh ky'i' 弗 犯 着° 去°; feh kch'-sön ky'i' 弗 合 算 去°; keh'-feh-djoh-ky'i' 合 弗 着°去°; *not worth* — *to do,* feh-zông -sön tso' 弗 上 算 做

WHILE, *during the time that,* pin, or i'-pin, used twice, thus; —*talk-ing he was crying,* pin kông' pin k'oh' 隨°講°隨° 哭; — *rowing his boat, he eats his rice,* i'-pin wô' jün', i'-pin ky'üoh-væn' 隨°划船 隨° 吃° 飯; — *I was eating,* ngô ky'üoh-væn' z-'eo' 我吃°飯時候

WHIMS, *a person full of* —, ang' nying 獨°幅°个°人°

WHIP, *to* tang 打; — *with a bamboo,* tang pæn'-ts 打 板 子; — *with a ferule,* tang kao'-fông 打 戒°方; — *on the palm,* tang siu'-ti-sing 打手心

WHIP, *lash,* pin'-ts 鞭 子 (ih-keng); *thin bamboo* —, pæn'-ts 板 子 (ih-keng)

WHIRL, *to* kwah'-lah-lah cün' 刮 轆° 轆° 轉

WHIRLPOOL, bun-shü' 盤 水°; jün-shü' 旋 水° (ih-yüing)

WHIRLWIND, yiang-koh'-fong 羊 角° 風; djün-fong' 旋 風

WHISKERS, *and beard,* wu-cü'黏嘴

WHISKEY, *Chinese* siao-tsiu' 燒酒

WHISPER, *to* ts'ih'-ts'ih-c'ih-c'ih' kông' 嗻嗻喳喳 講°; — *in the ear,* kyiao' deo tsih' r 交頭 接耳; ngao ng'-tô kông 齩°耳°朵 講°

WHISTLE, *toy* kyiao-kyü 燻°篦°; tiao-kyü' (ih-gu)

WHISTLE, *to* — (or blow) *a tune,* c'ü' ing-diao' 吹音調; — *loud* (as steam), c'ü-hyiang' 吹 響

WHITE, bah 白°; *to bleach* —, p'iao'-bah 漂 白°

WHITE, the — of the eye, ngæn'-bah 眼°白°;— of the egg, dæn-bah' 蛋白°

WHITE-WASH, shih'-bah 刷白°; zông-hwe'上灰: feng'-shih 粉刷

WHO? jü 誰°? — is there? jü' læ-kæn' 誰°在°彼°°? soh'-go nying læ-kæn' 甚°麼°人°在°彼°? who says so? jü'-wô 誰°話? (often equivalent to you don't say so!); — (the relative), sô 所; the one — just came, fông-dzæ' sô læ'-go nying 方纔所來个人°

WHOEVER, feh-leng' jü 弗論誰°; ze-bin' soh'-go nying 隨便甚°麼°人°; peh' kyü soh'-go nying 不拘甚°麼°人°

WHOLE, djün 全; djün-fu' 全副; tsing 正; 'eh 合; 'o 和; ih-gong' 一共; mun 滿; weng 渾; the whole night, djün-yia' 全夜°; tsing-yia' 正夜°; — family, 'eh-kô' 合家°; 'o-kô' 和家°; djün-kô' 全°家°; what is the — amount? ih-gong' to-siao' 一共多少? ih'-kæ to-siao' 一概多少? — body, mun'-sing 滿身; weng-sing' 渾身; — life, ih-sang' ih-si' 一生°一世°; ih-seng' 一生; the — earth, p'n' t'in-'ô 普天下°; 'en'-t'in-'ô 合天下°; shall the chicken be cut in pieces, or boiled — ? kyi' wa-z feng-k'æ'ts', tsing'-tsah-ts' 鷄還°是分開羹呢°正隻羹?* — piece (of meat

&c.), tsing-kw'e' 正塊: — potato, tsing-dön' fæn-jü'; the — lot (of goods), ih-kwu'-nao-r' 一總°; nen-ken'; buy the — lot, teng'-cü ma' 薹買

* Observe, that in the latter part of this sentence, the classifier is used instead of the noun.

WHOLESALE, to buy at — , do-tông' ma' 大°批°頭°買; tsing-p'iao' ma' 正票買'; teng-tông' ma 薹當買°

WIG, (such as is used in Chinese theatres), mông'-kying 網巾; to wear a —, or false hair, s kô'-deo 梳°假°頭

WILD, yia 野°; — beasts, yia'-siu 野°獸; — flowers, yia'-hwô 野花°; yia when applied to persons may signify rude, or savage.

WILDERNESS, kw'ông'-iæ di'-fông 曠野°地方

WILES, kwe-kyi' 詭計; many —, kwe-kyi' to'-tön 詭計多端

WILL, cü'-i 主意; — (of God, or of the Emperor), ts'-i 旨意; sing'-ts 聖旨; strong —, cü'-i do' 主意大°; good — (right intention), hao'-i 好意; me'-i 美意; ill —, tæ'-i 歹意: oh'-i 惡意: to harbor ill —, dzeng tæ'-i 存歹意; — or testament, yi-coh', or yi-tsoh 遺囑; to make a —, lih' yi-coh' 立遺囑

WILL, to determine, ding ih-go cü'-i 定一个主意; ding hao' 定好; — (sometimes the

sigu of the future), we 會; *I will
go*, ngô'we ky'i' 我會°去°; *I will
not go*, ngô kyüih'-i-feh-ky'i' 我
決意弗去°; *it — do*, hao'-s-
teh 好使得; k'o'-yi 可以

WILL-WITH-A-WISP, kyü teng-
long' 鬼°燈籠; ling-ho' 燐火

WILLFUL, *very* 'eo zi'-go 擅自°
个°; sang' 'eo-zi-'go 生°來°
擅°自个°

WILLING, k'eng 肯; ken-sing'
甘心; dzing-nyün' 情願; *are
you — or not?* ng' k'eng' feh
k'eng' 你肯弗肯; *— to work*,
tso sang-weh' ken-sing'-go 做
生°活甘心个°

WILLINGLY, dzing-nyün' 情願

WILLOW, yiang-liu' 楊柳; *weep-
ing —*, tao'-gwæn yiang-liu' 倒
撌楊柳 (ih-cü)

WILT, *to* pih 瞞; pih'-long-ky'i
瞞攏去°; *— in the sun*, sa'-
pih 曬°瞞

WILY, kæn-wah' 奸°滑

WIN, *to — a victory*, teh-sing' 得
勝; *the first to —*, sin sing' 先
勝; *— (in chess)*, tsiah'-ying
着贏

WINCE, *to* geo-soh' 勾縮

WIND, fong 風; *favorable —*,
jing fong' 順風; *contrary —*,
teo' fong 對風; *head —*, ting'
deo fong' 頂頭風; *strong —*,
mang' fong 猛風; *— has sub-
sided*, fong sih'-de 風息了°

WIND, *to* nyiao 繞; *ing*; dziu

紬; *— up*, nyiao-nyiao-tsing 繞°
上°; *to — off*, dziu-c'ih 紬出;
*— thread*, yüih siu' 繹°線, &c.;
*— a watch*, k'æ piao' 開表

WHOLESOME, hao yiang sing-t'i'
go 好養°身體个°

WHOSE, jü'-go? 誰°个°; soh'-go
nying'-go? 甚麼°人°个°

WHOSOEVER, See WHOEVER.

WHY, dza-we'? 何°爲°; *— so?*
dza-we' z-ka'? 何°爲°如°此°?
*— so badly off?* 'o-ts' ü-ts'' 何
至於此?

WICK, teng-sing' 燈芯; *pith —*,
teng-sing' ts'ao 燈芯草

WICKED, oh 惡; *— man*, oh'
nying 惡人°; *forsake the —*,
yün siao'-jing 遠小人

WIDE, kw'eh 闊

WIDEN, *to* tso k'æ-kw'eh' 做開
闊; *make a little wider*, long
kw'eh'-tin 弄闊些

WIDER, keng'-kô kw'eh' 更加°
闊; *to grow —*, kw'eh'-ky'i-læ
闊起來

WIDOW, sông-vn 媚婦; kwô kyü'
寡居; kwô'-vn 寡婦; kwu'-
sông ma'-ma 孤孀; kwu'-sông
lao'-nyüing; *— who remains pure*,
tsih'-vn 節婦

WIDOWED, *in a — state* kwô'-kyü-
tong 現°在°寡居

WIDOWER, kwæn'-fu 鰥夫; *living
as a —*, kwæn'-kyü-tong 現°在°
鰥居; dön-yin'-liao-go 斷絲了

WIFE, ts'i-ts' 妻子; nyü'-nying

女人°ᵃ; lao'-nyüing 婦'; (contemptuous), lao'-bo 老婆; *the
principal* —, tsing'-shih 正室;
kyih'-fah 結髮; do lao'-nyüing
*the inferior* —, tseh'-shih 側
室; p'in-vông' 偏房; siao lao-
nyüing' 姜; *how is your* —?
(to a gentleman), fu-nying' hao'
feh? 夫人°好否°; he replies,
*my* —, dzin-ne' 賤內 &c.; *your*
— (one gentleman to another),
tseng sao' 尊嫂; (to a stranger
or superior), tseng-fu' nying 尊
夫人°; (to a servant &c.), ng'-
go oh'-li nying 你°个°家°裏
人°; ng-go ne'-li'-hyiang你°个°
內裡向; (he replies), *my* —,
ah-lah ne-li 我°个°內裡; *have
you a* —? (to a servant), ng' yiu
dzing-kô' feh 你°有成家°否°?
ng yiu kô-siao' 由'-teh 你°有
家°小沒°有°? *newly married*
—, sing-vu' 新婦; *second* —
dzoh-yin' 續絃; dzoh-c'ü' 續
娶; *she is the second* — (the first
having died), gyi z dzoh'-go 其
是續娶°个°; gyi z in'-vông.
* Nyü-nying though used in the generic sense of woman, means properly
a wife. An unmarried lady of fifty is
not a nyü-nying, as we should suppose,
because she is not a wife.

WIFE'S *older brother*, do ah'-gyiu
大°阿舅; — *younger brother*,
siao' ah'-gyiu 小阿舅; — *elder
sister*, yi-mô' 姨媽; — *younger
sister*, siao'-yi 小姨; — *sister's*

*husband*, lin-kying' 連襟; yi-
dziang' 姨丈; *wife of an elder
brother*, hyüong-sao' 兄嫂; *do of
younger brother*, di-sing'-vu 弟媳°
婦; — *father*, dziang'-nying 丈°
人°; ngoh-vu' 岳父; — *mother*,
dziang'-vu 丈°父; ngoh-meo'
岳母

WINDING(as a road), wæn-ky'üoh'
go 彎曲个°; wæn-nyiao'-go 彎
繞°个°; *very* —, ts'ih'-wæn-
pah'-ky'üoh' 七彎八曲

WINDLASS, kao'-ts'ô 絞°車°; —
(for drawing boats over an inclined plane), ts'ô-dong' 車°筒
*to raise by a* —, ts'ô-zông'-ky'i
車上去°

WINDOW, ts'ông 牕; *glass* —,
po-li' ts'ông 玻璃牕; *paper* —,
ts ts'ông 紙牕; *small — for
ventilating*, c'ih-ky'i'-dong 出氣
洞; *oyster shell* —, ming-ngô',
ts'ông 明瓦°牕; *ditto in the
roof*, t'in-tsing'-pæn 天井板

WINDPIPE, ky'i'-kwun 氣管; hô'-
kwun 呼°吸°管

WINE, tsiu 酒

WINE-BIBBER, tsiu-weh-lu 酒崩°
蘆

WINE-CUP, tsiu-pe' 酒杯

WINE-JAR, tsiu-dzing' 酒壜°; *a
jar of wine*, (30 catties), ih-dzing
tsiu 一埕酒

WINE-SHOP, tsiu-tin 酒店(ih-bæn)

WING, yih-sao' or yiah-sao' 翅°
膀°, 翼稍 (ih-tsah)

WINK, to — the eyes, sah ngæn'-tsing 瞓° 眼° 睛; ngæn'-tsing sah'-sah 眼° 睛 瞓° 瞓°

WINK, as quick as a —, ngæn'-tsing ih-sah' 眼° 睛 一 瞓°; give him a —, tiu ngæn-seh' peh gyi 與° 伊° 丟 眼° 瞓°

WINK, to — at, or appear not to see, ngæn-k'æ ngæn-pi' 眼° 開 眼° 閉; tsông'-leh feh k'en'-kyin 裝 得° 弗 看 見; to appear to be unconscious of, tsông'-leh feh-dzæ'-i 裝 得° 弗 在 意

WINNOW, to — (by throwing up before the wind), po 播; po-yiang' 播 揚; po-long 播 弄; — grain, yiang koh 揚 穀

WINNOWING machine, fong-siang' 風 箱 (ih-bu)

WINTER, Tong-t'in' 冬 天; — season, Tong-kyi' 冬 季; to pass the —, ko Tong' 過 冬

WIPE, to k'a tsæ°; — dry, k'a sao' 揩° 燥; — clean, k'a ken-zing' 揩° 乾 淨; — away tears, k'a ngæn'-li 揩° 眼° 淚

WIRE, iron t'ih'-s 鐵 絲; brass —, dong s' 銅 絲

WISDOM, ts'ong-ming' 聰 明

WISE, ts'ong-ming' 聰 明; very —, ts'ong-ming cü-we' 聰 明 智 慧; naturally — (bright), t'in-ts'ong' t'in-ming' 天 聰 天 明

WISH, to want, iao 要; do you — to go, ng' iao ky'i' feh 你° 要 去° 否'! I — very much, pô'-feh

neng'-keo 巴 弗 能 殼; pô'-feh-teh' 巴 弗 得'; I — you a pleasant (i.e. peaceful) journey, dæn'-nyün ng'ih-lu' bing-en' 但 願 你° 一 路 平 安; —you well, pô'-feh-neng'-keo ng hao' 巴 弗 能 殼 你° 好

WISH, sing-siang' 心 想; sing-nyün 心 願; my — is to go in the Spring, ngô sing-siang' C'ing-t'in'-li ky'i 我 心 想 到° 春 季 裏 去°; exactly according to my —, jü-sing' ziang-i' 如 心 合° 意; obtained his—, gyi'-go sing-nyün' teh'-djoh-de 其 个° 心 願 得 若° 了°

WISTERIA, ts'-deng 紫 籐

WIT. See WITTY.

WITCH, sorceress, yüong zia-fah'-go nyü'-nying 用 邪° 法 个° 女 人°

WITCH-CRAFT, fah'-jih 法 術; zia-fah' 邪° 法

WITH, teng 與°; lin 連; 'o 和; go — me, teng ngô' dô-kô' ky'i 與° 我 一° 同 去°; eat — milk, lin na' ky'üoh' 連 嬭 吃°; na 'o'-leh ky'üoh' 嬭 和 了° 吃°; — a spoon, yüong diao-kang' 用 調 羹°; — a pen, yüong pih' 用 筆; to mix —, 'o-long' 和 攏

WITHDRAW, to t'e 退; —from, or out of, t'e'-c'ih 退 出; t'eng'-c'ih 褪 出; soh'-c'ih 縮 出; — (walking backward), tao'-t'e 倒 退; tao'-t'eng-bu 倒 退 步; — to another place, t'e'-bi 退 避

WITHER, to — (as if dying), kw'u

枯；— *and dry*, ken-kw'u'乾枯；
— *up*, kw'u-long'-ky'i 枯攏去°

WITHERED, *dried up*, ken'-de 乾
了°；kw'u'-de 枯了°；*flowers are*
— *and fallen*, hwô zia'-de 花謝°
了°；— *hand*, siu'-hyüih kw'u'-
de 手血枯了°

WITHHOLD, *to restrain from*, ts'-
djü 止住；lah-djü' 攔°住；*to*
*retain* —, siu-tsing' 收進

WITHIN, li-hyiang' 裡向°li'-deo
裏面°；ne 內；— *three days*,
sæn nyih' li-hyiang'三日°裡向；
sæn nyih' ts ne' 三日°之內

WITHOUT, *outside*, nga-deo' 外°
面°；nga-hyiang 外°向；—*wood*
*and rice*, ᴍ-za' ᴍ-mi'無°柴無°
米；— *a cash*, feng-veng' ᴍ'-
teh 分文沒°有°；ih'-go dong-
din' tu ᴍ'-neh；一個銅錢°都
沒°有°；*can't do* — *it*, ky'üih'-
gyi-feh-læ' 缺其弗來；siao'-
feh-teh 少弗得；hyih'-feh-læ'
歇弗來；*can do* — *it*, hao-
hyih'-go 好歇个°；hao-sang'-
go 好省个°；— *reason*, ᴍ-kao'
yün-kwn' 沒°有°緣故；vu-
yün' vu-kwu' 無緣無故；—
*day* (sine die), yiao-yiao' vu gyi
遙遙無期；*better* — *such a son*,
keh'-cü-ka ng-ts' feh-jü' ᴍ'-teh
如°此°兒°子倒°弗如沒°有°

WITHSTAND, *to* gyü-djih' 拒°
絕；— (an enemy), ti'-dih 抵敵；
dih-djü' 敵住

WITNESS, *to testify*, tso te'-tsing

做對証；*to testify to what one*
*has seen*, kyin'-tsing 見証

WITNESS, *eye* ts'ing-ngæn'-moh-
tu' 親眼°目睹

WITTY *words*, ky'iao'-tsong ka
shih-wô'；ky'iao'-wô 巧話；*quaint*
*words*, kwn'-li-kwu-tong'shih-wô'
言°有°古°風°；kwn'-tong lin'-
ky'i shih-wô' 古董臉氣說話

WITS, *frightened out of one's* —,
weh-ling' hah'-c'ih-de 魂°靈嚇
出了°

WOE, 'o 禍；'o'-se 禍祟

WOLF, za-lông' 豺°狼 (ih-tsah)

WOMAN, (married), nyü'-nying
女人°；lao-nyüing 婦°女；nyü
liu-ts-pe' 女流之輩；*ought*
*not to treat a* — *so*, nyü'-liu-ts-pe'
feh ing -kæ ka' dæ gyi' 女流之
輩弗應如°此°待伊；*old*
—, lao'-bo-bo 老婆婆；bo'-
bo 婆婆；lao-t'a-bun' 老太°婆°
(disrespectful)；*woman's work*,
nyü'-kong 女工；vu'-nyü sô'-
we' 婦女所會 See WIFE.

WOMANISH, ziang nyü'-nying ka'
像女人°一°樣°；nyü'-siang
女相

WOMB, t'æ 胎

WOMEN, (as a class), nyü'-nyiug-
lah' 女人°等

WONDER, *to be surprised*, hyi-gyi'
希奇；gyi-kwa' 奇怪°；*doubt*,
feh'-tsiao；liao feh tao 料°弗°
到°；*I* — *who is there*, feh'-tsiao
jü' læ'-kæn料°弗°到°誰°在°彼°

WONDERFUL, hyi-gyi′ 希奇;
gyi-kwa′ 奇怪; *very* —, hyi-
gyi′-leh-kying′ 甚° 希奇; hyi-
gyi′-sah-nying′ 希奇煞人°; hyi-
gyi′-kwu-kwa 希奇古怪°

WOOD, moh-deo′ 木頭; jü 樹;
(a piece of, ih-kwe); *hard* —,
ngang-moh′ 硬木; ngang-jü′ 硬
樹; *mixed* —, zeh-jü′ 雜° 樹;
(a log of, ih-dön); — *for burning*, za-bæn 柴° 爿; *a stick of*
—, ih-kw'e′ za-bæn′ 一塊柴°
爿; *a bundle of* —, ih-ky'iu za′
一籸柴°; *to split* —, p'ih za′
劈柴°; *to saw* —, ka za′鋸°柴°
WOODEN, moh-deo′ tso′-go 木頭
做 个°; jü′ tso′-go 樹做个°

WOOD-SHOP (for timber), jü-'ông′
樹行°; *small ditto*, zah-moh'′ông
雜°木行°; *fuel-shop*, za-'ông
柴° 行°; za-tin′ 柴°店 (ih-bæn)
WOOF, we 緯; yü-sô 緯°紗°
WOOL, yiang-mao′ 羊毛
WOOLEN, *made of wool*, yiang-
mao′ tso-go 羊毛做个°; —
*yarn*, nyüong sin′ 絨線
WORD, shih-wô′ 說話; — (often
in a bad sense), wô-deo′ 話頭
(ih-kyü); *to break one's* —, shih-
sing′ 失信; *keeps* (his) —,shih-wô′
hao tsoh-cing′ 說 話 好作凖;
shih-wô′ hao sön-su′ 說話好算
數; *left* — *there*, ih-kyü′shih-wô′
lin-c'ih′-kæn 一句說話關°照
出 了°; shih-wô′ t'oh′-c'ih-kæn
說°話′託出了°; *write a few*

*words*, sia liang′kyü shih-wô′ 寫°
兩句說話; *ditto* (or characters),
sia ko′-pô-z′ 寫°個巴字; *words
few, and easily understood*, shih-
wô′ ling-ts'ing 說話靈清
WORK, sang-weh′ 生° 活; kong
工; *hard* —, lao-kw'u′sang-weh′
勞苦生°活; kw'u′-kong 苦
工; djong-deo′ sang-weh′ 鄭重
生°活; *a day's* —, ih kong′ 一
工; *to stop* —, hyih kong′ 歇
工; *no* — *to do*, m-kao′sang-weh′
hao tso° 無° 甚°生°活好做;
*fond of eating, and lazy at* —,
t'en ky'üoh′, kæn tso° 貪吃°懶
做; *well executed* —, hao′ kong-
fu′好工夫; *needle* —, tsing-ts′
sang weh′ 針箬生° 活°; *em-
broidery* —, ts'æ′-tsông sang-
weh′ 彩裝生活
WORK, *to* tso sang-weh′做生°活;
tso kong′ 做工; yüong kong′
用工; *what* — *are you doing*,
(to a servant or laborer), ng tso
soh′-go sang-weh′? 你° 做甚°
麼° 生° 活; *ditto* (to a gentleman), ng yüong soh′-go kong′?
你°用甚° 麼功; *I* — *for a
living*, ngô yüong-kong′ du-nyih′
我儁工度日°; — *early and late*,
ky'i′-tsao loh-æn′ 起早落夜°; —
*by the day*, leng-kong′ tso 論工
做; leng-nyih′tso論日°做; *to —
with the hand* (as clay), nyiah揑;
— *between the palms*, tso做; — *a
miracle*, 'ang jing-tsih′ 行°神跡

WORK-BASKET, tsia-k'ong-kæn' 纔° 筐° 籃

WORKING *well* (as a machine), jing-dzeh' 光° 潤; *fermenting* (as honey *&c.*), la-tih fæn' 正在° 泛

WORKMAN, s-vu' 司務; tso siu-nyi-go 做手藝个°

WORKMANSHIP, siu'-dön 手段; *exquisite —*, siu'-dön tsing-cü' 手段精緻

WORLD, shü'-kæn-zông' 世界° 上; *the whole —*, p'u-t'in-'ô 普天下°; t'ong'-t'in-'ô 統天下°; 'en'-t'in-'ô 合° 天下°; *this —*, kying-si' 今世'; *while in this —*, we-nying' dzæ-shü' 爲人° 在世; *before one came into the —*, zin-si' 前° 世°; *the — hereafter*, 'ô'-si 下° 世°; *the invisible* (dark) *—*, ing-kæn' 陰間°; *has seen much of the —*, shü'-min tu kyin'-ko 世面都見過; *ditto* (still stronger), kyin'-kwông-sih-da' 見廣識大

WORLDLY *affairs*, shü'-z 世事; *— customs*, shü'-dzoh, or shü-djoh 世俗; *— pleasures*, shü'-zông-go kw'a'-loh 世上个° 快樂

WORM, djong 蟲; *earth —*, c'oh'-zin, tsoh'-zin, or c'ih'-zin 曲° 蟮 (ih-keng)

WORRIED, sing ông' 心煩°; sing-væn-tsao' 心煩嘈; væn-beh'-tsi-tsao' 煩白嘈嘈; ông-beh'-tsi-tsao' ; *can't help being —*, p'i'-leh-k'æ 譬弗開; *—, and anxious*, to-sing' to-z 多心多事;

*— to death*, væn-zeh'-sah-de 煩雜° 煞了°; *— and restless*, sing-li' tsiao-tsao' 心裡焦躁; *will not allow one's self to be —*, p'i'-leh-k'æ 譬得° 開

WORRY, *to* væn 煩; *— much, to* væn' 多煩; tsi-tseo' 嘈啁; *— by much talking*, or *by begging*, lo'-so 囉唆; *— by many things*, væn-zeh' 煩雜°

WORSE, yüih-fah wa' 越發孬°; yü'-kô wa 愈加° 孬°; keng'-kô wa 更加° 孬°; *— than before*, pi zin-deo' wa' 比前° 頭° 孬°; pi zin-deo' feh-jü 比前° 頭弗如; *—* (as disease), yü'-kô djong' 愈加° 重; yü-kô' li-'æ' 愈加° 利害; *grows — every day*, ih-nyih' feh jü' ih-nyih' 一日° 弗如一日°; nyih djong' ih-nyih' 日° 重一日°; nyih-nyih djong' 日° 日° 重

WORSHIP, li'-pa 禮拜°; *to perform —*, tso li'-pa 做禮拜°

WORSHIP, *to* pa 拜°; pa li'-pa; *— idols*, pa bu-sah' 拜² 菩薩; *— at the graves*, zông veng' 上墳; *— ancestors*, tsi tsu' 祭祖; *— sacred books* (a Buddhists do), pa kying' 拜° 經

WORST, wa-gyih' 孬° 極; tsæ'-m-tsæ-wa' 再無° 再孬°; wa' feh ko'-yi wa 孬° 而° 又孬°; peh'-k'æn wa' 不堪孬°; *at the —*, wa' tao toh' 孬° 到邊°; wa' tao gyih-deo' 孬° 到極頭

WORTHLESS, feh-dzih' dong-din' 弗 值 銅 錢°; — *thing*, æn-ho 次°貨; — *fellow*, fi'-veh 廢物, *ditto* (used in reviling), ts'æn'-deo.

WORTHY *to receive*, ing-teh'-go 應 得 個°; — *to bear*, kæ-tông'-go 該 當 個°

WOULD *that he might come again*, 'o'-feh gyi tsæ læ' 但°願° 其 再 來; — *rather die*, neng'-s si' 甯° 使 死°; — *not this be better?* feh'-z keh'-go hao'-tin ma 弗 是 這° 个°好點嗎°? — *like very much*, po'-feh-neng'-keo 巴 弗 能 彀

WOUND, *to* —, *injure, or bruise*, sông 傷; sông-'æ' 傷害; *tang'-sông* 打傷; — *with a knife*, tao' kah'-sông 刀 割傷; — *with a bullet*, dæn-ts' tang'-sông 彈子打傷; — *feelings*, sông ky'üoh'傷情°

WOUND, *received a severe* —, ziu djong'-sông de 受 重 傷 了°; *a fatal* —, cü-ming'-go sông 致 命 个° 傷; *the mark of a* —, sông-'eng' 傷 痕

WRANGLE, *to* k'eo'-kyüoh siang'-tseng 口 角 相 爭°

WRAP, *to* pao 包; ko 裹°; — *it in paper*, yüong ts', pao'-ih-pao 用 紙包一包; — *up*, pao-long' 包 攏; ko'-long 裹 攏; pao-ky'i'-læ 包 起 來

WRAPPED *within*, pao-tsing'-tih 包 進 的; *ditto* (as ideas), pao-kweh'-tih 包 括 的

WRAPPING, *coarse* pao-bi' 包皮;

*a large handkerchief used for* — *clothes, &c.*, pao-voh' 包 袱

WORTH, dzih 值; — *money*, dzih' dong-din' 值 銅 錢°; *how much is* (it) — ? dzih to-siao' 值 多 少°? — *the trouble*, dzih-teh'-go 值 得 个°; *is it* — (so much), *or not?* dzih feh dzih' 值 弗 值°; *while*. See WHILE.

WRATH, ô'-wông; nu 怒; *great*—, nu'-ky'i dzih-ts'ong 怒 氣 直 冲; nu'-fah ts'ong-kwun' 怒髮冲冠; nu'-ky'i ts'ong-t'in' 怒氣冲天

WREAK *vengeance, or wrath upon him*, læ gyi'-go sing-zông' nu'-fah ts'ong-kwun' 在° 其 个° 身 上 怒 髮 冲 冠

WRECKED, *a vessel* —, jün tso'-diao-de 船觸°壞°了°; *ditto capsized*, jün tao'-meh-de 船 倒 沒 了°; *split upon rocks*, ngô-tsiao'-de 觸° 礁 了

WRENCH, *to* — *out*, cih'-c'ih 折 出; — *round*, cih'-cün 折 轉; — *open*, cih'-k'æ 折 開

WREST *the meaning*, nyiao ka'-shih 拘° 泥° 解° 說°

WRESTLE, *to* sæ gyün' 賽 拳; pi gyün 比 拳; — (as children), k'ô tih 扳° 跌

WRETCHED, kw'u 苦; — *end*, kyih'-gyüoh wa' 結 局 孬°

WRIGGLE, *to* — (as a serpent), dzin-læ' dzin-ky'i' 纏 來 纏 去°

WRING, *to*—(as clothes), kao 絞; — *dry*, kao siao' 絞 燥;—*the neck*, deo-kying' cih'-cün 頭頸扭°轉

WRINKLE, tseo'-veng 皺紋; veng-lu' 紋路 ; *fold,* or *plait,* kæn 裙

WRINKLE, *to* tseo 皺 ; long-tseo' 弄皺 ; —*by folding badly,* tsih'-tseo 摺皺

WRINKLED (as cloth), tseo'-tseo 皺皺;—(as the face), yiu tseo'-veng 有皺紋 ; tang-kæn'-de 打裙°了

WRIST, siu'-bu-lu-deu' 手蒲蘆頭°

WRITE, *to* sia 寫° ; sia'-loh 寫°落 ; — *one's name,* sia ming-z' 寫°名字 ; loh ming-z' 錄名字 ; *ditto* (as in a register, &c.), zông ming-z' 上名字 ; — *char-acters,* sia z' 寫°字 ; — *a letter,* sia sing 寫°信

WRITER, sia-z'-go 寫字个° ; (on a vessel), t'iah'-sia-go 帖°寫°

WRITHING *in* *pain,* tông'-leh-ngao' tsin-feh-ko' 痛得°蒸煎弗過

WRITING, *penmanship,* shü-fah' 書法; pih'-fah 筆法; *hand—,* pih'-tsih 筆跡; (Chinese) —*materials,* pih'-moh-ts-nyin' 筆墨紙硯; veng-vông-s'-pao 文房四寶

WRONG, ts'o 錯 ; ngo 訛 ; *to be* —, yiu ts'o' 有錯 ; yiu feh-z' 有弗是 ; *to do* —, tso' ts'o 做錯 ; long ts'o' 弄錯 ; *under-stand* (or hear) —, t'ing' ts'o 聽錯 ; *put in the* — *place,* fông' ts'o 放錯 ; — *side out,* fæn-min' 反面 ; *to wear ditto,* c'ün'-leh

fæn'-min 反面穿了 ; —, (*i.e.* the wrong person receives),tsiang-kwun' li-ta' 張冠李戴 ; *can't distinguish right and—,* z'-fi bin'-feh-c'ih-læ' 是非辨弗出來 ; *to write a* — *character,* sia' bah-z' 寫°白字 ; *to be in the* —, *and tell others* —, yi'-ngo, djün-ngo' 以訛傳訛

WRONG, *injury,* we'-ky'üoh 委屈° ; ün-wông' 冤枉 ; *to receive* —, ziu ün-wông' 受冤枉

WRONG,*to* we'-ky'üoh 委屈° ; (in a stronger sense), ün-ky'üih' 冤屈

WROUGHT *iron,* joh-t'ih' 熟°鐵

WRY *face,* wæn-cü' wæn-teh ; *put on a* — *face,* tsông-leh wæn-cü' wæn-teh 裝得°環嘴環咭 ; *distorted, twisted face,* hwa-cü' hwa-lin 歪嘴歪臉

# Y

YAM, (Chinese), z-yiah' 蕌藥 ; sæn-yiah' 山藥

YARD, *a* ih-mô' 一碼 ; *a—of cotton cloth,* ih-mô pu' 一碼布 ; *space around a house,* yü-di' 餘°地

YAWN, *to* tang hô-hen' 打呵肝

YEAR, *a* ih-nyin' 一年 ; *beginning of the* —, nyin-deo' 年頭 ; *end of the* —, nyin-ti' 年底 ; sæn'-jih-nyin-yia' 大°年夜 ; nyiæn-kyiu' yia 小°年夜 ; *near the end of the* —, nyin-dzing'shü-pih 年近歲畢 ; *this* —, kying-nyin' 今年 ; peng'-nyin 本年 ; *this or the same* —, tông'-nyin 當

年; *next* —, ming-nyin' 明年; nen-nyin'; læ-nyin' 來 年; 'o'-nyin 下°年; *last* —, gyiu-nyin' 舊 年; ky'ü'-nyin 去年; zông-nyin' 上年; — *before last*, zin'-nyin 前°年; — *after* —, le'-nyin 屢 年; *once a* —, ih-nyin'ih-we' 一年一回; (of a young person), *how many years old is he*, gyi' kyi shü' 其幾歲°; (of one over 20), gyi' to-siao nyin'-kyi 其多少 年紀; *eight years old*, pah'-shü-de 八 歲° 了°; *a — old*, tsiu'-shü 週歲; *about a — old*, tsiu-pô-shü' 將° 近° 週 歲

YEARLY, nyin-nyin' 年 年; me'-nyin 每 年

YEARN *to see*, vông' gyi-we min' ziang k'eo-k'eh' ka 企 望 如 渴; — *for*, k'eh-k'eh-neng'-neng siang'-vông 刻 刻 時°時°想 望

YEAST, kao'-shü 酵 水°

YELLOW, wông 黃; *pale* —, dæn wông' 淡 黃

YELLOWISH, yiu-tin wông' 有點 黃; wông-shô'-shô; wông-bang'-bang; ta wông-seh'-go 帶° 黃 色 个°

YES, The Chinese often repeat a part of the question in affirmation; thus, *is he there?* gyi' læ-kæn''feh 其在°彼°否°? for yes, say, *it is there*, læ-kæn' 在°彼°? *can do or not?* hao-tso' feh 好做 否°? —, or *can do*, hao'-tso 好做; *is it so?* z-ka' feh 如°此°否°? —,

or *exactly so*, feh-ts'o' 弗錯; —, or *it is*, z'-go 是 个°

YESTERDAY, zô-nyih' 昨°日°; *day before* —, zin-nyih' 前°日°

YET, wa 還°; *not* —, feh-zing' 弗 曾°; vi'-dzeng 未 曾°; wa m-neh 還°沒°有°; — *here*, wa læ-tong' 還°在°; *not — come*, feh-zing' læ 弗 曾°來; vi'-dzing læ 未 曾 來

YIELD *fruit*, kyih ko'-ts 結果子; — *interest*, c'ih'-sih 出 息; *to — place*, nyiang 讓°; *to submit*, voh 服; shü-voh' 輸服; — *one's self up to justice*, zi deo'-tao 自° 投 到

YIELDING *to pressure*, nen'-tsi-tsi 軟°綿°綿°; *having no determination*, m-nô-neh'-go 無 拿 捺 个°; *too ready to listen to others*, ng'-tô nyün' 耳 朵 軟; *too ready to follow others*, ze-zông' ze-loh'-go 隨 上 隨 落 个°

YOKE, ah 軶 (ih-go); — (*for carrying*), pin'-tæn 扁 擔 (ih-ts)

YOLK *of an egg*, dæn-wông' 蛋 黃; dæn-wông 蛋 殼

YONDER, *there*, keh'-deo 那°邊°; nô; na 那; læ-kæn' 在°彼°

YOU, ng 你°; (the plural only), ng-lah' 你°等°; — *sir*, tseng kô' 尊 駕°; *respected* —, koh'-yüô 閣 下°; — *gentlemen*, ng-lah' cü-kong' 你°等°諸公; ng-lah' cü-we' 你°等°諸 位

YOUNG *and tender*, neng 嫩; —

(under sixteen), iu′-nyin nying 幼 年 人°; nyin-iu′-go 年 幼 个°; nyin-kyi′-siao′-go 年 紀 小 个°; nyin-kyi′ ky′ing′-go 年 紀 輕 个°; siao′-nyin nying 少 年 人°; — and strong, nyin-lih′ tsing-tsông′ 年 力 精 壯 (tsông or công); — man, tsông′-nyin-nying 壯 年 人°; — person, ‛eo′-sang 後 生°; ‛eo′-sang-kô ; — woman, (married),′ eo′-sang nyü′-nying 後 生 女 人°; — (unmarried) woman, do kwu′-nyiang 大° 姑 娘; both old and — were there, lao′-siao tu læ′-kæn 老 小 都 在° 彼°; when we were — , ah′-lah siao-læ′ z-‛eo 我 等° 小 的° 時 候; ah-lah iu′-nyin-kyin 我 等° 幼 年 間

YOUNGER than I, nyin-kyi′ pi ngô′ siao′ 年 紀 比 我 小; nyin-kyi′ pi ngô ky′ing′ 年 紀 比 我 輕

YOUNGEST, nyin-kyi′ ting ky′ing′ 年 紀 頂 輕; nyin-kyi′ ting siao 年 紀 頂 小

YOUR, ng-go′ 你 个°; (the plural), ng-lah′-go 你 等° 个°; — book, ng′-go shü′ 你° 个° 書; what is — age? ng′ to-siao′ nyin-kyi′ 你° 多 少 年 紀? (more respectful), ng kwe′-kang ni 你° 貴 庚° 呢? to-siao kwe′-kang 多 少 貴 庚°? what is — (family) name? kwe sing′ 貴 姓; — son, ling-lông′ 令 郎; — daughter, ling-æ′ 令 愛; — father, ling-

tseng′ 令 尊; tseng da′-jing 尊 大 人; t′a′ sin-sang 太° 先 生°; — mother, ling-dông′ 令 堂; t′a′ s-meo 太° 師 母; — country, kwe′ koh 貴 國

YOURSELF, zi 自°; did you go —? ng zi′ ky′i′-ko ma 你° 自° 去° 過 嗎°? ng ts′ing-sing′ ky′i′-ko ma 你° 親 身 去° 過 嗎°?

YOUTH, (male under sixteen), iu′-dong 幼 童; small — , mong-dong′ 蒙 童; precocious —, jing-dong′ 神 童; the doer of brave deeds must commence in —, ing-yüong′, c′ih siao′-nyin 英 雄 出 少 年; the time of — and strength, sing-công′lih gyin′z-‛eo′ 身 壯 力 健 之° 時°

YOUTHFUL, ing-nyin′ 英 年; ing-yüong′ pe 英 雄 輩; having a — appearance, sang′-leh neng-min′ 生° 得° 嫩 相°; how —! dza ‛eo′-sang 甚° 後 生°!

# Z

ZEALOUS, hyüih′-sing 血 心; he is very — , gyi ky′i hyüih′-sing 其 頂 用° 血 心

ZENITH, t′in-cong′ 天 中; the sun is in the —, nyih-deo′ læ t′in-cong′ 日° 在° 天 中

ZINC, bah-k′æn′ 白 鉛

ZONE, torrid nyih-dao′ 熱 道; frigid —, ‛en-dao′ 塞 道; north temperate —, poh′-weng dao 北 溫 道

# LIST OF GEOGRAPHICAL NAMES.

———— ◦–•–◦ ————

## A

| | | |
|---|---|---|
| Abyssinia | 阿比西尼亞 | Ah-pi-si-nyi-üô |
| Acheen | 亞齊 | Üô-dzi |
| Aden | 亞登 | Üô-teng |
| Adriatic (Sea) | 亞底亞海 | Üô-ti-üô Hæ |
| Afghanistan | 阿富汗 | Ah-fu-'en |
| Africa | 亞非利加 | Üô-fi-li-kyüô |
| Ajan | 亞然 | Üô-jün |
| Alabama | 雅邦 | Yüô-pông |
| Alaska | 阿拉斯恪 | Ah-lah-s-keh |
| Algeria | 亞利其亞 | Üô-li-gyi-üô |
| Algiers | 亞利及斯 | Üô-li-gyih-s |
| Alleghany | 押利結尼 | Iah-li-kyih-nyi |
| Alps | 亞卑斯 | Üô-pe-s |
| Altai (Great) | { 阿爾泰 <br> 金山 | { Ah-r-t'æ <br> Kying-sæn |
| Amazon | 亞馬孫 | Üô-mô-seng |
| America | 亞美利駕 | Üô-me-li-kyüô |
| America (Central) | 中亞美利駕 | Cong Üô-me-li-kyüô |
| Amoo | 阿牟 | Ah-meo |
| Amoor | 黑龍江 | Heh-long Kông |
| Amoy | 廈門 | 'Ô-meng |
| Amsterdam | 恩斯德爾敦 | Eng-s-teh-r-teng |
| Annam | 安南 | En-nen |
| Andalusia | 安特路西亞 | En-deh-lu-si-üô |
| Andes | 安地斯 | En-di-s |
| Antarctic (Ocean) | 南冰洋 | Nen-ping Yiang |
| Antioch | 安提阿 | En-di-ah |
| Antwerp | 安德回百 | En-teh-we-pah |

| | | |
|---|---|---|
| Apennines | 亞皁尼奴 | Ǖô-pe-nyi-nu |
| Arabia | { 大食國 <br> { 亞喇伯 | { Da-zih Koh <br> { Ǖô-lah-pah |
| Arabian (Sea) | 亞喇伯海 | Ǖô-lah-pah Hæ |
| Arracan | 阿喇喀 | Ah-lah-k'eh |
| Aral (Sea) | 鹹海 | 'Æn Hæ |
| Ararat | 亞喇묙 | Ǖô-lah-liah |
| Archipelago | 羣島 | Gyüing-tao |
| Arctic (Ocean) | 北氷洋 | Poh-ping Yiang |
| Armenia | 亞米尼亞 | Ǖô-mi-nyi-üô |
| Ascension (Is.) | 阿森森 | Ah-seng-seng |
| Asia | 亞細亞 | Ǖô-si-üô |
| Asia Minor | 小亞細亞 | Siao Ǖô-si-üô |
| Assam | 阿三 | Ah-sæn |
| Asuncion | 亞生生 | Ǖô-seng-seng |
| Athens | 雅典 | Ǖô-tin |
| Atlantic | 大西洋海 | Da Si-yiang Hæ |
| Atlas | 亞大蠟 | Ǖô-da-lah |
| Australasia | 澳大利西亞 | Ao-da-li-si-üô |
| Australia | 澳大利亞 | Ao-da-li-üô |
| Austria | 奧地利亞 | Ao-di-li-üô |
| Ava | 阿瓦 | Ah-wô |
| Azof or Azov (Sea) | 亞速海 | Ǖô-soh Hæ |
| Azure Sea | 青海 | Ts'ing Hæ |

# B

| | | |
|---|---|---|
| Babel Mandeb | 巴白曼德 | Pô-bah-mæn-teh |
| Babylon | 巴比倫 | Pô-pi-leng |
| Bactria | 大夏 | Da-yüô |
| Baffin (Bay) | 巴芬 | Pô-feng |
| Bahamas | 巴哈麻 | Pô-ha-mô |
| Bahia | 巴喜亞 | Pô-hyi-üô |
| Baikal | { 貝加耳 <br> { 北海 | { Pe-kyüô-r <br> { Poh Hæ |
| Balkan | 巴幹 | Pô-ken |
| Baltic | 波羅的 | Po-lo-tih |

| | | |
|---|---|---|
| Bangkok | 曼谷 | Mæn-koh |
| Barbadoes | 渤渤多斯 | Bah-bah-to-s |
| Barbary | 巴巴利 | Pô-pô-li |
| Barcelona | 巴西羅尼 | Pô-si-lo-nyi |
| Barkul | 鎭西 | Cing-si |
| Bashee Islands | 紅頭嶼 | 'Ong-deo-jü |
| Bass (Strait) | 巴斯海腰 | Pô-s Hæ-iae |
| Batavia | { 咖喇巴<br>噶喇巴 | { Gyia-liu-pô<br>Keh-lah-pô |
| Beersheba | 別士巴 | Bih-z-pô |
| Behring | 白令 | Bah-ling |
| Belgium | 比利時 | Pi-li-z |
| Belleisle | 北勒利 | Poh-leh-li |
| Beloochistan | 俾路芝 | Pe-lu-ts |
| Belur tagh | 葱嶺 | Ts'ong-ling |
| Benares | 波羅奈 | Po-lo-næ |
| Bengal | 孟加拉 | Meng-kyüô-lah |
| Berlin | 比耳林 | Pi-r-ling |
| Bermudas | 渤牟特 | Bah-meo-deh |
| Berne | 比爾尼 | Pi-r-nyi |
| Bethany | 伯大尼 | Pah-da-nyi |
| Bethel | 伯特利 | Pah-deh-li |
| Bethlehem | 伯利恒 | Pah-li-'eng |
| Beyrout | 貝路德 | Pe-lu-tch |
| Bhamo | 猛卯 | Meng-mao |
| Biscay | 比斯加 | Pi-s-kyüô |
| Black (Sea) | 黑海 | Heh Hæ |
| Blanco (Cape) | 罷蘭哥 | Bô-læn-ko |
| Bohemia | 婆喜彌亞 | Bo-hyi-mi-üô |
| Bokhara (Little) | { 天山南路<br>阿霸科爾 | { T'in-sæn Nen-lu<br>Ah-pô-k'o-r |
| Bombay | { 揮國<br>孟買 | { Tæn-koh<br>Meng-ma |
| Bootan | 不丹 | Peh-tæn |
| Borneo | { 婆羅<br>渤泥 | { Bo-lo<br>Bah-nyi |

| Bosphorus | { 均士淡丁<br>海腰 | { Kyüing-z-dæn-ting-<br>Hæ-iao |
|---|---|---|
| Boston | 波士頓 | Po-z-teng |
| Bothnia (Gulf) | 波的尼 | Po-tih-nyi |
| Bozrah | 破斯拉 | P'o-s-lah |
| Brahmaputra | 雅魯藏布 | Yüô-lu-dzông-pu |
| Brazil | 巴西 | Pô-si |
| Brazilian (Mts.) | 巴西山 | Pô-si Sæn |
| Bristol | 渤爾斯督 | Bah-r-s-toh |
| Britannia | 大英國 | Da-ing Koh |
| Brooklyn | 蒲葛令 | Bu-keh-ling |
| Brussels | 北律悉 | Poh-lih-sih |
| Buenos Ayres | 普納塞利斯 | P'u-neh-seh-li-s |
| Bussorah | 勿些 | Feh-sæ |

## C

| Cabul | { 加布利<br>安石國 | { Kyüô-pu-li<br>En-zih Koh |
|---|---|---|
| Cadiz | 加提士 | Kyüô-di-z |
| Caffraria | 加弗拉利亞 | Kyüô-feh-lah-li-üô |
| Cairo | 加義羅 | Kyüô-yi-lo |
| Calcutta | 加以各搭 | Kyüô-yi-koh-tah |
| Caledonia | 加利陀尼 | Kyüô-li-do-nyi |
| California | { 加利福尼<br>金山 | { Kyüô-li-foh-nyi<br>Kying-sæn |
| Calvary | 枯髏 (髑髏) | Kw'u-leo |
| Cambodia | 占臘 | Tsin-lah |
| Cambodia or Mei kong River, | 瀾滄江 | Læn-ts'ông Kông |
| Campeachy or Campeche | 堪比支 | K'æn-pi-ts |
| Canada | 加拿他 | Kyüô-nô-t'a |
| Canal (Grand) | 運糧河 | Yüing-liang 'O |
| Canary (Is.) | 加拿利 | Kyüô-nô-li |
| Cancer (Tropic) | 北日至線 | Poh-jih-ts-sin |
| Candia | 廣地亞 | Kwông-di-üô |
| Canton | 廣東 | Kwông-tong |
| Cape Colony | 岌哥洛尼 | Kyih-ko-loh-nyi |

| | | |
|---|---|---|
| Capricorn | 南日至線 | Nen-jih-ts-sin |
| Caraccas | 加拉克四 | Kyüô-lah-k'eh-s |
| Caribbean (Sea) | 加里比海 | Kyüô-li-pi Hæ |
| Carmel | 加密 | Kyüô-mih |
| Caroline | 加羅林 | Kyüô-lo-ling |
| Carpathian | 加伯旦 | Kyüô-pah-tæn |
| Carthage | 加德治 | Kyüô-teh-djü |
| Cashgar | 喀什噶爾 | K'eh-jih-keh r |
| Cashmere | 加濕彌羅 | Kyüô-sih-mi-lo |
| Caspian (Sea) | { 裏海<br>內海 | { Li Hæ<br>Nen Hæ |
| Cathay | 契丹 | Ky'ih-tæn |
| Cattegat | 加的牙 | Kyüô-tih-yüô |
| Caucasus | 高加索 | Kao-kyüô-soh |
| Cayenne | 基恒 | Kyi-'eng |
| Celebes | { 西利伯<br>西利窒 | { Si-li-pah<br>Si-li-cih |
| Celestial (Mts.) | 天山 | T'in Sæn |
| Cenis | 基尼斯 | Kyi-nyi-s |
| Ceylon | 錫蘭山 | Sih-læn Sæn |
| Chapoo | 乍浦 | Dzô-pu |
| Chefoo | { 之㬊<br>烟臺 | { Ts-veo<br>In-dæ |
| Chekiang | 浙江 | Tsih-kông |
| Chesapeake | 吉沙彼葛 | Kyih-sô-pe-keh |
| Chicago | 世加哥 | Shü-kyüô-ko |
| Chihli | 直隸 | Dzih-li |
| Chili | 智利 | Cü-li |
| China (proper) | 中國 | Cong-koh |
| China Sea | 南海 | Nen Hæ |
| China (Great wall of) | 萬里長城 | Væn-li-dziang-dzing |
| Chinchew | 泉州府 | Djün-tsiu-fu |
| Chinese Empire | 大清國 | Da Ts'ing Koh |
| Chinhai | 鎭海 | Cing-hæ |
| Chinkiang | 鎭江 | Cing-kông |
| Christiana | 基督亞尼亞 | Kyi-toh-üô-nyi-üô |

| | | |
|---|---|---|
| Chusan | 舟山 | Tsiu-sæn |
| Cincinnati | 鎮鎮那底 | Cing-cing-na-ti |
| Cochin China or | 交趾 | Kyiao-ts |
| Cambodia | 占城 | Tsin-dzing |
| Cologne | 哥羅尼 | Ko-lo-nyi |
| Colombia | 科倫比亞 | K'o-leng-pi-üô |
| Colorado | 各落拉多 | Koh-lôh-leh-to |
| Columbia (River) | 科倫比亞河 | K'o-leng-pi-üô 'O |
| Columbus | 科倫布 | K'o-leng-pu |
| Comorin | 哥摩令 | Ko-mo-ling |
| Congo | 港哥 | Kông-ko |
| Constantinople | 均士淡丁 | Kyüing-z-dæn-ting |
| Coomassie | 古麥西 | Kwu-mah-si |
| Copenhagen | 哥阜納給 | Ko-pe-neh-kyih |
| Corea | { 朝鮮 | { Dziao-sin |
| | 高麗 | Kao-li |
| Corea (Strait) | 高麗海腰 | Kao-li Hæ-iao |
| Corfu | 可兒夫 | K'o-r-fu |
| Corinth | 哥林多 | Ko-ling-to |
| Corsica | 哥塞牙 | Ko-seh-yüô |
| Costa Rica | 哥斯德黎各 | Ko-s-teh Li-koh |
| Crimea | 葛里彌亞 | Keh-li-mi-üô |
| Cuba | 古巴 | Kwu-pô |
| Cyprus | 居比路 | Kyü-pi-lu |
| Cyrene | 古利奈 | Kwu-li-næ |

# D

| | | |
|---|---|---|
| Dahomey | 大火米 | Da-ho-mi |
| Damascus | 大馬色 | Da-mô-seh |
| Danube | 多惱 | To-nao |
| Dardanelles | 他大尼里 | T'a-da-nyi-li |
| Darien | 大里尼 | Da-li-nyi |
| Davis (Strait) | 大比海腰 | Da-pi Hæ-iao |
| Deccan | 大境 | Da-kying |
| Delaware (State) | 特邦 | Deh-pông |
| Delhi | 特里 | Deh-li |

| | | |
|---|---|---|
| Denmark | { 嗹國<br>{ 黃旗國 | { Lìn Koh<br>{ Wông-gyi Koh |
| Dnieper | 尼百爾 | Nyi-pah-r |
| Domingo | 多名哥 | To-ming-ko |
| Don (River) | 唐江 | Dông Kông |
| Douro (River) | 斗羅河 | Teo-lo 'O |
| Dover (Straits) | 多非海腰 | To-fi Hæ-iao |
| Dresden | 特拉斯敦 | Deh-lah-s-teng |
| Dublin | 都彼林 | Tu-pe-ling |
| Dundee | 屯地 | Deng-di |
| Dunkirk | 屯葛爾 | Deng-keh-r |
| Dutch | 荷蘭人 | 'O-læn jing |
| Dwina | 土伊拿 | T'u-i-nô |

## E

| | | |
|---|---|---|
| Ecuador | 厄瓜多 | Eh-kwô-to |
| Eden | 挨田 | Yiæ-din |
| Edinburgh | 壹丁不爾格 | Ih-ting-peh-r-keh |
| Egypt | 埃及 | Yiæ-gyih |
| Elbe | 合利比 | 'Eh-li-pi |
| Elizabeth | 以利沙伯 | Yi-li-sô-pah |
| England | 英倫 | Ing-leng |
| English (Channel) | 英倫海岔 | Ing-leng Hæ-ts'ò |
| Ephesus | 以弗所 | Yi-feh-sò |
| Equator | 赤道 | Ts'ih-dao |
| Erie | 衣里 | I-li |
| Erzeroum | 合徐籠 | 'Eh-zi-long |
| Ethiopia | 古實國 | Kwu-jih-koh |
| Etna (Mt.) | 以底那山 | Yi-ti-nô Sæn |
| Euphrates | 百辣河 | Pah-lah 'O |
| Europe | 歐羅巴 | Eo-lo-pô |

## F

| | | |
|---|---|---|
| Falkland | 發哥蘭 | Fah-ko-læn |
| Fatshan | 佛山 | Veh-sæn |

| Finland (Gulf) | 芬蘭 | Feng-læn |
| Florida | 福落里得 | Foh-lôh-li-teh |
| Fohkien | 福建 | Foh-kyin |
| Foochow | 福州 | Foh-tsiu |
| Formosa | { 毗舍耶 臺灣 | { Bi-shæ-yiæ Dæ-ẇæn |
| France | 法郎西 | Fah-lông-si |
| Friendly (Is.) | 友羣島 | Yiu Gyüing-tao |
| Fung hwa | 奉化 | Vong-hwô |
| Fusiyama | 富士山 | Fu-z-sæn |

## G

| Galatia | 加拉忒 | Kyüô-lah-t'a |
| Galilee | 加利利 | Kyüô-li-li |
| Ganges | 恒河 | 'Eng 'O |
| Garonne | 咖羅尼 | Gyia-lo-nyi |
| Geelong | 雞籠 | Kyi-long |
| Geneva | 虢尼瓦 | Joh-nyi-wô |
| Genoa | 基那瓦 | Kyi-no-wô |
| Georgetown | 查爾治敦 | Dzô-r-djü-teng |
| Germany | 日耳曼 | Jih-r-mæn |
| Gibralter | 日巴拉大 | Jih-pô-lah-da |
| Gilboa | 吉坡 | Kyih-p'o |
| Gilead | 基列 | Kyi-lih |
| Girin | 吉林 | Kyih-ling |
| Glasgow | 格勒斯高 | Keh-leh-s-kao |
| Goa | 小西洋 | Siao Si-yiang |
| Good Hope (Cape) | 好望土角 | Hao-vông T'u-koh |
| Goshen | 坷山 | K'o-sæn |
| Great Britain | 大英國 | Da-ing Koh |
| Great Wall | 萬利長城 | Væn-li-dziang-dzing |
| Greece | 希利尼 | Hyi-li-nyi |
| Greenland | 哥里蘭 | Ko-li-læn |
| Greenwich | 葛理業治 | Keh-li-nyih-djü |
| Grenada | 加拉那大 | Kyüô-lah-no-da |

| | | |
|---|---|---|
| Guardafui | 瓜達夫 | Kwô-deh-fu |
| Guiana | 歪阿那 | Hwa-ah-nô |
| Guinea | 幾尼亞 | Kyi-nyi-üô |
| Gutslaff | 馬蹟 | Mô-tsih |

# H

| | | |
|---|---|---|
| Haarlem | 郝而倫 | Heh-r-leng |
| Hague | 海克 | Hæ-k'eh |
| Hakodadi | 箱館 | Siang-kwun |
| Hakkas | 客家 | K'ah-kyüô |
| Halifax | 哈勒法 | Ha-leh-fah |
| Halle | 黑利 | Heh-li |
| Hamburg | 恒不以革 | 'Eng-peh-yi-keh |
| Hangchow | 杭州 | 'Ong-tsiu |
| Hankow | 漢口 | Hen-k'eo |
| Han (River) | 漢水 | Hen-se |
| Hanover | 哈那惟爾 | Ha-nô-vi-r |
| Havana | 哈瓦那 | Ha-wô-nô |
| Havre | 黑法 | Heh-fah |
| Hayti | 海地 | Hæ-di |
| Hebrides | 黑皮地斯 | Heh-bi-di-s |
| Hebron | 希伯倫 | Hyi-pah-leng |
| Hecla | 挨哥拉 | A-ko-lah |
| Hermon | 黑門 | Heh-meng |
| Himalaya | { 喜馬拉<br>{ 雪山 | { Hyi-mô-lah<br>{ Shih-sæu |
| Hindookoosh | 縣度 | Yün-du |
| Hindoostan | { 印度國<br>{ 天竺國 | { Ing-du Koh<br>{ T'in-coh Koh |
| Honan | 河南 | 'O-nen |
| Holland | 荷蘭國 | 'O-læn Koh |
| Honduras | 鬨都拉 | 'Ong-tu-lah |
| Hongkong | 香港 | Hyiang-kông |
| Honolulu | 霍那盧盧 | Hoh-nô-lu-lu |
| Honque | 虹口 | 'Ong-k'eo |
| Hoogly | 呼葛理 | Hwu-keh-li |

| Hottentots | 合丁突 | 'Eh-ting-deh |
| Huchow | 湖州 | Wu-tsiu |
| Hudson (Strait) | 哈德孫海腰 | Ha-teh-seng Hæ-iao |
| Hue | 順化 | Jing-hwô |
| Hunan | 湖南 | Wu-nen |
| Hungary | 亨嘉利 | Heng-kyüô-li |
| Hupeh | 湖北 | Wu-poh |
| Huron | 休倫 | Hyiu-leng |
| Hwangho | 黃河 | Wông 'O |

## I

| Iceland | 義斯蘭 | Yi-s-læn |
| Ili | { 伊犂 <br> 惠遠城 | { I-li <br> We-yün-dzing |
| Illyria | 以利哩古 | Yi-li-li-kwu |
| India | 印度 | Ing-du |
| Indian (Ocean) | { 南海 <br> 印度洋 | { Nen Hæ <br> Ing-du Yiang |
| Indus | { 岡喝 <br> 印度河 | { Kông-heh <br> Ing-du 'O |
| Ionia | 亞尼亞 | Üô-nyi-üô |
| Ireland | 阿爾蘭 | Ah-r-læn |
| Irish (Sea) | 阿爾蘭海 | Ah-r-læn Hæ |
| Irrawaddy | { 伊犂瓦地 <br> 潞江 | { I-li-wô-di <br> Lu Kông |
| Italy | { 以大利 <br> 意大利亞 | { Yi-da-li' <br> I-da-li-üô |

## J

| Jaffa | 約帕 | Iah-p'ô |
| Jamaica | 牙買加 | Yüô-mæ-kyüô |
| Japan | 日本 | Jih-peng |
| Java | { 爪哇 <br> 加拉巴 | { Tsao-wô <br> Kyüô-lah-pô |
| Jehol | 熱河 | Jih 'O |
| Jericho | 耶利哥 | Yiæ-li-ko |
| Jersey | 耶爾歲 | Yiæ-r-se |

| Jerusalem | 耶路撒冷 | Yiæ-lu-sah-leng |
| Joppa | 約帕 | Iah-p'ô |
| Jordan | 約但 | Iah-dæn |

# K

| Kaifung | 開封 | K'æ-fong |
| Kalgan | 張家口 | Tsiang-kyüô-k'eo |
| Kamtschatka | 堪察加 | K'æn-ts'ah-kyüô |
| Kanagawa | 金川 | Kying-c'ün |
| Kansuh | 甘肅 | Ken-soh |
| Karens | 鈞町 | Keo-t'ing |
| Kashgar | 喀什噶爾 | K'eh-jih-keh-r |
| Kelat | 基拉 | Kyi-lah |
| Kelung | 雞籠 | Kyi-long |
| Khokan | 霍罕 | Hoh-hen |
| Khoten | 和闐 | 'O-din |
| Kiachta | 買賣鎮 | Mæ-mæ-cing |
| Kiahing | 嘉興 | Kyüô-hying |
| Kiangsi | 江西 | Kông-si |
| Kiangsu | 江蘇 | Kông-su |
| Kien Kiang | 贛江 | Ken-kông |
| Kirin | 吉林 | Kyih-ling |
| Kiukiang | 九江 | Kyiu-kông |
| Kiushiu | 九洲 | Kyiu-tsiu |
| Kobi | 神戶 | Jing Wu |
| Koko Nor | 青海 | Ts'ing Hæ |
| Kokand | 霍罕 | Hoh-hen |
| Kong (Mts.) | 港山 | Kông Sæn |
| Kowloong | 九龍 | Kyiu-long |
| Kuenlun | 崑崙 | Kweng-leng |
| Kuldja | 惠遠城 | We-yün-dzing |
| Kwang si | 廣西 | Kwông-si |
| Kwangtung | 廣東 | Kwông-tong |
| Kwei chow | 貴州 | Kwe-tsiu |

# L

| Labrador | 臘不拉多 | Lah-peh-lah-to |
| Ladrone (Is.) | 老萬山 | Lao-væn Sæn |
| Lands End | 蘭森角 | Læn-seng Koh |
| Lanchee | 蘭谿 | Læn-ky'i |
| Laos | 越裳 | Yüih-dzông |
| Lapland | 立蘭 | Lih-læn |
| Lassa | 拉薩 | Lah-sah |
| Lebanon | 利巴嫩 | Li-pô-neng |
| Leeds | 利達斯 | Li-deh-s |
| Lemnos | 里那士  · | Li-nô-z |
| Lena | 利拿 | Li-nô |
| Lew chew | { 中山<br>{ 琉球 | { Cong-sæn<br>{ Liu-gyiu |
| Liam po (Ningpo) | 甯波 | Nying-po |
| Liberia | 利卑利亞 | Li-pe-li-üô |
| Lima | 利瑪 | Li-mô |
| Lisbon | 力斯本 | Lih-s-peng |
| Liverpool | 立弗布立 | Lih-feh-pu-lih |
| Loire | 盧爾 | Lu-r |
| London | 倫敦 | Leng-teng |
| Long Island | 長島 | Dziang-tao |
| Lop | 羅布 | Lo-pu |
| Luzon | 小呂宋 | Siao Li-song |
| Lyons | 雷昂 | Le-ngông |
| Lyons (Gulf) | 雷昂海股 | Le-ngông Hæ-kwu |

# M

| Macao | 澳門 | Ao-meng |
| Mackenzie | 馬根些 | Mô-keng-siæ |
| Madagascar | 馬達加斯加 | Mô-dah-kyüô-s-kyüô |
| Madeira | 馬地膜 | Mô-di-lah |
| Madras | 麻打拉薩 | Mô-tang-lah-sah |
| Madrid | 馬特 | Mô-deh |
| Magellan | 麥折倫 | Mah-tsih-leng |

| Malaysia | 馬來西亞 | Mô-læ-si-üô |
|---|---|---|
| Malabar | 古俚國 | Kwu-li Koh |
| Malacca | 麻六呷 | Mo-loh-kyiah |
| Malta | 米利大 | Mi-li-da |
| Manchuria | 滿洲 | Mun-tsiu |
| Mandelay | { 緬京<br>緬都 | { Min-kying<br>Min-tu |
| Manilla | { 龜豆<br>馬尼喇 | { Kwe-deo<br>Mô-nyi-lah |
| Manweyn | 騰越 | Deng-yüih |
| Marmora | 馬馬拉 | Mô-mô-lah |
| Martaban | 馬爾達般 | Mô-r-deh-pæn |
| Massachusetts | 馬邦 | Mô-pông |
| Mauritius | 馬利底斯 | Mô-li-ti-s |
| Mecca | { 默克<br>麥加 | { Meh-k'eh<br>Mah-kyüô |
| Medina | 默德那 | Meh-teh-nô |
| Mediterranean (Sea) | 地中海 | Di-cong Hæ |
| Mei kong (River) | 九龍江 | Kyiu-long Kông |
| Meinam (River) | 湄南河 | Me-nen 'O |
| Melbourne | 麥利婆納 | Mah-li-bo-neh |
| Memphis | 孟非斯 | Meng-fi-s |
| Mesopotamia | 米所波大米 | Mi-sô-po-da-mi |
| Messina | 麥西拿 | Mah-si-nô |
| Mexico | 墨西哥 | Moh-si-ko |
| Michigan | 米邦 | Mi-pông |
| Mindanao | 民荅那莪 | Ming-teh-nô-ngô |
| Mississippi (State) | 密邦 | Mih-pông |
| Missouri (State) | 墨邦 | Moh-pông |
| Moluccas | 慕洛居 | Mo-lôh-kyü |
| Mongolia | 蒙古 | Mong-kwu |
| Montevideo | 蒙德惟多 | Mong-teh-vi-to |
| Montreal | 蒙德利阿 | Mong-teh-li-ah |
| Morocco | 摩洛哥 | Mo-lôh-ko |
| Moscow | 莫斯哥 | Moh-s-ko |
| Moukden | 奉天 | Vong-t'in |

| Moulmein | 騰越州 | Deng-yüih-tsiu |
| Mozambique | 莫三皮絟 | Moh-sæn-bi-kyih |
| Muscat | 莫斯葛 | Moh-s-keh |
| Mysore | 米瑣勒 | Mi-so-leh |

# N

| Nagasaki | 長崎 | Dziang-gyi |
| Nankin | 南京 | Nen-kying |
| Naples | 那不利斯 | Nô-peh-li-s |
| Natal | 那達爾 | Nô-deh-r |
| Nazareth | 拿撒拉 | Nô-sah-lah |
| Nepaul | 尼婆羅 | Nyi-bo-lo |
| Nestorians | 大秦人 | Da-dzing jing |
| New Brunswick | 新不倫瑞克 | Sing Peh-leng-ze-k'eh |
| Newchwang | 牛莊 | Nyiu-tsông |
| New Foundland | 新著大島 | Sing Cü-da Tao |
| New Granada | 新加拉那大 | Sing Kyüô-lah-no-da |
| New Orleans | 紐呵連尼斯 | Nyiu Ho-lin-nyi-s |
| New York | 紐約爾 | Nyiu Iah-r |
| New Zealand | 新西蘭 | Sing Si-læn |
| Niger (River) | 黑江 | Heh Kông |
| Nile | 尼羅江 | Nyi-lo Kông |
| Nineveh | 尼尼微 | Nyi-nyi-vi |
| Ninghai | 甯海 | Nying-hæ |
| Ningpo | 甯波 | Nying-po |
| Ningyuen | 鄞縣 | Nying-yün |
| Niphon | 葉半 | Yih-pun |
| Normandy | 拿孟地 | Nô-mang-di |
| North Cape | 北角 | Poh Koh |
| North Channel | 北岔 | Poh Ts'ô |
| North Sea | 北海 | Poh Hæ |
| Norway | 挪耳回 | Nô-r-we |
| Nova Scotia | 新蘇葛蘭 | Sing Su-keh-læn |
| Nubia | 努比阿 | Nu-pi-ah |

# O

| | | |
|---|---|---|
| Obi (River) | 猗比河 | Ho-pi 'O |
| Obi (Gulf) | 猗比海股 | Ho-pi Hæ-kwu |
| Ochotsk | 大拉該 | Da-lah-kæ |
| Odessa | 和達沙 | 'O-deh-sô |
| Ohio | 和喜和 | 'O-hyi-'O |
| Olives (Mt.) | 橄欖山 | Ken-læn Sæn |
| Olympus | 阿林卜斯 | 'O-ling-poh-s |
| Onega | 阿尼牙 | O-nyi-yüô |
| Ontario | 安迭里河 | En-dih-li-'o |
| Ophir | 阿妃 | O-fi |
| Oporto | 阿波爾多 | Ah-po-r-to |
| Orange (River) | 猗蘭日河 | Ho-læn-jih 'O |
| Oregon | 阿里昂 | O-li-ngông |
| Orinoco | 猗勒諾哥 | Ho-leh-noh-ko |
| Orissa | 烏稇國 | U-ts'ô Koh |
| Osaca | 大阪 | Da-pæn |
| Ouigour | 回鶻 | We-kweh |

# P

| | | |
|---|---|---|
| Pacific (Ocean) | 太平洋 | T'a-bing Yiang |
| Palem-bang | 亙港 | Gyü-kông |
| Palestine | { 不利斯底尼<br>拂林國 | { Peh-li-s-ti-nyi<br>Fah-ling Koh |
| Palmyra | 伯母拉 | Pah-meo-lah |
| Panama | 巴拿馬 | Pô-nô-mô |
| Papua | { 巴不亞<br>褻暴 | { Pô-peh-üô<br>Bao-bao |
| Paraguay | 巴拉圭 | Pô-lah-kwe |
| Paramaribo | 巴拉馬利波 | Pô-lah-mô-li-po |
| Paris | 巴勒 | Pô-leh |
| Parsees | 火神敎 | Ho-jing kyiao |
| Patagonia | 巴他莪尼 | Pô-t'a-ngo-nyi |
| Pechele | 北直隷 | Poh-dzih-li |
| Pegu | { 北揆<br>皮求 | { Poh-ngo<br>Bi-gyiu |
| Peiho | 北河 | Poh 'O |

| | | |
|---|---|---|
| Peking | 北京 | Poh-kying |
| Penang | 檳榔 | Ping-lông |
| Perouse (St.) | 北路西 | Poh-lu-si |
| Persia | 波斯 | Po-s |
| Peru | 秘魯 | Pi-lu |
| Peshawur | 布魯沙布羅 | Pu-lu-sô-pu-lo |
| Philadelphia | 非拉銤非 | Fi-lah-tʻih-fi |
| Philippi | 腓立比 | Fi-lih-pi |
| Piedmont | 秘達孟德 | Pi-deh-meng-teh |
| Pisgah | 比士迦 | Pi-z-kyüô |
| Pittsburg | 碧沘城 | Pih-ts-dzing |
| Po (River) | 波江 | Po Kông |
| Polynesia | 波里尼西亞 | Po-li-nyi-si-üô |
| Poonah | 波那 | Po-nô |
| Porto Rico | 波爾多黎谷 | Po-r-to Li-koh |
| Portugal | { 葡萄牙<br>西洋國 | { Bu-dao-yüô<br>Si-yiang Koh |
| Posen | 波遜 | Po-seng |
| Potomac | 波多麥 | Po-to-mah |
| Poyang | 鄱陽 | Bo-yiang |
| Prussia | { 普魯士<br>單鷹 | { Pʻu-lu-z<br>Tæn-ing |
| Punjaub | 本加渤 | Peng kyüô-bah |
| Pyrenees | 必爾尼斯 | Pih-nyi-nyi-s |

## Q

| | | |
|---|---|---|
| Quebec | 貴璧 | Kwe-pih |
| Quito | 基多 | Kyi-to |

## R

| | | |
|---|---|---|
| Rangoon | 藍哥尼 | Læn-ko-nyi |
| Red (Sea) | 紅海 | ʻOng Hæ |
| Rhine | 來尼 | Læ-nyi |
| Rhodes | 羅底 | Lo-ti |
| Rhone | 羅尼 | Lo-nyi |
| Rio de la Plata | 拉巴拉他 | Lah-pô-lah-tʻa |
| Rio Grande | 理阿骨蘭 | Li-ah-kweh-læn |

| | | |
|---|---|---|
| Rio Jeneiro | 里約熱內盧 | Li-iah-jih-nen-lu |
| Roanoke | 羅阿那機 | Lo-ah-no-kyi |
| Rocky (Mts.) | 落機山 | Lôh-kyi-sæn |
| Romania (Cape) | 羅馬尼 | Lo-mô-nyi |
| Rome | 羅馬 | Lo-mô |
| Rotterdam | 樂得屯 | Loh-teh-deng |
| Russia | 俄羅斯 | Ngo-lo-s |

## S

| | | |
|---|---|---|
| Sacramento | 撒葛孟多 | Sah-keh-meng-to |
| Saghalien | 庫頁 / 北蝦夷 | K'wu-yih / Poh-hyüô-yi |
| Sahara | 撒哈拉 | Sah-ha-lah |
| Saigon | 柴貢 / 西貢 | Za-kong / Si-kong |
| Salwen (River) | 怒江 | Nu Kông |
| Samarang | 三寶瓏 | Sæn-pao-long |
| Samarcand | 撒馬兒罕 | Sæn-mô-r-hen |
| Sandwich | 三維思 | Sæn-vi-s |
| San Francisco | 三法蘭西哥 | Sæn Fah-læn-si-ko |
| Santiago | 三底亞加 | Sæn-ti-üô-kyüô |
| Sardinia | 沙迷尼亞 | Sô-dih-nyi-üô |
| Sardis | 撒狄 | Sah-dih |
| Sarepta | 撒拉大 | Sah-lah-da |
| Savannah | 撒華尼 | Sah-wô-nyi |
| Savoy | 撒華 | Sah-wô |
| Saxony | 撒葛斯尼 | Sah-keh-s-nyi |
| Scotland | 蘇葛蘭 | Su-keh-læn |
| Seine | 西尼 | Si-nyi |
| Senegal | 塞內岡 | Seh-nen-kông |
| Senegambia | 塞內岡比亞 | Seh-nen-kông-pi-üô |
| Shanghai | 上海 | Zông-hæ |
| Shansi | 山西 | Sæn-si |
| Shantung | 山東 | Sæn-tong |
| Sharon | 撒崙 | Sah-leng |
| Shauhing | 紹興 | Ziao-hying |
| Shensi | 陝西 | Sin-si |

| Shing king | 盛京 | Zing-kying |
|---|---|---|
| Siam | 暹羅 | Sin-lo |
| Siberia | { 西比利亞 | { Si-pi-li-üô |
|  | 奚國 | Yi Koh |
| Sicily | 西西里 | Si-si-li |
| Sidney | 悉尼 | Sih-nyi |
| Sidon | 西頓 | Si-teng |
| Sierra Leone | 西爾拉里河尼 | Si-r-lah Li-ʻo-nyi |
| Sierra Madre | 西爾拉馬特 | Si-r-lah-mô-deh |
| Sierra Nevada | 西亞拉尼哇達 | Si-üô-lah Nyi-wô-dah |
| Si kok | 四國 | S Koh |
| Sinai | 西乃 | Si-nœ |
| Si Ngan | 西安 | Si-en |
| Singapore | { 息辣 | { Sih-lah |
|  | 新嘉坡 | Sing-kyüô-pʻo |
| Skagger Rack | 加惹拉 | Kyüô-jô-lah |
| Smyrna | 士每拿 | Z-me-nô |
| Snowy Valley | 雪寶 | Shih-deo |
| Society (Is.) | 會羣島 | We Gyüing-tao |
| Songaria | 天山北路 | Tʻin-sœn Poh-lu |
| Soochow | 蘇州 | Su-tsiu |
| Sooloo | 蘇六 | Su-loh |
| Soudan | 蘇丹 | Su-tœn |
| Spain | { 西班牙 | { Si-pœn-yüô |
|  | 大呂宋 | Do Li-song |
| St. Domingo | 三多名哥 | Sœn-to-ming-ko |
| St. George's (Channel) | 三若岔 | Sœn Ziah Tsʻô |
| St. Helena | 三厄里那 | Sœn Eh-li-nô |
| St. John | 新約翰 | Sing Iah-ʻen |
| St. Lawrence | 勞棱索 | Lao-leng-soh |
| Stockholm | 士篤恆 | Z-toh-ʻeng |
| St. Petersburg | 新彼得城 | Sing Pe-teh dzing |
| St. Roque | 羅克土角 | Lo-kʻeh Tʻu-koh |
| Suez | 蘇爾士 | Su-r-z |
| Sumatra | { 蘇門答臘 | { Su-meng-tah-lah |
|  | 三佛齊 | Sœn-veh-dzi |

| | | |
|---|---|---|
| Sumbawa | 巽備華 | Seng-be-wô |
| Sunda | 巽他 | Seng-t'a |
| Sungkiang | 松江 | Song-kông |
| Superior | 蘇必力耳 | Su-pih-li-r |
| Swatow | 汕頭 | Sæn-deo |
| Sweden | { 瑞典<br>瑞國 | { Ze-tin<br>Ze Koh |
| Switzerland | 瑞士 | Ze-z |
| Syria | 如利亞 | Jü-li-üô |
| Szechuen | 四川 | S-e'ün |

## T

| | | |
|---|---|---|
| Tabor | 大泊 | Da-boh |
| Tadmor | 達莫 | Dah-moh |
| Tagus | 德大 | Teh-da |
| Tai Hu | 太湖 | T'a-wu |
| Taku | 大沽 | Da-kwu |
| Talifoo | 大理府 | Da-li fu |
| Tamsiu | 淡水 | Dæn-se |
| Taranto | 推倫多 | T'e-leng-to |
| Tarim | 堆林 | Te-ling |
| Tarsus | 大數 | Da-su |
| Tartary | 大嚏地 | Da-deh-di |
| Taurus | 島拉斯 | Tao-lah-s |
| Teheran | 第希蘭 | Di-hyi-læn |
| Tenasserim | { 頓遜<br>地拿先廉 | { Teng-seng<br>Di-nô-sin-lin |
| Terra del Fuego | 鋳府衣勾 | T'ih-fu-i-keo |
| Thames | 達迷斯 | Dah-mi-s |
| Thibet | 西藏 | Si-dzóng |
| Tiber | 底拔 | Ti-bah |
| Tiendong | 天童 | T'in-dong |
| Tientai | 天台 | T'in-t'æ |
| Tientsin | 天津 | T'in-tsing |
| Tigris | 底格里 | Ti-keh-li |
| Tinghai | 定海 | Ding-hæ |
| Tobolsk | 多波爾斯科 | To-po-r-s-ko |

| | | |
|---|---|---|
| Tocantins | 多甘定 | To-ken-ding |
| Tokio | 東京 | Tong-kying |
| Tonquin | { 東京 / 明都 | { Tong-kying / Ming-tu |
| Toronto | 多倫多 | To-leng-to |
| Trieste | 的里斯的 | Tih-li-s-teh |
| Tripoli | 的波里 | Tih-po-li |
| Tsien tang | 錢塘 | Dzin-dông |
| Tsitsihar (Province) | 黑龍江 | Heh-long-kông |
| Tsinan | 濟南 | Tsi-nen |
| Tungchow | 登州 | Teng-tsiu |
| Tung ting | 洞庭 | Dong-ding |
| Tunis | 突尼斯 | Deh-nyi-s |
| Turin | 都靈 | Tu-ling |
| Turkistan | 西域 | Si-yüoh |
| Turkistan (Eastern) | 天山南路 | T'in-sæn Nen-lu |
| Turkey | 土耳其 | T'u-r-gyi |

## U

| | | |
|---|---|---|
| Uigurs | 回鶻 | We-kweh |
| Uliatsi | 烏理雅蘇臺 | U-li-yüô-su-dæ |
| United States | { 合衆國 / 大美國 | { 'Eh-cong Koh / Da-me Koh |
| Ural (River) | 烏拉江 | U-lah Kông |
| Ural (Mts.) | 烏拉山 | U-lah Sæn |
| Uruguay | 烏拉圭 | U-lah-kwe |
| Usuri (River) | 烏蘇里河 | U-su-li 'O |

## V

| | | |
|---|---|---|
| Valparaiso | 法巴雷瑣 | Fah-pô-le-so |
| Vancouver | 萬古福 | Væn-kwu-foh |
| Venice | 惟尼斯 | Vi-nyi-s |
| Verde | 威的 | We-tih |
| Vesuvius | 非蘇未斯 | Fi-su-vi-s |
| Vienna | 未伊拿 | Vi-i-nô |
| Virginia | 惟爾勤尼 | Vi-r-gying-nyi |
| Volga | 服拉加 | Voh-lah-kyüô |

# W

| | | |
|---|---|---|
| Wales | 威勒斯 | We-lah-s |
| Wampoa | 黃埔 | Wông-p'u |
| Warsaw | 華爾沙 | Wô-r-sô |
| Washington | 華盛頓 | Wô-zing-teng |
| Wenchow | 溫州 | W̆eng-tsiu |
| West Indies | 西印度 | Si Ing-du |
| White (Sea) | 白海 | Bah Hæ |
| Winnipeg | 維尼八 | Vi-nyi-pah |
| Wongpoo | 黃浦 | Wông-p'u |
| Wuchang | 武昌 | Vu-ts'ông |

# Y

| | | |
|---|---|---|
| Yang chow | 揚州 | Yiang-tsiu |
| Yiang tse Kiang | 揚子江 | Yiang-ts Kông |
| Yarkand | 頁爾羌 | Yih-r-ky'iang |
| Yedo | 也多 江戶 | Yiæ-to Kyüông-wu |
| Yellow (River) | 黃河 | Wông 'O |
| Yellow (Sea) | 東海 | Tong Hæ |
| Yenisei | 日尼塞 | Jih-nyi-seh |
| Yesso | 蝦夷 | Hyüô-yi |
| Yokohama | 橫濱 | Wang-ping |
| Yucatan | 如加敦 | Jü-kyüô-teng |
| Yung (River) | 甬江 | Üong Kông |
| Yunnan | 雲南 | Yüing-nen |

# Z

| | | |
|---|---|---|
| Zambeze | 散皮西 | Sæn-bi-si |
| Zanguibar | 桑給巴爾 | Sông-kyih-pô-r |
| Zealand | 西蘭 | Si-læn |
| Zion | 郇山 | Shing-sæn |
| Zulu | 蘇勞 | Su-lao |
| Zurich | 蘇力 | Su-lih |
| Z-ky'i | 慈谿 | Z-ky'i |